D1393783

CRABB'S ENGLISH SYNONYMS

CRABB'S
ENGLISH SYNONYMS

ARRANGED ALPHABETICALLY WITH
COMPLETE CROSS REFERENCES
THROUGHOUT

BY

GEORGE CRABB, M.A.

ROUTLEDGE & KEGAN PAUL
LONDON, BOSTON, MELBOURNE AND HENLEY

First published 1816
First Routledge edition 1884
Routledge & Kegan Paul Limited
39 Store Street
London WC1E 7DD 9, Park Street,
Boston, Mass, 02108, USA, 296, Beaconsfield
Parade, Middle Park, Melbourne, 3206,
Australia and Broadway House, Newtown Road,
Henley-on-Thames, Oxon, RG9 1EN
Reprinted seventeen times
Revised edition 1916
Reprinted eleven times
Reprinted 1974 (with corrections) 1977, 1979 and 1982

Printed in Great Britain by
Redwood Burn Limited
Trowbridge Wiltshire

ISBN 0 7100 1234 9

PREFACE TO THE 1916 EDITION

ONE hundred years ago George Crabb, an English philologist, then thirty-eight years old, published the first edition of his "English Synonymes Explained." This edition was arranged on the alphabetical plan. In a later one he adopted the classification plan, as being "more scientifick," but in a subsequent one he reverted to the alphabetical as being less perplexing to readers.

It is an exceptional tribute to Crabb's scholarship that during an entire century his masterful work has continued to hold the regard of the English-speaking world, and that to-day it is consulted with probably more appreciation than ever before.

Crabb found the study of words a fascinating diversion, and, familiar as any one may be with the general run of them, but little association is required to discover that they are very illusive creatures in a large family that is divided into four groups of progenies—*viz.*, *synonyms*, or words of similar meaning; *antonyms*, their opposites in meaning; *homonyms*, those alike in spelling but different in meaning; and *homophonous* ones, that differ in spelling and meaning but are alike in sound. Crabb confined himself to an exposition of the first group, and it was his purpose in explaining the most common members to indicate clearly the various meanings of words that bear a family resemblance by familiar comparisons, apposite historical allusions, and homely reflections.

It has been claimed by eminent philologists that every language the world has ever known has contributed to the formation of what is to-day called the English language. Single roots, meaning specific things, through local application, have been changed into idioms meaning other, though somewhat related, things. Then both roots and idioms have been adopted into more widely diffused forms, such as Hebrew, Greek, and Latin, and thence again into the specifically modern languages. Practically each new incorporation has undergone some change either in form or signification until, when a migratory word has found a lodgment in the English language, its appearance and meaning differ more or less from those of the primitive stock. It is this transmigration of words from language to language, losing some force here and gaining a new force there, that has given so many of them a variety of meanings, according to local usage and to other words with which they have become associated. Hence the large educational value of Crabb's synonymic explanations.

In the studious treatment of his subject, Crabb's work differs greatly from others, which, in the main, give only the generic, or key, words and some others that have a like significance. It will be observed that in many instances the author indicated the different shades of meaning of a single key word by separate paragraphs following the main application. This was to clarify the import of such words as *Fair* with its synonyms, as applied to the sky or weather, *Fair* with its synonyms, as applied to a person's conduct, reputation, and qualities, and *Fair* with its synonyms, as applied to an exhibition.

In this Centennial Edition of Crabb's most enduring work nothing has been eliminated from the master's explanations of his chosen words, and his style of presentation has been followed as closely as intervening conditions would permit. The entire body of the original words and explanations has been supplemented by a large number of words with their applications that have grown into the language within recent years, besides many that came to have a deeper significance than before because of the great European War.

And probably the most noteworthy feature of this edition is the exceedingly copious cross-references throughout the body of the work, binding closely related words together and so facilitating the location of a particular word that may be wanted without the tedious searching of a cumbersome index.

INTRODUCTION TO THE FIRST EDITION

It may seem surprising that the English, who have employed their talents successfully in every branch of literature, and in none more than in that of philology, should yet have fallen below other nations in the study of their synonymes. It cannot, however, be denied that, while the French and Germans have had several considerable works on the subject, we have not a single writer who has treated it in a scientific manner adequate to its importance: not that I wish by this remark to depreciate the labors of those who have preceded me, but simply to assign it as a reason why I have now been induced to come forward with an attempt to fill up what is considered a chasm in English literature.

In the prosecution of my undertaking, I have profited by everything which has been written in any language upon the subject; and although I always pursued my own train of thought, yet whenever I met with anything deserving of notice I adopted it, and referred it to the author in a note. I had not proceeded far before I found it necessary to restrict myself in the choice of my materials, and accordingly laid it down as a rule not to compare any words together which were sufficiently distinguished from each other by striking features in their signification, such as *abandon* and *quit*, which require a comparison with others, though not necessarily with themselves; for the same reason I was obliged to limit myself, as a rule, to one authority for each word, unless where the case seemed to require further exemplification. But, notwithstanding all my care in this respect, I was compelled to curtail much of what I had written, for fear of increasing the volume to an inconvenient size.

Although a work of this description does not afford much scope for system and arrangement, yet I laid down to myself the plan of arranging the words according to the extent or universality of their acceptation, placing those first which had the most general sense and application, and the rest in order. By this plan I found myself greatly aided in analyzing their differences, and I trust that the reader will thereby be equally benefited. . . .

For the sentiments scattered through this work I offer no

apology, although I am aware that they will not fall in with the views of many who may be competent to decide on its literary merits. I write not to please or displease any description of persons; but I trust that what I have written according to the dictates of my mind will meet the approbation of those whose good opinion I am most solicitous to obtain. Should any object to the introduction of morality in a work of science, I beg them to consider that a writer whose business it was to mark the nice shades of distinction between words closely allied could not do justice to his subject without entering into all the relations of society, and showing, from the acknowledged sense of many moral and religious terms, what has been the general sense of mankind on many of the most important questions which have agitated the world. My first object certainly has been to assist the philological inquirer in ascertaining the force and comprehension of the English language; yet I should have thought my work but half completed had I made it a mere register of verbal distinctions. While others seize every opportunity unblushingly to avow and zealously to propagate opinions destructive of good order, it would ill become any individual of contrary sentiments to shrink from stating his convictions when called upon, as he seems to be, by an occasion like that which has now offered itself. As to the rest, I throw myself on the indulgence of the public, with the assurance that, having used every endeavor to deserve their approbation, I shall not make an appeal to their candor in vain.

ENGLISH SYNONYMS

A

ABACK, Backward, Behind, Rearward, Retrograde, Surprise. *Aback*, in Anglo-Saxon, *on bæc*, at or on the back, is applied both to persons and localities. A person goes *aback*, *backward*, or *rearward*, or he *retrogrades* when in a movement opposite to forward or going ahead, and he goes *behind* when he passes from the front to the rear, and also when he fails to maintain a set gait in a movement or a course in a study. An object is *behind* or to the *rearward* of another object according as it is placed or becomes situated. In navigation, a sail is *aback* when pressed against a mast. A person *surprised*, taken unawares, or suddenly astonished, confused, or perplexed, is said to be *taken aback*.

ABAFT, Aft, Behind, Rearward, Astern. These words abound in nautical language, and, in relation to a given point forward or ahead of something on shipboard, imply localities. *Abaft*, from *a* (on) and Anglo-Saxon *be-æftan* (itself a combination of *be* (by) and *æftan*, an adverb meaning behind or back), is the opposite of *afore*. The original stem of the word appears in the phrase *fore and aft*.

ABANDON, Desert, Forsake, Relinquish. The idea of leaving or separating one's self from an object is common to these terms, which vary in the circumstances of the action. *Abandon*, from Old French *à bandon* (proscription, control, ban), meant originally to put under a public ban, to proscribe utterly. *Desert*, from Late Latin *deserto*, is derived from the privative *de* and the verb *sero*, meaning bind or join, the root of which also appears in the noun *series*. It therefore signified the breaking of ties, the severing of one's connection with something. *Forsake*, compounded of the prefix *for* and the Anglo-Saxon *sacan*, to strive, meant to strive against, to take the opposite side, hence to repudiate. *Abandoning* is a violation of the most sacred ties, and exposes the object to every misery; *desertion* is a breach of honor and fidelity; it deprives a person of the assistance or the countenance which he has a right to expect; by *forsaking*, the kindly feelings are hurt and the social ties are broken. A bad mother *abandons* her offspring; a soldier *deserts* his comrades; a man *forsakes* his companions.

Things as well as persons may be *abandoned*, *deserted*, or *forsaken;* things only are *relinquished*. To *abandon* may be an act of necessity or discretion, as a captain *abandons* a vessel when it is no longer safe to remain in it. *Desertion* is often a dereliction of duty, as to *desert* one's post; and often an indifferent action, particularly in the sense of leaving any place which has had one's care and attention bestowed upon it, as people *desert* a village, or any particular country where they have been established. *Forsaking* is an indifferent action, and implies simply the leaving something to which one has been attached in one form or another; a person *forsakes* a certain house which he has been accustomed to frequent; birds *forsake* their nests when they find them to have been discovered. To *relinquish* is an act of prudence or imprudence; men often inadvertently *relinquish* the fairest prospects in order to follow some favorite scheme which terminates in their ruin.

We may *desert* or *forsake* a place, but the former comprehends more than the latter; a place that is *deserted* is left by all, and left entirely. A place may be *forsaken* by individuals or to a partial extent.

Abandon, Resign, Renounce, Abdicate.—The idea of giving up is common to these terms, which signification, though analogous to the former, admits, however, of this distinction, that in the one case we separate ourselves from an object, in the other we send or cast it from us. *Abandon* (see above). *Resign,* from *re* and *signo,* signifies to sign away or back from one's self. *Renounce,* in Letin *renuntio,* from *nuntiare,* to tell or declare, is to declare off from a thing. *Abdicate,* from *ab,* from, and *dicere,* to speak, signifies likewise to call or cry off from a thing.

We *abandon* and *resign* by giving up to another; we *renounce* by sending away from ourselves; we *abandon* a thing by transferring it to another; in this manner a debtor *abandons* his goods to his creditors; we *resign* a thing by transferring our possession of it to another; in this manner we *resign* a place to a friend; we *renounce* a thing by simply ceasing to hold it; in this manner we *renounce* a claim or a profession. As to *renounce,* signified originally to give up by word of mouth, and to *resign* to give up by signature, the former is consequently a less formal action than the latter; we may *renounce* by implication; we *resign* in direct terms; we *renounce* the pleasures of the world when we do not seek to enjoy them; we *resign* a pleasure, a profit, or advantage, of which we expressly give up the enjoyment. To *abdicate* is a species of informal resignation. A monarch *abdicates* his throne who simply declares his will to cease to reign; but a minister *resigns* his office when he gives up the seals by which he held it. We *abandon* nothing but that over which we have had an entire control; we *abdicate* nothing but that which we have held by a certain right, but we may *resign* or *renounce* that which may be in our possession only by an act of violence; a usurper cannot be said properly to *abandon* his people or *abdicate* a throne, but he may *resign* his power or *renounce* his pretensions to a throne.

To *abandon* and *resign* are likewise used in a reflective sense; the former in the bad sense, to denote the giving up the understanding to the passion, or the giving up one's self, mind and body, to bad practices; the latter in the good sense, to denote the giving up one's will and desires to one's circumstances or whatever is appointed. The soldiers of Hannibal *abandoned* themselves to pleasure at Capua. A patient man *resigns* himself to his fate, however severe that may be. When *resign* is taken in the bad sense, it is not so complete a giving up of one's self as *abandonment,* which implies a yielding to a passion.

See also WAIVE.

ABANDONED. See PROFLIGATE.

ABASE, HUMBLE, DEGRADE, DISGRACE, HUMILIATE, DEPRESS, LOWER, REDUCE, DEBASE. To *abase* expresses the strongest degree of self-humiliation; like the French *abaisser,* it signifies literally to bring down or make low, *abaisser* being compounded of the intensive syllable *a* or *ad,* and *baisser,* from Low Latin *bassare,* to make low. The root appears in the Latin *basis,* Greek βάσις, the lowest part of the column, from the root βά, to go, hence, in some cases, to stand, the basis being that on which the rest of the column stands. It implies the laying aside all the high pretensions which distinguish us from our fellow-creatures—the descending to a state comparatively low and mean. To *humble,* in French *humilier,* from the Latin *humilis,* humble, and *humus,* the ground, naturally marks a prostration to the ground, and figuratively a lowering of the thoughts and feelings. According to the principles of Christianity whoever *abaseth* himself shall be exalted, and according to the same principles whoever reflects on his own littleness and unworthiness will daily *humble* himself before his Maker. The *abasement* consists in the greatest possible dejection of spirit which, if marked by an outward act, will lead to the utmost prostration of the body; *humbling,* in comparison with *abasement,* is an ordinary sentiment.

Abase and *humble* have regard to persons considered absolutely, *degrade* and *disgrace* to their relative situation. To *degrade* (see DISPARAGE) signifies to descend from one rank (Latin *gradus,* rank, English *grade*) to another. It supposes elevation either in outward circumstances or in public opinion. To *disgrace*, compounded of the privative *dis* and *grace*, or favor, properly implies to put out of favor, which is always attended with circumstances of more or less ignominy. To *abase* and *humble* one's self may be meritorious acts as suited to the infirmity and fallibility of human nature, but to *degrade* or *disgrace* one's self is always a culpable act. The penitent man *humbles* himself, the contrite man *abases* himself, the man of rank *degrades* himself by a too familiar deportment with his inferiors, he *disgraces* himself by his vices. The great and good man may also be abased and humbled without being *degraded* or *disgraced;* his glory follows him in his *abasement* or *humiliation*, his greatness protects him from *degradation*, and his virtue shields him from *disgrace*.

To *degrade* has most regard to the external rank and condition, *disgrace* to the moral estimation and character. Whatever is low and mean is *degrading* for those who are not of mean condition; whatever is immoral is *disgraceful* to all, but most so to those who ought to know better. It is *degrading* to a nobleman to associate with prize-fighters and jockeys, it is *disgraceful* for him to countenance a violation of the laws which he is bound to protect. The higher the rank of the individual, the greater is his *degradation;* the higher his previous character, or the more sacred his office, the greater his *disgrace* if his acts be inconsistent with its duties.

Persons may sometimes be *degraded* and *disgraced* at the will of others, but with a similar distinction of the words. He who is not treated with the outward honor and respect he deserves is *degraded;* he who is not regarded with the same kindness as before is *disgraced*.

These terms may be employed with a similar distinction in regard to things, and in that case they are comparable with *debase*. To *debase*, from the intensive syllable *de* and *base*, signifying to make *base*, is applied to whatever may lose its purity or excellence.

To *humiliate* a person implies the doing by another or the occurrence of something that produces mortification, vexation, chagrin, etc. To *depress*, in relation to a person, is to dispirit, discourage, cast down, debilitate; in relation to material objects, it is to press or thrust down, to flatten, from above or vertically; in relation to commerce, it is to bring about a diminution or dullness in trade. To *lower* is to lessen, bring down, change from a high price (or note in music) to a lesser one, to sink, to rebate. A person *lowers* himself in another's estimation by a wrongful or unfriendly act. To *reduce* is to bring into a lower state, to shorten, to condense, to abbreviate (see ABATE). A person is degraded or disgraced by being *reduced* from one station to a lower one.

ABASH, CONFOUND, CONFUSE. *Abash*, Old French *esbahir*, an onomatopœtic word formed from the interjection *bah* of astonishment, meant originally to amaze, astound, but it has been partly confused with the word *abase* and is sometimes used as an intensive of it. *Confound* and *confuse* are derived from different parts of the same Latin verb *confundo* and its participle *confusus*. *Confundo* is compounded of *con* and *fundo*, to pour together. To *confound* and *confuse* then signify properly to melt together or into one mass what ought to be distinct; and figuratively, to derange the thoughts so that they seem melted together.

Abash expresses more than *confound*, and *confound* more than *confuse*. *Abash* has regard to the spirit which is greatly abased and lowered, *confound* has regard to the faculties which are benumbed and crippled; *confuse* has regard to the feelings and ideas which are deranged and perplexed. The haughty man is *abashed* when he is humbled in the eyes of others; the wicked man is *confounded* when his villainy is suddenly detected; a modest person may be *confused* in the presence of his superiors.

Abash is always taken in a bad sense; neither the scorn of fools, nor the taunts of the oppressor, will *abash* him who has a conscience void of offence toward God and man. To be *confounded* is not always the consequence of guilt; superstition and ignorance are liable to be *confounded* by extraordinary phenomena; and Providence sometimes thinks fit to *confound* the wisdom of the wisest by signs and wonders, far above the reach of human comprehension. *Confusion* is at the best an infirmity more or less excusable according to the nature of the cause: a steady mind and a clear head are not easily *confused;* but persons of quick sensibility cannot always preserve a perfect collection of thought in trying situations; and those who have any consciousness of guilt, and are not very hardened, will be soon thrown into *confusion* by close interrogatories.

To Shame, Mortify, Disconcert, Discompose, Dishearten, Bewilder.—These words signify a something done by a person or an occurrence that unpleasantly affects another person. You may *shame* a person by exposing an act of crime, dishonor, impropriety, or breach of modesty or decorum on his part, and the person may bring the painful sensation of *shame* upon himself by his own premeditated or incautious action. The acts that *shame* a person may also *mortify* him, and in addition actions of himself or others that cause in him a sense of humiliation, vexation, chagrin, or guilt, may also do so. Various substances *mortify* when their vital functions are destroyed, the root of the word being derived from the Latin *mors, mortis*, death. Gangrene produces *mortification* of the flesh. Some acts of penance or austerities, imposed as a punishment, are said to *mortify* the body. To *disconcert* and *discompose* are closely allied to *confound* and *confuse*, specifically meaning to disturb one's composure or self-possession. To *dishearten* is to do that toward another that will disappoint, discourage, depress, dispirit him; also an untoward occurrence that produces the same effect. To *bewilder* (Eng. prefix *be*, and Prov. Eng. *wildern*, a wilderness; Ger. *verwildern*, to render wild) implies a stronger action than either *to confound* or *to confuse*, for it involves in addition to those distractions a sense of extreme perplexity, helplessness, stupefaction, such as would possess a person lost in a wilderness and not knowing which way to turn to get out.

ABATE, LESSEN, DIMINISH, DECREASE. *Abate*, fr~m the French *abattre*, signified originally to beat down, in the active sense; to come down, in the neuter sense. *Diminish*, from the Latin *de* and *minuere*, to lessen, and *minus*, less, expresses, like the verb *lessen*, the sense of either making less or becoming less. *Decrease* is compounded of the privative *de* and Latin *crescere*, to grow, signifying to grow less.

Abate, lessen, and *diminish* agree in the sense of becoming less and of making less; *decrease* implies only becoming less. *Abate* respects only vigor of action, and applies to that which is strong or violent, as a fever *abates*, pain, anger, etc., *abate; lessen* and *diminish* are applied to size, quantity, and number, but *lessen* is much seldomer used intransitively than *diminish;* things are rarely said to *lessen* of themselves, but to *diminish*. The passion of an angry man ought to be allowed to *abate* before any appeal is made to his understanding. Objects apparently *diminish* as they recede from the view.

Abate, transitively taken, signifies to bring down—*i. e.*, to make less in height or degree by means of force or a particular effort, as to *abate* pride or to *abate* misery; *lessen* and *diminish*, the former in the familiar, the latter in the grave style, signify to make less in quantity or magnitude by an ordinary process, as the size of a room is *lessened*, the credit of a person is *diminished*. We may *lessen* the number of our evils by not dwelling upon them; nothing *diminishes* the lustre of great deeds more than cruelty.

To *decrease* is to fall off; a retreating army will *decrease* rapidly when, exposed to all the privations and hardships attendant on forced marches, it is compelled to fight for its safety; some things *decrease* so gradually that it is some time before they are observed to be *diminished*.

The *decrease* is the process, the *diminution* is the result; as a *decrease* in the taxes causes a *diminution* in the revenue. The term *decrease* is peculiarly applicable to material objects which can grow less, *diminution* is applicable to objects generally which may become or be actually less from any cause.

To Remit, Rebate, Deduct, Decline, Slacken, Subside, Suppress, Subdue,

ABHOR

Allow, Mitigate, Alleviate, Quell, Calm.
—*Remit, rebate, deduct,* and *allow* are terms especially common in business transactions. A statement of an account is *remitted,* or sent, by the seller to the purchaser, and a specified discount or reduction in the amount of money called for in the statement is *remitted, rebated, deducted,* or *allowed* by the seller for a cash payment within a designated period of time. To *decline, slacken, subside* signify a decrease, a slowing-up, a settling. Stocks, bonds, commodities *decline* in prices from time to time for various reasons; a person's health *declines* as it becomes less vigorous than usual; winds, storms, and tides *slacken* as they diminish in severity and flow; and storms, disturbances, excitements, anxieties, alarms, fevers, and various physical conditions *subside* as their causes are brought under control or eliminated. *Suppress, quell,* and *subdue* are suggestive of riots and their ending; the crushing, overpowering, conquering of discordant or dangerous elements and conditions; all implying the use of force against force. *Subdue* is the rather stronger term of the trio, for while a disturbance may be *suppressed* or *quelled,* the resulting condition is not necessarily a finality, as the disturbance is liable to break out anew, whereas the elements of a disturbance that are *subdued* are presumably forced into submission.

A harsh legal sentence is *mitigated* when its severity is reduced in consideration of extenuating circumstances; sickness and untoward conditions are *alleviated* when made less painful or threatening. *Calm* stands for the most benevolent and inspiring condition in human life and nature, being indicative of peace, quiet, tranquillity, serenity, safety. A person, the ocean, the weather, the stock-markets, and countless activities are *calm* when undisturbed.

ABATEMENT. See DEDUCTION.
ABBREVIATE. See ABRIDGE.
ABDICATE. See ABANDON.
ABERRATION. See HALLUCINATION.
ABETTOR, ACCESSORY, ACCOMPLICE, CONFEDERATE. *Abettor,* or one that abets, gives aid and encouragement by counsel, promises, or rewards. An *accessory,* or one added and annexed, takes an active, though subordinate, part. An *accomplice,* not related to *accomplish,* implies the principal in any plot, who takes a leading part and brings it to perfection. *Abettors* propose, *accessories* assist, *accomplices* execute. The *abettor* and *accessory,* or the *abettor* and *accomplice,* may be one and the same person; but not so the *accessory* and *accomplice.* In every deep-laid scheme there must be *abettors* to set it on foot, *accessories* to co-operate, and *accomplices* to put it into execution; in the Gunpowder Plot there were many secret *abettors,* some noblemen who were *accessories,* and Guy Fawkes the principal *accomplice.* *Accomplice,* like the other terms, may be applied to other objects besides criminal offences. A *confederate* assists in an undertaking, and may do so openly or secretly, actively or passively. In criminal matters a *confederate* is equally guilty with a principal.

ABHOR, DETEST, ABOMINATE, LOATHE. These terms equally denote a sentiment of aversion. *Abhor,* in Latin *abhorreo,* compounded of *ab,* from, and *horrere,* to stiffen with horror, signifies to start from with a strong emotion of horror. *Detest,* in Latin *detestor,* compounded of *de,* from or against, and *testor,* I bear witness, signifies to condemn with indignation. *Abominate,* in Latin *abominatus,* participle of *abominor,* compounded of *ab,* from or against, and *ominor,* to fear something as being of ill omen, signifies to hold in religious abhorrence, to detest in the highest possible degree. *Loathe,* Anglo-Saxon *lathian,* is associated with the very common Anglo-Saxon adjective *lath,* hateful, and is allied with the German verb *leiden,* to suffer. It suggests a feeling of intense and even painful physical repulsion.

What we *abhor* is repugnant to our moral feelings; what we *detest* is opposed to our moral principles; what we *abominate* does violence to our religious and moral sentiments; what we *loathe* offends our physical taste. We *abhor* what is base and ungenerous, we *detest* hypocrisy; we *abominate* profanation and open impiety; we *loathe* food when we are sick.

In the moral acceptance *loathe* is a strong figure of speech to mark the abhorrence and disgust which the sight or thought of offensive objects produces.

ABIDE, Sojourn, Dwell, Live, Reside, Inhabit. *Abide,* in Anglo-Saxon *abidan,* signifies to await, to expect. *Sojourn,* in French *séjourner,* from *sub* and *diurnus,* in the daytime, signifies to pass the day—that is, a certain portion of one's time—in a place. *Dwell* is from a Teutonic root meaning to wander, to lead astray, to tarry. This was the meaning of the Anglo-Saxon *dwellan;* the present meaning of the word is a peculiar development in English paralleled only by some uses of the word in the Scandinavian tongues. At the present it implies a stay in a place by way of residence, which is expressed in common discourse by the word *live,* for passing one's life. *Reside,* from the Latin *re* and *sedere,* to sit down, conveys the full idea of a settlement. *Inhabit,* from the Latin *habito,* a frequentative of *habeo,* signifies to have or occupy for a permanency.

The length of stay implied in these terms is marked by a certain gradation. *Abide* denotes the shortest stay; to *sojourn* is of longer continuance; *dwell* comprehends the idea of perpetuity in a given place, but *reside* and *inhabit* are partial and local—we *dwell* only in one spot, but we may *reside* at or *inhabit* many places. These words have likewise a reference to the state of society. *Abide* and *sojourn* relate more properly to the wandering habits of men in a primitive state of society. *Dwell,* as implying a stay under a cover, is universal in its application; for we may *dwell* either in a palace, a house, a cottage, or any shelter. *Live, reside,* and *inhabit* are confined to a civilized state of society; the former applying to the abodes of the inferior orders, the latter to those of the higher classes. The word *inhabit* is never used but in connection with the place *inhabited.*

The Easterners *abode* with one another, *sojourned* in a country, and *dwelt* in tents. The angels *abode* with Lot that night; Abram *sojourned* in the land of Canaan; the Israelites *dwelt* in the land of Goshen. Savages either *dwell* in the cavities which nature has formed for them, or in some rude structure erected for a temporary purpose; but as men increase in cultivation they build places for themselves which they can *inhabit;* the poor have their cottages in which they can *live;* the wealthy provide themselves with superb buildings in which they *reside.*

ABILITY, Capacity. *Ability,* in French *habilité,* Latin *habilitas,* comes from *able, habile, habilis,* and *habeo,* to have, because possession and power are inseparable. *Capacity,* in French *capacité,* Latin *capacitas,* from *capax* and *capio,* to receive, marks the abstract quality of being able to receive or hold.

Ability is to *capacity* as the genus to the species. *Ability* comprehends the power of doing in general, without specifying the quality or degree; *capacity* is a particular kind of *ability.* *Ability* may be either physical or mental; *capacity,* when said of persons, is mental only. *Ability* respects action, *capacity* respects thought. *Ability* always supposes something able to be done; *capacity* is a mental endowment, and always supposes something ready to receive or hold.

Ability is no wise limited in its extent; it may be small or great; *capacity* of itself always implies a positive and superior degree of power, although it may be modified by epithets to denote different degrees; a boy of *capacity* will have the advantage over his school-fellows, particularly if he be classed with those of a dull *capacity.*

Abilities, when used in the plural only, is confined to the signification of mental endowments, and comprehends the operations of thought in general; *capacity,* on the other hand, is that peculiar endowment, that enlargement of understanding, that exalts the possessor above the rest of mankind. Many men have the *abilities* for managing the concerns of others who would not have the *capacity* for conducting a concern of their own. We should not judge highly of that man's *abilities* who could only mar the plans of others, but had no *capacity* for conceiving and proposing anything better in their stead.

Ability, Faculty, Talent. — These terms all agree in denoting a power. *Ability* is, as in the preceding case, the general term. *Faculty*, in Latin *facultas*, changed from *facilitas* and *facere*, to do, signifying an ability to do; and *talent*, in Latin *talentum*, a Greek coin exceeding one hundred pounds sterling, and employed figuratively, as in *Matthew* 25, 15, for a gift, possession, or power—denote definite kinds of power.

Ability relates to human power generally, by which a man is enabled to act; it may vary in degree and quality with times, persons, and circumstances; health, strength, and fortune are *abilities; faculty* is a gift of nature directed to a certain end and following a certain rule. An *ability* may be acquired, and consequently is properly applied to individuals, an *ability* to speak extempore or an *ability* to write; but a *faculty* belongs to the species, as a *faculty* of speech or of hearing, etc.

Ability being in general the power of doing, may be applied in its unqualified sense to the whole species, without any distinction. *Faculty* is always taken in a restricted sense, although applied to the species. *Faculty* and *talent* are both gifts of nature, but a *faculty* is supposed to be given in an equal degree to all, a *talent* in an unequal degree; as the *faculty* of seeing, the *talent* of mimicry, the *talent* for music; a *faculty* may be impaired by age, disease, or other circumstances; a *talent* is improved by exercise.

As all these terms may be applied to different objects, they are aptly enough used in the plural to denote so many distinct powers: *abilities* denote all our powers generally, corporeal and mental, but more especially the latter; *faculties* relate to the ordinary powers of body and mind, as when we speak of a person's retaining or losing his *faculties; talents* relate to the particular gifts or powers which may serve a beneficial purpose, as to employ one's *talents* usefully.

Ability, Dexterity, Address.—*Ability* is, as before observed, a general term, without any qualification. *Dexterity*, from *dexter*, the right hand, signifying mechanical or manual facility, and *address*, signifying a mode of address, in particular terms. *Ability* may be used to denote any degree, as to do according to the best of one's *ability;* and it may be qualified to denote a small degree of *ability*. *Dexterity* and *address* are positive degrees of *ability*.

Ability is, however, frequently taken in a restricted sense for a positive degree of *ability*, which brings it still nearer to the two other terms, from which it differs only in the application; *ability* in this case refers to intellectual endowment generally, *dexterity* relates to a particular power or facility of executing, and *address* to a particular mode or manner of addressing one's self on particular occasions. *Ability* shows itself in the most important transactions and the general conduct in the highest stations, as a minister of state displays his *ability; dexterity* and *address* are employed occasionally, the former in removing difficulties and escaping dangers, the latter in improving advantages and accommodating tempers; the former in directing the course of things, the latter in managing of men.

Able, Capable, Capacious. — These epithets, from which the preceding abstract nouns are derived, have distinctions peculiar to themselves. *Able* and *capable* are applied to ordinary actions, but not always indifferently, the one for the other: *able* is said of the abilities generally, as a child is *able* or not *able* to walk; *capable* is said of one's ability to do particular things, as to be *capable* of performing a great journey. *Able* is said of that which one can do, as to be *able* to write or read; *capable* is said of that which either a person or a thing can take, receive, or hold; a person is *capable* of an office, or *capable* of great things; a thing is *capable* of improvement. *Able* may be added to a noun by way of epithet when it denotes a positive degree of ability, as an *able* commander, an *able* financier. *Capable* may be used absolutely to express a mental power.

Capable and *capacious*, though derived from the same verb *capio*, to take or receive, are distinguished from each other in respect to the powers or properties of the objects to which they are applied, *capable* being said of powers generally, *capacious* only of the property of having amplitude of space or a power to take in or comprehend; and men are *capable* of thought or reason, of life or death, etc.; a hall may be said to be *capacious*, or, figuratively, a man has a *capacious* mind.

ABIOGENIC, LIFELESS, SOURCE-LESS. *Abiogenic* is a recently coined word that has no real synonyms; *abiogenic*, the adjective of *abiogenesis*, a compound of the Greek *a*, without, βιός, life, and γένεσις, origin, invented by Huxley, signifies, literally, spontaneous generation, the opposite of sexual generation and *biogenesis* (which see). *Abiogenic* pertains to the production of life or living beings under certain physical conditions without the intervention of antecedent living forms, Huxley having propounded the theory that living matter can be produced from that which in itself is not living matter. Hence, it is claimed, as the basis of *abiogenesis*, that certain material objects may be developed from other objects that in themselves are *lifeless* and, as far as known, *sourceless*.

Biologists at one time held the view that some of the lower animals or plants, or the primordial of one or the other, or both, of the animal and vegetable kingdoms may have sprung from *lifeless* matter without the intervention of any previously existing parent. On the demonstration that alleged instances of such spontaneous generation were unfounded, the early view was discarded till Haeckel and other evolutionists revived it and Huxley gave it a name.

ABJURE, RECANT, RETRACT, RECALL, REVOKE. *Abjure*, in Latin *abjuro*, is compounded of the privative *ab* and *juro*, swear, signifying to swear to the contrary, or give up with an oath. *Recant*, in Latin *recanto*, is compounded of the privative *re* and *canto*, to sing or declare, signifying to unsay, to contradict by a counter declaration. *Retract*, in Latin *retractus*, participle of *retraho*, is compounded of *re*, back, and *traho*, to draw, signifying to draw back what has been let go. *Revoke* and *recall* have the same original sense as *recant*, with this difference only, that the word *call*, which is expressed also by *voke*, or in Latin *voco*, implies an action more suited to a multitude than the word *canto*, to sing,

which may pass in solitude. We *abjure* a religion, we *recant* a doctrine, we *retract* a promise, we *revoke* a command, we *recall* an expression, and, where the initiative, referendum, and recall prevail, an incompetent or unfaithful official.

What has been solemnly professed is renounced by *abjuration;* what has been publicly maintained as a settled point of belief is as publicly given up by *recanting;* what has been pledged so as to gain credit is contradicted by *retracting;* what has been pronounced by an act of authority is rendered null by *revocation;* what has been misspoken through inadvertence or mistake is rectified by *recalling* the words.

Although Archbishop Cranmer *recanted* the principles of the Reformation, yet he soon after *recalled* his words, and died boldly for his faith. Henry IV. of France *abjured* Calvinism, but he did not *retract* the promise which he had made to the Calvinists of his protection. Louis XIV. drove many of his best subjects from France by *revoking* the Edict of Nantes. Interest but too often leads men to *abjure* their faith; the fear of shame or punishment leads them to *recant* their opinions; the want of principle dictates the *retracting* of one's promise; reasons of state occasion the *revoking* of decrees; a love of precision commonly induces a speaker or writer to *recall* a false expression.

ABOLISH, ABROGATE, REPEAL, REVOKE, ANNUL, CANCEL. *Abolish*, in French *abolir*, Latin *abolere*, to grow less, is compounded of *ab*, away, and *olere*, to grow. *Abrogate*, in French *abroger*, Latin *abrogatus*, participle of *abrogo*, compounded of *ab*, away, and *rogare*, to ask, signifies to ask away, or to ask that a thing may be done away; in allusion to the custom of the Romans, among whom no law was valid unless the consent of the people was obtained by asking, and in like manner no law was unmade without asking their consent. *Repeal*, in French *rappeller*, from the Latin words *re* and *appello*, signifies literally to call back or unsay what has been said, which is in like manner the original meaning of *re-*

ABOVE

9

voke. Annul, in French *annuller,* comes from Latin *nullus, ne-ullus,* not any, signifying to reduce to nothing. *Cancel,* in French *canceller,* comes from the Latin *cancello,* cut crosswise, signifying to strike out crosswise—that is, to cross out.

The word *abolish* conveys the idea of putting a total end to a thing, and is applied properly to those things which have been long in existence and firmly established: an *abolition* may be effected either by an act of power, as to *abolish* an institution or an order of men, and the like. Or it may be a gradual act, or effected by indirect means, as to *abolish* a custom, practice, etc.

All the other terms have respect to the partial acts of men, in undoing that which they have done. Laws are either *repealed* or *abrogated,* but *repealing* is a term of modern use, applied to the acts of public councils or assemblies, where laws are made or unmade by the consent or open declaration of numbers. *Abrogate* is a term of less definite import; to *abrogate* a law is to render it null by any act of the legislature; thus, the making of a new law may *abrogate* the old one.

Revoking is an act of individual authority—edicts are *revoked; annulling* is an act of discretion, as official proceedings or private contracts are *annulled; cancelling* is a species of annulling, as in the case of *cancelling* deeds, bonds, obligations, etc. None can *abrogate* but those who have the power to make. Any one who has the power to give his word may also *revoke* it, if he see reason so to do. Any one who can bind himself or others, by any deed or instrument, may *annul* or render this null and void, provided it be done for a reasonable cause, and in the proper manner. As *cancelling* serves to blot out or obliterate what has been written, it may be applied to what is blotted out of the memory. It is a voluntary resignation of right or demand which one person has upon another.

ABOMINABLE, DETESTABLE, EXECRABLE. The primitive idea of these terms, agreeable to their derivation (for which see ABOMINATE, MALEDICTION, and DETEST), is that of badness in the highest degree; conveying by themselves the strongest signification, and excluding the necessity for every other modifying epithet.

The *abominable* thing excites aversion; the *detestable* thing, hatred and revulsion; the *execrable* thing, indignation and horror.

These sentiments are expressed against what is *abominable* by strong ejaculations, against what is *detestable* by animadversion and reprobation, and against what is *execrable* by imprecations and anathemas.

In the ordinary acceptation of these terms, they serve to mark a degree of excess in a very bad thing; *abominable* expressing less than *detestable,* and that less than *execrable.* This gradation is sufficiently illustrated in the following example. Dionysius, the tyrant, having been informed that a very aged woman prayed to the gods every day for his preservation, and wondering that any of his subjects should be so interested for his safety, inquired of this woman respecting the motives of her conduct, to which she replied, "In my infancy I lived under an *abominable* prince, whose death I desired; but when he perished, he was succeeded by a *detestable* tyrant worse than himself. I offered up my vows for his death also, which were in like manner answered; but we have since had a worse tyrant than he. This *execrable* monster is yourself, whose life I have prayed for, lest, if it be possible, you should be succeeded by one even more wicked."

The exaggeration conveyed by these expressions has given rise to their abuse in vulgar discourse, where they are often employed indifferently to serve the humor of the speaker.

ABOMINATE. See ABHOR.

ABORIGINAL. See FIRST.

ABORTION. See FAILURE.

ABOVE, OVER, UPON, BEYOND. When an object is *above* another, it exceeds it in height; when it is *over* another, it extends along its superior surface; when it is *upon* another, it comes in contact with its superior surface; when it is *beyond* another, it lies at a greater distance. Trees frequently grow *above* a wall, and sometimes the branches hang *over* the wall, or rest *upon* it, but they seldom stretch much *beyond* it.

In the figurative sense, the first is mostly employed to convey the idea of superiority; the second, of authority; the third, of immediate influence; and the fourth, of extent. Every one should be above falsehood, but particularly those who are set *over* others, who may have an influence *on* their minds *beyond* all calculation.

ABRIDGE, ABBREVIATE, CURTAIL, CONTRACT. *Abridge*, in French *abréger*, Latin *abbreviare*, is compounded of the intensive syllable *ab* and *breviare*, from *brevis*, short, signifying to make short. *Abridge* and *abbreviate*, by derivation, have therefore exactly the same meaning, though they are used in different connections. We *abbreviate* a word; we *abridge* a book. *Curtail*, in French *court*, short, and *tailler*, to cut, signifies to diminish in length by cutting. *Contract*, in Latin *contractus*, participle of *contraho*, is compounded of *con* and *traho*, signifying to draw close together.

By *abridging*, in the figurative as well as the literal sense, the quantity is diminished; by *curtailing*, the measure or number is reduced; by *contracting*, the compass is reduced. Privileges are *abridged*, pleasures *curtailed*, and powers *contracted*. It is ungenerous to *abridge* the liberty of any one, or *curtail* him of his advantages, while it makes no improper use of them; otherwise it is advisable, in order to *contract* his means of doing mischief. See also DEPRIVE.

Abridgment, Compendium, Epitome, Digest, Summary, Abstract.—The first four terms are applied to a distinct work, the two latter to parts of a work. An *abridgment* is the reduction of a work into a smaller compass. A *compendium* is a general and concise view of any science, as geography or astronomy. An *epitome* is a compressed view of all the substantial parts of a thing, or, in other words, the whole of any matter brought into a small compass. A *digest* is any materials digested in order. A *summary* comprehends the heads and subdivisions of a work. An *abstract* includes a brief but comprehensive view of any particular proceeding. *Abridgments* often surpass the originals in values when they are made with judgment. *Compendiums* are fit-

ted for young persons to commit to memory on commencing the study of any science. There is perhaps not a better *epitome* than that of the Universal History by Bossuet, nor a better *digest* than that of the laws made by order of Justinian. Systematic writers give occasional *summaries* of what they have been treating upon. It is necessary to make *abstracts* of deeds or judicial proceedings. *Epitome* and *abstract* are taken for other objects, which contain within a small compass the essence of a thing.

ABROAD. See OUT.

ABROGATE. See ABOLISH.

ABRUPT, RUGGED, ROUGH. *Abrupt*, in Latin *abruptus*, participle of *abrumpere*, to break off, signifies the state of being broken off. *Rugged* is a Scandinavian word signifying hairy, hence unshaven, rough. *Rough*, from Anglo-Saxon *ruh*, hairy, rough, had the same meaning and development.

These words mark different degrees of unevenness. What is *abrupt* has greater cavities and protuberances than what is *rugged;* what is *rugged* has greater irregularities than what is *rough*. In the natural sense *abrupt* is *opposed* to what is unbroken, *rugged* to what is even, and *rough* to what is smooth. A precipice is *abrupt*, a path is *rugged*, a plank is *rough*. The *abruptness* of a body is generally occasioned by a violent concussion and separation of its parts; *ruggedness* arises from natural, but less violent, causes; *roughness* is mostly a natural property, although sometimes produced by friction.

In the figurative or extended application, the distinction is equally clear. Words and manners are *abrupt* when they are sudden and unconnected; the temper is *rugged* which is exposed to frequent ebullitions of angry humor; actions are *rough* when performed with violence and incaution. An *abrupt* behavior is the consequence of an agitated mind; a *rugged* disposition is inherent in the character; a *rough* deportment arises from an undisciplined state of feeling. An habitual steadiness and coolness of reflection is best fitted to prevent or correct any *abruptness* of manner; a cultivation of the

Christian temper cannot fail of smoothing down all *ruggedness* of humor; an intercourse with polished society will inevitably refine down all *roughness* of behavior.

See also SUDDEN.

ABSCOND, STEAL AWAY, SECRETE ONE'S SELF. *Abscond*, in Latin *abscondo*, is compounded of *abs* and *condo*, signifying to hide from the view, which is the original meaning of the other words; to *abscond* is to remove one's self for the sake of not being discovered by those with whom we are acquainted. To *steal away* is to get away so as to elude observation. To *secrete one's self* is to get into a place of secrecy without being perceived. Dishonest men *abscond*, thieves *steal away* when they dread detection, and fugitives *secrete themselves*. Those who *abscond* will have frequent occasion to *steal away*, and still more frequent occasion to *secrete themselves*.

ABSENT, ABSTRACTED, ABSTRACT, DIVERTED, DISTRACTED. *Absent*, in French *absent*, Latin *absens*, comes from *ab*, from, and *sum*, to be, signifying away or at a distance from all objects. *Abstracted*, or *abstract*, in French *abstrait*, Latin *abstractus*, participle of *abstraho*, or *abs*, from, and *traho*, to draw, signifies drawn or separated from all objects. *Diverted*, in French *divertir*, Latin *diverto*, compounded of *dis*, asunder, and *vertere*, to turn, signifies turned aside from the object that is present. *Distracted*, of course, implies drawn asunder by different objects.

A want of proper attention is implied in all these terms, but in different degrees and under different circumstances. *Absence* of mind is either a state or a habit; a man may be occasionally *absent*. Or a man may contract an habitual *absence*, either from profound study, or from any other less commendable cause. *Abstraction* denotes a state, and, for the most part, a temporary state.

The term *absent* simply implies not present with one's mind, not observant of present objects, but it does not necessarily imply thinking of anything; a man man be *absent* who is thinking of nothing.

Abstracted, on the other hand, denotes deep thought of something not present. *Abstract* may in poetry be used in the sense of *abstracted*.

Absent and *abstracted* denote an exclusion of present objects; *diverted* and *distracted*, a misapplied attention to present objects, or to such objects as do not demand attention. An *absent* man never has his body and mind in the same place; the *abstracted* man is lost in thinking; a man who is easily *diverted* seeks to take an interest in every passing object; a *distracted* man is unable to think properly of anything: it may be good to be sometimes *diverted*. It is bad at any time to be *distracted*, particularly when it arises from passion.

ABSOLUTE, DESPOTIC, ARBITRARY, TYRANNICAL. *Absolute*, in Latin *absolutus*, participle of *absolvo*, signifies absolved or set at liberty from all restraint as it regards persons; unconditional, unlimited, as it regards things. *Despotic*, from *despot*, in Greek δεσπότης, a master or lord (the same root appears in the word *potent*), implies being like a lord, uncontrolled. *Arbitrary*, in French *arbitraire*, from the Latin *arbitror*, act as an umpire, decide, implies independence of judgment and will. *Tyrannical* signifies being like a tyrant.

Absolute power is independent of and superior to all other power: an *absolute* monarch is uncontrolled not only by men, but things; he is above all law except what emanates from himself. When this absolute power is assigned to any one according to the constitution of a government, it is *despotic*. *Despotic* power is therefore something less than *absolute* power; a prince is *absolute* of himself; he is *despotic* by the consent of others. In the early ages of society monarchs were *absolute*, and among the Eastern nations they still retain the *absolute* form of government, though much limited by established usage. In the more civilized stages of society the power of *despots* has been considerably restricted by prescribed laws, in so much that *despotism* is now classed among the regular forms of government.

Absolute is a term of a general application in the sense of *absolved* or freed from all control or limit; in this sense God is said to be absolute. Sometimes it is applied either to the power itself or to the exercise of power, as *absolute* rule or dominion; *despotic* is likewise applied to the exercise of the power as well as the power itself, as *despotic* sway; *arbitrary* and *tyrannical* are used only in this last application: the latter is always taken in a bad sense, the former sometimes in an indifferent sense. With *arbitrariness* is associated the idea of caprice and selfishness. With *tyranny* is associated the idea of oppression and injustice. Among the Greeks the word τύραννος, a tyrant, implied no more than what we now understand by *despot*, or, more properly, one who gained the supreme power in a republic; but from the natural abuse of such power, it has acquired the signification now attached to it, namely, of exercising power to the injury of another. If *absolute* power come into the hands of any one man or body of men, it is fair to expect that it will be used arbitrarily. In *despotic* governments the *tyrannical* proceedings of the subordinate officers are often more intolerable than those of the prince.

ABSOLUTION. See FORGIVE.

ABSOLVE, ACQUIT. *Absolve*, in Latin *absolvo*, is compounded of *ab*, from, and *solvere*, to loose, signifying to loose from that with which one is bound. *Acquit*, in French *acquitter*, is compounded of the intensive syllable *ac* or *ad*, and *quit, quitter*, from Latin *quietus*, quiet, signifying to make easy by the removal of a charge.

These terms imply the setting free from guilt or its consequences. *Absolving* may sometimes be applied to offences against the laws of man, but more frequently to offences against God; *acquitting* applies solely to offences against man. The conscience is released by *absolution;* the body, goods, or reputation are set free by an *acquittal*.

See also FORGIVE.

Absolve, Acquit, Clear.—*Absolve* in this case, as distinguished from the former article, is extended to all matters affecting the conscience generally. *Acquit* and *clear*, in the sense of making *clear* or free from, are applied to everything which may call for blame, or the imputation of what is not right. A person may be *absolved* from his oath,

acquitted or pronounced quit of every charge, and *cleared* from every imputation.

ABSORB, SWALLOW UP, INGULF, ENGROSS, IMBIBE. *Absorb*, French *absorber*. Latin *absorbeo*, is compounded of *ab* and *sorbeo*, to sup up, in distinction from *swallow up*—the former denoting a gradual consumption; the latter, a sudden envelopment of the whole object. The excessive heat of the sun *absorbs* all the nutritious fluids of bodies, animal and vegetable. The gaming-table is a vortex in which the principle of every man is *swallowed up* with his estate. *Ingulf*, compounded of *in* and *gulf*, signifies to be enclosed in a great gulf, which is a strong figurative representation for being swallowed up. As it applies to grand and sublime objects, it is used only in the higher style.

Engross, which is compounded of the French words *en gros*, whole, signifies to purchase wholesale, so as to swallow up the profits of others. In the moral application therefore it is very analogous to *absorb*. The mind is *absorbed* in the contemplation of any subject when all its powers are so bent upon it as not to admit distraction. The mind is *engrossed* by any subject when the thoughts of it force themselves upon its contemplation to the exclusion of others which should engage the attention.

Absorb conveys the idea not only of taking from something, but also of taking to itself; *engross* conveys the idea of taking to itself, to the exclusion of others; a certain subject *absorbs* the faculties, and, metaphorically, the roots of plants *absorb* moisture; a person *engrosses* the conversation so that others cannot take part in it.

Absorb, and *imbibe*, from *in* and *bibo*, to drink, both imply the taking in by a gradual process; but the former includes the idea of being taken in so as to be lost, the latter that of being taken in so as to form a part of that by which it is received. So in the improper application, an idea *absorbs* the mind, and the mind *imbibes* the idea.

See also MONOPOLIZE.

ABSORBABLE. See ASSIMILABLE.

ABSTAIN, FORBEAR, REFRAIN. *Abstain*, in French *abstenir*, Latin *abstineo*, is compounded of *ab* or *abs*, from, and *tenere*, to keep, signifying to keep one's self from a thing. *Forbear* is compounded of the preposition for, or from, and the verb to bear or carry, signifying to carry or take one's self from a thing. *Refrain*, in French *refréner*, Latin *refræno*, is compounded of *re*, back, and *frænum*, a bridle, signifying to keep back as it were by a bridle, to bridle in.

All these terms imply the omission to do anything, but vary in the circumstances and in the motives for the omission. To *abstain* is the general term, to *forbear* and *refrain* are particular modes of *abstaining*. *Abstaining* is an act that may require no self-denial, nor oppose any inclination; *forbearing* and *refraining* both imply a certain degree of opposition to the will or inclination, the latter much more than the former. We *abstain* from doing indifferent things from motives of convenience, as to *abstain* from speaking upon a particular subject, or we *abstain* from important matters from a sense of duty, as "to *abstain* from the appearance of evil." We *forbear* from prudence or duty to do that which we have motives for doing; as we *forbear* to do an injury though in return for an injury. We *refrain*, from the same motives, from doing that which we are strongly inclined or impelled to do, as to *refrain* from expressing the feelings of the moment.

These words are often coupled with a negative, to show the inability of the agent to omit doing a thing, as when it is said, "I cannot *abstain* from the gratification," or "I cannot *forbear* mentioning," etc., or "she was so affected that she could not *refrain*" from tears.

Abstaining as a religious duty is mostly said of indulgences as to food or otherwise which are prohibited; as it is the part of the Mohammedan faith to *abstain* from wine; *forbearing* is mostly said of that which concerns others. Every one is too liable to offend, not to have motives for *forbearing* to deal harshly with the offences of others; for being patient, indulgent, long-suffering.

Abstinence, Fast, Abstinent, Sober, Abstemious, Temperate.—*Abstinence* is a general term, applicable to any ob-ject from which we abstain; *fast* is a species of *abstinence*, namely, an *abstaining* from food. The general term is likewise used in the particular sense, to imply a partial *abstinence* from particular food; but *fast* signifies an abstinence from food altogether.

Abstinent respects everything that acts on the senses, and in a limited sense applies particularly to solid food. *Sober*, from the Latin *sobrius*, compounded of *so* or *se*, expressing separation (cf. *se* in separation) and *ebrius*, drunk, implies an abstinence from excessive drinking. *Abstemious*, from the Latin *abstemius*, compounded of *abs* and *temetum*, wine, implies the abstaining from wine or strong liquor in general. *Temperate*, in Latin *temperatus*, participle of *tempero*, to moderate or regulate, implies a well-regulated abstinence in all manner of sensual indulgence.

The first of the last four terms is generic, the rest specific. We may be *abstinent* without being *sober*, *sober* without being *abstemious*, and all together without being *temperate*. An *abstinent* man does not eat or drink as much as he could enjoy; a *sober* man may drink much without being affected; an *abstemious* man drinks nothing strong; a *temperate* man enjoys all in a due proportion. A particular passion may cause us to be *abstinent* either partially or totally; *sobriety* may often depend upon the strength of the constitution, or be prescribed by prudence: necessity may dictate *abstemiousness*, but nothing short of a well-disciplined mind will enable us to be *temperate*.

ABSTRACT, SEPARATE, DISTINGUISH. *Abstract*, see ABRIDGE; ABSENT. *Separate*, in Latin *separatus*, participle of *separo*, is compounded of *se*, apart, and *parare*, to dispose, signifying to put things asunder, or at a distance from each other. *Distinguish*, in French *distinguer*, Latin *distinguo*, is compounded of the separative preposition *dis* and a root which appears in the Greek στίγγω, prick, and in the English *sting*, *stick*, etc. It may signify the giving of different marks to things, by which they may be known from each other.

Abstract, as compared with the other terms, is used in the moral sense only;

separate mostly in a physical sense: *distinguish* either in a moral or physical sense; we *abstract* what we wish to regard particularly and individually; we *separate* what we wish not to be united; we *distinguish* what we wish not to confound. The mind performs the office of *abstraction* for itself; *separating* and *distinguishing* are exerted on external objects. Arrangements, place, time, and circumstances serve to *separate:* the ideas formed of things, the outward marks attached to them, the qualities attributed to them, serve to *distinguish.* By the operation of *abstraction* the mind creates for itself a multitude of new ideas; in the act of *separation* bodies are removed from each other by distance of place; in the act of *distinguishing* objects are discovered to be similar or dissimilar. Qualities are *abstracted* from the subjects in which they are inherent; countries are *separated* by mountains or seas; their inhabitants are *distinguished* by their dress, language, or manners. The mind is never less *abstracted* from one's friends than when *separated* from them by immense oceans; it requires a keen eye to *distinguish* objects that bear a great resemblance to each other. Volatile persons easily *abstract* their minds from the most solemn scenes to fix them on trifling objects that pass before them: an unsocial temper leads some men to *separate* themselves from all their companions: an absurd ambition leads others to *distinguish* themselves by their eccentricities.

See also ABRIDGMENT.

Abstracted, Abstract, Abstraction, Alienation, Estrangement.—*Abstracted,* as in the former case (see ABSENT), is properly applied to persons or things personal. *Abstract,* which is but a contraction of the former, is most commonly used to denote the qualities of things. A person is said to be *abstracted* who is in a state of *abstraction;* or a person may lead an *abstracted* life or course of life, or follow an *abstracted* theory, when the mind is altogether *abstracted* from external or sensible objects; a thing is said to be *abstract* which is formed by the operation of *abstraction* or *abstracted* thinking, as an *abstract* idea, which is *abstracted* or separated by the mind from the ob-

jects to which they belong or inhere; whiteness is an *abstract* idea, because it is conceived in the mind *abstracted* from snow, a wall, or any other substance that is white.

Abstraction expresses the state of being abstracted as to one's mind or person from any object generally. *Alienation,* the state of being alienated as to one's affections from others. *Estrangement,* the state of being a stranger is unknown to others. *Abstraction* expresses less than *alienation* or *estrangement;* it is simply the abstaining to take a part with others in any matter, as an *abstraction* from the world, its cares, pursuits, and pleasures. *Alienation* and *estrangement* both suppose an altered state of mind toward any object; *alienation* is where the heart and affections become alien or strange to that on which they have been or ought to be fixed; *estrangement* is where the person becomes distant from that with which one has been or ought to be intimate. One is said to be *abstracted* from the thing, but *alienated* or *estranged* from the person or the thing.

See also ABSENT.

ABSURD. See FARCICAL; IRRATIONAL.

ABUNDANT. See PLENTIFUL.

ABUSE, MISUSE, *Abuse,* in Latin *abusus,* participle of *abutor,* compounded of *ab,* from, and *utor,* to use, signifies to use away or wear away with using; in distinction from *misuse,* which signifies to use amiss.

Everything is *abused* which receives any sort of injury; it is *misused* if not used at all, or turned to a wrong use. Young people are too prone to *abuse* books for want of setting a proper value on their contents; they do not always avoid *misusing* them in their riper years, when they read for amusement only instead of improvement. Money is *abused* when it is clipped or its value any way lessened; it is *misused* when it is spent in excess and debauchery.

Abuse, Invective.—*Abuse* is here taken in the metaphorical application for ill-treatment of persons by the use of harsh words. *Invective,* from the Latin *inveho,* signifies to bear upon or, in modern slang, to "sail into." Harsh and unseemly censure is the idea common to these terms; but the former is employed more properly against the person, the latter against the thing. *Abuse* is addressed to the individual, and mostly by word of mouth; *invective* is communicated mostly by writing. *Abuse* is dictated by anger, which throws off all constraint and violates all decency; *invective* is dictated by party spirit, or an intemperate warmth of feeling in matters of opinion. *Abuse* is always resorted to by the vulgar in their private quarrels; *invective* is the ebullition of zeal and ill-nature in public concerns. The more rude and ignorant the man, the more liable he is to indulge in *abuse;* the more restless and opinionated the partisans, whether in religion or politics, the more ready he is to deal in *invective.*

ABUSIVE. See REPROACHFUL.

ABUTTING. See SALIENT.

ABYSS. See GULF.

ACADEMIC, CLASSIC, SCHOLASTIC, PEDANTIC. These words all refer to formal learning, but there is a difference in their origin and their application. *Academic* is derived from Greek ἀκαδημέια, the name of the garden or grove where Plato taught. It referred at first to Plato's school, and then became a general designation. *Academic*, therefore, means according to the methods of the schools, and is sometimes used in a good sense with reference to the life of the scholar in the universities, and sometimes in a derogatory sense to characterize that which merely originates in books, and is unrelated to practical experience. *Classic,* from Latin *classis,* meant originally of the highest class, and referred especially to the works of the Greek and Latin authors as being the highest types of literature. It is usually contrasted with *modern* and *natural,* as *academic* is contrasted with *practical.* In a general way, therefore, it is associated with the idea conveyed in *academic,* though not strictly synonymous with it. *Scholastic,* Latin *scholasticus* (from Greek σχολάζειν. to devote one's leisure to learning, from σχολή, leisure), refers especially to the scholars of the Middle Ages, called the *scholastic*

philosophers. It means characterized by the methods of the schools, with special reference to logical procedure and minute analysis. *Pedantic,* from Italian *pedante,* a schoolmaster or *pedagogue,* comes from Greek παιδεύειν, to instruct youth, and means characteristic of the schoolmaster. It is used in a derogatory sense to characterize barren learning.

ACADEMY. See SCHOOL.

ACCEDE. See AGREE.

ACCELERATE. See HASTEN.

ACCENT. See STRESS.

ACCEPT. See TAKE.

ACCEPTABLE, GRATEFUL, WELCOME. *Acceptable* signifies worthy to be accepted. *Grateful,* from the Latin *gratus,* pleasing, signifies altogether pleasing; it is that which recommends itself. The *acceptable* is a relative good; the *grateful* is positive; the former depends upon our external condition, the latter on our feelings and taste; a gift is *acceptable* to a poor man, which would be refused by one less needy than himself; harmonious sounds are always *grateful* to a musical ear.

Welcome signifies come well or in season for us. *Acceptable* and *welcome* both apply to external circumstances, and are therefore relatively employed; but the former is confined to such things as are offered for our choice, the latter refers to whatever happens according to our wishes; we may not always accept that which is *acceptable,* but we shall never reject that which is *welcome;* it is an insult to offer anything by way of a gift to another which is not *acceptable;* it is a *grateful* task to be the bearer of *welcome* intelligence to our friends.

Acceptance, Acceptation. — Though both derived from the verb *accept,* these terms have this difference, that the former is employed to express the active sense of the verb, the latter the passive sense. *Acceptance* is the act of accepting, *acceptation* the state of being accepted, as the *acceptance* of a favor lays a person under an obligation. A book, or whatever else is offered to us, may be worthy of our *acceptance* or not; a word acquires its *acceptation* from the manner in which it is generally accepted by the learned.

ACCESS. See APPROACH.

ACCESSION. See INCREASE.
ACCESSORY. See ABETTOR.

ACCIDENT, CHANCE. *Accident*, in Latin *accidens*, from *ad* and *cadens*, falling, and *chance* (in French *chance*, also connected with *cadens*), both signify falling out (cf. English *befall*)—*i. e.*, without any design; but the former, by the force of the *ac* or *ad*, signifies falling out at a given time, or under given circumstances; *chance*, on the other hand, signifies falling out without any qualification or restriction. Both may be employed to denote either the manner or cause of things happening, or the things themselves that so happen; in the first sense, *accident* and *chance* may be used indifferently in the colloquial expressions to happen by *chance* or by *accident*, but otherwise *accident* is used only in respect to particular events as, it was pure *accident;* but *chance* is employed to denote a hidden senseless cause of things, as opposed to a positive intelligent cause. Atheists ascribe all things to *chance;* whatever happens by secondary causes hidden from our view we are accustomed to ascribe to *chance*, which is only a mode of confessing our ignorance as to how it happens.

When taken for the thing that happens, *accident* is said ordinarily of things that have been; *chance* of things that are to be. That is an *accident* which is done without intention; that is a *chance* which cannot be brought about by the use of means. It is an *accident* when a house falls; it is a *chance* when and how it may fall. *Accidents* cannot be prevented; *chances* cannot be calculated upon. *Accidents* may sometimes be remedied; *chances* can never be controlled. *Accidents* give rise to sorrow; they mostly occasion mischief: *chances* give rise to hope; they often produce disappointment; it is wise to dwell upon neither.

Sometimes *chance* is used without reference to time for any fortuitous event, and in that case it is more expressive than the word *accident*. The term *accident* may likewise sometimes be taken for what may happen in the future.

See also EVENT.

Accident, Contingency, Casualty, Accidental, Incidental, Casual, Contingent.

—*Accident* (see above). *Contingency*, in French *contingence*, Latin *contingens*, participle of *contingo*, compounded of *con*, together, and *tangere*, to touch one another, signifies the falling out or happening together, or the thing that happens in conjunction with another. *Casualty*, in French *casualité*, from the Latin *casualis*, and *cado*, to fall or happen, signifies the thing that happens in the course of events.

All these words imply whatever takes place independently of our intentions. *Accidents* express more than *contingencies;* the former comprehend events with their causes and consequences; the latter respect collateral actions, or circumstances appended to events; *casualties* have regard simply to circumstances. *Accidents* are frequently occasioned by carelessness, and *contingencies* by trivial mistakes; but *casualties* are altogether independent of ourselves. The overturning of a carriage is an *accident;* our situation in a carriage at the time is a *contingency*, which may occasion us to be more or less hurt; the passing of any one at the time is a *casualty*. We are all exposed to the most calamitous *accidents*, and our happiness or misery depends upon a thousand *contingencies;* the best-concerted schemes may be thwarted by *casualties*, which no human foresight can prevent.

Accidental, see under ACCIDENT. *Incidental*, from *incident*, in Latin *incidens* and *incido*, or *in*, on, and *cadere*, to fall upon, signifies belonging to a thing by chance. *Casual*, see CASUALTY above. *Contingent*, see CONTINGENCY above.

Accidental is opposed to what is designed or planned; *incidental* to what is premeditated; *casual* to what is constant and regular; *contingent* to what is definite and fixed. A meeting may be *accidental*, an expression *incidental*, a look, expression, etc., *casual*, an expense or circumstance *contingent*. We do not expect what is *accidental;* we do not suspect or guard against what is *incidental;* we do not heed what is *casual;* we are not prepared for what is *contingent*. Many of the most fortunate and important occurrences in our lives are *accidental;* many remarks, seemingly *incidental*, do in reality conceal a settled intent; a *casual* remark in the course of conversation will sometimes make a stronger impression on the minds of children than the most eloquent and impressive discourse or repeated counsel; in the prosecution of any plan we ought to be prepared for the numerous *contingencies* which we may meet with to interfere with our arrangements.

ACCLAMATION. See APPLAUSE.

ACCLIMATE. See NATURALIZE.

ACCOMMODATE. See FIT.

ACCOMMODATOR, ASSISTANT, HELPER. *Accommodator*, from the Latin *accommodatus* or *accommodo*, that from *ad*, to, and *commodo*, to adapt, signifies, literally, one who accommodates another, who adapts himself or herself to the wishes of another. While the accommodation may be rendered in any desired direction, the term *accommodator* has recently taken on a new application, and now implies a man or woman who makes a business of hiring out by the hour or day to render whatever assistance or help a housewife may require.

Assistant (for the derivation see *assist* under HELP) has a less specialized meaning. It designates any one whose office it is to aid another in his work—*assistant* secretary, *assistant* editor, *assistant* to the president, etc. *Helper* is more colloquial and informal. We speak of the helpers in any regularly organized business office as *assistants*, but an assistant in certain household duties is often called a "mother's *helper*," and country people speak of their "hired *help*" rather than of their "hired *assistants*."

ACCOMPANIMENT, COMPANION, CONCOMITANT. *Accompaniment* is properly a collective term to express what goes in company, and is applied only to things; *companion*, which also signifies what is in the company, is applied either to persons or to things. *Concomitant*, from the intensive syllable *con* and *comes*, a companion, implies what is attached to an object, or goes in its train, and is applied only to things.

When said in relation to things, *accompaniment* implies a necessary connection, *companion* an incidental connection; the former is as a part to a whole, the latter is as one whole to another; the *accompaniment* belongs to the thing accompanied, inasmuch as it serves to render it more or less complete; the *companion* belongs to the thing accompanied, inasmuch as they correspond: in this manner singing is an *accompaniment* to instrumental music; subordinate ceremonies are the *accompaniments* in any solemn service; but a picture may be the *companion* of another picture from their fitness to stand together. A *concomitant* is as much of an appendage as the *accompaniment*, but it is applied only to moral objects; thus morality is a *concomitant* to religion.

ACCOMPANY, ATTEND, ESCORT. *Accompany*, Old French *companie*, Low Latin *companiem*, is compounded of *con*, with, and *panis*, bread, and signifies the breaking of bread together, hence friendly intercourse and society. *Accompany* is compounded of *ad*, to, and *companiem*, and hence means to give one's society *to* another. *Attend*, in French *attendre*, compounded of *ad* and *tendere*, to tend or incline toward, signifies to direct one's notice or care toward any object. *Escort*, in French *escorter*, from the Latin *ex* and *corrigo* (set right or correct), meant to guide in the right direction, and referred especially to the band of armed attendants delegated to guide a traveler through a dangerous country.

We *accompany* those with whom we wish to go; we *attend* those whom we wish to serve; we *escort* those whom we are called upon to protect or guard. We *accompany* our equals, we *attend* our superiors, and *escort* superiors or inferiors. The desire of pleasing or being pleased actuates in the first case; the desire of serving or being served, in the second case; the fear of danger or the desire of security, in the last place. One is said to have a numerous *company*, a crowd of *attendants*, and a strong *escort;* but otherwise one person only may *accompany* or *attend*, though several are wanting for an *escort*. Friends *accompany* each other in their excursions; a servant *attends* his master on a journey; a strong *escort* is necessary in traveling through unfrequented and dangerous roads.

Accompany and *attend* may likewise be said of things as well as persons.

In this case the former is applied to what goes with an object so as to form a part of it; the latter to that which follows an object as a dependent upon it. Pride is often *accompanied* by meanness, and *attended* with much inconvenience to the possessor.

ACCOMPLICE. See ABETTOR; CONFEDERATE.

ACCOMPLISH, EFFECT, EXECUTE, ACHIEVE. *Accomplish*, in French *accomplir*, is compounded of the intensive syllable *ac* or *ad*, and *complir*, in Latin *compleo*, fill to the top, signifying to finish entirely. *Effect*, in Latin *effectus*, participle of *efficio*, compounded of *ex*, out of or up, and *facere*, to make, signifies to make until nothing remains to be done. (Compare the colloquial phrase "How did you *make out* with it?") *Execute*, in Latin *executus*, participle of *exsequor*, compounded of *ex* and *sequor*, follow, signifies to carry through to the end. (Compare the business slang *"follow-up* methods," etc.) *Achieve*, in French *achever*, from the phrase *venir à chef*, Latin *ad caput venire*, come to a head, expresses the same meaning by another and, to us also, a familiar metaphor.

To *accomplish* is properly a mode of effecting, namely, to effect completely, or to the utmost extent proposed; to *accomplish* an object, therefore, signifies more than simply to *effect* a purpose, both as to the thing aimed at and the means employed in bringing it about. Extraordinary means are requisite for *accomplishing*, and ordinary means for *effecting*. To *accomplish* is properly said of that which a person sets before himself; but to *effect, execute*, and *achieve* do not relate to the views of the person acting, but to the thing brought about. To *effect* expresses less than *execute* or *achieve;* whatever is brought about or into effect is *effected;* what is *executed* is complicated in its nature, as to *execute* a design or project; what is *achieved* is grand, as to *achieve* an enterprise. Practical abilities are requisite for *effecting*, skill for *executing*, spirit and talent for *achieving*. Some persons are always striving to attain an end without even *accomplishing* what they propose. It is the part of wisdom to suit the means to the end when we have any scheme to *effect*. Those who are readiest in forming projects are not always the fittest for carrying them into *execution*. That ardor of character which impels to the *achievement* of arduous undertakings belongs but to very few. We should never give up what we have the least chance of *accomplishing*, if it be worth the labor; nor pursue any plan which affords us no prospect of *effecting* what we wish; nor undertake what we do not feel ourselves competent to *execute*, particularly when there is anything extraordinary to *achieve*.

See also FULFIL.

Accomplished, Perfect, Accomplishment, Perfection.—These epithets express an assemblage of all the qualities suitable to the subject; and mark the qualification in the highest degree. *Accomplished* refers only to the artificial refinements of the mind; *perfect* is said of things in general, whether natural or artificial, mental or corporeal.

An acquaintance with modern languages and the ornamental branches of the arts and sciences constitutes a person *accomplished;* the highest possible degree of skill in any art constitutes a man a *perfect* artist.

An *accomplishment* is acquired; but a *perfection* is either acquired or natural.

See also QUALIFICATION.

ACCORD. See AGREE; TALLY.

ACCORDANCE. See MELODY.

ACCORDANT. See CONSONANT.

ACCORDINGLY. See THEREFORE.

ACCOST, SALUTE, ADDRESS, GREET, HAIL, WELCOME. *Accost*, in French *accoster*, is compounded of *ad*, and the Latin *costa*, a rib or side, signifying to come by the side of a person. *Salute*, in Latin *saluto*, from *salus*, health, signifies to bid good-speed. *Address*, in French *adresser*, compounded of *ad* and *dresser*, from the Low Latin *drictus*, a contracted form of *directus*, straight, signifies to direct one's discourse to a person.

See also under ABILITY.

To *accost* and *salute* are said of persons on their first meeting; *address* may be said of those who direct their discourse to others at any time. The leading idea of *accost* is that of speaking to a person on coming up to him; *salute* is to notice a person, which may be by words or otherwise; that of *address* is to direct one's words to the individual, which may either be personally or by writing. *Accosting* is an act of familiarity not warranted by anything but an intimate acquaintance, or for purposes of business; *saluting* is an act of courtesy between friends which cannot be dispensed with; *addressing* is a matter of convenience or discretion.

Greet, Anglo-Saxon *gretan*, to visit or address, implies a verbal and friendly salute between equals, conveying a good and kind wish. *Hail*, from *heal* and *health*, denotes a wish for the health and long life of the person addressed, which was a customary form of address among the Eastern nations on approaching their sovereign; the word is now used to denote a similar expression on solemn occasions, particularly by the poets. *Welcome* denotes an expression of good wishes and kind regards on a person's first arrival; it is therefore confined to strangers or those who have been absent for a time. See also under ACCEPTABLE.

ACCOUNT, RECKONING, BILL. *Account*, compounded of *ad* and *count*, signifies to count to a person; an account is the thing so counted. *Reckoning*, from the verb to *reckon*, signifies the thing reckoned up. *Bill*, Low Latin *billa*, is derived from Latin *bulla*, a sealed writing fastened with a *bulla* or a round seal like a knob, knob being the original meaning of the word. (The same root appears in the words *bulletin*, Papal *bull*, *billet-doux*, etc.) These words, which are very similar in signification, may frequently be substituted for one another.

Account is the generic, the others the specific terms; a *reckoning* and *bill* is an *account*, though not always *vice versa;* *account* expresses the details, with the sum of them counted up; *reckoning* implies the register and notation of the things to be reckoned up; *bill* denotes the details, with their particular charges. An *account* should be correct, containing neither more nor less than is proper; a *reckoning* should be explicit, leaving nothing unnoticed as to dates and names; a *bill* should be fair. We speak of keeping an *account*, of coming to a *reckoning*, of sending in a *bill*. Customers have an *account* with

their tradespeople; masters have a *reckoning* with their workpeople; tradesmen send in their *bills* at stated periods.

Account, from the extensive use of the term, is applicable to everything that is noted down, the particulars of which are considered worthy of notice, individually or collectively: merchants keep their *accounts;* an *account* is taken at the Custom-House of all that goes in and out of the kingdom; an *account* is taken of all transactions, of the weather, of natural phenomena, and whatever is remarkable. *Reckoning*, as a particular term, is more partial in its use; it is mostly confined to the dealings of men with one another; in which sense it is superseded by the preceding term, and now serves to express only an explanatory enumeration, which may be either verbal or written. *Bill*, as implying something charged or engaged, is used not only in a mercantile, but a legal sense; hence, we speak of a *bill* of lading, a *bill* of parcels, a *bill* of exchange, a *bill* of indictment, or a *bill* in Parliament, Congress, or a Legislature. See also RECKON; SAKE.

Account, Narrative, Description.— *Account* is the most general of these terms; whatever is noted as worthy of remark is an *account*. *Narrative*, from *narrate*, in Latin *narratus*, from *narus* or *gnarus*, knowing, signifies the thing made known. *Description*, from *describe*, in Latin *describo*, from *de*, down, and *scribere*, to write, signifies the thing written down.

Account has no reference to the person giving the account; a *narrative* must have a narrator; a *description* must have a describer. An *account* may come from one or several quarters, or no specified quarter; but a *narrative* and *description* bespeak themselves as the production of some individual. *Accounts* from the armies are anxiously looked for in time of war; he suddenly broke off his *narrative;* his book is full of *descriptions*.

An *account* may be given of political events, domestic occurrences, or natural phenomena, but more particularly of matters of temporary and immediate interest; it may be true or false; a *narrative* is mostly personal, respecting the proceedings, accidents, or adventures of individuals; it may be real or fictitious; a *description* does not so much embrace occurrences as local circumstances, properties, and characteristics; it is either correct or otherwise.

ACCOUNTABLE, See Answerable.

ACCUMULATE. See Absorb; Acquire; Collect; Gain; Gather; Heap.

ACCURATE, Exact, Precise. *Accurate*, in French *accurate*, Latin *accuratus*, participle of *accuro*, compounded of the intensive *ad* and *curare*, to take care of, signifies done with great care. *Exact*, in French *exacte*, Latin *exactus*, participle of *exigere*, to finish or complete, denotes the quality of completeness, the absence of defect. *Precise*, in French *précis*, Latin *præcisus*, participle of *præcidere*, to cut by rule after the manner of carpenters, signifies the quality of doing by rule.

Accurate refers to the care bestowed upon any matter to make it what it ought to be; *exact* and *precise* simply denote the quality of the thing, the former implying completeness, the latter nicety as to the manner of executing anything. From this difference in their meaning arises a difference in their application; a painting, on examination or on observation, is more properly said to be *accurate;* a model, figure, or measure, to be *exact;* a line, a rule, or a form, to be *precise.*

These epithets rise in sense upon each other, *exact* signifying more than *accurate*, and *precise* a greater degree of minuteness than either. With this distinction they may be applied to the same or similar objects: a description or view may be *accurate* and *exact*, but in the former case it is only just as far as it goes, in the latter it is fuller of particulars and details.

In denoting moral qualities or habits, *accuracy* may be applied to whatever men attempt to do; *exactness* to matters of economy, prudence, and duty; *precision*, in regard to manners, modes, and forms. *Accuracy* is indispensable in either business or science, but particularly in commercial and legal transactions; *exactness* is requisite in the payment of debts and the observance of all obligations. Some men may be very *accurate* in their particular line who are not very *exact* in fulfilling their engagements. In some cases, where great results may flow from trifling causes, the greatest *precision* becomes requisite; we may, however, be too *precise* when we dwell on unimportant particulars or adhere too tenaciously to forms and modes, but we never can be too *accurate* or *exact;* hence the epithet *precise* is sometimes taken for affectedly *exact.* A man may be *precise* in his dress who is not remarkable either for *accuracy* or *exactness* in his general conduct. A time or a period is said to be *exact*, an hour, a moment, or instant, *precise;* an expression *accurate;* the meaning of a word *precise.*

ACCUSATION. See Complaint.

ACCUSE, Charge, Impeach, Arraign. *Accuse*, in Latin *accuso*, compounded of *ad* and *causa*, a cause or trial, signifies to bring to trial. *Charge*, like *cargo*, is derived from Low Latin *carrico*, to load a car (Latin *carrus*). *Impeach*, in French *empêcher*, to hinder or disturb, compounded of *in* and *pes*, the foot, signifies to entangle the feet in anything. *Arraign*, Old French *aranier*, *areisnier*, from Latin *ad* and *ratio*, reason, meant to reason against, to bring a formal charge against another.

The idea of asserting something to the prejudice of another is common to these terms; but *accuse* is said of acts, *charge* of moral qualities constituting the character: we *accuse* a person of murder; we *charge* him with dishonesty. *Accuse* is properly a formal action; *charge* is an informal action: criminals are *accused*, and their *accusation* is proved in a court of judicature to be true or false; any person may be *charged*, and the *charge* may be either substantiated or refuted in the judgment of a third person.

Impeach and *arraign* are both species of *accusing;* the former in application to statesmen and state concerns, the latter in regard to the general conduct or principles; with this difference, that he who *impeaches* only asserts the guilt, but does not determine it; but those who *arraign* also take upon themselves to decide: statesmen are *impeached* for misdemeanors in the administration of government: kings *arraign* governors of provinces and subordinate princes, and in this manner kings are sometimes *arraigned* before mock tribunals: our Saviour was *arraigned* before Pilate; and creatures in the madness of presumption *arraign* their Creator.

Accuse, Censure.—*Accuse,* see above. *Censure,* in French *censure,* in Latin *censura,* is derived from *censor,* a Roman magistrate who took cognizance of the morals and manners of the citizens, as also of the domestic arrangements of the city. It signifies not only the office of censor, but, in an extended sense, the act of blaming or punishing offenders against morality, which formed a prominent feature in his office.

To *accuse* is only to assert that which is prejudicial to another; to *censure* is to take the fault for granted. We *accuse* only to make known the offence, to provoke inquiry; we *censure* in order to inflict a punishment. An *accusation* may be false or true; a *censure* mild or severe. It is extremely wrong to *accuse* another without sufficient grounds; but still worse to *censure* him without the most substantial grounds. Every one is at liberty to *accuse* another of offences which he knows him for a certainty to have committed; but none can *censure* who are not authorized by their age or station.

ACHIEVE. See ACCOMPLISH.

ACHIEVEMENT. See DEED.

ACKNOWLEDGE, OWN, CONFESS, AVOW. The first of these terms, compounded of *a* and *knowledge,* implies to bring to knowledge, to make known. *Own* is a familiar figure, signifying to take to one's self, to make one's own; it is a common substitute for *confess. Confess,* in French *confesser,* Latin *confessus,* participle of *confiteor,* compounded of *con,* together, and *fateor,* I speak, signifies to impart to any one. *Avow,* in French *avouer,* Latin *advoveo,* signifies to vow or protest to any one.

These words all denote the making known to others what relates to one's self, or that in which one has taken a part; *acknowledge* is used in this general sense in a diversity of applications; the other terms are partially employed, and with various modifications in their meaning. *Acknowledge* and *own* are employed either in matters of indifference or those which are blameworthy; *con-*

c.e.s.—2

fess mostly in such matters as are criminal or in a high degree culpable. A person *acknowledges* that he was present, or *owns* that he assisted another, he *confesses* a theft, or *confesses* his guilt, or a sinner *confesses* his sins. To *acknowledge* and *own,* when applied to culpable matters, may either have respect to particular transactions or general characteristics, as to *acknowledge* or *own* the fact, to *acknowledge* or *own* one's weakness, fallibility, incapacity, etc.; to *confess* is mostly said of particular transactions, as to *confess* the crime laid to one's charge. To *acknowledge,* being a voluntary act, may be either by words or actions, or tacitly without any outward expression; *confessing,* on the other hand, being mostly called for in consequence of an interrogatory or the necessities of the party, must always be by express words.

To *acknowledge* and *own* also signify to admit that a thing belongs to one, but the former denotes only a general relationship, the latter a special ownership; with this distinction we may speak of *acknowledging* or *owning* a son; but we may likewise *acknowledge* many things which we cannot properly *own,* as to *acknowledge* a woman as one's *wife,* or any particular person as a prince, or any particular state as independent.

To *acknowledge, own,* and *confess* are all used in the sense of expressing one's mind or what passes in one's mind, in which application they are comparable with *avow.* In this case to *acknowledge* is most properly applied to matters of opinion, *own* to matters of feeling, although they may in many such cases be indifferently employed.

To *acknowledge* is to declare in a general manner one's assent to anything; to *confess* is to declare in a solemn manner one's assent to matters of faith; to *avow* is to declare the motives or reasons of one's actions, particularly such as might with more propriety be concealed; as to *acknowledge* the justness of a remark, to *confess* the faith, to *avow* one's motives, contempt, scorn, etc.

See also RECOGNIZE.

ACME. See ZENITH.

ACQUAINT. See INFORM.

ACQUAINTANCE. FAMILIARITY,

INTIMACY. *Acquaintance*, from *acquaint*, is derived from the Old French *acointer* (Latin *ad* and *cognitus*, from the verb *cognosco* which is cognate with the English *know* and has the same meaning); it signifies being known to another. *Familiarity* comes from *familiar*, in Latin *familiaris* and *familia* (from *famulus*, a servant), signifying known as one of the household. *Intimacy*, from Latin *intimus*, innermost, signifies known to the innermost recesses of the heart. These terms mark different degrees of closeness in the social intercourse; *acquaintance* expressing less than *familiarity*, and that less than *intimacy*.

Acquaintance springs from occasional intercourse; *familiarity* is produced by a daily intercourse, which wears off all constraint and banishes all ceremony; *intimacy* arises not merely from frequent intercourse, but unreserved communication. An *acquaintance* will be occasionally a guest; but one that is on terms of *familiarity* has easy access to our table; and an *intimate* likewise lays claim to a share, at least, of our confidence. An *acquaintance* with a person affords but little opportunity for knowing his character; *familiarity* puts us in the way of *seeing* his foibles, rather than his virtues; but *intimacy* enables us to appreciate his worth.

A simple *acquaintance* is the most desirable footing on which to stand with all persons, however deserving. If it have not the pleasures of *familiarity* or *intimacy*, it can claim the privilege of being exempted from their pains. "Too much *familiarity*," according to the old proverb, "breeds contempt." The unlicensed freedom which commonly attends *familiarity* affords but too ample scope for the indulgence of the selfish and unamiable passions. *Intimacies* begun in love often end in hatred, as ill-chosen friends commonly become the bitterest enemies. A man may have a thousand acquaintances, and not one whom he should make his *intimate*.

These terms may be applied to things as well as persons, in which case they bear a similar analogy. An *acquaintance* with a subject is opposed to entire ignorance upon it; *familiarity* with it is the consequence of frequent repetition; and *intimacy* of a steady and thorough research. In our intercourse with the world we become daily *acquainted* with fresh subjects to engage our attention. Some men have by extraordinary diligence acquired a considerable *familiarity* with more than one language and science; but few, if any, can boast of having possessed an *intimate acquaintance* with all the particulars of even one language or science. When we can translate the authors of any foreign language, we may claim an *acquaintance* with it; when we can speak or write it freely, we may be said to be *familiar* with it; but an *intimate acquaintance* comprehends a thorough critical *intimacy* with all the niceties and subtleties of its structure.

ACQUIESCE. See AGREE.

ACQUIRE, OBTAIN, GAIN, WIN, EARN. *Acquire*, Old French *acquérir*, Latin *acquiro*, is compounded of *ad*, to, and *quærere*, to seek, signifying to seek or get for one's self. *Obtain*, in French *obtenir*, Latin *obtineo*, is compounded of *ob*, near, and *tenere*, to hold, signifying to lay hold or secure within one's reach. *Gain* comes from French *gagne*, from a Teutonic root signifying a pasture, hence something to be desired among shepherd-people, hence success, profit. *Win* comes from Anglo-Saxon *winnan*, to fight or struggle, hence to succeed in a struggle. *Earn* comes from Anglo-Saxon *earnian*, allied to German *ernte*, a harvest.

The idea of getting is common to these terms, but the circumstances of the action vary. We *acquire* by our own efforts; we *obtain* by the efforts of others as well as ourselves; we *gain* or *win* by striving; we *earn* by labor. Talents and industry are requisite for *acquiring*; what we *acquire* comes gradually to us in consequence of the regular exercise of our abilities; in this manner, knowledge, honor, and reputation are *acquired*. Things are *obtained* by all means, honest or dishonest; whatever comes into our possession agreeable to our wishes is *obtained*; favors and requests are always *obtained*. Fortune assists in both *gaining* and *winning*; but particularly in the latter case; a subsistence, a superiority, a victory, or battle, is *gained*; a game or a prize in the lottery is *won*. A good constitution and full employment are all that is necessary for *earning* a livelihood. Fortunes are *acquired* after a course of years; they are *obtained* by inheritance, or *gained* in trade.

What is *acquired* is solid, and produces lasting benefit; what is *obtained* may often be injurious to one's health, one's interest, or one's morals: what is *gained* or *won* is often only a partial advantage, and transitory in its nature; it is *gained* or *won* only to be lost; what is *earned* serves sometimes only to supply the necessity of the moment; it is hardly got and quickly spent. Scholars *acquire* learning, *obtain* rewards, *gain* applause, and *win* prizes, which are often hardly earned by the loss of health.

Acquire, Attain.—To *acquire* is a progressive and permanent action. To *attain*, in Latin *attingo*, compounded of *ad* and *tango*, touch, signifies to touch the goal, to reach the end, and represents a perfect and finished action. We always go on *acquiring;* but we stop when we have *attained.* What is *acquired* is something got into one's possession; what is *attained* is the point arrived at. We *acquire* a language; we *attain* to a certain degree of perfection. By abilities and perseverance we may *acquire* a considerable fluency in speaking several languages; but we can scarcely expect to *attain* to the perfection of a native in any foreign language. Ordinary powers coupled with diligence will enable a person to *acquire* whatever is useful; but we cannot *attain* to superiority without extraordinary talents and determined perseverance. *Acquirements* are always serviceable; *attainments* always creditable.

Acquirement, Acquisition.—Two abstract nouns, from the same verb, denoting the thing acquired. *Acquirement* implies the thing acquired for and by ourselves; *acquisition*, that which is acquired for the benefit of one's self or another. People can expect to make but slender *acquirements* without a considerable share of industry; and without them they will be no *acquisition* to the community to which they have attached themselves. *Acquirement* respects

rather the exertions employed; *acquisition* the benefit or gain accruing. To learn a language is an *acquirement;* to gain a class or a degree, an *acquisition.* The *acquirements* of literature far exceed in value the *acquisitions* of fortune.

ACQUIT. See ABSOLVE.

ACRIMONY, TARTNESS, ASPERITY, HARSHNESS. These epithets are figuratively employed to denote sharpness of feeling corresponding to the quality in natural bodies. *Acrimony,* in Latin *acrimonia,* from *acer,* sharp, is the characteristic of garlic, mustard, and pepper, that is, a biting sharpness. *Tartness,* from *tart,* Anglo-Saxon *teart,* sharp, from *teran,* tear, is associated with the idea of *tearing* as *bitter* is associated with that of *biting.* *Asperity* is derived from the Latin *asper,* a word of uncertain etymology signifying rough. *Harshness* is the substantive corresponding to *harsh,* a Scandinavian word signifying rank, unpleasant to the taste, and denotes especially the sharp, rough taste of unripe fruit.

A quick sense produces *acrimony;* it is too frequent among disputants, who embitter each other's feelings. An acute sensibility, coupled with quickness of intellect, produces *tartness;* it is too frequent among females. *Acrimony* is a transient feeling that discovers itself by the words; *tartness* is an habitual irritability that mingles itself with the tone and looks. An *acrimonious* reply frequently gives rise to much ill-will; a *tart* reply is often treated with indifference, as indicative of the natural temper, rather than of any unfriendly feeling.

Asperity and *harshness* respect one's conduct to inferiors; the latter expresses a strong degree of the former. *Asperity* is opposed to mildness and forbearance; *harshness* to kindness. A reproof is conveyed with *asperity,* when the words and looks convey strong displeasure; a treatment is *harsh* when it wounds the feelings and does violence to the affections. Mistresses sometimes chide their servants with *asperity;* parents sometimes deal *harshly* with their children.

ACT, Do, MAKE. *Act,* in Latin *actus,* participle of *ago,* Greek ἄγω, drive or impel, signifies literally to move or put in motion. *Do*, in German *thun*, like the Greek τίθημι, signifies to put or put in order, to bring to pass. *Make*, Anglo-Saxon *macian*, corresponds to German *machen*, and is allied to *match*.

All these terms imply to exert a power in a given form and manner: *act*, which is the general term, conveys this general idea without any further qualification; the other terms convey this idea with modifications. We always *act* when we *do*, but we do not always *do* when we *act*. To *act* is applied either to persons or things, as a spring or a lock *acts;* to *do* applies in this sense to persons only. To *act* is also mostly intransitive or reflective, as to *act* well or ill in this or that manner; to *do* is always transitive, as to *do* right or wrong, to *do* one's duty.

One may either *act* a part or *do* one's part, which are essentially different things; to *act* a part is either really or fictitiously to *act* in any part; but to *do* our part is to *do* that which is allotted to us as our part or duty.

To *do* and to *make*, in regard to persons, are both used in the sense of voluntarily exerting a power to bring a thing to pass; but *do* applies to the ordinary business of life or what is *done* by a given rule, as to *do* a work, to *do* justice; *make* applies to that which is *done* by a particular contrivance or for a particular purpose, as to *make* a pen or a table, etc. What is *done* once may have been *done* before, and may be *done* again; but what is *made* is at once brought into existence, and, if it be *made* again, it can only be by imitation.

To *do* and to *make*, as applied to things, signify to cause; but the former is used only in the expressions to *do* good or harm, the latter is ordinarily used, to *make* room, to *make* a thing easy, etc.

Act, Work, Operate.—To *act* is to exert a simple power, or by simple means, as a wire *acts*. *Work*, Anglo-Saxon *wyrcan*, like the German *wirken*, etc., is to exert complex powers, or exert power by a gradual process. A machine *works*, but each of its parts is said to *act;* so beer *works*, and bread *works; acting* may be accompanied with no particular effect or change in the body that *acts*, but that which *works* mostly undergoes a change and also produces changes, as medicine, which *works* in the system. Sometimes *act* as well as *work* is taken in the sense of exerting a power upon other bodies and producing changes, as the sun *acts* on the plants.

To *work* and *operate* both imply to *act*, or exert a power in order to bring about some end or purpose; but *operate* is applied to matters of a general nature in science or morals, as a measure *operates*, or words may *operate* on the mind, or reasons may *operate* on the understanding. To *work* is mostly applied to familiar matters and particular objects, as the hand *works*, the head *works*, the brain *works; operate* is always intransitive.

As nouns, *action* implies either the act of acting or the thing done; *work*, the act or state of working, or what results from the *work*, as to go to *work* or be at *work*, the *work* of one's hands; *operation*, either to the act of operating, as the *operation* of thought or the *operation* of vegetation, or the mode of operating, as the *operations* of time are various.

See also DEAL.

Act, Action, Deed.—The words *act*, *action*, and *deed*, though derived from the preceding verbs, have an obvious distinction in their meaning. *Act*, in French *acte*, Latin *actum*, denotes the thing done. *Action*, in French *action*, Latin *actio*, signifies doing. *Act* is a single exercise of power, as an *act of* the will or an *act* of the mind, the *act* of walking, speaking, and the like; *action* a continued exercise of power, or a state of exercising power, as to be in *action*, as opposed to rest; the *action* of walking is agreeable in fine weather.

When these words are taken in the sense of the thing done, they admit of a similar distinction. An *act* is the single thing done, or what is done by a single effort, as that is your *act* or his *act;* an *action* may consist of more *acts* than one, or embrace the causes and consequences of the action, as a bold *action*, to judge of *actions*, etc.

Hence it is that the term *act* is more proper than *action* where it is so defined as to imply what is single and simple, as an *act* of authority, an *act* of government, an *act* of folly, and the like; but otherwise the word *action* is to be preferred where the moral conduct or character is in question. We may enumerate particular *acts* of a man's life, as illustrative of certain traits in his character, or certain circumstances in his life; but to speak at large of his *actions* would be to describe his character.

Act and *deed* are both employed for what is done; but *act* refers to the power exerted, and *deed* to the work performed; as a voluntary or involuntary *act*, a good or bad *deed*.

Act is mostly employed either in an abstract or familiar application; *deed* is employed for whatever men do in the business of life, particularly in those things which are extraordinary.

Acts are either public or private, of individuals or of bodies, as *acts* of government, *acts* of Parliament; *deeds* are always private, or what is done by men individually.

Acts are in their proper sense informal; but *deeds* may sometimes be formal instruments: when you speak of a thing as a man's *act* and *deed*, this is not tautology; it is his *act* as far as he and no one else *acts* in it, it is his *deed* as far as it is that which is done completely or is accomplished.

Action, Gesture, Gesticulation, Posture, Attitude.—*Action*, see derivation in preceding group of words; also BATTLE. *Gesture*, Low Latin *gestura*, Latin *gestus*, participle of *gero*, carry, signifies the manner of carrying one's body. *Gesticulation*, in Latin *gesticulatio*, comes from *gesticulor*, to make many gestures. *Posture*, in French *posture*, Latin *positura*, a position, comes from *positus*, participle of *pono*, signifying the manner of placing one's self. *Attitude*, in French *attitude*, Italian *attitudine*, is a doublet of *aptitude*, signifying a propriety in the disposition of one's body.

All these terms are applied to the state of the body; the three former indicating a state of motion, the two latter a state of rest. *Action* respects the movements of the body in general; *gesture* is an *action* indicative of some particular state of mind; *gesticulation* is a species of artificial *gesture*. Raising the arm is an *action;* bowing is a *gesture*. *Actions* may be ungraceful; *gestures* indecent. A suitable *action* some-

times gives great force to the words that are uttered; *gestures* often supply the place of language between people of different nations. *Actions* characterize a man as vulgar or well-bred; *gestures* mark the temper of the mind. There are many *actions* which it is the object of education to prevent from growing into habits; savages express the vehement passions of the mind by vehement *gestures* on every occasion, even in their amusements. An extravagant or unnatural *gesture* is termed a *gesticulation;* a sycophant, who wishes to cringe into favor with the great, deals largely in *gesticulation* to mark his devotion; a buffoon who attempts to imitate the *gestures* of another will use *gesticulation;* and the monkey who apes the *actions* of human beings does so by means of *gesticulations*.

Posture and *attitude* both imply a mode of placing the body, but the *posture* is either natural or assumed; the *attitude* is always assumed or represented: natural *postures* are those in which the body places itself for its own conveniences, as sitting, standing, or lying *postures*.

A *posture*, when assumed, may be distorted or ridiculous, to suit the humor of the party, as mountebanks put themselves into ridiculous *postures;* or they may be artfully contrived to improve the carriage of the body, as the *postures* of a dancing-master; and, in graver matters, a person may put himself in a *posture* of defence.

An *attitude* is assumed in order to display some grace of the body, or some affection or purpose of the mind, as to stand in a graceful *attitude*, to represent any one in the *attitude* of prayer.

These terms may be applied to things personified, with precisely the same distinction. They may also be applied figuratively to other objects besides the body, as an army assumes a menacing *attitude*, a critical *posture* of affairs.

Action, Agency.—*Action* is the effect; *agency* the cause. *Action* is inherent in the subject; *agency* is something exterior; it is, in fact, putting a thing into *action:* in this manner the whole world is in *action* through the *agency* of the Divine Being.

ACTIVE, DILIGENT, INDUSTRIOUS, ASSIDUOUS, LABORIOUS. *Active*, from the verb to *act*, implies a propensity to act, to be doing something without regard to the nature of the object. *Diligent*, in French *diligent*, Latin *diligens*, participle of *diligo*, to choose or like, implies an attachment to an object, and consequent attention to it. *Industrious*, in French *industrieux*, Latin *industrius*, from *indu*, for *in*, and *struere*, to build, make, or do, signifies an inward or thorough inclination to be engaged in some serious work. *Assiduous*, in Latin *assiduus*, is compounded of *ad* and *siduus*, from *sedere*, to sit, signifying to sit close to a thing. *Laborious*, in French *laborieux*, Latin *laboriosus*, from *labor*, signifies the inclination to labor.

We are *active* if we are only ready to exert our powers, whether to any end or not; we are *diligent* when we are active for some specific end; we are *industrious* when no time is left unemployed in some serious pursuit; we are *assiduous* if we do not leave a thing until it is finished; we are *laborious* when the bodily or mental powers are regularly employed in some hard labor. A man may be *active* without being *diligent*, since he may employ himself in what is of no importance; but he can scarcely be *diligent* without being *active*, since *diligence* supposes some degree of activity in one's application to a useful object. A man may be *diligent* without being *industrious*, for he may diligently employ himself about a particular favorite object without employing himself constantly in the same way; and he may be *industrious* without being *diligent*, since *diligence* implies a free exercise of the mental as well as corporeal powers; but *industry* applies principally to manual labor. *Activity* and *diligence* are, therefore, commonly the property of lively or strong minds, but *industry* may be associated with moderate talents. A man may be *diligent* without being *assiduous;* but he cannot be *assiduous* without being *diligent*, for *assiduity* is a sort of persevering *diligence*. A man may be *industrious* without being *laborious*, but not *vice versa;* for *laboriousness* is a severer kind of *industry*.

Active, Brisk, Agile, Nimble.—*Active*, see preceding group. *Brisk* is of ob-

scure origin, possibly Celtic. *Agile*, in Latin *agilis*, comes from the same verb as active, signifying a fitness, a readiness to act or move. *Nimble* comes from Anglo-Saxon *niman* (German *nehmen*), to take, implying a capacity "to take hold," to "catch on," as we say to-day. Compare the name *Nym*, in *Henry V*, signifying thief.

Activity respects one's transactions; *briskness* one's sports: men are *active* in carrying on business; children are *brisk* in their play. *Agility* refers to the light and easy carriage of the body in springing; *nimbleness* to its quick and gliding movements in running. A rope-dancer is *agile;* a female moves *nimbly*. *Activity* results from ardor of mind; *briskness* from vivacity of feeling: *agility* is produced by corporeal vigor and habitual strong exertion; *nimbleness* results from an habitual effort to move lightly.

See also KINETIC.

Active, Busy, Officious.—*Active*, same as in the preceding groups. *Busy*, Anglo-Saxon *bysig*, signifies to be actively engaged in some work. *Officious*, in French *officieux*, Latin *officiosus*, from *officium*, duty or service, signifies a propensity to perform some service or office.

Active respects the habit or disposition of the mind; *busy* and *officious*, either the disposition of the mind, or the employment of the moment: the former regards every species of employment; the latter only particular kinds of employment. An *active* person is ever ready to be employed; a person is *busy* when he is actually employed in any object; he is *officious* when he is employed for others. *Active* is always taken in a good, or at least an indifferent sense; it is opposed to lazy: *busy*, as it respects occupation, is mostly in a good sense; it is opposed to being at leisure; as it respects disposition, it is always in a bad sense; *officious* is seldom taken in a good sense; it implies being *busy* without discretion. To an *active* disposition nothing is more irksome than inaction; but it is not concerned to inquire into the utility of the action. It is better for a person to be *busy* than quite unemployed; but a *busy* person will employ himself about the concerns of others when he has none of his own sufficiently important to engage his attention; an *officious* person is as unfortunate as he is troublesome; when he strives to serve he has the misfortune to annoy.

ACTOR, AGENT. These terms vary according to the different senses of the verb from which they are drawn. *Actor* is used for one who either acts a part, or who represents the actions and characters of others, whether real or feigned.

Agent is, in the general sense, an active or acting being, one possessing and exerting the faculty of action, as a free *agent*, a moral *agent*. The *agent* is properly opposed to the patient in the physical world. *Agent* is also taken generally for whatever puts in motion.

Actor, Player, Performer.—The *actor* and *player* both perform on a stage; but the former is said in relation to the part that is acted, the latter to the profession that is followed. We may be *actors* occasionally, without being players professionally, but we may be *players* without deserving the name of *actors*. Those who personate characters for their amusement are *actors*, but not *players;* those who do the same for a livelihood are *players* as well as *actors;* hence we speak of a company of *players*, not *actors*. So, likewise, in the figurative sense, whoever acts a part real or fictitious, that is, on the stage of life, or the stage of a theatre, is an *actor;* but he only is a *player* who performs the fictitious part; hence the former is taken in a bad or good sense, according to circumstances.

The *player* is always taken in a less favorable sense, from the artificiality which attaches to his profession.

Performer signifies, in its most general sense, one that performs any act or part; but in a limited sense, one who performs a part in a public exhibition, whether as a singer, actor, dancer, or otherwise.

ACTUAL, REAL, POSITIVE. *Actual*, in French *actuel*, Latin *actualis*, from *actio*, a deed, signifies belonging to the thing done. *Real*, in French *réel*, Latin *realis*, from *res*, signifies belonging to the thing as it is. *Positive*, in French *positif*, Latin *positivus*, from *pono*, place or fix, signifies the state or quality of being fixed, established.

What is *actual* has proof of its existence within itself, and may be exposed to the eye; what is *real* may be satisfactorily proved to exist; and what is *positive* precludes the necessity of a proof. *Actual* is opposed to the suppositious, conceived or reported; *real* to the feigned, imaginary; *positive* to the uncertain, doubtful. Whatever is the condition of a thing for the time being is the *actual* condition; sorrows are *real* which flow from a substantial cause; proofs are *positive* which leave the mind in no uncertainty. The *actual* state of a nation is not to be ascertained by individual instances of poverty, or the reverse; there are but few, if any, *real* objects of compassion among common beggars; many *positive* facts have been related of the deception which they have practised. By an *actual* survey of human life, we are alone enabled to form just opinions of mankind; it is but too frequent for men to disguise their *real* sentiments, although it is not always possible to obtain *positive* evidence of their insincerity.

See also OBJECTIVE.

ACTUATE, IMPEL, INDUCE. *Actuate*, from the Latin *actum*, an action, implies to call into action. *Impel*, in Latin *impello*, is compounded of *in*, toward, and *pellere*, to drive, signifying to drive toward an object. *Induce*, in Latin *induco*, is compounded of *in*, in, and *ducere*, to lead, signifying to lead into an object.

One is *actuated* by motives, *impelled* by passions, and *induced* by reason or inclination. Whatever *actuates* is the result of reflection; it is a steady and fixed principle: whatever *impels* is momentary and vehement, and often precludes reflection: whatever *induces* is not vehement, though often momentary. One seldom repents of the thing to which one is *actuated;* as the principle, whether good or bad, is not liable to change: but we may frequently be *impelled* to measures which cause serious repentance: the thing to which we are *induced* is seldom of sufficient importance to call for repentance.

ACUTE, KEEN, SHREWD, SHARP. *Acute*, in French *aigu*, Latin *acutus*, associated with *acus*, a needle, signifies the quality of sharpness and pointedness peculiar to a needle. *Keen* in Anglo-Saxon *cene*, is related to the German *kühn*, bold, and signified originally energy and activity of spirit, hence quickness of mind. *Shrewd*, from the verb *shrewen*, to curse, beshrew, is from Anglo-Saxon *screawa*, a shrewmouse, whose bite was venomous, and is allied to the word *shrew*, a scolding woman. It meant malicious, cunning, sharp, in the double sense—sharp of temper, and sharp of mind and tongue —hence the modern significance.

In the natural sense, a fitness to pierce is predominant in the word *acute;* and that of cutting, or a fitness for cutting, in the word *keen*. The same difference is observable in their figurative acceptation. An *acute* understanding is quick at discovering truth in the midst of falsehood; it fixes itself on a single point with wonderful celerity: a keen understanding cuts or removes away the artificial veil under which the truth lies hidden from the view: a *shrewd* understanding is rather quicker at discovering new truths than at distinguishing truth from falsehood. *Acuteness* is requisite in speculative and abstruse discussions; *keenness* in penetrating characters and springs of action; *shrewdness* in eliciting remarks and new ideas. The *acute* man detects errors, and the *keen* man falsehoods; the *shrewd* man exposes follies. Arguments may be *acute*, reproaches *keen*, and replies or retorts *shrewd*. A polemic, or a lawyer, must be *acute*, a satirist *keen*, and a wit *shrewd*.

Sharp primarily signifies a thin edge or fine point; also artful, crafty, subtle. A pain, ache, or retort in conversation may be distressingly *sharp*. An unscrupulous person is often guilty of *sharp practice* in dealing with others. See also SHARP.

ACUTENESS. See GUMPTION; PENETRATION.

ADAGE. See AXIOM.

ADAPT. See FIT.

ADD, JOIN, UNITE, COALESCE. *Add*, in Latin *addo*, compounded of *ad* and *do*, to give or put, signifies to put one thing to another. *Join*, in French *joindre*, and Latin *jungo*, is in all probability connected with, if not derived

from, the Greek, ξεύγω, to yoke, that is, to set one thing in juxtaposition with another. *Unite*, from the Latin *unus*, one, signifies to make into one. *Coalesce*, in Latin *coalesco*, from *con*, together, and *alescere*, to grow, signifies to grow together.

We *add* by putting a part to any body so as to form a whole; we *join* by attaching two whole bodies to each other; we *unite* by putting two bodies to or into one another, so that they may become one body; things *coalesce* when their parts mingle together so as to form one substance. *Additions* may be made to whatever admits of becoming greater in size or quantity; a wing may be *added* to a building, or a house may be *added* to a row of houses; *junctions* may be made of any two bodies which can touch each other in any part; thus two houses may be *joined*, or two countries, lands, kingdoms, etc., may be *joined; unions* may be formed of any things which admit of being made into one so as to lose their individuality; as, if two houses be made into one, they may be said to be *united;* things may be said to *coalesce*, the minutest parts of which will readily fall into one another; a *coalition* is properly a complete *union*, and is applied to the natural process of bodies. *Adding* is opposed to subtracting or diminishing, *joining* to separating, *uniting* to dividing, and *coalescing* to falling asunder.

They preserve this distinction in their moral application. One virtue or perfection may be *added* to another; persons *join* in matrimony, trade, or other particular act; they *unite* in families, in mind, or modes of living; qualities may be *joined* with others in the same substance, without any necessary connection between them; they are *united* when they belong to or are intimately connected with each other; nations *coalesce* when they adopt the same language, laws, and manners; parties *coalesce* when they lay aside their differences and *unite*.

See also INCREASE.

ADDICT, DEVOTE, APPLY. *Addict*, from *addico*, or *ad* and *dico*, to speak or declare in favor of a thing, signifies generally to apply one's self to it. *Devote*, from the Latin *devoveo*, or *de*, on account or behalf of, and *voveo*, to vow, signifies to make a solemn vow or resolution for a thing. *Apply*, in French *appliquer*, and Latin *applico*, from *ap* or *ad* and *plico*, signifies to knit or join one's self to a thing.

To *addict* is to indulge one's self in any particular practice; to *devote* is to direct one's powers and means to any particular pursuit; to *apply* is to employ one's time or attention about any object. Men are *addicted* to learning; they *devote* their talents to the acquirement of any art or science; they *apply* their minds to the investigation of a subject.

Addict is seldomer used in a good than in a bad sense; *devote* is mostly employed in a good sense; *apply* in an indifferent sense. We are *addicted* to a thing from an irresistible passion or propensity; we are *devoted* to a thing from a strong, but settled, attachment to it; we *apply* to a thing from a sense of its utility. We *addict* ourselves to study by yielding to our passion for it; we *devote* ourselves to the service of our king and country by employing all our powers to their benefit; we *apply* to business by giving it all the time and attention that it requires.

ADDITION. See INCREASE.

ADDRESS, APPLY. For the derivation of these words see ACCOST and ADDICT.

An *address* is immediately directed from one party to the other, either personally or by writing; an *application* may be made through the medium of a third person. An *address* may be made for an indifferent purpose or without any express object; but an *application* is always occasioned by some serious circumstance. We *address* those to whom we speak or write; but we *apply* to those to whom we wish to communicate some object of personal interest. An *address*, therefore, may be made without an *application;* and an *application* may be made by means of an *address.* An *address* may be rude or civil; an *application* may be frequent or urgent. It is impertinent to *address* any one with whom we are not acquainted, unless we have any reason for making an *application* to him. It is a privilege of the British Constitution that the subject may *address* the monarch, and *apply* for a redress of

grievances. A court is *addressed* by a suitor or counsel on his behalf; it is *applied* to by means of legal forms for the redress of grievances. We cannot pass through the streets of the metropolis without being continually *addressed* by beggars, who *apply* for the relief of artificial more than of real wants. Men in power are always exposed to be publicly *addressed* by persons who wish to obtrude their opinions upon them, and to have perpetual *applications* from those who solicit favors.

See also ABILITY; ACCOST; DIRECTION.

Address, Speech, Harangue, Oration. —*Address*, see preceding terms for derivation. *Speech*, from Anglo-Saxon *spæc*, the substantive corresponding to *speak*, signifies the thing spoken. *Harangue*, Old French *harangue*, comes from Old High German *hrinc*, whence *ring, rank*, etc., are derived, and signified an address to a circle or *ring* of listeners. *Oration*, from the Latin *oro*, to beg or entreat, signifies that which is said by way of entreaty.

All these terms denote a set form of words directed or supposed to be directed to some person: an *address* in this sense is always written, but the rest are really spoken, or supposed to be so; a *speech* is in general that which is addressed in a formal manner to one person or more; a *harangue* is a noisy, tumultuous *speech* addressed to many; an *oration* is a solemn *speech* for any purpose. *Addresses* are frequently sent up to the throne by public bodies. *Speeches* in Parliament, like *harangues* at elections, are often little better than the crude effusions of party spirit. The *orations* of Demosthenes and Cicero, which have been so justly admired, received a polish from the correcting hand of their authors before they were communicated to the public.

ADDUCE, ALLEGE, ASSIGN, ADVANCE. *Adduce*, in Latin *adducere*, compounded of *ad* and *ducere*, to lead, signifies to bring forward proofs or evidence in support of some statement or proposition already made. *Allege*, in French *alléguer*, in Latin *allegare*, compounded of *ad* and *legare*, from the stem *lex, legis*, law, signified to send with legal dispatches, hence to affirm authoritatively. *Assign*, in French *assigner,* Latin *assigno,* compounded of *as* or *ad* and *signo,* to sign or mark out, signifies to set apart for a purpose. *Advance,* Middle English *avancen,* from French *avant,* Low Latin *ab* (from) and *ante* (before), written *abante,* signified to come from the front ranks, to proceed from the front ranks forward.

An argument is *adduced;* a fact or a charge is *alleged;* a reason is *assigned;* a position or an opinion is *advanced.* What is *adduced* tends to corroborate or invalidate; what is *alleged* tends to criminate or exculpate; what is *assigned* tends to justify or support; what is *advanced* tends to explain and illustrate. Whoever discusses disputed points must have arguments to *adduce* in favor of his principles; censures should not be passed where nothing improper can be *alleged;* a conduct is absurd for which no reason can be *assigned;* those who *advance* what they cannot maintain expose their ignorance as much as their folly. We may controvert what is *adduced* or *advanced;* we may deny what is *alleged,* and question what is *assigned.* The reasoner *adduces* facts in proof of what he has *advanced;* the accuser *alleges* circumstances in support of his charge; the philosophical investigator *assigns* causes for particular phenomena.

ADEQUATE. See PROPORTIONATE.

ADHERE, ATTACH, ADHESION, ADHERENCE. *Adhere,* from the French *adhérer,* Latin *adhæro,* is compounded of *ad* and *hæro,* to stick close to. *Attach,* in French *attacher,* is compounded of *ad* and a root which is found in the English word *tack,* meaning peg or small nail, so that to *attach* was to fasten with a *tack.*

A thing is *adherent* by the union which nature produces; it is *attached* by arbitrary ties which keep it close to another thing. Glutinous bodies are apt to *adhere* to everything they touch; a smaller building is sometimes *attached* to a larger by a passage, or some other mode of communication. What *adheres* to a thing is closely joined to its outward surface; but what is *attached* may be fastened to it by the intervention of a third body. There is a universal *adhesion* in all the particles of matter one to another; the sails of a vessel are *attached* to a mast by means of ropes; or bodies are *attached* by bare locality, or being in the same enclosure.

In the improper and figurative application, *things* adhere from a fitness of their natures. Things are *attached* to each other by politicial ties.

Adherence and *attachment* are both applied to persons in a moral sense; the former as it respects matters of principle, the latter as it respects matters of inclination or interest. *Adherence* is always marked by a particular line of conduct; but *attachment* may exist without any particular expression. A person *adheres* to a prince or a community so long as he follows the one or co-operates with the other; he is *attached* to a person whenever the feeling or relation is created.

In the same manner, a person *adheres* to matters of opinion, by professing his belief; he is *attached* to objects from habit or private motives.

Adhesion and *adherence* are both derived from the verb *adhere,* one expressing the proper or figurative sense, and the other the moral sense or acceptation. There is a power of *adhesion* in all glutinous bodies, a disposition for *adherence* in steady minds.

See also STICK.

ADHERENT. See FOLLOWER.

ADJACENT, ADJOINING, CONTIGUOUS. *Adjacent,* in Latin *adjiciens,* participle of *adjicio,* is compounded of *ad* and *jacio,* to lie near. *Adjoining,* as the word implies, signifies being joined together. *Contiguous,* Latin *contiguus,* comes from *contingo,* or *con* and *tango,* signifying to touch close.

What is *adjacent* may be separated altogether by the intervention of some third object; what is *adjoining* must touch in some part; and what is *contiguous* must be fitted to touch entirely on one side. Lands are *adjacent* to a house or a town; fields are *adjoining* to each other; and houses *contiguous* to each other.

ADJECTIVE. See EPITHET.
ADJOINING. See ADJACENT.
ADJOURN. See PROROGUE.
ADJUST. See COUNTERPOISE; FIT.
ADMINISTER. See MINISTER.
ADMINISTRATION. See GOVERNMENT.

ADMIRE. See WONDER.

ADMISSION. See ADMIT.

ADMIT, RECEIVE. *Admit,* in French *admettre,* Latin *admitto,* compounded of *ad* and *mitto,* signifies to send or suffer to pass to. *Receive,* in French *recevoir,* Latin *recipio,* compounded of *re* and *capio,* signifies to take back or to one's self.

To *admit* is a general term, the sense of which depends upon what follows; to *receive* has a complete sense in itself: we cannot speak of *admitting* without associating with it an idea of the object to which one is *admitted;* but *receive* includes no relative idea of the *receiver* or the received. *Admitting* is an act of relative import; *receiving* is always a positive measure: a person may be *admitted* into a house, who is not prevented from entering; he is *received* only by the actual consent of some individual. We may be *admitted* in various capacities; we are *received* only as guests, friends, or inmates. Persons are *admitted* to the tables, and into the familiarity or confidence of others; they are hospitably *received* by those who wish to be their entertainers.

When applied to unconscious agents, the distinction is similar: rays of light are *admitted* into a room, or ideas into the mind, when they are suffered to enter at pleasure; but things *receive* each other for specific purposes, according to the laws of nature.

We *admit* willingly or reluctantly; we *receive* politely or rudely. Foreign ambassadors are *admitted* to an audience, and *received* at court. It is necessary to be cautious not to *admit* any one into our society who may not be an agreeable and suitable companion; but still more necessary not to *receive* any one into our houses whose character may reflect disgrace on ourselves. Whoever is *admitted* as a member of any community should consider himself as bound to conform to its regulations; whoever is *received* into the service of another should study to make himself valued and esteemed. A winning address and agreeable manners gain a person *admittance* into the most refined circles; the talent for affording amusement procures a person a good *reception* among the mass of mankind.

Admit, Allow, Permit, Suffer, Tolerate.—*Admit,* see key word preceding. *Allow,* in French *allouer,* from Latin *allaudare,* from *laus, laudis,* praise, signified to give approving consent. Compare *laudatory, laudable,* etc. *Permit,* in French *permettre,* Latin *permitto,* is compounded of *per,* through or away, and *mitto,* to send or let go, signifying to let go its way. *Suffer,* in French *souffrir,* Latin *suffero,* is compounded of *sub* and *fero* (cognate with English *bear*), signifying to bear with. *Tolerate,* in Latin *toleratus,* participle of *tolero,* sustain, signifies to bear or bear with.

To *admit* is an involuntary or negative act; to *allow* is voluntary and positive: we *admit* by simply not refusing or preventing; we *allow* by positively granting or complying with; we *admit* that which concerns ourselves or is done toward ourselves; we *allow* that which is for the convenience of others, or what they wish to do: one *admits* the freedoms or familiarities of those who choose to offer them; one *allows* an indulgence to a child. To *permit* is very nearly allied to *allow,* both in sense and application, with this difference, that *permit* is more formal and positive, being employed in respect to more important matters; as a father *permits* his son to travel; one man *permits* another to use his name. To *suffer* and *tolerate* are nearly allied to *admit,* but both are mere passive acts, and relate to matters which are more objectionable and serious: what is *admitted* may be at most but inconvenient; what is *suffered* may be burdensome to the sufferer, if not morally wrong; what is *tolerated* is bad in itself, and *suffered* only because it cannot be prevented: a parent frequently *suffers* in his children what he condemns in others; there are some evils in society which the magistrate finds it needful to *tolerate.*

A well-regulated society will be careful not to *admit* of any deviation from good order, which may afterward become injurious as a practice: it frequently happens that what has been *allowed* from indiscretion is afterward claimed as a right: no earthly power can *permit* that which is prohibited by the divine law: when abuses are *suffered* to creep in and to take deep root in any established institution, it is difficult to bring about a reform without endangering the existence of the whole; when abuses, therefore, are not very grievous, it is wiser to *tolerate* them than run the risk of producing a greater evil.

Admit, Allow, Grant.—These terms are here compared only in regard to matters of speculation; and in this case they rise in sense, *allow* being more voluntary and positive than *admit*, and *grant* more so than *allow*. What is *admitted* is that which it is either not easy or possible for a person to deny; certain facts are *admitted* which are too clearly proved to be disputed; what is *allowed* is that which is agreed to from the conviction or feelings of the party *allowing*; it is said mostly of that in which the interests as well as the opinions of men are concerned; he *allows* that it would be good, but thinks that it is not practicable; what is *granted* is agreed upon as true, and is said most properly of abstract or self-evident truths, as to *grant* that two and two make four, or to take that for *granted* which is the point in dispute.

Admittance, Admission. — These words differ according to the different acceptations of the primitive from which they are both derived; the former being taken in the proper sense or familiar style, and the latter in the figurative sense or in the grave style. The *admittance* to public places of entertainment is, on particular occasions, difficult. The *admission* of irregularities, however trifling in the commencement, is mostly attended with serious consequences.

Admittance is properly confined to the receiving a person or a thing into a given place; *admission* includes in itself the idea not only of receiving, but also the purpose of receiving. Whoever is *admitted*, or has the liberty of entering any place, whether with or without an object, has *admittance;* but a person has *admission* to places of trust, or into offices and the like.

See also APPROACH.

ADMITTANCE. See ADMIT.

ADMONISH, ADVISE. *Admonish,* in Latin *admoneo*, is compounded of the intensive *ad* and *monere*, to advise, signifying to put seriously in mind. *Advise* is compounded of the Latin *ad* and *visus*, participle of *videre*, to see, signifying to make to see or to show.

Admonish mostly regards the past; *advise* respects the future. We *admonish* a person on the errors he has committed, by representing to him the extent and consequences of his offence; we *advise* a person as to his future conduct, by giving him rules and instructions. Those who are most liable to transgress require to be *admonished;* those who are most inexperienced require to be *advised*. *Admonition* serves to put people on their guard against evil; *advise* to direct them in the choice of good.

Admonition, Warning, Caution.—*Admonition* (see ADMONISH). *Warning,* from Anglo-Saxon *warnian*, is allied with the words *wary, ward, guard*, etc., and hence it meant to tell another to *beware*, to be on his *guard*. *Caution,* from *caveo*, beware, signifies the making beware. A guarding against evil is common to these terms; but *admonition* expressed more than *warning*, and that more than *caution*.

An *admonition* respects the moral conduct; it comprehends reasoning and remonstrance: *warning* and *caution* respect the personal interest or safety; the former comprehends a strong, forcible representation of the evil to be dreaded; the latter a simple apprisal of a future contingency. *Admonition* may therefore frequently comprehend *warning;* and *warning* may comprehend *caution*, though not *vice versa*. We *admonish* a person against the commission of any offence; we *warn* him against danger; we *caution* him against any misfortune. *Admonitions* and *warnings* are given by those who are superior in age and station; *cautions* by any who are previously in possession of information. Parents give *admonitions;* ministers of the gospel give *warnings;* indifferent persons give *cautions*. It is necessary to *admonish* those who have once offended to abstain from a similar offence; it is necessary to *warn* those of the consequences of sin who seem determined to persevere in a wicked course; it is necessary to *caution* those against any false step who are going in a strange path. *Admonitions* should be given with mildness and gravity; *warnings* with impressive force and warmth; *cautions* with clearness and precision. The young require frequent *admonitions;* the ignorant and self-deluded solemn *warnings;* the inexperienced timely *cautions. Admonitions* ought to be listened to with sorrowful attention; *warnings* should make a deep and lasting impression; *cautions* should be borne in mind; but *admonitions* are too often rejected, *warnings* despised, and *cautions* slighted.

Admonitions are given by persons only; *warnings* and *cautions* are given by things as well as persons. The young are *admonished* by the old; the death of friends serves as a *warning* to the survivors; the unfortunate accidents of the careless serve as a *caution* to others to avoid the like error.

ADOPT. See ESPOUSE; NATURALIZE.

ADORE, WORSHIP. *Adore,* in French *adorer,* Latin *adoro*—that is, *ad* and *orare,* to pray to. *Worship,* in Anglo-Saxon *weorthscype,* is contracted from *worthship,* implying either the object that is worth, or the worth itself: whence it has been employed to designate the action of doing suitable homage to the object which has worth, and, by a just distinction, of paying homage to our Maker by religious rites.

Adoration is the service of the heart toward a Superior Being, in which we acknowledge our dependence and obedience by petition and thanksgiving; *worship* consists in the outward form of showing reverence to some supposed superior being. *Adoration* can with propriety be paid only to the one true God; but *worship* is offered by heathen to stocks and stones. We may *adore* our Maker at all times and in all places, whenever the heart is lifted up toward Him; but we *worship* Him only at stated times and according to certain rules. Outward signs are but secondary in the act of *adoration;* and in divine *worship* there is often nothing existing but the outward form. We may *adore* without *worshipping;* but we ought not to *worship* without *adoring.*

Adore, Reverence, Venerate, Revere. *Adore,* see key word preceding. *Reverence,* in Latin *reverentia,* reverence or

awe, implies to show reverence, from *revereor,* to stand in awe of; from *vereor,* I fear, allied with English *wary.* *Venerate,* in Latin *veneratus,* participle of *veneror,* is allied to *venus,* love, from a root *wan* signifying to love or win. *Revere* has the same etymology as *reverence.*

Adoration has been before considered only in relation to our Maker; it may, however, be employed in an improper and extended application to express in the strongest possible manner the devotion of the mind toward sensible objects. Good princes are frequently said to be *adored* by their subjects.

Reverence is equally engendered by the contemplation of superiority, whether of the Supreme Being as our Creator, or of any earthly being as our parent: it differs, however, from *adoration,* inasmuch as it has a mixture of fear, arising from the consciousness of weakness and dependence, or of obligations for favors received. *Adoration* in this case, as in the former, requires no external form; it is properly the homage of the mind: *reverencing* our Maker is also an inward sentiment; but *reverencing* our parents, who are invested with a sacred character, includes in it an outward expression of our sentiments by our deportment toward them.

As sentiments of the mind, there is this distinction between *reverence* and *veneration,* that the latter has none of the feeling of fear which forms a part of the former. The contemplation of a sacred edifice which combines grandeur with solemnity will awaken *reverence;* the contemplation of any place rendered sacred by its antiquity awakens *veneration.*

Between the verbs to *revere* and to *reverence* there is but a small shade of difference in the sense: the former denotes a sentiment of the mind only; the latter the expression of that sentiment, as well as the sentiment itself. Hence we say with more propriety, to *revere,* not to *reverence,* a name or memory of any one, etc.

ADORN, DECORATE, EMBELLISH. *Adorn,* in Latin, *adorno,* is compounded of the intensive syllable *ad* and *orno,* in Greek ὡραῖος beautiful, signifying to dispose for the purpose of ornament. *Decorate,* in Latin *decoratus,* participle of *decoro*, from *decus*, an ornament, signifies to make beautiful by the addition of something extraneous. *Embellish*, in French *embellir*, is compounded of the intensive syllable *em* or *in* and *bellir* or *bel*, in Latin *bellus*, handsome, signifying to make handsome.

We *adorn* by giving the best external appearance to a thing; we *decorate* by annexing something to improve its appearance; we *embellish* by giving a finishing stroke to a thing that is well executed, or adding to the beauty of a thing. Females *adorn* their persons by the choice and disposal of their dress; or gentlemen *adorn* their estates by giving them the appearance of tasteful cultivation: a head-dress is *decorated* with flowers, or a room with paintings: fine writing is *embellished* by suitable flourishes.

Adorn and *embellish* are figuratively employed; *decorate* only in the proper sense. Inanimate objects may be *adorned*, or the mind is *adorned* by particular virtues which are implanted in it; a narrative is *embellished* by the introduction of some striking incidents.

See also GARNISH; ORNATE.

ADROIT. See CLEVER.

ADROITNESS. See KNACK.

ADULATE, FLATTER, COMPLIMENT. *Adulate*, in Latin *adulatus*, participle of *adulor*, signified to wag the tail as a dog does, to fawn like a dog. *Flatter*, Old French *flater*, to stroke, to soothe, signified to calm with caressing words. *Compliment*, like *comply*, is derived through the Italian *complimento*, civility, from the Latin *compleo*, fill entirely, hence to fulfil expectations, to please.

We *adulate* by discovering in our actions as well as words an entire subserviency: we *flatter* directly by words expressive of admiration; indirectly by actions which convey the same sentiments: we *compliment* by fair language or respectful civilities. An *adulatory* address is couched in terms of feigned devotion to the object; a *flattering* address is filled with the fictitious perfections of the object; a *complimentary* address is suited to the station of the individual and the occasion which gives rise to it. Courtiers are guilty of *adulation;* lovers are addicted to *flattery;* people of fashion indulge themselves in a profusion of *compliments.*

Adulation can never be practised without falsehood; its means are hypocrisy and lying, its motive servile fear, its end private interest: *flattery* always exceeds the truth; it is extravagant praise dictated by an overweening partiality, or, what is more frequent, by a disingenuous temper: *compliments* are not incompatible with sincerity, unless they are dictated from a mere compliance with the prescribed rules of politeness or the momentary desire of pleasing. *Adulation* may be fulsome, *flattery* gross, *compliments* unmeaning. *Adulation* inspires a person with an immoderate conceit of his own importance; *flattery* makes him in love with himself; *compliments* make him in good-humor with himself.

ADVANCE, PROCEED. *Advance* (see ADDUCE). *Proceed*, in Latin *procedo*, signifies to go forward.

To *advance* is to go toward some point; to *proceed* is to go onward in a certain course. The same distinction is preserved between them in their figurative acceptation. A person *advances* in the world who succeeds in his transactions and raises himself in society; he *proceeds* in his business when he carries it on as he has done before. We *advance* by *proceeding*, and we *proceed* in order to *advance*. Some people pass their lives in the same situation without *advancing;* some are always doing without *proceeding*. Those who make considerable progress in learning stand the fairest chance of *advancing* to dignity and honor. See also ADDUCE; ENCOURAGE; GO; PROGRESS.

ADVANTAGE, BENEFIT, UTILITY. *Advantage*, French *avantage*, for the derivation of which see *advance* under ADDUCE, signifies that which *advances* one's interests, improves one's condition. *Benefit*, in French *bienfait*, Latin *benefactum*, compounded of *bene*, well, and *factum*, done, signifies done or made to one's wishes. *Utility*, in French *utilité*, Latin *utilitas*, and *utilis*, useful, from *utor*, to use, signifies the quality of being able to be used.

Advantage respects external or extrinsic circumstances of profit, honor, and convenience; *benefit* respects the consequences of actions and events;

utility respects the good which can be drawn from the use of any object. A large house or a particular situation may have its *advantages;* suitable exercise is attended with *benefit;* sun-dials have their *utility* in ascertaining the hour precisely by the sun. Things are sold to *advantage;* persons ride or walk for the *benefit* of their health; they purchase articles for their *utility.* A good education has always its *advantages,* although every one cannot derive the same *benefit* from the cultivation of his talents, as all have not the happy art of employing their acquirements to the right objects; riches are of no *utility* unless rightly employed. It is of great *advantage* to young people to form good connections on their entrance into life; it is no less *beneficial* to their morals to be under the guidance of the aged and experienced, from whom they may draw many *useful* directions for their future conduct.

See also GOOD.

Advantage, Profit. — *Advantage,* see above. *Profit,* in French *profit,* Latin *profectus,* participle of *proficio,* compounded of *pro* and *facio,* signifies to make an advance.

The idea common to these terms is of some good received by a person. *Advantage* is general; it respects everything which can contribute to the wishes, wants, and comforts of life; *profit* in its proper sense is applied to pecuniary *advantage.* Situations have their *advantages;* trade has its *profits.*

Advantage may be applied either to the good derived from a thing, as the *advantage* of dress—that is, the *advantage* derived from dress—or to the thing from which the good is derived, as, dress is an *advantage* to the person.

Profit is always taken for that good which is derived from a thing.

Advantage implies something annexed to or coming to a thing accidentally; or it may be what a man esteems to be an *advantage; profit* is that which is real, substantial, and permanent.

ADVENTURE. See EVENT.

ADVENTUROUS. See ENTERPRISING; FOOLHARDY.

ADVERSARY. See ENEMY.

ADVERSE, CONTRARY, OPPOSITE. *Adverse,* in French *adverse,* Latin *adversus,* participle of *adverto,* compounded of *ad* and *verto,* signifies turning toward or against. *Contrary,* in French *contraire,* Latin *contrarius,* comes from *contra,* against. *Opposite,* in Latin *oppositus,* participle of *oppono,* is compounded of *ob* and *pono,* signifying placed in the way.

Adverse respects the feelings and interests of persons; *contrary* regards their plans and purposes; *opposite* respects the situation and relative nature of things. Fortune is *adverse;* an event turns out *contrary* to what was expected; sentiments are *opposite* to each other. Circumstances are sometimes so *adverse* as to baffle the best concerted plans; facts often prove directly *contrary* to the representations given of them; people with *opposite* characters cannot be expected to act together with pleasure to either party.

Adverse, Inimical, Hostile, Repugnant.—*Adverse,* see above. *Inimical,* from the Latin *in amicus,* not friendly, and *hostile* from Latin *hostis,* an enemy (allied to English *guest,* a stranger), signify belonging to an enemy. *Repugnant,* in Latin *repugnans,* from *repugno,* or *re* and *pugnare,* to fight against, signifies warring with.

Adverse may be applied to either persons or things; *inimical* and *hostile* to persons or things personal; *repugnant* to things only. A person is *adverse,* or a thing is *adverse* to an object; a person, or what is personal, is either *inimical* or *hostile* to an object; one thing is *repugnant* to another. We are *adverse* to a proposition, or circumstances are *adverse* to our advancement; partisans are *inimical* to the proceedings of government, and *hostile* to the possessors of power. In respect to persons, *adverse* denotes merely the relation of being opposed; *inimical,* the spirit of the individual in private matters; and *hostile,* the situation, conduct, and temper of individuals or bodies in public matters. Those who are *adverse* to any undertaking are not likely to use their endeavors to insure success; traders will be *inimical* to the introduction of anything that threatens to be injurious to their trade; some persons are *hostile* to establishments in religion.

In respect to things, what is *adverse* acts to the hindrance or disadvantage ot the thing to which it is opposed; as *adverse* minds, *adverse* circumstances. Sickness is *adverse* to the improvement of youth; what is *inimical* acts directly to injury, as writings which are *inimical* to religion, a spirit *inimical* to learning; what is *repugnant* is in a state of positive opposition or contrariety, as slavery is *repugnant* to the mild spirit of Christianity.

Adverse, Averse. — *Adverse* (see above), signifying turned against or over against, denotes simply opposition of situation. *Averse,* from *a* and *versus.* signifying turned from or away from, denotes an active removal or separation from. *Adverse* is therefore as applicable to inanimate as to animate objects; *averse* only to animate objects. When applied to conscious agents, *adverse* refers to matters of opinion and sentiment; *averse* to matters of feeling. One is *adverse* to that which he thinks wrong; he is *averse* to that which opposes his inclinations, habits, or interests.

Adversity, Distress.—*Adversity* signifies adverse circumstances. *Distress,* from the Latin *distringo,* compounded of *dis,* asunder, and *stringo,* I pull, signified tearing to pieces, hence the state of a mind disorganized by grief or fear.

Adversity respects external circumstances, *distress* regards either external circumstances or inward feelings. *Adversity* is opposed to prosperity; *distress* to ease. *Adversity* is a general condition; *distress* a particular state. *Distress* is properly the highest degree of *adversity.* When a man's affairs go altogether *adverse* to his wishes and hopes, when accidents deprive him of his possessions or blast his prospects, he is said to be in *adversity;* but when in addition to this he is reduced to a state of want, deprived of friends and all prospect of relief, his situation is that of real *distress. Adversity* is trying, *distress* is overwhelming. Every man is liable to *adversity,* although few are reduced to *distress* but by their own fault.

ADVERTISE, PUBLISH. *Advertise,* from the Latin *adverto,* compounded of *ad* and *verto,* to turn to, signifies to turn the attention to a thing. *Publish,* in Latin *publico*—that is, *facere publicum* —signifies to make public.

Advertise denotes the means, and *publish* the end. To *advertise* is to direct the public attention to any event by means of a printed circular; *publish* is to make known either by oral or printed communication. We *publish* by *advertising,* but we do not always *advertise* when we *publish.* Mercantile and civil transactions are conducted by means of *advertisements.* Extraordinary circumstances are speedily *published* in a neighborhood by circulating from mouth to mouth. See also ANNOUNCE.

ADVICE, COUNSEL, INSTRUCTION. *Advice* (see ADMONISH). *Counsel,* in French *conseil,* Latin *consilium,* comes from *consilio* (compounded of *con* and a root which probably meant to sit), signified to come together to talk over something; and in an extended sense implies deliberation, or the thing deliberated upon, determined, and prescribed. *Instruction,* in French *instruction,* Latin *instructio,* building, signified to build up from within, and is used in this literal sense by Milton: "*Instruct* me, for Thou knowest," meaning "Enter into me and build up my spirit from within."

The end of all the actions implied by these words is the communication of knowledge, and all of them include the accessory idea of superiority, either of age, station, knowledge, or talent. *Advice* flows from superior professional knowledge, or an acquaintance with things in general; *counsel* regards superior wisdom, or a superior acquaintance with moral principles and practice; *instruction* respects superior local knowledge in particular transactions. A medical man gives *advice* to his patient; a father gives *counsel* to his children; a counsellor gives *advice* to his client in points of law; he receives *instructions* from him in matters of fact. *Advice* should be prudent and cautious; *counsel* sage and deliberative; *instructions* clear and positive. *Advice* is given on all the concerns of life, important or otherwise; *counsel* is employed for grave and weighty matters; *instruction* is used on official occasions. Men of business are best able to give *advice* in mercantile transactions. In all measures that involve our future happiness, it is prudent to take the *counsel* of those who are more experienced than ourselves.

An ambassador must not act without *instructions* from his court. See also INFORMATION.

ADVISE. See ADMONISH.

ADVOCATE. See DEFENDER.

AERIAL NAVIGATION. See AERONAUTICS.

AERIAL NAVIGATOR. See AERONAUT.

AERIAL PILOT. See AERONAUT.

AERONAUT, AERIAL NAVIGATOR, AERIAL PILOT, AVIATOR, BALLOONIST. *Aeronaut,* in French *aéronaute,* from Latin *aer,* the air, and *nauta,* a sailor, as a general term, any one who navigates the air. *Aerial navigator* and *aerial pilot* are terms used to distinguish the one who guides an aircraft from the crew having other duties. *Aviator* is applied to any one engaged in aerial flights, but is more akin to *aerial navigator.* *Balloonist,* strictly an aviator who makes ascensions in a balloon or a lighter-than-air craft, usually an elongated or spherical bag inflated with gas—the original flying-machine.

AERONAUTICS, AEROSTATICS, AEROSTATION, AVIATION, BALLOONING. *Aeronautics,* in French *aéronautique,* the science or art which treats of aerial navigation. *Aerostatic,* in German *aerostatik,* in French *aérostatique,* "standing in the air," and *aérostation* both relate to air at rest and specifically to the suspension and control of flying-craft in the air. *Aviation,* from the Latin *avis,* a bird, applies both to the science of aerial flight in general and particularly to the use of machines capable of rising and maintaining themselves in the air without the aid of gas or rarefied air. *Balloon,* allied to *ball,* meant originally a large spherical bag, and *ballooning* differs from *aviation* as here defined in that it applies to a machine deriving its ascending and sustaining power from gas or rarefied air contained in a huge bag. A *captive balloon* is one used for observation purposes over a limited area, and is attached by a rope or cable to a holding object on the ground. It was formerly used for scouting in warfare, but has given way to other forms of aircraft.

AEROPLANE. See AIRCRAFT.

AFFABLE, COURTEOUS. *Affable,* in Latin *affabilis,* from *af* or *ad,* to, and *fari,* to speak, signifies ready to speak or be spoken with, and is particularly applied to persons in a higher condition; princes and nobles are commonly said to be *affable* when they converse freely with those not in the same condition.

Affability is properly confined to verbal communications; but *courteousness,* from the word *court,* signifying after the manner of a court or courtier, refers to actions and manners; *affability* flows from the natural temper; *courteousness* from good breeding, or the acquired temper.

AFFAIR, BUSINESS, CONCERN. *Affair,* in French *affaire,* is formed from the phrase *à faire,* corresponding to English *do,* etc., in such phrases as "much *ado,*" "a great *to do,*" etc. *Business,* from *busy* (see ACTIVE), signifies the thing that makes or interests a person or with which he is busy or occupied. *Concern,* in French *concerner,* Latin *concerno,* compounded of *con* and *cernere,* to sift, cognate with Greek κρίνειν, whence our words *critic, criticism,* are derived, signifies the sifting out of things that belong together.

An *affair* is what happens; a *business* is what busies; a *concern* is what is felt. An *affair* is general; it respects one, many, or all: every *business* and *concern* is an *affair,* though not *vice versa.* *Business* and *concern* are personal; *business* is that which engages the attention; *concern* is that which interests the feelings, prospects, and condition, advantageously or otherwise. An *affair* is important; a *business* is serious; a *concern* momentous. The usurpation of power is an *affair* which interests a nation; the adjusting a difference is a *business* most suited to the ministers of religion; to make one's peace with one's Maker is the *concern* of every individual. *Affairs* are administered; *business* is transacted; *concerns* are managed. The *affairs* of the world are administered by a Divine Providence. Those who are in the practice of the law require peculiar talents to fit them for transacting the complicated *business* which perpetually offers itself. Some men are so involved in the *affairs* of this world as to forget the *concerns* of the next, which ought to be nearest and dearest to them.

AFFECT, Concern. *Affect,* in French *affecter,* Latin *affectum,* participle of *afficio,* compounded of *ad* and *facere,* to do or act, signifies to act upon. *Concern,* for derivation see under Affair.

Things *affect* us which produce any change in our outward circumstances; they *concern* us if connected with our circumstances in any shape. Whatever *affects* must *concern;* but all that *concerns* does not *affect.* The price of corn *affects* the interest of the seller; and therefore it concerns him to keep it up, without regard to the public good or injury. Things *affect* either persons or things; but they *concern* persons only. Rain *affects* the hay or corn; and these matters *concern* every one more or less.

Affect and *concern* have an analogous meaning likewise when taken for the influence on the mind. We are *affected* by things when our *affections* only are awakened by them: we are *concerned* when our understanding and wishes are engaged. We may be *affected* either with joy or sorrow: we are *concerned* only in a painful manner. People of tender sensibility are easily *affected:* irritable people are *concerned* about trifles. It is natural for every one to be *affected* at the recital of misfortunes; but there are people of so cold and selfish a character as not to be *concerned* about anything which does not immediately *affect* their own persons or property.

AFFECT, Assume. *Affect,* in this sense, derives its origin immediately from the Latin *affecto,* desire eagerly, signifying to aim at or aspire after. *Assume,* in Latin *assumo,* compounded of *ad* and *sumere,* to take, signifies to take to one's self.

To *affect* is to use forced efforts to appear to have that which one has not; to *assume* is to appropriate to one's self that which one has no right to have. One *affects* to have fine feelings, and *assumes* great importance. *Affectation* springs from the desire of appearing better than we really are; *assumption* from the thinking ourselves better than we really are. We *affect* the virtues which we have not; we *assume* the character which does not belong to us. An *affected* person is always thinking of others; an *assuming* person thinks only of himself. The *affected* man strives to gain applause by appearing to be what he is not; the *assuming* man demands respect upon the ground of what he supposes himself to be. Hypocrisy is often the companion of *affectation,* self-conceit always that of *assumption.*

To *affect* is always taken in a bad sense; but to *assume* may be sometimes an indifferent action at least, if not justifiable. Men always *affect* that which is supposed to please others, in order to gain their applause; but they sometimes *assume* a name or an authority which is no more than their just right.

Affect, Pretend.—Affect, see above. *Pretend,* in Latin *pretendo*—that is, *præ* and *tendo*—signifies to hold or stretch one thing before another by way of a blind.

These terms are synonymous only in the bad sense of setting forth to others what is not real: we *affect* by putting on a false air; we *pretend* by making a false declaration. Art is employed in *affecting;* assurance and self-complacency in *pretending.* A person *affects* not to hear what it is convenient for him not to answer; he *pretends* to have forgotten what it is convenient for him not to recollect. One *affects* the manners of a gentleman, and *pretends* to gentility of birth. One *affects* the character and habits of a scholar; one *pretends* to learning. To *affect* the qualities which we have not spoils those which we have; to *pretend* to attainments which we have not made obliges us to have recourse to falsehoods in order to escape detection.

See also Thrill.

Affected, Disposed.—Affected signifies moved or acted upon by any particular circumstance, as to be *affected* at any spectacle. *Disposed,* from *dispose,* to settle or put in order, signifies settled or determined as to one's purpose; as *disposed* to do a good turn.

Affected likewise signifies to be *affected* with a particular sentiment, which brings it nearer to the sense of *disposed* in denoting a state of mind, but *disposed* in this case implies a settled if not an habitual temper, *affection* a temporary and partial state:

subjects are either well or ill *affected* to their government; people are either well or ill *disposed* as regards their moral character or principles.

See also NAMBY-PAMBY.

AFFECTING. See MOVING.

AFFECTION, LOVE. *Affection*, from the verb *affect*, denotes the state of being kindly *affected* toward a person. *Love*, German *liebe*, like the English *lief*, German *lieb*, dear or pleasing, is connected with the Latin *libet*, it is pleasing, signifying the state of holding a person dear.

These two words are comparable, inasmuch as they denote a sentiment toward any object: they differ both in the nature of the object and the nature of the sentiment. *Affection* is private or confined to one or more particular individuals; *love* is either general or particular: it either embraces all objects capable of awakening the sentiment, or it is confined to particular objects: in the former case *love* expresses the sentiment of the Divine Being toward all His creatures, and also that of man to the rest of his fellow-creatures.

When applied to particular objects, *love* is a much warmer sentiment than *affection*. The latter subsists between persons of the same sex, the former in a particular manner between persons of a different sex. *Affection* is a tender and durable sentiment, a chastened feeling under the control of the understanding which promises no more pleasure than it gives; *love* is an ardent sentiment which, as between the sexes, has all the characteristics of a passion, being exclusive, restless, and fluctuating. *Love* may subsist before marriage, but it must terminate in *affection* in order to insure happiness after marriage.

Between the words *affection* and *love* there is this further distinction, that the former did not always imply a kindly or favorable sentiment; there may be an ill as well as a good *affection:* the *affections* of a people to a government may be various; the *affection* of a prince may change from favor to disfavor toward a subject.

See also ATTACHMENT.

Affectionate, Kind, Fond.—*Affectionate*, from *affection* (see above), denotes the quality of having *affection*. *Kind*, from the word *kind*, kindred or family, denotes the quality or feeling engendered by the family tie. *Fond* is the past participle of Middle English *fonnen*, to be weak, to act like a fool.

Affectionate characterizes the feeling; *kind* has mostly a reference to the action: *affectionate* is directed to a particular object; *kind* to objects generally. Relations are *affectionate* to one another, persons may be *kind* to any one, even to mere strangers.

So toward animals generally we may be *kind*, and toward favorite animals *affectionate*.

As epithets, these words observe the same distinction; a mother or a child is *affectionate*, a master *kind;* looks, or whatever serve to express *affection*, are said most appropriately to be *affectionate;* offices, or any actions prompted by the general sentiment of *kindness*, are called kind.

Affectionate and *kind* are always taken in the good sense for a proper sentiment; *fondness* is an excess of liking for any object, which, whether it be a person or a thing, is more or less reprehensible; children are always *fond* of whatever affords them pleasure or of whoever gives them indulgences.

AFFINITY. See ALLIANCE; KINDRED.

AFFIRM, ASSEVERATE, ASSURE, VOUCH, AVER, PROTEST. *Affirm*, in French *affirmer*, Latin *affirmo*, compounded of *ad* and *firmo*, strengthen, signifies to give strength to what has been said. *Asseverate*, in Latin *asseveratus*, participle of *assevero*, compounded of *ad* and *severus*, signifies to make a serious statement. *Assure*, in French *assurer*, is compounded of the intensive syllable *as* or *ad* and *securus* (English *secure*), safe, signifying to make sure. *Vouch* is probably changed from *vow*. *Aver*, in French *avérer*, is compounded of the intensive syllable *a* or *ad* and *verus*, true, signifying to bear testimony to the truth. *Protest*, in French *protester*, Latin *protesto*, is compounded of *pro* and *testor*, to call to witness as to what we think about a thing. All these terms indicate an expression of a person's conviction.

In one sense, to *affirm* is to declare that a thing is, in opposition to denying or declaring that it is not; in the sense here chosen, it signifies to declare a thing as a fact on our credit. To *asseverate* is to declare it with confidence. To *vouch* is to rest the truth of another's declaration on our own responsibility. To *aver* is to express the truth of a declaration unequivocally. To *protest* is to declare a thing solemnly, and with strong marks of sincerity. *Affirmations* are made of the past and present; a person *affirms* what he has seen and what he sees. *Asseverations* are strong *affirmations*, made in cases of doubt to remove every impression disadvantageous to one's sincerity. *Assurances* are made of the past, present, and future; they mark the conviction of the speaker as to what has been, or is, and his intentions as to what shall be; they are appeals to the estimation which another has in one's word. *Vouching* is an act for another; it is the supporting of another's *assurance* by our own. *Averring* is employed in matters of fact; we *aver* as to the accuracy of details; we *aver* on positive knowledge that sets aside all question. *Protestations* are stronger than either *asseverations* or *assurances*, they are accompanied with every act, look, or gesture that can tend to impress conviction on another.

Affirmations are employed in giving evidence, whether accompanied with an oath or not; liars deal much in *asseverations* and *protestations*. People *asseverate* in order to produce a conviction of their veracity; they *protest* in order to obtain a belief of their innocence; they *aver* where they expect to be believed. *Assurances* are altogether personal; they are always made to satisfy some one of what they wish to know and believe. We ought to be sparing of our *assurances* of regard for another. Whenever we *affirm* anything on the authority of another, we ought to be particularly cautious not to *vouch* for its veracity if it be not unquestionable.

See also SWEAR.

Affirm, Assert.—*Affirm* (see above). *Assert*, in Latin *assertus*, participle of *assero*, compounded of *ad* and *sero*, to connect, signifies to connect words into a proposition. To *affirm* is said of facts; to *assert*, of opinions; we *affirm* what we know; we *assert* what we believe. Whoever *affirms* what he does not know to be true is guilty of falsehood; whoever *asserts* what he cannot prove to be true is guilty of folly. We contradict an *affirmation;* we confute an *assertion*.

AFFIX, SUBJOIN, ATTACH, ANNEX. *Affix*, in Latin *affixus*, participle of *affigo*, compounded of *af* or *ad* and *figo*, to fix, signifies to fix to a thing. *Subjoin* comes from Latin *sub*, under, and *jungere*, to join, and means to join to the lower or farther extremity of a body. *Attach* (see ADHERE), to *adhere*. *Annex*, in Latin *annexus*, participle of *annecto*, compounded of *an* or *ad* and *necto*, to knit, signifies to knit or tie to a thing.

To *affix* is to put anything as an essential to any whole; to *subjoin* is to put anything as a subordinate part to a whole: in the former case, the part to which it is put is not specified; in the latter, the syllable *sub* specifies the extremity as the part: to *attach* is to make one person or thing *adhere* to another by a particular tie, mostly in the moral sense; to *annex* is to bring things into a general connection with each other. A title is *affixed* to a book; a few lines are *subjoined* to a letter by way of postscript; we *attach* blame to a person; a certain territory is *annexed* to a kingdom. Letters are *affixed* to words in order to modify their sense, or names are *affixed* to ideas; it is necessary to *subjoin* remarks to what requires illustration; we are apt from prejudice or particular circumstances to *attach* disgrace to certain professions which are not only useful, but important; papers are *annexed* by way of appendix to some important transaction.

AFFLICT, DISTRESS, TROUBLE. *Afflict*, in Latin *afflictus*, participle of *affligo*, compounded of *ad*, to, and *fligere*, to dash, signifies to strike to the ground. For *distress* see ADVERSITY. *Trouble* signifies to cause a tumult, from the Latin *turba*, Greek τύρβη, a tumult.

When these terms relate to outward circumstances, the first expresses more than the second, and the second more than the third. People are *afflicted* with grievous maladies. The mariner is *distressed* for want of water in the midst of the wide ocean; or an embarrassed tradesman is *distressed* for money to maintain his credit. The mechanic is *troubled* for want of proper tools, or the head of a family for want of good domestics.

When they respect the inward feelings *afflict* conveys the idea of deep sorrow; *distress* that of sorrow mixed with anxiety; *trouble* that of pain in a smaller degree. The death of a parent *afflicts;* the misfortunes of our family and friends *distress;* crosses in trade and domestic inconveniences *trouble*. In the season of *affliction* prayer affords the best consolation and surest support. The assistance and sympathy of friends serve to relieve *distress*. We may often help ourselves out of our *troubles*, and remove the evil by patience and perseverance. *Afflictions* may be turned to benefits if they lead a man to turn inwardly into himself and examine the state of his heart and conscience in the sight of his Maker. The *distresses* of human life often serve only to enhance the value of our pleasures when we regain them. Among the *troubles* with which we are daily assailed, many of them are too trifling for us to be *troubled* by them.

Affliction, Grief, Sorrow.—*Affliction* (see AFFLICT). *Grief*, Old French *grief*, comes from Latin *gravus*, heavy, burdensome, sad. *Sorrow*, in German *sorge*, etc., originally signified care, as well as sorrow.

All these words mark a state of suffering which differs either in the degree or the cause, or in both. *Affliction* is much stronger than *grief;* it lies deeper in the soul, and arises from a more powerful cause; the loss of what is most dear, the continued sickness of our friends, or a reverse of fortune, will all cause *affliction;* the misfortunes of others, the failure of our favorite schemes, the troubles of our country, will occasion us *grief*. *Sorrow* is less than grief; it arises from the untoward circumstances which perpetually arise in life. A disappointment, the loss of a game, our own mistake, or the negligence of others causes *sorrow*. *Affliction* lies too deep to be vehement; it discovers itself by no striking marks in the exterior; it is lasting, and does not cease when the external causes cease

to act; *grief* may be violent, and discover itself by loud and indecorous signs; it is transitory, and ceases even before the cause which gave birth to it: *sorrow* discovers itself by a simple expression; it is still more transient than *grief*, not existing beyond the moment in which it is produced. A person of a tender mind is *afflicted* at the remembrance of his sins; he is *grieved* at the consciousness of his fallibility and proneness to error; he is *sorry* for the faults which he has committed. *Affliction* is allayed: *grief* subsides: *sorrow* is soothed.

AFFLUENCE. See RICHES.

AFFORD, YIELD, PRODUCE. *Afford*, Anglo-Saxon *geforthian* (*a* being a corruption of *ge*, pronounced *ye*, a verbal prefix, added to *forth*, the present English *forth*), meant to cause to come forth, to promote, etc. *Yield*, German *gelten*, in Anglo-Saxon *gildan*, *gieldan*, means to give the value of something. *Produce*, in Latin *produco*, compounded of *pro*, forth, and *ducere*, to bring, signifies to bring out or into existence.

With *afford* is associated the idea of communicating a part or property of some substance to a person, by way of supply to his wants: meat *affords* nourishment to those who make use of it; the sun *affords* light and heat to all living creatures.

To *yield* is the natural operation of any substance to give up or impart the parts or properties inherent in it; it is the natural surrender which an object makes of itself: trees *yield* fruit; the seed *yields* grain; some sorts of grain do not *yield* much in particular soils, and in an extended application trees may be said to *yield* a shade.

Produce conveys the idea of one thing causing another to exist, or to spring out of it; it is a species of creation, the formation of a new substance: the earth *produces* a variety of fruits; confined air will *produce* an explosion.

In the moral application they are similarly distinguished: nothing *affords* so great a scope for ridicule as the follies of fashion; nothing *yields* so much satisfaction as religion; nothing *produces* so much mischief as the vice of drunkenness.

See also GIVE.

Afford, Spare.—*Afford* (see above).

Spare, in German *sparen,* Latin *parco,* signifies laying aside for some particular use.

The idea of deducting from one's property with convenience is common to these terms; but *afford* respects solely expenses which are no more than commensurate with our income; *spare* is said of things in general, which we may part with without any sensible diminution of our comfort. There are few so destitute that they cannot *afford* something for the relief of others who are more destitute. He who has two things of a kind may easily *spare* one.

AFFRAY. See QUARREL.

AFFRONT, INSULT, OUTRAGE. *Affront,* in French *affronte,* from the Latin *ad* and *frons,* the forehead, signifies flying in the face of a person. *Insult,* in French *insulte,* comes from the Latin *insulto,* meaning literally "to jump on." The former of these actions marks defiance, the latter scorn and triumph. *Outrage* is compounded of the French adverb *outre* and the suffix *rage,* and signifies to go beyond bounds.

An *affront* is a mark of reproach shown in the presence of others; it piques and mortifies: an *insult* is an attack made with insolence; it irritates and provokes: an *outrage* combines all that is offensive; it wounds and injures. An intentional breach of politeness is an *affront;* if coupled with any external indication of hostility, it is an *insult;* if it break forth into personal violence, it is an *outrage.* Captious people construe every innocent freedom into an *affront.* When people are in a state of animosity they seek opportunities of offering one another *insults.* Intoxication or violent passion impels men to the commission of *outrages.*

See also OFFENCE.

AFRAID, FEARFUL, TIMOROUS, TIMID. *Afraid* is changed from *afeard,* signifying in a state of fear. *Fearful,* as the words of which it is compounded imply, signifies full of fear. *Timorous* and *timid* come from the Latin *timidus,* fearful, *timor,* fear, and *timere,* to fear.

The first of these epithets denotes a temporary state, the last three a habit of the mind. *Afraid* may be used either in a physical or moral application, either as it relates to ourselves only or to others; *fearful* and *timorous* are applied only physically and personally; *timid* is mostly used in a moral sense. It is the character of the *fearful* or *timorous* person to be *afraid* of what he imagines would hurt himself; it is not necessary for the prospect of danger to exist in order to awaken fear in such a disposition; it is the characteristic of the *timid* person to be *afraid* of offending or meeting with something painful from others; a person of such a disposition is prevented from following the dictates of his own mind. Between *fearful* and *timorous* there is little distinction, either in sense or application, except that we say *fearful* of a thing, not *timorous* of a thing.

AFTER, BEHIND. *After* respects order; *behind* respects position. One runs *after* a person, or stands *behind* his chair. *After* is used either figuratively or literally; *behind* is used only literally. Men hunt *after* amusements; misfortunes come *after* one another; a garden lies *behind* a house; a thing is concealed *behind* a bush.

AGE. See GENERATION; TIME.

AGED. See ELDERLY; GLOAMING.

AGENCY. See ACT.

AGENT. See ACTOR; FACTOR.

AGGRAVATE, IRRITATE, PROVOKE, EXASPERATE, TANTALIZE. *Aggravate,* in Latin *aggravatus,* participle of *aggravo,* compounded of the intensive syllable *ad* and *gravo,* make heavy, signifies to make very heavy. *Irritate,* in Latin *irritatus,* participle of *irrito,* snarl, is a word of uncertain origin. It may be a frequentative of *irrire,* to snarl like a dog, which is possibly an imitative word. *Provoke,* in French *provoquer,* Latin *provoco,* compounded of *pro,* forth, and *voco,* call, signifies to challenge or defy. *Exasperate,* Latin *exasperatus,* participle of *exaspero,* is compounded of the intensive syllable *ex* and *asper,* rough, signifying to make things exceedingly rough. *Tantalize,* in French *tantaliser,* Greek ταντάλιζω, comes from *Tantalus,* a king of Phrygia, who, having offended the gods, was destined, by way of punishment, to stand up to his chin in water, with a tree of fair fruit hanging over his head, both of which, as he attempted to allay his hunger and thirst, fled from his touch.

All these words, except the first, refer to the feelings of the mind, and in familiar discourse that also bears the same signification, but otherwise respects the outward circumstances. The crime of robbery is *aggravated* by any circumstances of cruelty; whatever comes across the feelings *irritates;* whatever awakens anger *provokes;* whatever heightens this anger extraordinarily *exasperates;* whatever raises hopes in order to frustrate them *tantalizes.* An appearance of unconcern for the offence and its consequences *aggravates* the guilt of the offender; a grating, harsh sound *irritates,* if long continued and often repeated; angry words *provoke,* particularly when spoken with an air of defiance: when to this are added bitter taunts and multiplied provocations, they *exasperate;* the weather, by its frequent changes, *tantalizes* those who depend upon it for amusement. Wicked people *aggravate* their transgression by violence; susceptible and nervous people are most easily *irritated;* proud people are quickly *provoked;* hot and fiery people are soonest *exasperated;* those who wish for much, and wish for it eagerly, are oftenest *tantalized.*

See also HEIGHTEN.

AGGRESSOR, ASSAILANT. *Aggressor,* from the Latin *aggressus,* participle of *aggredior,* compounded of *ag* or *ad* and *gradi,* to step, signifies one stepping up to, falling upon, or attacking. *Assailant* comes from *assail,* in French *assaillir,* compounded of *ad* and the Latin *salio,* to leap upon, and signifies one leaping upon or attacking any one vehemently. Compare the origin of *insult.*

The characteristic idea of *aggression* is that of one person going up to another in a hostile manner, and by a natural extension of the sense commencing an attack: the characteristic idea of *assailing* is that of one committing an act of violence upon another. An *aggressor* offers to do some injury either by word or deed; an *assailant* actually commits some violence: the former commences a dispute; the latter carries it on with a vehement and direct attack. An *aggressor* is blamable for giving rise to quarrels: an *assailant* is culpable for the mischief

he does. Were there no *aggressors,* there would be no disputes; were there no *assailants,* those disputes would not be serious. An *aggressor* may be an *assailant,* or an *assailant* may be an *aggressor,* but they are as frequently distinct.

AGILE. See ACTIVE.

AGITATION, TREPIDATION, TREMOR, EMOTION. *Agitation,* in Latin *agitatio,* from *agito,* a frequentative of *ago,* act, signifies the state of being *agitated* or put into action. *Trepidation,* in Latin *trepidatio,* from *trepidare,* to tremble, signifies the condition of trembling in all one's limbs from head to foot. *Tremor,* from the Latin *tremor,* signifies originally the same state of trembling. *Emotion,* in Latin *emotio,* from *emotus,* participle of *emoveo,* compounded of *e,* out of, and *movere,* to move, signifies the state of being moved out of rest or put in motion.

Agitation is a violent action backward and forward and in different ways. It may be applied either to the body or the mind; the body may be *agitated* or thrown into violent and irregular motion, either by external action upon it, or by the operations of grief, terror, or any other passion; the mind is *agitated* when the thoughts or the feelings are put into any violent or irregular motion. *Trepidation,* like the former, is an irregular motion of the body, but differs both in the manner and cause of the motion; *trepidation* is the hurried trembling motion of the limbs in performing their functions, whence we speak of doing a thing with *trepidation,* or that there is a *trepidation* in a person's manner: in all cases it arises from a sentiment of fear or alarm.

Agitation and *trepidation* may be both applied to bodies of men as well as individuals, with a similar distinction.

Tremor is a trembling motion of the body, differing from the two former either in the force or the causes of the action: it is not violent nor confined to any particular part, like *trepidation,* and may, like *agitation,* arise either from physical or mental causes. There may be a *tremor* in the whole body, or a *tremor* in the voice, and the like.

Emotion refers solely to the movements of the mind, and is therefore to be compared only with *agitation*. *Emotion* is the movement of a single feeling, varying with the object that awakens it; there may be *emotions* of pleasure as well as of pain; *agitation* may be the movement of one or many feelings, but those always of the painful kind. *Emotions* may be strong, but not violent: *agitation* will always be more or less violent.

AGONY. See DISTRESS; PAIN.

AGREE, ACCEDE, CONSENT, COMPLY, ACQUIESCE. *Agree*, from the Old French phrase *à gre*, at pleasure, from Latin *gratia*, signifies to be in a pleasant relation to another, to like something. *Accede*, in Latin *accedo*, *ac* or *ad* and *cedo*, go or come, signifies to come toward another. *Consent*, from *consentio*, or *con, cum*, with, together, and *sentio*, think or feel, signifies to think or feel in unison. *Comply*, in French *complaire*, Latin *compleo* (for derivation see COMPLIMENT), signifies to fulfil all expectations, to satisfy the demands of another. *Acquiesce*, in Latin *acquiesco*, or *ac, ad*, to or with, and *qutesco*, be quiet, signifies rest contented with.

All of these terms denote the falling in of any one or more persons in any matter that comes before their notice. *Agree* expresses this general idea without any qualifications; all the other terms express different modes of *agreeing*. All may *agree* in the same thing, or one may *agree* to that which is proposed; *acceding, complying*, and *acquiescing* are the acts of persons individually; *consenting* is properly the act of numbers, but it is also the act of individuals; one *accedes* to, *complies* with, or *acquiesces* in a thing. *Agreeing* is often a casual act not brought about by the parties themselves; the other terms denote positive acts, varying in the motives and circumstances. We *accede* by becoming a party to a thing: those who *accede* are on equal terms; one objects to that to which one does not *accede*; we *consent* to a thing by authorizing it, we *comply* with a thing by allowing it; those who *consent* or *comply* are not on equal terms with those in whose favor the *consent* is given or *compliance* made; *consenting* is an act of authority, *complying*

an act of good nature or weakness; one refuses that to which one does not *consent*, or with which one does not *comply;* to *acquiesce* is quietly to admit; it is a passive act, dictated by prudence or duty; one opposes that in which one does not *acquiesce*.

To *agree* is to be of the same mind in matters of opinion or feeling; it is well for those who act together to be able to *agree*.

The term *agree* is, however, commonly used in regard to acting, as well as thinking, in the ordinary transactions of life.

To *accede* and the other terms are with very few exceptions employed in practical matters, but sometimes otherwise; to *accede* is mostly said in regard to that which is in a special manner proposed, if not recommended; as a private individual *accedes* to a proposition; a plenipotentiary *accedes* to a treaty.

To *consent*, as far as it is a universal act, is applied to moral objects; as customs are introduced by the *consent* of the community; but as the act of one or more individuals, it is applied to such practical matters as interest the parties for themselves or others; the parliament *consents* to the measures of the ministry; a parent *consents* to the marriage of a child. Equals *consent* to that in which they have a common interest.

Complying is used in the sense of yielding to the requests, demands, or wishes of another for the sake of conformity, and sometimes in the general sense of yielding to the wishes of the community.

To *acquiesce* is applied in the sense of yielding or agreeing to that which is decided upon by others. In this sense we *acquiesce* in the dispensations of Providence.

Agree, Accord, Suit.—*Agree* is here used in application to things only. *Accord*, in French *accord*, from the Latin *cors, cordis*, heart, signifies literally "heart to heart," in hearty agreement. *Suit*, from the Latin *secutus*, participle of *sequor*, follow, signifies to be in a line, in the order a thing ought to be.

An *agreement* between two things requires an entire sameness; an *accord-*

ance supposes a considerable resemblance; a *suitableness* implies an aptitude to coalesce. Opinions *agree*, feelings *accord*, and tempers *suit*. Two statements *agree* which are in all respects alike; that *accords* with our feelings which produces pleasurable sensations; that *suits* our taste which we wish to adopt, or, in adopting, gives us pleasure. Where there is no *agreement* in the essentials of any two accounts, their authenticity may be greatly questioned: if a representation of anything *accords* with what has been stated from other quarters, it serves to corroborate it: it is advisable that the ages and stations as well as tempers of the parties should be *suitable* who look forward for happiness in a matrimonial connection.

Agree, Coincide, Concur.—*Agree* is here taken in its application to both persons and things. It is as before the general term. *Coincide*, from the Latin *con*, together, and *incido*, fall, means literally "to fall in with." *Concur*, from *con*, together, and *curro*, run, implying a running in the same course, an acting together on the same principles, or modes of agreeing.

In respect to persons, they *agree* either in their general or particular opinions; they *coincide* and *concur* only in particular opinions. A person *coincides* in opinion with another in regard to speculative matters, but *concurs* with another in regard to practical matters; to *coincide* is only to meet at the same point, but to *concur* is to go together in the same road or in the same course of conduct.

In respect to things, they *agree* in one, many, or every point, as the accounts of different persons, times, modes, and circumstances *agree;* things *coincide* or meet at one point, as where two circumstances fall out at the same time; this is a *coincidence;* things *concur* if they have the same tendency or lead to the same point; several circumstances must sometimes *concur* to bring about any particular event. The *coincidence* is mostly accidental, the *concurrence* depends upon the nature of things.

See also TALLY.

AGREEABLE, PLEASANT, PLEASING. The first two of these epithets approach so near in sense and application that they can with propriety be used indifferently, the one for the other; yet there is an occasional difference which may be clearly defined. The *agreeable* is that which agrees with or suits the character, temper, and feelings of a person; the *pleasant* that which pleases; the *pleasing* that which is adapted to please. *Agreeable* expresses a feeling less vivid than *pleasant;* people of the soberest and gravest character may talk of passing *agreeable* hours, or enjoying *agreeable* society, if those hours were passed *agreeably* to their turn of mind, or that society suited their taste; but the young and the gay will prefer *pleasant* society, where vivacity and mirth prevail, suitable to the tone of their spirits. A man is *agreeable* who by a soft and easy address contributes to the amusement of others; a man is *pleasant* who to this softness adds affability and communicativeness. *Pleasing* marks a sentiment less vivid and distinctive than either. A *pleasing* voice has something in it which we like; an *agreeable* voice strikes with positive pleasure upon the ear. A *pleasing* countenance denotes tranquillity and contentment; it satisfies us when we view it: a *pleasant* countenance bespeaks happiness; it gratifies the beholder, and invites him to look upon it.

See also CONFORMABLE.

AGREEMENT, CONTRACT, COVENANT, COMPACT, BARGAIN. *Agreement* signifies what is agreed to. *Contract*, in French *contrat*, from the Latin *contractus*, participle of *contraho*, draw close together or bind, signifies the thing thus contracted or bound. *Covenant*, in Old French *covenant*, from the present participle of *convenio*, meet together, signifies the point at which several meet, that is, the thing agreed upon by many. *Compact*, in Latin *compactus*, participle of *compingo*, bind close, signifies the thing to which people bind themselves close. *Bargain* comes from Late Latin *barcaniare*, to change about. Its remote origin is unknown.

An *agreement* is general, and applies to transactions of every description, but particularly such as are made between single individuals, in cases where the other terms are not so applicable; a *contract* is a binding *agreement* between individuals; a simple *agreement* may be verbal, but a *contract* must be written and legally executed: *covenant*, in the technical sense, is an *agreement* by deed, but in the general sense a solemn *agreement;* a *compact* is an *agreement* among numbers; a *covenant* may be a national and public transaction; a *compact* respects individuals as members of a community, or communities with each other who are *compacted* together; a *bargain*, in its proper sense, is an *agreement* solely in matters of trade, but applies figuratively in the same sense to other objects. The simple consent of parties constitutes an *agreement;* certain solemnities are necessary to make a *contract* or *covenant* valid; a tacit sense of mutual obligation in all the parties gives virtue to a *compact;* an assent to stipulated terms of sale may form a *bargain.*

Friends make an *agreement* to meet at a certain time; two tradesmen enter into a *contract* to carry on a joint trade; and if it be under hand and seal, the stipulations therein contained are technically called *covenants;* in the Society of Freemasons, every individual is bound to secrecy by a solemn *compact;* the trading part of the community are continually striking *bargains.*

AGRICULTURIST. See FARMER.

AID. See HELP; UPHOLD.

AIDING. See AUXILIARY.

AIM, OBJECT, END, VIEW. *Aim* is mostly derived from the Latin *œstimare*, to put a value on, signifying the thing valued, consequently the particular point to which one's efforts are directed, which is held always in view, and to the attainment of which everything is made to bend. *Object*, from the Latin *objectus*, participle of *ob* and *jacio*, throw in the way, is more vague; it signifies the thing that lies before us; we pursue it by taking the necessary means to obtain it; it becomes the fruit of our labor. *End*, Anglo-Saxon *ende*, a Teutonic word meaning termination, is still more general, signifying the thing that ends one's wishes and endeavors; it is the result not only of action, but of combined action; it is the consummation of a scheme; we must take the proper measures to arrive at it.

The *aim* is that which the person has in his own mind: it depends upon the character of the individual whether it be good or bad, attainable or otherwise; the *object* lies in the thing; it is a matter of choice, it depends upon accident as well as design, whether it be worthy or unworthy; the *end* is that which follows or terminates any course or proceeding; it depends upon the means taken whether the *end* is arrived at or not. It is the *aim* of the Christian to live peaceably; it is a mark of dulness or folly to act without an *object;* it is sophistry to suppose that the *end* will justify the means.

Aim and *view*, from *video*, to see or look at, are both acts of the mind, but the *aim* is that which the mind particularly sets before itself as a thing to be obtained; the *view* is, generally speaking, whatever the mind sets before itself, whether by way of opinion or motive; a person's *views* may be interested or disinterested, correct or false. The *aim* is practical in its operations; the *view* is a matter rather of contemplation than of practice.

See also ENDEAVOR; TENDENCY; TENOR.

Aim, Point, Level.—*Aim,* signifying to take aim, is to direct one's aim toward a point. *Point*, Latin *punctum*, from *pungere*, to prick (compare *pungent*), signifies to direct the sharp end or point of an implement toward something. *Level* comes from Old French *livel*, from Latin *libella*, a diminutive of *libra*, a balance, and signified an instrument for determining that a thing is horizontal. *Level*, from the adjective *level*, signifies to put one thing on a level or in a line with another.

Aim expresses more than the other two words, inasmuch as it denotes a direction toward some minute point in an object, and the others imply direction toward the whole objects themselves. We *aim* at a bird; we *point* a cannon against a wall; we *level* a cannon at a wall. *Pointing* is of course used with most propriety in reference to instruments that have points; it is likewise a less decisive action than either *aiming* or *leveling*. A stick or a finger may be *pointed* at a person, merely out of derision; but a blow is *leveled* or *aimed* with an express intent of committing an act of violence.

The same analogy is kept up in their figurative application. The shafts of ridicule are but too often *aimed* with little effect against the follies of fashion: remarks which seem merely to *point* at others, without being expressly addressed to them, have always a bad tendency; it has hitherto been the fate of infidels to *level* their battery of sneers, declamation, and sophistry against the Christian religion, only to strengthen the conviction of its sublime truths in the minds of mankind at large.

Aim, Aspire.—*Aim* includes efforts as well as views, in obtaining an object. *Aspire*, from *as* or *ad*, to or after, and *spiro*, breathe, comprehends views, wishes, and hopes to obtain an object. We *aim* at a certain proposed point by endeavoring to gain it; we *aspire* after that which we think ourselves entitled to, and flatter ourselves with gaining. Many men *aim* at riches and honor: it is the lot of but few to *aspire* to a throne. We *aim* at what is attainable by ordinary efforts; we *aspire* after what is great and unusual, and often improper.

AIR, MANNER. *Air*, Latin *aer*, Greek ἀήρ, signifies the atmosphere; and thence, figuratively, the enveloping atmosphere of a personality created by appearance, manner, etc. *Manner*, Old French *maniere*, allied to the verb *manier*, to handle, from Latin *manus*, hand, signifies the way of handling something, hence a way of doing.

Air lies in the whole person; *manner* is confined to the action or the movement of a single limb. A man has the *air* of a common person; it discovers itself in all his *manners*. An *air* strikes at the first glance, whether the person be in motion or at rest; the *manner* can only be seen when the person is in action; it develops itself on closer observation. Some people have an *air* about them which displeases; but their *manners* afterward win upon those who have a further intercourse with them. An *air* is indicative of a state of mind; it may result either from a natural or habitual mode of thinking: a *manner* is indicative of the education; it is produced by external circumstances. An *air* is noble or simple, it marks an elevation or simplicity of character: a *manner* is rude, rustic, or awkward, for want of culture, good society, and good example. We assume an *air*, and affect a *manner*.

See also APPEARANCE.

Air, Mien, Look.—*Air* (see above). *Mien* is a word of unknown origin, possibly Celtic, adopted into English from the French. *Look* signifies properly a mode of looking or appearing (for derivation see LOOK).

The exterior of a person is comprehended in the sense of all these words. *Air* depends not only on the countenance, but the stature, carriage, and action: *mien* respects the whole outward appearance, not excepting the dress: *look* depends altogether on the face and its changes. *Air* marks any settled state of the mind: *mien* denotes any state of the outward circumstances: *look* any individual movement of the mind. We may judge by a person's *air* that he has a confident and fearless mind; we may judge by his sorrowful *mien* that he has substantial cause for sorrow; and by sorrowful *looks* that he has some partial or temporary cause for sorrow. We talk of doing anything with a particular *air;* of having a *mien;* of giving a *look*. An innocent man will answer his accusers with an *air* of composure; a person's whole *mien* sometimes bespeaks his wretched condition; a *look* is sometimes given to one who acts in concert by way of intimation.

AIRCRAFT, AEROPLANE, BALLOON, BIPLANE, DIRIGIBLE, FLYING-MACHINE, GYROPLANE, HELICOPTER, HYDROPLANE, MONOPLANE, MULTIPLANE, ORNITHOPTER, TAUBE, TRIPLANE, ZEPPELIN.

Aircraft is a compound of French *air*, Greek ἀήρ, from a root signifying to blow, meaning the lower atmosphere, and *craft*, a nautical term for vessel.

The European war which began in 1914 gave a new impetus to the designing and construction of aircraft as an offensive weapon. From the mechanism originally built for pleasure or scientific research there was speedily developed a variety of apparatus that in operation startled and shocked the world, especially those aeroplanes and the Zeppelins that were constructed to drop bombs on an enemy's territory and to carry rifled cannon with which to fight similar hostile craft.

An *aeroplane* is a heavier-than-air flying-machine with one or more planes or sustaining surfaces; a *balloon* is a lighter - than - air construction, elongated or spherical in shape, made of silk or other fabric, and inflated with gas; a *biplane* is an aeroplane with two sustaining surfaces; a *dirigible* is a balloon made to travel in any direction by means of a propeller operated by a motor; a *flying-machine* is the common but indefinite name of any form of aircraft; a *gyroplane* is a machine combining the features of an aeroplane and a helicopter; a *helicopter* is a machine that derives its ascending power from a fan wheel; a *hydroplane* is an aeroplane with a body that enables it to alight on or rise from a water surface; a *monoplane* is a machine with a single sustaining surface; a *multiplane* is a machine with two or more sustaining surfaces; an *ornithopter* is a machine with movable or flapping planes; a *Taube* is a German bomb-dropping aeroplane; a *triplane* is an aeroplane with three sustaining surfaces; a *Zeppelin* is a German dirigible and passenger-carrying apparatus constructed on the balloon principle, and used in the European war as a raiding bomb-dropper.

ALACRITY. See ALERTNESS.

ALARM, TERROR, FRIGHT, CONSTERNATION. *Alarm* is probably derived through French from the Italian *all' arme*, to arms, Latin *ad illa arma*, or Low Latin *ad illas armas*, to the arms. *Terror*, in Latin *terror*, comes from *terreo*, to cause to tremble. *Fright*, Anglo-Saxon *fyrhto*, allied to German *fürchten*, is a widely distributed Germanic word from a root signifying *fear*. *Consternation*, in Latin, *consternatus*, from *consterno*, strew, scatter on the ground, expresses the mixed emotion of terror and amazement which confounds.

Alarm springs from any sudden signal that announces the approach of danger. *Terror* springs from any event or phenomenon that may serve as a prognostic of some catastrophe. It supposes a less distinct view of danger than *alarm*, and affords room to the

imagination, which commonly magnifies objects. *Alarm* therefore makes us run to our defence, and *terror* disarms us. *Fright* is a less vivid emotion than either, as it arises from the simple appearance of danger. It is more personal than either *alarm* or *terror;* for we may be *alarmed* or *terrified* for others, but we are mostly *frightened* for ourselves. *Consternation* is stronger than either *terror* or *affright;* it springs from the view of some very serious evil, and commonly affects many. *Alarm* affects the feelings, *terror* the understanding, and *fright* the senses; *consternation* seizes the whole mind and benumbs the faculties. Cries *alarm;* horrid spectacles *terrify;* a tumult *frightens;* a sudden calamity fills with *consternation.* One is filled with *alarm*, seized with *terror*, overwhelmed with *fright* or *consternation*. We are *alarmed* for what we apprehend; we are *terrified* by what we imagine; we are *frightened* by what we see; *consternation* may be produced by what we learn.

ALERTNESS, ALACRITY. *Alertness*, from *ales*, a wing, designates corporeal activity or readiness for action. *Alacrity*, from *acer*, sharp, brisk, designates mental activity. We proceed with *alertness* when the body is in its full vigor; we proceed with *alacrity* when the mind is in full pursuit of an object.

ALIEN. See STRANGER.

ALIENATE. See TRANSFER; WEAN.

ALIENATION. See ABSTRACTION.

ALIKE. See EQUAL.

ALL, WHOLE. *All* is a Germanic word signifying *everything*. *Whole*, Anglo-Saxon *hal*, allied to German *heil*, and Greek καλός, excellent, beautiful, and the English words *hale, health, wholesome*, etc., signified to be sound, well, without fault or blemish. hence complete, entire.

All respects a number of individuals; *whole* respects a single body with its components: we have not *all*, if we have not the *whole* number; we have not the *whole*, if we have not all the parts of which it is composed. It is not within the limits of human capacity to take more than a partial survey of all the interesting objects which the *whole* globe contains. When applied to spiritual objects in a general sense, *all* is preferred to *whole:* but when the object is specific, *whole* is preferable: thus we say, *all* hope was lost; but, our *whole* hope rested in this.

All, Every, Each.—*All* is collective; *every* single or individual; *each*, distributive. *All* and *every* are universal in their signification; *each* is restrictive: the former are used in speaking of great numbers; the latter is applicable to small numbers. *All* men are not born with the same talent, either in degree or kind; but *every* man has a talent peculiar to himself; a parent divides his property among his children, and gives to *each* his due share.

ALLAY, Soothe, Appease, Mitigate, Assuage. To *allay*, Middle English *aleggen*, is properly no more than a French doublet of the word *alleviate*, derived from Latin *ad* and *levis*, light; hence it means to lighten a burden. *Soothe*, from Anglo-Saxon *soth*, true, which appears in the phrases "in sooth," "forsooth," etc., means to assent to something as being true, hence to humor. *Appease*, in French *apaiser*, is compounded of *ad* and *pax*, peace, signifying to quiet. *Mitigate*, from *mitis*, meek, gentle, signifies to make gentle or easy to bear. *Assuage*, from Old French *a* (Latin *ad*) and *suavis*, sweet, pleasant, cognate with the English *sweet* (compare the adjective *suave*), means literally to sweeten.

All these terms indicate a lessening of something painful. In a physical sense an irritating pain is *allayed;* a wounded part is *soothed* by affording ease and comfort. Extreme heat or thirst is *allayed;* extreme hunger is *appeased;* a punishment or sentence is *mitigated.*

In a moral sense one *allays* what is fervid and vehement; one *soothes* what is distressed or irritated; one *appeases* what is tumultuous and boisterous; one *mitigates* the pains of others, or what is rigorous and severe; one *assuages* grief or afflictions. Nothing is so calculated to *allay* the fervor of a distempered imagination as prayer and religious meditation: religion has everything in it which can *soothe* a wounded conscience by presenting it with the hope of pardon, that can *appease* the angry passions by giving us a sense of our own sinfulness and need of God's pardon, and that can *assuage* the bit-

terest griefs by affording us the brightest prospects of future bliss.

See also QUELL.

ALLEGE. See ADDUCE.

ALLEGORY. See FIGURE; PARABLE.

ALLEVIATE, RELIEVE. For the derivation of *alleviate* see ALLAY. *Relieve*, from the Latin *relevo*, is compounded of *re* and *levo*, lift up, signifying to take away or remove.

A pain is *alleviated* by making it less burdensome; a necessity is *relieved* by supplying what is wanted. *Alleviate* respects our internal feelings only; *relieve*, our external circumstances. That *alleviates* which affords ease and comfort; that *relieves* which removes the pain. It is no *alleviation* of sorrow to a feeling mind to reflect that others undergo the same suffering; a change of position is a considerable *relief* to an invalid, wearied with confinement. Condolence and sympathy tend greatly to *alleviate* the sufferings of our fellow-creatures; it is an essential part of the Christian's duty to *relieve* the wants of his indigent neighbor.

See also ABATE.

ALLIANCE, LEAGUE, CONFEDERACY. *Alliance*, in French *alliance*, from the Latin *alligo*, to tie to (compare *ligament*), signifies the state of being tied. *League*, in French *ligue*, comes from the same verb, *ligo*, bind. *Confederacy* or confederation, in Latin *confederatio*, from *con* and *fœdus*, an agreement, signifies a joining together under a certain pledge.

All these terms agree in expressing the union between two or more persons or bodies, but they differ in the nature of the union and the motive for entering into it. *Alliance* is the most general term, the other two are rather particular terms; an *alliance* may be entered into either on public grounds as between states, or on private grounds as between families or individuals; a *league* or *confederacy* is entered into upon public grounds or for common interests, as a *league* between nations or states, and a *confederacy* between smaller powers or between individuals. *Alliances* are formed for the mutual conveniences of parties, as between states to promote commerce; *leagues* and *confederacies* are entered into mostly for purposes of self-defence or common safety against the attacks of a common enemy; but a *league* is mostly a solemn act between two or more states and for general purposes of safety; and may, therefore, be both defensive and offensive; a *confederacy* is mostly the temporary act of several uniting in a season of actual danger to resist a common adversary.

Alliance, as regards persons, is always taken in a good sense, and as between families or individuals is mostly matrimonial. *League* and *confederacy* are frequently taken in a bad sense; we may speak of a wicked *league* or an unnatural *league* between persons of opposite characters for their own private purposes, or a *league* between beasts for savage purposes; there may be a *confederacy* between persons to resist a lawful demand or to forward any evil design.

Alliance, Affinity. — *Alliance* (see above). *Affinity*, in Latin *affinitas*, from *ad* and *finis*, a border, signifies a contiguity of borders.

An *alliance* is a union artificially formed between persons; an *affinity* is a relation which flows from that act as far as the *alliance* is matrimonial; the *affinity* is properly that which results from it; when an *alliance* is formed between persons of different sexes, this necessarily creates an *affinity* between the relatives of the two parties.

As respects things, *alliance* is used figuratively in the same sense to denote their union by an artificial tie; as an *alliance* between church and state; *affinity* in this case implies a relation between things by reason of their agreement or resemblance to each other; as an *affinity* of sounds or an *affinity* of languages.

ALL-KNOWING. See OMNISCIENT.

ALLOT, APPOINT, DESTINE. *Allot* is a hybrid word compounded of the Latin *ad* and the English word *lot*, a portion. *Appoint*, in French *appointer*, from *ad* and *pungo*, participle *punctus*, signifies to point out or set out in a particular manner for a particular purpose. *Destine*, in French *destiner*, Latin *destino*, compounded of *de* and a verb from the root *sta*, to stand, signifies to place apart for a particular object.

The idea of setting apart or selecting is common to these terms; but *allot* is used only for things, *appoint* and *destine* for persons or things. A space of ground is *allotted* for cultivation, a person is *appointed* as steward or governor; a youth is *destined* for a particular profession. *Allotments* and *appointments* are made for immediate purposes, *destinations* for a future purpose; time may be either *allotted, appointed,* or *destined*; but *allot* respects indefinite portions of time, as to *allot* a portion of one's time to religious meditations; *appoint* respects any particularly defined portion of time, as to *appoint* an hour of meeting; *destine* implies a future time purposely fixed, as the *destined* hour arrived. A space may be *allotted*, because space may be divided into portions; a particular place is *appointed* for a particular immediate object, or it is *destined* by some previous determination; as a person *appoints* the place where a house shall be built; he *destines* a house for a particular purpose.

See also DISTRIBUTE.

ALLOW, GRANT, BESTOW. *Allow* (see ABATE; ADMIT). *Grant*, Old French *graunter* or *creanter*, to assure, from Latin stem *credent*, from *credere*, to trust, is allied on the one hand to the word *guarantee*, on the other to such words as *credible, credulous, credence*, etc. *Bestow* is compounded of the prefix *be* and the Anglo-Saxon *stow*, a place, from the root *sta*, whence *stand* is also derived, and which is closely allied to the English verb *stow*. Hence to *bestow* signifies to dispose according to one's wishes and convenience.

That is *allowed* which may be expected, if not directly required; that is *granted* which is desired, if not directly asked for; that is *bestowed* which is wanted as a matter of necessity. What is *allowed* is a gift sometimes stipulated as to time and quantity, but frequently depends upon the will of the giver; what is *granted* is sometimes perfectly gratuitous on the part of the giver, but, when *granted*, is not always to be taken back; what is *bestowed* is occasional, altogether depending on circumstances and disposition of both giver and receiver. Many of the poor are *allowed* a small sum weekly from the parish. It is as improper to *grant* a person more than he asks, as it is to ask a person for more than he can *grant*. Alms are very ill *bestowed* which only serve to encourage beggary and idleness. A *grant* comprehends in it something more important than an *allowance*, and passes between persons in a higher station; what is *bestowed* is of less value than either. A father *allows* his son a yearly sum for his casual expenses, or a master *allows* his servant a maintenance; kings *grant* pensions to their officers; governments *grant* subsidies to one another; relief is *bestowed* on the indigent.

In a figurative application, things are *allowed* either out of courtesy or complaisance; they are *granted* by way of favor or indulgence; they are *bestowed* either from necessity or urgent reasons: merit is *allowed;* a request is *granted;* attention or applause is *bestowed.*

See also ADMIT; CONSENT.

Allowance, Stipend, Salary, Wages, Hire, Pay.—All these terms denote a stated sum paid according to certain stipulations. *Allowance*, from *allow* (see ADMIT), signifies the thing *allowed.* *Stipend*, in Latin *stipendium*, from *stips*, a piece of money, signifies money paid. *Salary*, in French *salaire*, Latin *salarium*, comes from *sal*, salt, and meant salt-money, money for salt. (Compare the word *pin-money* for a similar method of designation.) *Wages*, Old French *gage*, Low Latin *vadium*, signifies something paid for labor. *Hire* expresses the sum for which one is hired, and *pay* the sum that is to be *paid.*

An *allowance* is gratuitous; it ceases at the pleasure of the donor; all the rest are the requital for some supposed service; they cease with the engagement made between the parties. A *stipend* is more fixed and permanent than a *salary;* and that than *wages, hire,* or *pay;* a *stipend* depends upon the fulfilling of an engagement, rather than on the will of an individual; a *salary* is a matter of contract between the giver and receiver, and may be increased or diminished at will. An *allowance* may be given in any form, or at any stated times; a *stipend* and *salary* are paid yearly, or at even portions of a year; *wages, hire,* and *pay*

are estimated by days, weeks, or months, as well as years. An *allowance* may be made by, with, and to persons of all ranks; a *stipend* and *salary* are assignable only to persons of respectability; *wages* are given to laborers, *hire* to servants, *pay* to soldiers or such as are employed under government.

ALL-SEEING. See OMINISCIENT.

ALLUDE, REFER, HINT, SUGGEST. *Allude*, in Latin *alludo*, is compounded of *ad* and *ludo*, sport. It means to say anything in a cursory manner. *Refer*, in Latin *refero*, signifies to bring back—that is, to bring back a person's recollection to any subject by mentioning it. *Hint*, a verb formed from the noun *hint*, which is a contraction of the participle of a verb *hinten, hinted*, is allied to the words *hit, hurt*, etc., and originally meant taken, touched. To *hint* is to touch upon something. *Suggest*, in Latin *suggestus*, participle of *suggero*, is compounded of *sub* and *gero*, bring under or near, and signifies to bring forward in an indirect or casual manner.

To *allude* is not so direct as to *refer*, but it is more clear and positive than either *hint* or *suggest*. We *allude* to a circumstance by introducing it into one's discourse; we *hint* at a person's intentions by darkly insinuating what may possibly happen; we *suggest* an idea by some poetical expressions relative to it. There are frequent *allusions* in the Bible to the customs and manners of the East. It is necessary to *refer* to certain passages of a work when we do not expressly copy them. It is sometimes better to be entirely silent upon a subject than to *hint* at what cannot be fully explained. Many improvements have owed their origin to some ideas casually *suggested* in the course of conversation.

Allude and *refer* are always said with regard to things that have positively happened, and mostly such as are indifferent; *hint* and *suggest* have mostly a personal relation to things that are precarious. The whole drift of a discourse is sometimes unintelligible for want of knowing what is *alluded* to; although many persons and incidents are *referred* to with their proper names and dates. It is the part of the slanderer to *hint* at things discreditable to another when he does not dare to speak openly; and to *suggest* doubts of his veracity when he cannot positively charge him with falsehood.

See also GLANCE.

ALLURE, TEMPT, SEDUCE, ENTICE, DECOY. *Allure*, from the Old French *à leurre*, a word of possibly Germanic origin, signifying bait, meant to draw to a bait. *Tempt*, in French *tenter*, Latin *tento*, a frequentative of the verb *tendere*, to stretch, meant to draw out one's will, hence to try the strength of, hence to test. *Seduce*, in French *séduire*, Latin *seduco*, is compounded of *se*, apart, and *duco*, lead, signifying to lead any one aside. *Entice* comes from Old French *enticier*, based on *titio*, a firebrand. *Decoy*, from *de* and Old French *coi*, earlier *coit*, from Latin *quietus*, quiet, still, meant to render still or tame. (Compare the adjective *coy*.) But it is also influenced by provincial English *coy*, from Latin *cavea* (whence English *cage*), a trap for catching wild ducks.

We are *allured* by the appearances of things; we are *tempted* by the words of persons as well as the appearances of things; we are *enticed* by persuasions; we are *seduced* or *decoyed* by the influence and false arts of others. To *allure* and *tempt* are used either in a good or bad sense: *entice* sometimes in an indifferent, but mostly in a bad sense; *seduce* and *decoy* are always in a bad sense. The weather may *allure* us out-of-doors: the love of pleasures may *allure* us into indulgences that afterward cause repentance. We are sometimes *tempted* upon very fair grounds to undertake what turns out unfortunately in the end: our passions are our bitterest enemies; the devil uses them as instruments to *tempt* us to sin. When the wicked *entice* us to do evil, we should turn a deaf ear to their flattering representations: those who know what is right, and are determined to practise it, will not suffer themselves to be *enticed* into any irregularities. Young men are frequently *seduced* by the company they keep. Children are *decoyed* away by the evil-minded, who wish to get them into their possession. The country has its *allurements* for the contemplative mind; the metropolis is full of *temptations*. Those who have any evil project to execute will omit no *enticement* in order to *seduce* the young and inexperienced from their duty. The practice of *decoying* children or ignorant people into places of confinement was formerly more frequent than at present.

Allure does not imply such a powerful influence as *tempt;* what *allures* draws by gentle means; it lies in the nature of the thing that affects: what *tempts* acts by direct and continued efforts; it presents motives to the mind in order to produce decision; it tries the power of resistance. *Entice* supposes such a decisive influence on the mind as produces a determination to act; in which respect it differs from the two former terms. *Allure* and *tempt* produce actions on the mind, not necessarily followed by any result; for we may be *allured* or *tempted* to do a thing, without necessarily doing the thing; but we cannot be *enticed* unless we are led to take some step. *Seduce* and *decoy* have reference to the outward action, as well as the inward movements of the mind which give rise to them; they indicate a drawing aside of the person as well as the mind; it is a misleading by false representation. Prospects are *alluring*, offers are *tempting*, words are *enticing*, charms are *seductive*.

See also ATTRACT; TWEEDLE.

ALL-WISE. See OMNISCIENT.

ALLY, CONFEDERATE. Although derived from the preceding terms (see ALLIANCE), these are used only in part of their acceptations. An *ally* is one who forms an *alliance* in the political sense; a *confederate* is one who forms *confederacies* in general, but more particularly when such *confederacies* are unauthorized. William Tell had some few particular friends who were his *confederates;* but we should use the word with more propriety in its worst sense, for an associate in a rebellious faction, as in speaking of any bandit and his *confederates*.

ALMANAC. See CALENDAR.

ALONE, SOLITARY, LONELY. *Alone,* in Middle English often written as two words, *al one*, signifies altogether one, or single; that is, by one's self. *Soli-*

tary, in French *solitaire*, Latin *soli-tarius*, from *solus*, alone, signifies the quality of being *alone*. *Lonely* is a derivative of *lone*, which is a contraction of *all one*. *Alone* marks the state of a person; *solitary* the quality of a person or thing; *lonely* has more melancholy connotations than *solitary*, and may be used to indicate the state of mind of one dwelling *alone*. A person walks *alone*, or takes a *solitary* walk in a *lonely* place. Whoever likes to be much *alone* is of a *solitary* turn; wherever we can be most and oftenest *alone*, that is a *solitary* or *lonely* place; people who are forced to dwell *alone* may be often *lonely*.

ALSO, LIKEWISE, TOO. *Also*, compounded of *all* and *so*, signifies literally all in the same manner. *Likewise*, compounded of *like* and *wise*, or manner, signifies in like manner. *Too*, a variation of the numeral *two*, signifies what may be added or joined to another thing from its similarity.

These adverbial expressions obviously convey the same idea of including or classing certain objects together upon a supposed ground of affinity. *Also* is a more general term, and has a more comprehensive meaning, as it implies a sameness in the whole; *likewise* is more specific and limited in its acceptation; *too* is still more limited than either, and refers only to a single object. "He *also* was among the number," may convey the idea of totality both as respects the person and the event; "he writes *likewise* a very fine hand," conveys the idea of similar perfection in his writing as in other qualifications; "he said so, *too*," signifies he said so in addition to the others; "he said it *likewise*," would imply that he said the same thing or in the same manner.

ALTER. See CHANGE.

ALTERCATION. See DIFFERENCE.

ALTERNATE. See SUCCESSIVE.

ALTISCOPE. See PERISCOPE.

ALWAYS, AT ALL TIMES, EVER. *Always*, compounded of *all* and *ways*, is the same as, under all circumstances, through all the ways of life, that is, uninterruptedly. *At all times* means without distinction of time. *Ever* implies for a perpetuity, without end. A man must be *always* virtuous, that is, whether in adversity or prosperity; and *at all times* virtuous, that is, in his going out and coming in, his rising up and his lying down, by day and by night; he will then be *ever* happy, that is, in this life and the life to come.

See also AYE.

AMASS. See HEAP.

AMAZE. See WONDER.

AMBASSADOR, ENVOY, PLENIPOTENTIARY, DEPUTY. *Ambassador* is derived through French from Low Latin *ambactus*, by way of Italian. *Ambactus* is derived from an Old Gaulish (Celtic) root meaning servant, which also appears in the Anglo-Saxon *ombiht*, a servant. *Envoy*, Old French *envoyer*, to send, from Latin *inde*, and *via*, way, meant one sent on a mission. (Compare VOYAGE.) *Plenipotentiary*, from the Latin *plenus* and *potens*, signifies one invested with full powers. *Deputy* (for etymology see *depute* under ASSIGN) meant one deputed, one assigned to a particular mission.

Ambassadors, *envoys*, and *plenipotentiaries* speak and act in the name of their sovereigns, with this difference, that the first is invested with the highest authority, acting in all cases as the representative; the second appears only as a simple authorized minister acting for another, but not always representing him: the third is a species of *envoy* used by courts only on the occasion of concluding peace or making treaties: *deputies* are not deputed by sovereigns, although they may be *deputed* to sovereigns; they have no power to act or speak but in the name of some subordinate community or particular body. The functions of the first three belong to the minister, those of the latter to the agent.

An *ambassador* is a resident in a country during a state of peace; he must maintain the dignity of his court by a suitable degree of splendor: an *envoy* may be a resident, but he is more commonly employed on particular occasions; address in negotiating forms is an essential in his character: a *plenipotentiary* is not so much connected with the court immediately as with persons in the same capacity with himself; he requires to have integrity, coolness, penetration, loyalty, and patriotism. A *deputy* has little or no responsibility, and still less intercourse with those to whom he is *deputed;* he needs no more talent than is sufficient to maintain the respectability of his own character and that of the body to which he belongs.

AMBIGUOUS, EQUIVOCAL. *Ambiguous,* in Latin *ambiguus,* from *ambigo,* compounded of *ambo,* both, and *agere,* to act, signifies acting both ways or having two meanings. *Equivocal,* in French *équivoque,* Latin *equivocus,* composed of *œquus* and *vox,* signifies a word to be applied equally to two or more different objects.

An *ambiguity* arises from a too general form of expression, which leaves the sense of the author indeterminate; an *equivocation* lies in the power of particular terms used, which admit of a double interpretation, or an application to two different things: the *ambiguity* leaves us in entire incertitude as to what is meant; the *equivocation* misleads us in the use of a term in the sense which we do not suspect.

The *ambiguity* may be unintentional, arising from the nature both of the words and the things; or it may be employed to withhold information respecting our views; the *equivocation* is always intentional, and may be employed for purposes of fraud. The histories of heathen nations are full of confusion and *ambiguity;* the heathen oracles are mostly veiled by some *equivocation;* of this we have a remarkable instance in the oracle of the Persian mule, by which Crœsus was misled.

AMENABLE. See ANSWERABLE.

AMEND, CORRECT, EMEND, IMPROVE, MEND, BETTER. *Amend* and *emend,* in Latin *emendo,* from *menda,* the fault of a transcriber, signifies to remove faults generally. *Mend,* which is a contraction of *amend,* is similar in sense, but different in application. *Correct,* from *cum* and *regere,* to regulate, signifies to set right in a particular manner. *Improve,* from *probus,* good, signifies to make good, as *better* signifies to make *better.*

To *amend, emend, correct,* and *mend* imply the removing of an evil; *improve* and *better,* the increase of good.

Amend, emend, and *correct,* are all applied to works of the understanding, with this distinction, that *amend* signifies to remove faults or defects generally, either by adding, taking away, or altering, as to *amend* a law, to *amend* a passage in a book; this is the work of the author, or some one acting for him: to *emend* is to remove particular faults in any literary work by the alteration of letters or single words; this is the work of the critic: to *correct* is to remove gross faults, as to *correct* the press.

Amend and *correct* may be applied to moral objects with a similar distinction.

Mend is employed in respect to any works in the sense of putting that right which either is or has become faulty. It is a term in ordinary use, but may be employed in the higher style.

To *improve* is said either of persons or things which are made better; as to improve the mind, morals, etc.: to *better* is mostly applied to the outward condition on familiar occasions.

AMENDS. See COMPENSATION; RESTORATION.

AMIABLE, LOVELY, BELOVED. *Amiable,* in Latin *amabilis,* from *amare* to love, signifies fit to be loved. *Lovely,* compounded of *love* and *ly,* or *like,* signifies like that which we love, fit to produce love. *Beloved* signifies having or receiving love.

The two first express the fitness of an object to awaken the sentiment or love: the former by spiritual qualities, the latter by personal attractions. One is *amiable* from the qualities of the heart.

So also it is said of things personified. One has a *lovely* person, or is *lovely* in one's person. It may be applied to the attractions of other objects besides those of the person.

Beloved denotes the state of being loved, or being the object of love, which may arise from being *amiable* or *lovely,* or from other causes. Both persons and things may be *beloved.*

AMICABLE, FRIENDLY. *Amicable,* from *amicus,* a friend, signifies able or fit for a friend. *Friendly* signifies *like a friend.* The word *amicus* likewise comes from *amo,* to love, and *friend* from Anglo-Saxon *freogan,* to love. *Amicable* and *friendly,* therefore, both denote the tender sentiment of good-will which all men ought to bear one to another; but *amicable* rather implies a negative sentiment, a freedom from discordance; and *friendly* a positive feeling of regard, the absence of indifference. We make an *amicable* accommodation, and a *friendly* visit. It is a happy thing when people who have been at variance can *amicably* adjust all their disputes. Nothing adds more to the charms of society than a *friendly* correspondence. *Amicable* is always said of persons who have been in connection with each other; *friendly* may be applied to those who are perfect strangers. Neighbors must always endeavor to live *amicably* with each other. Travelers should always endeavor to keep up a *friendly* intercourse with the inhabitants wherever they come.

The abstract terms of the preceding qualities admit of no variation but in the signification of *friendship*, which marks an individual feeling only. To live *amicably*, or in *amity* with all men, is a point of Christian duty, but we cannot live in *friendship* with all men, since *friendship* must be confined to a few: so nations may be in *amity*, though not on terms of *friendship* with each other.

AMMUNITION, MUNITIONS. These words have been somewhat modified in application since the beginning of the European war. *Ammunition* was originally merely an army corruption of *munition*, from Latin *munitio* (from *munire*, to fortify with a wall). During the war, however, the word *munitions*, used in the plural, has been widely used to designate all the materials for shooting employed in warfare; *ammunition* has merely kept its meaning of material with which to load a gun which it had before the war, and in popular speech has been largely supplanted by the more general word *munitions*.

AMNESIA, BEWILDERMENT, FORGETFULNESS. *Amnesia* comes from the Greek ἀμνησία, and implies the loss of memory for words. The victim is apt to be an apparently aimless wanderer on the streets, and on being accosted appears to be in a high state of *bewilderment*, anxiety, perplexity.

While the affliction is in an acute stage the victim is unable to recall his or her name, place of residence, occupation, or present intentions.

Properly speaking, the word has no genuine synonym. *Bewilderment* and *forgetfulness* are general words which may be used to describe the state of mind of one afflicted by *amnesia*.

AMOROUS, LOVING, FOND. *Amorous*, from *amor*, and the ending, *ous*, which designates abundance, signifies full of love. *Loving* signifies the act of *loving*, that is, continually *loving*. *Fond* (for derivation see under *affectionate*) signifies an extreme or foolish attachment.

These epithets are all used to mark the excess or distortion of a tender sentiment. *Amorous* is taken in a criminal sense, *loving* and *fond* in a contemptuous sense; an indiscriminate and dishonorable attachment to the fair sex characterizes the *amorous* man; an overweening and childish attachment to any object marks the *loving* and *fond* person. *Loving* is less dishonorable than *fond:* men may be *loving;* children and brutes may be *fond*. Those who have not a well-regulated affection for each other will be *loving* by fits and starts; children and animals who have no control over their appetites will be apt to be *fond* of those who indulge them. An *amorous* temper should be suppressed; a *loving* temper should be regulated; a *fond* temper should be checked.

When taken generally, *loving* and *fond* may be used in a good or indifferent sense.

AMORTIZEMENT, AMORTIZATION. The term *amortizement*, in French *amortissement*, is derived from *amortize*, in French *amortir*, to extinguish, from Latin *mortis*, death, meaning in a general sense to make dead or render useless.

While *amortization* specifically means the right of alienating lands in mortmain, the term has of late come into vogue as synonymous with *amortizement*, especially in European countries burdened with debt.

Thus we read that certain revenues, or parts thereof, of a country have been assigned to the *amortization* or *amortizement* of the national debt, meaning a *payment* on account, or the extinction (payment in full), *liquidation* (partial or full payment), *reduction* (partial payment), or *redemption* (full payment) of outstanding obligations.

AMPLE, SPACIOUS, CAPACIOUS. *Ample* is in French *ample*, Latin *amplus*, large, full. *Spacious*, in French *spacieux*, from Latin *spatium*, allied to Greek σπάειν, to draw out, English *span*—all from a root *spa*, to spread or draw out. *Capacious*, in Latin *capax*, from *capio*, to hold, signifies the quality of being able to hold.

These epithets convey the analogous ideas of extent in quantity and extent in space. *Ample* is figuratively employed for whatever is extended in quantity; *spacious* is literally used for whatever is extended in *space; capacious* is literally and figuratively employed to express extension in both quantity and *space*. Stores are *ample*, room is *ample*, an allowance is *ample;* a room, a house, or a garden is *spacious;* a vessel or hollow of any kind is *capacious;* the soul, the mind, and the heart are *capacious. Ample* is opposed to scanty, *spacious* to narrow, *capacious* to small. What is *ample* suffices and satisfies; it imposes no constraint: what is *spacious* is free and open; it does not confine: what is *capacious* readily receives and contains; it is liberal and generous. Although sciences, arts, philosophy, and languages afford to the mass of mankind *ample* scope for the exercise of their mental powers without recurring to mysterious or fanciful researches, yet this world is hardly *spacious* enough for the range of the intellectual faculties: the *capacious* minds of some are no less capable of containing than they are disposed for receiving whatever spiritual good is offered them.

See also PLENTIFUL.

AMUSE, DIVERT, ENTERTAIN. To *amuse*, to cause to muse or wonder at, is derived from French *à* and *muser* (English verb *muse*), Italian *musare*, to gape idly about, from *muso*, a snout, a face. "The image is that of a dog snuffling idly about, and *musing* which way to take" (Skeat). Cf. *muzzle*. *Divert*, in French *divertir*, Latin *diverto*, is compounded of *dis*, apart, and *vertere*, to turn aside, signifying to turn the mind aside from an object. *Entertain*, in French *entretenir*, compounded of *entre*, Latin *inter*, and *tenir*, Latin *tenere*, to keep, signifies to keep the mind fixed on a thing.

We *amuse* or *entertain* by engaging the attention on some present occupation, we *divert* by drawing the attention from a present object; all this proceeds by means of that pleasure which the object produces, which in the first case is less vivid than in the second, and in the second case is less durable than in the third. Whatever *amuses* serves to kill time, to lull the faculties and banish reflection; it may be solitary, sedentary, and lifeless; whatever *diverts* causes mirth and provokes laughter; it will be active, lively, and tumultuous: whatever *entertains* acts on the senses and awakens the understanding; it must be rational, and is mostly social. The bare act of walking and changing place may *amuse;* the tricks of animals *divert;* conversation *entertains.* We sit down to a card-table to be *amused;* we go to a comedy or pantomime to be *diverted;* we go to a tragedy to be *entertained.* Children are *amused* with looking at pictures; ignorant people are *diverted* with shows; intelligent people are *entertained* with reading. The dullest and most vacant minds may be *amused;* the most volatile are *diverted;* the most reflective are *entertained;* the Emperor Domitian *amused* himself with killing flies; the Emperor Nero *diverted* himself with appearing before his subjects in the characters of the gladiator and charioteer; Socrates *entertained* himself by discoursing on the day of his execution with his friends on the immortality of the soul.

Amuse, Beguile.—As *amuse* denotes the occupation of the mind, so *beguile*, compounded of the English prefix *be* and Old French *guile* (English *wile*), (for the derivation of which see that key-word), signifying to overreach with guile, expresses an effect or consequence of amusement. When *amuse* and *beguile* express any species of deception, the former indicates what is effected by persons, and the latter that which is effected by things. The first is a fraud upon the understanding; the second is a fraud upon the memory and consciousness. We are *amused* by a false story; our misfortunes are *beguiled* by the charms of fine music or fine scenery. To suffer one's self to be *amused* is an act of weakness; to be *beguiled* is a relief and a privilege. Credulous people are easily *amused* by any idle tale, and thus prevented from penetrating the designs of the artful; weary travelers *beguile* the tedium of the journey by lively conversation.

Amusement, Entertainment, Diversion, Sport, Recreation, Pastime.—*Amusement* signifies here that which serves to *amuse*. *Entertainment*, that which serves to *entertain*. *Diversion*, that which serves to *divert*. *Sport*, that which serves to give *sport*. *Recreation*, that which serves to *recreate*, from *recreatus*, participle of *recreo*, or *re* and *creo*, means to create or make alive again, and was originally used of a recovery from illness. *Pastime* is that which serves to *pass time*.

The first four of these terms are either applied to objects which specifically serve the purposes of pleasure, or to such objects as may accidentally serve these purposes; the last two terms are employed only in the latter sense. The distinction between the first three terms is very similar in this as in the preceding case. *Amusement* is a general term, which comprehends little more than the common idea of pleasure, whether small or great; *entertainment* is a species of *amusement* which is always more or less of an intellectual nature; *diversions* and *sports* are a species of *amusements* more adapted to the young and the active, particularly the latter: the theatre or the concert is an *amusement;* fairs and public exhibitions are *diversions;* games of racing or cricket, hunting, shooting, and the like, are *sports*.

Recreation and *pastime* are terms of relative import: the former is of use for those who labor; the latter for those who are idle. A *recreation* must partake more or less of the nature of an *amusement*, but it is an occupation which owes its pleasure to the relaxation of the mind from severe exertion: in this manner gardening may be a *recreation* to one who studies; company is *recreation* to a man of business: the *pastime* is the *amusement* of the leisure hour; it may be alternately a *diversion*, a *sport*, or a simple *amusement*, as circumstances require.

ANATHEMA. See MALEDICTION.

ANATHEMATIZE. See EXCOMMUNICATE.

ANCESTORS. See FOREFATHERS.

ANCIENT. See OLD.

ANCIENTLY. See FORMERLY.

ANECDOTE, STORY. An *anecdote* has but little incident and no plot; a *story* (which, like Latin *historia*, English *history*, is derived from Greek ἱστορία, which originally referred to something learned by inquiry, being a derivative from a verb signifying to know) may have many incidents and an important catastrophe annexed to it: *anecdotes* are related of individuals, some of which are of a trifling nature, and others characteristic; *stories* are generally told to young people of ghosts and visions, which are calculated to act on their fears. An *anecdote* is pleasing and pretty; a *story* is frightful or melancholy; an *anecdote* always consists of some matter of fact; a *story* is sometimes founded on that which is real. *Anecdotes* are related of some distinguished persons, displaying their characters or the circumstances of their lives: *stories* from life, however striking and wonderful, will seldom impress so powerfully as those which are drawn from the world of spirits: *anecdotes* serve to amuse men, stories to amuse children.

Anecdotes, Memoirs, Chronicles, Annals.—*Anecdote*, Greek ἀνέκδοτος, meant literally unpublished, not given out, from ἐκ (*ex*) and δίδωμι, give. *Memoirs*, in French *mémoires*, from the word *memory*, signifies what serves to help the memory. *Chronicle*, in French *chronique*, from the Greek χρόνος, time, signifies an account of the times. *Annals*, from the French *annales*, from the Latin *annus*, signifies a detail of what passes in the year.

All these terms mark a species of narrative, more or less connected, that may serve as materials for a regular history. *Anecdotes* consist of personal or detached circumstances of a public or private nature, involving one subject or more. *Anecdotes* may be either moral or political, literary or biographical; they may serve as characteristics of any individual, or of any particular nation or age. *Memoirs* may include *anecdotes*, as far as they are connected with the leading subject on which they treat: *memoirs* are rather connected than complete; they are a partial narrative respecting an individual, comprehending matter of a public or private nature; they serve as *memorials* of what ought not to be forgotten, and lay the foundation either for a history or a life.

Chronicles and *annals* are altogether of a public nature; and approach the nearest to regular and genuine history. *Chronicles* register the events as they pass; *annals* digest them into order, as they occur in the course of successive years. *Chronicles* are minute as to the exact point of time; *annals* only preserve a general order within the period of a year. *Chronicles* detail the events of small as well as large communities, as of particular districts and cities; *annals* detail only the events of nations. *Chronicles* include domestic incidents, or such things as concern individuals; the word *annals*, in its proper sense, relates only to such things as affect the great body of the public, but it is frequently employed in an improper sense. *Chronicles* may be confined to simple matter of fact; *annals* may enter into the causes and consequences of events.

ANGER, RESENTMENT, WRATH, IRE, INDIGNATION. *Anger* comes from the Latin *angere*, Greek ἄγχειν, to strangle, Icelandic *angr*, grief, sorrow, Danish *anger*, compunction, etc., from which our words *anxious*, *anxiety*, etc., are also derived, and refers to the physical sensations accompanying anger or grief. *Resentment*, in French *ressentiment*, from *resentir*, is compounded of *re* and *sentir*, signifying to feel again, over and over, or for a continuance. *Wrath*, Anglo-Saxon *wrath*, English *wroth*, *angry*, and *ire*, Latin *ira*, are less obviously metaphorical than the preceding, the original roots in both cases having, apparently, the meaning of the present words. *Indignation*, in French *indignation*, in Latin *indignatio*, from *indignor*, to think or feel unworthy, marks the strong feeling which base conduct or unworthy treatment awakens in the mind.

An impatient agitation against any one who acts contrary to our inclinations or opinions is the characteristic of all these terms. *Resentment* is less vivid than *anger*, and *anger* than *wrath*, *ire*, or *indignation*. *Anger* is a sudden sentiment of displeasure; *resentment* is a continued *anger; wrath* is a heightened sentiment of *anger*, which is poetically expressed by the word *ire*. *Anger* may be either a selfish or a disinterested passion, it may be provoked by injuries done to ourselves, or injustice done to others: in this latter sense of strong displeasure God is *angry* with sinners, and good men may to a certain degree be *angry* with those under their control who act improperly. *Resentment* is a brooding sentiment altogether arising from a sense of personal injury; it is associated with a dislike of the offender, as much as the offence, and is diminished only by the infliction of pain in return; in its rise, progress, and effects, it is alike opposed to the Christian spirit. *Wrath* and *ire* are the sentiment of a superior toward an inferior, and when provoked by personal injuries discovers itself by haughtiness and a vindictive temper: as a sentiment of displeasure, *wrath* is unjustifiable between man and man; but the *wrath* of God may be provoked by the persevering impenitence of sinners; the *ire* of a heathen god, according to the gross views of pagans, was but the *wrath* of man associated with greater power: it was altogether unconnected with moral displeasure. *Indignation* is a sentiment awakened by the unworthy and atrocious conduct of others; as it is exempt from personality, it is not irreconcilable with the temper of a Christian: a warmth of constitution sometimes gives rise to sallies of *anger;* but depravity of heart breeds *resentment;* unbending pride is a great source of *wrath;* but *indignation* may flow from a high sense of honor and virtue.

See also DISPLEASURE.

Anger, Choler, Rage, Fury.—*Anger* (see above). *Choler*, in French *colère*, Latin *cholera*, Greek χολέρα, comes from χολή, bile, of which the English word *gall* is a cognate, because the overflowing of *bile* was supposed to be the physical accompaniment of anger.

Rage, in French *rage*, from Latin *rabies*, madness, and *rabio*, to rave like a madman, signifies madness, hence the loss of self-control in extreme anger. Compare the use of *mad* for angry among children. *Fury*, derived through French from Latin *furia*, is from a root signifying to rage, which refers especially to violent physical expression of anger, because one is carried or hurried away by the emotion of *fury*.

These words have a progressive force in their significance. *Choler* expresses something more sudden and virulent than *anger*; *rage* is a vehement ebullition of *anger*; and *fury* is an excess of *rage*. *Anger* may be so stifled as not to discover itself by any outward symptoms; *choler* is discoverable by the paleness of the visage; *rage* breaks forth into extravagant expressions and violent distortions; *fury* takes away the use of the understanding. *Anger* is an infirmity incident to human nature; it ought, however, to be suppressed on all occasions: *choler* is a malady too physical to be always corrected by reflection: *rage* and *fury* are distempers of the soul, which nothing but religion and the grace of God can cure.

ANGLE. See CORNER.

ANGRY, PASSIONATE, HASTY. *Angry* signifies either having *anger*, or prone to *anger*. *Passionate* signifies prone to *passion*. *Hasty* signifies prone to excess of *haste* from intemperate feeling.

Angry denotes either a particular state or a habit of the mind; *passionate* expresses a habit of the mind; *hastiness* is mostly a temporary feeling. An *angry* man is in a state of *anger*; a *passionate* man is habitually prone to be *passionate*. The *angry* has less that is vehement and impetuous in it than the *passionate*; the *hasty* has something less vehement, but more sudden and abrupt in it than either. The *angry* man is not always easily provoked, nor ready to retaliate; but he often retains his *anger* until the cause is removed: the *passionate* man is quickly roused, eager to repay the offence, and speedily appeased by the infliction of pain of which he afterward probably repents: the *hasty* man is very soon offended, but not ready to offend

in return; his *angry* sentiment spends itself in *angry* words.

See also SPLENETIC.

ANGUISH. See DISTRESS; PAIN.

ANIMADVERSION, CRITICISM, STRICTURE. *Animadversion*, in Latin *animadversio*, from *animadvertere*, that is *vertere animum ad*, signifies to turn the mind to a thing. *Criticism*, in French *critique*, Latin *criticus*, Greek κριτικός, from κρίνειν, to separate, hence to judge, signifies especially judgment founded on analysis. *Stricture*, Latin *strictura*, comes from the verb *stringere*, to draw tight, to urge, and signifies in Latin the exertion of pressure, oppression, etc. (Compare *strict*, *stringent*.)

Animadversion includes censure and reproof; *criticism* implies scrutiny and judgment, whether for or against; and *stricture* comprehends a partial investigation mingled with censure. We *animadvert* on a person's opinions by contradicting or correcting them; we *criticise* a person's works by minutely and rationally exposing their imperfections and beauties; we pass *strictures* on public measures by descanting on them cursorily and censuring them partially. *Animadversions* are too personal to be impartial, consequently they are seldom just; they are mostly resorted to by those who want to build up one system on the ruins of another: *criticism* is one of the most important and honorable departments of literature; a *critic* ought justly to weigh the merits and demerits of authors, but of the two his office is rather to blame than to praise; much less injury will accrue to the cause of literature from the severity than from the laxity of *criticism*; *strictures* are mostly the vehicles of party spleen; like most ephemeral productions, they are too superficial to be entitled to serious notice.

See also CENSURE.

ANIMAL, BRUTE, BEAST. *Animal*, Latin *animal*, from *anima*, life, which is derived from a root signifying to breathe, indicates a living thing—*i. e.*, one that breathes. *Brute*, Latin *brutus*, heavy, dull, was originally used as an adjective with beast, "a brute beast," and hence developed into a substantive. *Beast*, French *bête*, from Latin *bestia*, signified the lower animals, as distinguished from man.

Animal is the generic, *brute* and *beast* are the specific terms. The *animal* is the thing that lives and moves. If *animal* be considered as thinking, willing, reflecting, and acting, it is confined in its signification to the human species; if it be regarded as limited in all the functions which mark intelligence and will, if it be divested of speech and reason, it belongs to the *brute;* if *animal* be considered, moreover, as to its appetites, independent of reason, of its destination, and consequent dependence on its mental powers, it descends to the *beast. Man* and *brute* are opposed. To man an immortal soul is assigned; but we are not authorized by Scripture to extend this dignity to the *brutes.* "The *brutes* that perish" is the ordinary mode of distinguishing that part of the *animal* creation from the superior order of terrestrial beings who are destined to exist in a future world. *Animal,* when applied to man individually, is a term of reproach; the epithets *brute* and *beast* are still stronger terms of reproach, the perversion of the rational faculty being at all times more shocking and disgraceful than the absence of it by nature.

ANIMATE, INSPIRE, ENLIVEN, CHEER, EXHILARATE. *Animate,* in Latin *animatus,* from *animus,* the mind, and *anima,* the soul or vital principle, signifies in the proper sense to give life, and in the moral sense to give spirit. The connection between the idea of breathing and that of life found in *animate* (see derivation of *animal* above) is more obvious in the word *inspire,* from *in* and *spirare,* breathe into. *Enliven* means literally to put life into. *Cheer,* Old French *chere,* is derived from Low Latin *cara,* a face, Greek κάρα, the head (compare *cerebrum,* the brain, *cerebral,* etc.) The original meaning is seen in the phrase "be of good *cheer,*" literally put "a good *face* on the matter." It began to signify especially a glad face, and thence developed the verb to gladden, cheer. *Exhilarate,* in Latin *exhilaratus,* participle of *exhilaro,* from *hilaris,* Greek ἱλαρός, joyful, signifies to make glad.

Animate and *inspire* imply the communication of the vital or mental spark; *enliven, cheer,* and *exhilarate* signify actions on the mind or body. To be *animated* in its physical sense is simply to receive the first spark of animal life in however small a degree; for there are *animated* beings in the world possessing the vital power in an infinite variety of degrees and forms: to be *animated* in the moral sense is to receive the smallest portion of the sentient or thinking faculty, which is equally varied in thinking beings; the term *animation,* therefore, taken absolutely, never conveys the idea of receiving any strong degree of either physical or moral feeling. To *inspire,* on the contrary, expresses the communication of a strong moral sentiment or passion; hence, to *animate* with courage is a less forcible expression than to *inspire* with courage: we likewise speak of *inspiring* with emulation or a thirst for knowledge; not of *animating* with emulation or a thirst for knowledge. To *enliven* respects the mind; *cheer* relates to the heart; *exhilarate* regards the spirits, both animal and mental; they all denote an action on the frame by the communication of pleasurable emotions: the mind is *enlivened* by contemplating the scenes of nature; the imagination is *enlivened* by reading poetry; the benevolent heart is *cheered* by witnessing the happiness of others; the spirits are *exhilarated* by the convivialities of social life: conversation *enlivens* society; the conversation of a kind and considerate friend *cheers* the drooping spirits in the moments of trouble; unexpected good news is apt to *exhilarate* the spirits.

See also CHEER; ENCOURAGE; HEARTEN.

Animation, Life, Vivacity, Spirit.— *Animation* and *life* do not differ either in sense or application, but the latter is more in familiar use. They express either the particular or general state of the mind. *Vivacity* and *spirit* express only the habitual nature and state of the feelings.

A person of no *animation* is divested of the distinguishing characteristic of his nature, which is mind; a person of no *vivacity* is a dull companion; a person of no *spirit* is unfit to associate with others. A person with *animation* takes an interest in everything: a *vivacious* man catches at everything:

that is pleasant and interesting: a *spirited* man enters into plans, makes great exertions, and disregards difficulties. A speaker may address his audience with more or less *animation*, according to the disposition in which he finds it: a man of a *vivacious* temper diffuses his *vivacity* into all his words and actions: a man of *spirit* suits his measures to the exigency of his circumstances.

ANIMOSITY. See ENMITY.

ANNALS. See ANECDOTES.

ANNEX. See AFFIX.

ANNOTATION. See REMARK.

ANNOUNCE, PROCLAIM, PUBLISH. *Announce,* in Latin *annuncio,* is compounded of *an* or *ad* and *nuncio,* to tell to any one in a particular manner. *Proclaim,* in Latin *proclamo,* is compounded of *pro* and *clamo,* to cry before, or cry aloud. *Publish,* in Latin *publico,* from *publicus* and *populus,* signifies to make *public* or known to the people at large.

The characteristic sense of these words is the making of a thing known to numbers of individuals: a thing is *announced* in a formal manner to many or few; it is *proclaimed* to a neighborhood, and *published* to the world. We *announce* an event that is expected and just at hand; we *proclaim* an event that requires to be known by all the parties interested; we *publish* what is supposed likely to interest all who know it. *Announcements* are made verbally, or by some well-known signal; *proclamations* are made verbally and accompanied by some appointed signal; *publications* are ordinarily made through the press, or by oral communication from one individual to another. The arrival of a distinguished person is *announced* by the ringing of the bells; the *proclamation* of peace by a herald is accompanied with certain ceremonies calculated to excite notice; the *publication* of news is the office of the journalist.

See also ADVERTISE.

ANNOY. See HECTOR; INCONVENIENCE; WORRY.

ANNUL. See ABOLISH.

ANSWER, REPLY, REJOINDER, RESPONSE. *Answer,* Anglo-Saxon *ands-warian,* compounded of *and* (corresponding to Latin *ante,* Greek ἀντι) and *swerian,* to swear, means to swear in response to something, to take one's oath concerning the other side of the question. *Reply* comes from the French *répliquer,* Latin *replico,* unfold, signifying to unfold or enlarge upon by way of explanation. *Rejoin* is compounded of *re* and *jungere,* to join, signifying to join or add in return. *Response,* in Latin *responsus,* participle of *respondeo,* compounded of *re* and *spondeo,* promise (compare *sponsor*), signifies to promise in return, to give sanction to in return.

Under all these terms is included the idea of using words in return for other words, or returning a sound for a sound. An *answer* is given to a question; a *reply* is made to an assertion; a *rejoinder* is made to a *reply;* a *response* is made in accordance with the words of another. We *answer* either for the purpose of affirmation, information, or contradiction; we always *reply* or *rejoin,* in order to explain or confute; *responses* are made by way of assent or confirmation. It is impolite not to *answer* when we are addressed; arguments are maintained by the alternate *replies* and *rejoinders* of two parties; but such arguments seldom tend to the pleasure and improvement of society: the *responses* in the Liturgy are peculiarly calculated to keep alive the attention of those who take part in the devotion.

An *answer* may be either spoken or written, or delivered in any manner; *reply* and *rejoinder* are used in personal discourse only; a *response* may be said or sung, or delivered in a formal manner.

Animals as well as men may give *answers* or make *responses,* though not *replies* or *rejoinders.*

Answerable, Responsible, Accountable, Amenable.—*Answerable,* from *answer,* signifies ready or able to *answer* for. *Responsible,* from *respondeo,* to *answer,* has a similar meaning in its original sense. *Accountable,* from *account,* signifies able or ready to give an *account. Amenable,* from the French *amener,* to lead, signifies liable to be led or bound.

Between *answerable* and *responsible*

there is a close alliance in the sense, but some difference in the application. A person is *answerable* generally in respect to what he undertakes to pay or take charge of; he is *answerable* for his own debts, or for the debts of others to which he has made himself liable; he may also be *answerable* for things left in his charge: *responsible* is applied to higher matters of trust or duty; as an officer is *responsible* for the conduct of the men who are under him; so to hold a responsible position under government; and in an extended sense to be morally *responsible*—that is, *responsible* to society as a moral agent.

Answerable and *responsible* convey the idea of a pledge given for the performance of some act, or the fulfilment of some engagement, a breach of which subjects the defaulter to loss, punishment, or disgrace: *accountable* implies simply giving an account or explanation of one's proceedings. The two former have respect to the obligations only: the *accountability* results from the relation of the parties; a person is *accountable* to his employer for the manner in which he has conducted any business intrusted to him; a child is *accountable* to his parents for all his actions while he is under their control; and we are all *accountable* to the Great Judge of all. To be *amenable* is to be *accountable* as far as laws and regulations bind a person; one is *amenable* to the laws of society, or he is *amenable* to the rules of the house in which he is only an inmate.

See also CORRESPONDENT.

ANTAGONIST. See ENEMY.

ANTECEDENT, PRECEDING, FOREGOING, PREVIOUS, ANTERIOR, PRIOR, FORMER. *Antecedent*, in Latin *antecedens*—that is, *ante* and *cedens*, going before. *Preceding*, in Latin *precedens*, going before. *Foregoing*, literally going before. *Previous* is in Latin *prævius*, that is, *præ* and *via*, in the way before. *Anterior*, the comparative of the Latin in *ante*, before. *Prior*, in Latin *prior*, comparative of *primus*, first. *Former*, in English the comparative of first.

Antecedent, *preceding*, *foregoing*, *previous* are employed for what goes or happens before: *anterior*, *prior*, *former*, for what is or exists before. *Antecedent* marks priority of order, place, and position, with this peculiar circumstance, that it denotes the relation of influence, dependence, and connection established between two objects: thus, in logic the premises are called the *antecedent*, and the conclusion the consequent; in theology or politics, the *antecedent* is any decree or resolution which influences another decree or action; in mathematics it is that term from which any induction can be drawn to another; in grammar, the *antecedent* is that which requires a particular regimen from its subsequent. *Antecedent* and *preceding* both denote *priority* of time, or the order of events; but the former in a more vague and indeterminate manner than the latter. A *preceding* event is that which happens immediately before the one of which we are speaking; whereas *antecedent* may have events of circumstances intervening. An *antecedent* proposition may be separated from its consequent by other propositions; but a *preceding* proposition is closely followed by another. In this sense *antecedent* is opposed to *posterior*; *preceding* to *succeeding*.

Preceding respects simply the succession of times and things; but *previous* denotes the succession of actions and events, with the collateral idea of their connection with any influence upon each other: we speak of the *preceding* day, or the *preceding* chapter, merely as the day or chapter that goes before; but when we speak of a *previous* engagement or a *previous* inquiry, it supposes an engagement preparatory to something that is to follow: *previous* is opposed to subsequent: *foregoing* is employed to mark the order of things narrated or stated; as when we speak of the *foregoing* statement, the *foregoing* objections, or the *foregoing* calculation, etc.: *foregoing* is opposed to following.

Anterior, *prior*, and *former* have all a relative sense, and are used for things that are more before than others: *anterior* is a technical term to denote forwardness in place or time, but more commonly the former, as in anatomy; the *anterior* or fore part of the skull, in contradistinction to the posterior part; so likewise the *anterior* or fore front of a building, in opposition to the back front: *prior* is used in the sense of *previous* when speaking comparatively of two or more things when it implies anticipation; a *prior* claim invalidates the one that is set up; a *prior* engagement prevents the forming of any other that is proposed: *former* is employed either with regard to times, as *former* times, in contradistinction to later periods, or with regard to propositions, when the *former* or first thing mentioned is opposed to the latter or last mentioned.

ANTHRAX, MALIGNANT PUSTULE, SPLENIC FEVER, CARBUNCLE. *Anthrax*, Greek ἄνθραξ, a carbuncle or coal (compare *anthracite*), is the name for a disease attacking animals, and characterized by the appearance of *malignant boils*, or *carbuncles*. The various synonymes refer to the characteristics of the disease, but do not differ in application. *Splenic fever* refers to the enlargement of the spleen, caused by the disease. *Malignant pustule* refers especially to the inflammation and breaking of the boils. *Carbuncle* in itself does not indicate the disease as it is now known; it is the early name applied to boils in the skin.

The disease was long believed to affect the lower animals only, but late in 1915 several persons in the United States were attacked by it, some with fatal results. The Department of Agriculture placed at the disposal of the attending physicians a remedy it had been using with marked success among cattle, and in one case this proved effective, while in others the application was too late.

ANTICIPATE. See PREVENT.
ANTIPATHY. See AVERSION.
ANTIQUE. See OLD.
ANXIETY. See CARE; DISTRESS; WORRY.
ANY. See SOME.
APARTMENTS. See LODGINGS.
APATHY. See INDIFFERENCE.
APE. See IMITATE.
APERTURE. See OPENING.
APEX. See ZENITH.
APHORISM. See ANXIOUS.
APOLOGIZE, DEFEND, JUSTIFY, EXCULPATE, EXCUSE, PLEAD. *Apologize*, from the Greek ἀπολογία, and ἀπολογέομαι, compounded of ἀπό, from or away, and λέγω, speak, signifies to do away by speaking. *Defend*, in French *défendre*, is compounded of *de* and *fendo*, signifying to keep or ward off. *Justify*, in French *justifier*, Latin *justifico*, is compounded of *justus* and *facio*, signifying to do justice, or to put right. *Exculpate*, in Latin *exculpatus*, participle of *exculpo*, compounded of *ex* and *culpa*, signifies to get out of a fault. *Excuse*, in French *excuser*, Latin *excuso*, compounded of *ex* and *causa*, signifies to get out of any charge, *causa* being a legal term, found in the phrases "to plead one's *cause*," "make out a *case*," etc. *Plead*, in French *plaider*, is derived from *placere*, to please, like the words *plea, please, placate*, etc.

There is always some imperfection supposed or real which gives rise to an *apology*; with regard to persons it presupposes a consciousness of impropriety, if not of guilt; we *apologize* for an error by acknowledging ourselves guilty of it: a *defence* presupposes a consciousness of innocence more or less; we *defend* ourselves against a charge by proving its fallacy: a *justification* is founded on the conviction not only of entire innocence, but of strict propriety; we *justify* our conduct against any imputation by proving that it was blameless; *exculpation* rests on the conviction of innocence with regard to the fact: we *exculpate* ourselves from all blame by proving that we took no part in the transaction: *excuse* and *plea* are not grounded on any idea of innocence; they are rather appeals for favor resting on some collateral circumstance which serves to extenuate; a *plea* is frequently an idle or unfounded *excuse*, a frivolous attempt to lessen displeasure; we *excuse* ourselves for a neglect by alleging indisposition; we *plead* for forgiveness by solicitation and entreaty.

An *apology* mostly respects the conduct of individuals with regard to each other as equals; it is a voluntary act, springing out of a regard to decorum or the good opinion of others. To avoid misunderstandings it is necessary to *apologize* for any omission that wears the appearance of neglect. A *defence* respects matters of higher importance; the violations of laws or public morals: judicial questions decided in a court or matters of opinion which are offered to the decision of the public; no one *defends* himself but he whose conduct or opinions are called in question. A *justification* is applicable to all moral cases in common life, whether of a serious nature or otherwise: it is the act of individuals toward each other according to their different stations: no one can demand a *justification* from another without a sufficient authority, and no one will attempt to *justify* himself to another whose authority he does not acknowledge: men *justify* themselves either on principles of honor or from the less creditable motive of concealing their imperfections from the observation and censure of others. An *exculpation* is the act of an inferior; it respects the violations of duty toward the superior; it is dictated by necessity, and seldom the offspring of any higher motive than the desire to screen one's self from punishment: *exculpation* regards offences only of commission; *excuse* is employed for those of omission as well as commission: we *excuse* ourselves oftener for what we have not done than for what we have done: it is the act of persons in all stations, and arises from various motives, dishonorable or otherwise: a person may often have substantial reasons to *excuse* himself from doing a thing or for not having done it; an *excuse* may likewise sometimes be the refuge of idleness and selfishness. To *plead* is properly a judicial act, and extended in its sense to the ordinary concerns of life; it is mostly employed for the benefit of others rather than ourselves.

Excuse and *plea*, which are mostly employed in an unfavorable sense, are to *apology*, *defence*, and *exculpation* as the means to an end: an *apology* is lame when, instead of an honest confession of an unintentional error, an idle attempt is made at *justification; a defence* is poor when it does not contain sufficient to invalidate the charge; a *justification* is nugatory when it applies to conduct altogether wrong; an *excuse* or a *plea* is frivolous or idle which turns upon some falsehood, misrepresentation, or irrelevant point.

APOPHTHEGM or **APOTHEGM.** See AXIOM.

APOSTATE. See RECREANT.
APPALL. See DISMAY.
APPAREL, ATTIRE, ARRAY. *Apparel* comes from Old French *apareiller*, from Latin *ad*, to, and Medieval Latin *pariculus*, from *par*, equal, meaning to put together things that are alike, to arrange, hence to arrange the dress. *Attire* comes from Old French *atirier*, from *ad*, to, and Old French *tire* or *tiere*, a row (compare our word *tier*), possibly of Teutonic origin; it means to place in rows, hence to arrange. *Array* comes from Latin *ad* and Teutonic *rede*, ready; and meant at first to get ready.

These terms are all applicable to dress or exterior decoration. *Apparel* is the dress of every one; *attire* is the dress of the great; *array* is the dress of particular persons on particular occasions: it is the first object of every man to provide himself with *apparel* suitable to his station; but the desire of shining forth in gaudy *attire* is the property of little minds: in festivals and solemn occasions it may be proper for those who are to be conspicuous to set themselves out with a comely *array*. *Apparel* and *attire* respect the quality and fashion of the thing; but *array* has regard to the disposition of the things with their neatness and decorum: *apparel* may be costly or mean; *attire* may be gay or shabby; but *array* will never be otherwise than neat or comely.

APPARENT, VISIBLE, CLEAR, PLAIN, OBVIOUS, EVIDENT, MANIFEST. *Apparent*, in Latin *apparens*, participle of *appareo*, to appear, signifies the quality of appearing. *Visible*, in Latin *visibilis*, from *visus*, participle of *video*, to see, signifies capable of being seen. *Clear* is in French *clair*, German, Swedish, etc., *klar*, Latin *clarus*. *Plain*, in Latin *planus*, even, signifies what is so smooth and unencumbered that it can be seen. *Obvious* in Latin *obvius*, compounded of *ob* and *via*, signifies the quality of lying in one's way or before one's eyes. *Evident*, in French *évident*, Latin *evidens*, means something clearly seen or known, from *e* or *ex*, out, and *video*, see. The intensive force of *e* in this case is similar to that of the prepositions or adverb in English phrases like "see one's way out" of difficulty, "to see through" something, etc. *Manifest*, in French *manifeste*, Latin *manifestus*, compounded of *manus*, the hand, and *festus*, possibly from *fendo*, to strike, signifies the quality of being so near that it can be laid hold of by the hand.

These words agree in expressing various degrees in the capability of seeing; but *visible* is the only one used purely in a physical sense; *apparent, clear, plain*, and *obvious* are used physically and morally; *evident* and *manifest* solely in a moral acceptation. That which is simply an object of sight is *visible;* that which presents itself to our view in any form, real or otherwise, is *apparent;* the stars themselves are *visible* to us; but their size is *apparent.*

Visible is applied to that which merely admits of being seen; *apparent* and the other terms denote not only what is to be seen, but what is easily to be seen: they are all applied as epithets to objects of mental discernment; what is *apparent* strikes the view; what is *clear* is to be seen in all its parts and in its proper colors: it is opposed to that which is obscure; what is *plain* is seen by a plain understanding: it requires no deep reflection or severe study; it is opposed to what is intricate: what is *obvious* presents itself readily to the mind of every one; it is seen at the first glance, and is opposed to that which is abstruse: what is *evident* is seen forcibly, and leaves no hesitation on the mind; it is opposed to that which is dubious; *manifest* is a greater degree of the *evident;* it strikes on the understanding and forces conviction; it is opposed to that which is dark. A thing is *apparent* upon the face of it: a case is *clear;* it is decided on immediately: a truth is *plain;* it is involved in no perplexity; it is not multifarious in its bearings: a falsehood is *plain;* it admits of no question: a reason is *obvious;* it flows out of the nature of the case: a proof is *evident;* it requires no discussion, there is nothing in it that clashes or contradicts; the guilt or innocence of a person is *evident* when everything serves to strengthen the conclusion: a contradiction or absurdity is *manifest* which is felt by all as soon as it is perceived.

APPARITION. See Vision.

APPEAR. See Look; See; Seem; Transpire.

APPEARANCE, Air, Aspect. *Appearance* signifies the thing that appears or the manner of appearing. *Air* (see Air). *Aspect*, in Latin *aspectus*, from *aspicio*, from *ad* (to) and *specere*, look, cognate with English *spy*, signifies the thing that is looked upon or seen.

Appearance is the generic, the rest are specific terms. The whole external form, figure, or colors, whatever is visible to the eye, is its *appearance; air* is a particular *appearance* of any object as far as it is indicative of its quality or condition; an *air* of wretchedness or poverty: *aspect* is the partial *appearance* of a body as it presents one of its sides to view; a gloomy or cheerful *aspect.* It is not safe to judge of either persons or things altogether by *appearances;* the *appearance* and reality are often at variance: the *appearance* of the sun is that of a moving body, but astronomers assert that it has no motion round the earth: there are particular towns, habitations, or rooms which have always an *air* of comfort, or the contrary: this is a sort of appearance the most to be relied on: politicians of a certain stamp are always busy in judging for the future from the *aspect* of affairs; but their predictions, like those of astrologers who judge from the *aspect* of the heavens, frequently turn out to the discredit of the prophet.

See also Air; Show.

APPEASE, Calm, Pacify, Quiet, Still. For derivation of *appease* see Allay. *Calm* comes from Late Latin *cauma*, the heat of the sun, Greek καῦμα, modified by Latin *calere*, to grow hot, and signified rest during the day. *Pacify*, in Latin *pacifico*, compounded of *pax* and *facio*, signifies to make peaceable. *Quiet*, in French *quiet*, Latin *quietus*, from *quies*, rest, signifies to put to rest. *Still*, from Anglo-Saxon *stillan*, to remain in a *stall*, is allied with the German *stellen*, to place, and signifies to stop all movement, to place at rest.

To *appease* is to remove great agitation; to *calm* is to bring into a tranquil state. The wind is *appeased*, the sea is calmed. With regard to persons, it is necessary to *appease* those who are in transports of passion, and to *calm* those who are in trouble, anxiety, or apprehension. *Appease* respects matters of force or violence, *calm* those of inquietude and distress: one is *appeased* by a submissive behavior, and *calmed* by the removal of danger. *Pacify* corresponds to *appease*, and *quiet* to *calm;* in sense they are the same, but in application they differ; *appease* and *calm* are used only in reference to objects of importance; *pacify* and *quiet* to those of a more familiar nature: the uneasy humors of a child are *pacified* or its groundless fears are *quieted*. *Still* is a loftier expression than any of the former terms; serving mostly for the grave or poetic style: it is an onomatopæia for restraining or putting to silence that which is noisy and boisterous.

See also ALLAY; MOLLIFY.

APPELLATION. See NAME.

APPLAUD. See PRAISE.

APPLAUSE, ACCLAMATION. *Applause,* from the Latin *applaudo,* signifies, literally, to clap or stamp the feet to a thing. *Acclamation,* from *acclamo,* signifies a crying out to a thing.

These terms express a public demonstration; the former by means of a noise with the hands or feet; the latter by means of shouts and cries: the former being employed as a testimony of approbation; the latter as a sanction, or an indication of respect. An actor looks for *applause;* a speaker looks for *acclamation.* What a man does calls forth *applause,* but the person himself is mostly received with *acclamations.* At the hustings popular speeches meet with *applause,* and favorite members are greeted with loud *acclamations.*

APPLICATION. See ATTEND.

APPLY. See ADDED; ADDRESS.

APPOINT, ORDER, PRESCRIBE, ORDAIN. *Appoint* (see ALLOT). *Order,* in French *ordre,* Latin *ordino,* to arrange, dispose, *ordo,* order, signifies to place in regular position. *Prescribe,* in Latin *prescribo,* compounded of *præ,* before, and *scribere,* to write, signifies to draw a line for a person. *Ordain* is a variation of *order.*

To *appoint* is either the act of an equal or superior: we *appoint* a meeting with any one at a given time and place; a king *appoints* his ministers. To *order* is the act of one invested with partial authority: a customer *orders* a commodity from his tradesman: a master gives his *orders* to his servant. To *prescribe* is the act of one who is superior by virtue of his knowledge: a physician *prescribes* for his patient. To *ordain* is an act emanating from the highest authority: kings and councils *ordain;* but their *ordinances* must be conformable to what is *ordained* by the Divine Being. *Appointments* are made for the convenience of individuals or communities; but they may be altered or annulled at the pleasure of the contracting parties. *Orders* are dictated by the superior only, but they presuppose a discretionary obligation on the part of the individual to whom they are given. *Prescriptions* are binding on none but such as voluntarily admit their authority; but *ordinances* leave no choice to those on whom they are imposed to accept or reject them: the *ordinances* of man are not less binding than those of God, so long as they do not expressly contradict the divine law.

Appointments are kept, *orders* executed or obeyed, *prescriptions* followed, *ordinances* submitted to. It is a point of politeness or honor, if not of direct moral obligation, to keep the *appointments* which we have made. Interest will lead men to execute the *orders* which they receive in the course of business: duty obliges them to obey the *orders* of their superiors. It is a nice matter to *prescribe* to another without hurting his pride; this principle leads men often to regard the counsels of their best friends as *prescriptions;* with children it is an unquestionable duty to follow the *prescriptions* of those whose age, station, or experience authorizes them to *prescribe.* God has *ordained* all things for our good; it rests with ourselves to submit to His *ordinances* and be happy.

See also CONSTITUTE.

APPORTION. See DISTRIBUTE.

APPRAISE, APPRECIATE, ESTIMATE, ESTEEM. *Appraise* and *appreciate,* both from *appretio* and *appretiatus,* participle of *apprecio,* compounded of *ad* and *pretium,* a price, signify to set a price or value on a thing. *Estimate* comes from *estimatus*, participle of *estimo*, to value. To *esteem* is a variation of *estimate*.

Appraise and *appreciate* are used in precisely the same sense for setting a value on anything according to relative circumstances; but the one is used in the proper, and the other in the figurative sense: a sworn *appraiser appraises* goods according to the condition of the articles and their salable property; the characters of men are *appreciated* by others when their good and bad qualities are justly put in a balance.

To *estimate* a thing is to get the sum of its value by calculation; to *esteem* anything is to judge its actual and intrinsic value. *Estimate* is used either in a proper or a figurative acceptation; *esteem* only in a moral sense: the expense of an undertaking, losses by fire, gains by trade, are *estimated* at a certain sum; the *estimate* may be too high or too low: the moral worth of men is often *estimated* above or below the reality, according to the particular bias of the *estimator;* but there are individuals of such an unquestionable worth that they need only to be known in order to be *esteemed*.

APPRECIATE. See APPRAISE.

APPREHEND, CONCEIVE, SUPPOSE, IMAGINE. To *apprehend*, from the Latin *ad* and *prehendo*, I lay hold of, signifies to take. *Conceive*, from the Latin *con* and *capio*, to take together— that is, to put together in the mind. *Suppose*, from the Latin *suppono*, to put one thing in the place of another. *Imagine*, from *imago*, to have an *image* or figure of anything in the mind.

To *apprehend* is simply to take an idea into the mind; thus we may *apprehend* any object that we hear or see: to *conceive* is to form an idea in the mind, as to *conceive* the idea of doing anything, to *conceive* a design.

Apprehending is the first effort of the thinking faculty: *conceiving* is the act of a more matured understanding; the former belongs to children as well as grown persons, the latter more properly to grown persons. *Apprehending* is performed by the help of the senses; we may be quick or dull of *apprehension*. *Conceiving* is performed by reflection and combination: we may *conceive* properly or improperly.

That of which we can have no sensible impression is not to be *apprehended*, that which is above the reach of our thought is not to be *conceived*.

To *apprehend* and to *conceive* are applied only to reality, to *suppose* and *imagine* are applied to things which may exist only in the imagination; but the former being drawn from that which is real may be probable or improbable according to circumstances; the latter being the peculiar act of the imagination, more commonly exists in the imagination only.

These terms are all employed to denote one's opinion or belief in regard to ordinary matters with a like distinction. *Apprehend* expresses the weakest kind of belief, the having the least idea of the presence of a thing.

A man is said to *conceive* that on which he forms a direct opinion.

What one *supposes* may admit of a doubt; it is frequently only conjectural.

What one *imagines* may be altogether improbable or impossible, and that which cannot be *imagined* may be too improbable to admit of being believed.

Apprehend, Fear, Dread.—*Apprehend* signifies to have an idea of danger in one's mind, without necessarily implying any sentiment of fear. *Fear,* Anglo-Saxon *fær,* a sudden peril or danger, referred originally to the peril of travelling, and is allied to *faran,* modern *fare,* meaning to travel. *Dread,* Anglo-Saxon *drædan,* to be afraid, expresses the highest degree of fear.

What is possible may be *apprehended;* we may *apprehend* a change in the weather, or that an accident will take place by the way. What is probable may be *feared;* we may fear the consequences of a person's resentment. Not only the evil which is nigh, but that which is exceeding great, produces *dread*.

Apprehend is said only of things. *Fear* and *dread* are also applied to persons with the like distinction: *fear* is a salutary sentiment; it is the sentiment of a child toward a parent or instructor: *dread*, as toward a fellow-creature, is produced by harshness and oppression, but in regard to our Maker is produced by the consciousness of guilt.

APPREHENSION. See WORRY.

APPRISE. See INFORM.

APPRISED. See AWARE.

APPROACH, ACCESS, ADMITTANCE. *Approach,* Old French *aprochier,* from Latin *prope* near, signifies near to—that is, coming near to. *Access,* in Latin *accessus,* from *ac* or *ad,* and *cedere,* to go, is, properly, going to. *Admittance* (see ADMIT).

Approach signifies the coming near or toward an object, and consequently is an unfinished act, but *access* and *admittance* are finished acts; *access* is the coming to—that is, as close to an object as is needful; and *admittance* is the coming into any place or into the presence or society of any person. *Approach* expresses simply the act of drawing near, but *access* and *admittance* comprehend, in their signification, the liberty and power of coming to or into: an *approach* may be quick or slow, an *access* easy or difficult, an *admittance* free or exclusive.

Approach may sometimes be taken for a road or way of *approach,* which brings it nearer in sense to the other terms, as the *approaches* to a bridge or a town.

Access is used only in its proper sense for the act of persons; *approach* and *admittance* are employed figuratively, as the *approach* of winter, age, etc., or the *approach* to immortality, in the sense of coming near to it in similitude, the *admittance* of immoral thoughts into the mind.

Approach, Approximate.—*Approach* (see preceding use). *Approximate,* compound of *ap* and *proximus,* to come nearest or next, signifies either to draw near or bring near. To *approach* is intransitive only; a person *approaches* an object. To *approximate* is both transitive and intransitive; a person *approximates* two objects to each other. To *approach* denotes simply the moving of an object toward another, but to *approximate* denotes the gradual moving of two objects toward each other: that which *approaches* may come into immediate conjunction; but bodies may *approximate* for some time before they form a junction, or may never

form a junction. An equivocation *approaches* to a lie. Minds *approximate* by long intercourse.

APPROBATION. See ASSENT; CONSENT.

APPROPRIATE, USURP, ARROGATE, ASSUME, ASCRIBE. *Appropriate,* in French *approprier,* compounded of *ad* and *propriatus,* participle of *propriare,* an old verb, and *proprius,* proper or own (compare *proper*), signifies to make one's own. *Usurp,* in French *usurper,* Latin *usurpo,* from *usu rapere,* to seize for one's own use, signifies to make use of as one's own. *Arrogate,* in Latin *arrogatus,* participle of *arrogo,* signifies to ask or claim for one's self. *Assume,* in French *assumer,* Latin *assumo,* compounded of *as* or *ad* and *sumo,* to take, signifies to take to one's self. *Ascribe,* in Latin *ascribo,* compounded of *ad* and *scribo,* write, signifies here to write down to one's own account.

The idea of taking something to one's self by an act of one's own is common to all these terms. To *appropriate* is to take to one's self with or without right; to *usurp* is to take to one's self by violence or in violation of right. *Appropriating* is applied in its proper sense to goods in possession; *usurping* is properly applied to power, titles, rights. Individuals *appropriate* whatever comes to their hands which they use as their own; they *usurp* power when they exercise the functions of government without a legitimate sanction.

These words may be applied in the same sense to moral or spiritual objects.

Arrogate, assume, and *ascribe* denote the taking to one's self, but do not, like *appropriate* and *usurp,* imply taking from another. *Arrogate* is a more violent action than *assume,* and *assume* than *ascribe.* *Arrogate* and *assume* are employed either in the proper or figurative sense, *ascribe* only in the figurative sense. We *arrogate* distinctions, honors, titles; we *assume* names, rights, and privileges. In the moral sense we *arrogate* pre-eminence, *assume* importance, *ascribe* merit. To *arrogate* is a species of moral *usurpation;* it is always accompanied with haughtiness and contempt for others: that is *arrogated* to one's self to which one has not the smallest title: an *arrogant* temper is one of the most odious features in the human character; it is a compound of folly and insolence. To *assume* is a species of moral *appropriation;* its objects are of a less serious nature than those of *arrogating*, and it does less violence to moral propriety: we may *assume* in trifles, we *arrogate* only in important matters. To *ascribe* is oftener an act of vanity than of injustice: many men may be entitled to the merit which they *ascribe* to themselves; but by this very act they lessen the merit of their best actions.

Arrogating as an action, or *arrogance* as a disposition, is always taken in a bad sense: the former is always dictated by the most preposterous pride; the latter is associated with every unworthy quality. *Assumption* as an action varies in its character according to circumstances; it may be either good, bad, or indifferent: it is justifiable in certain exigencies to *assume* a command where there is no one else able to direct; it is often a matter of indifference what name a person *assumes* who does so only in conformity to the will of another; but it is always bad to *assume* a name as a mask to impose upon others. As a disposition *assumption* is always bad, but still not to the same degree as *arrogance*. An *arrogant* man renders himself intolerable to society: an *assuming* man makes himself offensive: *arrogance* is the characteristic of men; *assumption* is peculiar to youths: an *arrogant* man can be humbled only by silent contempt; an *assuming* youth must be checked by the voice of authority.

See also MONOPOLIZE; NAB; PECULIAR.

APPROVE. See RATIFY.

APPROXIMATE. See APPROACH.

APT. See FIT; READY.

APTITUDE. See KNACK.

ARBITER. See JUDGE.

ARBITRARY. See ABSOLUTE.

ARBITRATE, ADJUST, DECIDE, DETERMINE, MEDIATE, SETTLE. *Arbitrate* (for derivation see JUDGE) means to decide as an outsider, an impartial judge. *Adjust* (not derived from justice, but from *ad* and *juxta*, next to) meant originally to put side by side, to put something into a proper relation to something else. *Decide* is derived from *de* and *cædere*, to cut, and means to cut off, hence to end. *Determine* comes from Latin *de* and *terminare*, from *terminus*, limit, and meant to decide the limits of something. *Mediate*, from Latin *medius*, middle, meant to act as a go-between. *Settle* meant to cause to rest, from Anglo-Saxon *setl*, seat (compare the noun *settle*, a seat). It received the special sense of to establish peace between two combatants, from an association with the Anglo-Saxon *sæht*, the end of a suit, allied to the verb *sacan*, to contend, which appears in *forsake*. Of these terms *mediate* and *arbitrate* refer especially to the difficulties that arise between states or between other organized groups of individuals. To *mediate* involves an action prior to arbitration, for it is based upon a tender of the "good offices" of a neutral nation to others in a dispute or war. In case it is accepted the *mediating* nation may become the *arbitrator* or the dispute may be submitted to another form of *arbitration*—that is, final decision concerning the justice of the case by an impartial court. For an analysis of the difference between *decide* and *determine* see the article on *decide*. *Decide* and *determine* refer to purely intellectual operations. One may *decide* or *determine* the rights of a case without proceeding to *adjust* the difficulties or to *settle* the disturbance. *Adjust* and *settle* imply active participation. *Adjust* and *settle* differ mainly in the connotations suggested by their derivations. We *adjust* matters where the trouble is due to a lack of mutual understanding between two conflicting parties. We *settle* a disturbance where conflicting claims cannot be *adjusted* by superior force or authority.

ARBITRATOR. See JUDGE; PACIFIST.

ARCHITECT, BUILDER. *Architect*, from architecture, in Latin *architectus*, from *architectura*, Greek ἀρχιτέκτων, compounded of ἀρχός, the chief, and τέχνη, art or contrivance, signifies the chief of contrivers. *Builder*, from the verb to *build*, denotes the person concerned in buildings, who causes the structure of houses, either by his money or his personal service.

An *architect* is an artist, employed only to form the plans for large buildings; a *builder* is a simple tradesman, or even workman, who *builds* common dwelling-houses.

ARCHIVE. See RECORD.

ARDENT. See HOT; SANGUINE.

ARDOR. See FERVOR; ZEAL.

ARDUOUS. See HARD.

ARGUE, DISPUTE, DEBATE. *Argue* comes from Latin *arguere*, to make clear. *Dispute*, in French *disputer*, Latin *disputo*, compounded of *dis* and *puto*, signifies to think differently; in an extended sense, to assert a different opinion. *Debate*, in French *débattre*, compounded of the intensive syllable *de* and *battre*, to beat or fight, signifies to contend for and against.

To *argue* is to defend one's self; to *dispute*, to oppose another; to *debate*, to dispute in a formal manner. To *argue* on a subject is to explain the reasons or proofs in support of an assertion; to *argue* with a person is to defend a position against him: to *dispute* a thing is to advance objections against a position; to *dispute* with a person is to start objections against his positions, to attempt to refute them: a *debate* is a disputation held by many. To *argue* does not necessarily suppose a conviction on the part of the arguer that what he defends is true, nor a real difference of opinion in his opponent; for some men have such an itching propensity for an *argument* that they will attempt to prove what nobody denies: to *dispute* always supposes an opposition to some person, but not a sincere opposition to the thing; for we may *dispute* that which we do not deny, for the sake of holding a *dispute* with one who is of different sentiments: to *debate* presupposes a multitude of clashing or opposing opinions. Men of many words *argue* for the sake of talking: men of ready tongues *dispute* for the sake of victory: in parliament men often *debate* for the sake of opposing the ruling party, or from any other motive than the love of truth.

Argue, Evince, Prove.—*Argue* (see above). *Evince*, in Latin *evinco*, compounded of *vinco*, to *prove*, or make out, and *e*, forth, signifies to bring to light, to make to appear clear. *Prove*, in French *prouver*, in Latin *probo*, from *probus*, good, signifies to make good or to make to appear good.

These terms in general convey the idea of *evidence*, but with gradations: *argue* denotes the smallest, and *prove* the highest degree. To *argue* is to serve as an indication amounting to probability; to *evince* denotes an indication so clear as to remove doubt; to *prove* marks an *evidence* so positive as to produce conviction. It *argues* a want of candor in any man to conceal circumstances in his statement which are in any wise calculated to affect the subject in question: the tenor of a person's conversation may *evince* the refinement of his mind and the purity of his taste: when we see men sacrificing their peace of mind and even their integrity of character to ambition it *proves* to us how important it is even in early life to check this natural and in some measure laudable, but still insinuating and dangerous, passion.

Argument, Reason, Proof.—*Argument*, from *argue*, signifies either the thing that *argues*, or that which is brought forward in *arguing*. *Reason*, in French *raison*, Latin *ratio*, from *ratus*, participle of *reor*, think, signifies the faculty of mind which draws conclusions. *Proof*, like *prove*, is derived ultimately from Latin *probus*, good, excellent, and means that which tests and reveals the excellence of something.

An *argument* serves for defence; a *reason* for justification; a *proof* for conviction. *Arguments* are adduced in support of a hypothesis or proposition; *reasons* are assigned in matters of belief and practice; *proofs* are collected to ascertain a fact.

Arguments are either strong or weak; *reasons* solid or futile; *proofs* clear and positive, or vague and indefinite. We confute an *argument*, overpower a *reason*, and invalidate a *proof*. Whoever wished to defend Christianity will be in no want of *arguments;* the believer need never be at a loss to give a *reason* for the hope that is in him; but throughout the whole of Divine Revelation there is no circumstance that is substantiated with such irrefragable *proofs* as the resurrection of our Saviour.

ARISE, or RISE, MOUNT, ASCEND, CLIMB, SCALE. *Arise* or *rise*, derived from a root signifying to move, found in *river*, *rivulet*, etc., means specifically to move in an upward direction. *Ascend* is derived from *ad*, to, and *scandere*, to climb, from a root found in *scandal* (originally a stumbling-block), and means to climb to something. *Climb* means to ascend by grasping, and is derived from a Germanic root signifying to grasp, found in *clip*, *cleave*, *clamber*, etc. *Scale* is derived from Latin *scala* (from the same root found in *ascend*), that by which one *ascends*, and means to rise by a ladder.

The idea of going upward is common to all these terms; *arise* is used only in the sense of simply getting up, but *rise* is employed to express a continued motion upward: a person *arises* from his seat or his bed; a bird *rises* in the air; the silver of the barometer *rises;* the first three of these terms convey a gradation in their sense; to *arise* or *rise* denotes a motion to a less elevated height than to *mount*, and to *mount* that which is less elevated than *ascend;* a person *rises* from his seat, *mounts* a hill, and *ascends* a mountain. *Arise* and *rise* are intransitive only; the rest are likewise transitive: we *rise* from a point, we *mount* and *ascend* to a point, or we *mount* and *ascend* something: an air-balloon *rises* when it first leaves the ground; it *mounts* higher and higher until it is out of sight; but if it *ascends* too high it endangers the life of the aërial adventurer. *Climb* and *scale* express a species of rising: to *climb* is to *rise* step by step by clinging to a certain body; to *scale* is to rise by an escalade, or species of ladder, employed in *mounting* the walls of fortified towns: trees and mountains are *climbed;* walls are *scaled.*

Arise or *Rise, Proceed, Issue, Spring, Flow, Emanate.*—To *arise* (see above). *Proceed*, in Latin *procedo*, that is, *pro* and *cedere*, to go, signifies to go forth. *Issue* is French *issue*, participle of *issir* (from *ex*, out of, and *ire*, to go. *Spring*, in German *springen*, signifies to leap forth. *Flow*, Anglo-Saxon *flowan*, is derived from a Germanic root allied to the Latin *pluit*, it rains, and the Greek πλωειν, to float. It has no connection with the Latin *fluere*, to flow. *Emanate*, in Latin *emanatus*, participle of *emano*, from *ex*, out, and *manare*, to flow, means to flow out.

The idea of one object coming out of another is expressed by all these terms, but they differ in the circumstances of the action. What comes up out of a body and rises into existence is said to *arise*, as the mist which *arises* out of the sea: what comes forth as an effect, or comes forth in a particular manner, is said to *proceed;* thus the light *proceeds* from a certain quarter of the heavens, or from a certain part of a house: what comes out from a small aperture is said to *issue;* thus perspiration *issues* through the pores of the skin; water *issues* sometimes from the sides of rocks; what comes out in a sudden or quick manner, or comes from some remote source, is said to *spring;* thus blood *springs* from an artery which is pricked; water *springs* up out of the earth: what comes out in quantities or in a stream is said to *flow;* thus blood *flows* from a wound: to *emanate* is a species of *flowing* by a natural operation, when bodies send forth, or seem to send forth, particles of their own composition from themselves; thus light *emanates* from the sun.

This distinction in the signification of these terms is kept up in their moral acceptation, where the idea of one thing originating from another is common to them all; but in this case *arise* is a general term, which simply implies the coming into existence; *proceed* conveys also the idea of a progressive movement into existence. Every object, therefore, may be said to *arise* out of whatever produces it; but it *proceeds* from it only when it is gradually produced: evils are continually *arising* in human society for which there is no specific remedy: in complicated disorders it is not always possible to say precisely from what the complaint of the patient *proceeds*. *Issue* is seldom used but in application to sensible objects: yet we may say, in conformity to the original meaning, that words *issue* from the mouth: the idea of the distant source or origin is kept up in the moral application of the term *spring*, when we say that actions *spring* from a generous or corrupt principle: the idea of a quantity and a stream is preserved in the moral use of the terms *flow* and *emanate;* but the former may be said of that which is not inherent in the body; the latter respects that only which forms a component part of the body: God is the *spring* whence all our blessings *flow;* all authority *emanates* from God, who is the supreme source of all things; theologians, when speaking of God, say that the Son *emanates* from the Father, and the Holy Ghost from the Father and the Son, and that grace *flows* upon us incessantly from the inexhaustible treasures of Divine mercy.

ARMISTICE. See TRUCE.

ARMS, WEAPONS. *Arms,* from the Latin *arma,* literally fittings, equipments, from the root signifying to join or fashion found in *art, arm* (a part of the human body), etc., is now properly used for instruments of offence, and never otherwise except by a poetic license of *arms* for armor; but *weapon,* from a widespread Germanic root, may be used either for an instrument of offence or defence. We say fire-*arms,* but not fire-*weapons;* and *weapons* offensive or defensive, not *arms* offensive or defensive. *Arms,* likewise, agreeably to its origin, is employed for that only which is purposely made to be an instrument of offence; *weapon,* according to its extended and indefinite application, is employed for whatever may be accidentally used for this purpose: guns and swords are always *arms;* stones, brick-bats, and pitchforks, and also the tongue or words, may be occasionally *weapons.*

ARMY, HOST. An *army* is an organized body of *armed* men; a *host,* from *hostis,* an enemy, is properly a body of *hostile* men. An *army* is a limited body; a *host* may be unlimited, and is therefore generally considered a very large body.

The word *army* applies only to that which has been formed by the rules of art for purposes of war: *host* has been extended in its application not only to bodies, whether of men or angels, that were assembled for purposes of offence, but also in the figurative sense to whatever rises up to assail.

ARRAIGN. See ACCUSE.

ARRANGE. See CLASS; DISPOSE.

ARRAY. See APPAREL.

ARRIVE. See COME.

ARROGANCE, PRESUMPTION. *Arrogance,* in French *arrogance,* Latin *arrogantia,* signifies the disposition to *arrogate* (see APPROPRIATE). *Presumption,* from *presume,* Latin *præsumo,* compounded of *præ,* before, and *sumere,* itself compounded from *sub* and *emere,* to buy, and meaning to put or take, signifies the disposition to put one's self forward.

Arrogance is the act of the great; *presumption* that of the little: the *arrogant* man takes upon himself to be above others; the *presumptuous* man strives to be on a level with those who are above him. *Arrogance* is commonly coupled with haughtiness; *presumption* with meanness: men *arrogantly* demand as a right the homage which has perhaps before been voluntarily granted; the creature *presumptuously* arraigns the conduct of the Creator, and murmurs against the dispensations of His providence.

See also ASSUMPTION; HAUGHTINESS.

ARROGATE. See APPROPRIATE.

ART, CUNNING, DECEIT. *Art,* in Latin *ars,* from a root *ar,* to join (see *arms*), allied to Greek ἄρτιος, fit, exact, signifies literally the "putting of two and two together." *Cunning* is derived from Anglo-Saxon *cunnan,* to know, and therefore corresponds exactly to the colloquial adjective *knowing,* in such phrases as "a *knowing* look," "a *knowing* child," etc. *Deceit,* in Latin *deceptum,* participle of *decipio,* or *de* and *capio,* signifies to take by surprise or unawares.

Art implies a disposition of the mind to use circumvention or artificial means to attain an end: *cunning* marks the disposition to practise disguise in the prosecution of a plan: *deceit* leads to the practice of dissimulation and gross falsehood, for the sake of gratifying a desire. *Art* is the property of a lively mind; *cunning,* of a thoughtful and knowing mind; *deceit,* of an ignorant, low, and weak mind. *Art* is practised often in self-defence; as a practice, therefore, it is even sometimes justifiable, although not as a disposition: *cunning* has always self in view; the *cunning* man seeks his gratification without regard to others; *deceit* is often practised to the express injury of an-

ARTIFICE 73

other: the *deceitful* man adopts base
means for base ends. Animals practise *art* when opposed to their superiors
in strength; but they are not *artful*, as
they have not that versatility of power
which they can habitually exercise to
their own advantage like human beings;
animals may be *cunning*, inasmuch as
they can by contrivance and concealment seek to obtain the object of their
desire, but no animal is *deceitful* except
man; the wickedest and stupidest of
men have the power and the will of
deceiving and practising falsehood upon
others which is unknown to the
brutes.

See also BUSINESS.

Artful, Artificial, Fictitious.—*Artful,*
compounded of *art* and *full,* marks the
quality of being full of *art.* *Artificial,*
in Latin *artificialis,* from *ars* and *facio,*
to do, signifies done with *art.* *Fictitious,*
in Latin *fictitius,* from *fingere* to feign
(compare article on *feign*), signifies the
quality of being *feigned.*

Artful respects what is done with art
or design; *artificial* what is done by
the exercise of workmanship; *fictitious*
what is made out of the mind. *Artful*
and *artificial* are used either for natural
or moral objects; *fictitious* always for
those that are moral: *artful* is opposite
to what is *artless, artificial* to what is
natural, *fictitious* to what is real: the
ringlets of a lady's hair are disposed
in an *artful* manner; the hair itself
may be *artificial;* a tale is *artful* which
is told in a way to gain credit; manners are *artificial* which do not seem
to suit the person adopting them; a
story is *fictitious* which has no foundation whatever in truth and is the invention of the narrator. Children
sometimes tell their stories so *artfully*
as to impose on the most penetrating
and experienced. Those who have no
character of their own are induced to
take an *artificial* character in order to
put themselves on a level with their
associates. Beggars deal in *fictitious*
tales of distress in order to excite compassion.

See also SCHEMING.

ARTICLE, CONDITION, TERM. *Ar-
ticle,* in French *article,* Latin *articulus,*
a joint or a part of a member. *Condition* is usually believed to be derived
from the Latin *condere,* to build. Skeat

declares that this is incorrect. The
Latin *conditio* is derived from *con* and
a root found in *dicere,* to speak, meaning to point out. *Term* is derived
from Latin *terminus,* Greek τέρμα, from
the root meaning to cross over.

These words agree in their application to matters of compact, or understanding between man and man. *Article* and *condition* are used in both numbers: *terms* only in the plural in this
sense: the former may be used for
any point individually; the latter for
all the points collectively: *article* is
employed for all matters which are
drawn out in specific *articles* or *points;*
as the *articles* of an indenture, of a
capitulation, or an agreement. *Condition* respects any point that is admitted as a ground of obligation or
engagement: it is used for the general
transactions of men, in which they
reciprocally bind themselves to return
certain equivalents. The word *terms*
is employed in regard to mercantile
transactions; as the *terms* of any bargain, the *terms* of any agreement, the
terms on which anything is bought or
sold. *Articles* are mostly voluntary;
they are admitted by mutual agreement: *conditions* are frequently compulsory, sometimes hard; they are
submitted to from policy or necessity;
terms are dictated by interest or equity;
they are fair or unfair according to
the temper of the parties; they are
submitted or agreed to.

ARTICULATE. See UTTER.

ARTIFICE, TRICK, FINESSE, STRAT-
AGEM. *Artifice,* from French *artifice,*
Latin *artifex,* an *artificer,* and *artem
facio,* to execute an art, signifies the
performance of an art. *Trick* is derived from Dutch and originally meant
a clever contrivance. *Finesse,* a word
directly imported from France, with all
the meaning attached to it which is
characteristic of the nation itself,
means properly fineness; the word *fin*
in French is derived from Latin *finitus,*
meaning well finished. *Stratagem,* in
French *stratagème,* from the Greek
στρἄτήγημα and στρἄτηγέω, to lead an
army, signifies by distinction to head
them in carrying on any scheme.

All these terms denote the exercise of
an art calculated to mislead others.
Artifice is the generic term, the rest are

specific: the former has likewise a particular use and acceptation distinct from the others; it expresses a ready display of art for the purpose of extricating one's self from a difficulty, or securing to one's self an advantage. *Trick* includes in it more of design to gain something for one's self, or to act secretly to the inconvenience of others: it is rather a cheat on the senses than the understanding. *Finesse* is a species of artifice in which art and cunning are combined in the management of a cause: it is a mixture of invention, falsehood, and concealment. *Stratagem* is a display of art in plotting and contriving, a disguised mode of obtaining an end. Females who are not guarded by fixed principles of virtue and uprightness are apt to practise *artifices* upon their husbands. Men without honor, or an honorable means of living, are apt to practise various *tricks* to impose upon others to their own advantage: every trade, therefore, is said to have its *tricks;* and professions are not entirely clear from this stigma, which has been brought upon them by unworthy members. Diplomatic persons have most frequent recourse to *finesse*. Military operations are sometimes considerably forwarded by well-concerted and well-timed *stratagems* to surprise the enemy.

An *artifice* may be perfectly innocent when it serves to afford a friend an unexpected pleasure. A *trick* is childish which only serves to deceive or amuse children. *Stratagems* are allowable not in war only; the writer of a novel or a play may sometimes adopt a successful *stratagem* to cause the reader a surprise. *Finesse* is never justifiable; it carries with it too much of concealment and disingenuousness to be practised but for selfish and unworthy purposes.

ARTIFICER. See ARTIST.

ARTIFICIAL. See ARTFUL; THEATRICAL.

ARTISAN. See ARTIST.

ARTIST, ARTISAN, ARTIFICER, MECHANIC. *Artist* is the practicer of the fine arts (for derivation see ART); *artisan* the practicer of the vulgar arts. *Artificer* comes from *ars* and *facio*, one who does or makes according to art. *Mechanic*, from Greek μηχανική, a machine, a device, signifies one who works with machines.

The *artist* ranks higher than the *artisan*, the former requires intellectual refinement, the latter nothing but to know the common practice of art. The musician, painter, and sculptor are *artists;* the carpenter, the sign-painter, and the blacksmith are *artisans*. The *artificer* is an intermediate term between the *artist* and the *artisan;* manufacturers are *artificers;* and, in an extended sense, any one who makes a thing by his contrivance is an *artificer*. The *mechanic* is that species of artisan who works at arts purely *mechanical*, in distinction from those which contribute to the completion and embellishment of any objects; on this ground a shoemaker is a *mechanic*, but a common painter is a simple *artisan*.

ARTLESS. See NAÏVE.

AS. See BOTH.

ASCEND. See ARISE.

ASCENDANCY. See INFLUENCE.

ASCETIC, AUSTERE, RIGID, STERN. *Ascetic* in French *ascétique*, from ἀσκεῖν, to work, exercise, applied, literally, to the practice of an art, hence to an athlete, and, by extension, to the discipline practised by an athlete. In the schools of the stoics, the term that implied this discipline practised by the wrestlers was employed to designate the practice of mastering the desires and passions or of severe virtue, and in this sense it passed into the language of the early Christians: on this basis the modern meaning of a person unduly rigid or *austere* was derived.

Austere is derived from Latin *austerus*, harsh, sour, tart, from Greek αὐστηρός, making the tongue dry, harsh, bitter. It signifies a manner, a temperament, and does not so distinctly imply the mastering of the physical appetites as does the word *ascetic*. Similarly *stern*, from Anglo-Saxon *styrne*, of harsh mind, refers to a kind of temper. *Austerity* suggests both the habits of life indicated in *asceticism* and the kind of nature suggested by *sternness*. A man may be *stern* and, at the same time, be the opposite of *ascetic*. *Rigid*, from Latin *rigidus* (whence *rigorous* is also derived by way of French), comes from the Latin *rigere*, to be stiff or straight. It refers both to the property of physical things and, figuratively, to a certain habit of mind or of life. *Stern* refers to a kind of emotional temperament; *rigid* suggests an intellectual habit, an unbending mind, whence certain characteristics of temper and habits of living might develop.

ASCRIBE, IMPUTE, ATTRIBUTE. To *ascribe* signifies here generally to write or set down in one's own mind to a person (see APPROPRIATE)—that is, to assign anything in one's estimate as the possession or the property of another, as to *ascribe* honor or power. To *impute*, from *im* or *in* and *puto*, think, is to form an estimate of a person; as to *impute* a thing to a person's folly. To *attribute*, from *ad* and *tribuo*, bestow, is to assign a thing as a cause; as to *attribute* the loss of a vessel to the violence of the storm.

What is *ascribed* and *imputed* is mostly of a personal nature, either to honor or dishonor; *ascribe* more frequently for the former, *impute* for the latter. In the doxology of the church ritual, all honor, might, majesty, dominion, and power are *ascribed* to the three persons in the Holy Trinity; men of right minds cannot bear the slightest *imputation* on their honor, nor virtuous women the slightest *imputation* on their chastity.

Ascribe may, however, sometimes be employed in an unfavorable sense, and *impute* in a favorable sense. We may *ascribe* imperfection as well as perfection, and *impute* good as well as bad motives.

To *ascribe* may also denote to assign a cause, which brings it nearer in sense to *attribute;* but the former always refers to some characteristic of the person, and the latter, although applied to personal qualities, conveys no personal reflection.

To *ascribe* is always to assign to some individual person; but to *attribute* may either refer to no persons, or to none individually. Milton *ascribes* the first use of artillery to the devil: the Letters of Junius have been *ascribed* successively to many as the author; the death of many persons may be *attributed* to intemperance.

ASEPTIC, GERMLESS, NON-PUTRE-FYING. *Aseptic*, a compound of the Greek ἄσηπτος (from ἀ privative and σηπτικός, putrefying) and the English suffix *ic*, signifies that which is not liable to putrefaction, or that which is *germless* or free from septic matter, or any substance that produces or promotes putrefaction; in the substantive form, *asepsis*, the absence of toxinous or pathogenic bacteria which poison the blood. From the original Greek term we have *septicæmia*, an acute disease resembling pyæmia in its general characteristics, supposed to be caused by the introduction into the blood of putrid matter from the surface of a wound or ulcer, the putrefaction now being known, through the antiseptic researches of Pasteur and Lister, to be a fermentative change due to the presence of certain micro-organisms in the blood.

Antiseptic surgery is the operation of introducing antiseptic solutions into a wound whence the poisonous matter has been carried into the blood, or where the wound has not been promptly treated by antisepsis, or the exclusion of microbes or bacteria from wounds and open sores.

ASK, BEG, REQUEST. *Ask*, in Anglo-Saxon *ascian*, is derived from a Germanic root signifying to wish. *Beg* is derived, by a somewhat complicated process, from a frequentative of *bid*, and meant to bid often, to ask again and again. *Request*, in Latin *requisitus*, participle of *requiro*, is compounded of *re* and *quærere*, to seek or look after, with indications of desire to possess.

The expression of a wish to some one to have something is the common idea comprehended in these terms. As this is the simple signification of *ask*, it is the generic term; the other two are specific; we *ask* in *begging* and *requesting*, but not *vice versa*. *Asking* is peculiar to no rank or station; in consequence of our mutual dependence on each other, it is requisite for every man to *ask* something of another: the master *asks* of the servant, the servant *asks* of the master; the parent *asks* of the child, the child *asks* of the parent. *Begging* marks a degree of dependence which is peculiar to inferiors in station; we *ask* for matters of indifference; we *beg* that which we think is of importance: a child *asks* a favor of his parent; a poor man *begs* the assistance of one who is able to afford it: that is *asked* for which is easily granted; that is *begged* which is with difficulty obtained. To *ask*, therefore, requires no effort, but to *beg* is to *ask* with importunity: those who by merely *asking* find themselves unable to obtain what they wish, will have recourse to *begging*. As *ask* sometimes implies a demand, and *beg* a vehemence of desire or strong degree of necessity, politeness has adopted another phrase, which conveys neither the imperiousness of the one nor the urgency of the other; this is the word *request*. *Asking* carries with it an air of superiority; *begging* that of submission; *requesting* has the air of independence and equality. *Asking* borders too nearly on an infringement of personal liberty; *begging* imposes a constraint by making an appeal to the feelings; *requests* leave the liberty of granting or refusing unencumbered. It is the character of impertinent people to *ask* without considering the circumstances and situation of the person *asked;* they seem ready to take without permission that which is *asked*, if it be not granted: selfish and greedy people *beg* with importunity, and in a tone that admits of no refusal; men of good breeding tender their *requests* with moderation and discretion; they *request* nothing but what they are certain can be conveniently complied with.

Ask is altogether excluded from polite life, although *beg* is not. We may *beg* a person's acceptance of anything; we may *beg* him to favor or honor us with his company; but we can never talk of *asking* a person's acceptance, or *asking* him to do us an honor. *Beg* in such cases indicates a condescension which is sometimes not unbecoming, but on ordinary occasions *request* is with more propriety substituted in its place.

Ask, or Ask For, Claim, Demand.— *Ask* (see above). *Claim*, in Old French *claimer*, Latin *clamo*, to cry after, signifies to express an imperious wish for. *Demand*, in French *demander*, is derived from Old French *de* and *mander*, to order from the hands of another (from *manus*, hand), and hence to ask for that which has been intrusted.

Ask, in the sense of *beg*, is confined to the expression of wishes on the part of the *asker*, without involving any obligation on the part of the person *asked;* all granted in this case is voluntary, or complied with as a favor; but *ask for*, in the sense here taken, is involuntary, and springs from the forms and distinctions of society. *Ask* is here, as before, generic or specific; *claim* and *demand* are specific: in its specific sense it conveys a less peremptory sense than either *claim* or *demand*. To *ask for* denotes simply the expressed wish to have what is considered as due; to *claim* is to assert a right or to make it known;. to *demand* is to insist on having, without the liberty of a refusal. *Asking* respects obligation in general, great or small; *claim* respects obligations of importance. *Asking for* supposes a right not questionable; *claim* supposes a right hitherto unacknowledged; *demand* supposes either a disputed right or the absence of all right, and the simple determination to have: a tradesman *asks* for what is owed to him as circumstances may require; a person *claims* the property he has lost; people are sometimes pleased to make *demands* the legality of which cannot be proved. What is lent must be *asked for* when it is wanted; whatever has been lost and is found must be recovered by a *claim;* whatever a selfish person wants he strives to obtain by a *demand*, whether just or unjust.

Ask, Inquire, Question, Interrogate.— *Ask* (see above). *Inquire*, Latin *inquiro*, compounded of *in* and *quæro*, signifies to search after. *Question*, in French *questionner*, signifies to put a question, from the Latin *quæstio* and *quæro*, to seek or search, to look into. *Interrogate*, Latin *interrogatus*, participle of *interrogo*, compounded of *inter* and *rogo*, signifies to *ask*.

We perform all these actions in order to get information: but we *ask* for general purposes of convenience; we *inquire* from motives of curiosity; we *question* and *interrogate* from motives of discretion. To *ask* respects simply one thing; to *inquire* respects one or many subjects; to *question* and *interrogate* is to *ask* repeatedly, and in the fatter case more authoritatively than in the former. Indifferent people *ask* of each other whatever they wish to know: learners *inquire* the reasons of things which are new to them: masters *question* their servants, or parents their children, when they wish to ascertain the real state of any case: magistrates *interrogate* criminals when they are brought before them. It is very uncivil not to answer whatever is *asked* even by the meanest person: it is proper to satisfy every *inquiry*, so as to remove doubt: *questions* are sometimes so impertinent that they cannot with propriety be answered: *interrogations* from unauthorized persons are little better than insults.

ASKEW. See WRY.

ASPECT. See APPEARANCE.

ASPERITY. See ACRIMONY.

ASPERSE, DETRACT, DEFAME, SLANDER, CALUMNIATE. *Asperse*, in Latin *aspersus*, participle of *aspergere*, to sprinkle, allied to English *sprinkle*, signifies in a moral sense to stain with spots. *Detract*, in Latin *detractus*, participle of *detraho*, compounded of *de* and *traho*, to draw from, signifies to take from another that which is his due, or which he desires to retain; particularly to take from the merit of an action. *Defame*, in Latin *defamo*, compounded of the privative *de* and *fama*, from root *fari*, to speak, meaning reputation—that which others say about us—signifies to deprive of reputation. *Slander*, Middle English *sclandre*, is a doublet of *scandal* (see DISCREDIT), derived from Greek through Latin and French. *Calumniate* is derived from Latin *calumnia*, from *caluere*, to deceive.

All these terms denote an effort made to injure the character or estimation by some representation. *Asperse* and *detract* mark an indirect representation; *defame*, *slander*, and *calumniate*, a positive assertion. To *asperse* is to fix a moral stain on a character; to *detract* is to lessen its merits and excellences. *Aspersions* always imply something bad, real or supposed; *detractions* are always founded on some supposed good in the object that is *detracted;* to *defame* is openly to advance some serious charge against the character; to *slander* is to expose the faults of another in his absence; to *calumniate* is to communicate secretly, or otherwise, false circumstances to the injury of another. If I speak slightingly of my neighbor, and insinuate anything against the purity of his principles or the rectitude of his conduct, I *asperse* him: if he be a charitable man, and I ascribe his charities to a selfish motive, or otherwise take away from the merit of his conduct, I am guilty of *detraction;* if I publish anything openly that injures his reputation, I am a *defamer;* if I communicate to others the reports that are in circulation to his disadvantage, I am a *slanderer;* if I fabricate anything myself and spread it abroad, I am a *calumniator*.

ASPHYXIA, SYNCOPE, SUFFOCATION. *Asphyxia*, in French *asphyxie*, is from Latin *asphyxia*, Greek ἀσφυξία the latter a compound of ἀ, without, and σφύξις, the pulse, signifies, literally, a pulseless condition, the temporary or permanent cessation of the motions or throbbings of the heart, as in hanging, drowning, and suffocation, due to an interruption of the passage of the blood in the body which keeps it from its connection with the atmosphere by respiration, and so prevents a sufficiently free exchange of carbonic acid for oxygen. In its mild form we have *syncope*, from συγ and κόπτειν, to cut. This is a fainting brought on by a sudden fright, illness, or a more than ordinarily disturbing spectacle. In its most severe or fatal form it becomes *suffocation*, the effect of a stoppage of respiration.

The usual treatment of *asphyxia* has recently been supplemented, with marked success, by the invention of the pulmotor, an apparatus designed to resuscitate victims of poisoning by gases and noxious fumes, electric shocks, suspended animation from any cause, drowning, attempted suicide, collapse in narcosis, and other mishaps, by forcing oxygen into the lungs. Many of the large gas companies now keep pulmotors on hand to send out in cases of accidental or intentional asphyxiation by illuminating gas.

ASPIRE. See AIM.

ASSAIL. See ATTACK.

ASSAILANT. See AGGRESSOR.

ASSASSINATE. See KILL.
ASSAULT. See ATTACK.
ASSAY. See EXPERIENCE.
ASSEMBLAGE. See ASSEMBLY.
ASSEMBLE, MUSTER, COLLECT.
Assemble is derived through French
from Low Latin *assimulare*, from *ad*,
to, and *simul*, together, from a root
which also appears in *similar, same*,
etc. *Muster* comes from Latin *mon-
strari*, to show, and means specifically
a review of troops. *Collect* is derived
from Latin *con*, together, and *legere*,
to gather, from the root which also
appears in *college, colleague*, etc.

Assemble is said of persons only; *muster* and *collect* of persons or things. To
assemble is to bring together by a call or
invitation; to *muster* is to bring together by an act of authority, or a particular effort, into one point of view at
one time and from one quarter; to
collect is to bring together at different
times and from different quarters:
the parliament is *assembled;* soldiers
are *mustered* every day in order to ascertain their numbers; an army is
collected in preparation for war; a king
assembles his council in order to consult with them on public measures; a
general *musters* his forces before he undertakes an expedition, and *collects*
more troops if he finds himself too
weak.

Collect is used for everything which
can be brought together in numbers;
muster is used figuratively for bringing
together, for an immediate purpose,
whatever is in one's possession: books,
coins, curiosities, and the like are *collected;* a person's resources, his strength,
courage, resolution, etc., are *mustered;*
some persons have a pleasure in *collecting* all the pieces of antiquity which
fall in their way; on a trying occasion
it is necessary to *muster* all the fortitude of which we are master.

Assemble, Convene, Convoke.—*Assemble* (see above). *Convene*, in Latin *convenio*, signifies to come or bring together. *Convoke*, in Latin *convoco*,
signifies to call together.

The idea of collecting many persons
into one place, for a specific purpose, is
common to all these terms. *Assemble*
conveys this sense without any addition; *convene* and *convoke* include likewise some collateral idea: people are
assembled, therefore, whenever they
are *convened* or *convoked*, but not *vice
versa. Assembling* is mostly by the
wish of one; *convening* by that of several: a crowd is *assembled* by an individual in the streets; a meeting is
convened at the desire of a certain number of persons: people are *assembled*
either on public or private business;
they are always *convened* on a public
occasion. A king *assembles* his parliament; a particular individual *assembles* his friends; the inhabitants of a
district are *convened*. There is nothing
imperative on the part of those that
assemble or *convene*, and nothing binding on those *assembled* or *convened;* one
assembles or *convenes* by invitation or
request; one attends to the notice or
not, at pleasure. *Convoke*, on the
other hand, is an act of authority; it
is the call of one who has the authority
to give the call; it is heeded by those
who feel themselves bound to attend.

*Assembly, Assemblage, Group, Col-
lection.*—*Assembly, assemblage*, are collective terms derived from the verb *assemble. Group* comes through French
from Italian *groppo*, which among
painters signifies an *assemblage* of figures in one place. *Collection* expresses
the act of *collecting*, or the body *collected.*

Assembly respects persons only; *assemblage*, things only; *group* and *collection*, persons or things: an *assembly*
is any number either brought together
or coming together of themselves; an
assemblage is any number of things
standing together; a *group* is come
together by accident or put together
by design; a *collection* is mostly put or
brought together by design. A general alarm will cause an *assembly* to
disperse; an agreeable *assemblage* of
rural objects, whether in nature or in
representation, constitutes a landscape:
a painting will sometimes consist only
of a *group* of figures; but if they be
well chosen it will sometimes produce
a wonderful effect: a *collection* of evil-
minded persons ought to be immediately dispersed by the authority of the
magistrate. In a large *assembly* you
may sometimes observe a singular *assemblage* of characters, countenances,
and figures· when people come together in great numbers on any occasion, they will often form themselves

into distinct *groups;* the *collection* of scarce books and curious editions has become a passion, which is ridiculed under the title of Bibliomania.

Assembly, Company, Meeting, Congregation, Parliament, Diet, Congress, Convention, Synod, Convocation, Council.—An *assembly* (see ASSEMBLY) is simply the *assembling* together of any number of persons: this idea is common to all the rest of these terms, which differ in the object, mode, and other collateral circumstances of the action. *Company,* a body linked together (see ACCOMPANY), is an *assembly* for purposes of *amusement. Meeting,* a body met together, is an *assembly* for general purposes of business. *Congregation,* a body flocked or gathered together, from the Latin *grex,* a flock, is an *assembly* brought together from congeniality of sentiment and community of purpose. *Parliament* is derived through French *parler,* and a suffix from Latin *parabola,* Greek παραβολή, a speech in which two things are compared. (Compare *parable.*) *Diet,* from Greek δίαιτα, a mode of life, has the same etymology as the word *diet* applied to the mode of life in respect to food. The peculiar sense in which it is here used is due to a confusion of it in the popular mind with the Latin *dies,* day, especially a day set apart for public business; and so it came to mean an assembly which conducted public business. *Congress,* from the Latin *congredior,* to march in a body, is an *assembly* coming together in a formal manner from distant parts for special purposes. *Convention,* from the Latin *convenio,* come together, is an *assembly* coming together in an informal and promiscuous manner from a neighboring quarter. *Synod,* in Greek σύνοδος, compounded of σύν and ὁδός, signifies literally going the same road, and has been employed to signify an *assembly* for consultation on matters of religion. *Convocation* is an *assembly* convoked for an especial purpose. *Council* is an *assembly* for consultation either on civil or on ecclesiastical affairs.

An *assembly* is, in its restricted sense, public, and under certain regulations; a *company* is private, and confined to friends and acquaintances; a *meeting* is either public or private; a *congrega-tion* is always public. *Meetings* are held by all who have any common concern to arrange; *congregations* consist of those who pursue the same objects particularly in matters of religion, although extended in its application to other matters: all these different kinds of *assemblies* are formed by individuals in their private capacity; the other terms designate *assemblies* that come together for national purposes, with the exception of the word *convention,* which may be either domestic or political. A *parliament* and *diet* are popular *assemblies* under a monarchical form of government; *congress* and *convention* are *assemblies* under a republican government: of the first description is the *parliament* of England, the *diets* of Prussia and Finland *assembled* by the reigning prince to deliberate on the affairs of the nation. Of the latter description is the *congress* of the United States of America and the national *convention* of France; but there is this difference observable between a *congress* and a *convention,* that the former consists of deputies or delegates from higher authorities—that is, from independent governments already established; but a *convention* is a self-constituted *assembly,* which has no power but what it assumes to itself. A *synod* and *convocation* are in religious matters what a *diet* and *convention* are in civil matters: the former exists only under an episcopal form of government; the latter may exist under any form of church discipline, even where the authority lies in the whole body of the ministry. A *council* is more important than all other species of *assembly;* it consists of persons invested with the highest authority, who, in their consultations, do not so much transact ordinary concerns as arrange the forms and fashions of things. Religious *councils* used to determine matters of faith and discipline; political *councils* frame laws and determine the fate of empires.

ASSENT, CONSENT, APPROBATION, CONCURRENCE. *Assent,* in Latin *assentio,* is compounded of *as* or *ad* and *sentio,* to think, signifying to bring one's mind or judgment to a thing. *Consent* (see ACCEDE). *Approbation,* in Latin *approbatio,* is compounded of *ad* and *probo*, to prove, signifying to make a thing out good. *Concurrence* (see AGREE).

Assent respects matters of judgment; *consent* respects matters of conduct. We *assent* to what we admit to be *true;* we *consent* to what we allow to be done. *Assent* may be given to anything, whether positively proposed by another or not, but *consent* supposes that what is *consented* to is proposed by some other person. Some men give their hasty *assent* to propositions which they do not fully understand, and their hasty *consent* to measures which are very injudicious. It is the part of the true believer not merely to *assent* to the Christian doctrines, but to make them the rule of his life: those who *consent* to a bad action are partakers in the guilt of it.

Assent and *consent* may sometimes be both applied to matters of judgment or abstract propositions, but in that case *assent* is the act of an individual, *consent* is the act of many individuals: one *assents* to that which is offered to his notice; some things are admitted by the common *consent* of mankind.

Approbation is a species of *assent*, concurrence of consent. To *approve* is not merely to *assent* to a thing as right, but to determine upon it positively to be so; the word *assent* is applied therefore most properly to speculative matters, or matters of inference or deduction; *approbation* to practical matters or matters of conduct, as to give one's *assent* to a proposition in Euclid, to express one's *approbation* of a particular measure.

Concurrence is properly the *consent* of many: *consent* may pass between two individuals, namely, the party proposing and the party to whom the thing is proposed; but *concurrence* is always given by numbers: *consent* may be given by a party who has no personal interest in the thing *consented* to; *concurrence* is given by those who have a common interest in the thing proposed: *consent* therefore passes between persons individually, *concurrence* between communities or between men collectively.

Assent is given by equals or inferiors; it is opposed to contradiction or denial: *consent* is given by superiors, or those who have the power of preventing; it is opposed to refusal: *approbation* is given by equals or superiors, or those who have the power to withhold it; it is opposed to disapprobation: *concurrence* is given by equals; it is opposed to opposition or rejection.

ASSERT, MAINTAIN, VINDICATE. *Assert* (see AFFIRM). *Maintain*, in French *maintenir*, from the Latin *manus* and *teneo*, signifies to hold by the hand—that is, closely and firmly. *Vindicate*, in Latin *vindicatus*, participle of *vindico* (*vin*, a root signifying to wish, to claim, allied to *venerate*, *Venus*, etc., and *dicere*), signifies to express a wish or claim for ourselves or others.

To *assert* is to declare a thing as our own; to *maintain* is to abide by what we have so declared; to *vindicate* is to stand up for that which concerns ourselves or others. We *assert* anything to be true; we *maintain* it by adducing proofs, facts, or arguments; we *vindicate* our own conduct or that of another when it is called in question. We *assert* boldly or impudently; we *maintain* steadily or obstinately; we *vindicate* resolutely or insolently. A right or claim is *asserted* which is avowed to belong to any one; it is *maintained* when attempts are made to prove its justice or regain its possession; the cause of the *asserter* or *maintainer* is *vindicated* by another. Innocence is *asserted* by a positive declaration; it is *maintained* by repeated *assertions* and the support of testimony; it is *vindicated* through the interference of another. The most guilty persons do not hesitate to *assert* their innocence with the hope of inspiring credit; and some will persist in *maintaining* it even after their guilt has been pronounced; but the really innocent man will never want a friend to *vindicate* him when his honor or his reputation is at stake. *Assertions* which are made hastily and inconsiderately are seldom long *maintained* without exposing a person to ridicule; those who attempt to *vindicate* a bad cause expose themselves to as much reproach as if the cause were their own.

ASSESSMENT. See TAX.
ASSEVERATE. See AFFIRM.
ASSIDUOUS. See ACTIVF

ASSIGN. See ADDUCE; DISTRIBUTE.

ASSIGNEE, ADMINISTRATOR. *Assignee*, in French *assigné*, from the Latin *assigno* (*ad*, to, and *signum*, seal), signifies one to whom something is formally given over, either in trust or for his own use and enjoyment. An *assignee in deed* is one appointed by a person; an *assignee in law* is one appointed by a court or other competent authority; an *assignee in bankruptcy* is one to whom a bankrupt's estate is assigned and in whom it is vested for the benefit of his creditors.

The last is the most familiar application of the term. In his capacity as an *administrator* of another person's property (from Latin *ad* and *ministrare*, to serve, *administer* signifying public service applied in this case to a specific function) an *assignee*, after accepting the trust, is not at liberty to assign the property back again to the assignor. It is his duty to act as a faithful trustee for all concerned. He is to take immediate possession of all the property and effects and valuable interests of every kind of the insolvent, and demand and take any necessary steps to collect all outstanding debts. If he sells property of the insolvent he cannot buy it himself. Acting in the discharge of the ordinary duties of an administrator, an *assignee* is personally liable only for want of ordinary skill and care. See *administer* under MINISTER for further definition of the function of *administrator* in general.

ASSIMILABLE, ABSORBABLE, CONFORMABLE, CONVERTIBLE. *Assimilable*, in French the same form, from *assimilate*, derived from *ad* and *similis*, to make like, signifies that which is capable of being made like another thing, or changed into its own substance. As an adjective, it implies that which may be made in some particulars to resemble another thing; and as a substantive, that which is capable of being so changed.

In the sense of mixing together, or merging, either of persons or substances, we have the main act of bringing some one or some thing into conformity or agreement with other persons or things, of converting, changing, or incorporating some one or some thing with others. A substance may be readily *absorbable* (from *ab* and *sorbere*, to sup up, Greek ροφέειν) by another when the first will be so *conformable* to the second that both become one substance, and each of the two separately is *convertible* into a single substance as if individually homogeneous.

Persons of like temperament and taste are *assimilable* in association with others of like qualities; citizens are made *conformable* to the law by penalties for being otherwise; sound securities are readily *convertible* into cash when desired; certain kinds of food and drink are *assimilable*, or capable of being united or mixed in the stomach without causing distress.

Hence, in all of these terms we have the sense of a complete and agreeable union of separate things in a single body, because each constituent in itself possesses the qualities of the others.

ASSIST. See HELP.

ASSISTANT. See ACCOMMODATOR; COADJUTOR.

ASSISTING. See AUXILIARY.

ASSOCIATE, COMPANION. *Associate*, in Latin *associatus*, participle of *associo*, is derived from *ad* and *socius*, a companion, literally a follower (allied to *sequor*, I follow). *Companion*, from company (for derivation see ACCOMPANY), signifies one that bears company.

Associates are habitually together: *companions* are only occasionally in company. As our habits are formed from our *associates*, we ought to be particular in our choice of them: as our *companions* contribute much to our enjoyments, we ought to choose such as are suitable to ourselves. Many men may be admitted as *companions* who would not altogether be fit as *associates*.

An *associate* may take part with us in some business, and share with us in the labor: a *companion* takes part with us in some concern, and shares with us in the pleasure or the pain.

Association, Society, Company, Partnership.—All these terms denote a union of several persons into one body. *Association* is general, the rest are specific. Whenever we habitually or frequently meet together for some common object, it is an *association*. *Asso-*

ciations are therefore political, religious, commercial, and literary. A *society* is an *association* for some specific purpose, moral or religious, civil or political. A *company* is an *association* of many for the purpose of trade. A *partnership* is an *association* of a few for the same object.

Whenever *association* is used in distinction from the others, it denotes that which is partial in its object and temporary in its duration. It is founded on unity of sentiment as well as unity of object; but it is mostly unorganized, and kept together only by the spirit which gives rise to it. A *society* requires nothing but unity of object which is permanent in its nature; it is well organized, and commonly set on foot to promote the cause of humanity, literature, or religion. No country can boast such numerous and excellent *societies*, whether of a charitable, a religious, or a literary description, as England. *Companies* are brought together for the purpose of interest, and are dissolved when that object ceases to exist: their duration depends on the contingencies of profit and loss. The South Sea *Company*, which was founded on an idle speculation, was formed for the ruin of many, and dispersed almost as soon as it was formed. *Partnerships* are altogether of an individual and private nature. As they are without organization and system, they are more precarious than any other *association*. Their duration depends not only on the chances of trade, but the compatibility of individuals to co-operate in a close point of union. They are often begun rashly and end ruinously.

Association, Combination.—*Association* (see the preceding). *Combination*, from the Latin *combino*, or *con* and *binus*, signifies tying two into one.

An *association* is something less binding than a *combination; associations* are formed for purposes of convenience; *combinations* are formed to serve either the interests or passions of men. The word *association* is therefore always taken in a good or an indifferent sense; *combination* in an indifferent or bad sense. An *association* is public; it embraces all classes of men: a *combination* is often private, and includes only a particular description of persons. *Associations* are formed for some general purpose; *combinations* are frequently formed for particular purposes which respect the interest of the few to the injury of many. *Associations* are formed by good citizens; *combinations* by discontented mechanics, or low persons in general.

When used for things, *association* is a natural action; *combination* an arbitrary action. Things *associate* of themselves, but *combinations* are formed either by design or accident. Nothing will *associate* but what harmonizes; things the most opposite in their nature may be *combined* together. We *associate* persons with places, or events with names; discordant properties are *combined* in the same body. With the name of one's birthplace are *associated* pleasurable recollections; virtue and vice are so *combined* in the same character as to form a contrast. The *association* of ideas is a remarkable phenomenon of the human mind, but it can never be admitted as solving any difficulty respecting the structure and composition of the soul; the *combination* of letters forms syllables, and that of syllables forms words.

ASSUAGE. See ALLAY.

ASSUME. See AFFECT; APPROPRIATE.

ASSUMPTION, PRESUMPTION, ARROGANCE. *Assumption*, the act of assuming (see APPROPRIATE). *Presumption*, from presume, in Latin *præsumo*, from *præ*, before, and *sumo*, to take, signifies to take beforehand, to take for granted. *Arrogance* (see APPROPRIATE).

Assumption is a person's taking upon himself to act a part which does not belong to him. *Presumption* is the taking a place which does not belong to him. *Assumption* has to do with one's general conduct; *presumption* relates to matters of right and precedence. A person may be guilty of *assumption* by giving commands when he ought to receive them, or by speaking when he ought to be silent: he is guilty of *presumption* in taking a seat which is not fit for him. *Assumption* arises from self-conceit and self-suf-

ASTRONOMY

83

iciency, *presumption* from self-importance. *Assumption* and *presumption* both denote a taking to one's self merely, *arrogance* claiming from others. A person is guilty of *assumption* and *presumption* for his own gratification only, without any direct intentional offence to others; but a man cannot be *arrogant*, be guilty of *arrogance*, without direct offence to others. The arrogant man exacts deference and homage from others; his demands are as extravagant as his mode of making them is offensive. Children are apt to be *assuming*, low people to be *presuming;* persons among the higher orders, inflated with pride and bad passions, are apt to be arrogant.

ASSURANCE, CONFIDENCE. *Assurance* implies either the act of making another sure (see AFFIRM), or of being sure one's self. *Confidence* implies simply the act of the mind in *confiding*, which is equivalent to a feeling.

Assurance, as an action, is to *confidence* as the means to the end. We give a person an *assurance* in order to inspire him with *confidence. Assurance* and *confidence*, as a sentiment in ourselves, may respect either that which is external of us, or that which belongs to ourselves; in the first case they are both taken in an indifferent sense: but the feeling of *assurance* is much stronger than that of *confidence*, and applies to objects that interest the feelings; whereas *confidence* applies only to such objects as exercise the understanding: thus we have an *assurance* of a life to come; an *assurance* of a blessed immortality: we have a *confidence* in a person's integrity.

As respects ourselves exclusively, *assurance* is employed to designate either an occasional feeling or a habit of the mind; *confidence*, an occasional feeling mostly; *assurance*, therefore, in this sense, may be used indifferently, but in general it has a bad acceptation: *confidence* has an indifferent or a good sense.

Assurance is a self-possession of the mind, arising from the conviction that all in ourselves is right; *confidence* is that self-possession only in particular cases, and grounded on the reliance we have in our abilities or our char-

acter. The man of *assurance* never loses himself under any circumstances, however trying; he is calm and easy when another is abashed and confounded: the man who has *confidence* will generally have it in cases that warrant him to trust to himself. A liar utters falsehoods with an air of *assurance*, in order the more effectually to gain belief; conscious innocence enables a person to speak with *confidence* when interrogated. *Assurance* shows itself in the behavior, *confidence* in the conduct. Young people are apt to assert everything with a tone of *assurance;* no man should undertake anything without a *confidence* in himself.

Assurance, Impudence. — *Assurance* (see above). *Impudence* literally implies shamelessness, from *in*, a negative prefix, and *pudere*, to feel shame. They are so closely allied to each other that *assurance* is distinguished from *impudence* more in the manner than the spirit; for *impudence* has a grossness attached to it which does not belong to *assurance*. Vulgar people are *impudent*, because they have *assurance* to break through all the forms of society; but those who are more cultivated will have their *assurance* controlled by its decencies and refinements.

ASSURE. See AFFIRM.

ASTERN. See ABAFT.

ASTONISH. See WONDER.

ASTRONOMY, ASTROLOGY. *Astronomy* is compounded of the Greek ἄστρον, cognate with English *star*, and νόμος, law, and signifies the laws of the stars, or a knowledge of their laws. *Astrology*, from ἄστρον and γόλος, signifies a reasoning on the stars.

The *astronomer* studies the course and movement of the stars; the *astrologer* reasons on their influence. The former observes the state of the heavens, marks the order of time, the eclipses, and the revolutions which arise out of the established laws of motion in the immense universe: the latter predicts events, draws horoscopes, and announces all the vicissitudes of rain and snow, heat and cold, etc. The *astronomer* calculates and seldom errs, as his calculations are built on fixed rules and actual observations; the *astrologer* deals in conjectures, and his imagination often deceives him. The *astronomer* explains what he knows, and merits the esteem of the learned; the *astrologer* hazards what he thinks, and seeks to please.

ASYLUM, REFUGE, SHELTER, RETREAT. *Asylum*, in Latin *asylum*, in Greek ἄσυλον, compounded of *a*, privative, and σύλη, plunder, signifies a place exempt from plunder. *Refuge*, in Latin *refugium*, from *refugio*, to fly away, signifies the place one may fly away to. *Shelter* is a corruption of Middle English *sheld-trume*, Anglo-Saxon *scildtruma*, shield-troop, a band of armed men protecting something, and hence a protection in general. *Retreat*, in French *retraite*, Latin *retractus*, from *retraho*, or *re* and *traho*, to draw back, signifies the place that is situated behind or in the background.

Asylum, *refuge*, and *shelter* all denote a place of safety; but the former is fixed, the two latter are occasional: the *retreat* is a place of tranquillity rather than of safety. An *asylum* is chosen by him who has no home, a *refuge* by him who is apprehensive of danger: the French emigrants found a *refuge* in England, but very few will make it an *asylum*. The inclemencies of the weather make us seek a *shelter*. The fatigues and toils of life make us seek a *retreat*. It is the part of a Christian to afford an *asylum* to the helpless orphan and widow. The terrified passenger takes *refuge* in the first house he comes to, when assailed by an evil-disposed mob. The vessel shattered in a storm takes *shelter* in the nearest haven. The man of business, wearied with the anxieties and cares of the world, disengages himself from the whole, and seeks a *retreat* suited to his circumstances.

ATOMIC, INAPPRECIABLE, MINUTE, SMALL. *Atomic*, in French *atomique*, is in English a compound of *atom* and the suffix *ic; atom*, Latin *atomus*, is derived from Greek ἄτο τος, ᾰ, a negative prefix, and τέμνειν, to cut, and signifies that which cannot be cut, a particle of matter which cannot be made smaller. *Inappreciable* is compounded of *in*, a negative prefix, and *ad* and *pretium*, price, and signifies something too small to evaluate, too small to notice at all. *Minute* is

derived from the past participle of *minuere*, to make small, whence *minor*, *diminish*, etc., are also derived. *Small* is a Teutonic word meaning in most Germanic languages what it means in English.

Of these terms *atomic* is the most absolute and emphatic, and *small* the least so. *Small* is used relatively. We speak of a *small* man or a *small* army, though the man is gigantic compared with a mosquito, and the army may be many times the size of groups of people which at other times we call large. We mean that the man is *small* compared with other men, etc. The use of *small* is generally influenced by some specific standard of comparison. *Minute* suggests extreme smallness, but is not so absolute a term as *atomic*. A *minute* object is small compared with most of the things that we know, but it may nevertheless contain many atoms. *Inappreciable* is a relative term, but it differs from *small* in emphasizing the relation of the object to the mind perceiving it. While the degree of smallness indicated in the word *inappreciable* may vary with the circumstances, the fluctuation is not so great as in the word *small*, because the capacity of the mind to notice and appreciate remains fairly stable, and hence *inappreciable* has much the same meaning for one person as for another.

ATONE, EXPIATE. *Atone*, or *at one*, signifies to be at peace or good friends. *Expiate*, in Latin *expiatus*, participle of *expio*, compounded of *ex* and *pio*, signifies to put out or cancel by an act of piety.

Both these terms express a satisfaction for an offence; but *atone* is general, *expiate* is particular. We may *atone* for a fault by any species of suffering; we *expiate* a crime only by suffering a legal punishment. A woman often sufficiently *atones* for her violation of chastity by the misery she brings on herself; there are too many unfortunate wretches in England who *expiate* their crimes on the gallows.

Neither *atonement* nor *expiation* always necessarily requires punishment or even suffering from the offender. The nature of the *atonement* depends on the nature of the offence or will of the individual who is offended; *expiations* are frequently made by means of performing certain religious rites or acts of piety. Offences between man and man are sometimes *atoned* for by an acknowledgment of error; but offences toward God require an *expiatory* sacrifice, which our Saviour has been pleased to make of himself, that we, through him, might become partakers of eternal life. *Expiation*, therefore, in the religious sense, is to *atonement* as the means to the end: *atonement* is often obtained by an *expiation*, but there may be *expiations* where there is no *atonement*.

ATROCIOUS. See DIABOLIC; HEINOUS.

ATTACH. See ADHERE; AFFIX.

ATTACHE, ASSISTANT, INFORMANT. *Attaché*, though a purely French term, has been adopted in the vocabulary of practically all modern nations, implying, literally, a person attached to a thing or other person, and, specifically, one attached to an embassy. In the diplomatic world, an *attaché* is much less than an ambassador, and much more than a routine clerk. One may be an ordinary *attaché* who gathers information for his superior, a *military attaché*, who is usually an officer in the army of his own country, or a *naval attaché*, one holding a naval office at home.

Assistant (see HELP) and *informant* (see INFORM) are more general terms which may be specialized to refer to the functions of an *attaché* in *assisting* the work of his superiors, and *informing* them concerning conditions in the country where he serves.

In peaceful days the post of an *attaché* is a very pleasant one: in wartimes it may be a very difficult and unpleasant one, as, in carrying out instructions of his superior and secretly gaining some desired information, an *attaché* may become seriously involved with the authorities of the country to which he is assigned, though immune from arrest or other legal proceeding. In December, 1915, the United States Government demanded the recall of the military and naval *attachés* of the German embassy at Washington, because of their activities in fomenting local troubles during the European war. Both officers declared they had acted under orders, as they were bound to do.

ATTACHED. See ON.

ATTACHMENT, AFFECTION, INCLINATION. *Attachment* respects persons and things: *affection* regards persons only: *inclination*, denoting the act of inclining, has respect to things mostly, but may be applied to objects generally.

Attachment, as it regards persons, is not so powerful or solid as *affection*. Children are *attached* to those who will minister to their gratifications; they have an *affection* for their nearest and dearest relatives. *Attachment* is sometimes a tender sentiment between persons of different sexes; *affection* is an affair of the heart without distinction of sex. The passing *attachments* of young people are seldom entitled to serious notice; although sometimes they may ripen by a long intercourse into a laudable and steady *affection*. Nothing is so delightful as to see *affection* among brothers and sisters.

Attachment is a something more powerful and positive than *inclination;* the latter is a rising sentiment, a mere leaning of the mind toward an object; the former is a feeling already fixed so as to create a tie; an *attachment* is formed, an *inclination* arises in the mind of itself.

In respect to things, *attachment* and *inclination* admit of a similar distinction. We strive to obtain that to which we are *attached*, but a simple *inclination* rarely produces any effort for possession. Little minds are always betraying their *attachment* to trifles. It is the character of indifference not to show an *inclination* to anything. Interest, similarity of character, or habit gives rise to *attachment;* a natural warmth of temper gives birth to various *inclinations*. Suppress the first *inclination* to gaming, lest it grow into an *attachment*.

ATTACK, ASSAIL, ASSAULT, ENCOUNTER. *Attack* is a doublet of *attach*, derived from the same original word. (See ADHERE.) *Assail, assault,* in French *assaillir*, Latin *assilio, assaltum*, compounded of *ad* and *salio*, signify to leap upon. *Encounter*, in Old French *encontrer*, compounded of *en* or *in* and *contre*, in Latin *contra*, against, signifies to run or come against.

Attack is the generic, the rest are specific terms. To *attack* is to make an approach in order to do some violence to the person; to *assail* or *assault* is to make a sudden and vehement *attack;* to *encounter* is to meet the *attack* of another. One *attacks* by simply offering violence without necessarily producing an effect; one *assails* by means of missile weapons; one *assaults* by direct personal violence; one *encounters* by opposing violence to violence. Men and animals *attack* or *encounter;* men only, in the literal sense, *assail* or *assault*. Animals *attack* each other with the weapons nature has bestowed upon them: those who provoke a multitude may expect to have their houses or windows *assailed* with stones, and their persons *assaulted;* it is ridiculous to attempt to *encounter* those who are superior in strength and prowess.

They are all used figuratively. Men *attack* with reproaches or censures; they *assail* with abuse; they are *assaulted* by temptations; they *encounter* opposition and difficulties. A fever *attacks;* horrid shrieks *assail* the ear; dangers are *encountered*. The reputations of men in public life are often wantonly *attacked;* they are *assailed* in every direction by the murmurs and complaints of the discontented; they often *encounter* the obstacles which party spirit throws in the way, without reaping any solid advantage to themselves.

Attack, Assault, Encounter, Onset, Charge.—*Attack, assault, encounter*, denote the act of *attacking, assaulting, encountering*. *Onset* signifies a setting on or to, a commencing. *Charge* (see Accuse) signifies pressing upon.

An *attack* and *assault* may be made upon an unresisting object; *encounter, onset*, and *charge* require at least two opposing parties. An *attack* may be slight or indirect; an *assault* must always be direct, and mostly vigorous. An *attack* upon a town need not be attended with any injury to the walls or inhabitants; but an *assault* is commonly conducted so as to effect its capture. *Attacks* are made by robbers upon the person or property of another; *assaults* upon the person only. An

encounter generally respects an informal casual meeting between single individuals; *onset* and *charge* a regular *attack* between contending armies: *onset* is employed for the commencement of the battle; *charge* for an *attack* from a particular quarter. When knight-errantry was in vogue, *encounters* were perpetually taking place between the knights, which were sometimes fierce and bloody. Armies that make impetuous *onsets* are not always prepared to withstand a continued *attack* with perseverance and steadiness. A furious and well-directed *charge* from the cavalry will sometimes decide the fortune of the day.

See also Impugn.

ATTAIN. See Acquire.

ATTAINT, Corrupt, Stain, Taint. *Attaint* and *taint* are commonly confused in the popular mind, but, etymologically, they have nothing to do with each other. *Attaint* is the past participle of the verb *attain*, used in a technical sense in law. To *attain* meant to *convict*, to attain the end sought in a legal trial.

Under an act of the British parliament known as the *Act of Attainder*, an attainder is a decree involving the loss of civil rights and estate of one guilty of the crime of treason or other capital offence, and a *Bill of Attainder* is the designation of the foregoing act. Hence, in the popular mind, it was natural that *attaint* should be associated with *taint* (from Latin *tingere*, to color, whence *tint* is derived), and with *stain* (from *distingere*, literally to discolor), because the conviction by the court involved disgrace, or the *staining* and *tainting* of the character and reputation.

The Constitution of the United States declares that (1) "No bill of *attainder* or *ex post facto* laws shall be passed"; (2) "No state shall . . . pass any bill of *attainder, ex post facto* law, or law impairing the obligation of contracts"; and (3) ". . . but no *attainder* of treason shall work corruption of blood or forfeiture except during the life of the person *attained*."

Corrupt, as used in the phrase *corruption of blood*, implies that the blood of a person who has been *attainted* or is under an *attainder* has been legally corrupted, *tainted*, or *stained* by the disgrace. In old English law a jury that brought in a false verdict was liable to be *attainted* by another jury, and in case of conviction the members were pronounced infamous, their goods were forfeited, their families turned out of doors, and their houses razed. The later practice set aside verdicts and granted new trials, and an act of parliament put an end to the system of *attaints*.

ATTEMPT, TRIAL, ENDEAVOR, EFFORT, ESSAY. *Attempt*, in French *attenter*, Latin *attento*, from *ad* and *tento*, signifies to *try* at a thing. *Trial*, from French *trier*, *try*, comes from Late Latin *tritare*, to pound small; thence developing the meaning of culling, picking out. *Endeavor*, compounded of *en* and the French *devoir*, to owe, signifies to try according to one's duty. *Effort*, from Latin *ex* and *fortem* (accusative), strength, signifies the putting forth of strength. *Essay* comes from Latin *exagium*, a trial of weight, from *ex*, out, and *agere*, to drive or move; it is the same word as *assay*.

To *attempt* is to set about a thing with a view of effecting it; to *try* is to set about a thing with a view of seeing the result. An *attempt* respects the action with its object; a *trial* is the exercise of power. We always act when we *attempt*: we use the senses and the understanding when we *try*. We *attempt* by *trying*, but we may *try* without *attempting*; when a thief *attempts* to break into a house, he first *tries* the locks and fastenings, to see where he can most easily gain admittance. Men *attempt* to remove evils; they *try* experiments. *Attempts* are perpetually made by quacks to recommend some scheme of their own to the notice of the public, which are often nothing more than *trials* of skill to see who can most effectually impose on the credulity of mankind. Spirited people make *attempts;* persevering people make *trials;* players *attempt* to perform different parts, and *try* to gain applause An *endeavor* is a continued *attempt*. *Attempts* may be fruitless; *trials* may be vain; *endeavors*, though unavailing, may be well meant. Many *attempts* are made which exceed the abilities of the *attempter; attempts* at imitation expose the imitator to ridicule when they do not succeed;

trials are made in matters of speculation, the results of which are uncertain; *endeavors* are made in the moral concerns of life. People *attempt* to write books; they *try* various methods; and *endeavor* to obtain a livelihood.

An *effort* is to an *attempt* as a means to an end; it is the act of calling forth those powers which are required in an *attempt*. Great *attempts* frequently require great *efforts*, either of body or mind.

An *essay* is an imperfect *attempt*, or *attempt* to do something which cannot be done without difficulty. It is applied either to corporeal or intellectual matters.

Whence treatises which serve as *attempts* to illustrate any point in morals are termed *essays*.

Attempt, Undertaking, Enterprise.— *Attempt* signifies the thing *attempted*. *Undertaking*, from *undertake*, or take in hand, signifies the thing taken in hand. *Enterprise*, from the Old French *enterpris*, participle of *entreprendre*, to undertake, has the same original sense.

The idea of something set about to be completed is common to all these terms. An *attempt* is less complicated than an *undertaking;* and that less arduous than an *enterprise*. *Attempts* are the common exertions of power for obtaining an object; an *undertaking* involves in it many parts and particulars which require thought and judgment: an *enterprise* has more that is hazardous and dangerous in it; it requires resolution. *Attempts* are frequently made on the lives and property of individuals; *undertakings* are formed for private purposes; *enterprises* are commenced for some great national object. Nothing can be effected without making the *attempt; attempts* are therefore often idle and unsuccessful when they are made by persons of little discretion, who are eager to do something without knowing how to direct their powers: *undertakings* are of a more serious nature, and involve a man's serious interests; if begun without adequate means of bringing them to a conclusion, they too frequently bring ruin by their failure on those who are concerned in them: *enterprises* require personal sacrifices rather than those of interest; he who does not combine great resolution and perseverance with considerable bodily powers will be ill-fitted to take part in grand *enterprises*.

ATTEND, MIND, REGARD, HEED, NOTICE. *Attend*, in French *attendre*, Latin *attendo*, compounded of *ad* and *tendere*, to stretch, signifies to stretch or bend the mind to a thing. *Mind* comes from Anglo-Saxon *munan*, to think. *Regard*, in French *regarder*, compounded of *re* and *garder*, a word of German origin meaning to watch over, signifies to look upon again or with attention. *Heed*, Anglo-Saxon *hedan*, is allied to German *hüten*, to guard. *Notice*, from the Latin *notitia*, knowledge, signifies to bring to the knowledge of, or bring to one's mind.

The idea of fixing the mind on an object is common to all these terms. As this is the characteristic of *attention*, *attend* is the generic, the rest are specific terms. We *attend* in *minding, regarding, heeding*, and *noticing*, and also in many cases in which these words are not employed. To *mind* is to *attend to* a thing, so that it may not be forgotten; to *regard* is to look on a thing as of importance; to *heed* is to *attend to* a thing from a principle of caution; to *notice* is to think on that which strikes the senses. We *attend to* a speaker when we hear and understand his words; we *mind* what is said when we bear it in mind; we *regard* what is said by dwelling and reflecting on it; *heed* is given to whatever awakens a sense of danger; *notice* is taken of what passes outwardly. Children should always *attend* when spoken to, and *mind* what is said to them; they should *regard* the counsels of their parents, so as to make them the rule of their conduct, and *heed* their warnings so as to avoid the evil; they should *notice* what passes before them, so as to apply it to some useful purpose. It is a part of politeness to *attend* to every minute circumstance which affects the comfort and convenience of those with whom we associate: men who are actuated by any passion seldom pay any *regard* to the dictates of conscience, nor *heed* the unfavorable impressions which their conduct makes on others, for in fact they seldom think what is said of them to be worth their *notice*.

See also ACCOMPANY.

Attend, Wait On.—*Attend* is here employed in the improper sense for the devotion of the person to an object. To *wait on* is the same as to wait for the wishes of another. They may be either partial and temporary acts or permanent acts; in either case *attend* has a higher signification than *wait on*. *Attendance* is for the purpose of discharging some duty, as a physician *attends* his patient; a member *attends* in parliament; *waiting on* is either a matter of courtesy between equals, as one gentleman *waits on* another to whom he wishes to show a mark of respect; or a matter of business, as a tradesman *waits on* his customers to take orders.

In the sense of being permanently about the person of any one, to *attend* is to bear company or be in readiness to serve; to *wait on* is actually to perform some service. A nurse *attends* a patient in order to afford him assistance as occasion requires; the servant *waits on* him to perform the menial duties. *Attendants* about the great are always near the person; but men and women in *waiting* are always at call. People of rank and fashion have a crowd of *attendants;* those of the middle classes have only those who *wait on* them.

Attend, Hearken, Listen. — *Attend* (see above). *Hearken* comes from Anglo-Saxon *heorcnian*, to listen to, but is not directly allied to hear. *Listen* comes from Anglo-Saxon *hlystan*, to hear.

Attend is a mental action; *hearken*, both corporeal and mental; *listen* simply corporeal. To *attend* is to have the mind engaged on what we hear; to *hearken* and *listen* are to strive to hear. People *attend* when they are addressed; they *hearken* to what is said by others; they *listen* to what passes between others. It is always proper to *attend*, and mostly of importance to *hearken*, but frequently improper to *listen*. The mind that is occupied with another object cannot *attend;* we are not disposed to *hearken* when the thing does not appear interesting; curiosity often impels to *listening* to what does not concern the *listener*.

Listen is sometimes used figuratively in the sense of *hearkening* with the desire to profit by it; it is necessary at all times to *listen* to the dictates of reason.

Attention, Application, Study. — These terms indicate a direction of the thoughts to an object, but differing in the degree of steadiness and force. *Attention* marks the simple bending of the mind. *Application* (see ADDRESS) marks an envelopment or engagement of the powers; a bringing them into a state of close contact. *Study*, from the Latin *studeo*, to desire eagerly, marks a degree of *application* that arises from a strong desire of attaining the object.

Attention is the first requisite for making a progress in the acquirement of knowledge; it may be given in various degrees, and it rewards according to the proportion in which it is given: a divided *attention* is, however, more hurtful than otherwise; it retards the progress of the learner, while it injures his mind by improper exercise. *Application* is requisite for the attainment of perfection in any pursuit; it cannot be partial or variable, like *attention;* it must be the constant exercise of power or the regular and uniform use of means for the attainment of an end: youth is the period for *application*, when the powers of body and mind are in full vigor; no degree of it in after-life will supply its deficiency in younger years. *Study* is that species of *application* which is most purely intellectual in its nature; it is the exercise of the mind for itself and in itself, its native effort to arrive at maturity; it embraces both *attention* and *application*. The student *attends* to all he hears and sees; *applies* what he has learned to the acquirement of what he wishes to learn, and digests the whole by the exercise of reflection: as nothing is thoroughly understood or properly reduced to practice without *study*, the professional man must choose this road in order to reach the summit of excellence.

See also HEED.

Attentive, Careful.—Attentive marks a readiness to attend. *Careful* signifies full of care (see CARE, SOLICITUDE).

These epithets denote a fixedness of mind: we are *attentive* in order to understand and improve: we are *careful* to avoid mistakes. An *attentive* scholar profits by what is told him in learning his task: a *careful* scholar performs his exercises correctly. *Attention* respects matters of judgment; *care* relates to mechanical action: we listen *attentively;* we read or write *carefully.* A servant must be *attentive* to the orders that are given him, and *careful* not to injure his master's property. A translator must be *attentive;* a transcriber *careful.* A tradesman ought to be *attentive* to the wishes of his customers, and *careful* in keeping his accounts.

ATTENDANT. See CHAPERON.

ATTIRE. See APPAREL.

ATTITUDE. See ACT.

ATTRACT, ALLURE, INVITE, ENGAGE. *Attract*, in Latin *attractum*, participle of *attraho*, compounded of *ad*, to, and *traho*, signifies to draw toward. *Allure* (see ALLURE). *Invite*, in French *inviter*, Latin *invitare*, means to ask or request, the stem being allied to *vitus* in *invitus*, unwilling. *Engage*, compounded of *en* or *in* and the French *gage*, a pledge (from a Teutonic root), signifies to bind as by a pledge.

That is *attractive* which draws the thoughts toward itself; that is *alluring* which awakens desire; that is *inviting* which offers persuasion; that is *engaging* which takes possession of the mind. The attention is *attracted;* the senses are *allured;* the understanding is *invited;* the whole mind is *engaged.* A particular sound *attracts* the ear; the prospect of gratification *allures;* we are *invited* by the advantages which offer; we are *engaged* by those which already accrue. The person of a female is *attractive;* female beauty involuntarily draws all eyes toward itself; it awakens admiration: the pleasures of society are *alluring;* they create in the receiver an eager desire for still further enjoyment; but when too eagerly pursued they vanish in the pursuit, and leave the mind a prey to listless uneasiness: fine weather is *inviting;* it seems to persuade the reluctant to partake of its refreshments: the manners of a person are *engaging;* they not only occupy the attention, but they lay hold of the affections.

Attractions, Allurements, Charms.— *Attraction* signifies the thing that attracts. *Allurement* signifies the thing that allures. *Charm*, from the Latin *carmen,* a verse, signifies whatever acts by an irresistible influence, like poetry.

Besides the synonymous idea which distinguishes these words, they are remarkable for the common property of being used only in the plural when denoting the thing that *attracts, allures,* and *charms,* as applied to female endowments or the influence of persons on the heart: it seems that in *attractions* there is something natural; in *allurements* something artificial; in *charms* something moral and intellectual. *Attractions* and *charms* are always taken in a good sense; *allurements* mostly in a bad sense: *attractions* lead or draw; *allurements* win or entice; *charms* seduce or captivate. The human heart is always exposed to the power of female *attractions;* it is guarded with difficulty against the *allurements* of a coquette; it is incapable of resisting the united *charms* of body and mind.

When applied to other objects, an *attraction* springs from something remarkable and striking; it lies in the exterior aspect, and awakens an interest toward itself; a *charm* acts by a secret, all-powerful, and irresistible impulse on the soul; it springs from an accordance of the object with the affections of the heart; it takes hold of the imagination, and awakens an enthusiasm peculiar to itself: an *allurement* acts on the senses; it flatters the passions; it enslaves the imagination. The metropolis has its *attractions* for the gay; music has its *charms* for every one; fashionable society has too many *allurements* for youth, which are not easily withstood.

ATTRIBUTE. See ASCRIBE; QUALITY.

AUDACITY, EFFRONTERY, HARDIHOOD or HARDINESS, BOLDNESS. *Audacity,* from *audacious,* in French *audacieux,* Latin *audax* and *audere,* to dare, signifies literally the quality of daring. *Effrontery,* through French from *ef,* for *ex,* out, and *frons,* a face, signifies putting out the forehead. *Hardihood* or *hardiness,* from *hardy* or *hard,* signifies a capacity to endure or stand the brunt of difficulties, opposition, or shame. *Bold* comes from Anglo-Saxon *bald.*

The idea of disregarding what others regard is common to all these terms.

Audacity expresses more than *effrontery;* the first has something of vehemence, of defiance in it; the latter that of cool unconcern: *hardihood* expresses less than *boldness;* the first has more of determination, and the second more of spirit and enterprise. *Audacity* and *effrontery* are always taken in a bad sense; *hardihood,* in an indifferent, if not a bad sense; *boldness,* in a good, bad, or indifferent sense. *Audacity* marks haughtiness and temerity; effrontery the want of all modesty, a total shamelessness; *hardihood* indicates a firm resolution to meet consequences; *boldness,* a spirit and courage to commence action. An *audacious* man speaks with a lofty tone, without respect and without reflection; his haughty demeanor makes him forget what is due to his superiors. *Effrontery* discovers itself by an insolent air, a total unconcern for the opinions of those present, and a disregard of all the forms of civil society. A *hardy* man speaks with a resolute tone, which seems to brave the utmost evil that can result from what he says. A *bold* man speaks without reserve, undaunted by the quality, rank, or haughtiness of those whom he addresses. It requires *audacity* to assert false claims or vindicate a lawless conduct in the presence of accusers and judges; it requires *effrontery* to ask a favor of the man whom one has basely injured, or to assume a placid, unconcerned air in the presence of those by whom one has been convicted of flagrant atrocities; it requires *hardihood* to assert as a positive fact what is dubious, *boldness* to maintain the truth in spite of every danger with which one is threatened.

AUGMENTATION. See INCREASE.

AUGUR, PRESAGE, FOREBODE, BETOKEN, PORTEND. *Augur,* in French *augurer,* Latin *augurium,* comes from *avis,* a bird, as an *augury* was originally, and at all times principally, drawn from the song, the flight, or other actions of birds. *Presage,* in French *présage,* from the Latin *præ* and *sagio,* to be instinctively wise, signifies to be thus wise about what is to come. *Forebode* is compounded of *fore* and the Anglo-Saxon *bodian,* to declare, signifying to pronounce on futurity. *Betoken* signifies to serve as a token, from Anglo-Saxon *tacen* (from a root found also in *teach*). *Portend*, in Latin *portendo*, compounded of *por*, for, and *tendo*, signifies to set or show forth.

Augur signifies either to serve or make use of as an *augury;* to *forebode,* and *presage,* is to form a conclusion in one's own mind: to *betoken* or *portend* is to serve as a sign. Persons or things *augur;* persons only *forebode* or *presage;* things only *betoken* or *portend.* *Auguring* is a calculation of some future event, in which the imagination seems to be as much concerned as the understanding: *presaging* is rather a conclusion or deduction of what may be from what it is; it lies in the understanding more than in the imagination: *foreboding* lies altogether in the imagination. Things are said to *betoken* which present natural signs; those are said to *portend* which present extraordinary or supernatural signs. It *augurs* ill for the prosperity of a country or a state when its wealth has increased so as to take away the ordinary stimulus to industry and to introduce an inordinate love of pleasure. We *presage* the future greatness of a man from the indications which he gives of possessing an elevated character. A distempered mind is apt to *forebode* every ill from the most trivial circumstances. We see with pleasure those actions in a child which *betoken* an ingenuous temper: a mariner sees with pain the darkness of the sky which *portends* a storm; the moralist *augurs* no good to the morals of a nation from the lax discipline which prevails in the education of youth; he *presages* the loss of independence to the minds of men in whom proper principles of subordination have not been early engendered. Men sometimes *forebode* the misfortunes which happen to them, but they oftener *forebode* evils which never come.

AUGUST. See MAGISTERIAL; SUPERB.

AUSPICIOUS, PROPITIOUS. *Auspicious,* from the Latin *auspicium* and *auspex,* compounded of *avis* and *spicio,* to behold, signifies favorable according to the inspection of birds. *Propitious* is probably also a term in augury, meaning "flying forward," from *pro,* forward, and *petere,* to seek, originally to fly.

Auspicious is said only of things; *propitious* is said only of persons or things personified. Those things are *auspicious* which are casual or only indicative of good; persons are *propitious* to the wishes of others who listen to their requests and contribute to their satisfaction. A journey is undertaken under *auspicious* circumstances where everything incidental, as weather, society, and the like, bid fair to afford pleasure; it is undertaken under *propitious* circumstances when everything favors the attainment of the object for which it was begun. Whoever has any request to make ought to seize the *auspicious* moment when the person of whom it is asked is in a pleasant frame of mind; a poet in his invocation requests the muse to be *propitious* to him, or the lover conjures his mistress to be *propitious* to his vows.

See also OPPORTUNE.

AUSTERE, RIGID, SEVERE, RIGOROUS, STERN. For the derivations of *austere, rigid, rigorous,* and *stern* see ASCETIC. *Severe* comes from Latin *severus,* serious, grave.

Austere applies to ourselves as well as to others; *rigid* applies to ourselves only; *severe, rigorous, stern,* apply to others only. We are *austere* in our manner of living; *rigid* in our mode of thinking; *austere, severe, rigorous,* and *stern* in our mode of dealing with others. Effeminacy is opposed to *austerity,* pliability to *rigidity.* The *austere* man mortifies himself; the *rigid* man binds himself to a rule: the manners of a man are *austere* when he refuses to take part in any social enjoyments; his probity is *rigid*—that is, inaccessible to the allurements of gain or the urgency of necessity: an *austere* life consists not only in the privation of every pleasure, but in the infliction of every pain; *rigid* justice is unbiased, no less by the fear of loss than by the desire of gain: the present age affords no example of *austerity,* but too many of its opposite extreme, effeminacy: and the *rigidity* of former times, in modes of thinking, has been succeeded by a culpable laxity.

Austere, when taken with relation to others, is said of the behavior; *severe* of the conduct: a parent is *austere* in his looks, his manner, and his words to his child; he is *severe* in the restraints he imposes and the punishments he inflicts; an *austere* master speaks but to command, and commands so as to be obeyed; a *severe* master punishes every fault and punishes in an undue measure; an *austere* temper is never softened; the countenance of such a one never relaxes into a smile, nor is he pleased to witness smiles: a *severe* temper is ready to catch at the imperfections of others and to wound the offender: a judge should be a *rigid* administrator of justice between man and man, and *severe* in the punishment of offences as occasion requires; but never *austere* toward those who appear before him; *austerity* of manner would ill become him who sits as a protector of either the innocent or the injured. *Rigor* is a species of great *severity*, namely, in the infliction of punishment: toward enormous offenders, or on particular occasions where an example is requisite, *rigor* may be adopted, but otherwise it marks a cruel temper. A man is *austere* in his manners, *severe* in his remarks, and *rigorous* in his discipline. *Austerity*, *rigidity*, and *severity* may be habitual; *rigor* and *sternness* are occasional. *Sternness* is a species of severity more in manner than in direct action; a commander may issue his commands *sternly*, or a despot may issue his *stern* decrees.

See also ASCETIC; SEVERE.

AUTHOR. See WRITER.

AUTHORITATIVE. See COMMAND; ORACULAR.

AUTHORITY. See INFLUENCE; POWER.

AUTHORIZE. See COMMISSION.

AUTOCRACY, OLIGARCHY, ARISTOCRACY. *Autocracy* corresponds most nearly to words listed under ABSOLUTE, which see. *Autocracy*, from Greek αὐτός, self, and κρατέειν, to rule, refers to a state in which absolute power is in the hands of one man or a small group of men. *Oligarchy* is a form of *autocracy* in which the power is in the hands of a few—of a council of men or a group of nobles. It is derived from Greek ὀλίγος, few, and ἄρχειν, to rule. An *oligarchy*, therefore, is generally an *autocracy*, but an *autocracy* is not always an *oligarchy;* at least

nominally it is not, but practically it generally is, because the power even of an absolute monarch really resides in the group of his advisers. An *aristocracy* is an *oligarchy* in which the few are also the *best* men, from Greek ἄριστος, best. While the Greeks held an ideal of a state in which the power was in the hands of the wisest and the noblest, as a matter of fact there was, in practice, little difference between an *aristocracy* and an *oligarchy*, the "best" men being the self-assertive and the powerful who could get the government into their hands, with special reference to those of noble birth.

As adjectives *autocratic* corresponds very nearly to *absolute* (which see), and has the same synonymes — *despotic*, *tyrannical*, etc. *Autocratic* generally has reference to the assertion of the right to hold absolute rule, in action, speech, or manner; *despotic* and *tyrannical* to the actual exercise of that self-appointed right to the oppression of another. *Aristocratic*, like *autocratic*, is a more general word than *oligarchical*. *Oligarchical* means characteristic of an *oligarch*, one of a small group of autocratic rulers; *aristocratic* refers in general to the characteristics of men of hereditary importance in a state whose qualities of personality and gifts of fortune entitle them to a position of dignity. It is generally used in a good sense, while *oligarchical* is somewhat derogatory.

AUTOMOBILE, AUTO, CAR, MACHINE, MOTOR. These words do not differ in meaning or application; the only difference is the extent and dignity of their usage as designations for exactly the same thing. *Automobile* is the regular word; the rest are more or less colloquial substitutes. *Automobile* is a French word formed by adding Greek αὐτο, self, to French *mobile*, to indicate a self-moving vehicle, one propelled by its own machinery. *Auto* is a somewhat inelegant abbreviation usually frowned on in polite society in favor of *car* or *machine*, general words which have been given this special application. *Motor*, in America, is usually employed as a verb meaning to ride in an *automobile;* in England, however, *motor-car* is the common term for *automobile*.

AUXILIARY, Ancillary, Subsid-iary. *Auxiliary* comes from Latin *auxilium*, help, from *augere*, to increase. *Ancillary* comes from Latin *ancilla*, a handmaid, and means literally serving in the capacity of a handmaid. *Sub-sidiary* comes from Latin *subsidium*, a body of troops in reserve, from Latin *sub*, under, in reserve, and *sedere*, to sit. All these words mean aiding or assisting, and there is very little dif-ference in their application. What there is is mainly that suggested by the derivation. *Auxiliary* does not suggest the degree of subordination implied in *ancillary* and *subsidiary*. *Subsidiary* and *ancillary* differ slightly in the relation of the implied help to the person or object to be helped, *ancillary* suggesting merely subordinate aid, *sub-sidiary* aid held in reserve.

AVAIL. See Signify; Utility.

AVARICE. See Covetousness.

AVARICIOUS, Miserly, Parsimo-nious, Niggardly. *Avaricious*, from Latin *avarus*, and *avere*, to desire, signi-fies desiring money, from a love of it. *Miserly* signifies like a *miser*, or *miser-able* man; for none are so miserable as the lovers of money. *Parsimonious*, from the Latin *parcere*, to spare or save, signifies, literally, saving. *Niggardly* is a Scandinavian word signifying stingy.

The *avaricious* man and the *miser* are one and the same character, with this exception, that the *miser* carries his passion for money to a still greater excess. An *avaricious* man shows his love of money in his ordinary dealings, but the *miser* lives upon it, and suffers every privation rather than part with it. An *avaricious* man may sometimes be indulgent to himself and generous to others; the *miser* is dead to every-thing but the treasure which he has amassed. *Parsimonious* and *niggardly* are the subordinate characteristics of *avarice*. The *avaricious* man indulges his passion for money by *parsimony*—that is, by saving out of himself, or by *niggardly* ways in his dealings with others. He who spends a farthing on himself where others with the same means spend a shilling does it from *parsimony*: he who looks to every farthing in the bargains he makes gets the name of a *niggard*. *Avarice* some-times cloaks itself under the name of

prudence: it is, as Goldsmith says, often the only virtue which is left a man at the age of seventy-two. The *miser* is his own greatest enemy, and no man's friend; his ill-gotten wealth is generally a curse to him by whom it is inherited. A man is sometimes rendered *parsimonious* by circum-stances; but he who first saves from necessity too often ends with saving from inclination. The *niggard* is an object of contempt, and sometimes hatred; every one fears to lose by a man who strives to gain from all.

See also Greedy.

AVENGE, Revenge, Vindicate. *Avenge, revenge,* and *vindicate* all spring from the same source, namely, the Latin *vindicare*, from *vindex*, a claim-ant, signifying to pronounce justice or put justice in force.

The idea common to these terms is that of taking up some one's cause. To *avenge* is to punish in behalf of another; to *revenge* is to punish for one's self; to *vindicate* is to defend an-other. The wrongs of a person are *avenged* or *revenged;* his rights are *vin-dicated.* The act of *avenging,* though attended with the infliction of pain, is oftentimes an act of humanity, and always an act of justice; none are the sufferers but such as merit it for their oppression; while those are benefited who are dependent for support: this is the act of God Himself, Who always *avenges* the oppressed who look up to Him for support; and it ought to be the act of all His creatures who are in-vested with the power of punishing offenders and protecting the helpless. *Revenge* is the basest of all actions, and the spirit of *revenge* the most dia-metrically opposed to the Christian principles of forgiving injuries and re-turning good for evil; it is gratified only with inflicting pain without any prospect of advantage. *Vindication* is an act of generosity and humanity; it is the production of good without the infliction of pain: the claims of the widow and orphan call for *vindication* from those who have the time, talent, or ability to take their cause into their own hands: England can boast of many noble *vindicators* of the rights of hu-manity, not excepting those which con-cern the brute creation.

AVER. See AFFIRM.

AVERSE, UNWILLING, BACKWARD, LOATH, RELUCTANT. *Averse*, in Latin *aversus*, participle of *avertere*, compounded of *vertere*, to turn, and *a*, from, signifies the state of having the mind turned from a thing. *Unwilling* literally signifies not willing. *Backward* signifies having the will in a *backward* direction. *Loath*, from Anglo-Saxon *lath*, hateful, hostile, has developed a somewhat milder meaning. *Reluctant*, from the Latin *re* against, and *luctare*, to struggle, signifies struggling with the will against a thing.

Averse is positive, it marks an actual sentiment of dislike; *unwilling* is negative, it marks the absence of the will; *backward* is a sentiment between the two, it marks a leaning of the will against a thing; *loath* and *reluctant* mark strong feelings of *aversion*. *Aversion* is an habitual sentiment; *unwillingness* and *backwardness* are mostly occasional; *loath* and *reluctant* always occasional. *Aversion* must be conquered; *unwillingness* must be removed; *backwardness* must be counteracted or urged forward; *loathing* and *reluctance* must be overpowered. One who is *averse* to study will never have recourse to books; but a child may be *unwilling* or *backward* to attend to his lessons from partial motives, which the authority of the parent or master may correct; he who is *loath* to receive instruction will always remain ignorant; he who is *reluctant* in doing his duty will always do it as a task. A miser is *averse* to nothing so much as to parting with his money: he is even *unwilling* to provide himself with necessaries, but he is not *backward* in disposing of his money when he has the prospect of getting more; friends are *loath* to part who have had many years' enjoyment in each other's society; we are *reluctant* in giving unpleasant advice. Lazy people are *averse* to labor; those who are not paid are *unwilling* to work; and those who are paid less than others are *backward* in giving their services: every one is *loath* to give up a favorite pursuit, and when compelled to it by circumstances they do it with *reluctance*.

See also ADVERSE.

Aversion, Antipathy, Dislike, Hatred, *Repugnance.* — *Aversion* denotes the quality of being averse. *Antipathy*, in French *antipathie*, Latin *antipathia*, Greek ἀντιπάθεια, compounded of ἀντί, against, and παθεῖν, to suffer, to feel, feeling, signifies here a natural feeling against an object. *Dislike*, compounded of the privative *dis* and *like*, signifies not to like or be attached to. *Hatred* comes from Anglo-Saxon *hatian*, to hate. *Repugnance*, in French *répugnance*, Latin *repugnantia* and *repugnare*, compounded of *re*, against, and *pugnare*, to fight, signifies the resistance of the feelings to an object.

Aversion is in its most general sense the generic term to these and many other similar expressions, in which case it is opposed to attachment, the former denoting an alienation of the mind from an object; the latter a knitting or binding of the mind to objects: it has, however, more commonly a partial acceptation, in which it is justly comparable with the above words. The first four are used indifferently for persons and things, the last for things. *Aversion* and *antipathy* seem to be less dependent on the will, and to have their origin in the temperament or natural taste, particularly the latter, which springs from causes that are not always visible; it lies in the physical organization. *Antipathy* is, in fact, a natural *aversion* opposed to sympathy: *dislike* and *hatred* are, on the contrary, voluntary, and seem to have their root in the angry passions of the heart; the former is less deep-rooted than the latter, and is commonly awakened by slighter causes: *repugnance* is not an habitual and lasting sentiment, like the rest; it is a transitory but strong *dislike* to anything. People of a quiet temper have an *aversion* to disputing or argumentation; those of a gloomy temper have an *aversion* to society; *antipathies* mostly discover themselves in early life, and as soon as the object comes within the view of the person affected: men of different sentiments in religion or politics, if not of amiable tempers, are apt to contract *dislikes* to each other by frequent irritation in discourse: when men of malignant tempers come in collision, nothing but a deadly *hatred* can ensue from their repeated and complicated aggressions toward each other; any one who is under the influence of a misplaced pride is apt to feel a *repugnance* to acknowledge himself in error.

AVIATION. See AERONAUTICS.

AVIATOR. See AERONAUT.

AVIDITY. GREEDINESS, EAGERNESS are terms expressive of a strong desire. *Avidity*, in Latin *aviditas*, from *avere*, to desire, expresses very strong desire. *Greediness* comes from Anglo-Saxon *grædig*, *greedy*. *Eagerness*, through French from the Latin *acer*, sharp, signifies acuteness of feeling.

Avidity is in mental desires what *greediness* is in animal appetites: *eagerness* is not so vehement, but more impatient than *avidity* or *greediness*. *Avidity* and *greediness* respect simply the desire of possessing; *eagerness* the general desire of attaining an object. An opportunity is seized with *avidity;* the miser grasps at money with *greediness*, or the glutton devours with *greediness;* a person runs with *eagerness* in order to get to the place of destination: a soldier fights with *eagerness* in order to conquer; a lover looks with *eager* impatience for a letter from the object of his affection. *Avidity* is employed in the adverbial form to qualify an action: we seize with *avidity;* *greediness* marks the abstract quality or habit of the mind; *greediness* is the characteristic of low and brutal minds: *eagerness* denotes the transitory state of feeling; a person discovers his *eagerness* in his looks.

AVOCATION. See BUSINESS.

AVOID, ESCHEW, SHUN, ELUDE. *Avoid* comes from Old French *esvuidier*, to empty out, from French *es*, Latin *ex*, and *vuide*, *voide*, empty, a word of unknown origin. *Eschew* comes through French from Old High German *sciuhan*, to frighten. *Shun* comes from Anglo-Saxon *scunian*, to shun or avoid, whence *schooner* is derived. *Elude*, in French *éluder*, Latin *eludo*, compounded of *e*, out, and *ludere*, to play, to trick, signifies to get one's self out of a thing by a trick.

Avoid is both generic and specific; we *avoid* in *eschewing* or *shunning*, or we *avoid* without *eschewing* or *shunning*. Various contrivances are requisite for *avoiding;* *eschewing* and *shunning* consist only of going out of the way, of not

coming in contact; *eluding*, as its derivation denotes, has more of artifice in it than any of the former. We *avoid* a troublesome visitor under real or feigned pretences of ill-health, prior engagement, and the like; we *eschew* evil company by not going into any but what we know to be good; we *shun* the sight of an offensive object by turning into another road; we *elude* a punishment by getting out of the way of those who have the power of inflicting it. Prudence enables us to *avoid* many of the evils to which we are daily exposed: nothing but a fixed principle of religion can enable a man to *eschew* the temptations to evil which lie in his path: fear will lead us to *shun* a madman whom it is not in our power to bind: a want of all principle leads a man to *elude* his creditors whom he wishes to defraud. We speak of *avoiding* a danger and *shunning* a danger; but to *avoid* it is in general not to fall into it; to *shun* it is with care to keep out of the way of it.

AVOW. See ACKNOWLEDGE; SWEAR.

AWAIT. See WAIT.

AWAKEN, EXCITE, PROVOKE, ROUSE, STIR UP. To *awaken* is to make *awake* or alive. *Excite*, in Latin *excito*, compounded of the intensive syllable *ex*, and *citare*, to arouse, means to arouse very much. *Provoke* (see AGGRAVATE). To *rouse* is to cause to rise. *Stir* comes from Anglo-Saxon *styrian*, to move, which may be allied to *storm*. To *excite* and *provoke* convey the idea of producing something: *rouse* and *stir up* that of only calling into action that which previously exists; to *awaken* is used in either sense. To *awaken* is a gentler action than to *excite*, and this is gentler than to *provoke*. We *awaken* by a simple effort; we *excite* by repeated efforts or forcible means; we *provoke* by words, looks, or actions. The tender feelings are *awakened;* affections, or the passions in general, are *excited;* the angry passions are commonly *provoked*. Objects of distress *awaken* a sentiment of pity; competition among scholars *excites* a spirit of emulation; taunting words *provoke* anger. *Awaken* is applied only to the individual and what passes within him; *excite* is applicable to the outward circumstances of one or many; *provoke* is applicable to the conduct or temper of one or many. The attention is *awakened* by interesting sounds that strike upon the ear; the conscience is *awakened* by the voice of the preacher, or by passing events: a commotion, a tumult, or a rebellion is *excited* among the people by the active efforts of individuals; laughter or contempt is *provoked* by preposterous conduct.

To *awaken* is in the moral, as in the physical sense, to call into *consciousness* from a state of *unconsciousness;* to *rouse* is forcibly to bring into action that which is in a state of inaction; and *stir up* is to bring into a state of agitation or commotion. We are *awakened* from an ordinary state by ordinary means; we are *roused* from an extraordinary state by extraordinary means; we are *stirred up* from an ordinary to an extraordinary state. The mind of a child is *awakened* by the action on its senses as soon as it is born; there are some persons who are not *roused* from their stupor by anything but the most awful events; and there are others whose passions, particularly of anger, are *stirred up* by trifling circumstances. The conscience is sometimes *awakened* for a time, but the sinner is not *roused* to a sense of his danger, or to any exertions for his own safety, until an intemperate zeal is *stirred up* in him by means of enthusiastic preaching, in which case the vulgar proverb is verified, that the remedy is as bad as the disease. Death is a scene calculated to *awaken* some feeling in the most obdurate breast: the tears and sighs of the afflicted *excite* a sentiment of commiseration; the most equitable administration of justice may *excite* murmurs among the discontented; a harsh and unreasonable reproof will *provoke* a reply: oppression and tyranny mostly *rouse* the sufferers to a sense of their injuries; nothing is so calculated to *stir up* the rebellious spirits of men as the harangues of political demagogues.

AWARE, ON ONE'S GUARD, APPRISED, CONSCIOUS. *Aware* is a corruption of Anglo-Saxon *gewær*, from Anglo-Saxon *ge*, a common prefix, and *wær*, cautious, modern English *wary*. *Guard* comes through Old French from a Teutonic word cognate with English *ward*, and meant to *watch*, hence *guard*. *Apprise* is derived through French *appris*, the past participle of *apprendre*, from Latin *ad*, to, and *prehendere*, to take. *Conscious*, in Latin *conscius*, compounded of *con* and *scire*, to know, signifies knowing within one's self.

The idea of having the expectation or knowledge of a thing is common to all these terms. We are *aware* of a thing when we calculate upon it; we are *on our guard* against it when we are prepared for it; we are *apprised* of that of which we have had an intimation, and are *conscious* of that in which we have ourselves been concerned. To be *aware*, and *on one's guard*, respect the future; to be *apprised*, either the past or present; to be conscious, only the past. Experience enables a man to be *aware* of consequences; prudence and caution dictate to him the necessity of being *on his guard* against evils. Whoever is fully *aware* of the precarious tenure by which he holds all his goods in this world will be *on his guard* to prevent any calamities, as far as depends upon the use of means in his control. We are *apprised* of events, or what passes outwardly, through the medium of external circumstances; we are *conscious* only through the medium of ourselves, or what passes within.

AWE, REVERENCE, DREAD. *Awe* is a Scandinavian word allied to Gothic *agis*, fear, anguish. *Reverence* comes from Latin *re*, intensive, and *vereri*, to fear, allied to English *wary*. *Dread* comes from *drædan*, in Anglo-Saxon *ondrædan*, to fear.

Awe and *reverence* both denote a strong sentiment of respect, mingled with some emotions of fear; but the former marks the much stronger sentiment of the two: *dread* is an unmingled sentiment of fear for one's personal security. *Awe* may be awakened by the help of the senses and understanding; *reverence* by that of the understanding only; and *dread* principally by that of the imagination. Sublime, sacred, and solemn objects awaken *awe;* they cause the beholder to stop and consider whether he is worthy to approach them any nearer; they rivet his mind and body to a spot, and make him cautious lest by his presence he should contaminate that which is hallowed: exalted and noble objects produce *reverence;* they lead to every outward mark of obeisance and humiliation which it is possible for him to express; terrific objects excite *dread;* they cause a shuddering of the animal frame, and a revulsion of the mind which is attended with nothing but pain. When the creature places himself in the presence of the Creator—when he contemplates the immeasurable distance which separates himself, a frail and finite mortal, from his infinitely perfect Maker—he approaches with *awe;* even the sanctuary where he is accustomed thus to bow before the Almighty acquires the power of awakening the same emotions in his mind. Age, wisdom, and virtue, when combined in one person, are never approached without *reverence;* the possessor has a dignity in himself that checks the haughtiness of the arrogant, that silences the petulance of pride and self-conceit, that stills the noise and giddy mirth of the young, and communicates to all around a sobriety of mien and aspect. A grievous offender is seldom without *dread;* his guilty conscience pictures everything as the instrument of vengeance, and every person as pronouncing his merited sentence. The solemn stillness of the tomb will inspire *awe,* even in the breast of him who has no *dread* of death. Children should be early taught to have a certain degree of *reverence* for the Bible as a book, in distinction from all other books.

AWKWARD, CLUMSY. *Awkward* is composed of an English suffix *ward,* added to a Scandinavian word, and originally signified transversely or "in a backhanded manner." *Clumsy* comes through Middle English *clumsed,* benumbed, from the Scandinavian—*clumsy* being therefore the manner or action characteristic of benumbed hands.

These epithets denote what is contrary to rule and order, in form or manner. *Awkward* respects outward deportment; *clumsy* the shape and make of the object: a person has an *awkward* gait, is *clumsy* in his whole person. *Awkwardness* is the consequence of bad education; *clumsiness* is mostly a natural defect. Young recruits are *awkward* in marching and *clumsy* in their manual exercise.

They may be both employed figuratively in the same sense, and sometimes in relation to the same objects: when speaking of *awkward* contrivances, or *clumsy* contrivances, the latter expresses the idea more strongly than the former.

Awkward, Cross, Untoward, Crooked, Froward, Perverse.—*Awkward* (see above). *Cross,* from the noun *cross,* implies the quality of being *transverse,* hence contrary, like the arms of a cross. *Untoward* signifies the reverse of *toward. Crooked* signifies the quality of resembling a *crook,* a Scandinavian word meaning hook, angle, etc. *Froward* is composed of an English suffix added to a Scandinavian word—*fro* for English *from*—and means in the contrary direction. *Perverse,* Latin *perversus,* participle of *perverto,* compounded of *per* and *verto,* signifies turned aside.

Awkward, cross, untoward, and *crooked* are used as epithets in relation to the events of life or the disposition of the mind; *froward* and *perverse* respect only the disposition of the mind. *Awkward* circumstances are apt to embarrass; *cross* circumstances to pain; *crooked* and *untoward* circumstances to defeat. What is *crooked* springs from a *perverted* judgment; what is *untoward* is independent of human control. In our intercourse with the world there are always little *awkward* incidents arising which a person's good sense and good nature will enable him to pass over without disturbing the harmony of society. It is the lot of every one in his passage through life to meet with *cross* accidents that are calculated to ruffle the temper, but he proves himself to be the wisest whose serenity is not so easily disturbed. A *crooked* policy obstructs the prosperity of individuals, as well as of states. Many men are destined to meet with severe trials in the frustration of their dearest hopes, by numberless *untoward* events which call forth the exercise of patience; in this case the Christian can prove to himself and others the infinite value of his faith and doctrine.

When used with regard to the disposition of the mind, *awkward* expresses less than *froward*, and *froward* less than *perverse*. *Awkwardness* is an habitual frailty of temper; it includes certain weaknesses and particularities, pertinaciously adhered to: *crossness* is a partial irritation resulting from the state of the humors, physical and mental. *Frowardness* and *perversity* lie in the will: a *froward* temper is capricious; it wills or wills not to please itself without regard to others. *Perversity* lies deeper; taking root in the heart, it assumes the shape of malignity; a *perverse* temper is really wicked; it likes or dislikes by the rule of contradiction to another's will. *Untowardness* lies in the principles; it runs counter to the wishes and counsels of another. An *awkward* temper is connected with self-sufficiency; it shelters itself under the sanction of what is apparently reasonable; it requires management and indulgence in dealing with it. *Crossness* and *frowardness* are peculiar to children; indiscriminate indulgence of the rising will engenders those diseases of the mind which, if fostered too long in the breast, become incorrigible by anything but a powerful sense of religion. *Perversity* is, however, but too commonly the result of a vicious habit, which embitters the happiness of all who have the misfortune of coming in collision with it. *Untowardness* is also another fruit of these evil tempers. A *froward* child becomes an *untoward* youth, who turns a deaf ear to all the admonitions of an afflicted parent.

AWRY. See BENT.

AXIOM, MAXIM, APHORISM, APOPHTHEGM (old form; modern APOTHEGM), SAYING, ADAGE, PROVERB, BYWORD, SAW. *Axiom*, in French *axiome*, Latin *axioma*, comes from the Greek ἀξίωπα, worth, signifying the thing valued. *Maxim*, in French *maxime*, in Latin *maxima* for *maxima sentiarum*, the most important opinion. *Aphorism*, from Greek ἀφορίζειν, to define or limit, meant originally a definition. *Apothegm*, in Greek ἀπόφθεγμα, from ἀπό, from, and φθέγγεσθαι, to utter, to speak pointedly, signifies a pointed saying. *Saying* signifies literally what is said—that is, said habitually. *Adage*,

in Latin *adagium*, comes from Latin *ad*, to, to the point, and a stem signifying to say. *Proverb*, in French *proverbe*, Latin *proverbium*, compounded of *pro*, publicly, and *verbum*, a saying, signifies a common saying. *Byword* signifies a word by-the-by, or by-the-way, in the course of conversation. *Saw* comes from Anglo-Saxon *sagu*, a saying, from the verb to *say* in its older form.

A given sentiment conveyed in a specific sentence, or form of expression, is the common idea included in the signification of these terms. The *axiom* is a truth of the first value; a self-evident proposition which is the basis of other truths. A *maxim* is a truth of the first moral importance for all practical purposes. An *aphorism* is a truth set apart for its pointedness and excellence. *Apothegm* is, in respect to the ancients, what *saying* is in regard to the moderns; it is a pointed sentiment pronounced by an individual and adopted by others. *Adage* and *proverb* are vulgar sayings, the former among the ancients, the latter among the moderns. The *byword* is a casual saying originating in some local circumstance. The *saw*, which is a barbarous corruption of *saying*, is the *saying* formerly current among the ignorant.

Axioms are in science what *maxims* are in morals; self-evidence is an essential characteristic in both; the *axiom* presents itself in so simple and undeniable a form to the understanding as to exclude doubt and the necessity for reasoning. The *maxim*, though not so definite in its expression as the *axiom*, is at the same time equally parallel to the mind of man, and of such general application that it is acknowledged by all moral agents who are susceptible of moral truth; it comes home to the common sense of all mankind. "Things that are equal to one and the same thing are equal to each other"—"Two bodies cannot occupy the same space at the same time," are *axioms* in mathematics and metaphysics. "Virtue is the true source of happiness"—"The happiness of man is the end of civil government," are *axioms* in ethics and politics. "To err is human, to forgive divine"—"When our vices leave us, we flatter ourselves that we leave them," are among the number of *maxims*. Between *axioms* and *maxims* there is this obvious difference to be observed: that the former are unchangeable both in matter and manner and admit of little or no increase in number; but the latter may vary with the circumstances of human life, and admit of considerable extension.

An *aphorism* is a speculative principle either in science or morals, which is presented in a few words to the understanding; it is the substance of a doctrine, and many *aphorisms* may contain the abstract of a science. Of this description are the *aphorisms* of Hippocrates, and those of Lavater in physiognomy.

Sayings and *apothegms* differ from the preceding, inasmuch as they always carry the mind back to the person speaking; there is always one who says when there is a *saying* or an *apothegm*, and both acquire a value as much from the person who utters them as from the thing that is uttered: when Leonidas was asked why brave men prefer honor to life, his answer became an *apothegm;* namely, that "they hold life by fortune, and honor by virtue": of this description are the *apothegms* comprised by Plutarch, the *sayings* of Franklin's Poor Richard, or those of Dr. Johnson: they are happy effusions of the mind which men are fond of treasuring.

The *adage* and *proverb* are habitual as well as general *sayi..gs*, not repeated as the *sayings* of one, but of all; not adopted for the sake of the person, but for the sake of the thing; and they have been used in all ages for the purpose of conveying the sense of mankind on ordinary subjects. The *adage* of former times is tne *proverb* of the present time: if there be any difference between them, it lies in this, that the former are the fruit of knowledge and long experience, the latter of vulgar observations; the *adage* is therefore more refined than the *proverb*. Adversity is our best teacher, according to the Greek *adage*, "What hurts us instructs us." "Old birds are not to be caught with chaff" is a vulgar *proverb*.

Bywords rarely contain any important sentiment; they mostly consist of familiar similes, nicknames, and the like, as the Cambridge, *byword* of "Hobson's choice," signifying that or none: the name of Nazarene was a *byword* among the Jews for a Christian. A *saw* is vulgar in form and vulgar in matter: it is the partial *saying* of particular neighborhoods, originating in ignorance and superstition: of this description are the *sayings* which attribute particular properties to animals or to plants, termed old women's *sayings*.

AYE, AY. *Aye* and *ay* are words frequently confused—so often confused, indeed, that the distinction between them is not clearly maintained even in good writing; but the distinction exists. *Aye*, pronounced like *I*, seems to have been originally a different form from *ay;* it means yes, and is still used in poetry and in old-fashioned and humble colloquial speech, for yes— as well as in the parliamentary procedure of voting. *Ay*, which rhymes with day, gay, etc., from a Teutonic root meaning age, eternity, means ever, always, and continually. It should not be spelled or pronounced like *aye*.

B

BABBLE, CHATTER, CHAT, PRATTLE, PRATE. *Babble* is allied to German *bappeln*, Dutch *babbelen*, French *babiller*, etc. The suffix *le* is frequentative, and the verb means to keep on saying *ba*, *ba*, syllables imitative of a child trying to talk. *Chatter* and *chat* are imitative words. *Prate*, allied to Dutch *prat*, talk, Low German *praten*, etc., is possibly an imitative word. *Prattle* is the frequentative of *prate* and means to keep on prating.

All these terms mark a superfluous or improper use of speech: *babble* and *chatter* are onomatopœias drawn from the noise or action of speaking; *babbling* denotes rapidity of speech, which renders it unintelligible; hence the term is applied to all who make use of many words to no purpose: *chatter* is an imitation of the noise of speech properly applied to magpies or parrots, and figuratively to a corresponding vicious mode of speech in human beings. The vice of *babbling* is most commonly attached to men, that of *chattering* to women: the *babbler* talks much to impress others with his self-importance; the *chatterer* is actuated by self-conceit and a desire to display her volubility: the former cares not whether he is understood; the latter cares not if she be but heard. *Chatting* is both harmless and respectable; the winter's fireside invites neighbors to assemble and *chat* away many an hour which might otherwise hang heavy on hand, or be spent less inoffensively; *chatting* is the practice of adults; *prattling* and *prating* that of children, the one innocently, the other impertinently; the *prattling* of babes has an interest for every feeling mind, but for parents it is one of their highest enjoyments; *prating*, on the contrary, is the consequence of ignorance and childish assumption: a *prattler* has all the unaffected gayety of an uncontaminated mind; a *prater* is forward, obtrusive, and ridiculous.

BACCALAUREATE, BACHELOR. *Baccalaureate* is a term of uncertain derivation. *Baccalaureate* and *bachelor* are derived from the same Latin word, *baccalaureus*, the one directly, the other through the medium of French. *Baccalaureus* meant "cowherd," from *bacca*, cow; thence it became the term applied to any young man. *Bachelor* in the Middle Ages signified a young knight, one not old enough to display his own banner, and still fighting under the standard of another. In modern times it has been specialized to mean, on the one hand, an unmarried man, on the other, the recipient of the first degree at a university—the degree of *Bachelor* of Arts. The term *baccalaureate* has been similarly specialized to refer to the type of academic initiation into mature life that corresponds in modern times to the military initiation of the young *bachelor* at arms. *Baccalaureate* refers to the ceremony of receiving the *bachelor's* degree, and, in America, it refers especially to the farewell sermon preached to students on the Sunday preceding their graduation, which is called the *baccalaureate* sermon.

BACK, BACKWARD, BEHIND. *Back* and *backward* are used only as adverbs: *behind*, either as an adverb or a preposition—to go *back* or *backward*, to go *behind*, or *behind* the wall. *Back* denotes the situation of being and the direction of going; *backward* simply the manner of going; a person stands *back* who does not wish to be in the way; he goes *backward* when he does not wish to turn his *back* to an object. *Back* marks simply the situation of a place, *behind* the situation of one object with regard to another: a person stands *back* who stands in the *back* part of any place; he stands *behind* who has any one in front of him: the *back* is opposed to the front, *behind* to before.

See also ABACK; AFT; AVERSE.

BACKSLIDER. See RECREANT.

BAD, WICKED, EVIL. *Bad* is formed from Anglo-Saxon *bœddel*, a hermaphrodite, an effeminate man, hence a worthless fellow—thence *bad*, worthless. *Wicked*, Anglo-Saxon *wikke*, evil, is derived from the substantive *wikke*, a witch. *Wicked* means bewitched, possessed of an evil spirit. *Bad* respects moral and physical qualities in general; *wicked*, only moral qualities. *Evil*, Anglo-Saxon *yfel*, comes from a widely distributed Germanic root, the ultimate origin of which is unknown. *Evil*, in its full extent, comprehends both *badness* and *wickedness*.

Whatever offends the taste and sentiments of a rational being is *bad;* food is *bad* when it disagrees with the constitution; the air is *bad* which has anything in it disagreeable to the senses or hurtful to the body; books are *bad* which only inflame the imagination or the passions. Whatever is *wicked* offends the moral principles of a rational agent: any violation of the law is *wicked*, as law is the support of human society; an act of injustice or cruelty is *wicked*, as it opposes the will of God and the feelings of humanity. *Evil* is either moral or natural, and may be applied to every object that is contrary to good; but the term is employed only for that which is in the highest degree *bad* or *wicked*.

When used in relation to persons, both refer to the morals, but *bad* is more general than *wicked;* a *bad* man is one who is generally wanting in the performance of his duty; a *wicked* man is one who is chargeable with actual violations of the law, human or divine; such a one has an *evil* mind. A *bad* character is the consequence of immoral conduct; but no man has the character of being *wicked* who has not been guilty of some known and flagrant vices: the inclinations of the best are *evil* at certain times.

BADGE. See MARK.

BADLY, ILL. *Badly* means in the manner of *bad* (see above). *Ill* is a Scandinavian word, not a contraction of the word which appears in Anglo-Saxon as *yfel*, in Modern English as *evil*.

These terms are both employed to modify the actions or qualities of things, but *badly* is always annexed to the action, and *ill* to the quality: as to do anything *badly*, the thing is *badly* done, an *ill*-judged scheme, an *ill*-contrived measure, an *ill*-disposed person.

BAFFLE, DEFEAT, DISCONCERT, CONFOUND. *Baffle* is a Scotch word of doubtful origin meaning originally

to disgrace or vilify. Compare French *beffler*, and Middle High German *beffen*, to scold. It may be of imitative origin, like the slang *biff*, meaning to slap. *Defeat*, in French *défait*, participle of *défaire*, is derived from *dis*, apart, and *facere*, to do, and signifies to undo. *Disconcert* is compounded of the privative *dis* and *concert*, signifying to throw out of concert or harmony, to put into disorder. *Confound*, in French *confondre*, is compounded of *con* and *fundere*, to pour, and signifies to melt or mix together in general disorder.

When applied to the derangement of the mind or rational faculties, *baffle* and *defeat* respect the powers of argument; *disconcert* and *confound*, the thoughts and feelings: *baffle* expresses less than *defeat; disconcert* less than *confound;* a person is *baffled* in argument who is for the time discomposed and silenced by the superior address of his opponent; he is *defeated* in argument if his opponent has altogether the advantage of him in strength of reasoning and justness of sentiment: a person is *disconcerted* who loses his presence of mind for a moment, or has his feelings any way discomposed; he is *confounded* when the powers of thought and consciousness become torpid or vanish. A superior command of language or a particular degree of effrontery will frequently enable a person to *baffle* one who is advocating the cause of truth: ignorance of the subject, or a want of ability, may occasion a man to be *defeated* by his adversary, even when he is supporting a good cause: assurance is requisite to prevent any one from being *disconcerted* who is suddenly detected in any disgraceful proceedings: hardened effrontery sometimes keeps the daring villain from being *confounded* by any events, however awful.

When applied to the derangement of plans, *baffle* expresses less than *defeat*, *defeat* less than *confound*, and *disconcert* less than all. Obstinacy, perseverance. skill, or art *baffles;* superior force *defeats;* awkward circumstances *disconcert;* the visitation of God *confounds*. When wicked men strive to obtain their ends, it is a happy thing if their adversaries have sufficient skill and address to *baffle* all their arts, and sufficient power to *defeat* all their projects; but sometimes when our best endeavors fail in our own behalf, the devices of men are *confounded* by the interposition of Heaven. It frequently happens, even in the common transactions of life, that the best schemes are *disconcerted* by the trivial casualties of wind and weather. The obstinacy of a disorder may *baffle* the skill of the physician; the imprudence of the patient may *defeat* the object of his prescriptions; the unexpected arrival of a superior may *disconcert* the unauthorized plan of those who are subordinate; the miraculous destruction of his army *confounded* the project of the king of Assyria.

BALANCE. See COUNTERPOISE; POISE.

BALDERDASH. See TWADDLE.

BALL. See GLOBE.

BALLOON. See AIRCRAFT.

BALLOONIST. See AERONAUT.

BAN, CURSE, DENOUNCE, FORBID, PROHIBIT. These terms represent various types and degrees of social and spiritual ostracism. *Ban*, in Anglo-Saxon *bannan*, is a Germanic word which has entered most of the Romance languages and appears in the word *abandon*, derived in English from a French phrase. In ancient German law a *ban* was a sentence of outlawry pronounced against one who had escaped from justice or refused to submit to trial; the *ban of the empire* was a penalty imposed on refractory princes and even on cities, in Germany. *Ban* implies a formal *forbidding* or *prohibiting*. To *curse*, Anglo-Saxon *cursian*, is to attempt to cut souls off from all sources of spiritual life and health. It is a spiritual *ban*, as it were, and corresponds in the world of the spirit to the political outlawry suggested by the word *ban*. *Denounce*, from Latin *de*, fully, and *nuntiare*, to make a formal statement, suggests a public criticism or accusation which might lead to a *ban*, but which, in itself, does not imply that the person denounced is *forbidden* to enjoy any of his natural rights or *prohibited* from doing what he pleases. *Forbidden*, Anglo-Saxon *forbeodan*, from *for*, a privative prefix, and *beodan*, to bid, means to bid a person not to do some-

thing. It does not imply formal and public action, as does the word *ban*. *Prohibit*, from Latin *prohibere*, *pro* and *habere*, means to keep another from doing something, and implies an exertion of some force besides the purely verbal one expended in *forbidding*. It does not imply formal and public action.

BAND, COMPANY, CREW, GANG. *Crew*, is from *crue*, a shortened form of *accrue*, a reinforcement, from Old French *accroistre*, to increase, from Latin *accrescere*. *Gang*, from Anglo-Saxon *gangen*, to go, signifies a group of individuals who go together.

All these terms denote a small association for a particular object: a *band* is an association where men are bound together by some strong obligation, whether taken in a good or bad sense, as a *band* of soldiers, a *band* of robbers. A *company* marks an association for convenience, without any particular obligation, as a *company* of travellers, a *company* of strolling players. *Crew* marks an association collected together by some external power, or by coincidence of plan and motive: in the former case it is used for a ship's *crew;* in the latter and bad sense of the word it is employed for any number of evil-minded persons met together from different quarters and cooperating for some bad purpose. *Gang* is used in a bad sense for an association of thieves, murderers, and depredators in general; or in a technical sense for those who work together.

See also CHAIN.

BANE, PEST, RUIN. *Bane* is derived from Anglo-Saxon *bana*, a murderer, from a root found in Icelandic *bani*, death, Gothic *banja*, a wound, Greek φόνος, murder, etc. *Pest*, from Latin *pestis*, originally meant a deadly disease. *Ruin*, Latin *ruina*, is derived from *ruere*, to fall down. Milton uses *ruin* with special reference to its etymology to mean something rushing down, falling headlong.

These terms borrow their figurative signification from three of the greatest evils in the world: namely, poison, plague, and destruction. *Bane* is said of things only; *pest* of persons only: whatever produces a deadly corruption is the *bane;* whoever is as obnoxious as

BARE

the plague is a *pest;* luxury is the *bane* of civil society; gaming is the *bane* of all youth; sycophants are the *pests* of society. *Ruin* comprehends more than either *bane* or *pest,* these latter being comparatively partial mischiefs, but *ruin* extends to every part of that which it affects.

BANISH, EXILE, EXPEL. *Banish,* in French *bannair,* German *bannen,* signifies to put out of a community by a ban or civil interdict, which was formerly either ecclesiastical or civil. *Exile,* in French *exiler,* from the Latin *exilium,* banishment, and *exul,* an exile, compounded of *extra* and *solum,* the soil, signifies to put away from one's native soil or country. *Expel,* in Latin *expello,* compounded of *ex* and *pellere,* to drive, signifies to drive out.

The idea of exclusion, or of a coercive removal from a place, is common to these terms: *banishment* includes the removal from any place, or the prohibition of access to any place, where one has been or whither one is in the habit of going; *exile* signifies the removal from one's home; to *exile,* therefore, is to *banish,* but to *banish* is not always to *exile;* the Tarquins were *banished* from Rome never to return; Coriolanus was *exiled,* or driven from his home. *Banishment* follows from a decree of justice; *exile* either by the necessity of circumstances or an order of authority: *banishment* is a disgraceful punishment inflicted by tribunals upon delinquents; *exile* is a disgrace incurred without dishonor: *exile* removes us from our country; *banishment* drives us from it ignominiously: it was the custom in Russia to *banish* offenders to Siberia; Ovid was *exiled* by an order of Augustus. *Banishment* is an action, a compulsory exercise of power over another, which must be submitted to; *exile* is a state into which we may go voluntarily; many Romans chose to go into *exile* rather than await the judgment of the people, by whom they might have been *banished.* *Banishment* and *expulsion* both mark a disgraceful and coercive exclusion, but *banishment* is authoritative; it is a public act of government: *expulsion* is simply coercive; it is the act of a private individual or a small community. *Banishment* always supposes a removal to a distant spot, to another land; *expulsion* never reaches beyond a particular house or society: *expulsion* from the university, or any public school, is the necessary consequence of discovering a refractory temper or a propensity to insubordination.

Banishment and *expulsion* are likewise used in a figurative sense, although *exile* is not: in this sense, *banishment* marks a distant and entire removal; *expulsion* a violent removal: we *banish* that which it is not prudent to retain; we *expel* that which is noxious. Hopes are *banished* from the mind when every prospect of success has disappeared; fears are *banished* when they are altogether groundless; envy, hatred, and every evil passion should be *expelled* from the mind as disturbers of its peace: harmony and good-humor are best promoted by *banishing* from conversation all subjects of difference in religion and politics; good morals require that every unseemly word should be *expelled.*

See also PROSCRIBE.

BANKRUPTCY. See INSOLVENCY.

BANQUET. See FEAST.

BANTER. See DERIDE.

BAR. See TRIBUNAL.

BARBAROUS. See CRUEL.

BARE, NAKED, UNCOVERED. *Bare* and *naked* are both Anglo-Saxon words —the one being in Anglo-Saxon *bœr,* the other *nacod.* For the derivation of *uncover* see COVER.

Bare marks the condition of being without a particular covering; *naked* that of being without any covering; *bare* is therefore often substituted for *naked,* to a certain degree: we speak of *bareheaded, barefoot,* to expose the *bare* arm; but a figure is *naked,* or the body is *naked.*

When applied to other objects, *bare* conveys the idea of a particular want; *naked* of a general want: as the *bare* ground, *bare* walls, a *bare* house, where the idea of want in a certain particular is strongly conveyed; but *naked* walls, *naked* fields, a *naked* appearance, denote the absence of covering that is usual or general: *bare* in this sense is frequently followed by the object that is wanted; *naked* is mostly employed as an adjunct: a tree is *bare* of leaves: this constitutes it a *naked* tree.

They preserve the same analogy in their figurative application: a *bare* sufficiency is that which scarcely suffices; the *naked* truth is that which has nothing about it to intercept the view of it from the mind.

Naked and *uncovered* bear a strong resemblance to each other; to be *naked* is, in fact, to have the body *uncovered*, but many things are *uncovered* which are not *naked;* nothing is said to be *naked* but what in the nature of things, or according to the usages of men, ought to be covered; everything is *uncovered* from which the covering is removed. According to our natural sentiments of decency or our acquired sentiments of propriety, we expect to see the *naked* body covered with clothing: the *naked* tree covered with leaves; the *naked* walls covered with paper or paint; and the *naked* country covered with verdure or habitations: on the other hand, plants are left *uncovered* to receive the benefit of the sun or rain; furniture or articles of use or necessity are left *uncovered* to suit the convenience of the user; or a person may be *uncovered,* in the sense of *bareheaded,* on certain occasions; so in the moral application, what is *naked* is without the ordinary or necessary appendage; what is *uncovered* is simply without any covering.

Bare, Scanty, Destitute.—*Bare* (see above). *Scanty* is derived from *scant,* a Scandinavian word, from a root found in Icelandic *skamt,* short, brief, and in the somewhat colloquial verb *scamp,* in the phrase "to scamp work," etc. *Destitute,* in Latin *destitutus,* participle of *destituo,* compounded of *de,* privative, and *statuo,* appoint or provide for, signifies unprovided for or wanting.

All these terms denote the absence or privation of some necessary. *Bare* and *scanty* have a relative sense: *bare* respects what serves for ourselves; *scanty* that which is provided by others. A subsistence is *bare;* a supply is *scanty.* An imprudent person will estimate as a *bare* competence what would supply an economist with superfluities. A hungry person will consider as a *scanty* allowance what would more than suffice for a moderate eater.

Bare is said of those things which belong to our corporeal sustenance; *destitute* is said generally of whatever one wants. A person is *bare* of clothes or money; he is *destitute* of friends, of resources, or of comforts.

Bare, Mere.—*Bare* (see above). *Mere* is derived from Latin *merus,* pure, unmixed, used especially of wine.

Bare is used in a positive sense; *mere,* negatively. The *bare* recital of some events brings tears. The *mere* circumstance of receiving favors ought not to bind any person to the opinions of another. The *bare* idea of being in the company of a murderer is apt to awaken horror in the mind. The *mere* attendance at a place of worship is the smallest part of a Christian's duty.

BAREFACED. See GLARING.

BARGAIN. See AGREEMENT; BUY.

BARTER. See CHANGE; EXCHANGE.

BASE, VILE, MEAN. For the origin of *base* see ABASE. *Vile* is derived from Latin *vilis,* of small price, cheap, worthless. *Mean,* Anglo-Saxon *mæne,* usually found in *gemæne,* German *gemein,* instead of in its simple form, signifies common; hence low, ordinary, of little value, etc.

Base is a stronger term than *vile,* and *vile* than *mean.* *Base* marks a high degree of moral turpitude: *vile* and *mean* denote in different degrees the want of all that can be valued or esteemed. What is *base* excites our abhorrence, what is *vile* provokes disgust, what is *mean* awakens contempt. *Base* is opposed to magnanimous, *vile* to noble, *mean* to generous. Ingratitude is *base;* it does violence to the best affections of our nature: flattery is *vile;* it violates truth in the grossest manner for the lowest purposes of gain: compliances are *mean* which are derogatory to the rank, dignity, or responsibility of the individual. The more elevated a person's rank, the greater is his *baseness* who abuses his influence to the injury of those who repose confidence in him. The lower the rank of the individual and the more atrocious his conduct, the *viler* is his character. The more respectable the station of the person and the more extended his wealth, the greater is his *meanness* when he descends to practices fitted only for his inferiors. The schoolmaster of Falerii was guilty of the *basest* treachery in surrendering his helpless charge to the enemy: the Roman general, therefore, with true nobleness of mind, treated him as a *vile* malefactor. Sycophants are in the habit of practising every *mean* artifice to obtain favor.

BASHFUL. See MODEST.

BASIS. See FOUNDATION.

BATTLE, COMBAT, ENGAGEMENT, ACTION. *Battle,* in French *bataille,* comes from the Latin *batuere,* to beat, signifying a beating. *Combat* signifies literally a *battle,* one with the other, from *con,* with, and *batuere. Engagement* signified binding with a pledge, fighting under a pledge to defend some one or some cause, from French *en* and *gage,* a pledge—a word of Teutonic origin. *Action* signifies the state of acting and being acted upon by the way of fighting.

Battle is a general term; *combat, engagement,* and *action* are particular terms, having a modified signification. *Battle,* as an act of fighting, may be applied to what takes place either between bodies or individuals, as the *battles* between the Carthaginians and the Romans, or between Cæsar and Pompey; *combat* applies only to what takes place between individuals, as the *combat* between the Horatii and the Curiatii. *Battle* is taken for that which is premeditated and prepared, as *battles* between armies always are; *combats* are frequently accidental, if not unexpected, as the *combats* of Hercules or the combat between Menelaus and Paris.

Battle and *combat* are taken for the act of fighting generally; *engagement* and *action* are seldom used in any other acceptation. *Battle* in this case is taken without any qualification of time, circumstances, or manner, as armed for *battle,* wager of *battle,* and the like; *combat* refers to the act of individuals fighting with one another: to challenge to single *combat;* the *combat* was obstinate and bloody: *engagement* and *action,* which are properly abstract and general terms to denote engaging and acting, but here limited to the act of fighting, have always a reference to something actually passing or described as passing, and are therefore confined to descriptions, as in describing what passes during the *engagement*

or *action,* or the number of engagements or actions, in which an individual is present or takes a part. It is reported of the German women that whenever their husbands went to *battle* they used to go into the thickest of the *combat* to carry them provisions or dress their wounds; and that sometimes they would take part in the *engagement.*

BE, EXIST, SUBSIST. *Be,* with its inflections, is to be traced through the Northern languages to an original Aryan root signifying to live, to exist. *Exist,* in French *exister,* Latin *existo,* compounded of *e* or *ex* and *sisto,* signifies to "stand out" against the fortunes of life, hence simply to live, to keep on living. From this derivation of the latter verb arises the distinction in the use of the two words. The former is applicable either to the accidents of things or to the substances of things themselves; the latter only to substances or things that stand or *exist* of themselves. We say of qualities, of forms, of actions, of arrangement, of movement, and of every different relation, whether real, ideal, or qualificative, that they *are;* we say of matter, of spirit, of body, and of all substances, that they *exist.* Man *is* man, and will *be* man under all circumstances and changes of life: he *exists* under every known climate and variety of heat or cold in the atmosphere.

Being and *existence* as nouns have this further distinction, that the former is employed not only to designate the abstract action of *being,* but is metaphorically employed for the sensible object that *is;* the latter is confined altogether to the abstract sense. Hence we speak of human *beings; beings* animate or inanimate; the Supreme *Being:* but of the *existence* of a God; *existence* of innumerable worlds; the *existence* of evil.

Being may in some cases be indifferently employed for *existence,* particularly in the grave style: when speaking of animate objects, as the *being* of a God; our frail *being;* and when qualified in a compound form is preferable, as our *well-being.*

Subsist is properly a species of *existing;* from the Latin prepositive *sub,* signifying for a time, it denotes temporary or partial *existence*. Everything *exists* by the creative and preservative power of the Almighty; that which *subsists* depends for its *existence* upon the chances and changes of life. To *exist*, therefore, designates simply the event of *being* or *existing;* to *subsist* conveys the accessory ideas of the mode and duration of *existing.* Man *exists* while the vital or spiritual part of him remains; he *subsists* by what he obtains to support life. Friendships *exist* in the world, notwithstanding the prevalence of selfishness; but they cannot *subsist* for any length of time between individuals in whom this base temper prevails.

Be, Become, Grow.—*Be* (see above). *Become* signifies to *come* to *be*—that is, to *be* in course of time. *Grow* comes from Anglo-Saxon *growan*, to produce green shoots, and is allied to *green.*

Be is positive; *become* is relative: a person *is* what he *is* without regard to what he *was;* he *becomes* that which he *was* not before. We judge of a man by what he *is*, but we cannot judge of him as to what he will *become;* this year he *is* immoral and irreligious, but by the force of reflection on himself he may *become* the contrary in another year. To *become* includes no idea of the mode or circumstance of its *becoming;* to *grow* is to *become* by a gradual process: a man may *become* a good man from a vicious one, in consequence of a sudden action on his mind; but he *grows* in wisdom and virtue by means of an increase in knowledge and experience.

BEAM. See GLEAM; RAY.

BEAR, YIELD. *Bear*, Anglo-Saxon *beran*, is allied to Latin *ferre*, Greek φέρειν, to carry, hence to bring forth that which has been carried and nourished within a living organism or a life-giving substance. *Yield* (see AFFORD).

Bear conveys the idea of creating within itself; *yield*, that of giving from itself. Animals *bear* their young, inanimate objects *yield* their produce. An apple-tree *bears* apples; the earth *yields* fruits. *Bear* marks properly the natural power of bringing forth something of its own kind; *yield* is said of the result or quantum brought forth: shrubs *bear* leaves, flowers, or berries,

according to their natural properties; flowers *yield* seeds plentifully or otherwise, as they are favored by circumstances.

Bear, Carry, Convey, Transport.— *Carry* comes immediately from Latin *carrus*, a four-wheeled vehicle, and hence meant to bear about in a car. *Convey* is derived from *con*, with, and *via*, way, and means to bear with one on the way. *Transport*, in French *transporter*, Latin *transporto*, compounded of *trans*, over, and *portare*, to carry, signifies to *carry* to a distance.

To *bear* is simply to take the weight of any substance upon one's self, or to have the object about one: to *carry* is to remove a body from the spot where it was: we always *bear* in carrying, but we do not always *carry* when we *bear*. Both may be applied to things as well as persons: whatever receives the weight of anything *bears* it; whatever is caused to move with anything *carries* it. That which cannot be easily *borne* must be burdensome to *carry;* in extremely hot weather it is sometimes irksome to *bear* the weight even of one's clothing: Virgil praises the pious Æneas for having *carried* his father on his shoulders in order to save him from the sacking of Troy. Weak people or weak things are not fit to *bear* heavy burdens: lazy people prefer to be *carried* rather than to *carry* anything.

To *bear* is said either of persons or inanimate things; to *carry*, in its proper application, is said of persons only.

To *bear* supposes the bearer for the most part to be stationary, but it may be applied to one who is in motion, as the *bearer* of a letter. In poetry it is mostly used in such connection for *carry*.

To *carry* always supposes the *carrier* to be in motion, and that which is *carried* may either be about his person or resting on something, as to *carry* a thing in one's hand, or to *carry* it in a basket.

Bear and *carry* preserve this distinction in their figurative or moral application; *bear* is applied to that which for the most part remains with the person or thing *bearing; carry* to that which passes by means of the person; thus to *bear* or *carry* a name:

to *bear* a name is to have it without regard to time or place; to *carry* a name is to *carry* it down to posterity. So to *bear* a burden, to *carry* weight, authority, conviction, etc.; to *bear* a stamp, to *carry* a mark to one's grave.

Convey and *transport* are species of *carrying*. *Carry* in its particular sense is employed either for personal exertions or actions performed by the help of other means; *convey* and *transport* are employed for such actions as are performed not by immediate personal intervention or exertion: a porter *carries* goods on his knot (*i. e.*, shoulder-pad); goods are *conveyed* in a wagon; they are *transported* in a vessel. *Convey* expresses simply the mode of removing; *transport* annexes to this the idea of the place and the distance. Merchants get the goods *conveyed* into their warehouses which they have had *transported* from distant countries. Pedestrians take no more with them than what they can conveniently *carry;* could armies do the same, one of the greatest obstacles to the indulgence of human ambition would be removed; for many an incursion into a peaceful country is defeated for the want of means to *convey* provisions sufficient for such numbers; and when mountains or deserts are to be traversed, another great difficulty presents itself in the *transportation* of artillery.

Bear, Suffer, Endure, Support.— To *bear* (see above). *Suffer*, in Latin *suffero*, compounded of *sub*, under, and *ferre*, to bear, signifies to "bear up under" — an expression frequently heard in English, which, like several others cited in this book, literally translates the Latin word. *Endure*, from Latin *durus*, hard, lasting, signifies to harden one's self under trouble. *Support*, from *sub* and *portare*, to carry, has the same meaning as *suffer*, as far as its etymology is concerned.

The idea of receiving the weight or pressure of any object is common to these terms, which differ only in the circumstances of the action. To *bear* is the general term taken in the proper sense without any qualification; the other terms denote different modes of *bearing*. To *bear* may be said of that which is not painful, as to bear a burden, in the indifferent sense; so likewise the term to *support*, as to *support* a person who is falling; but for the most part these, as well as the other two terms, are taken in the bad sense. In this case to *bear* and to *suffer* are both involuntary acts as far as they relate to evils imposed upon us without our will; but *bear* is also voluntary, inasmuch as it denotes the manner of receiving the evil, so as to diminish the sense of it; and *suffer* is purely passive and involuntary. We are born to *suffer*—hence the necessity for us to learn to *bear* all the numerous and diversified evils which to us are obnoxious.

To *bear* is applied either to ordinary or extraordinary evils, and is either a temporary or a permanent act of the resolution; to *endure* is applied only to great evils requiring strong and lasting resolution: we *bear* disappointments and crosses; we *endure* hunger, cold, tortures, and provocations. The first object of education should be to accustom children to *bear* contradictions and crosses, that they may afterward be enabled to *endure* every trial.

To *bear* and *endure* signify to receive becomingly the weight of what befalls ourselves; to *support* signifies to bear either our own or another's evils, for we may either *support* ourselves or be *supported* by others, but in this former case we *bear* not so much from the resolution to *bear* as from the motives which are presented to the mind; a person *supports* himself in the hour of trial by the condolence of friends, but still more by the power of religion.

The words *suffer* and *endure* are said only of persons and personal matters: to *bear* and *support* are said also of things; the former in respect to things of any weight, large or small; the latter in respect to things of great weight, as the beams are cut according to the weight they have to *bear;* a building is *supported* by pillars.

See also Brook; Undergo; Waft.

BEAST. See Animal.

BEAT, Strike, Hit. *Beat* is derived from Anglo-Saxon *beatan*, from a Teutonic root signifying to push. The resemblance to Latin *batuere*, French *battre*, is merely accidental. *Strike* is derived from a Teutonic root meaning to give blows to. *Hit* is a

Scandinavian word meaning to light on, to attain to, hence to strike, and is allied to *hint*. For a similar relation between the idea of lighting upon and striking see the slang expression "He *lit* into me."

To *beat* is to redouble blows; to *strike* is to give one single blow; but the bare touching in consequence of an effort constitutes *hitting*. We never *beat* but with design, nor *hit* without an aim, but we may *strike* by accident. *Beating* was formerly resorted to as almost the only mode of punishment. He who brandishes a stick heedlessly may *strike* another to his serious injury. *Hitting* is the object of the marksman.

Beat, Defeat, Overpower, Rout, Overthrow.—*Beat* is here figuratively employed in the sense of the former section. *Defeat*, from the French *défaire*, implies to undo, and *overpower* to have the power over any one. To *rout* is derived from *rupta*, broken, from Latin *rumpere*, to break, and *overthrow*, to throw over or upside down.

Beat respects personal contests between individuals or parties; *defeat*, *rout, overpower,* and *overthrow* are employed mostly for contests between numbers. A general is *beaten* in important engagements; he is *defeated* and may be *routed* in partial attacks; he is *overpowered* by numbers, and *overthrown* in set engagements. To *beat* is an indefinite term expressive of no particular degree: the being *beaten* may be attended with greater or less damage. To be *defeated* is a specific disadvantage, it is a failure in a particular object of more or less importance. To be *overpowered* is a positive loss; it is a loss of the power of acting, which may be of longer or shorter duration; to be *routed* is a temporary disadvantage; a *rout* alters the *route* or course of proceeding, but does not disable: to be *overthrown* is the greatest of all mischiefs, and is applicable only to great armies and great concerns: an *overthrow* commonly decides a contest. *Beat* is a term which reflects more or less dishonor on the general or the army, or on both: *defeat* is an indifferent term; the best generals may sometimes be *defeated* by circumstances which are above human control; *over-powering* is coupled with no particular honor to the winner nor disgrace to the loser; superior power is oftener the result of good fortune than of skill. The bravest and finest troops may be *overpowered* in cases which exceed human power: a *rout* is always disgraceful, particularly to the army; it always arises from want of firmness: an *overthrow* is fatal rather than dishonorable; it excites pity rather than contempt.

BEATIFICATION, CANONIZATION. These acts emanate from the pontifical authority, by which the Pope declares a person, whose life had been exemplary and accompanied with miracles, as entitled to enjoy eternal happiness after his death, and determines in consequence the sort of worship which should be paid to him. In the act of *beatification* (*beare,* to make blessed) the Pope pronounces only as a private person, and uses his own authority only in granting to certain persons, or to a religious order, the privilege of paying a particular worship to a *beatified* object. In the act of *canonization,* the Pope speaks as a judge after a judicial examination on the state, and decides the sort of worship which ought to be paid by the whole church.

BEAU. See GALLANT.

BEAUTIFUL, FINE, HANDSOME, PRETTY. *Beautiful,* or full of *beauty,* in French *beauté,* comes from *beau, belle,* in Latin *bellus,* fair. *Fine* is derived from *finitus,* the past participle of *finire,* to finish, and meant *finished,* polished, finely wrought, hence, on the one hand, delicate, small; on the other hand, impressive, comely, the very opposite of delicate. *Handsome* originally meant dexterous, *handy,* and hence well formed, comely, good-looking. *Pretty* comes from Anglo-Saxon *prœtig,* deceitful, tricky, etc.; its ultimate origin and meaning are uncertain. It may have developed its present meaning through the same psychological process that has turned words like *cunning, cute,* etc., into endearing descriptive epithets.

Of these epithets, which denote what is pleasing to the eye, *beautiful* conveys the strongest meaning; it marks the possession of that in its fullest extent of which the other terms denote the possession in part only. *Fineness, handsomeness*, and *prettiness* are to *beauty* as parts to a whole. When taken in relation to persons, a woman is *beautiful* who in feature and complexion possesses a grand assemblage of graces; a woman is *fine* who with a striking figure unites shape and symmetry; a woman is *handsome* who has good features, and *pretty* if with symmetry of feature be united delicacy. The *beautiful* is determined by fixed rules; it admits of no excess or defect; it comprehends regularity, proportion, and a due distribution of color, and every particular which can engage the attention: the *fine* must be coupled with a certain grandeur of figure; it is incompatible with that which is small; a little woman can never be *fine;* the *handsome* is a general assemblage of what is agreeable; it is marked by no particular characteristic but the absence of all deformity: *prettiness* is always coupled with simplicity; it is incompatible with that which is large; a tall woman with masculine features cannot be *pretty*. *Beauty* is peculiarly a female perfection; in the male sex it is rather a defect; a man can scarcely be *beautiful* without losing his manly characteristics—boldness and energy of mind, strength and robustness of limb; but though a man may not be *beautiful* or *pretty*, he may be *fine* or *handsome*.

When said in relation to other objects, *beautiful*, *fine*, *pretty* have a strong analogy. With respect to the objects of nature, the *beautiful* is displayed in the works of creation, and wherever it appears it is marked by elegance, variety, harmony, proportion, but, above all, that softness which is peculiar to female *beauty;* the *fine*, on the contrary, is associated with the grand, and the *pretty* with the simple: the sky presents either a *beautiful* aspect or a *fine* aspect, but not a *pretty* aspect. A rural scene is *beautiful* when it unites richness and diversity of natural objects with superior cultivation; it is *fine* when it presents the bolder and more impressive features of nature, consisting of rocks and mountains; it is *pretty* when, divested of all that is extraordinary, it presents a smiling view of nature in the gay attire of shrubs, and many-colored flowers,

and verdant meadows, and luxuriant fields.

Beautiful, fine, and *pretty* are applied indifferently to works of nature and art; *handsome* mostly to those of art only: a *beautiful* picture, a *fine* drawing, a *pretty* cap, and *handsome* furniture.

In the moral application *beautiful* sentiments have much in them to interest the affections as well as the understanding; they make a vivid impression: *fine* sentiments mark an elevated mind and a loftiness of conception; they occupy the understanding and afford scope for reflection; they make a strong impression: *pretty* ideas are but pleasing associations or combinations that only amuse for the time being, without producing any lasting impression. We may speak of a *beautiful* poem, although not a *beautiful* tragedy; but a *fine* tragedy, and a *pretty* comedy. Imagery may be *beautiful* and *fine*, but seldom *pretty*.

Handsome conveys the idea not only of that which is agreeable in appearance, but also that which is agreeable to the understanding and the moral feelings from its fitness and propriety; it is therefore applied with this collateral meaning to moral circumstances and actions, as a *handsome* present, a *handsome* apology.

BECOME. See BE.

BECOMING, DECENT, SEEMLY, FIT, SUITABLE. *Becoming* comes from Anglo-Saxon *becuman*, to arrive, happen; hence to happen to fit. *Decent*, in French *décent*, in Latin *decens*, participle of *decere*, to beseem, is allied to *decus*, an ornament, honor, fame, etc. *Seemly* is derived from a root which appears in *same, similar*, etc., and *ly*, meaning like; it means literally "same like," just like, hence suitable, fitting, etc. *Fit* is a Scandinavian word meaning to knit together, to draw laces together, etc. *Suitable*, from *suit*, signifies able to *suit;* and *suit*, in French *suite*, Latin *secuta*, comes from *sequor*, to follow, signifying to follow.

What is *becoming* respects the manner of being in society such as it ought; as to person, time, and place. *Decency* regards the manner of displaying one's self so as to be approved and respected. *Seemliness* is very similar in sense to *de-*

cency, but is confined to such things as immediately strike the observer. *Fitness* and *suitableness* relate to the disposition, arrangement, and order of either being or doing, according to persons, things, or circumstances. The *becoming* consists of an exterior that is pleasing to the view: *decency* involves moral propriety; it is regulated by the fixed rules of good-breeding: *seemliness* is decency in the minor morals or in one's behavior; *fitness* is regulated by local circumstances, and *suitableness* by the established customs and usages of society. The dress of a woman is *becoming* that renders her person more agreeable to the eye; it is *decent* if it in no wise offends modesty; it is *unseemly* if it in any wise violates propriety; it is *fit* if it be what the occasion requires; it is *suitable* if it be according to the rank and character of the wearer. What is *becoming* varies for every individual; the age, the complexion, the stature, and the habits of the person must be consulted in order to obtain the appearance which is *becoming;* what *becomes* a young female, or one of fair complexion, may not *become* one who is further advanced in life, or who has dark features: *decency* and *seemliness* are one and the same for all; all civilized nations have drawn the exact line between the *decent* and the *indecent,* although fashion or false principles may sometimes draw persons aside from this line: *fitness* varies with the seasons, or the circumstances of persons; what is *fit* for the winter is *unfit* for the summer, or what is *fit* for dry weather is *unfit* for wet; what is *fit* for town is not *fit* for the country; what is *fit* for a healthy person is not *fit* for one that is infirm: *suitableness* accommodates itself to the external circumstances and conditions of persons; the house, the furniture, the equipage of a prince must be *suitable* to his rank; the retinue of an ambassador must be *suitable* to the character which he has to maintain, and to the wealth, dignity, and importance of the nation whose monarch he represents. Gravity *becomes* a judge or a clergyman at all times: an unassuming tone is *becoming* in a child when he addresses his superiors. *Decency* requires a more than ordinary

gravity when we are in the house of mourning or prayer; it is *indecent* for a child, on the commission of a fault, to affect a careless unconcern in the presence of those whom he has offended. *Seemliness* is an essential part of good manners; to be loud or disputative in company is *unseemly.* There is a *fitness* or *unfitness* in persons for one another's society: education *fits* a person for the society of the noble, the wealthy, the polite, and the learned. There is a *suitableness* in people's tempers for one another; such a *suitability* is particularly requisite for those who are destined to live together: selfish people, with opposite tastes and habits, can never be *suitable* companions.

Becoming, Comely, Graceful. — *Becoming* (see preceding). *Comely,* or *come like,* signifies coming or appearing as one would have it. *Graceful* signifies full of *grace.*

These epithets are employed to mark in general what is agreeable to the eye. *Becoming* denotes less than *comely,* and this less than *graceful;* nothing can be *comely* or *graceful* which is *unbecoming;* although many things are *becoming* which are neither *comely* nor *graceful.* *Becoming* respects the decorations of the person and the exterior deportment; *comely* respects natural embellishments; *graceful,* natural or artificial accomplishments: manner is *becoming;* figure is *comely;* air, figure, or attitude is *graceful.*

Becoming is a relative term depending on the circumstances and condition of the person: what is *unbecoming* in one case may not be so in another, and what is *becoming* in one person may not be so in another: what is *graceful* is so absolutely and at all times, although it may not be seen and acknowledged without the aid of cultivation.

BEDEW. See Sprinkle.

BEG, Desire. *Beg* (see Ask). *Desire,* Latin *desidero,* is probably allied to *sidus, sideris,* star, which also appears in *consider.* To *desire,* from *de,* from, and *sidus,* star, may mean to be turned away from the light of the stars.

To *beg* marks the wish; to *desire,* the will and determination. *Beg* is the act of an inferior, or one in a subordinate condition; *desire* is the act of a superior: we *beg* a thing as a favor; we *desire* it as a right: children *beg* their parents to grant them an indulgence; parents *desire* their children to attend to their business.

Beg, Beseech, Solicit, Entreat, Supplicate, Implore, Crave.—*Beg* (see above). *Beseech,* compounded of *be* and *seken,* seek, is an intensive verb, signifying to seek strongly. *Solicit,* in French *soliciter,* Latin *solicito,* is probably compounded of *sollus* and *citus,* aroused, signifying to rouse altogether. *Entreat,* compounded of *en* or *in* and *treat,* in French *traiter,* Latin *tracto,* to manage, signifies to act upon. *Supplicate,* in Latin *supplicatus,* participle of *supplico,* compounded of *sub* and *plicare,* to *fold,* signifies to bend the body down, in token of submission or distress, in order to awaken notice. *Implore,* in French *implorer,* Latin *imploro,* compounded of *in* and *plorare,* to weep or lament, signifies to act upon by weeping. *Crave,* from Anglo-Saxon *crafian,* to demand, means to long for earnestly.

All these terms denote a species of asking varied as to the person, the object, and the manner; the first four do not mark such a state of dependence in the agent as the last three: to *beg* denotes a state of want; to *beseech, entreat,* and *solicit,* a state of urgent necessity; *supplicate* and *implore,* a state of abject distress; *crave,* the lowest state of physical want: one *begs* with importunity; *beseeches* with earnestness; *entreats* by the force of reasoning and strong representation: one *solicits* by virtue of one's interests, *supplicates* by a humble address; *implores* by every mark of dejection and humiliation. *Begging* is the act of the poor when they need assistance: *beseeching* and *entreating* are resorted to by friends and equals when they want to influence or persuade, but *beseeching* is more urgent, *entreating* more argumentative: *solicitations* are employed to obtain favors, which have more respect to the circumstances than the rank of the solicitor: *supplicating* and *imploring* are resorted to by sufferers for the relief of their misery, and are addressed to those who have the power of averting or increasing the calamity: *craving* is the consequence of longing;

it marks an earnestness of *supplication,* an abject state of suffering dependence. Those who are too idle to work commonly have recourse to *begging;* a kind parent will sometimes rather *beseech* an undutiful child to lay aside his wicked courses than plunge him deeper into guilt by an ill-timed exercise of authority; when we are *entreated* to do an act of civility, it is a mark of unkindness to be heedless to the wishes of our friends; gentlemen in office are perpetually exposed to the *solicitations* of their friends, to procure for themselves, or their connections, places of trust and emolument; a slave *supplicates* his master for pardon when he has offended, and *implores* his mercy to mitigate, if not to remit, the punishment; a poor wretch, suffering with hunger, *craves* a morsel of bread.

BEGIN, COMMENCE, ENTER UPON. *Begin,* in German *beginnen,* is compounded of *be* and *ginnen,* signifying to do a thing first. *Commence* is derived through French from Low Latin *cominitiare,* from *con,* and *in,* into, and *ire,* to go, meaning to initiate, to enter upon something. *Enter,* in Latin *intro,* within, signifies, with the proposition *upon,* to go into a thing.

Begin and *commence* are so strictly allied in signification that it is not easy to discover the difference in their application, although a minute difference does exist. To *begin* respects the order of time; to *commence,* the exertion of setting about a thing: whoever *begins* a dispute is termed the aggressor; no one should *commence* a dispute unless he can calculate the consequences, and, as this is impracticable, it is better never to *commence* disputes. *Begin* is opposed to end; *commence* to complete: a person *begins* a thing with a view of ending it; he *commences* a thing with a view of completing it. To *begin* is either transitive or intransitive; to *commence* is mostly transitive: a speaker *begins* by apologizing; he *commences* his speech with an apology: happiness frequently ends where prosperity *begins;* whoever *commences* any undertaking, without estimating his own power, must not expect to succeed. To *begin* is used either for things or persons; to *commence* for persons only: all things have their *beginning;* in order to effect anything, we must make a *commencement;* a word *begins* with a particular letter, or a line *begins* with a particular word; a person *commences* his career. Lastly, *begin* is more colloquial than *commence;* thus we say, to *begin* the work, to *commence* the operation: to *begin* one's play; to *commence* the pursuit: to *begin* to write; to *commence* the letter.

To *commence* and *enter upon* are as closely allied in sense as the former words; they differ principally in application: to *commence* seems rather to denote the making an experiment; to *enter upon*, that of first doing what has not been tried before; we *commence* an undertaking; we *enter upon* an employment: speculating people are very ready to *commence* schemes; considerate people are always averse to *entering upon* any office until they feel themselves fully adequate to discharge its duties.

BEGINNING. See ORIGIN.

BEGUILE. See AMUSE.

BEHAVE. See DEAL.

BEHAVIOR, CONDUCT, CARRIAGE, DEPORTMENT, DEMEANOR. *Behavior,* from Anglo-Saxon *behæbban,* composed of the prefix *be* and the verb which now appears as *have,* signifies to have one's self, or have self-possession. *Conduct,* in Latin *conductus,* participle of *conduco,* compounded of *con* and *ducere,* to lead along, signifies, literally, leading one's self along, acting as a guide to one's self. *Carriage,* the abstract of *carry* (see BEAR), signifies the act of carrying one's body, or one's self. *Deportment* from Latin *de,* from, and *portare,* to carry, means, literally, what is expressed in our colloquial expression, "He *carried it off* well." *Demeanor* is a coined word from Middle English *demenen,* to demean or behave, which comes through Old French from Late Latin *minare,* to drive cattle, to conduct, signifying to conduct others, then to conduct one's self, to control or guard one's own action.

Behavior respects corporeal or mental actions; *conduct,* mental actions; *carriage, deportment,* and *demeanor* are different species of *behavior. Behavior* respects all actions exposed to the notice of others; *conduct,* the general line of a person's moral proceedings: we speak of a person's *behavior* at table or in company, in a ball-room, in the street, or in public; of his *conduct* in the management of his private concerns, in the direction of his family, or in his different relations with his fellow-creatures. *Behavior* applies to the minor morals of society; *conduct,* to those of the first moment: in our intercourse with others we may adopt a civil or polite, a rude or boisterous *behavior;* in our serious transactions we may adopt a peaceable, discreet, or prudent, a rash, dangerous, or mischievous *conduct.* The *behavior* of young people in society is of particular importance; it should, above all things, be marked with propriety in the presence of superiors and elders: the youth who does not learn betimes a seemly *behavior* in company will scarcely know how to *conduct* himself judiciously on any future occasion.

Carriage respects simply the manner of *carrying* the body; *deportment* includes both the action and the *carriage* of the body in performing the action: *demeanor* respects only the moral character or tendency of the action; *deportment* is said only of those exterior actions that have an immediate reference to others; *demeanor,* of the general *behavior* as it relates to the circumstances and situation of the individual: the *carriage* is that part of *behavior* which is of the first importance to attend to in young persons. A *carriage* should neither be haughty nor servile; to be graceful, it ought to have a due mixture of dignity and condescension: the *deportment* of a man should be suited to his station; a humble *deportment* is becoming in inferiors; a stately and forbidding *deportment* is very unbecoming in superiors: the *demeanor* of a man should be suited to his situation; the suitable *demeanor* of a judge on the bench, or of a clergyman in the pulpit, or when performing his clerical functions, adds much to the dignity and solemnity of the office itself. The *carriage* marks the birth and education: an awkward *carriage* stamps a man as vulgar: a graceful *carriage* evinces refinement and culture. The *deportment* marks either the habitual or the existing temper of the mind: whoever is really impressed with the solemnity and importance of public worship will evince his impressions by a gravity of *deportment:* the *demeanor* is most commonly used to denote the present temper of the mind; as a modest *demeanor* is particularly suitable for one who is in the presence of the person whom he has offended.

BEHIND. See ABACK; ABAFT; AFTER.

BEHOLD. See LOOK.

BEHOLDER. See LOOKER-ON.

BELIEF, CREDIT, TRUST, FAITH. In *belief* the *be* stands for an earlier *ge* which appears in the German *glauben,* originally *ge-lauben,* to believe. The root is the same as that which appears in the adjective *lief,* dear, and the Latin *libet,* it pleases, and, in this case, signifies the pleasure or assent of the mind. *Credit* is derived from the Latin *credere,* to believe, which also gives rise to the words *credulous, credible, creed,* etc. *Trust* is a Germanic word (German *trost,* consolation), from a root whence *true, truth, trow,* etc., are derived, meaning protection, confidence, consolation, etc. *Faith,* Old French *fei,* is derived from Latin *fidem* (accusative), Greek πιστις, faith, from πίθειν, to persuade.

Belief is the generic term, the others are specific; we *believe* when we *credit* and *trust,* but not always *vice versa. Belief* rests on no particular person or thing; but *credit* and *trust* rest on the authority of one or more individuals. Everything is the subject of *belief* which produces one's assent: the events of human life are *credited* upon the authority of the narrator: the words, promises, or the integrity of individuals are *trusted;* the power of persons and the virtue of things are objects of *faith. Belief* and *credit* are particular actions or sentiments: *trust* and *faith* are permanent dispositions of the *mind.* Things are entitled to our *belief;* persons are entitled to our *credit;* but people repose a *trust* in others, or have a *faith* in others. Our *belief* or *unbelief* is not always regulated by our reasoning faculties or the truth of things: we often *believe,* from presumption, ignorance, or passion, things to be true which are very false. With the bulk of mankind assurance goes further than anything else in obtaining *credit;* gross falsehoods, pronounced with confidence, will be *credited* sooner than plain truths told in an unvarnished style. There are no disappointments more severe than those which we feel on finding that we have *trusted* to men of base principles. Ignorant people have commonly a more implicit *faith* in any nostrum recommended to them by persons of their own class than in the prescriptions of professional men regularly educated

Belief, trust, and *faith* have a religious application, which *credit* has not. *Belief* is simply an act of the understanding; *trust* and *faith* are active moving principles of the mind. *Belief* does not extend beyond an assent of the mind to any given proposition; *trust* and *faith* impel to action. *Belief* is to *trust* and *faith* as cause to effect: there may be *belief* without either *trust* or *faith;* but there can be no *trust* or *faith* without belief; we *believe* that there is a God who is the creator and preserver of all His creatures; we therefore *trust* in Him for His protection of ourselves: we *believe* that Jesus Christ died for the sins of men; we have, therefore, *faith* in his redeeming grace to save us from our sins. *Belief* is common to all religions: *trust* is peculiar to the *believers* in Divine revelation: *faith* is employed by distinction for the Christian *faith. Belief* is purely speculative; and *trust* and *faith* are operative: the former operates on the mind, the latter on the outward conduct. *Trust* in God serves to dispel all anxious concern about the future. Theorists substitute *belief* for *faith;* enthusiasts mistake passion for *faith.* True *faith* must be grounded on a right *belief* and accompanied with a right practice.

BELIEVE. See THINK.

BELOVED. See AMIABLE.

BELOW. See UNDER.

BELT. See ZONE.

BEMOAN. See BEWAIL.

BENCH. See TRIBUNAL.

BEND, BENT. *Bend* and *bent* are both derived from a root found in the English *bind,* Anglo-Saxon *bindan,* Icelandic *benda,* to stretch, strain. *Bend* means to strain a bow by fastening the band or string, hence to curve it (Skeat). Both abstract nouns from the verb to *bend;* the one to express its proper, and the other its moral application: a stick has a *bend;* the mind has a *bent.* A *bend* in anything that should be straight is a defect; a *bent* of the inclination that is not sanctioned by religion is detrimental to a person's moral character and peace of mind. For a vicious *bend* in a natural body there are various remedies; but nothing will cure a corrupt *bent* of the will except religion.

See also DEFLECT; KNUCKLE; LEAN; TURN.

BENEATH. See UNDER.

BENEFACTION, DONATION. *Benefaction,* from the Latin *benefacio,* signifies the thing well done, or done for the good of others. *Donation,* from *dono,* to give or present, signifies the sum presented.

Both these terms denote an act of charity, but the former comprehends more than the latter: a *benefaction* comprehends acts of personal service in general toward the indigent; *donation* respects simply the act of giving and the thing given. *Benefactions* are for private use; *donations* are for public service. A *benefactor* to the poor does not confine himself to the distribution of money; he enters into all their necessities, consults their individual cases, and suits his *benefactions* to their exigencies; his influence, his counsel, his purse, and his property are employed for their good: his *donations* form the smallest part of the good which he does.

Beneficent, Bountiful or *Bounteous, Munificent, Generous, Liberal.*—*Beneficent* comes from *benefacio* (see above). *Bountiful* signifies full of *bounty* or goodness, from the French *bonté,* Latin *bonitas.* *Munificent,* in Latin *munificus,* from *munus,* present, gift, and *facio,* signifies the disposition to make presents. *Generous,* from Latin *generosus,* meant originally of high blood, of noble extraction, and consequently of a noble character. *Liberal,* in French *libéral,* Latin *liberalis,* from *liber,* free, signifies the quality of being like a freeman in distinction from a bondman, and, by a natural association, being of a free disposition, ready to communicate.

Beneficent respects everything done for the good of others: *bounty, munificence,* and *generosity* are species of *beneficence; liberality* is a qualification of all. The first two denote modes of action: the last three either modes of action or modes of sentiment. The sincere well-wisher to his fellow-creatures is *beneficent* according to his means; he is *bountiful* in providing for the comfort and happiness of others; he is *munificent* in dispensing favors; he is *generous* in imparting his property; he is *liberal* in all he does. *Beneficence* and *bounty* are characteristics of the Deity as well as of His creatures: *munificence, generosity,* and *liberality* are mere human qualities. *Beneficence* and *bounty* are the peculiar characteristics of the Deity: with Him the will and the act of doing good are commensurate only with His power; He was *beneficent* to us as our Creator, and continues His *beneficence* to us by His daily preservation and protection; to some, however, He has been more *bountiful* than to others, by providing them with an unequal share of the good things of this life. The *beneficence* of man is regulated by the *bounty* of Providence: to whom much is given, from him much will be required. Instructed by His word, and illumined by that spark of benevolence which was infused into their souls with the breath of life, good men are ready to believe that they are but stewards of all God's gifts, holden for the use of such as are less *bountifully* provided. They will desire, as far as their powers extend, to imitate this feature of the Deity by bettering with their *beneficent* counsel and assistance the condition of all who require it and by gladdening the hearts of many with their *bountiful* provisions

Princes are *munificent,* friends are *generous,* patrons *liberal. Munificence* is measured by the quality and quantity of the thing bestowed; *generosity* by the extent of the sacrifice made; *liberality* by the warmth and freedom of the spirit discovered. A monarch displays his *munificence* in the presents which he sends by his ambassadors to another monarch. A *generous* man will waive his claims, however powerful they may be, when the accommodation or relief of another is in question. A *liberal* spirit does not stop to inquire the reason for giving, but gives when the occasion offers. *Munificence* may spring either from ostentation or a becoming sense of dignity; *generosity* may spring either from a generous temper or an easy unconcern about property; *liberality* of conduct is dictated by nothing but a warm heart and an expanded mind. *Munificence* is confined simply to giving, but we may be *generous* in assisting, and *liberal* in rewarding.

BENEFIT, FAVOR, KINDNESS, CIVILITY.—*Benefit* signifies here that which is done to benefit (see ADVANTAGE). *Favor*, in French *faveur*, Latin *favor* and *favere*, to bear good-will, signifies the act flowing from good-will. *Kindness* signifies an action that is kind (see AFFECTIONATE). *Civility* signifies that which is *civil*.

The idea of an action gratuitously performed for the advantage of another is common to these terms. *Benefits* and *favors* are granted by superiors; *kindnesses* and *civilities* pass between equals. *Benefits* serve to relieve actual wants: the power of conferring and the necessity of receiving them constitute the relative difference in station between the giver and the receiver: *favors* tend to promote the interest or convenience; the power of giving and the advantage of receiving are dependent on local circumstances, more than on difference of station. *Kindnesses* and *civilities* serve to afford mutual accommodation by a reciprocity of kind offices on the many and various occasions which offer in human life: they are not so important as either *benefits* or *favors*, but they carry a charm with them which is not possessed by the former. *Kindnesses* are more endearing than *civilities*, and pass mostly between those who are known to each other: *civilities* may pass between strangers. *Benefits* tend to draw those closer to one another who by station of life are set at the greatest distance from each other: affection is engendered in him who *benefits*, and devoted attachment in him who is *benefited*: *favors* increase obligation beyond its due limits; if they are not asked and granted with discretion, they may produce servility on the one hand and haughtiness on the other.

Kindnesses are the offspring and parent of affection; they convert our multiplied wants into so many enjoyments: *civilities* are the sweets which we gather on the way as we pass along the journey of life.

Benefit, Service, Good Office.—*Benefit* (see above). *Service* (see ADVANTAGE). *Office*, in French *office*, Latin *officium*, duty, from *officio*, perhaps from *opi* (*opus*), work, and *facere*, to do, signifies the doing of one's work, the fulfilling of a duty or obligation.

These terms, like the former, agree in denoting some action performed for the good of another, but they differ in the principle on which the action is performed. A *benefit* is perfectly gratuitous, it produces an obligation; a *service* is not altogether gratuitous; it is that at least which may be expected, though it cannot be demanded: a *good office* is between the two; it is in part gratuitous, and in part such as one may reasonably expect. *Benefits* flow from superiors, or those who are in a situation to do good, and *service* from inferiors or equals: but *good offices* are performed by equals only. Princes confer *benefits* on their subjects; subjects perform *services* for their princes; neighbors do *good offices* for one another. *Benefits* are sometimes the reward of services; *good offices* produce a return from the receiver. *Benefits* consist of such things as serve to relieve the difficulties or advance the interests of the receiver: *services* consist in those acts which tend to lessen the trouble, or increase the ease and convenience, of the person served: *good offices* consist in the employ of one's credit, influence, and mediation for the advantage of another; it is a species of voluntary service. It is a great *benefit* to assist an embarrassed tradesman out of his difficulty: it is a great *service* for a soldier to save the life of his commander, or for a friend to open the eyes of another to see his danger: it is a *good office* for any one to interpose his mediation to settle disputes and heal divisions It is possible to be loaded with *benefits* so as to affect one's independence of character. *Services* are sometimes a source of dissatisfaction and disappointment when they do not meet with the remuneration or return which they are supposed to deserve. *Good offices* tend to nothing but the increase of good-will. Those who perform them are too independent to expect a return, and those who receive them are too sensible of their value not to seek an opportunity for making a return. Politically, they are tendered by a neutral nation to another or others in time of trouble.

See also ADVANTAGE; GOOD.

BENEVOLENCE, BENEFICENCE. *Benevolence* is literally well willing. *Beneficence* is literally well doing. The former consists of intention, the latter of action: the former is the cause, the latter the result. *Benevolence* may exist without *beneficence*, but *beneficence* always supposes *benevolence;* a man is not said to be *beneficent* who does good from sinister views. The *benevolent* man enjoys but half his happiness if he cannot be *beneficent;* yet there will still remain to him an ample store of enjoyment in the contemplation of others' happiness; that man who is gratified only with that happiness which he himself is the instrument of producing is not entitled to the name of *benevolent.* As *benevolence* is an affair of the heart, and *beneficence* of the outward conduct, the former is confined to no station, no rank, no degree of education or power: the poor may be *benevolent* as well as the rich, the unlearned as the learned, the weak as well as the strong: the latter, on the contrary, is controlled by outward circumstances, and is therefore principally confined to the rich, the powerful, the wise, and the learned.

Benevolence, Benignity, Humanity, Kindness, Tenderness.—*Benevolence* (see above). *Benignity,* in Latin *benignitas,* from *bene* and *gigno,* beget, signifies the quality or disposition for producing good. *Humanity,* in French *humanité,* Latin *humanitas,* from *humanus* and *homo,* man signifies the quality of belonging to a man, or having what is common to man. *Kindness,* from *kind* (see AFFECTIONATE). *Tenderness,* from *tender,* is in Latin *tener,* allied to *tenuis,* thin—hence soft, gentle, mild, etc.

Benevolence lies in the will, *benignity* in the disposition or frame of mind; *humanity* lies in the heart; *kindness* and *tenderness* in the affections: *benev-*olence indicates a general good-will to all mankind; *benignity* particular goodness or *kindness* of disposition; *humanity* is a general tone of feeling; *kindness* and *tenderness* are particular modes of feeling. *Benevolence* consists in the wish or intention to do good; it is confined to no station or object: the *benevolent* man may be rich or poor, and his *benevolence* will be exerted wherever there is an opportunity of doing good; *benignity* is mostly associated with the power of doing good, and is actually exerted or displayed in the actions or looks. *Benevolence* in its fullest sense is the sum of *moral* excellence, and comprehends every other virtue; when taken in this acceptation, *benignity, humanity, kindness,* and *tenderness* are but modes of *benevolence. Benevolence* and *benignity* tend to the communicating of happiness; *humanity* is concerned in the removal of evil. *Benevolence* is common to the Creator and His creatures; it differs only in degree; the former has the knowledge and power as well as the will to do good; man often has the will to do good, without having the power to carry it into effect. *Benignity* is ascribed to the stars, to Heaven, or to princes; ignorant and superstitious people are apt to ascribe their good fortune to the *benign* influence of the stars rather than to the gracious dispensations of Providence. *Humanity* belongs to man only; it is his peculiar characteristic, and ought at all times to be his boast; when he throws off this, his distinguishing badge, he loses everything valuable in him; it is a virtue that is indispensable in his present suffering condition: *humanity* is as universal in its application as *benevolence;* wherever there is distress, *humanity* flies to its relief. *Kindness* and *tenderness* are partial modes of affection, confined to those who know or are related to one another; we are *kind* to friends and acquaintances, *tender* toward those who are near and dear: *kindness* is a mode of affection most fitted for social beings; it is what every one can show, and every one is pleased to receive: *tenderness* is a state of feeling that is occasionally acceptable: the young and the weak demand *tenderness* from those who stand in the closest connection with them, but this feeling may be carried to an excess, so as to injure the object on which it is fixed.

BENIGNITY. See BENEVOLENCE.

BENT, CURVED, CROOKED, AWRY. For *bent* see the derivation of *bend*. *Curved* is derived from Latin *curvus*, allied to *circus*, and means bent so as to form the arc of a circle. *Awry* is derived from Anglo-Saxon *wrigian*, to turn, whence *wriggle* is also derived. *Crooked* (see AWKWARD).

Bent is here the generic term, all the rest are but modes of the *bent;* what is *bent* is opposed to that which is straight; things may therefore be *bent* to any degree, but when *curved* they are *bent* only to a small degree; when *crooked* they are *bent* to a great degree: a stick is *bent* any way; it is *curved* by being *bent* one specific way; it is *crooked* by being *bent* different ways. Things may be *bent* by accident or design; they are *curved* by design or according to some rule; they are *crooked* by accident or in violation of some rule: a stick is *bent* by the force of the hand; a line is *curved* so as to make a mathematical figure; it is *crooked* so as to lose all figure: *awry* marks a species of *crookedness*, but *crooked* is applied as an epithet, and *awry* is employed to characterize the action; hence we speak of a *crooked* thing and of sitting or standing *awry*.

Bent, Bias, Inclination, Prepossession.—*Bent* (see above). *Bias*, in French *biais*, at first signified a slope; its origin is unknown. *Inclination*, in French *inclination*, Latin *inclinatio*, from *inclino*, Greek κλίνω, signifies a leaning toward. *Prepossession*, compounded of *pre* and *possession*, signifies the taking *possession* of the mind previously or beforehand.

All these terms denote a preponderating influence on the mind. *Bent* is applied to the will, affection, and power in general: *bias* solely to the judgment: *inclination* and *prepossession*, to the state of the feelings. The *bent* includes the general state of the mind, and the object on which it fixes a regard: *bias*, the particular influential power which sways the judging faculty: the one is absolutely considered with regard to itself; the other relatively to its results and the object it acts upon. *Bent* is sometimes, with regard to *bias*, as cause is to effect; we may frequently trace in the particular *bent* of a person's likes and dislikes the principal *bias* which determines his opinions. *Inclination* is a faint kind of *bent; prepossession* is a weak species of *bias;* an *inclination* is a state of something—namely, a state of the feelings: *prepossession* is an actual something—namely, the thing that *prepossesses*.

We may discover the *bent* of a person's mind in his gay or serious moments, in his occupations, and in his pleasures; in some persons it is so strong that scarcely an action passes which is not more or less influenced by it, and even the exterior of a man will be under its control; in all disputed matters the support of a party will operate more or less to *bias* the minds of men for or against particular men or particular measures; when we are attached to the part that espouses the cause of religion and good order, this *bias* is in some measure commendable and salutary; a mind without *inclination* would be a blank, and where *inclination* is there is the groundwork for *prepossession*. Strong minds will be strongly *bent* and labor under a strong *bias;* but there is no mind so weak and powerless as not to have its *inclinations*, and none so perfect as to be without its *prepossessions;* the mind that has virtuous *inclinations* will be *prepossessed* in favor of everything that leans to virtue's side: it were well for mankind were this the only *prepossession;* but in the present mixture of truth and error it is necessary to guard against *prepossessions* as dangerous anticipations of the judgment: if their object be not perfectly pure, or their force be not qualified by the restrictive powers of the judgment, much evil springs from their abuse.

See also BEND; TURN.

BENUMBED. See NUMB.

BEQUEATH. See DEVISE.

BEREAVE, DEPRIVE, STRIP. *Bereave*, in Anglo-Saxon *bereafian*, is compounded of the verbal prefix *be* and a root found also in *rob, rove*, etc., which suggests the idea of taking by violence. *Deprive*, compounded of *de* and *prive*, French *priver*, Latin *privo*, from *privus*, private, signifies to cause a thing to be no longer a man's own. *Strip* is a Germanic word meaning to tear off, to make bare.

To *bereave* expresses more than *deprive,* but less than *strip,* which denotes a total and violent *bereavement;* one is *bereaved* of children, *deprived* of pleasures, and *stripped* of property: we are *bereaved* of that on which we set most value; the act of *bereaving* does violence to our inclination: we are *deprived* of the ordinary comforts and conveniences of life; they cease to be ours: we are *stripped* of the things which we most want; we are thereby rendered, as it were, naked. *Deprivations* are preparatory to *bereavements;* if we cannot bear the one patiently, we may expect to sink under the other: common prudence should teach us to look with unconcern on our *deprivations:* Christian faith should enable us to consider every *bereavement* as a step to perfection; that when *stripped* of all worldly goods we may be invested with those more exalted and lasting honors which await the faithful disciple of Christ.

Bereave and *deprive* are applied only to persons, *strip* may be figuratively applied to things.

BESEECH. See BEG.

BESET. See BESIEGE.

BESIDES, MOREOVER. *Besides*—that is, by the *side,* next to—marks simply the connection which subsists between what goes before and what follows. *Moreover*—that is, more than all else—marks the addition of something particular to what has already been said. Thus, in enumerating the good qualities of an individual, we may say "he is, *besides,* of a peaceable disposition." On concluding any subject of question, we may introduce a further cause by a *moreover.* "*Moreover,* we must not forget the claims of those who will suffer by such a change."

Besides, Except.—*Besides,* which is here taken as a preposition, expresses the idea of addition. *Except* expresses that of exclusion. There were many there *besides* ourselves; no one *except* ourselves will be admitted.

BESIEGE, BESET, ENCOMPASS, INVEST. *Besiege,* a compound of the Anglo-Saxon *be* by, and the Old French *siege,* a seat, signifies, as a transitive, to surround any place with soldiers, as a city or town, in order to take possession of it by force; literally, to sit down before a place with the view of capturing it; and, figuratively, to surround a person or place, as excited depositors making a run on a bank, a crowd pressing the gate-keepers at a game of baseball or football between favorite players.

To *beset* a person or place is to surround him or it with or without hostile intent, to press upon him or it on all sides, and, as applied to a city or fortification, to entangle it with obstructions, to prevent those within from escaping. To *encompass,* from Latin *cum,* with, and *passus,* pace or step, whence *compass,* a route that comes together and joins itself—a circular object—means to encircle, like a body of troops between hostile forces or placed about an objective point, so as to cut off means of communication, relief, or retreat; and to *invest* is to blockade, beleaguer, take possession of the outskirts of a place or army with forces, so as to intercept succor by men or provisions.

These terms are all used here in a military sense, and indicate movements intended to force the surrender of an army, a fortification, a strategic point, or a city by, literally, sitting down and waiting. For applications to other purposes see the articles on INVEST and SURROUND.

BESPEAK, BETOKEN, ENGAGE, SOLICIT. *Bespeak,* a compound of the Anglo-Saxon *be,* by, and *sprecan,* to speak, German *besprechen,* signifies to speak for or on behalf of a person or thing beforehand, in advance, as to *engage* an article ahead of the time when it will be wanted. For the derivation of *engage* see *engagement* under BATTLE, *engage* always being suggestive of a *pledge,* however it is used. To *betoken* is to point out something in the future that is likely to occur from things or conditions known now, to foreshow a result from present indications, to predict or prognosticate, as indications tonight *betoken* a fair day to-morrow.

We *engage* now to buy or do a thing or go somewhere at a future time, pledge or bind a future undertaking by a contract or oath, promise or assume now an obligation for a future transaction, and we *solicit* to-day a favor, benefit, or other advantage from another that we expect to obtain some other day when it is needed. For the derivation of *solicit* see BEG.

BESTOW. See ALLOW; CONFER; GIVE.

BETIMES. See SOON.

BETOKEN. See AUGUR; BESPEAK.

BETROTH. See ESPOUSE.

BETTER. See AMEND.

BEWAIL, BEMOAN, LAMENT. For the derivation of *bewail* see *wail*. *Bemoan* is derived from the verbal prefix *be* and Anglo-Saxon *mænan*, to *mean*, intend. *Moan* in Middle English means both a communication and a complaint; its significance is no doubt influenced by the accidental effect of the sound, which makes it seem like an onomatopœtic word. *Lament* is formed with the suffix *mentum* from the base *la*, meaning to utter a cry (Latin *lamentum*).

All these terms mark an expression of pain by some external sign. *Bewail* is not so strong as *bemoan*, but stronger than *lament; bewail* and *bemoan* are expressions of unrestrained grief or anguish: a wretched mother *bewails* the loss of her child; a person in deep distress *bemoans* his hard fate: *lamentation* may arise from simple sorrow or even imaginary grievances: a sensualist *laments* the disappointment of some expected gratification. *Bewail* and *bemoan* are always indecorous if not sinful expressions of grief which are inconsistent with the profession of a Christian; they are common among the uncultivated, who have not a proper principle to restrain the intemperance of their feelings. There is nothing temporal which is so dear to any one that he ought to *bewail* its loss; nor any condition of things so distressing or desperate as to make a man *bemoan* his lot. *Lamentations* are sometimes allowable; the miseries of others, or our own infirmities and sins, may justly be *lamented*.

BEWILDER. See ABASH.

BEWILDERMENT. See AMNESIA.

BEWITCHED. See SPELLBOUND.

BEYOND. See ABOVE; OUT; YONDER.

BIAS, PREPOSSESSION, PRUDENCE. *Bias, prepossession* (see BENT). *Prej-*udice, in French *préjudice*, Latin *præjudicium*, compounded of *præ*, before, and *judicium*, judgment, signifies a judgment beforehand—that is, before examination.

Bias marks the state of the mind, as leaning to this or that side, so as to determine one's feelings or opinions generally; *prepossession* denotes the previous occupation of the mind with some particular idea or feeling, so as to preclude the admission of any other; *prejudice* is a prejudging or predetermining a matter without knowing its merits. We may be *biased* for or against; we are always *prepossessed* in favor and mostly *prejudiced* against; the feelings have mostly to do with the *bias* and *prepossession*, and the understanding or judgment with the *prejudice*. *Bias* and *prepossession* suppose a something real, whether good or otherwise, which determines the inclination of the mind, but *prejudice* supposes a something unreal or false, which misleads the judgment: *bias* and *prepossession* may therefore be taken in an indifferent, if not a good sense; *prejudice* always in a bad sense: interest or personal affection may *bias*, but not so as to pervert either the integrity or judgment; *prepossessions* may be formed of persons at first sight, but they may be harmless, even although they may not be perfectly correct; *prejudices* prevent the right exercise of the understanding, and consequently favor the cause of falsehood, as when a person has a *prejudice* against another, which leads him to misinterpret his actions.

See also BENT.

BICKER, CONTEND, DISPUTE, QUARREL. *Bicker* is derived from a Celtic source, and is probably allied to *peck* and the word *beak*, that with which a bird *pecks*. *Bikere* in Middle English meant a skirmish. In Scottish speech it means to fight by throwing stones, to indulge in strife or contention by word of mouth. *Contend* is derived from Latin *contendere*, from *con*, against, and *tendere*, to stretch; it means to stretch against, to exert one's strength against.

To *contend* is to strive physically or verbally with another, to vie with or against another, to engage in more or less protracted disputes, to take part in a debate by opposing another in speech, to support an opinion or statement against another. To *dispute* is to attempt to maintain by argument an opinion different from one that has been advanced by another, to call in question or deny the correctness or justness of any statement or conclusion. For a critical comparison of the cognate terms *contend*, *contest*, and *dispute* see the article on the former term.

A *quarrel*, in French *querelle*, an altercation, from the Latin *querela*, a complaint, is, literally, an angry dispute, an open variance between parties, a ground or reason of dispute, something that gives right to angry reprisal. It is the result of a breach of friendship or concord between persons or nations, a falling out or disagreement between parties, and may lead to a war between nations, or a judicial settlement of the questions in dispute, or a common brawl or petty fight between individuals. The term *quarrel* is further considered in connection with *difference*, *dispute*, and *altercation* in the article on DIFFERENCE.

BID. See CALL; OFFER.

BIG. See GREAT.

BIGOT. See DEVOTEE.

BIKE. See CYCLE.

BILL. See ACCOUNT.

BILLOW. See WAVE.

BIND, TIE. *Bind* is a Germanic word, allied to *bundle*, *bend*, etc. *Tie* is a Germanic word from the root also found in *tug*, so that to *tie* is to *tug* or draw things tightly together.

The species of fastening denoted by these two words differ both in manner and degree. *Binding* is performed by circumvolution round a body; *tying*, by involution within itself. Some bodies are *bound* without being *tied;* others are *tied* without being *bound:* a wounded leg is *bound*, but not *tied;* a string is *tied*, but not *bound;* a ribbon may sometimes be *bound* round the head, and *tied* under the chin. *Binding*, therefore, serves to keep several things in a compact form together; *tying* may serve to prevent one single body separating from another: a criminal is *bound* hand and foot; he is *tied* to a stake. *Binding* and *tying* likewise differ in degree; *binding* serves to produce adhesion in all the parts of a body; *tying* only to produce contact in a single part: thus, when the hair is *bound*, it is almost enclosed in an envelope: when it is *tied* with a string, the ends are left to hang loose.

A similar distinction is preserved in the figurative use of the terms. A *bond* of union is applicable to a large body with many component parts; a *tie* of affection marks an adhesion between individual minds.

Bind, Oblige, Engage.—*Bind* (see above). *Oblige*, in French *obliger*, Latin *obligo*, compounded of *ob*, to, and *ligo*, signifies to tie up. *Engage*, in French *engager*, compounded of *en* or *in* and *gage*, a pledge, signifies to *bind* by means of a pledge.

Bind is more forcible and coercive than *oblige; oblige* than *engage*. We are *bound* by an oath, *obliged* by circumstances, and *engaged* by promises.

Conscience *binds*, prudence or necessity *obliges*, honor and principle *engage*. A parent is *bound* no less by the law of his conscience than by those of the community to which he belongs to provide for his helpless offspring. Politeness *obliges* men of the world to preserve a friendly exterior toward those for whom they have no regard. When we are *engaged* in the service of our king and country, we cannot shrink from our duty without exposing ourselves to the infamy of all the world. We *bind* a man by a fear of what may befall him; we *oblige* him by some immediate urgent motive; we *engage* him by alluring offers and the prospect of gain. A debtor is *bound* to pay by virtue of a written instrument in law; he is *obliged* to pay in consequence of the importunate demands of the creditor; he is *engaged* to pay in consequence of a promise given. A *bond* is the strictest deed in law; an *obligation* binds under pain of a pecuniary loss; an *engagement* is mostly verbal, and rests entirely on the rectitude of the parties.

See also RATIFY.

BIPLANE. See AIRCRAFT.

BISHOPRIC, DIOCESE. *Bishopric* is derived from *bishop*, and the Anglo-Saxon *rice*, meaning dominion, realm. *Bishop* comes from Greek ἐπίσκοπος, overseer, whence *episcopal* is directly, taken over into English. *Diocese*, in Greek διοίκησις, compounded of δία and οἰκέω, administer throughout, signifies the district within which a government is administered.

Both these words describe the extent of an episcopal jurisdiction; the first with relation to the person who officiates, the second with relation to the charge. There may, therefore, be a *bishopric* either where there are many *dioceses* or no *diocese;* but according to the import of the term, there is properly no *diocese* where there is no *bishopric*. When the jurisdiction is merely titular, as in countries where the Catholic religion is not recognized, it is a *bishopric*, but not a *diocese*. On the other hand, the *bishopric* of Rome, or that of an archbishop, comprehends all the *dioceses* of the subordinate bishops. Hence it arises that when we speak of the ecclesiastical distribution of a country, we term the divisions *bishoprics;* but when we speak of the actual office, we term it a *diocese*. England is divided into a certain number of *bishoprics*, not *dioceses*. Every bishop visits his *diocese*, not his *bishopric*, at stated intervals.

BITE. See Nip.

BLAME, Censure, Condemn, Reprove, Reproach, Upbraid. *Blame*, Old French *blasmer*, is derived from Latin *blasphemare*, Greek βλασφημεῖν, to speak ill, whence the word *blaspheme*, to speak ill of things sacred, is directly taken. *Censure* (see Accuse). *Condemn*, in Latin *condemno*, from *con* and *damnum*, loss or damage, signifies literally to inflict a penalty or to punish by a sentence. *Reprove*, from the Latin *reprobo*, signifies the contrary of *probo*, approve. *Reproach*, derived through French, from Latin *repropriare* and *proprius*, near, signifies to cast back upon or against another. *Upbraid* comes from Anglo-Saxon *up* and *bregdan*, to braid or weave, and also to pull, draw. The original sense of *upbraid* was probably to lay hands on, hence to attack, to lay to some one's charge.

The expression of an unfavorable opinion of a person or thing is the common idea in the signification of these terms. To *blame* is simply to ascribe a fault to; to *censure* is to express disapprobation: the former is less personal than the latter. The thing more than the person is *blamed;* the person more than the thing is *censured*. The action or conduct of a person in any particular may be *blamed*, without reflecting on the individual; but the person is directly *censured* for that which is faulty in himself.

Venial or unquestionable faults, or even things that are in themselves amiable, may be the subject of *blame*, but positive faults are the subject of *censure*. A person may be *blamed* for his good-nature and *censured* for his negligence.

Persons are *blamed* in general or qualified terms, but are *censured* in terms more or less harsh.

Condemn, like *blame*, though said of personal matters, has more reference to the thing than the person; but that which is *condemned* is of a more serious nature, and produces a stronger and more unfavorable expression of displeasure or disapprobation, than that which is *blamed*.

Blame and *condemn* do not necessarily require to be expressed in words, but *censure* must always be conveyed in direct terms.

Reprove is even more personal than *censure*. A *reproof* passes from one individual to another, or to a certain number of individuals; *censure* may be public or general.

Censure is frequently provoked by ill-nature or some worse feeling, or dictated by ignorance, as the *censures* of the vulgar.

Reproaching and *upbraiding* are as much the acts of individuals as *reproving*, but the former denote the expression of personal feelings, and may be just or unjust; the latter is presumed to be divested of all personal feelings.

Reproaches are frequently dictated by resentment or self-interest, *upbraidings* by contempt or wounded feelings.

Blame, *condemn*, *reproach*, and *upbraid* are applied to ourselves with the same distinction.

Reproof and *censure* are most properly addressed to others: in the following example, *censure*, as applied to one's self, is not so suitable as *blame* or *condemn*. See also Find Fault.

Blameless, Irreproachable, Unblemished, Unspotted, or *Spotless.*—*Blameless* signifies literally void of *blame. Irreproachable,* that is, not able to be *reproached. Unblemished,* that is, without *blemish. Unspotted,* that is, without *spot* (see BLEMISH).

Blameless is less than *irreproachable;* what is *blameless* is simply free from *blame,* but that which is *irreproachable* cannot be *blamed,* or have any *reproach* attached to it. It is good to say of a man that he leads a *blameless* life, but it is a high encomium to say that he leads an *irreproachable* life: the former is but the negative praise of one who is known only for his harmlessness; the latter is the positive commendation of a man who is well known for his integrity in the different relations of society.

Unblemished and *unspotted* are applicable to many objects besides that of personal conduct; and when applied to this, their original meaning sufficiently points out their use in distinction from the former two. We may say of a man that he has an *irreproachable* or an *unblemished* reputation, and *unspotted* or *spotless* purity of life.

BLASPHEME. See SWEAR.

BLAZE. See FLAME.

BLEMISH, STAIN, SPOT, SPECK, FLAW. *Blemish* is derived through French, possibly from Icelandic *blamen,* the livid color of a wound, cognate with English *blue. Stain* comes from Old French *desteindre,* from Latin *dis,* apart, and *tingere,* to color, and means to discolor. *Spot* means literally a thing spat out, hence a wet blot. *Speck* has a similar origin. *Flaw* is a Scandinavian word and originally signified a crack or break.

In the proper sense *blemish* is the generic, the rest specific: a *stain,* a *spot, speck,* and *flaw* are *blemishes,* but there are likewise many *blemishes* which are neither *stains, spots, specks,* nor *flaws.* Whatever takes off from the seemliness of appearance is a *blemish.* In works of art the slightest dimness of color or want of proportion is a *blemish.* A *stain* or *spot* sufficiently characterizes itself as that which is superfluous and out of its place. A *speck* is a small *spot;* and a *flaw,* which is confined to hard substances, mostly con-

sists of a faulty indenture on the outer surface. A *blemish* tarnishes; a *stain* spoils; a *spot, speck,* or *flaw* disfigures. A *blemish* is rectified, a *stain* wiped out, a *spot* or *speck* removed.

All these terms are employed figuratively. Even an imputation of what is improper in our moral conduct is a *blemish* on our reputation: the failings of a good man are so many *spots* or *specks* in the bright hemisphere of his virtue: there are some vices which affix a *stain* on the character of nations, as well as of the individuals who are guilty of them. In proportion to the excellence or purity of a thing, so is any *flaw* the more easily to be discerned.

Blemish, Defect, Fault.—*Blemish* (see above). *Defect* is derived from the past participle of *deficere,* Latin, from *de* and *facere,* and means *undone,* something not made or made in the wrong way. *Fault,* French *faillir,* is derived from Latin *fallere,* to deceive, and signifies that which is wanting in truth and propriety.

Blemish respects the exterior of an object: *defect* consists in the want of some specific propriety in an object; *fault* conveys the idea not only of something wrong, but also of its relation to the author. There is a *blemish* in fine china; a *defect* in the springs of a clock; and a *fault* in the contrivance. An accident may cause a *blemish* in a fine painting; the course of nature may occasion a *defect* in a person's speech; but the carelessness of the workman is evinced by the *faults* in the workmanship. A *blemish* may be easier remedied than a *defect* is corrected or a *fault* repaired.

BLEND. See MIX.

BLIND. See CLOAK.

BLOCKADE. See SURROUND.

BLOCKHEAD. See NINNY.

BLONDE, GOLDEN, FLAXEN, FAIR, XANTHOUS. All these words indicate a type of fair hair and coloring opposed to *brunette* or dark. *Blonde,* a word of unknown origin which appears in Medieval Latin and French, signified "a colour midway between golden and light chestnut" (Littré). *Golden* signifies the color of gold; *flaxen* of the color of flax, which is lighter than gold and not so bright. *Fair* is extended from its meaning of beautiful to indicate the coloring considered most beautiful—*i. e.*, the *blonde* coloring, and is, next to *blonde*, the word most generally applied to signify, not the hair alone, but the whole coloring. *Xanthous*, Greek, ζανθός, yellow is the ethnological term indicating the blonde races.

BLOODTHIRSTY. See SANGUINARY.

BLOODY. See SANGUINARY.

BLOT, EXPUNGE, RASE, or ERASE, EFFACE, CANCEL, OBLITERATE. *Blot*, signifying a spot, is derived from Old French *blotte*, a clot of earth, probably of Teutonic origin. *Expunge*, in Latin *expungo*, compounded of *ex* and *pungere*, to prick, signifies to put out by pricking with any sharp instrument. *Erase*, in Latin *erasus*, participle of *erado*—that is, *e* and *rado* found in *abrade*, to scratch out. *Efface*, from *ex*, out, and *facies*, face, means to remove the face of something. *Cancel*, in French *canceller*, Latin *cancello*, from *cancelli*, lattice-work, signifies to strike out with cross-lines. *Obliterate*, in Latin *obliteratus*, participle of *oblitero*, compounded of *ob* and *litera*, letter, signifies to cover over letters.

All these terms obviously refer to characters that are impressed on bodies; the first three apply in the proper sense only to that which is written with the hand, and bespeak the manner in which the action is performed. Letters are *blotted out*, so that they cannot be seen again; they are *expunged*, so as to signify that they cannot stand for anything; they are *erased*, so that the space may be re-occupied with writing. The last three are extended in their application to other characters formed on other substances: *efface* is general, and does not designate either the manner or the object: inscriptions on stone may be *effaced*, which are rubbed off so as not to be visible: *cancel* is principally confined to written or printed characters; they are *cancelled* by striking through them with the pen; in this manner leaves or pages of a book are *cancelled* which are no longer to be reckoned: *obliterate* is said of all characters, but without defining the mode in which they are put out; letters are *obliterated*

which are in any way made illegible. *Efface* applies to images, or the representations of things; in this manner the likeness of a person may be *effaced* from a statue; *cancel* respects the subject which is written or printed; *obliterate* respects the single letters which constitute words. *Efface* is the consequence of some direct action on the thing which is *effaced;* in this manner writing may be *effaced* from a wall by the action of the elements: *cancel* is the act of a person, and always the fruit of design: *obliterate* is the fruit of accident and circumstances in general; time itself may *obliterate* characters on a wall or on paper.

The metaphorical use of these terms is easily deducible from the preceding explanation; what is figuratively described as written in a book may be said to be *blotted;* thus our sins are *blotted out* of the book by the atoning blood of Christ: when the contents of a book are in part rejected, they are aptly described as being *expunged;* in this manner the freethinking sects *expunge* everything from the Bible which does not suit their purpose, or they *expunge* from their creed what does not humor their passions. When the memory is represented as having characters impressed, they are said to be *erased* when they are, as it were, directly taken out and occupied by others; in this manner, the recollection of what a child has learned is easily *erased* by play; and with equal propriety sorrows may be said to *efface* the recollection of a person's image from the mind. From the idea of striking out or *cancelling* a debt in an account-book, a debt of gratitude, or an obligation, is said to be *cancelled*. As the lineaments of the face corresponded to written characters, we may say that all traces of his former greatness are *obliterated*.

BLOW, STROKE. *Blow* is a word of obscure history from a Teutonic root meaning to strike. *Stroke*, from the word *strike*, is a substantive allied to the verb *strike*, and denotes the act of striking.

Blow is used abstractedly to denote the effect of violence; *stroke* is employed relatively to the person producing that effect. A *blow* may be received by the carelessness of the receiver or by a pure accident; but *strokes* are dealt out according to the design of the giver. Children are always in the way of getting *blows* in the course of their play, and of receiving *strokes* by way of chastisement. A *blow* may be given with the hand, or with any flat substance; a *stroke* is rather a long-drawn *blow* given with a long instrument, like a stick. *Blows* may be given with the flat part of a sword, and *strokes* with a stick.

Blow is seldom used but in the proper sense; *stroke* sometimes figuratively, as a *stroke* of death or a *stroke* of fortune.

See also KNOCK.

BLUNDER. See ERROR.

BLUNT. See OBTUSE.

BLUSTER. See GASCONADE.

BOAST. See GLORY.

BODILY. See CORPORAL.

BODY, CORPSE, CARCASS. *Body,* Anglo-Saxon *bodig,* is derived from the root meaning to bind, and signifies that which confines the life or spirit. It is here taken in the special sense of dead body. *Corpse,* from Latin *corpus,* body, represents the same kind of specialization—the general word for body being limited to the body in a single state. *Carcass* has been introduced through French from Italian *carcassa,* a kind of shell, the dead body being an empty shell. The word is ultimately derived from Persian.

Body is applicable either to men or brutes, *corpse* to men only, and *carcass* to brutes only, unless when taken in a contemptuous sense. When speaking of any particular person who is deceased, we should use the simple term *body;* the *body* was suffered to lie too long unburied: when designating its condition as lifeless, the term *corpse* is preferable: he was taken up as a *corpse;* when designating the body as a lifeless lump separated from the soul, it may be characterized (though contemptuously) as a *carcass;* the fowls devour the *carcass.*

BOISTEROUS. See VIOLENT.

BOLD, FEARLESS, INTREPID, UN-DAUNTED. *Bold* (see AUDACITY). *Fearless* signifies without fear (see APPREHEND). *Intrepid,* compounded of *in,* privative, and *trepidus,* trembling, marks the total absence of fear. *Un-*daunted is the opposite of *daunted,* daunt being derived from the Latin verb *domitare,* to tame, allied to English *tame.*

Boldness is a positive characteristic of the spirit; *fearlessness* is a negative state of the mind, that is, simply an absence of fear. A person may be *bold* through *fearlessness,* but he may be *fearless* without being *bold;* he may be *fearless* where there is no apprehension of danger or no cause for apprehension, but he is *bold* only when he is conscious or apprehensive of danger, and prepared to encounter it. A man may be *fearless* in a state of inaction; he is *bold* only in action, or when in a frame of mind for action.

Intrepidity is properly a mode of *fearlessness, undauntedness* a mode of *boldness* in the highest degree, displayed only on extraordinary occasions; he is *intrepid* who has no fear where the most fearless might tremble; he is *undaunted* whose spirit is unabated by that which would make the stoutest heart yield. *Intrepidity* may be shown either in the bare contemplation of dangers or in the actual encountering of dangers in opposing esistance to force.

Undauntedness is the opposing actual resistance to a force which is calculated to strike with awe.

See also DARING; STALWART; STRENUOUS.

BOLDNESS. See AUDACITY.

BOMBASTIC. See HIGH-FLOWN; TURGID.

BONDAGE. See S E R V I T U D E; THRALDOM.

BOOTY, SPOIL, PREY. *Booty* comes through Old French *butin,* from Low German, signifying prey. *Spoil* is derived from Latin *spolium,* meaning skin stripped off, referring to the stripping off of the dress of a slain warrior. *Prey* is derived from Latin *præda,* that which is taken or carried off.

Booty and *spoil* are used as military terms in attacks on an enemy, *prey* in cases of particular violence. The soldier gets his *booty,* the combatant his *spoils,* the carnivorous animal his *prey. Booty* respects what is of personal service to the captor; *spoils,* whatever serves to designate his triumph; *prey* includes whatever gratifies the appetite and is to be consumed. When a town is taken, soldiers are too busy in the work of destruction and mischief to carry away much *booty;* in every battle the arms and personal property of the slain enemy are the lawful *spoils* of the victor; the hawk pounces on his *prey* and carries it up to his nest. Greediness stimulates to take *booty;* ambition produces an eagerness for *spoils;* a ferocious appetite impels to a search for *prey.* Among the ancients the prisoners of war who were made slaves constituted a part of their *booty;* and even in later periods such a capture was good *booty* when ransom was paid for those who could liberate themselves. Among some savages the head or limb of an enemy constituted part of their *spoils.* Among cannibals the prisoners of war are the *prey* of the conquerors.

Booty and *prey* are often used in an extended and figurative sense. Plunderers obtain a rich *booty;* the diligent bee returns loaded with his *booty.* It is necessary that animals should become a *prey* to man, in order that man may not become a *prey* to them; everything in nature becomes a *prey* to another thing, which in its turn falls a *prey* to something else. All is changed but order. Man is a *prey* to the diseases of his body or his mind, and after death to the worms.

BORDER, EDGE, RIM or BRIM, BRINK, MARGIN, VERGE. *Border,* in French *bord* or *bordure,* Teutonic *bord,* is probably connected with *bret,* board, signifying a strip in shape like a board. *Edge* comes from Anglo-Saxon *ecg,* border; and *rim* from Anglo-Saxon *rima,* which has the same meaning. *Brim* is a Middle English word which does not appear in Anglo-Saxon, though it has Teutonic parallels. *Brink* comes from the Scandinavian. *Margin* is derived from Latin *margo,* a border or brink, cognate with English *mark,* a boundary. *Verge,* French *verge,* from Latin *virga,* at first signified a rod, wand, or hoop; from the sense of rod it came to mean hoop (a bent rod—bent to form a circle), a ring, hence rim or edge.

Of these terms, *border* is the least definite point; *edge* the most so; *rim* and *brink* are species of *edge; margin*

and *verge* are species of *border.* A *border* is a stripe, an *edge* is a line. The *border* lies at a certain distance from the *edge;* the *edge* is the exterior termination of the surface of any substance. Whatever is wide enough to admit of any space round its circumference may have a *border,* whatever comes to a narrow extended surface has an *edge.* Many things may have both a *border* and an *edge;* of this description are caps, gowns, carpets, and the like; others have a *border,* but no *edge,* as lands; and others have an *edge,* but no *border,* as a knife or a table. A *rim* is the *edge* of any vessel; and *brim* is the exterior *edge* of a cup; a *brink* is the *edge* of any precipice or deep place; a *margin* is the *border* of a book or a piece of water; a *verge* is the extreme *border* of a place.

Border, Boundary, Frontier, Confine, Precinct.—*Border* (see above). *Boundary,* from Old French *bonne,* a limit, Low Latin *bodina,* is derived from a Celtic word signifying limit, and is allied to *bourne. Frontier,* French *frontière,* from the Latin *frons,* a forehead, signifies the fore part, or the commencement of anything. *Confine,* in Latin *confinis,* compounded of *con* or *cum* and *finis,* an end, signifies an end next to an end. *Precinct,* in Latin *præcinctum,* participle of *præcingo*— that is, *præ* and *cingere,* to enclose— signifies any enclosed place.

Border, boundary, frontier, and *confines* are all applied to countries or tracts of land: the *border* is the outer edge or tract of land that runs along a country; it is mostly applied to countries running on a line with each other, as the *borders* of England and Scotland; the *boundary* is that which bounds or limits, as the *boundaries* of countries or provinces; the *frontier* is that which lies in the front or forms the entrance into a country, as the *frontiers* of Germany or the *frontiers* of France; the *confines* are the parts lying contiguous to others, as the *confines* of different states or provinces. The term *border* is employed in describing those parts which form the *borders,* as to dwell on the *borders,* or to run along the *borders.* The term *boundary* is used in speaking of the extent or limits of places; it belongs to the science of geography to describe the *boundaries* of countries. The *frontiers* are mostly spoken of in relation to military matters, as to pass the *frontiers*, to fortify *frontier* towns, to guard the *frontiers*, or in respect to one's passage from one country to another, as to be stopped at the *frontiers*. The term *confines*, like that of *borders*, is mostly in respect to two places; the *border* is mostly a line, but the *confines* may be a point: we therefore speak of going along the *borders*, but meeting on the *confines*.

The term *border* may be extended in its application to any space, and *boundary* to any limit. *Confines* is also figuratively applied to any space included within the *confines*, as the *confines* of the grave; *precinct* is properly any space which is encircled by something that serves as a girdle, as to be within the *precincts* of a court—that is, within the space which belongs to or is under the control of a court.

BORE. See PENETRATE.

BOTCH. See BUNGLE.

BOTH, PAIR, TWAIN, TWO. *Both* is a Scandinavian word—a compound of two words. *Bo*, meaning two, corresponds to *bo* in Latin *ambo*, both, and Greek ἄμφω. The *th* originally stood for the definite article, as in Gothic *ba tho skipa*, "the two ships." *Pair* is derived from Latin *par*, equal, a *pair* being two equal things that belong together, or that form one single whole. The difference between *two* and *twain* was originally one of gender only. All of these words signify two, but there is a difference in their meaning corresponding to the difference in their derivation. *Two* is the general term; it merely conveys the idea of number. *Twain* was originally merely another form of *two;* it is now a poetic word, a trifle more specific than *two*, perhaps. *Both* contains the idea of the definite article or the demonstrative. It suggests two specific ideas, consciously comprehended in one general statement. To say that there are *two* books on the table suggests merely the general idea of number. To say that *both* books are on the table suggests that there are two particular books, distinguished in the mind of the speaker from all other books, and deliberately combined, as it were, in the general idea indicated in the verb. *Pair* suggests two objects, equal or alike, comprehended in one general idea—two separate and similar things which, taken together, make one whole, such as a *pair* of gloves, a *pair* of skates.

BOUND, LIMIT, CONFINE, CIRCUMSCRIBE, RESTRICT. *Limit*, from the Latin *limes*, a landmark, signifies to draw a line which is to be the exterior line or limit. *Confine* signifies to bring within *confines*. *Circumscribe*, in Latin *circumscribo*, is compounded of *circum* and *scribo*, to write round—that is, to describe a line round. *Restrict*, in Latin *restrictum*, participle of *restringo*, compounded of *re* and *stringo*, signifies to keep fast back.

The first four of these terms are employed in the proper sense of parting off certain spaces. *Bound* applies to the natural or political divisions of the earth: countries are *bounded* by mountains and sea; kingdoms are often *bounded* by each other; Spain is *bounded* on one side by Portugal, on the other side by the Mediterranean, and on a third side by the Pyrenees. *Limit* applies to any artificial boundary: as landmarks in fields serve to show the *limits* of one man's ground from another's; so may walls, palings, hedges, or any other visible sign, be converted into a *limit*, to distinguish one spot from another, and in this manner a field is said to be *limited*, because it has *limits* assigned to it. To *confine* is to bring the *limits* close together; to part off one space absolutely from another: in this manner we *confine* a garden by means of walls. To *circumscribe* is literally to surround: in this manner a circle may *circumscribe* a square: there is this difference, however, between *confine* and *circumscribe*, that the former may not only show the *limits*, but may also prevent egress and ingress; whereas the latter, which is only a line, is but a simple mark that *limits*.

From the proper acceptation of these terms, we may easily perceive the ground on which their improper acceptation rests: to *bound* is an action suited to the nature of things, or to some given rule; in this manner our views are *bounded* by the objects which intercept our sight.

Or we *bound* our desires according to the principles of propriety.

To *limit, confine,* and *circumscribe* all convey the idea of an action more or less involuntary, and controlled either by circumstances or by persons. To *limit* is an affair of discretion or necessity; we *limit* our expenses because we are *limited* by circumstances.

Things may be *limited* to one or many points or objects.

Confine conveys the same idea to a still stronger degree: what is *confined* is not only brought within a *limit,* but is kept to that *limit,* which it cannot pass; in this manner a person *confines* himself to a diet which he finds absolutely necessary for his health, or he is *confined* in the size of his house, in the choice of his situation, or in other circumstances equally uncontrollable; hence the term *confined* expresses also the idea of the *limits* being made narrow as well as impassable or unchangeable. Therefore to *confine* is properly to bring within narrow *limits;* it is applied either to space or to the movements of the body or the mind.

To *circumscribe* is to *limit* arbitrarily, or to bring within improper or inconvenient *limits.*

Sometimes *circumscribing* is a matter of necessity resulting from circumstances, as a person is *circumscribed* in his means of doing good who cannot do all the good he wishes.

To *restrict* is to exercise a stronger degree of control, or to impose a harder necessity, than either of the other terms: a person is *restricted* by his physician to a certain portion of food in the day.

BOUNDARY. See BORDER; BOUNDS; TERM.

BOUNDLESS, UNBOUNDED, UNLIMITED, INFINITE. *Boundless,* or without *bounds,* is applied to objects which admit of no *bounds* to be made or conceived by us. *Unbounded,* or *not bounded,* is applied to that which might be *bounded. Unlimited,* or not *limited,* applies to that which might be *limited. Infinite,* or not *finite,* applies to that which in its nature admits of no *bounds.*

The ocean is a *boundless* object so long as no *bounds* to it have been discovered; desires are often *unbounded* which ought always to be *bounded; power* is sometimes *unlimited* which would be better *limited;* nothing is *infinite* but that Being from whom all *finite* beings proceed.

BOUNDS, BOUNDARY. *Bounds* and *boundary,* from the verb *bound,* signify the line which sets a *bound* or marks the extent to which any spot of ground reaches.

Bounds is employed to designate the whole space, including the outer line that confines: *boundary* comprehends only this outer line. *Bounds* are made for a local purpose; *boundary* for a political purpose: the master of a school prescribes the *bounds* beyond which the scholar is not to go; the parishes throughout England have their *boundaries,* which are distinguished by marks; fields have likewise their *boundaries,* which are commonly marked out by a hedge or a ditch. *Bounds* are temporary and changeable; *boundaries* permanent and fixed: whoever has the authority of prescribing *bounds* for others may in like manner contract or extend them at pleasure; the *boundaries* of places are seldom altered but in consequence of great political changes.

In the figurative sense *bound* or *bounds* is even more frequently used than *boundary;* we speak of setting *bounds* or keeping within *bounds,* but to know a *boundary:* it is necessary occasionally to set *bounds* to the inordinate appetites of the best disposed children, who cannot be expected to know the exact *boundary* for indulgence.

BOUNTEOUS. See BENEFICENT.
BOUNTIFUL. See BENEFICENT.
BRACE. See COUPLE.
BRAG. See GASCONADE.
BRAVE, GALLANT. *Brave,* French *brave,* originally signified *fine, proud,* inclined to be a braggart; then valiant, allied to Italian *bravo.* The origin is unknown. *Gallant,* Old French *galant,* is a participle of *galer,* to make merry, allied to Italian and Spanish *gala,* which appears in the expression "*gala* day," "*gala* attire." The early meaning of dashing, spirited, bold, associated with this word is now obsolete

in French, but survives in English together with the common French meaning—courteous, courtly, etc.

These epithets, whether applied to the person or the action, are alike honorable; but the latter is a much stronger expression than the former. *Gallantry* is extraordinary *bravery*, or *bravery* on extraordinary occasions: the *brave* man goes willingly where he is commanded; the *gallant* man leads on with vigor to the attack. *Bravery* is common to vast numbers and whole nations; *gallantry* is peculiar to individuals or particular bodies: the *brave* man *bravely* defends the post assigned him; the *gallant* man volunteers his services in cases of peculiar danger: a man may feel ashamed in not being considered *brave;* he feels a pride in being looked upon as *gallant*. To call a hero *brave* adds little or nothing to his character; but to entitle him *gallant* adds a lustre to the glory he has acquired.

See also STALWART.

Brave, Defy, Dare, Challenge.—*Brave*, from the epithet *brave*, signifies to act the part of a fearless man. *Defy*, in French *défier*, from Late Latin *diffidare*, from Latin *dis*, apart, and *fides*, faith, means to renounce faith. *Dare*, Anglo-Saxon *ic dearr*, I dare, is allied to Greek θαρσεῖν, to be bold. *Challenge*, Middle English *chalenge*, was often used in the sense of *claim;* it is derived from Latin *calumnia*, a false accusation, whence the word *calumny* is also derived. A *challenge* meant an invitation to defend one's honor against an accusation by fighting.

To *brave* is with bravery to resist or meet the force of any opposing power: as the sailor *braves* the tempestuous ocean, or, in the bad sense, a man *braves* the scorn and reproach of the world; so things personified may *brave*.

To *defy* is to hold cheap that which opposes itself as it respects persons; there is often much insolent resistance in *defiance*, as a man *defies* the threats of his superior.

In respect to things it denotes a resolution to bear whatever may be inflicted.

To *dare* and to *challenge* have more of provocation than resistance in them; he who *dares* and *challenges* provokes or calls on another to do something. To *dare* is an informal act, performed either by words or deeds; as to *dare* a person to come out, to *dare* him to leave his place of retreat: to *challenge* is a formal act, performed by words; as to *challenge* another to fight, or to engage in any contest.

Daring may sometimes be performed by actions, and *braving* sometimes by words; so that by the poets they are occasionally used one for the other.

Bravery, Courage, Valor.—*Bravery* denotes the abstract quality of *brave*. *Courage*, in French *courage*, comes from *cœur*, in Latin *cor*, the heart, which is the seat of *courage*. *Valor*, in French *valeur*, Latin *valor*, from *valere*, to be strong, signifies by distinction strength of mind.

Bravery lies in the blood; *courage* lies in the mind; the latter depends on the reason, the former on the physical temperament: the first is a species of instinct; the second is a virtue: a man is *brave* in proportion as he is without thought; he has *courage* in proportion as he reasons or reflects. *Bravery* is of utility only in the hour of attack or contest; *courage* is of service at all times and under all circumstances: *bravery* is of avail in overcoming the obstacle of the moment; *courage* seeks to avert the distant evil that may possibly arrive. *Bravery* is a thing of the moment—that is or is not, as circumstances may favor; it varies with the time and season: *courage* exists at all times and on all occasions. The *brave* man who fearlessly rushes to the mouth of the cannon may tremble at his own shadow as he passes through a churchyard or turn pale at the sight of blood: the *courageous* man smiles at imaginary dangers, and prepares to meet those that are real. It is as possible for a man to have *courage* without *bravery* as to have *bravery* without *courage*. Cicero showed no marks of personal *bravery* as a commander, but he displayed his *courage* when he laid open the treasonable purposes of Catiline to the whole senate, and charged him to his face with the crimes of which he knew him to be guilty.

Valor is a higher quality than either *bravery* or *courage*, and seems to partake of the grand characteristics of both; it combines the fire of *bravery* with the determination and firmness of *courage:* *bravery* is most fitted for the soldier and all who receive orders; *courage* is most adapted for the general and all who give command; *valor* for the leader and framer of enterprises and all who carry great projects into execution: *bravery* requires to be guided; *courage* is equally fitted to command or obey; *valor* directs and executes. *Bravery* has most relation to danger; *courage* and *valor* include in them a particular reference to action: the *brave* man exposes himself; the *courageous* man advances to the scene of action which is before him; the *valiant* man seeks for occasions to act. The three hundred Spartans who defended the Straits of Thermopylæ were *brave*. Socrates drinking the hemlock, Regulus returning to Carthage, Titus tearing himself from the arms of the weeping Berenice, Alfred the Great going into the camp of the Danes, were *courageous*. Hercules destroying monsters, Perseus delivering Andromeda, Achilles running to the ramparts of Troy, and the knights of more modern date who have gone in quest of extraordinary adventures, are all entitled to the peculiar appellation of *valiant*.

BRAWNY. See HERCULEAN.

BREACH, BREAK, GAP, CHASM. *Breach* and *break* are both derived from the same verb *break* (see BREAK), to denote what arises from being broken, in the figurative sense of the verb itself. *Gap* is a Scandinavian word allied to *gape*, signifying that which gapes or stands open. *Chasm* (Latin *chasma*, a gulf, which is a transliteration of Greek χάσμα, a yawning cleft, allied to χαός, chaos) has a similar meaning.

The idea of an opening is common to these terms, but they differ in the nature of the opening. A *breach* and a *gap* are the consequence of a violent removal which destroys the connection; a *break* and a *chasm* may arise from the absence of that which would form a connection. A *breach* in a wall is made by means of cannon; *gaps* in fences are commonly the effect of some violent effort to pass through; a *break* is made in a page of printing by leaving off in the middle of a line; a *chasm* is left in writing when any words in

the sentence are omitted. A *breach* and a *chasm* always imply a larger opening than a *break* or *gap*. A *gap* may be made in a knife; a *breach* is always made in the walls of a building or for- tification: the clouds sometimes sepa- rate so as to leave small *breaks;* the ground is sometimes so convulsed by earthquakes as to leave frightful *chasms*.

Breach, *chasm*, and *gap* are figura- tively applied to other objects with the same distinction; as a *breach* of friend- ship or of domestic harmony; a *gap* in nature or time; and a *chasm* in our enjoyments.

BREAK, RACK, REND, TEAR. *Break*, Anglo-Saxon *brecan*, is a Ger- manic word signifying to crack with a noise. *Rack* is a variant of *wrack*, allied to Anglo-Saxon *wrecan* (Mod- ern English *wreck*), to drive, urge: it refers especially to something driven ashore, hence to anything broken in pieces, like a ship crushed on the rocks in a storm. *Rend*, North- ern French *renne*, to tear apart, has few cognates outside of English. *Tear* comes from Anglo-Saxon *teran*, to rend.

The forcible division of any sub- stance is the common characteristic of these terms. *Break* is the generic term, the rest are specific: everything *racked*, *rent*, or *torn* is broken, but not *vice versa*. *Break* has, however, a specific meaning, in which it is comparable with the others. *Breaking* requires less violence than either of the others: brittle things may be *broken* with the slightest touch, but nothing can be *racked* without intentional violence of an extraordinary kind. Glass is quick- ly *broken;* a table is *racked*. Hard sub- stances only are *broken* or *racked;* but everything of a soft texture and com- position may be *rent* or *torn*. *Breaking* is performed by means of a blow; *rack- ing* by that of a violent concussion or straining; but *rending* and *tearing* are the consequences of a pull or a sudden snatch. Anything of wood or stone is *broken;* anything of a complicated structure, with hinges and joints, is *racked;* cloth is *rent*, paper is *torn*. *Rend* is sometimes used for what is done by design; a *tear* is always faulty. *Cloth* is sometimes *rent* rather than cut when it is wanted to be divided; but when it is *torn* it is injured. To *tear* is also used in the sense not only of dividing by violence that which ought to remain whole, but by separating one object from another; as to *tear* anything off or out, etc.

In the moral or figurative application, *break* denotes in general a division or separation more or less violent of that which ought to be united or bound; as to *break* a tie, to *break* an engagement or promise. To *rack* is a continued action; as to *rack* the feelings, to place them in a violent state of tension. To *rend* is figuratively applied in the same sense as in the proper application, to denote a sudden division of what has been before whole; as to *rend* the heart, to have it pierced or divided, as it were, with grief; so likewise to *rend* the air with shouts. To *tear* is metaphorically separating objects from one another which are united; as to *tear* one's self from the company of a friend.

Break, Bruise, Squeeze, Pound, Crush. —*Break* (see above). *Bruise,* Anglo-Saxon *brysan* in the compound *to-brysan,* to bruise, is also found in Old French *bruiser,* to break. It may be a Celtic word. *Squeeze,* Late Middle English *queisan,* is derived from *ex,* and Anglo-Saxon *cwiesan,* to crush. *Pound,* from Anglo-Saxon *punian,* to pound, is allied to Dutch *puin,* rubbish, hash, or "a cyment of stones," and Low German *pun,* chips of stones. *Crush,* Old French *crusir,* to crack or break, is derived from a Teutonic root signifying to gnash with the teeth.

Break always implies the separation of the component parts of a body; *bruise* denotes simply the destroying the continuity of the parts. Hard, brittle substances, as glass, are *broken;* soft, pulpy substances, as flesh or fruits, are *bruised.* The operation of *bruising* is performed either by a violent blow or by pressure; that of *squeezing* by compression only. Metals, particularly lead and silver, may be *bruised;* fruits may be either *bruised* or *squeezed.* In this latter sense *bruise* applies to the harder substances, or indicates a violent compression; *squeeze* is used for soft substances or a gentle compression. The kernels of nuts are *bruised;* oranges or apples are *squeezed.* To

pound is properly to *bruise* in a mortar, so as to produce a separation of parts; to *crush* is the most violent and destructive of all operations, which amounts to the total dispersion of all the parts of a body. What is *broken* may be made whole again; what is *bruised* or *squeezed* may be restored to its former tone and consistency; what is *pounded* is only reduced to smaller parts for convenience; but what is *crushed* is destroyed. When the wheel of a carriage passes over any body that yields to its weight, it *crushes* it to powder.

In the figurative sense, *crush* marks a total annihilation: if a conspiracy be not *crushed* in the bud, it will prove fatal to the power which has suffered it to grow.

Break, Burst, Crack, Split. —*Break* (see preceding). *Burst,* Anglo-Saxon *berstan,* is a Teutonic word signifying to break asunder. *Crack,* Anglo-Saxon *cracian,* to crack, is apparently an imitative word representing a sudden breaking asunder. *Split* is apparently borrowed from Middle Dutch *splitten;* it signifies a form of breaking.

Break is the general term, denoting any separation or coming apart with more or less force; the rest are particular modes, varied either in the circumstances of the action or the object acted upon. To *break* does not specify any particular manner or form of action; what is *broken* may be *broken* in two or more pieces, *broken* short or lengthwise, and the like: to *burst* is to *break* suddenly and with violence, frequently also with noise.

Everything that is exposed to external violence, particularly hard substances, are said to be *broken;* but hollow bodies, or such as are exposed to tension, are properly said to *burst.*

In the sense of making way or opening the same distinction is preserved.

To *crack* and *split* are modes of *breaking* lengthwise: the former in application to hard or brittle objects, as clay, or the things made of clay; the latter in application to wood, or that which is made of wood. *Breaking* frequently causes an entire separation of the component parts so as to destroy the things; *cracking* and *splitting* are but partial separations.

BREAKER. See WAVE.

BREED, ENGENDER. *Breed* signifies to produce or cherish a *brood*, a Teutonic word from a root meaning heat or warmth, *breed* being suggestive of fostering warmth. *Engender*, from Latin *in*, in, and *generare*, from *gener*, stem of *genus*, race, means to produce a race.

These terms are properly employed for the act of procreation. To *breed* is to bring into existence by a slow operation: to *engender* is to be the author or prime cause of existence. So, in the metaphorical sense, frequent quarrels are apt to *breed* hatred and animosity: the leveling and inconsistent conduct of the higher classes in the present age serves to *engender* a spirit of insubordination and assumption of the inferior order. Whatever *breeds* acts gradually; whatever *engenders* produces immediately as cause and effect. Uncleanliness *breeds* diseases of the body; want of occupation *breeds* those of the mind; playing at chance games *engenders* a love of money.

See also RACE.

BREEDING. See EDUCATION.

BREEZE, GALE, BLAST, GUST, STORM, TEMPEST, HURRICANE. All these words express the action of the wind, in different degrees and under different circumstances. *Breeze*, in Italian *brezza*, is in all probability an onomatopœia for that kind of wind peculiar to Southern climates. *Gale* is a Scandinavian word possibly allied to Danish *gal*, furious, and derived from the root found in Modern English *yell*. *Blast*, Anglo-Saxon *blœst*, signifies a blowing. *Gust* is allied to the verb *gush*, signifying a wind which *gushes* out, a sudden blast. *Storm* is a Germanic word from the root whence *stir* is also derived, and signifies a great stirring up of the elements. *Tempest*, in Latin *tempestas*, or *tempus*, a time or season, describes that season or sort of weather which is most remarkable, but at the same time most frequent, in Southern climates. *Hurricane* has been introduced by the Spaniards into European languages from the Caribbee Islands, where it describes that species of *tempestuous* wind most frequent in tropical climates.

A *breeze* is gentle; a *gale* is brisk, but steady; we have *breezes* in a calm summer's day; the mariner has favorable *gales*, which keep the sails on the stretch. A *blast* is impetuous: the exhalations of a trumpet, the breath of bellows, the sweep of a violent wind, are *blasts*. A *gust* is sudden and vehement; *gusts* of wind are sometimes so violent as to sweep everything before them while they last. *Storm, tempest,* and *hurricane* include other particulars besides wind. A *storm* throws the whole atmosphere into commotion; it is a war of the elements, in which wind, rain, hail, and the like conspire to disturb the heavens. *Tempest* is a species of *storm* which has also thunder and lightning to add to the confusion. *Hurricane* is a species of *storm* which exceeds all the rest in violence and duration.

Gust, storm, and *tempest*, which are applied figuratively, preserve their distinction in this sense. The passions are exposed to *gusts* and *storms*, to sudden bursts, or violent and continued agitations; the soul is exposed to *tempests* when agitated with violent and contending emotions.

BRIEF. See LACONIC; SHORT.

BRIGHT. See CLEAR; ORIENT.

BRIGHTNESS, LUSTRE, SPLENDOR, BRILLIANCY. *Brightness*, from Anglo-Saxon *beorht*, shining, is allied to Greek φορκός, white. *Lustre* is derived from Late Latin *lustrum*, a window, Italian *lustro*, "a lustre, a glasse, a shining" (Florio), which comes ultimately from Latin *lucere*, to shine. *Splendor*, in French *splendeur*, is derived from Latin *splendor*, from *splendere*, to shine. *Brilliancy*, from French *briller*, to shine, comes from the Latin of the Middle Ages *beryllus*, a crystal.

Brightness is the generic, the rest are specific terms: there cannot be *lustre, splendor,* and *brilliancy* without *brightness;* but there may be *brightness* where these do not exist. These terms rise in sense; *lustre* rises on *brightness, splendor* on *lustre,* and *brilliancy* on *splendor*. *Brightness* and *lustre* are applied properly to natural lights; *splendor* and *brilliancy* have been more commonly applied to that which is artificial or unusual: there is always more or less *brightness* in the sun or moon; there is an occasional *lustre* in all the heavenly bodies when they shine in their unclouded *brightness;* there is *splendor* in the eruptions of flame from a volcano or an immense conflagration; there is *brilliancy* in a collection of diamonds. There may be both *splendor* and *brilliancy* in an illumination: the *splendor* arises from the mass and richness of light; the *brilliancy* from the variety and *brightness* of the lights and colors. *Brightness* may be obscured, *lustre* may be tarnished, *splendor* and *brilliancy* diminished.

The analogy is closely preserved in the figurative application. *Brightness* attaches to the moral character of men in ordinary cases, *lustre* attaches to extraordinary instances of virtue and greatness, *splendor* and *brilliancy* attach to the achievements of men. Our Saviour is strikingly represented to us as the *brightness* of his Father's glory and the express image of His person. The humanity of the English in the hour of conquest adds a *lustre* to their victories, which are either *splendid* or *brilliant,* according to the number and nature of the circumstances which render them remarkable.

BRILLIANCY. See BRIGHTNESS; RADIANCE.

BRILLIANT. See GORGEOUS.

BRIM. See BORDER.

BRING, FETCH, CARRY. *Bring,* Anglo-Saxon *bringan,* is a widely distributed Germanic word. *Fetch,* Anglo-Saxon *feccan,* to fetch, is allied to *fæt,* a pace, a step, and Latin *pes,* a foot; and meant to go to get something. *Carry* (see BEAR; CARRY).

To *bring* is simply to take with one's self from the place where one is; to *fetch* is to go first to a place and then *bring* a thing; to *fetch,* therefore, is a species of *bringing;* whatever is near at hand is *brought;* whatever is at a distance must be *fetched:* the porter at an inn *brings* a parcel, a servant who is sent for it *fetches* it. *Bring* always respects motion toward the place in which the speaker resides; *fetch,* a motion both to and from; *carry,* always a motion directly from the place or at a distance from the place. A servant *brings* the parcel home which his master has sent him to *fetch;* he *carries* a parcel from home. A *carrier carries* parcels to and from a place, but he does not *bring* parcels to and

from any place. *Bring* **is an action** performed at the option of the agent; *fetch* and *carry* are mostly done at the command of another. Hence the old proverb, "He who will *fetch* will *carry,*" to mark the character of the gossip and tale-bearer, who reports what he hears from two persons in order to please both parties.

BRINK. See BORDER.

BRISK. See ACTION.

BRITTLE. See FRAGILE.

BROAD. See LARGE.

BROIL. See QUARREL.

BROOK, BEAR, ENDURE, STAND. *Brook* is derived from Anglo-Saxon *brucan,* to enjoy. For the derivations of *bear* and *endure,* see BEAR. For the derivation of *stand* see that key-word. The term applies generally to the attitude of a person toward others. We *bear* with the company or actions of another whom we may dislike, from the impulse of politeness or policy, with conditions that are uncongenial because they are forced upon us or are unavoidable by us; we *endure,* or put up with, people, conditions, and objects because we are obliged to do so, or because it would not be convenient or prudent for us to do otherwise: and for similar reasons we permit or allow things to be said or done that are distasteful. The term *stand,* colloquially, has a very intimate relation to *brook,* as we say we will *brook* no delay, interference, postponement, and the like, in matters that concern us closely, implying that we will not *stand,* permit, or put up with any such actions.

BRUISE. See BREAK.

BRUTAL. See HEARTLESS.

BRUTE. See ANIMAL.

BUD. See GERM; SPROUT.

BUFFOON. See FOOL.

BUILD, ERECT, CONSTRUCT. *Build,* Anglo-Saxon *byldan,* is allied to *bold,* a house, Icelandic *bol,* a house, etc., and signifies the making of a house. *Erect,* in French *ériger,* Latin *erectus,* participle of *erigere,* means to set up straight. *Construct,* in Latin *constructus,* participle of *construo,* compounded of *con,* together, and *struere,* to pile or put, signifies to build by piling stones one on top of another, etc.

The word *build* by distinction expresses the purpose of the action; *erect* indicates the mode of the action; *construct* indicates contrivance in the action. What is *built* is employed for the purpose of receiving, retaining, or confining; what is *erected* is placed in an elevated situation; what is *constructed* is put together with ingenuity. All that is *built* may be said to be *erected* or *constructed;* but all that is *erected* or *constructed* is not said to be *built;* likewise what is *erected* is mostly *constructed*, though not *vice versa*. We *build* from necessity; we *erect* for ornament; we *construct* for utility and convenience. Houses are *built*, monuments *erected*, machines are *constructed*.

See also FOUND.

BUILDER. See ARCHITECT.

BULK. See SIZE.

BULKY, MASSIVE. *Bulky* denotes having *bulk*, from a root signifying to swell, which appears in *bowl*, *bulge*, *belly*, etc. It is a Scandinavian word. *Massive*, in French *massif*, from *mass*, signifies having a mass or being like a *mass*, which is in the German *masse*, Latin *massa*, Greek μᾱζα, dough, from μάσσειν, to knead, signifying made into a solid substance.

Whatever is *bulky* has a prominence of figure; what is *massive* has compactness of matter. The *bulky*, therefore, though larger in size, is not so weighty as the *massive*. Hollow bodies frequently have *bulk;* none but solid bodies can be *massive*. A vessel is *bulky* in its form; lead, silver, and gold are *massive*.

BULLY. See HECTOR.

BUNGLE, BOTCH, MISMANAGE, SPOIL. *Bungle*, a word of imitative origin, signifies in ordinary language to do anything clumsily, to mismanage, or execute badly an affair through ignorance, clumsiness, or awkwardness. *Botch*, a word of imitative origin allied to *patch*, a piece of work, means to put together carelessly, as a patch on anything, or a part of any work so finished that it looks worse than the rest or unbecoming to it. *Spoil* means to render useless, to disfigure beyond recognition, to mar, damage, or ruin anything, or by careless work to cause an object to deteriorate in appearance or value.

BUOYANT. See SANGUINE.

BURDEN. See FREIGHT; WEIGHT.

BURDENSOME. See HEAVY.

BURIAL, INTERMENT, SEPULTURE. *Burial*, allied to *bury*, Anglo-Saxon *byrigan*, is derived from *beorgan*, to hide, and means to hide in the ground. *Interment*, from *inter*, compounded of *in*, and *terra*, signifies the putting into the ground. *Sepulture*, in French *sépulture*, Latin *sepultura*, is derived from *sepelire*, to bury.

Under *burial* is comprehended simply the purpose of the action; under *interment* and *sepulture*, the manner as well as the motive of the action. We *bury* in order to conceal; *interment* and *sepulture* are accompanied with religious ceremonies. *Bury* is confined to no object or place; we *bury* whatever we deposit in the earth, and wherever we please; but *interment* and *sepulture* respect only the bodies of the deceased when deposited in a sacred place. *Burial* requires that the object be concealed under ground; *interment* may be used for depositing in vaults. Self-murderers were formerly *buried* in the highways; Christians in general are *buried* in the churchyard; but the kings of England were formerly *interred* in Westminster Abbey. *Burial* is a term in familiar use; *interment* serves frequently as a more elegant expression; *sepulture* is an abstract term confined to particular cases, as in speaking of the rites and privileges of *sepulture*.

BURIAL-GROUND. See NECROPOLIS.

BURLESQUE. See CARICATURE; TRAVESTY; WIT.

BURNING. See HOT.

BURST. See BREAK.

BUSINESS, OCCUPATION, EMPLOYMENT, ENGAGEMENT, AVOCATION. *Business* signifies that which makes *busy* (see ACTIVE). *Occupation*, from Latin *occupare*, compounded of *ob*, near, and *capere*, to take, signifies that which serves or takes possession of a person or thing to the exclusion of other things. *Employment*, in French *emploi*, is derived from Latin *implico* (whence *implicate*), signifying to enfold, *employment* being that which enfolds one, shuts one off from other activities; compare the phrase "wrapped up in his work" for a similar metaphor. *Engagement* (see ATTRACT). *Avocation*, in Latin *avocatio*, from *a*, away, and *vocare,* to call, signifies the thing that calls off from another thing.

Business occupies all a person's thoughts as well as his time and powers; *occupation* and *employment* occupy only his time and strength: the first is mostly regular, it is the object of our choice; the second is casual, it depends on the will of another. *Engagement* is a partial *employment, avocation* a particular *engagement:* an *engagement* prevents us from doing anything else; an *avocation* calls off or prevents us from doing what we wish. Every tradesman has a *business,* on the diligent prosecution of which depends his success in life; every mechanic has his daily *occupation,* by which he maintains his family; every laborer has an *employment* which is fixed for him. *Business* and *occupation* always suppose a serious object. *Business* is something more urgent and important than *occupation:* a man of independent fortune has no occasion to pursue *business,* but as a rational agent he will not be contented to be without an *occupation.*

Employment, engagement, and *avocation* leave the object undefined. An *employment* may be a mere diversion of the thought and a wasting of the hours in some idle pursuit; a child may have its *employment,* which may be its play in distinction from its *business:* an *engagement* may have no higher object than that of pleasure; the idlest people have often the most *engagements;* the gratification of curiosity and the love of social pleasure supply them with an abundance of *engagements.* *Avocations* have seldom a direct trifling object, although it may sometimes be of a subordinate nature, and generally irrelevant: numerous *avocations* are not desirable; every man should have a fixed pursuit, as the *business* of his life, to which the principal part of his time should be devoted: *avocations,* therefore, of a serious nature are apt to divide the time and attention to a hurtful degree.

A person who is *busy* has much to attend to, and attends to it closely: a person who is *occupied* has a full share of *business* without any pressure; he is opposed to one who is idle: a person who is *employed* has the present moment filled up; he is not in a state of inaction: the person who is *engaged* is not at liberty to be otherwise *employed;* his time is not his own; he is opposed to one at leisure.

Business, Trade, Profession, Art.—Business (see above). *Trade* signifies that which employs the time by way of *trade. Profession* signifies that which one professes to do. *Art* signifies that which is followed in the way of the *arts*.

These words are synonymous in the sense of a calling for the purpose of a livelihood: *business* is general, *trade* and *profession* are particular; all *trade* is *business,* but all *business* is not *trade.* Buying and selling of merchandise is inseparable from *trade;* but the exercise of one's knowledge and experience for purposes of gain constitutes a *business:* when learning or particular skill is required, it is a *profession;* and when there is a peculiar exercise of *art,* it is an *art;* every shopkeeper and retail dealer carries on a *trade;* brokers, manufacturers, bankers, and others carry on *business;* clergymen, medical or military men follow a *profession;* musicians and painters follow an *art.*

Business, Office, Duty.—Business (see above). *Office* (see BENEFIT). *Duty* signifies what is due or owing one, based on French *du,* Latin *debitum,* participle of *debere,* to owe.

Business is that which engages the time, talents, and interest of a man; it is what a man proposes to himself: *office* is that which a man is called upon to do for another; it is consequently prescribed by others: *duty* is that which duty prescribes: one follows *business,* fills or discharges an *office,* and performs or discharges a *duty.* As *business* is the concern of the individual, and *duty* is his duty, these terms properly apply to private matters as the *business* or *duties* of life: *office,* on the other hand, being that which is done for the benefit or by the direction of others, is properly applied to public matters.

But the terms may be so qualified that the former may be applied to public, and the latter to private matters.

Business and *office* are frequently applied to that part which a man is called to perform; in which sense *busi-*

ness and *office* come still nearer to the term *duty;* what belongs to a person to do or see done, that is properly his *business:* a person is bound, either by the nature of his engagements or by private and personal engagements or private and personal motives, to perform a service for another, as the *office* of a prime minister, the *office* of a friend; that is his *office. Duty* in this application expresses a stronger obligation than either of the other terms; where the service is enjoined by law, or commanded by the person, that is a *duty,* as the clerical *duties,* the *duty* of a soldier. See also AFFAIR.

BUSTLE, TUMULT, UPROAR. *Bustle* is a Scandinavian word, a frequentative of the Norwegian *busta,* to be violent, and related to Icelandic *bustla,* to splash about like a fish, and to English *boast, boisterous,* etc. *Tumult,* Latin *tumultus,* is derived from Latin *tumere,* to swell, surge up, whence *tumor* is also derived. *Uproar* is derived from Dutch *op,* up, and *roeren,* to excite, stir, move, and signified originally a stirring up; but its meaning has been influenced by its similarity to English *roar.*

Bustle has most of hurry in it; *tumult* most of disorder and confusion; *uproar* most of noise: the hurried movements of one, or many, cause a *bustle;* the disorderly struggles of many constitute a *tumult;* the loud elevation of many opposing voices produces an *uproar. Bustle* is frequently not the effect of design, but the natural consequence of many persons coming together; *tumult* commonly arises from a general effervescence in the minds of a multitude; *uproar* is the consequence either of general anger or mirth. A crowded street will always be in a *bustle;* contested elections are always accompanied with a great *tumult;* drinking-parties make a considerable *uproar,* in the indulgence of their intemperate mirth.

BUSY. See ACTIVE.

BUT, EXCEPT. As a conjunction *but* implies something more to supply, unless, yet, nevertheless, than, and otherwise than, and is used where a second sentence or clause is in opposition to the one preceding it, to arrest an inference which the first sentence or clause would otherwise have sug-

gested. As an adverb, it implies only; as a proposition, technically, a term of separation or exclusion, it signifies excepting; as an interjection it expresses surprise or dissent; as a substantive, a hindrance or impediment, also the outer room of a house of two or more apartments where the inner room is entered from the other. In logic, *but* is the connecting word which introduces the minor term of a syllogism; in mathematics, it denotes what is assumed or proved.

As a conjunction *but* is a synonyme of *yet. Yet* denotes a stronger degree of opposition than *but.* As a preposition *but* is a synonyme of *except.* There is little difference in meaning between the two prepositions. *Except* is somewhat clearer and more emphatic, and may be used to introduce not merely a noun but a noun clause.

BUTCHERY. See CARNAGE.

BUTT. See MARK.

BUY, PURCHASE, BARGAIN, CHEAPEN. *Buy* is derived from Anglo-Saxon *bycgan,* to buy. *Purchase* comes from Old French *pour* (Latin *pro*) and *chacer,* to chase, and signifies to hunt for eagerly. *Bargain* is derived from Late Latin *barcaniare,* to change about, to chaffer; its remoter origin is unknown. *Cheapen,* from Anglo-Saxon *ceap,* price, meant to price, and then to seek to obtain for a small price.

Buy and *purchase* have a strong resemblance to each other, both in sense and application; but the latter is a term of more refinement than the former: *buy* may always be substituted for *purchase* without impropriety; but *purchase* would be sometimes ridiculous in the familiar application of *buy:* the necessaries of life are *bought;* luxuries are *purchased.* The characteristic idea of *buying* is that of expending money according to a certain rule and for a particular purpose; that of *purchasing* is the procuring the thing by any means; some things, therefore, may more properly be said to be *purchased* than *bought,* as to *purchase* friends, ease, and the like.

Buying implies simply the exchange of one's money for a commodity; *bargaining* and *cheapening* have likewise respect to the price: to *bargain* is to make a specific agreement as to the price; to *cheapen* is not only to lower the price asked, but to deal in such things as are *cheap:* trade is supported by *buyers; bargainers* and *cheapeners* are not acceptable customers: mean people are prone to *bargaining,* poor people are obliged to *cheapen.*

BYGONE, PAST. *Bygone,* a compound of the English *by,* near, from, after, and *gone,* departed, moved, as an adjective implies gone by, passed or past, and as a substantive, things that have disappeared, passed away, become lost to sight and, in a sense, to memory. From this we have the familiar phrase *let bygones be bygones,* implying let the past be forgotten, doubtless from the old form, *byganes suld be byganes,* the past should not be brought up against one. As an adjective *bygone* does not really differ in meaning from *past.* But *past* is a prosaic word; it merely indicates a fact or a condition. *Bygone* has a pensive, poetic, slightly archaic quality.

BYWORD. See AXIOM.

C

CABAL. See COMBINATION.

CAJOLE. See COAX.

CALAMITOUS. See INFELICITOUS.

CALAMITY, DISASTER, MISFORTUNE, MISCHANCE, MISHAP. *Calamity* comes from Latin *calamitas*, misfortune; its ultimate origin is unknown. *Disaster*, in French *désastre*, is compounded of the privative *des* or *dis* and *astre*, in Latin *astrum*, a star, signifying what comes from the adverse influence of the stars. *Misfortune*, *mischance*, and *mishap* naturally express what comes amiss by fortune or chance.

The idea of a painful event is common to all these terms, but they differ in the degree of impatience. A *calamity* is a great *disaster* or *misfortune;* a *misfortune*, a great *mischance* or *mishap:* whatever is attended with destruction is a *calamity;* whatever is accompanied with a loss of property, or the deprivation of health, is a *misfortune;* whatever diminishes the beauty or utility of objects is a *mischance* or *mishap:* the devastation of a country by hurricanes or earthquakes, and the desolation of its inhabitants by famine or plague, are great *calamities;* the overturning of a carriage, and the fracture of a limb, are *disasters;* losses in trade are *misfortunes;* the spoiling of a book is, to a greater or less extent, a *mischance* or *mishap.* A *calamity* seldom arises from the direct agency of man; the elements, or the natural course of things, are mostly concerned in producing this source of misery to men; the rest may be ascribed to chance, as distinguished from design: *disasters* mostly arise from some specific known cause, either the carelessness of persons or the unfitness of things for their use; as they generally serve to derange some preconcerted scheme or undertaking, they seem as if they were produced by some secret influence: *misfortune* is frequently assignable to no specific cause; it is the bad fortune of an individual; a link in the chain of his destiny; an evil independent of himself, as distinguished from a fault: *mischance* and *mishap* are

misfortunes of comparatively so trivial a nature that it would not be worth while to inquire into their cause or to dwell upon their consequences. A *calamity* is dreadful, a *disaster* melancholy, a *misfortune* grievous or heavy, a *mischance* or *mishap* slight or trivial.

CALCULATE, RECKON, COMPUTE, COUNT. *Calculate*, in Latin *calculatus*, participle of *calculo*, comes from *calculus*, Greek κάλιξ, a pebble; because the Greeks gave their votes, and the Romans made out their accounts, by little stones; hence it denotes the action itself of *reckoning*. *Reckon* is derived from Anglo-Saxon *gerecnian*, to explain, from *reccan* to rule, order, direct, and refers to an orderly process of thought —to the directing and ordering of one's thoughts or plans. *Compute*, in French *computer*, Latin *computo*, compounded of *com* and *puto*, signifies to put together in one's mind. *Count*, in French *compter*, is but a contraction of *computer*.

These words indicate the means by which we arrive at a certain result in regard to quantity. To *calculate* is the generic term; the rest denote modes of *calculating:* to *calculate* denotes any numerical operation in general, but is particularly applicable to the abstract science of figures; the astronomer *calculates* the motions of the heavenly bodies; the mathematician makes algebraic *calculations:* to *reckon* is to enumerate and set down things in detail; *reckoning* is applicable to the ordinary business of life: tradesmen keep their accounts by *reckoning;* children learn to *reckon* by various simple processes. *Calculation* is therefore the science, *reckoning* the practical art of enumerating.

To *compute* is to come at the result by *calculation;* it is a sort of numerical estimate drawn from different sources: historians and chronologists *compute* the times of particular events by comparing them with those of other known events. An almanac is made by *calculation*, *computation*, and *reckoning.* The rising and setting of the heavenly bodies are *calculated;* from given astronomical tables is *computed* the moment on which any celestial phenomenon may return; and by *reckoning* are determined the days on which holidays, or other periodical events, fall.

To *count* is as much as to take account of, and when used as a mode of *calculation* it signifies the same as to *reckon* one by one; as to *count* one by one, to *count* the hours or minutes.

These words are all employed in application to moral objects, to denote the estimate which the mind takes of things. To *calculate* is to look to future events and their probable consequences; we *calculate* on a gain, on an undertaking, or any enterprise: to *compute* is to look to that which is past and what results from any past event, as to *compute* a loss, or the amount of any mischief done: to *reckon* is either to look at that which is present, and to set an estimate upon it; as to *reckon* a thing cheap; or to look to that which is future as something desirable, as to *reckon* on a promised pleasure. To *count* is to look on the thing that is present, and to set a value upon it according to circumstances, as to *count* a thing for nothing. A spirit of *calculation* arises from the cupidity engendered by trade; it narrows the mind to the mere prospect of accumulation and self-interest. *Computations* are inaccurate that are not founded upon exact numerical *calculations.* Inconsiderate people are apt to *reckon* on things that are very uncertain, and then lay up to themselves a store of disappointments. Those who have experienced the instability of human affairs will never *calculate* on an hour's enjoyment beyond the moment of existence. It is difficult to *compute* the loss which an army sustains upon being defeated, especially if it be obliged to make a long retreat. Those who know the human heart will never *reckon* on the assistance of professed friends in the hour of adversity. Men often *count* their lives as nothing in the prosecution of a favorite scheme.

CALENDAR, ALMANAC, EPHEMERIS. *Calendar,* Latin *calendarium,* was originally an account book kept by money-changers, so called because in-terest was due on the first of the month, which was termed the *Calendæ. Almanac* is a word of unknown origin which appears in Latin in the thirteenth century, and shortly after that in most of the Romance languages. It may be derived from an Arabic root signifying to reckon. *Ephemeris,* in Greek ἐφημερίς, from ἐπι and ἡμέρα, the day, implies that which happens by the day.

These terms denote a date-book, but the *calendar* is a book which registers events under every month: the *almanac* is a book which registers times, or the divisions of the year: and an *ephemeris* is a book which registers the planetary movements every day. An *almanac* may be a *calendar* and an *ephemeris* may be both an *almanac* and a *calendar;* but every *almanac* is not a *calendar,* nor every *calendar* an *almanac.* The Gardener's *Calendar* is not an *almanac,* and the sheet *almanacs* are seldom *calendars:* likewise the Nautical *Ephemeris* may serve as an *almanac,* although not as a *calendar.*

CALL, CRY, EXCLAIM. *Call* is a word of Scandinavian origin, and signifies simply the raising of the voice. *Cry,* French *crier,* Italian *gridare,* is derived from Latin *quiritare,* to shriek or lament, originally signifying to implore the aid of the *Quirites,* or Roman citizens. *Exclaim* is derived from the Latin *ex* and *clamare,* to cry out; both denote a raising the voice louder than a simple call. *Call* is used on all ordinary occasions in order to draw a person to a spot, or for any other purpose, when one wishes to be heard; to *cry* is to *call* loudly on particular occasions: a *call* draws attention; a *cry* awakens alarm.

To *cry* is for general purposes of convenience, as the *cry* of the hunter, or the *cries* of persons to or among numbers; to *exclaim* is an expression of some particular feeling.

See also ALARM; NAME.

Call, Invite, Bid, Summon.—*Call,* in its abstract and original sense, signifies simply to give an expression of the voice. *Bid* is derived from Anglo-Saxon *beodan,* to command. *Invite* comes from Latin *invitus,* unwilling, the unwilling person being one who must be especially requested or *invited* to do something. *Summon* is derived from Latin *submoneo*, from *sub* and *monere*, to warn, and signifies to give special notice.

The idea of signifying one's wish to another to do anything is included in 'all these terms. In the act of *calling*, any sounds may be used; we may *call* by simply raising the voice; *inviting* may be a direct or indirect act; we may *invite* by looks or signs as well as by words, by writing as well as by speaking.

To *bid* and *summon* require the express use of words; the former is always directly addressed to the person, the latter may be conveyed by an indirect channel.

As the action of *calling* requires no articulate sounds, it may be properly applied to animals; as sheep *call* their young.

So likewise to inanimate objects when made to sound by way of signal or for the purpose of *calling*.

So likewise *invite* may be said not only of unconscious, but spiritual agents.

Calling is the act of persons of all ranks, superiors, inferiors, or equals; it may therefore be either a command, a demand, or a simple request. Parents and children, masters and servants, *call* to each other as the occasion requires.

Bidding is always the act of a superior by way of command or entreaty.

Inviting is an act of courtesy or kindness between equals.

To *summon* is an act of authority, as to *summon* witnesses.

When these words are employed in the sense of causing any one to come to a place, *call* and *summon* are most nearly allied, as are also *bid* and *invite*. In this case to *call* is an act of discretion on ordinary occasions, and performed in an ordinary manner; as to *call* a meeting, to *call* together, to *call* home: to *summon* is a formal act, and more or less imperative according to the occasion; as to *summon* a jury.

Bidding and *inviting*, though acts of kindness, are distinguished as before according to the condition of the person; *bid* is properly the act of a superior, and *invite* of an equal, or one entitled to the courtesies of life.

These terms may all be used in tue figurative application with a similar distinction in sense. Things personified may be said to *call, summon, bid, invite*.

Things personified may also be said to be *called, invited, bidden*, or *summoned*.

CALLING. See VOCATION.
CALLOUS. See HARD.
CALM, COMPOSED, COLLECTED. *Calm* (see APPEASE). *Composed*, from the verb *compose*, marks the state of being *composed;* and *collected*, from *collect*, the state of being *collected*.

These terms agree in expressing a state; but *calm* respects the state of the feelings, *composed* the state of the thoughts and feelings, and *collected* the state of the thoughts more particularly. *Calmness* is peculiarly requisite in seasons of distress, and amidst scenes of horror: *composure*, in moments of trial, disorder, and tumult: *collectedness*, in moments of danger. *Calmness* is the companion of fortitude; no one whose spirits are easily disturbed can have strength to bear misfortune: *composure* is an attendant upon clearness of understanding; no one can express himself with perspicuity whose thoughts are any way deranged: *collectedness* is requisite for a determined promptitude of action; no one can be expected to act promptly who cannot think fixedly. It would argue a want of all feeling to be *calm* on some occasions, when the best affections of our nature are put to a severe trial. *Composedness* of mind associated with the detection of guilt evinces a hardened conscience and an insensibility to shame. *Collectedness* of mind has contributed in no small degree to the preservation of some persons' lives in moments of the most imminent peril.

See also ABATE; PEACE; QUELL; UNRUFFLED.

Calm, Placid, Serene.—*Calm* (see above). *Placid*, in Latin *placidus*, from *placeo*, please, signifies the state of being pleased, or free from uneasiness. *Serene* is derived from Latin *serenus*, bright, clear.

Calm and *serene* are applied to the elements; *placid* only to the mind. *Calmness* respects only the state of the winds, *serenity* that of the air and heavens; the weather is *calm* when it is free from agitation: it is *serene* when free from noise and vapor. *Calm* respects the total absence of all perturbation; *placid*, the ease and contentment of the mind; *serene*, clearness and composure of the mind.

As in the natural world a particular agitation of the wind is succeeded by a *calm*, so in the mind of man, when an unusual effervescence has been produced, it commonly subsides into a *calm; placidity* and *serenity* have more that is even and regular in them; they are positively what they are. *Calm* is a temporary state of the feelings; *placid* and *serene* are habits of the mind. We speak of a *calm* state, but a *placid* and *serene* temper. *Placidity* is more of a natural gift; *serenity* is acquired: people with not very ardent desires or warmth of feeling will evince *placidity;* they are pleased with all that passes inwardly or outwardly: nothing contributes so much to *serenity* of mind as a pervading sense of God's good providence, which checks all impatience, softens down every asperity of humor, and gives a steady current to the feelings.

CALUMNIATE. See ASPERSE.

CAMOUFLAGE, DISGUISE, MASK. *Camouflage* is a bit of trench slang which bids fair to become a naturalized English word. It is said to have been originally applied to the actor's make-up, and is derived through French *camoufler,* to disguise, from Latin *caput,* head, and Low Latin *muffulare,* to muffle. It referred to the covering of the head or disguising of the features in such a way as to escape recognition. It is now applied to the art of concealing or disguising guns, trenches, etc., in such a way that they appear to the enemy to be innocuous features of the natural scenery.

In meaning *camouflage* does not really differ from *disguise;* in most instances *disguise* may be substituted for it. But it is a much fresher and more picturesque term, and carries with it a definite suggestion of the romance and adventure of warfare. *Mask* is a word which also has the fundamental meaning of *disguise,* and suggests an image similar to that originally implied by *camouflage.* But it has not the vividness and timeliness of the new word.

CAN, MAY. *Can,* in the Northern languages *können,* etc., is derived, most probably, from *kennen,* to know, from the natural intimacy which subsists between knowledge and power. *May* is in German *mögen,* to desire or wish, its present meaning having developed from the connections between wishing and complying with a wish. *Can* denotes possibility, *may* liberty and probability: he who has sound limbs *can* walk; but he *may* not walk in places which are prohibited.

CANCEL. See ABOLISH; BLOT.

CANDID, OPEN, SINCERE. *Candid,* Latin *candidus,* from *candere,* to shine, signifies to be pure as truth itself. *Open,* Anglo-Saxon *ofen,* is possibly allied to *up,* and may have signified the lifting up of the tent door. *Sincere* comes from Latin *sincerus,* pure, unaffected.

Candor arises from a conscious purity of intentions; *openness,* from a warmth of feeling and love of communication; *sincerity,* from a love of truth.

Candor obliges us to acknowledge even that which may make against ourselves; it is disinterested: *openness* impels us to utter whatever passes in the mind; it is unguarded: *sincerity* prevents us from speaking what we do not think; it is positive. A *candid* man will have no reserve when *openness* is necessary; an *open* man cannot maintain a reserve at any time; a *sincere* man will maintain a reserve only as far as it is consistent with truth. *Candor* wins much upon those who come in connection with it; it removes misunderstandings and obviates differences; the want of it occasions suspicion and discontent. *Openness* gains as many enemies as friends; it requires to be well regulated not to be offensive; there is no mind so pure and disciplined that all the thoughts and feelings which it gives birth to may or ought to be made public. *Sincerity* is an indispensable virtue; the want of it is always mischievous, frequently fatal.

See also FRANK.

CANONIZATION. See BEATIFICATION.

CAPABLE. See ABLE.

CAPACIOUS. See ABLE; AMPLE.

CAPACITY, CAPACIOUSNESS. *Capacity* (see ABILITY) is the abstract of *capax*, receiving or apt to hold; it is therefore applied to the contents of hollow bodies. *Capaciousness* (see AMPLE) is the abstract of *capacious*, and is therefore applied to the plane surface comprehended within a given space. Hence we speak of the *capacity* of a vessel, and the *capaciousness* of a room.

Capacity is an indefinite term designating the property of being fit to hold or receive, as applied to bodies generally; but *capaciousness* denotes a fulness of this property as belonging to a particular object in a great degree. Measuring the *capacity* of vessels belongs to the science of mensuration: the *capaciousness* of a room is to be observed by the eye. They are marked by the same distinction in their moral application: men are born with various *capacities;* some are remarkable for the *capaciousness* of their minds.

CAPRICE. See HUMOR.

CAPRICIOUS. See FANCIFUL; HUMORSOME.

CAPTIOUS, CROSS, PEEVISH, PETULANT, FRETFUL. *Captious* is derived from Latin *captio,* a sophistical argument, from *capere,* to hold. *Cross,* after the noun *cross,* Latin *crux,* signifies a temper which is contrary to the wishes of others. *Peevish* is a word of imitative origin; the leading idea seems to have been to make a whining cry. *Fret,* Anglo-Saxon *fretan,* from *fra,* from, and *etan,* eat, signifies to eat away, hence a wearing and gnawing grief or anger. *Petulant,* Latin *petulans,* comes from the root found in *petere,* to seek, to fly toward, and signified originally a dissatisfied temper, one which was continually seeking something not in its possession.

All these terms indicate an unamiable working and expression of temper. *Captious* marks a readiness to be offended or come *across* the wishes of others; *peevish* expresses a strong degree of *crossness; fretful,* a complaining impatience; *petulant,* a quick or sudden impatience. *Captiousness* is the consequence of misplaced pride; *crossness,* of ill-humor; *peevishness* and *fretfulness,* of a painful irritability; *petu-lance* is either the result of a naturally hasty temper or of a sudden irritability: adults are most prone to be *captious;* they have frequently a self-importance which is in perpetual danger of being offended: an undisciplined temper, whether in young or old, will manifest itself on certain occasions by *cross* looks and words toward those with whom they come in connection: spoiled children are most apt to be *peevish;* they are seldom thwarted in any of their unreasonable desires without venting their ill-humor by an irritating and offending action: sickly children are mostly liable to *fretfulness,* their unpleasant feelings vent themselves in a mixture of crying, complaints, and *crossness:* the young and ignorant are most apt to be *petulant* when contradicted.

See also CYNICAL.

CAPTIVATE. See CHARM; ENSLAVE.

CAPTIVITY. See CONFINEMENT.

CAPTURE, SEIZURE, PRIZE. *Capture,* Latin *captura,* from *captus,* participle of *capere,* to take, signifies either the act of taking or the thing taken, but mostly the former. *Seizure,* in French *saisir,* comes from Late Latin *sacire,* to put, to place. *Prize,* French *prise,* the thing taken, from Latin *prehendere,* to take, signifies only the thing taken.

Capture and *seizure* differ in the *mode:* a *capture* is made by force of arms; a *seizure* by direct and personal force. The *capture* of a town or an island requires an army; the *seizure* of property is effected by the exertions of an individual.

A *seizure* always requires some force, but a *capture* may be effected without force on unresisting objects. Merchant vessels are *captured;* contraband goods are *seized,* or there may be an unlawful *seizure* of another's property.

Capture and *seizure* relate to the act of taking as well as the thing taken: *prize* relates only to the thing taken, and its value to the captor. There are many *captures* made at sea which never become *prizes;* the term *prize* is therefore applied to whatever valuable comes into our possession by our own efforts.

CARBUNCLE. See ANTHRAX.

CARCASS. See BODY.

CARDINAL, CHIEF, LEADING, MAIN. *Cardinal,* in Latin *cardinalis,* from *cardo,* a hinge, French *cardinal,* principal. The implication of a hinge in the term is said to have been derived from a letter erroneously attributed to Pope Anacletus I., in the first century, in which the apostolic chair was declared "the hinge and head of all the Churches and, as a door is controlled by its hinge, so all Churches are governed by this Holy Chair."

For the difference between *chief* and *main* see CHIEF. *Cardinal* differs from these two words mainly in the image that it suggests. *Chief* and *main* indicate objects, people, or ideas that are prominent by reason of position or size; *cardinal* indicates something that is important by reason of its relation to something else.

CARE, SOLICITUDE, ANXIETY. *Care,* Anglo-Saxon *caru,* anxiety, is allied to Old Saxon *kara,* sorrow, Old High German *chara,* a lament. *Solicitude,* from the same root as *solicit,* meant originally the state of being aroused or stirred up. *Anxiety,* from Latin *angere* (whence *anger* is also derived), to suffocate or torment, signifies a state of mental discomfort caused by uncertainty.

These terms express the application of the mind to any object. *Care* is the most indefinite of the three; it may be accompanied with pain or not, according to the nature of the object or the intensity of the application: *solicitude* and *anxiety* are accompanied with a positive degree of pain, the latter still more than the former. When *care* is employed in the discharge of any office, it may be without any feeling, but it is always accompanied with active exertions, as the *care* which a subordinate takes of a child. *Solicitude* and *anxiety* lie together in the mind, unaccompanied with any other action: *solicitude* has desire, mixed with fear; *anxiety* has distress for the present, mixed with fear for the future.

Care is inseparable from the business of life; there is nothing which is done but what requires *care* for it to be well done: *solicitude* and *anxiety* are produced by the events and circumstances of life, with this difference, that, as

solicitude has so much of desire in it, it is more under our control or may be more easily restrained than *anxiety,* which is forced upon us.

Care by its intensity and duration, and *anxiety* by its violence, may produce injurious effects; as worn out with *care,* overwhelmed with *anxiety.*

Solicitude is awakened only by ordinary events, and never rises to excess: there may be a *solicitude* to please, or a tender *solicitude* for the health of a person.

See also HEAL.

Care, Concern, Regard.—*Care* (see above). *Concern* (see AFFAIR) and *regard,* from Latin *re,* back, and French *garder,* to look at (from an Old High German root signifying to watch, or guard, found in *wary, ward,* etc., meaning to look back upon or look at attentively), are nearly allied to each other in denoting the application of the mind to any object.

Care, as in the former article, is either coupled with active exertions or is employed in the right doing of things; we take *care* to do a thing, or we bestow *care* upon a thing: *concern* and *regard* both lie in the mind, but in the former case the feelings as well as the thoughts, and in the latter case the thoughts only, have a part. *Concern* is particularly applied to that which awakens a painful interest in the mind, as to express or show a *concern* for another's troubles or distress; *regard* is applied to that which one values sufficiently to bestow one's thoughts upon.

Care and *concern* are also used to denote the object of caring or concerning, but *regard* is only employed for the action of regarding. The *care* is that which requires *care* to be bestowed upon it; *concern* is that in which one is concerned, or has a share or interest.

Care, Charge, Management.—*Care* (see above). *Charge,* in French *charge,* is derived from Late Latin *carricare,* to load a car, whence *cargo* is also derived. It is figuratively employed in the sense of a burden. *Management,* in French *ménagement,* is ultimately derived from Latin *manus,* hand, and signifies the doing or directing of something with the hand.

Care will include both *charge* and *management;* but, in the strict sense, it comprehends personal labor: *charge* involves responsibility: *management* includes regulation and order. A gardener has the *care* of a garden; a nurse has the *charge* of children; a steward has the *management* of a farm: we must always act in order to take *care;* we must always look in order to take *charge;* we must always think in order to *manage. Care* is employed generally in all matters, high and low, which require mental application or active exertion; *charge,* in matters of trust and confidence; *management,* in matters of business and experience: the servant has the *care* of the cattle; an *instructor* has the *charge* of youth; a clerk has the *management* of a business.

Careful, Cautious, Provident.—Careful, or full of care, that is, having *care,* is the general term. *Cautious,* that is, having *caution,* and *provident,* that is, literally foreseeing, are modes of the *careful.* To be *cautious* is to be *careful* in guarding against danger; to be *provident* is to be *careful* in preventing straits and difficulties. One is *careful* either in doing or in omitting to do: one is *cautious* in abstaining from doing, as to be *careful* in writing, or in the disposition of things; to be *cautious* not to offend, not to say anything.

When the terms *careful* and *cautious* are applied to what is to be avoided, the former is used in ordinary cases, where the difficulty of avoiding the evil is not great; the latter on extraordinary occasions, where the danger of falling into the evil is great.

The term *careful* is applied for the most part to present matters, but *provident* only to that which is future. One is *careful* of his money or his books, but *provident* toward a time of need.

These words are all employed to denote a habit of the mind or a characteristic of the person with a similar distinction, except that *caution,* being properly a virtue of the occasion, becomes excessive if it be always employed whether it be necessary or not.

See also ATTENTION.

CARELESS. See INDOLENT; NEGLIGENT.

CARESS, FONDLE. Both these terms mark a species of endearment. *Caress,* like *cherish,* and the French *chérir* and *cher,* comes from the Latin *carus,* dear, signifying the expression of a tender sentiment. *Fondle,* from *fond* (for derivation see under AFFECTION), is a frequentative verb, signifying to become *fond* of, or express one's *fondness* for.

We *caress* by words or actions; we *fondle* by actions only: *caresses* are not always unsuitable; but *fondling,* which is the extreme of *caressing,* is not less unfit for the one who receives than for the one who gives: animals *caress* each other, as the natural mode of indicating their affection; *fondling,* which is the expression of perverted feeling, is peculiar to human beings, who alone abuse the faculties with which they are endowed.

CARICATURE, BURLESQUE, EXAGGERATION, PARODY. *Caricature,* in Italian *caricatura,* a satirical picture, from *caricare,* to load, Low Latin *carrico,* load, from *carrus,* a cart, signifies literally, a picture that is overloaded with exaggeration, and, specifically, a twisted or distorted resemblance to a person or object, a figure, drawing, or description of a person or thing in which defects or peculiarities are greatly exaggerated in order to make the subject appear ludicrous. *Burlesque* is derived from Latin *burræ,* trifles, Italian *burlesco,* ludicrous, and signifies a trifling or ludicrous representation. *Exaggeration,* from Latin *ex,* an intensive prefix, and *agger,* heap, means a heaping up, hence a heightening by over - statement, over - coloring, etc. *Parody, parodia,* from Greek παρωδία (παρά, besides, and ὠδή, song, English *ode*), signified a song sung in imitation of another. All of these terms signify a humorous imitation, but they differ somewhat in their usual applications. *Caricature* generally refers to a humorous imitation of a person; *burlesque* to the imitation of an action or an occasion; and *parody* to the imitation of a literary production— of words either spoken or written. *Caricature* and *burlesque* are almost interchangeable, however. *Exaggeration* is a more general word. It signifies a humorous imitation which depends for its effect upon the heightening of certain features. An *exaggeration* may not be a *caricature* or a *burlesque*, though *caricatures* and *burlesques* usually depend upon *exaggeration* for the creation of the humorous effect.

CARGO. See FREIGHT.

CARNAGE, SLAUGHTER, MASSACRE, BUTCHERY. *Carnage,* from the Latin *caro, carnis,* flesh, implies properly a collection of dead flesh; that is, the reducing to the state of dead flesh. *Slaughter,* from *slay,* is the act of taking away life. *Massacre,* in French *massacre,* comes from Old French *maçacre,* shambles, slaughterhouse, the origin of which is unknown. *Butchery,* Old French *bochier,* signified originally the killing of goats, from Old French *boc,* a goat, German *bock,* English *buck.*

Carnage respects the number of dead bodies made; it may be said either of men or animals, but more commonly of the former: *slaughter* respects the act of taking away life, and the circumstances of the agent: *massacre* and *butchery* respect the circumstances of the objects who are the sufferers of the action; the last three are said of human beings only. *Carnage* is the consequence of any impetuous attack from a powerful enemy; soldiers who get into a besieged town, or a wolf that breaks into a sheepfold, commonly make a dreadful *carnage: slaughter* is the consequence of warfare; in battles the *slaughter* will be very considerable where both parties defend themselves pertinaciously: a *massacre* is the consequence of secret and personal resentment between bodies of people; it is always a stain upon the nation by whom it is practised, as it cannot be effected without a violent breach of confidence and a direct act of treachery; of this description was the *massacre* of the Danes by the original Britons: *butchery* is the general accompaniment of a *massacre;* defenceless women and children are commonly *butchered* by the savage furies who are most active in this work of blood.

CAROUSAL. See FEAST.

CARP. See CENSURE.

CARRIAGE, GAIT, WALK. *Carriage,* from the verb to *carry* (see BEAR), signifies the act of *carrying* in general, but here that of *carrying* the body.

Gait, allied to *go,* signifies the manner of going. *Walk* signifies the manner of *walking.*

Carriage is here the most general term; it respects the manner of *carrying* the body, whether in a state of motion or rest: *gait* is the mode of *carrying* the limbs and body whenever we move: *walk* is the manner of *carrying* the body when we move forward to *walk.* A person's *carriage* is somewhat natural to him; it is often an indication of character, but admits of great change by education; we may always distinguish a man as high or low, either in mind or station, by his *carriage; gait* is artificial; we may contract a certain *gait* by habit; the *gait* is therefore often taken for a bad habit of going, as when a person has a limping *gait* or an unsteady *gait: walk* is less definite than either, as it is applicable to the ordinary movements of men; there is a good, a bad, or an indifferent *walk;* but it is not a matter of indifference which of these kinds of *walk* we have; it is the great art of the dancing-master to give a good *walk.*

See also BEHAVIOR.

CARRY. See BEAR; BRING.

CASE, CAUSE. *Case,* in Latin *casus,* from *cadere,* to fall, happen, signifies the thing falling out. *Cause,* in French *cause,* comes from Latin *causa,* a cause.

The *case* is matter of fact; the *cause* is matter of question: a *case* involves circumstances and consequences; a *cause* involves reasons and arguments: a *case* is something to be learned; a *cause* is something to be decided. A *case* needs only to be stated; a *cause* must be defended: a *cause* may include *cases,* but not *vice versa:* in all *causes* that are to be tried there are many legal *cases* that must be cited: whoever is interested in the *cause* of humanity will not be heedless of those *cases* of distress which are perpetually presenting themselves.

See also SITUATION.

CASH. See MONEY.

CAST, THROW, HURL. *Cast* is a Scandinavian word signifying to throw. *Throw,* Anglo-Saxon *thrawan,* originally meant to twist. *Hurl* is a Scandinavian word of imitative origin.

These terms all express the idea of sending one object from another. To *cast* is often a negative act, to *throw* is always positive. We *cast* off clothes by simply ceasing to wear them, but we *throw off* clothes by removing them from the person with an actual effort. Hence the word *cast* is most aptly applied when the manner of the action is left undefined, and the word *throw* when it is intended to be expressly defined; as to *cast* anchor, which may either be done by simply letting it down or by sending it forth from one with force: so to *cast* seed into the ground may be simply to let it fall in, or to *cast* anything into a box; but to *throw* anything into the sea, or to *throw* seed into the ground, implies a specific act done in a specific manner.

For the same reason *casting* is applied to what is done by a process of nature, as animals *cast* their young, or *cast* their coats, or to what is acted on by unconscious agents; as a ship or a person is *cast* on a shore.

Throwing is not merely an act of direct purpose, but frequently of a violent or offensive purpose; as to *throw* stones or dust at a person, to *throw* down the gauntlet.

So to *cast* a glance may be simply to direct the eye to an object, but to *throw* an angry look is the result of anger.

The word *cast*, from the generality of its meaning, is properly employed in the higher style of writing, and in reference to higher subjects: when *throw* is used in respect to any but familiar subjects, it is taken figuratively; as to *throw* a veil over a matter, to *throw* light upon a subject.

When applied to similar objects, they preserve the same distinction; *throwing* requires a greater effort or more violence than *casting*, as to *cast* away prejudices, to throw off habits, etc.

To *hurl* is a violent species of *throwing*, employed only on extraordinary occasions. Sometimes it denotes the vehemence of the agent: but still oftener the magnitude of the occasion or the extremity of the occasion. The giants, who made war against heaven, are feigned to have been *hurled* by the thunderbolts of Jupiter down to the earth.

Cast, Turn, Description.—*Cast*, from the verb to *cast* (see above), signifies that which is *cast*, and here, by an ex-

tension of the sense, the form in which it is *cast*. *Turn*, from the verb to *turn*, signifies also the act of *turning* or the manner of being *turned*. *Description* signifies the act of *describing*, or the thing which is to be *described*.

What is *cast* is artificial; what *turns* is natural: the former is the act of some foreign agent; the latter is the act of the subject itself: hence *cast*, as applicable to persons, respects that which they are made by circumstances; *turn*, that which they are by themselves: thus there are religious *castes* in India, that is, men *cast* in a certain form of religion; and men of a particular moral *cast*, that is, such as are *cast* in a particular mould as respects their thinking and acting: so in like manner men of a particular *turn*, that is, as respects their inclinations and tastes.

The *cast* is that which marks a man to others; the *turn* is that which may be known only to a man's self; the *description* is that by which he is *described* or made known to others.

CASUAL. See ACCIDENTAL; OCCASIONAL.

CASUALTY. See ACCIDENT.

CATALOGUE. See LIST.

CATEGORICAL, UNQUALIFIED, POSITIVE. *Categorical* is derived from Greek καταγορία, an accusation, and is in logic an unconditional statement, one which does not depend upon a hypothesis or any modifying qualification. Hence the word has been extended to mean in general an *unqualified* or *positive* statement. These two adjectives, though synonymous here, have different original meanings. *Unqualified* comes from Latin *qualis*, how much, and means not questioning or indicating how much—not modified in accordance with any possible standard of measurement. *Positive*, from *positus*, the past participle of *ponere*, means placed, ready to stand, unmovable.

CAUCUS, PRIVATE MEETING. In this case *caucus* represents a species of the *genus* indicated in the words *private meeting*. *Caucus* is a purely American term, possibly of American Indian origin, from the Algonkin *kaw-kaw-asu*, a counsellor. It has, strictly speaking, no real synonymes. The term applies chiefly to political gatherings, or private meetings of representatives of a party, faction, or interest, called to consider a situation and to plan a programme for action.

A *caucus* by different political parties is generally held prior to an election, at which candidates for office are selected and arrangements perfected for the ensuing campaign. Members of the Congress, of State legislatures, of municipal bodies, and even of smaller organizations, meet in *caucus* prior to the opening sessions, or when deemed necessary, at any time during a session. Members who are entitled to attend a *caucus* and, from dissatisfaction or other cause fail to do so, are said to *bolt the caucus*—that is, they won't be bound to any action on which the *caucus* has decided.

CAUSE, REASON, MOTIVE. *Cause* is supposed to signify originally the same as case; it means, however, now, by distinction, the case or thing happening before another as its *cause*. *Reason*, in French *raison*, Latin *ratio*, from *ratus*, participle of *reor*, to think, signifies the thing thought, estimated, or valued in the mind. *Motive*, in French *motif*, from the Latin *motus*, participle of *movere*, to move, signifies the thing that brings into action.

Cause respects the order and connection of things; *reason*, the movements and operations of the mind; *motives*, the movements of the mind and body. *Cause* is properly the generic term; *reason* and *motive* are specific: every *reason* or *motive* is a *cause*, but every *cause* is not a *reason* or *motive*. *Cause* is said of all inanimate objects; *reason* and *motive*, of rational agents: whatever happens in the world happens from some *cause* mediate or immediate; the primary or first *cause* of all is God: whatever opinions men hold, they ought to be able to assign a substantial *reason* for them; and for whatever they do, they ought to have a sufficient *motive*.

As the *cause* gives birth to the effect, so does the *reason* give birth to the conclusion, and the *motive* gives birth to the action. Between *cause* and effect there is a necessary connection: whatever in the natural world is capable of giving birth to another thing is an adequate *cause;* but in the moral world there is not a necessary connection between *reasons* and their results, or *motives* and their actions; the state of the agent's mind is not always such as to be acted upon according to the nature of things: every adequate *reason* will not be followed by its natural conclusion, for every man will not believe who has *reasons* to believe, nor yield to the *reasons* that would lead to a right belief; and every *motive* will not be accompanied with its corresponding action, for every man will not act who has a *motive* for acting, nor act in the manner in which his *motives* ought to dictate.

Cause, Occasion, Create.—To *cause*, from the substantive *cause*, naturally signifies to be the *cause* of. *Occasion*, from the noun *occasion*, signifies to be the *occasion* of. *Create* is, in Latin, *creatus*, participle of *creare*, to make.

What is *caused* seems to follow naturally; what is *occasioned* follows incidentally; or what *occasions* may be incidental, but necessary: what is *created* receives its existence arbitrarily. A wound *causes* pain; accidents *occasion* delay; busybodies *create* mischief. The misfortunes of children *cause* great affliction to their parents; business *occasions* a person's late attendance at a place; disputes and misunderstandings *create* animosity and ill-will. The *cause* of a person's misfortune may often be traced to his own misconduct: the improper behavior of one person may *occasion* another to ask for an explanation: jealousies are *created* in the minds of relatives by an unnecessary reserve and distance.

CAUTION. See ADMONISH; CAVEAT.

CAUTIOUS, WARY, CIRCUMSPECT. For *cautious* see CAREFUL. *Wary*, Anglo-Saxon *wær*, is allied to *ward*, *guard*, etc., and to the Greek ὁράω, I see. *Circumspect*, from *circumspicio*, look about, signifies literally looking on all sides. The idea of using great care for the preventing of evil is common to these terms, but they vary in the degree and object of the care. *Cautious* expresses less than *wary:* we must be *cautious* on all occasions where there is danger, but we must be *wary* where there is great danger. A tradesman must be cautious in his dealings with all men, but he must be *wary* when he has to deal with designing men.

Cautious and *wary* are used in reference to practical matters, or the common matters of business, where the senses or bodily powers are more exercised than the mind: *circumspect* is used in reference to matters of theory or contemplation, when the mind is principally employed. A traveler must be *cautious* in passing along a road that is not familiar to him; he must be *wary* in passing over slippery and dangerous places. A man must be *circumspect* when he transacts business of particular importance and delicacy. Hence it is that *cautious* and *wary* may be said of the brute creation; *circumspect* only of rational beings.

CAVEAT, CAUTION, WARNING. *Caveat*, in Latin the same form, implying let him beware, from *cavere*, to beware, signifies, in law, a judicial warning or caution, an intimation to stay proceedings, an intimation or notice by a party interested in an approaching procedure to the proper officer, to prevent the latter from taking any action without an intimation or notice being given to the said party to enable him to appear and object. A *caveat* is commonly filed with the proper officer against the probating of a will by an interested party to enable him to contest it or file objections against its probate. Until the *caveat* is withdrawn by the person who filed it, the probating process is halted.

Hence *caveat* represents a species of the genus indicated in *caution* (from the same Latin verb, *caveo*), and *warning* (allied to *wary*). Of these two words *warning* is a stronger word than *caution*. We *caution* others against something which may prove annoying or inconvenient; we *warn* them against something really dangerous.

CAVIL. See CENSURE.

CAVITY. See OPENING.

CEASE, LEAVE OFF, DISCONTINUE. *Cease*, in French *cesser*, Latin *cessare*, a frequentative of *cedere*, to yield, signifies to give up or put an end to. *Leave*, from Anglo-Saxon *leaf*, permission, is derived from the same root found in the adjective *lief*, dear or pleasing. *Discontinue*, with the priva-tive *dis*, expresses the opposite of *continue*.

To *cease* is neuter; to *leave off* and *discontinue* are active: we *cease* from doing a thing; we *leave off* or *discontinue* a thing. *Cease* is used either for particular actions or general habits: *leave off* more usually and properly for particular actions; *discontinue* for general habits. A restless, spoiled child never *ceases* crying until it has obtained what it wants; it is a mark of impatience not to *cease* lamenting when one is in pain. A laborer *leaves off* his work at any given hour. A delicate person *discontinues* his visits when they are found not to be agreeable. It should be our first endeavor to *cease* to do evil. It is never good to *leave off* working while there is anything to do and time to do it in. The *discontinuing* a good practice without adequate grounds evinces great instability of character.

CEDE. See GIVE UP.

CELEBRATE, COMMEMORATE. *Celebrate*, in Latin *celebratus*, participle of *celebrare*, from *celeber*, populous, signifies to gather a big assembly for some festive purpose. *Commemorate*, in Latin *commemoratus*, participle of *commemoro*, compounded of *com* or *cum* and *memoro*, to keep in mind, signifies to keep in the memory of a number.

Commemorate is a species of *celebrating;* we always *commemorate* when we *celebrate*, but not *vice versa*. Everything is *celebrated* which is distinguished by any marks of attention, without regard to the time of the event, whether present or past; but nothing is *commemorated* but what has been past. A marriage or a birthday is *celebrated;* the anniversary of any national event is *commemorated*. *Celebrating* is not limited to any species of events or circumstances; whatever interests any number of persons is *celebrated: commemorating* is confined to whatever is thought of sufficient importance to be borne in mind, whether of a public or private nature. The election of a favorite member is *celebrated* by those who have contributed to his success: a remarkable preservation, whether national or individual, sometimes demands some signal act of *commemoration*.

Celebrating is a festive as well as social act; it may be sometimes serious, but it is mostly mingled with more or less of gayety and mirth: *commemorating* is a solemn act; it may be sometimes festive and social, but it is always mingled with what is serious, and may be altogether solitary; it is suited to the occasion, and calculated to revive in the mind suitable impressions of what is just. The birthday of our sovereign is always *celebrated* by his people with such marks of honor and congratulation as are due from subjects to a prince: the providential escape of our nation from destruction by the Gunpowder Plot is annually *commemorated* by a public act of devotion, as also by popular demonstrations of joy. The Jews *celebrate* their feast of the Passover: as Christians, we *commemorate* the sufferings and death of our Saviour by partaking of the Lord's Supper.

CELEBRATED. See FAMOUS.

CELERITY. See QUICKNESS.

CELESTIAL, HEAVENLY. *Celestial* and *heavenly* derive their difference in signification from their different origin: they both literally imply belonging to heaven; but the former, from the Latin *cœlum*, signifies belonging to the *heaven* of heathens; the latter, which has its origin among believers in the true God, has acquired a superior sense, in regard to *heaven* as the habitation of the Almighty. This distinction is pretty faithfully observed in their application: *celestial* is applied mostly in the natural sense of the *heavens; heavenly* is employed more commonly in a spiritual sense. Hence we speak of the *celestial* globe as distinguished from the terrestrial; of the *celestial* bodies; of Olympus, as the *celestial* abode of Jupiter; of the *celestial* deities.

But, on the other hand, of the *heavenly* habitation, of *heavenly* joys or bliss, of *heavenly* spirits, and the like. See also ETHEREAL.

CEMETERY. See NECROPOLIS.

CENSOR, CRITIC, EXAMINER, INSPECTOR. These terms all signify an official whose duty it is to see documents, publications, public performances, etc., and to pass judgment upon them. But *examiner* and *inspector* emphasize the act of seeing; *censor* and *critic* that of judging.

Examiner (for the derivation of *examine* see DISCUSS) is a stronger word than *inspector*. *Examine* means to *inspect* with particular care, with the intention of passing a judgment. Similarly *critic* is a milder and more general term than *censor* (from Latin *censere*, to rate). To *censor* is not merely to judge, but to abolish that which proves to be contrary to the *censor's* judgment. These terms differ also in their applications. *Censor* is applied particularly to the examining and judging of literary material—letters and cables in time of war, books, newspapers, etc.—and of artistic public productions. A rigorous *censorship* of mail, etc., was maintained in all belligerent countries during the European war. The term *inspector* is applied to various public officials whose duty it is to detect any violation of the laws—health - *inspectors*, milk-*inspectors*, customs-*inspectors*, etc. The terms *critic* and *examiner* are less frequently used to refer to public officials.

CENSURE, ANIMADVERT, CRITICISE. *Censure* (see ACCUSE). *Animadvert* and *criticise* (see ANIMADVERSION).

To *censure* expresses less than to *animadvert* or *criticise;* one may always *censure* when one *animadverts* or *criticises.* To *censure* and *animadvert* are both personal, the one direct, the other indirect; *criticism* is directed to things, and not to persons only. *Censuring* consists in finding some fault, real or supposed: it refers mostly to the conduct of individuals. *Animadvert* consists in suggesting some error or impropriety; it refers mostly to matters of opinion and dispute; *criticism* consists in minutely examining the intrinsic characteristics and appreciating the merits of each individually or the whole collectively; it refers to matters of science and learning. To *censure* requires no more than simple assertion; its justice or propriety often rests on the authority of the individual: *animadversions* require to be accompanied with reasons; those who *animadvert* on the proceedings or opinions of others must state some grounds for their objections. *Criticism* is altogether argumentative and illustrative; it takes nothing for granted, it analyzes and decomposes, it compares and combines, it asserts and supports the assertions. The office of the *censurer* is the easiest and least honorable of the three; it may be assumed by ignorance and impertinence, it may be performed for the purpose of indulging an angry or imperious temper. The task of *animadverting* is delicate; it may be resorted to for the indulgence of an overweening self-conceit. The office of a *critic* is both arduous and honorable; it cannot be filled by any one incompetent for the charge without exposing his arrogance and folly to merited contempt.

See also BLAME; LASH.

Censure, Carp, Cavil.—Censure (see above). *Carp*, a Scandinavian word, appears in Middle English with the meaning of to talk (in Icelandic it meant to boast). The present sinister sense is apparently due to a confusion with Latin *carpere*, to pluck. *Cavil*, in French *caviller*, Latin *cavillor*, from *cavilla*, a taunt, and *cavus*, hollow, signifies to be unsound or unsubstantial in speech.

To *censure* respects positive errors; to *carp* and *cavil* have regard to what is trivial or imaginary: the former is employed for errors in persons; the latter for supposed defects in things. *Censures* are frequently necessary from those who have the authority to use them; a good father will *censure* his children when their conduct is *censurable*. *Carping* and *cavilling* are resorted to only to indulge ill-nature or self-conceit: whoever owes another a grudge will be most disposed to *carp* at all he does, in order to lessen him in the esteem of others: those who contend more for victory than truth will be apt to *cavil* when they are at a loss for fair argument: party politicians *carp* at the measures of administration; infidels *cavil* at the evidences of Christianity, because they are determined to disbelieve.

CEREMONIAL. See FORMAL.

CEREMONIOUS. See FORMAL; THEATRICAL.

CEREMONY. See ETIQUETTE; FORM.

CERTAIN, SURE, SECURE. *Certain*, in French *certain*, Latin *certus*, comes from *cernere*, to discriminate. *Sure* and *secure* are variations of the same word, in French *sûr*, German *sicher*, Latin *securus;* this is compounded of *se* (sine), apart, and *cura*, care, signifying without care, requiring no care.

Certain and *sure* have regard to a person's convictions; *secure* to his interests or condition: one is *certain* from actual knowledge or from a belief in others; one is *sure* from a reliance upon others; one is *secure* when free from danger. We can be *certain* of nothing future but death; we may be *sure* that God will fulfil His promises in His own way; we may be *secure* against any loss or mischief if we use proper precautions. In respect to things the distinction is similar: facts, principles, and rules are *certain* which are certainly known and admitted: rules, methods, guides, etc., are *sure* which guard against error and may be depended upon; a place may be *secure* which serves to *secure* or preserve with certainty from mischief or danger.

See also INFALLIBLE; TANGIBLE.

CERTAINLY. See AYE.

CESSATION, STOP, INTERMISSION. *Cessation*, from the verb to *cease*, marks the condition of leaving off. *Stop*, from to *stop*, marks that of being *stopped* or prevented from going on. *Rest*, from to *rest*, marks the state of being quiet; and *intermission*, from *intermit*, marks that of *ceasing* occasionally.

To *cease* respects the course of things; whatever does not go on has *ceased;* things *cease* of themselves: *stop* respects some external action or influence; nothing *stops* but what is supposed to be *stopped* or hindered by another: *rest* is a species of *cessation* that regards labor or exertion; whatever does not move or exert itself is at *rest: intermission* is a species of *cessation* only for a time or at certain intervals. That which *ceases* or *stops* is supposed to be at an end; *rest* or *intermission* supposes a renewal. A *cessation* of hostilities is at all times desirable; to put a *stop* to evil practices is sometimes the most difficult and dangerous of all undertakings: *rest* after fatigue is indispensable, for labor without *intermission* exhausts the frame. The rain *ceases*, a person or a ball *stops* running, the laborer *rests* from his toil, a fever is *intermittent*.

There is nothing in the world which does not *cease* to exist at one point or another: death *stops* every one sooner or later in his career: whoever is vexed with the cares of getting riches will find no *rest* for his mind or body; he will labor without *intermission* oftentimes only to heap troubles on himself.

CHAFE. See RUB.

CHAGRIN. See VEXATION.

CHAIN, FETTER, BAND, SHACKLE. *Chain*, in French *chaîne*, Latin *catena*, signifies that which takes or holds. *Fetter*, Anglo-Saxon *fetor*, meant a shackle for the *foot*, and is allied to the word *foot*, *feet*. *Band*, from *bind*, signifies that which *binds*. *Shackle*, Anglo-Saxon *sceacul*, bond, fetter, was originally a loose band which shook when the captive moved, *shackle* being from the same root as *shake*.

All these terms designate the instrument by which animals or men are confined. *Chain* is general and indefinite; all the rest are species of *chains:* but there are many *chains* which do not come under the other names; a *chain* is indefinite as to its make; it is made generally of iron rings, but of different sizes and shapes: *fetters* are larger; they consist of many stout *chains: bands* are in general anything which confines the body or the limbs; they may be either *chains* or even cords: *shackle* is that species of *chain* which goes on the legs to confine them; malefactors of the worst order have *fetters* on different parts of their bodies, and *shackles* on their legs.

These terms may all be used figuratively. The substantive *chain* is applied generally to whatever confines like a *chain*, and the verb to *chain* signifies to confine as with a *chain:* thus the mind is *chained* to rules, according to the opinions of the freethinkers, when men adhere strictly to rule and order: the noun *fetter* is seldom used except in the proper sense, but the verb to *fetter* signifies to control or prevent the proper exercise of the mind, as to be *fettered* by systems. *Band*, in the figurative sense, is applied, particularly in poetry, to everything which is supposed to serve the purpose of a *band;* thus love is said to have its silken *bands*. *Shackle*, whether as a substantive or a verb, retains the idea of impeding the progress of a person, not in his body only, but also in his mind and in his moral conduct; thus a man who commences life with a borrowed capital is *shackled* in his commercial concerns by the interest he has to pay and the obligations he has to discharge.

CHALLENGE. See BRAVE.

CHAMPION. See COMBATANT.

CHANCE, FORTUNE, FATE. *Chance* (see ACCIDENT) is here considered as the cause of what falls out. *Fortune*, in French *fortune*, Latin *fortuna*, comes from *fors*, chance, allied to *ferre*, to bear —fortune being that which is brought to one, borne in upon the sufferer. *Fate*, in Latin *fatum*, from *fatum*, participle of *fari*, to speak or decree, signifies that which is decreed, or the power of decreeing.

These terms have served at all times as cloaks for human ignorance; and before mankind was favored by the light of Divine Revelation they had an imaginary importance which has now happily vanished. Believers in Divine Providence no longer conceive the events of the world as left to themselves, or as under the control of any unintelligent or unconscious agent, but ascribe the whole to an overruling mind, which, though invisible to the bodily eye, is clearly to be traced by the intellectual eye wherever we turn ourselves. In conformity, however, to the preconceived notions attached to these words, we now employ them in regard to the agency of secondary causes. But how far a Christian may use them, without disparagement to the majesty of the Divine Being, it is not so much my business to inquire as to define their ordinary acceptation. In this ordinary sense *chance* is the generic, *fortune* and *fate* are specific terms: *chance* applies to all things, personal or otherwise; *fortune* and *fate* are mostly said of that which is personal. *Chance* neither forms, orders, nor designs; neither knowledge nor intention is attributed to it; its events are uncertain and variable: *fortune* forms plans and designs, but without choice; we attribute to it an intention without discernment; it is said to be blind: *fate* forms plans and chains of causes; intention, knowledge, and power are attributed to it; its views are fixed, its results decisive. A person goes as *chance* directs him when he has no express object to determine his choice one way or other; his *fortune* favors him if without any expectation he gets the thing he wishes; his *fate* wills it if he reaches the desired point contrary to what he intended. Men's success in their undertakings depends oftener on *chance* than on their ability; we are ever ready to ascribe to ourselves what we owe to our good *fortune;* it is the *fate* of some men to fail in everything they undertake. When speaking of trivial matters this language is unquestionably innocent, and any objection to its use must spring from an overscrupulous conscience. If I suffer my horse to direct me in the road I take to London, I may fairly attribute it to *chance* if I take the right instead of the left; and if in consequence I meet with an agreeable companion by the way, I shall not hesitate to call it my good *fortune;* and if, in spite of any previous intention to the contrary, I should be led to take the same road repeatedly, and as often meet with an agreeable companion, I shall immediately say that it is my *fate* to meet with an agreeable companion whenever I go to London.

See also HAPPEN.

Chance, Probability. — *Chance* (see above). *Probability*, in French *probabilité*, Latin *probabilitas*. from *probabilis* and *probare*, to prove, signifies the quality of being able to be proved or made good.

These terms are both employed in forming an estimate of future events; but the *chance* is either for or against, the *probability* is always for a thing. *Chance* is but a degree of *probability;* there may in this latter case be a *chance* where there is no *probability*. A *chance* affords a possibility; many *chances* are requisite to constitute a *probability*. What has been once may, under similar circumstances, be again; for that there is a *chance;* what has fallen to one man may fall to another; so far he has a *chance* in his favor; but in all the *chances* of life there will be no *prob-*

ability of success where a man does not unite industry with integrity. *Chance* cannot be calculated upon; it is apt to produce disappointment; *probability* justifies hope; it is sanctioned by experience.

Chance, Hazard. — *Chance* (see above). *Hazard* comes from Spanish *azar*, an unlucky throw at dice, possibly allied to Arabian *al zahr*, but the ultimate origin is doubtful.

Both these terms are employed to mark the course of future events, which is not discernible by the human eye. With the Deity there is neither *chance* nor *hazard;* His plans are the result of omniscience: but the designs and actions of men are all dependent on *chance* or *hazard*. *Chance* may be favorable or unfavorable, more commonly the former: *hazard* is always unfavorable; it is properly a species of *chance*. There is a *chance* either of gaining or losing; there is a *hazard* ot losing. In most speculations the *chance* of succeeding scarcely outweighs the *hazard* of losing.

CHANGE, ALTER, VARY. *Change,* in French *changer*, is probably derived from the Middle Latin *cambio, exchange*, signifying to take one thing for another. *Alter*, from the Latin *alter*, another, signifies to make a thing otherwise. *Vary*, in Latin *vario*, make various, from *varius*, doubtful.

We *change* a thing by putting another in its place; we *alter* a thing by making it different from what it was before; we *vary* it by *altering* it in different manners and at different times. We *change* our clothes whenever we put on others: the tailor *alters* clothes which are found not to fit; and he *varies* the fashion of making them whenever he makes new. A man *changes* his habits, *alters* his conduct, and *varies* his manner of speaking and thinking, according to circumstances. A thing is *changed* without *altering* its kind; it is *altered* without destroying its identity; and it is *varied* without destroying the similarity. We *change* our habitation, but it still remains a habitation; we *alter* our house, but it still remains the same house; we *vary* the manner of painting and decoration, but it may strongly resemble the manner in which it has been before executed.

Change, Exchange, Barter, Substitute. —*Change* (see preceding). *Exchange* is compounded of *e* or *ex* and *changer*, signifying to *change* in the place of another. *Barter* is supposed to come from the French *barater*, to cheat or beguile, the ultimate origin of which is doubtful. *Substitute*, in French *substitut*, Latin *substitutus*, from *sub*, instead of, and *statuere*, to place, signifies to place one thing in the room of another.

The idea of putting one person or thing in the place of another is common to all these terms, which varies in the manner and the object. *Change* is the generic, the rest are specific terms: whatever is *exchanged*, *bartered*, or *substituted* is changed, but not *vice versa*. To *change* in respect to persons is to take one for another, without regard to whether they are alike or different, as a king *changes* his ministers; to *exchange* is to take one person in return for another who is in like condition, as prisoners are *exchanged* in time of war.

In respect to things, to *change* is to take anything new or fresh, whether alike or different. Clothes may be *changed*, or books may be *changed*, or things may be *changed* for others quite different; to *exchange* is to take one thing for another, that is, either of the same kind or equivalent in value, as to *exchange* one commodity for another, one house, or one piece of land, for another. To *change* may often be the result of caprice, but to *exchange* is always an act either of discretion or necessity.

To *barter* is a species of *exchanging*, namely, the giving of any commodity for others of the same or a different kind; it is confined properly to what passes by way of commerce, as, in dealing with savages, to *barter* toys or knives for provisions.

To *substitute* is to put one person in the place of another for the purpose of doing any service or filling any office, as to *substitute* one for another who has been drawn for the militia.

In the moral application these terms bear the same analogy to each other, with this difference, that the word *barter* is taken in a bad sense. A person *changes* his opinions; but a proneness to such *changes* evinces a want of firmness in the character. A good king at his death *exchanges* a temporal for an eternal crown. The mercenary trader *barters* his conscience for paltry pelf. Men of dogmatical tempers *substitute* assertion for proof, and abuse for argument.

Change, Variation, Vicissitude. —*Change* and *variation* (see preceding). *Vicissitude*, in French *vicissitude*, Latin *vicissitudo*, from *vicissim*, by turns, signifies changing alternately.

Change is, both to *vicissitude* and *variation*, as the genus to the species. Every *variation* or *vicissitude* is a *change*, but every *change* is not a *variation* or *vicissitude*. *Change* consists simply in ceasing to be the same: *variation* consists in being different at different times; *vicissitude*, in being alternately or reciprocally different and the same. All created things are liable to *change*; old things pass away, all things become new: the humors of men, like the elements, are exposed to perpetual *variations*: human affairs, like the seasons, are subject to frequent *vicissitudes*. *Changes* in societies or families are seldom attended with any good effect. *Variations* in the state of the atmosphere are indicated by the barometer or thermometer. *Vicissitudes* of a painful nature are less dangerous than those which elevate men to an unusual state of grandeur. By the former they are brought to a sense of themselves, by the latter they are carried beyond themselves.

Changeable, Mutable, Variable, Inconstant, Fickle, Versatile. —*Changeable*, ready to change. *Mutable*, from the Latin *mutare*, to change, is the same as *changeable*. *Variable* means liable to *vary*. *Inconstant*, compounded of the privative *in* and *constant*, in Latin *constans*, from *con* and *stare*, to stand together or remain the same, signifies not remaining the same for any long continuance. *Fickle*, Anglo-Saxon *ficol*, is allied to *fœcne*, deceitful, and *facen*, fraud. *Versatile*, in Latin *versatilis*, from *verto*, to turn, signifies easy to be turned.

Changeable is said of persons or things; *mutable* is said of things only: human beings are *changeable*, human affairs are *mutable*.

Changeable respects the sentiments

and opinions of the mind; *variable*, the state of the feelings; *inconstant*, the affections; *fickle*, the inclinations and attachments; *versatile*, the application of the talents. A *changeable* person rejects what he has once embraced in order to take up something new; a *variable* person likes and dislikes alternately the same thing; an *inconstant* person likes nothing long; a *fickle* person likes many things successively or at the same time; a *versatile* person has a talent for whatever he likes. *Changeableness* arises from a want of fixed principles; *variableness*, from a predominance of humor; *inconstancy*, from a selfish and unfeeling temper; *fickleness*, from a lightness of mind; *versatility*, from a flexibility of mind. Men are the most *changeable* and *inconstant;* women are the most *variable* and *fickle:* the former offend from an indifference for objects in general or a diminished attachment for any object in particular; the latter from an excessive warmth of feeling that is easily biassed and ready to seize new objects. People who are *changeable* in their views and plans are particularly unfit for the government of a state; those who are *variable* in their humors are unsuitable as masters; people of an *inconstant* character ought to be shunned as lovers; those of a *fickle* disposition ought not to be chosen as friends. *Changeable, variable, inconstant,* and *fickle,* as applied to persons, are taken in the bad sense; but *versatility* is a natural gift which may be employed advantageously.

CHANNEL. See TRENCH.

CHAPERON, ATTENDANT, GUIDE. Of these terms *attendant* is the general word: *guide* and *chaperon* indicate particular kinds of attendants. For the meaning and derivation of *attendant* see ACCOMPANY. A *chaperon,* French *chaperon,* Italian *capperone,* the wearer of a hooded *cape,* signifies a woman who accompanies a young girl in public places to *guide* her, and protect her from annoyance. The term *guide* is applied to attendants whose function it is to point out the way to others— such as mountain-*guides, guides* in large museums or public galleries, etc.

CHARACTER, LETTER. *Character* comes from the Greek χάρακτήρ, signifying an impression or mark, from χαράσσειν, to imprint or stamp. *Letter* is derived from Latin *littera,* a letter.

Character is to *letter* as the genus to the species: every *letter* is a *character;* but every *character* is not a *letter. Character* is any written or printed mark that serves to designate something; a *letter* is a species of *character* which is the constituent part of a word. Shorthand and hieroglyphics consist of *characters,* but not of *letters. Character* is employed figuratively, but *letter* is not. A grateful person has the favors which are conferred upon him written in indelible *characters* upon his heart.

Character, Reputation. — From the natural sense of a stamp or mark. *Character* (see above) is figuratively employed for the moral mark which distinguishes one man from another. *Reputation,* from the French *réputer,* Latin *reputare,* to think, signifies what is thought of a person.

Character lies in the man; it is the mark of what he is; it shows itself on all occasions: *reputation* depends upon others; it is what they think of him. A *character* is given particularly: a *reputation* is formed generally. Individuals give a *character* of another from personal knowledge: public opinion constitutes the *reputation. Character* has always some foundation; it is a positive description of something: *reputation* has more of conjecture in it; its source is hearsay. It is possible for a man to have a fair *reputation* who has not in reality a good *character,* although men of really good *character* are not likely to have a bad *reputation.*

CHARACTERIZE. See NAME.

CHARGE. See ACCUSE; ATTACK; CARE; COST; OFFICE.

CHARM, ENCHANT, FASCINATE, ENRAPTURE, CAPTIVATE. *Charm* (see ATTRACTION). *Enchant,* French *enchanter,* is derived from Latin *in,* in, and *cantare,* to sing, whence *incantation* is also derived. It signified to sing to another until the music entered *into* the hearer, as it were, and had some magical or hypnotic effect upon his soul. *Fascinate* is derived from Latin *fascinum,* a spell. *Enrapture,* compounded of *en* and *rapture*, signifies to put into a *rapture;* and *rapture*, from the Latin *rapio*, to seize or carry away, signifies the state of being carried away; whence to *enrapture* signifies to put into that state. *Captivate*, in Latin *captivatus*, participle of *captivo*, from *capere*, to take, signifies to take, as it were, prisoner.

To *charm* expresses a less powerful effect than to *enchant;* a *charm* is simply a magical verse used by magicians and sorcerers: *incantation* or *enchantment* is the use not only of verses, but of any mysterious ceremonies, to produce a given effect. To *charm* and *enchant* in this sense denotes an operation by means of words or motions; to *fascinate* denotes an operation by means of the eyes or tongue: the two former are less powerful acts than the latter: the superstitious have always had recourse to *charms* or *enchantments*, for the purpose of allaying the passions of love or hatred; the Greeks believed that the malignant influence passed by *fascination* from the eyes or tongues of envious persons, which infected the ambient air, and through that medium penetrated and corrupted the bodies of animals and other things. *Charms* and *enchantments* are performed by persons; *fascinations* are performed by animals: the former have always some supposed good in view; the latter have always a mischievous tendency: there are persons who pretend to *charm* away the toothache, or other pains of the body: some serpents are said to have a *fascinating* power in their eyes by which they can kill the animals on which they have fixed them.

To *charm, enchant,* and *fascinate* are taken in the improper sense to denote moral as well as natural operations; *enrapture* and *captivate* have a moral application only, in reference to those things which act more on the imagination or the moral feelings than on the senses. To *charm* in this case is to act as a charm; to *enchant*, to act by enchantment; and to *fascinate*, to act by the power of fascination; all which, as in the former case, denote a secret or involuntary influence. To *enrapture* and *captivate*, on the other hand, denote a direct but irresistible influence. To *charm, enchant,* and *enrapture*, when

applied to the same objects, rise in their sense; to *enchant* expresses a stronger effect than to *charm*, and to *enrapture* than to *enchant*. Music ordinarily *charms*, delightful music *charms* a delicate ear: the finest music only is calculated to *enrapture*, or the finest ears to be *enraptured*.

Beauty or fine scenery may in the same manner *charm*, *enchant*, or *enrapture*, according to the circumstances of the case.

To *fascinate* and *captivate* are, according to their original import, oftener used in a bad sense than a good one: we may sometimes speak indifferently of *fascinating* manners or a *captivating* address; but for the most part what *fascinates* and *captivates* acts on the passions to the injury of the understanding: a bad woman may have more power to *fascinate* than a modest woman, and flowery language may *captivate* when plain speech would not be heeded.

See also GRACE; PLEASURE.

CHARMED. See SPELLBOUND.

CHARMING. See DELIGHTFUL.

CHARMS. See ATTRACTIONS.

CHASE. See HUNT.

CHASM. See BREACH.

CHASTEN, CHASTISE. *Chasten, chastise,* both come through the French *châtier*, from the Latin *castigare*, to make pure.

Chasten has most regard to the end, *chastise* to the means; the former is an act of the Deity, the latter a human action: God *chastens* His faithful people, to cleanse them from their transgressions; parents *chastise* their children, to prevent the repetition of faults: afflictions are the means which God adopts for *chastening* those whom He wishes to make more obedient to his will; stripes are the means by which offenders are *chastised*.

CHASTITY, CONTINENCE. *Chastity,* in French *chastité*, Latin *castitas*, comes from *castus*, pure, and the Hebrew *kedish*, sacred. *Continence*, in French *continence*, Latin *continentia*, from *continens* and *contineo*, signifies the act of keeping one's self within bounds. These two terms are equally employed in relation to the pleasures of sense: both are virtues, but sufficiently distinct in their characteristics.

Chastity prescribes rules for the indulgence of these pleasures; *continence* altogether interdicts their use. *Chastity* extends its views to whatever may bear the smallest relation to the object which it proposes to regulate; it controls the thoughts, words, looks, attitudes, food, dress, company, and, in short, the whole mode of living: *continence* simply confines itself to the privation of the pleasures themselves; it is possible, therefore, to be *chaste* without being *continent*, and *continent* without being *chaste*. *Chastity* is suited to all times, ages, and conditions; *continence* belongs only to a state of celibacy; the Christian religion enjoins *chastity* as a positive duty on all its followers; the Romish religion enjoins *continence* on its clerical members.

See also VIRTUOUS.

CHATTELS. See GOODS.

CHATTER. See BABBLE; JABBER.

CHEAPEN. See BUY.

CHEAT, DEFRAUD, TRICK. *Cheat* comes from *escheat*, Middle English *eschete*, Old French *eschete*, rent, that which falls to the landlord, from *ex*, out, and *cadere*, to fall. As Skeat says, the lords of the manor or the *escheaters* "were often cheats in our sense," hence the verb." *Defraud*, from *de* and *fraud*, is either to practise fraud or get from a person by fraud. *Trick*, Norman French *trigue*, is probably influenced by Dutch *trik*, a pull, a stroke, a touch, the development of meaning is a little uncertain.

These terms convey the idea of practising deception, but in different ways. One *cheats* by direct and gross falsehood or artifice; one *defrauds* by a settled plan or contrivance; one *tricks* by a sudden invention. *Cheating* and *tricking* are resorted to in the common dealings of men; both may be equally low in their ends, but not equally base in their means. *Tricking* requires ingenuity, which is not wanted in the practice of *cheating*. *Defrauding* applies to the more serious concerns of life, and for the most part involves a breach of confidence, as to *defraud* one's creditors.

Cheating has respect to the delusion practised on the person, and may therefore be applied to whatever produces the delusion. *Defrauding* respects the thing wrongfully got, and may therefore be applied to persons, animals, or things which may suffer from fraud: as to *defraud* the state, the revenue, or animals of their food. *Tricking* properly passes only between men in their dealings with one another.

See also JUGGLE.

CHECK, CURB, CONTROL. All these terms express a species of restraining. *Check* and *curb* derive their meaning from natural objects. To *check*, in French *checé* (from the Persian word for king found in *shah*, king), in reference to the movement in the game of chess by which the king is prevented moving, implies generally to impede the course. *Curb*, from Latin *curvare*, to bend, refers to the binding of the horse's neck by pulling on the bit. To *check* is properly applied to bodies in motion, but *curb* may be applied to those which are at rest or in motion: a horse with a tender mouth is easily *checked* with a touch of the bridle; a young horse requires to be *curbed*.

To *check* and to *curb* have also a moral application; to *control*, contracted from *counter-roll*, or to keep one roll or account against another, has only a moral application. To *check* is, as before, an act of much less restraint than to *curb*. Every feeling, however good, may sometimes require to be *checked*; the passions, or will, require to be *curbed*.

To *check* is applied to individual acts, frequently to the act or circumstance of the moment, as to *check* the forwardness of youth; to *curb* and *control*, to the general conduct; the former in respect to bodies of men as well as individuals; the latter in respect to individuals, as to *curb* a people by laws, to *control* youth until they are enabled to act for themselves.

The act of *checking* is applied to one's self; a person may *check* himself when he is going to speak: to *curb* and *control* are properly applied to the acts of others.

Check, Chide, Reprimand, Reprove, Rebuke.—*Check* (see above). *Chide* is a word peculiar to English. It is not found in any other language. *Reprimand* is derived from the gerundive of

Latin *reprimere*, to repress, and so indicates something that ought to be repressed, hence the attempt to repress it by an expression of opinion. *Reprove*, in French *réprouver*, Latin *reprobo*, is compounded of the privative syllable *re* and *probo*, signifying to find the contrary of good, that is, to find bad, to blame. *Rebuke* is derived from Old French *busche*, a log, and meant originally to lop, to cut back.

The idea of expressing one's disapprobation of a person's conduct is common to all these terms. A person is *checked* that he may not continue to do what is offensive; he is *chidden* for what he has done, that he may not repeat it: impertinent and forward people require to be *checked*, that they may not become intolerable; thoughtless people are *chidden* when they give hurtful proofs of their carelessness. People are *checked* by actions and looks as well as words; they are *chidden* by words only: a timid person is easily *checked:* the want even of due encouragement will serve to damp his resolution: the young are perpetually falling into irregularities which require to be *chidden*.

To *chide* marks a stronger degree of displeasure than *reprimand*, and *reprimand* than *reprove* or *rebuke;* a person may *chide* or *reprimand* in anger, he *reproves* and *rebukes* with coolness: great offences call forth *chidings;* omissions or mistakes occasion or require a *reprimand:* irregularities of conduct give rise to *reproof;* and improprieties of behavior demand *rebuke*. *Chiding* and *reprimanding* are employed for offences against the individual, and in cases where the greatest disparity exists in the station of the parties; a child is *chidden* by his parent; a servant is *reprimanded* by his master. *Reproving* and *rebuking* have less to do with the relation or station of the parties than with the nature of the offence: wisdom, age, and experience, or a spiritual mission, give authority to *reprove* or *rebuke* those whose conduct has violated any law, human or divine: the prophet Nathan *reproved* King David for his heinous offences against his Maker; our Saviour *rebuked* Peter for his presumptuous mode of speech.

See also SNUB.

Check, Stop.—*Check*, as before, signifies to impede the course of a body in motion, that is, to cause it to move slowly; to *stop* (see CESSATION) is to cause it not to move at all: the growth of a plant is *checked* when it does not grow so fast as usual; its growth is *stopped* when it ceases altogether to grow: the water of a river is *stopped* by a dam; the rapidity of its course is *checked* by the intervention of rocks and sands.

These words admit of a similar distinction when applied to the conduct or condition of men and things: if an evil be *checked*, it is diminished in extent; if it be *stopped*, it is altogether put an end to; so a person may be *checked* in his career, or *stopped* in his career, with the like distinction.

CHEER, ENCOURAGE, COMFORT. *Cheer* (see ANIMATE). *Encourage*, compounded of *en* and *courage*, signifies to inspire with courage. *Comfort* is compounded of *com* or *cum*, and *fortis*, strong, signifying to invigorate or strengthen.

To *cheer* regards the spirits; to *encourage*, the resolution: the sad require to be *cheered;* the timid to be *encouraged*. Mirthful company is suited to *cheer* those who labor under any depression; the prospect of success *encourages* those who have any object to obtain.

To *cheer* and *comfort* have both regard to the spirits, but the latter differs in degree and manner: to *cheer* expresses more than to *comfort*, the former signifying to produce a lively sentiment, the latter to lessen or remove a painful one: we are *cheered* in the moments of despondency, whether from real or imaginary causes; we are *comforted* in the hour of distress.

Cheering may be effected either by the direct effort of others or by anything passing outward or inward; a discourse or voice *cheers*, a prospect or a reflection *cheers: comforting* is often properly effected by external objects, whether personal or otherwise. *Cheering* is purely a mental operation, but *comforting* may act on the body as well as on the mind.

See also ANIMATE; HEARTEN.

Cheerful, Merry, Sprightly, Gay.— *Cheerful* signifies full of *cheer*, or of that which *cheers. Merry,* Anglo-Saxon *myrge,* meant originally "lasting a short time," fragile, evanescent; hence that which makes the time pass quickly. *Sprightly* should be spelled *spritely,* from *sprite,* Old French *esprit,* a spirit (Latin *spiritus*), or the *spirit.* It signifies full of life, animated. *Sprightly* is contracted from *spiritedly. Gay* is from Old High German *wahi,* fine, beautiful.

Cheerful marks an unruffled flow of spirits; with *mirth* there is more of tumult and noise; with *sprightliness* there is more buoyancy; *gayety* comprehends *mirth* and indulgence. A *cheerful* person smiles; a *merry* person laughs; a *sprightly* person dances; a *gay* person takes his pleasure. The *cheerful* countenance is permanently so; it marks the contentment of the heart and its freedom from pain: the *merry* face will often look sad; a trifle will turn *mirth* into sorrow: the *sprightliness* of youth is often succeeded by the listlessness of bodily infirmity or the gloom of despondency: *gayety* is as transitory as the pleasures upon which it subsists; it is often followed by sullenness and discontent. *Cheerfulness* is a habitual state of the mind; *mirth* is an occasional elevation of the spirits; *sprightliness* lies in the temperature and flow of the blood; *gayety* depends altogether on external circumstances. Religion is the best promoter of *cheerfulness;* it makes its possessor pleased with himself and all around him; company and wine are but too often the only promoters of *mirth;* youth and health will naturally be attended with *sprightliness;* a succession of pleasures, an exemption from care, and the banishment of thought will keep *gayety* alive.

Sprightliness and *mirth* are seldom employed but in the proper sense as respects persons; but *cheerful* and *gay* are extended to different objects which affect the senses or the mind: *cheerful* objects are such as cheer the spirits; *gay* objects please or delight the senses; as a *cheerful* prospect, a *cheerful* room, *gay* attire, a *gay* scene, *gay* colors, etc.

See also GLAD; OPTIMISTIC; SANGUINE.

CHERISH. See FOSTER; NOURISH.

CHICANERY, PETTIFOGGERY. *Chicanery* and *pettifoggery* are both words of obscure origin meaning the abuse of legal forms—trickery, sophistry, and subterfuge in conducting a case. *Pettifoggery* comes from *pettifogger,* a legal practitioner of inferior status who gets up or conducts petty cases. Apart from this suggestion of particular attorneys of rascally practices in the development of the word *pettifoggery,* instead of the general habit of quibbling and cavilling in law-courts suggested in *chicanery,* there is really no difference between the words, and they can be used interchangeably. *Chicane* was applied long ago to the game of pall-mall, then to a dispute arising in that game, and latterly to sharp practice, especially in law-suits.

CHIDE. See CHECK.

CHIEF, PRINCIPAL, MAIN. *Chief,* in French *chef,* from the Latin *caput,* the head, signifies belonging to the uppermost part. *Principal,* in French *principal,* Latin *principalis,* comes from *princeps,* a chief or prince, signifying belonging to a prince. *Main,* from the Scandinavian, Icelandic *megn,* strong, signifies to a great degree.

Chief respects order and rank; *principal* has regard to importance and respectability; *main,* to degree or quantity. We speak of a *chief* clerk; a commander in *chief;* the *chief* person in a city; but the *principal* people in a city; the *principal* circumstances in a narrative, and the *main* object. The *chief* cities, as mentioned by geographers, are those which are classed in the first rank; the *principal* cities generally include those which are the most considerable for wealth and population; these, however, are not always technically comprehended under the name of *chief* cities: the *main* end of men's exertions is the acquirement of wealth.

See also CARDINAL.

Chief, Leader, Chieftain, Head.—Chief and *chieftain* signify him who is *chief. Leader,* from to *lead,* and *head,* from the *head,* sufficiently designate their own signification.

Chief respects precedency in civil matters; *leader* regards the direction of enterprises: *chieftain* is a species of *leader;* and *head* is the superior in general concerns. Among savages the *chief* of every tribe is a despotic prince within his own district, acting or directing in particular cases. Factions and parties in a state, like savage tribes, must have their *leaders*, to whom they are blindly devoted and by whom they are instigated to every desperate proceeding. Robbers have their *chieftains*, who plan and direct everything, having an unlimited power over the band. The *heads* of families were, in the primitive ages, the *chiefs*, who in conjunction regulated the affairs of state. *Chiefs* have a permanent power, which may descend by inheritance, to branches of the same families: *leaders* and *chieftains* have a deputed power with which they are invested as the time and occasion require: *heads* have a natural power springing out of the nature of their birth, rank, talents, and situation; it is not hereditary, but successive. *Chiefs* ought to have superiority of birth combined with talents for ruling; *leaders* and *chieftains* require a bold and enterprising spirit; *heads* should have talents for directing.

See also SUPREME.

CHIEFLY. See ESPECIALLY.

CHILDISH. INFANTINE. *Childish* is in the manner of an *infant*.

What *children* do is frequently simple or foolish; what *infants* do is commonly pretty and engaging; therefore *childish* is taken in the bad, and *infantine* in the good sense. *Childish* manners are very offensive in those who have ceased, according to their years, to be children; the *infantine* actions of some children evince a simplicity of character.

CHILL, COLD. *Chill* and *cold* are but variations of the same word, in German *kalt*, etc.

Chill expresses less than *cold;* that is to say, it expresses a degree of *cold*. The weather is often *chilly* in summer, but it is *cold* in winter. We speak of taking the *chill* off water when the *cold* is in part removed; and of a *chill* running through the frame when the *cold* begins to penetrate the frame that is in a state of warmth.

CHIMERICAL. See UTOPIAN.

CHOICE. See OPTION.

CHOKE. See SUFFOCATE.

CHOLER. See ANGER.

CHOOSE, PREFER. *Choose,* Anglo-

Saxon *ceósan*, is allied to Latin *gustare*, to taste, Greek γεόομαι, I taste. *Prefer*, in French *préférer*, Latin *præfero*, compounded of *præ* and *ferre*, to take before, signifies to take one thing rather than another.

To *choose* is to *prefer* as the genus to the species: we always *choose* in *preferring*, but we do not always *prefer* in *choosing*. To *choose* is to take one thing from among others; to *prefer* is to take one thing before or rather than another. We sometimes *choose* from the bare necessity of *choosing;* but we never *prefer* without making a positive and voluntary *choice*.

When we *choose* from a specific motive, the acts of *choosing* and *preferring* differ in the nature of the motive. The former is absolute, the latter relative. We *choose* a thing for what it is, or what we esteem it to be of itself; we *prefer* a thing for what it has, or what we suppose it has, superior to another. Utility or convenience are grounds for *choosing;* comparative merit occasions the *preference:* we *choose* something that is good, and are contented with it until we see something better which we *prefer*. We calculate and pause in *choosing;* we decide in *preferring;* the judgment determines in making the *choice;* the will or the affections determine in giving the *preference*. We *choose* things from an estimate of their merits or their fitness for the purpose proposed; we *prefer* them from their accordance with our tastes, habits, and pursuits. Books are *chosen* by those who wish to read; romances and works of fiction are *preferred* by general readers; learned works by the scholar. One who wants instruction *chooses* a master, but he will mostly *prefer* a teacher whom he knows to a perfect stranger. Our *choice* is good or bad according to our knowledge; our *preference* is just or unjust according as it is sanctioned by reason or otherwise. Our *choice* may be directed by our own experience or that of others; our *preference* must be guided by our own feelings. We make our *choice;* we give our *preference:* the first is the settled purpose of the mind, it fixes on the object; the latter is the inclining of the will, it yields to the object.

Choosing must be employed in all

the important concerns of life; *preferring* is admissible in subordinate matters only. There is but one thing that is right, and that ought to be *chosen* when it is discovered: there are many indifferent things that may suit our tastes and inclinations; these we are at liberty to *prefer*. But to *prefer* what we ought not to *choose* is to make our reason bend to our will. The path of life should be *chosen;* but the path to be taken in a walk may be *preferred*. It is advisable for a youth in the *choice* of a profession to consult what he *prefers*, as he has the greatest chance of succeeding when he can combine his pleasure with his duty. A friend should be *chosen:* a companion may be *preferred*. A wife should be *chosen;* but unfortunately lovers are most apt to give a *preference* in a matter where a good or bad *choice* may determine one's happiness or misery for life. A wise prince is careful in the *choice* of his ministers; but a weak prince has mostly favorites whom he *prefers*.

Choose, Pick, Select.—To *choose* is here, as in the foregoing article, a general and indefinite term, signifying to take one out of two or more. To *pick* is allied to *peck*. In Middle English *pikken*, to pick, and *pekken*, to peck, are equivalent words. They are derived from *pic*, a sharp point, and signify to take anything up with a beak or a pointed thing; hence to take things one by one. *Select*, in Latin *selectus*, from *seligo*, or *se*, apart, and *lego*, to gather, signifies properly to set apart. We may *choose* whatever comes in our way without regard to the number of the objects to be *chosen* from, but we *pick* or *select* out of a number only; as to *pick* or *select* books from a library: we may *pick* one or many out of a number, but we mostly *select* a number. Choosing is not always an act of particular design or discrimination; but to *pick* and *select* signify to *choose* with care, the latter with still greater care than the former. What is *picked* and *selected* is always the best of its kind; but the former is commonly something of a physical nature, the latter of a moral or intellectual description. Soldiers are sometimes *picked* to form a particular regiment; pieces are *selected* in prose or verse for general purposes.

Choose, Elect.—*Choose* (see above). *Elect*, in Latin *electus*, participle of *eligo*, is compounded of *e* and *lego*, signifying to gather or take out from.

Both these terms are employed in regard to persons appointed to an office; the former in a general, the latter in a particular sense. *Choosing* is the act either of one man or of many; *election* is always that of a number; it is performed by the concurrence of many voices. A prince *chooses* his ministers; the constituents *elect* members of parliament. A person is *chosen* to serve the office of sheriff; he is *elected* by the corporation to be mayor. *Choosing* is an act of authority; it binds the person *chosen: election* is a voluntary act; the *elected* has the power of refusal. People are obliged to serve in some offices when they are *chosen*, although they would gladly be exempt. The circumstances of being *elected* is an honor after which they eagerly aspire, and for the attainment of which they risk their property and use the most strenuous exertions.

To *elect* may sometimes be extended in its application to persons or things for general purposes, which brings it nearer to the word *choose;* but *election* in this case signifies the *choosing* one out of two or more specific objects; as where one has several friends and makes his *election* of one to be his constant companion, or a person makes his *election* where he has several alternatives set before him.

CHRONICLES. See ANECDOTES.

CHURCH. See TEMPLE.

CIPHER. See ZERO.

CIRCLE, SPHERE, ORB, GLOBE. *Circle* comes from Latin *circulus*, a diminutive of *circus*, a ring. *Sphere* is derived from Latin *sphœra*, a transliteration of Greek σφαίρα, a ball. *Orb* is derived from Latin *orbis*, a round disk or ring. *Globe* comes from Latin *globus*, a ball.

Rotundity of figure is the common idea expressed by these terms; but the *circle* is that figure which is represented on a plane superficies; the others are figures represented by solids. We draw a *circle* by means of compasses; the *sphere* is a round body, conceived to be formed according to the rules of geometry by the circumvolution of a *circle* round about its diameter; hence the whole frame of the world is denominated a *sphere*. An *orb* is any body which describes a *circle;* hence the heavenly bodies are termed *orbs:* a *globe* is any solid body the surface of which is in every part equidistant from the centre; of this description is the terrestrial *globe*.

A *circle* may be applied in the improper sense to any round figure which is formed or supposed to be formed by circumscribing a space; simple rotundity constitutes a *circle:* in this manner a *circle* may be formed by real objects, as persons, or by moral objects, as pleasures. To the idea of *circle* is annexed that of extent around, in the signification of a *sphere*, as a *sphere* of activity, whether applied in the philosophical sense to natural bodies or in the moral sense to men. Hollowness, as well as rotundity, belongs to an *orb;* hence we speak of the *orb* of a wheel. Of a *globe*, solidity is the peculiar characteristic; hence any ball, like the ball of the earth, may be represented as a *globe*.

CIRCUIT, TOUR, ROUND. *Circuit,* in French *circuit,* Latin *circuitus,* participle of *circumeo,* signifies either the act of going round or the extent gone. *Tour* is derived from Latin *tornum* (acc.), Greek τόρνος, a lathe. *Round* comes from Latin *rotundus,* indicating the motion of a wheel, from *rota,* wheel.

A *circuit* is made for a specific end of a serious kind; a *tour* is always made for pleasure; a *round*, like a *circuit*, is employed in matters of business, but of a more familiar and ordinary kind. A judge goes his *circuit* at particular periods of time: gentlemen, in times of peace, consider it as an essential part of their education to make what is termed the grand *tour:* tradesmen have certain *rounds*, which they take on certain days. We speak of making the *circuit* of a place; of taking a *tour* in a given country; and going a particular *round*. A *circuit* is wide or narrow; a *tour* and a *round* are great or little. A *circuit* is prescribed as to extent; a *tour* is optional; a *round* is prescribed or otherwise.

Circuit is seldom used but in a specific sense; *tour* is seldom employed but in regard to travelling; *round* may be taken figuratively, as when we speak of going one's *round* of pleasure.

CIRCULATE. See SPREAD.

CIRCUMSCRIBE, INCLOSE. *Circumscribe,* from the Latin *circum,* about, and *scribere,* to write, marks simply the surrounding with a line. *Inclose,* from the Latin *inclusus,* participle of *includo,* based on *in* and *claudere,* to shut, marks a species of confinement.

The extent of any place is drawn out to the eye by a *circumscription;* its extent is limited to a given point by an *inclosure.* A garden is *circumscribed* by any ditch, line, or posts that serve as its boundaries; it is *inclosed* by wall or fence. An *inclosure* may serve to *circumscribe;* but that which *circumscribes* is frequently imaginary, and will not serve to *inclose.*

See also BOUND.

CIRCUMSPECT. See CAUTIOUS.

CIRCUMSTANCE, SITUATION. *Circumstance,* in Latin *circumstantia,* from *circum* and *sto,* signifies what stands about a thing, or belongs to it as its accident. *Situation,* in French *situation,* comes from the Latin *situs,* a place.

Circumstance is to *situation* as a part to a whole: many *circumstances* constitute a *situation:* a *situation* is an aggregate of *circumstances.* A person is said to be in *circumstances* of affluence who has an abundance of everything essential for his comfort; he is in an easy *situation* when nothing exists to create uneasiness. *Circumstance* respects that which externally affects us; *situation* is employed both for the outward *circumstances* and the inward feelings. The success of any undertaking depends greatly on the *circumstances* under which it is begun; the particular *situation* of a person's mind will give a cast to his words or actions. *Circumstances* are critical, a *situation* is dangerous.

Circumstance, Incident, Fact.—Circumstance is, as before, a general term. *Incident,* in Latin *incidens,* participle of *incido,* or *in* and *cadere,* to fall, signifying what falls upon or to another thing, and *fact,* in Latin *factus,* participle of *facere*, to do, signifying the thing done, are species of *circumstances*. *Incident* is what happens; *fact* is what is done; *circumstance* is not only what happens and is done, but whatever is or belongs to a thing. To everything are annexed *circumstances*, either of time, place, age, color, or other collateral appendages, which changes its nature. Everything that moves and operates is exposed to *incidents;* effects are produced, results follow, and changes are brought about; these are *incidents:* whatever moves and operates does, and what it produces is done or is the *fact:* when the artificer performs any work of art, it depends not only on his skill, but on the excellence of his tools, the time he employs, the particular frame of his mind, the place where he works, with a variety of other *circumstances*, whether he will succeed in producing anything masterly. Newspapers abound with the various *incidents* which occur in the animal or the vegetable world, some of which are surprising and singular; they likewise contain a number of *facts* which serve to present a melancholy picture of human depravity.

Circumstance is as often employed with regard to the operations or properties of things, in which case it is most analogous to *incident* and *fact;* it may then be employed for the whole affair, or any part of it whatever that can be distinctly considered. *Incidents* and *facts* either are *circumstances* or have *circumstances* belonging to them. A remarkably abundant crop in any particular part of a field is for the agriculturist a singular *circumstance* or *incident;* this may be rendered more surprising if associated with unusual sterility in other parts of the same field. A robbery may either be a *fact* or a *circumstance;* its atrocity may be aggravated by the murder of the injured parties, the savageness of the perpetrators, and a variety of *circumstances*. *Circumstance* comprehends in its signification whatever may be said or thought of anything; *incident* carries with it the idea of whatever may befall or be said to befall anything; *fact* includes in it nothing but what really is or is done. A narrative, therefore, may contain many *circum-*

stances and *incidents* without any *fact*, when what is related is either fictitious or not positively known to have happened: it is necessary for a novel or play to contain much *incident*, but not *facts*, in order to render it interesting; history should contain nothing but *facts*, as authenticity is its chief merit.

Circumstantial, Particular, Minute.— *Circumstantial*, from *circumstance*, signifies consisting of *circumstances*. *Particular* comes from Latin *particula*, a double diminutive of *partem* (acc.), part; hence a very little part. *Minute*, in French *minute*, Latin *minutus*, participle of *minuere*, to diminish, signifies diminished or reduced to a very small point.

Circumstantial expresses less than *particular*, and that less than *minute*. A *circumstantial* account contains all leading events; a *particular* account includes every event and movement, however trivial; a *minute* account omits nothing as to person, time, place, figure, form, and every other trivial *circumstance* connected with the events. A narrative may be *circumstantial, particular*, or *minute;* an inquiry, investigation, or description may be *minute*. An event or occurrence may be *particular*, a circumstance or particular may be *minute*.

CITE, QUOTE. *Cite* is derived from Latin *citare*, a frequentative of *ciere*, to arouse (compare *excite*, *incite*, etc.). As applied to persons it means to arouse, to summon; it was figuratively applied to things in a similar sense. To *cite* a passage in a book or an instance in history meant to summon it to bear witness. *Quote* is derived from Latin *quotare*, to mark off into chapters or verses for reference, from *quotus*, how much (compare *quota*); from the significance to mark off it came to mean the repeating of the words marked off.

To *cite* is employed for persons or things; to *quote* for things only: authors are *cited*, passages from their works are *quoted:* we *cite* only by authority; we *quote* for general purposes of convenience. Historians ought to *cite* their authority in order to strengthen their evidence and inspire confidence; controversialists must *quote* the objectionable passages in those works which they wish to confute: it is prudent to *cite* no one whose authority is questionable; it is superfluous to *quote* anything that can be easily perused in the original.

Cite, Summon.—The idea of calling a person authoritatively to appear is common to these terms. *Cite* is used in a general sense, *summon* in a particular and technical sense: a person may be *cited* to appear before his superior; he is *summoned* to appear before a court: the station of the individual gives authority to the act of *citing;* the law itself gives authority to that of *summoning.* When *cite* is used in a legal sense, it is mostly employed for witnesses, and *summon* for every occasion: a person is *cited* to give evidence; he is *summoned* to answer a charge. *Cite* is seldomer used in the legal sense than in that of calling by name, in which general acceptation it is employed with regard to authors, as specified in the preceding article, and in some few other connections: the legal is the ordinary sense of *summon;* it may, however, be extended in its application to a military *summons* of a fortified town, or to any call for which there may be occasion; as when we speak of the *summons* which is given to attend the death-bed of a friend; or, figuratively, death is said to *summon* mortals from this world.

CIVIL, POLITE. *Civil,* in French *civil,* Latin *civilis,* from *civis,* a citizen, signifies belonging to or becoming a citizen. *Polite,* in French *poli,* Latin *politus,* participle of *polire,* to polish, signifies properly polished.

These two epithets are employed to denote different modes of acting in social intercourse: *polite* expresses more than *civil;* it is possible to be *civil* without being *polite: politeness* supposes *civility* and something in addition. *Civility* is confined to no rank, age, condition, or country; all have an opportunity with equal propriety of being *civil,* but not so with *politeness;* that requires a certain degree of equality, at least the equality of education; it would be contradictory for masters and servants, rich and poor, learned and unlearned, to be *polite* to one another. *Civility* is a Christian duty;

there are times when every man ought to be *civil* to his neighbor: *politeness* is rather a voluntary devotion of ourselves to others: among the inferior orders *civility* is indispensable; an *uncivil* person in a subordinate station is an obnoxious member of society: among the higher orders *politeness* is often a substitute; and, where the form and spirit are combined, it supersedes the necessity of *civility: politeness* is the sweetener of human society; it gives a charm to everything that is said and done. *Civility* is contented with pleasing when the occasion offers: *politeness* seeks the opportunity to please; it prevents the necessity of asking by anticipating the wishes; it is full of delicate attentions, and is an active benevolence in the minor concerns of life. *Civil* is therefore most properly applied to what passes from and to persons of inferior condition; as the peasantry are very *civil.*

Or it may be applied to the ordinary transactions of life without distinction of rank.

Polite is applied to those who are in a condition to have good-breeding.

Civility is rather a negative than a positive quality, implying the absence of rudeness. *Politeness* requires positive and peculiar properties of the head and heart, natural and acquired. To be *civil,* therefore, is the least that any one can be to another if he do not wish to offend; but *politeness,* where it is real, is as strong an indication of kindness in the outward behavior as the occasion calls for.

The term *civil* may be applied figuratively, but *politeness* is a characteristic of real persons only.

See also TEMPORAL.

Civil, Obliging, Complaisant.—*Civil* is more general than *obliging,* which signifies ready to oblige. One is always *civil* when one is *obliging,* but not always *obliging* when one is *civil.* *Civil* applies to words or manner as well as to the action; *obliging,* to the action only. As *civil* is indefinite in its meaning, so it is indiscriminate in its application; *obliging,* on the other hand, is confined to what passes between particular persons or under particular circumstances. Strangers may be *civil,* and persons may frequently be *civil* who from their situation may be expected to be otherwise; one friend is *obliging* to another.

Civil and *obliging* both imply a desire to do a kindness; but *complaisant*, which is a variation of *complacent*, from *complaceo*, to be highly pleased, signifies the desire of receiving pleasure, which is a refined mode of doing a kindness.

Civility, lying very much in the manner, may be put on, and *complaisance*, implying a concern to please by being pleased, may be bad if it lead one to consult the humors of others to the sacrifice of duty or propriety.

CIVILITY. See BENEFIT.

CIVILIZATION. See CULTIVATION.

CLAIM. See ASK; PRETENSION; RIGHT.

CLAMOR. See NOISE.

CLAMOROUS. See LOUD.

CLANDESTINE, SECRET. *Clandestine*, in Latin *clandestinus*, comes from *clam*, secretly. *Secret*, in French *secret*, Latin *secretus*, participle of *secernere*, to separate, signifies remote from observation.

Clandestine expresses more than *secret*. To do a thing *clandestinely* is to elude observation; to do a thing *secretly* is to do it without the knowledge of any one: what is *clandestine* is unallowed, which is not necessarily the case with what is *secret*. With the *clandestine* must be a mixture of art; with *secrecy* caution and management are requisite: a *clandestine* marriage is effected by a studied plan to escape notice; a *secret* marriage is conducted by the forbearance of all communication; conspirators have many *clandestine* proceedings and *secret* meetings: an unfaithful servant *clandestinely* conveys away his master's property from his premises; a thief *secretly* takes a purse from the pocket of a bystander.

CLASP, HUG, EMBRACE. *Clasp* is a word confined to English. It first appears in the fourteenth century; it means to fasten by two interlocking parts. *Hug* may be a Scandinavian word related to Icelandic *hugga*, to soothe; *hugna*, to please. *Embrace*, in French *embrasser*, is compounded of *en* and *bras*, arm, Latin *brachia*, arms, signifying to take or lock in one's arms.

All these terms are employed to express the act of inclosing another in one's arms: *clasp* marks this action when it is performed with the warmth of true affection; *hug* is a ludicrous sort of *clasping*, which is the consequence of ignorance or extravagant feeling; *embrace* is simply a mode of ordinary salutation: a parent will *clasp* his long-lost child in his arms on their re-meeting; a peasant in the excess of his raptures would throw his body, as well as his arms, over the object of his joy, and stifle with *hugging* him whom he meant to *embrace*; in the Continental parts of Europe *embracing* between males, as well as females, is universal on meeting after a long absence, or on taking leave for a length of time; *embraces* are sometimes given in England between near relatives, but in no other case.

Clasp and *embrace* may be applied to other objects besides persons in the same sense.

CLASS, ORDER, RANK, DEGREE. *Class* is derived from Latin *classis*, a faction, a division, a fleet. *Order*, Latin *ordo*, is allied to Latin *oriri*, to begin, from *oriri*, to rise. *Rank*, Old French *reng*, comes from Old High German *hrinc*, a ring of men. *Degree*, in French *degré*, comes from the Latin *gradus*, a stop.

Class is more general than *order; degree* is more specific than *rank. Class* and *order* are said of the persons who are distinguished; *rank* and *degree* of the distinction itself: men belong to a certain *class* or *order;* they hold a certain *rank;* they are of a certain *degree:* among the Romans all the citizens were distinctly divided into *classes* according to their property; but in the modern constitution of society *classes* are distinguished from one another on general, moral, or civil grounds; there are reputable or disreputable *classes;* the laboring *class*, the *class* of merchants, mechanics, etc.; *order* has a more particular signification; it is founded upon some positive civil privilege or distinction: the general *orders* are divided into higher, lower, and middle, arising from the unequal distribution of wealth and power; the particular *orders* are those of the nobility, of the clergy, of freemasonry, and the like: *rank* distinguishes one individual from another; it is peculiarly applied to the nobility and the gentry, although every man in the community holds a certain *rank* in relation to those who are above or below him: *degree*, like *rank*, is applicable to the individual, but only in particular cases; literary and scientific *degrees* are conferred upon superior merit in different departments of science; there are likewise *degrees* in the same *rank*, whence we speak of men of high and low *degree*.

Class, Arrange, Range.—To *class*, from the noun *class*, signifies to put in a *class*. *Arrange* and *range* both come from the Old French *rangier*, from *reng*, Old High German *hrinc*, a ring, a row—*arrange* being formed by the addition of Latin *ad* (to) to the French verb.

The general qualities and attributes of things are to be considered in *classing;* their fitness to stand by each other must be considered in *arranging;* their capacity for forming a line is the only thing to be attended to in *ranging*. *Classification* serves the purposes either of public policy or science; *arranging* is a matter of convenience to the individual himself; *ranging* is a matter of convenience for others: men are *classed* into different bodies according to some certain standard of property, power, education, occupation, etc.; furniture is *arranged* in a room according as it answers in color, shade, convenience of situation, etc.; men are *ranged* in order whenever they make a procession. All these words require more or less exercise of the intellectual faculty, but *classing* is a more abstract and comprehensive act than either *arranging* or *ranging*. All objects, external or internal, may admit of *classification*, according to their similitudes and differences; but *arranging* and *ranging* are particular acts employed in regard to familiar objects, and the order in which they ought to be placed. Ideas are *classed* by the logician into simple and complex, abstract and concrete; an individual *arranges* his own ideas in his mind: words are *classed* by the grammarian into different parts of speech: words are *arranged* by the writer in a sentence, so as to be suitable. To *arrange* is a more complex proceeding than simply to *range;* a merchant or tradesman *arranges* his affairs when they are got into confusion, but a shopkeeper *ranges* his goods in such manner as best to set them out to view.

These words are applied figuratively in the same sense.

CLASSIC. See ACADEMIC.

CLEAN, CLEANLY, PURE. *Clean* and *cleanly* come from Anglo-Saxon *clœne*, pure, bright, which in German developed the special sense of little—German *klein*. *Pure*, in French *pur*, Latin *purus*.

Clean expresses a freedom from dirt or soil; *cleanly* the disposition or habit of being *clean*. A person who keeps himself *clean* is *cleanly;* a *cleanly* servant takes care to keep other things *clean*. *Clean* is employed either in the proper or the figurative sense; *pure*, mostly in the moral sense: the hands should be *clean;* the heart should be *pure;* it is the first requisite of good writing that it should be *clean;* it is of the first importance for the morals of youth to be kept *pure*.

CLEANSE, See SANCTIFY.

CLEAR, LUCID, BRIGHT, VIVID. *Clear*, see ABSOLVE. *Lucid*, in Latin *lucidus*, from *lucere*, to shine, and *lux*, light, signifies having light. *Bright*, see BRIGHTNESS. *Vivid*, Latin *vividus*, from *vivere*, to live, signifies being in a state of life.

These epithets mark a gradation in their sense; the idea of light is common to them, but *clear* expresses less than *lucid*, *lucid* than *bright*, and *bright* less than *vivid;* a mere freedom from stain or dulness constitutes the *clearness;* the return of light, and consequent removal of darkness, constitutes *lucidity; brightness* supposes a certain strength of light; *vividness* a freshness combined with the strength, and even a degree of brilliancy: a sky is *clear* that is divested of clouds: the atmosphere is *lucid* in the day, but not in the night; the sun shines *bright* when it is unobstructed by anything in the atmosphere; lightning sometimes presents a *vivid* redness, and sometimes a *vivid* paleness: the light of the stars may be *clear*, and sometimes *bright*, but never *vivid;* the light of the sun is rather *bright* than *clear* or *vivid;* the light of the moon is either *clear, bright,* or *vivid.* These epithets may with equal propriety be applied to color as well as to light: a *clear* color is unmixed with any other; a *bright* color has something striking and strong in it; a *vivid* color something lively and fresh in it.

In their moral application they preserve a similar distinction: a conscience is said to be *clear* when it is free from every stain or spot; a deranged understanding may have *lucid* intervals; a *bright* intellect throws light on everything around it; a *vivid* imagination glows with every image that nature presents.

See also APPARENT; DIAPHANOUS; EUPHONIOUS; FAIR.

Clearly, Distinctly.—That is seen *clearly* of which one has a *clear* view independent of anything else; that is seen *distinctly* which is seen so as to distinguish it from other objects. We see the moon *clearly* whenever it shines, but we cannot see the spots in the moon *distinctly* without the help of glasses. What we see *distinctly* must be seen *clearly,* but a thing may be seen *clearly* without being seen *distinctly.* A want of light, or the intervention of other objects, prevents us from seeing *clearly;* distance, or a defect in the sight, prevents us from seeing *distinctly.* Old men often see *clearly,* but not *distinctly;* they perceive large or luminous objects at a distance, but they cannot distinguish such small objects as the characters of a book without the help of convex glasses; short-sighted persons, on the contrary, see near objects *distinctly,* but they have no *clear* vision of distant ones, unless they are viewed through concave glasses.

Clearness, Perspicuity. — *Clearness,* from *clear,* is here used figuratively to mark the degree of light by which one sees things distinctly. *Perspicuity,* in French *perspicuité,* Latin *perspicuitas,* from *perspicuus* and *perspicere,* to look through, signifies the quality of being able to be seen through.

These epithets denote qualities equally requisite to render a discourse intelligible, but each has its peculiar character. *Clearness* respects our ideas and springs from the distinction of the things themselves that are discussed: *perspicuity* respects the mode of expressing the ideas, and springs from the good qualities of style. It requires a *clear* head to be able to see a subject in all its bearings and relations; to distinguish all the niceties and shades of difference between things that bear a strong resemblance, and to separate it from all irrelevant objects that intermingle themselves with it. But whatever may be our *clearness* of conception, it is requisite, if we would communicate our conceptions to others, that we should observe a purity in our mode of diction, that we should be particular in the choice of our terms, careful in the disposition of them, and accurate in the construction of our sentences; that is *perspicuity* which, as it is the first, so, according to Quintilian, it is the most important part of composition.

Clearness of intellect is a natural gift; *perspicuity* is an acquired art: although intimately connected with each other, yet it is possible to have *clearness* without *perspicuity,* and *perspicuity* without *clearness.* People of quick capacities will have *clear* ideas on the subjects that offer themselves to their notice, but for want of education they may often use improper or ambiguous phrases; or by errors of construction render their phraseology the reverse of *perspicuous:* on the other hand, it is in the power of some to express themselves *perspicuously* on subjects far above their comprehension, from a certain facility which they acquire of catching up suitable modes of expression. The study of the classics and mathematics is most fitted for the improvement of *clearness;* the study of grammar, and the observance of good models, will serve most effectually for the acquirement of *perspicuity.*

CLEAVE. See STICK.

CLEFT. See JAGGED.

CLEMENCY, LENITY, MERCY. *Clemency* is in Latin *clementia,* signifying mildness. *Lenity* is in Latin *lenitas,* from *lenis,* soft. *Mercy* is derived from Latin *merces,* pay, which has developed into words of curiously diverse meanings — *mercenary, merchant,* French *merci,* thanks, etc. In this connection it signifies that which brings a reward in heaven, and is influenced by the Latin *misericordia*, pitiful of heart.

All these terms agree in denoting the disposition or act of forbearing to inflict pain by the exercise of power. *Clemency* and *lenity* are employed only toward offenders; *mercy* toward all who are in trouble, whether from their own fault or any other cause. *Clemency* lies in the disposition; *lenity* and *mercy*, in the act; the former as respects superiors in general, the latter in regard to those who are invested with civil power: a monarch displays his *clemency* by showing *mercy;* a master shows *lenity* by not inflicting punishment where it is deserved. *Clemency* is arbitrary on the part of the dispenser, flowing from his will, independent of the object on whom it is bestowed: *lenity* and *mercy* are discretionary, they always have regard to the object and the nature of the offence or misfortunes; *lenity*, therefore, often serves the purposes of discipline, and *mercy* those of justice, by forgiveness instead of punishment; but *clemency* sometimes defeats its end by forbearing to punish where it is needful. A mild master, who shows *clemency* to a faithless servant by not bringing him to justice, often throws a worthless wretch upon the public to commit more atrocious depredations. A well-timed *lenity* sometimes recalls an offender to himself, and brings him back to good order. Upon this principle the English constitution has wisely left in the hands of the monarch the discretionary power of showing *mercy* in all cases that do not demand the utmost rigor of the law.

CLERGYMAN, PARSON, PRIEST, MINISTER. *Clergyman* is derived from Latin *clericus*, from Greek κληρικός, κλῆρος, a lot); in Late Greek it signifies the consecrated members of a Christian society, whose lot or portion "is in the Lord." *Parson* is derived from Latin *persona*, a person of rank, and meant a person of rank in a Christian society. *Priest* comes from the Greek πρεσβύτερος, signifying an elder who holds the sacerdotal office. *Minister*, in Latin *minister*, a servant, from *minor*, less or inferior, signifies literally one who performs a subordinate office.

It acquired a special significance because of the Christian emphasis upon humility. The Pope called himself the "servant of the servants of Jesus Christ."

The word *clergyman* applies to such as are regularly bred according to the forms of the national religion, and applies to none else. In this sense we speak of the English, the French, and Scotch *clergy* without distinction. A *parson* is a species of *clergyman* who ranks the highest in the three orders of inferior *clergy*, that is, *parson*, vicar, and curate; the *parson* being a technical term for the rector, or he who holds the living: in its technical sense it has now acquired a definite use, but in general conversation it is become almost a nickname. The word *clergyman* is always substituted for *parson* in polite society. When *priest* respects the Christian religion it is a species of *clergyman*, that is, one who is ordained to officiate at the altar in distinction from the deacon, who is only an assistant to the *priest*. But the term *priest* has likewise an extended meaning in reference to such as hold the sacerdotal character in any form of religion, as the *priests* of the Jews, or those of the Greeks, Romans. Indians, and the like. A *minister* is one who actually or habitually officiates. *Clergymen* are therefore not always strictly *ministers*, nor are all *ministers clergymen*. If a *clergyman* delegates his functions altogether he is not a *minister;* nor is he who presides over a dissenting congregation a *clergyman*. In the former case, however, it would be invidious to deprive the *clergyman* of the name of *minister* of the Gospel, but in the latter case it is a misuse of the term *clergyman* to apply it to any *minister* who does not officiate according to the form of an established religion.

CLEVER, SKILFUL, EXPERT, DEXTEROUS, ADROIT. *Clever*, Middle English *cliver*, ready to seize, is allied to Middle English *cliver*, a claw. *Skilful* comes from *skill*, a Scandinavian word which meant originally intelligent, discerning. *Expert*, in French *expert*, Latin *expertus*, participle of *experior*, to search or try, signifies searched and tried. *Dexterous*, in Latin *dexter*, signifies the quality of doing rightly, as with the right hand. *Adroit* is derived from the French phrase *à droit*, from Latin *ad* (to) and *directum*, right, justice, *ultimately* from *regere*, to order or rule. *Cleverness* is mental power employed in the ordinary concerns of life: a person is *clever* in business. *Skill* is both a mental and corporeal power, exerted in mechanical operations and practical sciences: a physician, a lawyer, or an artist is *skilful:* one may have a *skill* in divination, or a *skill* in painting. *Expertness* and *dexterity* require more corporeal than mental power exerted in minor arts and amusements: one is *expert* at throwing the quoit: *dexterous* in the management of horses. *Adroitness* is altogether a corporeal talent, employed only as occasion may require: one is *adroit* at eluding the blows aimed by an adversary. *Cleverness* is rather a natural gift; *skill* is *cleverness* improved by practice and extended knowledge; *expertness* is the effect of long practice; *dexterity* arises from habit combined with agility; *adroitness* is a species of *dexterity* arising from a natural agility. A person is *clever* at drawing who shows a taste for it, and executes it well without much instruction: he is *skilful* in drawing if he understands it both in theory and practice; he is *expert* in the use of the bow if he can use it with expedition and effect; he is *dexterous* at any game when he goes through the manœuvres with celerity and an unerring hand; he is *adroit* if, by a quick, sudden, and well-directed movement of his body, he effects the object he has in view.

CLEVERNESS. See GUMPTION.

CLIMACTERIC, CRITICAL, DANGEROUS. These words all suggest a time of suspense, when some misfortune may be about to fall. Of the three words *climacteric* is the most specific. *Climacteric*, from the Greek κλῖμακτήρ, a round or step of a ladder, pertains to one of the supposed critical and dangerous steps or periods in human life, in which some great change is by some believed to take place in the human constitution. The numbers 7 and 9 are thought by many to mark the years of age when such steps or periods are reached, and when dangerous attacks of sickness may be

expected. The most critical period of all, according to belief, and known as the *grand climacteric*, is within the 63d year, that is 7x9, of a man's life, when his constitution is said to decline rapidly, involving him in critical illness till the year has passed and old age begins.

Critical (see CRITICAL) and *dangerous* (see DANGER) are less limited in their application. *Dangerous* is a stronger word than *critical*. *Critical* suggests the possibility of misfortune; *dangerous* the probability.

CLIMB. See ARISE.

CLOAK, MASK, BLIND, VEIL. These are figurative terms, expressive of different modes of intentionally keeping something from the view of others. They are borrowed from those familiar objects which serve similar purposes in common life. *Cloak* and *mask* express figuratively and properly more than *blind* or *veil*. The two former keep the whole object out of sight; the two latter only partially intercept the view. In this figurative sense they are all employed for a bad purpose. The *cloak*, the *mask*, and the *blind* serve to deceive others; the *veil* serves to deceive one's self. The whole or any part of a character may be concealed by a *blind;* a part, though not the whole, may be concealed by a *mask*. A *blind* is not only employed to conceal the character, but the conduct or proceedings. We carry a *cloak* and a *mask* about with us; but a *blind* is something external. The *cloak*, as the external garment, is the most convenient of all coverings for entirely keeping concealed what we do not wish to be seen; a good outward deportment serves as a *cloak* to conceal a bad character. A *mask* hides only the face; a *mask*, therefore, serves to conceal only as much as words and looks can effect. A *blind* is intended to shut out the light and prevent observation; whatever, therefore, conceals the real truth, and prevents suspicion by a false exterior, is a *blind*. A *veil* prevents a person from seeing as well as being seen; whatever, therefore, obscures the mental sight acts as a *veil* to the mind's eye. Religion is unfortunately the object which may serve to *cloak* the worst of purposes and the worst of characters: its importance in the eyes of all men makes it the most effectual passport to their countenance and sanction; and its external observances render it the most convenient mode of presenting a false profession to the eyes of the world: those, therefore, who set an undue value on the ceremonial part of religion do but encourage this most heinous of all sins, by suffering themselves to be imposed upon by a *cloak* of religious hypocrisy. False friends always wear a *mask;* they cover a malignant heart under the smiles and endearments of friendship. Illicit traders mostly make use of some *blind* to facilitate the carrying on their nefarious practices. Among the various arts resorted to in the metropolis by the needy and profligate, none is so bad as that which is made to be a *blind* for the practice of debauchery. Prejudice and passion are the ordinary *veils* which obscure the judgment and prevent it from distinguishing the truth.

CLOG, LOAD, ENCUMBER. *Clog* in Middle English means the wooden sole of a shoe; hence a hindrance. For the derivation of *load* see FREIGHT. *Encumber* is from French *encombrer,* Latin *in* and Late Latin *combrus,* an obstacle.

Clog is figuratively employed for whatever impedes the motion or action of a thing, drawn from the familiar object which is used to impede the motion of animals: *load* is used for whatever occasions an excess of weight or materials. A wheel is *clogged,* or a machine is *clogged;* a fire may be *loaded* with coals, or a picture with coloring. The stomach and memory may be either *clogged* or *loaded:* in the former case by the introduction of improper food, and in the second case by the introduction of an improper quantity. A memory that is *clogged* becomes confused, and confounds one thing with another; that which is *loaded* loses the impression of one object by the introduction of another. *Clog* and *encumber* have the common signification of interrupting or troubling by means of something irrelevant. Whatever is *clogged* has scarcely the liberty of moving at all; whatever is *encumbered* moves and acts, but with difficulty. When the roots of plants are *clogged*

with mould, or any improper substance, their growth is almost stopped; weeds and noxious plants are *encumbrances* in the ground where flowers should grow.

CLOISTER, CONVENT, MONASTERY. *Cloister,* Latin *claustrum,* means literally an enclosure, and signifies a certain close place in a convent, or an enclosure of houses for canons, or, in general, a religious house. *Convent,* from the Latin *conventus,* a meeting, and *convenire,* to come together, signifies a religious assembly. *Monastery,* in French *monastère,* signifies a habitation for monks, from the Greek μόνος, alone.

The proper idea of *cloister* is that of seclusion; the proper idea of *convent* is that of community; the proper idea of a *monastery* is that of solitude. One is shut up in a *cloister,* put into a *convent,* and retires to a *monastery.* Whoever wishes to take an absolute leave of the world shuts himself up in a *cloister;* whoever wishes to attach himself to a community that has renounced all commerce with the world goes into a *convent;* whoever wishes to shun all human intercourse retires to a *monastery.* In the *cloister* our liberty is sacrificed; in the *convent* our worldly habits are renounced, and, those of a regular religious community being adopted, we submit to the yoke of established orders: in a *monastery* we impose a sort of voluntary exile upon ourselves; we live with the view of living only to God. In the ancient and true *monasteries* the members divided their time between contemplation and labor; but as population increased and towns multiplied *monasteries* were, properly speaking, succeeded by *convents.* In ordinary discourse *cloister* is employed in an absolute and indefinite manner: we speak of the *cloister* to designate a *monastic* state; as entering a *cloister;* burying one's self in a *cloister;* penances and mortifications are practised in a *cloister.* It is not the same thing when we speak of the *cloister* of the Benedictines and of their *monastery;* or the *cloister* of the Capuchins and their *convent.*

CLOSE, COMPACT. *Close* is from the French *clos,* and Latin *clausus,* the participle of *claudere,* to shut. *Compact* is derived from Latin *compactus, cum,* together, and *pangere*, to fasten, to fit, and signifies fitted, close, form.

Proximity is expressed by both these terms; the former in a general and the latter in a restricted sense. Two bodies may be *close* to each other, but a body is *compact* with regard to itself. Contact is not essential to constitute *closeness;* but a perfect adhesion of all the parts of a body is essential to produce *compactness.* Lines are *close* to each other that are separated but by a small space; things are rolled together in a *compact* form that are brought within the smallest possible space.

Close, Near, Nigh. — *Close* (see above). *Near* is the comparative of *nigh.*

Close is more definite than *near:* houses stand *close* to each other which are almost joined; men stand *close* when they touch each other; objects are *near* which are within sight; persons are *near* each other when they can converse together. *Near* and *nigh*, which are but variations of each other in etymology, admit of little or no difference in their use; the former, however, is the most general. People live *near* each other who are in the same street; they live *close* to each other when their houses are adjoining. *Close* is annexed as an adjective; *near* is employed only as an adverb or preposition. We speak of *close* ranks or *close* lines; but not *near* ranks or *near* lines.

See also END; SEQUEL.

Close, Shut. — *Close* (see above). *Shut,* Anglo-Saxon *scyttan,* meant originally to fasten a door with a bolt, and is allied to *shoot.* We still say "shoot the bolt" (Skeat).

To *close* signifies simply to put *close* together; *shut* to stop or prevent admittance; *closing* is therefore a partial *shutting,* and *shutting* a complete *closing;* as to *close* a door or window is to put it partially to, as distinguished from *shutting* it, *i. e., shutting* it *close.* The eyes are *shut* by *closing* the eyelids, and the mouth is *shut* by *closing* the lips; and by the figure of metonymy to *close* may therefore often be substituted for *shut:* as to *close* the eyes, to *close* the mouth, particularly in poetry.

There is, however, a further distinction between these two words: to *close* properly denotes the bringing anything *close,* and may, therefore, be applied to any opening or cavity which may thus be filled up or covered over for a permanency; as to *close* a wound, to *close* the entrance to any place; but *shutting* implies merely an occasional stoppage of an entrance by that which is movable: whatever is *shut* may be opened in this sense; not only a door, a book, or a box may be *shut,* but also the ears may be *shut.* In familiar language it is usual to speak of *closing* a scene, for putting an end to it; but in poetry the term *shut* may without impropriety be used in the same sense.

See also BLOCKADE.

Close, Conclude, Finish. — To *close* is to bring toward an end; to *conclude,* from *con* and *claudere,* to shut, *i. e.,* to shut together, signifies to bring actually to an end; *finish,* in Latin *finio* and *finis,* an end, signifies also literally to bring to an end. The idea of putting an end to a thing is common to these terms, but they differ in the circumstances of the action. To *close* is the most indefinite of the three. We may *close* at any point by simply ceasing to have any more to do with it; but we *conclude* in a definite and positive manner. Want of time may compel us to *close* a letter before we have said all we wish to say; a letter is commonly *concluded* with expressions of kindness or courtesy. Whatever admits of being discontinued is properly said to be *closed;* as to *close* a procession, entertainment, and the like.

Whatever is brought to the last or the desired point is properly said to be *concluded;* as to *conclude* a speech, a narrative, a business, and the like.

To *conclude* is to bring to an end by determination; to *finish* is to bring to an end by completion: what is settled by arrangement and deliberation is properly *concluded;* what is begun on a certain plan is said to be *finished.*

CLOWN. See COUNTRYMAN.

CLOY. See SATISFY.

CLUE. See KEY.

CLUMSY. See AWKWARD.

CLUTCH. See NAB.

COADJUTOR, ASSISTANT. *Coadju-*

tor, compounded of *von* and *adjutor*, a helper, signifies a fellow-laborer. *Assistant* signifies properly one that *assists* or takes a part.

A *coadjutor* is more noble than an *assistant:* the latter is mostly in a subordinate station, but the former is an equal; the latter performs menial offices in the minor concerns of life, and a subordinate part at all times; the former labors conjointly in some concern of common interest and great importance. An *assistant* is engaged for a compensation; a *coadjutor* is a voluntary fellow-laborer. In every public concern where the purposes of charity or religion are to be promoted *coadjutors* often effect more than the original *promoters*: in the medical and scholastic professions *assistants* are indispensable to relieve the pressure of business. *Coadjutors* ought to be zealous and unanimous; *assistants* ought to be assiduous and faithful.

COALESCE. See ADD.

COALITION. See UNION.

COARSE, ROUGH, RUDE. *Coarse* was formerly *course*, and developed as an adjective from the phrase *in course*, to denote anything of ordinary character. *Rough* comes from Anglo-Saxon *ruh*, rough, hairy. *Rude* is derived from Latin *rudis*, raw, rough.

These epithets are equally applied to what is not polished by art. In the proper sense *coarse* refers to the composition and materials of bodies, as *coarse* bread, *coarse* meat, *coarse* cloth; *rough* respects the surface of bodies, as *rough* wood and *rough* skin; *rude* respects the make or fashion of things, as a *rude* bark, a *rude* utensil. *Coarse* is opposed to fine, *rough* to smooth, *rude* to polished.

In the figurative application they are distinguished in a similar manner: *coarse* language is used by persons of naturally *coarse* feeling; *rough* language, by those whose tempers are either naturally or occasionally *rough; rude* language, by those who are ignorant of any better.

See also GROSS.

COAX, WHEEDLE, CAJOLE, FAWN. *Coax* is a comparatively recent word of uncertain origin. Dr. Johnson, 1755–73, describes it as "a low word." The original meaning seems to have been to make a *cokes* of, from *cokes*, a simpleton, a dupe. *Wheedle* may be derived from Anglo-Saxon *wædlian*, to beg, originally to be poor, from *wædl*, poverty. *Cajole* meant formerly to chatter like a jay. It may be of imitative origin. *Fawn* is derived from Anglo-Saxon *fahnian*, to rejoice, from *fægen*, fain, glad, and means to rejoice servilely, hence to cringe.

The idea of using mean arts to turn people to one's selfish purposes is common to all these terms: *coax* has something childish in it; *wheedle* and *cajole* that which is knavish; *fawn* that which is servile. The act of *coaxing* consists of urgent entreaty and whining supplication; the act of *wheedling* consists of smooth and winning entreaty; *cajoling* consists mostly of trickery and stratagem, disguised under a soft address and insinuating manners; the act of *fawning* consists of supplicant grimace and antics, such as characterize the little animal from which it derives its name: children *coax* their parents in order to obtain their wishes; the greedy and covetous *wheedle* those of any easy temper; knaves *cajole* the simple and unsuspecting; parasites *fawn* upon those who have the power to contribute to their gratifications: *coaxing* is mostly resorted to by inferiors toward those on whom they are dependent; *wheedling* and *cajoling* are low practices confined to the baser sort of men with one another; *fawning*, though not less mean and disgraceful than the above-mentioned vices, is commonly practised only in the higher walks, where men of base character, though not mean education, come in connection with the great.

COERCE, RESTRAIN. *Coerce*, in Latin *coerceo*, that is, *con* and *arceo*, from *arca*, a chest, signifies to drive into *conformity*, with the under meaning of enclosing. *Restrain* is a variation of *restrict* (see BIND).

Coercion is a species of *restraint:* we always *restrain* or intend to *restrain* when we *coerce;* but we do not always *coerce* when we *restrain; coercion* always comprehends the idea of force; *restraint*, that of simply keeping under or back: *coercion* is always an external application; *restraint* either external or internal: a person is *coerced* by others only; he may be *restrained* by himself as well as others. *Coercion* acts by a direct application: it opposes force to resistance: *restraint* acts indirectly to the prevention of an act: the law *restrains* all men in their actions more or less; it *coerces* those who attempt to violate it; the unruly will is *coerced;* the improper will is *restrained. Coercion* is exercised; *restraint* is imposed: punishment, threats, or any actual exercise of authority, *coerces;* fear, shame, or a remonstrance from others, *restrains.*

COEVAL, CONTEMPORARY. *Coeval,* from the Latin *ævum,* an age, signifies of the same age. *Contemporary,* from *tempus,* signifies of the same time.

An age is a specifically long space of time; a time is indefinite; hence the application of the terms to things in the first case and to persons in the second: the dispersion of mankind and the confusion of languages with *coeval* with the building of the tower of Babel; Addison was *contemporary* with Swift and Pope.

COGENT, FORCIBLE, STRONG. *Cogent,* from the Latin *cogere,* to compel; and *forcible,* from the verb to *force* (see COMPEL), have equally the sense of acting by *force. Strong* is here figuratively employed for that species of strength which is connected with the mind (for derivation see STRONG).

Cogency applies to reasons individually considered; *force* and *strength,* to modes of reasoning or expression: *cogent* reasons impel to decisive conduct; *strong* conviction is produced by *forcible* reasoning conveyed in *strong* language: changes of any kind are so seldom attended with benefit to society that a legislator will be cautious not to adopt them without the most *cogent* reasons; the important truths of Christianity cannot be presented from the pulpit too *forcibly* to the minds of men. Accuracy and *strength* are seldom associated in the same mind; those who accustom themselves to *strong* language are not very scrupulous about the correctness of their assertions.

COINCIDE. See AGREE; TALLY.

COLD. See CHILL; COOL.

COLLEAGUE, PARTNER. *Colleague,* in French *collègue,* Latin *col-*

lega, compounded of *ligare,* to bind, signifies united in the same work. *Partner,* from Latin *partem* (acc.), part, whence our word *part* is derived, signifies one having a *part* or share.

Colleague is more noble than *partner:* men in the highest offices are *colleagues;* tradesmen, mechanics, and subordinate persons are *partners:* every Roman consul had a *colleague;* every workman had commonly a *partner. Colleague* is used only with regard to community of office; *partner* is most generally used with regard to community of interest: whenever two persons are employed to act together on the same business they stand in the relation of *colleagues* to each other; whenever two persons unite their endeavors either in trade or in games, or the business of life, they are denominated *partners:* ministers, judges, commissioners, and plenipotentiaries are *colleagues;* bankers, chess-players, card-players, and the like, have *partners.*

COLLECT. See ASSEMBLE; GARNER.

COLLECTED. See CALM.

COLLECTION. See ASSEMBLY.

COLLOQUY. See CONVERSATION.

COLOR, DYE, TINGE, STAIN. To *color,* in Latin *color,* signifies to put *color* on or give *color* to a thing. To *dye,* in Anglo-Saxon *deagian,* signifies to imbue with a *color.* To *tinge,* in Latin *tingo,* and Greek τέγγειν, to sprinkle, signifies to touch lightly with a *color. Stain,* in French *déteindre,* comes from Latin *dis,* apart, and *tingere,* color, signifies to put a *color* on in a bad manner, or give a bad *color.*

To *color,* which is the most indefinite of these terms, is employed technically for putting a *color* on a thing; as to *color* a drawing.

But to *color,* in the general sense of giving *color,* may be applied to physical objects; as to *color* the cheeks. More commonly, however, to moral objects, as to *color* a description with the introduction of strong figures, strong facts, or strong descriptions, etc.

To *dye* is a process of art, as in the *dyeing* of cloth, but the term is applied to objects generally in the sense of imbuing with any substance so as to change the *color.*

To *tinge* may be applied to ordinary objects; as to *tinge* a painting with blue by way of intermixing *colors;* but it is most appropriately used in poetry.

To *stain* is used in its proper sense when applied to common objects; as to *stain* a painting by putting blue instead of red, or to *stain* anything by giving it an unnatural *color.*

Whence it has also a moral application in the sense of taking away the purity from a thing; as to *stain* the reputation or character.

Color, Hue, Tint.—*Hue* and *tint*, from *tinge*, are but modes of *color;* the former of which expresses a faint or blended *color;* the latter a shade of *color.* Between the *colors* of black and brown, as of all other leading *colors*, there are various *hues* and *tints*, by the due intermixture of which natural objects are rendered beautiful.

Colorable, Specious, Ostensible, Plausible, Feasible.—*Colorable*, from to *color* or *tinge*, expresses the quality of being able to give a fair appearance. *Specious*, from the Latin *species*, appearance, from the root *spec*, to see, signifies the quality of looking as it ought. *Ostensible*, from the Latin *ostendere*, to stretch before the eyes, signifies the quality of being able or fit to be shown or seen. *Plausible*, from *plaudo*, to clap or make a noise, signifies something deserving of applause or approval. *Feasible*, from the French *faire*, and Latin *facere*, to do, signifies literally *doable*, and denotes seemingly practicable.

The first three of these words are figures of speech drawn from what naturally pleases the eye; *plausible* is drawn from what pleases the ear: *feasible* takes its signification from what meets the judgment or conviction. What is *colorable* has an aspect or face upon it that lulls suspicion and affords satisfaction; what is *specious* has a fair outside when contrasted with that which it may possibly conceal; what is *ostensible* is that which presents such an appearance as may serve for an indication of something real: what is *plausible* is that which meets the understanding merely through the ear; that which is *feasible* recommends itself from its intrinsic value rather than from any representation given of it. A pretence is *colorable* when it has the *color* of truth impressed upon it; it is *specious* when its fallacy is easily discernible through the thin guise it wears; a motive is *ostensible* which is the one soonest to be discovered; an excuse is *plausible* when the well-connected narrative of the maker impresses a belief of its justice: a plan is *feasible* which recommends itself as fit to be put in execution.

COMBAT, Oppose. *Combat*, from the French *combattre*, from Latin *con*, together, and *batuere*, to beat, to fight together, is used figuratively in the same sense with regard to matters of opinion. *Oppose*, through French *opposer*, from Latin *ob* and Late Latin *pansare*, for *pono*, to place one's self in the way, signifies to set one's self against another.

Combat is properly a species of *opposing;* one always *opposes* in *combating*, though not *vice versa*. To *combat* is used in regard to speculative matters; *oppose* in regard to private and personal concerns. A person's positions are *combated*, his interests or his measures are *opposed*. The Christian *combats* the erroneous doctrines of the infidel with no other weapon than that of argument: the sophist *opposes* Christianity with ridicule and misrepresentation. The most laudable use to which knowledge can be converted is to *combat* error wherever it presents itself; but there are too many, particularly in the present day, who employ the little pittance of knowledge which they have collected to no better purpose than to *oppose* everything that is good, and excite the same spirit of *opposition* in others.

See also BATTLE; CONFLICT.

COMBATANT, Champion. *Combatant*, from to *combat*, marks any one that engages in a *combat*. *Champion*, French *champion*, signifies originally a soldier or fighter, from the Latin *campus*, a field, especially a field of battle.

A *combatant* fights for himself and for victory; a *champion* fights either for another or in another's cause. The word *combatant* has always relation to some actual engagement; *champion* may be employed for one ready to be engaged or in the habit of being engaged. The *combatants* in the Olympic games used to contend for a prize; the Roman gladiators were *combatants* who fought for their lives: when knight-errantry was in fashion there were *champions* of all descriptions, *champions* in behalf of distressed females, *champions* in behalf of the injured and oppressed, or *champions* in behalf of aggrieved princes. The mere act of fighting constitutes a *combatant;* the act of standing up in another's defence at a personal risk constitutes the *champion.* Animals have their *combats,* and consequently are *combatants;* but they are seldom *champions.* There may be *champions* for causes as well as persons, and for bad as well as good causes; as *champions* for liberty, for infidelity, and for Christianity.

COMBINATION, CABAL, PLOT, CONSPIRACY. *Combination* (see ASSO-CIATION). *Cabal,* in French *cabale,* comes from the Hebrew *kabala,* signifying a secret science pretended to by the Jewish rabbi, whence it is applied to any association that has a pretended secret. *Plot,* in French *complot,* is a word of unknown origin. *Plot* in the sense of *plan* may have developed from *plot,* a small portion, to *plot* being to lay out in portions; from this familiar significance of the word may have developed its sinister meaning. *Conspiracy,* in French *conspiration,* from *con* and *spirare,* to breathe together, signifies the having one spirit.

An association for a bad purpose is the idea common to all these terms, and peculiar to *combination.* A *combination* may be either secret or open, but secrecy forms a necessary part in the signification of the other terms; a *cabal* is secret as to its end; a *plot* and *conspiracy* are secret both as to the means and the end. *Combination* is the close adherence of many for their mutual defence in obtaining their demands or resisting the claims of others. A *cabal* is the intrigue of a party or faction, formed by cunning practices in order to give a turn to the course of things to their own advantage: the natural and ruling idea in *cabal* is that of assembling a number and manœuvring secretly with address. A *plot* is a clandestine union of some persons for the purpose of mischief: the ruling idea in a *plot* is that of a complicated enterprise formed in secret, by two or more persons. A *conspiracy* is a general intelligence among persons united to effect some serious change: the ruling and natural idea in this word is that of unanimity and concert in the prosecution of a plan.

Combination, Cabal, Junto.— A special term applied to a *combination* or *cabal* for political purposes is found in the word *junto,* from Spanish *junta* (Latin *jungere,* to join), signifying a secret council or assembly, a select body of men combined secretly to effect some political aim. The form *junta* refers specifically to the Grand Council of the State of Spain, and was adopted in 1895 by the Cuban insurgents to designate the representation of their cause in foreign countries. The form *junto* is applicable to any secret gathering of men of a political character. It does not have the sinister significance of *cabal,* but, like *cabal,* it adds the idea of secrecy to that of *combination.*

See also ASSOCIATION.

COMBINE. See CONNECT; MERGE.

COMBINED. See SYNTHETIC.

COME, ARRIVE. *Come* is general; *arrive* is particular.

Persons or things *come;* persons only, or what is personified, *arrives.* To *come* specifies neither time nor manner; *arrival* is employed with regard to some particular period or circumstance. The *coming* of our Saviour was predicted by the prophets; the *arrival* of a messenger is expected at a certain hour. We know that evils must *come,* but we do wisely not to meet them by anticipation; the *arrival* of a vessel in the haven, after a long and dangerous voyage, is a circumstance of general interest in the neighborhood where it happens.

COMELY. See BECOMING.

COMFORT, PLEASURE. *Comfort* (see CHEER). *Pleasure,* from to *please,* signifies what *pleases.*

Comfort describes a state of quiet enjoyment, a freedom from trouble, pain, or disquiet. It is applied also to the relief or strength afforded in time of weakness, oppression, or danger. The grand feature in *comfort* is substantiality; in that of *pleasure* is warmth. *Pleasure* is quickly succeeded by pain; it is the lot of humanity that to every *pleasure* there should be an alloy: *comfort* is that portion of *pleasure* which seems to lie exempt from this disadvantage; it is the most durable sort of *pleasure*. *Comfort* must be sought for at home; *pleasure* is pursued abroad: *comfort* depends upon a thousand nameless trifles which daily arise; it is the relief of a pain, the heightening of a gratification, the supply of a want, or the removal of an inconvenience. *Pleasure* is the companion of luxury and abundance: it dwells in the palaces of the rich and the abodes of the voluptuary. *Comfort* is less than *pleasure* in the detail; it is more than *pleasure* in the aggregate.

See also CHEER; CONSOLE; HEARTEN.

COMICAL. See LAUGHABLE.

COMMAND, ORDER, INJUNCTION, PRECEPT. *Command* is compounded of *con*, together, and *mandare*, or *dare in manus*, to give into the hand, signifying to give or appoint as a task. *Order*, in the extended sense of regularity, implies what is done in the way of *order* or for the sake of regularity. *Injunction* comes from *in* and *jungo*, which signifies literally to join or bring close to; figuratively, to impress on the mind. *Enjoin* is derived from the same Latin word. *Precept*, in French *précepte*, Latin *præceptum*, participle of *præcipio*, compounded of *præ* and *capere*, to take before, signifies the thing proposed to the mind.

A *command* is an exercise of power or authority; it is imperative and must be obeyed: an *order* serves to direct; it is instructive and must be executed.

Command is properly the act of a superior or of one possessing power: *order* has more respect to the office than to the person. A sovereign issues his *commands*: *orders* may be given by a subordinate or by a body; as *orders* in council, or *orders* of a court.

A *command* may be divine or given from heaven; an *order* or *injunction* is given by men only.

Order is applied to the common concerns of life; *injunction* and *precept* to the moral conduct or duties of men. *Injunction* imposes a duty by virtue of the authority which enjoins: the

precept lays down or teaches such duties as already exist.

See also PRAISE.

COMMANDING, IMPERATIVE, IMPERIOUS, AUTHORITATIVE. *Commanding* signifies having the force of a *command* (see above). *Imperative*, from Latin *imperare*, is derived from Latin *in*, and *parare*, to prepare, hence to order, arrange, command. *Imperious*, also from *imperare*, signifies in the way of, or like a command. *Authoritative* signifies having authority, or in the way of *authority* (for the derivation of which see INFLUENCE).

Commanding is either good or bad, according to circumstances; a *commanding* voice is necessary for one who has to command; but a *commanding* air is offensive when it is affected: *imperative* is applied to things, and used in an indifferent sense; *imperious* is used for persons or things in the bad sense: any direction is *imperative* which comes in the shape of a command, and circumstances are likewise *imperative* which act with the force of a command: persons are *imperious* who exercise their power oppressively; in this manner underlings in office are *imperious*; necessity is *imperious* when it leaves us no choice in our conduct. *Authoritative* is mostly applied to persons or things personal in the good sense only; magistrates are called upon to assume an *authoritative* air when they meet with any resistance.

COMMEMORATE. See CELEBRATE.

COMMENCE. See BEGIN.

COMMENDABLE. See LAUDABLE.

COMMENSURATE. See PROPORTIONATE.

COMMENT. See REMARK.

COMMENTARY. See REMARK.

COMMERCE. See INTERCOURSE; TRADE.

COMMERCIAL. See MERCANTILE.

COMMISERATION. See SYMPATHY.

COMMISSION, AUTHORIZE, EMPOWER. *Commission*, from Latin *cum*, with, and *mittere*, to send, signifies the act of sending some one with authority, or putting into the hands of another. To *authorize* signifies to give *authority*; to *empower*, to put in possession of *power*.

The idea of transferring some business to another is common to these terms; the circumstances under which this is performed constitute the difference. We *commission* in ordinary cases; we *authorize* and *empower* in extraordinary cases. We *commission* in matters where our own will and convenience are concerned; we *authorize* in matters where our personal *authority* is requisite; and we *empower* in matters where the *authority* of the law is required. A *commission* is given by the bare communication of one's wishes; we *authorize* by a positive and formal declaration to that intent; we *empower* by the transfer of some legal document. A person is *commissioned* to make a purchase; he is *authorized* to communicate what has been confided to him; he is *empowered* to receive money. *Commissioning* passes mostly between equals; the performance of *commissions* is an act of civility; *authorizing* and *empowering* are as often directed to inferiors; they are frequently acts of justice and neecssity. Friends give one another *commissions;* servants and subordinate persons are sometimes *authorized* to act in the name of their employers; magistrates *empower* the officers of justice to apprehend individuals or enter houses. We are *commissioned* by persons only; we are *authorized* sometimes by circumstances; we are *empowered* by law.

COMMIT. See CONSIGN; PERPETUATE.

COMMODIOUS, CONVENIENT. *Commodious,* from the Latin *commodus,* or *con* and *modus,* according to the measure and degree required. *Convenient,* from the Latin *conveniens,* participle of *con* and *venire,* to come together, signifies that which comes together with something else as it ought.

The *commodious* is a species of the *convenient,* namely, that which men contrive for their convenience. *Commodious* is therefore mostly applied to that which contributes to the bodily ease and comfort, *convenient* to whatever suits the purposes of men in their various transactions: a house, a chair, or a place is *commodious;* a time, an opportunity, a season, or the arrival of a person is *convenient.*

What is *commodious* is rendered so by design; what is *convenient* is so from the nature of the thing: in this sense arguments may be termed *commodious* which favor a person's ruling propensity or passion.

COMMODITY, GOODS, MERCHANDISE, WARE. These terms agree in expressing articles of trade under various circumstances. *Commodity,* in Latin *commoditas,* signifies in its abstract sense *convenience,* and in an extended application anything that is *convenient* or fit for use. This being also salable, the word has been applied to things that are sold. *Goods,* from Anglo-Saxon *god,* fit, which denotes the thing that is good, has derived its use from the same analogy in its sense. *Merchandise,* from Latin *merx,* pay, Greek μάρπτειν, to seize, signifies salable things. (Compare the derivation of *mercy* under the key-word CLEMENCY.) *Ware,* Anglo-Saxon *waru,* originally meant valuables, being allied to *waru,* signifying protection, guard, custody, etc.

Commodity is employed only for articles of the first necessity; it is the source of comfort and object of industry: *goods* is applied to everything belonging to tradesmen for which there is a stipulated value; they are sold retail, and are the proper objects of trade: *merchandise* applies to what belongs to merchants; it is the object of commerce: *wares* are manufactured, and may be either goods or *merchandise;* a country has its *commodities,* a shopkeeper his *goods,* a merchant his *merchandise,* a manufacturer his *wares.*

COMMON, VULGAR, ORDINARY, MEAN. *Common,* in French *commun,* Latin *communis,* from *con* and *munus,* the joint office or property of many, has regard to the multitude of objects. *Vulgar,* in French *vulgaire,* Latin *vulgaris,* from *vulgus,* the people, has regard to the number and quality of the persons. *Ordinary,* in French *ordinaire,* Latin *ordinarius,* from *ordo,* the order or regular practice, has regard to the repetition or disposition of things. *Mean* is derived from Anglo-Saxon *mæne,* which usually appears in the word *gemæne,* common (German *gemein);* its meaning has been influenced by Latin *medius,* moderate, and by the English *mean,* the middle place, derived from that Latin word. Familiar use renders things *common*, *vulgar*, and *ordinary;* but what is *mean* is so of itself: the *common*, *vulgar*, and *ordinary* are therefore frequently, though not always, *mean;* and, on the contrary, what is *mean* is not always *common*, *vulgar*, or *ordinary;* consequently in the primitive sense of these words the first three are not strictly synonymous with the last: monsters are *common* in Africa; *vulgar* reports are little to be relied on; it is an *ordinary* practice for men to make light of their word.

In the figurative sense in which they convey the idea of low value they are synonymous with *mean;* what is to be seen, heard, and enjoyed by everybody is *common* and naturally of little value, since the worth of objects frequently depends upon their scarcity and the difficulty of obtaining them. What is peculiar to *common* people is *vulgar* and consequently worse than *common;* it is supposed to belong to those who are ignorant and depraved in taste as well as in morals: what is done and seen *ordinarily* may be done and seen easily; it requires no abilities or mental acquirements; it has nothing striking in it, it excites no interest: what is *mean* is even below that which is *ordinary;* there is something defective in it. *Common* is opposed to rare and refined; *vulgar*, to polite and cultivated; *ordinary*, to the distinguished; *mean*, to the noble: a *common* mind busies itself with *common* objects; *vulgar* habits are easily contracted from a slight intercourse with *vulgar* people; an *ordinary* person is seldom associated with elevation of character; and a *mean* appearance is a certain mark of a degraded condition if not of a degraded mind. See also PUBLIC.

Commonly, Generally, Frequently, Usually.—*Commonly*, in the form of *common* (see above). *Generally*, from *general*, and the Latin *genus*, the kind, respects a whole body in distinction to an individual. *Frequently*, from *frequent*, Latin *frequens*, is derived from a lost Latin verb, *frequere*, to cram, and signifies, properly, in a crowding manner. *Usually*, from Latin *usualis*, from *usus*, use, signifies according to *use* or custom.

What is *commonly* done is an action *common* to all; what is *generally* done is the action of the greatest part; what is *frequently* done is either the action of many or an action many times repeated by the same person; what is *usually* done is done regularly by one or many. *Commonly* is opposed to rarely; *generally* and *frequently*, to occasionally or seldom; *usually*, to casually: men *commonly* judge of others by themselves; those who judge by the mere exterior are *generally* deceived; but notwithstanding every precaution one is *frequently* exposed to gross frauds; a man of business *usually* repairs to his counting-house every day at a certain hour.

COMMON - CARRIER, SHIPPER, TRANSPORTER. *Common-carrier* is one of two conspicuous legal and commercial terms applied to a person or company engaged in the business of carrying goods from one place to another for the general public and for pay; the other term being *private-carrier*, one who carries only for a particular customer and not for the general public, and who incurs no responsibility beyond that of ordinary diligence.

A *common-carrier* by land may be a railroad corporation, express company, stage-coach proprietor, a truckman, teamster, or porter, and a *common-carrier* by water may be a steamship company, the master or owner of other ships and vessels engaged in transportation of goods, a lighterman, canal-boatman, ferryman, and others employed in like manner.

A *shipper* is one who puts goods on board the *ship;* and is extended to refer to any one whose business it is to put goods on some means of conveyance for *transportation* to another place. The *transporter* (from Latin *trans*, across, and *portare*, to carry) is, strictly speaking, the person who carries the goods from one spot to another. A *common-carrier* in America is a public *transporter*, and as such is bound by strict legal obligations defined by the Interstate Commerce Commission.

COMMONWEALTH. See STATE.

COMMOTION, DISTURBANCE. *Commotion*, compounded of *cum*, together, and *movere*, signifying properly a motion of several together, expresses more than *disturbance*, which denotes the state of being *disturbed* (see TROUBLE). When applied to physical objects, *commotion* denotes the violent motion of several objects or of the several parts of any individual thing; *disturbance* denotes any motion or noise which puts a thing out of its natural state. We speak of the *commotion* of the elements, or the stillness of the night being *disturbed* by the rustling of the leaves.

In respect to men or animals, *commotion* and *disturbance* may be either inward or outward with a like distinction in their signification. A *commotion* supposes a motion of all the feelings; a *disturbance* of the mind may amount to no more than an interruption of the quiet to an indefinite degree.

So in regard to external circumstances: a *commotion* in public is occasioned by extraordinary circumstances, and is accompanied with unusual bustle and movement; whatever interrupts the peace of a neighborhood is a *disturbance:* political events occasion a *commotion;* drunkenness is a common cause of *disturbances* in the streets or in families.

COMMUNICATE, IMPART. To *communicate*, from the Latin *communis*, common, signifies to make common, or give a joint possession or enjoyment: to *impart*, from *in* and *part*, signifies to give in part or make partaker. Both these words denote the giving some part of what one has in his power or possession; but the former is more general and indefinite in its signification and application than the latter. A thing may be *communicated* directly or indirectly, and to any number of persons; as to *communicate* intelligence by signal or otherwise. *Impart* is a direct action that passes between individuals; as to *impart* instruction.

What is *communicated* may be a matter of interest to the person *communicating* or otherwise; but what is *imparted* is commonly and properly that which interests both parties. A man may *communicate* the secrets of another as well as his own; he *imparts* his sentiments and feelings to a friend.

Communion, Converse.—Communion, from *commune* and *common*, signifies the act of making common. *Converse*, from Latin *con* and *versari*, to dwell, from *vertere*, to turn, signifies the intercourse of those dwelling together.

Both these terms imply a communication between minds; but the former may take place without corporeal agency, the latter never does; spirits hold *communion* with one another; people hold *converse*. For the same reason a man may hold *communion* with himself; he holds *converse* always with another.

See also LORD'S SUPPER.

COMMUNISM. See SOCIALISM.

COMMUNITY, SOCIETY. Both these terms are employed for a body of rational beings. *Community*, from *communitas* and *communis*, common, signifies abstractly the state of being *common*, and in an extended sense those who are in a state of common possession. *Society*, in Latin *societas*, from *socius*, a companion, signifies the state of being companions, or those who are in that state.

Community in anything constitutes a *community;* a common interest, a common language, a common government, is the basis of that *community* which is formed by any number of individuals; the coming together of many and keeping together under given laws and for given purposes constitutes a *society*; *societies* are either public or private, according to the purpose: friends form *societies* for pleasure, indifferent persons form *societies* for business. The term *community* is therefore appropriately applied to indefinite numbers, and *society* in cases where the number is restricted by the nature of the union.

The term *community* may likewise be applied to a small body, and in some cases be indifferently used for *society;* but as it always retains its generality of meaning, the term *society* is more proper where the idea of a close union, a tie, or obligation is to be expressed; as, every member of the *community* is equally interested; every member of the *society* is bound to contribute.

See also PUBLIC.

COMMUTE. See EXCHANGE.

COMPACT. See AGREEMENT; CLOSE.

COMPANION. See ACCOMPANIMENT; ASSOCIATE.

COMPANY. See ASSEMBLY; ASSO-CIATION; BAND; SOCIETY; TROOP.

COMPARISON, CONTRAST. *Comparison*, Latin *comparo*, or *con*, together, and *par*, equal, signifies the putting together of equals. *Contrast*, in French *contraster*, Latin *contrasto*, or *contra*, against, and *stare*, to stand, signifies the placing one thing opposite to another.

Likeness in the quality and difference in the degree are requisite for a *comparison;* likeness in the degree and opposition in the quality are requisite for a *contrast:* things of the same color are *compared;* those of an opposite color are *contrasted:* a *comparison* is made between two shades of red: a *contrast* between black and white. *Comparison* is of a practical utility, it serves to ascertain the true relation of objects; *contrast* is of utility among poets, it serves to heighten the effect of opposite qualities: things are large or small by *comparison;* they are magnified or diminished in one's mind by *contrast:* the value of a coin is best learned by *comparing* it with another of the same metal; the generosity of one person is most strongly felt when *contrasted* with the meanness of another.

See also SIMILE.

COMPASSION. See PITY; SYMPATHY.

COMPATIBLE, CONSISTENT. *Compatible*, compounded of *com* or *cum*, with, and *pati*, to suffer, signifies a fitness to be suffered together. *Consistent*, in Latin *consistens*, participle of *consisto*, compounded of *con* and *sistere*, to cause to stand, to please, signifies the fitness to be placed together.

Compatibility has principally a reference to plans and measures; *consistency*, to character, conduct, and station. Everything is *compatible* with a plan which does not interrupt its prosecution; everything is *consistent* with a person's station by which it is neither degraded nor elevated. It is not *compatible* with the good discipline of a school to allow of foreign interference; it is not *consistent* with the elevated and dignified character of a clergyman to engage in the ordinary pursuits of other men.

COMPEL, FORCE, OBLIGE, NECESSITATE. All these terms denote the application of force either on the body or the mind in order to influence the conduct. To *compel*, from the Latin *con* and *pello*, drive, signifying to drive to a specific point, denotes rather moral than physical force; but to *force*, from Latin *fors*, strong, signifying to effect by force, is properly applied to the use of physical force or a violent degree of moral force. A man may be *compelled* to walk if he have no means of riding; he may be *forced* to go at the will of another.

These terms may, therefore, be applied to the same objects to denote different degrees of force.

Compel expresses a direct and powerful force on the will which leaves no choice. *Oblige*, from *ob* and *ligare*, to bind, signifying to bind or keep down to a particular point, expresses only an indirect influence, which may be resisted or yielded at discretion; we are *compelled* to do that which is repugnant to our will and our feelings; that which one is *obliged* to do may have the assent of the judgment if not of the will. Wants *compel* men to do many things which are inconsistent with their station and painful to their feelings. Honor and religion *oblige* men scrupulously to observe their word one to another.

Compel, force, and *oblige* are mostly the acts of persons in the proper sense. *Necessitate*, which signifies to lay under a necessity, is properly the act of things. We are *necessitated* by circumstances, or by anything which puts it out of our power to do otherwise.

Compel, Impel, Constrain, Restrain.—To *compel* and *impel* are both derived from the verb *pello*, to drive; the former, by the force of the preposition *com*, is to drive to any particular action or for a given purpose; but the latter, from the preposition *im* or *in*, into, is to force into action generally. A person, therefore, is *compelled* by outward circumstances, but he is *impelled* from within: he is *compelled* by another to go farther than he wished, he is *impelled* by curiosity to go farther than he intended. *Constrain* and *restrain* are from *stringere*, to bind or oblige. The former, by force of the *con* or *com*, to force in a particular manner or for a particular purpose; the latter by the *re*, back or again, is to keep back from anything. To *constrain*, like to *compel*, is to force to act; to *restrain*, to prevent from acting. *Constrain* and *compel* differ only in the degree of force used, *constrain* signifying a less degree of force than *compel*. A person who is *compelled* has no choice whatever left to him; but when he is only *constrained* he may do it or not at discretion.

Constraint is put on the actions or movements of the body only, *restraint* on the movements of both body and mind: a person who is in a state of *constraint* shows his want of freedom in the awkwardness of his movements; he who is in a state of *restraint* may be unable to move at all. *Constraint* arises from that which is inherent in the person, *restraint* is imposed upon him.

See also CONSTRAINT.

COMPENDIUM. See ABRIDGMENT.

COMPENSATION, AMENDS, SATISFACTION, RECOMPENSE, REMUNERATION, REQUITAL, REWARD. All these terms imply some return or equivalent for something else, good or bad. *Compensation*, from *cum* and *pendere*, to weigh, signifies literally what is weighed with or against something else, hence paid for another thing. *Amends*, signifies that which amends or makes good. *Satisfaction*, that which satisfies or makes up something wanted. *Recompense*, from *pensum*, participle of *pendo*, that which pays back. *Remuneration*, from *munus*, a gift or reward, that which is given back by way of reward. *Requital*, from to *quit*, that which acquits in return. The first three of these terms denote a return or equivalent for something amiss or wanting; the last three a return for some good.

A *compensation* is a return for a loss or damage sustained; justice requires that it should be equal in value, although not alike in kind.

Amends is a return for anything that is faulty in ourselves or toward others. A person may make *amends* for idleness at one time by double portion of diligence at another.

A man may make another *amends* for any hardship done to him by showing him some extra favor another way.

Satisfaction is that which satisfies the individual requiring it; it is given for personal injuries, and may be made either by a slight return or otherwise, according to the disposition of the person to be satisfied. As regards man and man, affronts are often unreal, and the *satisfaction* demanded is still oftener absurd and unchristian-like. As regards man and his Maker, *satisfaction* is for our offences, which Divine Justice demands and Divine Mercy accepts.

Compensation and *amends* may both denote a simple equivalent without any reference to that which is personal. A *compensation* in this case may be an advantage one way to counterbalance a disadvantage another way. Or it may be the putting one desirable thing of equal value in the place of another. An *amends* supplies a defect by something superabundant in another part.

Compensation is sometimes taken for a payment or some indefinite return for a service or good done: this brings it nearer in sense to the words *recompense* and *remuneration*, with this difference, that the *compensation* is given for bodily labor, or inferior services; *recompense* and *remuneration*, for that which is done by persons in a superior condition. The time and strength of a poor man ought not to be used without his receiving a *compensation*.

A *recompense* is a voluntary return for a voluntary service; it is made from a generous feeling, and derives its value not so much from the magnitude of the service or return as from the intentions of the parties toward each other; and it is received not so much as a matter of right as of courtesy; there are a thousand acts of civility performed by others which may be entitled to some *recompense*.

Remuneration is not so voluntary as *recompense*, but it is equally indefinite, being estimated rather according to the condition of the person and the dignity of the service than its positive worth. Authors often receive a *remuneration* for their works according to the reputation they have previously acquired, and not according to the real merit of the work.

Requital is the return of a kindness, the making it is an act of gratitude.

Reward, from *ward,* and the German *währen,* to see, signifies properly a looking back upon—*i. e.,* a return that has respect to something else. A *reward* conveys no idea of an obligation on the part of the person making it; whoever *rewards* acts optionally. It is the conduct which produces the *reward,* and consequently this term, unlike all the others, denotes a return for either good or evil. Whatever accrues to a man and the consequences of his conduct, be it good or bad, is a *reward.* The *reward* of industry is ease and content.

When a deceiver is caught in his own snare, he meets with the *reward* which should always attend deceit.

A *compensation, recompense, requital,* and *reward* may be a bad as well as a good return. That which ill supplies the thing wanted is a bad *compensation;* honor is but a poor *compensation* for the loss of health.

That which does not answer one's expectations is a bad *recompense;* there are many things which people pursue with much eagerness that do not *recompense* the trouble bestowed upon them.

When evil is returned for good, that is a bad *requital,* and, as a proof of ingratitude, wounds the feelings. Those who befriend the wicked may expect to be ill *requited.*

A *reward* may be a bad return when it is inadequate to the merits of the person.

COMPETENT, Fitted, Qualified. *Competent,* from *con,* together, and *petere,* to seek, signifies suitable (literally, seeking that which belongs to one). *Fitted,* from *fit* (see Becoming). *Qualified,* participle of *qualify,* from the Latin *qualis,* how much, and *facere,* to make, signifies made as much as it ought to be, measured up to a standard.

Competency mostly respects the mental endowments and attainments; *fitness,* the disposition and character; *qualification* the artificial acquirements or natural qualities. A person is *competent* to undertake an office; *fitted* or *qualified* to fill a situation. Familiarity with any subject aided by strong mental endowments gives *competency:* suitable habits and temper constitute the *fitness:* acquaintance with the business to be done, and expertness in the mode of performing it, constitute the *qualification:* none should pretend to give their opinions on serious subjects who are not *competent* judges; none but lawyers are *competent* to decide in cases of law; none but medical men are *competent* to prescribe medicines: none but divines of sound learning, as well as piety, to determine on doctrinal questions: men of sedentary and studious habits, with a serious temper, are most *fitted* to be clergymen: and those who have the most learning and acquaintance with the Holy Scriptures are the best *qualified* for the important and sacred office of instructing the people. Many are *qualified* for managing the concerns of others who would not be *competent* to manage a concern for themselves. Many who are *fitted,* from their turn of mind, for any particular charge may be unfortunately *incompetent* for want of the requisite *qualifications.*

COMPETITION, Emulation, Rivalry. *Competition,* from the Latin *competo,* compounded of *con* and *peto,* signifies to sue or seek together, to seek for the same object. *Emulation* comes from Latin *æmulus,* which means striving to be equal. *Rivalry,* from the Latin *rivus,* the bank of a stream, signifies the undivided or common enjoyment of any stream, which in olden times was a natural source of discord and led to *rivalry*

Competition is properly an act, *emulation* is a feeling or temper of mind which incites to action, and *emulation,* therefore, frequently furnishes the motive for *competition;* the bare action of seeking the same object constitutes the *competition;* the desire of excelling is the principal characteristic in *emulation.* *Competition,* therefore, applies to matters either of interest or honor where more than one person strive to gain a particular object, as *competition* for the purchase of a commodity or for a prize. *Emulation* is confined to matters that admit of superiority and distinction.

Rivalry resembles *emulation* as far as it has most respect to the feeling, and *competition* as far as it has respect to the action. But *competition* and *emulation* have for the most part a laudable object, and proceed in the attainment of it by honest means; *rivalry* has always a selfish object, and is often but little scrupulous in the choice of the means: a *competitor* may be unfair, but a *rival* is very rarely generous. There are *competitors* for office, or *competitors* at public games, and *rivals* for the favor of others.

When *emulation* degenerates into a desire for petty distinctions it is akin to *rivalry*.

Competitors must always come in close collision, as they seek for the same individual thing; but *rivals* may act at a distance, as they only work toward the same point: there may be *rivalry* between states which vie with one another in greatness or power, but there cannot properly be *competition*.

COMPLAIN, LAMENT, REGRET. *Complain*, French *complaindre* or *plaindre*, Latin *plango*, to beat the breast as a sign of grief. *Lament* (see BEWAIL). *Regret* comes through French from Latin *re* and a Scandinavian verb found in Anglo-Saxon *grætan*, to bewail.

Complaint marks most of dissatisfaction; *lamentation*, most of grief; *regret*, most of pain. *Complaint* is expressed verbally; *lamentation*, either by words or signs; *regret* may be felt without being expressed. *Complaint* is made of personal grievances; *lamentation* and *regret* may be made on account of others as well as ourselves. We *complain* of our ill health, of our inconveniences, or of troublesome circumstances; we *lament* our inability to serve another; we *regret* the absence of one whom we love. Selfish people have the most to *complain* of, as they demand most of others and are most liable to be disappointed; anxious people are the most liable to *lament*, as they feel everything strongly; the best-regulated mind may have occasion to *regret* some circumstances which give pain to the tender affections of the heart.

We may *complain* without any cause, and *lament* beyond what the cause requires; but *regret* is always founded on some real cause, and never exceeds in measure.

Complain, Murmur, Repine.—*Complain* (see above). *Murmur* is a word of imitative origin, from Latin *murmur*, Sanskrit *marmara*, the rustling sound of the wind; hence a low complaining. *Repine* is compounded of *re* and *pine*, from Anglo-Saxon *pin*, pain, Latin *pœna*, punishment, and Greek ποινή, penalty, signifying to think on with pain.

The idea of expressing displeasure or dissatisfaction of what is done by others is common to these terms. *Complaint* is not so loud as *murmuring*, but more so than *repining*. We *complain* or *murmur* by some audible method; we may *repine* secretly. *Complaints* are always addressed to some one; *murmurs* and *repinings* are often addressed only to one's self. *Complaints* are made of whatever creates uneasiness, without regard to the source from which they flow; *murmurings* are a species of *complaints* made only of that which is done by others for our inconvenience; when used in relation to persons, *complaint* is the act of a superior, or of one who has a right to express his dissatisfaction; *murmuring*, that of an inferior, or one who is subject to another. When the conduct of another offends, it calls for *complaint;* when a superior aggrieves by the imposition of what is burdensome, it occasions *murmuring* on the part of the aggrieved.

Complain and *murmur* may sometimes signify to be dissatisfied simply, without implying any direct expression which brings them nearer to the word *repine;* in this case *complain* expresses a less violent dissatisfaction than *murmur*, and both more than *repine*, which implies what is deep-seated. With this distinction they may all be employed to denote the dissatisfaction produced by events that inevitably happen. Men may be said to *complain, murmur,* or *repine* at their lot.

Complaint, Accusation.—*Complaint* (see preceding term). *Accusation* (see ACCUSE). Both these terms are employed in regard to the conduct of others, but a *complaint* is mostly made in matters that personally affect the *complainant;* an *accusation* is made of matters in general, but especially those of a moral nature. A *complaint* is made for the sake of obtaining redress; an *accusation* is made for the sake of ascertaining a fact or bringing to punishment. A *complaint* may be frivolous, an *accusation* false. People in subordinate stations should be careful to give no cause for *complaint:* the most guarded conduct will not protect any person from the unjust *accusations* of the malevolent.

COMPLAISANCE, DEFERENCE, CONDESCENSION. *Complaisance,* from the present participle of French *complaire* (Latin *complacere,* please), signifies the act of complying with, or pleasing others. *Deference,* in French *déférence,* from the Latin *defero,* to bear down, marks the inclination to defer, or acquiesce in the sentiments of another in preference to one's own. *Condescension,* from Latin *con,* with, and *descendere,* to descend, means the *descending* from one's own height to comply with the wishes of others.

The necessities, the conveniences, the accommodations and allurements of society, of familiarity, and of intimacy lead to *complaisance:* it makes sacrifices to the wishes, tastes, comforts, enjoyments, and personal feelings of others. Age, rank, dignity, and personal merit call for *deference:* it enjoins compliance with respect to our opinions, judgments, pretensions, and designs. The infirmities, the wants, the defects and foibles of others call for *condescension:* it relaxes the rigor of authority and removes the distinction of rank or station. *Complaisance* is the act of an equal; *deference,* that of an inferior; *condescension,* that of a superior. *Complaisance* is due from one well-bred person to another; *deference* is due to all superiors in age, knowledge, or station whom one approaches; *condescension* is due from all superiors to such as are dependent on them for comfort and enjoyment. All these qualities spring from a refinement of humanity; but *complaisance* has most of genuine kindness in its nature; *deference,* most of respectful submission; *condescension,* most of easy indulgence.

COMPLAISANT. See CIVIL; COURTEOUS.

COMPLETE, PERFECT, FINISHED. *Complete,* in French *complet,* Latin *completus,* participle of *complere,* to fill up, signifies the quality of being filled, or having all that is necessary. *Perfect,* in Latin *perfectus,* participle of *perficere,* from *per,* through, and *facere,* to do, signifies the state of being done thoroughly. *Finished,* from *finish* (see CLOSE), marks the state of being *finished.*

That is *complete* which has no deficiency: that is *perfect* which has positive excellence; and that is *finished* which has no omission in it. That to which anything can be added is *incomplete;* when it can be improved, it is *imperfect;* when more labor ought to be bestowed upon it, it is *unfinished.* A thing is *complete* in all its parts; *perfect* as to the beauty and design of the construction; and *finished* as it comes from the hand of the workman and answers his intention. A set of books is not *complete* when a volume is wanting: there is nothing in the proper sense *perfect* which is the work of man, but the term is used relatively for whatever makes the greatest approach to *perfection:* a *finished* performance evinces care and diligence on the part of the workman. These terms admit of the same distinction when applied to moral or intellectual objects.

See also WHOLE.

Complete, Finish, Terminate. — We *complete,* that is, make complete, what is undertaken by continuing to labor at it. We *finish* what is begun in a state of forwardness by putting the last hand to it. We *terminate* what ought not to last by bringing it to a close, from *terminus,* a term, a boundary, signifying to set bounds to a thing.

The characteristic idea of *completing* is that of making a thing altogether what it ought to be; that of *finishing* the doing all that is intended to be done toward a thing; and that of *terminating,* simply putting an end to a thing. *Completing* has properly relation to permanent works only, whether mechanical or intellectual; we desire a thing to be *completed* from a curiosity to see it in its entire state. To *finish* is employed for passing occupations; we wish a thing *finished* from an anxiety to proceed to something else, or a dislike to the thing in which we are engaged. *Terminating* respects space or time: a view may be *terminated,* a life may be *terminated,* or that to which one may put a term, as to *terminate* a dispute. Light minds undertake many things without *completing* any. Children and unsteady people set about many things without *finishing* any. Litigious people *terminate* one dispute only to commence another.

COMPLETELY. See QUITE.

COMPLETION. See CONSUMMATION.

COMPLEX. See COMPOUND.

COMPLEXITY, COMPLICATION, INTRICACY. *Complexity* and *complication,* in French *complication,* compounded of *con,* with, and *plectere,* to plait, allied to *plicare,* to twine, signifies a plaiting together of two different things—an interweaving. *Intricacy,* Latin *intricatio* and *intrico,* compounded of *in* and *tricæ,* perplexities, signifies a state of entanglement.

Complexity expresses the abstract quality or state; *complication* the act: they both convey less than *intricacy; intricate* is that which is very *complicated. Complexity* arises from a multitude of objects and the nature of these objects; *complication,* from an involvement of objects; and *intricacy,* from a winding and confused involution. What is *complex* must be decomposed; what is *complicated* must be developed; what is *intricate* must be unraveled. A proposition is *complex,* affairs are *complicated;* the law is *intricate.* The *complexity* of a subject often deters young persons from application to their business. There is nothing embarrasses a physician more than a *complication* of disorders, where the remedy for one impedes the cure for the other. Some affairs are involved in such a degree of *intricacy* as to exhaust the patience and perseverance of the most laborious.

COMPLIMENT. See ADULATE.

COMPLY, CONFORM, YIELD, SUBMIT. *Comply* (see AGREE). *Conform,* compounded of *con* and *formare,* signifies to put into the same *form. Yield* (see AGREE). *Submit,* in Latin *submitto,* compounded of *sub,* under, and *mittere,* to send, signifies to put under, that is to say, to put one's self under another person. *Compliance* and *conformity* are voluntary; *yielding* and *submission* are involuntary. *Compliance* is an act of the inclination; *conformity* an act of the judgment: *compliance* is altogether optional; we com-

ply with a thing or not, at pleasure; *conformity* is binding on the conscience; it relates to matters in which there is a right and a wrong. *Compliance* with the fashions and customs of those we live with is a natural propensity of the human mind that may be mostly indulged without impropriety; *conformity* in religious matters, though not to be enforced by human law, is not on that account less binding on the consciences of every member of the community; the violation of this duty on trivial grounds involves in it that of more than one breach of the moral law.

Compliance and *conformity* are produced by no external action on the mind; they flow spontaneously from the will and understanding: *yielding* is altogether the result of foreign agency. We *comply* with a wish as soon as it is known; it accords with our feelings so to do: we *yield* to the entreaties of others; it is the effect of persuasion, a constraint upon or at least a direction of the inclination. We *conform* to the regulations of a community, it is a matter of discretion; we *yield* to the superior judgment of another, we have no choice or alternative. We *comply* cheerfully; we *conform* willingly; we *yield* reluctantly. A cheerful *compliance* with the requests of a friend is the sincerest proof of friendship: the wisest and most learned of men have ever been the readiest to *conform* to the general sense of the community in which they live: the harmony of social life is frequently disturbed by the reluctance which men have to *yield* to one another.

To *yield* is to give way to another, either with one's will, judgment, or outward conduct; *submission* is the giving up of one's self altogether; it is the substitution of another's will for one's own. *Yielding* is partial; we may *yield* in one case or in one action, though not in another: *submission* is general; it includes a system of conduct.

We *yield* when we do not resist; this may sometimes be the act of a superior: we *submit* only by adopting the measures and conduct proposed to us; this always is the act of an inferior. *Yielding* may be produced by means more or less gentle, by enticing or insinuating arts, or by the force of argument; *submission* is made only to power or positive force: one *yields* after a struggle; one *submits* without resistance: we *yield* to ourselves or others; we *submit* to others only: it is a weakness to *yield* either to the suggestions of others or our own inclinations to do that which our judgments condemn; it is a folly to *submit* to the caprice of any one where there is not a moral obligation: it is obstinacy not to *yield* when one's adversary has the advantage; it is sinful not to *submit* to constituted authorities.

See also AGREE.

Compliant, Yielding, Submissive.— These epithets from the preceding verbs serve to designate a propensity to the respective actions, which may be excessive or otherwise. A *compliant* temper *complies* with every wish of another, good or bad: a *yielding* temper leans to every opinion, right or wrong; a *submissive* temper *submits* to every demand, just or unjust. A *complaint* person may want command of feeling; a *yielding* person may want fixedness of principle; a *submissive* person may want resolution: a too *complaint* disposition will be imposed upon by the selfish and unreasonable; a too *yielding* disposition is most unfit for commanding; a too *submissive* disposition exposes a person to the exactions of tyranny.

COMPOSE, SETTLE. *Compose* is derived through French from Greek παῦσις, a pause. "One of the most remarkable facts of French etymology is the extraordinary substitution whereby Late Latin *pausare*, from Greek, coming to mean to cause to rest, usurped the place of Latin *ponere*, with which it had no etymological connection at all; so that the compounds of *pausare* (*compausare*, French *composer*, for example) usurped the place of the compounds of Latin *ponere*, like *componere*, throughout" (Skeat). *Settle* is derived from Anglo-Saxon *setlan*, to fix, from *setl*, a seat, Modern English *settle*, a seat.

We *compose* that which has been disjointed and separated by bringing it together again; we *settle* that which has been disturbed and put in motion by making it rest: we *compose* our thoughts when they have been deranged and thrown into confusion: we *settle* our mind when it has been fluctuating and distracted by contending desires; the mind must be *composed* before we can think justly; it must be *settled* before we can act consistently.

Differences are *composed* where there are jarring and discord; it is effected by conciliation, differences are *settled* when they are brought to a final arrangement by consultation or otherwise. In this manner a person may be said to *compose* himself, his thoughts, his dress, and the like; to *settle* matters, points, questions, etc. It is a good thing to *compose* differences between friends; it is not always easy to *settle* questions where either party is obstinate.

See also COMPOUND; FORM.

Composed, Sedate.—*Composed* signifies the state or quality of being in order, or free from confusion or perturbation; it is applied either to the mind or to the air, manner, or carriage. *Sedate*, in Latin *sedatus*, from Latin *sedare*, to make calm, causative of *sedere*, to sit (compare *sedative*), signifies properly the quality of being settled (see COMPOSE), *i. e.*, free from irregular motion, and is applied either to the carriage or the temper. *Composed* is opposite to ruffled or hurried, and is a temporary state; *sedate* is opposed to buoyant or volatile, and is a permanent habit of the mind or body. A person may be *composed* or his carriage may be *composed* in moments of excitement. Young people are rarely *sedate*.

See also CALM; SYNTHETIC.

COMPOUND, COMPLEX. *Compound* comes from the present of *componere*, to place together. *Complex* (see COMPLEXITY).

The *compound* consists of similar and whole bodies put together; the *complex* consists of various parts linked together: adhesion is sufficient to constitute a *compound*; involution is requisite for the *complex*; we distinguish the whole that forms the *compound*; we separate the parts that form the *complex*; what is *compound* may consist only of two; what is *complex* consists always of several. *Compound* and *complex* are both commonly opposed

to the simple; but the former may be opposed to the single, and the latter to the simple: words are *compounded*, sentences are *complex*.

Compound, Compose.—*Compound* and *compose* (see COMPOSE). *Compound* is used in the physical sense only; *compose* in the proper or the moral sense; words are *compounded* by making two or more into one; sentences are *composed* by putting words together so as to make sense: a medicine is *compounded* of many ingredients; society is *composed* of various classes.

COMPREHEND. See COMPRISE; CONCEIVE.

COMPREHENSIVE, EXTENSIVE. *Comprehensive*, from *comprehend*, in Latin *comprehendo*, from *con*, together, and *prehendere*, to take, signifies the quality of putting together. *Extensive*, from *extend*, in Latin *extendo*, or *ex* and *tendere*, to stretch out, signifies the quality of reaching to a distance.

Comprehensive respects quantity, *extensive* regards space: that is *comprehensive* which *extends* into a wide field: a *comprehensive* view of a subject includes all branches of it; an *extensive* view of a subject enters into minute details: the *comprehensive* is associated with the concise; the *extensive* with the diffuse: it requires a capacious mind to take a *comprehensive* survey of any subject; it is possible for a superficial thinker to enter very *extensively* into some parts, while he passes over others. *Comprehensive* is employed only with regard to intellectual objects; *extensive* is used both in the proper or the improper sense: the signification of a word is *comprehensive*, or the powers of the mind are *comprehensive*: a plain is *extensive*, or a field of inquiry is *extensive*.

COMPRISE, COMPREHEND, EMBRACE, CONTAIN, INCLUDE. *Comprise*, through the French *compris*, participle of *comprendre*, comes from the same source as *comprehend*. *Embrace* (see CLASP). *Contain*, in French *contenir*, Latin *contineo*, compounded of *con* and *teneo*, signifies to hold together within one place. *Include*, in Latin *includo*, compounded of *in* and *cludo* or *claudo*, signifies to shut in or within a given space.

Comprise, comprehend, and *embrace* have regard to the aggregate value, quantity, or extent; *include*, to the individual things which form the whole; *contain*, either to the aggregate or to the individual, being in fact a term of more ordinary application than any of the others. *Comprise* and *contain* are used either in the proper or the figurative sense; *comprehend, embrace*, and *include* in the figurative sense only: a stock *comprises* a variety of articles; a library *comprises* a variety of books; the whole is *comprised* within a small compass; rules *comprehend* a number of particulars; laws *comprehend* a number of cases; countries *comprehend* a certain number of districts or divisions; terms *comprehend* a certain meaning: a discourse *embraces* a variety of topics; a plan, project, scheme, or system *embraces* a variety of objects; a house *contains* one, two, or more persons; a city *contains* a number of houses; a book *contains* much useful matter; a society *contains* very many individuals; it *includes* none but of a certain class; or it *includes* some of every class.

COMPULSION. See CONSTRAINT.

COMPUNCTION. See REPENTANCE.

COMPUTE. See CALCULATE; ESTIMATE.

CONCEAL, DISSEMBLE, DISGUISE. *Conceal* is compounded of Latin *con* and *celare*, to hide. *Dissemble*, in French *dissimuler*, compounded of *dis*, negative prefix, and *similis*, like, signifies to make a thing appear unlike what it is. *Disguise*, in French *déguiser*, compounded of the privative *dis* or *de* and *guise*, in Old High German *wise*, a manner or fashion, signifies to take a form opposite to the reality.

To *conceal* is simply to abstain from making known what we wish to keep secret; to *dissemble* and *disguise* signify to *conceal* by assuming some false appearance: we *conceal* facts; we *dissemble* feelings; we *disguise* sentiments. Caution only is requisite in *concealing*; it may be effected by simple silence: art and address must be employed in *dissembling*; it mingles falsehood with all its proceedings; labor and cunning are requisite in *disguising*; it has nothing but falsehood in all its movements. The *concealer* watches over himself that he may not be betrayed into any indiscreet communication; the *dissembler* has an eye to others, so as to prevent them from discovering the state of his heart; *disguise* assumes altogether a different face from reality, and rests secure under this shelter. It is sufficient to *conceal* from those who either cannot or will not see; it is necessary to *dissemble* with those who can see without being shown; but it is necessary to *disguise* from those who are anxious to discover and use every means to penetrate the veil that intercepts their sight.

Conceal, Hide, Secrete.—*Conceal* (see above). *Hide*, Anglo-Saxon *hydan*, is allied to Greek κεύθειν, to cover or put out of sight. *Secrete*, in Latin *secretus*, participle of *secerno*, or *se*, apart, and *cernere*, to separate, means to take away and hide in a place apart.

Concealing has simply the idea of not letting come to observation; *hiding*, that of putting under cover; *secreting*, that of setting at a distance or in unfrequented places: whatever is not seen is *concealed*, but whatever is *hidden* or *secreted* is intentionally put out of sight: a person *conceals* himself behind a hedge; he *hides* his treasures in the earth; he *secretes* what he has stolen under his cloak. *Conceal* is more general than either *hide* or *secrete:* all things are *concealed* which are *hidden* or *secreted*, but they are not always *hidden* or *secreted* when they are *concealed:* both mental and corporeal objects are *concealed;* corporeal objects mostly, and sometimes mental ones, are *hidden;* corporeal objects only are *secreted:* we *conceal* in the mind whatever we do not make known: that is *hidden* which may not be discovered or cannot be discerned; that is *secreted* which may not be seen. Facts are *concealed*, truths are *hidden*, goods are *secreted*. Children should never attempt to *conceal* from their parents or teachers any error they have committed when called upon for an acknowledgment; we are told in Scripture, for our consolation, that nothing is *hidden* which shall not be revealed; people seldom wish to *secrete* anything but with the intention of *concealing* it from those who have a right to demand it back.

Concealment, Secrecy.—*Concealment* is itself an action; *secrecy*, from *secret*, is the quality of an action: *concealment* may respect the state of things; *secrecy* the conduct of persons; things may be *concealed* so as to be known to no one; but *secrecy* supposes some person to whom the thing *concealed* is known. *Concealment* has to do with what concerns others; *secrecy*, with that which concerns ourselves: what is *concealed* is kept from the observation of others; what is *secret* is known only to ourselves: there may frequently be *concealment* without *secrecy*, although there cannot be *secrecy* without *concealment:* *concealment* is frequently practised to the detriment of others; *secrecy* is always adopted for our own advantage or gratification: *concealment* is essential in the commission of crimes; *secrecy* in the execution of schemes: many crimes are committed with impunity when the perpetrators are protected by *concealment;* the best-concerted plans are often frustrated for want of observing *secrecy.*

See also CAMOUFLAGE.

CONCEDE. See GIVE UP.

CONCEIT, FANCY. *Conceit* comes immediately from the Latin *conceptus*, participle of *concipere*, from *con*, together, and *capere*, take, and means to take and put together, to conceive or form in the mind. *Fancy*, in French phantasie. Latin *phantasia*, Greek φἄντασία, from φαντάζω, make appear, and φαίνω, appear.

These terms equally express the working of the imagination in its distorted state; but *conceit* denotes a much greater degree of distortion than *fancy:* our *conceits* are preposterous; what we *fancy* is unreal or only apparent. *Conceit* applies only to internal objects: it is mental in the operation and the result; it is a species of invention: *fancy* is applied to external objects, or whatever acts on the senses: nervous people are subject to strange *conceits;* timid people *fancy* they hear sounds or see objects in the dark which awaken terror. Those who are apt to *conceit* oftener *conceit* that which is painful than otherwise; *conceiting* either that they are always in danger of dying, or that all the world is their enemy.

There are, however, insane people who *conceit* themselves to be kings and queens: and some, indeed, who are not called insane, who *conceit* themselves very learned while they know nothing, or very wise and clever while they are exposing themselves to perpetual ridicule for their folly, or very handsome while the world calls them plain, or very peaceable while they are always quarrelling with their neighbors, or very humble while they are tenaciously stickling for their own: it would be well if such *conceits* afforded a harmless pleasure to their authors, but unfortunately they only render them more offensive and disgusting than they would otherwise be. Those who are apt to *fancy* never *fancy* anything to please themselves; they *fancy* that things are too long or too short, too thick or too thin, too cold or too hot, with a thousand other *fancies* equally trivial in their nature, thereby proving that the slightest aberration of the mind is a serious evil, and productive of evil.

When taken in reference to intellectual objects, *conceit* is always in a bad sense; but *fancy* may be employed in a good sense.

See also PRIDE.

CONCEITED. See OPINIONATED.

CONCEIVE, UNDERSTAND, COMPREHEND. *Conceive* has the same derivation as *conceit*. *Understand* signifies to stand under, or near to the mind. *Comprehend*, in Latin *comprehendo*, compounded of *con*, together, and *prehendere*, to sieze, signifies to seize or embrace within the mind.

These terms indicate the intellectual operations of forming ideas, that is, ideas of the complex kind, in distinction from the simple ideas formed by the act of perception. *Conception* is the simplest operation of the three; when we *conceive* we may have but one idea; when we *understand* or *comprehend* we have all the ideas which the subject is capable of presenting. We cannot *understand* or *comprehend* without *conceiving;* but we may often *conceive* that which we neither *understand* nor *comprehend*. That which we cannot *conceive* is to us nothing; but the *conception* of it gives it an existence, at least in our minds; but *understanding* and *comprehending* is not essential to the belief of a thing's existence. So long as we have reasons sufficient to *conceive* a thing as possible or probable, it is not necessary either to *understand* or *comprehend* it in order to authorize our belief. The mysteries of our holy religion are objects of *conception*, but not of *comprehension*. We *conceive* that a thing may be done without *understanding* how it is done; we *conceive* that a thing may exist without *comprehending* the nature of its existence. We *conceive* clearly, *understand* fully, *comprehend* minutely.

Conceiving is a species of invention; it is the fruit of the mind's operation within itself. *Understanding* and *comprehension* are employed solely on external objects; we *understand* and *comprehend* that which actually exists before us and presents itself to our observation. *Conceiving* is the office of the imagination as well as the judgment; *understanding* and *comprehension* are the office of the reasoning faculties exclusively.

Conceiving is employed with regard to matters of taste, to arrangements, designs, and projects; *understanding* is employed on familiar objects which present themselves in the ordinary discourse and business of men; *comprehending* respects principles, lessons, and speculative knowledge in general. The artist *conceives* a design, and he who will execute it must *understand* it; the poet *conceives* that which is grand and sublime, and he who will enjoy the perusal of his *conceptions* must have refinement of mind, and capacity to *comprehend*, the grand and sublime. The builder *conceives* plans, the scholar *understands* languages, the metaphysician attempts to explain many things which are not to be *comprehended*.

See also APPREHEND.

Conception, Notion. — *Conception*, from *conceive*, signifies the thing *conceived*. *Notion*, in French *notion*, Latin *notio*, from *notus*, the participle of *noscere*, to know, signifies the thing known.

Conception is the mind's own work, what it pictures to itself from the exercise of its own powers; *notion* is the representation of objects as they are drawn from observation. *Conceptions* are the fruit of the understanding and imagination; *notions* are the result of experience and information. *Conceptions* are formed; *notions* are entertained. *Conceptions* are either grand or mean, gross or sublime; either clear or indistinct, crude or distinct; *notions* are either true or false, just or absurd. Intellectual culture serves to elevate men's *conceptions;* the extension of knowledge serves to correct and refine their *notions.*

Some heathen philosophers had an indistinct *conception* of the Deity, whose attributes and character are unfolded to us in His revelation: the ignorant have often false *notions* of their duty and obligations to their superiors. The unenlightened express their gross and crude *conceptions* of a Superior Being by some material and visible object: the vulgar *notion* of ghosts and spirits is not entirely banished from the most cultivated parts of any country.

See also PERCEPTION.

CONCERN. See AFFAIR; AFFECT; CARE; INTEREST.

CONCERT, CONTRIVE, MANAGE. *Concert* is derived from Latin *concertare*, from *con*, together, and *certare*, to strive, and signified to strive together, to vie. *Contrive* comes from Old French *controver*, to find together. *Manage*, in French *ménager*, comes from Latin *manus*, hand, and means to control with the hand.

There is a secret understanding in *concerting;* invention in *contriving;* execution in *managing.* There is mostly *contrivance* and *managing* in *concerting;* but there is not always *concerting* in *contrivance* or *management.* Measures are *concerted;* schemes are *contrived;* affairs are *managed.* Two parties at least are requisite in *concerting,* one is sufficient for *contriving* and *managing. Concerting* is always employed in all secret transactions; *contrivance* and *management* are used indifferently. Robbers who have determined on any scheme of plunder *concert* together the means of carrying their project into execution; they *contrive* various devices to elude the vigilance of the police; they *manage* everything in the dark. Those who are debarred the opportunity of seeing one

another unrestrainedly *concert* measures for meeting privately. The ingenuity of a person is frequently displayed in the *contrivances* by which he strives to help himself out of his troubles. Whenever there are many parties interested in a concern, it is never so well *managed* as when it is in the hands of one individual suitably qualified.

CONCILIATE, RECONCILE. *Conciliate*, in Latin *conciliatus*, and *reconcile*, in Latin *reconcilio*, both come from *conciliare*, to bring together, whence *council* is also derived, and denote an achieving of unity and harmony.

Conciliate and *reconcile* are both employed in the sense of uniting men's affections, but under different circumstances. The *conciliator* gets the good-will and affections for himself; the *reconciler* unites the affections of two persons to each other. The *conciliator* may either gain new affections or regain those which are lost; the *reconciler* always either renews affections which have been once lost or fixes them where they ought to be fixed. The best means of *conciliating* esteem is by *reconciling* all that are at variance. *Conciliate* is mostly employed for men in public stations; *reconcile* is indifferently employed for those in public or private stations. Men in power have sometimes the happy opportunity of *conciliating* the good-will of those who are most averse to their authority, and thus *reconciling* them to measures which would otherwise be odious. Kindness and condescension serve to *conciliate;* a friendly influence, or a well-timed exercise of authority, is often successfully exerted in *reconciling.*

Conciliate is mostly employed in the sense of bringing persons into unison with each other who have been at variance; but *reconcile* may be employed to denote the bringing a person into unison or acquiescence with that which would be naturally disagreeable.

CONCISE. See LACONIC; SHORT.

CONCLUDE. See CLOSE; DECIDE.

CONCLUSION, INFERENCE, DEDUCTION. *Conclusion*, from Latin *concludere*, compounded of *con*, together, and *claudere*, close, signifies the closing up of all arguments and reasoning. *Inference*, from *infer*, in Latin *infero*, signifies what is brought in. *Deduction*, from Latin *deducere*, compounded of *de*, from, and *ducere*, lead, to bring out, signifies the bringing or drawing one conclusion from another.

A *conclusion* is full and decisive; an *inference* is partial and indecisive: a *conclusion* leaves the mind in no doubt or hesitation; it puts a stop to all further reasoning: *inferences* are special *conclusions* from particular circumstances; they serve as links in the chain of reasoning. *Conclusion* in the technical sense is the concluding proposition of a syllogism, drawn from the two others, which are called the premises.

Conclusions are drawn from real facts; *inferences* are drawn from the appearances of things; *deductions* only from arguments or assertions. *Conclusions* are practical, *inferences* ratiocinative, *deductions* are final. We *conclude* from a person's conduct or declarations what he intends to do or leave undone; we *infer* from the appearance of the clouds or the thickness of the atmosphere that there will be a heavy fall of rain or snow; we *deduce*, from a combination of facts, *inferences*, and assertions, that a story is fabricated. Hasty *conclusions* betray a want of judgment or of firmness of mind: contrary *inferences* are frequently drawn from the same circumstances to serve the purpose of party and support a favorite position; the *deductions* in such cases are not unfrequently true when the *inferences* are false.

Conclusive, Decisive, Convincing.— *Conclusive* applies either to practical or argumentative matters; *decisive*, to what is practical only; *convincing*, to what is argumentative only. It is necessary to be *conclusive* when we deliberate, and *decisive* when we command. What is *conclusive* puts an end to all discussions and determines the judgment; what is *decisive* puts an end to all wavering and determines the will. Negotiators have sometimes an interest in not speaking *conclusively*; commanders can never retain their authority without speaking *decisively*. *Conclusive*, when compared to *convinc-*

ing, is general; the latter is particular: an argument is *convincing*, a chain of reasoning *conclusive*. There may be much that is *convincing* where there is nothing *conclusive*: a proof may be *convincing* of a particular circumstance, but *conclusive* evidence will bear upon the main question.

See also FINAL.

CONCOMITANT. See ACCOMPANIMENT.

CONCORD, HARMONY. *Concord*, in French *concorde*, Latin *concordia*, is compounded from *con*, together, and *cors*, heart, having the same heart and mind. *Harmony*, in French *harmonie*, Latin *harmonia*, Greek ἁρμονία, from ἁρμός, a joining, signifies the state of fitting or suiting.

The idea of union is common to both these terms, but under different circumstances. *Concord* is generally employed for the union of wills and affections; *harmony* respects the aptitude of minds to coalesce. There may be *concord* without *harmony*, and *harmony* without *concord*. Persons may live in *concord* who are at a distance from one another; but *harmony* is mostly employed for those who are in close connection and obliged to cooperate. *Concord* should never be broken by relations under any circumstances; *harmony* is indispensable in all members of a family that dwell together. Interest will sometimes stand in the way of brotherly *concord*; a love of rule and a dogmatical temper will sometimes disturb the *harmony* of a family.

These terms are both applied to music, the one in a particular, the other in a general sense; there is *concord* between two or more single sounds, and *harmony* in any number or aggregate of sounds.

Harmony may be used in the sense of adaptation to things generally.

See also UNION.

CONCUR. See AGREE.

CONCURRENCE. See ASSENT.

CONCUSSION. See SHOCK.

CONDEMN. See BLAME; PROSCRIBE; REPROBATE; SENTENCE.

CONDESCENSION. See COMPLAISANCE.

CONDITION, STATION. *Condition,*

in French *condition*, Latin *conditio*, from *con*, together, and *dicere*, to talk, signifies the agreement arrived at as a result of talking a matter over—something granted as a prerequisite to granting something else. *Station*, in French *station*, Latin *statio*, from *stare*, to stand, signifies a standing place or point.

Condition has most relation to circumstances, education, birth, and the like; *station* refers rather to the rank, occupation, or mode of life which is marked out. Riches suddenly acquired are calculated to make a man forget his original *condition* and to render him negligent of the duties of his *station*. The *condition* of men in reality is often so different from what it appears that it is extremely difficult to form an estimate of what they are or what they have been. It is the folly of the present day that every man is unwilling to keep the *station* which has been assigned to him by Providence: the rage for equality destroys every just distinction in society; the low aspire to be, in appearance at least, equal with their superiors; and those in elevated *stations* do not hesitate to put themselves on a level with their inferiors.

See also ARTICLE; ESTATE; SITUATION.

CONDITIONAL. See PROVISIONAL.

CONDOLENCE. See SYMPATHY.

CONDUCE, CONTRIBUTE. *Conduce*, Latin *conduco*, compounded of *con* and *duco*, signifies to bring together for one end. *Contribute*, in Latin *contributus*, participle of *contribuo*, compounded of *con* and *tribuere*, to divide and assign, signifies to bestow for the same end.

To *conduce* signifies to serve the full purpose; to *contribute* signifies only to serve a secondary purpose: the former is always taken in a good sense, the latter in a bad or good sense. Exercise *conduces* to the health; it *contributes* to give vigor to the frame. Nothing *conduces* more to the well-being of any community than a spirit of subordination among all ranks and classes. A want of firmness and vigilance in the government or magistrates *contributes* greatly to the spread of disaffection and rebellion. Schemes of ambition never *conduce* to tranquillity of mind. A single failure may *contribute* sometimes to involve a person in perpetual trouble.

CONDUCT, MANAGE, DIRECT. *Conduct*, in Latin *conductus*, participle of *conduco*, signifies to lead in some particular manner or for some special purpose. To *manage* (see CARE; CHARGE). To *direct*, in Latin *directus*, participle of *dirigo*, or *dis*, apart, and *regere*, to rule, signifies to regulate distinctly or put each in its right place.

Conducting requires most wisdom and knowledge; *managing* most action; *direction* most authority. A lawyer *conducts* the cause intrusted to him; a steward *manages* the mercantile concerns for his employer; a superintendent *directs* the movements of all the subordinate agents. *Conducting* is always applied to affairs of the first importance: *management* is a term of familiar use to characterize a familiar employment: *direction* makes up in authority what it wants in importance; it falls but little short of the word *conduct*. A *conductor* conceives, plans, arranges, and disposes; a *manager* acts or executes; a *director* commands.

It is necessary to *conduct* with wisdom; to *manage* with diligence, attention, and skill; to *direct* with promptitude, precision, and clearness. A minister of state requires peculiar talents to *conduct* with success the various and complicated concerns which are connected with his office; he must exercise much skill in *managing* the various characters and clashing interests with which he becomes connected; and possess much influence to *direct* the multiplied operations by which the grand machine of government is kept in motion. When a general undertakes to *conduct* a campaign, he will intrust the *management* of minor concerns to persons on whom he can rely; but he will *direct* in person whatever is likely to have any serious influence on his success.

See also BEHAVIOR; LEAD.

CONFEDERACY. See ALLIANCE.

CONFEDERATE, ACCOMPLICE. *Confederate* (see ALLY) and *accomplice* (see ABETTOR) both imply a partner in some proceeding, but they differ as to the nature of the proceeding: in the former case it may be lawful or unlawful; in the latter unlawful only. In this latter sense a *confederate* is a partner in a plot or secret association: an *accomplice* is a partner in some active violation of the laws. Guy Fawkes retained his resolution, till the last extremity, not to reveal the names of his *confederates:* it is the common refuge of all robbers and desperate characters to betray their *accomplices* in order to screen themselves from punishment.

CONFER, BESTOW. *Confer*, in French *conférer*, Latin *confero*, compounded of *con* and *fero*, signifies to bring something toward a person or place it upon him. *Bestow* is compounded of *be*, a verbal prefix, and Anglo-Saxon *stow*, a place, and signifies to put in a place. *Conferring* is an act of authority; *bestowing* that of charity or generosity. Princes and men in power *confer;* people in a private station *bestow.* Honors, dignities, privileges, and rank are the things *conferred;* favors, kindnesses, and pecuniary relief are the things *bestowed.* Merit, favor, interest, caprice, or intrigue give rise to *conferring;* necessity, solicitation, and private affection lead to *bestowing.*

In the moral application, what is *conferred* or *bestowed* is presumed to be deserved, but with the distinction that the one is gratuitous, the other involuntary.

CONFERENCE. See CONVERSATION.

CONFESS. See ACKNOWLEDGE.

CONFIDE, TRUST. *Confide*, in Latin *confido* (or *cum*, with, and *fidere*, to *trust*), signifying to be united by trust with another, is to *trust* (see BELIEF) as the species to the genus: we always *trust* when we *confide*, but not *vice versa*. *Confidence* is an extraordinary *trust*, but *trust* is always ordinary unless the term be otherwise qualified. *Confidence* involves communication of a man's mind to another, but *trust* is confined to matters of action.

Confidence may be sometimes limited in its application, as *confidence* in the integrity or secrecy of a man; but *trust* is in its signification limited to matters of personal interest. A breach of *trust* evinces a want of that common principle which keeps human society

together; but a breach of *confidence* betrays a more than ordinary share of baseness and depravity.

Confident, Dogmatical, Positive.— *Confident*, from *confide*, marks the temper of *confiding* in one's self. *Dogmatical*, from Greek δόγμα (English *dogma*), an opinion, signifies the temper of dealing in unqualified assertions. *Positive*, in Latin *positivus*, from *positus*, signifies fixed to a point.

The first two of these words denote an habitual or permanent state of mind; the last either a partial or an habitual temper. There is much of *confidence* in *dogmatism* and *positivity*, but it expresses more than either. *Confidence* implies a general reliance on one's abilities in whatever we undertake; *dogmatism* implies a reliance on the truth of our opinions; *positivity*, a reliance on the truth of our assertions. A *confident* man is always ready to act, as he is sure of succeeding; a *dogmatical* man is always ready to speak, as he is sure of being heard; a *positive* man is determined to maintain what he has asserted, as he is convinced that he has made no mistake. *Confidence* is opposed to diffidence; *dogmatism*, to scepticism; *positivity*, to hesitation. A *confident* man mostly fails for want of using the necessary means to insure success; a *dogmatical* man is mostly in error, because he substitutes his own partial opinions for such as are established; a *positive* man is mostly deceived, because he trusts more to his own senses and memory than he ought. Self-knowledge is the most effectual cure for *self-confidence;* an acquaintance with men and things tends to lessen *dogmatism;* the experience of one's self having been deceived, and the observation that others are perpetually liable to be deceived, ought to check the folly of being *positive* as to any event or circumstance that is past. *Confidence* is oftener expressed by actions than words; *dogmatism* and *positivity* always by words; the former denotes only the temper of the speaker, but the latter may influence the temper of others; a *positive* assertion may not only denote the state of the person's mind who makes it, but also may serve to make another *positive.*

See also SANGUINE.

CONFINE. See BORDER; BOUND; INTERN.

CONFINED. See CONTRACTED.

CONFINEMENT, IMPRISONMENT, CAPTIVITY. *Confinement* (see BOUND). *Imprisonment,* compounded of Latin *in* and *prensionem* (acc.), a seizure, French *prison,* from *pris,* participle of *prendre,* Latin *prehendere,* to take, signifies the act or state of being taken or laid hold of. *Captivity,* in French *captivité,* Latin *captivitas,* from *capere,* to take, signifies likewise the state of being, or being kept, in possession by another.

Confinement is the generic, the other two are specific terms. *Confinement* and *imprisonment* both imply the abridgment of one's personal freedom, but the former specifies no cause, which the latter does. We may be *confined* in a room by ill health or *confined* in any place by way of punishment; but we are never *imprisoned* but in some specific place appointed for the *confinement* of offenders, and always for some supposed offence. We are *captives* by the rights of war when we fall into the hands of the enemy. *Confinement* does not specify the degree or manner as the other terms do; it may even extend to the restricting the body of its free movements; while *imprisonment* simply *confines* the person within a certain extent of ground or the walls of a *prison;* and *captivity* leaves a person at liberty to range within a whole country or district.

Confinement is so general a term as to be applied to animals and even inanimate objects; *imprisonment* and *captivity* are applied in the proper sense to persons only, but they admit of a figurative application. Poor stray animals, which are found trespassing on unlawful ground, are doomed to a wretched *confinement,* rendered still more hard and intolerable by the want of food: the *confinement* of plants within too narrow a space will stop their growth for want of air. There is many a poor *captive* in a cage who, like Sterne's starling, would say, if it could, "I want to get out."

CONFIRM, CORROBORATE. To *confirm,* in Latin *confirmo,* or *con* and *firmare,* to make firm, signifies to make firm in a special manner. *Corroborate,* from Latin *robur,* strength, whence our adjective *robust* is derived, signifies to give additional strength.

The idea of strengthening is common to these terms, but under different circumstances; *confirm* is used generally, *corroborate* only in particular instances. What *confirms* serves to *confirm* the mind; what *corroborates* gives weight to the thing. An opinion or a story is *confirmed;* an evidence or the representation of a person is *corroborated.* What *confirms* removes all doubt; what *corroborates* only gives more strength than the thing had before. When the truth of a thing is *confirmed,* nothing more is necessary: the testimony of a person may be so little credited that it may want much *corroboration.*

Confirm, Establish. — *Confirm* (see above). *Establish,* from Latin *stabilis,* English *stable,* from *stare,* to stand, signifies to make stable, or able to stand.

The idea of strengthening is common to these as to the former terms, but with a different application: to *confirm* is applied to what is partial, if not temporary; to *establish* to that which is permanent and of importance, as to *confirm* a report, to *establish* a reputation, to *confirm* a treaty or alliance, to *establish* a trade or government.

So in respect to the mind and its operations: a belief, opinion, suspicion, or resolution is *confirmed;* principles, faith, hopes, etc., are *established.*

See also RATIFY.

CONFLICT, COMBAT, CONTEST. *Conflict,* in Latin *conflictus,* participle of *confligo,* compounded of *con* and *fligere,* to flip or strike, signifies to strike against each other. *Combat* (see BATTLE). *Contest,* in French *contester,* Latin *contestor,* compounded of *con* and *testor,* from *testes,* a witness (compare English *testify*), signifies to call or set witness against witness.

A striving for the mastery is the common idea in the signification of these terms, which is varied in the manner and spirit of the action. A *conflict* has more of violence in it than a *combat,* and a *combat* than a *contest.* A *conflict* supposes a violent collision, a meeting of force against force; a *combat* supposes a contending together in fighting or battle. A *conflict* may be the unpremeditated meeting of one or more persons in a violent or hostile manner; a *combat* is frequently a concerted engagement between two or more particular individuals, as a sudden and violent *conflict* ensued upon their coming up; they engaged in single *combat*.

Conflict is applied to whatever comes in violent collision, whether animate or inanimate, as the *conflicts* of wild beasts or of the elements; *combat* is applied to animals as well as men, particularly where there is a trial of skill or strength, as the *combats* of the gladiators either with one another or with beasts; *contest* is applied only to men.

Conflict and *contest* are properly applied to moral objects, and *combat* sometimes figuratively so, and all with a like distinction; violent passions produce *conflicts* in the mind; there may be a *combat* between reason and any particular passion; there may be a *contest* for honors as well as posts of honor; reason will seldom come off victorious in the *combat* with ambition.

CONFORM. See COMPLY.

CONFORMABLE, AGREEABLE, SUITABLE. *Conformable* signifies able to *conform* (see COMPLY), that is, having a sameness of form. *Agreeable* signifies the quality of being able to *agree*. *Suitable* signifies able to *suit* (see AGREE).

Conformable is employed for matters of obligation; *agreeable*, for matters of choice; *suitable*, for matters of propriety and discretion: what is *conformable* accords with some prescribed form or given rule of others; what is *agreeable* accords with the feelings, tempers, or judgments of ourselves or others; what is *suitable* accords with outward circumstances: it is the business of those who act for others to act *conformably* to their directions; it is the part of a friend to act *agreeably* to the wishes of a friend; it is the part of every man to act *suitably* to his station. The decisions of a judge must be strictly *conformable* to the letter of the law; he is seldom at liberty to consult general views of equity: the decision of a partisan is always *agreeable* to the temper of his party: the style of a writer should be *suitable* to his subject.

See also ASSIMILABLE.

CONFORMATION. See FORM.

CONFOUND, CONFUSE. *Confound* and *confuse* are both derived from different parts of the same verb, namely, *confundo*, and its participle *confusus*, signifying to pour or mix together without design that which ought to be distinct.

Confound has an active sense; *confuse* a neuter or reflective sense: a person *confounds* one thing with another; objects become *confused*, or a person *confuses* himself: it is a common error among ignorant people to *confound* names, and among children to have their ideas *confused* on commencing a new study. The present age is distinguished by nothing so much as by *confounding* all distinctions, which is a great source of *confusion* in men's intercourse with one another, both in public and private life.

Confuse is sometimes used transitively in the sense of causing *confusion*, as to *confuse* an account; but in this case it is as much distinguished from *confound* as in the other case. A person *confounds* one account with the other when he takes them to be both the same; but he *confuses* any particular account when he mingles different items under one head or brings the same item under different heads.

See also ABASH; BAFFLE; MIX.

CONFRONT, FACE. *Confront,* from the Latin *frons*, a forehead, implies to set *face* to *face;* and *face,* from Latin *facies*, English *face,* signifies to set the *face* toward any object. The former of these terms is always employed for two or more persons with regard to one another; the latter for a single individual with regard to objects in general. Witnesses are *confronted;* a person *faces* danger, or *faces* an enemy: when people give contrary evidence, it is sometimes necessary, in extra-judicial matters, to *confront* them in order to arrive at the truth; the best evidence which a man can give of his courage is to evince his readiness for *facing* his enemy whenever the occasion requires.

CONFUSE. See ABASH; CONFOUND.

CONFUSED. See INDISTINCT.

CONFUSION, DISORDER. *Confusion* signifies the state of being *confounded* or *confused* (see CONFOUND).

Disorder, compounded of *dis*, privative, and Latin *ordo*, English *order*, signifies the reverse of order.

Confusion is to *disorder* as the species to the genus: *confusion* supposes the absence of all order; *disorder* the derangement of order where it exists, or is supposed to exist: there is always *disorder* in *confusion*, but not always *confusion* in *disorder*. The greater the multitude the more they are liable to fall into *confusion* if they do not act in perfect concert, as in the case of a routed army or a tumultuous mob.

Where there is the greatest order, the smallest circumstance is apt to produce *disorder*, the consequences of which will be more or less serious.

See also JUMBLE.

CONFUTE, REFUTE, DISPROVE, OPPUGN. *Confute* and *refute*, in Latin *confuto* and *refuto*, are compounded of *con*, against, *re* privative, and a verb stem *futa*, which is probably from the same root as Latin *fundere*, to pour out, overthrow, and is allied to English *futile*, Latin *futilis*, etc. *Disprove*, compounded of *dis*, privative, and *probare*, to prove, signifies to prove the contrary. *Oppugn* comes from Latin *oppugnare*, to fight against.

To *confute* respects what is argumentative; *refute*, what is practical and personal; *disprove*, whatever is represented or related; *oppugn*, what is held or maintained. An argument is *confuted* by proving its fallacy; a charge is *refuted* by proving the innocence of the party charged; an assertion is *disproved* by proving that it is incorrect; a doctrine is *oppugned* by a course of reasoning. Paradoxes may be easily *refuted;* calumnies may be easily *refuted;* the marvellous and incredible stories of travellers may be easily *disproved;* heresies and sceptical notions ought to be *oppugned*. The pernicious doctrines of sceptics, though often *confuted*, are as often advanced with the same degree of assurance by the free-thinking, and I might say the unthinking, few who imbibe their spirit: it is the employment of libellists to deal out their malicious aspersions against the objects of their malignity in a manner so loose and indirect as to preclude the possibility of *refutation:* it would be a fruitless and unthankful task to attempt to *disprove* all the statements which are circulated in a common newspaper. It is the duty of the ministers of the Gospel to *oppugn* all doctrines that militate against the established faith of Christians.

CONGRATULATE. See FELICITATE.

CONGREGATION. See ASSEMBLE.

CONGRESS. See ASSEMBLE.

CONJECTURE, SUPPOSITION, SURMISE. *Conjecture*, in French *conjecture*, Latin *conjectura*, from *con*, together, and *jacere*, to throw, signifies the thing put together or framed in the mind without design or foundation. *Supposition*, in French *supposition*, from Latin *supponere*, compounded of *sub*, in place of, and *ponere*, to place, signifies to put one's thoughts in place of reality. *Surmise* is compounded of Old French *sur*, Latin *super*, above, and *mettre* (Latin *mittere*), to put; it very nearly corresponds in its original meaning to the modern slang "put it over."

All these terms convey an idea of something in the mind independent of the reality; but *conjecture* is founded less on rational inference than *supposition;* and *surmise* less than either: any circumstance, however trivial, may give rise to a *conjecture;* some reasons are requisite to produce a *supposition;* a particular state of feeling or train of thinking may of itself create a *surmise*. Although the same epithets are generally applicable to all these terms, yet we may with propriety say that a *conjecture* is idle, a *supposition* false, a *surmise* fanciful. *Conjectures* are employed on events, their causes, consequences, and contingencies: *supposition;* on speculative points; *surmise*, on personal concerns. The secret measures of government give rise to various *conjectures:* all the *suppositions* which are formed respecting comets seem at present to fall short of the truth: the behavior of a person will often occasion a *surmise* respecting his intentions and proceedings, let them be ever so disguised. Antiquarians and etymologists deal much in *conjectures;* they have ample scope afforded them for asserting what can be neither proved nor denied: religionists are pleased to build many *suppositions* of a doctrinal nature on the Scriptures, or, more properly, on their own partial and forced interpretations of the Scriptures: it is the part of prudence, as well as justice, not to express any *surmises* which we may entertain, either as to the character or conduct of others, which may not redound to their credit.

See also GUESS.

CONJUNCTURE, CRISIS. *Conjuncture,* in Latin *conjunctura,* from *con,* together, and *jungere,* to join, signifies the joining together of circumstances. *Crisis,* in Latin *crisis,* Greek κρίσις, from κρίνειν, to separate, signified a judgment founded upon analysis; hence simply a judgment, or anything which decides, or turns the scale.

Both these terms are employed to express a period of time marked by the state of affairs. A *conjuncture* is a joining or combination of corresponding circumstances tending toward the same end: a *crisis* is the high-wrought state of any affair which immediately precedes a change: a *conjuncture* may be favorable, a *crisis* alarming. An able statesman seizes the *conjuncture* which promises to suit his purpose, for the introduction of a favorite measure: the abilities, firmness, and perseverance of Alfred the Great, at one important *crisis* of his reign, saved England from destruction.

CONJURE. See JUGGLE.

CONNECT, COMBINE, UNITE. *Connect,* Latin *connecto,* compounded of *con* and *necto,* signifies to knit together. *Combine* (see ASSOCIATION). *Unite* (see ADD).

The idea of being put together is common to these terms, but with different degrees of proximity. *Connected* is more remote than *combined,* and this than *united.* What is *connected* and *combined* remains distinct, but what is *united* loses all individuality. Things the most dissimilar may be *connected* or *combined;* things of the same kind only can be *united.* Things or persons are *connected* more or less remotely by some common property or circumstance that serves as a tie; they are *combined* by a species of juncture; they are *united* by a coalition: houses are *connected* by means of a common passage; the armies of two nations are *combined;* two armies of the same nation are *united.* Trade, marriage, or general intercourse create a *connection* between individuals; co-operation and similarity of tendency are grounds for *combination;* entire accordance leads to a *union.* It is dangerous to be *connected* with the wicked in any way; our reputation, if not our morals, must be the sufferers thereby. The most obnoxious members of society are those in whom wealth, talents, influence, and a lawless ambition are *combined.* *United* is an epithet that should apply to nations and families; the same obedience to laws should regulate every man who lives under the same government; the same heart should animate every breast; the same spirit should dictate every action of every member in the community who has a common interest in the preservation of the whole.

Connection, Relation. — *Connection* (see above). *Relation,* from *relate,* in Latin *relatus,* participle of *refero,* to bring back, signifies carrying back to some point.

These words are applied to two or more things to denote the manner in which they stand in regard to one another. A *connection* denotes that which binds two objects, or the situation of being so bound by some tie; but *relation* denotes the situation of two or more objects in regard to one another, yet without defining what it is; a *connection* is therefore a species of *relation,* but a *relation* may be something which does not amount to a *connection.* Families are *connected* with each other by the ties of blood or marriage; persons are *connected* with each other in the way of trade or business; objects stand in a certain *relation* to each other, as persons stand in the *relation* of giver and receiver; or of debtor and creditor; there is a *connection* between Church and State, or between morality and religion; men stand in the *relation* of creatures to their Creator.

The word *relation* is sometimes taken in a limited sense for one *connected* by family ties, which denotes something nearer in that case than *connection;* as when speaking of a man's *relations,* or of a person being *related* to another, or to leave one's property to one's *relations*.

See also INTERCOURSE.

CONQUER, VANQUISH, SUBDUE, OVERCOME, SURMOUNT. *Conquer*, in French *conquérir*, Latin *conquiro*, compounded of *con* and *quærere*, to search after diligently, signifies in an extended sense to obtain by searching. *Vanquish* is in French *vaincre*, Latin *vincere*. *Subdue*, Latin *subdere*, signifies to give or put under. *Overcome* signifies to come over or get the mastery over one. *Surmount*, in French *surmonter*, compounded of *sur* (Latin *super*), above, and *monter* (from Latin *montem*, hill), to climb a hill, or simply to climb, signifies to rise above any one. The leading idea in the word *conquer* is that of getting; the leading idea in *vanquish* and *subdue* is that of getting the better of, the former partially, the latter thoroughly, so as to prevent any future resistance: a country is *conquered;* an enemy is *vanquished;* in the field of battle a people is *subdued.*

Conquer may sometimes also signify to get the better of, but in that case it does not define the mode or extent of the action; we may *conquer* another in any contest and in any manner; but we *vanquish* and *subdue* persons only by force, and mostly by force of arms. When *overcome* is applied to persons it has precisely the same indefinite and general meaning as *conquer*.

But *overcome*, as well as *conquer*, *subdue*, and *vanquish*, are applied also to moral objects, and *surmount* has for the most part no other application. To *conquer* is said of the person himself, his likes, dislikes, and feelings generally; *subdue* of what relates either to the person himself or some other person, as to *subdue* the will or the passions. What is *conquered* makes less resistance and requires less force than what is *subdued.* It is likewise not so thoroughly subjugated or destroyed. We may *conquer* an aversion at one time which may return at another time; if the will be *subdued* in childhood, it will not prevail in riper years.

To *vanquish* is applied figuratively to particular objects as in the proper sense.

To *overcome* is applied to objections, scruples, prejudices, difficulties, and the

like; *surmount*, to difficulties, obstacles, impediments, etc. What is *overcome* requires less exertion than that which is *surmounted*. We may *overcome* by patience or forbearance; but determination, or the application of more or less force, is necessary in *surmounting* obstacles.

Conqueror, Victor. — These terms, though derived from the preceding verbs, have, notwithstanding, characteristics peculiar to themselves. A *conqueror* is always supposed to add something to his possessions; a *victor* gains nothing but the superiority: there is no *conquest* where there is not something gotten; there is no *victory* where there is no contest: all *conquerors* are not *victors*, nor all *victors conquerors:* those who take possession of other men's lands by force of arms make a *conquest;* those who excel in any trial of skill are the *victors.* Monarchs when they wage a successful war are mostly *conquerors;* combatants who compel their adversaries to yield are *victors.*

CONQUEST. See TRIUMPH
CONSANGUINITY. See KINDRED.
CONSCIENTIOUS. SCRUPULOUS.
Conscientious, ultimately from Latin *con*, intensive prefix, and *scire*, to know, signifies the possession of moral intelligence, the perception of right and wrong. *Scrupulous*, from *scruple*, signifies the quality of having scruples. *Scruple*, in Latin *scrupulus*, signifies a little hard stone, which in walking gives pain.

Conscientious is to *scrupulous* as a whole to a part. A *conscientious* man is so altogether; a *scrupulous* man may have only particular *scruples:* the one is therefore always taken in a good sense; and the other at least in an indifferent, if not a bad sense. A *conscientious* man does nothing to offend his *conscience;* but a *scrupulous* man has often his *scruples* on trifling or minor points; the Pharisees were *scrupulous* without being *conscientious:* we must therefore strive to be *conscientious* without being over-*scrupulous.*

CONSCIENTIOUSLY. See ETHICAL.

CONSCIOUS. See AWARE; FEEL.
CONSECRATE. See DEDICATE; SANCTIFY.

CONSENT, PERMIT, ALLOW. *Consent* (see AGREE). *Permit* and *allow* (see ADMIT).

The idea of determining the conduct of others by some authorized act of one's own is common to these terms, but under various circumstances. They express either the act of an equal or a superior. As the act of an equal we *consent* to that in which we have a common interest with others: we *permit* or *allow* what is for the accommodation of others: we *allow* by abstaining to oppose; we *permit* by a direct expression of our will; contracts are formed by the *consent* of the parties who are interested. The proprietor of an estate *permits* his friends to sport on his grounds; he *allows* of a passage through his premises. It is sometimes prudent to *consent*, complaisant to *permit*, good-natured or weak to *allow*.

Consent respects matters of serious importance; *permit* and *allow* regard those of an indifferent nature: a parent *consents* to the establishment of his children; he *permits* them to read certain books; he *allows* them to converse with him familiarly. We must pause before we give our *consent;* it is an express sanction to the conduct of others; it involves our own judgment and the future interests of those who are under our control. This is not always so necessary in *permitting* and *allowing;* they are partial actions, which require no more than the bare exercise of authority, and involve no other consequence than the temporary pleasure of the parties concerned. Public measures are *permitted* and *allowed*, but never *consented* to. The law *permits* or *allows;* or the person who is authorized *permits* or *allows*. *Permit* in this case retains its positive sense; *allow*, its negative sense, as before. Government *permits* individuals to fit out privateers in time of war: when magistrates are not vigilant, many things will be done which are not *allowed*. A judge is not *permitted* to pass any sentence but what is strictly conformable to law: every man who is accused is *allowed* to plead his own cause, or intrust it to another, as he thinks fit.

These terms are similarly distinguished in the moral application.

See also ASSENT.

CONSEQUENCE, EFFECT, RESULT, ISSUE, EVENT. *Consequence*, in French *conséquence*, Latin *consequentia*, from *consequor*, follow, signifies that which follows in connection with something else. *Effect* is the thing effected (see ACCOMPLISHED). *Result*, in French *résulte*, Latin *resulto*, or *resultus* and *resilire*, to rebound, signifies that which springs or bounds back from another thing. *Issue* is that which issues or flows out (see ARISE). *Event*, in Latin *eventus*, participle of *evenio*, from *e*, forth, and *venire*, to come, is that which comes forth.

All these terms are employed to denote that which follows something else; they vary according to the different circumstances under which they follow, or the manner of their following. A *consequence* is that which follows of itself, without any qualification or restriction; an *effect* is that which is effected or produced, or which follows from the connection between the thing effecting, as a cause, and the thing effected. In the nature of things causes will have *effects*, and for every *effect* there will be a cause, although it may not be visible. *Consequences*, on the other hand, are either casual or natural; they are not always to be calculated upon. *Effect* applies to physical or moral objects; *consequences* to moral objects only: diseases are the *effects* of intemperance; the loss of character is the general *consequence* of an irregular life.

Consequences follow either from the actions of men or from things where there is no direct agency or design; *results* follow from the actions or efforts of men: *consequences* are good or bad; *results* are favorable or unfavorable. We endeavor to avert *consequences* and to produce *results*. Not to foresee the *consequences* which are foreseen by others evinces a more than ordinary share of indiscretion and infatuation. To calculate on a favorable *result* from an ill-judged or ill-executed enterprise only proves a consistent blindness in the projector.

A *consequence* may be particular or follow from a part; a *result* is general, following from a whole: there may be many *consequences* from the same thing, and but one *result* only.

As *results* follow from actions or *efforts*, there is this further distinction; that in regard to intellectual operations *results* may be drawn by the act of the mind, as the *results* of reasoning or calculation.

Consequences may be intermediate or final; *issue* and *event* are always final: the former is that which flows from particular efforts; the latter from complicated undertakings where chance may interpose to bring about that which happens; hence we speak of the *issue* of a negotiation or a battle, and the *event* of a war. The fate of a nation sometimes hangs on the *issue* of a battle. The measures of government are often unjustly praised or blamed according to the *event*.

See also IMPORTANCE.

CONSEQUENTLY. See NATURALLY; THEREFORE.

CONSERVE. See HUSBAND.

CONSIDER, REFLECT. *Consider* is derived from Latin *con*, together, and *sidus*, star, signifying to contemplate the stars, then simply to contemplate or think. *Reflect*, in Latin *reflecto*, compounded of *re* and *flecto*, bend, signifies to turn back or upon itself.

The operation of thought is expressed by these two words, but it varies in the circumstances of the action. *Consideration* is employed for practical purposes; *reflection* for matters of speculation or moral improvement. Common objects call for *consideration;* the workings of the mind itself, or objects purely spiritual, occupy *reflection*. It is necessary to *consider* what is proper to be done before we take any step; it is consistent with our natures, as rational beings, to *reflect* on what we are, what we ought to be, and what we shall be. Without *consideration* we shall naturally commit the most flagrant errors; without *reflection* we shall never understand our duty to our Maker, our neighbor, and ourselves.

Consider, Regard.—To *consider* signifies to take a view of a thing in the mind which is the result of thought. To *regard* (see CARE) is properly to look back upon or to look at with concern. There is more caution or thought in *considering*, more personal interest in *regarding*. To *consider* is to bear in

mind all that prudence or propriety suggests; to *regard* is to bear in mind all that our wishes or interests suggest. It is most usual to *consider* the means or matters in detail, and to *regard* the end or object at large: a man will *consider* whether a thing is good or bad, proper or improper, out of the *regard* which he has for his reputation, his honor, his conscience, and the like. Where he has no *consideration* he cannot possibly have a *regard*, but he may have a *regard* where *considerations* are not necessary. A want of *consideration* as to the circumstances and capacity of another may lead one to form a wrong judgment of his conduct. A want of *regard* for the person himself may lead one to be regardless of his comfort and convenience.

So, in application to things not expressly connected with one's interests or inclinations, to *consider* is to look at things simply as they are; to *regard* is to look at them with a certain degree of interest.

Consideration, Reason. — *Consideration*, or that which enters into a person's *consideration*, has a reference to the person considering. *Reason* (see CAUSE), or that which influences the reason, is taken absolutely. *Considerations* are therefore, for the most part, partial, as affecting particular interests, or dependent on particular circumstances. *Reasons*, on the contrary, may be general, and vary according to the subject.

The *consideration* influences particular actions; the *reason* determines a line of conduct: no *consideration* of profits should induce a person to forfeit his word; the *reasons* which men assign for their conduct are often as absurd as they are false.

In matters of argument, the *consideration* is that which one offers to the *consideration* of another; the *reason* is that which lies in the nature of the thing.

CONSIGN, COMMIT, INTRUST. *Consign*, in French *consigner*, Latin *consigno*, compounded of *con* and *signare*, to seal, signifies to seal for a specific purpose, also to deposit. *Commit*, in French *commettre*, Latin *committo*, compounded of *con*, together, and *mittere*, to send or put, signifies to put into a person's hands. *Intrust* signifies to put in trust.

The idea of transferring from one's self to the care of another is common to these terms, differing in the nature and object of the action. To *consign* is a more formal act, a more absolute giving from ourselves to another, than to *commit:* a merchant *consigns* his goods to another to dispose of them for his advantage; he *commits* the management of his business to his clerk: a child is *consigned* to another, for him to take the whole charge of his education, maintenance, and the like; but when he is *committed* to the charge of another, it is mostly with limitations. To *intrust* refers to the degree of trust or confidence which is reposed in the individual; a child may be *intrusted* to the care of a servant for a short time; a person may be *intrusted* with the property or secrets of another; or individuals may be *intrusted* with power.

In the figurative application, to *consign* is to deliver over so as to become the property of another thing; to *commit* is to give over for the purpose of taking charge of. Death *consigns* many to an untimely grave; a writer *commits* his thoughts to the press.

Consign may thus be used in the sense of assign, and *commit* in the sense of trusting at all hazards.

CONSISTENT. See COMPATIBLE; CONSONANT.

CONSOLE, SOLACE, COMFORT. *Console* and *solace* are derived from the same source, in French *consoler*, Latin *consolari*, to comfort. *Comfort* (see COMFORT).

Console and *solace* denote the relieving of pain; *comfort* marks the communication of positive pleasure. We *console* others with words; we *console* or *solace* ourselves with reflections; we *comfort* by words or deeds. *Console* is used on more important occasions than *solace*. We *console* our friends when they meet with afflictions; we *solace* ourselves when we meet with disasters; we *comfort* those who stand in need of comfort. The greatest *consolation* which we can enjoy on the death of our friends is derived from the hope that they have exchanged a state of imperfection and sorrow for one that is full of pure and unmixed felicity. It is no small *solace* to us, in the midst of all our troubles, to consider that they are not so bad that they might not have been worse. The *comforts* which a person enjoys may be considerably enhanced by the comparison with what he has formerly suffered.

CONSONANT, ACCORDANT, CONSISTENT. *Consonant*, from the Latin *consonans*, participle of *con*, together, and *sonare*, to sound, signifies to sound, or be, in unison or harmony. *Accordant*, from *accord*, signifies the quality of according (for derivation see *accord* under the key-word AGREE). *Consistent*, from the Latin *consistens*, participle of *consisto*, from *con*, together, and *sistere*, to place, signifies the quality of being able to stand in unison together.

Consonant is employed in matters of representation; *accordant*, in matters of opinion or sentiment; *consistent*, in matters of conduct. A particular passage is *consonant* with the whole tenor of the Scriptures; a particular account is *accordant* with all one hears and sees on a subject; a person's conduct is not always *consistent* with his station. *Consonant* is opposed to dissonant; *accordant*, to discordant; *consistent*, to inconsistent. *Consonance* is not so positive a thing as either *accordance* or *consistency*, which respects real events, circumstances, and actions. *Consonance* may serve to prove the truth of a thing, but *dissonance* does not prove its falsehood until it amounts to direct *discordance* or *inconsistency*. There is a *dissonance* in the accounts given by the four Evangelists of our Saviour, which serves to prove the absence of all collusion and imposture, since there is neither *discordance* nor *inconsistency* in what they have related or omitted.

CONSPICUOUS. See DISTINGUISHED; PROMINENT.

CONSPIRACY. See COMBINATION.

CONSTANCY, STABILITY, STEADINESS, FIRMNESS. *Constancy*, in French *constance*, Latin *constantia*, from *constans* and *consto*, compounded of *con* and *stare*, to stand by or close to a thing, signifies the quality of adhering to the thing that has been once chosen. *Stability*, in French *stabilité*, Latin *stabilitas*, from *stabilis* and *stare*, to stand, signifies the quality of being able to stand. *Steadiness*, the quality of being *steady*, is derived from Anglo-Saxon *stede*, a place, found in words like *homestead*, *instead*, etc. *Steady* signifies standing in one place. *Firm* comes from Latin *firmus*, unmoved.

Constancy respects the affections; *stability*, the opinions; *steadiness*, the action or the motives of action; *firmness*, the purpose or resolution. *Constancy* prevents from changing, and furnishes the mind with resources against weariness or disgust of the same object; it preserves and supports an attachment under every change of circumstances; *stability* prevents from varying; it bears up the mind against the movements of levity or curiosity, which a diversity of objects might produce; *steadiness* prevents from deviating; it enables the mind to bear up against the influence of humor, which temperament or outward circumstances might produce; it fixes on one course, and keeps to it: *firmness* prevents from yielding; it gives the mind strength against all the attacks to which it may be exposed; it makes a resistance, and comes off triumphant. *Constancy* among lovers and friends is the favorite theme of poets; the word has, however, afforded but few originals from which they could copy their pictures: they have mostly described what is desirable rather than what is real. *Stability* of character is essential for those who are to command, for how can they govern others who cannot govern their own thoughts? *Steadiness* of deportment is a great recommendation to those who have to obey: how can any one perform his part well who suffers himself to be perpetually interrupted? *Firmness* of character is indispensable in the support of principles: there are many occasions in which this part of a man's character is likely to be put to a severe test. *Constancy* is opposed to fickleness; *stability*, to changeableness; *steadiness*, to flightiness; *firmness*, to pliancy.

CONSTANT. See CONTINUED; DURABLE; UNSWERVING.

CONSTERNATION. See ALARM.

CONSTITUENT. See ELEMENTARY.

CONSTITUTE, APPOINT, DEPUTE.

Constitute, in Latin *constitutus*, participle of *constituto*, that is, *con*, together, and *statuo*, place, signifies here to put or place for a specific purpose. *Appoint* (see APPOINT). *Depute,* in French *députer*, Latin *deputo*, compounded of *de*, from, and *putare*, to esteem or assign, signifies to assign a certain office to a person.

The act of choosing some person or persons for an office is comprehended under all these terms: *constitute* is a more solemn act than *appoint*, and this than *depute:* to *constitute* is the act of a body; to *appoint* and *depute*, either of a body or an individual: a community *constitutes* any one their leader; a monarch *appoints* his ministers; an assembly *deputes* some of its members. To *constitute* implies the act of making as well as choosing; the office as well as the person is new: in *appointing*, the person, but not the office, is new. A person may be *constituted* arbiter or judge as circumstances may require; a successor is *appointed*, but not *constituted*.

Whoever is *constituted* is invested with supreme authority derived from the highest sources of power; whoever is *appointed* derives his authority from the authority of others, and has consequently but limited power: no individual can *appoint* another with authority equal to his own: whoever is *deputed* has private and not public authority; his office is partial, often confined to the particular transaction of an individual, or a body of individuals. According to the Romish religion, the Pope is *constituted* supreme head of the Christian Church throughout the whole world; governors are *appointed* to distant provinces; persons are *deputed* to present petitions or make representations to government.

See also FORM.

CONSTITUTION. See FRAME.

CONSTRAIN. See COMPEL.

CONSTRAINT, COMPULSION. *Constraint*, from *constrain*, Latin *constringo*, compounded of *con*, together, and *stringere*, to draw tight, signifies the act of straining or tying together. *Compulsion* signifies the act of compelling. (See COMPEL.)

There is much of binding in *con-*

straint: of violence in *compulsion:* *constraint* prevents from acting agreeably to the will; *compulsion* forces to act contrary to the will: a soldier in the ranks moves with much *constraint,* and is often subject to much *compulsion* to make him move as is desired. *Constraint* may arise from outward circumstances; *compulsion* is always produced by some active agent: the forms of civil society lay a proper *constraint* upon the behavior of men, so as to render them agreeable to one another; the arm of the civil power must ever be ready to *compel* those who will not submit without *compulsion:* in the moments of relaxation, the actions of children should be as free from *constraint* as possible; those who know and wish to do what is right will always be ready to discharge their duty without *compulsion.*

Constraint,   Restraint. — *Constraint* (see above). *Restraint* (see COERCE).

Constraint respects the movements of the body only; *restraint,* those of the mind and the outward actions: when they both refer to the outward actions, we say a person's behavior is *constrained;* his feelings are *restrained;* he is *constrained* to act or not to act, or to act in a certain manner; he is *restrained* from acting at all, or he may be *restrained* from feeling: the conduct is *constrained* by certain prescribed rules, by discipline and order; it is *restrained* by particular motives: whoever learns a mechanical exercise is *constrained* to move his body in a certain direction; the fear of detection often *restrains* persons from the commission of vices more than any sense of their enormity.

CONSTRUCT.   See BUILD.

CONSULT, DELIBERATE. *Consult,* in French *consulter,* Latin *consulto,* is a frequentative of *consulo,* signifying to counsel together (see ADVICE). The root of *consulo* is uncertain; it may be allied to *sedere,* to sit. *Deliberate,* in French *délibérer,* Latin *delibero,* compounded of *de* and *libra,* a balance, signifies to weigh as in a balance.

Consultations always require two persons at least; *deliberations* may be carried on either with a man's self or with numbers: an individual may *consult* with one or many; assemblies commonly *deliberate:* advice and informa-

tion are given and received in *consultations;* doubts, difficulties, and objections are started and removed in *deliberations.* We communicate and hear when we *consult;* we pause and hesitate when we *deliberate:* those who have to co-operate must frequently *consult* together; those who have serious measures to decide upon must coolly *deliberate.*

CONSUME.   See DESTROY.

CONSUMMATION, COMPLETION. *Consummation,* Latin *consummatio,* compounded of *con,* together, and *summa,* the top, the sum, from *supmus* (superlative of words whose comparative is *super,* above), signifying the very top, means the summing or winding up of the whole—the putting a final period to any concern. *Completion* signifies either the act of completing or the state of being completed (see COMPLETE).

The arrival at a conclusion is comprehended in both these terms, but they differ principally in application; wishes are *consummated;* plans are *completed:* we often flatter ourselves that the *completion* of all our plans will be the *consummation* of all our wishes, and thus expose ourselves to grievous disappointments

As epithets, *consummate* and *complete* admit of a similar distinction. *Consummate* is said of that which rises absolutely to the highest possible degree, as *consummate* wisdom, or *consummate* felicity: *complete* is said of that which is so relatively; a thing may be *complete* which fully answers the purpose.

CONSUMPTION.   See DECAY.

CONTACT, TOUCH. *Contact,* in Latin *contactus,* participle of *contingo,* compounded of *con* and *tangere,* to touch together, is distinguished from the simple word *touch* (derived through French *toucher* from a Teutonic root allied with Anglo-Saxon *teon,* to pull or draw, and Latin *ducere,* to lead), not so much in sense as in grammatical construction; the former expressing a state, and referring to two bodies actually in that state; the latter, on the other hand, implying the abstract act of *touching:* we speak of things coming or being in *contact,* but not of the *contact* instead of the *touch* of a thing: the poison which comes from the poison-tree is so powerful in its nature that it is not necessary to come in *contact* with it in order to feel its baneful influence; some insects are armed with stings so inconceivably sharp that the smallest *touch* possible is sufficient to produce a puncture in the flesh.

CONTAGION, INFECTION. Both these terms imply the power of communicating something bad, but *contagion*, from the Latin *con*, and *tag*, from *tango*, to come in contact, proceeds from a simple touch; and *infection*, from the Latin *inficio*, or *in*, in, and *facere*, to make, proceeds by receiving something inwardly or having it infused. We consider *contagion* as to the manner of spreading from one body to another; we consider *infection* as to the act of its working itself into the system. Whatever acts by *contagion* acts immediately by direct personal contact; whatever acts by *infection* acts gradually and indirectly, or through the medium of a third body, as clothes, or the air when *infected*. The word *contagion* is, therefore, properly applied only to particular diseases, but *infection* may be applied to every disease which is communicable from one subject to another. Whatever, therefore, is *contagious* is also *infectious*, but not *vice versa.*

So, in application to other things besides diseases, *contagion* is employed to denote that species of communication which is effected by a direct action on the senses.

Infection is employed to denote the communication which takes place by the gradual process of being *infected* with anything.

So, in the moral application, whatever is outward acts by *contagion*, as to shun the *contagion* of bad example or bad manners. Whatever acts inwardly acts by *infection*, as to shun the *infection* of bad principles.

Contagious, Epidemical, Pestilential. —*Contagious* signifies having or causing *contagion. Epidemical*, in Latin *epidemicus* (Greek ἐπίδημος, that is, ἐπί and δῆμος, among the people), signifies universally spread. *Pestilential*, from the Latin *pestis*, the plague, signifies having the plague, or a similar disorder.

The *contagious* applies to that which is capable of being caught, and ought not, therefore, to be touched; the *epidemical*, to that which is already caught or circulated, and requires, therefore, to be stopped; the *pestilential*, to that which may breed an evil, and is, therefore, to be removed: diseases are *contagious* or *epidemical;* the air or breath is *pestilential.*

They may all be applied morally or figuratively in the same sense. We endeavor to shun a *contagious* disorder, that it may not come near us; we endeavor to purify a *pestilential* air, that it may not be inhaled to our injury; we endeavor to provide against *epidemical* disorders, that they may not spread any farther. Vicious example is *contagious;* certain follies or vices of fashion are *epidemical* in almost every age; the breath of infidelity is *pestilential.*

CONTAIN, HOLD. *Contain* (see COMPRISE). *Hold* is derived from Anglo-Saxon *healdan*, which appears in some form in most of the Teutonic languages with the significance that it now has in English.

These terms agree in sense, but differ in application; the former is by comparison noble, the latter is ignoble in its use: *hold* is employed only for the material contents of hollow bodies; *contain* is employed for moral or spiritual contents: in familiar discourse a cask is said to *hold*, but in more polished language it is said to *contain* a certain number of gallons. A coach *holds* or *contains* a given number of persons; a room *holds* a given quantity of furniture; a house or city *contains* its inhabitants.

CONTAMINATE, DEFILE, POLLUTE, TAINT, CORRUPT. *Contaminate* has the same derivation as *contagion;* it comes from Latin *contaminare*, from the prefix *con*, together, and the root *tag*, touch. *Defile* is compounded of Latin *de*, from, and Anglo-Saxon *fylan*, to make foul, from *ful*, Modern English *foul. Pollute* is derived from Latin *pol*, allied to Old Latin *por*, toward, and *luere*, to wash, allied to *lave*, and meant originally to wash over, like a flooded river. *Taint*, in French *teint*, participle of *teindre*, in Latin *tingere*, to dye or stain. *Corrupt*, in Latin *corruptus*, participle of *corrumpo*, compounded of *con*, together, and *rumpere*, to break, signifies to break to pieces.

Contaminate is not so strong an expression as *defile* or *pollute;* but it is stronger than *taint:* these terms are used in the sense of injuring purity: *corrupt* has the idea of destroying it. Whatever is impure *contaminates;* what is gross and vile in the natural sense *defiles*, and in the moral sense *pollutes;* what is contagious or infectious *corrupts;* and what is *corrupted* may *taint* other things. Improper conversation or reading *contaminates* the mind of youth; lewdness and obscenity *defile* the body and *pollute* the mind; loose company *corrupts* the morals; the coming in contact with a *corrupted* body is sufficient to give a *taint.* If young people be admitted to a promiscuous intercourse with society, they must unavoidably witness objects that are calculated to *contaminate* their thoughts, if not their inclinations. They are thrown in the way of seeing the lips of females *defiled* with the grossest indecencies, and hearing or seeing things which cannot be heard or seen without *polluting* the soul: it cannot be surprising if after this their principles are found to be *corrupted* before they have reached the age of maturity.

CONTEMN, DESPISE, SCORN, DISDAIN. *Contemn* comes from Latin *contemnere*, compounded of *con*, intensive prefix, and *temnere*, to despise. *Despise*, in Latin *despicio*, compounded of *de*, from, and *specere*, to look, signifies to look down upon, which is a strong mark of *contempt*. *Scorn*, from Old French *escorner*, meant originally to deprive of horns (Latin *ex*, from, and *cornu*, horn), hence to humiliate or dishonor. It has been influenced by the Old High German *scernon*, to deride. *Disdain* is compounded of *dis*, privative, and Old French *degnier*, from Latin *dignare*, to think worthy; accordingly it means to think unworthy.

The above elucidations sufficiently evince the feeling toward others which gives birth to all these actions. But the feeling of *contempt* is not quite so strong as that of *despising*, nor that of *despising* so strong as those of *scorning* and *disdaining*, the latter of which expresses the strongest sentiment of all. Persons are *contemned* for their moral qualities; they are *despised* on account of their outward circumstances, their characters, or their endowments. Superiors may be *contemned;* inferiors only, or those who degrade themselves, are *despised*. *Contempt*, as applied to persons, is not incompatible with a Christian temper when justly provoked by their character; but *despising* is distinctly forbidden and seldom warranted. Yet it is not so much our business to *contemn* others as to *contemn* that which is *contemptible;* but we are not equally at liberty to *despise* the person, or anything belonging to the person, of another. Whatever springs from the free-will of another may be a subject of *contempt*, but the casualties of fortune or the gifts of Providence, which are alike independent of personal merit, should never expose a person to be *despised*. We may, however, *contemn* a person for his impotent malice, or *despise* him for his meanness.

Persons are not *scorned* or *disdained*, but they may be treated with *scorn* or *disdain;* they are both improper expressions of *contempt* or *despite:* *scorn* marks the sentiment of a little, vain mind: *disdain* of a haughty and perverted one. A beautiful woman looks with *scorn* on her whom she *despises* for the want of this natural gift. The wealthy man treats with *disdain* him whom he *despises* for his poverty.

In speaking of things independently of others, or as immediately connected with ourselves, all these terms may be sometimes employed in a good or an indifferent sense. When we *contemn* a mean action, and *scorn* to conceal by falsehood what we are called upon to acknowledge, we act the part of the gentleman as well as the Christian; but it is inconsistent with our infirm and dependent condition that we should feel inclined to *despise* anything that falls in our way; much less are we at liberty to *disdain* to do anything which our station requires; we ought to think nothing unworthy of us, nothing degrading to us, but that which is inconsistent with the will of God: there are, however, too many who affect to *despise* small favors as not reaching their fancied deserts, and others who *disdain* to receive any favors at all, from mistaken notions about dependence and obligation.

CONTEMPLATE, MEDITATE, MUSE. *Contemplate,* from Latin *contemplari,* was used at first of the observations and meditations of the augurs, and was derived from *templum,* English *temple,* the consecrated place open to the sky, where the augurs made their observations. *Meditate,* in Latin *meditatus,* participle of *meditor,* from Greek μέδομαι, I attend to, meant to devote the thoughts to something. For the derivation of *muse* see AMUSE.

Different species of reflection are marked by these terms. We *contemplate* what is present or before our eyes; we *meditate* on what is past or absent. The heavens and all the works of the Creator are objects of *contemplation;* the ways of Providence are fit subjects for *meditation.* One *muses* on events or circumstances which have been just passing.

We may *contemplate* and *meditate* for the future, but never *muse.* In this case the two former terms have the sense of contriving or purposing: what is *contemplated* to be done is thought of more indistinctly than when it is *meditated* to be done: many things are bad in *contemplation* which are never seriously *meditated* upon: between *contemplating* and *meditating* there is oftener a greater distance than between *meditating* and executing.

Meditating is a permanent and serious action; *musing* is partial and unimportant; *meditation* is a religious duty, it cannot be neglected without injury to a person's spiritual improvement; *musing* is a temporary employment of the mind on the ordinary concerns of life, as they happen to excite an interest for the time. *Contemplative* and *musing,* as epithets, have a strong analogy to each other. *Contemplative* is a habit of the mind; *musing* is a particular state of the mind. A person may have a *contemplative* turn, or be in a *musing* mood.

CONTEMPORANEOUS. See SYNCHRONOUS.

CONTEMPORARY. See COEVAL.

CONTEMPTIBLE, CONTEMPTU-

OUS. These terms are very frequently, though very erroneously, confounded in common discourse. *Contemptible* is applied to the thing deserving *contempt; contemptuous,* to that which is expressive of *contempt.* Persons, or what is done by persons, may be either *contemptible* or *contemptuous.* A production is *contemptible;* a sneer or look is *contemptuous.*

Contemptible, Despicable, Pitiful.— *Contemptible* is not so strong as *despicable* or *pitiful.* A person may be *contemptible* for his vanity or weakness; but he is *despicable* for his servility and baseness of character; he is *pitiful* for his want of manliness and becoming spirit. A lie is at all times *contemptible;* it is *despicable* when it is told for purposes of gain or private interest; it is *pitiful* when accompanied with indications of unmanly fear. It is *contemptible* to take credit to one's self for the good action one had not performed; it is *despicable* to charge another with the faults which we ourselves have committed; it is *pitiful* to offend others, and then attempt to screen ourselves from their resentment under any shelter which offers. It is *contemptible* for a man in a superior station to borrow of his inferiors; it is *despicable* in him to forfeit his word; it is *pitiful* in him to attempt to conceal anything by artifice.

Contemptuous, Scornful, Disdainful. —These epithets rise in sense by a regular gradation. *Contemptuous* is general, and applied to whatever can express *contempt: scornful* and *disdainful* are particular; they apply only to outward marks: one is *contemptuous* who is *scornful* or *disdainful,* but not *vice versa.* Words, actions, and looks are *contemptuous:* looks, sneers, and gestures are *scornful* and *disdainful.* *Contemptuous* expressions are always unjustifiable; whatever may be the *contempt* which a person's conduct deserves, it is unbecoming in another to give him any indications of the sentiment he feels. *Scornful* and *disdainful* smiles are resorted to by the weakest or the worst of mankind.

CONTEND, CONTEST, DISPUTE. *Contend,* from *tendo,* stretch, and *contra,* against, signifies to strive against. *Contest,* from *con,* against, and *testor,* from *testis*, a witness, signifying to call to witness against; and *dispute*, from *dis* and *puto*, signifying to think diversely, are modes of *contending*.

To *contend* is simply to exert a force against a force; to *contest* is to struggle together for an object.

To *contend* and *contest* may be both applied to that which is claimed and striven for; but *contending* is the act of the individual without reference to others, where success depends upon personal efforts or prowess, as when one *contends* at games. To *contest* is to set up rival pretensions to be determined by the suffrage of others, as to *contest* an election, to *contest* a prize.

Opinions may likewise be both *contended* and *contested*, with this distinction, that to *contend* is to maintain any opinion; to *contest* is to maintain different opinions: the person is said to *contend* and the thing to be *contested*.

To *dispute*, according to its original meaning, applies to opinions only, and is distinguished from *contend* in this, that the latter signifies to maintain one's own opinion, and the former to call in question the opinion of another. In respect to matters of personal interest, *contend* and *dispute* are employed with a like distinction, the former to denote striving for something desired by one's self, the latter to call in question something relating to others, as to *contend* for a victory, to *dispute* a person's right; and when the idea of striving for a thing in *dispute* is to be expressed, this word may be employed indifferently with *contend* for, as to *dispute* or *contend* for a prize.

Contention, *contest*, and *dispute*, as nouns, admit of a further distinction. *Contention* is always of a personal nature, whether as regards interests or opinions, and is always accompanied with more or less ill feeling.

Contests may be as personal as *contentions*, but the objects in a *contest* being higher, and the *contesting* parties coming less into direct collision, there is less ill feeling produced.

As differences of opinion have a tendency to create ill feeling, *disputes* are rarely conducted without acrimony; but sometimes there may be *disputes* for that which is honorable, where there is no personal animosity.

See also BICKER; STRIVE.

CONTENTION. See DISSENSION; STRIFE.

CONTENTMENT, SATISFACTION. *Contentment*, in French *contentement*, from *content*, in Latin *contentus*, participle of *contenere*, to contain or hold, signifies the keeping one's self to a thing. *Satisfaction*, in Latin *satisfactio*, compounded of *satis*, enough, and *facere*, to do, signifies the making or having enough.

Contentment lies in ourselves: *satisfaction* is derived from external objects. One is *contented* when one wishes for no more: one is *satisfied* when one has obtained all one wishes. The *contented* man has always enough; the *satisfied* man has only enough for the time being. The *contented* man will not be *dissatisfied;* but he who looks for *satisfaction* will never be *contented*. *Contentment* is the absence of pain; *satisfaction* is positive pleasure. *Contentment* is accompanied with the enjoyment of what one has; *satisfaction* is often quickly followed with the alloy of wanting more. A *contented* man can never be miserable; a *satisfied* man can scarcely be long happy. *Contentment* is a permanent and habitual state of mind; it is the restriction of all our thoughts, views, and desires within the compass of present possession and enjoyment: *satisfaction* is a partial and turbulent state of the feelings, which awakens rather than deadens desire. *Contentment* is suited to our present condition; it accommodates itself to the vicissitudes of human life; *satisfaction* belongs to no created being; one *satisfied* desire engenders another that demands *satisfaction*. *Contentment* is within the reach of the poor man, to whom it is a continual feast; but *satisfaction* has never been procured by wealth, however enormous, or ambition, however boundless and successful. We should therefore look for the *contented* man where there are the fewest means of being *satisfied*. Our duty bids us be *contented;* our desires ask to be *satisfied:* but our duty is associated with our happiness; our desires are the sources of our misery.

When taken in a partial application

to particular objects, there are cases in which we ought not to be *contented*, and where we may with propriety look for permanent *satisfaction*. We cannot be *contented* to do less than our duty requires; we may justly be *satisfied* with the consciousness of having done our duty.

CONTEST. See CONFLICT; CONTEND.

CONTIGUOUS. See ADJACENT.

CONTINENCE. See CHASTITY.

CONTINGENCY. See ACCIDENT.

CONTINGENT. See ACCIDENTAL; PROVISIONAL.

CONTINUAL, PERPETUAL, CONSTANT. *Continual*, in French *continuel*, Latin *continuus*, from *continere*, to hold or keep together, signifies keeping together without intermission. *Perpetual*, in French *perpétuel*, Latin *perpetualis*, from *perpeto*, compounded of *per*, meaning thoroughly, and *petere*, to seek, to seek thoroughly, signifies going on everywhere and at all times. *Constant* (see CONSTANCY).

What is *continual* admits of no interruption: what is *perpetual* admits of no termination. There may be an end to that which is *continual*, and there may be intervals in that which is *perpetual*. Rains are *continual* in the tropical climates at certain seasons: complaints among the lower orders are *perpetual*, but they are frequently without foundation. There is a *continual* passing and repassing in the streets of the metropolis during the day; the world and all that it contains are subject to *perpetual* change.

Constant, like *continual*, admits of no interruption, and it also admits of no change; what is *continual* may not always *continue* in the same state, but what is *constant* remains in the same state: *continual* is therefore applied to that which is expected to cease, and *constant* to that which ought to last. A nervous person may fancy he hears *continual* noises. It will be the *constant* endeavor of a peaceable man to live peaceably.

Continual may sometimes have a moral application; as when we say, *contentment* is a *continual* feast; to have a *continual* enjoyment in anything: *constant* is properly applied to moral objects.

Continual, Continued. — *Continual* and *continued* both mark length of duration, but the former admits of a certain degree of interruption, which the latter does not. What is *continual* may have frequent pauses; what is *continued* ceases only to terminate. Rains are continual which are frequently repeated; so noises in a tumultuous street are *continual*: the bass in music is said to be *continued;* the mirth of a drunken party is one *continued* noise. *Continual* interruptions abate the vigor of application and create disgust: in countries situated near the poles, there is one *continued* darkness for the space of five or six months, during which time the inhabitants are obliged to leave the place.

Continual respects the duration of actions only; *continued* is likewise applied to the extent or course of things: rumors are *continual;* talking, walking, running, and the like, are *continual;* but a line, a series, a scene, or a stream of water is *continued*.

Continuance, Continuation, Duration. —*Continuance*, from the intransitive verb to *continue*, denotes the state of continuing or being carried on further. *Continuation*, from the transitive verb *continue*, denotes the act of continuing or carrying on further. The *continuance* is said of that which itself *continues;* the *continuation*, of that which is *continued* by some other agency: as the *continuance* of the rain; the *continuation* of a history, work, line, etc. As the species is said to be *continued*, the word *continuation* is most properly applied in this case.

Continuance and *duration* are both employed for the time of *continuing;* things may be of long *continuance* or of long *duration;* but *continuance* is used only with regard to the action; *duration* with regard to the thing and its existence. Whatever is occasionally done, and soon to be ended, is not for a *continuance;* whatever is made, and soon destroyed, is not of long *duration:* there are many excellent institutions in England which promise to be of no less *continuance* than utility. *Duration* is with us a relative term; things are of long or short *duration* by comparison: the *duration* of the world, and all sublunary objects, is nothing in regard to eternity.

Continuation, Continuity.—Continuation signifies either the act of continuing, as to undertake the *continuation* or *continuing* of a history; or the thing *continued;* as to read the *continuation* of a history—that is, the history *continued.*

Continuity denotes the quality of bodies holding together without interruption; there are bodies of so little *continuity* that they will crumble to pieces on the slightest touch.

Continue, Remain, Stay.—Continue (see CONTINUAL). *Remain,* in Latin *remaneo,* is compounded of *re,* behind, and *manere,* to stay, and signifies to stay behind. *Stay* is derived through French from Middle Dutch *stade,* which is allied to English *stead,* in *steadfast, steady,* etc., signifying place; it means to *remain* in one place.

The idea of keeping to an object is common to these terms. To *continue* is associated with a state of action; to *remain,* with a state of rest: we are said to *continue* to speak, walk, or do anything, to *continue* in action or motion; to *remain* stationary, or in a position.

So likewise in application to the outward condition or the state of mind, *continue* denotes that which is active and positive; *remain,* that which is quiescent and tranquil; to *continue* in a course or in a belief; to *continue* steadfast: to *remain* in doubt.

The same distinction exists between these words when things are the subjects: a war *continues;* a stone *remains* in the place where it is put.

Continue is frequently taken absolutely for continuing in action; *remain,* from the particle *re,* has a relative signification to something else: the sickness or the rain *continues;* I will use my utmost endeavors as long as health *remains.*

Continue and *remain* are used in respect of place; *stay* is used in that of connection only. *Continue* is indefinite in its application and signification; as to *continue* in town or in the country: to *remain* is an involuntary act; as a soldier *remains* at his post, or a person *remains* in prison: *stay* is a voluntary act; as to *stay* at a friend's or with a friend.

Continue, Persevere, Persist, Pursue, Prosecute.—Continue (see above). *Persevere,* in French *persévérer,* Latin *perseverare,* compounded of *per,* through, and *severus,* strict and steady, signifies to be steady throughout or to the end. *Persist,* in French *persister,* Latin *persisto,* is compounded of *per,* through, and *sistere,* to put, and corresponds to the modern phrase "to put it through." *Pursue* and *prosecute,* in French *poursuivre,* come from the Latin *prosequor* and its participle *prosecutus,* signifying to follow after or keep on with.

The idea of not setting aside is common to these terms, which is the sense of *continue* without any qualification; the other terms, which are all species of *continuing,* include likewise some collateral idea which distinguishes them from the first, as well as from one another. *Continue* is comparable with *persevere* and *persist* in the neuter sense, with *pursue* and *prosecute* in the active sense. To *continue* is simply to do as one has done hitherto; to *persevere* is to *continue* without wishing to change or from a positive desire to attain an object; to *persist* is to *continue* from a determination or will not to cease. The act of *continuing,* therefore, specifies no characteristic of the agent; that of *persevering* or *persisting* marks a direct temper of mind; the former is always used in a good sense, the latter in an indifferent or bad sense. We *continue* from habit or casualty; we *persevere* from reflection and the exercise of our judgment; we *persist* from attachment. It is not the most exalted virtue to *continue* in a good course merely because we have been in the habit of so doing: what is done from habit merely, without any fixed principle, is always exposed to change from the influence of passion or evil counsel; there is real virtue in the act of *perseverance,* without which many of our best intentions would remain unfulfilled and our best plans would be defeated: those who do not *persevere* can do no essential good; and those who do *persevere* often effect what has appeared to be impracticable; of this truth the discoverer of America is a remarkable proof, who, in spite of every mortification, rebuff, and disappointment, *persevered* in calling the attention of monarchs to his project, until he at length obtained the assistance requisite for effecting the discovery of a new world.

The Romans have not observed this distinction between *perseverare* and *persistere;* for they say, "In errore *perseverare:*" CICERO. "Ad ultimum *perseverare:*" LIVY. "In eadem impudentiâ *persistere:*" LIVY. "In proposito *persistere:*" CICERO. Probably in imitation of them, examples are to be found in English writers of the use of *persevere* in the bad sense, and of *persist* in the good sense; but the distinction is now invariably observed. *Persevere* is employed only in matters of some moment, in things of sufficient importance to demand a steady purpose of the mind; *persist* may be employed in that which is trifling, if not bad: a learner *perseveres* in his studies, in order to arrive at the necessary degree of improvement; a child *persists* in making a request until he has obtained the object of his desire: there is always wisdom in *perseverance*, even though unsuccessful; there is mostly folly, caprice, or obstinacy in *persistence:* how different the man who *perseveres* in the cultivation of his talents from him who only *persists* in maintaining falsehoods or supporting errors!

Continue, when compared with *persevere* or *persist*, is always coupled with modes of action: but in comparison with *pursue* or *prosecute*, it is always followed by some object: we *continue* to do, *persevere* or *persist* in doing something: but we *continue, pursue*, or *prosecute* some object which we wish to bring to perfection by additional labor. *Continue* is equally indefinite as in the former case; *pursue* and *prosecute* both comprehend collateral ideas respecting the disposition of the agent and the nature of the object: to *continue* is to go on with a thing as it has been begun; to *pursue* and *prosecute* is to *continue* by some prescribed rule, or in some particular manner: a work is *continued;* a plan, measure, or line of conduct is *pursued;* an undertaking or a design is *prosecuted:* we may *continue* the work of another in order to supply a deficiency: we may *pursue* a plan that emanates either from ourselves or another; we *prosecute* our own work only in order to obtain some

peculiar object: *continue*, therefore, expresses less than *pursue*, and this less than *prosecute:* the history of England has been *continued* down to the present period by different writers; Smollett has *pursued* the same plan as Hume in the *continuation* of his history; Captain Cook *prosecuted* his work of discovery in three several voyages. To *continue* is itself altogether an indifferent action; to *pursue* and *prosecute* are commendable actions; the latter still more than the former: it is a mark of great instability not to *continue* anything that we begin; it betrays a great want of prudence and discernment not to *pursue* some plan on every occasion which requires method; it is the characteristic of a *persevering* mind to *prosecute* whatever it has deemed worthy to enter upon.

CONTINUITY. See CONTINUATION.

CONTRABAND, FORBIDDEN, PROHIBITED. *Contraband* is derived through Spanish and Italian from Latin *contra*, against, and Italian *bando*, Late Latin *bannum*, a word of Teutonic origin found in *abandon, ban*, etc. It means literally a *ban* against something, and refers to a special kind of *forbidding* or *prohibiting*. McCulloch, in the "Commercial Dictionary," gives the following succinct definition of the perplexing phrase *contraband of war:*

"When two nations are engaged in war, if there be any foreign article or articles necessary for the defence or subsistence of either of them, and without which it would be difficult for it to carry on the contest, the other may legitimately exert every means in its power to prevent its opponent being supplied with such article or articles."

Such goods are called *contraband of war*. After *forbidding* the importation of such goods by a legal proclamation, a nation may use every means to *prohibit* the enemy from obtaining the *contraband* articles. For a further definition of the difference between *forbid* and *prohibit* see BAN and FORBID.

CONTRACT. See ABRIDGE; AGREEMENT.

CONTRACTED, CONFINED, NARROW. These words agree in denoting a limited space; but *contracted*, from *contraho*, draw together, signifying drawn into a smaller compass than it might otherwise be in, and *confined* (see BOUND), signifying brought within unusually small bounds, are said of that which is made or becomes so by circumstances. *Narrow* comes from Anglo-Saxon *nearu*, closely drawn. A limb is said to be *contracted* which is drawn up by disease; a situation is *confined* which has not the necessary or usual degree of open space; a road or a room is *narrow*.

These terms are figuratively applied to moral objects with the same distinction: the mind is *contracted* by education or habit; a person's views are *confined* by reason of his ignorance; people have for the most part a temper *narrow* by nature.

CONTRADICT, DENY, OPPOSE. *Contradict*, from the Latin *contra*, against, and *dictum*, speech, signifies a speech against a speech. *Deny* is derived from Latin *de* and *negare*, to say "no," from the negative particle *ne*, and signifies to say "no." *Oppose* comes from Latin *ob*, in the way of, and French *poser* (see COMPOSE), and signifies to place in the way of.

To *contradict*, as the origin of the word sufficiently denotes, is to set up one assertion against another, but it does not necessarily imply an intentional act. The *contradiction* may lie in the force of the terms, whence logicians call those propositions *contradictory* which in all their terms are directly opposed to each other: as, "All men are liars"; "No men are liars." A person may *contradict* himself, or two witnesses may *contradict* each other who have had no communication.

To *deny* is to assert the falsehood of another's assertion, and is therefore a direct and personal act; as to *deny* any one's statement.

Contradictions may be given at the pleasure or for the convenience of the parties; *denials* are made in support either of truth or falsehood, in matters of fact or matters of opinion.

One *contradicts* in direct terms by asserting something contrary; one *denies* by advancing arguments or suggesting doubts or difficulties. These terms

may therefore both be used in reference to disputations. We may *deny* the truth of a position by *contradicting* the assertions that are advanced in its support.

Contradiction and *denial* are commonly performed by words only; *opposition*, by any kind of action or mode of expression. We may therefore sometimes *oppose* by *contradiction*, although not properly by *denial*; *contradicting* and *opposing* being both voluntary acts, *denying* frequently a matter of necessity or for self-defence.

CONTRARY. See ADVERSE; HETEROGENEOUS.

CONTRAST. See COMPARISON.

CONTRIBUTE. See CONDUCE; MINISTER.

CONTRIBUTION. See TAX.

CONTRITION. See REPENTANCE.

CONTRIVE, DEVISE, INVENT. *Contrive* in Old French *controver*, compounded of Latin *con*, together, and a stressed stem of Old French *trover*, to find, signifies to find out by putting together. *Devise*, compounded of *de* and Latin *visus*, seen, signifies to show or present to the mind. *Invent*, in Latin *inventus*, participle of *invenire*, compounded of *in*, in, and *venire*, to come, signifies to come or bring into the mind.

Contriving requires less exercise of the thoughts than *devising*: we *contrive* on familiar and common occasions; we *devise* in seasons of difficulty and trial. A *contrivance* is simple and obvious to a plain understanding: a *device* is complex and far-fetched; it requires a ready conception and a degree of art. *Contrivances* serve to supply a deficiency or increase a convenience; *devices* are employed to extricate from danger, to remove an evil, or forward a scheme: the history of Robinson Crusoe derives considerable interest from the relation of the various *contrivances* by which he provided himself with the first articles of necessity and comfort; the history of robbers and adventurers is full of the various *devices* by which they endeavor to carry on their projects of plunder or elude the vigilance of their pursuers.

To *contrive* and *devise* do not express so much as to *invent*: we *contrive* and *devise* in small matters; we *invent* in those of greater moment. *Contriving* and *devising* respect the manner of doing things; *inventing* comprehends the action and the thing itself; the former are but the new fashioning of things that already exist; the latter is, as it were, the creation of something new: to *contrive* and *devise* are intentional actions, the result of a specific effort; *invention* naturally arises from the exertion of an inherent power: we require thought and combination to *contrive* or *devise;* ingenuity is the faculty which is exerted in *inventing.* A *device* is often employed for bad and fraudulent purposes; *contrivances* mostly serve the innocent purposes of life; *inventions* are mostly good, unless they are stories *invented,* which are always false.

See also CONCERT.

CONTRIVING. See SCHEMING.

CONTROL. See CHECK.

CONTROVERT, DISPUTE. *Controvert,* compounded of the Latin *contra,* against, and *vertere,* to turn, signifies to turn against another in discourse, or direct one's self against another. *Dispute* (see ARGUE).

To *controvert* has regard to speculative points; to *dispute* respects matters of fact: there is more of opposition in *controversy;* more of doubt in *disputing:* a sophist *controverts;* a sceptic *disputes:* the plainest and sublimest truths of the Gospel have been all *controverted* in their turn by the self-sufficient inquirer: the authenticity of the Bible itself has been *disputed* by some few individuals: the existence of a God by still fewer. *Controversy* is worse than an unprofitable task; instead of eliciting truth, it does but expose the failings of the parties engaged: *disputing* is not so personal, and consequently not so objectionable: we never *controvert* any point without seriously and decidedly intending to oppose the notions of another; we may sometimes *dispute* a point for the sake of friendly argument or the desire of information: theologians and politicians are the greatest *controversialists:* it is the business of men in general to *dispute* whatever ought not to be taken for granted.

CONTUMACIOUS. See OBSTINATE.

CONTUMACY, REBELLION. *Contumacy,* from the Latin *contumax,* compounded of *contra,* against, and *tumere,* to swell, signifies the swelling one's self up by way of resistance. *Rebellion,* in Latin *rebellio,* compounded of *re,* in return, and *bellum,* war, signifies carrying on war against those to whom we owe, and have before paid, a lawful subjection.

Resistance to lawful authority is the common idea included in the signification of both these terms, but *contumacy* does not express so much as *rebellion:* the *contumacious* resist only occasionally; the *rebel* resists systematically: the *contumacious* stand only on certain points, and oppose the individual; the *rebel* sets himself up against the authority itself: the *contumacious* thwart and contradict, they never resort to open violence: the *rebel* acts only by main force; *contumacy* shelters itself under the plea of equity and justice; *rebellion* sets all law and order at defiance.

CONTUMELY. See REPROACH.

CONVENE. See ASSEMBLE.

CONVENIENT, SUITABLE. *Convenient* (see COMMODIOUS). *Suitable* (see CONFORMABLE).

Convenient regards the circumstances of the individual; *suitable* respects the established opinions of mankind, and is closely connected with moral propriety: nothing is *convenient* which does not favor one's purpose: nothing is *suitable* which does not suit the person, place, and thing: whoever has anything to ask of another must take a *convenient* opportunity in order to insure success; his address on such an occasion would be very *unsuitable* if he affected to claim as a right what he ought to solicit as a favor.

CONVENT. See CLOISTER.

CONVENTION, AGREEMENT, COMPACT, TREATY. *Convention,* in French the same form, from Latin *con,* together, and *venire,* to come, in the diplomatic sense in which it is here used signifies literally an agreement as distinguished from an assembly of a political character. In international disputes or warfare it has frequently been the custom for the disputants to seek a peaceable solution of the trouble between them, the first step being a meeting of mutual delegates to ascertain what demands and concessions are likely to be made.

This meeting may formulate terms, which are usually of a tentative character, and afterward plenipotentiaries are appointed to negotiate a formal *agreement*, *compact*, and sometimes a *treaty* itself. The final engagement becomes effective only on its ratification by each disputant. The plenipotentiaries, instructed on general lines by their respective governments, give and take, and their agreement is almost always accepted as binding by their governments.

See also ASSEMBLY.

CONVERSABLE. See FACETIOUS.

CONVERSANT, FAMILIAR. *Conversant*, from *con*, together, and *versari*, to dwell, signifies dwelling together, hence familiar with, consequently becoming acquainted. *Familiar*, from the Latin *familiaris*, to be of the same family, signifies the closest connection.

An acquaintance with things is implied in both these terms, but the latter expresses something more particular than the former. A person is *conversant* in matters that come frequently before his notice; he is *familiar* with such as form the daily routine of his business: one who is not a professed lawyer may be *conversant* with the questions of law which occur on ordinary occasions; but one who is skilled in his profession will be *familiar* with all cases which may possibly be employed in support of a cause: it is advisable to be *conversant* with the ways of the world; but to be *familiar* with the greater part of them would not redound to one's credit or advantage.

Conversation, Dialogue, Conference, Colloquy.—*Conversation* denotes the act of holding *converse* (see COMMUNION). *Dialogue*, in French *dialogue*, Latin *dialogus*, Greek διάλογος, compounded of διά and λόγος, signifies a speech between two. *Conference*, from the Latin *con*, together, and *ferre*, to bring, signifies consulting together on subjects. *Colloquy*, in Latin *colloquium*, from *con*, together, and *loquor*, speak, signifies the art of talking together.

A *conversation* is always something actually held between two or more persons; a *dialogue* is mostly fictitious,

and written as if spoken: any number of persons may take part in a *conversation*, but a *dialogue* always refers to the two persons who are expressly engaged: a *conversation* may be desultory; a *dialogue* is formal, in which there will always be reply and rejoinder: a *conversation* may be carried on by any signs besides words, which are addressed personally to the individual present; a *dialogue* must always consist of express words: a prince holds frequent *conversations* with his ministers on affairs of state; Cicero wrote *dialogues* on the nature of the gods, and many later writers have adopted the *dialogue* form as a vehicle for conveying their sentiments: a *conference* is a species of *conversation;* a *colloquy* is a species of *dialogue:* a *conversation* is indefinite as to the subject or the parties engaged in it: a *conference* is confined to particular subjects and descriptions of persons: a *conversation* is mostly occasional: a *conference* is always specifically appointed: a *conversation* is mostly on indifferent matters; a *conference* is mostly on national or public concerns: we have a *conversation* as friends; we have a *conference* as ministers of state. The *dialogue* naturally limits the number to two; the *colloquy* is indefinite as to number: there may be *dialogues*, therefore, which are not *colloquies;* but every *colloquy* may be denominated a *dialogue*.

CONVERSE. See COMMUNION; SPEAK.

CONVERT, PROSELYTE. *Convert*, from the Latin *converto*, signifies changed to something in conformity with the views of another. *Proselyte*, from the Greek πρός, to, and ἤλυθον, second aorist of ἔρχομαι, I come, signifies come over to the side of another.

Convert is more extensive in its sense and application than *proselyte: convert* in its full sense includes every change of opinion, without respect to the subject; *proselyte*, in its original application, denoted changes only from one religious belief to another: there are many *converts* to particular doctrines of Christianity, and *proselytes* from the Pagan, Jewish, or Mohammedan to the Christian faith; but the word *proselyte* has since acquired an application which distinguishes it from *convert*.

Conversion is a more voluntary act than *proselytism;* it emanates entirely from the mind of the agent, independently of foreign influence; it extends not merely to the abstract or speculative opinions of the individual, but to the whole current of his feelings and spring of his actions: it is the *conversion* of the heart and soul. *Proselytism* is an outward act, which need not extend beyond the conformity of one's words and actions to a certain rule: *convert* is therefore always taken in a good sense; it bears on the face of it the stamp of sincerity: *proselyte* is a term of more ambiguous meaning; the *proselyte* is often the creature and tool of a party: there may be many *proselytes* where there are no *converts.* The *conversion* of a sinner is the work of God's grace, either by His special interposition or by the ordinary influence of His Holy Word on the heart: partisans are always anxious to make *proselytes* to their own party.

CONVERTIBLE. See ASSIMILATE.

CONVEY. See BEAR; WAFT.

CONVICT, DETECT. *Convict,* from the Latin *convictus,* participle of *convinco,* I make manifest, signifies to make guilt clear. *Detect,* from the Latin *detectus,* participle of *detego,* compounded of the privative *de* and *tegere,* to cover, signifies to uncover or lay open guilt.

A person is *convicted* by means of evidence; he is *detected* by means of ocular demonstration. One is *convicted* of having been the perpetrator of some evil deed; one is *detected* in the very act of committing the deed. Whatever serves to prove the guilt of another is said to *convict,* whether the *conviction* be by others or by one's self: a man may be *convicted* in his own mind, as well as in the opinion of others, before a public tribunal or by private individuals; *detection* is confined to the act of the individual, which is laid open to others.

See also CRIMINAL.

Convict, Convince, Persuade.—To *convict* is to satisfy a person of another's guilt or error. To *convince* is to satisfy the person himself of the truth or falsehood of a thing.

A person may be *convicted* of heresy, if it be proved to the satisfaction of others; he may be *convinced* that the opinion which he has held is heretical. So a person may be *convicted* who is involuntarily *convinced* of his error, but he is *convinced* if he is made sensible of his error without any force on his own mind. One is *convicted* only of that which is false or bad, but one is *convinced* of that which is true as well as that which is false. The noun *conviction* is used in both the senses of *convict* and *convince.*

What *convinces* binds; what *persuades* attracts. We are *convinced* by arguments; it is the understanding which determines: we are *persuaded* by entreaties and personal influence; it is the imagination or will which decides. Our *conviction* respects solely matters of belief or faith; our *persuasion* respects matters of belief or practice: we are *convinced* that a thing is true or false; we are *persuaded* that it is either right or wrong, advantageous or the contrary. A person will have half effected a thing who is *convinced* that it is in his power to effect it; he will be easily *persuaded* to do that which favors his own interests.

Conviction respects our most important duties; *persuasion* is applied to matters of indifference, or of temporary personal interest. The first step to true repentance is a thorough *conviction* of the enormity of sin. The cure of people's maladies is sometimes promoted to a surprising degree by their *persuasion* of the efficacy of the remedy.

As *conviction* is the effect of substantial evidence, it is solid and permanent in its nature; it cannot be so easily changed and deceived: *persuasion,* depending on our feelings, is influenced by external objects, and exposed to various changes; it may vary both in the degree and in the object. *Conviction* answers in our minds to positive certainty; *persuasion* answers to probability. We ought to be *convinced* of the propriety of avoiding everything which can interfere with the good order of society; we may be *persuaded* of the truth of a person's narrative or not, according to the representation made to us; we may be *persuaded* to pursue any study or lay it aside.

CONVINCING. See CONCLUSIVE.

CONVIVIAL, SOCIAL. *Convivial,* in

Latin *convivialis*, from *con*, together, and *vivere*, to live, signifies being entertained together. *Social*, from *socius*, a companion, signifies pertaining to company.

The prominent idea in *convivial* is that of sensual indulgence; the prominent idea in *social* is that of enjoyment from an intercourse with society. *Convivial* is a species of the *social*, it is the *social* in matters of festivity. What is *convivial* is social, but what is *social* is something more; the former is excelled by the latter as much as the body is excelled by the mind. We speak of *convivial* meetings, *convivial* enjoyments, or the *convivial* board; but *social* intercourse, *social* pleasure, *social* amusements, and the like.

CONVOCATION. See ASSEMBLE.

CONVOKE. See ASSEMBLE.

COOL, COLD, FRIGID. In the natural sense, *cool* is simply the absence of warmth; *cold* and *frigid* are positively contrary to warmth; the former in regard to objects in general, the latter to moral objects: in the figurative sense the analogy is strictly preserved. *Cool* is used as it respects the passions and the affections; *cold* only with regard to the affections; *frigid* only in regard to the inclinations. With regard to the passions, *cool* designates a freedom from agitation, which is a desirable quality. *Coolness* in a time of danger, and *coolness* in an argument, are alike commendable. As *cool* and *cold* respect the affections, the *cool* is opposed to the friendly, the *cold* to the warm-hearted, the *frigid* to the animated; the former is but a degree of the latter. A reception is said to be *cool*, an embrace to be *cold*, a sentiment *frigid*. *Coolness* is an enemy to social enjoyments; *coldness* is an enemy to affection; *frigidity* destroys all force of character. *Coolness* is engendered by circumstances; it supposes the previous existence of warmth; *coldness* lies often in the temperament, or is engendered by habit; it is always something vicious; *frigidity* is occasional, and is always a defect. Trifling differences produce *coolness* sometimes between the best friends: trade sometimes engenders a *cold*, calculating temper in some minds: those who are remarkable for apathy will often express themselves with *frigid*

indifference on the most important subjects.

See also DISPASSIONATE.

COPIOUS. See PLENTIFUL.

COPIOUSLY. See LARGELY.

COPY, TRANSCRIBE. *Copy* is derived from the Latin *copia*, abundance, and signifies to create an abundance of some article by duplicating it or *copying*. *Transcribe*, in Latin *transcribo*, that is, *trans*, over, and *scribere*, to write, signifies literally to write over from something else, to make to pass over in writing from one paper or substance to the other.

To *copy* respects the matter; to *transcribe* respects simply the act of writing. What is *copied* must be taken immediately from the original, with which it must exactly correspond; what is *transcribed* may be taken from the *copy*, but not necessarily in an entire state. Things are *copied* for the sake of getting the contents; they are often *transcribed* for the sake of clearness and fair writing. A *copier* should be very exact; a *transcriber* should be a good writer. Lawyers *copy* deeds, and have them afterward frequently *transcribed* as occasion requires.

See also SUITABLE.

Copy, Model, Pattern, Specimen.— *Copy*, from the verb to *copy*, marks either the thing from which we *copy* or the thing *copied*. *Model*, in French *modèle*, Latin *modulus*, a little mode or measure, signifies the thing that serves as a measure or that is made after a measure. *Pattern*, which is a variation of *patron*, from the Latin *patronus*, whence English *patron* is derived, signifies the thing that directs. *Specimen*, in Latin *specimen*, from *specere*, to behold, signifies what is looked at for the purpose of forming one's judgment by it.

A *copy* and a *model* imply either that which is *copied* or taken from something, as when we speak of a *copy* in distinction from an original, and of making a *model* of anything.

Or they imply that from which anything is *copied* or taken, as to follow a *copy*, to choose a *model*.

The term *copy* is applied to that which is delineated, as writings or pictures, which must be taken faithfully and literally; the *model*, to that which may be represented in wood or stone, and which serves as a guide.

In application to other objects, a *copy* may be either that which is made or done in imitation, or it may be that which is imitated.

A *model* is that which may be used as a guide or rule.

Pattern and *specimen* serve, like the *model*, to guide or regulate, but differ in the nature of the objects; the *pattern* regards solely the outward form or color of anything that is made or manufactured, as the *pattern* of a carpet; a person fixes on having a thing according to a certain *pattern;* the *specimen* is any portion of a material which serves to show the quality of that of which it forms a part, as the *specimen* of a printed work; the value of things is estimated by the *specimen.*

In the moral application *pattern* respects the whole conduct or behavior which may deserve imitation; *specimen* only the detached parts by which a judgment may be formed of the whole: the female who devotes her whole time and attention to the management of her family and the education of her offspring is a *pattern* to those of her sex who depute the whole concern to others. A person gives but an unfortunate *specimen* of his boasted sincerity who is found guilty of an evasion.

COQUETTE, FLIRT, JILT. *Coquette* is in French the feminine form of *coquet,* a little cock, and signified a proud and strutting little creature, hence a woman who seeks admiration and attention. *Flirt* is an imitative word which originally meant to jerk lightly away, hence to tease, mock, gibe. *Jilt* is a diminutive of *Jill,* a girl's name, contracted from Latin *Juliana,* and frequently found in old rhymes and proverbs—"Every Jack must have his Jill," "Jack and Jill went up the hill," etc. Of these words the more recent term, *flirt,* has partly replaced the older words, *coquette* and *jilt. Flirt* is a more vulgar term than *coquette.* There is something of a fine lady in the *coquette.* The *flirt* uses the natural arts of an ordinary girl; the *coquette* is the product of a refined and sophisticated society. The *coquette* has more daintiness and apparently more reserve than the *flirt,* but she may be more heartless and less innocent. *Jilt* is a word which formerly was much more commonly employed than at present; now it survives mainly in the verb to *jilt,* to break one's engagement. The older distinction between *coquette* and *jilt* is expressed by Crabb as follows: *Coquetry* is contented with employing little arts to excite notice; *jilting* extends to the violation of truth and honor, in order to awaken a passion which it afterward disappoints. Vanity is the mainspring by which *coquettes* and *jilts* are impelled to action; but the former indulges her propensity mostly at her own expense only, while the latter does no less injury to the peace of others than she does to her own reputation. The *coquette* makes a traffic of her own charms by seeking a multitude of admirers; the *jilt* sports with the sacred passion of love, and barters it for the gratification of any selfish propensity. *Coquetry* is a fault which should be guarded against by every female as a snare to her own happiness; *jilting* is a vice which cannot be practised without some depravity of the heart.

CORDIAL. See HEARTY.

CORNER, ANGLE. *Corner* comes from Latin *cornu,* signifying a horn or projection. *Angle,* in Latin *angulus,* comes in all probability from ἄγκυλος, the elbow.

Corner properly implies the outer extreme point of any solid body; *angle,* on the contrary, the inner extremity produced by the meeting of two right lines or plane surfaces. When speaking, therefore, of solid bodies, *corner* and *angle* may be both employed; but in regard to simple right lines, or plane surfaces, the word *angle* only is applicable; in the former case a *corner* is produced by the meeting of the different parts of a body, whether inwardly or outwardly; but an *angle* is produced by the meeting of two bodies; inwardly one house has many *corners;* two houses, or two walls at least, are requisite to make an *angle.*

CORPORAL, CORPOREAL, BODILY. *Corporal, corporeal,* and *bodily,* as their origin bespeaks, have all relation to the same object, the *body;* but the two former are employed to signify relating or appertaining to the *body,* the latter to denote containing or forming part of the *body.* Hence we say *corporal* punishment, *bodily* vigor or strength, *corporeal* substances; the Godhead *bodily,* the *corporeal* frame, *bodily* exertion. *Corporal* is only employed for the animal frame in its proper sense; *corporeal* is used for animal substance in an extended sense; hence we speak of *corporal* sufferance and *corporeal* agents. *Corporeal* is distinguished from spiritual; *bodily* from mental. It is impossible to represent spiritual beings any other way than under a *corporeal* form; *bodily* pains, however severe, are frequently overpowered by mental pleasures.

Corporeal, Material. — Corporeal is properly a species of *material;* whatever is *corporeal* is *material,* but not *vice versâ. Corporeal* respects animated bodies; *material* is used for everything which can act on the senses, animate or inanimate. The world contains *corporeal* beings, and consists of *material* substances.

See also TANGIBLE.

Corpulent, Stout, Lusty.—Corpulent, from *corpus,* the body, signifies having fulness of body. *Stout,* Anglo-Saxon *stolt,* is allied to German *stolz,* proud, and possibly to Latin *stultus,* foolhardy; it signifies strength and self-assertion resulting from a large physical frame; hence, in some cases, the large physique itself. *Lusty,* in German, etc., *lustig,* merry, cheerful, implies here a vigorous state of body.

Corpulent respects the fleshy state of the body; *stout* respects also the state of the muscles and bones: *corpulence* is therefore an incidental property; *stoutness* is a natural property: *corpulence* may come upon us according to circumstances; *stoutness* is the natural make of the body which is born with us. *Corpulence* and *lustiness* are both occasioned by the state of the health; but the former may arise from disease, the latter is always the consequence of good health: *corpulence* consists of an undue proportion of fat; *lustiness* consists of a due and full proportion of all the solids in the body.

CORRECT, RECTIFY, REFORM. *Correct* (see AMEND) is more definite in its meaning, and more general in its application, than *rectify,* which, from

rectus and *facio,* signifies simply to make right or as it should be.

To *correct* is an act of necessity or discretion; to *rectify,* an act of discretion only. What is *corrected* is substantially faulty; what is *rectified* may be faulty by accident or from inadvertence. Faults in the execution are *corrected;* mistakes are *rectified.*

To *reform,* from *re,* again, and *formare,* to form, signifies to form again, or put into a new form; it expresses, therefore, more than *correct,* which removes that which is faulty in a thing without altering the thing itself. *Correction* may produce only a partial change, but what is *reformed* assumes a new form and becomes a new thing.

They are employed also in respect to public matters with a like distinction: abuses are *corrected,* the state is *reformed.*

Correct, Accurate.—Correct is equivalent to *corrected,* or set to rights. *Accurate,* from Latin *ad,* to, and *cura,* care, signifies done with care, or by the application of care. *Correct* applies to that which is done according to rules which either a man prescribes to himself or are prescribed for him; *accurate,* to that which is done by application of the mind or attention to an object: the result in both cases will be nearly the same—namely, that the thing will be as it ought or is intended to be, but there is a shade of difference in the meaning and application. What is done by the exercise of the judgment is said to be *correct,* as a *correct* style, a *correct* writer, a *correct* way of thinking; what is done by the effort of the individual is more properly *accurate,* as *accurate* observations, an *accurate* survey, and the like.

When applied to the same objects, *correct* is negative, it is opposed to *incorrect* or faulty; *accurate* is positive, it is opposed to *inaccurate* or loose: it is sufficient to be free from fault to be *correct;* it must contain every minute particular to be *accurate:* information is *correct* which contains nothing but facts; it is *accurate* when it contains all the details of dates, persons, and circumstances given *accurately.*

Correction, Discipline, Punishment.— As *correction* and *discipline* have commonly required *punishment* to render them efficacious, custom has affixed to them a strong resemblance in their application, although they are distinguished from each other by obvious marks of difference. The prominent idea in *correction* is that of making right what has been wrong. In *discipline*, from the Latin *disciplina* and *discere*, to learn, the leading idea is that of instructing or regulating. In *punishment*, from the Latin *punio*, and the Greek ποινή, penalty, the leading idea is that of inflicting pain as a penalty for wrong-doing.

We remove an evil by *correction;* we prevent it by *discipline. Correction* extends no further than to the *correcting* of particular faults; but *discipline* serves to train, guide, and instruct generally.

When *correction* and *discipline* are taken in the sense of *punishment*, they mean *punishment* for the purpose of *correction* and *discipline: punishment,* on the other hand, means the infliction of pain as the consequence of any particular conduct. *Correction* and *discipline* are personal acts, and mostly acts of authority. A parent inflicts *correction,* a master exercises *discipline: punishment* may either be inflicted by persons or result from things: the want of proper *discipline* may be *punished* by insubordination.

CORRECTNESS. See JUSTNESS.

CORRESPOND. See TALLY.

CORRESPONDENT, ANSWERABLE, SUITABLE. *Correspondent,* from Latin *cum*, together, and *respondere,* to answer, signifies to answer in unison or in uniformity. *Answerable* and *suitable,* from *answer* and *suit,* mark the quality or capacity of *answering* or *suiting. Correspondent* supposes a greater agreement than *answerable,* and *answerable* requires a greater agreement than *suitable.* Things that *correspond* must be alike in size, shape, color, and in every minute particular; those that *answer* must be fitted for the same purpose; those that *suit* must have nothing disproportionate or discordant. In the artificial dispositions of furniture, or all matters of art and ornament, it is of considerable importance to have some things made to *correspond,* so that they be placed in *suitable* directions to *answer* to each other.

In the moral application, actions are said not to *correspond* with professions; the success of an undertaking does not *answer* the expectations; particular measures do not *suit* the purpose of individuals. It ill *corresponds* with a profession of friendship to refuse assistance to a friend in the time of need; wild schemes undertaken without thought will never *answer* the expectations of the projectors; it never *suits* the purpose of the selfish and greedy to contribute to the relief of the necessitous.

CORROBORATE. See CONFIRM; RATIFY.

CORRUPT. See ATTAINT; CONTAMINATE; DEBAUCH; ROT.

CORRUPTION. See DEPRAVITY.

COSMOS, EARTH, UNIVERSE, WORLD. These words all indicate the world in which we live, but they differ considerably in their application and connotations. *Cosmos,* from Greek κόσμος, order, ornament, was so called by Pythagoras or his disciples from its "perfect order and arrangement." *Cosmos* corresponds very nearly to *universe* (from Latin *unus,* and *vertere,* meaning turned into one, combined into a whole), with the additional suggestion of harmonious system. *Universe* refers to the whole infinite extent of life and form; *cosmos* to the whole orderly scheme of things as they are. *World* and *earth* are Anglo-Saxon terms. *World,* from *wer,* man, and *eld,* age, meant originally a lifetime, a course of life, and age; and referred to the whole of the present creation, which was thought of as having been brought into existence at a particular time, and doomed to extinction at some future time. It is a more extensive word than earth, but less extensive than *universe* or *cosmos. Earth,* Anglo-Saxon *eorth,* signifies the ground under our feet—as distinguished from the heavens above—and now refers to the particular globe on which we live.

COST, EXPENSE, PRICE, CHARGE. *Cost* is derived through Old French *coster,* from Latin *con,* together, and *stare,* to stand, and signified, literally, to support, and, in an extended sense, what is given for support. *Expense* is compounded of *ex* and Latin *pensus,* participle of *pendere,* to weigh, signifying the thing paid or given out. *Price*, from the Latin *pretium*, price, signifies the thing given for what is bought. *Charge*, from Latin *carricare*, to load a car, signifies the thing laid on as a burden in return for something received.

The *cost* is what a thing *costs*, or what is to be laid out for it; the *expense* is that which a person actually lays out; the *price* is that which a thing may fetch or which it may be worth; the *charge* is that which a person or thing is *charged* with. As a *cost* commonly comprehends an *expense*, the terms are on various occasions used indifferently for each other: we speak of counting the *cost* or counting the *expense* of doing anything; at a great *cost* or at a great *expense:* on the other hand, of doing a thing to one's *cost*, of growing wise at other people's *expense*. The *cost* and the *price* have respect to the thing and its supposed value; the *expense* and the *charge* depend on the option of the persons. The *cost* of a thing must precede the *price*, and the *expense* must succeed the *charge:* we can never set a *price* on anything until we have ascertained what it has *cost* us; nor can we know or defray the *expense* until the *charge* be made. There may, however, frequently be a *price* where there is no *cost*, and *vice versâ:* there may also be an *expense* where there is no *charge;* but there cannot be a *charge* without an *expense:* what *costs* nothing sometimes fetches a high *price*, and other things cannot obtain a *price* equal to the first *cost*. *Expenses* vary with modes of living and men's desires; whoever wants much, or wants that which is not easily obtained, will have many *expenses* to defray; when the *charges* are exorbitant, the *expenses* must necessarily bear a proportion.

Between the epithets *costly* and *expensive* there is the same distinction. Whatever is *costly* is naturally *expensive*, but not *vice versâ*. Articles of furniture, of luxury, or indulgence are *costly*, either from their variety or their intrinsic value; everything is *expensive* which is attended with much *expense*, whether of little or great value. Jewels are *costly;* travelling is *expensive*. The *costly* treasures of the East are imported into Europe for the gratification of those who cannot be contented with the produce of their native soil: those who indulge themselves in such *expensive* pleasures often lay up in store for themselves much sorrow and repentance in the time to come.

In the moral acceptation, the attainment of an object is said to *cost* much pains; a thing is persisted in at the *expense* of health, of honor, or of life. The sacrifice of a man's quiet is the *price* which he must pay for the gratification of his ambition.

COSTLY. See VALUABLE.

COUNCIL. See ASSEMBLE.

COUNSEL. See ADVICE.

COUNT. See CALCULATE; RECKON.

COUNTENANCE, SANCTION, SUPPORT. *Countenance* comes from Latin *con*, together, and *tenere*, to hold together, to control, referring to the personal demeanor, hence to the face. To *countenance* means to keep in *countenance*. *Sanction*, in French *sanction*, Latin *sanctio*, from *sanctus*, sacred, signifies to ratify a decree or ordinance; in an extended sense, to make anything binding. *Support*, in French *supporter*, Latin *supporto*, compounded of *sub* and *porto*, to bear, signifies to bear from underneath, to bear up.

Persons are *countenanced;* things are *sanctioned;* persons or things are *supported:* persons are *countenanced* in their proceedings by the apparent approbation of others; measures are *sanctioned* by the consent or approbation of others who have due authority; measures or persons are *supported* by every means which may forward the object. There is most of encouragement in *countenancing;* it consists of some outward demonstration of regard or good-will toward the person: there is most of authority in *sanctioning;* it is the lending of a name, an authority, or an influence, in order to strengthen and confirm the thing: there is most of assistance and co-operation in *support;* it is the employment of means to an end. Superiors only can *countenance* or *sanction;* persons in all conditions may *support:* those who *countenance* evil-doers give a *sanction* to their evil deeds; those who *support* either an individual or a cause ought to be satisfied that they are entitled to *support*.

See also FACE.

COUNTERFEIT. See IMITATE; SPURIOUS.

COUNTERPOISE, BALANCE, POISE, WEIGH. These terms all indicate methods of *weighing*. *Counterpoise* is derived from Latin *contra*, against, and *pensare*, to weigh, and signifies to *weigh* one thing against another. *Poise* is derived from *pensare*, also; it signifies to weigh, and refers especially to the adjusting of one part of a balance to the other. *Balance* comes through Italian from *bilanx*, Latin, from *bis*, double, and *lanx*, a dish or platter, and refers to a pair of scales with two plates suspended from a cross-bar. *Weigh*, Anglo-Saxon *wegan*, to carry or bear, meant at first to move in any direction; then to lift up, then to lift up two things, *balancing* one against the other. Hence these words have practically the same meaning, but differ in the vividness with which they suggest the actual performance of weighing—*balance* and *counterpoise* being more suggestive in this respect than *poise* and *weigh*. The substantives corresponding to these words have figurative meanings which differ somewhat more vividly. *Poise* and *balance* are both applied to a kind of self-control, which enables its possessor to remain quiet and reasonable, and uninfluenced either by outward events or violent emotion. *Poise*, in this sense, is a general attribute; *balance* is applied to specific cases in which *poise* has been displayed. We say that a lady has *poise*, meaning that she is almost uniformly unruffled and self-controlled—that she resembles a pair of scales in which the weight on one side exactly corresponds to the weight on the other. We say that a man kept his *balance*, when we mean that in a particular instance he did not let himself be absolutely controlled by only one feeling or one consideration. *Weight* has a figurative meaning of another sort; it corresponds to heaviness, and signifies that which *weighs* heavily. A man of *weight* is a man who can bring much force or influence to bear upon a situation.

COUNTRY. See LAND.

COUNTRYMAN, PEASANT, SWAIN, HIND, RUSTIC, CLOWN. *Countryman*, that is, a man of the country, or one belonging to the *country*, is the general term applicable to all inhabiting the *country*, in distinction from a townsman. *Peasant*, from Old French *pais* (French *pays*), the country, signified originally the inhabitant of a *pagus* (Latin) village—*pagus* being the word whence *pagan* is also derived. *Peasant* is employed in the same sense for any *countryman* among the inhabitants of the Continent, and is in consequence used in poetry or the grave style for a *countryman*. *Swain*, in Anglo-Saxon *swan*, signified literally a *swineherd*, but it has acquired, from its use in poetry, the higher signification of a shepherd, or husbandman. *Hind* is derived from Anglo-Saxon *hina*, a domestic, and *hiwen*, a family; compare the relation of Latin *famulus*, servant, to the word *family*. It signified a servant in the household. *Rustic*, from *rus*, the country, signifies one born and bred in the country. *Clown* is a Scandinavian word meaning a clumsy, boorish fellow, allied to *clump*.

All these terms are employed as epithets to persons, and principally to such as live in the *country:* the terms *countryman* and *peasant* are taken in an indifferent sense, and may comprehend persons of different descriptions; they designate nothing more than habitual residence in the *country:* the other terms are employed for the lower orders of *countrymen*, but with collateral ideas favorable or unfavorable annexed to them: *swain, hind,* both convey the idea of innocence in a humble station, and are therefore always employed in poetry in a good sense: the *rustic* and *clown* both convey the idea of that uncouth rudeness and ignorance which is in reality found among the lowest orders of *countrymen*.

COUPLE, PAIR, BRACE. *Couple* comes from Latin *con*, together, and Old Latin *apere*, to join, preserved in *aptus*, English *apt*. It signifies things joined together; and as two things are with most convenience bound together, it has by custom been confined to this number. *Pair*, in French *paire*, Latin *par*, equal, signifies things that are equal, which can with propriety be said only of two things with regard to each other. *Brace*, from the French *bras*, arm, signifies things locked together after the manner of the folded arms, which on that account are confined to the number of two.

From the above illustration of these terms, it is clear that the number of two, which is included in all of them, is, with regard to the first, entirely arbitrary; that with regard to the second it arises from the nature of the junction; and with regard to the third it arises altogether from the nature of the objects; *couples* and *braces* are made by *coupling* and *bracing;* *pairs* are either so of themselves or are made so by others: *couples* and *braces* always require a junction in order to make them complete; *pairs* require similarity only to make them what they are: *couples* are joined by a foreign tie; even the being in company is sufficient to make a *couple;* *braces* are produced by a close junction, or what is supposed to be so, which requires them to go together. *Couple* is applied to objects generally.

Pair is applied to things that naturally go in *pairs*.

Brace is applied to particular things, either themselves joined together or serving to join others together; as birds that are shot and are usually linked together are termed a *brace;* whence in poetry the term is applied to animals or other objects in a close state of junction.

Couple is applied to persons of different sex who are bound to each other by the ties of affection or by the marriage tie.

Pair is also applied to persons similarly situated, but refers more to the moral tie from similarity of feeling: whence the newly married *couple* is in ordinary discourse called the happy *pair*.

Pair is applied to persons in no other connection, and *brace* never except in the burlesque style.

COURAGE, FORTITUDE, RESOLUTION. *Courage* (see BRAVERY). *Fortitude,* in French *fortitude,* Latin *fortitudo,* is the abstract noun from *fortis,* strong. *Resolution,* from Latin *re,* again, and *solvere,* to loose, signifies to divide something into its component parts; hence to decide; and marks the act of *resolving,* or the state of being *resolved.*

Courage respects action, *fortitude* respects passion: a man has *courage* to meet danger, and *fortitude* to endure pain. *Courage* is that power of the mind which bears up against the evil that is in prospect; *fortitude* is that power which endures the pain that is felt: the man of *courage* goes with the same coolness to the mouth of the cannon as the man of *fortitude* undergoes the amputation of a limb. Horatius Cocles displayed his *courage* in defending a bridge against the whole army of the Etruscans: Caius Mutius displayed no less *fortitude* when he thrust his hand into the fire in the presence of King Porsena, and awed him as much by his language as his action.

Courage seems to be more of a manly virtue; *fortitude* is more distinguishable as a feminine virtue: the former is at least most adapted to the male sex who are called upon to act, and the latter to the females, who are obliged to endure: a man without *courage* would be as ill prepared to discharge his duty in his intercourse with the world as a woman without *fortitude* would be to support herself under the complicated trials of body and mind with which she is liable to be assailed.

Resolution is a minor species of *courage,* or it is *courage* in the minor concerns of life: *courage* comprehends under it a spirit to advance; *resolution* simply marks the will not to recede: we require *courage* to bear down all the obstacles which oppose themselves to us; we require *resolution* not to yield to the first difficulties that offer.

COURSE, RACE, PASSAGE. *Course,* from *currere,* to run, signifies either the act of running or the space run over. *Race* comes from Scandinavian *ras,* a running, and signifies the same act. *Passage,* Latin *passus,* a step, signifies either the act of stepping, or the space passed over.

Course and *race* as acts imply the act of walking or running; *passage,* the act of passing or going generally: as swift in the *course,* to win the *race,* to be lost in the *passage.* The *course* in this case may be the act of one alone; the *race* is always the act of one in competition with others.

In the sense of the space gone over,

course is to be compared with *passage* in the proper application, and with *race* in the improper. The *course* is the direction taken or chosen by any object, and applies to persons or things personified; as a person pursues a *course*.

Passage is the way either through or over an object, and applies only to inanimate objects.

Course, in the moral application, signifies the direction taken in the business of life; as to pursue a right or wrong *course*.

The *race* is that course of life which a person is supposed to run with others toward a certain object. It is used mostly in the spiritual sense.

See also ROUTE; SERIES; WAY.

COURT. See HOMAGE; TRIBUNAL.

COURTEOUS, COMPLAISANT, COURTLY. *Courteous*, from *court*, denotes properly belonging to a *court*, and, by a natural extension of the sense, suitable to a *court*. *Complaisant* (see COMPLAISANCE).

Courteous in one respect comprehends in it more than *complaisant;* it includes the manner as well as the action; it is, properly speaking, polished *complaisance:* on the other hand, *complaisance* includes more of the disposition in it than *courteousness;* it has less of the polish, but more of the reality of kindness. *Courteousness* displays itself in the address and manners; *complaisance*, in direct good offices: *courteousness* is practised between strangers; *complaisance*, among friends.

See also AFFABLE; WELL-BRED.

Courtly, though derived from the same word as *courteous*, is in some degree opposed to it in point of sense; it denotes a likeness to a *court*, but not a likeness which is favorable: *courtly* is to *courteous* as the form to the reality; the *courtly* consists of the exterior only, the latter of the exterior combined with the spirit; the former, therefore, seems to convey the idea of insincerity when contrasted with the latter, which must necessarily suppose the contrary: a *courtly* demeanor, or a *courtier*-like demeanor, may be suitable on certain occasions; but a *courteous* demeanor is always desirable.

Courtly may likewise be employed in relation to things, as belonging to a *court;* but *courteous* has always respect to persons: we may speak of a *courtly* style, or *courtly* grandeur; but we always speak of *courteous* behavior, *courteous* language, and the like.

COVENANT. See AGREEMENT.

COVER, HIDE. *Cover*, in French *couvrir*, Italian *coprire*, Latin *cooperio*, is compounded of *con*, intensive, and *operio*, to conceal, and signifies to conceal thoroughly. *Hide* (see CONCEAL).

Cover is to *hide* as the means to the end: we commonly *hide* by *covering;* but we may easily *cover* without *hiding*, as also *hide* without *covering*. The ruling idea in the word *cover* is that of throwing or putting something over a body: in the word *hide* is that of keeping carefully to one's self, from the observation of others. In most civilized countries it is common to *cover* the head: in the Eastern countries females commonly wear veils to *hide* the face.

Cover sometimes, particularly in the moral application, signifies to conceal; but in that case it denotes the manner of concealing, namely, by overspreading; but *hide* denotes either the intention or desire to conceal or the concealing what ought not to be seen.

Cover, Shelter, Screen.—*Cover* properly denotes what serves as a *cover*, in the literal sense of the verb from which it is derived (see above). *Shelter* comes from Anglo-Saxon *scild-truma*, literally *shield-troop*, a band of men with shields set to guard a place; hence any protection. *Screen* is derived through French from Teutonic *schranne*, a railing or a grate.

Cover is literally applied to many particular things which are employed in *covering;* but in the general sense which makes it analogous to the other terms it includes the idea of concealing: *shelter* comprehends that of protecting from some immediate or impending evil: *screen* includes that of warding off some trouble. A *cover* always supposes something which can extend over the whole surface of a body; a *shelter* or a *screen* may merely interpose to a sufficient extent to serve the intended purpose. Military operations are sometimes carried on under *cover* of the night; a bay is a convenient *shelter* for vessels against the violence of the winds; a chair may be used as a *screen* to prevent the violent action of the heat or the external air.

In the moral sense, a fair reputation is sometimes made the *cover* for the commission of gross irregularities in secret. When a person feels himself unable to withstand the attacks of his enemies, he seeks a *shelter* under the sanction and authority of a great name. Bad men sometimes use wealth and power to *screen* them from the punishment which is due to their offences.

COVERING. See TEGUMENT.

COVET. See DESIRE.

COVETOUSNESS, CUPIDITY, AVARICE. *Covetousness*, from *covet*, and Latin *cupere*, to desire, signifies having a desire. *Cupidity* is a more immediate derivative from the Latin, signifying the same thing. *Avarice* (see AVARICIOUS).

All these terms are employed to express an illicit desire after objects of gratification; but *covetousness* is applied to property in general, or to whatever is valuable; *cupidity* and *avarice*, only to money or possessions. A child may display its *covetousness* in regard to the playthings which fall in its way; a man shows his *cupidity* in regard to the gains that fall in his way; we should, therefore, be careful to check a *covetous* disposition in early life, lest it show itself in the more hateful character of *cupidity* in advanced years. *Covetousness* is the natural disposition for having or getting; *cupidity* is the acquired disposition. As the love of appropriation is an innate characteristic in man, that of accumulating or wanting to accumulate, which constitutes *covetousness*, will show itself, in some persons, among the first indications of character: where the prospect of amassing great wealth is set before a man, as in the case of a governor of a distant province, it will evince great virtue in him if his *cupidity* be not excited. The *covetous* man seeks to add to what he has; the *avaricious* man only strives to retain what he has: the *covetous* man sacrifices others to indulge himself; the *avaricious* man will sometimes sacrifice himself to indulge others; for generosity, which is opposed to *covetousness*, is sometimes associated with *avarice*.

COWARD. See RECREANT.

COWER. See QUAIL.

CRACK. See BREAK.

CRAFTY. See CUNNING.

CRAVE. See BEG; YEARN.

CREATE. See CAUSE; MAKE.

CREDIT, FAVOR, INFLUENCE. *Credit*, from the Latin *creditus*, participle of *credere*, to believe or trust, marks the state of being believed or trusted. *Favor*, from the Latin *favere*, to befriend or please, marks an agreeable or pleasant state of feeling toward an object. *Influence*, in French *influence*, Latin *influentia*, from *in*, in, and *fluere*, to flow, marks the state or power of acting upon any object so as to direct or move it.

These terms mark the state we stand in with regard to others as flowing out of their sentiments toward ourselves: *credit* arises out of esteem: *favor*, out of good-will or affection; *influence*, out of either *credit* or *favor*, or external circumstances: *credit* depends altogether on personal merit, real or supposed; *favor* may depend on the caprice of him who bestows it. The *credit* which we have with others is marked by their confidence in our judgment; by their disposition to submit to our decisions; by their reliance on our veracity or assent to our opinions: the *favor* we have with others is marked by their readiness to comply with our wishes, their subserviency to our views, attachment to our society: men of *talent* are ambitious to gain *credit* with their sovereigns by the superiority of their counsel: weak men or men of ordinary powers are contented with being the *favorites* of princes and enjoying their patronage and protection. *Credit* redounds to the honor of the individual, and stimulates him to noble exertions; it is beneficial in its results to all mankind, individually or collectively: *favor* redounds to the personal advantage, the selfish gratification of the individual; it is apt to inflame pride and provoke jealousy.

Credit and *favor* are the gifts of others; *influence* is a possession which we derive from circumstances: there will always be *influence* where there is *credit* or *favor*, but it may exist independently of either: we have *credit* and *favor* for ourselves; we exert *influence* over others: *credit* and *favor* serve one's own purposes; *influence* is employed in directing others: weak people easily give their *credit*, or bestow their *favor*, by which an *influence* is gained over them to bend them to the will of others; the *influence* itself may be good or bad, according to the views of the person by whom it is exerted. See also BELIEF; NAME.

CREED. See FAITH.

CREMATION, INCINERATION. *Cremation*, in Latin *crematio* through *crematus* from *cremare*, to burn, and *incineration*, in Low Latin *incineratio* from *incinerare*, to reduce to ashes, both refer to the method of disposing of the dead by burning, instead of earth burial. *Cremation* is the more common term in the United States.

CREW. See BAND.

CRIME, VICE, SIN. *Crime*, in Latin *crimen*, Greek κρίνειν, to judge, signifies a sentence, or punishment; and also the cause of the sentence or punishment, in which latter sense it is here taken. *Vice*, in Latin *vitium*, a blemish, signifies that which destroys the perfection of something. *Sin*, Anglo-Saxon *synn*, is allied to one form of the verb *to be* (Latin *sum, sunt,* etc.). "Language regards the guilty man as *the man who it was*" (CURTIUS).

A *crime* is a social offence; a *vice* is a personal offence: every action which does injury to others, either individually or collectively, is a *crime;* that which does injury to ourselves is a *vice*. *Crime* consists in a violation of human laws; *vice*, in a violation of the moral law: *sin*, in a violation of the divine law: *sin*, therefore, comprehends both *crime* and *vice;* but there are many *sins* which are not *crimes* nor *vices: crimes* are tried before a human court, and punished agreeably to the sentence of the judge; *vices* and *sins* are brought before the tribunal of the conscience; the former are punished in this world, the latter will be punished in the world to come, by the sentence of the Almighty: treason is one of the most atrocious *crimes;* drunkenness one of the most dreadful *vices;* religious hypocrisy one of the most heinous *sins.*

Crime, Misdemeanor. — *Crime* (see above). *Misdemeanor* signifies literally a wrong demeanor.

The former of these terms is to the latter as the genus to the species: a *misdemeanor* is in the technical sense a minor *crime*. Housebreaking is under all circumstances a *crime;* but shoplifting or pilfering amounts only to a *misdemeanor.* Corporal punishments are most commonly annexed to *crimes;* pecuniary punishments frequently to *misdemeanors.* In the vulgar use of these terms, *misdemeanor* is moreover distinguished from *crime* by not always signifying a violation of public law, but only of private morals; in which sense the former term implies what is done against the state, and the latter that which offends individuals or small communities.

Criminal, Guilty.—*Criminal*, from *crime*, signifies belonging or relating to a *crime*. *Guilty*, from *guilt* (in Anglo-Saxon *gylt*, a trespass and a fine for trespass, possibly allied to *geldan*, to pay, whence our word *yield* is derived), signifies having *guilt.*

Criminal respects the character of the offence; *guilty* respects the fact of committing the offence. The *criminality* of a person is estimated by all the circumstances of his conduct which present themselves to observation; his *guilt* requires to be proved by evidence. The *criminality* is not a matter of inquiry, but of judgment; the *guilt* is often doubtful, if not positively concealed. The higher the rank of a person the greater his *criminality* if he does not observe an upright and irreproachable conduct: where a number of individuals are concerned in any unlawful proceeding, the difficulty of attaching the *guilt* to the real offender is greatly increased.

Criminal may be applied as an epithet either to the person or that which is personal: *guilty* is properly applied only to the person: a person, or his actions, looks, thought, intentions, may be *criminal:* the person himself is *guilty* of whatever he actually commits. What is *criminal* is against good morals; but a person may be *guilty* of trivial errors in indifferent matters.

Criminal, Culprit, Malefactor, Felon, Convict.—All these terms are employed for a public offender; but the first conveys no more than this general idea; while the others comprehend some accessory idea in their signification. *Criminal* is a general term, and the rest are properly species of *criminals*. *Culprit* comes from Anglo-French *cul* (for Latin *culpa*, fault) and *prest*, ready to prove it, signifying that the clerk of the crown was ready to prove the indictment. *Malefactor*, compounded of the Latin terms *male* and *factor*, signifies an evil-doer—that is, one who does evil, in distinction from him who does good. *Felon* is derived from Late Latin *felonem* (accusative), a traitor, allied to *fell*, meaning cruel, dire. *Convict*, in Latin *convictus*, participle of *convinco*, to convince or prove, signifies one proved or found guilty.

When we wish to speak in general of those who by offences against the laws or regulations of society have exposed themselves to punishment, we denominate them *criminals:* when we consider them as already brought before a tribunal, we call them *culprits:* when we consider them in regard to the moral turpitude of their character, as the promoters of evil rather than of good, we entitle them *malefactors:* when we consider them as offending by the grosser violations of the law, they are termed *felons:* when we consider them as already under the sentence of the law, we denominate them *convicts*. The punishments inflicted on *criminals* vary according to the nature of their crimes and the spirit of the laws by which they are judged: a guilty conscience will give a man the air of a *culprit* in the presence of those who have no authority to be either his accusers or judges; it gratified the malice of the Jews to cause our blessed Saviour to be crucified between two *malefactors:* it is an important regulation in the internal economy of a prison to have *felons* kept distinct from one another, particularly if their crimes are of an atrocious nature: it has not unfrequently happened that, when the sentence of the law has placed *convicts* in the lowest state of degradation, their characters have undergone so entire a reformation as to enable them to attain a higher pitch of elevation than they had ever enjoyed before.

CRINGE. See KNUCKLE.

CRISIS. See CONJUNCTURE.

CRITERION, STANDARD. *Criterion*, in Greek κριτήριον, from κρίνειν, to judge, signifies the mark or rule by which one may judge. *Standard* signified originally an ensign, a flag fixed on a large standing-pole, and is derived from *extendere*, to extend, though influenced by the verb *stand*. The pole bearing the flag came to indicate a standard of measurement, symbolizing the ideals of the people whom it represented, and the action expected of them.

The *criterion* is employed only in matters of judgment; the *standard* is used in the ordinary concerns of life. The former serves for determining the characters and qualities of things; the latter for defining quantity and measure. The language and manners of a person are the best *criterion* for forming an estimate of his station and education. In order to produce a uniformity in the mercantile transactions of mankind one with another, it is the custom of governments to fix a certain *standard* for the regulation of coins, weights, and measures.

The word *standard* may likewise be used figuratively in the same sense. The Bible is a *standard* of excellence, both in morals and religion, which cannot be too closely followed. It is impossible to have the same *standard* in the arts and sciences, because all our performances fall short of perfection and will admit of improvement.

See also SHIBBOLETH; TEST.

CRITICAL, CRUCIAL, IMPORTANT, VITAL. These words all suggest a state of uncertainty, or something necessary to decide the welfare or success of a person or a project. *Critical*, from the Greek κρίνειν, to judge, and *crucial*, from Latin *crux*, a cross, referring to the cross placed at the fork in a road to point the way, have a similar meaning. A *critical* moment is a moment in which the decision hangs in the balance. A *crucial* instance is the instance on which the decision depends. The use of *crucial* is partly influenced by its relation to *crux*, which also suggests an instrument of torture—so that the word has a certain intensity of meaning that *critical* does not have. It has also a more limited and specific application. *Important*, from *in*, in, and *portare*, to bring, is a more general word. It signifies, literally, "bringing in" much, having weighty results; it does not suggest the making of a decision. *Vital* (from *vita*, life) means essential to the life of something.

See also CENSOR; CLIMACTERIC.

CRITICISE. See CENSURE.

CRITICISM. See ANIMADVERSION.

CROOKED. See AWKWARD; BENT; WRY.

CROSS. See AWKWARD; CAPTIOUS; QUERULOUS.

CROTCHET. See VAGARY.

CROWD. See MULTITUDE.

CRUCIAL. See CRITICAL.

CRUEL, INHUMAN, BARBAROUS, BRUTAL, SAVAGE. *Cruel*, from the Latin *crudelis* and *crudus*, raw, rough, or untutored; *inhuman*, compounded of the privative *in* and *human*, signifying not human; *barbarous*, from the Greek βάρβαρος, foreigner, in imitation of the sound of a strange language—"bar, bar"—all these mark a degree of bad feeling which is uncontrolled by culture or refinement. *Brutal*, signifying like the *brute* (see ANIMAL), and *savage*, from Old French *salvage*, from Latin *silva*, woods, signifying a dweller in the woods—these mark a still stronger degree of this bad passion.

Cruel is the most familiar and the least powerful epithet of all these terms; it designates the ordinary propensity which, if not overpowered by a better principle, will invariably show itself by the desire of inflicting positive pain on others, or abridging their comfort: *inhuman* and *barbarous* are higher degrees of *cruelty; brutal* and *savage* rise so much in degree above the rest as almost to partake of another nature. A child gives early symptoms of his natural *cruelty* by his ill-treatment of animals; but we do not speak of his *inhumanity*, because this is a term confined to men, and more properly to their treatment of their own species, although extended in its sense to their treatment of the *brutes: barbarity* is but too common among children and persons of riper years. A person is *cruel* who neglects the creature he should protect and take care of: he is *inhuman* if he withhold from him the common

marks of tenderness or kindness which are to be expected from one *human* being to another; he is *barbarous* if he find amusement in inflicting pain; he is *brutal* or *savage* according to the circumstances of aggravation which accompany the act of torturing.

See also HARD-HEARTED; HEARTLESS.

CRUSH. See BREAK; OVERWHELM; QUELL.

CRUTCH. See STAFF.

CRY, WEEP. An outward indication of pain is expressed by both these terms, but *cry* (see CALL) comprehends an audible expression accompanied with tears or otherwise. *Weep*, Anglo-Saxon *wepan*, signified originally to make an outcry; it now refers to the silent shedding of tears. *Crying* arises from an impatience in suffering corporeal pains; children and weak people commonly *cry*: *weeping* is occasioned by mental grief; the wisest and best of men will not disdain sometimes to *weep*. *Crying* is as selfish as it is weak; it serves to relieve the pain of the individual to the annoyance of the hearer; *weeping*, when called forth by others' sorrows, is an infirmity which no man could wish to be without: as an expression of generous sympathy, it affords essential relief to the sufferer.

Cry, Scream, Shriek.—To *cry* indicates the utterance of an articulate or an inarticulate sound. *Scream* is a Scandinavian word meaning to *cry* aloud. *Shriek* is an imitative word, like *screech*, which tries to represent by its sound a certain kind of *cry*. *Crying* is an ordinary mode of loud utterance resorted to on common occasions; one *cries* in order to be heard: *screaming* is an intemperate mode of *crying*, resorted to from an impatient desire to be heard or from a vehemence of feeling. People *scream* to deaf people from the mistaken idea of making themselves heard; whereas a distinct articulation will always be more efficacious. It is frequently necessary to *cry* when we cannot render ourselves audible by any other means; but it is never necessary nor proper to *scream*. *Shriek* may be compared with *cry* and *scream* as expressions of pain; in this case to *shriek* is more than to *cry*, and less than to *scream*. They both signify to *cry* with a violent effort. We may *cry* from the slightest pain or inconvenience; but one *shrieks* or *screams* only on occasions of great agony, either corporeal or mental. A child *cries* when it has hurt its finger; it *shrieks* in the moment of terror at the sight of a frightful object, or *screams* until some one comes to its assistance. See also WAIL.

CUFF. See KNOCK.

CULPABLE, FAULTY. *Culpable*, in Latin *culpabilis*, comes from *culpa*, a fault or blame, signifying worthy of blame, fit to be blamed. *Faulty*, from *fault*, is ultimately derived from Latin *fallere*, to deceive.

We are *culpable* from the commission of one fault; we are *faulty* from the number of *faults: culpable* is a relative term; *faulty* is absolute: we are *culpable* with regard to a superior whose intentions we have not fulfilled; we are *faulty* whenever we commit any *faults*. A master pronounces his servant as *culpable* for not having attended to his commands; an indifferent person pronounces another as *faulty* whose *faults* have come under his notice. It is possible, therefore, to be *faulty* without being *culpable*, but not *vice versâ*.

CULPRIT. See CRIMINAL.

CULTIVATED. See WELL-BRED.

CULTIVATION, CULTURE, CIVILIZATION, REFINEMENT. *Cultivation* is derived from Latin *cultus*, from *colere*, to till, and denotes the act of *cultivating*, or state of being *cultivated*. *Culture*, from *cultus*, signifies the state only of being *cultivated*. *Civilization* signifies the act of *civilizing*, or state of being *civilized*, from *civis*, a citizen, one who lives with others on comfortable terms in a city or state. *Refinement* denotes the act of *refining*, or the state of being *refined*.

Cultivation is with more propriety applied to the thing that grows; *culture* to that in which it grows. The *cultivation* of flowers will not repay the labor unless the soil be prepared by proper *culture*. In the same manner, when speaking figuratively, we say the *cultivation* of any art or science: the *cultivation* of one's taste or inclination may be said to contribute to one's own skill or the perfection of the thing itself; but the mind requires *culture* previously to this particular exertion of the powers.

Civilization is the first stage of *cultivation; refinement* is the last; we *civilize* savages by divesting them of their rudeness and giving them a knowledge of such arts as are requisite for *civil* society; we *cultivate* people in general by calling forth their powers into action and independent exertion; we *refine* them by the introduction of the liberal arts. The introduction of Christianity has been the best means of *civilizing* the rudest nations. The *cultivation* of the mind in serious pursuits tends to refine the sentiments without debilitating the character; but the *cultivation* of the liberal arts may be pursued to a vicious extent, so as to introduce an excessive *refinement* of feeling that is incompatible with real manliness.

Cultivation, Tillage, Husbandry.— *Cultivation* has a much more comprehensive meaning than either *tillage* or *husbandry*. *Tillage* comes from Anglo-Saxon *tilian*, to labor, from *til*, beneficial, and signifies to make land useful. It is a mode of *cultivation* that extends no further than the preparation of the ground for the reception of the seed; *cultivation* includes the whole process by which the produce of the earth is brought to maturity. We may *till* without *cultivating;* but we cannot *cultivate*, as far as respects the soil, without *tillage*. *Husbandry* (see HUSBAND) is more extensive in its meaning than *tillage*, but not so extensive as *cultivation*. *Tillage* respects the act only of *tilling* the ground; *husbandry* is employed for the office of *cultivating* for domestic purposes. A *cultivator* is a general term, defined only by the object that is *cultivated*, as the *cultivator* of the grape or the olive; a *tiller* is a laborer in the soil that performs the office for another: a *husbandman* is a humble species of *cultivator* who himself performs the whole office of *cultivating* the ground for domestic purposes.

CULTURE. See CULTIVATION.

CUNNING, CRAFTY, SUBTLE, SLY, WILY. *Cunning* (see ART). *Crafty* signifies having *craft*, from Anglo-Saxon *cræft*, German *kraft*, meaning power or energy, hence, specifically, power of mind; hence, in a still more specific sense, a particular kind of skill. (Compare the development of *keen*, from Anglo-Saxon *cene*, German *kuhn*, bold.) *Subtle*, in French *subtil*, and Latin *subtilis*, thin, from *sub* and *tela*, a thread drawn to be fine; hence in the figurative sense in which it is here taken, fine or acute in thought. *Sly* is a Scandinavian word originally meaning handy, dexterous, possibly allied to *slay*. *Wily*, full of wiles, may be derived from Anglo-Saxon *wiglian*, to practise sorcery.

All these epithets agree in expressing an aptitude to employ peculiar and secret means to the attainment of an end; they differ principally in the secrecy of the means or the degree of circumvention that is employed. The *cunning* man shows his dexterity simply in concealing; this requires little more than reservedness and taciturnity: the *crafty* man goes further; he shapes his words and actions so as to lull suspicion; hence it is that a child may be *cunning*, but an old man will be *crafty*: a *subtle* man has more acuteness of invention than either, and all his schemes are hidden by a veil that is impenetrable to common observation: the *cunning* man looks only to the concealment of an immediate object; the *crafty* and *subtle* man has a remote object to conceal: thus men are *cunning* in their ordinary concerns; politicians are *crafty* or *subtle:* the former are more so as to the end, and the latter as to the means. A man is *cunning* and *crafty* by deeds; he is *subtle* mostly by means of words alone, or words and actions combined. *Slyness* is a vulgar kind of *cunning;* the *sly* man goes cautiously and silently to work. *Wiliness* is a species of *cunning* or *craft*, applicable only to cases of attack or defence.

See also ART.

CUPIDITY. See COVETOUSNESS.

CURB. See CHECK.

CURE, HEAL, REMEDY. *Cure*, in Latin *curo*, signifies to take care of, that is, by distinction, to take care of that which requires particular care, in order to remove an evil. *Heal* signifies to make whole that which is unsound. *Remedy*, in Latin *remedium*, is compounded of *re* and *medere*, to heal. The particle *re* is here an intensive.

To *cure* is employed for what is out of order; to *heal*, for that which is broken: diseases are *cured*, wounds are *healed;* the former is a complex, the latter is a simple process. Whatever requires to be *cured* is wrong in the system; it requires many and various applications internally and externally: whatever requires to be *healed* is occasioned externally by violence, and requires external applications. In a state of refinement men have the greatest number of disorders to be *cured*; in a savage state there is more occasion for the *healing* art.

Cure is used as properly in the moral as the natural sense; *heal* in the moral sense is altogether figurative. The disorders of the mind are *cured* with greater difficulty than those of the body. The breaches which have been made in the affections of relatives toward each other can be *healed* by nothing but a Christian spirit of forbearance and forgiveness.

To *remedy*, in the sense of applying *remedies*, has a moral application, in which it accords most with *cure*. Evils are either *cured* or *remedied*, but the former are of a much more serious nature than the latter. The evils in society require to be *cured;* an omission, a deficiency, or a mischief requires to be *remedied*. When bad habits become inveterate, they are put out of the reach of *cure*. It is an exercise for the ingenuity of man to attempt to *remedy* the various troubles and inconveniences which are daily occurring.

Cure, Remedy.—Cure denotes either the act of *curing* or the thing that *cures*. *Remedy* is mostly employed for the thing that *remedies*. In the former sense the *remedy* is to the *cure* as the means to the end; a *cure* is performed by the application of a *remedy*. That is *incurable* for which no *remedy* can be found; but a *cure* is sometimes performed without the application of any specific *remedy*. The *cure* is complete when the evil is entirely removed; the *remedy* is sure which by proper application never fails of effecting the *cure*. The *cure* of disorders depends upon the skill of the physician and the state of the patient; the efficacy of *remedies* depends upon their suitable choice and application: but a *cure* may be defeated, or a *remedy* made of no avail, by a variety of circumstances independent of either.

A *cure* is sometimes employed for the thing that *cures*, which brings it nearer in sense to the word *remedy*, the former being applied to great matters, the latter to small. Quacks always hold forth their nostrums as infallible *cures*, not for one, but for every sort of disorder; experience has, however, fatally proved that the *remedy* in most cases is worse than the disease.

CURING. See SANITARY.

CURIOUS, INQUISITIVE, PRYING. *Curious*, in French *curieux*, Latin *curiosus*, from *cura*, care, signifying full of care. *Inquisitive*, in Latin *inquisitus*, from *inquirere*, to inquire or search into, signifies a disposition to investigate thoroughly. *Prying*, from *pry*, is derived from Old French *prier*, to pillage, from Late Latin *predare*, to prey upon, hence to search out prey, or simply to search out.

The disposition to interest one's self in matters not of immediate concern is the idea common to all these terms. *Curiosity* is directed to all objects that can gratify the inclination, taste, or understanding; *inquisitiveness*, to such things only as satisfy the understanding. The *curious* person interests himself in all the works of nature and art; he is *curious* to try effects and examine causes: the *inquisitive* person endeavors to add to his store of knowledge. *Curiosity* employs every means which falls in its way in order to procure gratification; the *curious* man uses his own powers or those of others to serve his purpose: *inquisitiveness* is indulged only by means of verbal inquiry; the *inquisitive* person collects all from others. A traveller is *curious* who examines everything for himself; he is *inquisitive* when he minutely questions others. *Inquisitiveness* is therefore to *curiosity* as a means to an end; whoever is *curious* will naturally be *inquisitive*, but he who is *inquisitive* may be so either from *curiosity* or from other motives.

Curious and *inquisitive* may both be used in a bad sense; *prying* is never used otherwise than in a bad sense. *Inquisitive*, as in the former case, is a mode of *curiosity*, and *prying* is a species of eager *curiosity*. A *curious* person takes unallowed means of learning that which he ought not to wish to know; an *inquisitive* person puts many impertinent and troublesome questions: a *prying* temper is unceasing in its endeavors to get acquainted with the secrets of others. *Curiosity* is a fault most frequent among females; *inquisitiveness* is most general among children; a *prying* temper belongs only to people of low character. A well-disciplined mind checks the first risings of idle *curiosity:* children should be taught early to suppress an *inquisitive* temper, which may so easily become burdensome to others: those who are of a *prying* temper are insensible to everything but the desire of unveiling what lies hidden; such a disposition is often engendered by the unlicensed indulgence of *curiosity* in early life, which becomes a sort of passion in riper years.

CURRENT. See STREAM.

CURSE. See BAN; MALEDICTION; SWEAR.

CURSORY, HASTY, SLIGHT, DESULTORY. *Cursory*, from the Latin *curro*, signifies run over or done in running. *Hasty* signifies done in *haste*, from Anglo-Saxon *hæst*, violence. *Slight* meant originally even or flat; then plain, smooth, simple, trivial. *Desultory*, from *desilo*, to leap, signifies leaped over.

Cursory includes both *hasty* and *slight;* it includes *hasty* inasmuch as it expresses a quick motion; it includes *slight* inasmuch as it conveys the idea of a partial action: a view may be either *cursory* or *hasty*, as the former is taken by design, the latter from carelessness: a view may be either *cursory* or *slight;* but the former is not so imperfect as the latter: an author will take a *cursory* view of those points which are not necessarily connected with his subject; an author who takes a *hasty* view of a subject will mislead by his errors; he who takes a *slight* view will disappoint by the shallowness of his information. Between *cursory* and *desultory* there is the same difference as between running and leaping: we run in a line, but we leap from one part to another; so remarks that are *cursory* have still more or less connection, but remarks that are *desultory* are without any coherence.

CURTAIL. See ABRIDGE.

CURVED. See BENT.

CUSTODY. See KEEPING.

CUSTOM, HABIT. *Custom,* in French *coûtume,* from Latin *consuetudinem,* based on Latin *consuetum,* participle of *consuescere,* to accustom. *Habit,* in French *habit,* Latin *habitudo,* from *habere,* to have, marks the state of having or holding.

Custom is a frequent repetition of the same act; *habit,* the effect of such repetition: the *custom* of rising early in the morning is conducive to the health, and may in a short time become such a *habit* as to render it no less agreeable than it is useful. *Custom* supposes an act of the will; *habit* implies an involuntary movement: *custom* is followed; a *habit* is acquired.

Custom is applicable to bodies of men; *habit* is confined to the individual; every nation has *customs* peculiar to itself; and every individual has *habits* peculiar to his age, station, and circumstances.

Customary and *habitual,* the epithets derived from these words admit of a similar distinction: the *customary* action is that which is repeated after the manner of a *custom;* the *habitual* action is that which is done by the force of *habit.*

See also TAX; USAGE.

Custom, Fashion, Manner, Practice.— *Customs, fashions,* and *manners* are all employed for communities of men; *custom* respects established and general modes of action: *fashion,* in French *façon,* from *factio,* a making or doing, regards partial and transitory modes of making or doing things: *manner,* in the limited sense in which it is here taken, signifies the *manner* or mode of men's living or behaving in their social intercourse.

Custom is authoritative; it stands in the place of law and regulates the conduct of men in the most important concerns of life: *fashion* is arbitrary and capricious, it decides in matters of trifling import: *manners* are rational; they are the expressions of moral feelings. *Customs* have most force in a simple state of society; *fashions* rule most where luxury has made the great-

est progress; *manners* are most distinguishable in a civilized state of society. *Customs* are in their nature as unchangeable as *fashions* are variable; *manners* depend on cultivation and collateral circumstances; *customs* die away or are abolished; *fashions* pass away and new ones take their place; *manners* are altered either for the better or the worse.

Practice, in Latin *practica,* Greek πρακτική, from πράσσειν, to do, signifies actual doing or the thing done, that is, by distinction, the regularly doing, or the thing regularly done, in which sense it is most analogous to *custom;* but the former simply conveys the idea of actual performance; the latter includes also the accessory idea of repetition at stated periods: a *practice* may be defined as frequent or unfrequent, regular or irregular; but a *custom* does not require to be qualified by any such epithets: it may be the *practice* of a person to do acts of charity, as the occasion requires; but, when he uniformly does a particular act of charity at any given period of the year, it is properly denominated his *custom.*

Both *practice* and *custom* are general or particular, but the former is absolute, the latter relative: a *practice* may be adopted by a number of persons without reference to one another; but a *custom* is always followed either by imitation or prescription: the *practice* of gaming has always been followed by the vicious part of society; but it is to be hoped for the honor of man that it will never become a *custom.*

CUT. See NIP; TRENCH.

CUTTING. See TRENCHANT.

CYCLE, BICYCLE, TRICYCLE, HYDROCYCLE, MOTORCYCLE, TANDEM, SOCIABLE. *Cycle,* from the Greek κύκλος, a circle, in the sense of a vehicle, is a shortened term for a variety of constructions, outgrowths of the old French velocipede and dandy-horse of two and three wheels.

The *bicycle* and *tricycle,* as their names denote, are supplied with two and three wheels respectively; the *hydrocycle* is an adaptation for use on a water surface; the *motorcycle* is a bicycle propelled by an electric motor or other contrivance instead of by pedals on the front wheel, a form of cycle much used by the police; a *tandem* has two wheels farther separated than the ordinary bicycle, with seats for two persons, one in the rear of the driver; and the *sociable* is one of several names applied to a *tricycle* having a more or less fancy rear seat for a second person, a form also used for light delivery vehicles.

Bike is a new slang term given by both professional and amateur wheelmen to their machines.

CYNICAL. See MISANTHROPICAL.

D

DABBLE, Dip, Splash. *Dabble* exactly agrees in form and sense with Dutch *dabbelen*. *Dip* comes from Anglo-Saxon *dyppan*. *Splash* is formed by adding *s*, French *es*, Latin *ex*, to *plash* (from a Teutonic root meaning to strike) for added emphasis. *Dip* means to immerse in water and then to withdraw the immersed object quickly—indicating a light, decided, comparatively noiseless action. *Splash* means to *dip* in such a way as to fling the water about and make considerable noise. *Dabble* means to keep *dipping lightly*, making each time a little *splash*. It indicates a purposeless action; *dip* indicates an action not lacking in purpose, but in continuity and endurance.

DAILY, Diurnal. *Daily*, from *day* and *like*, signifies after the manner or in the time of the *day*, *day* being derived from a Teutonic root signifying to burn, day being the bright, hot time, as opposed to night. *Diurnal*, from *dies*, day, signifies belonging to the *day*. *Daily* is the colloquial term which is applicable to whatever passes in the *day*-time; *diurnal* is the scientific term, which applies to what passes within or belongs to the astronomical *day*: the physician makes *daily* visits to his patients; the earth is said by astronomers to have a *diurnal* motion on its own axis.

DAINTY, Delicacy. These terms, which are in vogue among epicures, have some shades of difference not altogether undeserving of notice. *Dainty*, through French from Latin *dignitatem*, worthy, is applied to that which is of worth or value—of course only to such things as have a superior value in the estimation of epicures, and consequently conveys a more positive meaning than *delicacy*; inasmuch as a *dainty* may be that which is extremely *delicate*, a *delicacy* is sometimes a species of *dainty*; but there are many *delicacies* which are altogether suited to the most *delicate* appetite that are neither costly nor rare, two qualities which are almost inseparable from a *dainty:* those who indulge themselves freely in *dainties* and *delicacies* scarcely know what it is to eat with an appetite; but those who are temperate in their use of the enjoyments of life will be enabled to derive pleasure from ordinary food.

DALLY, Toy. *Dally* comes from Old French *dalier*, to converse, to pass one's time in light social converse. *Toy* is derived from Dutch *tuig*, tools, utensils. A *toy* is a device to give amusement, a plaything for children, especially. To *toy* is to treat as a plaything—as a matter of no consequence; to amuse one's self as with a game. *Dally* and *toy* have substantially the same meaning, indicating frivolous or playful self-indulgence. Such difference as there is is that suggested by their derivation—*dally* emphasizing a certain lightness and frivolousness, *toy* a more positive playing with something. Both words are used to refer to amorous caresses with the slight difference in meaning above suggested. *Dally* means also to delay, to put off by trifling, and *toy* a purposeless handling, as when we say "He *toyed* with his watch-chain."

DAMAGE. See Injury; Loss; Scathe.

DAMPNESS. See Moisture.

DAMSEL. See Virgin.

DANGER, Peril, Hazard. *Danger*, Old French *dongier*, from Late Latin *dominum*, power, from Late Latin *domnus*, lord—one who has absolute authority. *Peril* is derived from Latin *periculum*, from the verb *periri*, to try, Greek πεῖρα, an attempt. *Hazard* (see Chance).

The idea of chance or uncertainty is common to all these terms; but the two former may sometimes be foreseen and calculated upon; the latter is purely contingent. *Dangers* are far and near, ordinary and extraordinary: they meet us if we do not go in search of them; *perils* are always distant and extraordinary: we must go out of our course to expose ourselves to them; in the quiet walk of life, as in the most busy and tumultuous, it is the lot of man to be surrounded by *danger;* the mariner, and the traveller who goes in search of unknown countries, put themselves in the way of undergoing *perils* both by sea and land.

Danger and *peril* are applied to positive evils; *hazard* respects the possibilities of good as well as of evil. When we are involved in *danger* we are in a situation to lose what we wish to retain; when we run the *hazard* of a battle we may either win or lose. The same distinction exists between the epithets that are derived from these terms.

It is *dangerous* for a youth to act without the advice of his friends; it is *perilous* for a traveler to explore the wilds of Africa; it is *hazardous* for a merchant to speculate in time of war: experiments in matters of policy or government are always *dangerous;* a journey through deserts that are infested with beasts of prey is *perilous;* a military expedition conducted with inadequate means is *hazardous.*

DANGEROUS. See CLIMACTERIC.

DARE. See BRAVE.

DARING, BOLD. *Daring* signifies having the spirit to *dare. Bold* (see AUDACITY).

These terms may both be taken in a bad sense, but *daring* much oftener than *bold;* in either case *daring* expresses much more than *bold:* he who is *daring* provokes resistance and courts *danger;* but the *bold* man is contented to overcome the resistance that is offered to him: a man may be *bold* in the use of words only, he must be *daring* in actions: he is *bold* in the defence of truth; he is *daring* in military enterprise.

See also STALWART.

DARK, OBSCURE, DIM, MYSTERIOUS. *Dark,* Anglo-Saxon *deorc,* is connected with Old High German *tarchanjan,* to hide. *Obscure* comes from Latin *obscurus,* from *ob,* over, and *scurus,* covered. *Dim* comes from Anglo-Saxon *dim,* and is allied to Swedish *dimma,* a fog or haze.

Darkness expresses more than *obscurity;* the former denotes the total privation of light; the latter only the diminution of light. *Dark* is opposed to light; *obscure* to bright; what is *dark* is altogether hidden; what is *obscure* is not to be seen distinctly or without an effort.

Darkness may be used either in a natural or moral sense; *obscurity* only in the latter; in which case the former conveys a more unfavorable idea: *darkness* serves to cover that which ought not to be hidden; *obscurity* intercepts our view of that which we would wish to see: the former is the consequence of design; the latter of neglect or accident: the letter sent by the conspirator in the gunpowder plot to his friend was *dark;* all passages in ancient writers which allude to circumstances no longer known must necessarily be *obscure;* a corner may be said to be *dark* or *obscure,* but the former is used literally and the latter figuratively; the owl is obliged from the weakness of its visual organs to seek the *darkest* corners in the daytime; men of distorted minds often seek *obscure* corners only from disappointed ambition.

Dim expresses a degree of *darkness,* but it is employed more in relation to the person seeing than to the object seen. The eyes are said to grow *dim,* or the sight *dim.* The light is said to be *dim* by which things are but *dimly* seen.

Mysterious denotes a species of the *dark,* in relation to the actions of men; where a veil is intentionally thrown over any object so as to render it as incomprehensible as that which is sacred. *Dark* is an epithet taken always in the bad sense, but *mysterious* is always in an indifferent sense. We are told in the Sacred Writings that men love *darkness* rather than light, because their deeds are evil. Whatever, therefore, is *dark* in the ways of men is naturally presumed to be evil; but things may be *mysterious* in the events of human life without the express intention of an individual to render them so. The speeches of an assassin and conspirator will be *dark;* any intricate affair, which involves the characters and conduct of men may be *mysterious.* The same distinction exists between these terms when applied to the ways of Providence, which are said to be sometimes *dark,* inasmuch as they present a cloudy aspect; and mostly *mysterious,* inasmuch as they are past finding out.

See also OPAQUE.

DART. See SHOOT.
DASH. See SALLY.
DASTARD. See RECREANT.
DATE. See TIME.
DAUB. See SMEAR.
DAUNT. See DISMAY; OVERAWE.
DAY OF REST. See SABBATH.
DAZZLING. See GORGEOUS.
DEAD. See LIFELESS.

DEADLY, MORTAL, FATAL. *Deadly* or *dead-like* signifies like death itself in its effects. *Mortal*, in Latin *mortalis*, signifies belonging to *death*. *Fatal*, in Latin *fatalis*, signifies according to *fate*.

Deadly is applied to what is productive of death; *mortal* to what terminates in or is liable to death; *fatal* applies not only to death, but everything which may be of great mischief. A poison is *deadly;* a wound or a wounded part is *mortal;* a step in walking, or a step in one's conduct, may be *fatal*. Things only are *deadly;* creatures are *mortal*. Hatred is *deadly;* whatever has life is *mortal*. There may be remedies sometimes to counteract that which is *deadly;* but that which is *mortal* is past all cure; and that which is *fatal* cannot be retrieved.

DEAL, QUANTITY, PORTION. *Deal*, Anglo-Saxon *dæl*, a part, and German *theil*, from *dælen, theilen*, etc., to divide, signifies literally the thing divided or taken off. *Quantity*, in Latin *quantitas*, comes from *quantus*, signifying how much. *Portion* comes from Latin *portio*, allied to *parare*, to prepare, signifying a part prepared.

Deal always denotes something great, and cannot be coupled with any epithet that does not express much: *quantity* is a term of relative import; it either marks indefinitely the how much or so much of a thing, or may be defined by some epithet to express much or little: *portion* is of itself altogether indefinite, and admits of being qualified by any epithet to express much or little: *deal* is a term confined to familiar use, and sometimes substituted for *quantity*, and sometimes for *portion*. It is common to speak of a *deal* or a *quantity* of paper, a great *deal* or a great *quantity* of money; likewise of a great *deal* or a great *portion* of pleasure, a great *deal* or a great *portion* of wealth: and in some cases *deal* is more usual

than either *quantity* or *portion*, as a *deal* of heat, a *deal* of rain, a *deal* of frost, a *deal* of noise, and the like; but it is admissible only in the familiar style.

Portion is employed only for part of that which is detached from the whole; *quantity* may sometimes be employed for a number of wholes. We may speak of a large or a small *quantity* of books; a large or a small *quantity* of plants or herbs; but a large or small *portion* of food, a large or small *portion* of color.

Deal, Act, Behave, Trade.—In an extended sense, *deal* relates to a business transaction, and also implies to *behave* well or ill, to *act* or practise, and one's conduct or behavior toward others. In business concerns a *deal* may be an ordinary buying and selling of a commodity, more generally a bargain resulting from dickering between interested parties, a *trade* or exchange of one commodity for another, or a transaction more or less discreditable to those engaged in it.

As applied to persons, we have political *deals*, the trading of supposed or actual influence for votes, the disposition of a public measure according to the wishes of certain interested parties, as opposed to the authors and promoters of the measure, the side-tracking, pigeonholing, or defeat of a legislative bill as payment for services rendered in other directions, and the like. We say *deal gently with the erring*, meaning to *act* kindly toward them; *that was an unfriendly deal*, a questionable, unfortunate, or indiscreet transaction; *to deal with*, to trade with or be a customer of another: *to deal by*, to treat well or ill; *to deal out*, to distribute or give in small quantities, doles; *to deal the cards*, to give each player the proper number; and *a great deal*, meaning very much, a large quantity.

DEALING. See TRADE.
DEARTH. See SCARCITY.
DEATH, DEPARTURE, DECEASE, DEMISE, PASSING OVER. *Death* signifies the act of *dying*. *Departure* signifies the act of *departing*. *Decease*, from the Latin *de*, away, and *cedere*, to go, signifies the act of going away. *Demise*, from *demittere*, to lay down, signifies literally resigning possession.

Death is a general or a particular term; it marks, in the abstract sense, the extinction of life, and is applicable to men or animals, to one or many. *Departure, decease,* and *demise* are particular expressions suited only to the condition of human beings. We speak of *death* in reference to what happens before or at the time; we speak of the *death* of men generally, or of the *death* of individuals; we speak of the circumstances of *death,* its causes and effects. *Departure* is a Christian term which carries with it an idea of a passage from one life to another. *Death* of itself has always something terrific in it; but the Gospel has divested it of its terrors: the hour of *departure,* therefore, for a Christian, is often the happiest period of his mortal existence.

Decease presents only the idea of leaving life to the survivors. It is either a technical term in law for *death* or it is used in common discourse for the falling off from the number of the living. Property is in perpetual occupancy; at the *decease* of one possessor it passes into the hands of another.

Demise signifies properly a putting off, and in this acceptation the putting off of mortality; it is therefore appropriately used for princes, to denote that they at the same time put off or resign an earthly crown.

As an epithet, *dead* is used collectively; *departed* is used with a noun only; *deceased,* generally without a noun, to denote one or more, according to the connection. There is a respect due to the *dead* which cannot be violated without offence to the living. It is a pleasant reflection to conceive of *departed* spirits as taking an interest in the concerns of those whom they have left. All the marks on the body of the *deceased* indicated that he had met with his death by some violence.

Passing over is the term used by Christian Scientists for dying.

DEBAR. See DEPRIVE.

DEBASE. See ABASE.

DEBATE, DELIBERATE. These terms equally mark the acts of pausing or withholding the decision, whether applicable to one or many. To *debate* (see ARGUE) supposes always a contrariety of opinion; to *deliberate* (see CONSULT) supposes simply the weigh-ing or estimating the value of the opinion that is offered. Where many persons have the liberty of offering their opinions, it is natural to expect that there will be *debating;* when any subject offers that is complicated and questionable, it calls for mature *deliberation.* It is lamentable when passion gets such an ascendancy in the mind of any one as to make him *debate* which course of conduct he shall pursue between virtue and vice; the want of *deliberation,* whether in private or public transactions, is a more fruitful source of mischief than almost any other.

DEBAUCH, SEDUCE, POLLUTE. These words all indicate the act of enticing or corrupting, or both. *Debauch* comes from French *débaucher,* to mar, seduce, mislead, probably of Teutonic origin. *Seduce* comes from Latin *se,* apart, and *ducere,* to lead, and means to lead astray, to entice into reprehensible action. *Pollute* comes from Old Latin *por* or *pol,* toward, and *luere,* to wash, referring to the overflowing of a river; hence it came to mean to defile—as the washing over of the turbid flood destroys the cleanness and beauty of the shores. *Debauch* is the strongest of these three words and the most specific in its application. It includes the idea of *seducing* or leading astray and of *polluting,* and connotes unrestrained sensual indulgence. *Debauch* has always a moral application; *pollute* may have either a moral or physical application. *Seduce* suggests trickery and persuasion in attaining an unhallowed end; *debauch* suggests violence and moral ruin.

DEBILITATE. See WEAKEN.

DEBILITY, INFIRMITY, IMBECILITY. *Debility* comes from Latin *debilis,* weak. *Infirmity,* in Latin *infirmitas,* from *in-firmus,* or *in,* privative, and *firmus,* strong, signifies the absence of strength. *Imbecility* comes from Latin *imbecilius,* weak.

All these terms denote a species of weakness, but the former two, particularly the first, respect that which is either physical or mental. *Debility* is constitutional or otherwise; *imbecility* is always constitutional; *infirmity* is accidental, and results from sickness or a decay of the frame. *Debility* may be either general or local; *infirmity* is always local; *imbecility* always general. *Debility* prevents the active performance of the ordinary functions of nature; it is a deficiency in the muscular power of the body: *infirmity* is a partial want of power which interferes with, but does not necessarily destroy, the activity; *imbecility* lies in the whole frame, and renders it almost entirely powerless. Young people are frequently troubled with *debilities* in their ankles or legs, of which they are never cured. Old age is most exposed to *infirmities;* but there is no age at which human beings are exempt from *infirmity* of some kind or another. The *imbecility* natural to youth, both in body and mind, would make them willing to rest on the strength of their elders if they were not too often misled by a mischievous confidence in their own strength.

DEBT, DUE. *Debt* and *due*, in French *dû*, are both derived from the Latin *debere*, to owe. *Debt* is used only as a substantive; *due* either as a substantive or an adjective. As a substantive, *debt* is commonly applied to that which is owing from the person spoken of; *due* is always applied to that which is owing to the person: to pay one's *debts*, and receive one's *due*. So in the moral application to pay the *debt* of nature, that is, what is *due* or owing to nature; to give every man his *due*.

DECAY, DECLINE, CONSUMPTION. *Decay*, in French *déchoir*, from the Latin *decado*, signifies literally to fall off or away. *Decline*, from the Latin *declino*, or *de*, away, and *clino*, a root meaning to lean, signifies to turn away or lean aside. The direction expressed by both these actions is very similar; it is a downward movement, but *decay* expresses more than *decline*. What is *decayed* is fallen or gone; what *declines* leads toward a fall, or is going; when applied, therefore, to the same objects, a *decline* is properly the commencement of a *decay*. The health may experience a *decline* at any period of life from a variety of causes, but it naturally experiences a *decay* in old age.

Consumption, in general, implies a rapid decay. By *decay* things lose their perfection, their greatness, and their consistency; by *decline* they lose their strength, their vigor, and their lustre; by *consumption* they lose their existence. *Decay* brings to ruin; *decline* leads to an end or expiration. There are some things to which *decay* is peculiar, and some things to which *decline* is peculiar, and other things to which both *decay* and *decline* belong. The corruption to which material substances are particularly exposed is termed *decay:* the close of life, when health and strength begin to fall away, is termed the *decline:* the *decay* of states in the moral world takes place by the same process as the *decay* of fabrics in the natural world; the *decline* of empires, from their state of elevation and splendor, is a natural figure drawn from the *decline* of the setting sun. *Consumption* is seldom applied to anything but animal bodies except figuratively.

See also DEGENERATE; PERISH.

DECEASE. See DEATH.

DECEIT, DECEPTION. *Deceit* and *deception* are both associated with the verb *deceive*, from, *decipere*, to take away, and both imply the act of deceiving; with this difference, that the *deceit* is practised from an expressly bad motive, but *deception* may be from either bad or indifferent motives. A person is therefore said to be guilty of *deceit* who has sought to deceive another for his own purposes; but *deceptions* may be practised in a diversity of ways, and from a diversity of motives. *Deceit* is always a personal act, and if there be an habitual propensity to deceiving, the *deceit* is then a characteristic of the person; a deceiver is full of *deceit*. *Deception* frequently denotes the state of being deceived; it is the effect of any agency, whether from accident or from design. *Deceit* is applied to cases where the understanding is intentionally deceived; but there may be a *deception* on the senses as well as on the understanding.

Deceitful and *deceptive* are employed with this distinction: a person is said to be *deceitful*, and a thing *deceptive*.

See also SOPHISTRY.

Deceit, Duplicity, Double-dealing.—Deceit (see above). *Duplicity* signifies *doubleness* in dealing, the same as *double-dealing.* The former two may be applied either to habitual or particular actions, the latter only to particular actions. There may be much *deceit* or *duplicity* in a person's character or in his proceedings; there is *double-dealing* only where dealing goes forward. The *deceit* may be more or less veiled; the *duplicity* lies very deep, and is always studied whenever it is put into practice. *Duplicity,* in reference to actions, is mostly employed for a course of conduct; *double-dealing* is but another term for *duplicity* on particular occasions. Children of reserved characters are frequently prone to *deceit,* which grows into consummate *duplicity* in riper years: the wealthy are often exposed to much *duplicity* when they choose their favorites among the low and ignorant.

Deceit, Fraud, Guile.—*Deceit* is allied to *fraud* in reference to actions; to *guile* in reference to the character.

Deceit is here, as in the preceding article, indeterminate when compared with *fraud,* which is a specific mode of deceiving; *deceit* is practised only in private transactions; *fraud* is practised toward bodies as well as individuals, in public as well as private: a child practises *deceit* toward its parents; *frauds* are practised upon government, on the public at large, or on tradesmen: *deceit* involves the violation of moral law, *fraud* that of the criminal law. A servant may *deceive* his master as to the time of his coming or going, but he *defrauds* him of his property if he obtains it by any false means.

Deceit as a characteristic is indefinite in magnitude; *guile* marks a strong degree of moral turpitude in the individual. The former is displayed in petty concerns: the latter, which contaminates the whole character, displays itself in inextricable windings and turnings that are suggested in a peculiar manner by the author of all evil. *Deceitful* is an epithet commonly and lightly applied to persons in general; but *guileless* is applied to characters which are the most diametrically opposed to, and at the greatest possible distance from, that which is false.

See also ART.

DECEITFUL. See FALLACIOUS.

DECEIVE, DELUDE, IMPOSE UPON. *Deceive,* in French *décevoir,* Latin *decipere,* compounded of *de,* privative, and *capere,* to take, signifies to take wrong. *Delude,* in Latin *deludo,* compounded of *de* and *ludere,* signifies to play upon or to mislead by a trick. *Impose* comes from Latin *in,* on, and French *poser,* from Latin *pausare.*

Falsehood is the leading feature in all these terms; they vary, however, in the circumstances of the action. To *deceive* is the most general of the three; it signifies simply to produce a false conviction; the other terms are properly species of *deceiving,* including accessory ideas. *Deception* may be practised in various degrees; *deluding* is always something positive, and considerable in degree. Every false impression produced by external objects, whether in trifles or important matters, is a *deception;* but *delusion* is confined to errors in matters of opinion. We may be *deceived* in the color or the distance of an object: we are *deluded* in what regards our principles or moral conduct.

A *deception* does not always suppose a fault on the part of the person *deceived,* but a *delusion* does. A person is sometimes *deceived* in cases where *deception* is unavoidable; he is *deluded* through a voluntary blindness of the understanding: artful people are sometimes capable of *deceiving* so as not even to excite suspicion; their plausible tales justify the credit that is given to them: when the ignorant enter into nice questions of politics or religion, it is their ordinary fate to be *deluded.*

Deception is practised by an individual on himself or others; a *delusion* is commonly practised on one's self; an *imposition* is always practised on another. Men *deceive* others from a variety of motives; they always *impose upon* them for purposes of gain or the gratification of ambition. Men *deceive* themselves with false pretexts and false confidence; they *delude* themselves with vain hopes and wishes.

Deceiver, Impostor. — Between the words *deceiver* and *impostor* there is a similar distinction. A *deceiver* is any one who practises any sort of deception; but an *impostor* is a *deceiver* who studiously deceives by putting on a false appearance. The *deceiver* practises *deception* on individuals or the public; the *impostor* most commonly on the public at large. The false friend and the faithless lover are *deceivers;* the assumed nobleman who practises frauds under his disguise, and the pretended prince who lays claim to a crown to which he was never born, are *impostors*.

DECENCY, DECORUM. Though *decency* and *decorum* are both derived from the same word (see BECOMING), they have acquired a distinction in their sense and application. *Decency* respects a man's conduct; *decorum* his behavior: a person conducts himself with *decency:* he behaves with *decorum*. *Indecency* is a vice; it is the violation of public or private morals: *indecorum* is a fault; it offends the feelings of those who witness it. Nothing but a depraved mind can lead to *indecent* practices; indiscretion and thoughtlessness may sometimes give rise to that which is *indecorous*. *Decency* enjoins upon all relatives, according to the proximity of their relationship, to show certain marks of respect to the memory of the dead: regard for the feelings of others enjoins a certain outward *decorum* upon every one who attends a funeral.

DECENT. See BECOMING.

DECEPTION. See DECEIT.

DECIDE, DETERMINE, CONCLUDE. *Decide*, from the Latin *decido*, compounded of *de*, from, and *cœdere*, to cut, signifies to cut off or cut short a business. For the derivation of *determine* see ARBITRATE. *Conclude* (see CLOSE).

The idea of bringing a thing to an end is common in the signification of all these words; but to *decide* expresses more promptitude than to *determine:* we may *decide* instantaneously, but we must take more or less time to *determine;* we may *decide* any single point either by an act of external force or by a sudden act of the mind; but, in *determining* any question, its extent, limits, and every circumstance must be taken into consideration; *determining* is therefore an act of deliberation To *decide* is an act of greater authority: a parent *decides* for a child,

but subordinates sometimes *determine* in the absence of their employers. Points of law are *decided* by the judge, points of fact are *determined* by the jury. To *decide* is therefore properly applied to all matters of dispute where more or less power or force is required to bring it to an end; to *determine*, to all matters of conduct which may more easily be brought to an end.

To *determine* and *decide* are applied to practical matters; to *conclude* to speculative as well as practical matters, as to *decide* the fate of persons, to *determine* anything that interests one, to *conclude* that a thing is right or wrong, just or unjust, and the like.

In respect to practical matters, to *determine* is either said of that which is subordinate or it is a partial act of the mind; to *conclude* is said of the grand result; it is a complete act of the mind. Many things may be *determined on* which are either never put into execution or remain long unexecuted; but that which is *concluded on* is mostly followed by immediate action. To *conclude* is properly to come to a final *determination*.

Decided, Determined, Resolute. — A man who is *decided* remains in no doubt: he who is *determined* is uninfluenced by the doubts or questions of others: he who is *resolute* (see DETERMINED) is uninfluenced by the consequences of his actions. A *decided* character is at all times essential for a prince or a minister, but particularly so in an unsettled period; a *determined* character is essential for a commander or any one who has to exercise authority; a *resolute* character is essential for one who is engaged in dangerous enterprises. Pericles was a man of a *decided* temper, which was well fitted to direct the affairs of government in a season of turbulence and disquietude: Titus Manlius Torquatus displayed himself to be a man of a *determined* character when he put to death his victorious son for a breach of military discipline. Brutus, the murderer of Cæsar, was a man of a *resolute* temper.

Decided, Decisive. — *Decided* marks that which is actually *decided: decisive*, that which appertains to *decision*.

Decided is employed for persons or things; *decisive* only for things. A person's aversion or attachment is *decided;* a sentence, a judgment, or a victory is *decisive.* A man of a *decided* character always adopts *decisive* measures. It is right to be *decidedly* averse to everything which is immoral: we should be cautious not to pronounce *decisively* on any point where we are not perfectly clear and well grounded in our opinion. In every popular commotion it is the duty of a good subject to take a *decided* part in favor of law and order: such is the nature of law that if it were not *decisive* it would be of no value.

Decision, Judgment, Sentence.—Decision signifies literally the act of *deciding,* or the thing *decided* upon. *Judgment* signifies the act of *judging* or *determining* in general. *Sentence,* in Latin *sententia,* from *sentire,* to think, signifies the opinion held or maintained.

These terms, though very different in their original meaning, are now employed so that the two latter are species of the former: a final conclusion of any business is comprehended in them all; but *decision* conveys none of the collateral ideas which are expressed by *judgment* and *sentence:* a *decision* has no respect to the agent; it may be said of one or many; it may be the *decision* of the court, of the nation, of the public, of a particular body of men, or of a private individual; but a *judgment* is given in a public court or among private individuals: a *sentence* is passed in a court of law or at the bar of the public. A *decision* specifies none of the circumstances of the action: it may be a legal or an arbitrary *decision;* it may be a *decision* according to one's caprice or after mature deliberation: a *judgment* is always passed either in a court of law, and consequently by virtue of authority, or it is passed by an individual by the authority of his own *judgment:* a *sentence* is passed either by the authority of law or at the discretion of an individual or of the public.

A *decision* is given; it is that which decides, and, by putting an end to all dispute and doubt, enables a person to act. A *judgment* is formed; it respects the guilt or innocence, the moral excellence or defects, of a person or thing; it enables a person to think. A *sentence* is pronounced or passed; it respects all matters generally, and determines what are the sentiments of those by whom it is pronounced. Some points are of so complicated a nature that no *decision* can be given upon them; some are of so high a nature that they can be *decided* only by the highest authority; men are forbidden by the Christian religion to be severe in their *judgments* upon one another; the works of an author must sometimes await the *sentence* of impartial posterity before their value can be duly appreciated.

DECISIVE. See CONCLUSIVE; DECIDED.

DECLAIM, INVEIGH. *Declaim,* in Latin *declamo,* that is, *de* and *clamo,* signifies literally to cry aloud in a set form of words. *Inveigh* (see ABUSE; INVECTIVE).

The sense in which these words agree is that of using the language of displeasure against any person or thing: *declaim* is used generally, *inveigh* particularly: public men and public measures are subjects for the *declaimer;* private individuals afford subjects for *inveighing* against: the former is under the influence of particular opinions or prejudices; the latter is the fruit of personal resentment or displeasure: politicians *declaim* against the conduct of those in power or the state of the nation; they *inveigh* against individuals who have offended them. A *declaimer* is noisy; he is a man of words; he makes long and loud speeches: an *inveigher* is virulent and personal; he enters into private details, and often indulges his malignant feelings under an affected regard for morality.

DECLARE, PUBLISH, PROCLAIM. *Declare,* in Latin *declaro,* compounded of *de* and *clarus,* clear, signifies literally to make clear or show plainly to a person. *Publish* (see ANNOUNCE). *Proclaim,* in Latin *proclamo,* compounded of *pro* and *clamo,* signifies to cry before or in the ears of others.

The idea of making known is common to all these terms: this is simply the signification of *declare,* but the other two include accessory ideas. The word *declare* does not express any particular mode or circumstance of making known, as is implied by the others: we may *declare* publicly or privately; we *publish* and *proclaim* only in a public manner: we may declare by word of mouth or by writing; we *publish* or *proclaim* by any means that will render the thing most generally known. In *declaring*, the leading idea is that of speaking out that which passes in the mind; in *publishing*, the leading idea is that of making public or common; in *proclaiming*, the leading idea is that of crying aloud; we may, therefore, often *declare* by *publishing* and *proclaiming*: a *declaration* is a personal act; it concerns the person *declaring*, or him to whom it is *declared;* its truth or falsehood depends upon the veracity of the speaker: a *publication* is of general interest; the truth or falsehood of it does not always rest with the *publisher:* a *proclamation* is altogether a public act, in which no ᴑne's veracity is implicated. Facts and opinions are *declared;* events and circumstances are *published;* the measures of government are *proclaimed:* it is folly for a man to *declare* anything to be true which he is not certain to be so, and wickedness in him to *declare* that to be true which he knows to be false: whoever *publishes* all he hears will be in great danger of *publishing* many falsehoods; whatever is *proclaimed* is supposed to be of sufficient importance to deserve the notice of all who may hear or read.

A *declaration* is always a personal act, whether relating to public or private matters: a *publication* and a *proclamation* may be both indirect actions made by any channel the fittest to make a wide communication. In cases of war or peace, princes are expected to *declare* themselves on one side or the other; in the political world intelligence is quickly *published* through the medium of the public papers; in private life domestic occurrences are *published* with equal celerity through the medium of tale-bearers; *proclaiming* is not confined to political matters: whatever is made known after the manner of a *proclamation* is said to be *proclaimed:* joyful news is *proclaimed*, and where private matters which ought not to be known are *published* to the world people are said to *proclaim* their own shame.

See also DISCOVER; EXPRESS; PROFESS.

DECLINE. See DECAY; DEGENERATE; REFUSE.

DECORATE. See ADORN; GARNISH.

DECORATED. See ORNATE.

DECORUM. See DECENCY; ETIQUETTE.

DECOY. See ALLURE; TWEEDLE.

DECREASE. See ABATE.

DECREE, EDICT, PROCLAMATION. *Decree*, in French *décret*, Latin *decretus*, from *decernere*, to give judgment or pass sentence, signifies the sentence or resolution that is passed. *Edict*, in Latin *edictus*, from *edico*, to say out, signifies the thing spoken out or sent forth. *Proclamation* (see DECLARE).

A *decree* is a more solemn and deliberative act than an *edict;* on the other hand, an *edict* is more authoritative than a *decree*. A *decree* is the decision of one or many; an *edict* speaks the will of an individual: councils and senates, as well as princes, make *decrees;* despotic rulers issue *edicts*. *Decrees* are passed for the regulation of public and private matters; they are made known as occasion requires, but are not always public; *edicts* and *proclamations* contain the commands of the sovereign authority, and are directly addressed by the prince to his people. An *edict* is peculiar to a despotic government; a *proclamation* is common to a monarchical and aristocratic form of government: the *ukase* in Russia was a species of *edict*, by which the emperor made known his will to his people; the king of England communicates to his subjects the *determinations* of himself and his council by means of a *proclamation*.

The term *decree* is applied figuratively; the other terms are used, for the most part, in their proper sense only.

See also ORDINANCE.

DECRY. See DISPARAGE.

DEDICATE, DEVOTE, CONSECRATE, HALLOW. *Dedicate*, in Latin *dedicatus*, participle from *de* and *dicare*, signifies to set apart by a promise. *Devote*, in Latin *devotus*, participle from *devoveo*, signifies to vow for an express purpose. *Consecrate*, in Latin *consecratus*, from *consecro,* or *con* and *sacrare,* signifies to make sacred by a special act. *Hallow,* from Anglo-Saxon *halig,* holy, signifies to make holy.

There is something more solemn in the act of *dedicating* than in that of *devoting;* but less so than in that of *consecrating.* To *dedicate* and *devote* may be employed in both temporal and spiritual matters; to *consecrate* and *hallow* only in the spiritual sense: we may *dedicate* or *devote* anything that is at our disposal to the service of some object; but the former is employed mostly in regard to superiors, and the latter to persons without distinction of rank: we *dedicate* a house to the service of God; or we *devote* our time to the benefit of our friends or the relief of the poor: we may *dedicate* or *devote* ourselves to an object; but the former always implies a solemn setting apart springing from a sense of duty; the latter an entire application of one's self from zeal and affection; in this manner he who *dedicates* himself to God abstracts himself from every object which is not immediately connected with the service of God; he who *devotes* himself to the ministry pursues it as the first object of his attention and regard. To *consecrate* is a species of formal *dedication* by virtue of a religious observance; it is applicable mostly to places and things connected with religious works: *hallow* is a species of informal *consecration* applied to the same objects: the church is *consecrated;* particular days are *hallowed.*

DEDUCE. See **DERIVE.**

DEDUCT, SUBTRACT. *Deduct,* from the Latin *deductus,* participle of *deducere,* to lead away, and *subtract,* from *subtractum,* participle of *subtrahere,* to draw away, have both the sense of taking from, but the former is used in a general, and the latter in a technical sense. He who makes an estimate is obliged to *deduct;* he who makes a calculation is obliged to *subtract.* The tradesman *deducts* what has been paid from what remains due; the accountant *subtracts* small sums from the gross amount.

Deduction, Abatement. — Both these words imply a taking off from something, but the *deduction* is made at the discretion of the person deducting; while the *abatement* is made for the convenience or at the desire of the person for whom it is made. A person may make a *deduction* in an account for various reasons, but he makes an *abatement* in a demand when it is objected to as excessive; so an *abatement* may be made in a calculation when it is supposed to be higher than it ought to be.

See also CONCLUSION.

DEED, EXPLOIT, ACHIEVEMENT, FEAT. *Deed,* allied to *do,* expresses the thing done. *Exploit,* in French *exploit,* was most probably changed from *explicatus,* signifying the thing unfolded or displayed. *Achievement* comes from French *à chef,* to a head, meaning something brought to a head or finished. *Feat,* in French *fait,* Latin *factum,* from *facio,* signifies the thing done.

The first three words rise progressively on one another: *deeds,* compared with the others, is employed for that which is ordinary or extraordinary; *exploit* and *achievement* are used only for the extraordinary; the latter in a higher sense than the former. *Deeds* must always be characterized as good or bad, magnanimous or atrocious, and the like, except in poetry, when the term becomes elevated.

Exploit and *achievement* do not necessarily require such epithets; they are always taken in the proper sense for something great. *Exploit,* when compared with *achievement,* is a term used in plain prose; it designates not so much what is great as what is real: *achievement* is most adapted to poetry and romance; an *exploit* is properly a single act, and refers to the efforts of the individual performing it; an *achievement* may involve many acts and circumstances; in the execution it refers us to the point gained, as also to the difficulties of gaining it. An *exploit* marks only personal bravery in action; an *achievement* denotes elevation of character in every respect, grandeur of design, promptitude in execution, and valor in action. An *exploit* may be executed by the design and at the will of another; a common soldier or an army may perform *exploits.* An *achievement* is designed and executed by the *achiever:* Hercules is distinguished for his *achievements;* and in the same manner we speak of the *achievements* of knights-errant or of great commanders.

Feat approaches nearest to *exploit* in signification; the former marks skill, and the latter resolution. The *feats* of chivalry displayed in jousts and tournaments were in former times as much esteemed as warlike *exploits.*

Exploit and *feat* are often used in derision, to mark the absence of skill or bravery in the actions of individuals. The soldier who affects to be foremost in situations where there is no danger cannot be more properly derided than by terming his action an *exploit;* he who prides himself on the display of skill in the performance of a paltry trick may be laughed at for having performed a *feat.* The same words may also be applied in an indifferent sense to familiar objects, as the *exploits* of a freebooter, or *feats* of horsemanship.

See also ACT.

DEEM. See THINK.

DEFACE, DISFIGURE, DEFORM. *Deface, disfigure,* and *deform* signify literally to spoil the *face, figure,* and *form. Deface* expresses more than either *deform* or *disfigure.* To *deface* is an act of destruction; it is the actual destruction of that which has before existed: to *disfigure* is either an act of destruction or an erroneous execution, which takes away the figure: to *deform* is altogether an imperfect execution, which renders the *form* what it should not be. A thing is *defaced* by design; it is *disfigured* either by design or accident; it is *deformed* either by an error or by the nature of the thing. Persons only *deface;* persons or things *disfigure;* things are most commonly *deformed* of themselves. That may be *defaced,* the face or external surface of which may be injured or destroyed; that may be *disfigured* or *deformed,* the figure or form of which is imperfect or may be rendered imperfect. A fine painting or piece of writing is *defaced* which is torn or besmeared with dirt: a fine building is *disfigured* by any want of symmetry in its parts: a building is *deformed* that is made contrary to all form. A statue may be *defaced, disfigured,* and *deformed:* it is *defaced* when

any violence is done to the face or any outward part of the body; it is *disfigured* by the loss of a limb; it is *deformed* if made contrary to the perfect form of the person or thing to be represented. Inanimate objects are mostly *defaced* or *disfigured,* but seldom *deformed;* animate objects are either *disfigured* or *deformed,* but seldomer *defaced.* A person may *disfigure* himself by his dress; he is *deformed* by the hand of nature.

DEFAME. See ASPERSE.

DEFEAT, FOIL, DISAPPOINT, FRUSTRATE. *Defeat* (see BEAT). *Foil* comes from Late Latin *fullare,* to full cloth, a method of cleaning. It originally meant to trample on, then to defeat by less obvious physical action. *Frustrate,* in Latin *frustratus,* from *frustra,* vain, signifies to make vain. *Disappoint,* from the privative *dis* and the verb *appoint,* signifies literally to do away with what has been appointed.

Defeat and *foil* are both applied to matters of enterprise; but that may be *defeated* which is only planned, and that is *foiled* which is in the act of being executed. What is rejected is *defeated:* what is aimed at or purposed is *frustrated:* what is calculated on is *disappointed.* The best concerted schemes may sometimes be easily *defeated:* where art is employed against simplicity, the latter may be easily *foiled:* when we aim at what is above our reach, we must be *frustrated* in our endeavors: when our expectations are extravagant, it seems to follow, of course, that they will be *disappointed.* Design or accident may tend to *defeat,* design only to *foil,* accident only to *frustrate* or *disappoint.* The superior force of the enemy, or a combination of untoward events which are above the control of the commander, will serve to *defeat* the best concerted plans of the best generals: men of upright minds can seldom *foil* the deep-laid schemes of knaves: when we see the perversity of men is liable to *frustrate* the kind intentions of others in their behalf, it is wiser to leave them to their folly: the cross accidents of human life are a fruitful source of *disappointment* to those who suffer themselves to be affected by them.

See also BAFFLE.

DEFECT. See BLEMISH; IMPERFECTION.

DEFECTION, REVOLT. *Defection,* from the Latin *de,* negative, and *facere,* to do, signifies literally an undoing. *Revolt* comes from French *re* and the verb *volvere,* to roll, meaning to roll back, to overturn, to turn against.

Defection is a general, *revolt* a specific term, that is, it denotes a species of *defection. Defection* is applicable to any person or thing to which we are bound by any obligation; *revolt* is applicable only to the government to which one is bound. There may be a *defection* from religion, or any cause that is held sacred: a *revolt* is only against a monarch or the supreme authority.

Defection does not designate the mode of the action; it may be quietly made or otherwise: a *revolt* is an act of violence, and always attended with violence. The *defection* may be the act of one; a *revolt* is properly the act of many. A general may be guilty of a *defection* who leaves the party to which he has hitherto adhered; a nation or a community may commit an act of *revolt* by shaking off the authority under which they have lived. A *defection,* being mostly the act of an individual, or one part of a community against the whole, is mostly a culpable act; but a *revolt* may be a justifiable measure when one nation *revolts* against another, under whose power it has been brought by force of arms: the Roman people were guilty of a *defection* when they left the senate and retired to Mount Aventine; the Germans frequently attempted to recover their liberty by *revolting* against the Romans.

DEFECTIVE, DEFICIENT. *Defective* expresses the quality or property of having a *defect* (see BLEMISH); *deficient* is employed with regard to the thing itself that is wanting. A book may be *defective* in consequence of some leaves being *deficient;* a child may de *defective* because of some mental *deficiency.* A *deficiency* is therefore often what constitutes a *defect.* Many things, however, may be *defective* without having any *deficiency,* and *vice versâ.* Whatever is misshapen, and fails either in beauty or utility, is *defective;* that

which is wanted to make a thing complete is *deficient.* It is a *defect* in the eye when it is so constructed that things are not seen at their proper distances; there is a *deficiency* in a tradesman's accounts when one side falls short of the other. That which is *defective* is most likely to be permanent; but a *deficiency* may be only occasional and easily rectified.

DEFEND, PROTECT, VINDICATE. *Defend* (see APOLOGIZE). *Protect,* in Latin *protectum,* participle of *protegere,* compounded of *pro,* before, and *tegere,* to cover, signifies to put anything before a person as a covering. *Vindicate* (see ASSERT).

Defend is a general term; it defines nothing with regard to the degree and manner of the action: *protect* is a particular and positive term, expressing an action of some considerable importance. Persons may *defend* others without distinction of rank or station: none but superiors or persons having power can *protect* others. *Defence* is an occasional action; *protection* is a permanent action. A person may be *defended* in any particular case of actual danger or difficulty; he is *protected* from what may happen as well as what does happen. *Defence* respects the evil that threatens; *protection* involves the supply of necessities and the affording comforts.

Defence requires some active exertion either of body or mind; *protection* may consist only of the extension of power in behalf of any particular individual. A *defence* is successful or unsuccessful; a *protection,* weak or strong. A soldier *defends* his country; a counsellor *defends* his client; a prince *protects* his subjects.

In a figurative and extended sense things may either *defend* or *protect* with a similar distinction: a coat *defends* us from the inclemencies of the weather; houses are a *protection* not only against the changes of the seasons, but also against the violence of men.

To *vindicate* is a species of *defence* only in the moral sense of the word. Acts of importance are *defended:* those of trifling import are commonly *vindicated.* Cicero *defended* Milo against the charge of murder, in which he was implicated by the death of Clodius; a child or a servant *vindicates* himself when any blame is attached to him. *Defence* is employed either in matters of opinion or conduct; *vindicate* only in matters of conduct. Some opinions are too absurd to be openly *defended;* he who *vindicates* the conduct of another should be fully satisfied of the innocence of the person whom he *defends.*

See also ESPOUSE; GARNISH; GUARD.

Defendant, Defender.—The *defendant* defends himself; the *defender* defends another. We are *defendants* when any charge is brought against us which we wish to refute: we are *defenders* when we undertake to rebut or refute the charge brought against any person or thing.

Defender, Advocate, Pleader.—A *defender* exerts himself in favor of one who wants support: an *advocate,* from the Latin *ad,* to, and *vocare,* to call, signifies one who is called to speak in favor of another; he exerts himself in favor of any cause that offers: a *pleader,* from *plea* or *excuse,* signifies him who pleads in behalf of one who is accused or in distress. A *defender* attempts to keep off a threatened injury by rebutting the attack of another: an *advocate* states that which is to the advantage of the person or thing *advocated;* a *pleader* throws in *pleas* and extenuations; he blends entreaty with argument. Oppressed or accused persons and disputed opinions require *defenders;* that which falls in with the humors of men will always have *advocates;* the unfortunate and the guilty require *pleaders.*

An official, known as the *public defender,* has been appointed recently in, a number of cities in the United States, to defend in courts persons unable to pay lawyers' fees.

The term *pleader* is used sometimes like that of *defender,* in the general sense. Valeria and Volumnia, the mother and wife of Coriolanus, were powerful and successful *pleaders* in behalf of the Roman republic.

Defensible, Defensive.—*Defensible* is employed for the thing that is to be *defended; defensive,* for the thing that *defends.* An opinion or a line of conduct is *defensible;* a weapon or a military operation is *defensive.* The *defensible* is opposed to the *indefensible;* and the *defensive* to the *offensive.* It is the height of folly to attempt to *defend* that which is *indefensible;* it is sometimes prudent to act on the *defensive* when we are not in a condition to commence the offensive.

DEFER. See DELAY.

DEFERENCE. See COMPLAISANCE.

DEFICIENT. See DEFECTIVE; FAIL.

DEFILE. See CONTAMINATE.

DEFINITE, POSITIVE. *Definite,* in Latin *definitum,* participle of *definire,* compounded of *de* and *finis,* signifies that which is bounded by a line or limit. *Positive,* in Latin *positivus,* from *ponere,* to place, signifies that which is placed or fixed.

Definite signifies that which is defined, or has the limits drawn or marked out; *positive* that which is placed or fixed in a particular manner: *definite* is said of things as they present themselves or are presented to the mind, as a *definite* idea, a *definite* proposal; *positive* is said of a person's temper of mind; a person is *positive* as to his opinions, or an assurance is *positive* which serves to make one *positive.* In respect to a man's self, his views ought to be *definite* to prevent him from being misled, but he ought not to be *positive* in matters that admit of doubt. In respect to others, the more *definite* the instructions which are given the less danger there is of mistake; the more *positive* the information communicated the greater reliance which is placed upon it.

DEFINITION, EXPLANATION. A *definition* is properly a species of *explanation.* The former is used scientifically, the latter on ordinary occasions; the former is confined to words, the latter is employed for words or things. A *definition* is correct or precise; an *explanation* is general or ample. The *definition* of a word defines or limits the extent of its signification; it is the rule for the scholar in the use of any word: the *explanation* of a word may include both definition and illustration: the former admits of no more words than will include the leading features in the meaning of any term; the latter admits of an unlimited scope for diffuseness on the part of the explainer.

DEFLECT, BEND, DIVERGE, SWERVE. *Deflect* is the Latin term; *bend*, the Anglo-Saxon word. *Bend*, Anglo-Saxon *bendan*, allied to *band*, *bind*, etc., means to curve as a bow is curved when the string is fastened. *Deflect*, from *de*, from, and *flectere*, to bend, means to bend from the straight course, especially to turn to one side. *Diverge*, from Latin *dis*, apart, and *vergere*, to bend, is the intransitive corresponding to the transitive *deflect*. We *deflect* another's course; we *diverge* from that which we have marked out for ourselves. *Bend* is a more general word than *deflect* or *diverge*. It indicates the physical act of bending, and suggests any kind of departure from the condition of straightness. *Deflect* suggests a turning from a straight line contrary to all apparent intention or purpose. *Swerve*, Anglo-Saxon *sweorfan*, suggests a very sudden turning, a jerky and unpremeditated movement, emphasizing the idea of action contrary to apparent purpose, barely suggested in *deflect*. All these words may be used either with the physical or with a moral application.

DEFORM. See DEFACE.

DEFORMED. See WRY.

DEFRAUD. See CHEAT.

DEFY. See BRAVE.

DEGENERATE, DETERIORATE. *Degenerate* signifies to fall from race or kind, to lose ancestral quality, from Latin *degenerare*, compounded of *de*, from, and the stem of *genus*, race. *Deteriorate* comes from Latin *deteriorare*, to grow worse, from the comparative of an obsolete adjective connected with *de*, down. Both these words mean to grow worse, but *degenerate* adds to the idea contained in *deteriorate* a definite indication that the deterioration is a departure from the standard of the individual's race or natural endowment. It is therefore more specific in its implications.

DEGRADE. See ABASE; DISPARAGE; HUMBLE.

DEGREE. See CLASS.

DEITY, DIVINITY. *Deity*, from *deus*, a god, signifies a divine person. *Divinity*, from *divinus*, signifies the divine essence or power; the *deities* of the heathens had little of *divinity* in them; the *divinity* of our Saviour is a fundamental article in the Christian faith.

DEJECTION, DEPRESSION, MELANCHOLY. *Dejection*, from *dejicere*, to cast down, and *depression*, from *deprimere*, to press or sink down, have both regard to the state of the animal spirits. *Melancholy*, from the Greek μελαγχολία, black bile, originally referred to the state of the humors in general, or of the particular humor called the bile.

Dejection and *depression* are occasional, and depend on outward circumstances; *melancholy* is permanent, and lies in the constitution. *Depression* is but a degree of *dejection*: slight circumstances may occasion a *depression*; distressing events occasion a *dejection*: the death of a near and dear relative may be expected to produce *dejection* in persons of the greatest equanimity; lively tempers are most liable to *depressions*; *melancholy* is a disease which nothing but clear views of religion can possibly correct.

DELAY, DEFER, POSTPONE, PROCRASTINATE, PROLONG, PROTRACT, RETARD. *Delay*, compounded of *de* and *lay*, signifies to lay or keep back. *Defer*, compounded of *de* and *ferre*, to bring, signifies to put off. *Postpone*, compounded of *post* and the Latin *ponere*, to place, signifies to place behind or after. *Procrastinate*, from *pro*, for, and *cras*, to-morrow, signifies to put off until to-morrow. *Prolong* signifies to lengthen out the time, and *protract* to draw out the time. *Retard*, from *re*, intensive, and *tardum*, slow, to make a thing go slowly.

To *delay* is simply not to commence action; to *defer* and *postpone* are to fix its commencement at a more distant period: we may *delay* a thing for days, hours, and minutes; we *defer* or *postpone* it for months or weeks. *Delays* mostly arise from the fault of the person *delaying*; they are seldom reasonable or advantageous: *deferring* and *postponing* are discretionary acts, which are justified by the circumstances; indolent people are most prone to *delay*; when a plan is not maturely digested, it is prudent to *defer* its execution until everything is in an entire state of preparation. *Procrastination* is a culpable *delay* arising solely from the fault of the *procrastinator:* it is the part of a dilatory man to *procrastinate* that which it is both his interest and duty to perform.

We *delay* the execution of a thing; we *prolong* or *protract* the continuation of a thing; we *retard* the termination of a thing: we may *delay* answering a letter, *prolong* a contest, *protract* a lawsuit, and *retard* a publication.

Delay, Laches, Moratorium.—*Laches* and *moratorium* are two special applications of the idea of *delay.* They are not synonymous with each other at all, but they are connected through the general idea expressed in the key-word. *Laches* is a legal term (from Latin *laxus,* loose), signifying inexcusable delay in meeting the terms of a contract, or taking up and paying a promissory note. *Moratorium,* on the other hand, signifies a delay granted by a government, corporation, or other large body to persons to *delay* making payment of their obligations beyond the time of their maturity.

DELEGATE, DEPUTE; **DELEGATE,** DEPUTY. *Delegate,* in Latin *delegatus,* from *delegare,* signifies to send on a mission; *depute* comes from *deputare,* to assign a business to. To *delegate* is applied to the power or office which is given; *depute* to the person employed. Parents *delegate* their office to the instructor; persons are *deputed* to act for others.

As nouns, *delegate* and *deputy* are applied only to persons. The *delegate* is the person commissioned, who is bound to act according to his commission; the *deputy* is the person *deputed,* who acts in the place of another, but may act according to his own discretion or otherwise, as circumstances require. A *delegate* is mostly chosen in public matters and on particular occasions: as *delegates* sent from a besieged town to the camp of the besiegers; *deputies* are those who are *deputed* to act officially and regularly for others, as *deputies* sent to any public assembly.

DELIBERATE. See CONSENT; DEBATE; THOUGHTFUL.

DELICACY. See DAINTY.

DELICATE. See FINE.

DELIGHT. See PLEASURE.

DELIGHTFUL, CHARMING. *De-*

lightful is applied either to material or spiritual objects; *charming,* mostly to objects of sense. When they both denote the pleasure of the sense, *delightful* is not so strong an expression as *charming:* but the latter rises to a degree that carries the senses away captive. Of music we should rather say that it was *charming* than *delightful,* as it acts on the senses in so powerful a manner; on the other hand, we should with more propriety speak of a *delightful* employment to relieve distress, or a *delightful* spectacle to see a family living together in love and harmony.

DELINEATE, SKETCH *Delineate,* in Latin *delineatus,* participle of *delineare,* from *de,* down, and *linea,* line, means literally to put down lines on paper. *Sketch,* Dutch and Italian *schizzo,* a first rough draft, comes from Latin *schedium,* a thing made hastily, from Greek σχέδιος, hastily.

Both these terms are properly employed in the art of drawing, and figuratively applied to moral subjects to express a species of descriptions: a *delineation* expresses something more than a *sketch;* the former conveying not merely the general outlines or more prominent features, but also as much of the details as would serve to form a whole; the latter, however, seldom contains more than some broad touches by which an imperfect idea of the subject is conveyed. A *delineation,* therefore, may be characterized as accurate, and a *sketch* as hasty or imperfect: an attentive observer who has passed some years in a country may be enabled to give an accurate *delineation* of the laws, customs, manners, and character of its inhabitants; a traveller who merely passes through can give only a hasty *sketch* from what passes before his eyes.

DELINQUENT. See OFFENDER.

DELIVER, RESCUE, SAVE. *Deliver,* in French *délivrer,* from the Latin *de,* and *liberare,* from *liber,* free, signifies to make free. *Rescue* comes from Late Latin *rescutere,* from *re,* again, and *excutere,* to drive. *Save* signifies literally to make safe, from Latin *salvus,* safe.

The idea of taking or keeping from any evil is common to these terms; but to *deliver* and *rescue* signify most properly to take, and *save* to keep from evil. To *deliver* is a general term, not defining either the mode or object of the action. One may be *delivered* from any evil, whether great or small, and in any manner: to *rescue* is to *deliver* from a great impending danger or immediate evil; as to *rescue* from the hands of robbers or from the jaws of a wild beast.

One is *delivered* mostly by some active effort; but we may be *saved* either by active or passive means. A person is *delivered* from the hands of an enemy by force or stratagem: he *saves* his life by flying.

See also FILL; GIVE UP.

Deliverance, Delivery.—Both words are drawn from the same verb (see above) to express its different senses of taking from or giving to: the former denotes the taking something from one's self; the latter implies giving something to another. To wish for a *deliverance* from that which is hurtful or painful is to a certain extent justifiable: the careful *delivery* of property into the hands of the owner will be the first object of concern with a faithful agent.

See also SALVATION.

DELUDE. See DECEIVE.

DELUGE. See OVERFLOW.

DELUSION, ILLUSION. Both these words, being derived from the Latin *ludere*, to play, are applied to such matters as act upon the imagination; but *delude*, by the force of the preposition *de*, signifies to carry away from the right line, to cause to deviate into error; while *illude*, from the preposition *il*, *im*, in or upon, signifies simply to act on the imagination. The former is therefore taken in a bad sense, but the latter in an indifferent sense. A deranged person falls into different kinds of *delusions:* as when he fancies himself poor while he is very rich, or that every one who comes in his way is looking at him, or having evil designs against him, and the like; but there may be optical *illusions*, when an object is made to appear brighter or larger than it really is.

See also FALLACY; HALLUCINATION.

DEMAND, REQUIRE. *Demand* (see ASK). *Require*, in Latin *requiro*, compounded of *re*, again, and *quærere*, to

C.E.S.—9

seek, signifies to seek for or to seek to get back.

We *demand* that which is owing and ought to be given; we *require* that which we wish and expect to have done. A *demand* is more positive than a *requisition;* the former properly admits of no question; the latter is liable to be both questioned and refused: the creditor makes a *demand* on the debtor; the master *requires* a certain portion of duty from his servant: it is unjust to *demand* of a person what he has no right to give; it is unreasonable to *require* of him what it is not in his power to do. A thing is commonly *demanded* in express words; it is *required* by implication: a person *demands* admittance when it is not voluntarily granted; he *requires* respectful deportment from those who are subordinate to him.

In the figurative application the same sense is preserved: things of urgency and moment *demand* immediate attention; difficult matters *require* a steady attention.

See also ASK.

DEMEANOR. See BEHAVIOR.

DEMISE. See DEATH.

DEMOLISH, RAZE, DISMANTLE, DESTROY. The throwing down what has been built up is the common idea included in all these terms. *Demolish*, from the Latin *demolior*, and *moles*, a mass or structure, signifies to decompound what has been fabricated into a mass. *Raze*, like *erase* (see BLOT), signifies the making smooth or even with the ground. *Dismantle*, in French *démanteler*, signifies to deprive a thing of its mantle or guard. *Destroy*, from the Latin *destruo*, compounded of the privative *de* and *struo*, to build, signifies properly to pull down.

A fabric is *demolished* by scattering all its component parts; it is mostly an unlicensed act of caprice; it is *razed* by way of punishment, as a mark of public vengeance; a fortress is *dismantled* from motives of prudence, in order to render it defenceless; places are *destroyed* by various means and from various motives, that they may not exist any longer. Individuals may *demolish;* public authority causes an edifice to be *razed* with the ground; a general orders towers to be *dismantled* and fortifications to be *destroyed*.

DEMON. See Devil.

DEMONSTRATE. See Prove.

DEMONSTRATIVE. See Categorical.

DEMUR, Hesitate, Pause. *Demur*, in French *demeurer*, Latin *demorari*, signifies to keep back. *Hesitate*, in Latin *hæsitatum*, participle of *hæsito*, a frequentative from *hæreo*, signifies to stick or remain a long time back. *Pause*, in Latin *pausa*, from the Greek παύω, cease, signifies to make a stand.

The idea of stopping is common to these terms, to which signification is added some distinct collateral idea for each: we *demur* from doubt or difficulty; we *hesitate* from an undecided state of mind; we *pause* from circumstances. *Demurring* is a matter of prudence, it is always grounded on some reason; *hesitating* is rather a matter of feeling and is oftener faulty than otherwise: when a proposition appears to be unjust, we *demur* in supporting it, on the ground of its injustice; when a request of a dubious nature is made to us, we *hesitate* in complying with it: prudent people are most apt to *demur;* but people of a wavering temper are apt to *hesitate:* demurring may be often unnecessary, but it is seldom injurious; *hesitating* is mostly injurious when it is not necessary. *Demurring* and *hesitating* are both employed as acts of the mind; *pausing* is an external action: we *demur* and *hesitate* in determining; we *pause* in speaking or doing anything.

Demur, Doubt, Hesitation, Objection. —*Demur* (see above). *Doubt*, in Latin *dubito*, from *duo*, two, and *itus*, past participle of *ire*, to go, signifies to go two ways. *Hesitation* (see above). *Objection*, from *objicio*, or *ob*, in the way, and *jacere*, to throw, to throw in the way, signifies what is thrown in the way so as to stop our progress.

Demurs often occur in matters of deliberation; *doubt* in regard to matters of fact; *hesitation* in matters of ordinary conduct; and *objections* in matters of common consideration. Artabanes made many *demurs* to the proposed invasion of Greece by Xerxes.

Doubts have been suggested respecting the veracity of Herodotus as a historian.

It is not proper to ask that which cannot be granted without *hesitation;* and it is not the part of an amiable disposition to make a *hesitation* in complying with a reasonable request.

There are but few things which we either attempt to do or recommend to others that are not liable to some kind of an *objection.*

A *demur* stops the adjustment of any plan or the *determination* of any question.

A *doubt* interrupts the progress of the mind in coming to a state of satisfaction and certainty.

The last two words are both applied to abstract questions, or such as are of general interest. *Hesitation* and *objection* are more individual and private in their nature. *Hesitation* lies mostly in the state of the will; *objection* is rather the offspring of the understanding. A *hesitation* interferes with the action; an *objection* affects the measure or the mode of action.

DENOMINATION. See Name.

DENOTE, Signify. *Denote*, in Latin *denoto* or *noto*, from *notum*, participle of *nosco*, signifies to cause to know. *Signify*, from the Latin *signum*, a sign, and *facere*, to make, is to become or be made a sign or guide for the understanding.

Denote is employed with regard to things and their characters; *signify*, with regard to the thoughts or movements. A letter or character may be made to *denote* any number, as words are made to *signify* the intentions and wishes of the person. Among the ancient Egyptians hieroglyphics were very much employed to *denote* certain moral qualities; in many cases looks or actions will *signify* more than words. Devices and emblems of different descriptions, drawn either from fabulous history or the natural world, are likewise now employed to *denote* particular circumstances or qualities: the cornucopia *denotes* plenty; the beehive *denotes* industry; the dove *denotes* meekness, and the lamb gentleness: he who will not take the trouble to *signify* his wishes otherwise than by nods or signs must expect to be frequently misunderstood.

DENOUNCE. See Ban; Excommunicate; Proscribe.

DENSE. See THICK.

DENTICULATED. See JAGGED.

DENY, REFUSE. *Deny,* in Latin *de,* from, and *negare,* to say no, from *ne,* not, signifies to say no to a thing. *Refuse,* in Latin *refusus,* from *re* and *fundere,* to pour or cast, signifies to throw off from one.

To *deny* respects matters of fact or knowledge; to *refuse,* matters of wish or request. We *deny* what immediately relates to ourselves; we *refuse* what relates to another. We *deny* as to the past; we *refuse* as to the future: we *deny* our participation in that which has been; we *refuse* our participation in that which may be: to *deny* must always be expressly verbal; a *refusal* may sometimes be signified by actions or looks as well as words. A *denial* affects our veracity; a *refusal* affects our good-nature.

But to *deny* signifies in this case simply to withhold; and *refuse* signifies to cast off from one, which is a more positive act: to *deny* one's self a pleasure is simply to *abstain* from it; but to *refuse* one's food is to cast it from one with a positive indisposition. What is *denied* may be *denied* by circumstances or by Providence; and it may be *denied* to one, many, or all; but what is *refused* is *refused* by and to particular individuals.

See also CONTRADICT; DISAVOW.

DEPART. See GO.

DEPARTED, See BYGONE.

DEPARTURE. See DEATH; EXIT.

DEPENDENCE, RELIANCE. *Dependence,* from *depend,* from Latin *de,* from, and *pendere,* to hang, signifies, literally, to rest one's weight by hanging from that which is held. *Rely,* compounded of *re* and *lie,* signifies likewise to rest one's weight by lying or hanging back from the object held.

Dependence is the general term; *reliance* is a species of *dependence:* we *depend* either on persons or things; we *rely* on persons only: *dependence* serves for that which is immediate or remote; *reliance* serves for the future only. We *depend* upon a person for that which we are obliged to receive or led to expect from him: we *rely* upon a person for that which he has given us reason to expect from him. *Dependence* is an outward condition or the state of ex-

ternal circumstances; *reliance* is a state of the feelings with regard to others. We *depend* upon God for all that we have or shall have; we *rely* upon the word of man for that which he has promised to perform. We may *depend* upon a person's coming from a variety of causes; but we *rely* upon it only in reference to his avowed intention.

DEPICT. See PAINT.

DEPLORE, LAMENT. *Deplore* comes from Latin *deplorare,* from *de,* intensive, and *plorare,* to weep. *Lament,* see BEWAIL.

Deplore is a much stronger expression than *lament;* the former calls forth tears from the bitterness of the heart; the latter excites a cry from the warmth of feeling. *Deploring* indicates despair; to *lament* marks only pain or distress. Among the poor we have *deplorable* instances of poverty, ignorance, vice, and wretchedness combined; among the higher classes we have often *lamentable* instances of extravagance and consequent ruin. A field of battle or a city overthrown by an earthquake is a spectacle truly *deplorable:* it is *lamentable* to see beggars putting on all the disguises of wretchedness in order to obtain by deceit what they might earn by honest industry. The condition of a dying man suffering under the agonies of an awakened conscience is *deplorable;* the situation of the relative or friend who witnesses the agony, without being able to afford consolation to the sufferer, is truly *lamentable.*

See also WAIL.

DEPONENT, EVIDENCE, WITNESS. *Deponent,* from *deponere,* to lay down or set forth, signifies he who declares or substantiates anything. The *evidence,* from *evident,* is that which makes *evident;* and the *witness,* from the Anglo-Saxon *witan,* to know, signifies he who makes known.

All these words are properly applied to judicial proceedings, where the *deponent* deposes generally to facts either in causes or otherwise: the *evidence* consists either of persons or things, which are brought before the court for the purpose of making a doubtful matter clear; the *witness* is always a person who bears witness to any fact for or against another.

Evidence is applied to moral objects, in the proper sense, and *witness* in the figurative application.

DEPORTMENT. See BEHAVIOR.

DEPOSE. See SWEAR.

DEPOSIT, PLEDGE, SECURITY. *Deposit* is a general term, from the Latin *depositus*, participle of *deponere*, signifying to lay down, or put into the hands of another. *Pledge* comes through French from Old Low German *plegan*, to promise. *Security*, the substantive corresponding to *secure*, comes from Latin *se*, privative, and *cura*, care, signifying free from care.

The term *deposit* has most regard to the confidence we place in another; *pledge* has most regard to the security we give for ourselves; *security* is a species of *pledge*. A *deposit* is always voluntarily placed in the hands of an indifferent person; a *pledge* and *security* are required from the parties who are interested. A person may make a *deposit* for purposes of charity or convenience; he gives a *pledge* or *security* for a temporary accommodation or the relief of a necessity. Money is *deposited* in the hands of a friend in order to execute a commission: a *pledge* is given as an equivalent for that which has been received: a *security* is given by way of security for the performance of some agreement. A *deposit* must consist of something movable, as money, papers, or jewels, which can be deposited or placed in the hands of another. It may sometimes serve as a *pledge* or *security* where it is intended to bind the party *depositing* to anything. A *pledge* may, properly speaking, be anything which serves to *pledge* or bind a person by motives of interest, affection, or honor; it may consist of anything which is given to another for that purpose. A *security* is whatever makes a person *secure* against a loss, and in the ordinary acceptation consists of any instrument or written document which legally binds a person. In this sense, the person who binds himself for another becomes a *security*.

These words are all applied in this sense to moral objects.

See also GARNER.

DEPRAVITY, DEPRAVATION, CORRUPTION. *Depravity*, from the Latin *pravitas* and *pravus*, crooked or not straight, marks the quality of being crooked. *Depravation*, in Latin *depravatio*, signifies a making crooked, or not as it should be. *Corruption*, in Latin *corruptio*, *corrumpo*, from *rumpere*, to break, marks the disunion and decomposition of the parts of anything.

All these terms are applied to objects which are contrary to the order of Providence, but the term *depravity* characterizes the thing as it is; the terms *depravation* and *corruption* designate the making or causing it to be so; *depravity*, therefore, excludes the idea of any cause; *depravation* always carries us to the cause or external agency: hence we may speak of *depravity* as natural, but we speak of *depravation* as the result of circumstance: there is a *depravity* in man which nothing but the grace of God can correct; the introduction of obscenity on the stage tends greatly to the *depravation* of morals; bad company tends to the *corruption* of a young man's morals.

Depravity or *depravation* implies crookedness or a distortion from the regular course; *corruption* implies a *dissolution*, as it were, in the component parts of bodies. Cicero says (2 *De Finibus*) that *depravity* is applicable only to the mind and heart; but we say a *depraved* taste, and *depraved* humors in regard to the body. A *depraved* taste loathes common food, and longs for that which is unnatural and hurtful. *Corruption* is the natural process by which material substances are disorganized. In the figurative application of these terms they preserve the same signification. *Depravity* is characterized by being directly opposed to order and an established system of things; *corruption* marks the vitiation or spoiling of things, and the ferment that leads to destruction. *Depravity* turns things out of their ordinary course; *corruption* destroys their essential qualities. *Depravity* is a vicious state of things, in which all is deranged and perverted: *corruption* is a vicious state of things, in which all is sullied and polluted. That which is *depraved* loses its proper manner of acting and existing; that which is *corrupted* loses its virtue and essence.

That is a *depraved* state of morals in

which the gross vices are openly practised in defiance of all decorum: that is a *corrupt* state of society in which vice has secretly insinuated itself into all the principles and habits of men, and concealed its deformity under the fair semblance of virtue and honor. The manners of savages are most likely to be *depraved;* those of civilized nations to be *corrupt,* when luxury and refinement are risen to an excessive pitch. Cannibal nations present us with the picture of human *depravity;* the Roman nation, during the time of the emperors, affords us an example of almost universal *corruption.*

From the above observations it is clear that *depravity* is best applied to those objects to which common usage has annexed the epithets of right, regular, fine, etc.; and *corruption,* to those which may be characterized by the epithets of sound, pure, innocent, or good. Hence we prefer to say *depravity* of mind and *corruption* of heart; *depravity* of principle and *corruption* of sentiment or feeling: a *depraved* character; a *corrupt* example; a *corrupt* influence.

In reference to the arts or belles-lettres we say either *depravity* or *corruption* of taste, because taste has its rules, is liable to be disordered, is or is not conformable to natural order, is regular or irregular; and, on the other hand, it may be so intermingled with sentiments and feelings foreign to its own native purity as to give it justly the title of *corrupt.* The last thing worthy of notice respecting the two words *depravity* and *corruption* is that the former is used for man in his moral capacity, but the latter for man in a political capacity: hence we speak of human *deparvity,* but the *corruption* of government.

DEPRECIATE. See DISPARAGE.

DEPREDATION, ROBBERY. *Depredation,* in Latin *deprædatio,* from *præda,* a prey, conveys the idea of taking by way of prey. *Rob* is allied to Anglo-Saxon *reaf,* the root found in *bereave,* and *robe, i. e.,* that stripped from the slain; it signified to strip, despoil, take away. Both these words denote the taking what belongs to another, but differ in the circumstances of the action. *Depredation* is not so lawless an act as *robbery;* it may be

excused, if not justified, by the laws of war or the hostile situation of parties to each other. The borderers on the confines of England and Scotland used to commit *depredations* on each other. *Robbery* is in direct violation of every law, it is committed only by those who set all laws at defiance. *Depredations* may be committed in any manner short of direct violence; those who commit *depredations* do so mostly in the absence of those on whom they are committed: *robberies* are commonly committed on the persons, and mostly accompanied with violence. *Depredation* taken absolutely refers us to that which the *depredator* gains or gets to himself by the act; *robbery* refers us to that which the person loses who is *robbed:* the one goes away loaded with his plunder, the other goes away stripped of that which is most valuable to him.

In the extended application of these words this distinction is kept up: birds commit *depredations* on cornfields, bees *rob* flowers of their honey.

DEPRESSED. See HYPOCHONDRIACAL.

DEPRESSION. See DEJECTION.

DEPRIVATION. See SPOLIATION.

DEPRIVE, DEBAR, ABRIDGE. *Deprive,* from *de,* from, and Latin *privus,* one's own, signifies to make not one's own what one has or expects to have. *Debar,* from *de* and *bar,* signifies to prevent by means of a *bar.* *Abridge* (see ABRIDGE).

Deprive conveys the idea of either taking away that which one has or withholding that which one may have; *debar* conveys the idea only of withholding; *abridge* conveys that also of taking away. *Depriving* is a coercive measure; *debar* and *abridge* are merely acts of authority. We are *deprived* of that which is of the first necessity; we are *debarred* of privileges, enjoyments, opportunities, etc.; we are *abridged* of comforts, pleasures, conveniences, etc. Criminals are *deprived* of their liberty; their friends are in extraordinary cases *debarred* the privilege of seeing them; thus men are often *abridged* of their comforts in consequence of their own faults. *Deprivations* and *debarring* sometimes arise from things as well as persons; *abridging* is always the voluntary act of conscious agents. Religion teaches men to be resigned under the severest *deprivations;* it is painful to be *debarred* the society of those we love, or to *abridge* others of any advantage which they have been in the habit of enjoying.

When used as reflective verbs they preserve the same analogy in their signification. An extravagant person *deprives* himself of the power of doing good. A person may *debar* himself of any pleasure from particular motives of prudence. A miser *abridges* himself of every enjoyment in order to gratify his ruling passion.

See also BEREAVE.

DEPTH, PROFUNDITY. *Depth* comes from Anglo-Saxon *deop,* and contains the same root as that found in `dip, dive,* etc. *Profundity,* from *profound,* in Latin *profundus,* compounded of *pro,* far, and *fundus,* the bottom, signifies remoteness from the lower surface of anything.

These terms do not differ merely in their derivation; but *depth* is indefinite in its signification; and *profundity* is a positive and considerable degree of *depth.* Moreover, the word *depth* is applied to objects in general; *profundity* is confined in its application to moral objects: thus we speak of the *depth* of the sea, or the *depth* of a person's learning, but his *profundity* of thought.

DEPUTE. See CONSTITUTION; DELEGATE.

DEPUTY. See AMBASSADOR.

DERANGE. See DISORDER.

DERANGEMENT, INSANITY, LUNACY, MADNESS, MANIA. *Derangement,* from the verb to *derange,* implies the first stage of disordered intellect. *Insanity,* or unsoundness, from *in,* negative, and Latin *sanus,* whole, implies positive disease, which is more or less permanent. *Lunacy* is a violent sort of *insanity,* which was supposed to be influenced by the moon, and is derived from Latin *luna,* the moon. Cf. Shakespeare's "moon - struck calf. " *Madness,* allied to Anglo-Saxon *gemœdan,* to drive mad, from a root meaning severely injured, and *mania,* Latin *mania,* Greek μανία, mental excitement, allied to μένος, mind, both imply insanity in its most furious and confirmed stage. *Deranged* persons may sometimes be perfectly sensible about everything but particular subjects. *Insane* persons are sometimes entirely restored. *Lunatics* have their lucid intervals, and *maniacs* their intervals of repose. *Derangement* may sometimes be applied to the temporary confusion of a disturbed mind which is not in full possession of all its faculties: *madness* may sometimes be the result of violently inflamed passions: and *mania* may be applied to any vehement attachment which takes possession of the mind.

DERIDE, MOCK, RIDICULE, RALLY, BANTER. *Deride* and *ridicule* are both derived from Latin *ridere,* to smile at. *Mock* comes from Late Latin *muccare,* to blow the nose (compare *mucus*), indicating a scoffing, coarse gesture. *Rally* is allied to *rail,* perhaps; its real origin is unknown. The origin of *banter* is also obscure.

Strong expressions of contempt are designated by all these terms. *Derision* and *mockery* evince themselves by the outward actions in general; *ridicule* consists more in words than actions; *rallying* and *bantering* almost entirely in words. *Deride* is not so strong a term as *mock,* but much stronger than *ridicule.* There is always a mixture of hostility in *derision* and *mockery,* but *ridicule* is frequently unaccompanied with any personal feeling of displeasure. *Derision* is often deep, not loud; it discovers itself in suppressed laughter, contemptuous sneers or gesticulations, and cutting expressions: *mockery* is mostly noisy and outrageous; it breaks forth in insulting buffoonery and is sometimes accompanied with personal violence: the former consists of real but contemptuous laughter; the latter often of affected laughter and grimace. *Derision* and *mockery* are always personal; *ridicule* may be directed to things as well as persons. *Derision* and *mockery* are a direct attack on the individual, the latter still more so than the former; *ridicule* is as often used in writing as in personal intercourse.

Rally and *banter,* like *derision* and *mockery,* are altogether personal acts, in which application they are very analogous to *ridicule.* *Ridicule* is the most general term of the three; we often *rally* and *banter* by *ridiculing.* There is more exposure in *ridiculing,* reproof in *rallying,* and provocation in *bantering.* A person may be *ridiculed* on account of his eccentricities; he is *rallied* for his defects; he is *bantered* for accidental circumstances: the former two actions are often justified by some substantial reason; the last is an action as puerile as it is unjust, it is a contemptible species of *mockery.* Self-conceit and extravagant follies are oftentimes best corrected by good-natured *ridicule;* a man may deserve sometimes to be *rallied* for his want of resolution; those who are of an ill-natured turn of mind will *banter* others for their misfortunes, or their personal defects, rather than not say something to their annoyance.

DERIVE, Trace, Deduce. *Derive,* from the Latin *de* and *rivus,* a river, signifies to draw, after the manner of water, from a source. *Trace,* Middle French *tracer,* is drawn ultimately from Latin *tractus,* the past participle of *trahere,* to draw or drag; and originally signified the mark left by drawing something across the surface, or the act of making such a mark. *Deduce,* in Latin *de,* from, and *ducere,* to lead, signifies to bring from.

The idea of drawing one thing from another is included in all the actions designated by these terms. The act of *deriving* is immediate and direct; that of *tracing* a gradual process; that of *deducing* a ratiocinative process. We discover causes and sources by *derivation;* we discover the course, progress, and commencement of things by *tracing;* we discover the grounds and reasons of things by *deduction.* A person *derives* his name from a given source; he *traces* his family up to a given period; principles or powers are *deduced* from circumstances or observations. The Trojans *derived* the name of their city from Tros, a king of Phrygia; ·they *traced* the line of their kings up to Dardanus.

DEROGATE. See Disparage.

DESCRIBE. See Relate.

DESCRIPTION. See Account; Cast.

DESCRY. See Find.

DESECRATING. See Sacrilegious.

DESERT, Merit, Worth. *Desert,* from *deserve,* in Latin *deservio,* signifies to do service or to be serviceable. *Merit,* in Latin *meritus,* participle of *mereor,* comes from the Greek μέρος, a share, because he who *merits* anything has a right to share in it. *Worth,* in German *werth,* seems to come from a root found in Latin *vereri,* to respect.

Desert is taken for that which is good or bad; *merit* for that which is good only. We *deserve* praise or blame: we *merit* a reward. *Desert* consists in the action, work, or service performed; *merit* has regard to the character of the agent or the nature of the action. A person does not *deserve* a recompense until he has performed some service; he does not *merit* approbation if he have not done his part well. *Deserve* is a term of ordinary import; *merit* applies to objects of greater moment: the former includes matters of personal and physical gratification; the latter those altogether of an intellectual nature. Criminals cannot always be punished according to their *deserts;* a noble mind is not contented with barely obtaining, it seeks to *merit* what it obtains.

The idea of value, which is prominent in the signification of the term *merit,* renders it closely allied to that of *worth.* *Merit* is that on which mankind set a value; it is sought for on account of the honor or advantages it brings: *worth* is that which is absolutely valuable; it must be sought for on its own account.

From these words are derived the epithets *deserved* and *merited,* in relation to what we receive from others; and *deserving, meritorious, worthy,* and *worth,* in regard to what we possess in ourselves: a treatment is *deserved* or *undeserved;* reproofs are *merited* or *unmerited:* the harsh treatment of a master is easier to be borne when it is *undeserved* than when it is *deserved;* the reproaches of a friend are very severe when *unmerited.*

A laborer is *deserving* on account of his industry; an artist is *meritorious* on account of his professional abilities; a citizen is *worthy* on account of his benevolence and uprightness. The ·first person *deserves* to be well paid and encouraged; the second *merits* the applause which is bestowed on him; the third is *worthy* of confidence and esteem from all men. Between *worthy* and *worth* there is this difference, that the former is said of intrinsic and moral qualities, the latter of extrinsic ones: a *worthy* man possesses that which calls for the esteem of others; but a man is *worth* the property which he can call his own: so in like manner a subject may be *worthy* the attention of a writer, or a thing may not be *worth* the while to consider.

See also ABANDON; SOLITARY.

DESIGN, PURPOSE, INTEND, MEAN. *Design*, from the Latin *de*, down, and *signare*, to make a sign, signifies to mark out as with a pen or pencil. *Purpose*, like *propose*, comes through French from the Latin *pro* and *pansare*, signifying to set before one's mind as an object of pursuit. *Intend*, in Latin *in*, to, and *tendere*, to stretch, signifies the bending of the mind toward an object. *Mean*, in Anglo-Saxon *mænen*, German *meinen*, is probably connected with the word mind, signifying to have in the mind.

Design and *purpose* are terms of higher import than *intend* and *mean*, which are in familiar use; the latter still more so than the former. A *design* embraces many objects; a *purpose* consists of only one: the former supposes something studied and methodical, it requires reflection; the latter supposes something fixed and determinate, it requires resolution. A *design* is attainable; a *purpose* is steady. We speak of the *design* as it regards the thing conceived; we speak of the *purpose* as it regards the temper of the person. Men of a sanguine or aspiring character are apt to form *designs* which cannot be carried into execution; whoever wishes to keep true to his *purpose* must not listen to many counsellors.

A *purpose* is the thing proposed or set before the mind; an *intention* is the thing to which the mind bends or inclines: *purpose* and *intend* differ, therefore, both in the nature of the action and the object; we *purpose* seriously; we *intend* vaguely: we set about that which we *purpose;* we may delay that which we have only *intended:* the execution of one's *purpose* rests mostly with one's self; the fulfilment of an *intention* depends upon circumstances: a man of a resolute temper is not to be diverted from his *purpose* by trifling objects: we may be disappointed in our *intentions* by a variety of unforeseen but uncontrollable events. *Purpose* is always applied to some proximate or definite object; *intend*, to that which is indefinite or remote. *Mean*, which is a term altogether of colloquial use, differs but little from *intend*, except that it is used for matters requiring but little thought; to *mean* is simply to have in the mind, to *intend* is to stretch with the mind to a thing.

Design and *purpose* are taken sometimes in the abstract sense; *intend* and *mean*, always in connection with the agent who *intends* or *means:* we see a *design* in the whole creation which leads us to reflect on the wisdom and goodness of the Creator; whenever we see anything done, we are led to inquire the *purpose* for which it is done; or are desirous of knowing the *intention* of the person in so doing: things are said to be done with a *design*, in opposition to that which happens by chance; they are said to be done for a *purpose* in reference to the immediate *purpose* which is expected to result from them. *Design*, when not expressly qualified by a contrary epithet, is used in a bad sense in connection with a particular agent; *purpose*, *intention*, and *meaning*, taken absolutely, have an indifferent sense: a *designing* person is full of latent and interested *designs;* there is nothing so good that it may not be made to serve the *purposes* of those who are bad; the *intentions* of a man must always be taken into the account when we are forming an estimate of his actions: ignorant people frequently *mean* much better than they do.

Design, *Plan*, *Scheme*, *Project.*—*Design* (see preceding). *Plan*, in French *plan*, comes from Latin *planus*, smooth or even, signifying a drawing on a flat surface, a preliminary drawing of something to be constructed. *Scheme*, in Latin *schema*, Greek σχῆμα, a form or figure, signifies the thing drawn out in the mind. *Project*, in Latin *projectus*, from *projicio*, compounded of *pro* and *jacio*, signifies to cast or put forth something, hence to propose.

Arrangement is the idea common to those terms: the *design* includes the thing that is to be brought about; the *plan* includes the means by which it is to be brought about: a *design* was formed in the time of James I. for overturning the government of the country; the *plan* by which this was to have been realized consisted in placing gunpowder under the Parliament House and blowing up the assembly. A *design* is to be estimated according to its intrinsic worth; a *plan* is to be estimated according to its relative value, or fitness for the *design*: a *design* is noble or wicked, a *plan* is practicable; every founder of a charitable institution may be supposed to have a good *design;* but ne may adopt an erroneous *plan* for obtaining the end proposed.

Scheme and *project* respect both the end and the means, which makes them analogous to *design* and *plan*: the *design* stimulates to action; the *plan* determines the mode of action; the *scheme* and *project* consist most in speculation: the *design* and *plan* are equally practical, and suited to the ordinary and immediate circumstances of life; the *scheme* and *project* are contrived or conceived for extraordinary or rare occasions: no man takes any step without a *design;* a general forms the *plan* of his campaign; adventurous men are always forming *schemes* for gaining money; ambitious monarchs are full of *projects* for increasing their dominions. *Scheme* and *project* differ principally in the magnitude of the objects to which they are applied, the former being much less vast and extensive than the latter: a *scheme* may be formed by an individual for attaining any trifling advantage; *projects* are mostly conceived in matters of great moment involving deep interests.

DESIGNATE. See NAME.

DESIGNING. See SCHEMING.

DESIRE, WISH, LONG FOR, HANKER AFTER, COVET. *Desire,* in Latin *desidero,* is a word of obscure origin; it may be allied to *sidus,* star, like *consider,* which see. *Wish* is derived from a Germanic root which is derived from the Aryan root whence the word *win,* and Latin *ven,* in *Venus, venerate,* etc., are also drawn. *Long* comes from Anglo-Saxon *langian,* to crave or desire. *Hanker* signifies to hang on an object with one's mind. *Covet* (see COVETOUS).

Desire is imperious, it demands gratification; *wish* is less vehement, it consists of a strong inclination; *longing* is an impatient and continued species of *desire; hankering* is a *desire* for that which is set out of one's reach; *coveting* is a *desire* for that which belongs to another, or what it is in his power to grant: we *desire* or *long for* that which is near at hand or within view; we *wish* for and *covet* that which is more remote or less distinctly seen; we *hanker after* that which has been once enjoyed: a discontented person *wishes* for more than he has; he who is in a strange land *longs* to see his native country; vicious men *hanker after* the pleasures which are denied them; ambitious men *covet* honors, avaricious men *covet* riches. *Desires* ought to be moderated, *wishes* to be limited, *longings, hankerings,* and *covetings* to be suppressed: uncontrolled *desires* become the greatest torments; unbounded *wishes* are the bane of all happiness; ardent *longings* are mostly irrational and not entitled to indulgence; *coveting* is expressly prohibited by the Divine law.

Desire, as it regards others, is not less imperative than when it respects ourselves; it lays an obligation on the person to whom it is expressed: a *wish* is gentle and unassuming; it appeals to the good-nature of another: we act by the *desire* of a superior or of one who has a right to ask; we act according to the *wishes* of an equal, or of one who can only request: the *desire* of a parent will amount to a command in the mind of a dutiful child: his *wishes* will be anticipated by the warmth of affection.

See also BEG; YEARN.

DESIST, LEAVE OFF. *Desist,* from the Latin *desistere,* signifies to take one's self off. *Desist* is applied to actions good, indifferent, or offensive to some person; *leave off,* to actions that are indifferent; the former is voluntary or involuntary, the latter voluntary: we are frequently obliged to *desist;* but we *leave off* at our option: it is prudent to *desist* from using our endeavors when we find them ineffectual; it is natural for a person to *leave off* when he sees no further occasion to continue his labor: he who annoys another must be made to *desist;* he who does not wish to offend will *leave off* when requested.

DESOLATE. See Solitary.

DESOLATION. See Ravage.

DESPAIR, Desperation, Despondency. *Despair, desperation,* from the French *désespoir,* compounded of the privative *de* and the Latin *spes,* hope, signifies the absence or the annihilation of all hope. *Despondency,* from *despond,* in Latin *despondeo,* compounded of the privative *de* and *spondere,* to promise, signifies literally to deprive in a solemn manner, or cut off from every gleam of hope.

Despair is a state of mind produced by the view of external circumstances; *desperation* and *despondency* may be the fruit of the imagination; the former, therefore, always rests on some ground, the latter are sometimes ideal: *despair* lies mostly in reflection; *desperation* and *despondency* in the feelings: the former marks a state of vehement and impatient feeling, the latter that of fallen and mournful feeling. *Despair* is often the forerunner of *desperation* and *despondency,* but it is not necessarily accompanied with effects so powerful: the strongest mind may have occasion to *despair* when circumstances warrant the sentiment; men of an impetuous character are apt to run into a state of *desperation;* a weak mind full of morbid sensibility is most liable to fall into *despondency. Despair* interrupts or checks exertion; *desperation* impels greater exertions; *despondency* unfits for exertion: when a physician *despairs* of making a cure, he lays aside the application of remedies; when a soldier sees nothing but death or disgrace before him, he is driven to *desperation,* and redoubles his efforts; when a tradesman sees before him nothing but failure for the present and want for the future he may sink into *despondency: despair* is justifiable as far as it is a rational calculation into futurity from present appearances; *desperation* may arise from extraordinary circumstances or the action of strong passions; in the former case it is unavoidable, and may serve to rescue from great distress; in the latter case it is mostly attended with fatal

consequences: *despondency* is a disease of the mind, which nothing but a firm trust in the goodness of Providence can obviate.

Desperate, Hopeless.—*Desperate* (see above) is applicable to persons or things; *hopeless* to things only: a person makes a *desperate* effort; he undertakes a *hopeless* task. *Desperate,* when applied to things, expresses more than *hopeless;* the latter marks the absence of hope as to the attainment of good, the former marks the absence of hope as to the removal of an evil: a person who is in a *desperate* condition is overwhelmed with actual trouble for the present and the prospect of its continuance for the future; he whose case is *hopeless* is without the prospect of effecting the end he has in view: gamesters are frequently brought into *desperate* situations when bereft of everything that might possibly serve to lighten the burdens of their misfortunes: it is a *hopeless* undertaking to endeavor to reclaim men who have plunged themselves deep into the labyrinths of vice.

See also Deter.

DESPICABLE. See Contemptible.

DESPISE. See Contemn.

DESPOIL. See Sack.

DESPONDENCY. See Despair.

DESPONDING. See Pessimistic.

DESPOTIC. See Absolute.

DESTINE. See Allot.

DESTINY, Fate, Lot, Doom. *Destiny,* from *destine* (see Appoint) signifies either the power that *destines* or the thing *destined. Fate* (see Chance). *Lot,* Anglo-Saxon *hlot,* signifies a ticket, die, or any other thing by which the casual distribution of things is determined; and, in an extended sense, it expresses the portion thus assigned by chance. *Doom* comes from a Teutonic root meaning that which is put up or set up—irrevocably decreed and established.

All these terms are employed with regard to human events which are not under one's control: among the heathens *destiny* and *fate* were considered as deities, who each in his way could direct human affairs and were both superior even to Jupiter himself: the *Destinies,* or Parcæ, as they were termed, presided only over life and death; but *Fate* was employed in ruling the general affairs of men. Since revelation has instructed mankind in the nature and attributes of the true God, those blind powers are now not acknowledged to exist in the overruling providence of an all-wise and an all-good Being; the terms *destiny* and *fate*, therefore, have now only a relative sense as to what happens without the will or control of man.

Destiny is used in regard to one's station and walk in life; *fate*, in regard to what one suffers; *lot*, in regard to what one gets or possesses; and *doom* to the final *destiny* which terminates unhappily and depends mostly upon the will of another: *destiny* is marked out; *fate* is fixed; a *lot* is assigned; a *doom* is passed. It is the *destiny* of some men to be always changing their plan of life; it is but too frequently the *fate* of authors to labor for the benefit of mankind and to reap nothing for themselves but poverty and neglect; it is the *lot* of but very few to enjoy what they themselves consider a competency; a man sometimes seals his own *doom* by his imprudence or vices.

Destiny, Destination.—Both *destiny* and *destination* are used for the thing *destined;* but the former is said in relation to a man's important concerns, the latter only of particular circumstances; in which sense it may likewise be employed for the act of *destining. Destiny* is the point or line marked out in the walk of life; *destination* is the place fixed upon in particular: as every man has his peculiar *destiny*, so every traveller has his particular *destination. Destiny* is altogether set above human control; no man can determine, though he may influence, the *destiny* of another: *destination* is, however, the specific act of an individual, either for himself or another: we leave the *destiny* of a man to develop itself; but we may inquire about his own *destination* or that of his children: it is a consoling reflection that the *destinies* of short-sighted mortals like ourselves are in the hands of One who both can and will overrule them to our advantage if we place full reliance in Him; in the *destination* of

children for their several professions or callings, it is of importance to consult their particular turn of mind as well as inclination.

DESTITUTE. See BARE; FORSAKEN.

DESTROY, CONSUME, WASTE. *Destroy,* in Latin *destruo,* from *de,* privative, and *struere,* to build, is to undo that which has been built or done. *Consume,* in French *consumer,* Latin *consumo, i. e., con* or *cum,* together, and *sumere,* to take, signifies to take away altogether. *Waste* comes from Latin *vastus,* desolate, English *waste,* and signifies to make desolate.

To *destroy* is to reduce to nothing that which has been artificially raised or formed; as to *destroy* a town or a house: to *consume* is to use up; as to *consume* food, or to *consume* articles of manufacture: to *destroy* is an immediate act mostly of violence; *consume* is a gradual and natural process, as oil is *consumed* in a lamp.

To *destroy* is always taken in the bad sense for putting an end to that which one wishes to preserve; *consume* is also taken in a similar sense, but with the above distinction as to the mode of the action: as a hurricane *destroys* the crops; rust *consumes* iron: to *waste* is to *consume* by a misuse; as to *waste* provisions by throwing them away or suffering them to spoil; or to fall away or lose its substance, as the body *wastes* from disease.

In the figurative application they are used with precisely the same distinction: happiness or peace is *destroyed;* time is *consumed* in an indifferent sense; time or strength is *wasted* in the bad sense.

See also DEMOLISH.

DESTROYER. See UNDERSEACRAFT.

DESTRUCTION, RUIN. *Destruction,* from *destroy,* and the Latin *destruo,* signifies literally to unbuild that which is raised up. *Ruin,* from the Latin *ruere,* to fall, signifies that which is fallen into pieces.

Destruction is an act of immediate violence; *ruin* is a gradual process; a thing is *destroyed* by some external action upon it; a thing falls to *ruin* of itself: we witness *destruction* wherever war or the adverse elements rage; we witness *ruin* whenever the works of man are exposed to the effects of time; nevertheless, if *destruction* be more forcible and rapid, *ruin* is, on the other hand, more sure and complete: what is *destroyed* may be rebuilt or replaced; but what is *ruined* is mostly lost forever, it is past recovery: when houses or towns are *destroyed*, fresh ones rise up in their place; but when commerce is *ruined* it seldom returns to its old course. *Destruction* admits of various degrees; *ruin* is something positive and general. The property of a man may be *destroyed* to a greater or less extent without necessarily involving his *ruin*. The *ruin* of a whole family is oftentimes the consequence of *destruction* by fire. Health is *destroyed* by violent exercises or some other active cause; it is *ruined* by a course of imprudent conduct. The happiness of a family is *destroyed* by broils and discord; the morals of a young man are *ruined* by a continued intercourse with vicious companions.

Both words are used figuratively with the same distinction. The *destruction* of both body and soul is the consequence of sin; the *ruin* of a man, whether in his temporal or spiritual concerns, is inevitable if he follow the dictates of misguided passion.

Destructive, Ruinous, Pernicious.— *Destructive* signifies producing *destruction*. *Ruinous* signifies either having or causing *ruin*. *Pernicious*, from the Latin *pernicies*, or *per*, intensive, and stem *neci* of *nex*, slaughter, signifies causing violent and total dissolution.

Destructive and *ruinous*, as the epithets of the preceding terms, have a similar distinction in their sense and application; fire and sword are *destructive* things; a poison is *destructive:* consequences are *ruinous;* a condition or state is *ruinous;* intestine commotions are *ruinous* to the prosperity of a state. *Pernicious* approaches nearer to *destructive* than to *ruinous;* both the former imply a tendency to produce dissolution, which may be more or less gradual; but the latter refers us to the result itself, to the *dissolution* as already having taken place: hence we speak of the instrument or cause as being *destructive* or *pernicious*, and the action, event, or result as *ruinous: destructive*

is applied in the most extended sense to every object which has been created or supposed to be so; *pernicious* is applicable only to such objects as act only in a limited way: sin is equally *destructive* to both body and soul; certain food is *pernicious* to the body; certain books are *pernicious* to the mind.

See also SPOLIATION.

DESULTORY. See CURSORY.

DETACH. See SEGREGATE; SEPARATE; WEAN.

DETAIN. See HOLD.

DETECT, DISCOVER. *Detect*, from the Latin *de*, privative, and *tegere*, to cover, and *discover*, from the privative *dis* and *cover*, both originally signify to deprive of a covering; see COVER.

Detect is always taken in a bad sense: *discover* in an indifferent sense. A person is *detected* in what he wishes to conceal; a person or a thing is *discovered* that has unintentionally lain concealed. Thieves are *detected* in picking pockets; a lost child is *discovered* in a wood or in some place of security. *Detection* is the act of the moment; it relates to that which is passing: a *discovery* is either a gradual or an immediate act, and may be made of that which has long since passed. A plot is *detected* by any one who communicates what he has seen and heard; many murders have been *discovered* after a lapse of years by ways the most extraordinary.

See also CONVICT.

DETER, DISCOURAGE, DISHEARTEN. *Deter*, in Latin *deterreo*, compounded of *de* and *terrere*, signifies to frighten away from a thing. *Discourage* and *dishearten*, by the privative *dis*, signify to deprive of courage or heart. One is *deterred* from commencing anything; one is *discouraged* or *disheartened* from proceeding. A variety of motives may *deter* any one from an undertaking; but a person is *discouraged* or *disheartened* mostly by the want of success or the hopelessness of the case. The prudent and the fearful are alike easily to be *deterred;* impatient people are most apt to be *discouraged;* fainthearted people are easily *disheartened*. The foolhardy and the obdurate are the least easily *deterred* from their object; the persevering will not suffer themselves to be *discouraged* by particular failures; the resolute and self-confident will not be *disheartened* by trifling difficulties.

DETERIORATE. See DEGENERATE.

DETERMINE, RESOLVE. To *determine* (see DECIDE) is more especially an act of the judgment; to *resolve* (see COURAGE) is an act of the will: we *determine* how or what we shall do; this requires examination and choice: we *resolve* that we will do what we have *determined* upon; this requires a firm spirit. Our *determinations* should be prudent, that they may not cause repentance; our *resolutions* should be fixed, in order to prevent variation. There can be no co-operation with a man who is *undetermined;* it will be dangerous to co-operate with a man who is *irresolute.* In the ordinary concerns of life we have frequent occasions to *determine* without *resolving;* in the discharge of our moral duties, or the performance of any office, we have occasion to *resolve* without *determining.* A master *determines* to dismiss his servant; the servant *resolves* on becoming more diligent. Personal convenience or necessity gives rise to the *determination;* a sense of duty, honor, fidelity, and the like gives birth to the *resolution.* A traveller *determines* to take a certain route; a learner *resolves* to conquer every difficulty in the acquirement of learning. Humor or change of circumstances occasions a person to alter his *determination;* timidity, fear, or defect in principle occasions the *resolution* to waver. Children are not capable of *determining;* and their best *resolutions* fall before the gratification of the moment.

In matters of knowledge, to *determine* is to fix the mind, or to cause it to rest in a certain opinion; to *resolve* is to lay open what is obscure, to clear the mind from doubt and hesitation. We *determine* points of question; we *resolve* difficulties. It is more difficult to *determine* in matters of rank or precedence than in cases where the solid and real interests of men are concerned; it is the business of the teacher to *resolve* the difficulties which are proposed by the scholar. Every point is not proved which is *determined,* nor is every difficulty *resolved* which is answered.

See also DECIDE; FIX.

DETERMINED. See UNSWERV-ING.

DETEST. See ABHOR; HATE

DETESTABLE. See ABOMINABLE.

DETRACT. See ASPERSE; DISPARAGE.

DETRIMENT. See DISADVANTAGE; LOSS.

DEVASTATE. See SACK.

DEVASTATION. See RAVAGE.

DEVELOP. See UNFOLD.

DEVELOPMENT. See EVOLUTION.

DEVIATE, WANDER, SWERVE, STRAY. *Deviate,* from *devious,* and the Latin *de viâ,* signifies, literally, to run out of the way. *Wander* is a frequentative of *wend* and is connected with Anglo-Saxon *windan,* to wind; it meant originally to keep winding in and out—indicating a purposeless going. For the derivation of *swerve* see DEFLECT. *Stray* comes from Old French *estraier,* to wander out into the streets, from Latin *strata,* street, whence our word *street* is derived.

Deviate always supposes a direct path which is departed from; *wander* includes no such idea. The act of *deviating* is commonly faulty, that of *wandering* is different: they may frequently exchange significations; the former being justifiable by necessity, and the latter arising from an unsteadiness of mind. *Deviate* is mostly used in the moral acceptation; *wander* may be used in either sense. A person *deviates* from any plan or rule laid down; he *wanders* from the subject in which he is engaged. As no rule can be laid down which will not admit of an exception, it is impossible but the wisest will find it necessary in their moral conduct to *deviate* occasionally; yet every wanton *deviation* from an established practice evinces a culpable temper on the part of the *deviator.* Those who *wander* into the regions of metaphysics are in great danger of losing themselves; it is with them as with most *wanderers,* that they spend their time at best but idly.

See also DIGRESS.

DEVIL, DEMON. *Devil,* in Anglo-Saxon *deofal,* French *diable,* etc., is connected with the Greek διάβολος, from διαβάλλειν, to traduce, literally to throw something at another (cf. the slang phrase to "sling mud" for meaning to slander). It signifies properly a calumniator, and is always taken in the bad sense for the spirit which incites to evil and tempts men through the medium of their evil passion. *Demon*, in Latin *dæmon*, Greek δαίμων, a being of divine nature, is taken either in a bad sense or good sense for the power that acts within us and controls our actions. Since the *devil* is represented as the father of all wickedness, associations have been connected with the name that render its pronunciation in familiar discourse offensive to the chastened ear; it is therefore used in the grave style only.

Among Jews and Christians the term *demon* is always taken in a bad sense for an evil spirit generally; but the Greeks and Romans understood by the word *dæmon* any genius or spirit, but particularly the good spirit or guardian angel who was supposed to accompany a man from his birth. Socrates professed to be always under the direction of such a *dæmon*, who is alluded to very much by the ancients in their writings and on their medals; hence it is that in figurative language the word may still be used in a good sense.

In general, the word is taken for an evil spirit, as the *demon* of discord.

DEVISE, BEQUEATH. *Devise*, compounded of *de* and *visus*, participle of *videre*, to see or show, signifies to point out specifically. *Bequeath* comes from Anglo-Saxon *becwethan*, from *cwethan*, to say (whence *quoth*), and means to give over to a person by saying or by word of mouth.

In the technical sense, to *devise* is to give lands by a will duly attested according to law; to *bequeath* is to give personality after one's death by a less formal instrument; whence the term *bequeath* may also be used figuratively, as to *bequeath* one's name to posterity.

DEVOID. See EMPTY.

DEVOTE. See ADDICT: DEDICATE; SANCTIFY.

DEVOTEE. See ENTHUSIAST.

DEVOUT. See HOLY.

DEXTERITY. See ABILITY; KNACK.

DEXTEROUS. See CLEVER.

DIABOLIC, DEVILISH, FIENDISH, SATANIC. These words all mean resembling the devil or the powers of evil, and differ very little in meaning. *Devilish* and *diabolical* both come ultimately from Greek διάβολος, devil, literally slanderer, hater. *Fiendish* comes from Anglo-Saxon *feond*, an enemy, from *feogan*, to hate. *Satanic* comes originally from the Hebrew designation of the "Prince of the Powers of Darkness," which meant "Adversary." All the words signify the highest degree of wickedness and maliciousness, characteristic of the opponent of all good. Though *devilish* and *diabolical* have the same derivation, *devilish* has been so largely and carelessly used in colloquial speech to signify anything unpleasant that it has somewhat lost its force and dignity; *diabolical* expresses more definitely the idea of resemblance to the devil with special reference to malicious skill and ingenuity. *Fiendish* has the same meaning with special emphasis on malignity and cruelty. *Satanic* means characteristic of Satan, the prince of devils, and sometimes has special reference to size and daring in malignant action, or to Satan's distinguishing characteristic of pride. However, the words are really well-nigh interchangeable.

DIALECT. See LANGUAGE.

DIALOGUE. See CONVERSATION.

DIAPHANOUS, CLEAR, PELLUCID, TRANSLUCENT. *Diaphanous*, in French *diaphane*, from the Greek διαφανής, that a compound of διά, through, and φαίνειν, to show, pertains to that which permits light to pass through or has the quality of transmitting light. *Clear* and *pellucid* apply to substances, as air and water, when free from anything that would obstruct a view through them; but *diaphanous* implies a *translucent* quality in distinction from a *transparent* one. A substance is *translucent* that permits rays of light to pass through it without rendering the form or color of objects on the other side distinguishable; hence so nearly opaque that objects are scarcely, if at all, visible through it; while *transparent* applies to a substance that can be seen through clearly or allows light to pass through without diminution. A *diaphanous* substance, therefore, is *translucent* or only partially *transparent*.

Translucency implies that property of

certain minerals, as well as other substances, which permits light to pass through them, but in a subdued degree. *Diaphanous* has been of late especially applied to semi-transparent textures such as lace and chiffon. There is nothing in the history of the word to support such a limitation of its meaning, but this is its most frequent application. A veil is *diaphanous;* a piece of smoked glass for viewing the sun and spectacles worn by people motoring or exposed to strong light are *translucent;* window-glass is *transparent.*

DICTATE, PRESCRIBE. *Dictate,* from the Latin *dictatus* and *dictum,* a word, signifies to make a word for another; and *prescribe* literally signifies to write down for another (see APPOINT), in which sense the former of these terms is used technically for a principal who gets his secretary to write down his words as he utters them; and the latter for a physician who writes down for his patient what he wishes him to take as a remedy.

They are used figuratively for a species of counsel given by a superior; to *dictate* is, however, a greater exercise of authority than to *prescribe.* To *dictate* amounts even to more than to command; it signifies commanding with a tone of unwarrantable authority, or still oftener a species of commanding by those who have no right to command; it is therefore mostly taken in a bad sense. To *prescribe* partakes altogether of the nature of counsel, and nothing of command; it serves as a rule to the person *prescribed,* and is justified by the superior wisdom and knowledge of the person *prescribing;* it is therefore always taken in an indifferent or a good sense. He who *dictates* speaks with an adventitious authority; he who *prescribes* has the sanction of reason. To *dictate* implies an entire subserviency in the person *dictated* to; to *prescribe* carries its own weight with it in the nature of the thing *prescribed.* Upstarts are ready to *dictate* even to their superiors on every occasion that offers; modest people are often fearful of giving advice lest they should be suspected of *prescribing.*

Dictate, Suggestion.—*Dictate* signifies the thing *dictated,* and has an imperative sense, as in the former case. *Suggestion* signifies the thing *suggested,* and conveys the idea of its being proposed secretly or in a gentle manner.

These terms are both applied with this distinction to acts of the mind. When conscience, reason, or passion presents anything forcibly to the mind, it is called a *dictate;* when anything enters the mind in a casual manner, it is called a *suggestion.* The *dictate* is obeyed or yielded to; the *suggestion* is followed or listened to. It is the part of a Christian at all times to obey the *dictates* of reason. He who yields to the *dictates* of passion renounces the character of a rational being. It is the characteristic of a weak mind to follow the *suggestions* of envy.

Dictate is employed only for what passes inwardly; *suggestion* may be used for any action on the mind by external objects. No man will err essentially in the ordinary affairs of life who is guided by the *dictates* of plain sense. It is the lot of sinful mortals to be drawn to evil by the *suggestions* of Satan as well as their own evil inclinations.

DICTION, STYLE, PHRASE, PHRASEOLOGY. *Diction,* from the Latin *dictio,* saying, is put for the mode of expressing ourselves. *Style* comes from the Latin *stylus,* the bodkin with which the Latins wrote and corrected what they had written on their waxen tablets; whence the word has been used for the manner of writing in general. *Phrase,* in Greek φράσις, from φράζειν, to speak; and *phraseology,* from φράσις, and λόγος, both signify the manner of speaking.

Diction expresses much less than *style:* the former is applicable to the first efforts of learners in composition; the latter only to the original productions of a matured mind. Errors in grammar, false construction, a confused disposition of words, or an improper application of them constitutes bad *diction;* but the niceties, the elegancies, the peculiarities, and the beauties of composition which mark the genius and talent of the writer are what is comprehended under the name of *style.* *Diction* is a general term, applicable alike to a single sentence or a connected composition; *style* is used in regard to a regular piece of composition. As *diction* is a term of inferior import, it is of course mostly confined to ordinary subjects, and *style* to the productions of authors. We should speak of a person's *diction* in his private correspondence, but of his *style* in his literary works. *Diction* requires only to be pure and clear; *style* may likewise be terse, polished, elegant, florid, poetic, sober, and the like.

Diction is said mostly in regard to what is written; *phrase* and *phraseology* are said as often of what is spoken as what is written; as that a person has adopted a strange *phrase* or *phraseology*. The former respects single words; the latter comprehends a succession of *phrases*.

DICTIONARY, ENCYCLOPÆDIA. *Dictionary,* Late Latin *dictionarium,* from the Latin *dictum,* a saying or word, is a register of words. *Encyclopædia,* from the Greek ἐγκυκλοπαιδεία, or ἐν, in, κύκλος, a circle, and παιδεία, learning, signifies a book containing the whole circle of knowledge.

The definition of words, with their various changes, modifications, uses, acceptations, and applications, are the proper subjects of a *dictionary;* the nature and properties of things, with their construction, uses, powers, etc., are the proper subjects of an *encyclopædia.* A general acquaintance with all arts and sciences as far as respects the use of technical terms, and a perfect acquaintance with the classical writers in the language, are essential for the composition of a *dictionary;* an entire acquaintance with all the minutiæ of every art and science is requisite for the composition of an *encyclopædia.* A single individual may qualify himself for the task of writing a *dictionary;* but the universality and diversity of knowledge contained in an *encyclopædia* render it necessarily the work of many. The term *dictionary* has been extended in its application to any work alphabetically arranged, as biographical, medical, botanical *dictionaries,* and the like, but still preserving this distinction, that a *dictionary* always contains only a general or partial illustration of the subject proposed, while an *encyclopædia* embraces the whole circuit of science.

Dictionary, Lexicon, Vocabulary, Glossary, Nomenclature.—*Dictionary* is a general term; *lexicon,* from λέγειν, to say; *vocabulary,* from *vox,* a word; *glossary,* from gloss, to explain, from γλῶσσα, the tongue; and *nomenclature,* from *nomen,* are all species of the *dictionary.*

Lexicon is a species of *dictionary* appropriately applied to the dead languages. A Greek or Hebrew lexicon is distinguished from a *dictionary* of the French or English language. A *vocabulary* is a partial kind of *dictionary,* which may comprehend a simple list of words, with or without explanation, arranged in order or otherwise. A *glossary* is an explanatory *vocabulary,* which commonly serves to explain the obsolete terms employed in any old author. A *nomenclature* is literally a list of names, and in particular a reference to proper names.

DIDACTIC, PEDAGOGIC. *Didactic,* in Greek διδακτικός, from διδάσκειν, to teach, cognate with the Latin *doceo,* in French *didactique,* signifies, specifically, whatever pertains to teaching, conveying instruction, or containing precepts or rules. In the plural and substantive form the term implies the science of teaching, the best methods of systematic instruction. *Didactic poetry* is a kind which aims, or seems to aim, at instruction, making pleasure entirely subservient to this. The "Georgics" of Virgil have been the model according to which such poems have generally been composed. *Pedagogic* has in recent years become a more conspicuous term than *didactic,* because of the great advance in educational methods. The term is from the Greek παιδαγωγός, compounded of παῖς, or παιδ-, a child, and ἀγωγός, leading, and originally applied to a slave who led his master's children to school and places of amusement while they were too young to go alone, and, in exceptional instances, such pedagogues acted also as teachers. Latterly the term *pedagogue* came to be used in contempt or ridicule to designate a pedant or a supercilious instructor.

Now *pedagogy,* the science of teaching, has become conspicuous among the learned arts, and has its special colleges with degree-granting privileges, besides the many state and municipal normal schools.

DIE, EXPIRE, PASS OVER. *Die* is a Scandinavian word from a Teutonic base whence *dead, death,* etc., are also derived. *Expire,* from *ex,* out, and *spirare,* to breathe, means giving up the breath of life.

There are beings, such as trees and plants, which are said to live, although they have not breath; these *die,* but do not *expire;* there are other beings which absorb and emit air, but do not live; such as the flame of a lamp which does not *die,* but it *expires.* By a natural metaphor, the time of being is put for the life of objects; and hence we speak of the date *expiring,* the term *expiring,* and the like; and as life is applied figuratively to moral objects, so may death to objects not having physical life.

To *pass over* is the Christian Science equivalent for *to die.*

See also PERISH.

DIET. See ASSEMBLY; FOOD.

DIFFER, VARY, DISAGREE, DISSENT. *Differ,* in Latin *differo,* or *dis,* apart, and *ferre,* to bear, signifies to make into two. *Vary* (see CHANGE). *Disagree* is literally not to *agree.* *Dissent,* in Latin *dissentio,* or *dis* and *sentire,* to think or feel, signifies to think or feel apart or differently.

Differ, vary, and *disagree* are applicable either to persons or things; *dissent* to persons only. First as to persons: to *differ* is the most general and indefinite term, the rest are but modes of *difference:* we may *differ* from any cause, or in any degree, we *vary* only in small matters: thus persons may *differ* or *vary* in their statements. There must be two at least to *differ,* and there may be an indefinite number: one may *vary,* or an indefinite number may *vary;* thus two or more may *differ* in an account which they give; one person may *vary* at different times in the account which he gives. To *differ* may be either in fact or matters of speculation; to *disagree,* mostly in matters of practice or personal interest; to *dissent,* mostly in matters of speculation or opinion. Philosophers may *differ* in accounting for any phenomenon; politicians may *differ* as to the conduct of public affairs; people may *disagree* who have to act together; a person may *dissent* from any opinion which is offered or prescribed.

Differences may occasion discordant feeling or otherwise, according to the nature of the difference. *Differences* in regard to claims or matters of interest are rarely unaccompanied with some asperity. *Disagreements, variances,* and *dissensions* are always accompanied with more or less ill-humor or ill-feeling. *Disagreements* between those who ought to *agree* and to co-operate are mostly occasioned by opposing passions; *variance* is said of whatever disturbs the harmony of those who ought to live in love and harmony. *Dissensions* arise not merely from diversity of opinion, but also from diversity of interest, and always produce much acrimony of feeling. They arise mostly among bodies of men.

In regard to things, *differ* is said of two things with respect to each other; *vary* of one thing in respect to itself: thus two tempers *differ* from each other, and a person's temper *varies* from time to time. Things *differ* in their essences, they *vary* in their accidents; thus the genera and species of things *differ* from each other, and the individuals of each species *vary: differ* is said of everything promiscuously, but *disagree* is only said of such things as might agree; thus two trees *differ* from each other by the course of things, but two numbers *disagree* which are intended to agree.

Difference, Variety, Diversity, Medley.—Difference signifies the cause or the act of differing. *Variety,* from *various* or *vary,* in Latin *varius,* different, signifies a continual difference. *Diversity,* in Latin *diversitas,* comes from *diverto,* compounded of *dis,* apart, and *vertere,* to turn, and signifies to turn asunder. *Medley* has the same derivation as *middle,* for which see *intermeddle* under INTERCEDE.

Difference and *variety* seem to lie in the things themselves; *diversity* and *medley* are created either by accident or design; a *difference* may lie in two objects only; a *variety* cannot exist without an assemblage: a *difference* is discovered by means of a comparison which the mind forms of objects to prevent confusion; *variety* strikes on the mind and pleases the imagination with many agreeable images; it is opposed to dull uniformity: the acute observer traces *differences*, however minute, in the objects of his research, and by this means is enabled to class them under their general or particular heads; nature affords such an infinite *variety* in everything which exists that if we do not perceive it the fault is in ourselves.

Diversity arises from an assemblage of objects naturally contrasted; a *medley* is produced by an assemblage of objects so ill suited as to produce a ludicrous effect. *Diversity* exists in the tastes or opinions of men; a *medley* is produced by the concurrence of such tastes or opinions as can in no wise coalesce. A *diversity* of sounds heard at a suitable distance in the stillness of the evening will have an agreeable effect on the ear; a *medley* of noises, whether heard near or at a distance, must always be harsh and offensive.

Difference, Distinction. — *Difference* lies in the thing; *distinction* is the act of the person: the former is, therefore, to the latter as the cause to the effect; the *distinction* rests on the *difference:* those are equally bad logicians who make a *distinction* without a *difference*, or who make no *distinction* where there is a *difference*.

Sometimes *distinction* is put for the ground of *distinction*, which brings it nearer in sense to *difference*, in which case the former is a species of the latter: a *difference* is either external or internal: a *distinction* is always external, the former lies in the thing, the latter is designedly made: we have *differences* in character and *distinctions* in dress; the *difference* between profession and practice, though very considerable, is often lost sight of by the professors of Christianity; in the sight of God there is no rank or *distinction* that will screen a man from the consequences of unrepented sins.

Difference, Dispute, Altercation, Quarrel.—*Difference* (see DIFFER). *Dispute* (see ARGUE). *Altercation*, in Latin *altercatio*, from *alter*, the other of two people, signifies to dispute in turns, first one speaking and then the other—suggesting also a decided difference of opinion. *Quarrel*, in French *querelle*, from the Latin *queri*, to complain, signifies having a complaint against another.

All these terms are here taken in the general sense of a *difference* on some personal question; the term *difference* is here as general and indefinite as in the former case: a *difference*, as distinguished from the others, is generally of a less serious and personal kind; a *dispute* consists not only of angry words, but much ill blood and unkind offices; an *altercation* is a wordy *dispute*, in which *difference* of opinion is drawn out into a multitude of words on all sides; *quarrel* is the most serious of all *differences*, which leads to every species of violence; a *difference* may sometimes arise from a misunderstanding, which may be easily rectified; *differences* seldom grow to *disputes* but by the fault of both parties; *altercations* arise mostly from pertinacious adherence to, and obstinate defence of, one's opinions; *quarrels* mostly spring from injuries real or supposed: *differences* subsist between men in an individual or public capacity; they may be carried on in a direct or indirect manner; *disputes* and *altercations* are mostly conducted in a direct manner between individuals; *quarrels* may arise between nations or individuals, and be carried on by acts of offence directly or indirectly.

Different, Distinct, Separate.—*Different* (see DIFFER). *Distinct*, in Latin *distinctus*, participle of *distinguo*, and *separate* (see ABSTRACT for both).

Difference is opposed to similitude; there is no *difference* between objects absolutely alike: *distinctness* is opposed to identity; there can be no *distinction* where there is only one and the same being: *separation* is opposed to unity; there can be no *separation* between objects that coalesce or adhere: things may be *different* and not *distinct*, or *distinct* and not *different: different* is said altogether of the internal properties of things; *distinct* is said of things as objects of vision, or as they appear either to the eye or to the mind: when two or more things are seen only as one they may be *different*, but they are not *distinct;* but whatever is seen as two or more things, each complete in itself, is *distinct*, although it may not be *different:* two roads are said to be *different* which run in *different* directions, but they may not be *distinct* when seen on a map: on the other hand, two roads are said to be *distinct* when they are observed as two roads to run in the same direction, but they need not in any particular to be *different:* two stars of *different* magnitudes may, in certain directions, appear as one, in which case they are *different* but not *distinct;* two books on the same subject, and by the same author, but not written in continuation of each other, are *distinct* books, but not *different.*

What is *separate* must in its nature be generally *distinct;* but everything is not *separate* which is *distinct:* when houses are *separate* they are obviously *distinct;* but they may frequently be distinct when they are not positively *separated:* the *distinct* is marked out by some external sign which determines its beginning and its end; the *separate* is that which is set apart and to be seen by itself: *distinct* is a term used only in determining the singularity or plurality of objects; the *separate* only in regard to their proximity to or distance from each other: we speak of having a *distinct* household, but of living in *separate* apartments; of dividing one's subject into *distinct* heads, or of making things into *separate* parcels: the body and soul are *different,* inasmuch as they have *different* properties; they are *distinct,* inasmuch as they have marks by which they may be *distinguished,* and at death they will be *separate.*

Different, Several, Divers, Sundry, Various.—All these terms are employed to mark a number, but *different* is the most indefinite of all these terms, as its office is rather to define the quality than the number, and is equally applicable to few and many; it is opposed to singularity, but the other terms are employed positively to express many. *Several,* from to *sever,* signifies split or made into many; they may be either *different* or alike: there may be *several* different things, or *several* things alike; but we need not say *several* divers things, for the word *divers* signifies properly many *different.* *Sundry,* from Anglo-Saxon adverb *sundor,* apart, signifies many things scattered or at a distance, whether as it regards time or space *Various* expresses not only a greater number, but a greater *diversity* than all the rest.

The same thing often affects *different* persons *differently:* an individual may be affected *several* times in the same way; or particular persons may be affected at *sundry* times and in *divers* manners; the ways in which men are affected are so *various* as not to admit of enumeration; it is not so much to understand *different* languages as to understand *several different* languages; *divers* modes have been suggested and tried for the good education of youth, but most are of too theoretical a nature to admit of being reduced successfully to practice; an incorrect writer omits *sundry* articles that belong to a statement; we need not wonder at the misery which is introduced into families by extravagance and luxury when we notice the infinitely *various* allurements for spending money which are held out to the young and the thoughtless.

Different, Unlike.—*Different* is positive, *unlike* is negative: we look at what is *different,* and draw a comparison; but that which is *unlike* needs no comparison: a thing is said to be *different* from every other thing, or *unlike* to anything seen before; which latter mode of expression obviously conveys less to the mind than the former.

DIFFICULT. See HARD; HERCULEAN; KNOTTY.

DIFFICULTIES, EMBARRASSMENTS, TROUBLES. These terms are all applicable to a person's concerns in life; but *difficulties* relate to the *difficulty* of conducting a business; *embarrassments* relate to the confusion attending a state of debt; and *trouble* to the pain which is the natural consequence of not fulfilling engagements or answering demands. Of the three, the term *difficulties* expresses the least, and that of *troubles* the most. A young man on his entrance into the world will unavoidably experience *difficulties* if not provided with ample means in the outset. But let his means be ever so ample, if he have not prudence and talents fitted for business he will hardly keep himself free from *embarrassments,* which are the greatest *troubles* that can arise to disturb the peace of a man's mind.

Difficulty, Obstacle, Impediment.—

Difficulty, in Latin *difficultas,* and *difficilis,* compounded of the privative *dis* and *facilis,* easy, from *facere,* to do, signifies not easy to be done. *Obstacle,* in Latin *obstaculum,* from *ob,* in the way, and *stare,* to stand, signifies the thing that stands in the way between a person and the object he has in view. *Impediment,* in Latin *impedimentum,* from *impedio,* compounded of *in,* in, and *pedes,* feet, signifies something that entangles the feet.

All these terms include in their signification that which interferes either with the actions or views of men: the *difficulty* lies most in the nature and circumstances of the thing itself; the *obstacle* and *impediment* consist of that which is external or foreign: a *difficulty* interferes with the completion of any work; an *obstacle* interferes with the attainment of any end; an *impediment* interrupts the progress and prevents the execution of one's wishes: a *difficulty* embarrasses, it suspends the powers of acting or deciding; an *obstacle* opposes itself, it is properly met in the way, and intervenes between us and our object; an *impediment* shackles and puts a stop to our proceedings: we speak of encountering a *difficulty,* surmounting an *obstacle,* and removing an *impediment:* the disposition of the mind often occasions more *difficulties* in negotiations than the subjects themselves; the eloquence of Demosthenes was the greatest *obstacle* which Philip of Macedon experienced in his political career; ignorance of the language is the greatest *impediment* which a foreigner experiences in the pursuit of any object out of his own country.

See also OBJECTION.

DIFFIDENCE. See DISTRUST.

DIFFIDENT. See MODEST.

DIFFUSE, PROLIX. Both mark defects of style opposed to brevity. *Diffuse,* in Latin *diffusus,* participle of *diffundere,* to pour out or spread wide, marks the quality of being extended in space. *Prolix* comes from Latin *pro,* beyond, and *liquere,* to flow (whence *liquid, liquor,* etc.), and means flowing beyond bounds, overflowing.

The *diffuse* is properly opposed to the precise; the *prolix* to the concise or laconic. A *diffuse* writer is fond of amplification, he abounds in epithets, tropes, figures, and illustrations; the *prolix* writer is fond of circumlocution, minute details, and trifling particulars. *Diffuseness* is a fault only in degree and according to circumstances; *prolixity* is a positive fault at all times. The former leads to the use of words unnecessarily; the latter to the use of phrases, as well as words, that are altogether useless: the *diffuse* style has too much of repetition: the *prolix* style abounds in tautology. *Diffuseness* often arises from an exuberance of imagination; *prolixity* from the want of imagination; on the other hand, the former may be coupled with great superficiality and the latter with great solidity. Modern writers have fallen into the error of *diffuseness.* Lord Clarendon and many English writers preceding him are chargeable with *prolixity.*

See also SPREAD.

DIGEST. See ABRIDGMENT; DISPOSE.

DIGNIFIED. See MAGISTERIAL.

DIGNITY. See HONOR; PRIDE.

DIGRESS, DEVIATE. Both in the original and the accepted sense, these words express going out of the ordinary course; but *digress* is used only in particular, and *deviate* in general cases. We *digress* only in a narrative, whether written or spoken; we *deviate* in actions as well as in words, in our conduct as well as in writings. *Digress* is mostly taken in a good or indifferent sense, *deviate* in an indifferent or bad sense. Although frequent *digressions* are faulty, yet occasionally it is necessary to *digress* for the purpose of explanation; every *deviation* is bad which is not sanctioned by the necessity of circumstances.

DILATE, EXPAND. *Dilate,* in Latin *dilato,* from *dis,* apart, and *latus,* wide, that is, to make very wide. *Expand,* in Latin *expando,* compounded of *ex* and *pandere,* to spread, to appear or show, signifying to set forth or lay open to view by spreading out.

The idea of drawing anything out so as to occupy a greater space is common to these terms in opposition to contracting. A bladder *dilates* on the admission of air, or the heart *dilates* with joy; knowledge *expands* the mind, or a person's views *expand* with circumstances.

DILATORY. See SLOW.

DILIGENT, EXPEDITIOUS, PROMPT. All these terms mark the quality of quickness in a commendable degree. *Diligent,* from *diligere,* to love, marks the interest one takes in doing something; he is *diligent* who loses no time, who keeps close to the work from inclination. *Expeditious* comes from the Latin *expedio,* from *ex,* out, and *pes, pedis,* foot, which meant originally to get one's foot out, to set off with speed. He who is *expeditious* applies himself to no other thing that offers; he finishes everything in its turn. *Prompt,* from the Latin *promo,* to draw out or make ready, marks one's desire to get ready; he is *prompt* who sets about a thing without delay, so as to make it ready. Idleness, dilatoriness, and slowness are the three defects opposed to these three qualities. The *diligent* man goes to his work willingly, and applies to it assiduously; the *expeditious* man gets it finished quickly; the *prompt* man sets about it readily and gets it finished immediately. It is necessary to be *diligent* in the concerns which belong to us, to be *expeditious* in any business that requires to be terminated, to be *prompt* in the execution of orders that are given to us.

See also ACTIVE; SEDULOUS.

DIM. See DARK.

DIMINISH. See ABATE.

DIMINUTIVE. See LITTLE.

DIOCESE. See BISHOPRIC.

DIP. See DABBLE.

DIPLOMACY. See TACT.

DIRECT, REGULATE, DISPOSE. We *direct* for the instruction of individuals; we *regulate* for the good order or convenience of many.

To *direct* is personal, it supposes authority; to *regulate* is general, it supposes superior information. An officer *directs* the movements of his men in military operations; the steward or master of the ceremonies *regulates* the whole concerns of an entertainment: the *director* is often a man in power; the *regulator* is always the man of business; the latter is frequently employed to act under the former.

To *direct* is always used with regard to others; to *regulate,* frequently with regard to ourselves. One person *di-*

rects another according to his better judgment: he *regulates* his own conduct by principles or circumstances.

But sometimes the word *direct* is taken in the sense of giving a direction to an object, and it is then distinguished from *regulate,* which signifies to determine the measure and other circumstances.

To *dispose,* from Latin *dis,* and French *poser,* for derivation of which see COMPOSE, signifying to put apart for a particular purpose, supposes superior power like *direct,* and superior wisdom like *regulate;* whence the term has been applied to the Almighty, who is styled the Supreme *Disposer* of events, and by the poets to the heathen deities.

See also CONDUCT; STRAIGHT.

Direction, Address, Superscription.— *Direction* marks that which directs. *Address* is that which addresses. *Superscription,* from *super,* above, and *scribere,* to write, signifies that which is written over.

Although these terms may be used promiscuously for one another, yet they have a peculiarity of signification by which their proper use is defined: a *direction* may serve to direct to places as well as to persons: an *address* is never used but in direct application to the person: a *superscription* has more respect to the thing than the person. A *direction* may be written or verbal; an *address* in this sense is always written; a *superscription* must not only be written, but either on or over some other thing: a *direction* is given to such as go in search of persons and places; it ought to be clear and particular: an *address* is put either on a card and a letter or in a book; it ought to be suitable to the station and situation of the person *addressed:* a *superscription* is placed at the head of other writings, or over tombs and pillars; it ought to be appropriate.

Direction, Order. — *Direction* (see DIRECT). *Order* (see COMMAND).

Direction contains most of instruction in it; *order,* most of authority. *Directions* should be followed, *orders* obeyed. It is necessary to direct those who are unable to act for themselves: it is necessary to *order* those whose business it is to execute the *orders*. *Directions* given to servants and children must be clear, simple, and precise; *orders* to tradespeople may be particular or general. *Directions* extend to the moral conduct of others, as well as the ordinary concerns of life; *orders* are confined to the personal convenience of the individual. A parent *directs* a child as to his behavior in company, or as to his conduct when he enters life; a teacher *directs* his pupil in the choice of books, or in the distribution of his studies: the master gives *orders* to his attendants to be in waiting for him at a certain hour; or he gives *orders* to his tradesmen to provide what is necessary.

See also KEY.

Directly, Immediately, Instantly, Instantaneously.—Directly signifies in a *direct* or straight manner. *Immediately* signifies without any medium or intervention. *Instantly* and *instantaneously*, from *instant*, signifies in an instant.

Directly is most applicable to the actions of men; *immediately* and *instantly* to either actions or events. *Directly* refers to the interruptions which may intentionally delay the commencement of any work; *immediately* in general refers to the space of time that intervenes. A diligent person goes *directly* to his work; he suffers nothing to draw him aside: good news is *immediately* spread abroad upon its arrival; nothing intervenes to retard it. *Immediately* and *instantly*, or *instantaneously*, both mark a quick succession of events, but the latter in a much stronger degree than the former. *Immediately* is negative; it expresses simply that nothing intervenes; *instantly* is positive, signifying the very existing moment in which the thing happens. A person who is of a willing disposition goes or runs *immediately* to the assistance of another; but the ardor of affection impels him to fly *instantly* to his relief, as he sees the danger. A surgeon does not proceed *directly* to dress a wound: he first examines it in order to ascertain its nature: men of lively minds *immediately* see the source of their own errors: people of delicate feelings are *instantly* alive to the slightest breach of decorum. A course

of proceeding is *direct*, the consequences are *immediate*, and the effects *instantaneous*.

DIRIGIBLE. See AIRCRAFT.

DIRTY. See SQUALID.

DISABILITY. See INABILITY.

DISADVANTAGE, INJURY, HURT, DETRIMENT, PREJUDICE. *Disadvantage* implies the absence of an *advantage*, which see. *Injury*, in Latin *injuria*, from *in*, not, and *jus, juris*, right, properly signifies what is contrary to right or justice, but extends in its sense to every loss or deficiency which is occasioned. *Hurt*, Middle English *hurten*, from Old French *hurter*, meant to strike or dash against, hence to injure. *Detriment*, in Latin *detrimentum*, from *detritum* and *deterrere*, to wear away, signifies the effect of being worn out. *Prejudice*, in the improper sense of the word (see BIAS), implies the ill which is supposed to result from *prejudice*.

Disadvantage is rather the absence of a good; *injury* is a positive evil: the want of education may frequently be a *disadvantage* to a person by retarding his advancement; the ill word of another may be an *injury* by depriving him of friends. *Disadvantage*, therefore, is applied to such things as are of of an *adventitious* nature: the *injury*, to that which is of essential importance.

Hurt, detriment, and *prejudice* are all species of *injuries*. *Injury*, in general, implies whatever ill befalls an object by the external action of other objects, whether taken in relation to physical or moral evil, to persons or to things; *hurt* is that species of *injury* which is produced by more direct violence; too close an application to study is *injurious* to the health; reading by an improper light is *hurtful* to the eyes; so in a moral sense, the light reading which a circulating library supplies is often *injurious* to the morals of young people; all violent affections are *hurtful* to the mind.

Detriment and *prejudice* are species of *injury* which affect only the outward circumstances of a person or thing, the former implying what may lessen the value of an object, the latter what may lower it in the esteem of others. Whatever affects the stability of a merchant's credit is highly *detrimental* to his interests: whatever is *prejudicial* to the character of a man should not be made the subject of indiscriminate conversation.

DISAFFECTION, DISLOYALTY. *Disaffection* is general: *disloyalty* is particular; it is a species of *disaffection*. Men are *disaffected* to the government, *disloyal* to their prince. *Disaffection* may be said with regard to any form of government; *disloyalty*, only with regard to monarchy. Although both terms are commonly employed in a bad sense, yet the former does not always convey the unfavorable meaning which is attached to the latter. A man may have reasons to think himself justified in *disaffection*, but he will never attempt to offer anything in justification of *disloyalty*. A usurped government will have many *disaffected* subjects with whom it must deal leniently; the best king may have *disloyal* subjects, upon whom he must exercise the rigor of the law. Many were *disaffected* to the usurpation of Oliver Cromwell, because they would not be *disloyal* to their king.

DISAGREE. See DIFFER.

DISAPPEAR, VANISH. To *disappear* signifies not to *appear* (see AIR). *Vanish*, in French *évanouir*, Latin *evaneo* or *evanesco*, compounded of *e* and *vanescere*, to become empty, from *vanus*, empty, signifies to go out of sight.

To *disappear* comprehends no particular mode of action; to *vanish* includes in it the idea of a rapid motion. A thing *disappears* either gradually or suddenly; it *vanishes* on a sudden; it *disappears* in the ordinary course of things; it *vanishes* by an unusual effort, a supernatural or a magic power. Any object that recedes or moves away will soon *disappear*; in fairy tales things are made to *vanish* the instant they are beheld. To *disappear* is often a temporary action; to *vanish* generally conveys the idea of being permanently lost to the sight. The stars *appear* and *disappear* in the firmament; lightning *vanishes* with a rapidity that is unequalled.

DISAPPOINT. See DEFEAT.

DISAPPROBATION. See DISPLEASURE.

DISAPPROVE, DISLIKE. To *disapprove* is not to approve, or to think not good. To *dislike* is not to like, or to find unlike or unsuitable to one's wishes.

Disapprove is an act of the judgment; *dislike* is an act of the will or the affection. To *approve* or *disapprove* is peculiarly the part of a superior, or one who determines the conduct of others; to *dislike* is altogether a personal act, in which the feelings of the individual are consulted. It is a misuse of the judgment to *disapprove* where we need only *dislike;* it is a perversion of the judgment to *disapprove* because we *dislike.*

DISASTER. See CALAMITY.

DISAVOW, DENY, DISOWN. To *disavow*, from *dis* and *avow* (see ACKNOWLEDGE), is to avow that a thing is not: *deny* is to assert that a thing is not: *disown*, from *dis* and *own*, is to assert that a person or thing is not one's own or does not belong to one. A *disavowal* is a general declaration; a *denial* is a particular assertion; the former is made voluntarily and unasked for, the latter is always in direct answer to a charge: we *disavow* in matters of general interest where truth only is concerned; we *deny* in matters of personal interest where the character or feelings are implicated. What is *disavowed* is generally in support of truth; what is *denied* may often be in direct violation of truth: an honest mind will always *disavow* whatever has been erroneously attributed to it; a timid person sometimes *denies* what he knows to be true from a fear of the consequences.

Deny is said of things that concern others as well as ourselves; *disown* only of things in which one is personally concerned or supposed to be so. *Denial* is employed for events or indifferent matters; *disowning* extends to whatever one can own or possess: a person *denies* that there is any truth in the assertion of another; he *disowns* all participation in any affair. Our veracity or judgment is often the only thing implicated in the *denial:* our guilt or innocence, honor or dishonor, is implicated in what we *disown.*

DISAVOWED. See NEUTRAL.

DISBELIEF, UNBELIEF. *Disbelief*

properly implies the *believing* that a thing is not, or refusing to *believe* that it is. *Unbelief* expresses properly a *believing* the contrary of what one has *believed* before: *disbelief* is most applicable to the ordinary events of life; *unbelief* to serious matters of opinion: our *disbelief* of the idle tales which are told by beggars is justified by the frequent detection of their falsehood; our Saviour had compassion on Thomas for his *unbelief*, and gave him such evidences of His identity as dissipated every doubt.

DISCARD. See Dismiss.

DISCERN. See Perceive.

DISCERNMENT, Penetration, Discrimination, Judgment. *Discernment* expresses the power of *discerning* (see Perceive). *Penetration* denotes the act or power of *penetrating*, from *penetrate*, in Latin *penetratus*, participle of *penetrare*, from *penitus*, within, and *penus*, the inner part of a sanctuary, signifying to see into the interior. *Discrimination* denotes the act or power of *discriminating*, from *discriminate*, in Latin *discriminatus*, participle of *discrimino*, to make a difference. *Judgment* denotes the power of *judging*, from *judge*, in Latin *judico*, compounded of *jus*, right, and *dicere*, signifying to pronounce right.

The first three of these terms do not express different powers, but different modes of the same power; namely, the power of seeing intellectually, or exerting the intellectual sight. *Discernment* is not so powerful a mode of intellectual vision as *penetration;* the former is a common faculty, the latter is a higher degree of the same faculty; it is the power of seeing quickly, and seeing in spite of all that intercepts the sight and keeps the object out of view: a man of common *discernment* discerns characters which are not concealed by any particular disguise; a man of *penetration* is not to be deceived by any artifice, however thoroughly cloaked or secured, even from suspicion. *Discernment* and *penetration* serve for the discovery of individual things by their outward marks; *discrimination* is employed in the discovery of differences between two or more objects; the former consists of simple observation, the latter combines also comparison: *dis-*

cernment and *penetration* are great aids toward *discrimination;* he who can *discern* the springs of human action or *penetrate* the views of men will be most fitted for *discriminating* between the characters of different men.

Although *judgment* derives much assistance from the three former operations, it is a totally distinct power: these only discover the things that are acting on external objects by seeing them: the *judgment* is creative; it produces by deduction from that which passes inwardly. *Discernment* and the others are speculative; they are directed to that which is to be known, and are confined to present objects; they serve to discover truth and falsehood, perfections and defects, motives and pretexts: the *judgment* is practical; it is directed to that which is to be done, and extends its views to the future; it marks the relations and connections of things; it foresees their consequences and effects.

Of *discernment*, we say that it is clear; it serves to remove all obscurity and confusion: of *penetration* we say that it is acute; it pierces every veil which falsehood draws before truth, and prevents us from being deceived: of *discrimination* we say that it is nice; it renders our ideas accurate and serves to prevent us from confounding objects; of *judgment* we say that it is solid or sound; it renders the conduct prudent and prevents us from committing mistakes or involving ourselves in embarrassments.

When the question is to estimate the real qualities of either persons or things, we exercise *discernment;* when it is required to lay open that which art or cunning has concealed, we must exercise *penetration;* when the question is to determine the proportions and degrees of qualities in persons or things, we must use *discrimination;* when called upon to take any step or act any part, we must employ *judgment.* *Discernment* is more or less indispensable for every man in private or public stations; he who has the most promiscuous dealings with men has the greatest need of it: *penetration* is of peculiar importance for princes and statesmen: *discrimination* is of great utility for all who have to determine the characters and merits of others: *judgment* is an absolute requisite for all to whom the execution or management of concerns is intrusted.

See also GUMPTION.

DISCHARGE. See DISMISS.

DISCIPLE. See SCHOLAR.

DISCLAIM, DISOWN. *Disclaim* and *disown* are both personal acts respecting the individual who is the agent; to *disclaim* is to throw off a *claim*, as to *disown* (see DISAVOW) is not to admit as one's own; as *claim*, from the Latin *clamo*, signifies to declare with a loud tone what we want as our own; so to *disclaim* is, with an equally loud or positive tone, to give up a *claim:* this is a more positive act than to *disown*, which may be performed by insinuation or by the mere abstaining to own. He who feels himself disgraced by the actions that are done by his nation or his family will be ready to *disclaim* the very name which he bears in common with the offending party; an absurd pride sometimes impels men to *disown* their relationship to those who are beneath them in external rank and condition: an honest mind will *disclaim* all right to praise which it feels not to belong to itself; the fear of ridicule sometimes makes a man *disown* that which would redound to his honor.

DISCLOSE. See PUBLISH; UNCOVER; UNVEIL.

DISCOMPOSE. See ABASH; DISORDER.

DISCONCERT. See ABASH; BAFFLE; DISORDER; SNUB.

DISCONTINUE. See CEASE.

DISCORD, STRIFE. *Discord* comes from Latin *dis*, apart, and the stem *cord*, heart, signifying a lack of harmony between two people; but now it is consciously used as a metaphor in which it derives its signification from the harshness produced in music by the clashing of two strings which do not suit with each other; whence, in the moral sense, the chords of the mind which come into an unsuitable collision produce a *discord. Strife* comes from the word *strive*, to denote the action of *striving*, that is, in any angry manner (see CONTEND); where there is *strife* there must be *discord;* but there may be *discord* without *strife;*

discord consists most in the feeling; *strife* consists most in the outward action. *Discord* evinces itself in various ways; by looks, words, or actions: *strife* displays itself in words or acts of violence. *Discord* is fatal to the happiness of families; *strife* is the greatest enemy to peace between neighbors; *discord* arose between the goddesses on the apple being thrown into the assembly; Homer commences his poem with the *strife* that took place between Agamemnon and Achilles. *Discord* may arise from mere difference of opinion; *strife* is in general occasioned by some matter of personal interest; *discord* in the councils of a nation is the almost certain forerunner of its ruin; the common principles of politeness forbid *strife* among persons of good breeding.

See also DISSENSION.

DISCOURAGE. See DETER.

DISCOURSE. See SPEAK.

DISCOVER, MANIFEST, DECLARE. The idea of making known is conveyed by all these terms; but *discover*, which signifies simply to take off the covering from anything, expresses less than *manifest* (see APPARENT), and that than *declare* (see DECLARE): we *discover* by any means direct or indirect; we *manifest* by unquestionable marks; we *declare* by express words: talents and dispositions *discover* themselves; particular feelings and sentiments *manifest* themselves; facts, opinions, and sentiments are *declared;* children early *discover* a turn for some particular art or science; a person *manifests* his regard for another by unequivocal proofs of kindness; a person of an open disposition is apt to *declare* his sentiments without disguise.

Animals or unconscious agents may be said to *discover*, as things *discover* symptoms of decay; but persons only, or things personified, *manifest* or *declare;* cruelty may be *manifested* by actions; the works of the creation *declare* the wisdom of the Creator.

See also DETECT; FIND; SPY; UNCOVER.

DISCREDIT, DISGRACE, REPROACH, SCANDAL. *Discredit* signifies the loss of *credit; disgrace*, the loss of grace, favor, or esteem; *reproach* stands for the thing that deserves to be *reproached,* and *scandal* comes from *Greek σκάνδαλον*, Latin *scandalum*, a stumbling-block, from the root found in *ascend*, signifying to step or jump. The conduct of men in their various relations with one another may give rise to the unfavorable sentiment which is expressed in common by these terms. Things are said to reflect *discredit* or *disgrace*, or to bring *reproach* or *scandal* on the individual. These terms seem to rise in sense one upon the other: *disgrace* is a stronger term than *discredit*, *reproach* than *disgrace*, and *scandal* than *reproach*.

Discredit interferes with a man's *credit* or respectability; *disgrace* marks him out as an object of unfavorable distinction; *reproach* makes him a subject of *reproachful* conversation; *scandal* makes him an object of offence or even abhorrence. As regularity in hours, regularity in habits or modes of living, regularity in payments, are a *credit* to a family, so is any deviation from this order to its *discredit*: as moral rectitude, kindness, charity, and benevolence serve to insure the good-will and esteem of men, so do instances of unfair dealing, cruelty, inhumanity, and an unfeeling temper tend to the *disgrace* of the offender: as a life of distinguished virtue or particular instances of moral excellence may cause a man to be spoken of in strong terms of commendation, so will flagrant atrocities or a course of immorality cause his name and himself to be the general subject of *reproach*: as the profession of a Christian with a consistent practice is the greatest ornament which a man can put on, so is the profession with an inconsistent practice the greatest deformity that can be witnessed; it is calculated to bring a *scandal* on religion itself in the eyes of those who do not know and feel its intrinsic excellences.

Discredit and *disgrace* are negative qualities, and apply properly to the outward and adventitious circumstances of a person; but *reproach* and *scandal* are something positive and have respect to the moral character. A man may bring *discredit* or *disgrace* upon himself by trivial or indifferent things; but *reproach* or *scandal* follows only the violation of some positive law, moral or divine.

The term *reproach* is also taken for the object of reproach, and *scandal* for the object of scandal.

See also DISGRACE.

DISCRETION. See JUDGMENT.

DISCRIMINATE. See DISTINGUISH.

DISCRIMINATION. See DISCERNMENT.

DISCUSS, EXAMINE. *Discuss*, in Latin *discussus*, participle of *discutio*, from *dis*, apart, and *quatere*, to shake, signifies to shake asunder or to separate thoroughly so as to see the whole composition. *Examine*, in Latin *examino*, comes from *examen*, the middle beam, or thread, by which the poise of the balance is held, because the judgment holds the balance in examining.

The intellectual operation expressed by these terms is applied to objects that cannot be immediately discerned or understood, but they vary both in mode and degree. *Discussion* is altogether carried on by verbal and personal communication; *examination* proceeds by reading, reflection, and observation; we often examine, therefore, by *discussion*, which is properly one mode of *examination*; a *discussion* is always carried on by two or more persons; an *examination* may be carried on by one only: politics are a frequent though not always a pleasant subject of *discussion* in social meetings; complicated questions cannot be too thoroughly *examined*.

DISDAIN. See CONTEMN; HAUGHTINESS.

DISDAINFUL. See CONTEMPTUOUS.

DISEASE. See DISORDER.

DISEASED. See SICK.

DISENGAGE, DISENTANGLE, EXTRICATE. *Disengage* signifies to make free from an *engagement*. *Disentangle* is to get rid of an *entanglement*. *Extricate*, in Latin *extricatus*, from *ex* and *tricæ*, difficulties, impediments. As to *engage* signifies simply to bind, and *entangle* signifies to bind in an involved manner (for derivation and meaning see EMBARRASS), to *disentangle* is naturally applied to matters of greater difficulty and perplexity than to *disengage;* and as the term *extricate* includes the idea of that which would hold fast and keep within a tight involvement, it is employed with respect to matters of the greatest possible embarrassment and intricacy: we may be *disengaged* from an oath; *disentangled* from pecuniary difficulties; *extricated* from a perplexity; it is not right to expect to be *disengaged* from all the duties which attach to men as members of society; he who enters into metaphysical disquisitions must not expect to be soon *disentangled:* when a general has committed himself by coming into too close a contact with a very superior force, he sometimes may be able to *extricate* himself from his awkward situation by his generalship.

DISENTANGLE. See DISENGAGE.

DISFIGURE. See DEFACE.

DISGRACE. See ABASE; DISCREDIT; DISHONOR.

DISGUISE. See CONCEAL.

DISGUST, LOATHING, NAUSEA. *Disgust,* from *dis* and *gustare,* to taste, from Latin *gustus,* the taste, denotes the aversion of the taste to an object. *Loathing* (see ABHOR). *Nausea,* in Latin *nausea,* from the Greek ναῦς, a ship, properly denotes seasickness.

Disgust is less than *loathing,* and that than *nausea.* When applied to sensible objects, we are *disgusted* with dirt; we *loathe* the smell of food if we have a sickly appetite; we *nauseate* medicine; and when applied metaphorically we are *disgusted* with affectation; we *loathe* the endearments of those who are offensive; we *nauseate* all the enjoyments of life after having made an intemperate use of them and discovered their inanity.

See also DISLIKE.

DISHEARTEN. See ABASH; DETER.

DISHONEST, KNAVISH. *Dishonest* marks the contrary to *honest; knavish* marks the likeness to a *knave, from* Anglo-Saxon *cnapa,* a boy, German *knabe,* a boy, a boy-servant; hence some one as mischievous and unreliable as boy-servants were likely to be. *Dishonest* characterizes simply the mode of action; *knavish* characterizes the agent as well as the action: what is *dishonest* violates the established laws of man; what is *knavish*

supposes peculiar art and design in the accomplishment. It is *dishonest* to take anything from another which does not belong to one's self; it is *knavish* to get it by fraud or artifice, or by imposing on the confidence of another. We may prevent *dishonest* practices by ordinary means of security; but we must not trust ourselves in the company of *knavish* people if we do not wish to be overreached.

DISHONOR, DISGRACE, SHAME. *Dishonor* signifies what does away honor. *Disgrace* (see DEGRADE). *Shame* signifies what produces *shame.* *Dishonor* deprives a person of those outward marks of honor which men look for according to their rank and station, or it is the state of being *dishonored* or less thought of and esteemed than one wishes. *Disgrace* deprives a man of the favor and kindness which he has heretofore received from others, or it is the state of being positively cast off by those who have before favored him or by whom he ought to be looked upon with favor. It is the fault of the individual that causes the *disgrace.* *Shame* expresses more than *disgrace;* it is occasioned by direct moral turpitude or that of which one ought to be ashamed. The fear of *dishonor* acts as a laudable stimulus to the discharge of one's duty; the fear of *disgrace* or *shame* serves to prevent the commission of vices or crimes. A soldier feels it a *dishonor* not to be placed at the post of danger, but he is not always sufficiently alive to the *disgrace* of being punished, nor is he deterred from his irregularities by the open *shame* to which he is sometimes put in the presence of his fellow-soldiers.

As epithets they likewise rise in sense and are distinguished by other characteristics: a *dishonorable* action is that which violates the principles of honor; a *disgraceful* action is that which reflects *disgrace;* a *shameful* action is that of which one ought to be fully *ashamed:* it is very *dishonorable* for a man not to keep his word; very *disgraceful* for a gentleman to associate with those who are his inferiors in station and education; very *shameful* for him to use his rank and influence over the lower orders only to mislead them from their duty. The sense of what is *dishonorable* is to the superior what the sense of the *disgraceful* is to the inferior, but the sense of what is *shameful* is independent of rank or station, and forms a part of that moral sense which is inherent in the breast of every rational creature. Whoever, therefore, cherishes in himself a lively sense of what is *dishonorable* or *disgraceful* is tolerably secure of never committing anything that is *shameful*. See also DISGRACE.

DISINCLINATION. See DISLIKE.

DISJOIN. See SEPARATE.

DISJOINT, DISMEMBER. *Disjoint* signifies to separate at the joint. *Dismember* signifies to separate the members.

The terms here spoken of derive their distinct meaning and application from the signification of the words *joint* and *member*. A limb of the body may be *disjointed* if it be so put out of the *joint* that it cannot act; but the body itself is *dismembered* when the different limbs or parts are separated from one another.

So in the metaphorical sense our ideas are said to be *disjointed* when they are so thrown out of their order that they do not fall in with one another: and kingdoms are said to be *dismembered* where any part or parts are separated from the rest.

DISLIKE, DISPLEASURE, DISSATISFACTION, DISTASTE, DISGUST. *Dislike* (see AVERSION). *Displeasure* signifies the opposite to pleasure. *Dissatisfaction* is the opposite to satisfaction. *Distaste* is the opposite to an agreeable taste.

Dislike and *dissatisfaction* denote the feeling or sentiment produced either by persons or things: *displeasure*, that produced by persons only: *distaste* and *disgust*, that produced by things only. In regard to persons, *dislike* is the sentiment of equals and persons unconnected; *displeasure* and *dissatisfaction*, of superiors, or such as stand in some particular relation to one another. Strangers may feel a *dislike* upon seeing each other: parents or masters may feel *displeasure* or *dissatisfaction:* the former sentiment is occasioned by supposed faults in the moral conduct of the child or servant; the latter by supposed defective services. I *dislike* a person for his assumption or loquacity;

I am *displeased* with him for his carelessness, and *dissatisfied* with his labor. *Displeasure* is awakened by whatever is done amiss: *dissatisfaction* is caused by what happens amiss or contrary to our expectation. Accordingly, the word *dissatisfaction* is not confined to persons of a particular rank, but to the nature of the connection which subsists between them. Whoever does not receive what he thinks himself entitled to from another is *dissatisfied*. A servant may be *dissatisfied* with the treatment he meets with from his master; and may be said, therefore, to express *dissatisfaction*, though not *displeasure*.

In regard to things, *dislike* is a casual feeling not arising from any specific cause. A *dissatisfaction* is connected with our desires and expectations: we *dislike* the performance of an actor from one or many causes, or from no apparent cause; but we are *dissatisfied* with his performance if it fall short of what we were led to expect. In order to lessen the number of our *dislikes* we ought to endeavor not to *dislike* without a cause; and in order to lessen our *dissatisfaction* we ought to be moderate in our expectation.

Dislike, distaste, and *disgust* rise on one another in their signification. *Distaste* expresses more than *dislike*, and *disgust* more than *distaste*. *Dislike* is a partial feeling, quickly produced and quickly subsiding; *distaste* is a settled feeling, gradually produced and permanent in its duration: *disgust* is either transitory or otherwise; momentarily or gradually produced, but stronger than either of the two others. Caprice has a great share in our likes and *dislikes: distaste* depends upon the changes to which the constitution physically and mentally is exposed: *disgust* owes its origin to the nature of things and their natural operation on the minds of men. A child likes and *dislikes* his playthings without any apparent cause for the change of sentiment: after a long illness a person will frequently take a *distaste* to the food or the amusements which before afforded him much pleasure: what is indecent or filthy is a natural object of *disgust* to every person whose mind is not depraved. It is good to suppress un-

founded *dislikes;* it is difficult to overcome a strong *distaste;* it is advisable
to divert our attention from objects
calculated to create *disgust.*

See also AVERSION; DISAPPROVE.

Dislike, Disinclination.—Dislike (see
above). *Disinclination* is the reverse of
inclination (see ATTACHMENT). *Dislike*
applies to what one has or does; *disinclination* only to what one does: we
dislike the thing we have, or *dislike* to
do a thing; but we are *disinclined* only
to do a thing. They express a similar
feeling that differs in degree. *Disinclination* is but a small degree of *dislike;
dislike* marks something contrary; *disinclination* does not amount to more
than the absence of an inclination.
None but a disobliging temper has a
dislike to comply with reasonable requests; but the most obliging disposition may have an occasional *disinclination* to comply with a particular request.

DISLOYALTY. See DISAFFECTION.

DISMAL. See DULL.

DISMANTLE. See DEMOLISH.

DISMAY, DAUNT, APPAL. *Dismay*
comes from the Old French participle
form, *dismayé,* of a verb compounded
from Latin *dis,* privative, and Old
High German *magan,* might or power.
Daunt comes from Latin *domare* to
tame, English *tame* being probably
the same word originally. *Appal,*
compounded of the intensive *ad* and
pallere, to grow pale, signifies to make
pale with fear.

The effect of fear on the spirit is
strongly expressed by all these terms;
but *dismay* expresses less than *daunt,*
and this than *appall.* We are *dismayed*
by alarming circumstances; we are
daunted by terrifying; we are *appalled*
by horrid circumstances. A severe defeat will *dismay* so as to lessen the force
of resistance: the fiery glare from the
eyes of a ferocious beast will *daunt* him
who was venturing to approach: the
sight of an apparition will *appall* the
stoutest heart.

DISMEMBER. See DISJOINT

DISMISS, DISCHARGE, DISCARD.
Dismiss, in Latin *dismissus,* participle
of *dimitto,* compounded of *dis,* away,
and *mittere,* to send, signifies to send
away. *Discharge* signifies to release
from a charge. *Discard,* in Spanish

descartar, compounded of *des* and *cartar,*
signifies to lay *cards* out or aside, to cast
them off.

The idea of removing to a distance is
included in all these terms, but with
various collateral circumstances. *Dismiss* is the general term; *discharge* and
discard are modes of dismissing: *dismiss*
is applicable to persons of all stations,
but used more particularly for the
higher orders: *discharge,* on the other
hand, is confined to those in a subordinate station. A clerk is *dismissed;* a menial servant is *discharged;*
an officer is *dismissed;* a soldier is
discharged.

Neither *dismiss* nor *discharge* defines
the motive of the action; they are used
indifferently for that which is voluntary or the contrary: *discard,* on the
contrary, always marks a *dismissal* that
is not agreeable to the party *discarded.*
A person may request to be *dismissed*
or *discharged,* but never to be *discarded.*
The *dismissal* or *discharge* frees a person
from the obligation or necessity of
performing a certain duty; the *dis-
carding* throws him out of a desirable
rank or station.

They are all applied to things in the
moral sense: we are said to *dismiss* our
fears, to *discharge* a duty, and to *discard*
a sentiment from the mind.

DISORDER, DERANGE, DISCON-
CERT, DISCOMPOSE. *Disorder* signifies
to put out of order. *Derange,* from *de*
and *range* or *rank,* signifies to put out
of the rank in which it was placed.
Disconcert, to put out of the concert or
harmony. *Discompose,* to put out of a
state of composure.

All these terms express the idea of
putting out of order; but the latter
three vary as to the mode or object
of the action. The term *disorder* is
used in a perfectly indefinite form, and
might be applied to any object. As
everything may be in order, so may
everything be *disordered;* yet it is
seldom used except in regard to such
things as have been in a natural order.
Derange and *disconcert* are employed
in speaking of such things as have
been put into an artificial order. To
derange is to *disorder* that which has
been systematically arranged or put
in a certain range; and to *disconcert*
is to *disorder* that which has been put

together by concert or contrivance: thus the body may be *disordered;* a man's affairs or papers *deranged;* a scheme *disconcerted.* To *discompose* is a species of *derangement* in regard to trivial matters: thus a tucker, a frill, or a cap may be *discomposed.* The slightest change of diet will *disorder* people of tender constitutions: misfortunes are apt to *derange* the affairs of the most prosperous: the unexpected return of a master to his home *disconcerts* the schemes which have been formed by the domestics: those who are particular as to their appearance are careful not to have any part of their dress *discomposed.*

When applied to the mind, *disorder* and *derange* are said of the intellect; *disconcert* and *discompose* of the ideas or spirits, the former denoting a permanent state, the latter a temporary or transient state. The mind is said to be *disordered* when the faculty of ratiocination is in any degree interrupted; the intellect is said to be *deranged* when it is brought into a positive state of incapacity for action: persons are sometimes *disordered* in their minds for a time by particular occurrences who do not become actually *deranged;* a person is said to be *disconcerted* who suddenly loses his collectedness of thinking: he is said to be *discomposed* who loses his regularity of feeling. A sense of shame is the most apt to *disconcert:* the more irritable the temper the more easily one is *discomposed.*

See also JUMBLE.

Disorder, Disease, Distemper, Malady. —*Disorder* signifies the state of being out of order. *Disease* signifies the state of being ill at ease, from Old French *des,* privative, and *aise,* ease. *Distemper* signifies the state of being out of temper or out of a due temperament. *Malady* is derived from the Latin *male habitus,* badly settled, in a bad condition.

All these terms agree in their application to the state of the animal body. *Disorder* is, as before, the general term, and the other specific. In this general sense *disorder* is altogether indefinite; but in its restricted sense it expresses less than all the rest: it is the mere commencement of a *disease: disease* is also more general than the other terms, for it comprehends every serious and permanent *disorder* in the animal economy, and is therefore of universal application. The *disorder* is slight, partial, and transitory: the *disease* is deep-rooted and permanent. The *disorder* may lie in the extremities: the *disease* lies in the humors and the vital parts. Occasional headaches, colds, and what is merely cutaneous are termed *disorders;* fevers, dropsies, and the like are *diseases.* *Distemper* is used for such particularly as throw the animal frame most completely out of its temper or course, and is consequently applied properly to virulent *disorders,* such as the smallpox. *Malady* has less of a technical sense than the other terms; it refers more to the suffering than to the state of the body. There may be many *maladies* where there is no *disease;* but *diseases* are themselves in general *maladies.* Our *maladies* are frequently born with us, but our *diseases* may come upon us at any time of life. Blindness is in itself a *malady* and may be produced by a *disease* in the eye. Our *disorders* are frequently cured by abstaining from those things which caused them; the whole science of medicine consists in finding out suitable remedies for our *diseases;* our *maladies* may be lessened with patience, although they cannot always be alleviated or removed by art.

The terms *disorder, disease,* and *distemper* may be applied with a similar distinction to the mind as well as the body. The *disorders* are either of a temporary or a permanent nature, but, unless specified to the contrary, are understood to be temporary: *diseases* consist in vicious habits: our *distempers* arise from the violent operations of passion; our *maladies* lie in the injuries which the affections occasion. Any perturbation in the mind is a *disorder:* avarice is a *disease:* melancholy is a *distemper* as far as it throws the mind out of its bias; it is a *malady* as far as it occasions suffering.

DISORDERED. See TOPSY-TURVY.

DISORDERLY. See IRREGULAR.

DISOWN. See DISAVOW; DISCLAIM.

DISPARAGE, DETRACT, TRADUCE, DEPRECIATE, DEGRADE, DECRY. *Dis-*

parage, compounded of *dis* and Late Latin *paraticum,* from *par,* equal, signifies to make a thing unequal or below what it ought to be. *Detract* (see ASPERSE). *Traduce,* from Latin *trans,* across, and *ducere,* to lead, signifies to carry from one to another that which is unfavorable. *Depreciate,* from the Latin *pretium,* a price, signifies to bring down the price. *Degrade* (see ABASE). *Decry* signifies literally to cry down.

The idea of lowering the value of an object is common to all these words, which differ in the circumstances and object of the action. *Disparagement* is the most indefinite in the manner: *detract* and *traduce* are specific in the forms by which an object is lowered: *disparagement* respects the mental endowments and qualifications: *detract* and *traduce* are said of the moral character, the former, however, in a less specific manner than the latter. We *disparage* a man's performance by speaking slightingly of it: we *detract* from the merits of a person by ascribing his success to chance; we *traduce* him by handing about tales that are unfavorable to his reputation: thus authors are apt to *disparage* the writings of their rivals; or a soldier may *detract* from the skill of his commander, or he may *traduce* him by relating scandalous reports.

To *disparage, detract,* and *traduce* can be applied only to persons or that which is personal; *depreciate, degrade,* and *decry,* to whatever is an object of esteem; we *depreciate* and *degrade,* therefore, things as well as persons, and *decry* things: to *depreciate* is, however, not so strong a term as to *degrade,* for the language which is employed to *depreciate* will be mild compared with that used for *degrading:* we may *depreciate* an object by implication or in indirect terms, but harsh and unseemly epithets are employed for *degrading:* thus a man may be said to *depreciate* human nature who does not represent it as capable of its true elevation; he *degrades* it who sinks it below the scale of rationality. We may *depreciate* or *degrade* an individual, a language, and the like; we *decry* measures and principles: the former two are an act of an individual; the latter is properly the act of many. Some men have such

perverted notions that they are always *depreciating* whatever is esteemed excellent in the world: they whose interests have stifled all feelings of humanity have *degraded* the poor Africans in order to justify the enslaving of them: political partisans commonly *decry* the measures of one party in order to exalt those of another.

Disparage, Derogate, Degrade.—Disparage (see above). *Derogate,* in Latin *derogatus,* from *de,* from, away, and *rogare,* to ask, meaning to "ask away," to repeal in part, signifies to take from a thing that which is claimed. *Degrade* (see ABASE).

Disparage is here employed, not as the act of persons, but of things, in which case it is allied to *derogate,* but retains its indefinite and general sense as before: circumstances may *disparage* the performances of a writer, or they may *derogate* from the honors and dignities of an individual: it would be a high *disparagement* to an author to have it known that he had been guilty of plagiarism; it *derogates* from the dignity of a magistrate to take part in popular measures. To *degrade* is here, as in the former case, a much stronger expression than the other two: whatever *disparages* or *derogates* does but take away a part from the value: but whatever *degrades* a thing sinks it many degrees in the estimation of those in whose eyes it is *degraded;* in this manner religion is *degraded* by the low arts of its enthusiastic professors: whatever tends to the *disparagement* of learning or knowledge does injury to the cause of truth; whatever *derogates* from the dignity of a man in any office is apt to *degrade* the office itself.

DISPARITY, INEQUALITY. *Disparity,* from *dis,* negative, and *par,* equal, means to be unequal. *Inequality,* from the Latin *in,* negative, and *æquus,* even, signifies having no regularity.

Disparity applies to two objects which should meet or stand in coalition with each other: *inequality* is applicable to those who are compared with each other: the *disparity* of age, situation, and circumstances is to be considered with regard to persons entering into a matrimonial connection: the *inequality* in the portion of labor which is to be performed by two persons is a ground for the *inequality* of their recompense: there is a great *inequality* in the chance of success where there is a *disparity* of acquirements in rival candidates: the *disparity* between David and Goliath was such as to render the success of the former more strikingly miraculous; the *inequality* in the conditions of men is not attended with a corresponding *inequality* in their happiness.

DISPASSIONATE, COOL. *Dispassionate* is taken negatively, it marks merely the absence of passion; *cool* is taken positively, it marks an entire freedom from passion.

Those who are prone to be passionate must learn to be *dispassionate;* those who are of a *cool* temperament will not suffer their passions to be roused. *Dispassionate* solely respects angry or irritable sentiments; *cool* respects any perturbed feeling: when we meet with an angry disputant it is necessary to be *dispassionate* in order to avoid quarrels; in the moment of danger our safety often depends upon our *coolness.*

DISPEL, DISPERSE. *Dispel,* from the Latin *pellere,* to drive, signifies to drive away. *Disperse* comes from Latin *dis,* apart, and *spargere,* to scatter, and means to scatter in all directions.

Dispel is a more forcible action than to *disperse:* we destroy the existence of a thing by *dispelling* it; we merely destroy the junction or cohesion of a body by *dispersing* it; the sun *dispels* the clouds and darkness; the wind *disperses* the clouds or a surgeon *disperses* a tumor.

DISPENSE, DISTRIBUTE. *Dispense,* from *dis,* asunder, and *pendere,* to weigh, to weigh out money, to bestow, signifies to bestow in different directions; and *distribute,* from the Latin *tribuere,* to assign, signifies the same thing. *Dispense* is an indiscriminate action; *distribute* is a particularizing action: we *dispense* to all; we *distribute* to each individually: nature *dispenses* her gifts bountifully to all the inhabitants of the earth; a parent *distributes* among his children different tokens of his parental tenderness. *Dispense* is an indirect action that has no immediate reference to the receiver;

distribute is a direct and personal action communicated by the giver to the receiver: Providence *dispenses* His favors to those who put a sincere trust in Him; a prince *distributes* marks of his favor and preference among his courtiers.

DISPERSE. See DISPEL; SPREAD.

DISPLAY. See SHOW.

DISPLEASE, OFFEND, VEX. *Displease* (see DISLIKE) naturally marks the contrary of pleasing. *Offend,* from Latin *ob,* against, and *fendere,* to strike, means, literally, to strike against. *Vex,* in Latin *vexo,* is a frequentative of *vehere,* to carry (whence *vehicle),* signifying literally to toss up and down.

These words express the painful sentiment which is felt by the supposed impropriety of another's conduct. *Displease* is not always applied to that which personally concerns ourselves; although *offend* and *vex* have always more or less of what is personal in them: a superior may be *displeased* with one who is under his charge for improper behavior toward persons in general; he will be *offended* with him for disrespectful behavior toward himself or neglect of his interests: circumstances as well as actions serve to *displease;* a supposed intention or design is requisite in order to *offend;* we may be *displeased* with a person or at a thing; one is mostly *offended* with the person; a child may be *displeased* at not having any particular liberty or indulgence granted to him; he may be *offended* with his playfellow for an act of incivility or unkindness.

Displease respects mostly the inward state of feeling; *offend* and *vex* have most regard to the outward cause which provokes the feeling: a humorsome person may be *displeased* without any apparent cause, but a captious person will at least have some avowed trifle for which he is *offended.* *Vex* expresses more than *offend;* it marks, in fact, frequent efforts to *offend,* or the act of *offending* under aggravated circumstances: we often unintentionally *displease* or *offend,* but he who *vexes* has mostly that object in view in so doing: any instance of neglect *displeases;* any marked instance of neglect *offends;* any aggravated instance of neglect *vexes.* The feeling of *displeasure* is more perceptible and vivid than that of *offence,* but it is less durable: the feeling of *vexation* is as transitory as that of *displeasure*, but stronger than either. *Displeasure* and *vexation* betray themselves by an angry word or look; *offence* discovers itself in the whole conduct: our *displeasure* is unjustifiable when it exceeds the measure of another's fault; it is a mark of great weakness to take *offence* at trifles; persons of the greatest irritability are exposed to the most frequent *vexations*.

These terms may all be applied to the acts of unconscious agents on the mind.

As epithets they admit of a similar distinction: it is very *displeasing* to parents not to meet with the most respectful attentions from children when they give them counsel; and such conduct on the part of children is highly *offensive* to God: when we meet with an *offensive* object we do most wisely to turn away from it: when we are troubled with *vexatious* affairs our best and only remedy is patience.

Displeasure, Anger, Disapprobation. —*Displeasure* (see DISLIKE). *Anger* (for derivation see ANGER). *Disapprobation* is the reverse of *approbation* (see ASSENT).

Between *displeasure* and *anger* there is a difference in the degree, the cause, and the consequence of the feeling: *displeasure* is always a softened and gentle feeling; *anger* is always a harsh feeling, and sometimes rises to vehemence and madness. *Displeasure* is always produced by some adequate cause, real or supposed; but *anger* may be provoked by every or any cause, according to the temper of the individual: *displeasure* is mostly satisfied with a simple, verbal expression; but *anger*, unless kept down with great force, always seeks to return evil for evil. *Displeasure* and *disapprobation* are to be compared, inasmuch as they respect the conduct of those who are under the direction of others: *displeasure* is an act of the will, it is an angry sentiment; *disapprobation* is an act of the judgment, it is an opposite opinion: any mark of self-will in a child is calculated to excite *displeasure;* a mistaken choice in matrimony may produce *disapprobation* in the parent.

Displeasure is always produced by
c.e.s.—10

that which is already come to pass; *disapprobation* may be felt upon that which is to take place; a master feels *displeasure* at the carelessness of his servant; a parent expresses his *disapprobation* of his son's proposal to leave his situation; it is sometimes prudent to check our *displeasure*, and mostly prudent to express our *disapprobation;* the former cannot be expressed without inflicting pain; the latter cannot be withheld when required without the danger of misleading.

See also DISLIKE.

DISPOSAL, DISPOSITION. These words derive their different meanings from the verb to *dispose*, to which they owe their common origin. *Disposal* is a personal act; it depends upon the will of the individual: *disposition* is an act of the judgment; it depends upon the nature of the things. The removal of a thing from one's self is involved in a *disposal;* the good order of the things is comprehended in their *disposition*. The *disposal* of property is in the hands of the rightful owner; the success of a battle often depends upon the right *disposition* of an army.

Dispose, Arrange, Digest.—*Dispose*, in French *disposer*, from Latin *dis*, apart, and French *poser*, is derived from Greek παῦσις, a pause, not from Latin *ponere* (see COMPOSE). *Arrange* (see CLASS). *Digest*, in Latin *digestus*, participle of *digero*, or *dis*, apart, and *gerere*, past participle *gestus*, to carry, signifies to gather apart with design.

The idea of a systematic laying apart is common to all, and proper to the word *dispose*. We *dispose* when we *arrange* and *digest;* but we do not always *arrange* and *digest* when we *dispose;* they differ in the circumstances and object of the action. There is less thought employed in *disposing* than in *arranging* and *digesting;* we may *dispose* ordinary matters by simply assigning a place to each; in this manner trees are *disposed* in a row, but we *arrange* and *digest* by an intellectual effort; in the first case by putting those together which ought to go together, and in the latter case by both separating that which is dissimilar and bringing together that which is similar; in this manner books are *arranged* in a library according to their size or their subject; the materials for a literary production are *digested*, or the laws of the land are *digested*. What is not wanted should be neatly *disposed* in a suitable place: nothing contributes so much to beauty and convenience as the *arrangement* of everything according to the way and manner in which they should follow; when writings are involved in great intricacy and confusion, it is difficult to *digest* them.

In an extended and moral application of these words we speak of a person's time, talent, and the like being *disposed* to a good purpose; of a man's ideas being properly *arranged*, and of being *digested* into form. On the *disposition* of a man's time and property will depend in a great measure his success in life; on the *arrangement* of accounts greatly depends his facility in conducting business; on the habit of *digesting* our thoughts depends in a great measure correctness of thinking.

See also DIRECT; PLACE.

Disposition, Temper. — *Disposition,* from *dispose,* signifies here the state of being *disposed.* *Temper,* like *temperament,* from the Latin *temperare,* to temper or manage, signifies the thing modelled or formed.

These terms are both applied to the mind and its bias; but *disposition* respects the whole frame and texture of the mind; *temper* respects only the bias or tone of the feelings.

Disposition is permanent and settled; *temper* may be transitory and fluctuating. The *disposition* comprehends the springs and motives of actions; the *temper* influences the action of the moment: it is possible and not infrequent to have a good *disposition* with a bad *temper,* and *vice versâ.*

A good *disposition* makes a man a useful member of society, but not always a good companion; a good *temper* renders him acceptable to all and peaceable with all, but essentially useful to none: a good *disposition* will go far toward correcting the errors of *temper;* but where there is a bad *disposition* there are no hopes of amendment. The *disposition* is properly said to be natural, the *temper* is rather acquired or formed by circumstances.

If the *temper* be taken for what is natural, it implies either the physical temperament or tnat frame of mind which results from or is influenced by it.

Disposition, Inclination. — *Disposition* in the former section is taken for the general frame of the mind; in the present case for its particular frame. *Inclination* (see ATTACHMENT).

Disposition is more positive than *inclination.* We may always expect a man to do that which he is *disposed* to do; but we cannot always calculate upon his executing that to which he is merely *inclined.* We indulge a *disposition;* we yield to an *inclination.* The *disposition* comprehends the whole state of the mind at the time; an *inclination* is particular, referring always to a particular object. After the performance of a serious duty, no one is expected to be in a *disposition* for laughter or merriment: it is becoming to suppress our *inclination* to laughter in the presence of those who wish to be serious; we should be careful not to enter into controversy with one who shows a *disposition* to be unfriendly. When a young person discovers any *inclination* to study, there are hopes of his improvement.

DISPOSED. See AFFECTED.

DISPROVE. See CONFUTE.

DISPUTE. See ARGUE; BICKER; CONTEND; CONTROVERT; DIFFERENCE.

DISQUISITION. See TOPIC.

DISREGARD, NEGLECT, SLIGHT. *Disregard* signifies properly not to *regard.* *Neglect,* in Latin *neglectus,* participle of *negligo,* is compounded of *nec,* not, and *legare,* to gather or choose out, signifying not to choose, to pay no attention to. *Slight* comes from an Old Low German word which originally meant flat, smooth, and developed in English through a series of meanings, smooth, simple, etc., into the meaning of trivial, unimportant. The verb *slight* means to treat as if of no importance.

We *disregard* the warnings, the words, or opinions of others; we *neglect* their injunctions or their precepts. To *disregard* results from the settled purpose of the mind; to *neglect,* from a temporary forgetfulness or oversight. What is *disregarded* is seen and passed over; what is *neglected* is generally not thought of at the time required. What is *disregarded* does not strike the mind at all; what is *neglected* enters the mind only when it is before the eye: what we *disregard* is not esteemed; what we *neglect* is often esteemed, but not sufficiently to be remembered or practised: a child *disregards* the prudent counsels of a parent; he *neglects* to use the remedies which have been prescribed to him.

Disregard and *neglect* are frequently not personal acts; they respect the thing more than the person; *slight* is altogether an intentional act toward an individual or toward any object which one has heretofore esteemed or ought to esteem.

DISSATISFACTION. See DISLIKE.

DISSATISFYING. See UNSATISFACTORY.

DISSEMBLE. See CONCEAL.

DISSEMINATE. See SPREAD.

DISSENSION, CONTENTION, DISCORD. *Dissension* marks either the act or the state of *dissenting*. *Contention* marks the act of *contending*. *Discord* (see CONTENTION).

A collision of opinions produces *dissension;* a collision of interests produces *contention;* a collision of humors produces *discord*. A love of one's own opinion, combined with a disregard for the opinion of others, gives rise to *dissension;* selfishness is the main cause of *contention,* and an ungoverned temper that of *discord*.

Dissension is peculiar to bodies or communities of men; *contention* is applicable mostly, and *discord* always, to individuals. A Christian temper of conformity to the general will of those with whom one is in connection would do away with *dissension;* a limitation of one's desire to that which is attainable by legitimate means would put a stop to *contention;* a correction of one's impatient and irritable humor would check the progress of *discord*. *Dissension* tends not only to alienate the minds of men from one another, but to dissolve the bonds of society; *contention* is accompanied by anger, ill-will, envy, and many evil passions; *discord* interrupts the progress of the kind affections, and bars all tender intercourse.

DISSENT. See DIFFER.

DISSENTER. See HERETIC.

DISSERTATION. See ESSAY.

DISSIMILAR. See HETEROGENEOUS.

DISSIMULATION. See SIMULATION.

DISSIPATE. See SPEND.

DISSOLUTE. See LOOSE.

DISTANT, FAR, REMOTE. *Distant* is employed as an adjunct or otherwise; *far* is used only as an adverb. We speak of *distant* objects, or objects being *distant;* but we speak of things only as being *far*. *Distant,* in Latin *distans,* compounded of *dis,* apart, and the participle *stans,* standing, from the verb *stare,* to stand, means standing apart, and is employed only for bodies at rest. *Far* comes from a Germanic and ultimately an Aryan root meaning beyond, found in Greek πέραν, beyond; and is employed for bodies either stationary or otherwise; hence we say a thing is *distant,* or it goes, runs, or flies *far*. *Distant* is used to designate great space; *far* only that which is ordinary: astronomers estimate that the sun is ninety-four millions of miles *distant* from the earth; a person lives not very *far* off, or a person is *far* from the spot. *Distant* is used absolutely to express an intervening space. *Remote,* in Latin *remotus,* participle of *removere,* to move back or away, rather expresses the relative idea of being gone out of sight. A person is said to live in a *distant* country, or in a *remote* corner of any country.

They bear a similar analogy in the figurative application; when we speak of a *remote* idea it designates that which is less liable to strike the mind than a *distant* idea. A *distant* relationship between individuals is never altogether lost sight of; when the connection between objects is very *remote* it easily escapes observation.

DISTASTE. See DISLIKE.

DISTEMPER. See DISORDER.

DISTINCT. See CATEGORICAL; DIFFERENT.

DISTINCTION. See DIFFERENCE; FASHION.

DISTINCTLY. See CLEAR.

DISTINGUISH, DISCRIMINATE. To *distinguish* (see ABSTRACT) is the general, to *discriminate* (see DISCERNMENT) is the particular term: the former is an indefinite, the latter a definite action. To *discriminate* is in fact to *distinguish* specifically; hence we speak of a *distinction* as true or false, but of a *discrimination* as nice. We *distinguish* things as to their divisibility or unity; we *discriminate* them as to their inherent properties; we *distinguish* things that are alike or unlike, in order to separate or collect them; we *discriminate* those that are different, for the purpose of separating one from the other: we *distinguish* by means of the senses as well as the understanding; we *discriminate* by the understanding only: we *distinguish* things by their color or we *distinguish* moral objects by their truth or falsehood; we *discriminate* the characters of men or we *discriminate* their merits according to circumstances.

See also ABSTRACT; PERCEIVE; SIGNALIZE.

Distinguish, Conspicuous, Noted, Eminent, Illustrious. — *Distinguished* signifies having a mark of *distinction* by which a thing is to be *distinguished* (see ABSTRACT). *Conspicuous*, in Latin *conspicuus*, from *con*, intensive, and *spicere*, to see, signifies easily to be seen. *Noted* comes from *notus*, known, well known. *Eminent*, in Latin *eminens*, from *emineo*, or *e* and a stem *min*, signifying to project, found in English *prominent*, means projecting out. *Illustrious* is a badly coined word from the root of *lux*, light, meaning full of light, shining out.

The idea of an object having something attached to it to excite notice is common to all these terms. *Distinguished* in its general sense expresses little more than this idea; the rest are but modes of the *distinguished*. A thing is *distinguished* in proportion as it is distinct or separate from others; it is *conspicuous* in proportion as it is easily seen; it is *noted* in proportion as it is widely known. In this sense a rank is *distinguished;* a situation is *conspicuous;* a place is *noted.* Persons are *distinguished* by external marks or by characteristic qualities; persons or things are *conspicuous* mostly from some external mark; persons or things are *noted* mostly by collateral circum-

stances. A man may be *distinguished* by his decorations, or he may be *distinguished* by his manly air, or by his abilities: a person is *conspicuous* by the gaudiness of his dress; a house is *conspicuous* that stands on a hill: a person is *noted* for having performed a wonderful cure; a place is *noted* for its fine waters.

We may be *distinguished* for things good, bad, or indifferent: we may be *conspicuous* for our singularities or that which only attracts vulgar notice: we may be *noted* for that which is bad, and mostly for that which is the subject of vulgar discourse: we can be *eminent* and *illustrious* only for that which is really good and praiseworthy; the former applies, however, mostly to those things which set a man high in the circle of his acquaintance; the latter to that which makes him shine before the world. A man of *distinguished* talent will be apt to excite envy if he be not also *distinguished* for his private virtue: affection is never better pleased than when it can place itself in such a *conspicuous* situation as to draw all eyes upon itself: lovers of fame are sometimes contented to render themselves *noted* for their vices or absurdities: nothing is more gratifying to a man than to render himself *eminent* for his professional skill: it is the lot of but few to be *illustrious*, and those few are very seldom to be envied.

In an extended and moral application these terms may be employed as epithets to heighten the character of an object: valor may be said to be *distinguished*, piety *eminent*, and a name *illustrious*.

DISTORT. See TURN.

DISTORTED. See WRY.

DISTRACTED. See ABSENT.

DISTRESS, ANXIETY, ANGUISH, AGONY. *Distress* (see ADVERSITY). *Anxiety* is allied to Latin *angustus*, narrow, and *angere*, to choke, from a root found also in *anger*. *Agony*, in French *agonie*, Latin *agonia*, Greek ἀγωνία, a struggle, signifies a severe struggle with pain and suffering.

Distress is the pain felt when in a strait from which we see no means of extricating ourselves; *anxiety* is that pain which one feels on the prospect of an evil. *Distress* always depends upon some outward cause; *anxiety* often lies in the imagination. *Distress* is produced by the present but not always immediate evil; *anxiety* respects that which is future; *anguish* arises from the reflection on the evil that is past; *agony* springs from witnessing that which is immediate or before the eye.

Distress is not peculiar to any age; where there is a consciousness of good and evil, pain and pleasure, *distress* will inevitably exist from some circumstance or another. *Anxiety, anguish,* and *agony* belong to riper years: infancy and childhood are deemed the happy periods of human existence because they are exempt from the *anxieties* attendant on every one who has a station to fill and duties to discharge. *Anguish* and *agony* are species of distress, of the severer kind, which spring altogether from the maturity of reflection and the full consciousness of evil. A child is in *distress* when it loses its mother, and the mother is also in *distress* when she misses her child. The station of a parent is, indeed, that which is most productive, not only of *distress*, but of *anxiety, anguish,* and *agony:* the mother has her peculiar *anxieties* for her child while rearing it in its infant state: the father has his *anxiety* for its welfare on its entrance into the world: they both suffer the deepest *anguish* when their child disappoints their dearest hopes by running a career of vice; not unfrequently they are doomed to suffer the *agony* of seeing a child encircled in flames from which he cannot be snatched, or sinking into a watery grave from which he cannot be rescued.

See also AFFLICT.

Distress, Harass, Perplex.—*Distress* (see above). *Harass*, in French *harasser*, is possibly derived from Old French *harer*, to set a dog on, from an Old High German word to call out. *Perplex*, in Latin *perplexus*, participle of *perplector*, compounded of *plectere*, to plait, with the prefix *per*, through, meaning to braid in and out, hence to make something difficult to unravel or to understand.

A person is *distressed* either in his outward circumstances or his feelings; he is *harassed* mentally or corporeally; he is *perplexed* in his understanding more than in his feelings: a deprivation *distresses;* provocations and hostile measures *harass;* stratagems and ambiguous measures *perplex:* a besieged town is *distressed* by the cutting off its resources of water and provisions; the besieged are *harassed* by perpetual attacks; the besiegers are *perplexed* in all their manœuvres and plans by the countermanœuvres and contrivances of their opponents: a tale of woe *distresses;* continual alarms and incessant labor *harass;* unexpected obstacles and inextricable difficulties *perplex.*

DISTRIBUTE, ALLOT, ASSIGN, APPORTION. *Distribute*, in Latin *distributus*, participle of *distribuo*, from *dis*, apart, and *tribuere*, to bestow, signifies to portion out to several. *Allot* (for derivation see ALLOT). *Assign*, in French *assigner*, Latin *assigno*, from *ad*, to, and *signare*, to set a seal to, signifies, by signing or marking, to set out for a particular purpose. *Apportion*, from *ad*, to, and *portio*, a part prepared, signifies to give by way of portion for a particular purpose.

The idea of giving to several is common to these terms; this is the proper signification of *distribute;* but to that of the other terms is annexed some qualification. *Distributing* is always applied to a number of individuals, but *allotting, assigning,* or *apportioning* is the giving either to one or several: a sum of money is *distributed* among a number of poor people; it is *allotted, assigned,* or *apportioned* to a particular individual, or to each individual out of a number. *Distribute* is said properly of that which is divided, or divisible into any number of parts, as bread is *distributed* in loaves, or money is *distributed* in the way of shillings; *allotted* is applied to that which is divisible into lots, and *apportion* to that which is formed into certain proportional parts or portions, as to *allot* land, to give a lot of land; to *apportion* a sum of money—that is, to give it in certain proportions. *Assign* is applied to any distinct whole, not considered either as divided or divisible, as to *assign* a house, place, etc. To *distribute* is to give promiscuously, without reference to the nature of objects or the purpose for which they are given; things may be *distributed* to the worthy or the unworthy, to those who want it or those who do not, at the will of the *distributor* or otherwise. To *allot* is to give according to the lots into which the thing is divided for a given purpose, as to *allot* land to each cottager; to *assign* is to set apart something that is suited to the person or adapted for the object proposed, as a prize is *assigned* to the most meritorious; a house is *assigned* for the reception of the houseless wanderer; to *apportion* is to give in a certain proportion according to a certain rule, as to *apportion* rent to different houses according to their size and value.

So in the figurative or moral application, the goods or ills of life are *distributed* by a wise Providence, but often in ways or for purposes that are hidden from our view.

Particular portions of that which is desirable, or the contrary, is *allotted* to each according to the circumstances of the case.

Offices, duties, properties, and the like are *assigned* according as they really are or are supposed to be suitable.

Labor, happiness, misery, or anything of which only parts can be had, may be *apportioned*.

See also DISPENSE; DIVIDE.

DISTRICT, REGION, TRACT, QUARTER. *District* is derived from the past participle of the verb *distringere*, from *dis*, apart, and *stringere*, to pull. It means to pull asunder, to vex, hence to force or rule; a *district* was a section in which a lord has power to enforce justice. *Region*, in Latin *regio*, from *regere*, to rule, signifies a portion that is within rule. *Tract*, in Latin *tractus*, from *trahere*, to draw, signifies a part drawn out. *Quarter*, from Latin *quartus*, signifies literally a fourth part.

These terms are all applied to portions of country, the former two comprehending divisions marked out on political grounds; the latter a geographical or an indefinite division: *district* is smaller than a *region;* the former refers only to part of a country, the latter frequently applies to a whole country: a *quarter* is indefinite, and may be applied either to a *quarter* of the world or a particular neighborhood: a *tract* is the smallest portion of all, and comprehends frequently no more than

what may fall within the compass of the eye. We consider a *district* only with relation to government; every magistrate acts within a certain *district:* we speak of a *region* when considering the circumstances of climate, or the natural properties which distinguish different parts of the earth; as the *regions* of heat and cold: we speak of the *quarter* simply to designate a point of the compass; as a person lives in a certain *quarter* of the town that is north or south, east or west, etc.; and so also, in an extended application, we say to meet with opposition in an unexpected *quarter:* we speak of a *tract* to designate the land that runs on in a line; as a mountainous *tract*.

DISTRUST, SUSPICION, DIFFIDENCE. *Distrust* signifies not putting trust in (see BELIEF). *Suspicion*, from the Latin *suspicio*, or *sub* and *specere*, signifies looking at askance, or with a *wry* mind. *Diffidence*, from the Latin *diffido* or *disfido*, signifies having no faith.

Distrust is said of either ourselves or others; *suspicion* is said only of others; *diffidence* only of ourselves: to be *distrustful* of a person is to impute no good to him; to be *suspicious* of a person is to impute positive evil to him: he who is *distrustful* of another's honor or prudence will abstain from giving him his confidence; he who is *suspicious* of another's honesty will be cautious to have no dealings with him.

Distrust is a particular state of feeling having a specific object; *suspicion* is an habitual state of feeling, and has indefinite objects.

As regards one's self, a person may *distrust* his own powers for the execution of a particular office, or a *distrust* of himself in company; he has a general *diffidence*, or he is naturally *diffident*.

DISTURB, INTERRUPT. *Disturb* (see COMMOTION). *Interrupt*, from the Latin *inter*, between, and *rumpere*, to break, signifies to break in between so as to stop the progress.

We may be *disturbed* either inwardly or outwardly; we are *interrupted* only outwardly: our minds may be *disturbed* by disquieting reflections, or we may be *disturbed* in our rest or in our business by unseemly noises; but we can be *interrupted* only in our business or pursuits: the *disturbance*, therefore, depends upon the character of the person; what *disturbs* one man will not *disturb* another: an *interruption* is, however, something positive: what *interrupts* one person will *interrupt* another: the smallest noises may *disturb* one who is in bad health; illness or the visits of friends will *interrupt* a person in any of his business.

The same distinction exists between these words when applied to things as to persons: whatever is put out of its order or proper condition is *disturbed;* thus water which is put into motion from a state of rest is *disturbed:* whatever is stopped in the evenness or regularity of its course is *interrupted;* thus water which is turned out of its ordinary channel is *interrupted*.

See also TROUBLE; WORRY.

DISTURBANCE. See COMMOTION.

DITCH. See TRENCH.

DIURNAL. See DAILY.

DIVE. See PLUNGE.

DIVERGE. See DEFLECT.

DIVERS. See DIFFERENT.

DIVERSION. See AMUSEMENT.

DIVERSITY. See DIFFERENCE.

DIVERT. See AMUSE.

DIVERTED. See ABSENT.

DIVIDE, SEPARATE, PART. *Divide* comes from Latin *dis,* apart, and a lost verb meaning to separate. *Separate* (see ABSTRACT). *Part* signifies to make into *parts*.

That is said to be *divided* which has been or is conceived to be a whole, that is *separated* which might be joined: an army may be *divided* into two or three divisions or portions: the *divisions* are frequently *separated* in their march. Things may be *divided* by anything which distinguishes the parts from one another; they are *separated* by disjunction of space only.

Things may be mentally divided, but they are separated only corporeally: the minds of men are often most *divided* when in person they are least *separated*.

To *part* has an intermediate sense between *divide* and *separate; to divide* is properly to make any whole into two *parts; to part* is to destroy the cohesion of two or more wholes when joined together: a loaf is *divided* when it is cut into two or more pieces; two loaves are *parted*. Sometimes things are both *divided* and *parted* in order to be distributed; in this case the distinction is the same; solid things, or what is in a mass, is *divided;* but things which do not lose their integrity are *parted:* an estate is *divided;* goods or effects are *parted*.

As disjunction is the common idea attached to both *separate* and *part,* they are frequently used in relation to the same objects; things are mostly said to be *parted* which are made to be apart for any temporary purpose or by any means, however slight or trivial; thus rooms may be *parted* by a partition; that is said to be *separated* which is intended to be kept permanently separate, or which ought not to be joined; thus fields are *separated* by hedges.

With regard to persons, *part* designates the actual leaving of the person; *separate* is used in general for that which lessens the society; the former is often casual, temporary, or partial; the latter is positive and serious; the *parting* is momentary; the *separation* may be longer or shorter: two friends *part* in the streets after a casual meeting; two persons *separate* on the road who had set out to travel together; men and their wives often *part* without coming to a positive *separation:* some couples are *separated* from each other in every respect but that of being directly *parted;* the moment of *parting* between friends is often more painful than the *separation* which afterward ensues.

Divide, Distribute, Share. — *Divide* (see above). *Distribute,* in Latin *distributus,* from *distribuere,* or *dis* and *tribuere,* signifies to bestow apart. *Share,* allied to the word *shear,* and the German *scheeren,* signified originally to cut.

The act of *dividing* does not extend beyond the thing *divided;* that of *distributing* and *sharing* comprehends also the purpose of the action: we *divide* the thing; we *distribute* to the person: we may *divide,* therefore, without *distributing;* or we may *divide* in order to *distribute:* thus we *divide* our land into distinct fields for our private convenience; or we *divide* a sum of money into so many parts, in order to *distribute* it among a given number of persons: on the other hand, we may *distribute* without *dividing;* for money, books, fruit, and many other things may be *distributed* which require no *division.*

To *share* is to make into parts, the same as *divide,* and it is to give those parts to some persons, the same as *distribute;* but the person who *shares* takes a part himself; he who *distributes* gives it all to others; a loaf is *divided* in order to be eaten, bread is *distributed* in loaves among the poor; the loaf is *shared* by a poor man with his poorer neighbor, or the profits of a business are *shared* by the partners.

To *share* may imply either to give or to receive; to *distribute* implies giving only: we *share* our own with another, or another *shares* what we have; but we *distribute* our own to others.

DIVINE. See ECCLESIASTIC; GODLIKE; GUESS; HOLY.

DIVINITY. See DEITY.

DIVISION. See PART.

DIVORCE, SEPARATION. *Divorce,* in French the same form, from the Latin *divortium,* compounded of *dis,* apart, and *vertere,* to turn, means the legal dissolution of the marriage contract, with a complete severance of all mutual claims and the right to remarry. A *separation,* often called a *legal separation* or a *judicial separation,* is a separation countenanced or required by a court of law, but not implying a complete severance of the marriage tie or the right to remarry. *Divorce* is often used, in a figurative sense, to refer to any disunion of things which have been closely united, and *separation,* of course, has also a wider application. See SEPARATE.

DIVULGE. See PUBLISH.

DO. See ACT.

DOCILE, TRACTABLE, DUCTILE. *Docile,* in Latin *docilis,* from *docere,* to teach, means ready to be taught. *Tractable,* from *tractare,* the frequentative of *trahere,* to draw, denotes the readiness to be drawn. One is *docile* as a scholar; one is *tractable* as a child or a servant. Where anything is to be learned, *docility* is necessary; where anything is to be done at the call of another, *tractability* is required. *Duc-*

tility, from *duco,* to lead, signifies aptness to be led, and is applied to the mind or its powers, which yield readily to impressions.

Animals may be said to be *docile* and *tractable* with a like distinction; inanimate objects, as metals, etc., may be *ductile.*

DOCTRINE, PRECEPT, PRINCIPLE. *Doctrine,* in French *doctrine,* Latin *doctrina,* from *docere,* to teach, signifies the thing taught; *precept,* from the Latin *præ,* before, and *capere,* to take, signifies the thing placed before one as a guide to conduct. *Principle* comes from French *principe,* Latin *principium,* the beginning of things, their first or original component parts.

A *doctrine* requires a teacher; a *precept* requires a superior with authority; a *principle* requires only a maintainer or holder. A *doctrine* is always framed by some one; a *precept* is enjoined or laid down by some one; a *principle* lies in the thing itself. A *doctrine* is composed of *principles;* a *precept* rests upon *principles* or *doctrines.* Pythagoras taught the *doctrine* of metempsychosis, and enjoined many *precepts* on his disciples for the regulation of their conduct, particularly that they should abstain from eating animal food and be only silent hearers for the first five years of their scholarship: the former of these rules depended upon the preceding *doctrine* of the soul's transmigration to the bodies of animals; the latter rested on that simple *principle* of education, the entire devotion of the scholar to the master. We are said to believe in *doctrines,* to obey *precepts,* to imbibe or hold *principles.* *Doctrine* is that which constitutes our faith; *precepts* are that which directs the practice: both are the subjects of rational assent, and suited only to the matured understanding: *principles* are often admitted without examination, and imbibed as frequently from observation and circumstances as from any direct personal efforts; children as well as men acquire *principles.*

Doctrine, Dogma, Tenet.—A *doctrine* originates with an individual. *Dogma,* from the Greek δόγμα, and δοκέω, think, signifies something thought, admitted, or taken for granted; this lies with a body or number of individuals. *Tenet*, from the Latin *tenet*, he holds, signifies the thing held or maintained, and is a species of principle specifically maintained in matters of opinion by persons in general. A *doctrine* rests on the authority of the individual by whom it is framed; the *dogma*, on the authority of the body by whom it is maintained; a *tenet* rests on its own intrinsic merits. Many of the *doctrines* of our blessed Saviour are held by faith in him; they are subjects of persuasion by the exercise of our rational powers; the *dogmas* of the Romish Church are admitted by none but such as admit its authority: every sect has its peculiar *tenets*.

DOGMA. See DOCTRINE.

DOGMATICAL. See CONFIDENT; ORACULAR.

DOLEFUL. See PITEOUS.

DOMESTIC. See SERVANT.

DOMICILE, HABITATION, HOME, HOUSE, RESIDENCE. These words all signify a dwelling-place, but they differ in their application and in the dignity of their usage. *Domicile*, from Latin *domus*, home, is the Latin term corresponding to the native English *home*, Anglo-Saxon *ham*. *Home* is the familiar and homely word, carrying with it all the emotional and imaginative connotations of the intimate communal life of those bound together by ties of birth and affection. *Domicile* is the corresponding intellectual and "learned" word, meaning more than the mere externals of *home* indicated in *habitation* or *residence*, for instance, but emptied of all emotional content, and sometimes employed, like many Latin words in English, with a slightly humorous assumption of dignity. *Domicile* is also used as a verb meaning "to make one's self at home." *Habitation*, from Latin *habitare*, a frequentative of *habere*, to have, means simply a dwelling-place. *House* also signifies a dwelling-place, but it is a more specific term than *habitation*, indicating a certain kind of permanent shelter, built for warmth and comfort. A *house* is a *habitation;* but a *habitation* is not necessarily a *house*. Tents, dug-outs, caves, etc., may be *habitations*. Many people have a sentimental habit of substituting *home* for the word *house*, when they mean merely the

structure that may contain a *home*. "We have bought a new *home*," they say, meaning merely that they have bought a new *house* to contain the old *home*. A *house* is the outside shell of a *home*. *Residence* is used to indicate a *house* of some pretension and stateliness. We speak of a spacious *residence*, a handsome *residence*, etc. It may also be extended to refer simply in a general way to one's dwelling-place, as when we speak of *residence* in the city, etc., not referring to any specific habitation, but merely the general idea of living or dwelling.

DOMINEERING. See IMPERIOUS.

DOMINION. See EMPIRE; POWER; TERRITORY.

DONATION. See BENEFACTION; GIFT.

DOOM. See DESTINY; SENTENCE.

DOUBT, QUESTION. *Doubt*, in French *douter*, Latin *dubito*, from *duo*, two, and *ire*, past participle *itus*, to go, signifies a state in which the mind is going in two directions, as it were, or does not know which direction to take. *Question*, in Latin *quæstio*, from *quærere*, to inquire, signifies to make a question.

Both these terms express the act of the mind in staying its decision. *Doubt* lies altogether in the mind; it is a less active feeling than *question:* by the former we merely suspend decision; by the latter we actually demand proofs in order to assist us in deciding. We may *doubt* in silence: we cannot *question* without expressing it, directly or indirectly. He who suggests *doubts* does it with caution: he who makes a *question* throws in difficulties with a degree of confidence. *Doubts* insinuate themselves on the part of the *doubter; questions* are always made with an express design. We *doubt* in matters of general interest, on abstruse as well as common subjects: we *question* mostly in ordinary matters that are of a personal interest: we *doubt* the truth of a position; we *question* the veracity of an author. When the practicability of any plan is *questioned*, it is unnecessary to enter any further into its merits.

The *doubt* is frequently confined to the individual; the *question* frequently respects others. We *doubt* whether we shall be able to succeed; we *question* another's right to interfere: we *doubt* whether a thing will answer the end proposed; we *question* the utility of any one making the attempt. There are many *doubtful* cases in medicine, where the physician is at a loss to decide; there are many *questionable* measures proposed by those who are in or out of power which demand consideration. A disposition to *doubt* everything is more inimical to the cause of truth than the readiness to believe everything; a disposition to *question* whatever is said or done by others is much more calculated to give offence than to prevent deception.

See also DEMUR.

Doubt, Suspense. — *Doubt* respects that which we should believe; *suspense* that which we wish to know or ascertain. We are in *doubt* for the want of evidence; we are in *suspense* for the want of certainty. *Doubt* interrupts our progress in the attainment of truth; *suspense* impedes us in the attainment of our objects: the former is connected principally with the understanding; the latter acts altogether upon the hopes. We have our *doubts* about things that have no regard to time; we are in *suspense* about what is to happen in the future. Those are the least inclined to *doubt* who have the most thorough knowledge of a subject; those are the least exposed to the unpleasant feeling of *suspense* who confine their wishes to the present.

See also QUANDARY.

Doubtful, Dubious, Uncertain, Precarious.—The *doubtful* admits of *doubt;* the *dubious* creates doubt or suspense. The *doubtful* is said of things in which we are required to have an opinion; the *dubious* respects events and things that must speak for themselves. In *doubtful* cases it is advisable for a judge to lean to the side of mercy; while the issue of a contest is *dubious*, all judgment of the parties, or of the case, must be carefully avoided.

Doubtful and *dubious* have always a relation to the person forming the opinion on the subject in question; *uncertain* and *precarious* are epithets which designate the qualities of the things themselves. Whatever is *uncertain* may from that very circum-

stance be *doubtful* or *dubious* to those who attempt to determine upon them; but they may be designated for their *uncertainty*, without any regard to the opinions which they may give rise to. A person's coming may be *doubtful* or *uncertain*, the length of his stay is oftener described as *uncertain* than as *doubtful*. The *doubtful* is opposed to that on which we form a positive conclusion, the *uncertain* to that which is definite or prescribed. The efficacy of any medicine is *doubtful;* the manner of its operation may be *uncertain*. While our knowledge is limited, we must expect to meet with many things that are *doubtful;* as everything in the world is exposed to change, and all that is future is entirely above our control, we must naturally expect to find everything *uncertain* but what we see passing before us.

Precarious, from the Latin *precarius*, and *precare*, to pray, signifies granted to entreaty, depending on the will or humor of another, whence it is applicable to whatever is obtained from others. *Precarious* is the highest species of *uncertainty*, applied to such things as depend on future casualties in opposition to that which is fixed and determined by design. The weather is *uncertain;* the subsistence of a person who has no stated income or source of living must be *precarious*. It is *uncertain* what day a thing may take place until it is determined; there is nothing more *precarious* than what depends upon the favors of princes.

DOWNFALL. See FALL.

DOZE. See SLEEP.

DRAIN. See SPEND.

DRAMATIC. See THEATRICAL.

DRAW, DRAG, HAUL or HALE, PULL, PLUCK, TUG. *Draw* comes from Anglo-Saxon *dragan,* German *tragen,* to draw, and *drag* is the Scandinavian form of the same word. *Haul* or *hale* comes through French from an Old High German word signifying to require or get. *Pull* comes from Anglo-Saxon *pullian,* to pull or pluck. *Pluck* is a Teutonic word which may possibly be borrowed from Late Latin *piluccare,* Italian *piluccare,* from *pilus,* hair (English *pile*), meaning to pluck out hairs. *Tug* is a Scandinavian word; compare Icelandic *tog,* a rope to pull by.

Draw expresses here the idea common to the first three terms, namely, of putting a body in motion from behind one's self or toward one's self; to *drag* is to *draw* a thing with violence, or to *draw* that which makes resistance; to *haul* is to *drag* it with still greater violence. We *draw* a cart; we *drag* a body along the ground; or *haul* a vessel to the shore. To *pull* signifies only an effort to *draw* without the idea of motion: horses *pull* very long sometimes before they can *draw* a heavily laden cart uphill. To *pluck* is to *pull* with a sudden twitch, in order to separate; thus feathers are *plucked* from animals. To *tug* is to *pull* with violence; thus men *tug* at the oar.

In the moral application of the words we may be said to be *drawn* by anything which can act on the mind to bring us near to an object; we are *dragged* only by means of force; we *pull* a thing toward us by a direct effort. To *haul*, *pluck*, and *tug* are seldom used but in physical application.

DREAD. See APPREHEND; AWE.

DREADFUL. See FEARFUL; FORMIDABLE.

DREAM, REVERY. *Dream* is a word of uncertain origin apparently unrelated to the Anglo-Saxon *dream*, which meant joy, and allied to Old Norse *drauge*, a ghost, the radical meaning being a deceptive appearance, an illusion. Compare German *trügen*, to deceive. *Revery*, in French *rêverie*, like the English *rave* and the Latin *rabies*, madness, originally signified something wandering or incoherent.

Dreams and *reveries* are alike opposed to the reality, and have their origin in the imagination; but the former commonly passes in sleep, and the latter when awake; the *dream* may and does commonly arise when the imagination is in a sound state; the *revery* is the fruit of a heated imagination: *dreams* come in the course of nature; *reveries* are the consequence of a peculiar ferment.

When the term *dream* is applied to the act of one that is awake it admits of another distinction from *revery*. They both designate what is confounded, but the *dream* is less extravagant than the *revery*. Ambitious men please themselves with *dreams* of future greatness; enthusiasts debase the purity of the Christian religion by blending their own wild *reveries* with the doctrines of the Gospel. He who indulges himself in idle *dreams* lays up a store of disappointment for himself when he recovers his recollection, and finds that it is nothing but a *dream:* a love of singularity operating on an ardent mind will too often lead men to indulge in strange *reveries*.

DREGS, SEDIMENT, DROSS, SCUM, REFUSE. *Dregs* is a Scandinavian word; it is the plural form of a word which in Middle English means mire. *Sediment*, from *sedere*, to sit, signifies that which settles at the bottom. *Dross* is a Germanic word; compare German *drusen*, meaning husks of grapes. *Scum* comes from a Scandinavian word meaning froth or foam, and referred especially to the *scum* thrown off from metals in the process of melting. *Refuse* comes from Latin *re*, away, and *fundere*, to pour, signifying that which is poured out, thrown away.

All these terms designate the worthless part of any body; but *dregs* is taken in a worse sense than *sediment*, for the *dregs* is that which is altogether of no value; but the *sediment* may sometimes form a necessary part of the body. The *dregs* are mostly a *sediment* in liquors, but many things are a *sediment* which are not *dregs*. After the *dregs* are taken away, there will frequently remain a *sediment;* the *dregs* are commonly the corrupt part which separates from compound liquids, as wine or beer; the *sediment* consists of the heavy particles which belong to all simple liquids, not excepting water itself. The *dregs* and *sediment* separate of themselves, but the *scum* and *dross* are forced out by a process; the former from liquids, and the latter from solid bodies rendered liquid or otherwise. *Dross* is applied to solid bodies in the same sense as *scum*, being that which remains after the purifying, as the *dross* of corn after threshing and cleaning. *Refuse*, as its derivation implies, is always said of that which is intentionally separated to be thrown away, and agrees with the former terms only inasmuch as they express what is worthless. With this distinction they are figuratively applied to moral objects.

DRENCH. See SOAK.

DRIFT. See TENDENCY; TENOR.

DROLL. See FARCICAL; LAUGHABLE.

DROOP. See FALL.

DROSS. See DREGS.

DROWSE. See SLEEP.

DRUDGE. See SERVANT.

DRUMMER, COMMERCIAL-TRAVELLER, SALESMAN, SOLICITOR. *Drummer* is a pure Americanism, supposed to have been derived from the old custom of having a man beat a drum to attract people to a circus, fair, show, recruiting-place, and the like, and signifies, literally one who drums up or summons people for a special purpose. Its general application is to a person employed by a manufacturer or merchant to solicit or "drum up trade," to secure new customers, to open up new lines of business. The professional *drummer* is not regarded in the same light as a *salesman*. The latter may be a graduated *drummer*, but his business is more particularly to keep in touch with the customers he has secured for his employer, ascertain the condition or amount of their stock of commodities he is interested in, and make such sales as he can.

The *commercial - traveller* and the *salesman* are quite similar in quality, but with this difference: the former travels extensively and at regular seasons to meet his customers at their places of business, and the latter usually remains at the home house to meet the customers from other cities who come to his house for purchases, though he, too, may travel. Again, a *salesman* may be an ordinary employee in a retail store who waits on and sells to ordinary patrons. The *drummer* and *solicitor* are also quite similar in quality, as both seek orders for goods from any one likely to buy, whether regular customers or strangers.

DUBIOUS. See DOUBTFUL.

DUCTILE. See DOCILE.

DULL, GLOOMY, SAD, DISMAL. *Dull* comes from Anglo-Saxon *dol*, foolish, German *toll*, mad. *Gloomy* is in Middle English *gloumen*, to lower, and is allied to Norwegian *glyma*, an overcast sky;

compare the adjective *glum*. *Sad*, Anglo-Saxon *sæd*, meant originally *sated;* hence tired, dispirited, grieved. *Dismal* comes from Latin *diesmali*, bad days, unlucky days.

When applied to natural objects, *dull* and *gloomy* denote the want of necessary light or life: in this sense metals are more or less *dull* according as they are stained with dirt: the weather is either *dull* or *gloomy* in different degrees, that is, *dull* when the sun is obscured by clouds, and *gloomy* when the atmosphere is darkened by fogs or thick clouds. *Dismal* denotes not merely the want of that which is necessary, but also the presence of that which is repugnant to the senses; as a glare of light or a sound may be *dismal*. A room is *dull, gloomy*, or *dismal*, according to circumstances: it is *dull* if the usual quantity of light and sound be wanting; it is *gloomy* if the darkness and stillness be very considerable; it is *dismal* if it have only light enough to show its wretchedness; in this sense a dungeon is a *dismal* abode. *Sad* is not applied so much to sensible as to moral objects, in which sense the distressing events of human life, as the loss of a parent or a child, is justly denominated *sad*.

In regard to the frame of mind which is designated by these terms, it will be easily perceived from the above explanation. As slight circumstances produce *dulness*, any change, however small, in the usual flow of spirits may be termed *dull*. *Gloom* weighs heavy on the mind, and gives a turn to the reflections and the imagination: desponding thoughts of futurity will spread a *gloom* over every other object. *Sad* indicates a wounded state of the heart, feelings of unmixed pain.

See also OBTUSE; STUPID.

DUMB. See SILENT.

DUNCE. See NINNY.

DUPLICITY. See DECEIT.

DURABLE, LASTING, PERMANENT. *Durable* is said of things that are intended to remain a shorter time than that which is *lasting;* and *permanent* expresses less than *durable*. *Durable*, from the Latin *durus*, hard, respects the texture of bodies and marks their capacity to hold out. *Lasting* is the participle of the verb *last* from the

Anglo-Saxon *læstan,* to observe, perform, originally to follow in the track of, from *last,* a foot-track (found in the shoemaker's term—*last* of a shoe). It is applicable to that which is of the longest duration. *Permanent,* from the Latin *per,* through, and *manere,* to remain, signifies remaining to the end.

Durable is naturally said of material substances, and *lasting* of those which are spiritual, although in ordinary discourse sometimes they exchange offices: *permanent* applies more to the affairs of men. That which perishes quickly is not *durable;* that which ceases quickly is not *lasting;* that which is only for a time is not *permanent.* Stone is more *durable* than iron, and iron than wood: in the feudal times animosities between families used to be *lasting;* a clerk has not a *permanent* situation in an office.

Durable, Constant. — *Durability* lies in the thing. *Constancy* lies in the person. What is *durable* is so from its inherent property; what is *constant* is so by the power of the mind. No *durable* connections can be formed where avarice or lust prevails.

DURATION, TIME. In the philosophical sense, according to Locke, *time* is that mode of *duration* which is formed in the mind by its own power of observing and measuring the passing objects. In the vulgar sense, in which *duration* is synonymous with *time,* it stands for the time of *duration,* and is more particularly applicable to the objects which are said to last; *time* being employed in general for whatever passes in the world.

Duration comprehends the beginning and end of any portion of *time,* that is, the how long of a thing; *time* is employed more frequently for the particular portion itself, namely, the *time* when: we mark the *duration* of a sound from the *time* of its commencement to the *time* that it ceases; the *duration* of a prince's reign is an object of particular concern to his subjects if he be either very good or the reverse; the *time* in which he reigns is marked by extraordinary events: the historian computes the *duration* of reigns and of events in order to determine the antiquity of a nation; he fixes the exact *time* when each person begins to reign and when he dies, in order to determine the number of years that each reigned.

See also CONTINUANCE.

DUTIABLE. See ETHICAL.

DUTIFUL, OBEDIENT, RESPECTFUL. *Dutiful* signifies full of a sense of duty or full of what belongs to duty. *Obedient* signifies ready to obey. *Respectful* signifies literally full of respect.

The *obedient* and *respectful* are but modes of the *dutiful:* we may be *dutiful* without being either *obedient* or *respectful;* but we are so far *dutiful* as we are either *obedient* or *respectful.* *Duty* denotes what is due from one being to another: it is independent of all circumstances: *obedience* and *respect* are relative *duties* depending upon the character and station of individuals: as we owe to no one so much as to our parents, we are said to be *dutiful* to no earthly being besides; and in order to deserve the name of *dutiful* a child, during the period of his childhood, ought to make a parent's will to be his law, and at no future period ought that will ever to be an object of indifference: we may be *obedient* and *respectful* to others besides our parents, although to them *obedience* and *respect* are in the highest degree and in the first case due; yet servants are enjoined to be *obedient* to their masters, wives to their husbands, and subjects to their king. *Respectful* is a term of still greater latitude than either; for as the characters of men as much as their stations demand *respect,* there is a *respectful* deportment due toward every superior.

Duty, Obligation.—*Duty,* as we see in the preceding section, consists altogether of what is right or due from one being to another. *Obligation,* from the Latin *obligo,* to bind, signifies the bond or necessity which lies in the thing.

All *duty* depends upon moral *obligation* which subsists between man and man or man and his Maker; in this abstract sense, therefore, there can be no *duty* without a previous *obligation,* and where there is an *obligation* it involves a *duty;* but in the vulgar acceptation, *duty* is applicable to the conduct of men in their various relations; *obligation* only to particular circumstances or modes of action: we have *duties* to perform as parents and children, as husbands and wives, as rulers and subjects, as neighbors and citizens: the debtor is under an *obligation* to discharge a debt; and he who had promised is under an *obligation* to fulfil his promise: a conscientious man, therefore, never loses sight of the *obligations* which he has at different times to discharge. The *duty* is not so peremptory as the *obligation; the obligation* is not so lasting as the *duty:* our affections impel us to the discharge of *duty;* interest or necessity impels us to the discharge of an *obligation:* it may therefore sometimes happen that the man whom a sense of *duty* cannot actuate to do that which is right will not be able to withstand the *obligation* under which he has laid himself.

See also BUSINESS; TAX.

DWELL. See ABIDE.

DYE. See COLOR.

E

EACH. See ALL.

EAGER, EARNEST, SERIOUS. *Eager* (see AVIDITY.) *Earnest*, Anglo-Saxon *eornest*, meaning earnestness, comes from a root found in Greek ὄρνυμι, to excite, and in Icelandic *arnbrick*, implying intensity of spirit; not the same as *pledge* (see below). Serious, Latin *serius*, grave, earnest, may possibly be allied to German *schwer*, heavy.

Eager is used to qualify the desires or passions; *earnest*, to qualify the wishes or sentiments; the former has either a physical or moral application, the latter altogether a moral application: a child is *eager* to get a plaything; a hungry person is *eager* to get food; a covetous man is *eager* to seize whatever comes within his grasp: a person is *earnest* in solicitation, *earnest* in exhortation, *earnest* in devotion. *Eagerness* is mostly faulty; it cannot be too early restrained in children. Whence this term is with particular propriety applied to brutes.

Earnestness is always taken in the good sense for the inward conviction of the mind, accompanied with the warmth of the heart in a good cause. A person is said to be *earnest*, or in *earnest;* a person or thing is said to be *serious:* the former characterizes the temper of the mind, the latter characterizes the object itself. In regard to persons, in which alone they are to be compared, *earnest* expresses more than *serious;* the former is opposed to lukewarmness, the latter to unconcernedness: we are *earnest* as to our wishes or our persuasions; we are *serious* as to our intentions: the *earnestness* with which we address another depends upon the force of our conviction; the *seriousness* with which we address them depends upon our sincerity and the nature of the subject: the preacher *earnestly* exhorts his hearers to lay aside their sins; he *seriously* admonishes those who are guilty of irregularities.

Earnest, Pledge. — In the proper sense, the *earnest*, compounded of Old French *erres*, *arres*, from Latin *arrha* and a diminutive, is given as a token of our being in *earnest* in the promise we have made; the *pledge*, in all probability from *plico*, to fold or implicate, signifies a security by which we are engaged to indemnify for a loss. When a contract is only verbally formed, it is usual to give *earnest;* whenever money is advanced, it is common to give a *pledge.*

In the figurative application the terms bear the same analogy: a man of genius sometimes, though not always, gives an *earnest* in youth of his future greatness; children are the dearest *pledges* of affection between parents.

EAGERNESS. See AVIDITY.

EARLY. See SOON.

EARN. See ACQUIRE.

EARNESTNESS. See UNCTION.

EARTH. See COSMOS.

EASE, QUIET, REST, REPOSE. *Ease* comes from the French *aise*, a word of unknown origin. *Quiet* is derived from Latin *quietus*, quiet. *Rest* comes from Anglo-Saxon *rest*, originally, perhaps, a halting-place. *Repose* comes from Latin *re*, back, and French *poser*, to place, from Late Latin *pausare*, allied to *pause;* it means to place one's self backward in an easy posture.

The idea of a motionless state is common to all these terms: *ease* and *quiet* respect action on the body; *rest* and *repose* respect the action of the body: we are *easy* or *quiet* when freed from any external agency that is painful; we have *rest* or *repose* when the body is no longer in motion. *Ease* denotes an exemption from any painful agency in general; *quiet* denotes an exemption from that in particular which noise, disturbance, or the violence of others may cause: we are *easy* or at *ease* when the body is in a posture agreeable to itself, or when no circumjacent object presses unequally upon it; we are *quiet* when there is an agreeable stillness around: our ease may be disturbed either by internal or external causes; our *quiet* is most commonly disturbed by external objects.

Rest simply denotes the cessation of motion; *repose* is that species of *rest* which is agreeable after labor: we *rest* as circumstances require; in this sense, our Creator is said to have *rested* from the work of creation: *repose* is a circumstance of necessity; the weary seek *repose;* there is no human being to whom it is not sometimes indispensable. We may *rest* in a standing posture; we can *repose* only in a lying position: the dove which Noah first sent out could not find *rest* for the sole of its foot; soldiers who are hotly pursued by an enemy have no time or opportunity to take *repose:* the night is the time for *rest;* the pillow is the place for *repose.*

Rest may be as properly applied to things as to persons; *repose* is figuratively applied to things.

Ease, Easiness, Facility, Lightness.— *Ease* denotes either the abstract state of a person or quality of a thing; *easiness,* from *easy,* signifying having *ease,* denotes simply an abstract quality which serves to characterize the thing; a person enjoys *ease,* or he has an *easiness* of disposition.

Ease is said of that which is borne, or that which is done; *easiness* and *facility,* from the Latin *facilis,* easy, from *facere,* to do, most commonly of that which is done; the former in application to the thing as before, the latter either to the person or the thing: we speak of the *easiness* of the task, but of a person's *facility* in doing it: we judge of the *easiness* of a thing by comparing it with others more difficult; we judge of a person's *facility* by comparing him with others who are less skilful.

Ease and *lightness* are both said of what is to be borne; the former in a general, the latter in a particular sense. Whatever presses in any form is not *easy;* that which presses by excess of weight is not *light:* a coat may be *easy* from its make; it can be *light* only from its texture. A work is *easy* which requires no particular effort either of body or of mind from any one performing it; a work is *light* as far

as it requires no bodily effort, or not more than what the individual can easily make who has to perform it.

The same distinction exists between their derivatives, to *ease, facilitate,* and *lighten;* to *ease* is to make *easy* or free from pain, as to *ease* a person of his labor; to *facilitate* is to render a thing more practicable or less difficult, as to *facilitate* a person's progress; to *lighten* is to take off an excessive weight, as to *lighten* a person's burdens.

Easy, Ready.—*Easy* signifies here a freedom from obstruction in ourselves. *Ready* is derived from *ræde,* which meant literally equipped for *riding,* prepared for a *raid*—all these words coming from the same root.

Easy marks the freedom of being done; *ready,* the disposition or willingness to do; the former refers mostly to the thing or the manner, the latter to the person; the thing is *easy* to be done: the person is *ready* to do it; it is *easy* to make professions of friendship in the ardor of the moment; but every one is not *ready* to act up to them when it interferes with his convenience or interest. As epithets, both are opposed to difficult, but agreeably to the above explanation of the terms; the former denotes a freedom from such difficulties or obstacles as lie in the nature of the thing itself; the latter an exemption from such as lie in the temper and character of the person; hence we say a person is *easy* of access whose situation, rank, employments, or circumstances do not prevent him from admitting others to his presence; he is *ready* to hear when he himself throws no obstacles in the way, when he lends a willing ear to what is said. So likewise a task is said to be *easy;* a person's wit, or a person's reply, to be *ready.*

EASTERN. See ORIENT.

EBULLITION, EFFERVESCENCE, FERMENTATION, FERMENT. These technical terms have a strong resemblance in their signification, but they are not strictly synonymous; they have strong characteristic differences. *Ebullition,* from the Latin *ebullitio* and *ebullio,* compounded of *e* and *bullire,* to bubble, boil, marks the commotion of a liquid acted upon by fire, and in chemistry it is said of two substances which, by penetrating each other, occasion bubbles to rise up. *Effervescence*, from the Latin *effervescentia*, and *effervescere*, to grow hot, marks the commotion which is excited in liquors by a combination of substances, such as of acids, which are mixed and commonly produce heat. *Ferment*, or *fermentation*, from the Latin *fermentatio* and *fermentum* or *fervimentum*, from *fervere*, to grow hot, marks the internal movement which is excited in a liquid of itself, by which its components undergo such a change or decomposition as to form a new body.

Ebullition is a more violent action than *effervescence; ferment* and *fermentation* are more gradual and permanent than either. Water is exposed to *ebullition* when acted upon by any powerful degree of external heat; iron in aqua-fortis occasions *effervescence;* beer and wine undergo a *ferment* or *fermentation* before they reach a state of perfection. These terms are applied figuratively to moral objects. The passions are exposed to *ebullitions;* the heart and affections to *effervescence* when powerfully awakened by particular objects. The minds or spirits, particularly of numbers, may be in a *ferment* or *fermentation*. If the angry humors of an irascible temper be not restrained in early life, they but too frequently break forth in the most dreadful *ebullitions* in maturer years; religious zeal, when not constrained by the sober exercise of judgment and corrected by sound knowledge, is an unhappy *effervescence* that injures the cause which it espouses and often proves fatal to the individual by whom it is indulged: the *ferment* produced by public measures may often endanger the public peace.

ECCENTRIC. See ERRATIC; PARTICULAR.

ECCLESIASTIC, DIVINE, THEOLOGIAN. An *ecclesiastic* derives his title from the office which he bears in the *ecclesia*, or church; a *divine* and *theologian*, from his pursuit after or engagement in *divine* or *theological* matters. An *ecclesiastic* is connected with an episcopacy; a *divine* or *theologian* is unconnected with any form of church government. An *ecclesiastic* need not in his own person perform any office,

although he fills a station; a *divine* not only fills a station, but actually performs the office of teaching; a *theologian* neither fills any particular station nor discharges any specific duty, but merely follows the pursuit of studying *theology*. An *ecclesiastic* is not always a *divine*, nor a *divine* an ecclesiastic; a *divine* is always more or less a *theologian*, but every *theologian* is not a *divine*. Among the Roman Catholics all monks, and in the Church of England the various dignitaries who perform the episcopal functions, are entitled *ecclesiastics*. There are but few denominations of Christians who have not appointed teachers who are called *divines*. Professors or writers on *theology* are peculiarly denominated *theologians*.

ECLIPSE, OBSCURE. *Eclipse*, from Greek ἐκ, out, and λείπειν, to leave, means the leaving out or vanishing of light. *Obscure*, from the adjective *obscure* (see DARK), signifies to cause the intervention of a shadow.

In the natural as well as the moral application *eclipse* is taken in a particular and relative signification; *obscure* is used in a general sense. Heavenly bodies are *eclipsed* by the intervention of other bodies between them and the beholder; things are in general *obscured* which are in any way rendered less striking or visible. To *eclipse* is therefore a species of *obscuring*: that is always *obscured* which is *eclipsed;* but everything is not *eclipsed* which is *obscured*. So, figuratively, real merit is *eclipsed* by the intervention of superior merit; it is often *obscured* by an ungracious exterior in the possessor or by his unfortunate circumstances.

ECONOMICAL, SAVING, SPARING, THRIFTY, PENURIOUS, NIGGARDLY. The idea of not spending is common to all these terms; but *economical* signifies not spending unnecessarily or unwisely. *Saving* is keeping and laying by with care; *sparing* is keeping out of that which ought to be spent; *thrifty* or *thriving* is accumulating by means of *saving; penurious* is suffering as from *penury* by means of *saving; niggardly*, after the manner of a *niggard*, nigh or close person, is not spending or letting go but in the smallest possible quantities. To be *economical* is a virtue in those who have but narrow means; all the other epithets, however, are employed in a sense more or less unfavorable; he who is *saving* when young will be avaricious when old; he who is *sparing* will generally be *sparing* out of the comforts of others; he who is *thrifty* commonly adds the desire of getting with that of *saving;* he who is *penurious* wants nothing to make him a complete miser; he who is *niggardly* in his dealings will be mostly avaricious in his character.

Economy, Frugality, Parsimony.— *Economy,* from the Greek οἰκονομία, the management of a house, is derived from Greek οἶκος, house, and νέμειν, to deal out. *Frugality,* from the Latin *fruges,* fruits, means subsisting on the fruits of the earth, hence temperance. *Parsimony* (see AVARICIOUS) implies simply forbearing to spend, which is in fact the common idea included in these terms; but the *economical* man spares expense according to circumstances; he adapts his expenditure to his means and renders it by contrivance as effectual to his purpose as possible; the *frugal* man spares expense on himself or on his indulgences; he may, however, be liberal to others while he is *frugal* toward himself as well as others; he has no other object than saving. By *economy* a man may make a limited income turn to the best account for himself and his family; by *frugality* he may with a limited income be enabled to lay by money; by *parsimony* he may be enabled to accumulate great sums out of a narrow income; hence it is that we recommend a plan for being *economical;* we recommend a diet for being *frugal;* we condemn a habit or a character for being *parsimonious.*

Economy, Management. — *Economy* has a more comprehensive meaning than *management;* for it includes the system of science and of legislation as well as that of domestic arrangements: as the *economy* of agriculture; the internal *economy* of a government; political, civil, or religious *economy:* or the *economy* of one's household. *Management,* on the contrary, is an action that is very seldom abstracted from its agent, and is always taken in a partial sense, namely, as a part of *economy.* The internal *economy* of a family depends principally on the prudent *management* of the female: the *economy* of every well-regulated community requires that all the members should keep their station and preserve a strict subordination; the *management* of particular branches of this *economy* should belong to particular individuals.

ECONOMIZE. See HUSBAND.

ECSTASY, RAPTURE, TRANSPORT. There is a strong resemblance in the meaning and application of these words. They all express an extraordinary elevation of the spirits or an excessive tension of the mind. *Ecstasy* marks a passive state, from the Greek ἔκστασις, from ἐκ, out, and ἵσταμαι, I stand, means to be out of one's mind, out of one's self. *Rapture,* from the Latin *rapere,* to seize or carry away; and *transport,* from *trans* and *portare,* to carry beyond one's self, rather designate an active state, a violent impulse with which it hurries itself forward. *Ecstasy* and *rapture* are always pleasurable, or arise from pleasurable causes; *transport* respects either pleasurable or painful feelings: joy occasions *ecstasies* or *raptures;* joy and anger have their *transports.* An *ecstasy* benumbs the faculties; it will take away the power of speech and often of thought; it is commonly occasioned by sudden and unexpected events: *rapture,* on the other hand, often invigorates the powers and calls them into action; it frequently arises from deep thought: the former is common to all persons of ardent feelings, but more particularly to children, ignorant people, or to such as have not their feelings under control; *rapture,* on the contrary, is applicable to persons with superior minds and to circumstances of peculiar importance. *Transports* are sudden bursts of passion which, from their vehemence, may lead to intemperate actions: a reprieve from the sentence of death will produce an *ecstasy* or delight in the pardoned criminal. Religious contemplation is calculated to produce holy *raptures* in a mind strongly imbued with pious zeal: in *transports* of rage men have committed enormities which have cost them bitter tears of repentance ever after: youth is the period in which *transports* of delight are mostly felt.

EDGE. See BORDER.

EDICT. See DECREE; ORDINANCE.

EDIFICE, STRUCTURE, FABRIC. *Edifice,* in Latin *œdificium,* from *œdifico,* or *œdes,* a house, and *facere,* to make, signifies properly the house made. *Structure,* from the Latin *structura,* and *struere,* to heap together, signifies the raising a thing or the thing raised. *Fabric* comes from Latin *faber,* a workman, from a base signifying skill, and means something made by skill.

Edifice in its proper sense is always applied to a building; *structure* and *fabric* are either employed as abstract actions or the results and fruits of actions: in the former case they are applied to many objects besides buildings, *structure* referring to the act of raising or setting up together, *fabric* to that of framing or contriving. As *edifice* bespeaks the thing itself, it requires no modification, since it conveys of itself the idea of something superior: the word *structure* must always be qualified; it is employed only to designate the mode of action; *fabric* is itself a species of epithet, it designates the object as something contrived by the power of art or by design. *Edifices* dedicated to the service of religion have in all ages been held sacred: it is the business of the architect to estimate the merits or demerits of any *structure;* when we take a survey of the vast *fabric* of the universe, the mind becomes bewildered with contemplating the infinite power of its Divine author.

When employed in the abstract sense of actions, *structure* is limited to objects of magnitude, or such as consist of complicated parts; *fabric* is extended to everything in which art or contrivance is requisite; hence we may speak of the *structure* of vessels, and the *fabric* of cloth, ironware, or the *fabric* of states, the universe, etc.

EDUCATION, INSTRUCTION, BREEDING. *Instruction* and *breeding* are to *education* as parts to a whole: *instruction* respects the communication of knowledge, and *breeding* respects the manners or outward conduct; but *education* comprehends not only both these, but the formation of the mind, the regulation of the heart, and the establishment of the principles: good *instruction* makes one wiser; good *breeding* makes one more polished and agreeable; good *education* makes one really good. A want of *education* will always be to the injury, if not to the ruin, of the sufferer: a want of *instruction* is of more or less inconvenience, according to circumstances; a want of *breeding* only unfits a man for the society of the cultivated. *Education* belongs to the period of childhood and youth; *instruction* may be given at different ages; *good-breeding* is best learned in the early part of life.

EFFACE. See BLOT.

EFFECT, PRODUCE, PERFORM. The latter two are in reality included in the former; what is *effected* is both *produced* and *performed;* but what is *produced* or *performed* is not always *effected.* To *effect,* in Latin *effectus,* participle of *efficio,* compounded of *ex,* out, and *facere,* to make, signifies to make out anything. To *produce,* from the Latin *pro,* forth, and *ducere,* to draw, signifies literally to draw forth. To *perform,* Old French *parfournir,* from Latin *per,* through, and Old High German *frumjan,* to provide, French *fournir,* English *furnish,* signifies to do or provide everything necessary.

To *produce* signifies to bring something forth or into existence; to *perform* to do something to the end: to *effect* is to *produce* an effect by *performing;* whatever is *effected* is the consequence of a specific design; it always requires, therefore, a rational agent to *effect:* what is *produced* may follow incidentally, or arise from the action of an irrational agent or an inanimate object; what is *performed* is done by specific efforts; it is, therefore, like *effect,* the consequence of design, and requires a rational agent. To *effect* respects both the end and the means by which it is brought about; to *produce* respects the end only; to *perform* the means only. No person ought to calculate on *effecting* a reformation in the morals of men without the aid of religion; changes both in individuals and communities are often *produced* by trifles.

To *effect* is said of that which emanates from the mind of the agent himself; to *perform,* of that which is marked out by rule or prescribed by another. We *effect* a purpose, we *perform* a part, a duty, or office. A true Christian is always happy when he can *effect* a reconciliation between parties who are at variance: it is a laudable ambition to strive to *perform* one's part creditably in society.

See also ACCOMPLISH; CONSEQUENCE.

Effective, Efficient, Effectual, Efficacious.—*Effective* signifies capable of *effecting; efficient* signifies, literally, *effecting; effectual* and *efficacious* signify having the *effect*, or possessing the power to *effect. Effective* and *efficient* are used only in regard to physical objects: an army or a revenue is *effective* that can be employed to *effect* any object: a cause is *efficient* that is adequate to produce an *effect.*

Effectual and *efficacious* are said of operations and intellectual objects: an end or result is *effectual;* the means are *efficacious:* a remedy or cure is *effectual* that is in reality effected; a medicine is *efficacious* that effects a cure. No *effectual* stop can be put to the vices of the lower orders while they have a vicious example from their superiors: a seasonable exercise of severity on an offender is often very *efficacious* in quelling a spirit of insubordination. When a thing is not found *effectual,* it is requisite to have recourse to further measures; that which has been proved to be *inefficacious* should never be adopted.

EFFECTS. See GOODS.

EFFEMINATE. See FEMALE.

EFFERVESCENCE. See EBULLITION.

EFFICACIOUS. See EFFECT.

EFFIGY. See LIKENESS.

EFFORT. See ATTEMPT; ENDEAVOR.

EFFRONTERY. See AUDACITY.

EFFUSION, EJACULATION. *Effusion* signifies the thing poured out, from *ex,* out, and *fundere,* to pour, and *ejaculation,* the thing ejaculated or thrown out, from *ex,* out, and *iacere,* to throw, both indicating a species of verbal expression; the former either by utterance or in writing; the latter only by utterance. The *effusion* is not so vehement or sudden as the *ejaculation;* the *ejaculation* is not so ample or diffuse as the *effusion; effusion* is seldom taken in a good sense; *ejaculation* rarely otherwise. An *effusion* commonly flows from a heated imagination uncorrected by the judgment; it is, therefore, in general not only incoherent, but extravagant and senseless: an *ejaculation* is produced by the warmth of the moment, but never without reference to some particular circumstance. Enthusiasts are full of extravagant *effusions;* contrite sinners will often express their penitence in pious *ejaculations.*

EGOISTICAL. See MISANTHROPICAL; OPINIONATED.

EJACULATION. See EFFUSION.

ELATED. See SANGUINE.

ELDER. See SENIOR.

ELDERLY, AGED, OLD. These three words rise by gradation in their sense; *aged* denotes a greater degree of *age* than *elderly,* and *old* still more than either. The *elderly* man has passed the meridian of life; the *aged* man is fast approaching the term of our existence; the *old* man has already reached this term or has exceeded it. In conformity, however, to the vulgar prepossession against *age* and its concomitant infirmities, the term *elderly* or *aged* is always more respectful than *old,* which latter word is often used by way of reproach, and can seldom be used free from such an association unless qualified by an epithet of praise, as good or venerable.

ELECT. See CHOOSE.

ELECTRIC, MAGNETIC. *Electric* comes from Latin *electrum,* Greek ἤλεκτρον, amber; and derives its present meaning from the fact that amber developed electricity when excited by friction. *Magnetic* referred to a similar property observed in the magnesian stone, so called because it was found in large quantities in magnesia. This stone had the power to attract iron and steel. Both words originally referred to the attractive power associated with certain substances under certain conditions. But, as the science of electricity has developed, *magnetic* has been associated with the properties of the *magnet* and *electric* with a force or current existent or generated under certain conditions. When used figuratively *electric* refers to the swift and thrilling quality of *electricity,* *magnetic* to a quality of attractiveness associated with the mysterious thrill of electrical force.

ELEGANT. See SUPERB.

ELEMENTARY, CONSTITUENT, PRIMARY, RUDIMENTARY. *Elementary* is the adjective corresponding to *element,* Latin *elementum,* a word whose etymology and primary meaning are uncertain, but which is used to indicate one of the simple substances of which all material bodies are compounded. *Constituent,* from Latin *con,* together, and *statuere,* to set up, indicates that which when joined to something else goes to make up a complex whole. But it does not indicate a simple or uncompounded substance, as does *elementary.* *Primary,* from Latin *primus,* first, means the first elements, the things absolutely necessary to form a contemplated whole; but it does not definitely suggest the combination of substances as does *constituent.* *Rudimentary,* from Latin *rudimentum,* from *rudis,* rough, indicates the first rude state of things. These words, therefore, all mean characteristic of that which is necessary to the formation of a complex whole; but they differ in the emphasis upon the character of the thing indicated, and its relation to a larger whole.

ELEVATE. See LIFT.

ELIGIBLE, PREFERABLE. *Eligible,* or fit to be elected, and *preferable,* fit to be preferred, serve as epithets in the sense of choose and prefer (see CHOOSE; PREFER); what is *eligible* is desirable in itself, what is *preferable* is more desirable than another. There may be many *eligible* situations, out of which perhaps there is but one *preferable.* Of persons, however, we say rather that they are *eligible* to an office than *preferable.*

ELOCUTION, ELOQUENCE, ORATORY, RHETORIC. *Elocution* and *eloquence* are derived from the same Latin verb, *eloqui,* from *ex,* out, and *loqui,* to speak, to speak out. *Oratory,* from *orare,* to implore, signifies the art of making a set speech.

Elocution consists in the manner of delivery; *eloquence* in the matter that is delivered. We employ *elocution* in repeating the words of another; we employ *eloquence* to express our own thoughts and feelings. *Elocution* is requisite for an actor; *eloquence* for a speaker.

Eloquence lies in the person: it is a natural gift: *oratory* lies in the mode of expression; it is an acquired art. *Rhetoric* is properly the theory of that art of which *oratory* is the practice. But the term *rhetoric* may be sometimes employed in an improper sense for the display of *oratory* or scientific speaking. *Eloquence* speaks one's own feelings; it comes from the heart and speaks to the heart: *oratory* is an imitative art; it describes what is felt by another. *Rhetoric* is either in the technical sense the science of *oratory,* or *oratory* reduced to rule, or, in the vulgar acceptation, it is the affectation of *oratory.*

ELUCIDATE. See EXPLAIN.

ELUDE. See ESCAPE.

EMANATE. See ARISE.

EMANCIPATE, ENFRANCHISE, UNSHACKLE. *Emancipate* comes from Latin *emancipare, e manibus capere,* to take out of the hands of, and referred to the provision made in Roman law for freeing a child or a wife from the power of the father or husband. It also referred to the freeing of slaves. *Enfranchise* comes from Old French *franchise,* privileged liberty, and referred especially to the admitting of a slave or a serf to personal freedom. The two words have therefore almost exactly the same meaning, but *enfranchise* has also been given the special significance of to admit to the full rights of a citizen, especially to grant the right to vote. Hence when we speak of the *emancipation* of the negro slaves, we refer to the decree of the President delivering them from the power of their masters. When we speak of their *enfranchisement,* we refer to the passing of the amendment to the Constitution of the United States granting them the right to vote. *Unshackle* is a figurative word from *shackle* (see CHAIN), meaning to deliver from shackles, and may be used to mean either *emancipate* or *enfranchise* or *free* in a still larger sense. See FREE.

EMBARGO, BAN, PROHIBITION. *Embargo,* Spanish *embargo,* from *barra,* a bar, means a prohibiting order, forbidding the ships of a foreign power to enter or leave the ports of a country or native ships to proceed there, generally issued in anticipation of war. It also indicates a suspension of commerce by municipal law. *Ban* is an older term of Germanic origin signifying a formal edict—a call to arms, an announcement of intention to marry, or an ecclesiastical excommunication. *Prohibition* (for derivation see BAN) is used in a special sense to refer to the forbidding of the sale of alcoholic liquor by the law of a community. It refers to a special embargo on alcoholic drink. See also INTERN.

EMBARRASS, PERPLEX, ENTANGLE. *Embarrass* (see DIFFICULTY) respects a person's manners or circumstances, *perplex* (see DISTRESS), his views and conduct; *entangle* (see DISENGAGE) is said of particular circumstances. *Embarrassments* depend altogether on ourselves; the want of prudence and presence of mind is the common cause; *perplexities* depend on extraneous circumstances as well as ourselves; extensive dealings with others are mostly attended with *perplexities; entanglements* arise mostly from the evil designs of others. That *embarrasses* which interrupts the even course or progress of one's actions: that *perplexes* which interferes with one's decisions: that *entangles* which binds a person in his actions. Pecuniary difficulties *embarrass,* or contending feelings produce *embarrassment;* contrary counsels or interests *perplex;* the artifices of cunning *entangle.* Steadiness of mind prevents *embarrassment* in the outward behavior. Firmness of character is requisite in the midst of *perplexities;* caution must be employed to guard against *entanglements.*

EMBARRASSMENT. See QUANDARY.

EMBARRASSMENTS. See DIFFICULTIES.

EMBELLISH. See ADORN; GARNISH.

EMBLEM. See FIGURE.

EMBOLDEN. See ENCOURAGE.

EMBRACE. See CLASP; COMPRISE.

EMBRYO, FŒTUS. *Embryo,* in French *embryon,* Greek ἔμβρυον, from βρύειν, to swell out or germinate, signifies the thing germinated. *Fœtus;* Latin *fœtus,* comes from an obsolete Latin verb signifying to generate or produce, and signifies the thing cherished. Both words refer to what is formed in the womb of the mother; but *embryo* properly implies the first-fruit of conception, and the *fœtus* that which is arrived to a maturity of formation. Anatomists tell us that the *embryo* in the human subject assumes the character of the *fœtus* about the forty-second day after conception.

Fœtus is applicable only in its proper sense to animated beings: *embryo* has a figurative application to plants and fruits when they remain in a confused and imperfect state, and also a moral application to plans, or whatever is roughly conceived in the mind.

See also GERM.

EMEND. See AMEND.

EMERGE. See RISE.

EMERGENCE. See EXIGENCY.

EMINENT. See DISTINGUISHED.

EMISSARY, SPY. *Emissary,* in Latin *emissarius,* from *emittere,* to send forth, signifies one sent out. *Spy* is a shortened form of *espy,* which comes through French *espier,* from Old High German *spehon,* German *spähen,* to spy.

Both these words designate a person sent out by a body on some public concern among their enemies; but they differ in their office according to the etymology of the words. The *emissary* is by distinction sent forth; he is sent so as to mix with the people to whom he goes, to be in all places, and to associate with every one individually as may serve his purpose; the *spy,* on the other hand, takes his station wherever he can best perceive what is passing; he keeps himself at a distance from all but such as may particularly aid him in the object of his search. Although the offices of *emissary* and *spy* are neither of them honorable, yet that of the former is more disgraceful than that of the latter. The *emissary* is generally employed by those who have some illegitimate object to pursue; *spies,* on the other hand, are employed by all regular governments in a time of warfare. Nations that are at war sometimes send *emissaries* into the states of the enemy to excite civil commotions. At Sparta, the trade of a *spy* was not so vile as it has been generally esteemed; it was considered as a self-devotion for the public good, and formed a part of their education.

These terms are applied to other objects figuratively.

See also SPY.

EMIT, EXHALE, EVAPORATE. *Emit,* from the Latin *emittere,* expresses properly the act of sending out: *exhale,* from *halitus,* the breath, and *evaporate,* from *vapor,* vapor or steam, are both modes of *emitting.*

Emit is used to express a more positive effort to send out; *exhale* and *evaporate* designate the natural and progressive process of things; volcanoes *emit* fire and lava; the earth *exhales* the damps, or flowers *exhale* perfumes; liquids *evaporate.* Animals may *emit* by an act of volition; things *exhale* or *evaporate* by an external action upon them; they *exhale* that which is foreign to them; they *evaporate* that which constitutes a part of their substance. The skunk *emits* such a stench from itself when pursued as to keep its pursuers at a distance from itself: bogs and fens *exhale* their moisture when acted upon by the heat: water *evaporates* by means of steam when put into a state of ebullition.

See also TRANSPIRE.

EMOLUMENT. See GAIN.

EMOTION. See AGITATION.

EMPHASIS. See STRESS.

EMPIRE, KINGDOM, REPUBLIC. Although the first two words obviously refer to two species of states, where the princes assume the title of either emperor or king, yet the difference between them is not limited to this distinction.

The word *empire* carries with it the idea of a state that is vast and composed of many different people; that of *kingdom* marks a state more limited in extent and united in its composition. In *kingdoms* there is a uniformity of fundamental laws, the difference in regard to particular laws or modes of jurisprudence being merely variations from custom, which do not affect the unity of political administration. From this uniformity, indeed, in the functions of government, we may trace the origin of the words *king* and *kingdom,* since

there is but one prince or sovereign ruler, although there may be many employed in the administration. With *empires* it is different: one part is sometimes governed by fundamental laws very different from those by which another part of the same *empire* is governed, which diversity destroys the unity of government and makes the union of the state to consist in the submission of certain chiefs in the commands of a superior general or chief. From this very right of commanding, then, it is evident that the words *empire* and *emperor* derive their origin; and hence it is that there may be many princes or sovereigns, and *kingdoms,* in the same *empire.* Rome, therefore, was first a *kingdom* while it was formed of only one people: it acquired the name of *empire* as soon as other nations were brought into subjection to it and became members of it, not by losing the distinctive character as nations, but by submitting themselves to the supreme command of their conquerors. For the same reason the German *empire* was so denominated because it consisted of several states independent of one another, yet all subject to one ruler or emperor; so likewise the Russian *empire,* the Ottoman *empire,* and the former Mogul *empire,* which were composed of different nations: and, on the other hand, the *kingdom* of Spain and of England, both of which, though divided into different provinces, were, nevertheless, one people, having but one ruler. While France, however, included many distinct countries within its jurisdiction, it properly assumed the name of an *empire,* and, with Portugal later, took the name of *republic;* and England, having by a legislative act united to itself a country distinct both in its laws and customs, has likewise, with equal propriety, been denominated the British *empire.*

The term *republic* applies both to countries as vast as the United States, Brazil, and Mexico, as several in Europe, and also to smaller ones, as those in Central and South America and some parts of Europe; and the term represents the form of government, the supreme authority being chosen or delegated by the people instead of being hereditary in a single family.

Empire, Reign, Dominion.—In the preceding article *empire* has been considered as a species of state: in the present case it conveys the idea of power or an exercise of sovereignty. In this sense it is allied to the word *reign,* which, from the verb to *reign,* signifies the act of *reigning;* and to the word *dominion,* which, from the Latin *dominus,* a lord, signifies either the power or the exercise of the power of a lord.

As *empire* signifies command, or the power exercised in commanding, it properly refers to the country or people commanded; and as *reign* signifies the act of reigning, it refers to the individual who reigns. If we speak of an extended *empire,* it has regard to the space over which it extends; if of an extended *reign,* it has regard either to the country reigned over or to the length of time that a prince reigns.

From this distinction of the terms the epithets vast, united, dismembered, and the like are most appropriately applied to *empire;* the epithets peaceful, warlike, glorious, prosperous, and the like, to *reign.* *Empire* and *reign* are properly applied to civil government or the exercise of regular power; *dominion* signifies either the act of ruling by a sovereign or a private individual, or the power exercised in ruling, which may be either regular or irregular; a sovereign may have *dominion* over many nations by force of arms; he holds his *reign* by force of law.

If *empire* and *reign* be extended in their application to other objects, it is figurative; thus a female may be said to hold her *empire* among her admirers, or fashions may be said to have their *reign.* *Dominion* may be applied in the proper sense to the power which man exercises over the brutes or inanimate objects, and figuratively to the power of the passions.

In countries under the republican form of government the entire body of citizens constitute the sovereignty. They choose the Congress, which is the highest lawmaking authority, and elect the President, who is the chief executive of the laws.

EMPIRICAL, EXPERIMENTAL, HYPOTHETICAL, PROVISIONAL, TENTATIVE. All these words mean "not yet established as an absolute fact, but serving as a working basis" for further discovery. But the failure to establish as an absolute fact or law is indicated under somewhat different conditions. *Empirical,* from Greek ἐν, on, in, and πεῖρα, trial, experience, refers to knowledge gained simply from observation and experience, not based on any thorough study of cause and effect or even on scientific experiment. *Experimental,* on the other hand, coming from Latin *experiri,* to make a thorough trial of, means the process of discovering laws or facts through systematized observation; *experimental* simply suggests an incomplete process of discovery. *Hypothetical,* from Greek ὑπό, under, and θέσις, a placing; it is the adjective corresponding to *hypothesis.* A *hypothesis* is a formulation of a possible law which has not yet been fully demonstrated by experience. That which is *experimental* may be as yet unformulated; that which is *hypothetical* may be formulated, but not yet proved by *experiment.* *Provisional,* from *pro,* forward, and *videre,* to see, means taken as truth or right until a better way can be discovered; it is a formulation of a principle or method of action with the distinct expectation that it will be superseded; and is intended to serve as a means to an end. *Tentative,* from Latin *tentare,* to try, also means experimental, but it refers to informal rather than formal and systematic experiment, and partly suggests the meaning of *provisional.* That which is *tentative* is tried as an experiment till something better can be discovered.

EMPLOY, USE. *Employ,* from the Latin *in,* in, and *plicare,* to fold, signifies to implicate or apply for any special purpose. *Use,* from the Latin *usus,* past participal of *utor,* signifies to enjoy or derive benefit from.

Employ expresses less than *use;* it is in fact a species of partial *using:* we always *employ* when we *use;* but we do not always *use* when we *employ.* We *employ* whatever we take into our service or make subservient to our convenience for a time; we *use* whatever we entirely devote to our purpose. Whatever is *employed* by one person may, in its turn, be *employed* by another, or at different times be *employed* by the same person; but what is *used* is frequently consumed or rendered unfit for a similar *use*. What we *employ* may frequently belong to another; but what one *uses* is supposed to be his exclusive property. On this ground we may speak of *employing* persons as well as things: but we speak of *using* things only, and not persons, except in the most degrading sense. Persons, time, strength, and power are *employed;* houses, furniture, and all materials, of which either necessities or conveniences are composed, are *used.* It is a part of wisdom to *employ* well the short portion of time which is allotted to us in this sublunary state, and to *use* the things of this world so as not to abuse them. No one is exculpated from the guilt of an immoral action by suffering himself to be *employed* as an instrument to serve the purposes of another: we ought to *use* our utmost endeavors to abstain from all connections with such as wish to implicate us in their guilty practices.

EMPLOYMENT. See BUSINESS; VOCATION.

EMPOWER. See COMMISSION.

EMPTY, VACANT, VOID, DEVOID. *Empty* is in Anglo-Saxon *œmta, œmetta,* meaning leisure. *Void* and *devoid* come from Old French *voide,* of unknown origin, meaning empty.

Empty is the term in most general use; *vacant, void,* and *devoid* are employed in particular cases; *empty* and *vacant* have either a proper or an improper application; *void* or *devoid* only a moral acceptation. *Empty,* in the natural sense, marks an absence of that which is substantial, or adapted for filling: *vacant* designates or marks the absence of that which should occupy or make use of a thing. That which is hollow may be *empty:* that which respects an even space may be *vacant.* A house is *empty* which has no inhabitants; a seat is *vacant* which is without an occupant; a room is *empty* which is without furniture; a space on paper is *vacant* which is free from writing.

In their figurative application *empty* and *vacant* have a similar analogy: the *empty* is opposed to that which is substantial: the *vacant* to that which is or ought to be occupied; a dream is

said to be *empty,* or a title *empty;* a stare is said to be *vacant,* or an hour *vacant.*

Void and *devoid* are used in the same sense as *vacant,* as qualifying epithets, but not prefixed as adjectives, and always followed by some object; thus we speak of a creature as *void* of reason, and of an individual as *devoid* of common sense.

See also HOLLOW.

EMULATION. See COMPETITION.

ENCHANT. See CHARM.

ENCHANTED. See SPELLBOUND.

ENCIRCLE. See SURROUND.

ENCOMIUM, EULOGY, PANEGYRIC. *Encomium* comes from Greek ἐν, in, and κῶρος, revelry, and signifies a set form of verses used on festive occasions for the purposes of praise. *Eulogy,* in Greek εὐλογία, from εὖ and λόγος, signifies, literally, speaking well of any one. *Panegyric,* in Greek πανηγυρικόν, from πάν, the whole, and ἀγορά, an assembly, signifies that which is spoken before an assembly, a solemn oration.

The idea of praise is common to all these terms; but the first seems more properly applied to the thing, or the unconscious object; the second to persons in general, their characters and actions; the third to the person of some particular individual: thus we bestow *encomiums* upon any work of art or production of genius, without reference to the performer; we bestow *eulogies* on the exploits of a hero, who is of another age or country; but we write *panegyrics* either in a direct address or in direct reference to the person who is *panegyrized:* the *encomium* is produced by merit, real or supposed; the *eulogy* may spring from admiration of the person *eulogized;* the *panegyric* may be mere flattery, resulting from servile dependence: great *encomiums* have been paid by all persons to the constitution of England; our naval and military heroes have received the *eulogies* of many besides their own countrymen; authors of no mean reputation have condescended to deal out their *panegyrics* pretty freely, in dedications to their patrons.

ENCOMPASS. See BESIEGE.

ENCOUNTER. See ATTACK.

ENCOURAGE, ANIMATE, INCITE, IMPEL, URGE, STIMULATE, INVESTI-

GATE. *Encourage* (see CHEER). *Animate* (see ANIMATE). *Incite*, from the Latin *citare*, to stir up, signifies to put into motion toward an object. *Impel* (see ACTUATE). *Urge* comes from Latin *urgere*, to drive. *Stimulate*, from the Latin *stimulus*, a spur or goad, and *instigate*, from the Latin *stigo*, signify literally to goad. The idea of actuating or calling into action is common to these terms, which vary in the circumstances of the action.

Encouragement acts as a persuasive: *animate*, as an *impelling* or enlivening cause: those who are weak require to be *encouraged;* those who are strong become stronger by being *animated:* the former require to have their difficulties removed, their powers renovated, their doubts and fears dispelled; the latter may have their hopes increased, their prospects brightened, and their powers invigorated; we are *encouraged* not to give up or slacken in our exertions; we are *animated* to increase our efforts: the sinner is *encouraged* by offers of pardon, through the merits of a Redeemer, to turn from his sinful ways; the Christian is *animated* by the prospect of a blissful eternity, to go on from perfection to perfection.

What *encourages* and *animates* acts by the finer feelings of our nature; what *incites* acts through the medium of our desires: we are *encouraged* by kindness; we are *animated* by the hope of reward: we are *incited* by the desire of distinction.

What *impels*, *urges*, *stimulates*, and *instigates* acts forcibly, be the cause internal or external: we are *impelled* and *stimulated* mostly by what is internal; we are *urged* and *instigated* by both the internal and the external, but *particularly* the latter: we are *impelled* by motives; we are *stimulated* by appetites and passions; we are *urged* and *instigated* by the representations of others: a benevolent man is *impelled* by motives of humanity to relieve the wretched; an ardent mind is *stimulated* by ambition to great efforts; we are *urged* by entreaties to spare those who are in our power; one is *instigated* by malicious representations to take revenge on a supposed enemy.

We may be *impelled* and *urged*, though not properly *stimulated* or *in-*stigated, by circumstances; in this case the former two differ only in the degree of force in the *impelling* cause: less constraint is laid on the will when we are *impelled* than when we are *urged*, which leaves no alternative or choice: a monarch is sometimes *impelled* by the state of the nation to make a peace less advantageous than he would otherwise do; he is *urged* by his desperate condition to throw himself upon the mercy of the enemy: a man is *impelled* by the mere necessity of choosing to take one road in preference to another; he is *urged* by his pecuniary embarrassments to raise money at a great loss.

We may be *impelled*, *urged*, and *stimulated* to that which is bad; we are never *instigated* to that which is good; we may be *impelled* by curiosity to pry into that which does not concern us; we may be *urged* by the entreaties of those we are connected with to take steps of which we afterward repent; we may be *stimulated* by a desire of revenge to many foul deeds; but those who are not hardened in vice require the *instigation* of persons more abandoned than themselves before they will commit any desperate act of wickedness.

Encouragement and *incitement* are the abstract nouns either for the act of *encouraging* or *inciting*, or the thing that *encourages* or *incites:* the *encouragement* of laudable undertakings is itself laudable; a single word or look may be an *encouragement:* the *incitement* of passion is at all times dangerous, but particularly in youth; money is said to be an *incitement* to evil. *Incentive*, which is another derivative from *incite*, has a higher application for things that *incite* than the word *incitement;* the latter being mostly applied to sensible, and the former to spiritual objects: savory food is an *incitement* to sensualists to indulge in gross acts of intemperance: a religious man wants no *incentives* to virtues; his own breast furnishes him with those of the noblest kind. *Impulse* is the derivative from *impel*, which denotes the act of *impelling; stimulus*, which is the root of the word *stimulate*, naturally designates the instrument, namely, the spur or goad, with which one is *stimulated:* hence, we speak of acting by a blind *impulse*, or wanting a *stimulus* to exertion.

See also HEARTEN.

Encourage, Advance, Promote, Prefer, Forward.—To *encourage* (see above). *Advance* (see ADVANCE). *Promote*, from the Latin *pro*, forward, and *movere*, to move, signifies to move forward. *Prefer*, from the Latin *præfero*, from *præ*, before, and *ferre*, to carry, signifies to set up before others. To *forward* is to put forward.

The idea of exerting an influence to the advantage of an object is included in the signification of all these terms, which differ in the circumstances and mode of the action: to *encourage, advance*, and *promote* are applicable to both persons and things; *prefer*, to persons only; *forward*, to things only.

First as to persons, *encourage* is partial as to the end, and indefinite as to the means: we may *encourage* a person in anything, however trivial, and by any means; thus we may *encourage* a child in his rudeness by not checking him; or we may *encourage* an artist or man of letters in some great national work; but to *advance, promote*, and *prefer* are more general in their end and specific in the means; a person may *advance* himself, or may be *advanced* by others; he is *promoted* and *preferred* only by others: a person's *advancement* may be the fruit of his industry, or result from the efforts of his friends; *promotion* and *preferment* are the work of one's friends; the former in regard to offices in general, the latter mostly in regard to ecclesiastical situations: it is the duty of every one to *encourage*, to the utmost of his power, those among the poor who strive to obtain an honest livelihood; it is every man's duty to *advance* himself in life by every legitimate means; it is the duty and the pleasure of every good man in the state to *promote* those who show themselves deserving of *promotion*; it is the duty of a minister to accept of *preferment* when it offers, but it is not his duty to be solicitous for it.

When taken in regard to things, *encourage* is used in an improper or figurative acceptation; the rest are applied properly: if we *encourage* an undertaking, we give courage to the undertaker; but when we speak of *advancing*

a cause, or *promoting* an interest, or *forwarding* a purpose, these terms properly convey the idea of keeping things alive or in a motion toward some desired end: to *advance* is, however, generally used in relation to whatever admits of extension and aggrandizement; *promote* is applied to whatever admits of being brought to a point of maturity or perfection; *forward* is but a partial term, employed in the sense of *promote* in regard to particular objects: thus we *advance* religion or learning; we *promote* an art or an invention; we *forward* a plan.

Encourage, Embolden.—To *encourage* is to give courage, and to *embolden* to make bold, the former impelling to action in general, the latter to that which is more difficult or dangerous: we are *encouraged* to persevere; the resolution is thereby confirmed: we are *emboldened* to begin; the spirit of enterprise is roused. Success *encourages;* the chance of escaping danger *emboldens.*

ENCROACH, INTRENCH, INTRUDE, INVADE, INFRINGE. *Encroach* comes through Old French *en crochier*, from French *en* (Latin *in*), and Middle Dutch *kroke*, hook (corresponding to English *crook*), and means literally to hook in. *Intrench*, from Latin *in* and *trencare* for *truncare*, to cut, from *truncus*, the trunk of a tree, signifies to cut into another's territory. *Intrude* comes from Latin *in*, and *trudere*, to thrust, meaning, literally, in the slang phrase, "to butt in." *Invade*, from *in*, in, and *vadere*, to go, signifies to march in upon. *Infringe*, from the Latin *infringo*, compounded of *in* and *frangere*, to break, signifies to break in upon.

All these terms denote an unauthorized procedure; but the first two designate gentle or silent actions, the latter violent if not noisy actions. *Encroach* is often an imperceptible action, performed with such art as to elude observation; it is, according to its derivation, an insensible creeping into: *intrench* is, in fact, a species of *encroachment*, namely, that perceptible species which consists in exceeding the boundaries in marking out the ground or space.

In an extended and figurative application of the terms one is said to *encroach* on a person or on a person's time, etc.; to *intrench* on the sphere or privilege of another.

Intrude and *invade* designate an unauthorized entry, the former in violation of right, equity, or good manners, the latter in violation of public law: the former is more commonly applied to individuals; the latter to nations or large communities: unbidden guests *intrude* themselves sometimes into families to their no small annoyance; an army never *invades* a country without doing some mischief.

They are figuratively applied to other objects: *intrude*, in the sense of going in without being invited, as unwelcome thoughts *intrude* themselves into the mind: *invade*, in the sense of going in by force, as sounds *invade* the ear.

To *invade* and *infringe* are both violent acts; but there is more violation of good faith in *infringing* than in *invading*, as the *infringement* of a treaty. A privilege may be either *invaded* or *infringed;* but to *invade* in this sense is applied to any privilege, however obtained; but *infringe* properly applies to that which persons hold under some grant, compact, or law.

ENCUMBER. See CLOG.

ENCYCLOPÆDIA. See DICTIONARY.

END, TERMINATE, CLOSE. To *end* is either to come to an end or put an end to. To *terminate*, either to come to a term or set a term to. To *close*, to come or bring to a close. To *end* is indefinite in its meaning and general in its application; *terminate* and *close* are modes of *ending:* to *terminate* is to end finally; to *close*, to end gradually. Whatever is begun will *end*, and it may *end* in any way; but what *terminates* is that which has been designedly brought to an *end;* a string, a line, a verse, etc., may *end*, but a road is said properly to *terminate*.

Things may *end* abruptly or at once, but they *close* by a process or by bringing the parts or points together; a scene may *close*, or several lines may *close*.

Any period of time, as a day, a life, may *end* or *close*.

See also AIM; SAKE.

End, Extremity.—Both these words imply the last of those parts which constitute a thing; but the *end* designates that part generally; the *extremity* marks the particular point. The *extremity* is from the Latin *extremus*, the very last *end*, that which is outermost. Hence *end* may be said of that which bounds anything, but *extremity* of that which extends farthest from us: we may speak of the *ends* of that which is circular in its form, or of that which has no specific form; but we speak of the *extremities* of that only which is supposed to project lengthwise. The *end* is opposed to the beginning; the *extremity* to the centre or point from which we reckon. When a man is said to go to the *end* of a journey or the *end* of the world, the expression is in both cases indefinite and general: but when he is said to go to the *extremities* of the earth or the *extremities* of a kingdom, the idea of relative distance is manifestly implied. He who goes to the *end* of a path may possibly have a little farther to go in order to reach the *extremity*. In the figurative application, *end* and *extremity* differ so widely as not to admit of any just comparison.

ENDEAVOR, AIM, STRIVE, STRUGGLE. To *endeavor* is general in its object, *aim* is particular; we *endeavor* to do whatever we set about; we *aim* at doing something which we have set before ourselves as a desirable object. To *strive* is to *endeavor* earnestly; to *struggle* is to *strive* earnestly. An *endeavor* springs from a sense of duty (from French *en devoir*, on duty); we *endeavor* to do that which is right and avoid that which is wrong: *aiming* is the fruit of an aspiring temper; the object *aimed* at is always something superior either in reality or in imagination, and calls for particular exertion: *striving* is the consequence of an ardent desire; the thing *striven* for is always conceived to be of importance: *struggling* is the effect of necessity; it is proportioned to the difficulty of attainment and the resistance which is opposed to it; the thing *struggled* for is indispensably necessary. Those only who *endeavor* to discharge their duty to God and their fellow-creatures can expect real tranquillity of mind. Whoever *aims* at the acquirement of great wealth or much power opens the door for much misery to himself. As our passions are acknowledged to be our greatest enemies when they obtain the ascendency, we should always *strive* to keep them under our control. There are some men who *struggle* through life to obtain a mere competence, and yet die without succeeding in their object.

Endeavor, Effort, Exertion.—Endeavor (see ATTEMPT and above). *Effort* comes from Latin *ex*, out, and *fortis*, strong, and means to bring force to bear upon. *Exertion* is derived from Latin *ex*, out, and *serere*, to join, or put, meaning to put forth the strength and apply it to something.

The idea of calling our powers into action is common to these terms; *endeavor* expresses little more than this common idea, being a term of general import: *effort* and *exertion* are particular modes of *endeavor;* the former being a special strong *endeavor*, the latter a continued strong *endeavor*. An *endeavor* is called forth by ordinary circumstances; *effort* and *exertion*, by those which are extraordinary. An *endeavor* flows out of the condition of our being and constitution; as rational and responsible agents we must make daily *endeavors* to fit ourselves for a hereafter; as willing and necessitous agents we use our *endeavors* to obtain such things as are agreeable or needful for us: when a particular emergency arises we make a great *effort*. An *endeavor* may call forth one or many powers; an *effort* calls forth but one power: the *endeavor* to please in society is laudable if it do not lead to vicious compliances; it is a laudable *effort* of fortitude to suppress our complaints in the moment of suffering.

The *exertion* is as indefinite as the *endeavor* is to the means, but, like the *effort*, is definite as to the object: when a serious object is to be obtained, suitable *exertions* must be made. The *endeavor* is mostly applied to individuals, but the *exertion* may frequently be the combined *endeavors* of numbers.

ENDLESS. See ETERNAL.

ENDOW. See INVEST.

ENDOWMENT. See GIFT.

ENDURANCE. See PATIENCE.

ENDURE. See BEAR; BROOK; TOLERATE; UNDERGO.

ENEMY, FOE, ADVERSARY, OPPONENT, ANTAGONIST. *Enemy*, in Latin *inimicus*, compound of *in*, privative, and *amicus*, a friend, signifies one that is unfriendly. *Foe* comes from Anglo-Saxon *fah*, hostile. *Adversary*, in Latin *adversarius* from *adversus*, against, signifies one that takes part against another; *adversarius* in Latin was particularly applied to those who contested a point in law with another. *Opponent*, in Latin *opponens*, participle of *opponere*, from *ob*, in the way of, and *ponere*, to place, signifies one pitted against another. *Antagonist*, in Greek ἀνταγωνιστής, compounded of ἀντί, against, and ἀγωνίζομαι, I struggle, signifies one struggling against another.

An *enemy* is not so formidable as a *foe;* the former may be reconciled, but the latter always retains a deadly hate. An *enemy* may be so in spirit, in action, or in relation; a *foe* is always so in spirit, if not in action likewise: a man may be an *enemy* to himself, though not a *foe*. Those who are national or political *enemies* are often private friends, but a *foe* is never anything but a *foe*. A single act may create an *enemy*, but continued warfare creates a *foe*.

Enemies are either public or private, collective or personal; in the latter sense the word *enemy* is most analogous in signification to that of *adversary, opponent, antagonist*. The term *enemy* is always taken in a larger sense than the other terms: a private *enemy* is never inactive; he seeks to do mischief from the desire of so doing. An *adversary*, *opponent*, and *antagonist* may be so simply from the relation which they stand in to others: the *adversary* is one who is adverse either in his claims, his opinions, his purposes, or his endeavors; he is active against others only as far as his interests and views require. An *opponent* is one who stands or acts in opposition to another: an *opponent* opposes the opinions, principles, conduct, and writings of others. An *adversary* is always personal, and sets himself up immediately against another; but an *opponent* has nothing to do with the person, but with the thing that emanates from or is connected with the person. A man can have no *adversaries* except while he is living, but he may have *opponents* after he is dead; partisans are always *opponents* to each other. An *antagonist* is a particular species of *opponent* either in combat or in action; it is personal or otherwise, according to circumstances: there may be *antagonists* who contend for victory without any feeling of animosity; such were the Horatii and Curiatii among the Romans: or they may engage in a personal and bloody conflict, as the gladiators who fought for their lives: in this sense wild beasts are *antagonists* when they engage in battle; there are also literary *antagonists* who are directly pitted against each other: as Scaliger and Petavius among the French; Boyle and Bentley among the English.

Enemy and *foe* are figuratively applied to moral objects, the first in a general, the second in a particular sense: our passions are our *enemies* when indulged; envy is a *foe* to happiness. The word *antagonist* may also be applied metaphorically to other objects.

ENERGY, Force, Vigor. *Energy* comes from Greek ἐνέργεια, from Greek ἐν, in, and ἔργον, work, meaning work put into something. *Force* (see Compel). *Vigor*, from the Latin *vigere*, to flourish, signifies unimpaired power, or that which belongs to a subject in a sound or flourishing state.

With *energy* is connected the idea of activity; with *force*, that of capability; with *vigor*, that of health. *Energy* lies only in the mind; *force* and *vigor* are the property of either body or mind. Knowledge and freedom combine to produce *energy* of character; *force* is a gift of nature that may be increased by exercise: *vigor*, both bodily and mental, is an ordinary accompaniment of youth, but is not always denied to old age.

ENERVATE. See Weaken.

ENFEEBLE. See Weaken.

ENFRANCHISE. See Emancipation.

ENGAGE. See Attract; Bespeak; Bind.

ENGAGEMENT. See Battle; Business; Promise.

ENGENDER. See Breed.

ENGRAVE. See Imprint.

ENGRAVING. See Picture.

ENGROSS. See Absorb; Monopolize.

ENIGMA, Paradox, Riddle. All these words indicate something puzzling, hard to understand or solve, but the character of the implied intellectual difficulty varies. *Enigma* comes from Greek αἴνιγμα, meaning an obscure speech, and referred to a short composition in prose or verse in which something was described by intentionally obscure metaphors, in order to afford an exercise for the ingenuity of the reader in guessing what was meant. *Riddle*, Anglo-Saxon *rædels*, is the native English term for exactly the same sort of thing. A *paradox*, from Greek παρά, contrary to, and δόξα, opinion, is a statement contrary to received opinion, a statement which on the face of it seems self-contradictory, absurd, or at variance with common sense, though it may be essentially true. An *enigma*, therefore, is not a *paradox*, but a *paradox*, not being intelligible, may seem like an *enigma*. Between *enigma* and *riddle* there is no essential difference. *Enigma*, being the Greek term and the learned word, less clearly suggests its exact character to the popular mind than the familiar native term *riddle*. Accordingly it is at once more vague and more dignified. *Paradox* has an essentially different meaning from *enigma* and *riddle*, but it is included because it shares with them the general implication of obscurity—something puzzling to the mind, difficult to solve.

ENJOYMENT, Fruition, Gratification. *Enjoyment*, from *enjoy*, to have the joy or pleasure, signifies either the act of *enjoying* or the pleasure itself derived from that act. *Fruition*, from *frui*, to *enjoy*, is employed only for the act of *enjoying*; we speak either of the *enjoyment* of any pleasure or of the *enjoyment* as a pleasure: we speak of those pleasures which are received from the *fruition*, in distinction from those which are had in expectation. *Enjoyment* is either corporeal or spiritual, as the *enjoyment* of music or the *enjoyment* of study: but the *fruition* of eating or any other sensible, or at least external, object: hope intervenes between the desire and the *fruition.*

Gratification, from the verb to *gratify,* to make grateful or pleasant, signifies either the act of giving pleasure or the pleasure received. *Enjoyment* springs from every object which is capable of yielding pleasure; by distinction, however, and in the latter sense, from moral and rational objects: but *gratification,* which is a species of *enjoyment,* is obtained through the mediu of the senses. *Enjoyment* is not so vivid as *gratification: gratification* is not so permanent as *enjoyment.* Domestic life has its peculiar *enjoyments;* brilliant spectacles afford *gratification.* Our capacity for *enjoyment* depends upon our intellectual endowments; our *gratification* depends upon the tone of our feelings and the nature of our desires.

ENLARGE, INCREASE, EXTEND. *Enlarge* signifies literally to make large or wide, and is applied to dimension and extent. *Increase,* from the Latin *increscere,* from *in,* in, and *crescere,* to grow, means to grow from within, and is applicable to quantity, signifying to become greater in size by natural development. *Extend,* in Latin *extendo,* or *ex,* out, and *tendere,* to stretch, signifies to stretch out, that is, to make greater in space. We speak of *enlarging* a house, a room, premises, or boundaries; of *increasing* an army or property, capital, expense, etc.; of *extending* the boundaries of an empire. We say the hole or cavity *enlarges,* the head or bulk *enlarges;* the number *increases,* the swelling, inflammation, and the like *increase:* so likewise in the figurative sense, the views, the prospects, the powers, the ideas, and the mind are *enlarged;* pain, pleasure, hope, fear, anger, or kindness is *increased;* views, prospects, connections, and the like are *extended.*

ENLIGHTEN. See ILLUMINATE.

ENLIST. See ENROLL.

ENLIVEN. See ANIMATE.

ENMITY, ANIMOSITY, HOSTILITY. *Enmity* lies in the heart; it is deep and malignant. *Animosity,* from *animus,* a spirit, lies in the passions; it is fierce and vindictive: *hostility,* from *hostis,* a political enemy, lies in the action; it is mischievous and destructive.

Enmity is something permanent; *animosity* is partial and transitory: in the feudal ages, when the darkness and ignorance of the times prevented the mild influence of Christianity, *enmities* between particular families were handed down as an inheritance from father to son; in free states party spirit engenders greater *animosities* than private disputes.

Enmity is altogether personal; *hostility* respects public or private measures. *Enmity* often lies concealed in the heart and does not betray itself by any open act of *hostility.*

See also HATRED.

ENORMOUS, HUGE, IMMENSE, VAST. *Enormous,* from *e* and *norma,* a rule, signifies out of rule or order. *Huge* comes from Anglo-French *ahoge,* the origin of which is unknown. *Immense,* in Latin *immensus,* compounded of *in,* privative, and *mensus,* measured, signifies not to be measured. *Vast,* in French *vaste,* Latin *vastus,* waste, signifies characteristic of a great open space, of a *waste* or wilderness.

Enormous and *huge* are peculiarly applicable to magnitude; *immense* and *vast* to extent, quantity, and number. *Enormous* expresses more than *huge,* as *immense* expresses more than *vast:* what is *enormous* exceeds in a very great degree all ordinary bounds; what is *huge* is great only in the superlative degree. The *enormous* is always out of proportion; the *huge* is relatively extraordinary in its dimensions. Some animals may be made *enormously* fat by a particular mode of feeding: to one who has seen nothing but level ground common hills will appear to be *huge* mountains. The *immense* is that which exceeds all calculation: the *vast* comprehends only a very great or unusual excess. The distance between the earth and sun may be said to be *immense:* the distance between the poles is *vast.*

Of all these terms *huge* is the only one confined to the proper application and in the proper sense of size: the rest are employed with regard to moral objects. We speak only of a *huge* animal, a *huge* monster, a *huge* mass, a *huge* size, a *huge* bulk, and the like; but we speak of an *enormous* waste, an *immense* difference, and a *vast* number.

Enormous, Prodigious, Monstrous.—
Enormous (see above). *Prodigious*
comes from *prodigy,* in Latin *prodigium,*
signifying, literally, breaking out in
excess or extravagance. *Monstrous,*
from *monster,* in Latin *monstrum,* and
monstro, show or make visible, signifies
remarkable, or exciting notice.

The *enormous* contradicts our rules of
estimating and calculating; the *prodig-*
ious raises our minds beyond their ordinary standard of thinking: the *mon-*
strous contradicts nature and the course
of things. What is *enormous* excites
our surprise or amazement: what is
prodigious excites our astonishment:
what is *monstrous* does violence to our
senses and understanding. There is
something *enormous* in the present
scale upon which property, whether
public or private, is amassed and expended: the works of the ancients in
general, but the Egyptian pyramids in
particular, are objects of admiration,
on account of the *prodigious* labor
which was bestowed on them: ignorance and superstition have always
been active in producing *monstrous*
images for the worship of its blind
votaries.

ENOUGH, SUFFICIENT. *Enough,*
Anglo-Saxon *genoh,* German *genug,*
probably comes from a root signifying
to attain to. *Sufficient,* in Latin
sufficiens, participle of *sufficio,* compounded of *sub* and *facere,* to make, signifies made or suited to the purpose.

He has *enough* whose desires are satisfied; he has *sufficient* whose wants are
supplied. We may therefore frequently have *sufficiency* when we have not
enough. A greedy man is commonly in
this case, who has never *enough,* although he has more than a *sufficiency.*
Enough is said only of physical objects
of desire: *sufficient* is employed in a
moral application for that which serves
the purpose. Children and animals
never have *enough* food, nor the miser
enough money: it is requisite to allow
sufficient time for everything that is to
be done, if we wish it to be done well.

ENRAPTURE. See CHARM.

ENROLL, ENLIST or LIST, REGIS-
TER, RECORD. *Enroll,* compounded of
French *en,* Latin *in,* and *role,* from
rotula, a little wheel, signifies to place in
a roll, that is, in a roll of paper or a

book. *Enlist* is compounded of French
en and *liste* from Old High German *lista,*
a border or strip, signifying a long strip
of paper on which names were written;
the verb meaning to put on a *list.*
Register comes from Latin *re,* back,
and *gestum,* past participle of *gerere,* to
carry, and means a thing carried back, a
memorandum brought back; the verb
means to write the memorandum.
Record, in Latin *recorder,* compounded
of *re,* back or again, and *cors,* the heart,
signifies to bring back to the heart or
call to mind by a memorandum.

Enroll and *enlist* respect persons only;
register respects persons and things;
record respects things only. *Enroll* is
generally applied to the act of inserting
names in an orderly manner into any
book; *enlist* is a species of *enrolling* applicable only to the military. The *en-*
rolment is an act of authority; the
enlisting is the voluntary act of an
individual. Among the Romans it was
the office of the censor to *enroll* the
names of all the citizens, in order to
ascertain their number and estimate
their property: in modern times soldiers are mostly raised by means of
enlisting.

In the moral application of the terms,
to *enroll* is to assign a certain place or
rank; to *enlist* is to put one's self under
a leader or attach one's self to a party.
Hercules was *enrolled* among the gods;
the common people are always ready to
enlist on the side of anarchy and rebellion.

To *enroll* and *register* both imply
writing down in a book; but the former
is a less formal act than the latter.
The insertion of the bare name or
designation in a certain order is enough
to constitute an *enrolment;* but *regis-*
tering comprehends the birth, family,
and other collateral circumstances of
the individual. The object of *register-*
ing likewise differs from that of *enroll-*
ing: what is *registered* serves for future
purposes and is of permanent utility to
society in general; but what is *enrolled*
often serves only a particular or temporary end. Thus in numbering the
people it is necessary simply to *enroll*
their names; but when in addition to
this it was necessary, as among the
Romans, to ascertain their rank in the
state, everything connected with their

property, their family, and their connection required to be *registered;* so in like manner, in more modern times, it has been found necessary for the good government of the state to *register* the births, marriages, and deaths of every citizen: it is manifest, therefore, that what is *registered,* as far as respects persons, may be said to be *enrolled;* but what is *enrolled* is not always *registered.* Persons only, or things personal, are *enrolled,* and that properly for public purposes only; but things as well as persons are *registered* for private as well as public purposes.

To *register* in its proper sense is to place in writing; to *record* is to make a memorial of anything, either by writing, printing, engraving, or otherwise: *registering* is for some specific and immediate purpose; as to *register* decrees or other proceedings in a court: *recording* is for general and oftentimes remote purposes: to *record* events in history.

In an extended and figurative application, things may be said to be *registered* in the memory; or events *recorded* in history. We have a right to believe that the actions of good men are *registered* in heaven; the particular sayings and actions of princes are *recorded* in history, and handed down to the latest posterity.

ENSAMPLE. See EXAMPLE.

ENSLAVE, CAPTIVATE. To *enslave* is to bring into a state of *slavery.* To *captivate* is to make a *captive.*

There is as much difference between these terms as between *slavery* and *captivity:* he who is a *slave* is fettered both body and mind; he who is a *captive* is only constrained as to his body: hence to *enslave* is always taken in the bad sense; *captivate,* in a good or bad sense: *enslave* is employed literally or figuratively; *captivate* only figuratively: we may be *enslaved* by persons or by our gross passions; we are *captivated* by the charms or beauty of an object.

ENSUE. See FOLLOW.

ENTANGLE. See EMBARRASS; INSNARE.

ENTER. See BEGIN.

ENTERPRISE. See ATTEMPT.

ENTERPRISING, ADVENTUROUS. These terms mark a disposition to engage in that which is extraordinary and hazardous; but *enterprising,* from *en-*

c.e.s.—11

terprise (see ATTEMPT), is connected with the understanding; and *adventurous,* from *adventure* (from Latin *ad,* to, and *venire,* to come, meaning a coming to, an attempt or trial), is a characteristic of the passions. The *enterprising* character conceives great projects, and pursues objects that are difficult to be obtained; the *adventurous* character is contented with seeking that which is new and placing himself in dangerous and unusual situations. An *enterprising* spirit belongs to the commander of an army or the ruler of a nation; an *adventurous* disposition is suitable to men of low degree. Peter the Great possessed, in a peculiar manner, an *enterprising* genius; Robinson Crusoe was a man of an *adventurous* turn. *Enterprising* characterizes persons only, but *adventurous* is also applied to things, to signify containing *adventures;* hence a journey, or a voyage, or a history may be denominated *adventurous.*

ENTERTAIN. See AMUSE.

ENTERTAINMENT. See AMUSEMENT; FEAST.

ENTHUSIAST, FANATIC, VISIONARY, DEVOTEE. The *enthusiast, fanatic,* and *visionary* have disordered imaginations; but the *enthusiast* is only affected inwardly with an extraordinary fervor, the *fanatic* and *visionary* betray that fervor by some outward mark; the former by singularities of conduct, the latter by singularities of doctrine. *Fanatics* and *visionaries* are therefore always more or less *enthusiasts;* but *enthusiasts* are not always *fanatics* or *visionaries.* ’Ενθουσιάσταί, among the Greeks, from ἐν, in, and θεός, God, signified those supposed to have, or pretending to have, divine inspiration. *Fanatici* were so called among the Latins from *fana* (temples), in which they spent an extraordinary portion of their time; they, like the ἐνθουσιάσται of the Greeks, pretended to revelations and inspirations, during the influence of which they indulged themselves in many extravagant tricks, cutting themselves with knives, and distorting themselves with every species of antic, gesture, and grimace.

In the modern acceptation of these terms the *fanatic* is one who fancies himself inspired, and, rejecting the use of his understanding, falls into every kind of extravagance; it is mostly applied to a man's religious conduct and belief, but may be applied to any extravagant conduct founded on false principles.

An *enthusiast* is one who is under the influence of any particular fervor of mind, more especially where it is a religious fervor.

There may be *enthusiasm* in other matters, where it is less mischievous. There may be *enthusiasts* in the cause of humanity, or in the love of one's country, or in any other matter in which the affections may be called into exercise.

The *visionary* is properly one that sees or professes to see visions, and is mostly applied to those who pretend to supernatural visions, but it may be employed in respect to any one who indulges in fantastical theories.

A *devotee* is one who is extravagantly and, it may be, superstitiously devoted to a cause. The word expresses exaggerated interest, and, so far, is synonymous with the other terms, but it does not suggest disordered imagination, as does *fanatic*.

ENTHUSIASTIC. See SANGUINE.

ENTICE. See ALLURE; PERSUADE; TWEEDLE.

ENTIRE. See WHOLE.

ENTIRELY. See QUITE.

ENTITLE. See NAME.

ENTRAP. See INSNARE.

ENTREAT. See BEG.

ENTREATY. See PRAYER.

ENVIOUS. See INVIDIOUS.

ENVIRON. See SURROUND.

ENVOY. See AMBASSADOR.

ENVY. See JEALOUSY.

EPHEMERAL. See EVANESCENT.

EPHEMERIS. See CALENDAR.

EPICURE. See SENSUALIST.

EPIDEMICAL. See CONTAGIOUS.

EPITHET, ADJECTIVE. *Epithet* is the technical term of the rhetorician; *adjective* that of the grammarian. The same word is an *epithet* as it qualifies the sense; it is an *adjective* as it is a part of speech: thus, in the phrase "Alexander the Great," great is an epithet, inasmuch as it designates Alexander in distinction from all other persons: it is an *adjective* as it expresses a quality in distinction from the noun Alexander, which denotes a thing.

The *epithet* (ἐπίθητον, from ἐπί, beside, and τίθημι, I place) is the word added by way of ornament to the diction; the *adjective*, from *adjectivum*, is the word added to the noun as its appendage, and made subservient to it in all its inflections. When we are estimating the merits of any one's style or composition, we should speak of the *epithets* he uses; when we are talking of words, their dependencies and relations, we should speak of *adjectives:* an *epithet* is either gentle or harsh, an *adjective* is either a noun or a pronoun *adjective*. All *adjectives* are *epithets*, but all *epithets* are not *adjectives;* thus, in Virgil's Pater Æneas, the *pater* is an *epithet*, but not an *adjective*.

EPOCHA. See TIME.

EQUAL, EVEN, EQUABLE, LIKE or ALIKE, UNIFORM. *Equal,* in Latin *æqualis,* comes from *æquus. Even* is in Anglo-Saxon *efen. Equable,* in Latin *equabilis,* signifies susceptible of *equality. Like,* Anglo-Saxon *lic,* comes from a Teutonic base meaning resembling in form. *Uniform,* compounded of *unus,* one, and *forma,* form, bespeaks its own meaning.

All these *epithets* are opposed to difference. *Equal* is said of degree, quantity, number, and dimensions, as *equal* in years; of an *equal* age; an *equal* height: *even* is said of the surface and position of bodies; a board is made *even* with another board; the floor or the ground is *even: like* is said of accidental qualities in things, as *alike* in color or in feature: *uniform* is said of things only as to their fitness to correspond; those which are *unlike* in color, shape, or make are not *uniform,* and cannot be made to match as pairs: *equable* is used only in the moral acceptation, in which all the others are likewise employed.

As moral qualities admit of degree, they admit of *equality:* justice is dealt out in *equal* portions to the rich and the poor; God looks with an *equal* eye on all mankind. As the natural path is rendered uneven by high and low ground, so the *evenness* of the temper, in the figurative sense, is destroyed by changes of humor, by elevations and depressions of the spirits; and the *equability* of life, from prosperous to adverse.

Even and *equable* are applied to the same object in regard to itself, as an *even* path or *equable* course; *like* or *alike* is applied to two or more objects in regard to one another, as two persons are *alike* in disposition, taste, opinions, etc.; *uniform* is said, either of one object in regard to itself, as to be *uniform* in conduct, or of many objects in regard to one another, as modes are *uniform*.

EQUIP. See FIT.

EQUITABLE. See FAIR.

EQUITY. See JUSTICE.

EQUIVOCAL. See AMBIGUOUS.

EQUIVOCATE. See EVADE.

EQUIVOCATION. See SOPHISTRY.

ERA. See TIME.

ERADICATE, EXTIRPATE, EXTERMINATE. To *eradicate*, from *radix*, the root, is to get out by the root: *extirpate*, from *ex* and *stirps*, the stem, is to get out the stock, to destroy it thoroughly. In the natural sense we may *eradicate* noxious weeds whenever we pull them from the ground; but we can never *extirpate* all noxious weeds, as they always disseminate their seeds and spring up afresh. These words are seldomer used in the physical than in the moral sense; where the former is applied to such objects as are conceived to be plucked up by the roots, as habits, vices, abuses, evils; and the latter to whatever is united or supposed to be united into a race or family, and is destroyed root and branch. Youth is the season when vicious habits may be thoroughly *eradicated;* by the universal deluge the whole human race was *extirpated* with the exception of Noah and his family.

Exterminate, in Latin *exterminatus,* participle of *extermino,* from *ex* or *extra* and *terminus,* boundary, signifies to expel beyond the boundary (of life), that is, out of existence. It is used only in regard to such things as have life, and designates a violent and immediate action: *extirpate,* on the other hand, may designate a progressive action: the former may be said of individuals, but the latter is employed in the collective sense only. Plague, pestilence, famine, *extirpate:* the sword *exterminates.*

ERASE. See BLOT.

ERECT. See BUILD; INSTITUTE; LIFT.

ERRAND. See MESSAGE.

ERRATIC, ECCENTRIC. *Erratic* comes from French *erratique,* Latin *erraticus,* prone to wander, from *errare,* to wander. *Eccentric* comes through French from Greek ἐκ, out, and κέντρον, circle, meaning not *concentric* with another circle, or, in astronomy, moving in an orbit deviating more or less from a center. These words have similar meanings. Both were astronomical terms; both indicate motion deviating from a fixed course; and both have been employed, in a figurative sense, to indicate that which does not correspond to a set standard. *Erratic,* however, refers to a more active departure from a fixed course than does *eccentric.* The *eccentric* person does not do as others do; the *erratic* person fails to do as others do, but acts in a particularly irregular and jerky and unsystematic fashion.

ERROR, MISTAKE, BLUNDER. *Error,* in French *erreur,* Latin *error,* from *errare,* to wander, marks the act of wandering, as applied to the rational faculty. A *mistake* is a taking amiss or wrong, and is derived from the Scandinavian. *Blunder* is a Scandinavian word formed as a frequentative from Icelandic *blunda,* to doze or slumber, allied to *blind.*

Error in its universal sense is the general term, since every deviation from what is right in rational agents is termed *error,* which is strictly opposed to truth; *error* is the lot of humanity; into whatever we attempt to do or think *error* will be sure to creep: the term, therefore, is of unlimited use; the very mention of it reminds us of our condition: we have *errors* of judgment, *errors* of calculation, *errors* of the head, and *errors* of the heart. The other terms designate *modes* of *error,* which mostly refer to the common concerns of life: *mistake* is an *error* of choice; *blunder* an *error* of action: children and careless people are most apt to make *mistakes;* ignorant, conceited, and stupid people commonly commit *blunders:* a *mistake* must be rectified; in commercial transactions it may be of serious consequence: a *blunder* must be set right; but *blunderers* are not always to be set right; and *blunders* are frequently so ridiculous as only to excite laughter.

See also SOPHISTRY.

Error, Fault.—*Error* respects the act; *fault*, from Latin *fallere*, to deceive, English *fail*, respects the agent: an *error* may lie in the judgment or in the conduct; but a *fault* lies in the will or intention: the *errors* of youth must be treated with indulgence; but their *faults* must on all accounts be corrected: *error* is said of that which is individual and partial; *fault* is said likewise of that which is habitual: it is an *error* to use intemperate language at any time; it is a *fault* in the temper of some persons that they cannot restrain their anger.

See also LAPSE.

ERST. See ONCE.

ERUDITION. See KNOWLEDGE.

ERUPTION, EXPLOSION. *Eruption,* from *e*, out, and *rumpere*, to break, signifies the breaking forth, that is, the coming into view, by a sudden bursting; *explosion,* from *ex*, out, and *plaudere*, to clap, meant to drive off the stage by clapping; and now signifies bursting out with a noise: hence of flames there will be properly an *eruption*, but of gunpowder an *explosion*: volcanoes have their *eruptions* at certain intervals, which are sometimes attended with *explosions*: on this account *eruptions* are applied to the human body for whatever comes out as the effects of humor, and may be applied in the same manner to any indications of humor in the mind; *explosions* are also applied to the agitations of the mind which burst out.

ESCAPE, ELUDE, EVADE. *Escape* means literally to slip out from under one's cape, from French *es*, out, Latin *ex*, and *cappa*, cape. *Elude* (see AVOID). *Evade*, from the Latin *evado*, compounded of *e*, out, and *vadere*, to go, signifies to go or get out of a thing.

The idea of being disengaged from that which is not agreeable is comprehended in the sense of all these terms; but *escape* designates no means by which this is effected; *elude* and *evade* define the means, namely, the efforts which are used by one's self: we are simply disengaged when we *escape*,

but we disengage ourselves when we *elude* and *evade*: we *escape* from danger; we *elude* search: our *escapes* are often providential and often narrow; our success in *eluding* depends on our skill: there are many bad men who *escape* punishment by the mistake of a word; there are many who *escape* detection by the art with which they *elude* observation and inquiry.

Elude and *evade* both imply the practice of art on trying occasions; but the former is employed to denote a more ready and dexterous exercise of art than the latter; the former consists mostly of that which is done by a trick, the latter consists of words as well as actions: a thief *eludes* those who are in pursuit of him by dexterous modes of concealment; he *evades* the interrogatories of the judge by equivocating replies. One is said to *elude* a punishment and to *evade* a law.

ESCORT. See ACCOMPANY.

ESPECIALLY, PARTICULARLY, PRINCIPALLY, CHIEFLY. *Especially* and *particularly* are exclusive or superlative in their import; they refer to one object out of many that is superior to all; *principally* and *chiefly* are comparative in their import; they designate in general the superiority of some objects over others. *Especially* is a term of stronger import than *particularly*, and *principally* expresses something less general than *chiefly*: we ought to have God before our eyes at all times, but *especially* in those moments when we present ourselves before Him in prayer: the heat is very oppressive in all countries under the torrid zone, but *particularly* in the deserts of Arabia, where there is a want of shade and moisture: it is *principally* among the higher and lower orders of society that we find vices of every description to be prevalent; robberies happen *chiefly* by night.

ESPOUSE, BETROTH. *Espouse*, in old French *espouser*, modern French *épouser*, a spouse or wife, from the Latin *sponso*, to betroth, that from *spondere*, to promise, old Spanish *esposar*, Italian *sposare*, has two very different significations. In the present and more common one the term implies to promise, or engage in marriage, usually by a written contract, sometimes by word of mouth with or without witnesses, and *espousal* implies the act of contracting a man and woman to each other in marriage.

Betroth, a compound of the English *be* and the Old English *troth*, truth, signifies the act of plighting or pledging one's *troth*, a token of faith, truth, or earnest intention: in this application a pledge or agreement of marriage. To *espouse* is to wed; to *betroth* is to give a pledge that the man and woman will wed. A father or *sponsor* gives a woman to a man to be his *spouse*, or wife, and a bridegroom takes the woman as his *spouse*.

Espouse is also used figuratively, meaning to make one's own entirely, as in the phrase to *espouse* a cause.

ESPY. See FIND.

ESSAY, TREATISE, TRACT, DISSERTATION. All these words are employed by authors to characterize compositions varying in their form and contents. *Essay*, which signifies a trial or attempt, is here used to designate in a specific manner an author's attempt to illustrate any point: it is most commonly applied to small detached pieces, which contain only the general thoughts of a writer on any given subject, and afford room for amplification into details also: though, by Locke, in his "*Essay* on the Understanding," Beattie, in his "*Essay* on Truth," and other authors, it is modestly used for their connected and finished endeavors to elucidate a doctrine. A *treatise* is more systematic than an *essay;* it treats on the subject in a methodical form, and conveys the idea of something labored, scientific, and instructive. A *tract* is only a species of a small *treatise*, drawn up upon particular occasions, and published in a separate form; they are both derived from the Latin *tractus*, participle of *traho*, draw, manage, or handle. *Dissertation*, from Latin *disserere*, compounded of *dis*, apart, and *serere*, to join, means the taking up of a subject part by part, suggesting a thorough and exhaustive analysis.

Essays are either moral, political, philosophical, or literary: they are the crude attempts of the youth to digest his own thoughts or they are the more mature attempts of the man to communicate his thoughts to others: of the former description are the prize *essays* in schools; and of the latter are the innumerable *essays* which have been published on every subject since the time of Bacon to the present day: *treatises* are mostly written on ethical, political, or speculative subjects such as Fénelon's, Milton's, or Locke's *treatise* on education; De Lolme's *treatise* on the constitution of England; Colquhoun's *treatise* on the police: *dissertations* are employed on disputed points of literature, as Bentley's *dissertation* upon the epistles of Phalaris; De Pauw's *dissertations* on the Egyptians and Chinese: *tracts* are ephemeral productions, mostly on political and religious subjects, which seldom survive the occasion which gave them birth; of this description are the pamphlets which daily issue from the press, for or against the measures of government or the public measures of any particular party.

See also ATTEMPT.

ESSENTIAL. See NECESSARY.

ESTABLISH. See CONFIRM; FIX; INSTITUTE.

ESTATE, PROPERTY, RANK. *Estate*, Old French *estat*, from Latin *status*, meant originally condition in general or a good condition, with special reference to worldly prosperity. Out of its original sense it developed several different meanings, characterized in each case, however, by a certain formality and legal stiffness in its application. In one sense *estate* is a synonyme of *property*, from Latin *proprius*, one's own, meaning that which is one's own. *Property* is the general and familiar term applied to all that one owns; *estate* a legal term applied to the interest that any one has in lands, tenements, or other effects. Again *property* may indicate a piece of land owned by an individual or a corporation; *estate* that same piece of land if it is sufficiently large and sumptuously developed. We speak of the farmer's *property;* the rich man's *estate*.

Estate, *Rank*. — *Estate* is also a synonyme of *rank* (see CLASS), from which it differs in suggesting not merely a division into *ranks*, but something of its original reference to worldly condition; as well as in being a somewhat more formal and specific word with distinctly French associations. In Great Britain the *estates of the realm* mean the lords spiritual, the lords temporal, and the commons—the first two being represented in the House of Lords, the last in the House of Commons.

ESTEEM, RESPECT, REGARD. *Esteem* (see APPRAISE). *Respect*, from the Latin *respicere*, signifies to look back upon, to look upon with attention. *Regard* (see ATTEND).

A favorable sentiment toward particular objects is included in the meaning of all these terms. *Esteem* and *respect* flow from the understanding; *regard* springs from the heart as well as the head: *esteem* is produced by intrinsic worth; *respect* by extrinsic qualities; *regard* is affection blended with *esteem:* it is in the power of every man, independently of all collateral circumstances, to acquire the *esteem* of others; but *respect* and *regard* are within the reach of a limited number only: the high and the low, the rich and the poor, the equal and the unequal are each, in their turn, the objects of *esteem;* those only are objects of *respect* who have some mark of distinction or superiority of either birth, talent, acquirements, or the like; *regard* subsists only between friends, or those who stand in close connection with one another: industry and sobriety excite our *esteem* for one man, charity and benevolence our *esteem* for another; superior learning or abilities excite our *respect* for another; a long acquaintance or a reciprocity of kind offices excites a mutual *regard*.

See also VALUE.

ESTIMATE, COMPUTE, RATE. *Estimate* (see APPRAISE). *Compute* (see CALCULATE). *Rate*, in Latin *ratus*, participle of *reor*, to think, signifies to weigh in the mind.

All these terms mark the mental operations by which the sum, amount, or value of things is obtained: to *estimate* is to obtain the aggregate sum in one's mind, either by an immediate or a progressive act; to *compute* is to obtain the sum by the gradual process of putting together items; to *rate* is to fix the relative value in one's mind by deduction and comparison; a builder *estimates* the expense of building a house on a given plan; a proprietor of houses *computes* the probable diminution in the value of his property in consequence of wear and tear; the surveyor *rates* the present value of lands or houses.

In the moral acceptation they bear the same analogy to each other: some men are apt to *estimate* the adventitious privileges of birth or rank too high; it would be a useful occupation for men to *compute* the loss they sustain by the idle waste of time, on the one hand, and its necessarily unprofitable consumption, on the other: he who *rates* his abilities too high is in danger of despising the means which are essential to secure success; and he who *rates* them too low is apt to neglect the means, from despair of success.

ESTRANGEMENT. See ABSTRACTION.

ETERNAL, ENDLESS, EVERLASTING. The *eternal* is set above time, the *endless* lies within time; it is therefore by a strong figure that we apply *eternal* to anything sublunary; although *endless* may with propriety be applied to that which is heavenly; that is properly *eternal* which has neither beginning nor end; that is *endless* which has a beginning but no end: God is, therefore, an *eternal*, but not an *endless* being: there is an *eternal* state of happiness or misery which awaits all men, according to their deeds in this life; but their joys or sorrows may be *endless* as regards the present life. That which is *endless* has no cessation; that which is *everlasting* has neither interruption nor cessation: the *endless* may be said of existing things; the *everlasting* naturally extends itself into futurity: hence we speak of *endless* disputes, an *endless* warfare; an *everlasting* memorial, an *everlasting* crown of glory.

ETHEREAL, CELESTIAL, HEAVENLY, SPIRITUAL. *Ethereal*, derived from the same source as *ether*, *viz.*, the Greek αἰθήρ, the sky, from αἴθω, to light up, cognate with the Latin *æstas*, summer, or *æstus*, heat, in Italian *etere*, implies, literally, that which pertains to, or is formed of, ether, the fluid that is believed to pervade all space beyond the atmosphere of the earth, and, figuratively, the high heavens or home of the gods. *Ethereal*, in chem-

EUPHONIOUS

istry, applies to whatever contains ether, but in ordinary language it has a strong poetical and religious significance.

Celestial specifically implies that which pertains to the sky or heavens, and, commonly, that which is *exquisite* or supremely excellent or which relates to the empire or people of China. Whatever is *heavenly* pertains to or resembles heaven, the firmament or sky, the abode of God and the blessed, and implies the state or condition of absolute bliss. Because of the general religious and the mythological belief that heaven is the abode of the redeemed and the gods who controlled the destinies of mankind, the term has come to designate the *spiritual* or incorporeal part of humanity, the state of being pure, holy, and heavenly-minded.

ETHICAL, MORAL. *Moral*, from Latin *mos, moris*, meaning custom, was Cicero's translation of the Greek ἠθικός, indicating habitual conduct. Both words, therefore, were meant to refer to a habit of right action habitual with the individual and sanctioned by the custom of the society in which he lived. But *ethical* has come to refer to the principles of right in the abstract, with reference to the individual character and its complete development in accordance with general human laws; *moral* refers to action as affecting the community and sanctioned by social and religious law. *Ethical* has philosophical connotations; *moral* practical and religious ones. When we speak of something as being *ethically* right, we suggest that we are going back to first principles and judging it as a matter of abstract right and wrong. When we speak of something as *morally* wrong, we are thinking especially of the act in relation to society and social judgments.

ETIQUETTE, CEREMONY, DECORUM, FASHION, MANNERS. *Etiquette*, in Old French *estiquet*, a little note, from the German *stichen*, to stick, is really a doublet of *ticket*, and signifies, literally, a ticket on which the forms to be observed on particular occasions were inscribed. Originally, the term was applied to a little piece of paper or note stuck up on the gate of a court. On state or very formal occasions it was customary to send small tickets to invited guests, informing them concerning the parts they were expected to take in the ceremony. From this practice the present meaning of the term doubtless arose, and the word came to signify the forms that should be observed in the ceremonial intercourses of life.

Of the words included in this article as synonymes of *etiquette, manners* is the most general, for the derivation and definition of which see MANNERS. It means simply ways of doing things. *Decorum* (see DECENCY) means *manners*, with special reference to that which is suitable and graceful. *Fashion* (see FASHION) signifies *manners* with special reference to the habits that happen to prevail in society at the minute. *Etiquette* indicates the *manners* that prevail in formal society considered as a well-defined system, in which every detail of conduct is regulated. *Ceremony* is the *etiquette* of particular formal occasions, with special reference to external dignity and form (see FORM).

EUGENICS, BREEDING. There is no real synonyme for *eugenics*, but the general word *breeding*, which it has partly replaced, may serve the purpose. *Eugenics*, from Greek εὖ, well, and γένος, race, means the science of producing a good race of human beings, and all that pertains thereto. *Breeding* (see BREED) means simply the production of animals or plants, but it has been specialized among raisers of stock, etc., to refer to the production of a good stock or particular kinds of stock, and hence as applied to the development of the lower orders of being it has much the same meaning as *eugenics*.

EULOGY. See ENCOMIUM.

EUPHONIOUS, HARMONIOUS. *Euphonious*, from Greek εὖ, well, and φονή, a sound, meaning a pleasant sound, and *harmonious* (see MELODY), both mean "agreeable to the ear," but *harmonious* is a more positive word than *euphonious*. *Harmonious* suggests the presence of sounds whose combination is delightful; *euphonious* the absence of all sounds which might be unpleasant. *Euphonious* refers especially to the juxtaposition of sounds in speaking;

harmonious to the juxtaposition of musical sounds, in singing, playing, etc.

EUTHANASIA, EASY DEATH. *Euthanasia*, from Greek *εὖ*, well, and *θάνατος*, death, being a technical word, has no exact synonymes except phrases like *easy death*, *painless death*, which are simply translations of the Greek term into familiar English. It refers to an easy or painless death, especially one attained through the administration of a drug by a physician in cases of mortal and painful illness.

EVADE, EQUIVOCATE, PREVARICATE. *Evade* (see ESCAPE). *Equivocate* (see AMBIGUITY). *Prevaricate* comes from Latin *prevaricari*, from *præ*, especially, very, and *varus*, crooked, and originally meant to say something very crooked, to tell a lie.

These words designate an artful mode of escaping the scrutiny of an inquirer: we *evade* by artfully turning the subject or calling off the attention of the inquirer; we *equivocate* by the use of *equivocal* expressions; we *prevaricate* by the use of loose and indefinite expressions; we avoid giving satisfaction by *evading;* we give a false satisfaction by *equivocating:* we give dissatisfaction by *prevaricating.* *Evading* is not so mean a practice as *equivocating:* it may be sometimes prudent to *evade* a question which we do not wish to answer; but *equivocations* are employed for the purposes of falsehood and interest: *prevarications* are still meaner; and are resorted to mostly by criminals in order to escape detection.

Evasion, Shift, Subterfuge.—*Evasion* is here taken only in the bad sense; *shift* and *subterfuge* are modes of *evasion:* the former signifies that gross kind of *evasion* by which one attempts to *shift* off an obligation from one's self; the *subterfuge*, from *subter*, under, and *fugio*, to fly, is a mode of *evasion* in which one has recourse to some screen or shelter. The *evasion*, in distinction from the others, is resorted to for the gratification of pride or obstinacy: whoever wishes to maintain a bad cause must have recourse to *evasions;* candid minds despise all *evasions;* the *shift* is the trick of a knave, it always serves a paltry, low purpose; he who has not courage to turn open thief will use any *shifts* rather than not get money dishonestly: the *subterfuge* is the refuge of one's fears; it is not resorted to from the hope of gain, but from the fear of a loss; but for purposes of interest, but for those of character; he who wants to justify himself in a bad cause has recourse to *subterfuge.*

EVANESCENT, EPHEMERAL, TRANSITORY. These words all indicate that which endures for only a little space, but there is some difference in the image conveyed in each word. *Evanescent*, from Latin *e*, away, and *vanescere*, about to vanish, means about to vanish away. *Ephemeral*, from Greek *ἐπί* and *ἡμέρα*, for a day, means enduring but for a day. *Transitory*, from Latin *trans*, beyond, and *itus*, the past participle of *ire*, to go, means about to pass beyond our sight. *Ephemeral* indicates that which by its very nature cannot endure; *transitory* that which, as a matter of fact but not of necessity, is not enduring. *Evanescent* indicates a higher degree of transitoriness suggesting that which is disappearing into thin air, as it were, before our very eyes.

EVANGELICAL, GOSPEL, ORTHODOX. *Gospel*, used as an adjective, is a translation of the Greek *εὐαγγελικός* (from *εὖ*, well, and *ἀγγελία*, tidings), into Anglo-Saxon *god*, good, and *spell*, story or tale. Both referred specifically to the original documents of the Christian faith, the biographies of Christ, and the message therein delivered. But, as in the case of many other similar pairs of words, the Greek has been specialized to refer to particular sects and tenets. *Evangelical* means like the original *gospel*, and has been adopted by certain sects, to characterize their attempts to carry out the precepts of the New Testament more literally. *Gospel* perfection means the standard of perfection enjoined in the Christian gospel; *evangelical* teaching may refer to the teaching of the New Testament or to the particular teaching of the *evangelical* sects. *Orthodox*, from Greek *ὀρθός*, straight, *δόξα*, opinion, means holding the right opinion concerning matters of Christian faith, and refers to matters of intellectual belief, rather than the active practice or emotional faith suggested in *evangelical*. It also refers to the whole body of Christian teaching founded upon the gospel rather than to the gospel itself.

EVEN, Smooth, Level, Plain. *Even* (see Equal). *Smooth*, Anglo-Saxon *smethe*, comes from a Teutonic base signifying creamy. *Level*, Late Latin *libella*, from *libra*, balance, was originally simply the name of a carpenter's instrument for determining that a thing is horizontal. *Plain* (see Apparent).

Even and *smooth* are both opposed to roughness; but that which is *even* is free only from great roughness or irregularities; that which is *smooth* is free from every degree of roughness, however small: a board is *even* which has no knots or holes; it is not *smooth* unless its surface be an entire plane: the ground is said to be *even*, but not *smooth*; the sky is *smooth*, but not *even*. *Even* is to *level*, when applied to the ground, what *smooth* is to *even*; the *even* is free from protuberances and depressions on its exterior surface; the *level* is free from rises or falls: a path is said to be *even*; a meadow is *level*: ice may be *level*, though it is not *even*; a walk up the side of a hill may be *even*, although the hill itself is the reverse of a *level*: the *even* is said of that which unites and forms one uninterrupted surface; but the *level* is said of things which are at a distance from each other, and are discovered by the eye to be in a parallel line; hence the floor of a room is *even* with regard to itself; it is *level* with that of another room. *Evenness* respects the surface of bodies; *plainness* respects their direction and freedom from external obstructions: a path is *even* which has no indentures or footmarks; a path is *plain* which is not stopped up or interrupted by wood, water, or any other thing intervening.

When applied figuratively, these words preserve their analogy: an *even* temper is secured from all violent changes of humor; a *smooth* speech is divested of everything which can ruffle the temper of others; but the former is always taken in a good sense, and the latter mostly in a bad sense, as evincing an illicit design or a purpose to deceive: a *plain* speech,

on the other hand, is divested of everything obscure or figurative, and is consequently a speech free from disguise and easy to be understood.

Even and *level* are applied to conduct or condition, the former as regards ourselves, the latter as regards others: he who adopts an *even* course of conduct is in no danger of putting himself upon a *level* with those who are otherwise his inferiors.

EVENING. See Gloaming.

EVENT, Incident, Accident, Adventure, Occurrence. *Event*, in Latin *eventus*, participle of *evenire*, to come out, signifies that which falls out or turns up. *Incident*, in Latin *incidens*, from *incidere*, signifies that which falls in or forms a collateral part of anything. *Accident* (for derivation see Accident). *Adventure*, from the Latin *advenire*, to come to, signifies what comes to or befalls one. *Occurrence*, from the Latin *ob*, in the way, and *currere*, to learn, signifies that which runs or comes in the way.

These terms are expressive of what passes in the world, which is the sole signification of the term *event*; while to that of the other terms are annexed some accessory ideas: an *incident* is a personal *event*; an *accident*, an accidental *event* which happens by the way; an *adventure*, an extraordinary *event*; an *occurrence*, an ordinary or domestic *event*: *event*, in its ordinary and limited acceptation, excludes the idea of chance; *accident* excludes that of design; *incident*, *adventure*, and *occurrence* are applicable in both cases.

Events affect nations and communities as well as individuals; *incidents* and *adventures* affect particular individuals; *accidents* and *occurrences* affect persons or things particularly or generally, individually or collectively: the making of peace, the loss of a battle, and the death of a prince are national *events*; the forming a new acquaintance and the revival of an old one are *incidents* that have an interest for the parties concerned; an escape from shipwreck, an encounter with wild beasts or savages, are *adventures* which individuals are pleased to relate and others to hear; a fire, the fall of a house, the breaking of a limb, are *accidents* **or** *occurrences;* a robbery and the death of individuals are properly *occurrences* which afford subject for a newspaper and excite an interest in the reader.

Event, when used for individuals, is always of greater importance than an *incident.* The settlement of a young person in life, the adoption of an employment, or the taking a wife, are *events,* but not *incidents;* while, on the other hand, the setting out on a journey or the return, the purchase of a house, and the despatch of a vessel are characterized as *incidents,* and not *events.*

It is further to be observed that *accident, event,* and *occurrence* are said only of that which is supposed really to happen: *incidents* and *adventures* are often fictitious; in this case the *incident* cannot be too important, nor the *adventure* too marvellous. History records the *events* of nations; plays require to be full of *incident* in order to render them interesting; romances and novels derive most of their charms from the extravagance of the *adventures* which they describe; periodical works supply the public with information respecting daily *occurrences.*

See also CONSEQUENCE.

EVER. See ALWAYS.

EVERLASTING. See ETERNAL.

EVERY. See ALL.

EVERYWHERE. See UBIQUITOUS.

EVIDENCE. See DEPONENT; PROOF.

EVIDENT. See APPARENT.

EVIL or **ILL, MISFORTUNE, HARM, MISCHIEF.** *Evil,* in its full sense, comprehends every quality which is not good, and consequently the other terms express only modifications of *evil.* The word is, however, more limited in its application than its meaning, and admits, therefore, of a just comparison with the other words here mentioned. They are all taken in the sense of *evils* produced by some external cause, or *evils* inherent in the object and arising out of it. The *evil,* or, in its contracted form, the *ill,* befalls a person; the *misfortune* comes upon him; the *harm,* originally Anglo-Saxon *hearm,* is taken, or one receives the *harm; mischief* is compounded of French *mes,*

Latin *minus,* lacking in, less, and *chef,* Latin *caput,* head, and means foolishness, something lacking in sense and wit, hence something harmful or annoying to others.

Evil, in its limited application, is taken for *evils* of the greatest magnitude; it is that which is *evil* without any mitigation or qualification of circumstances. The *misfortune* is a minor *evil;* it depends upon the opinion and circumstances of the individual; what is a *misfortune* in one respect may be the contrary in another respect. An untimely death, the fracture or loss of a limb, are denominated *evils;* the loss of a vessel, the overturning of a carriage, and the like are *misfortunes,* inasmuch as they tend to the diminution of property; but as all the casualties of life may produce various consequences, it may sometimes happen that that which seems to have come upon us by our *ill* fortune turns out ultimately of the greatest benefit; in this respect, therefore, *misfortune* is but a partial *evil:* of *evil* it is likewise observable that it has no respect to the sufferer as a moral agent; but *misfortune* is used in regard to such things as are controllable or otherwise by human foresight. The *evil* which befalls a man is opposed only to the good which he in general experiences; but the *misfortune* is opposed to the good fortune or the prudence of the individual. Sickness is an *evil,* let it be endured or caused by whatever circumstances it may; it is a *misfortune* for an individual to come in the way of having this *evil* brought on himself: his own relative condition in the scale of being is here referred to.

Harm and *mischief* are species of minor *evils,* the former of which is much less specific than the latter both in the nature and cause of the *evil.* A person takes *harm* from circumstances that are not known; the *mischief* is done to him from some positive and immediate circumstance. He who takes cold takes *harm,* the cause of which, however, may not be known or suspected: a fall from a horse is attended with *mischief* if it occasion a fracture or any *evil* to the body. *Evil* and *misfortune* respect persons only as the objects; *harm* and *mischief* are said of inanimate things as the object. A tender plant takes *harm* from being exposed to the cold air; *mischief* is done to it when its branches are violently broken off or its roots are laid bare.

See also BAD.

EVINCE. See ARGUE; PROVE.

EVOLUTION, DEVELOPMENT. *Evolution*, from Latin *e*, out, and *volvere*, to roll, unfold, and *development*, from *de*, down, and *volvere*, to roll, have originally the same meaning, but *evolution* has become a somewhat technical term referring to what in a more general way is indicated in *development*. *Development* refers to the orderly unfolding of plant or animal life or to the courses of history, *evolution* to this same orderly unfolding with specific reference to the doctrines and laws of *development* formulated by the natural scientists of the nineteenth century, especially Darwin, and extended from the field of natural science to all fields.

EXACT, EXTORT. *Exact*, in Latin *exactus*, participle of *exigere*, to drive out, signifies the exercise of simple force; but *extort*, from *extortus*, participle of *extorquere*, to wring out, marks the exercise of unusual force. In the application, therefore, to *exact* is to demand with force—it is commonly an act of injustice: to *extort* is to get with violence—it is an act of tyranny. The collector of the revenue *exacts* when he gets from the people more than he is authorized to take: an arbitrary prince *extorts* from his conquered subjects whatever he can grasp at. In the figurative sense, deference, obedience, applause, and admiration are *exacted:* a confession, an acknowledgment, a discovery, and the like are *extorted*.

Exact, Nice, Particular, Punctual.— *Exact* (see ACCURATE). *Nice* in Middle English means foolish or simple, from Old French *nice*, lazy, simple, Latin *nescius*, ignorant, compounded of *ne*, not, and *scius*, knowing. From the earlier meaning of simple the meaning of fastidious, careful in little things, developed. *Particular* means attentive to each little *particle*. *Punctual*, from the Latin *punctum*, a point, signifies keeping to a point.

Exact and *nice* are to be compared in their application either to persons or to things: *particular* and *punctual*, only in application to persons. To be *exact* is to arrive at perfection; to be *nice* is to be free from faults; to be *particular* is to be *nice* in certain *particulars;* to be *punctual* is to be *exact* in certain points. We are *exact* in our conduct or in what we do, *nice* and *particular* in our mode of doing it, *punctual* as to the time and season for doing it. It is necessary to be *exact* in our accounts; to be *nice* as an artist in the choice and distribution of colors; to be *particular* as a man of business, in the number and the details of merchandises that are to be delivered out; to be *punctual* in observing the hour of the day that has been fixed upon.

Exactness and *punctuality* are always taken in a good sense; they designate an attention to that which cannot be dispensed with: they form a part of one's duty: *niceness* and *particularity* are not always taken in the best sense; they designate an excessive attention to things of inferior importance, to matters of taste and choice. Early habits of method and regularity will make a man very *exact* in the performance of all his duties, and *particularly punctual* in his payments: an over-*niceness* in the observance of mechanical rules often supplies the want of genius; it is the mark of a contracted mind to amuse itself with *particularities* about dress, personal appearance, furniture, and the like.

When *exact* and *nice* are applied to things, the former expresses more than the latter; we speak of an *exact* resemblance and a *nice* distinction. The *exact* point is that which we wish to reach; the *nice* point is that which it is difficult to keep.

EXAGGERATION. See CARICATURE.

EXALT. See LIFT.

EXAMINATION, SEARCH, INQUIRY, RESEARCH, INVESTIGATION, SCRUTINY. *Examination* (see DISCUSS). *Search* comes from Old French *cercher*, Latin *circare*, to go around in a circle, to look everywhere. *Inquiry* (see ASK). *Research* is an intensive of *search*. *Investigation*, from the Latin *vestigium*, a track, signifies seeking by the tracks or footsteps. *Scrutiny*, from the Latin *scrutor*, to search, and *scruta*, broken pieces, signifies looking for among rubbish, to ransack.

Examination is the most general of these terms, which all agree in expressing an active effort to find out that which is unknown. An *examination* may be made without any particular effort, and may be made of things that are open to the observation, as to *examine* the face or features of a person, or anatomically to *examine* the body: a *search* is a close *examination* into matters that are hidden or less obvious: as to *search* the person or papers of one that is suspected, to *search* a house for stolen goods.

Examinations may be made by putting questions; an *inquiry* is always made in this manner. We may *examine* persons or things; we *inquire* of persons and into things: an *examination* of persons is always done for some specific and public purpose; one person *inquires* of another only for private purposes; a student is *examined* for the purpose of ascertaining his progress in learning; an offender is *examined* in order to ascertain his guilt; a person *inquires* as to the residence of another, or the road to be taken, and the like.

In the moral application of these terms, the *examination* is, as before, a general and indefinite action, which may either be confined simply to those matters which present themselves to the mind of the *examiner* or it may be extended to all points: the *search* is a laborious *examination* into that which is remote; the *inquiry* is extended to *examination* into that which is doubtful.

A *research* is a remote *search;* an *investigation* is a minute *inquiry;* a *scrutiny* is a strict *examination.* Learned men of inquisitive tempers make their *researches* into antiquity: magistrates *investigate* doubtful and mysterious affairs; physicians *investigate* the causes of diseases; men *scrutinize* the actions of those whom they hold in suspicion. Acuteness and penetration are peculiarly requisite in making *researches,* patience and perseverance are the necessary qualifications of the *investigator;* a quick discernment will essentially aid the *scrutinizer.*

Examine, Search, Explore.—Examine

and *search* (see above for both). *Explore,* in Latin *exploro,* compounded of *ex,* out, and *plorare,* to flow, signifies to make to flow out, to look for something until it is found.

These words are here considered as they designate the looking upon places or objects, in order to get acquainted with them. To *examine* expresses a less effort than to *search,* and this expresses less than to *explore.* We *examine* objects that are near; we *search* those that are hidden or removed at a certain distance; we *explore* those that are unknown or very distant. The painter *examines* a landscape in order to take a sketch of it; the botanist *searches* after curious plants; the inquisitive traveller *explores* unknown regions. An author *examines* the books from which he intends to draw his authorities; the antiquarian *searches* every corner in which he hopes to find a monument of antiquity; the classic scholar *explores* the learning and wisdom of the ancients.

EXAMINE. See ASSAY; DISCUSS.
EXAMINER. See CENSOR.
EXAMPLE, PATTERN, ENSAMPLE. *Example,* in Latin *exemplum,* from Latin *ex,* from, and *emere,* to take, means that from which something is to be imitated or taken. *Pattern* (see COPY). *Ensample* is an Anglo-French corruption of Latin *exemplum.*

All these words are taken for that which ought to be followed: but the *example* must be followed generally; the *pattern* must be followed particularly, not only as to what, but how a thing is to be done: the former serves as a guide to the judgment; the latter to guide the actions. The *example* comprehends what is either to be followed or to be avoided; the *pattern* only that which is to be followed or copied: the *ensample* is a species of *example,* the word being employed only in the solemn style. The *example* may be presented either in the object itself or the description of it; the *pattern* displays itself most completely in the object itself; the *ensample* exists only in the description. Those who know what is right should set the *example* of practising it; and those who persist in doing wrong must be made an *example* to deter others from doing the same: every one, let his age and station be what it may, may afford a *pattern* of Christian virtue; the child may be a *pattern* to his playmates of diligence and dutifulness; the citizen may be a *pattern* to his fellow-citizens of sobriety, and conformity to the laws; the soldier may be a *pattern* of obedience to his comrades: our Saviour has left us an *example* of Christian perfection which we ought to imitate, although we cannot copy it: the Scripture characters are drawn as *ensamples* for our learning.

Example, Precedent.—*Example* (see above). *Precedent,* from the Latin *precedens,* preceding, signifies by distinction that preceding which is entitled to notice. Both these terms apply to that which may be followed or made a rule; but the *example* is commonly present or before our eyes; the *precedent* is properly something past; the *example* may derive its authority from the individual; the *precedent* acquires its sanction from time and common consent: we are led by the *example,* or we copy the *example;* we are guided or governed by the *precedent.* The former is a private and often a partial affair; the latter is a public and often a national concern; we quote *examples* in literature and *precedents* in law.

Example, Instance.—*Example* refers in this case to the thing. *Instance,* from the Latin *instans,* standing on or in, signifies that which stands or serves as a resting-point.

The *example* is set forth by way of illustration or instruction; the *instance* is adduced by way of evidence or proof. Every *instance* may serve as an *example,* but every *example* is not an *instance.* The *example* consists of moral or intellectual objects; the *instance* consists of actions only, or of what serves as a proof. Rules are illustrated by *examples;* characters are illustrated by *instances:* the best mode of instructing children is by furnishing them with *examples* for every rule that is laid down; the Roman history furnishes us with many extraordinary *instances* of self-devotion for their country.

EXASPERATE. See AGGRAVATE.

EXCEED, EXCEL, SURPASS, TRANSCEND, OUTDO. *Exceed,* from the Latin *excedo,* compounded of *ex,* out, and *cedere,* to pass, means to pass out of, or beyond, the line, and is the general term. *Surpass,* compounded of French *sur,* Latin *super,* beyond, and French *passer,* to pass, from Latin *passus,* step, is one species of exceeding. *Excel,* compounded of *ex* and *cellere,* to lift or move over, found only in compounds, is another species.

Exceed is applied mostly to things in the sense of going beyond in measure, degree, quantity, and quality; one thing *exceeds* another in magnitude, height, or any other dimensions; a person's success *exceeds* his expectations.

It is taken either in an indifferent or in a bad sense, particularly in regard to persons, as a person *exceeds* his instructions or *exceeds* the due measure.

To *excel* and *surpass* signify to *exceed,* or be superior in that which is good. To *excel* may be used with reference to all persons generally, as a person strives to *excel;* to *surpass* is used in regard to particular objects, as to *surpass* another in any trial of skill.

When *excel* is used in respect of particular objects, it is more general in its sense than *surpass:* the Dutch and Italians formerly *excelled* the English in painting; one person may *surpass* another in bravery, or a thing may *surpass* one's expectations. Men *excel* in learning, arts, or arms; competitors *surpass* one another in feats of agility.

The derivatives *excessive* and *excellent* have this obvious distinction between them, that the former always signifies *exceeding* in that which ought not to be *exceeded;* and the latter *exceeding* in that where it is honorable to *exceed:* he who is habitually *excessive* in any of his indulgences must be insensible to the *excellence* of a temperate life.

Transcend, from *trans,* beyond, *scandere,* to climb, signifies to climb beyond; and *outdo*—that is, to do out of the ordinary course, are particular modes of *excelling* or *exceeding.* The genius of Homer *transcends* that of almost every poet; Heliogabalus *outdid* every other emperor in extravagance.

EXCELLENCE, SUPERIORITY. *Excellence* is an absolute term; *superiority* is a relative term; many may have *excellence* in the same degree, but they must have *superiority* in different degrees; *superiority* is often superior *excellence*, but in many cases they are applied to different objects. There is a moral *excellence* attainable by all who have the will to strive after it; but there is an intellectual and physical *superiority* which is above the reach of our wishes and is granted to a few only.

EXCEPT. See BESIDES; BUT; UNLESS.

EXCEPTION. See OBJECTION.

EXCESS, SUPERFLUITY, REDUNDANCY. *Excess* is that which exceeds any measure; *superfluity*, from *super*, over, and *fluere*, to flow, and *redundancy*, from *re*, back, and *unda*, a wave, to stream back or over, signify an *excess* of a good measure. We may have an *excess* of heat or cold, wet or dry, when we have more than the ordinary quantity, but we have a *superfluity* of provisions when we have more than we want. *Excess* is applicable to any object, but *superfluity* and *redundancy* are species of *excess*, the former applicable in a particular manner to that which is an object of our desire, and *redundancy* to matters of expression or feeling. We may have an *excess* of prosperity or adversity, a *superfluity* of good things, and a *redundancy* of speech or words.

Excessive, Immoderate, Intemperate.— The *excessive* is beyond measure; the *immoderate*, from *modus*, a mode or measure, is without measure; the *intemperate*, from *tempus*, a time or term, is that which is not kept within bounds.

Excessive designates *excess* in general; *immoderate* and *intemperate* designate *excess* in moral agents. The *excessive* lies simply in the thing which exceeds any given point: the *immoderate* lies in the passions which range to a boundless extent: the *intemperate* lies in the will which is under no control. Hence we speak of an *excessive* thirst physically considered, an *immoderate* ambition or lust of power, an *intemperate* indulgence, an *intemperate* warmth. *Excessive* admits of degrees; what is *excessive* may exceed in a greater or less degree: *immoderate* and *intemperate* mark a positively great degree of *excess*,

the former still higher than the latter: *immoderate* is in fact the highest conceivable degree of *excess*. The *excessive* use of anything will always be attended with some evil consequence: the *immoderate* use of wine will rapidly tend to the ruin of him who is guilty of the *excess:* the *intemperate* use of wine will proceed by a more gradual but not less sure process to his ruin.

See also UNREASONABLE.

EXCHANGE, BARTER, TRUCK, COMMUTE. To *exchange* (see CHANGE) is the general term signifying to take one for another, or put one thing in the place of another; the rest are but modes of *exchanging*. To *barter* is to *exchange* one article of trade for another, from Old French *barater*, to cheat, beguile, a word of doubtful origin, possibly Celtic. To *truck* is a familiar term to express a familiar action for *exchanging* one article of private property for another. *Commute*, from the Latin syllable *cum*, with, and *mutare*, to change, signifies an *exchanging* one mode of punishment for another, or one mode of payment for another: we may *exchange* one book for another; traders *barter* trinkets for gold-dust; coachmen or stablemen *truck* a whip for a handkerchief; government *commutes* the punishment of death for that of banishment.

Commute is now used, in a special sense, to refer to the travelling to and fro of people who dwell in the suburb of a city and do their business and find their pleasure within the city itself.

EXCITE, INCITE, PROVOKE. To *excite* (see AWAKEN) is said more particularly of the inward feelings; *incite* (see ENCOURAGE) is said of the external actions; *provoke* (see AGGRAVATE) is said of both. A person's passions are *excited;* he is *incited* by any particular passion to a course of conduct; a particular feeling is *provoked*, or he is *provoked* by some feeling to a particular step. Wit and conversation *excite* mirth; men are *incited* by a lust for gain to fraudulent practices; they are *provoked* by the opposition of others to *intemperate* language and intemperate measures. To *excite* is very frequently used in a physical acceptation; *incite* always, and *provoke* mostly, in a moral application. We speak of *exciting* hunger, thirst, or perspiration; of *inciting* to noble actions; of *provoking* impertinence, *provoking* scorn or resentment. When *excite* and *provoke* are applied to similar objects, the former designates a much stronger action than the latter. A thing may *excite* a smile, but it *provokes* laughter; it may *excite* displeasure, but it *provokes* anger; it may *excite* joy or sorrow, but it *provokes* to madness.

EXCITING. See ELECTRIC.

EXCLAIM. See CALL.

EXCLUDE. See COMPRISE; SEGREGATE.

EXCLUDING. See BUT.

EXCLUSION. See LOCKOUT.

EXCOMMUNICATE, ANATHEMATIZE. *Excommunicate* and *anathematize* are used in similar connections to refer to the denunciation of individuals by the Catholic Church, but they differ somewhat in meaning. *Excommunicate*, from Latin *ex*, out, and *communis*, common, means to banish from the common society and privileges of the church and the good graces and services of all Christian people. *Anathematize*, from Greek ἀνάθημα, means to denounce formally and publicly, and may refer to opinions and actions as well as individuals. It does not necessarily include, however, the formal act of excommunication. Both terms may be extended to refer to punishment by any society, or formal denunciation of any sort.

EXCORIATE. See SKIN.

EXCULPATE. See APOLOGIZE; EXONERATE.

EXCURSION, RAMBLE, TOUR, TRIP, JAUNT. *Excursion* signifies going out of one's course, from the Latin *ex* and *cursus*, the course or prescribed path: a *ramble* is a going without any course or regular path (see *ramble* under WANDER). A *tour* is a circuitous course: a *trip*, Middle English *trippen*, from base *trap*, meaning tread, found in tramp, means as a verb to tread lightly, and, as a substantive, a pleasant walk or, at present, any journey; *jaunt* comes from Old French *jaunts*, meaning toil, exercise. To go abroad in a carriage is an idle *excursion*, or one taken for mere pleasure: travellers who are not contented with what is not to be seen from a high-road make frequent *excursions* into the interior of the country. Those who are fond of rural scenery, and pleased to follow the bent of their inclinations, make frequent *rambles*. Those who set out upon a sober scheme of enjoyment from travelling are satisfied with making the *tour* of some one country or more. Those who have not much time for pleasure take *trips*. Those who have no better means of spending their time make *jaunts*.

EXCUSE, PARDON. We *excuse* (see APOLOGIZE) a person or thing by exempting him from blame. We *pardon* (from Late Latin *perdonare*, to give entirely or freely) by remitting the punishment for the offence one has committed.

We *excuse* a small fault, we *pardon* a great fault; we excuse that which is personally affects ourselves; we *pardon* that which offends against morals: we may *excuse* as equals: we can *pardon* only as superiors. We exercise good-nature in *excusing*: we exercise generosity or mercy in *pardoning*. Friends *excuse* one another for the unintentional omission of formalities; it is the prerogative of the king to *pardon* criminals whose offences will admit of *pardon:* the violation of good manners is *inexcusable* in those who are cultivated; falsehood is *unpardonable* even in a child.

See also PRETENCE.

EXECRABLE. See ABOMINABLE.

EXECRATION. See MALEDICTION.

EXECUTE, FULFIL, PERFORM. *Execute* (see ACCOMPLISH) in Latin *executus*, participle of *exsequi*, compounded of *ex*, out, and *sequi*, to follow, is to follow up to the end. To *fulfil* is to fill up to the full of what is wanted. *Perform* comes from Old French *parfournir*, from Latin *per*, thoroughly, and Old French *fournir*, to furnish, Old High German *frumjan*, to provide; and meant to furnish completely, to carry through to the end.

To *execute* is more than to *fulfil*, and to *fulfil* than to *perform*. To *execute* is to bring about an end; it involves active measures and is peculiarly applicable to that which is extraordinary or that which requires particular spirit and talents; schemes of ambition are executed: to *fulfil* is to satisfy a moral obligation; it is applicable to those duties in which rectitude and equity are involved; we *fulfil* the duties of citizens: to *perform* is to carry through by simple action or labor; it is more particularly applicable to the ordinary and regular business of life; we *perform* a work or a task. One *executes* according to one's own intentions or those of others; the soldier *executes* the orders of his general; the merchant *executes* the commissions of his correspondent: one *fulfils* according to the wishes and expectations of one's self or others; it is the part of an honest man to enter into no engagements which he cannot *fulfil;* it is the part of a dutiful son, by diligence and assiduity, to endeavor to *fulfil* the expectations of an anxious parent: one *performs,* according to circumstances, what suits one's own convenience and purposes; every good man is anxious to *perform* his part in life with credit and advantage to himself and others.

EXEMPT. See FREE.

EXEMPTION. See PRIVILEGE.

EXERCISE, PRACTICE. *Exercise,* in Latin *exercere,* from Latin *ex,* out, and *arcere,* to enclose, meant originally to drive out of an enclosure, to set at work. *Practice,* from the Greek πράσσειν, to do, signifies to perform a part.

These terms are equally applied to the actions and habits of men; but we *exercise* in that where the powers are called forth; we *practice* in that where frequency and habitude of action are requisite: we *exercise* an art; we *practice* a profession: we may both *exercise* and *practice* a virtue; but the former is that which the particular occurrence calls forth, and which seems to demand a peculiar effort of the mind; the latter is that which is done daily and ordinarily: thus we in a peculiar manner are said to *exercise* patience, fortitude, or forbearance; to *practice* charity, kindness, benevolence, and the like.

A similar distinction characterizes these words as nouns, the former applying solely to the powers of the body or mind, the latter solely to the mechanical operation: the health of the body and the vigor of the mind are alike impaired by the want of *exercise;*

in every art *practice* is an indispensable requisite for acquiring perfection: the *exercise* of the memory is of the first importance in the education of children; constant *practice* in writing is almost the only means by which the art of penmanship is acquired.

EXERT, EXERCISE. The employment of some power or qualification that belongs to one's self is the common idea conveyed by these terms; but *exert* (see ENDEAVOR) may be used for what is internal or external of one's self; *exercise* (see above) only for that which forms an express part of one's self; hence we speak of *exerting* one's strength, or *exerting* one's voice, or *exerting* one's influence: of *exercising* one's limbs, *exercising* one's understanding, or *exercising* one's tongue. *Exert* is often used only for an individual act of calling forth into action; *exercise* always conveys the idea of repeated or continued *exertion;* thus a person who calls to another *exerts* his voice; he who speaks aloud for any length of time *exercises* his lungs.

EXERTION. See ENDEAVOR.

EXHALE. See EMIT.

EXHAUST. See SPEED.

EXHIBIT. See GIVE; SHOW.

EXHILARATE. See ANIMATE.

EXHORT, PERSUADE. *Exhort,* in Latin *exhorter,* compounded of *ex,* intensive, and *hortari,* to persuade, meant to persuade earnestly. *Persuade* (see CONVICTION).

Exhortation has more of impelling in it; *persuasion,* more of drawing: a superior *exhorts;* his words carry authority with them, and rouse to action: a friend and an equal *persuades;* he wins and draws by the agreeableness or kindness of his expressions. *Exhortations* are employed only in matters of duty or necessity; *persuasions* are employed in matters of pleasure or convenience.

EXIGENCY, EMERGENCY. Necessity is the idea which is common to the signification of these terms: *exigency,* from the Latin *exigere,* to force out, to demand, expresses what the case demands; and *emergency,* from *emergere,* to arise out of, denotes what rises out of the case.

The *exigency* is more common, but less pressing; the *emergency* is imperious when it comes, but comes less frequently: a prudent traveller will never carry more money with him than what will supply the *exigencies* of his journey; and in case of an *emergency* will rather borrow of his friends than risk his property.

EXILE. See BANISH; PROSCRIBE.

EXIST, LIVE. *Live,* Anglo-Saxon *libban,* is the native English word corresponding to the Latin *exist,* for which see BE.

Existence is the property of all things in the universe; *life,* which is the inherent power of motion, is the particular property communicated by the Divine Being to some parts only of His creation: *exist,* therefore, is the general, and *live* the specific term: whatever *lives, exists* according to a certain mode; but many things *exist* without *living:* when we wish to speak of things in their most abstract relation, we say they *exist;* when we wish to characterize the form of *existence* we say they *live.*

Existence, in its proper sense, is the attribute which we commonly ascribe to the Divine Being, and it is that which is immediately communicable by Himself; *life* is that mode of *existence* which He has made to be communicable by other objects besides Himself: *existence* is taken only in its strict and proper sense, independent of all its attributes and appendages; but *life* is regarded in connection with the means by which it is supported, as animal life, or vegetable life. In like manner, when speaking of spiritual objects, *exist* retains its abstract sense, and *live* is employed to denote an active principle: animosities should never *exist* in the mind; and everything which is calculated to keep them *alive* should be kept at a distance.

EXIT, DEPARTURE. Both these words are metaphorically employed for death or a passage out of this life; the former is borrowed from the act of going off the stage; the latter from the act of setting off on a journey. *Exit* seems to convey the idea of volition; for we speak of making our *exit; departure* designates simply the event; the hour of a man's *departure* is not made known to him. When we speak of an *exit,* we think only of the place

left; when we speak of a *departure,* we think of the place gone to: the unbeliever may talk of his *exit;* the Christian most commonly speaks of his *departure.*

EXONERATE, EXCULPATE. *Exonerate,* from *onus,* a burden, signifies to take off the burden of a charge or of guilt; to *exculpate,* from *culpa,* a fault or blame, is to throw off the blame: the first is the act of another; the second is one's own act: we *exonerate* him upon whom a charge has lain, or who has the load of guilt; we *exculpate* ourselves when there is any danger of being blamed: circumstances may sometimes tend to *exonerate;* the explanation of some person is requisite to *exculpate:* in a case of dishonesty, the absence of an individual at the moment when the act was committed will altogether *exonerate* him from suspicion; it is fruitless for any one to attempt to *exculpate* himself from the charge of faithlessness who is detected in conniving at the dishonesty of others.

EXPAND. See DILATE; SPREAD.

EXPECT. See WAIT.

EXPECTATION. See HOPE.

EXPEDIENT, RESOURCE. The *expedient* is an artificial means; the *resource* is a natural means: a cunning man is fruitful in *expedients;* a fortunate man abounds in *resources:* Robinson Crusoe adopted every *expedient* in order to prolong his existence at a time when his *resources* were at the lowest ebb.

Expedient, Fit.—*Expedient,* from the Latin *expedire,* present participial stem, *expedient* (compounded of *ex,* out, and *pedem,* foot, and meaning to take one's feet out, to be ready to start) supposes a certain degree of necessity from circumstances; *fit* for the purpose signifies simply an agreement with, or suitability to, the circumstances: what is *expedient* must be *fit,* because it is called for; what is *fit* need not be *expedient,* for it may not be required. The *expediency* of a thing depends altogether upon the outward circumstances; the *fitness* is determined by a moral rule: it is imprudent not to do that which is *expedient;* it is disgraceful to do that which is *unfit:* it is *expedient* for him who wishes to prepare for death occasionally to take an account of his life; it is not *fit* for him who is about to die to dwell with anxiety on the things of this life.

See also NECESSARY.

EXPEDITE. See HASTEN.

EXPEDITIOUS. See DILIGENT.

EXPEL. See BANISH; PROSCRIBE.

EXPEND. See SPEND.

EXPENSE. See COST.

EXPERIENCE, EXPERIMENT, TRIAL, PROOF, TEST. *Experience* and *experiment*, from the Latin *ex*, intensive, and *periri*, to make a trial of, mean that which is learned through personal trial. *Try* comes from Old French *trier*, originally from Late Latin *tritare*, to rub, pulverize, separate, purify. *Proof* signifies either the act of *proving*, from the Latin *probare*, to make good, or the thing made good, *proved* to be good. *Test* comes from the Italian *testa*, a vessel in which metals are tried.

By all the actions implied in these terms we endeavor to arrive at a certainty respecting some unknown particular: *experience* is that which has been tried; an *experiment* is the thing to be tried; *experience* is certain, as it is a deduction from the past for the service of the present; the *experiment* is uncertain and serves a future purpose: *experience* is an unerring guide, which no man can desert without falling into error; *experiments* may fail, or be superseded by others more perfect.

Experience serves to lead us to moral truth; *experiments* aid us in ascertaining speculative truth: we profit by *experience* to rectify practice; we make *experiments* in theoretical inquiries: he, therefore, who makes *experiments* in matters of *experience* rejects a steady and definitive mode of coming at the truth of one that is variable and uncertain, and that, too, in matters of the first moment.

The *experiment*, *trial*, and *proof* have equally the character of uncertainty; but the *experiment* is employed only in matters of an intellectual nature; the *trial* is employed in matters of a personal nature, on physical as well as mental objects; the *proof* is employed in moral subjects: we make an *experiment* in order to know whether a thing be true or false; we make a *trial* in order to know whether it be capable or incapable, convenient or inconvenient, useful or the contrary; we put a thing to the *proof* in order to determine whether it be good or bad, real or unreal: *experiments* tend to confirm opinions; the philosopher doubts every position which cannot be demonstrated by repeated *experiments*; *trials* are of absolute necessity in directing our conduct, our taste, and our choice; we judge of our strength or skill by *trials*; we judge of the effect of colors by *trials*, and the like: the *proof* is the *trial* that proves; it determines the judgment in the knowledge of men and things; the *proof* of men's characters and merits is best made by observing their conduct. The *test* is the most decisive kind of *proof*, whence the phrase "to stand the *test*."

The *proof* and *test* may be taken for that which serves to prove, with the same distinction: to give *proofs* of sincerity; ridicule is not the *test* of truth.

See also ATTEMPT.

EXPERIMENTAL. See EMPIRICAL.

EXPERT. See CLEVER.

EXPIATE. See ATONE.

EXPIRE. See DIE.

EXPLAIN, EXPOUND, INTERPRET. *Explain* signifies to make *plain* (see APPARENT). *Expound*, from the Latin *expono*, compounded of *ex*, out, and *ponere*, to place or set, signifies to set forth in detail. *Interpret*, in Latin *interpres*, an agent, a broker, is compounded of *inter*, between, and possibly *pretium*, price, indicating a go-between in business and financial transactions; then a go-between in other affairs, especially between people speaking different languages.

To *explain* is the generic, the rest are specific: to *expound* and *interpret* are each modes of *explaining*. Single words or sentences are *explained;* a whole work, or considerable parts of it, are *expounded;* the sense of any writing or symbolical sign is *interpreted*. It is the business of the philologist to *explain* the meaning of words by a suitable definition; it is the business of the divine to *expound* Scripture; it is the business of the antiquarian to *interpret* the meaning of old inscriptions or of hieroglyphics. An *explanation* serves to assist the understanding to supply a deficiency, and remove obscurity; an *exposition* is an ample *explanation*, in which minute particulars are detailed and the connection of events in the narrative is kept up; it serves to assist the memory and awaken the attention: both the *explanation* and *exposition* are employed in clearing up the sense of things as they are, but the *interpretation* is more arbitrary; it often consists of affixing or giving a sense to things which they have not previously had; hence it is that the same passages in authors admit of different *interpretations,* according to the character or views of the commentator.

To *explain* and *interpret* are not confined to what is written or said, they are employed likewise with regard to the actions of men; *exposition* is, however, used only with regard to writings. The major part of the misunderstandings and animosities which arise among men might easily be obviated by a timely *explanation;* it is the characteristic of good-nature to *interpret* the looks and actions of men as favorably as possible. The *explanation* may sometimes flow out of circumstances; the *interpretation* is always the act of a voluntary and rational agent. The discovery of a plot or secret scheme will serve to *explain* the mysterious and strange conduct of such as were previously acquainted with it. According to an old proverb, "Silence gives consent"; for thus at least they are pleased to *interpret* it who are interested in the decision.

Explain, Illustrate, Elucidate.—Explain (see above). *Illustrate,* in Latin *illustratus,* participle of *illustrare,* to throw light on, signifies to make a thing bright, or easy to be surveyed and examined. *Elucidate,* in Latin *elucidatus,* participle of *elucido,* from *lux,* light, signifies to bring forth into the light.

To *explain* is simply to render intelligible; to *illustrate* and *elucidate* are to give additional clearness: everything requires to be *explained* to one who is ignorant of it; but the best informed will require to have abstruse subjects *illustrated* and obscure subjects *elucidated.* We always *explain* when we *illustrate* or *elucidate,* and we always *elucidate* when we *illustrate,* but not *vice versâ.* We *explain* by reducing compounds to simples, and generals to particulars; we *illustrate* by means of examples, similes, and allegorical figures; we *elucidate* by commentaries or the statement of facts. Words are the common subject of *explanation;* moral truths require *illustration;* poetical allusions and dark passages in writers require *elucidation.*

Explanatory, Explicit, Express.—Explanatory signifies containing or belonging to *explanation. Explicit,* in Latin *explicatus,* from *explicare,* to unfold, signifies unfolded or laid open. *Express,* in Latin *expressus,* the past participle of *exprimere,* to press out, signifies the same as expressed or delivered in specific terms.

The *explanatory* is that which is superadded to clear up difficulties or obscurities. A letter is *explanatory* which contains an *explanation* of something preceding, in lieu of anything new. The *explicit* is that which of itself obviates every difficulty; an *explicit* letter, therefore, will leave nothing that requires *explanation:* the *explicit* admits of a free use of words; the *express* requires them to be unambiguous. A person ought to be *explicit* when he enters into an engagement; he ought to be *express* when he gives commands.

EXPLOIT. See DEED.

EXPLORE. See EXAMINE; RUMMAGE.

EXPLOSION. See ERUPTION.

EXPOSED. See SUBJECT; VULNERABLE.

EXPOSTULATE, REMONSTRATE. *Expostulate,* from *postulare,* to demand, signifies to demand reasons for a thing. *Remonstrate,* from *monstrare,* to show, signifies to show reasons against a thing.

We *expostulate* in a tone of authority; we *remonstrate* in a tone of complaint. He who *expostulates* passes a censure and claims to be heard; he who *remonstrates* presents his case and *requests* to be heard. *Expostulation* may often be the precursor of violence; *remonstrance* mostly rests on the force of reason and representation: he who admits of *expostulation* from an inferior undermines his own authority; he who is deaf to the *remonstrances* of his friends is far gone in folly; the *expostulation* is mostly on matters of personal interest; the *remonstrance* may as often be made on matters of propriety. The Scythian ambassadors *expostulated* with Alexander against his invasion of their country; King Richard *expostulated* with Wat Tyler on the subject of his insurrection; Artabanes *remonstrated* with Xerxes on the folly of his projected invasion.

EXPOUND. See EXPLAIN.

EXPRESS, DECLARE, SIGNIFY, TESTIFY, UTTER. All these terms are taken in the sense of communicating to others. To *express*, from the Latin *exprimere*, or *ex*, out, and *premere*, to press, signifying to bring out by a particular effort, is the general term. To *declare* and the other terms are different modes of *expressing*, varying in the manner and circumstances of the action. To *express* is the simple act of communication, resulting from our circumstances as social agents; to *declare* is to *express* clearly and openly. A person may *express* his opinions to an individual, but to *declare* is to make clear or known to several. We may *express* directly or indirectly; we *declare* directly and sometimes loudly. Words, looks, gestures, or movements serve to *express;* actions and things may sometimes *declare:* sometimes we cannot *express* our contempt in so strong a manner as by preserving a perfect silence when we are required to speak; an act of hostility on the part of a nation is as much a *declaration* of war as if it were *expressed* in positive terms.

To *express* is to convey to another by any means that which passes in one's mind. To *signify*, from *signum*, a sign, and *facere*, to make, is to convey by some outward sign. To *express* is said generally of one's opinions and feelings; to *signify* is to make one's particular wishes known to an individual: we *express* mostly in positive terms; we may *signify* in any manner, either by looks or words.

Words may both *express* and *signify:* they *express* the commonly received meaning affixed to them; but they *signify* more or less according to circumstances or the intention of the speaker; the word "no" *expresses* simple negation, but it may be made to *signify* very differently by any one using it.

As epithets, *expressive* and *significant* admit of a similar distinction: an *expressive* look is that which is fitted to *express* what is intended; a *significant* look is that which is calculated to *signify* the particular feeling of the individual.

To *signify* and *testify*, from *testis*, a witness, and *facere*, to make, like the word *express*, are employed in general for any act of communication otherwise than by words; but *express* is used in a stronger sense than either of the former. The passions and strongest movements of the soul are *expressed;* the simple intentions or transitory feelings of the mind are *signified* or *testified.* A person *expresses* his joy by the sparkling of his eye and the vivacity of his countenance; he *signifies* his wish by a nod; he *testifies* his approbation by a smile. People of vivid sensibility must take care not to *express* all their feelings; those who expect a ready obedience from their inferiors must not adopt a haughty mode of *signifying* their will: nothing is more gratifying to an ingenuous mind than to *testify* its regard for merit, wherever it may discover itself.

Utter, from the preposition *out*, signifying to bring out, differs from *express* in this, that the latter respects the thing which is communicated, and the former the means of communication. We *express* from the heart; we *utter* with the lips: to *express* an uncharitable sentiment is a violation of Christian duty; to *utter* an unseemly word is a violation of good manners: those who say what they do not mean *utter*, but not *express;* those who show by their looks what is passing in their hearts *express*, but do not *utter*.

See also EXPLANATORY.

EXPRESSION. See WORD.

EXPRESSIVE. See SIGNIFICANT.

EXPUNGE. See BLOT.

EXTEMPORANEOUS. See UNPREMEDITATED.

EXTEND, STRETCH, REACH. These words are nearly allied to one another in the sense of drawing out so as to enlarge the dimensions, particularly that of length. *Extend*, from *ex*, out, and *tendere*, to stretch, signifying to tend outward or away from an object, is the most general of these terms

Stretch comes from Anglo-Saxon *stræc*, hard, rigid; *stretch* being to make stiff or hard, as in straining a string. *Reach*, Anglo-Saxon *ræcan*, conveys the idea of attaining a point or an object by *stretching*. Things may *extend* in any manner, either by simply passing over or occupying a certain space; as a piece of water *extends* into a country.

They may also be *extended* by adding to their dimensions; as to *extend* the garden beyond the house.

Things are *stretched* or *extended* lengthwise as far as they will admit of extension; as to *stretch* one's neck; to lie *stretched* on the ground.

Wherefore these words may be applied to the same objects with this distinction: to *extend* the arm or hand is simply to put it out; to *stretch* the arm is to extend it its full length.

A country is said to *extend* in its ordinary application, but it is only said figuratively to *stretch* when it seems to *extend* itself by an effort to its utmost length.

To *extend* is indefinite as to the distance; it may be shorter or longer, and requires, therefore, to be expressly defined: to *reach* is defined by the point arrived at, which may be either expressed or implied; as the road *extends* many miles; it will not *reach* so far, *i. e.*, as the house or other objects implied.

Persons *extend* things, as one *extends* a field, boundary, etc.; persons or things *reach* things; a person *reaches* a place; a sound *reaches* the ear.

In the moral and extended application they are distinguished in a similar manner: influence, power, observations, etc., may be *extended* in an indefinite manner as before, but they are said to be *stretched* when they are carried as far as they can be, and sometimes farther than is convenient.

One *reaches* a certain age, or one *reaches* a goal; the understanding *reaches* an object of contemplation.

See also ENLARGE.

EXTENSIVE. See COMPREHENSIVE.

EXTENT. See LIMIT.

EXTENUATE, PALLIATE. *Extenuate*, from the Latin *tenuis*, thin, small, signifies literally to make small. *Palliate*, in Latin *palliatus*, participle of *pallio*, from *pallium*, a cloak, signifies to throw a cloak over a thing so that it may not be seen.

These terms are both applicable to the moral conduct, and express the act of lessening the guilt of any impropriety.

To *extenuate* is simply to lessen guilt without reference to the means; to *palliate* is to lessen it by means of art. To *extenuate* is rather the effect of circumstances: to *palliate* is the direct effort of an individual. Ignorance in the offender may serve as an *extenuation* of his guilt, although not of his offence: it is but a poor *palliation* of a man's guilt to say that his crimes have not been attended with the mischief which they were calculated to produce.

EXTERIOR. See OUTWARD.

EXTERMINATE. See ERADICATE.

EXTERNAL. See OBJECTIVE; OUTWARD.

EXTINGUISHED. See OUT.

EXTIRPATE. See ERADICATE.

EXTOL. See PRAISE.

EXTORT. See EXACT.

EXTRANEOUS, EXTRINSIC, FOREIGN. *Extraneous*, from *ex* or *extra*, signifies out of the land, not belonging to it. *Extrinsic*, in Latin *extrinsecus*, compounded of *extra* and *secus*, beside, signifies outward, external. *Foreign*, from the Latin *foris*, out-of-doors, signifies not belonging to the household.

The *extraneous* is that which forms no necessary or natural part of anything: the *extrinsic* is that which forms a part or has a connection, but only in an indirect form; it is not an inherent or component part: the *foreign* is that which forms no part whatever and has no kind of connection. A work is said to contain *extraneous* matter which contains much matter not necessarily belonging to, or illustrative of, the subject: a work is said to have *extrinsic* merit when it borrows its value from local circumstances, in distinction from the intrinsic merit, or that which lies in the contents.

Extraneous and *extrinsic* have a general and abstract sense, but *foreign* has a particular signification; they always pass over to some object either expressed or understood: hence we say *extraneous* ideas or *extrinsic* worth, but that a particular mode of acting is *foreign* to the general plan pursued. Anecdotes of private individuals would be *extraneous* matter in a general history: the respect and credit which men gain from their fellow-citizens by an adherence to rectitude is the *extrinsic* advantage of virtue; the peace of a good conscience and the favor of God are its *intrinsic* advantages: it is *foreign* to the purpose of one who is making an abridgment of a work to enter into details in any particular part.

EXTRAORDINARY, REMARKABLE, are epithets both opposed to the ordinary; and in that sense the *extraordinary* is that which in its own nature is *remarkable:* but things, however, may be *extraordinary* which are not *remarkable,* and the contrary. The *extraordinary* is that which is out of the ordinary course, but it does not always excite remark, and is not, therefore, *remarkable,* as when we speak of an *extraordinary* loan, an *extraordinary* measure of government: on the other hand, when the *extraordinary* conveys the idea of what deserves notice, it expresses much more than *remarkable.* There are but few *extraordinary* things; many things are *remarkable:* the *remarkable* is eminent; the *extraordinary* is supereminent: the *extraordinary* excites our astonishment; the *remarkable* only awakens our interest and attention. The *extraordinary* is unexpected; the *remarkable* is sometimes looked for: every instance of sagacity and fidelity in a dog is *remarkable,* and some *extraordinary* instances have been related which would almost stagger our belief.

EXTRAVAGANT, PRODIGAL, LAVISH, PROFUSE. *Extravagant,* from *extra* and *vagans,* participle of *vagari,* to wander, signifies in general wandering from the line; and *prodigal,* from the Latin *prodigus,* from *prod-,* forth, and *agere,* to drive, signifies in general sending forth, or giving out in great quantities. *Lavish,* from Anglo-Saxon *lafian,* to wash, was probably borrowed from Latin *lavare,* to wash, at an early time, signifying to wash away in waste. *Profuse,* from the Latin *profusus,* participle of *profundere,* to pour forth, signifies pouring out freely.

The idea of using immoderately is implied in all these terms, but *extrava-*

gant is the most general in its meaning and application. The *extravagant* man spends his money without reason; the *prodigal* man spends it in excesses: one may be *extravagant* with a small sum where it exceeds one's means; one can be *prodigal* only with large sums.

Extravagant and *prodigal* designate habitual as well as particular actions: *lavish* and *profuse* are properly applied to particular actions, the former to denote an expenditure more or less wasteful or superfluous, the latter to denote a full supply without any sort of scant. He who is *lavish* consumes without considering the value of what is spent; but *profuseness* may sometimes arise from an excess of liberality.

As *extravagance* has respect to the disorder of the mind, it may be employed with equal propriety to other objects; as to be *extravagant* in praises, requests, etc. As *prodigal* refers to excess in the measure of consumption, it may be applied to other objects than worldly possessions; as to be *prodigal* of one's time, treasure, strength, and whatever is near and dear to us. *Lavish* may be applied to any objects which may be dealt out without regard to their value; as to be *lavish* of one's compliments by scattering them indiscriminately. *Profuse* may be applied to whatever may be given in superabundance, but mostly in a good or indifferent sense.

EXTREME. See UTTERMOST.

EXTREME UNCTION. See UNCTION.

EXTREMITY, EXTREME. *Extremity* is used in the proper or the improper sense; *extreme,* in the improper sense: we speak of the *extremity* of a line or an avenue, the *extremity* of distress, but the *extreme* of the fashion. In the moral sense, *extremity* is applicable to the outward circumstances; *extreme,* to the opinions and conduct of men: in matters of dispute between individuals it is a happy thing to guard against coming to *extremities;* it is the characteristic of volatile tempers to be always in *extremes,* either the *extreme* of joy or the *extreme* of sorrow.

See also END.

EXTRICATE. See DISENGAGE.

EXTRINSIC. See EXTRANEOUS.

EXUBERANT, LUXURIANT. *Exuberant*, from the Latin *exuberans*, or *ex* and *uber*, udder, signifies very fruitful or superabundant: *luxuriant*, in Latin *luxurians*, from *luxus*, pomp, excess, signifies expanding with unrestrained freedom. These terms are both applied to vegetation in a flourishing state; but *exuberance* expresses the excess, and *luxuriance* the perfection: in a fertile soil, where plants are left unrestrainedly to themselves, there will be *exuberance;* plants are to be seen in their *luxuriance* only in seasons that are favorable to them.

In the moral application *exuberance* of intellect is often attended with a restless ambition that is incompatible both with the happiness and advancement of its possessor; *luxuriance* of imagination is one of the greatest gifts which a poet can boast of.

EXULTATION. See TRIUMPH.

EYE. See LOOK.

F

FABLE, TALE, NOVEL, ROMANCE.
Fable, in Latin *fabula,* from *fari,* to
speak or tell, and *tale,* from to tell,
both designate a species of narration;
novel, from the Italian *novella,* comes
from Latin *novellus,* a diminutive of
novus, new, and signifies news from real
life, or simply something new in the
way of a story; *romance* meant a tale
in verse, embodying the adventures of
some hero of chivalry, written in the
vernacular—*i. e.,* Italian or Old French
—instead of Latin, and derives its name
from *Romanicus,* Roman, the general
designation of the various Latin dialects, French, Italian, etc., as opposed
to classical Latin. Different species of
composition are expressed by the above
words: the *fable* is allegorical; its actions are natural, but its agents are
imaginary: the *tale* is fictitious but not
imaginary; both the agents and actions are drawn from the passing scenes
of life. Gods and goddesses, animals
and men, trees, vegetables, and inanimate objects in general may be made
the agents of a *fable;* but of a *tale,*
properly speaking, only men or supernatural spirits can be the agents: of the
former description are the celebrated
fables of Æsop, and of the latter the
tales of Marmontel, the *tales* of the
Genii, the Chinese *tales,* etc.: *fables*
are written for instruction, *tales* principally for amusement: *fables* consist
mostly of only one incident or action,
from which a *novel* may be drawn;
tales, always of many which excite an
interest for an individual.

The *tale,* when compared with the
novel, is a simple kind of fiction, and
consists of but few persons in the
drama; while the *novel,* on the contrary, admits of every possible variety
in characters; the *tale* is told without
much art or contrivance to keep the
reader in suspense, without any depth
of plot or importance in the catastrophe; the *novel* affords the greatest
scope for exciting an interest by the
rapid succession of events, the involve-
ments of interest, and the unravelling
of its plot. If the *novel* awakens the
attention, the *romance* rivets the whole
mind and engages the affections; it
presents nothing but what is extraordinary and calculated to fill the imagination; "of the former description,
Cervantes, Le Sage, and Fielding have
given us the best specimens; and of the
latter we have the best modern specimens from the pen of Mrs. Radcliffe."

FABRIC. See EDIFICE.

FABRICATE. See INVENT.

FABRICATION. See FICTION.

FABULOUS. See LEGENDARY.

FACE, FRONT, figuratively designate the particular parts of bodies
which bear some sort of resemblance
to the human *face* or forehead. *Face* is
applied to that part of bodies which
serves as an index or rule and contains
certain marks to direct the observer;
front is employed for that part which
is most prominent or foremost: hence
we speak of the *face* of a wheel or clock,
the *face* of a painting, or the *face* of
nature: but the *front* of a house or
building, and the *front* of a stage:
hence, likewise, the propriety of the
expressions, to put a good *face* on a
thing, to show a bold *front.*

See also CONFRONT.

Face, Countenance, Visage. — *Face,*
in Latin *facies,* appearance, signifies
that which first strikes the attention
in the general appearance of another—
i. e., the *face. Countenance,* in French
contenance, from the Latin *continere,*
to control, meant method of acting or
controlling one's self, gestures, demeanor — hence *face. Visage,* from
visus, sight, look, signifies the particular form of the *face* as it presents itself
to view; properly speaking, a kind of
countenance. The *face* consists of a
certain set of features; the *countenance*
consists of the general aggregate of
looks produced by the mind upon the
features; the *visage* consists of the whole
assemblage of features and looks in
particular cases: the *face* is the work
of nature; the *countenance* and *visage*
are the work of the mind: the *face* re-

mains the same, but the *countenance* and *visage* are changeable.

The *face* properly belongs to brutes as well as men, the *countenance* is the peculiar property of man, although sometimes applied to the brutes; the *visage* is peculiarly applicable to superior beings: the last term is employed only in the grave or lofty style.

FACETIOUS, CONVERSABLE, PLEASANT, JOCULAR, JOCOSE. All these epithets designate that companionable quality which consists in liveliness of speech. *Facetious* was in Latin *facetus*, signifying fine, witty, courteous. *Conversable* is literally able to hold a conversation. *Pleasant* (see AGREEABLE) signifies making ourselves *pleasant* with others, or them pleased with us. *Jocular* signifies after the manner of a *joke*, from *joculus*, a little joke; *jocose*, using or having *jokes*, from *iocus*, joke.

Facetious may be employed either for writing or for conversation; the rest only in conversation: the *facetious* man deals in that kind of discourse which may excite laughter; a *conversable* man may instruct as well as amuse; the *pleasant* man says everything in a *pleasant* manner; his *pleasantry* even on the most delicate subject is without offence: the person speaking is *jocose;* the thing said, or the manner of saying it, is *jocular;* it is not for any one to be always *jocose*, although sometimes one may assume a *jocular* air when we are not at liberty to be serious. A man is *facetious* from humor; he is *conversable* by means of information; he indulges himself in occasional *pleasantry*, or allows himself to be *jocose*, in order to enliven conversation; a useful hint is sometimes conveyed in *jocular* terms.

FACILITY. See EASE.

FACT. See CIRCUMSTANCE.

FACTION, PARTY. These two words equally suppose the union of many persons, and their opposition to certain views different from their own: but *faction*, from *factio*, making, denotes an activity and secret machination against those whose views are opposed; and *party*, from the verb to part or split, expresses only a division of opinion.

The term *party* has of itself nothing odious; that of *faction* is always so: any man, without distinction of rank, may have a *party* either at court or in the army, in the city or in literature, without being himself immediately implicated in raising it; but *factions* are always the result of active efforts: one may have a *party* for one's merit, from the number and ardor of one's friends; but a *faction* is raised by busy and turbulent spirits for their own purposes: Rome was torn by the intestine *factions* of Cæsar and Pompey. *Faction* is the demon of discord, armed with the power to do endless mischief, and intent alone on destroying whatever opposes its progress; woe to that state into which it has found an entrance: *party* spirit may show itself in noisy debate; but while it keeps within the legitimate bounds of opposition it is an evil that must be endured.

FACTIOUS, SEDITIOUS. *Factious,* in Latin *factiosus,* from *facere,* to do, signifies the same as busy or intermeddling; ready to take an active part in matters not of one's own immediate concern. *Seditious,* in Latin *seditiosus,* signifies prone to sedition (see INSURRECTION).

Factious is an epithet to characterize the tempers of men; *seditious* characterizes their conduct: the *factious* man attempts to raise himself into importance, he aims at authority, and seeks to interfere in the measures of government; the *seditious* man attempts to excite others, and to provoke their resistance to established authority: the first wants to be a lawgiver; the second does not hesitate to be a law-breaker: the first wants to direct the state; the second, to overturn it: the *factious* man is mostly in possession of either power, rank, or fortune; the *seditious* man is seldom elevated in station or circumstances above the mass of the people. The Roman tribunes were in general little better than *factious* demagogues, such, in fact, as abound in all republics; Wat Tyler was a *seditious* disturber of the peace. *Factious* is mostly applied to individuals; *seditious* is employed for bodies of men: hence we speak of a *factious* nobleman, a *seditious* multitude.

FACTOR, Agent. Though both these terms, according to their origin, imply a maker or doer, yet, at present, they have a distinct signification; the word *factor* is used in a limited, and the word *agent* in a general sense: the *factor* only buys and sells on the account of others; the *agent* transacts every sort of business in general: merchants and manufacturers employ *factors* abroad to dispose of goods transmitted; lawyers are frequently employed as *agents* in the receipt and payment of money, the transfer of estates, and various other pecuniary concerns.

FACULTY. See Ability.

FAIL, Fall Short, Be Deficient. *Fail*, in French *faillir*, is derived from the Latin *fallere*, to deceive. To *fail* marks the result of actions or efforts; a person *fails* in his undertaking: *fall short* designates either the result of actions or the state of things; a person *falls short* in his calculation or in his account; the issue *falls short* of the expectation: to *be deficient* marks only the state or quality of objects; a person is *deficient* in good manners. People frequently *fail* in their best endeavors for want of knowing how to apply their abilities; when our expectations are immoderate, it is not surprising if our success *falls short* of our hopes and wishes: there is nothing in which people discover themselves to be more *deficient* than in keeping ordinary engagements. To *fail* and *be deficient* are both applicable to the characters of men; but the former is mostly employed for the moral conduct, the latter for the outward behavior; hence a man is said to *fail* in his duty, in the discharge of his obligations, in the performance of a promise, and the like: but to *be deficient* in politeness, in attention to his friends, in his address, in his manner of entering a room, and the like.

Failure, Failing.—*Failure* bespeaks the action or the result of the action; a *failing* is the habit or the habitual *failure:* the former is said of our undertakings, the latter of our moral character. *Failure* is opposed to success, a *failing* to a perfection. The merchant must be prepared for *failures* in his speculations; the statesman for *failures* in his projects, the result of which depends upon contingencies that are above human control. With our *failings*, however, it is somewhat different; we must never rest satisfied that we are without them, nor contented with the mere consciousness that we have them.

See also Imperfection.

Failure, Miscarriage, Abortion.— *Failure* has always a reference to the agent and his design; *miscarriage*, that is, the carrying or going wrong, is applicable to all sublunary concerns, without reference to any particular agent; *abortion*, from the Latin *aboriri*, to deviate from the rise, or to pass away before it comes to maturity, is in the proper sense applied to the process of animal nature, and in the figurative sense to the thoughts and designs which are conceived in the mind.

Failure is more definite in its signification and limited in its application; we speak of the *failures* of individuals, but of the *miscarriages* of nations or things: a *failure* reflects on the person so as to excite toward him some sentiment, either of compassion, displeasure, or the like; a *miscarriage* is considered mostly in relation to the course of human events: hence the *failure* of Xerxes's expedition reflected disgrace upon himself; but the *miscarriage* of military enterprises in general are attributable to the elements or some such untoward circumstance. The *abortion*, in its proper sense, is a species of *miscarriage*, and in application a species of *failure*, as it applies only to the designs of conscious agents; but it does not carry the mind back to the agent, for we speak of the *abortion* of a scheme with as´little reference to the schemer as when we speak of the *miscarriage* of an expedition.

See also Insolvency.

FAILING. See Fail; Imperfection.

FAINT, Languid. *Faint* comes from Latin *fingere*, to feign, Old French *feint*, pretended, hence weak; thence developed the general idea of weakness or unreality, to grow *faint*, or to *faint* meaning to be weak. *Languid*, in Latin *languidus*, from *languere*, is allied to Greek λαγαρός, slack, and English *lag*.

Faint is less than *languid; faintness*

is, in fact, in the physical application, the commencement of *languor;* we may be *faint* for a short time, and if continued and extended through the limbs it becomes *languor;* thus we say, to speak with a *faint* tone, and have a *languid* frame. In the figurative application, to make a *faint* resistance, to move with a *languid* air, to form a *faint* idea, to make a *languid* effort.

FAIR, CLEAR. *Fair,* in Anglo-Saxon *fœger,* beautiful, is allied to Gothic *fagrs,* fit. *Clear* (for derivation see CLEAR).

Fair is used in a positive sense, *clear* in a negative sense: there must be some brightness in what is *fair;* there must be no spots in what is *clear.* The weather is said to be *fair* which is not only free from what is disagreeable, but somewhat enlivened by the sun; it is *clear* when it is free from clouds or mists. A *fair* skin approaches to white; a *clear* skin is without spots or irregularities.

In the moral application, a *fair* fame speaks much in praise of a man; a *clear* reputation is free from faults. A *fair* statement contains everything that can be said *pro* and *con;* a *clear* statement is free from ambiguity or obscurity. *Fairness* is something desirable and inviting; *clearness* is an absolute requisite, it cannot be dispensed with.

See also BLONDE.

Fair, Honest, Equitable, Reasonable. —*Fair* (see above). *Honest,* in Latin *honestus,* comes from *honos,* honor. *Equitable* signifies having *equity,* or according to *equity,* from Latin *æquus,* equal. *Reasonable* signifies having *reason,* or according to *reason.*

Fair is said of persons or things; *honesty* mostly characterizes the person, either as to his conduct or his principle. When *fair* and *honest* are both applied to the external conduct, the former expresses more than the latter: a man may be *honest* without being *fair;* he cannot be *fair* without being *honest.* *Fairness* enters into every minute circumstance connected with the interests of the parties, and weighs them alike for both; *honesty* is contented with a liberal conformity to the law, it consults the interest of one party; the *fair* dealer looks to his neighbor as well as himself, he wishes only for an equal share of advantage; a man may be an *honest* dealer while he looks to no one's advantage but his own: the *fair* man always acts from a principle of right; the *honest* man may be so from a motive of fear.

When *fair* is employed as an epithet to qualify things, or to designate their nature, it approaches very near in signification to *equitable* and *reasonable;* they are all opposed to what is unjust: *fair* and *equitable* suppose two objects put in collision; *reasonable* is employed abstractly; what is *fair* and *equitable* is so in relation to all circumstances, what is *reasonable* is so of itself. An estimate is *fair* in which profit and loss, merit and demerit, with every collateral circumstance, is duly weighed; a judgment is *equitable* which decides suitably and advantageously for both parties; a price is *reasonable* which does not exceed the limits of reason or propriety. A decision may be either *fair* or *equitable;* but the former is said mostly in regard to trifling matters, even in our games and amusements, and the latter in regard to the important rights of mankind. It is the business of the umpire to decide *fairly* between the combatants or the competitors for a prize; it is the business of the judge to decide *equitably* between men whose property is at issue. A demand, a charge, a proposition, or an offer may be said to be either *fair* or *reasonable;* but the former term always bears a relation to what is right between man and man; the latter, to what is right in itself according to circumstances.

FAITH, CREED. *Faith* (see BELIEF) denotes either the principle of trusting or the thing trusted. *Creed,* from the Latin *credere,* to believe, denotes the thing believed.

These words are synonymous when taken for the thing trusted in or believed; but they differ in this, that *faith* has always a reference to the principle in the mind; *creed* only respects the thing which is the object of *faith:* *faith* is the general and *creed* the particular term, for a *creed* is a set form of *faith:* hence we say to be of the same *faith,* or to adopt the same *creed.* The holy martyrs died for the *faith* as it is in Christ Jesus; every established form of religion will have its peculiar *creed*. The Church of England has adopted that *creed* which it considers as containing the purest principles of Christian *faith*.

Faith, Fidelity. — Though derived from the same source, they differ widely in meaning: *faith* here denotes a mode of action, namely, in acting true to the *faith* which others repose in us; *fidelity*, a disposition of the mind to adhere to that *faith* which others repose in us. We keep our *faith*, we show our *fidelity*. *Faith* is a public concern, it depends on promises; *fidelity* is a private or personal concern, it depends upon relationships and connections. A breach of *faith* is a crime that brings a stain on a nation, for *faith* ought to be kept even with an enemy. A breach of *fidelity* attaches disgrace to the individual, for *fidelity* is due from a subject to a prince, or from a servant to his master, or from married people one to another. No treaty can be made with him who will keep no *faith;* no confidence can be placed in him who discovers no *fidelity*.

Faithful, Trusty.—*Faithful* signifies full of *faith* or *fidelity*. *Trusty* signifies fit or worthy to be *trusted*.

Faithful respects the principle altogether; it is suited to all relations and stations, public and private; *trusty* includes not only the principle, but the mental qualifications in general; it applies to those in whom particular *trust* is to be placed. It is the part of a Christian to be *faithful* to all his engagements; it is a particular excellence in a servant to be *trusty*.

Faithful is applied in the improper sense to an unconscious *agent; trusty* may be applied with equal propriety to things as to persons. We may speak of a *faithful* saying or a *faithful* picture; a *trusty* sword or a *trusty* weapon.

In the United States the term *trusty* has of late come to apply to an inmate of an institution for the insane whose condition has so far improved that he or she is relieved of ordinary restraint and is permitted to go about the grounds and vicinity; to a prisoner whose conduct has won for him a relaxation of rules and permission to go beyond the prison walls without a guard; and to one committed to a correctional institution who is allowed similar privileges.

Faithless, Unfaithful. — *Faithless* is mostly employed to denote a breach of *faith*, and *unfaithful* to mark the want of *fidelity*. The former is positive; the latter is rather negative, implying a deficiency. A prince, a government, a people, or an individual is said to be *faithless;* a husband, a wife, a servant, or any individual, *unfaithful*. Mettus Fuffetius, the Alban Dictator, was *faithless* to the Roman people when he withheld his assistance in the battle and strove to go over to the enemy: a man is *unfaithful* to his employer who sees him injured by others without doing his utmost to prevent it. A woman is *faithless* to her husband who breaks the marriage vow; she is *unfaithful* to him when she does not discharge the duties of a wife to the best of her abilities.

Faithless, Perfidious, Treacherous.— *Faithless* is the generic term, the rest are specific terms; a breach of good *faith* is expressed by them all, but *faithless* expresses no more: the others include accessory ideas in their signification. *Perfidious*, in Latin *perfidiosus*, signifies literally breaking through *faith* in a great degree, and now implies the addition of hostility to the breach of *faith*. *Treacherous* is derived from Old French *trechier*, to trick, Latin *tricare*, from *tricœ*, difficulties, wiles, and is allied to *intricate*, etc.

A *faithless* man is *faithless* only for his own interest; a *perfidious* man is expressly so to the injury of another. A friend is *faithless* who consults his own safety in time of need; he is *perfidious* if he profits by the confidence reposed in him to plot mischief against the one to whom he has made vows of friendship. *Faithlessness* does not suppose any particular efforts to deceive: it consists of merely violating that *faith* which the relation produces; *perfidy* is never so complete as when it has most effectually assumed the mask of sincerity.

Perfidy may lie in the will to do; *treachery* lies altogether in the thing done; one may therefore be *perfidious* without being *treacherous*. A friend is *perfidious* whenever he evinces his *perfidy;* but he is said to be *treacherous* only in the particular instance in which he betrays the confidence and interests of another. I detect a man's *perfidy*, or his *perfidious* aims, by the manner in which he attempts to draw my secrets from me; I am not made acquainted with his *treachery* until I discover that my confidence is betrayed and my secrets are divulged. On the other hand, we may be *treacherous* without being *perfidious*. *Perfidy* is an offence mostly between individuals; it is rather a breach of fidelity (see FAITH) than of faith; *treachery*, on the other hand, includes breaches of private or public faith. A servant may be both *perfidious* and *treacherous* to his master; a citizen may be *treacherous*, but not *perfidious*, toward his country. It is said that in the South Sea Islands, when a chief wants a human victim, their officers will sometimes invite their friends or relations to come to them when they take the opportunity of suddenly falling upon them and despatching them; here is *perfidy* in the individual who acts this false part, and *treachery* in the act of betraying him who is murdered. When the school-master of Falerii delivered his scholars to Camillus, he was guilty of *treachery* in the act and of *perfidy* toward those who had reposed confidence in him. When Romulus ordered the Sabine women to be seized, it was an act of *treachery*, but not of *perfidy:* so, in like manner, when the daughter of Tarpeius opened the gates of the Roman citadel to the enemy.

FALL, DOWNFALL, RUIN. *Fall* comes from Anglo-Saxon *feallan*, possibly allied to Latin *fallere*, to deceive. *Ruin* (see DESTRUCTION).

Whether applied to physical objects or the condition of persons, *fall* expresses less than *downfall*, and this less than *ruin*. *Fall* applies to that which is erect; *downfall*, to that which is elevated: everything which is set up, although as trifling as a stick, may have a *fall;* but we speak of the *downfall* of the loftiest trees or the tallest spires. A *fall* may be attended with more or less mischief, or even with none at all; but *downfall* and *ruin* are accompanied with the dissolution of the bodies that *fall*. The higher a body is raised, and the greater the art that is employed in the structure, the completer the *downfall;* the greater the structure the more extended the *ruin*. In the figurative application we may speak of the *fall* of man from a state of innocence, a state of ease, or a state of prosperity, or his *downfall* from greatness or high rank. He may recover from his *fall*, but his *downfall* is commonly followed by the entire *ruin* of his concerns, and often of himself. The *fall* of kingdoms and the *downfall* of empires must always be succeeded by their *ruin* as an inevitable result.

Fall, Drop, Droop, Sink, Tumble.— *Fall* (see above). *Drop* and *droop* were originally the same word, *drop* being the Anglo-Saxon form, and *droop* the Scandinavian form. *Sink* comes from Anglo-Saxon *sincan*, to sink. *Tumble* is in Anglo-Saxon *tumbian*, meaning to turn heels over head, allied to Old High German *tumon*, to turn over and over, whence French *tomber*, to fall, is derived.

Fall is the generic, the rest specific terms: to *drop* is to *fall* suddenly, and mostly in the form of a drop; to *droop* is to *drop* in part; to *sink* is to *fall* gradually; to *tumble* is to *fall* awkwardly or contrary to the usual mode. In cataracts the water *falls* perpetually and in a mass: in rain it *drops* partially; in ponds the water *sinks* low. The head *droops*, but the body may *fall* or *drop* from a height, it may *sink* down to the earth, it may *tumble* by accident.

Fall, drop, and *sink* are extended in their application to moral or other objects; *droop* and *tumble*, in the physical sense. A person *falls* from a state of prosperity; words *drop* from the lips and *sink* into the heart. Corn, or the price of corn, *falls;* a subject *drops;* a person *sinks* into poverty or in the estimation of the world.

FALLACIOUS, DECEITFUL, FRAUDULENT. *Fallacious* comes from the Latin *fallax* and *fallere*, to deceive, signifying the property of misleading. *Deceitful* (see DECEIVE). *Fraudulent* signifies after the manner of a *fraud*.

The *fallacious* has respect to falsehood in opinion; *deceitful* to that which is externally false: our hopes are often *fallacious;* the appearances of things are often *deceitful. Fallacious,* as characteristic of the mind, excludes the idea of design; *deceitful* excludes the idea of mistake; *fraudulent* is a gross species of the *deceitful.* It is a *fallacious* idea for any one to imagine that the faults of others can serve as any extenuation of his own; it is a *deceitful* mode of acting for any one to advise another to do that which he would not do himself; it is *fraudulent* to attempt to get money by means of a falsehood.

Fallacy, Delusion, Illusion. — The *fallacy* is that which has the tendency to deceive; the *delusion* is that which deludes, or the state of being *deluded;* the *illusion* is that which has the power of illuding or sporting with the mind, or the state of being so played upon. We endeavor to detect the *fallacy* which lies concealed in a proposition: we endeavor to remove the *delusion* to which the judgment has been exposed, and to dissipate the *illusion* to which the senses or fancy are liable. In all the reasonings of freethinkers there are *fallacies* against which the ignorant cannot always be on their guard. The ignorant are perpetually exposed to *delusions* when they attempt to speculate on matters of opinion. The ideas of ghosts and apparitions are mostly attributable to the *illusions* of the senses and the imagination.

See also SOPHISTRY.

FALL SHORT. See FAIL.

FALSEHOOD. See FICTION; UN-TRUTH.

FALSITY. See UNTRUTH.

FALTER. See HESITATE.

FAME, REPUTATION, RENOWN. *Fame* (from Latin *fari,* to speak) is the most noisy and uncertain; it rests upon report: . *reputation* (see CHARACTER) is silent and solid; it lies more in the thoughts and is derived from observation. *Renown,* in French *re-nommée,* from Latin *re,* again, and *nomen,* name, meaning named again and again, signifies the reverberation of a name; it is as loud as *fame,* but more substantial and better founded: hence we say that a person's *fame* is gone abroad, his *reputation* is established, and he has got *renown.*

Fame may be applied to any object, good, bad, or indifferent; *reputation* is

applied only to real eminence in some department; *renown* is employed only for extraordinary men and brilliant exploits. The *fame* of a quack may be spread among the ignorant multitude by means of a lucky cure; the *reputation* of a physician rests upon his tried skill and known experience; the *renown* of a general is proportioned to the magnitude of his achievements.

Fame, Report, Rumor, Hearsay. — *Fame* has a reference to the thing which gives birth to it; it goes about of itself without any apparent instrumentality. *Report* (from *re* and *portare,* to carry back, or away from an object) has always a reference to the *reporter. Rumor,* in Latin *rumor,* from a root which signifies to make a humming noise, has a reference to the buzzing nature of words that are carried; it is therefore properly a buzzing *report. Hearsay* refers to the receiver of that which is said: it is limited, therefore, to a small number of speakers or reporters. *Fame* serves to form or establish a character either of a person or a thing; it will be good or bad, according to circumstances; the *fame* of our Saviour's miracles went abroad through the land; a *report* serves to communicate information of events; it may be more or less correct according to the veracity or authenticity of the *reporter; reports* of victories mostly precede the official confirmation: a *rumor* serves the purposes of fiction; it is more or less vague, according to the temper of the times and the nature of the events; every battle gives rise to a thousand *rumors:* the *hearsay* serves for information or instruction, and is seldom so incorrect as it is familiar.

FAMILIAR. See CONVERSANT; FREE.

FAMILIARITY. See ACQUAINT-ANCE.

FAMILY, HOUSE, LINEAGE, RACE. Divisions of men, according to some rule of relationship or connection, is the common idea in these terms. *Family* is the most general in its import (from the Latin *familia,* a family, *famulus,* a servant). It is applicable to those who are bound together upon the principle of dependence. *House* figuratively denotes those who live in the same *house* (Anglo-Saxon *hūs,* German *haus,* possibly from a root meaning to hide), and is commonly extended in its signification to all that passes under the same roof: hence we rather say that a woman manages her *family;* that a man rules his *house.* The *family* is considered as to its relationships— the number, union, condition, and quality of its members: the *house* is considered more as to what is transacted within its walls. We speak of a numerous *family,* a united or affectionate *family;* a mercantile *house,* and *the House,* meaning the members of the *House* of Parliament or *House* of Representatives, sometimes called the *Lower House* to distinguish it from the *House* of Lords or the Senate, familiarly called the *Upper House.* If a man cannot find happiness in the bosom of his *family,* he will seek for it in vain elsewhere; the credit of a *house* is to be kept up only by prompt payments.

In an extended application of these words they are made to designate the quality of the individual, in which case *family* bears the same familiar and indiscriminate sense as before: *house* is employed as a term of grandeur. When we consider the *family* in its domestic relations, in its habits, manners, connections, and circumstances, we speak of a genteel *family,* a respectable *family,* the royal *family:* but when we consider it with regard to its political and civil distinctions, its titles and its power, then we denominate it a *house,* as an illustrious *house;* the *House* of Bourbon, of Brunswick, or of Hanover; the imperial *House* of Austria. Any subject may belong to an ancient or noble *family:* princes are said to be descended from ancient *houses.* A man is said to be of *family* or of no *family:* we may say likewise that he is of a certain *house;* but to say that he is of no *house* would be superfluous. In republics there are *families,* but not *houses,* because there is no nobility; in China, likewise, where the private virtues only distinguish the individual or his *family,* the term *house* is altogether inapplicable.

Family includes in it every circumstance of connection and relationship; *lineage* respects only consanguinity: *family* is employed mostly for those who are coeval; *lineage* is generally used for those who have gone before. When the Athenian general Iphicrates, son of a shoemaker, was reproached by Harmodius with his birth, he said, I had rather be the first than the last of my *family:* David was of the *lineage* of Abraham, and our Saviour was of the *lineage* of David. *Race,* from the Latin *radix,* a root, denotes the origin, or that which constitutes the original point of resemblance. A *family* supposes the closest alliance; a *race* supposes no closer connection than what a common property creates. *Family* is confined to a comparatively small number; *race* is a term of extensive import, including all mankind, as the human *race,* or particular nations, as the *race* of South Sea Islanders; or a particular *family,* as the *race* of the Heraclides: from Hercules sprang a *race* of heroes.

FAMOUS, CELEBRATED, RENOWNED, ILLUSTRIOUS. *Famous* signifies literally having *fame* or the cause of *fame;* it is applicable to that which causes a noise or sensation; to that which is talked of, written upon, discussed, and thought of; to that which is reported of far and near; to that which is circulated among all ranks and orders of men. *Celebrated* signifies literally kept in the memory by a *celebration* or memorial, and is applicable to that which is praised and honored with solemnity. *Renowned* signifies literally possessed of a name, and is applicable to whatever extends the name or causes the name to be often repeated. *Illustrious* signifies literally what has or gives a lustre: it is applicable to whatever confers dignity.

Famous is a term of indefinite import; it conveys of itself frequently neither honor nor dishonor, since it is employed indifferently as an epithet for things praiseworthy or otherwise; it is the only one of these terms which may be used in a bad sense. The others rise in a gradually good sense. The *celebrated* is founded upon merit, and the display of talent in the arts and sciences; it gains the subject respect: the *renowned* is founded upon the possession of rare or extraordinary qualities, upon successful exertions and an accordance with public opinion; it brings great honor or glory to the subject: the *illustrious* is founded upon those solid qualities which not only render one known, but distinguished; it insures regard and veneration. A person may be *famous* for his eccentricities; *celebrated* as an artist, a writer, or a player; *renowned* as a warrior or a statesman; *illustrious* as a prince, a statesman, or a senator. The Maid of Orleans, who was decried by the English and idolized by the French, is equally *famous* in both nations. There are *celebrated* authors whom to censure, even in that which is censurable, would endanger one's reputation. The *renowned* heroes of antiquity have, by the perusal of their exploits, given birth to a race of modern heroes not inferior to themselves. Princes may shine in their lifetime, but they cannot render themselves *illustrious* to posterity except by the monuments of goodness and wisdom which they leave after them.

FANATIC. See ENTHUSIAST.

FANCIFUL, FANTASTICAL, WHIMSICAL, CAPRICIOUS. *Fanciful* signifies full of *fancy* (see CONCEIT). *Fantastical* signifies belonging to the fantasy, which is the immediate derivative from the Greek φαντασία, Latin *fantasia*, a vision, from root meaning to shine. *Whimsical* signifies either like a whim or having a whim, from a Scandinavian word meaning freak. *Capricious* means having *caprice*.

Fanciful and *fantastical* are both employed for persons and things; *whimsical* and *capricious* are mostly employed for persons, or what is personal. *Fanciful* is said of that which is irregular in the taste or judgment; *fantastical* is said of that which violates all propriety as well as regularity: the former may consist of a simple deviation from rule; the latter is something extravagant. A person may, therefore, sometimes be advantageously *fanciful*, although he can never be *fantastical* but to his discredit. Lively minds will be *fanciful* in the choice of their dress, furniture, or equipage: the affectation of singularity frequently renders people *fantastical* in their manners as well as their dress.

Fanciful is said mostly in regard to

errors of opinion or taste; it springs from an aberration of the mind: *whimsical* is a species of the *fanciful* in regard to one's likes or dislikes; *capricious* respects errors of temper or irregularities of feeling. The *fanciful* does not necessarily imply instability; but the *capricious* excludes the idea of fixedness. One is *fanciful* by attaching a reality to that which only passes in one's own mind; one is *whimsical* in the inventions of the *fancy;* one is *capricious* by acting and judging without rule or reason that which admits of both.

See also UTOPIAN.

Fancy, Imagination. — From what has already been said the distinction between *fancy* and *imagination,* as operations of thought, will be obvious. *Fancy,* considered as a power, simply brings the object to the mind or makes it appear; but *imagination,* from *image,* in Latin *imago,* from the root found in *imitari,* English *imitate,* is a power which presents the images or likenesses of things. The *fancy,* therefore, only employs itself about things without regarding their nature; but the *imagination* aims at tracing a resemblance and getting a true copy. The *fancy* consequently forms combinations, either real or unreal, as chance may direct; but the *imagination* is seldomer led astray. The *fancy* is busy in dreams or when the mind is in a disordered state: but the *imagination* is supposed to act when the intellectual powers are in full play.

The *fancy* is employed on light and trivial objects which are present to the senses; the *imagination* soars above all vulgar objects and carries us from the world of matter into the world of spirits, from time present to the time to come.

A milliner or mantua-maker may employ her *fancy* in the decorations of a cap or gown; but the poet's *imagination* depicts everything grand, everything bold, and everything remote.

Although Mr. Addison has thought proper, for his convenience, to use the words *fancy* and *imagination* promiscuously when writing on this subject, yet the distinction, as above pointed out, has been observed both in familiar discourse and in writing. We say that we *fancy*, not that we *imagine*, that we see or hear something; the pleasures of the *imagination*, not of the *fancy*.

See also CONCEIT; VAGARY.

FANTASTIC. See QUIXOTIC.

FANTASTICAL. See FANCIFUL.

FAR. See DISTANT.

FARCICAL, COMIC. *Farcical*, the adjective of *farce* (in French the same form, from *farcer*, to stuff, Latin *farcio*, Italian *farso*), signifies, literally, the stuffing in meat, and, in ordinary language, whatever pertains to a farce, anything stuffed with foreign matters, specifically a dramatic piece of a humorous character, full of exaggeration and drollery; hence, anything absurdly exaggerated.

Farce differs from *comedy* proper in degree, but not in kind. The aim of both is to excite mirth, but while the *comedy* does so by a comparatively faithful adherence to nature and truth, the *farce* takes much greater license and does not scruple to make use of any extravagance or improbability that may serve its purpose. At one time a *farce* was a petty show exhibited in the streets, then it was a short after-piece on the stage following a more serious performance, and latterly it supplied the entire performance.

FARE, PROVISION. *Fare*, from Anglo-Saxon *faran*, to go, signifies in general the condition or thing that comes to one or is provided for a journey. *Provision*, from *provide*, signifies the thing provided for one.

These terms are alike employed for the ordinary concerns of life, and may either be used in the limited sense for the food one procures or in general for whatever necessity or convenience is procured: to the term *fare* is annexed the idea of accident; *provision* includes that of design: a traveller on the Continent must frequently be contented with humble *fare*, unless he takes the precaution of carrying his *provisions* with him.

FARMER, HUSBANDMAN, AGRICULTURIST. *Farmer* comes from Anglo-French *ferme*, Late Latin *firma*, from *firmus*, a fixed rent, a farmer being one who paid a fixed rent to a landlord; *husbandman* is one following *husbandry*,

that is, the tillage of land by manual labor; the *farmer*, therefore, conducts the concern, and the *husbandman* labors under his direction: *agriculturist*, from the Latin *ager*, a field, and *colere*, to till, signifies any one engaged in the art of cultivation. The *farmer* is always a practitioner; the *agriculturist* may be a mere theorist: the *farmer* follows *husbandry* solely as a means of living: the *agriculturist* follows it as a science; the former tills the land upon given admitted principles; the latter frames new principles or alters those that are established. Between the *farmer* and the *agriculturist* there is the same difference as between practice and theory: the former may be assisted by the latter so long as they can go hand in hand; but in the case of a collision the *farmer* will be of more service to himself and his country than the *agriculturist; farming* brings immediate profit from personal service; *agriculture* may only promise future, and consequently contingent, advantages.

Husbandman is now obsolete in prose, though it is still used in poetry.

FARRAGO. See OLIO.

FARTHEST. See UTTERMOST.

FASCINATE. See CHARM.

FASCINATED. See SPELLBOUND.

FASHION, QUALITY, DISTINCTION. These epithets are employed promiscuously in colloquial discourse, but not with strict propriety: by men *of fashion* are understood such men as live in the fashinable world and keep the best company; by men *of quality* are understood men of rank or title; by men *of distinction* are understood men of honorable superiority, whether by wealth, office, or pre-eminence in society. Gentry and merchants, though not men *of quality*, may, by their mode of living, be men *of fashion;* and by the office they hold in the state they may likewise be men *of distinction*.

See also CUSTOM; ETIQUETTE; FORM; VOGUE.

FAST. See ABSTINENCE.

FASTEN. See FIX.

FASTIDIOUS, SQUEAMISH. *Fastidious* comes from Latin *fastidium*, loathing, perhaps from *fastus*, arrogance, and *tædium*, disgust, *fastidium* meaning arrogant disgust; *squeamish* is in Middle English *skeymous*, disdainful, from Anglo-French *escoymous*, delicate, nice as to food, from Greek σχῆμα, English *scheme*, meaning form, air, mien, manners—hence literally full of airs; in a moral sense it signifies foolishly sickly, easily disgusted. *Squeamish* implies a stronger physical shrinking than *fastidious*. The *fastidious* man avoids or rejects what he does not like; a *squeamish* person reacts more obviously against it with a kind of nervous horror. Whoever examines his own imperfections will cease to be *fastidious;* whoever restrains humor and caprice will cease to be *squeamish*.

FATAL. See DEADLY.

FATE. See CHANCE; DESTINY.

FATIGUE, WEARINESS, LASSITUDE. *Fatigue*, from the Latin *fatigare*, possibly from a root meaning to yawn, is the Latin word corresponding to the English *weariness*. *Weariness* is the substantive corresponding to *weary*, Anglo-Saxon *werig*, from *worian*, to tramp about in a swampy place, from *wor*, swamp; hence the state of feeling produced by walking over swampy ground. *Lassitude*, from the Latin *lassus*, weary, marks a state without specifying a cause.

Fatigue is an exhaustion of the animal or mental powers; *weariness* is a wearing out the strength or breaking the spirits; *lassitude* is a general relaxation of the animal frame: the laborer experiences *fatigue* from the toils of the day; the man of business, who is harassed by the multiplicity and complexity of his concerns, suffers *fatigue;* and the student who labors to fit himself for a public exhibition of his acquirements is in like manner exposed to *fatigue: weariness* attends the traveller who takes a long or pathless journey; *weariness* is the lot of the petitioner who attends in the antechamber of a great man; the critic is doomed to suffer *weariness* who is obliged to drag through the shallow but voluminous writings of a dull author. *Lassitude* is the consequence of a distempered system, sometimes brought on by an excess of *fatigue*, sometimes by sickness, and frequently by the action of the external air.

FAULT. See BLEMISH; ERROR; IMPERFECTION; LAPSE.

FAULTLESS. See ORIENT; UNOFFENDING.

FAULTY. See CULPABLE.

FAVOR. See BENEFIT; CREDIT; GRACE.

FAVORABLE, PROPITIOUS. In a former paragraph (see AUSPICIOUS) I have shown *propitious* to be a species of the *favorable*, namely, the *favorable* as it springs from the design of an agent; what is *propitious*, therefore, is always *favorable*, but not *vice versâ:* the *favorable* properly characterizes both persons and things; the *propitious*, in the proper sense, characterizes the person only: as applied to persons, an equal may be *favorable;* a superior only is *propitious:* the one may be *favorable* only in inclination; the latter is *favorable* also in granting timely assistance. Cato was *favorable* to Pompey; the gods were *propitious* to the Greeks: we may all wish to have our friends *favorable* to our projects; none but heathens expect to have a blind destiny *propitious*. In the improper sense, *propitious* may be applied to things with a similar distinction: whatever is well disposed to us, and seconds our endeavors, or serves our purpose, is *favorable;* whatever efficaciously protects us, speeds our exertions, and decides our success is *propitious* to us: on ordinary occasions, a wind is said to be *favorable* which carries us to the end of our voyage; but it is said to be *propitious* if the rapidity of our passage forwards any great purpose of our own.

See also OPPORTUNE.

FAWN. See COAX.

FEALTY. See HOMAGE.

FEAR. See APPREHEND; WORRY.

FEARFUL, DREADFUL, FRIGHTFUL, TREMENDOUS, TERRIBLE, TERRIFIC, HORRIBLE, HORRID. *Fearful* here signifies full of that which causes *fear* (see ALARM); *dreadful*, full of what causes *dread* (see APPREHENSION); *frightful*, full of what causes *fright* (see AFRAID); *tremendous*, that which causes *trembling; terrible* or *terrific*, causing *terror; horrible* or *horrid*, causing *horror*. The application of these terms is easily to be discovered by these definitions: the first two affect the mind more than the senses; all the others affect the senses more than the mind: a contest is *fearful* when the issue is important but the event doubtful; the thought of death is *dreadful* to one who feels himself unprepared. The *frightful* is ·less than the *tremendous*, the *tremendous* than the *terrible*, the *terrible* than the *horrible:* shrieks may be *frightful;* thunder and lightning may be *tremendous;* the roaring of a lion is *terrible;* the glare of his eye *terrific;* the actual spectacle of killing is *horrible* or *horrid*. In their general application these terms are often employed promiscuously to characterize whatever produces very strong impressions: hence we may speak of a *frightful, dreadful, terrible,* or *horrid* dream; or *frightful, dreadful,* or *terrible* tempest; *dreadful, terrible,* or *horrid* consequences.

FEARLESS. See Bold.

FEASIBLE. See Colorable.

FEAST, Banquet, Carousal, Entertainment, Treat. As *feasts,* in the religious sense, being derived from *festus,* joyful, are always days of leisure and frequently of public rejoicing, this word has been applied to any social meal for the purposes of pleasure: this is the idea common to the signification of all these words, of which *feast* seems to be the most general; and for all of which it may frequently be substituted, although they have each a distinct application: *feast* conveys the idea merely of enjoyment: *banquet* is a splendid *feast,* attended with pomp and state; it is a term of noble use, particularly adapted to poetry and the high style: *carousal,* French *carous,* from the German *garaus* (from *gar,* entirely, and *aus,* out), means the emptying out of the glass, a drinking-bout; *entertainment* and *treat* convey the idea of hospitality.

· *Feast, entertainment,* and *treat* are taken in a more extended sense, to express other pleasures besides those of the table: *feast* retains its signification of a vivid pleasure, such as voluptuaries derive from delicious viands; *entertainment* and *treat* retain the idea of being granted by way of courtesy: we speak of a thing as being a *feast* or high delight; and of a person contributing to one's *entertainment,* or giving

one a *treat*. To a benevolent mind the spectacle of an afflicted man relieved and comforted is a *feast;* to a mind ardent in the pursuit of knowledge, an easy access to a well-stocked library is a continued *feast:* men of a happy temper give and receive *entertainment* with equal facility; they afford *entertainment* to their guests by the easy cheerfulness which they impart to everything around them; they in like manner derive *entertainment* from everything they see or hear or observe: a *treat* is given or received only on particular occasions; it depends on the relative circumstances and tastes of the giver and receiver; to one of a musical turn one may give a *treat* by inviting him to a musical party; and to one of an intelligent turn it will be equally a *treat* to be of the party which consists. of the enlightened and conversable.

Feast, Festival, Holiday.—*Feast,* in Latin *festum,* or *festus,* changed most probably from *fesiæ* and *feriæ,* which latter, in all probability, comes from the Greek ἱερεια, sacred, because these days were kept sacred or vacant from all secular labor: *festival* and *holiday,* as the words themselves denote, have precisely the same meaning in their original sense, with this difference, that the former derives its origin from heathenish superstition, the latter owes. its rise to the establishment of Christianity in its reformed state.

A *feast,* in the Christian sense of the word, is applied to every day which is. regarded as sacred and observed with particular solemnity, except Sundays; a *holyday,* or, according to its modern orthography, a *holiday,* is simply a day on which ordinary business is suspended: among the Roman Catholics there are many days which are kept holy, and consequently by them denominated *feasts,* which in the English reformed church are only observed as. *holidays,* or days of exemption from public business; of this description are the saints' days, on which the public offices are shut: on the other hand, Christmas, Easter, and Whitsuntide are regarded in both churches more as. *feasts* than as *holidays*. There are, therefore, many *feasts* where there are no *holidays,* and many *holidays* where there are no *feasts*.

A *feast* is altogether sacred; a *holiday* has frequently nothing sacred in it, not even in its cause; it may be a simple ordinary transaction, the act of an individual: a *festival* has always either a sacred or a serious object. A *feast* is kept by religious worship; a *holiday* is kept by idleness; a *festival* is kept by mirth and festivity: some *feasts* are *festivals*, as in the case of the carnival at Rome; some *festivals* are *holidays*, as in the case of weddings and public thanksgivings.

See also SATURNALIA.

FEAT. See DEED.

FEEBLE. See WEAK.

FEEL, BE SENSIBLE, CONSCIOUS. From the simple idea of a sense, the word *feel* has acquired the most extensive signification and application in our language, and may be employed indifferently for all the other terms, but not in all cases: to *feel* is said of the whole frame, inwardly and outwardly; it is the accompaniment of existence: to *be sensible*, from the Latin *sentio*, is said only of the senses. It is the property of all living creatures to *feel* pleasure and pain in a greater or less degree: those creatures which have not the sense of hearing will not *be sensible* of sounds. In the moral application, to *feel* is peculiarly the property or act of the heart; to *be sensible* is that of the understanding: an ingenuous mind *feels* pain when it is *sensible* of having committed an error: one may, however, *feel* as well as *be sensible* by means of the understanding: a person *feels* the value of another's service; is *sensible* of his kindness: one *feels* or is *sensible* of what passes outwardly; one is *conscious* only of what passes inwardly, from *con* or *cum* and *scio*, to know to one's self: we *feel* the force of another's remark; we are *sensible* of the evil which must spring from the practice of vice; we are *conscious* of having fallen short of our duty.

Feeling, Sense, Sensation.—*Feeling*, from Anglo-Saxon *felan*, is allied to Anglo-Saxon *folm*, the palm of the hand—the hand being that with which one *feels*. *Sensation* is taken only in a particular sense. *Feeling* and *sense* are either physical or moral properties; *sensation* is a particular act of physical or moral feeling.

Feeling, physically considered, is but a mode of *sense; anatomists reckon five senses*, of which *feeling* is one: *sense* is the abstract faculty of perceiving through the medium of the sense, as to be deprived of *sense* when stunned by a blow; to be without *sense* when divested of the ordinary faculties. As all creatures which have life have *feeling*, the expression, creatures without *feeling*, may be applied to inanimate objects; but in general the term *feeling* is taken for the sense of *feeling*.

Feeling, in its limited acceptation, is either a state of *feeling* or an act of *feeling: sense* is a mode of sense, *i. e.*, a mode of perceiving through the medium of any particular organ of sense, or a state of perceiving particular objects. In this acceptation *feeling* is applied to moral as well as physical objects, *sense*, to intellectual as well as sensible objects: *feeling* has its seat in the heart, *sense* in the understanding; *feeling* is transitory and fluctuating, *sense* is permanent and regular. There are *feelings* of love, charity, compassion, etc.; there is a *sense* of justice, rectitude, propriety, etc.

As the *sensation* denotes a particular act of *feeling*, it differs from *feeling* only in application: the term *feeling* is most adapted to ordinary discourse on familiar matters; *sensation*, to the grave and scientific style: a child may talk of an unpleasant or pleasant *feeling*, a *feeling* of cold or hunger; the professional man talks of the *sensation* of giddiness, a gnawing *sensation*, and the like.

Feeling, Sensibility, Susceptibility.— *Feeling*, in the present case, is taken for a positive characteristic, namely, the property of *feeling* in a strong degree; in this sense *feeling* expresses either a particular act or a habitual property of the mind. *Sensibility* is always taken in the sense of a habit. Traits of *feeling* in young people are happy omens in the estimation of the preceptor: an exquisite *sensibility* is not a desirable gift; it creates an infinite disproportion of pain. *Feeling* and *sensibility* are here taken as moral properties, which are awakened as much by the operations of the mind within itself as by external objects: *susceptibility*, from the Latin *suscipere*, and *capere*, to take, designates that property of the body or the mind which consists in being ready to be influenced by external objects; hence we speak of a person's *susceptibility* to take cold or his *susceptibility* to be affected with grief, joy, or any other passion: if an excess of *sensibility* be an evil, an excess of *susceptibility* is a still greater evil; it makes us slaves to every circumstance, however trivial, which comes under our notice.

FEIGN, PRETEND. *Feign*, in Latin *fingo* or *figo*, meant originally to fashion with the hands. *Pretend*, in Latin *præ*, before, and *tendere*, to stretch, signifies properly to stretch before, that is, to put on the outside.

These words may be used for either doing or saying; they are both opposed to what is true, but they differ from the motives of the agent: to *feign* is taken in either a bad or an indifferent sense; to *pretend*, always in a bad sense: one *feigns* in order to gain some future end; a person *feigns* sickness in order to be excused from paying a disagreeable visit: one *pretends* in order to serve a present purpose; a child *pretends* to have lost his book who wishes to excuse himself for his idleness. To *feign* consists often of a line of conduct; to *pretend* consists mostly of words, sometimes coupled with assumed looks and manners: Ulysses *feigned* madness in order to escape from going to the Trojan war: according to Virgil, the Grecian Sinon *pretended* to be a deserter come over to the Trojan camp.

In matters of speculation, to *feign* is to invent by force of the imagination; to *pretend* is to set up by force of self-conceit or false opinion: it is *feigned* by the poets that Orpheus went down into hell and brought back Eurydice, his wife; infidel philosophers *pretend* to account for the most mysterious things in nature upon natural or, as they please to term it, rational principles.

See also INVENT; UNFEIGNED.

FELICITATE, CONGRATULATE. *Felicitate*, from the Latin *felix*, happy, signifies to make happy, and is applicable only to ourselves; *congratulate* from *gratus*, pleasant or agreeable, is to make agreeable, and is applicable to either ourselves or others: we *felicitate* ourselves on having escaped the danger; we *congratulate* others on their good fortune.

FELLOWSHIP, SOCIETY. Both these terms are employed to denote a close intercourse; but *fellowship* is said of men as individuals, *society* of them collectively: we should be careful not to hold *fellowship* with any one of bad character, or to join the *society* of those who profess bad principles.

FELON. See CRIMINAL.

FEMALE, FEMININE, EFFEMINATE. *Female* is said of the sex itself, and *feminine* of the characteristics of the sex. *Female* is opposed to male, *feminine* to masculine.

In the *female* character we expect to find that which is *feminine*. The *female* dress, manners, and habits have engaged the attention of all essayists from the time of Addison to the present period. The *feminine* is natural to the *female;* the *effeminate* is unnatural to the male. A *feminine* air and voice, which is truly grateful to the observer in the one sex, is an odious mark of *effeminacy* in the other. Beauty and delicacy are *feminine* properties; robustness and vigor are masculine properties; the former, therefore, when discovered in a man, entitle him to the epithet *effeminate*.

FENCE, GUARD, SECURITY. *Fence* is a contraction of *defence*. *Guard* comes from Anglo-Saxon *weardian*, to watch, allied to ward, wary, etc.; *gu* is the French form corresponding to Germanic *w*—as in *guise* and *vise*, for example. *Security* implies that which secures or prevents injury, mischief, and loss. A *fence*, in the proper sense, is an inanimate object; a *guard* is a living agent; the former is of permanent utility, the latter acts to a partial extent: in the figurative sense they retain the same distinction. Modesty is a *fence* to a woman's virtue; the love of the subject is the monarch's greatest *safeguard*. There are prejudices which favor religion and subordination, and act as *fences* against the introduction of licentious principles into the juvenile or unenlightened mind; a proper sense of an overruling Providence will serve as a *guard* to prevent the admission of improper thoughts. The *guard* only stands at the entrance to prevent the ingress of evil: the *security* stops up all the avenues, it locks up with firmness. A *guard* serves to prevent the ingress of everything that may have an evil intention or tendency: the *security* rather secures the possession of what one has and prevents a loss. A king has a *guard* about his person to keep off all violence.

FERMENT. See EBULLITION; FERMENTATION.

FEROCIOUS, FIERCE, SAVAGE. *Ferocious* and *fierce* are both derived from the Latin *ferox*, from *ferus*, wild. *Savage* (see CRUEL).

Ferocity marks the untamed character of a cruel disposition: *fierceness* has a greater mixture of pride and anger in it, the word *fier* in French being taken for haughtiness: *savageness* marks a more permanent, but not so violent, a sentiment of either cruelty or anger as the former two. *Ferocity* and *fierceness* are in common applied to the brutes to designate their natural tempers: *savage* is mostly employed to designate the natural tempers of man when uncontrolled by the force of reason and a sense of religion. *Ferocity* is the natural characteristic of wild beasts; it is a delight in blood that needs no outward stimulus to call it into action; but it displays itself most strikingly in the moment when the animal is going to grasp, or when in the act of devouring, its prey: *fierceness* may be provoked in many creatures, but it does not discover itself unless roused by some circumstance of aggravation; many animals become *fierce* by being shut up in cages and exposed to the view of spectators: *savageness* is as natural a temper in the uncivilized man as *ferocity* or *fierceness* in the brute; it does not wait for an enemy to attack, but is restless in search of some one whom it may make an enemy and have an opportunity of destroying. It is an easy transition for the savage to become the *ferocious* cannibal, glutting himself in the blood of his enemies, or the *fierce* antagonist to one who sets himself up in opposition to him.

In an extended application of these terms, they bear the same relation to one another: the countenance may be either *ferocious*, *fierce*, or *savage*, according to circumstances. A robber who spends his life in the act of unlawfully shedding blood acquires a *ferocity* of countenance: a soldier who follows a predatory and desultory mode of warfare betrays the licentiousness of his calling and his undisciplined temper in the *fierceness* of his countenance; the tyrant whose enjoyment consists in inflicting misery on his dependants or subjects evinces the *savageness* of his temper by the *savage* joy with which he witnesses their groans and tortures.

FERTILE, FRUITFUL, PROLIFIC. *Fertile*, in Latin *fertilis*, from *ferre*, to bear, signifies capable of bearing or bringing to light. *Fruitful* signifies full of *fruit*, or containing within itself much *fruit*. *Prolific* is compounded of *proles* and *facere*, to make a progeny.

Fertile expresses in its proper sense the faculty of sending forth from itself that which is not of its own nature, and is peculiarly applicable to the ground which causes everything within itself to grow up. *Fruitful* expresses a state containing or possessing abundantly that which is of the same nature; it is, therefore, peculiarly applicable to trees, plants, vegetables, and whatever is said to bear *fruit*. *Prolific* expresses the faculty of generating; it conveys, therefore, the idea of what is creative, and is peculiarly applicable to animals. We may say that the ground is either *fertile* or *fruitful*, but not so properly *prolific*: we may speak of a female of any species being *fruitful* and *prolific*, but not *fertile*; we may speak of nature as being *fruitful*, but neither *fertile* nor *prolific*. A country is *fertile* as it respects the quality of the soil; it is *fruitful* as it respects the abundance of its produce: it is possible, therefore, for a country to be *fruitful* by the industry of its inhabitants which was not *fertile* by nature. An animal is said to be *fruitful* as it respects the number of young which it has; it is said to be *prolific* as it respects its generative power. Some women are more *fruitful* than others; but there are many animals more *prolific* than human creatures.

FIGURE 347

In the figurative application they admit of a similar distinction. A man is *fertile* in expedients who readily contrives upon the spur of the occasion; he is *fruitful* in resources who has them ready at his hand; his brain is *prolific* if it generates an abundance of new conceptions. A mind is *fertile* which has powers that admit of cultivation and expansion: an imagination is *fruitful* that is rich in stores of imagery; a genius is *prolific* that is rich in invention. Females are *fertile* in expedients and devices; ambition and avarice are the most *fruitful* sources of discord and misery in public and private life; novel-writers are the most *prolific* class of authors.

FERVOR, ARDOR. *Fervor*, from *fervere*, to boil, is not so violent a heat as *ardor*, from *ardere*, to burn. The affections are properly *fervent:* the passions are *ardent:* we are *fervent* in feeling, and *ardent* in acting; the *fervor* of devotion may be rational, but the *ardor* of zeal is mostly intemperate. The first martyr, Stephen, was filled with a holy *fervor;* St. Peter, in the *ardor* of his zeal, promised his Master to do more than he was able to perform.

See also UNCTION.

FESTIVAL. See FEAST.

FESTIVITY, M I R T H. There is commonly *mirth* and *festivity*, but there may be frequently *mirth* without *festivity*. The *festivity* lies in the outward circumstances, *mirth* in the temper of the mind. *Festivity* is rather the producer of *mirth* than the *mirth* itself. *Festivity* includes the social enjoyments of eating, drinking, dancing, cards, and other pleasures: *mirth* includes in it the buoyancy of spirits which is engendered by a participation in such pleasures.

FETCH. See BRING.

FETTER. See CHAIN.

FEUD. See QUARREL.

FICKLE. See CHANGEABLE.

FICTION, FABRICATION, FALSEHOOD. *Fiction* is opposed to what is real; *fabrication* and *falsehood* to what is true. *Fiction* relates what may be, though not what is: *fabrication* and *falsehood* relate what is not as what is, and *vice versâ*. *Fiction* serves for amusement and instruction: *fabrication* and *falsehood* serve to mislead and deceive. *Fiction* and *fabrication* both require invention: *falsehood* consists of simple contradiction. The fables of Æsop are *fictions* of the simplest kind, but yet such as require a peculiarly lively fancy and inventive genius to produce: the *fabrication* of a play, as the production of Shakespeare's pen, was once executed with sufficient skill to impose for a time upon the public credulity: a good memory is all that is necessary in order to avoid uttering *falsehoods* that can be easily contradicted and confuted. In an extended sense of the word *fiction*, it approaches still nearer to the sense of *fabricate*, when said of the *fictions* of the ancients, which were delivered as truth, although admitted now to be false: the motive of the narrator is what here constitutes the difference, namely, that in the former case he believes what he relates to be true, in the latter he knows it to be false. The heathen mythology consists principally of the *fictions* of the poets: newspapers commonly abound in *fabrication*.

Fabrication may sometimes be used in a good sense: in this case it denotes not the thing *fabricated*, but the act of *fabricating*.

As epithets, *fictitious* and *false* are very closely allied; for what is *fictitious* is *false*, though all that is *false* is not *fictitious:* the *fictitious* is that which has been feigned, or *falsely* made by some one; the *false* is simply that which is *false* by the nature of the thing; the *fictitious* account is therefore the invention of an individual, whose veracity is thereby impeached; but there may be many *false* accounts unintentionally circulated.

FICTITIOUS. See ARTFUL.

FIDELITY. See FAITH.

FIENDISH. See DIABOLIC.

FIERCE. See FEROCIOUS.

FIGURE, METAPHOR, ALLEGORY, EMBLEM, SYMBOL, TYPE. *Figure*, in Latin *figura*, from *fingere*, to fashion or shape, signifies anything painted or feigned by the mind. *Metaphor*, in Greek μεταφορά, from μεταφέρειν, to transfer, signifies a transfer of one object to another. *Allegory*, in Greek ἀλληγορία, from ἄλλος, another, and ἀγορένειν, to relate, signifies the relation of something under a borrowed term. *Emblem*, in Greek ἔμβλημα, from ἐμβάλλειν, to impress, signifies the thing stamped on as a mark. *Symbol*, from the Greek συμβάλλειν, to consider attentively, signifies the thing cast or conceived in the mind, from its analogy to represent something else. *Type*, in Greek τύπος, from τύπτειν, to strike or stamp, signifies an image of something that is stamped on something else.

Likeness between two objects, by which one is made to represent the other, is the common idea in the signification of these terms. *Figure* is the most general of these terms, comprehending everything which is figured by means of the imagination; the rest are but modes of the *figure*. The *figure* consists either in words or in things generally: we may have a *figure* in expression, a *figure* on paper, a *figure* on wood or stone, and the like. It is the business of the imagination to draw *figures* out of anything; the *metaphor* and *allegory* consist of a representation by means of words only: the *figure*, in this case, is any representation which the mind makes to itself of a resemblance between objects, which is properly a *figure* of thought, which when clothed in words is a *figure* of speech: the *metaphor* is a *figure* of speech of the simplest kind, by which a word acquires other meanings besides that which is originally affixed to it; as when the term head, which properly signifies a part of the body, is applied to the leader of an army. The *allegory* is a continued *metaphor*, where attributes, modes, and actions are applied to the objects thus *figured*, as in the *allegory* of sin and death in Milton.

The *emblem* is that sort of *figure* of thought by which we make corporeal objects to stand for moral properties; thus the dove is represented as the *emblem* of meekness, or the beehive is made the *emblem* of industry: the *symbol* is that species of *emblem* which is converted into a constituted sign among men; thus the olive and laurel are the *symbols* of peace, and have been recognized as such among barbarous as well as enlightened nations.

The *type* is that species of *emblem* by which one object is made to represent another mystically; it is, therefore, only employed in religious matters, particularly in relation to the coming, the office, and the death of our Saviour; in this manner the offering of Isaac is considered as a *type* of our Saviour's offering himself as an atoning sacrifice.

See also FORM.

FINAL, CONCLUSIVE. *Final*, in French *final*, Latin *finalis*, from *finis*, the end, signifies having an end. *Conclusive* signifies shutting up, or coming to a conclusion.

Final designates simply the circumstance of being the last; *conclusive* the mode of finishing or coming to the last: a determination is *final* which is to be succeeded by no other; a reasoning is *conclusive* that puts a stop to further question. The *final* is arbitrary; it depends upon the will to make it so or not: the *conclusive* is relative; it depends upon the circumstances and the understanding: a person gives a *final* answer at option; but in order to make an answer *conclusive* it must be satisfactory to all parties.

See also LAST.

FINAL WORD. See ULTIMATUM.

FIND, FIND OUT, DISCOVER, ESPY, DESCRY. *Find* is in Anglo-Saxon *findan*, German *finden*, etc. *Discover* (see DETECT). *Espy* comes through French from the Old High German *spehon*, to spy. *Descry* comes from Latin *describere*, from *de*, down, and *scribere*, to write, meaning to make a note of, hence to see and notice.

To *find* signifies simply to come within sight of a thing, which is the general idea attached to all these terms: they vary, however, either in the mode of the action or in the object. What we *find* may become visible to us by accident, but what we *find out* is the result of an effort. We may *find* anything as we pass along in the streets: but we *find out* mistakes in an account by carefully going over it, or we *find out* the difficulties which we meet with in learning by redoubling our diligence. What is *found* may have been lost to ourselves, but visible to others   What is *discovered* is always remote and unknown, and when *discovered* is something new. A piece of money may be *found* lying on the ground; but a mine is *discovered* underground. When Captain Cook *discovered* the islands in the South Sea, many plants and animals were *found*. What is not *discoverable* may be presumed not to exist; but that which is *found* may be only what has been lost. What has once been *discovered* cannot be *discovered* again; but what is *found* may be many times *found*. *Find out* and *discover* differ principally in the application, the former being applied to familiar, and the latter to scientific objects: scholars *find out* what they have to learn; men of research *discover* what escapes the notice of others.

To *espy* is a species of *finding out*, namely, to *find out* what is very secluded or retired; and *descry* is a species of *discovering* or observing at a distance or among a number of objects. An astronomer *discovers* fresh stars or planets; he *finds out* those on particular occasions which had been already *discovered*. A person *finds out* by continued inquiry any place to which he had been wrongly directed: he *espies* an object which lies concealed in a corner or secret place; he *descries* a horseman coming down a hill. *Find* and *discover* may be employed with regard to objects, either of a corporeal or intellectual kind; *espy* and *descry*, only with regard to sensible objects of corporeal vision: *find*, for those that are either external or internal; *discover*, only for those that are external. The distinction between them is the same as before; we *find* by simple inquiry; we *discover* by reflection and study: we *find* or *find out* the motives which influence a person's conduct; we *discover* the reasons or causes of things: the *finding* serves the particular purpose of the *finder;* the *discovery* serves the purpose of science, by adding to the stock of general knowledge.

When *find* is used as a purely intellectual operation, it admits of a new view, in relation both to *discover* and to *invent*, as may be seen in the following article.

Find, Find Out, Discover, Invent.—
To *find* or *find out* is said of things which do not exist in the forms in which a person *finds* them: to *discover* is said of that which exists in an entire state:

invent, from *invenire,* signifying literally to come upon, is said of that which is newly made or modelled. The merit of *finding* or *inventing* consists in newly applying or modifying the materials which exist separately; the merit of *discovering* consists in removing the obstacles which prevent us from knowing the real nature of the thing: imagination and industry are requisite for *finding* or *inventing;* acuteness and penetration for *discovering*. *Find* is applicable to the operative arts, *invent* to the mechanical, *discover* to the speculative. We speak of *finding* modes for performing actions and effecting purposes: of *inventing* machines, instruments, and various matters of use or elegance; of *discovering* the operations and laws of nature. Many fruitless attempts have been made to *find* the longitude: men have not been so unsuccessful in *finding out* various arts for communicating their thoughts, commemorating the exploits of their nations, and supplying themselves with luxuries. Harvey *discovered* the circulation of the blood: the geometrician *finds* by reasoning the solution of any problem; or by investigating he *finds out* a clearer method of solving the same problem; or he *invents* an instrument by which the proof can be deduced from ocular demonstration.

Find Fault With, Blame, Object To.—
All these terms denote not simply feeling, but also expressing, dissatisfaction with some person or thing. To *find fault with* signifies here to point out a *fault*, either in some person or thing; to *blame* is said only of the person; *object* is applied to the thing only: we *find fault with* a person for his behavior; we *find fault with* our seat, our conveyance, and the like; we *blame* a person for his temerity or his improvidence; we *object* to a measure that is proposed. We *find fault with* or *blame* that which has been done; we *object to* that which has been or is to be done. *Finding fault* is a familiar action applied to matters of personal convenience or taste; *blame* and *object to*, particularly the latter, are applied to serious objects. *Finding fault* is often the fruit of a discontented temper; there are some whom nothing will

please, and who are ever ready to *find fault with* whatever comes in their way: *blame* is a matter of discretion; we *blame* frequently in order to correct: *objecting to* is an affair either of caprice or discretion; some capriciously *object to* that which is proposed to them merely from a spirit of opposition; others *object to* a thing from substantial reasons.

FINE, DELICATE, NICE. It is remarkable of the word *fine* (see BEAUTIFUL) that it is equally applicable to large and small objects: *delicate*, in Latin *delicatus*, from *deliciæ*, delights, and *delicere*, to allure, is applied only to small objects. *Fine*, in the natural sense, denotes smallness in general. *Delicate* denotes a degree of *fineness* that is agreeable to the taste. Thread is said to be *fine*, as opposed to the coarse and thick; silk is said to be *delicate* when to fineness of texture it adds softness. The texture of a spider's web is remarkable for its *fineness;* that of the ermine's fur is remarkable for its *delicacy.* In writing, all up-strokes must be *fine;* but in superior writing they will be *delicately fine.* When applied to colors, the *fine* is coupled with the bold and strong; *delicate,* with what is faint, soft, and fair: black and red may be *fine* colors; white and pink *delicate* colors. The tulip is reckoned one of the *finest* flowers; the white moss-rose is a *delicate* flower. A *fine* painter delineates with boldness; but the artist who has a *delicate* taste throws *delicate* touches into the grandest delineations.

In their moral application these terms admit of the same distinction: the *fine* approaches either to the strong or to the weak; the *delicate* is a high degree of the *fine;* as a *fine* thought, which may be lofty; or *fine* feeling, which is acute and tender; and *delicate* feeling, which exceeds the former in *fineness.* The French use their word *fin* only in the latter sense, of acuteness, and apply it merely to the thoughts and designs of men, answering either to our word *subtle*, as *un homme fin,* or *neat,* as *une satire fine.*

Delicate is said of that which is agreeable to the sense and the taste; *nice,* to what is agreeable to the appetite: the former is a term of refinement, the latter of epicurism and sensual indulgence. The *delicate* affords pleasure only to those whose thoughts and desires are purified from what is gross; the *nice* affords pleasure to the young, the ignorant, and the sensual: thus *delicate* food, *delicate* colors, *delicate* shapes and forms, are always acceptable to the cultivated; a meal, a show, a color, and the like, which suits its appetite or meets its fancy, will be *nice* to a child.

When used in a moral application, *nice,* which is taken in a good sense, approaches nearer to the signification of *delicate.* A person may be said to have a *delicate* ear in music whose ear is offended with the smallest discordance; he may be said to have a *nice* taste or judgment in music who scientifically discriminates the beauties and defects of different pieces. A person is *delicate* in his choice who is guided by taste and feeling; he is *nice* in his choice who adheres to a strict rule. A point in question may be either *delicate* or *nice;* it is *delicate* as it is likely to touch the tender feelings of any party; it is *nice* as it involves contrary interests and becomes difficult of determination. There are *delicacies* of behavior which are learned by good-breeding, but which minds of a refined cast are naturally alive to without any particular learning; there are *niceties* in the law which none but men of superior intellect can properly enter into and discriminate.

Fine, Mulct, Penalty, Forfeiture.—Fine, from the Latin *finis,* the end or purpose, signifies, by an extended application, satisfaction by way of amends for an offence. *Mulct,* in Latin, *mulcta,* comes from *mulcare,* to injure. *Penalty,* in Latin *pœnalitas,* from *pœna,* a pain, signifies what gives pain by way of punishment. *Forfeiture,* from *forfeit,* comes through French from Late Latin *foris factum,* a trespass, from *foris,* beyond, and *facere,* to do, signifying an action beyond the bounds of law, hence a penalty for illegal action.

The *fine* and *mulct* are always pecuniary; a *penalty* may be pecuniary; a *forfeiture* consists of the deprivation of any right or property: the *fine* and *mulct* are imposed; the *penalty* is inflicted or incurred; the *forfeiture* is incurred. The violation of a rule or law is attended with a *fine* or *mulct*, but the former is a term of general use; the latter is rather a technical term in law: a criminal offence incurs a *penalty;* negligence of duty occasions the *forfeiture*. A *fine* or *mulct* serves either as punishment to the offender or as an amends for the offence: a *penalty* always inflicts some kind of pain as a punishment on the offender: a *forfeiture* is attended with loss as a punishment to the delinquent. Among the Chinese all offences are punished with *fines* or flogging: the Roman Catholics were formerly subject to *penalties* if detected in the performance of their religious worship: societies subject their members to *forfeitures* for the violation of their laws.

Finical, Spruce, Foppish.—These epithets are applied to such as attempt at finery by improper means. The *finical* is insignificantly fine; the *spruce* is laboriously and artfully fine; the *foppish* is fantastically and affectedly fine. The *finical* is said mostly of manners and speech: the *spruce* is said of the dress; the *foppish,* of dress and manners.

A *finical* gentleman clips his words and screws his body into as small a compass as possible, to give himself the air of a delicate person: a *spruce* gentleman strives not to have a fold wrong in his frill or cravat, nor a hair of his head to lie amiss: a *foppish* gentleman seeks, by extravagance in the cut of his clothes and by the tawdriness in their ornaments, to render himself distinguished for finery. A little mind, full of conceit of itself, will lead a man to be *finical:* a vacant mind that is anxious to be pleasing will not object to the employment of rendering the person *spruce:* a giddy, vain mind, eager after applause, impels a man to every kind of *foppery*.

FINISH. See CLOSE.

FINISHED. See COMPLETE; OUT.

FINITE, LIMITED. *Finite,* from *finis,* an end, is the natural property of things; and *limited,* from *limes,* a boundary, is the artificial property: the former is opposite only to the *infinite;* but the latter, which lies within the *finite,* is opposed to the *unlimited* or the *infinite.* This world is *finite,* and space *infinite;* the power of a prince is *limited.* It is not in our power to extend the bounds of the *finite,* but the *limited* is mostly under our control. We are *finite* beings, and our capacities are variously *limited* either by nature or circumstances.

FIRE, HEAT, WARMTH, GLOW. In the proper sense these words are easily distinguished, but not so easily in the improper sense; and as the latter depends principally upon the former, it is not altogether useless to enter into some explanation of their physical meaning.

Fire is with regard to *heat* as the cause to the effect; it is itself an inherent property in some material bodies, and when in action communicates *heat: fire* is perceptible to us by the eye as well as the touch; *heat* is perceptible only by the touch; we distinguish *fire* by means of the flame it sends forth or by the changes which it produces upon other bodies; but we discover *heat* only by the sensations which it produces in ourselves.

Heat and *warmth* differ principally in degree, the latter being a gentle degree of the former. The term *heat* is, however, in its most extensive sense, applicable to that universal principle which pervades all nature, animate and inanimate, and seems to vivify the whole; it is this principle which appears either under the form of *fire* or under the more commonly conceived form of *heat,* as it is generally understood and as I have here considered it. *Heat* in this limited sense is less active than *fire* and more active than *warmth:* the former is produced in bodies, either by the violent action of *fire,* as in the boiling of water, the melting of lead, or the violent friction of two hard bodies; the latter is produced by the simple expulsion of cold, as in the case of feathers, wool, and other substances which produce and retain *warmth. Glow* is a partial *heat* or *warmth* which exists, or is known to exist, mostly in the human frame; it is commonly produced in the body when it is in its most vigorous state and its nerves are firmly braced by the cold.

From the above analysis the figurative application of these terms, and the grounds upon which they are so employed, will be easily discerned. As *fire* is the strongest and most active principle in nature, which seizes everything within its reach with the greatest possible rapidity, genius is said to be possessed of *fire*, which flies with rapidity through all the regions of thought and forms the most lively images and combinations; but when *fire* is applied to the eye or the looks, it borrows its meaning from the external property of the flame, which is very aptly depicted in the eye or the looks of lively people. As *heat* is always excessive and mostly violent, those commotions and fermentations of the mind which flow from the agitation of the passions, particularly of the angry passions, are termed *heat*. As *warmth* is a gentle and grateful property, it has with most propriety been ascribed to the affections. As *glow* is a partial but vivid feeling of the body, so is friendship a strong but particular affection of the mind: hence the propriety of ascribing a *glow* to friendship. Age damps the *fire* of the poet. Disputants in the *heat* of the contest are apt to forget all the forms of good-breeding. A man of tender moral feelings speaks with *warmth* of a noble action, or takes a *warm* interest in the concerns of the innocent and the distressed. A youth in the full *glow* of friendship feels himself prepared to make any sacrifices in supporting the cause of his friend.

FIRM, FIXED, SOLID, STABLE. *Firm* (see CONSTANCY). *Fixed* denotes the state of being *fixed*. *Solid*, in Latin *solidus*, comes from *solum*, the ground, which is the most solid thing existing. *Stable* (see CONSTANCY).

That is *firm* which is not easily shaken; that is *fixed* which is fastened to something else and not easily torn; that is *solid* which is able to bear, and does not easily give way; that is *stable* which is able to make a stand against resistance or the effects of time. A pillar which is *firm* on its base, *fixed* to a wall made of *solid* oak, is likely to be *stable*. A man stands *firm* in battle who does not flinch from the attack: he is *fixed* to a spot by the order of his commander.

In the moral sense, *firmness* is used only for the purpose, or such actions as depend on the purpose; *fixed* is used either for the mind or for outward circumstances; *solid* is applicable to things in general, in an absolute sense; *stable* is applicable to things in a relative sense. Decrees are more or less *firm*, according to the source from which they spring; none are *firm*, compared with those which arise from the will of the Almighty: laws are *fixed* in proportion as they are connected with a constitution in which it is difficult to innovate. That which is *solid* is so of its own nature, but does not admit of degrees: a *solid* reason has within itself an independent property, which cannot be increased or diminished. That which is *stable* is so by comparison with that which is of less duration: the characters of some men are more *stable* than those of others; youth will not have so *stable* a character as manhood. A friendship is *firm* when it does not depend upon the opinion of others; it is *fixed* when the choice is made and grounded in the mind; it is *solid* when it rests on the only *solid* basis of accordancy in virtue and religion; it is *stable* when it is not liable to decrease or die away with time.

See also HARD; STALWART.

FIRMNESS. See CONSTANCY.

FIRST, ABORIGINAL, ORIGINAL, PRIMARY. All these words signify holding the *first* place, but to the general idea of being simply number one in any counting which is indicated in *first*, *aboriginal*, *original*, and *primary* add certain subsidiary notions. *Original*, from Latin *oriri*, to rise, means the first to appear or arise, and refers to the beginning of something, considered with reference to that which follows after the beginning or develops out of it. When we speak of the *first* language spoken in England, we are thinking of this language simply as number one in a series; when we speak of the *original* language of the Aryan peoples, we are thinking of it with reference to the languages which followed after it or developed out of it. The difference is not of meaning, but of emphasis. *Aboriginal*, from the phrase *ab origine*, meaning from the beginning, has the meaning of *original* specifically applied to the first tribes or peoples inhabiting a given land. *Primary*, from Latin *primus*, first, means *first*, not merely with respect to numbers, but with respect to relation. It differs from *original* in emphasizing, not the idea of the beginning, but the idea of the relation of the things designated as *primary* to something else of which they are considered a part.

See also SUPREME.

FIT, APT, MEET. *Fit* (see BECOMING) is either an acquired or a natural property; *apt*, in Latin *aptus*, from the Old Latin *apere*, to fit or join together, is a natural property; *meet*, from Anglo-Saxon *metan*, signifying measured, is a moral quality. A house is *fit* for the accommodation of the family according to the plan of the builder; the young mind is *apt* to receive either good or bad impressions. *Meet* is a term of rare use, except in spiritual matters or in poetry: it is *meet* to offer our prayers to the Supreme Disposer of all things.

Fit, Equip, Prepare, Qualify.—To *fit* signifies to adopt means in order to make *fit*, and conveys the general sense of all the other terms; they differ principally in the means and circumstances of *fitting*: to *equip* is to *fit* out by furnishing the necessary materials: to *prepare*, from the Latin *præparare*, compounded of *præ* and *parare*, to get beforehand, is to take steps for the purpose of *fitting* in future: to *qualify*, from the Latin *qualifacere*, or *qualis* and *facere*, to make a thing as it should be, is to *fit* or furnish with any requisites.

To *fit* is employed for ordinary cases; to *equip* is employed only for expeditions: a house is *fitted* up for the residence of a family; a vessel is *equipped* with everything requisite for a voyage; to *fit* may be for an immediate or a remote purpose; to *prepare* is for a remote purpose; to *fit* does not define the means; to *prepare* requires for the most part labor, time, and expense. A persons *fits* himself for taking orders when he is at the university: he *prepares* for an examination by going over what he has already learned.

To *fit* is said of everything, both in a natural and a moral sense: to *qualify* is used only in a moral sense. *Fit* is employed mostly for acquirements which are gained by physical exertions; *qualify* for those which are gained by

intellectual exertion: a youth *fits* himself for a mechanical business by working at it; a youth *qualifies* himself for a profession by following a particular course of studies.

See also EXPEDIENT; PREPAREDNESS; RIGHT.

Fit, Suit, Adapt, Accommodate, Adjust.—*Fit* signifies to make or be *fit*. *Suit* signifies to make or be *suitable* (see AGREE). *Adapt*, from *aptus*, fit, signifies to make *fit* for a specific purpose. *Accommodate* signifies to make commodious. *Adjust* signifies to make a thing just as it is desired to be.

To *fit*, in the transitive sense, is to make of like proportions, so that one thing may join with another as it ought: as to *fit* one board to another; to *fit* clothes to the body: to *suit* is to make things agreeable to one another, and is mostly applied to moral objects: as to *suit* one's actions or language to the occasion.

Fit may likewise be figuratively applied to moral objects, in the sense of making one object fit for another, as to *fit* a person by his education for a particular walk of life; to *fit* the mind for the reception of truth.

In the transitive sense these words have precisely the same distinction: as the shoe *fits*, or *fits* the foot, which is made to the same size; things *suit* which agree in essential qualities or produce an agreeable effect when placed together; as furniture is made to *suit*.

In the moral sense, the *fitness* of things is what we term just, right, or decent: that which *suits* falls in with our ideas and feelings.

To *adapt* is a species of *fitting;* to *accommodate* is a species of *suiting;* both applied to the moral actions of conscious beings. *Adaptation* is an act of the judgment; *accommodation* is an act of the will; we *adapt* by an exercise of discretion; we *accommodate* by a management of the humors: an *adaptation* does not interfere with our interests; but an *accommodation* always supposes a sacrifice: we *adapt* our language to the understandings of our hearers; we *accommodate* ourselves to the humors of others. The mind of an infinitely wise Creator is clearly evinced in the world by the universal *adaptation* of means to their ends: a spirit of *accommodation* is not merely a characteristic of politeness: it is of sufficient importance to be ranked among the Christian duties.

Accommodate and *adjust* are both applied to the affairs of men which require to be kept, or put, in right order: but the former implies the keeping as well as putting in order; the latter simply the putting in order. Men *accommodate* each other, that is, make things commodious for one another; but they *adjust* things either for themselves or for others. Thus they *accommodate* one another in pecuniary matters; or they *adjust* the ceremonial of a visit. *Accommodate* likewise always supposes a certain sacrifice or yielding on the part of the person *accommodating* for the convenience of the person *accommodated*. On this ground we may say that a difference is either *accommodated* or *adjusted;* for it is *accommodated,* inasmuch as the parties yield to each other so as to make it *commodious* to both; it is *adjusted,* inasmuch as that which was wrong is set right.

FITTED. See COMPETENT.

FIX, FASTEN, STICK. *Fix* is a generic term; *fasten, i. e.,* to make fast, and *stick, i. e.,* to make to stick, are but modes of *fixing:* we *fix* whatever we make to remain in a given situation; we *fasten* if we *fix* it firmly; we *stick* when we *fix* a thing by means of *sticking.* A post is *fixed* in the ground; it is *fastened* to a wall by a nail; it is *stuck* to another board by means of glue. Shelves are *fixed:* a horse is *fastened* to a gate; bills are *stuck.* What is *fixed* may be removed in various ways: what is *fastened* is removed by main force: what is *stuck* must be separated by contrivance.

See also FIRM.

Fix, Settle, Establish.—*Fix,* in Latin *fixi,* perfect of *figo,* signifies simply to make to keep its place. *Settle,* from Anglo-Saxon *setl,* seat, allied to *sit,* signifies to make to sit or be at rest. *Establish,* from the Latin *stabilis,* signifies to make stable.

Fix is the general and indefinite term: to *settle* and *establish* are to fix strongly. *Fix* and *settle* are applied either to material or spiritual objects, *establish* only to moral objects. A post

may be *fixed* in the ground in any manner, but it requires time for it to *settle.* A person may either *fix* himself, *settle* himself, or *establish* himself: the first case refers simply to his taking up his abode or choosing a certain spot; the second refers to his permanency of stay; and the third to the business which he raises or renders permanent.

The same distinction exists between these words in their further application to the conduct of men. We may *fix* one or many points, important or unimportant—it is a mere act of the will; we *settle* many points of importance—it is an act of deliberation; thus we *fix* the day and hour of doing a thing; we *settle* the affairs of our family: so likewise to *fix* is properly the act of one; to *settle* may be the joint act of many; thus a parent *fixes* on a business for his child, or he *settles* the marriage contract with another parent.

To *fix* and *settle* are personal acts, and the objects are mostly of a private nature: but *establish* is an indirect action, and the object mostly of a public nature: thus we *fix* our opinions; we *settle* our minds; or we are instrumental in *establishing* laws, institutions, and the like. It is much to be lamented that any one should remain *unsettled* in his faith; and still more so, that the best form of faith is not universally *established.*

Fix, Determine, Settle, Limit.—To *fix* is here the general term; to *determine* (see DECIDE); to *settle* (see PRECEDING); to *limit* (see BOUND), are here modes of *fixing.* They all denote the acts of conscious agents, but differ in the object and circumstances of the action; we may *fix* any object by any means and to any point; we may *fix* material objects or spiritual objects; we may *fix* either by means of our senses or our thoughts; but we can *determine* only by means of our thoughts. To *fix,* in distinction from the rest, is said in regard to a single point or a line; but to *determine* is always said of one or more points or a whole: we *fix* where a thing shall begin; but we *determine* where it shall begin and where it shall end, which way and how far it shall go, and the like: thus, we may *fix* our eye upon a star, or we *fix* our minds upon a particular branch of astronomy; but we *determine* the distance of the heavenly bodies, or the specific gravity of bodies, and the like, upon philosophical principles.

So in respect to other objects, to *fix* is a positive and immediate act; as to *fix* the day, hour, or minute, etc.; to *determine* requires consideration; as to *determine* times and seasons, or modes of doing things, and the like.

Determine is to *settle* as a means to the end; we commonly *determine* all subordinate matters in order to *settle* a matter finally: thus, the *determination* of a single cause will serve to *settle* all other differences. The *determination* respects the act of the individual who *fixes* certain points and brings them to a term; the *settlement* respects simply the conclusion of the affair or the termination of all dispute and question.

To *determine* and *limit* both signify to *fix* boundaries; but to *determine* or *fix* a term to a thing respects such *boundaries* or terms as are formed by the nature of things: to *limit* is the act of a conscious agent; a question is *determined* by removing the doubt; the price is *limited* by law, or the command of the magistrate, or the agreement of the parties.

FIXED. See FIRM.

FLAG, DROOP, LANGUISH, PINE. *Flag* comes from a Teutonic base found in Anglo-Saxon *flacor,* flying, roving, and Icelandic *flaka,* originally an imitative syllable found in *flap, flicker,* etc.; it means here to be weary after roving, to cease to rove, etc. *Droop* (see FALL). To *languish* is to become or continue languid (see FAINT). *Pine,* Middle English *pinen,* to suffer, more frequently to torment (from Anglo-Saxon *pin,* borrowed from Latin *pœna,* pain, penalty), means to languish with suffering.

In the proper application nothing *flags* but that which can be distended and made to flutter by the wind, as the leaves of plants when they are in want of water or in a weakly condition; hence figuratively the spirits are said to *flag:* nothing is said to *droop* but that the head of which *flags* or *drops;* the snow-drop *droops,* and flowers will generally *droop* from excess of drought or heat: the spirits in the same manner

are said to *droop,* which expresses more than to *flag;* the human body also *droops* when the strength fails: *languish* is a still stronger expression than *droop,* and is applicable principally to persons; some *languish* in sickness, some in prison, and some in a state of distress: to *pine* is to be in a state of wearing pain which is mostly of a mental nature; a child may *pine* when absent from all its friends and supposing itself deserted.

FLAGITIOUS. See HEINOUS.

FLAGRANT. See HEINOUS.

FLAME, BLAZE, FLASH, FLARE, GLARE. *Flame,* in Latin *flamma,* from the Greek φλέγειν, to burn, signifies the luminous exhalation emitted from fire. *Blaze,* Anglo-Saxon *blǣse,* torch, signifies a flame blown up, that is, an extended *flame: flash* comes from Middle English *flaschen,* to dash, Icelandic *flas,* a swift rushing, and refers to a sudden rush of light. *Flare* is only a variant of Swedish *flasa,* to burn violently. *Flash* and *flare,* which are but variations of *flame,* denote different species of *flame;* the former, a sudden *flame,* the second, a dazzling, unsteady *flame. Glare,* Anglo-Saxon *glœr,* amber, is possibly allied to glass; it refers to a sharp and shining flight, a strong *flame,* that emits a strong light: a candle burns only by *flame,* paper commonly by a *blaze,* gunpowder by a *flash,* a torch by a *flare,* and a conflagration by a *glare.*

FLAT, LEVEL. *Flat* is a Scandinavian word of uncertain origin. *Level,* in all probability from *libella* and *libra,* a balance, signifies the evenness of a balance. *Flat* is said of a thing with regard to itself; it is opposed to the round or protuberant; *level,* as it respects another thing; it is opposed to the uneven: a country is *flat* which has no elevation; a country is *level* as contrasted with that which is mountainous, or a wall is *level* with the roof of a house when it rises to the height of the roof.

In the moral application they differ too widely to render comparison necessary.

See also INSIPID.

FLATTER. See ADULATE.

FLATTERER, SYCOPHANT, PARASITE. *Flatterer* (see ADULATE). *Syco-*

phant, in Greek σῡκοφάντης, signified originally an informer on the matter of figs, but has now acquired the meaning of an obsequious and servile person. *Parasite*, in Greek παράσῑτος, from παρά and σῑτος, corn or meat, originally referred to the priests who attended feasts, but it is now applied to a hanger-on at the tables of the great.

The *flatterer* is one who flatters by words; the *sycophant* and *parasite* is therefore always a *flatterer*, and something more, for the *sycophant* adopts every mean artifice by which he can ingratiate himself, and the *parasite* submits to every degradation and servile compliance by which he can obtain his base purpose. These terms differ more in the object than in the means, the former having general purposes of favor, and the latter particular and still lower purposes to answer. Courtiers may be *sycophants* in order to be well with their prince and obtain preferment; but they are seldom *parasites*, who are generally poor and in want of a meal.

FLAVOR. See TASTE.
FLAW. See BLEMISH.
FLAY. See SKIN.
FLEETING. See TEMPORARY.
FLEETNESS. See QUICKNESS.
FLEXIBLE, PLIABLE, PLIANT, SUPPLE. *Flexible,* in Latin *flexibilis,* from *flectere,* to bend, signifies able to be bent. *Pliable* signifies able to be *plied* or folded: *pliant* signifies literally *plying,* bending, or folding. *Supple,* in French *souple,* comes from Latin *supplicem* (accusative), in the old sense of bending under; compare *supplicate.*

Flexible is used in a natural or moral sense; *pliable,* in the familiar sense only; *pliant,* in the higher and moral application only: what can be bent in any degree as a stick is *flexible;* what can be bent as wax, or folded like cloth, is *pliable.* *Supple,* whether in a proper or a figurative sense, is an excess of *pliability;* what can be bent backward and forward, like osier twig, is *supple.*

In the moral application, *flexible* is indefinite both in degree and application; it may be greater or less in point of degree; whereas *pliant* supposes a great degree of *pliability,* and *supple-*ness a great degree of *pliancy* or *pliability;* it applies likewise to the outward actions, to the temper, the resolution, or the principles; but *pliancy* is applied to the principles or the conduct dependent upon those principles; *suppleness,* to the outward actions and behavior only. A temper is *flexible* which yields to the entreaties of others; the person or character is *pliant* when it is formed or moulded easily at the will of another; a person is *supple* who makes his actions and his manners bend according to the varying humors of another: the first belongs to one in a superior station who yields to the wishes of the applicant; the latter two belong to equals or inferiors who yield to the influence of others. *Flexibility* is frequently a weakness, but never a vice; it always consults the taste of others, sometimes to its own inconvenience and often in opposition to its judgment; *pliancy* is often both a weakness and a vice: it always yields for its own pleasure, though not always in opposition to its sense of right and wrong: *suppleness* is always a vice, but never a weakness; it seeks its gratification to the injury of another by flattering his passions. *Flexibility* is opposed to firmness, *pliancy* to steadiness, *suppleness* to rigidity.

FLICKERING. See LAMBENT.
FLIGHT. See SITUATION.
FLIGHTINESS. See LIGHTNESS.
FLIMSY. See SUPERFICIAL.
FLOAT. See WAFT.
FLOATING. See UNFUNDED.
FLOURISH, THRIVE, PROSPER. *Flourish,* in French *fleurir, florissant,* Latin *floresco,* or *floreo,* from *flos,* a flower, is a figure of speech borrowed from the action of flowers which grow in full vigor and health. *Thrive* is a Scandinavian word from a root signifying to seize, meaning to seize for one's self, hence to prosper. *Prosper,* in Latin *prosper, prosperus,* compounded of *pro* and *spes,* hope, signifies to be agreeable to the hopes.

To *flourish* expresses the state of being that which is desirable: to *thrive* the process of becoming so. In the proper sense, *flourish* and *thrive* are applied to vegetation: the former to that which is full grown, the latter to that which is in the act of growing: the oldest trees are said to *flourish* which put forth their leaves and fruits in full vigor; young trees *thrive* when they increase rapidly toward their full growth.

Flourish and *thrive* are taken likewise in the moral sense; *prosper* is employed only in this sense; *flourish* is said either of individuals or of communities of men; *thrive* and *prosper* only of individuals. To *flourish* is to be in full possession of powers, physical, intellectual, and incidental: an author *flourishes* at a certain period; an institution *flourishes;* literature or trade *flourishes;* a nation *flourishes.* To *thrive* is to carry on one's concerns to the advantage of one's circumstances; it is a term of familiar use for those who gain by positive labor: the industrious tradesman *thrives.* To *prosper* is to be already in advantageous circumstances: men *prosper* who accumulate wealth agreeably to their wishes and beyond their expectations.

FLOW, STREAM, GUSH. For the derivation of *flow* see ARISE. *Stream* is, in Anglo-Saxon, *stream,* from a root signifying to flow. *Gush* comes from a Teutonic root and is allied to Icelandic *gjota,* to pour.

Flow is here the generic term: the other two are specific terms, expressing different modes: water may *flow* either in a large body or in a long, but narrow course; the *stream,* in a long, narrow course only: thus, waters *flow* in seas, rivers, rivulets, or in a small pond; they *stream* only out of spouts or small channels: they *flow* gently or otherwise; they *stream* gently; but they *gush* with violence: thus, the blood *flows* from a wound which comes from it in any manner; it *streams* from a wound when it runs, as it were, in a channel; it *gushes* from a wound when it runs with impetuosity and in as large quantities as the cavity admits. See also ARISE.

FLUCTUATE, WAVER. *Fluctuate,* in Latin *fluctuatus,* participle of *fluctuare,* from *fluctus,* a wave, signifies to move backward and forward like a wave. *Waver* comes from Anglo-Saxon *wæfre,* restless, wandering; it is not, however, the same word as wave, which is allied to *wag.*

To *fluctuate* conveys the idea of strong agitation; to *waver,* that of constant motion backward and forward: when applied in the moral sense, to *fluctuate* designates the action of the spirits or the opinions; to *waver* is said only of the will or opinions: he who is alternately merry and sad in quick succession is said to be *fluctuating;* or he who has many opinions in quick succession is said to *fluctuate;* but he who cannot form an opinion or come to a resolution is said to *waver.*

See also WAG.

FLUENT. See VOLUBLE.

FLUID, LIQUID, LIQUIDATE. *Fluid,* from *fluere,* to flow, signifies that which from its nature flows; *liquid,* from *liquere,* to be clear, signifies that which is melted. These words may be employed as epithets to the same objects; but they have a distinct office which they derive from their original meaning: when we wish to represent a thing as capable of passing along in a stream or current, we should denominate it a *fluid;* when we wish to represent it as passing from a congealed to a dissolved state, we should name it a *liquid;* water and air are both represented as *fluids* from their general property of flowing through certain spaces; but ice, when thawed, becomes a *liquid* and melts; melted lead is also termed a *liquid:* the humors of the animal body and the juices of trees are *fluids;* what we drink is a *liquid,* as opposed to what we eat, which is solid. We *liquidate* an obligation or debt when we settle it or pay it off.

FLUTTER. See PALPITATE.

FLYING-MACHINE. See AIRCRAFT.

FOE. See ENEMY.

FŒTUS. See EMBRYO.

FOIBLE. See IMPERFECTION.

FOIL. See DEFEAT.

FOLKS. See PEOPLE.

FOLLOW, SUCCEED, ENSUE. *Follow* comes from Anglo-Saxon *folgian.* *Succeed* is compounded of Latin *sub,* next, and *cedere,* to go, meaning to go after. *Ensue* comes from French *suivre,* Latin *sequi,* to follow.

Follow and *succeed* are said of persons and things; *ensue,* of things only: *follow,* in respect of persons, denotes the going in order, in a trace or line; *succeed* denotes the going or being in the same place immediately after another; many persons may *follow* one another at the same time; but only one individual properly *succeeds* another. *Follow* is taken literally for the motion of the physical body in relation to another; *succeed* is taken in the moral sense for taking the place of another: people *follow* one another in a procession, or one *follows* another to the grave; a king *succeeds* to a throne, or a son *succeeds* to the inheritance of his father. To *follow* may also be to go in the same course, though not at the same time, as to *follow* a person to the grave in the sense of dying after him: to *succeed* is always to go in the place of another, whether living or dead, as one minister of state *succeeds* another, or a son *succeeds* his father.

Persons may *follow* things, but things only *succeed* things: as to *follow* a rule or *follow* a course of conduct.

To *follow*, in relation to things, is said either simply of the order in which they go or of such as go by a connection between them; to *succeed* implies simply to take the place after another; to *ensue* is to *follow* by a necessary connection: as in a natural tempest one wave of the sea *follows* another in rapid succession, so in the moral tempest of political revolutions one mad convulsion is quickly *succeeded* by another: nothing can *ensue* from popular commotions but bloodshed and misery. *Follow* is used in general propositions; *ensue* is used in specific cases: sin and misery *follow* each other as cause and effect; quarrels too often *ensue* from the conversations of violent men who differ either in religion or politics.

Follow, Pursue.—The idea of going after any object in order to reach or obtain it is common to these terms, but under different circumstances: to *follow* a person is mostly with a friendly intention; to *pursue* (see CONTINUE), with a hostile intention: a person *follows* his fellow-traveller whom he wishes to overtake; the officers of justice *pursue* the criminal whom they wish to apprehend; so likewise the huntsmen and hunters *follow* the dogs in the chase; the dogs *pursue* the hare.

In application to things, *follow* is taken more in the passive, and *pursue* more in the active sense: a man *follows* the plan of another, and *pursues* his own plan; he *follows* his inclinations, and *pursues* an object.

Follow, Imitate.—*Follow* (see above). *Imitate* is in Latin *imitatus*, participle of *imitare*, from a root also found in *imago*.

Both these terms denote the regulating our actions by something that offers itself to us or is set before us; but we *follow* that which is either internal or external; we *imitate* that only which is external: we either *follow* the dictates of our own minds or the suggestions of others; but we *imitate* the conduct of others: in regard to external objects, we *follow* either a rule or an example; but we *imitate* an example only: we *follow* the footsteps of our forefathers; we *imitate* their virtues and their perfections: it is advisable for young persons as closely as possible to *follow* the good example of those who are older and wiser than themselves; it is the bounden duty of every Christian to *imitate* the example of our blessed Saviour to the utmost of his power.

To *follow* and *imitate* may both be applied to that which is good or bad: the former to any action, but the latter only to the behavior or the mode of doing anything: we may *follow* a person in his career of virtue or vice; we *imitate* his gestures, tone of voice, and the like.

Follower, Adherent, Partisan.—A *follower* is one who *follows* a person generally; and *adherent* is one who *adheres* to his cause; a *partisan* is the *follower* of a party; the *follower* follows either the person, the interests, or the principles of any one; thus the retinue of a nobleman, or the friends of a statesman, or the friends of any man's opinions, may be styled his *followers;* but the *adherent* is that kind of *follower* who espouses the interests of another, as the *adherents* of Charles I.: a *follower* follows near or at a distance; but the *adherent* is always near at hand; the *partisan* hangs on or keeps at a certain distance; the *follower* follows from various motives; the *adherent* adheres from a personal motive; the *partisan*, from a partial motive: Charles I. had as many *adherents* as he had *followers;* the rebels had as many *partisans* as they had *adherents.*

FOLLY, FOOLERY. *Folly* is the abstract of foolish, and characterizes the thing; *foolery,* the abstract of fool, and characterizes the person: we may commit an act of *folly* without being chargeable with weakness or *folly;* but none are guilty of *fooleries* who are not themselves fools, either habitually or temporarily: young people are perpetually committing *follies* if not under proper control; fashionable people lay aside one *foolery* only to take up another.

FOND. See AFFECTIONATE; AMOROUS; INDULGENT.

FONDLE. See CARESS; DALLY.

FOOD, DIET, REGIMEN. *Food,* Anglo-Saxon *foda,* signifying what one eats, comes from a root which appears in Latin *panis,* bread (English *pantry*), *pasture,* etc., *p* in Latin corresponding to *f* in the Teutonic languages, as in *pater* and *father, pedem* and *foot. Diet,* from δαιτάω, to live medicinally, signifies any particular mode of living. *Regimen,* in Latin *regimen,* from *rego,* signifies a system or practice by rule.

All these terms refer to our living, or that by which we live: *food* is here the general term; the others are specific. *Food* specifies no circumstances; whatever is taken to maintain life is *food:* diet is properly prescribed or regular *food:* it is the hard lot of some among the poor to obtain with difficulty *food* and clothing for themselves and their families; an attention to the *diet* of children is an important branch of their early education. *Food* is an unqualified term applicable to either man or beast; *diet* is applied to man only, not merely to individuals in the limited sense, but to the species in the sense of their daily and regular *food. Food* has also a figurative application which *diet* has not.

Diet and *regimen* are both particular modes of living; but the former respects the quality of *food,* the latter the quantity as well as quality: *diet* is confined to modes of taking nourishment; *regimen* often respects the abstinence from *food,* bodily exercise, and whatever may conduce to health: *diet* is generally the consequence of an immediate prescription from a physician, and during the period of sickness; *regimen* commonly forms a regular part of a man's system of living: *diet* is in certain cases of such importance for the restoration of a patient that a single deviation may defeat the best medicine; it is the misfortune of some people to be troubled with diseases from which they cannot get any exemption but by observing a strict *regimen.*

FOOL, IDIOT, BUFFOON. *Fool* comes from Latin *follis,* a wind-bag, and *folles,* puffed cheeks. *Idiot* comes from the Greek ἰδιώτης, signifying either a private person or one that is rude and unskilled in the ways of the world. *Buffoon* comes from French *bouffer,* to puff.

The *fool* is either naturally or artificially a *fool;* the *idiot* is a natural *fool;* the *buffoon* is an artificial *fool:* whoever violates common sense in his actions is a *fool;* whoever is unable to act according to common sense is an *idiot;* whoever intentionally violates common-sense is a *buffoon.*

See also NINNY.

Foolhardy, Adventurous, Rash.—*Foolhardy* signifies having the hardihood of a *fool. Adventurous* signifies ready to *venture. Rash* comes from a Germanic root signifying quick, sudden.

Foolhardy expresses more than the *adventurous,* and *adventurous* than *rash.* The *foolhardy* man *ventures* in defiance of consequences: the *adventurous* man *ventures* from a love of the arduous and the bold; the *rash* man *ventures* for want of thought: courage and boldness become *foolhardihood* when they lead a person to run a fruitless risk; an *adventurous* spirit sometimes leads a man into unnecessary difficulties; but it is a necessary accompaniment of greatness. There is not so much design, but there is more violence and impetuosity in *rashness* than in *foolhardihood:* the former is the consequence of an ardent temper which will admit of correction by the influence of the judgment; but the latter comprehends the perversion of both the will and the judgment. An infidel is *foolhardy,* who risks his future salvation for the mere gratification of his pride; Alexander was an *adventurous* prince who delighted in enterprises in proportion as they presented difficulties; he was likewise a *rash* prince, as was evinced by his jumping into the river Cydnus while he was hot, and by his leaping over the wall of Oxydracæ and exposing himself singly to the attack of the enemy.

FOOLISH. See IRRATIONAL; SIMPLE.

FOOTSTEP. See MARK.

FOPPISH. See FINICAL.

FORBEAR. See ABSTAIN.

FORBID, PROHIBIT, INTERDICT. The *for* in *forbid*, like the German *ver*, is negative, signifying to bid not to do. The *pro* in *prohibit*, and *inter* in *interdict*, have both a similarly negative sense: the former verb, from *habere*, to have, signifies to have or hold that a thing shall not be done, to restrain from doing; the latter, from *dicere*, to say, signifies to say that a thing shall not be done.

Forbid is the ordinary term; *prohibit* is the judicial term; *interdict* the moral term. To *forbid* is a direct and personal act; to *prohibit* is an indirect action that operates by means of extended influence: both imply the exercise of power or authority by any person; but the former is more applicable to the power of private persons, and the latter to the authority of government. A parent *forbids* his child marrying when he thinks proper: the government *prohibits* the use of spirituous liquors. *Interdict* is a species of *forbidding* applied to more serious concerns, as to *interdict* the use of any one strong drink. To *forbid* or *interdict* is opposed to command; to *prohibit*, to allow. As nothing is *forbidden* to Christians which is good and just in itself, so nothing is commanded that is hurtful and unjust. As no one is *prohibited* in our own country from writing that which can tend to the improvement of mankind, so on the other hand he is not allowed to indulge his private malignity by the publication of injurious personalities.

Forbid and *interdict*, as personal acts, are properly applicable to persons only, but by an improper application are extended to things; *prohibit*, however, in the general sense of restraining, is applied with equal propriety to things as to persons: shame *forbids* us doing a thing; law, authority, and the like, *prohibit*.

See also BAN.

FORCE, VIOLENCE. Both these terms imply an exertion of strength; but the former in a much less degree than the latter. *Force* (see COMPEL) is ordinarily employed to supply the want of a proper will; *violence*, in Latin *violentia*, from *vis*, and the Greek, βία, strength, is used to counteract an opposing will. The arms of justice must exercise *force* in order to bring offenders to a proper account; one nation exercises *violence* against another in the act of carrying on war. *Force* is mostly conformable to reason and equity; *violence* is always resorted to for the attainment of that which is unattainable by law. All who are invested with authority have occasion to use *force* at certain times to subdue the unruly will of those who should submit: *violence* and rapine are inseparable companions; a robber could not subsist by the latter without exercising the former.

In an extended and figurative application to things, these terms convey the same general idea of exerting strength. That is said to have *force* that acts with *force;* and that to have *violence* that acts with *violence.* A word, an expression, or a remark has *force* or is *forcible;* a disorder, a passion, a sentiment, has *violence* or is *violent.* *Force* is always something desirable; *violence* is always something hurtful. We ought to listen to arguments which have *force* in them; we endeavor to correct the *violence* of all angry passions.

See also ENERGY; POWER; STRAIN.

FORCIBLE. See COGENT.

FOREBODE. See AUGUR.

FORECAST. See FORESIGHT.

FOREFATHERS, PROGENITORS, ANCESTORS. *Forefathers* signifies our *fathers before* us, and includes our immediate parents. *Progenitors*, from *pro* and *gignere*, to beget, signifies those begotten before us, exclusive of our immediate parents. *Ancestors*, contracted from *antecessors*, or those going before, is said of those from whom we are remotely descended. *Forefathers* is a partial and familiar term for the preceding branches of any family.

Progenitors is a higher term in the same sense applied to families of distinction: we speak of the *forefathers* of a peasant, but the *progenitors* of a nobleman.

Forefathers and *progenitors*, but particularly the latter, are said mostly of individuals, and respect the regular line of succession in a family; *ancestors* is employed collectively as well as individually and regards simply the order of succession: we may speak of the *ancestors* of a nation as well as of any particular person.

FOREGO. See GIVE UP; WAIVE.

FOREGOING. See ANTECEDENT.

FOREIGN. See EXTRANEOUS.

FOREIGNER. See STRANGER.

FORERUNNER, PRECURSOR, MESSENGER, HARBINGER. *Forerunner* and *precursor* signify literally the same thing, namely, one *running before;* but the term *forerunner* is properly applied only to one who runs before to any spot to communicate intelligence; and it is figuratively applied to things which in their nature, or from a natural connection, precede others; *precursor* is only employed in this figurative sense: thus imprudent speculations are said to be the *forerunners* of a man's ruin; the ferment which took place in men's minds was the *precursor* of the revolution.

Messenger signifies literally one bearing *messages:* and *harbinger,* from the Old French *herberger,* Old High German *heri-berga,* from *heri,* an army, and *bergan,* to shelter, signified, one who provided a shelter for an army. Both terms are employed for persons: but the *messenger* states what has been or is; the *harbinger* announces what is to be. Our Saviour was the *messenger* of glad tidings to all mankind: the prophets were the *harbingers* of the Messiah. A *messenger* may be employed on different offices; a *harbinger* is a *messenger* who acts in a specific office. The angels are represented as *messengers* on different occasions. John the Baptist was the *harbinger* of our Saviour, who prepared the way of the Lord. They are both applied figuratively to other objects.

FORESIGHT, FORETHOUGHT, FORECAST, PREMEDITATION. *Foresight,* from *seeing before,* and *forethought,* from *thinking beforehand,* denote the simple act of the mind in seeing a thing before it happens: *forecast,* from casting the thoughts onward, signifies coming at the knowledge of a thing beforehand by means of calculation: *premeditation,* from *meditate,* signifies obtaining the same knowledge by force of meditating, reflecting deeply. *Foresight* and *forethought* are general and indefinite terms; we employ them on either ordinary or extraordinary occasions; but *forethought* is, of the two, the most familiar term; *forecast* and *premeditation,* mostly in the latter case: all business requires *foresight;* state concerns require *forecast; foresight* and *forecast* respect what is to happen; they are the operations of the mind in calculating futurity: *premeditation* respects what is to be said or done; it is a preparation of the thoughts and designs for action: by *foresight* and *forecast* we guard against evils and provide for contingencies; by *premeditation* we guard against errors of conduct. A man betrays his want of *foresight* who does not provide against losses in trade; he shows his want of *forecast* who does not provide against old age; he shows his want of *premeditation* who acts or speaks on the impulse of the moment: the man, therefore, who does a wicked act without *premeditation* lessens his guilt.

FOREST, CHASE, PARK, are all habitations for animals of venery; but the *forest* is of the first magnitude and importance, it being a franchise and the property of the king; the *chase* and *park* may be either public or private property. The *forest* is so formed of wood, and covers such an extent of ground, that it may be the haunt of wild beasts; of this description are the *forests* in Germany: the *chase* is an indefinite and open space that is allotted expressly for the *chase* of particular animals, such as deer; the *park* is an enclosed space that serves for the preservation of domestic animals.

FORETELL, PREDICT, PROPHESY, PROGNOSTICATE. To *foretell* is compounded of *fore* and *tell; predict* comes from *præ,* before, and *dicere,* to say; *prophesy,* in French *prophétiser,* Latin *prophetiso,* Greek προφῆτης, from προ, Latin *pro,* before, and φημί, to speak, meaning to speak before the event, conveys the same idea; *prognosticate*, from the Greek προγιγνώσκειν, to know beforehand, to bode or imagine to one's self beforehand, denotes the action of feeling or knowing, rather than speaking of things to come.

Foretell is the most general in its sense and familiar in its application; we may *foretell* common events, although we cannot *predict* or *prophesy* anything important: to *foretell* is an ordinary gift; one *foretells* by a simple calculation or guess: to *predict* and *prophesy* are extraordinary gifts; one *predicts* by a supernatural power, real or supposed; one *prophesies* by means of inspiration. Men of discernment and experience easily *foretell* the events of undertakings which fall under their notice. The priests among the heathens, like the astrologers and conjurers of more modern times, pretended to *predict* events that affected nations and empires. The gift of *prophecy* was one among the number of the supernatural gifts communicated to the primitive Christians by the Holy Ghost.

Prediction, as a noun, is employed for both the verbs *foretell* and *predict;* it is, therefore, a term of less value than *prophecy*. We speak of a *prediction* being verified and a *prophecy* fulfilled: the *predictions* of almanacmakers respecting the weather are as seldom verified as the *prophecies* of visionaries and enthusiasts are fulfilled respecting the death of princes or the affairs of governments.

To *prognosticate* is an act of the understanding; it is guided by outward symptoms, as a rule; it is only stimulated, and not guided, by outward objects; a physician *prognosticates* the crisis of a disorder by the symptoms discoverable in the patient.

FORFEITURE. See FINE.

FORGE. See INVENT.

FORGETFULNESS, OBLIVION. *Forgetfulness* characterizes the person or that which is personal; *oblivion*, the state of the thing: the former refers to him who *forgets*, the latter to that which is *forgotten:* we blame a person for his *forgetfulness;* but we sometimes bury things in *oblivion*.

See also AMNESIA.

FORGIVE, ABSOLVE, **P**ARDON, **R**E-MIT. *Forgive*, Anglo - Saxon *forgefan*, compounded of the privative *for* and *gifan*, Modern English *give*, and *pardon* (see EXCUSE) both signify not to give the punishment that is due, to relax from the rigor of justice in demanding retribution. *Forgive* is the familiar term; *pardon* is adapted to the serious style. Individuals *forgive* one another personal offences; they *pardon* offences against law and morals: the former is an act of Christian charity: the latter an act of clemency: the former is an act that is confined to no condition; the latter is peculiarly the act of a superior. He who has the right of being offended has an opportunity of *forgiving* the offender; he who has the authority of punishing the offence may *pardon*.

Pardon, when compared with *remission*, is the consequence of offence; it respects principally the person offending; it depends upon him who is offended; it produces reconciliation when it is sincerely granted and sincerely demanded. *Remission* is the consequence of the crime; it has more particular regard to the punishment; it is granted by either the prince or the magistrates; it arrests the execution of justice. *Remission*, like *pardon*, is peculiarly applicable to the sinner with regard to his Maker. *Absolution* is taken in no other sense: it is the consequence of the fault or the sin, and properly concerns the state of the culprit; it properly loosens him from the tie with which he is bound; it is pronounced either by the civil judge or by the ecclesiastical minister; and it re-establishes the accused or the penitent in the rights of innocence.

FORGOTTEN. See BYGONE.

FORLORN. See FORSAKEN.

FORM, FIGURE, **C**ONFORMATION. *Form*, in Latin *forma*, signifies properly the life within which gives shape and individuality to anything. *Figure* signifies the image feigned or conceived. *Conformation*, in French *conformation*, in Latin *conformatio*, from *conform*, signifies the image disposed or put together.

Form is the generic term; *figure* and *conformation* are special terms. The *form* is the work either of nature or art; it results from the arrangement of the parts: the *figure* is the work of design: it includes the general contour or outline: the *conformation* includes such a disposition of the parts of the body as is adapted for performing certain functions. *Form* is the property of every substance; and the artificial *form* approaches nearest to perfection as it is most natural; the *figure* is the fruit of the imagination; it is the representation of the actual *form* that belongs to things; it is more or less just as it approaches to the *form* of the thing itself: *conformation* is said only with regard to animal bodies; nature renders it more or less suitable according to the accidental concurrence of physical causes. The erect *form* of man is one of the distinguishing marks of his superiority over every other terrestrial being: the human *figure* when well painted is an object of admiration: the turn of the mind is doubtless influenced by the *conformation* of the organs. A person's *form* is said to be handsome or ugly, common or uncommon, his *figure* to be correct or incorrect; a *conformation*, to be good or bad. Heathens have worshipped the Deity under various *forms:* mathematical *figures* are the only true *figures* with which we are acquainted: the craniologist affects to judge of characters by the *conformation* of the skull.

Form and *figure* are used in a moral application, although *conformation* is not. We speak of adopting a *form* of faith, a *form* of words, a *form* of godliness; cutting a showy, a dismal, or ridiculous *figure*.

Form, Fashion, Mould, Shape.—To *form* is to put into a *form*, which is here as before the generic term: to *fashion* is to put into a particular or distinct *form;* to *mould* is to put into a set *form;* to *shape* is to *form* simply as it respects the exterior. As everything respects a *form* when it receives existence, so to *form* conveys the idea of producing. When we wish to represent a thing as *formed* in any distinct or remarkable way, we may speak of it as *fashioned*. God *formed* man out of the dust of the ground; He *fashioned* him after His own image. When we wish to represent a thing as *formed* according to a precise rule, we should

say it was *moulded;* thus the habits of a man are *moulded* at the will of a superior. When we wish to represent a thing as receiving the accidental qualities which distinguish it from others, we talk of *shaping* it: the potter *shapes* the clay; the milliner *shapes* a bonnet; a man *shapes* his actions to the humors of another.

See also MAKE.

Form, Compose, Constitute.—*Form* is a generic and indefinite term, signifying to give a *form*. To *compose* and *constitute* are modes of forming. These words may be employed either to designate modes of action or to characterize things. Things may be *formed* either by persons or things; they are *composed* and *constituted* only by conscious agents: thus persons *form* things, or things *form* one another: thus we *form* a circle, or the reflection of the light after rain *forms* a rainbow. Persons *compose* and *constitute:* thus a musician *composes* a piece of music, or men *constitute* laws.

To *form*, in regard to persons, is simply to put into a form; to *compose* is to put together into a form; and to *constitute* is to make to stand together in a form; to *form*, therefore, does not qualify the action: one *forms* a thing without defining how, whether at once or by degrees, whether with one or several materials; to *compose* and *constitute* are both modes of forming by the help of several materials, with device and contrivance; *compose* is said of that which only requires to be put together; *constitute*, of that to which a certain degree of stability must be given. God *formed* man, man *forms* a cup or a vessel; he *composes* a book; he *constitutes* offices, bodies politic, and the like.

When employed to characterize things, *form* signifies simply to have a *form*, be it either simple or complex; *compose* and *constitute* are said only of those things which have complex *forms;* the former as respecting the material, the latter the essential parts of an object: thus we may say that an object *forms* a circle, or a semicircle, or the segment of a circle: a society is *composed* of individuals; but law and order *constitute* the essence of society: so letters and syllables *compose* a word; but sense is essential to *constitute* a word.

Form, Ceremony, Rite, Observance.— *Form* (see above). *Ceremony*, in Latin *ceremonia*, signifies a formal celebration. *Rite*, Latin *ritus*, means a going, a way, a way of doing, from a root *ri*, meaning to flow, to move. *Observance* signifies the thing observed, from Latin *observare*, to heed, to observe.

All these terms are employed with regard to particular modes of action in civil society. *Form* is here, as in the preceding sections, the most general in its sense and application; *ceremony*, *rite*, and *observance* are particular kinds of *form*, suited to particular occasions. *Form*, in its distinct application, respects all determinate modes of acting and speaking that are adopted by society at large in every transaction of life; *ceremony* respects those *forms* of outward behavior which are made the expressions of respect and deference; *rite* and *observance* are applied to national *ceremonies* in matters of religion. A certain *form* is requisite for the sake of order, method, and decorum, in every social matter, whether in affairs of state, in a court of law, in a place of worship, or in the private intercourse of friends. So long as distinctions are admitted in society, and men are agreed to express their sentiments of regard and respect to one another, it will be necessary to preserve the *ceremonies* of politeness which have been established. Administering oaths by the magistrate is a necessary *form* in law; kissing the king's hand is a *ceremony* practiced at court.

As far as *form*, *ceremonies*, *rites*, and *observances* respect religion, the first is used in the most universal and unqualified sense in respect to religion generally or any particular *form*: the second may be said either of an individual or a community; the third only of a community; and the last, more properly, of an individual either in public or in private. There can be no religion without some *form*, but there may be different *forms* which are equally good. Every country has adopted certain *rites* founded upon its peculiar religious faith, and prescribed certain *observances* by which individuals can make a public profession of their faith: baptism is one *rite* of initiation into the Christian church; kneeling at prayer is a *ceremony*, prayer itself is an *observance*.

Formal, Ceremonious, Ceremonial.— *Formal* and *ceremonious*, from *form* and *ceremony*, are either taken in an indifferent sense with respect to what contains *form* and *ceremony*, or in a bad sense, expressing the excess of *form* and *ceremony*. A person expects to have a *formal* dismissal before he considers himself as dismissed; people of fashion pay one another *ceremonious* visits, by way of keeping up a distant intercourse.

Ceremonial is employed in the sense of appertaining to prescribed *ceremonies;* and *formal* implies appertaining to prescribed forms in public matters, as *formal* communications from one government to another: it is the business of the church to regulate the *ceremonial* part of religion.

Ceremonious was formerly used in the same sense as *ceremonial*.

Formal, in the bad sense, is opposed to easy: *ceremonious*, to the cordial. A *formal* carriage prevents a person from indulging himself in the innocent familiarities of friendly intercourse; *ceremonious* carriage puts a stop to all hospitality and kindness. Princes, in their *formal* intercourse with one another, know nothing of the pleasures of society; *ceremonious* visitants give and receive entertainments without tasting any of the enjoyments which flow from the reciprocity of kind offices.

FORMER. See ANTECEDENT.

FORMERLY, IN TIMES PAST or OLD TIMES, DAYS OF YORE, ANCIENTLY or ANCIENT TIMES. *Formerly* supposes a less remote period than *in times past:* and that less remote than *in days of yore* and *anciently*. The first two may be said of what happens within the age of man; the last two are extended to many generations and ages. Any individual may use the word *formerly* with regard to himself: thus, we enjoyed our health better *formerly* than now. An old man may speak of *times past*, as when he says he does not enjoy himself as he did *in times past*. *Old times, days of yore*, and *anciently* are more applicable to nations than to individuals; and all these express different degrees of *remoteness*. With respect to our present period, the age of Queen Elizabeth may be called *old times;* the days of Alfred, and, still later, the *days of yore:* the earliest period in which Britain is mentioned may be termed *ancient times*.

See also ONCE.

FORMIDABLE, DREADFUL, TERRIBLE, SHOCKING. *Formidable* is applied to that which is apt to excite fear (see APPREHEND). *Dreadful*, to what is calculated to excite dread; *terrible* (see ALARM), to that which excites *terror;* and *shocking* (from Middle English *shokken*, to jolt) is applied to that which violently shakes or agitates (see AGITATE). The *formidable* acts neither suddenly nor violently; the *dreadful* may act violently but not suddenly: thus the appearance of an army may be *formidable;* but that of a field of battle is *dreadful*. The *terrible* and *shocking* act both suddenly and violently; but the former acts both on the senses and on the imagination, the latter on the moral feelings: thus, the glare of a tiger's eye is *terrible;* the unexpected news of a friend's death is *shocking*.

FORSAKE. See ABANDON.

FORSAKEN, FORLORN, DESTITUTE. To be *forsaken* is to be deprived of the company and assistance of those we have looked to; to be *forlorn*, Anglo-Saxon *forloren* (German *verloren*), past participle of *forleosan*, to lose entirely, signifying lost, is to be *forsaken* in time of difficulty, to be without a guide in an unknown road; to be *destitute*, from the Latin *destitutus*, from Latin *de*, away, and *statuere*, to place, meaning taken away from, is to be deprived of the first necessaries of life. To be *forsaken* is a partial situation; to be *forlorn* and *destitute* is a permanent condition. We may be *forsaken* by a fellow-traveller on the road; we are *forlorn* when we get into a deserted path with no one to direct us; we are *destitute* when we have no means of subsistence, nor the prospect of obtaining the means. It is particularly painful to be *forsaken* by the friend of our youth and the sharer of our fortunes; the orphan who is left to travel the road of life without counsellor or friend is, of all others, in the most

forlorn condition; if to this be added poverty, his misery is aggravated by his becoming *destitute*.

FORSWEAR, PERJURE, SUBORN. *Forswear* is Anglo-Saxon; *perjure* is Latin; the prepositions *for* and *per* are both privative, and the words signify literally to swear contrary to the truth; this is, however, not their only distinction: to *forswear* is applied to all kinds of oaths; to *perjure* is employed only for such oaths as have been administered by the civil magistrate. A soldier *forswears* himself who breaks his oath of allegiance by desertion; and a subject *forswears* himself who takes an oath of allegiance to his sovereign which he afterward violates; a man *perjures* himself in a court of law who swears to the truth of that which he knows to be false. *Forswear* is used only in the proper sense: *perjure* may be used figuratively with regard to lover's vows; he who deserts his mistress to whom he has pledged his affections is a *perjured* man.

Forswear and *perjure* are the acts of individuals; *suborn*, from the Latin *sub*, secretly, and *ornare*, to adorn, to enrich, meaning to enrich secretly, to bribe, and hence to make to *forswear;* a *perjured* man has all the guilt upon himself; but he who is *suborned* shares his guilt with the *suborner*.

FORTIFY. See STRENGTHEN.

FORTITUDE. See COURAGE.

FORTUITOUS. See FORTUNATE.

FORTUNATE, LUCKY, FORTUITOUS, PROSPEROUS, SUCCESSFUL. *Fortunate* signifies having *fortune* (see CHANCE). *Lucky* is the adjective corresponding to *luck*, which is not found in Anglo-Saxon, but is a late borrowing from Dutch and German. (Compare German *Glück*.) *Fortuitous*, from *fors*, chance, signifies according to chance. *Prosperous* (see FLOURISH). *Successful* signifies full of *success*, enabled to *succeed*.

The *fortunate* and *lucky* are both applied to that which happens without the control of man; but the latter, which is a collateral term, describes the capricious goddess *Fortune* in her most freakish humors, while *fortunate* represents her in her more sober mood: in other words, the *fortunate* is more according to the ordinary course of things; the *lucky* is something sudden, unaccountable, and singular: a circumstance is said to be *fortunate* which turns up suitably to our purpose; it is said to be *lucky* when it comes upon us unexpectedly, at the moment that it is wanted: hence we speak of a man as *fortunate* in his business and the ordinary concerns of life, but *lucky* in the lottery or in games of chance: a *fortunate* year will make up for the losses of the past year; a *lucky* hit may repair the ruined spendthrift's *fortune*, only to tempt him to still greater extravagances.

Fortunate and *lucky* are applied to particular circumstances of good *fortune* and *luck*, but *fortuitous* is employed only in matters of chance generally and indifferently.

Prosperous and *successful* seem to exclude the idea of what is *fortuitous*, although *prosperity* and *success* are both greatly aided by good *fortune*. *Fortunate* and *lucky* are applied as much to the removal of evil as to the attainment of good; *prosperous* and *successful* are concerned only in what is good, or esteemed as such: we may be *fortunate* in making our escape; we are *prosperous* in the acquirement of wealth. *Fortunate* is employed for single circumstances; *prosperous* only for a train of circumstances; a man may be *fortunate* in meeting with the approbation of a superior; he is *prosperous* in his business. *Prosperity* is extended to whatever is the object of our wishes in this world; *success* is that degree of *prosperity* which immediately attends our endeavors; wealth, honors, children, and all outward circumstances constitute *prosperity;* the attainment of any object constitutes *success:* the *fortunate* and *lucky* man can lay no claim to merit, because they preclude the idea of exertion; the *prosperous* and *successful* man may claim a share of merit proportioned to the exertion.

The epithet *prosperous* may be applied to those things which promote *prosperity* or ultimate success.

See also HAPPY.

FORTUNE.　See CHANCE.

FORWARD.　See ENCOURAGE; ON; ONWARD.

FOSTER, CHERISH, HARBOR, INDULGE.　To *foster* comes from Anglo-Saxon *fostor*, nourishment, allied to *foda*, food; to *cherish*, through French from Latin *carus*, dear, is to hold affection; to *harbor*, from a *harbor* or *haven*, is to provide with a shelter and protection; to *indulge* comes from Latin *indulgere*, to be courteous to, of unknown origin. These terms are all employed here in the moral acceptation, to express the idea of giving nourishment to an object. To *foster* in the mind is to keep with care and positive endeavors; as when one *fosters* prejudices by encouraging everything which favors them: to *cherish* in the mind is to hold dear or set a value upon; as when one *cherishes* good sentiments by dwelling upon them with inward satisfaction: to *harbor* is to allow room in the mind, and is generally taken in the worst sense for giving admission to that which ought to be excluded; as when one *harbors* resentment by permitting it to have a resting-place in the heart: to *indulge* in the mind is to give the whole mind to it, to make it the chief source of pleasure: as when one *indulges* an affection, by making the will and the outward conduct bend to its gratification.

FOUL.　See SQUALID.

FOUND, GROUND, REST, BUILD. *Found*, in French *fonder*, Latin *fundo*, comes from *fundus*, the ground, and, like the verb *ground*, properly signifies to make firm in the *ground*, to make the *ground* the support. To *found* implies the exercise of art and contrivance in making a support; to *ground* signifies to lay a thing so deep that it may not totter; it is merely in the moral sense that they are here considered, as the verb to *ground* with this signification is never used otherwise. *Found* is applied to outward circumstances; *ground*, to what passes inwardly: a man *founds* his charge against another upon certain facts that are come to his knowledge; he *grounds* his belief upon the most substantial evidence: a man should be cautious not to make any accusations which are not well *founded*, nor to indulge any expectations which are not well *grounded:* monarchs commonly *found* their claims to a throne upon the right of primogeniture; Christians *ground* their hopes of immortality on the word of God.

To *found* and *ground* are said of things which demand the full exercise of the mental powers; to *rest* is an action of less importance: whatever is *founded* requires and has the utmost support; whatever is *rested* is more by the will of the individual: a man *founds* his reasoning upon some unequivocal fact; he *rests* his assertion upon mere hearsay. The words *found*, *ground*, and *rest* have always an immediate reference to the thing that supports; to *build* has an especial reference to that which is supported, to the superstructure that is raised: we should not say that a person *founds* an hypothesis without adding something, as observations, experiments, and the like, upon which it was *founded;* but we may speak of his simply *building* systems, supposing them to be the mere fruit of his distempered imagination; or we may say that a system of astronomy has been *built* upon the opinion of Copernicus respecting the motion of the earth. See also INSTITUTE.

Foundation, Ground, Basis.—*Foundation* and *ground* derive their meaning and application from the preceding article: a report is said to be without any *foundation* which has taken its rise in mere conjecture or in some arbitrary cause independent of all fact; a man's suspicion is said to be without *ground* which is not supported by the shadow of external evidence: *unfounded* clamors are frequently raised against the measures of government; *groundless* jealousies frequently arise between families to disturb the harmony of their intercourse.

Foundation and *basis* may be compared with each other, either in the proper or the improper signification: both *foundation* and *basis* are the lowest parts of any structure; but the former lies under *ground*, the latter stands above: the *foundation* supports some large and artificially erected pile; the *basis* supports a simple pillar: hence we speak of the *foundation* of St. Paul's, and the *base* or *basis* of the Monument.

This distinction is likewise preserved in the moral application of the terms: disputes have too often their *foundation* in frivolous circumstances; trea-ties have commonly their *basis* in some acknowledged general principle; with governments that are at war pacific negotiations may be commenced on the *basis* of the *uti possidetis*.

FOUNTAIN. See SPRING.

FOURIERISM. See SOCIALISM.

FRACTURE. See RUPTURE.

FRAGILE, FRAIL, BRITTLE. *Fragile* and *frail*, in French *frêle*, both come from the Latin *fragilis*, signifying breakable; but the former is used in the proper sense only, and the latter more generally in the improper sense: man, corporeally considered, is a *fragile* creature, his frame is composed of *fragile* materials; mentally considered, he is a *fragile* creature, for he is liable to every sort of *frailty*.

Brittle comes from the Anglo-Saxon *breotan*, to break, and means breakable; but it conveys a stronger idea of this quality than *fragile:* the latter applies to whatever will break from the effects of time; *brittle* to that which will not bear a temporary violence: in this sense all the works of men are *fragile*, and, in fact, all sublunary things; but glass, stone, and ice are peculiarly denominated *brittle*.

FRAGRANCE. See SMELL.

FRAIL. See FRAGILE.

FRAILTY. See IMPERFECTION.

FRAME, TEMPER, TEMPERAMENT, CONSTITUTION. *Frame*, Anglo-Saxon *framian*, to further, is allied to *from*, the preposition, and means literally the outside of anything; it is also allied to *fram*, meaning strong, and German *fromm*, good; it is applied to man physically or mentally, as denoting that constituent portion of him which seems to hold the rest together; which by an extension of the metaphor is likewise put for the whole contents, the whole body, or the whole mind. *Temper* and *temperament*, in Latin *temperamentum*, from *temperare*, to govern or dispose, signify the particular modes of being disposed or organized. *Constitution*, from *constitute* or appoint, signifies the particular mode of being *constituted* or formed.

Frame, when applied to the body, is taken in its most universal sense: as when we speak of the *frame* being violently agitated, or the human *frame* being wonderfully constructed: when applied to the mind, it will admit either of a general or restricted signification. *Temper*, which is applicable only to the mind, is taken in the general or particular state of the individual. The *frame* comprehends either the whole body of mental powers or the particular disposition of those powers in individuals; the *temper* comprehends the general or particular state of feeling as well as thinking in the individual. The mental *frame* which receives any violent concussion is liable to derangement; it is necessary for those who govern to be well acquainted with the *temper* of those whom they govern. By reflection on the various attributes of the Divine Being, a man may easily bring his mind into a *frame* of devotion: by the indulgence of a fretful, repining *temper*, a man destroys his own peace of mind and offends his Maker.

Temperament and *constitution* mark the general state of the individual; the former comprehends a mixture of the physical and mental; the latter has a purely physical application. A man with a warm *temperament* owes his warmth of character to the rapid impetus of the blood; a man with a delicate *constitution* is exposed to great fluctuations in his health; the whole *frame* of a new-born infant is peculiarly tender. Men of fierce *tempers* are to be found in all nations; men of sanguine *tempers* are more frequent in warm climates; the *constitutions* of females are more tender than those of the male, and their *frames* are altogether more susceptible.

See also INVENT.

FRANK, CANDID, INGENUOUS, FREE, OPEN, PLAIN. *Frank*, in French *franc*, Old High German *franko*, a Frank, from a weapon, was originally the name of a Germanic tribe which gave its name to France; the word signified a free-born German, as distinguished from those whom the Germans conquered, and hence the liberal and fearless manners of the man who calls no man master. *Candid* (for derivation see CANDID). *Ingenuous* comes from the Latin *ingenuus*, which signifies literally free-born, as distinguished from the *liberti*, who were afterward made *free:* hence the term has been employed by a figure of speech to denote nobleness of

birth or character. *Free*, Anglo-Saxon *freo*, originally meant dear, and was applied to the free-born children of a household, distinguished from the child-slaves. Compare Latin *liberi*, free, which also meant children. *Open* (see CANDID). *Plain* (see APPARENT).

All these terms convey the idea of a readiness to communicate and be communicated with; they are all opposed to concealment, but under different circumstances. The *frank* man is under no constraint; his thoughts and feelings are both set at ease, and his lips are ever ready to give utterance to the dictates of his heart; he has no reserve: the *candid* man has nothing to conceal; he speaks without regard to self-interest or any partial motive; he speaks nothing but the truth: the *ingenuous* man throws off all disguise; he scorns all artifice and brings everything to light; he speaks the whole truth. *Frankness* is acceptable in the general transactions of society; it inspires confidence and invites communication: *candor* is of peculiar use in matters of dispute; it serves the purposes of equity and invites to conciliation: *ingenuousness* is most wanted where there is most to conceal; it courts favor and kindness by an acknowledgment of that which is against itself.

Frankness is associated with unpolished manners, and frequently appears in men of no rank or education; sailors have commonly a deal of *frankness* about them: *candor* is the companion of uprightness; it must be accompanied with some refinement, as it acts in cases where nice discriminations are made: *ingenuousness* is the companion of a noble and elevated spirit: it exists most frequently in the unsophisticated period of youth. *Frankness* displays itself in the outward behavior; we speak of a *frank* air and *frank* manner: *candor* displays itself in the language which we adopt and the sentiments we express; we speak of a *candid* statement, a *candid* reply: *ingenuousness* shows itself in all the words, looks, or actions; we speak of an *ingenuous* countenance, an *ingenuous* acknowledgment, an *ingenuous* answer.

Free, *open*, and *plain* have not so high an office as the first three; *free* and *open* may be taken either in a good, bad, or indifferent sense; but seldomer in the first than in the last two senses.

The *frank, free,* and *open* men all speak without constraint; but the *frank* man is not impertinent, like the *free* man, nor indiscreet, like the *open* man. The *frank* man speaks only of what concerns himself; the *free* man speaks of what concerns others: a *frank* man may confess his own faults or inadvertencies; the *free* man corrects those which he sees in another: the *frank* man opens his heart from the warmth of his nature; the *free* man opens his mind from the conceit of his temper, and the *open* man says all he knows and thinks, from the inconsiderate levity of his temper.

Plainness, the last quality to be here noticed, is a virtue which, though of the humbler order, is not to be despised: it is sometimes employed, like *freedom,* in the task of giving counsel; but it does not convey the idea of anything unauthorized either in matter or manner. A *free* counsellor is more ready to display his own superiority than to direct the wanderer in his way; he rather aggravates faults than instructs how to amend them; he seems more like a supercilious enemy than a friendly monitor: the *plain* man is *free* from these faults: he speaks *plainly* but truly; he gives no false coloring to his speech; it is not calculated to offend, and it may serve for improvement: it is the part of a true friend to be *plain* with another whom he sees in imminent danger. A *free* speaker is in danger of being hated; a *plain* dealer must at least be respected.

FRAUD. See Deceit.

FRAUDULENT. See Fallacious.

FRAY. See Quarrel.

FREAK, Whim. *Freak* comes from Anglo-Saxon *frec,* meaning bold, rash. *Whim* is a Scandinavian word, allied to Icelandic *hvima,* to wander with the eyes, to be foolish. *Freak* has more of childishness and humor than boldness in it, a *whim* more of eccentricity than of childishness. Fancy and fortune are both said to have their *freaks,* as they both deviate most widely in their movements from all rule; but *whims* are at most but singular devia-

tions of the mind from its ordinary and even course. Females are most liable to be seized with *freaks,* which are in their nature sudden and not to be calculated upon: men are apt to indulge themselves in *whims* which are in their nature strange and often laughable. We should call it a *freak* for a female to put on the habit of a male, and so accoutred to sally forth into the streets: we term it a *whim* in a man who takes a resolution never to shave himself any more.

FREE, Liberal. In the section on Frank, *free* is considered only as it respects communication by words; in the present case it respects actions and sentiments. In all its acceptations, *free* is a term of dispraise, and *liberal* that of commendation. To be *free* signifies to act or think at will; to be *liberal* is to act according to the dictates of an enlarged heart and an enlightened mind. A clown and a fool may be *free* with his money, and may squander it away to please his humor or gratify his appetite; but the nobleman and the wise man will be *liberal* in rewarding merit, in encouraging industry, and in promoting whatever can contribute to the ornament, the prosperity, and improvement of his country.

A man who is *free* in his sentiments thinks as he pleases; the man who is *liberal* thinks according to the extent of his knowledge. The *free*thinking man is wise in his own conceit, he despises the opinions of others; the *liberal*-minded thinks modestly on his own personal attainments, and builds upon the wisdom of others.

Free, Set Free, Deliver, Liberate.— To *free* is properly to make *free,* in distinction from *set free;* the first is employed in what concerns ourselves, and the second in that which concerns another. A man *frees* himself from an engagement; he *sets* another *free* from his engagement: we *free,* or *set* ourselves *free,* from that which has been imposed upon us by ourselves or by circumstances; we are *delivered* or *liberated* from that which others have imposed upon us; the former from evils in general, the latter from the evil of confinement. I *free* myself from a burden; I *set* my own slave *free* from his slavery; I *deliver* another man's slave from a state of bondage; I *liberate* a man from prison. A man *frees* an estate from rent, service, taxes, and all encumbrances; a king *sets* his subjects *free* from certain imposts or tributes, he *delivers* them from a foreign yoke, or he *liberates* those who have been taken in war.

See also EMANCIPATE.

Free, Familiar.—*Free* has already been considered as it respects words, actions and sentiments; in the present case it is coupled with *familiarity*, inasmuch as they respect the outward behavior or conduct in general of men one to another. To be *free* is to be disengaged from all the constraints which the ceremonies of social intercourse impose; to be *familiar* is to be upon the footing of a *familiar*, of a relative, or one of the same family.

Neither of these terms can be admitted as unexceptionable; *freedom* is authorized only by particular circumstances and within certain limitations; *familiarity* sometimes shelters itself under the sanction of long, close, and friendly intercourse. *Free* is a term of much more extensive import than *familiar;* a man may be *free* toward another in a thousand ways; but he is *familiar* toward him only in his manners and address. A man who is *free* makes *free* with everything as if it were his own; a *familiar* man only wants to share with another, and to stand upon an equal footing in his social intercourse. No man can be *free* without being in danger of infringing upon what belongs to another, nor *familiar* without being in danger of obtruding himself to the annoyance of others, or of degrading himself.

Free, Exempt.—*Free* (see preceding terms). *Exempt*, in Latin *exemptus*, from *ex*, out, and *emere*, to take, signifies set out or disengaged from anything.

The condition and not the conduct of men is here considered. *Freedom* is either accidental or intentional; the *exemption* is always intentional; we may be *free* from disorders, or *free* from troubles; we are *exempt*, that is, *exempted* by government, from serving in the militia. *Free* is applied to everything from which any one may wish to be *free;* but *exempt*, on the contrary, to those burdens which we should share with others: we may be *free* from imperfections, *free* from inconveniences, *free* from the interruptions of others, but *exempt* from any office or tax. We may likewise be said to be *exempt* from troubles when speaking of these as the dispensations of Providence to others.

Freedom, Liberty.—*Freedom*, the abstract noun of *free*, is taken in all the senses of the primitive. *Liberty*, from the Latin *liber*, free, is only taken in the sense of *free* from external constraint, from the action of power.

Freedom is personal and private; *liberty* is public. The *freedom* of the city is the privilege granted by the city to individuals; the *liberties* of the city are the immunities enjoyed by the city. By the same rule of distinction we speak of the *freedom* of the will, the *freedom* of manners, the *freedom* of conversation, or the *freedom* of debate; but the *liberty* of conscience, the *liberty* of the press, the *liberty* of the subject.

Freedom serves, moreover, to qualify the action; *liberty* is applied only to the agent; hence we say, to speak or think with *freedom;* but to have the *liberty* of speaking, thinking, or acting.

Freedom and *liberty* are likewise employed for the private conduct of individuals toward one another; but the former is used in a qualified good sense, the latter often in an unqualified bad sense. A *freedom* may sometimes be licensed or allowed; a *liberty*, if it be taken, may be something not agreeable or allowed. A *freedom* may be innocent and even pleasant; a *liberty* may do more or less violence to the decencies of life or the feelings of individuals. There are little *freedoms* which may pass between youth of different sexes, so as to heighten the pleasures of society; but a modest woman will be careful to guard against any *freedoms* which may admit of misinterpretation, and resent every *liberty* offered to her as an insult.

FREIGHT, BURDEN, CARGO, LADING, LOAD. *Freight* is a word which has come from Dutch or Low German through French into English; it originally signified the earnings or the hire of a ship. *Cargo* comes through Spanish from the Late Latin *carricare*, to load a car. *Lading,* from *lade,* is derived from Anglo-Saxon *hladan,* to heap, to heap together. *Load* comes from Anglo-Saxon *lad,* a way or journey, allied to Modern English *lead,* and signifies that which is carried on a journey. *Burden,* from *bear,* conveys the idea of weight which is borne by the vessel.

A captain speaks of the *freight* of his ship as that which is the object of his voyage, by which all who are interested in it are to make their profit; he speaks of the *lading* as the thing which is to fill the ship; the quantity and weight of the *lading* are to be taken into the consideration: he speaks of the *cargo* as that which goes with the ship, and belongs, as it were, to the ship; the amount of the *cargo* is that which is first thought of: he speaks of the *burden* as that which his vessel will bear; it is the property of the ship which is to be estimated. The ship-broker regulates the *freight:* the captain and the crew dispose of the *lading:* the agent sees to the procuring of the *cargo:* the ship-builder determines the *burden:* the carrier looks to the *load* which he has to carry.

FRENZY. See MADNESS.

FREQUENT, RESORT TO, HAUNT. *Frequent* comes from French *fréquent,* in Latin *frequens,* crowded, signifying to come in numbers, or come often to the same place. *Resort* comes from Late Latin *resortere,* from *re,* again, and *sors,* a lot, and meant to go to a tribunal, to re-obtain by appeal. *Haunt,* from Old French *hanter,* is a word whose ultimate origin and meaning are disputed.

Frequent is more commonly used of an individual who goes often to a place; *resort* and *haunt,* of a number of individuals. A man is said to *frequent* a public place; but several persons may *resort* to a private place: men who are not fond of home *frequent* taverns; in the first ages of Christianity, while persecution raged, its professors used to *resort* to private places for purposes of worship. *Frequent* and *resort* are indifferent actions; but *haunt* is always used in a bad sense. A man may *frequent* a theatre, a club, or any other social meeting, innocent or otherwise; people

from different quarters may *resort to* a fair, a church, or any other place where they wish to meet for a common purpose; but those who *haunt* any place go to it in privacy for some bad purpose.

FREQUENTLY. See COMMONLY; OFTEN.

FRESH. See NEW.

FRET. See RUB.

FRETFUL. See CAPTIOUS; QUERULOUS; SPLENETIC.

FRIENDLY. See AMICABLE.

FRIENDSHIP. See LOVE.

FRIGHT. See ALARM.

FRIGHTEN, *Intimidate.* Between *frighten* and *intimidate* there is the same difference as between *fright* (see ALARM) and *fear* (see APPREHEND): the danger that is near or before the eyes *frightens;* that which is seen at a distance *intimidates:* hence females are oftener *frightened* and men are oftener *intimidated:* noises will *frighten;* threats may *intimidate:* we may run away when we are *frightened;* we waver in our resolution when we are *intimidated;* we fear immediate bodily harm when we are *frightened;* we fear harm to our property as well as our persons when we are *intimidated; frighten,* therefore, is always applied to animals, but *intimidate* never.

See also OVERAWE.

FRIGHTFUL. See FEARFUL.

FRIGID. See COOL.

FRIVOLOUS. See TRIFLING.

FROLIC, GAMBOL, PRANK. *Frolic* is a Dutch word, allied to German *froh,* merry. *Gambol* is derived through French from Italian *gambata,* a kick, Italian *gamba,* a leg (French *jambe*), from Late Latin *gamba,* a joint of the leg. *Prank* comes from Middle English *pranken,* to trim; compare *prink,* to arrange one's clothes before a mirror. The *frolic* is a merry, joyous entertainment; the *gambol* is a dancing, light entertainment; the *prank* is a freakish, wild entertainment. Laughing, singing, noise, and feasting constitute the *frolic* of the careless mind; it belongs to a company; conceit, levity, and trick, in movement, gesture, and contrivance, constitute the *gambol;* it belongs to the individual: adventure, eccentricity, and humor constitute the *prank;* it belongs to one or many.

One has a *frolic;* one plays a *gambol* or a *prank.*

FRONT. See FACE.

FRONTIER. See BORDER.

FROWARD. See AWKWARD.

FRUGALITY. See ECONOMY.

FRUITFUL. See FERTILE.

FRUITION. See ENJOYMENT.

FRUITLESS. See VAIN.

FRUSTRATE. See DEFEAT.

FULFIL, ACCOMPLISH, REALIZE. To *fulfil* is literally to fill quite full, that is, to bring about *full* to the wishes of a person; *accomplish* is to bring to perfection, but without reference to the wishes of any one; to *realize* is to make *real,* namely, whatever has been aimed at. The application of these terms is evident from their explanations: the wishes, the expectations, the intentions and promises of an individual are appropriately said to be *fulfilled;* national projects, or undertakings, prophecies, and whatever is of general interest are said to be *accomplished:* the fortune or the prospects of an individual, or whatever results successfully from specific efforts, is said to be *realized:* the *fulfilment* of our wishes may be as much the effect of good fortune as of design; the *accomplishment* of projects mostly results from extraordinary exertion, as the *accomplishment* of prophecies results from a miraculous exertion of power; the *realization* of hopes results more commonly from the slow process of moderate well-combined efforts than from anything extraordinary.

See also EXECUTE; KEEP.

FULL. See QUITE.

FULLY. See LARGELY.

FULNESS, PLENITUDE. Although *fulness* is simply the Anglo-Saxon translation of Latin *plenitude* (from *plenus,* full), yet the latter is used either in the proper sense to express the state of objects that are *full,* or in the improper sense to express great quantity, which is the accompaniment of *fulness;* the former only in the higher style and in the improper sense: hence we say in the *fulness* of one's heart, in the *fulness* of one's joy, or the *fulness* of the Godhead bodily; but the *plenitude* of power.

FULSOME, FLORID, RANK. All these words indicate an overgrowth, over-development, especially as applied figuratively to language or manners. *Fulsome* originally meant over *full,* indicating a *fulness* of growth—animal or vegetable growth—offensive to the taste. It is now almost obsolete except as applied figuratively to speech, to refer to exaggerated flattery or over-demonstrative affection. *Florid,* from *florem* (accusative), flower, means literally flowery, and is applied figuratively to speech, but it has different connotations; it refers simply to the elaborate and ornamental phraseology without the suggestion of flattery or demonstrativeness. *Rank,* Anglo-Saxon *rank,* strong, proud, like *fulsome,* applies to coarse, luxuriant growth, and by extension to a kind of speech—as when we say "rank flattery"—with an emphasis upon offensiveness.

FUNCTION. See OFFICE.

FUNDED. See UNFUNDED.

FUNERAL, OBSEQUIES. *Funeral* is in Latin *funus,* a burial; the term *funeral,* therefore, denotes the ordinary solemnity which attends the consignment of a body to the grave. *Obsequies,* from Latin *ob,* near, and *sequi,* to follow, means literally following the corpse, and refers to *funerals* attended with more than ordinary solemnity.

We speak of the *funeral* as the last sad office which we perform for a friend; it is accompanied by nothing but by mourning and sorrow: we speak of *obsequies* as the greatest tribute of respect which can be paid to the person of one who was high in station or public esteem: the *funeral,* by its frequency, becomes so familiar an object that it passes by unheeded; *obsequies* which are performed over the remains of the great attract our notice from the pomp and grandeur with which they are conducted.

FURIOUS. See VIOLENT.

FURNISH. See PROVIDE.

FURNITURE. See GOODS.

FURROW. See TRENCH.

FURY. See ANGER; MADNESS.

FUTILE. See TRIFLING.

G

GABBLE. See JABBER.

GAIN, PROFIT, EMOLUMENT, LUCRE. *Gain* signifies in general what is gained (see ACQUIRE; GET). *Profit* (see ADVANTAGE). *Emolument*, from *emoliri*, from *e*, out, and *moliri*, to work, signifies to work out or get by working. *Lucre* is in Latin *lucrum*, gain.

Gain is here a general term, the other terms are specific: the *gain* is that which comes to a man; it is the fruit of his exertions, or agreeable to his wish: the *profit* is that which accrues from the thing. Thus, when applied to riches, that which increases a man's estate is his *gains;* that which flows out of his trade or occupation is his *profits;* that is, they are his *gains* upon dealing. *Emolument* is a species of *gain* from labor, or a collateral *gain;* of this description are a man's *emoluments* from an office: a man estimates his *gains* by what he receives in the year; he estimates his *profits* by what he receives on every article; he estimates his *emoluments* according to the nature of the service which he has to perform: the merchant talks of his *gains*, the retail dealer of his *profits*, the placeman of his *emoluments*.

Gain and *profit* are also taken in an abstract sense; *lucre* is never used otherwise; but the latter always conveys a bad meaning; it is, strictly speaking, unhallowed *gain:* an immoderate thirst for *gain* is the vice of men who are always calculating *profit* and loss; a thirst for *lucre* deadens every generous feeling of the mind.

Gain and *profit* may be extended to other objects, and sometimes opposed to each other; for as that which we *gain* is what we wish only, it is often the reverse of *profitable*.

GAIT. See CARRIAGE.

GALL. See RUB.

GALLANT, BEAU, SPARK. These words convey nothing respectful of the person to whom they are applied; but the first, as is evident from its derivation, has something in it to recommend it to attention above the others: as true valor is ever associated with a regard for the fair sex, a *gallant* man will always be a *gallant* when he can render a female any service; sometimes, however, his *gallantries* may be such as to do them harm rather than good: insignificance and effeminacy characterize the *beau* or fine gentleman; he is the woman's man—the humble servant to supply the place of a lackey: the *spark* has but a *spark* of that fire which shows itself in impertinent puerilities; it is applicable to youth who are just broke loose from school or college and eager to display their manhood.

See also BRAVE.

GAMBOL. See FROLIC.

GAME. See PLAY.

GAMESOME. See PLAYFUL.

GANG. See BAND.

GAP. See BREACH.

GAPE, STARE, GAZE. *Gape* is a Scandinavian word meaning to look with an open or wide mouth. *Stare*, Anglo-Saxon *starian*, is allied to *sta*, the root of *stand, station, statue*, etc.; and signifies to look with fixed eyes. *Gaze*, Middle English *gasen*, is a Scandinavian word meaning to look at earnestly.

Gape and *stare* are taken in a bad sense, the former indicating the astonishment of gross ignorance, the latter not only ignorance, but impertinence: *gaze* is taken always in a good sense, as indicating a laudable feeling of astonishment, pleasure, or curiosity: a clown *gapes* at the pictures of wild beasts which he sees at a fair; an impertinent fellow *stares* at every woman he looks at, and *stares* a modest woman out of countenance: a lover of the fine arts will *gaze* with admiration and delight at the productions of Raphael or Titian; when a person is stupefied by affright he gives a vacant *stare:* those who are filled with transport *gaze* on the object of their ecstasy.

GARNER, DEPOSIT, HOARD. *Gar-*

ner comes from Latin *granaria*, a place in which the *grain* (*granum*) is gathered. *Deposit* is derived from *depositus*, the past participle of Latin *deponere*, to lay down. *Hoard* comes from Anglo-Saxon *hord*, from a root signifying to *hide*. These words have in common the general idea of gathering and stowing away, but they differ widely in their application. In one sense *garner* is synonymous with *gather*, which see. It signified originally to gather and put away the grain, and is used figuratively always with a distinct and poetic reminiscence of its original meaning. *Deposit* emphasizes not the gathering, but the putting away; it is given a special application nowadays in business. A *deposit* of money is a sum of money paid down against a debt that may be incurred, or simply the putting away of money in a bank. *Hoard* adds to the idea of gathering and stowing away the special suggestion ·of *hiding secretly*. A miser *hoards* his money; selfish people, in time of war, *hoard* foodstuffs, etc.

GARNISH, TRIM. *Garnish*, Old French *garnis*, comes from Old High German *warnon*, to defend one's self, to provide one's self with. It shares with *trim* the general idea of adorning by the addition of something external, especially of small and pretty decorations; but it has now a somewhat more limited application than *trim*. We speak of *garnishing* when we wish to refer especially to an ephemeral and perishable *trimming*. We *garnish* dishes served at the table, for instance; we may speak of *garnishing* a room with flowers. *Trim* is used in this connection, but it is extended to refer to all sorts of ornamental additions, including those of a more permanent nature—as *trimming* a hat, a dress, etc. It is a less dignified word than *adorn* and its synonymes (see ADORN), with which it has something in common.

GARRULOUS. See TALKATIVE.

GASCONADE. See GLORY.

GASP. See PALPITATE.

GATHER, COLLECT. To *gather* is in Anglo-Saxon *gaderian*, to bring things together, from the root also found in *together*. To *collect* (see ASSEMBLE) annexes also the idea of binding or forming into a whole; we *gather* that which is scattered in different parts: thus stones are *gathered* into a heap; vessels are *collected* so as to form a fleet. *Gathering* is a mere act of necessity or convenience; *collecting* is an act of design or choice: we *gather* apples from a tree, or a servant *gathers* books from off a table; the antiquarian *collects* coins, and the bibliomaniac *collects* rare books.

See also GARNER.

GAUDY. See SHOWY.

GAUNT. See HAGGARD.

GAY. See CHEERFUL; SHOWY.

GAYETY. See GLEE.

GAZE. See GAPE.

GENDER, SEX. *Gender*, in Latin *genus*, signifies properly a *genus*, or kind. *Sex* comes from Latin *sexus*. "Was it originally 'division,' from *secare*, to cut?" (Skeat.) *Gender* is that distinction in words which marks the distinction of *sex* in things; there are, therefore, three *genders*, but only two *sexes*. By the inflections of words is denoted whether things are of this or that *sex* or of no *sex*. The *genders*, therefore, are divided in grammar into *masculine*, *feminine*, and *neuter;* and animals are divided into male and female *sex*.

GENERAL, UNIVERSAL. The *general* is to the *universal* what the part is to the whole. What is *general* includes the greater part or number; what is *universal* includes every individual or part. The *general* rule admits of many exceptions; the *universal* rule admits of none. Human government has the *general* good for its object; the government of Providence is directed to *universal* good. *General* is opposed to particular, and *universal* to individual. A scientific writer will not content himself with *general* remarks when he has it in his power to enter into particulars; the *universal* complaint which we hear against men for their pride shows that in every individual it exists to a greater or less degree. It is a *general* opinion that women are not qualified for scientific pursuits, but many females have proved themselves honorable exceptions to this rule: it is a *universal* principle that children ought to honor their parents; the intention of the Creator in this respect is manifested in such a variety of forms as to admit of no question.

See also PUBLIC.

GENERALLY. See COMMONLY.

GENERATION, AGE. *Generation* is said of the persons who live during any particular period; and *age* is said of the period itself.

Those who are born at the same time constitute the *generation;* that period of time which comprehends the age of man is the *age:* there may, therefore, be many *generations* spring up in the course of an *age;* a fresh *generation* is springing up every day, which in the course of an *age* pass away and are succeeded by fresh *generations.* We consider man in his *generation* as to the part which he has to perform. We consider the *age* in which we live as to the manners of men and the events of nations.

See also RACE.

GENEROUS. See BENEFICENT.

GENIUS. See INTELLECT; TASTE.

GENTEEL, POLITE. *Genteel,* in French *gentil,* Latin *gentilis,* signifies literally one belonging to the same family, or the next akin to whom the estate would fall if there were no children; hence by an extended application it denoted to be of a good family. *Polite* (see CIVIL).

Gentility respects rank in life; *politeness,* the refinement of the mind and outward behavior. A *genteel* education is suited to the station of a gentleman; a *polite* education fits for polished society and conversation, and raises the individual among his equals. There may be *gentility* without *politeness,* and *vice versâ.* A person may have *genteel* manners, a *genteel* carriage, a *genteel* mode of living as far as respects his general relation with society; but a *polite* behavior and a *polite* address, which may qualify him for every relation in society and enable him to shine in connection with all orders of men, is independent of either birth or wealth; it is in part a gift of nature, although it is to be acquired by art. His equipage, servants, house, and furniture may be such as to entitle a man to the name of *genteel,* although he is wanting in all the forms of real good-breeding; while fortune may sometimes frown upon the polished gentleman, whose *politeness* is a recommendation to him wherever he goes.

GENTILE, HEATHEN, PAGAN. The Jews comprehended all strangers under the name of Goim, nations or *gentiles:* among the Greeks and Romans they were designated by the name of barbarians. By the name *gentile* was understood especially those who were not of the Jewish religion, including, in the end, even the Christians. Some learned men pretend that the *Gentiles* were so named from their having only a natural law, and such as they imposed on themselves, in opposition to the Jews and Christians, who have a positive revealed law to which they are obliged to submit. *Heathen,* Anglo-Saxon *hœthen,* meant originally a dweller on the heath; *pagan* comes from Latin *pagus,* village, and means a dweller in the village, because when Constantine banished idolaters from the towns they repaired to the villages, and secretly adhered to their religious worship, whence they were termed by the Christians of the fourth century *Pagani,* which was translated literally into the German *heidener,* a villager or worshipper in the field. Be this as it may, it is evident that the word *pagan* is in our language more applicable than *heathen* to the Greeks, the Romans, and the cultivated nations who practiced idolatry; and, on the other hand, *heathen* is more properly employed for rude and uncivilized people who worship false gods.

The *Gentile* does not expressly believe in a Divine Revelation; but he either admits of the truth in part or is ready to receive it: the *heathen* adopts a positively false system that is opposed to the true faith: the *pagan* is a species of *heathen,* who obstinately persists in a worship which is merely the fruit of his own imagination. The *heathens* and *pagans* are *Gentiles;* but the *Gentiles* are not all either *heathens* or *pagans.* Confucius and Socrates, who rejected the plurality of gods, and the followers of Mohammed, who adore the true God, are, properly speaking, *Gentiles.* The worshippers of Jupiter, Juno, Minerva, and all the deities of the ancients are termed *pagans.* The worshippers of Fo, Brahma, Xaca, and all the deities of savage nations are termed *heathens.*

The *Gentiles* were called to the true faith, and obeyed the call: many of the illustrious *pagans* would have doubtless done the same had they enjoyed the same privilege: there are to this day many *heathens* who reject this advantage, to pursue their own blind imaginations.

GENTLE, TAME. *Gentleness* lies rather in the natural disposition; *tameness* is the effect either of art or circumstances. Any unbroken horse may be *gentle*, but not *tame;* a horse that is broken in will be *tame*, but not always *gentle*. *Gentle*, as before observed (see GENTEEL), signifies literally well-born, and is opposed either to the fierce or the rude: *tame* is allied to Latin *domare*, to tame, whence *daunt* is also derived, and is opposed either to the wild or the spirited. Animals are in general said to be *gentle* who show a disposition to associate with man and conform to his will; they are said to be *tame* if, either by compulsion or habit, they are brought to mix with human society. Of the first description there are individuals in almost every species which are more or less entitled to the name of *gentle;* of the latter description are many species, as the dog, the sheep. the hen, and the like.

In the moral application, *gentle* is always employed in the good, and *tame* in the bad, sense: a *gentle* spirit needs no control, it amalgamates freely with the will of another: a *tame* spirit is without any will of its own; it is alive to nothing but submission; it is perfectly consistent with our natural liberty to have *gentleness*, but *tameness* is the accompaniment of slavery. The same distinction marks the use of these words when applied to the outward conduct or the language: *gentle* bespeaks something positively good; *tame* bespeaks the want of an essential good: the former is allied to the kind, the latter to the abject and mean qualities which naturally flow from the compression or destruction of energy and will in the agent. A *gentle* expression is devoid of all acrimony and serves to turn away wrath: a *tame* expression is devoid of all force or energy, and ill calculated to inspire the mind with any feeling whatever. In giving counsel to an irritable and conceited temper it is necessary to be *gentle: tame* expressions are nowhere such striking deformities as in a poem or an oration.

See also SOFT.

GENUINE. See INTRINSIC.

GERM, BUD, EMBRYO, SEED. These words all indicate the original or rudimentary state of a living organism— either animal or plant. *Germ* and *seed* represent the first beginnings, as it were, of life; *embryo* and *bud*, an early stage of development. *Germ* is a word of doubtful origin, probably allied to the root *ger* in *gerere*, to bear; it signifies that portion of an organic being which is capable of developing into the likeness of that from which it sprang. *Seed*, from Anglo-Saxon *sawan*, to sow, indicates that portion of a plant which is sown in the ground, and from which the new plant springs; it is the *germ* of the plant with a protective covering. *Embryo*, Greek ἔμβρυον, Greek ἐν and βρύον, neuter of the present participle of βρύειν, to be full, to swell out. It refers to the first stage of new animal life. *Bud*, Middle English *budde*, is not found in Anglo-Saxon. It refers to the first stage of a new flower or the group of new leaves folded together in a hard little bundle, as it were.

GESTICULATION. See ACTION.

GESTURE. See ACTION.

GET, GAIN, OBTAIN, PROCURE. To *get* signifies simply to cause to have or possess; it is generic, and the rest specific: to *gain* is to *get* the thing one wishes or that is for one's advantage: to *obtain* is to *get* the thing aimed at or striven after: to *procure*, from *pro*, for, and *curare*, to care, to care for, is to *get* the thing wanted or sought for.

Get is not only the most general in its sense, but in its application; it may be substituted in almost every case for the other terms, for we may say to *get* or *gain* a prize, to *get* or *obtain* a reward, to *get* or *procure* a book; and it is also employed in numberless familiar cases, where the other terms would be less suitable, for, what this word gains in familiarity it loses in dignity: hence we may with propriety talk of a servant's *getting* some water, or a person *getting* a book off a shelf or *getting* meat from the butcher, with numberless similar cases in which the other terms could not be employed without losing their dignity. Moreover, *get* is promiscuously used for whatever comes to the hand, whether good or bad, desirable or not desirable, sought for or not; but *gain, obtain,* and *procure* always include either the wishes or the instrumentality of the agent, or both together. Thus a person is said to *get* a cold or a fever, a good or an ill name, without specifying any of the circumstances of the action; but he is said to *gain* that approbation which is gratifying to his feelings; to *obtain* a recompense which is the object of his exertions; to *procure* a situation which is the end of his endeavors.

The word *gain* is peculiarly applicable to whatever comes to us fortuitously; what we *gain* constitutes our good fortune; we *gain* a victory or we *gain* a cause; the result in both cases may be independent of our exertions. To *obtain* and *procure* exclude the idea of chance, and suppose exertions directed to a specific end: but the former may include the exertions of others, the latter is particularly employed for one's own personal exertions. A person *obtains* a situation through the recommendation of a friend: he *procures* a situation by applying for it. *Obtain* is likewise employed only in that which requires particular efforts, that which is not immediately within our reach; *procure* is applicable to that which is to be *got* with ease, by the simple exertion of a walk, or of asking for.

GHASTLY. See HIDEOUS.

GHOST. See VISION.

GHOSTLY. See SPIRITUOUS.

GIBE. See SCOFF.

GIDDINESS. See LIGHTNESS.

GIFT, PRESENT, DONATION. *Gift* is derived from Anglo-Saxon *gifan,* to give (the hard *g* sound being due to Scandinavian influence), in the sense of what is communicated to another gratuitously of one's property. *Present* is derived from to *present,* signifying the thing *presented* to another. *Donation,* in French *donation,* from the Latin *donare,* to *present* or *give,* is a species of *gift.*

The *gift* is an act of generosity or condescension; it contributes to the benefit of the receiver: the *present* is an act of kindness, courtesy, or respect; it contributes to the pleasure of the receiver. The *gift* passes from the rich to the poor, from the high to the low, and creates an obligation; the *present* passes either between equals or from the inferior to the superior. Whatever we receive from God, through the bounty of His providence, we entitle a *gift;* whatever we receive from our friends, or whatever princes receive from their subjects, are entitled *presents.* We are told by all travellers that it is a custom in the East never to approach a great man without a *present;* the value of a *gift* is often heightened by being given opportunely. The value of a *present* often depends upon the esteem we have for the giver; the smallest *present* from an esteemed friend is of more worth in our eyes than the costliest *presents* that monarchs receive.

The *gift* is private, and benefits the individual: the *donation* is public, and serves some general purpose: what is given to relieve the necessities of any poor person is a *gift;* what is given to support an institution is a *donation.* The clergy are indebted to their patrons for the livings which are in their *gift:* it has been the custom of the pious and charitable in all ages to make *donations* for the support of almshouses, hospitals, infirmaries, and such institutions as serve to diminish the sum of human misery.

Gift, Endowment, Talent.—*Gift* (see above). *Endowment* signifies the thing with which one is endowed. *Talent* (see ABILITY).

Gift and *endowment* both refer to the act of *giving* and *endowing,* and of course include the idea of something given and something received: the word *talent* conveys no such collateral idea. When we speak of a *gift,* we refer in our minds to a *giver;* when we speak of an *endowment,* we refer in our minds to the receiver; when we speak of a *talent,* we only think of its intrinsic quality. A *gift* is either supernatural or natural; an *endowment* is only natural. The primitive Christians received various *gifts* through the inspiration of the Holy Spirit, as the *gift* of tongues, the *gift* of healing, etc. There are some men who have a peculiar *gift* of utterance; beauty of person and corporeal agility are *endowments* with which some are peculiarly invested.

The word *gift* excludes the idea of anything acquired by exertion; it is that which is communicated to us altogether independently of ourselves, and enables us to arrive at that perfection in any art which could not be attained any other way. Speech is denominated a general *gift*, inasmuch as it is given to the whole human race in distinction from the brutes; but the *gift* of eloquence is a peculiar *gift* granted to a few individuals, in distinction from others, and one which may be exerted for the benefit of mankind. *Endowments*, though inherent in us, are not independent of our exertions; they are qualities which admit of improvement by being used; they are, in fact, the *gifts* of nature, which serve to adorn and elevate the possessor when employed for a good purpose. *Talents* are either natural or acquired, or in some measure of a mixed nature; they denote powers without specifying the source from which they proceed; a man may have a *talent* for music, for drawing, for mimicry, and the like; but this *talent* may be the fruit of practice and experience as much as of nature. It is clear from the above that an *endowment* is a *gift*, but a *gift* is not always an *endowment;* and that a *talent* may also be either a *gift* or an *endowment*, but that it is frequently distinct from both. The terms *gift* and *talent* are applicable to corporeal as well as spiritual actions; *endowment* to corporeal or mental qualities. To write a superior hand is a *gift*, inasmuch as it is supposed to be unattainable by any force of application and instruction; it is a *talent*, inasmuch as it is a power or property worth our possession, but it is never an *endowment*. On the other hand, courage, discernment, a strong imagination, and the like are both *gifts* and *endowments;* and when the intellectual *endowment* displays itself in any creative form, as in the case of poetry, music, or any art, so as to produce that which is valued and esteemed, it becomes a *talent* to the possessor.

GIRDLE. See ZONE.
GIRL. See VIRGIN.
GIVE, GRANT, BESTOW. For the derivation of *give* see GIFT; *grant* and *bestow* (see ALLOW).

The idea of communicating to another what is our own or in our power is common to these terms; this is the whole signification of *give;* but *grant* and *bestow* include accessory ideas in their meaning. To *grant* is to *give* at one's pleasure; to *bestow* is to give from a certain degree of necessity. *Giving* is confined to no object; whatever property we transfer into the hands of another, that we *give;* we *give* money, clothes, food, or whatever is transferable: *granting* is confined to such objects as afford pleasure or convenience; they may consist of transferable property or not; *bestowing* is applied to such objects only as are necessary to supply wants, which always consist of that which is transferable. We *give* what is liked or not liked, asked for or unasked for: we *grant* that only which is wished for and requested. One may *give* poison or medicine; one *grants* a sum of money by way of loan: we *give* what is wanted or not wanted; we *bestow* that only which is expressly wanted: we *give* with an idea of a return or otherwise: we *grant* voluntarily, without any prospect of a return: we give for a permanency or otherwise; we *bestow* only in particular cases which require immediate notice. To *give* has no respect to the circumstances of the action or the agent; it is applicable to persons of all conditions: to *grant* bespeaks not only the will, but the power and influence of the *grantor:* to *bestow* bespeaks the necessitous condition of the receiver. Children may *give* to their parents and parents to their children, kings to their subjects or subjects to their kings; but monarchs only *grant* to their subjects, or parents to their children; and superiors in general *bestow* upon their dependents that which they cannot provide for themselves.

In an extended application of the terms to moral objects or circumstances they strictly adhere to the same line of distinction. We *give* our consent; we *give* our promise; we *give* our word; we *give* credit; we *give* in all cases that which may be simply transferred from one to another. Liberties, rights, privileges, favors, indulgences, permissions, and all things are *granted* which are in the hands of only a few but are acceptable to many. Blessings, care, concern, and the like, are *bestowed* upon those who are dependent upon others for whatever they have.

Give and *bestow* are likewise said of things as well as of persons; *grant* is said only of persons. *Give* is here equally general and indefinite; *bestow* conveys the idea of *giving* under circumstances of necessity and urgency. One *gives* a preference to a particular situation; one *gives* a thought to a subject that is proposed; one *gives* time and labor to any matter that engages one's attention: but one *bestows* pains on that which demands particular attention; one *bestows* a moment's thought on one particular subject out of the number which engage attention.

Give, Afford.—*Give* and *afford* are allied to each other in the sense of sending forth; but the former denotes an unqualified and unconditional action, as in the preceding article; the latter bears a relation to the circumstances of the agent. A person is said to *give* money without any regard to the state of his finances: he is said to *afford* what he *gives*, when one wishes to define his pecuniary condition. The same idea runs through the application of these terms to all other cases, in which inanimate things are made the agents. When we say a thing *gives* satisfaction, we simply designate the action; when we say it *affords* pleasure, we refer to the nature and properties of the thing thus specified —that is to say, its capacity to give satisfaction; the former is employed only to declare the fact, the latter to characterize the object. Hence, in certain cases, we should say this or that posture of the body *gives* ease to a sick person; but, as a moral sentiment, we should say nothing *affords* such ease to the mind as a clear conscience. Upon the same grounds the use of these terms is justified in the following cases: to *give* rise; to *give* birth; to *give* occasion; to *afford* an opportunity; to *afford* a plea or a pretext; to *afford* ground, and the like.

Give, Present, Offer, Exhibit.—These terms have a common signification, inasmuch as they designate the manual act of transferring something from one's self to another. The first is, here as elsewhere, the most indefinite and extensive in its meaning; it denotes the complete act: the latter two refer rather to the preliminaries of *giving* than to the act itself. What is *given* is actually transferred: what is *presented*, that is, made a *present* to any one, or *offered*, that is, brought in his way, is put in the way of being transferred: we *present* in *giving*, and *offer* in order to *give;* but we may *give* without presenting or offering; and, on the other hand, we may *present* or *offer* without *giving*, if the thing presented or *offered* be not received.

To *give* is the familiar term which designates the ordinary transfer of property: to *present* is a term of respect; it includes in it the formality and ceremony of setting before another that which we wish to *give:* to *offer* is an act of humility or solemnity; it bespeaks the movement of the heart, which impels to the making a transfer or *gift*. We *give* to our domestics; we *present* to princes; we *offer* to God: we *give* to a person what we wish to be received; we *present* to a person what we think agreeable; we *offer* what we think acceptable; what is *given* is supposed to be ours; what we *offer* is supposed to be at our command; what we *present* need not be either our own or at our command: we *give* a person not only our external property, but our esteem, our confidence, our company, and the like: an ambassador *presents* his credentials at court; a subject *offers* his services to his king.

They bear the same relation to each other when applied to words or actions, instead of property: we speak of *giving* a person an assurance or a contradiction; of *presenting* an address and *offering* an apology: of *giving* a reception, *presenting* a figure, or *offering* an insult. They may likewise be extended in their application, not only to personal and individual actions, but also to such as respect the public at large: we *give* a description in writing, as well as by word of mouth; one *pre-*

sents the public with the fruit of one's labors; we *offer* remarks on such things as attract notice and call for animadversion.

These terms may also be employed to designate the actions of unconscious agents, by which they are characterized: in this sense they come very near to the word *exhibit*, which, from *exhibeo*, signifies to hold or put forth. Here the word *give* is equally indefinite and general, denoting simply to send from one's self, and applies mostly to what proceeds from another, by a natural cause: thus, a thing is said to *give* pain or to *give* pleasure. Things are said to *present* or *offer:* thus, a town is said to *present* a fine view, or an idea *presents* itself to the mind; an opportunity *offers*, that is, *offers* itself to our notice. To *exhibit* is properly applied in this sense of setting forth to view; but expresses, likewise, the idea of attracting notice also: that which is *exhibited* is more striking than what is *presented* or *offered*, thus a poem is said to *exhibit* marks of genius.

Give Up, Deliver, Surrender, Yield, Cede, Concede.—We *give up* that which we wish to retain; we *deliver* that which we wish not to retain. *Deliver* does not include the idea of a transfer; but *give up* implies both the *giving* from and the *giving* to: we *give up* our house to the accommodation of our friends; we *deliver* property into the hands of the owner. To *give up* is a colloquial substitute for either *surrender* or *yield*, as it designates no circumstance of the action; it may be employed in familiar discourse, in almost every case, for the other terms: where the action is compulsory we may either say an officer *gives up* or *surrenders* his sword; when the action is discretionary, we may either say he *gives up* or *yields* a point of discussion: *give up* has, however, an extensiveness of application which gives it an office distinct from either *surrender* or *yield*. When we speak of familiar and personal subjects, *give up* is more suitable than *surrender*, which is confined to matters of public interest or great moment: a man *gives up* his place, his right, his claim, and the like; he *surrenders* a fortress, a vessel, or his property to his creditors. When *give up* is com-

pared with *yield*, they both respect personal matters; but the former expresses a much stronger action than the latter: a man *gives up* his whole judgment to another; he *yields* to the opinion of another in particular cases: he *gives* himself *up* to sensual indulgences; he *yields* to the force of temptation.

Cede, from the Latin *cedere*, to come to, to yield, to give, is properly to *surrender* by virtue of a treaty: we may *surrender* a town as an act of necessity; but the *cession* of a country is purely a political transaction: thus, generals frequently *surrender* such towns as they are not able to defend; and governments *cede* such countries as they find it not convenient to retain. To *concede*, which is but a variation of *cede*, is a mode of *yielding* which may be either an act of discretion or courtesy; as when a government *concedes* to the demands of the people certain privileges, or when an individual *concedes* any point in dispute for the sake of peace.

Give Up, Abandon, Resign, Forego.— These terms differ from the preceding ones, inasmuch as they designate actions entirely free from foreign influence. A man *gives up*, *abandons*, and *resigns* from the dictates of his own mind, independently of all control from others. To *give up* and *abandon* both denote a positive decision of the mind; but the former may be the act of the understanding or the will; the latter is more commonly the act of the will and the passions: to *give up* is applied to familiar cases; *abandon* to matters of importance: one *gives up* an idea, an intention, a plan, and the like; one *abandons* a project, a scheme, a measure of government.

To *give up* and *resign* are applied either to outward actions or merely to inward movements; but the former is active and determinately fixes the conduct; the latter seems to be rather passive—it is the leaning of the mind to the circumstances: a man *gives up* his situation by a positive act of his choice; he *resigns* his office when he feels it inconvenient to hold it; so, likewise, we *give up* expectations and *resign* hopes. In this sense, *forego*, which signifies to let go, is comparable with *resign*, inasmuch as it expresses a passive action; but we *resign* that which we have, and we *forego* that which we might have: thus, we *resign* the claims which we have already made; we *forego* the claims which we might make: the former may be a matter of prudence; the latter is always an act of virtue and forbearance.

When applied to the state of a person's mind, or the actions flowing from that state, to *give up* is used either in a good, bad, or indifferent sense; *abandon* always in a bad sense; *resign* always in a good sense: a man may *give* himself *up* either to studious pursuits, to idle vagaries, or vicious indulgences; he *abandons* himself to gross vices; he *resigns* himself to the will of Providence, or to the circumstances of his condition: a man is said to be *given up* to his lusts who is without any principle to control him in their gratification; he is said to be *abandoned* when his outrageous conduct bespeaks an entire insensibility to every honest principle; he is said to be *resigned* when he discovers composure and tranquillity in the hour of affliction; so one is said to *resign* a thing to another when one is contented with what one has.

GLAD, PLEASED, JOYFUL, CHEERFUL. *Glad* comes from Anglo-Saxon *glæd*, smooth, bright, allied to German *glatt*, smooth, polished. *Pleased*, from to *please*, marks the state of being *pleased*. *Joyful* bespeaks its own meaning either as full of *joy* or productive of great *joy*, from Latin *gaudium*, joy. *Cheerful* (see CHEERFUL).

Glad denotes either a partial state or a permanent and habitual sentiment: in the former sense it is most nearly allied to *pleased;* in the latter sense, to *joyful* and merry. *Glad* and *pleased* are both applied to the ordinary occurrences of the day; but the former denotes rather a lively and momentary sentiment, the latter a gentle but rather more lasting feeling: we are *glad* to see a friend who has been long absent; we are *glad* to have good intelligence from our friends and relatives; we are *glad* to get rid of a troublesome companion; we are *pleased* to have the approbation of those we esteem: we are *pleased* to hear our friends well spoken of; we are *pleased* with

the company of an intelligent and communicative person.

Glad, joyful, and *cheerful* all express more or less lively sentiments; but *glad* is less vivid than *joyful,* and more so than *cheerful. Gladness* seems to arise as much from physical as mental causes; wine is said to make the heart *glad: joy* has its source in the mind, as it is influenced by external circumstances; instances of good fortune, for either ourselves, our friends, or our country, excite *joy: cheerfulness* is an even tenor of the mind, which it may preserve of itself independently of all external circumstances; religious contemplation produces habitual *cheerfulness. Glad* is seldom employed as an epithet to qualify things, except in the scriptural or solemn style, as *glad* tidings of great *joy: joyful* is seldomer used to qualify persons than things; hence we speak of *joyful* news, a *joyful* occurrence, *joyful* faces, *joyful* sounds, and the like: *cheerful* is employed either to designate the state of the mind or the property of the thing; we either speak of a *cheerful* disposition, a *cheerful* person, a *cheerful* society, or a *cheerful* face, a *cheerful* sound, a *cheerful* aspect, and the like.

When used to qualify one's actions they all bespeak the temper of the mind; *gladly* denotes a high degree of willingness as opposed to aversion: one who is suffering under excruciating pains *gladly* submits to anything which promises relief: *joyfully* denotes unqualified *pleasure,* unmixed with any alloy or restrictive consideration; a convert to Christianity *joyfully* goes through all the initiatory ceremonies which entitle him to all its privileges, spiritual and temporal; *cheerful* denotes the absence of unwillingness, it is opposed to reluctantly; the zealous Christian *cheerfully* submits to every hardship to which he is exposed in the course of his religious profession.

See also JOY.

GLANCE AT, ALLUDE TO. *Glance* is a nasalized form of Old French *glacier,* to slip, slide; it indicated a sliding beam of light. *Allude* (see ALLUDE).

These terms are nearly allied in the sense of indirectly referring to any object, either in written or verbal discourse: but *glance* expresses a cursory and latent action; *allude,* simply an indirect but undisguised action: ill-natured satirists are perpetually *glancing* at the follies and infirmities of individuals; the Scriptures are full of *allusions* to the manners and customs of the Easterns: he who attempts to write an epitome of universal history must take but a hasty *glance* at the most important events.

See also GLIMPSE; LOOK.

GLARE.   See FLAME; SHINE.

GLARING, BAREFACED.   *Glaring* is here used in the figurative sense, drawn from its natural signification of broad light, which strikes powerfully upon the senses. *Barefaced* signifies literally having a *bare* or *uncovered face,* which denotes the absence of all disguise or all shame.

Glaring designates the thing; *barefaced* characterizes the person: a *glaring* falsehood is that which strikes the observer in an instant to be falsehood; a *barefaced* lie or falsehood betrays the effrontery of him who utters it. A *glaring* absurdity will be seen instantly without the aid of reflection; a *barefaced* piece of impudence characterizes the agent as more than ordinarily lost to all sense of decorum.

GLEAM, GLIMMER, RAY, BEAM. *Gleam* comes from Anglo-Saxon *glæm,* from a root signifying brightness, whence *glimmer,* a frequentative, is also derived. *Ray* comes from Latin *radius,* a ray—a beam of light issuing from a centre of light. *Beam,* Anglo-Saxon *beam,* from Teutonic root cognate with Greek φαῦσις, a light, which appears in *phosphorus.*

Certain portions of light are designated by all these terms, but *gleam* and *glimmer* are indefinite; *ray* and *beam* are definite. A *gleam* is properly the commencement of light, or that portion of opening light which interrupts the darkness: a *glimmer* is an unsteady *gleam: ray* and *beam* are portions of light which emanate from some luminous body; the former from all luminous bodies in general, the latter more particularly from the sun: the former is, as its derivation denotes, a row of light issuing in a greater or less degree from any body; the latter is a great row of light, like a pole issuing from a body. There may be a *gleam* of light

visible on the wall of a dark room, or a *glimmer* if it be movable; there may be *rays* of light visible at night on the back of a glow-worm, or *rays* of light may break through the shutters of a closed room; the sun in the height of its splendor sends forth its *beams.*

GLEAMING.   See LAMBENT.

GLEE, GAYETY, JOVIALITY, MERRIMENT, MIRTH.   *Glee,* Anglo-Saxon *gleo,* joy, mirth, and music, signifies in ordinary language an expression of joy, gladness, happiness, gratification over some pleasing occurrence. *Gayety* implies the state of being exuberant or having a superabundance of good-humor, liveliness, cheerfulness, blitheness; *joviality,* the state of being jolly, convivial, festive, joyous; *merriment,* the state of being full of fun and good-humor, sportive, frolicsome, loudly cheerful, gay of heart; and *mirth,* the state of being playful, festive, vivacious, witty, facetious, fond of merry-making, and the like.

In another application the term *glee* implies a musical composition sung in parts as a series of interwoven melodies for three or more voices, each part being limited to one voice; may be composed in any style and rendered with or without instrumentation.

GLIB.   See VOLUBLE.

GLIDE.   See SLIP.

GLIMMER.   See GLEAM.

GLIMPSE, GLANCE.   A *glimpse* is the action of the object appearing to the eye; a *glance* is the action of the eye seeking the object: one catches a *glimpse* of an object; one casts a *glance* at an object: the latter, therefore, is properly the means for obtaining the former, which is the end: we get a *glimpse* by means of a *glance.* The *glimpse* is the hasty, imperfect, and sudden view which we get of an object; the *glance* is the hasty and imperfect view which we take of an object: the former may depend upon a variety of circumstances; the latter depends upon the will of the agent. We can seldom do more than get a *glimpse* of objects in a carriage that is going with rapidity: when we do not wish to be observed to look, we take but a *glance* at an object.

GLITTER.   See SHINE.

GLOAMING, EVENING, TWILIGHT. Of these three terms *evening* is the term which simply denotes the time of day—the beginning of night. The other two terms add to the denotation of time certain special connotations. *Gloaming* is a poetic word found in the Anglo-Saxon compound *œfen-glommung*, literally evening-glow, from Anglo-Saxon *glowan*, to glow. It indicates the time just after sunset, when there is still a *glow* of light in the western sky, but when the *gloom* of night is fast falling. The word *gloaming* has this double suggestion of both *gloom* and *glow*. *Twilight* signifies literally the time of half light, the space between day and night when light has not entirely given way to darkness. Compare Middle Dutch *tweelicht*.

GLOBE, BALL. *Globe* comes from Latin *globus*, ball. *Ball*, Teutonic *ball*, is doubtless connected with the words *bowl*, *boil*, and the like, signifying that which is turned or rounded.

Globe is to *ball* as the species to the genus; a *globe* is a *ball*, but every *ball* is not a *globe*. The *globe* does not in its strict sense require to be of an equal rotundity in all its parts; it is properly an irregularly round body: a *ball*, on the other hand, is generally any round body, but particularly one that is entirely, regularly round; the earth itself is therefore properly denominated a *globe* from its unequal rotundity: and for the same reason the mechanical body, which is made to represent the earth, is also denominated a *globe:* but in the higher style of writing the earth is frequently denominated a *ball*, and in familiar discourse every solid body which assumes a circular form is entitled a *ball*.

See also CIRCLE.

GLOOM, HEAVINESS. *Gloom* has its source internally, and is often independent of outward circumstances; *heaviness* is a weight upon the spirits produced by a foreign cause: the former belongs to the constitution; the latter is occasional. People of a melancholy habit have a particular *gloom* hang over their minds which pervades all their thoughts; those who suffer under severe disappointments for the present, and have *gloomy* prospects for the future, may be expected to be *heavy* at heart; we may sometimes dispel the *gloom* of the mind by the force of reflec-

tion, particularly by the force of religious contemplation: *heaviness* of spirits is itself a temporary thing, and may be succeeded by vivacity or lightness of mind when the pressure of the moment has subsided.

Gloomy, Sullen, Morose, Splenetic.—All these terms denote a temper of mind the reverse of easy or happy: *gloomy* lies either in the general constitution or in the particular frame of the mind; *sullen* lies in the temper: a man of a *gloomy* disposition is an involuntary agent; it is his misfortune, and renders him in some measure pitiable: the *sullen* man yields to his evil humors; *sullenness* is his fault, and renders him offensive. The *gloomy* man distresses himself most; his pains are all his own: the *sullen* man has a great share of discontent in his composition; he charges his sufferings upon others, and makes them suffer in common with himself. A man may be rendered *gloomy* for a time by the influence of particular circumstances; but *sullenness* creates pains for itself when all external circumstances of a painful nature are wanting.

Sullenness and *moroseness* are both the inherent properties of the temper; but the former discovers itself in those who have to submit, and the latter in those who have to command: *sullenness* therefore betrays itself mostly in early life; *moroseness* is the peculiar characteristic of age. The *sullen* person has many fancied hardships to endure from the control of others; the *morose* person causes others to endure many real hardships by keeping them under too severe a control. *Sullenness* shows itself mostly by an unseemly reserve: *moroseness* shows itself by the hardness of the speech and the roughness of the voice. *Sullenness* is altogether a sluggish principle that leads more or less to inaction; *moroseness* is a harsh feeling, that is, not contented with exacting obedience unless it inflicts pain.

Moroseness is a defect of the temper; but *spleen* is a defect in the heart: the one betrays itself in behavior, the other more in conduct. A *morose* man is an unpleasant companion; a *splenetic* man is a bad member of society; the former is ill-natured to those about him, the latter is ill-humored with all the world. *Moroseness* vents itself in temporary expressions; *spleen* indulges itself in perpetual bitterness of expression.

See also DULL; HYPOCHONDRIACAL; PESSIMISTIC.

GLORY, HONOR. *Glory* is something dazzling and widely diffused, from Latin *gloria*. That the moral idea of *glory* is best represented by light is evident from the *glory* which is painted round the head of our Saviour. *Honor* is something less splendid, but more solid. It is derived from Latin *honorem*, honor, reputation.

Glory impels to extraordinary efforts and to great undertakings. *Honor* induces to a discharge of one's duty. Excellence in the attainment and success in the exploit bring *glory;* a faithful exercise of one's talents reflects *honor*. *Glory* is connected with everything which has a peculiar public interest; *honor* is more properly obtained within a private circle. *Glory* is not confined to the nation or life of the individual by whom it is sought; it spreads over all the earth and descends to the latest posterity: *honor* is limited to those who are connected with the subject of it and eye-witnesses to his actions. *Glory* is attainable but by few, and may be an object of indifference to any one; *honor* is more or less within the reach of all and must be disregarded by no one. A general at the head of an army goes in pursuit of *glory;* the humble citizen who acts his part in society so as to obtain the approbation of his fellow-citizens is in the road for *honor*. A nation acquires *glory* by the splendor of its victories and its superiority in arts as well as arms; it obtains *honor* by its strict adherence to equity and good faith in all its dealings with other nations.

Glory is a sentiment selfish in its nature, but salutary or pernicious in its effect, according as it is directed; *honor* is a principle disinterested in its nature and beneficial in its operations. A thirst for *glory* is seldom indulged but at the expense of others, as it is not attainable in the plain path of duty; there are but few opportunities of acquiring it by elevated acts of goodness, and still fewer who have the virtue to embrace the opportunities that offer:

a love of *honor* can never be indulged but to the advantage of others; it is restricted by fixed laws; it requires a sacrifice of every selfish consideration and a due regard to the rights of others; it is associated with nothing but virtue.

Glory, Boast, Gasconade, Vaunt.—To *glory* is to hold as one's *glory*. To *boast*, or *gasconade*, is to set forth to one's advantage. To *vaunt* is to set one's self up before others. The first two terms denote the value which the individual sets upon that which belongs to himself; the last term may be employed in respect to others.

To *glory* is more particularly the act of the mind, the indulgence of the internal sentiment: to *boast* denotes rather the expression of the sentiment. To *glory* is applied only to matters of moment; *boast* is rather suitable to trifling points: the former is seldom used in a bad sense, the latter still seldomer in a good one. A Christian martyr *glories* in the cross of Christ; a soldier *boasts* of his courage and his feats in battle. To *vaunt* is properly to proclaim praises aloud, and is taken either in an indifferent or bad sense.

GLOSS, VARNISH, PALLIATE. *Gloss* and *varnish* are figurative terms, which borrow their signification from the act of making the outer surface of any physical object shine. To *gloss* comes from a Scandinavian word signifying lustre, from a root meaning to glow; it means to give a glow or brightness to anything by means of friction, as in the case of japan or mahogany: to *varnish* is to give an artificial *gloss* by means of applying a foreign substance. Hence, in the figurative use of the terms, to *gloss* is to put the best face upon anything by various artifices; but to *varnish* is to do the same thing by means of direct falsehood; to *palliate*, which likewise signifies to give the best possible outside to a thing (see EXTENUATE), requires still less artifice than either. One *glosses* over that which is bad by giving it a soft name, as when a man's vices are *glossed* over with the name of indiscretion or a man's mistress is termed his friend one *varnishes* a bad character by ascribing good motives to his bad actions, by withholding many facts that are to his discredit, and fabricating other circumstances in his favor; an *unvarnished* tale contains nothing but the simple truth; the *varnished* tale, on the other hand, contains a great mixture of falsehood: to *palliate* is to diminish the magnitude of an offence by making an excuse in favor of the offender, as when an act of theft is *palliated* by considering the starving condition of the thief.

GLOSSARY. See DICTIONARY.

GLOW. See FIRE.

GLUT. See SATISFY.

GO, ADVANCE, DEPART, PROCEED, TRAVEL. *Go* is a widely distributed Teutonic word. It is the generic term signifying to move in any direction. The other terms indicate particular kinds of going. *Advance* and *proceed* mean to *go* forward (see ADVANCE). *Depart*, from Latin *de*, from, and *pars*, part, a separation, means to go away. *Travel* means to go about for the sake of pleasure or sightseeing.

GODLIKE, DIVINE, HEAVENLY. *Godlike* bespeaks its own meaning, as like *God*, or after the manner of *God*, from the Teutonic word corresponding in meaning to Latin *Deus*, possibly signifying the being worshipped from a root meaning to worship. *Divine*, in Latin *divinus*, from *divus* or *Deus*, signifies appertaining to *God*. *Heavenly*, or *heaven-like*, signifies like or appertaining to *heaven*, Anglo-Saxon *heofon*.

Godlike is a more expressive but less common term than *divine:* the former is used only as an epithet of peculiar praise for an individual; *divine* is generally employed for that which appertains to a superior being, in distinction from that which is human. Benevolence is a *godlike* property: the *Divine* image is stamped on the features of man, whence the face is called by Milton "the human face *divine.*" As *divine* is opposed to human, so is *heavenly* to earthly; the term *Divine* Being distinguishes the Creator from all other beings; but a *heavenly* being denotes the agents or inhabitants of *heaven*, in distinction from earthly beings, or the inhabitants of earth. A *divine* influence is to be sought for only by prayer to the Giver of all good things; but a *heavenly* temper may be acquired by a steady contemplation of *heavenly* things and an abstraction from those which

are earthly: the *Divine* will is the foundation of all moral law and obligation; *heavenly* joys are the fruit of all our labors in this earthly course. These terms are applied to other objects with similar distinction.

Godly, Righteous.—*Godly* is a contraction of *godlike*. *Righteous* signifies conformable to *right* or truth.

These epithets are both used in a spiritual sense, and cannot, without an indecorous affectation of religion, be introduced into any other discourse than that which is properly spiritual. *Godliness*, in the strict sense, is that outward deportment which characterizes a heavenly temper; prayer, reading of the Scriptures, public worship, and every religious act enters into the signification of *godliness*, which at the same time supposes a temper of mind, not only to delight in, but to profit by such exercises: *righteousness*, on the other hand, comprehends Christian morality, in distinction from that of the heathen or unbeliever; a *righteous* man does *right*, not only because it is *right*, but because it is agreeable to the will of his Maker and the example of his Redeemer; *righteousness* is therefore to *godliness* as the effect to the cause. The *godly* man goes to the sanctuary and by converse with his Maker assimilates all his affections to the character of that Being whom he worships; when he leaves the sanctuary he proves the efficacy of his *godliness* by his *righteous* converse with his fellow-creatures. It is easy, however, for men to mistake the means for the end and to rest content with *godliness* without *righteousness*, as too many are apt to do who seem to make their whole duty to consist in an attention to religious observances and in the indulgence of extravagant feelings.

GOLD, GOLDEN. These terms are both employed as epithets, but *gold* is the substantive used in composition, and *golden*, the adjective, in ordinary use. The former is strictly applied to the metal of which the thing is made, as a *gold* cup or a *gold* coin; but the latter to whatever appertains to *gold*, whether properly or figuratively, as the *golden* lion, the *golden* crown, the *golden* age, or a *golden* harvest.

GOOD, GOODNESS. *Good* is a word

which, under different forms, runs through all the Northern languages.

Good and *goodness* are abstract terms, drawn from the same word; the former to denote the thing that is *good*, the latter the inherent *good* property of persons or things. All *good* comes from God, whose *goodness* toward His creatures is unbounded. The good we do is determined by the tendency of the action; but our *goodness* in doing it is determined by the motive of our actions. *Good* is of a twofold nature, physical and moral, and is opposed to evil; *goodness* is applicable either to the disposition of moral agents or to the qualities of inanimate objects; it is opposed to badness. By the order of Providence the most horrible convulsions are made to bring about *good;* the *goodness* or badness of any fruit depends upon its fitness to be enjoyed.

See also VIRTUOUS.

Good, Benefit, Advantage.—*Good* is an abstract universal term which, in its unlimited sense, comprehends everything that can be conceived of as suited in all its parts to the end proposed. In this sense *benefit* and *advantage* are modifications of *good;* but the term *good* has likewise a limited application, which brings it to a just point of comparison with the other terms here chosen: the common idea which allies these words to one another is that of *good* as it respects a particular object. *Good* is here employed indefinitely; *benefit* and *advantage* are specified by some collateral circumstances. *Good* is done without regard to the person who does it, or him to whom it is done; but *benefit* has always respect to the relative condition of the giver and receiver, who must be both specified. Hence we say of a charitable man that he does much *good*, or that he bestows *benefits* upon this or that individual. In like manner, when speaking of particular communities or society at large, we may say that it is for the *good* of society or for the *good* of mankind that every one submits to the sacrifice of some portion of his natural liberty; but it is for the *benefit* of the poorer orders that the charitably disposed employ their money in charity.

Good is limited to no mode or manner, no condition of the person or the thing; it is applied indiscriminately: *benefit* is more particularly applicable to the external circumstances of a person, as to his health, his improvement, his pecuniary condition, and the like; it is also confined in its application to persons only: we may counsel another for his *good*, although we do not counsel him for his *benefit;* but we labor for the *benefit* of another when we set apart for him the fruits of our labor: exercise is always attended with some *good* to all persons; it is of particular *benefit* to those who are of a lethargic habit: an indiscreet zeal does more harm than *good* to the cause of religion; a patient cannot expect to derive *benefit* from a medicine when he counteracts its effects.

A *benefit* is a positive and direct *good*, an *advantage* is an adventitious and indirect *good:* the *benefit* serves to supply some want, to remove some evil and afford some sort of relief: an *advantage* serves to promote some ulterior object. An *advantage*, therefore, will not be a *benefit* unless it be turned to a *good* use. Education may be a *benefit* to a person if it enable him to procure a competence; a polite education is of *advantage* to one who associates with the great.

GOOD - NATURE, GOOD - HUMOR. *Good-nature* and *good-humor* both imply the disposition to please and be pleased; but the former is habitual and permanent, the latter is temporary and partial: the former lies in the nature and frame of the mind, the latter in the state of the humors or spirits. A *good-natured* man recommends himself at all times for his *good-nature;* a *good-humored* man recommends himself particularly as a companion: *good-nature* displays itself by a readiness in doing kind offices; *good-humor* is confined mostly to the ease and cheerfulness of one's outward deportment in social converse: *good-nature* is apt to be guilty of weak compliances; *good-humor* is apt to be succeeded by fits of peevishness and depression. *Good-nature* is applicable only to the character of the individual; *good-humor* may be said of a whole company: it is a mark of *good-nature* in a man not to disturb the *good-humor* of the company he is in by resenting the affront that is offered him by another.

GOODNESS. See GOOD.

GOOD OFFICE. See BENEFIT.

GOODS, FURNITURE, CHATTELS, MOVABLES, EFFECTS. All these terms are applied to such things as belong to an individual: the first term is the most general, both in sense and application; all the rest are species.

Furniture comprehends all household goods; wherefore in regard to an individual, supposing the house to contain all he has, the general is put for the specific term, as when one speaks of a person's moving his *goods* for his *furniture:* but in the strict sense *goods* comprehends more than *furniture,* including not only that which is adapted for the domestic purposes of a family, but also everything which is of value to a person: the chairs and tables are a part of *furniture;* papers, books, and money are included among his *goods:* it is obvious, therefore, that *goods,* even in its most limited sense, is of wider import than *furniture.*

Chattels, Old French *chatel,* comes from Late Latin *capitale,* capital, meaning property, and is a technical term in law, and therefore not so frequent in ordinary use, but still sufficiently employed to deserve notice. It comprehends that species of *goods* which is in a special manner separated from one's person and house; a man's cattle, his implements of husbandry, the partial rights which he has in land or buildings, are all comprehended under *chattels:* hence the propriety of the expression to seize a man's *goods* and *chattels,* as denoting the disposable property which he has about his person or at a distance. *Movables* comprehends all the other terms in the limited application to property, as far as it admits of being removed from one place to the other; it is opposed either to fixtures, when speaking of *furniture,* or to land as contrasted with *goods* and *chattels.*

Effects is a term of nearly as extensive a signification as *goods,* but not so extensive in its application: whatever a man has that is of any supposed value, or convertible into money, is entitled his *goods;* whatever a man has that can effect, produce, or bring forth money by sale is entitled his *effects; goods,* therefore, is applied only to that which a man has at his own disposal; *effects* more properly to that which is left at the disposal of others. A man makes a sale of his *goods* on his removal from any place; his creditors or executors take care of his *effects* either on his bankruptcy or decease; *goods,* in this case, is seldom employed but in the limited sense of what is removable, but *effects* includes everything real as well as personal.

Goods, Possessions, Property. — All these terms are applicable to such things as are the means of enjoyment; but the former term respects the direct quality of producing enjoyment, the latter two have regard to the subject of the enjoyment; we consider *goods* as they are real or imaginary, adapted or not adapted for the producing of real happiness; those who abound in the *goods* of this world are not always the happiest; *possessions* must be regarded as they are lasting or temporary; he who is anxious for earthly *possessions* forgets that they are but transitory and dependent upon a thousand contingencies: *property* is to be considered as it is legal or illegal, just or unjust; those who are anxious for great *property* are not always scrupulous about the means by which it is to be obtained. The purity of a man's Christian character is in danger from an overweening attachment to earthly *goods;* no wise man will boast the multitude of his *possessions* when he reflects that if they do not leave him the time is not far distant when he must leave them; the validity of one's claim to *property* which comes by inheritance is better founded than any other.

GORGEOUS, BRILLIANT, DAZZLING. *Gorgeous* has a curious derivation. It comes from the Old French *gorge,* throat (compare the slang phrase "Get my gorge"), and originally meant proud, with reference to the swelling of the throat in pride. *Gorge* itself comes from Latin *gurges,* a whirlpool, whence in Late Latin it came to signify the gullet, into which everything disappears as if into a whirlpool. *Gorgeous* now signifies brightly colored with special reference to splendor and richness of effect. *Brilliant* (for derivation see BRIGHTNESS) also means very bright, but it suggests light primarily rather than color, or color in so far as it also has the qualities of light. *Dazzling* indicates brightness of color or especially of light with special reference to the psychological effect upon the spectator. *Dazzle* refers to the sudden blurring of the rays of light to the eye when it faces something very bright. A *dazzling* light is something this side of a *blinding* light.

GOVERN, RULE, REGULATE. *Govern* is in French *gouverner*, Latin *guberno*, Greek κῦβερνάω. *Rule* and *regulate* signify to bring under a *rule* or make by *rule*.

The exercise of authority enters more or less into the signification of these terms; but to *govern* implies the exercise likewise of judgment and knowledge. To *rule* implies rather the unqualified exercise of power, the making the will the *rule:* a king *governs* his people by means of wise laws and an upright administration: a despot *rules* over a nation according to his arbitrary decision; if he have no principle, his *rule* becomes an oppressive tyranny. These terms are applied either to persons or to things: persons *govern* or *rule* others; or they *govern, rule* or *regulate* things.

In regard to persons *govern* is always in a good sense, but *rule* is sometimes taken in a bad sense; it is frequently associated with an abuse of power: to *govern* is so perfectly discretionary that we speak of *governing* ourselves; but we speak only of *ruling* others: nothing can be more lamentable than to be *ruled* by one who does not know how to *govern* himself: it is the business of a man to *rule* his house by keeping all its members in due subjection to his authority: it is the duty of a person to *rule* those who are under him in all matters wherein they are incompetent to *govern* themselves.

In application to things, *govern* and *rule* admit of a similar distinction: a minister *governs* the state and a pilot *governs* the vessel: the movements of the machine are in both cases directed by the exercise of the judgment; a person *rules* the times, seasons, fashions, and the like; it is an act of the individual will. *Regulate* is a species of *governing* simply by judgment; the word is applicable to things of minor moment, where the force of authority is not so requisite: one *governs* the affairs of a nation or a large body where great interests are involved; we *regulate* the concerns of an individual, or we *regulate* in cases where good order or convenience only is consulted: so likewise in regard to ourselves, we *govern* our passions, but we *regulate* our affections.

These terms are all properly used to denote the acts of conscious agents, but by a figure of personification they may be applied to inanimate or moral objects: the price of one market *governs* the price of another, or *governs* the seller in his demand; fashion and caprice *rule* the majority, or particular fashions *rule* them: the time of one clock *regulates* that of many others.

Government, Administration. — Both these terms may be employed either to designate the act of *governing* and *administering* or the persons *governing* and *administering.* In both cases *government* has a more extensive meaning than *administration:* the former includes every exercise of authority, while *administration* implies only that exercise of authority which consists in putting the laws or will of another in force.

When we speak of the *government* as it respects the persons, it implies the whole body of constituted authorities; and the *administration*, only that part which puts in execution the intentions of the whole: the *government* of a country, therefore, may remain unaltered, while the *administration* undergoes many changes: it is the business of the *government* to make treaties of peace and war; and without a *government* it is impossible for any people to negotiate: it is the business of the *administration* to *administer* justice, to regulate the finances, and to direct all the complicated concerns of a nation; without an *administration* all public business would be at a stand.

Government, Constitution. — *Government* is here, as in the former article, the general term; *constitution* the specific. *Government* implies generally the act of *governing*, or exercising authority under any form whatever; *constitution*

GRACE

implies any *constituted* or fixed form of *government:* we may have a *government* without a *constitution;* we cannot have a *constitution* without a *government.* In the first formation of society, *government* was placed in the hands of individuals who exercised authority according to discretion rather than any positive rule or law; here then was *government* without a *constitution:* as time and experience proved the necessity of some established form, and the wisdom of enlightened men discovered the advantages and disadvantages of different forms, *government* in every country assumed a more definite shape and became the *constitution* of the country; hence then the union of *government* and *constitution.* *Governments* are divided by political writers into three classes, monarchical, aristocratic, and republican; but these three general forms have been adopted with such variations and modifications as to impart to the *constitution* of every country something peculiar. The term *constitution* is now particularly applied to any popular form of *government,* or any *government* formed at the pleasure of the people, and in a still more restricted sense to the *government* of England.

See also EMPIRE.

GRACE, FAVOR. *Grace,* in French *grâce,* Latin *gratia,* comes from *gratus,* kind, because a *grace* results from pure kindness, independently of the merit of the receiver; but *favor* is that which is granted voluntarily and without hope of recompense, independently of all obligation.

Grace is never used but in regard to those who have offended and made themselves liable to punishment; *favor* is employed for actual good. An act of *grace,* in the spiritual sense, is that merciful influence which God exerts over His most unworthy creatures from the infinite goodness of His Divine nature; it is to His special *grace* that we attribute every good feeling by which we are prevented from committing sin: the term *favor* is employed indiscriminately with regard to man or his Maker; those who are in power have the greatest opportunity of conferring *favors;* but all we receive at the hands of our Maker must be acknowledged as a *favor.*

Grace, Charm.—*Grace* is altogether corporeal; *charm* is either corporeal or mental: the *grace* qualifies the action of the body; the *charm* is an inherent quality in the body itself. A lady moves, dances, and walks with *grace;* the *charms* of her person are equal to those of her mind.

Graceful, Comely, Elegant.—A *graceful* figure is rendered so by the deportment of the body. A *comely* figure has that in itself which pleases the eye. *Gracefulness* results from nature improved by art; *comeliness* is mostly the work of nature. It is possible to acquire *gracefulness* by the aid of the dancing-master, but for a *comely* form we are indebted to nature aided by circumstances. *Grace* is a quality pleasing to the eye; but *elegance,* from the Latin *e,* out, and *legere,* to choose, meaning worthy of being chosen out, is a quality of a higher nature, that inspires admiration; *elegant* is applicable, like *graceful,* to the motion of the body, or like *comely* to the person, and is extended in its meaning also to language, and even to dress. A person's step is *graceful;* his air or his movements are *elegant;* the *grace* of an action lies chiefly in its adaptation to the occasion.

See also BECOMING.

Gracious, Merciful, Kind.—*Gracious,* when compared with *merciful,* is used only in the spiritual sense; the latter is applicable to the conduct of man as well as of the Deity. *Grace* is exerted in doing good to an object that has merited the contrary; *mercy* is exerted in withholding the evil which has been merited. God is *gracious* to His creatures in affording them not only an opportunity to address Him, but every encouragement to lay open their wants to Him; their unworthiness and sinfulness are not made impediments of access to Him. God is *merciful* to the vilest of sinners, and lends an ear to the smallest breath of repentance; in the moment of executing vengeance He stops His arm at the voice of supplication: He expects the same *mercy* to be extended by man toward his offending brother. An act of *grace* in the largest sense, as not only independent of, but opposite to, the merits of the person, is properly ascribable to

God alone, but by analogy it has also been considered as the prerogative of earthly princes: thus we speak of acts of *grace*, by which insolvent debtors are released: in like manner, the *grace* of the sovereign may be exerted in various ways.

Gracious, when compared with *kind*, differs principally as to the station of the persons to whom it is applied. *Gracious* is altogether confined to superiors; *kind* is indiscriminately employed for superiors and equals: a king gives a *gracious* reception to the nobles who are presented to him; one friend gives a *kind* reception to another by whom he is visited. *Gracious* is a term in peculiar use at court and among princes. *Kindness* is a domestic virtue; it is found mostly among those who have not so much ceremonial to dispense with.

GRAND. See GREAT; NOBLE; SUPERB.

GRANDEUR, M A G N I F I C E N C E. *Grandeur* comes from *grand*, in French *grand*, great, Latin *grandis*, great. *Magnificence*, in Latin *magnificentia*, from *magnus*, great, and *facere*, to make, signifies making or acting on a large scale.

An extensive assemblage of striking qualities in the exterior constitutes the common signification of these terms, of which *grandeur* is the genus and *magnificence* the species. *Magnificence* cannot exist without *grandeur*, but *grandeur* exists without *magnificence:* the former is distinguished from the latter both in degree and in application. When applied to the same objects, they differ in degree, *magnificence* being the highest degree of *grandeur*. As it respects the style of living, *grandeur* is within the reach of subjects; *magnificence* is mostly confined to princes.

GRANT. See ADMIT; ALLOW; GIVE.

GRASP. See NAB.

GRASPING. See GREEDY.

GRATEFUL. See ACCEPTABLE.

GRATIFICATION. See ENJOYMENT.

GRATIFY, INDULGE, HUMŌR. To *gratify*, make *grateful* or *pleasant* (see ACCEPTABLE), is a positive act of the choice. To *indulge* (for derivation see FOSTER) is a negative act of the will,

a yielding of the mind to circumstances. One *gratifies* his desires or appetites and *indulges* his humors, or *indulges* in pleasures: by the former, one seeks to get the pleasure which the desire promises; by the latter, one yields to the influences which the humor or passion exercises. *Gratifying* as a habit becomes a vice, and *indulging* as a habit is a weakness. In this sense of the words, *gratification* is mostly applied to mental objects, as to *gratify* one's curiosity; *indulgence*, to matters of sense or partial feeling, as to *indulge* one's palate. A person who is in search of pleasure *gratifies* his desires as they rise; he lives for the *gratification*, and depends upon it for his happiness. He who has higher objects in view than the momentary *gratification* will be careful not to *indulge* himself too much in such things as will wean him from his purpose.

As occasional acts, *gratify* and *indulge* may be both innocent.

We *gratify* and *indulge* others as well as ourselves, and mostly in the good sense: to *gratify* is for the most part in return for services; it is an act of generosity: to *indulge* is to yield to the wishes or be lenient to the infirmities of others; it is an act of kindness or good-nature. To *humor* is mostly taken in a bad sense.

See also SATISFY.

GRATITUDE. See THANKFULNESS.

GRATUITOUS, VOLUNTARY. *Gratuitous* is opposed to that which is obligatory. *Voluntary* is opposed to that which is compulsory or involuntary. A gift is *gratuitous* when it flows entirely from the free will of the giver, independently of right: an offer is *voluntary* which flows from the free will independently of all external constraint. *Gratuitous* is therefore to *voluntary* as a species to the genus. What is *gratuitous* is *voluntary*, although what is *voluntary* is not always *gratuitous*. The *gratuitous* is properly the *voluntary* in regard to the disposal of one's property; and the *voluntary* is applicable to all other actions.

Gratuity, Recompense.—The distinction between these terms is very similar to the above. They both imply a gift, and a gift by way of return for some supposed service; but the *gratuity* is independent of all expectation as well as right: the *recompense* is founded upon some admissible claim. Those who wish to confer a favor in a delicate manner will sometimes do it under the shape of a *gratuity:* those who overrate their services will in all probability be disappointed in the *recompense* they receive.

GRAVE, SERIOUS, SOLEMN. *Grave,* in Latin *gravis,* heavy, denotes the weight which keeps the mind or person down and prevents buoyancy; it is opposed to the light. *Serious,* Latin *serius,* possibly allied to German *schwer,* heavy, marks the quality of slowness or considerateness, either in the mind or that which occupies the mind: it is opposed to the jocose.

Grave expresses more than *serious;* it does not merely bespeak the absence of mirth, but that heaviness of mind which is displayed in all the movements of the body; *seriousness,* on the other hand, bespeaks no depression, but simply steadiness of action and a refrainment from all that is jocular. A man may be *grave* in his walk, in his tone, in his gesture, in his looks, and all his exterior; he is *serious* only in his general air, his countenance, and demeanor. *Gravity* is produced by some external circumstance, *seriousness* springs from the operation of the mind itself or from circumstances. Misfortunes or age will produce *gravity: seriousness* is the fruit of reflection. *Gravity* is, in the proper sense, confined to the person, as a characteristic of his temper; *serious,* on the other hand, is a characteristic either of persons or of things: hence we should speak of a *grave* assembly, not a *serious* assembly, of old men; *grave* senators, not *serious* senators; of a *grave* speaker, not a *serious* speaker: but a *serious,* not a *grave* sermon; a *serious,* not a *grave* writer; but *grave* is sometimes extended to things in the sense of weight, as when we speak of *grave* matters of deliberation, a *grave* objection, sentiment. *Gravity* is peculiarly ascribed to a judge, from the double cause that much depends upon his deportment, in which there ought to be *gravity,* and that the weighty concerns which press on his mind are most apt to produce

gravity: on the other hand, both *gravity* and *seriousness* may be applied to the preacher; the former only as it respects the manner of delivery; the latter as it respects especially the matter of his discourse: the person may be *grave* or *serious;* the discourse only is *serious.*

Solemn expresses more than either *grave* or *serious,* from the Latin *solennis,* yearly; as applied to the stated religious festivals of the Romans, it has acquired the collateral meaning of religious *gravity:* like *serious,* it is employed not so much to characterize either the person or the thing: a judge pronounces the *solemn* sentence of condemnation in a *solemn* manner; a preacher delivers many *solemn* warnings to his hearers. *Gravity* may be the effect of corporeal habit, and *seriousness* of mental habit; but *solemnity* is something occasional and extraordinary. Some children exhibit a remarkable *gravity* as soon as they begin to observe; a regular attention to religious worship will induce a habit of *seriousness;* the admonitions of a parent on his death-bed will have peculiar *solemnity.*

See also SOBER.

Grave, Tomb, Sepulchre.—All these terms denote the place where bodies are deposited. *Grave,* in this sense, comes from Anglo-Saxon *grafan,* to cut or dig, and signifies something cut or dug out, especially the hollow made in the earth. *Tomb,* Latin *tumba,* Greek τύμβα, is allied to *tumulus,* a mound, and *tumere,* to swell, and has reference to the rising above a grave. *Sepulchre,* from *sepelio,* bury, has a reference to the use for which it is employed. From this explanation it is evident that these terms have a certain propriety of application: "To sink into the *grave*" is an expression that carries the thoughts where the body must rest in death, consequently to death itself: "To inscribe on the *tomb,* or to encircle the *tomb* with flowers," carries our thoughts to the external of that place in which the body is interred. To inter in a *sepulchre,* or to visit or enter a *sepulchre,* reminds us of a place in which bodies are deposited, or, by a figure, where anything may be buried.

GRAVEYARD. See NECROPOLIS.

GRAVITY. See WEIGHT.

GREAT, LARGE, BIG. *Great*, in Anglo-Saxon *great*, is applied to all kinds of dimensions in which things can grow or increase. *Large*, in Latin *largus*, wide, is properly applied to space, extent, and quantity. *Big*, Middle English *big*, is probably of Scandinavian origin; it denotes *great* as to expansion or capacity. A house, a room, a heap, a pile, an army, etc., are *great* or *large;* an animal or a mountain is *great* or *big:* a road, a city, a street, and the like, are termed rather *great* than *large.*

Great is used generally in the improper sense; *large* and *big* are used only occasionally: a noise, a distance, a multitude, a number, a power, and the like, are termed *great*, but not *large:* we may, however, speak of a *large* portion, a *large* share, a *large* quantity; or of a mind *big* with conception, or of an event *big* with the fate of nations.

Great, Grand, Sublime.—These terms are synonymous only in their moral applications. *Great* simply designates extent; *grand* includes likewise the idea of excellence and superiority. A *great* undertaking characterizes only the extent of the undertaking; a *grand* undertaking bespeaks its superior excellence: *great* objects are seen with facility; *grand* objects are viewed with admiration. It is a *great* point to make a person sensible of his faults; it should be the *grand* aim of all to aspire after moral and religious improvement.

Grand and *sublime* are both superior to *great;* but the former marks the dimensions of *greatness;* the latter, from the Latin *sublimis*, designates that of height. A scene may be either *grand* or *sublime:* it is *grand* as it fills the imagination with its immensity; it is *sublime* as it elevates the imagination beyond the surrounding and less important objects. There is something *grand* in the sight of a vast army moving forward, as it were, by one impulse; there is something peculiarly *sublime* in the sight of huge mountains and craggy cliffs of ice shaped into various fantastic forms. *Grand* may be said of the works of either art or nature; *sublime* is peculiarly applicable to the works of nature. The Egyptian pyra-mids and the ocean are both *grand* objects; a tempestuous ocean is a *sublime* object. *Grand* is sometimes applied to the mind; *sublime* is applied both to the thoughts and to the expressions.

GREATEST. See SUPREME.

GREATNESS. See SIZE.

GREEDINESS. See AVIDITY.

GREEDY, AVARICIOUS, GRASPING, RAPACIOUS, SELFISH. *Greedy*, in Anglo-Saxon *grædig*, from a Teutonic root meaning to be hungry, signifies the state of a person or animal that has a keen appetite for food or drink or an eagerness for anything earnestly desired. The latter implication is the most common one in the relation of the term to persons, and, with the possible exception of being *greedy* or intensely anxious to obtain useful knowledge, the term *greedy* indicates a wholly reprehensible quality, though it is to be admitted that many persons are born into that quality or state and in later life fail to escape from it. Such may be more pardonable than those of maturity who knowingly enter that state.

The *avaricious* person is one who is possessed, nay, controlled, by an inordinate or insatiable desire for gain, without any consideration of the element of need. He wants something because he has none of it now, because his neighbor has it, because he wants to increase the quantity of it that he already possesses, and for all manner of reasons, but decidedly because he *wants* it.

The *grasping* person is not only *avaricious*, that quality giving him a motive, but he is covetous of the possessions of others, desirous of obtaining them, jealous of the possessor because of his possessions, and very apt to reach out, stretch forth, commit some underhand act, or take a mean advantage of another to accomplish his desire. The *rapacious* person is more of an extremist, for he is addicted to plunderings, forcible seizures, severe exactions, heartless extortions, and preposterous demands for whatever he desires.

The *selfish* person lives only for one person—himself; is attentive only to his own interests; is influenced in his actions by motives of personal advantage only; and, to use a familiar colloquialism, "Wants the whole earth and everything in it." He, too, is jealous of others who have more of this world's goods than himself, covets whatever others have, and is the only person on earth to be considered under all circumstances—in his own estimation.

GREEN, VERDANT. *Green*, in Anglo-Saxon *grene*, is allied to grow, and signifies the color of growing things—of grass and herbage. *Verdant*, Old French *verd*, green, Latin *viridus*, green, is the Latin corresponding to Anglo-Saxon *green*. *Green* denotes simply the color green. *Verdant* suggests lusty and flourishing vegetable life. *Green* makes a clearer impression upon the sensuous imagination; *verdant* suggests more to the mind. It is a less definite word, but richer in associations. Both terms are applied figuratively to some one who is ignorant or young—*green* with a definite implied comparison with unripe fruits or vegetable growth; *verdant* as a humorous substitute for *green*.

GREET. See ACCOST.

GREETING. See SALUTE.

GRIEF. See AFFLICTION.

GRIEVANCE, HARDSHIP. *Grievance*, from the Latin *gravis*, heavy or burdensome, implies that which lies heavy at heart. *Hardship*, from the adjective *hard*, denotes that which presses or bears violently on the person. *Grievance* is in general taken for that which is done by another to *grieve* or distress: *hardship* is a particular kind of *grievance* that presses upon individuals. There are national *grievances*, though not national *hardships*. An infraction of one's rights, an act of violence or oppression, are *grievances* to those who are exposed to them, whether as individuals or bodies of men: an unequal distribution of labor, a partial indulgence of one to the detriment of another, constitute the *hardship*. A weight of taxes, levied in order to support an unjust war, will be esteemed a *grievance*: the partiality and caprice of the collector in making it fall with unequal weight upon particular persons will be regarded as a peculiar *hardship*. Men seek a redress of their *grievances* from some higher power than that by which they are inflicted: they endure their *hardships* until an opportunity offers of getting them removed.

Grieve, Mourn, Lament.—To *grieve* (see AFFLICTION) is the general term; *mourn*, like *murmur*, being an imitation of the sound produced by pain, is a particular term. To *grieve*, in its limited sense, is an inward act; to *mourn* is an outward act: the *grief* lies altogether in the mind; the *mourning* displays itself by some outward mark. A man *grieves* for his sins; he *mourns* for the loss of his friends. One *grieves* for that which immediately concerns one's self, or that which concerns others; one *mourns* for that which concerns others; one *grieves* over the loss of property; one *mourns* the fate of a deceased relative.

Grieve, from Old French *grever*, Latin *gravis*, is the act of an individual; *mourn* may be the common act of many: a nation *mourns*, though it does not *grieve*, for a public calamity. To *grieve* is applicable to domestic troubles; *mourn* may refer to public or private ills. The distractions of a state will cause many to *grieve* for their own losses and *mourn* the misfortunes of their country.

Grieve and *mourn* are permanent sentiments; *lament* (see BEWAIL) is a transitory feeling: the former are produced by substantial causes, which come home to the feelings; the latter respects things of a more partial, oftentimes of a more remote and indifferent, nature. A real widow *mourns* all the remainder of her days for the loss of her husband; we *lament* a thing to-day which we may forget to-morrow. *Mourn* and *lament* are both expressed by some outward sign; but the former is composed and free from all noise; the latter displays itself either in cries or simple words. In the moment of trouble, when the distress of the mind is at its height, it may break out into loud *lamentation*, but commonly *grieving* and *mourning* commence when *lamentation* ceases.

As epithets, *grievous, mournful*, and *lamentable* have a similar distinction. What presses hard or unjustly on persons, their property, connections, and circumstances, is *grievous;* what touches the tender feelings, and tears asunder the ties of kindred and friendship, is *mournful;* whatever excites a painful sensation in our mind is *lamentable.* Famine is a *grievous* calamity for a nation; the violent separation of friends by death is a *mournful* event at all times, but particularly so for those who are in the prime of life and the fulness of expectation; the ignorance which some persons discover even in the present cultivated state of society is truly *lamentable.*

See also WAIL.

GRIEVED. See SORRY.

GRIM. See HIDEOUS.

GRIPE. See PRESS.

GRISLY. See HIDEOUS.

GROAN, MOAN. *Groan,* in Anglo-Saxon *granian,* may be allied to *grin. Groan* and *moan,* however, both have the effect of onomatopœtic words. *Groan* is a deep sound produced by hard breathing: *moan* is a plaintive, long-drawn sound produced by the organs of utterance. The *groan* proceeds involuntarily as an expression of severe pain, either of body or of mind: the *moan* proceeds often from the desire of awakening attention or exciting compassion. Dying *groans* are uttered in the agonies of death: the *moans* of a wounded sufferer are sometimes the only resource he has left to make his destitute case known.

GROSS, COARSE. *Gross* comes from Latin *grossus,* thick, fat. *Coarse* (see COARSE).

These terms are synonymous in the moral application. *Grossness* of habit is opposed to delicacy; *coarseness* to softness and refinement. A person becomes *gross* by an unrestrained indulgence of his sensual appetites, particularly in eating and drinking; he is *coarse* from the want of polish as to either his mind or his manners. A *gross* sensualist approximates very nearly to the brute; he sets aside all moral considerations; he indulges himself in the open face of day in defiance of all decency: a *coarse* person approaches nearest to the savage, whose roughness of humor and inclination has not been refined down by habits of restraining his own will and complying with the will of another. A *gross* expression conveys the idea of that which should be kept from the view of the mind which shocks the moral feeling; a *coarse* expression conveys the idea of an unseemly sentiment in the mind of the speaker. The representations of the Deity by any sensible image is *gross,* because it gives us a low and grovelling idea of a superior being; the doing a kindness, and making the receiver at the same time sensible of your superiority and his dependence, indicates great *coarseness* in the character of the favorer.

Gross, Total.—From the idea of size which enters into the original meaning of *gross* is derived that of quantity. *Total,* from the Latin *totus,* signifies literally the whole: the *gross* implies that from which nothing has been taken: the *total* signifies that to which nothing need be added: the *gross* sum includes everything without regard to what it may be; the *total* includes everything which one wishes to include; we may, therefore, deduct from the *gross* that which does not immediately belong to it; but the *total* is that which admits of no deduction. The *gross* weight in trade is applicable to any article the whole of which, good or bad, pure or dross, is included in opposition to the net weight; the *total* amount supposes all to be included which ought to form a part, in opposition to any smaller amount or subdivisions; when employed in the improper sense, they preserve the same distinction: things are said to be taken or considered in the *gross,* that is, in the large and comprehensive way, one with another; things are said to undergo a *total* change.

GROUND. See FOUND.

GROUP. See ASSEMBLY.

GROW. See BE; INCREASE.

GRUDGE. See MALICE.

GUARANTEE, BE SECURITY, BE RESPONSIBLE, WARRANT. *Guarantee* and *warrant* are both derived from Old High German *werent,* present participle of *weren,* to certify to, to warrant; *security,* from *secure* (see CERTAIN), has the same original meaning; *responsible* (see AMENABLE).

To *guarantee* and *be security* have respect to what is done for others; to *be responsible* respects what is done by one's self or others; to *warrant,* what is done by one's self only. To *guarantee* is applied to matters of public or private interest; to *be security,* to private matters only. The larger governments frequently *guarantee* for the performance of stipulations entered into by minor powers; one man becomes *security* to another for the payment of a sum of money by a third person. *Guarantee* may be taken for the person or thing that guarantees.

One is *security* for another in pecuniary concerns, but he is *responsible* for his own conduct or that of others; he becomes a *security* by virtue of his contract, as one tradesman becomes *security* for another—he is *responsible* by virtue of his relative office or situation; masters are *responsible* for the conduct of their servants; a jailer is *responsible* for the safe custody of the prisoner; every man is *responsible* for that which is placed under his charge. To *warrant* is applied to commercial transactions: one *warrants* the goodness of any commodity that is sold.

The *warrant* serves to indemnify against loss, or, in a moral sense, to protect against censure, to give a sanction to.

GUARD, DEFEND, WATCH. *Guard* comes from Anglo-Saxon *weardian,* to watch, the *gu* being due to French influence. *Defend* (see APOLOGIZE and DEFEND). *Watch* and *wake* come from Anglo-Saxon *wacan,* to wake.

To *guard,* in its largest sense, comprehends both *watching* and *defending,* that is, both the preventing the attack and the resisting it when it is made. In the restricted sense, to *guard* is properly to keep off an enemy; to *defend* is to drive him away when he makes the attack. The soldier *guards* the palace of the king in time of peace, and *defends* his country in time of war.

Watch, like *guard,* consists in looking to the danger, but it does not necessarily imply the use of any means to prevent the danger: he who *watches* may only give an alarm.

In the improper application they have a similar sense: modesty *guards* female honor; clothing *defends* against the inclemency of the weather: a person who wants to escape *watches* his opportunity to slip out unobserved.

See also FENCE.

Guard, Sentinel.—These terms are used to designate those who are employed for the protection of either persons or things. *Guard* has been explained above. *Sentinel,* in French *sentinelle,* Italian *sentinella,* a watch, possibly from *Latin sentire,* to perceive, signifies a military *guard* in the time of a campaign; any one may be set as *guard* over property, who is empowered to keep off every intruder by force; but the *sentinel* acts in the army as the watch in the police, rather to observe the motions of the enemy than to repel any force.

They are figuratively applied to other objects; the *guard* in this case acts on ordinary occasions, the *sentinel* in the moments of danger.

Guard, Guardian.—These words are derived from the verb *guard;* but they have acquired a distinct office. *Guard* is used either in the literal or figurative sense; *guardian* only in the improper sense. *Guard* is applied either to persons or to things; *guardian* only to persons. In application to persons, the *guard* is temporary; the *guardian* is fixed and permanent: the *guard* only *guards* against external evils; the *guardian* takes upon him the office of parent, counsellor, and director: when a house is in danger of being attacked, a person may sit up as a *guard;* when a parent is dead, a *guardian* supplies his place: we expect from a *guard* nothing but human assistance; but from our *guardian* angel we may expect supernatural assistance.

Guard Against, Take Heed. — Both these terms imply express care on the part of the agent; but the former is used with regard to external or internal evils, the latter only with regard to internal or mental evils: in an enemy's country it is essential to be particularly on one's *guard,* for fear of a surprise; in difficult matters, where we are liable to err, it is of importance to *take heed* lest we run from one extreme to another: young men, on their entrance into life, cannot be too much on their *guard against* associating with those who would lead them into expensive pleasures; in slippery paths, whether physically or morally understood, it is necessary to *take heed* how we go.

GUARDIAN. See GUARD.

GUESS, CONJECTURE, DIVINE. *Guess* is a Scandinavian word. *Conjecture* (see that word). *Divine*, from the Latin *divinus* and *deus*, a god, signifies to think and know as a god.

We *guess* that a thing actually is; we *conjecture* that which may be; we *guess* that it is a certain hour; we *conjecture* as to the meaning of a person's actions. *Guessing* is opposed to the certain knowledge of a thing; *conjecturing* is opposed to the full conviction of a thing: a child *guesses* at that portion of his lesson which he has not properly learned; a fanciful person employs *conjecture* where he cannot draw any positive conclusion.

To *guess* and *conjecture* are natural acts of the mind: to *divine*, in its proper sense, is a supernatural act; in this sense the heathens affected to *divine* that which was known only to an Omniscient Being; and impostors in our time presume to *divine* in matters that are set above the reach of human comprehension. The term is, however, employed to denote a species of *guessing* in different matters, as to *divine* the meaning of a mystery.

GUEST, VISITOR, VISITANT. *Guest* is a Scandinavian word from the same root as Latin *hostes*, signifying a stranger or an enemy; *visitor* or *visitant* is the one who pays the visit. The *guest* is to the *visitor* as the species to the genus: every *guest* is a *visitor*, but every *visitor* is not a *guest;* the *visitor* simply comes to see the person and enjoy social intercourse; but the *guest* also partakes of hospitality: we are *visitors* at the tea-table, at the card-table, and round the fire; we are *guests* at the festive board.

GUIDE, RULE. *Guide* is to *rule* as the genus to the species: every *rule* is a *guide* to a certain extent; but the *guide* is often that which exceeds the *rule*. The *guide*, in the moral sense, as in the proper sense, goes with us and points out the exact path; it does not permit us to err either to the right or left: the *rule* marks out a line beyond which we may not go; but it leaves us to trace the line, and consequently to fail either on the one side or on the other. The Bible is our best *guide* for moral practice; its doctrines, as interpreted in the articles of the Christian Church, are the best *rule* of faith.

See also CHAPERON; LEAD; SYLLABUS.

GUILE. See DECEIT.

GUILTLESS, INNOCENT, HARMLESS. *Guiltless*, without *guilt*, is more than *innocent: innocence*, from *nocere*, to hurt, extends no further than the quality of not hurting by any direct act; *guiltless* comprehends the quality of not intending to hurt: it is possible, therefore, to be *innocent* without being *guiltless*, though not *vice versâ;* he who wishes for the death of another is not *guiltless*, though he may be *innocent* of the crime of murder. *Guiltless* seems to regard a man's general condition, *innocent* his particular condition: no man is *guiltless* in the sight of God, for no man is exempt from the guilt of sin; but he may be *innocent* in the sight of men, or *innocent* of all such intentional offences as render him obnoxious to his fellow-creatures. *Guiltlessness* was that happy state of perfection which men lost at the fall; *innocence* is that relative or comparative state of perfection which is attainable here on earth: the highest state of *innocence* is an ignorance of evil.

Guiltless is in the proper sense applicable only to the condition of man, and, when applied to things, it still has a reference to the person: *innocent* is equally applicable to persons or things; a person is *innocent* who has not committed any injury or has not any direct purpose to commit any injury; or a conversation is *innocent* which is free from what is hurtful. *Innocent* and *harmless* both recommend themselves as qualities negatively good; they designate a freedom either in the person or in the thing from injuring, and differ only in regard to the nature of the injury: *innocence* respects moral injury, and *harmless* physical injury: a person is *innocent* who is free from moral impurity and wicked purposes; he is *harmless* if he have not the power or disposition to commit any violence; a diversion is *innocent* which has nothing in it likely to corrupt the morals; a game is *harmless* which is not likely to inflict any wound or endanger the health.

GUILTY. See CRIMINAL.

GUISE, HABIT. *Guise* is the French form of English *wise*, both from a Teutonic root, and both signifying the manner. *Habit*, from the Latin *habitus*, a habit, fashion, or form, is taken for a settled or permanent mode of dress.

The *guise* is that which is unusual and often only occasional; the *habit* is that which is usual among particular classes: a person sometimes assumes the *guise* of a peasant, in order the better to conceal himself; he who devotes himself to the clerical profession puts on the *habit* of a clergyman.

GULF, ABYSS. *Gulf*, French *golfe*, Italian *golfo*, comes from Greek κόλπος, hollow, and is applied literally in the sense of a deep concave receptacle for water, as the *gulf* of Venice, *gulf* of Mexico, etc. *Abyss*, in Greek ἄβυσσος, compounded of ἀ- and βυσσός, a bottom, signifies literally a bottomless pit.

One is overwhelmed in a *gulf;* it carries with it the idea of liquidity and profundity, into which one inevitably sinks never to rise: one is lost in an *abyss;* it carries with it the idea of immense profundity, into which he who is cast never reaches a bottom, nor is able to return to the top; an insatiable voracity is the characteristic idea in the signification of this term.

A *gulf* is a capacious bosom, which holds within itself and buries all objects that suffer themselves to sink into it, without allowing them the possibility of escape; hell is represented as a fiery *gulf*, into which evil spirits are plunged, and remain perpetually overwhelmed: a guilty mind may be said, figuratively, to be plunged into a *gulf* of woe or despair when filled with the horrid sense of its enormities. An *abyss* presents nothing but an interminable space which has neither beginning nor end; he does wisely who does not venture in, or who retreats before he has plunged too deep to retrace his footsteps; as the ocean, in the natural sense, is a great *abyss*, so are metaphysics an immense *abyss* into which the human mind precipitates itself only to be bewildered.

GUMPTION, ACUTENESS, CLEVERNESS, DISCERNMENT, SHREWDNESS. *Gumption* is a Scandinavian word. The term is one of colloquial usage, implying, as a substantive, a quickness of perception, the possession of much common sense, and, in painting, the art of preparing colors. We say that a person is possessed of *gumption* who exhibits a quick-acting intellectuality, who perceives the drift, heart, spirit, of things speedily, whose mental activities evidence sharpness, keenness, *acuteness*.

Cleverness expresses more than *acuteness*, for it is that state or quality which enables its possessor to exercise a special skill or ability on certain lines, to be dexterous, expert, handy, adroit, to act expeditiously and efficiently with mind and body, and in intercourse with his fellow-men to be good-natured and obliging. *Shrewdness*, in a proper sense, implies sagacity, ingenuity, intelligence, "mother-wit," and cleverness in practical matters; in an improper sense, craftiness, cunning, slyness, depravity, and iniquity.

Discernment is an act of perception, an acuteness or sharpness in judgment, a penetrative ability, and, specifically, the quality of discrimination, the mental condition of being able to weigh, analyze, segregate, and classify objects so that each may be considered by itself, and the relation of a part to the whole may be clearly determined.

GUSH. See FLOW.

GUSTO. See ZEST.

GYROPLANE. See AIRCRAFT.

H

HABIT. See CUSTOM; GUISE.
HABITATION. See DOMICILE.
HACKNEYED. See TRITE.
HAGGARD, GAUNT. These words signify a wasted appearance. *Haggard* originally was applied to a hawk "that preyed for herself long before she was taken," and meant wild. It was applied to a person with special reference to a wild look in the eyes, but its meaning has been distinctly influenced by the resemblance in form to *hag*, so that it came to signify *hag-like*. It differs from *gaunt*, an East Anglian word meaning lean, in referring primarily to the wasted appearance of the face, especially the hollows under the eyes caused by illness or weariness. *Gaunt* refers both to the whole face and the whole figure. It means thin, angular, bony, with hollows where rounded flesh would naturally be. *Haggard* is always an abnormal condition caused by illness or some physical or emotional strain. *Gaunt* may apply under the same conditions, but it may also indicate the usual or normal appearance of an individual.

HAIL. See ACCOST.
HALE. See DRAW.
HALLOW. See DEDICATE; SANCTIFY.
HALLUCINATION, ABERRATION, DELUSION. *Hallucination*, in French the same form, from the Latin *hallucinatio*, that from *hallucinor*, to wander in the mind, signifies, in common language, a perception without a real object to be perceived, an erroneous or insane belief in the reality of things which have no existence. Specifically, the term implies a morbid condition of the mind in which a perception of something occurs where no impression has been made upon the external organs of the special senses, yet where the object is believed to be real and existent.

In a sense this state is a *delusion*, but *delusion* differs from *hallucination* in that it originates at the other extremity of the chain of consciousness in the mind itself, and consists of erroneous interpretations of real sensations. Thus we recognize in another an aberration, a departure from a customary course, a wandering from fact to fancy; a fallacy in a deceptive or false appearance, in an unsound method of reasoning; a phantasm, a vision of something that does not exist, a spectre that appears visible to the victim only. A victim of *hallucination* imagines that which is wholly erroneous, non-existent, but believes implicitly that it is real.

An *aberration*, from Latin *ab*, away, and *errare*, to wander, means a wandering out of the accustomed or normal course, with reference both to thought and to conduct. As applied to the activity of the mind, it differs from *hallucination* and *delusion* in emphasizing not the false vision or interpretation, but the abnormal action of the mind itself.

HANDLE. See WIELD.
HANDSOME. See BEAUTIFUL.
HANKER. See DESIRE.
HAPLESS, ILL-FATED, LUCKLESS. *Hapless* is a negative of *hap*, a Scandinavian word signifying good luck, whence *happy, happen,* etc., are derived. *Hapless*, accordingly, implies the condition that is contrary to the *hap* events—hence, misfortune and its attendant vicissitudes.

We say that a person is *ill-fated* who seems destined to misfortune. This is the strongest of the above group of terms, for it implies the recognition of a condition in which a person may have been born or one into which he has fallen, and from which apparently he cannot extricate himself—a condition to which he was doomed at birth and in which he remains through life. *Luckless*, on the contrary, implies a condition that may be similar to *ill-fated*, but in the most common usage it suggests not a permanent, but a temporary misfortune, as a venture may be *luckless* that is without an anticipated advantage; some proceedings out of many may be unfortunate in their results, while the others may turn out according to our desires.

HAPPEN, CHANCE. To *happen*, that is, to fall out by a *hap*, is to *chance* as the genus to the species; whatever *chances happens*, but not *vice versâ*. *Happen* respects all events, without including any collateral idea; *chance* comprehends likewise the idea of the cause and order of events: whatever comes to pass *happens*, whether regularly in the course of things or particularly and out of the order; whatever *chances happens*, altogether without concert, intention, and often without relation to any other thing. Accidents *happen* daily which no human foresight could prevent; the newspapers contain an account of all that *happens* in the course of the day or week: listeners and busybodies are ready to catch every word that *chances* to fall in their hearing.

HAPPINESS, FELICITY, BLESSEDNESS, BEATITUDE, BLISS. *Happiness* signifies the state of being *happy*. *Felicity* comes from Latin *felicitas*, happiness. *Bliss* is in Anglo-Saxon *bliths*, happiness, literally *blitheness*, from Anglo-Saxon *blithe*, English *blithe*. The original sense of *blessedness* may have been to consecrate with blood, either by sacrifice or the sprinkling of blood, as the word can be clearly traced back to *blood;* hence it may have meant to be consecrated, holy; then simply *happiness*. It retains a religious suggestion still. *Beatitude*, from the Latin *beatus*, signifies the property of being *happy* in a superior degree.

Happiness comprehends that aggregate of pleasurable sensations which we derive from external objects. It is the ordinary term which is employed alike in the colloquial or the philosophical style: *felicity* is a higher expression, comprehending inward enjoyment, or an aggregate of inward pleasure, without regard to the source whence either is derived: *bliss* is a still higher term, expressing more than either *happiness* or *felicity*, both as to the degree and nature of the enjoyment. *Happiness* is the thing adapted to our present condition and to the nature of our being, as a compound of body and soul; it is impure in its nature and variable in degree; it is sought for by various means and with great eagerness; but it often lies much more within our reach than we are apt to imagine: it is not to be found in the possession of great wealth, of great power, of great dominions, of great splendor, or the unbounded indulgences of any one appetite or desire; but in moderate possessions with a heart tempered by religion and virtue for the enjoyment of that which God has bestowed upon us: it is, therefore, not so unequally distributed as some have been led to conclude.

Happiness admits of degrees, since every individual is placed in different circumstances, either of body or of mind, which fit him to be more or less *happy*. *Felicity* is not regarded in the same light; it is that which is positive and independent of all circumstances: domestic *felicity* and conjugal *felicity* are regarded as moral enjoyments, abstracted from everything which can serve as an alloy. *Bliss* is that which is purely spiritual; it has its source in the imagination and rises above the ordinary level of human enjoyments: of earthly *bliss* little is known but in poetry; of heavenly *bliss* we form but an imperfect conception from the utmost stretch of our powers. *Blessedness* is a term of spiritual import, which refers to the *happy* condition of those who enjoy the Divine favor, and are permitted to have a foretaste of heavenly *bliss* by the exaltation of their minds above earthly *happiness*. *Beatitude* denotes the quality of *happiness* only which is most exalted, namely, heavenly *happiness*.

See also WELL-BEING.

Happy, Fortunate.—*Happy* and *fortunate* are both applied to the external circumstances of a man; but the former conveys the idea of that which is abstractly good, the latter implies rather what is agreeable to one's wishes. A man is *happy* in his marriage, in his children, in his connections, and the like: he is *fortunate* in his trading concerns. *Happy* excludes the idea of chance; *fortunate* excludes the idea of personal effort: a man is *happy* in the possession of what he gets; he is *fortunate* in getting it.

In another sense, they bear a similar analogy. A *happy* thought, a *happy* expression, a *happy* turn, a *happy* event, and the like, denote a degree of positive excellence; a *fortunate* idea, a *fortunate* circumstance, a *fortunate* event, are all relatively considered with regard to the wishes and views of the individual.

HARANGUE. See ADDRESS.

HARASS. See DISTRESS; WEARY; WORRY.

HARBINGER. See FORERUNNER.

HARBOR, HAVEN, PORT. The idea of a resting-place for vessels is common to these terms, of which *harbor* is general and the two others specific in their significance. *Harbor* is Scandinavian, from Icelandic *herbergi*, a shelter for an army, compounded of *heri*, army, German *heer*, and *bergen*, to hide; it carries with it little more than the common idea of affording a resting or anchoring place. *Haven* is also a Scandinavian word possibly allied to Anglo-Saxon *heaf*, sea. *Port*, from the Latin *portus*, a harbor, allied to *porta*, a gate, and to English *ford*, conveys the idea of an enclosure. A *haven* is a natural *harbor;* a *port* is an artificial *harbor.* We characterize a *harbor* as commodious, a *haven* as snug and secure; a *port* as safe and easy of access. A commercial country profits by the excellence and number of its *harbors;* it values itself on the security of its *havens,* and increases the number of its *ports* accordingly. A vessel goes into a *harbor* only for a season; it remains in a *haven* for a permanency; it seeks a *port* as the destination of its voyage. Merchantmen are perpetually going in and out of a *harbor;* a distressed vessel, at a distance from home, seeks some *haven* in which it may winter; the weary mariner looks to the *port*, not as the termination of his labor, but as the commencement of all his enjoyments.

Harbor, Shelter, Lodge.—The idea of giving a resting-place is common to these terms; but *harbor* (see FOSTER) is used mostly in a bad sense, *shelter* (see ASYLUM) in an indefinite sense;

lodge, Old French *loge,* Italian *loggia,* comes from Old High German *loube,* an arbor, from *loub,* a leaf—an arbor being a leafy shelter. *Lobby* is a doublet of *lodge.* One *harbors* that which ought not to find room anywhere; one *shelters* that which cannot find security elsewhere; one *lodges* that which wants a resting-place. Thieves, traitors, conspirators, are *harbored* by those who have an interest in securing them from detection: either the wicked or the unfortunate may be *sheltered* from the evil with which they are threatened: travellers are *lodged* as occasion may require.

As the word *harbor* does not, in its original sense, mean anything more than affording a temporary entertainment, it may be taken in a good sense for an act of hospitality.

Harbor and *shelter* are said of things in the sense of giving a harbor or shelter; *lodge* in the sense of being a resting-place: furniture *harbors* vermin, trees *shelter* from the rain, a ball *lodges* in the breast; so in the moral sense a man *harbors* resentment, ill-will, evil thoughts, and the like; he *shelters* himself from a charge by retorting it upon his adversary; or a particular passion may be *lodged* in the breast or ideas *lodged* in the mind.

HARD, FIRM, SOLID. The close adherence of the component parts of a body constitutes *hardness*. The close adherence of different bodies to one another constitutes *firmness* (see FIXED). That is *hard* which will not yield to a closer compression; that is *firm* which will not yield so as to produce a separation. Ice is *hard*, as far as it respects itself, when it resists every pressure; it is *firm*, with regard to the water which it covers, when it is so closely bound as to resist every weight without breaking.

Hard and *solid* respect the internal constitution of bodies and the adherence of the component parts; but *hard* denotes a much closer degree of adherence than *solid:* the *hard* is opposed to the soft; the *solid* to the fluid; every *hard* body is by nature *solid;* although every *solid* body is not *hard.* Wood is always a *solid* body, but it is sometimes *hard* and sometimes soft; water, when congealed, is a *solid* body, and admits of different degrees of *hardness.*

In another application, *hardness* is allied to insensibility; *firmness* to fixedness; *solidity* to substantiality; a *hard* man is not to be acted upon by any tender motives; a *firm* man is not to be turned from his purpose; a *solid* man holds no purposes that are not well-founded. A man is *hardened* in that which is bad by being made insensible to that which is good; a man is *confirmed* in anything good or bad by being rendered less disposed to lay it aside; his mind is *consolidated* by acquiring fresh motives for action.

Hard, Callous, Hardened, Obdurate.— *Hard* is here, as in the former case, the general term, and the rest particular: *hard*, in its most extensive physical sense, denotes the property of resisting the action of external force, so as not to undergo any change in its form or separation in its parts: *callous* is that species of the *hard*, in application to the skin, which arises from its dryness and the absence of all nervous susceptibility. *Hard* and *callous*, from Latin *callosus*, thick-skinned, are likewise applied in the moral sense: but *hard* denotes the absence of tender feeling, or the property of resisting any impression which tender objects are apt to produce; *callous* denotes the property of not yielding to the force of motives to action. A *hard* heart cannot be moved by the sight of misery, let it be presented in ever so affecting a form: a *callous* mind is not to be touched by any persuasions, however powerful. *Hard* does not designate any circumstance of its existence or origin: we may be *hard* from a variety of causes; but *callousness* arises from the indulgence of vices, passions, and the pursuit of vicious practices. When we speak of a person as *hard*, it simply determines what he is: if we speak of him as *callous*, it refers also to what he was, and from what he is become so.

Callous, hardened, and *obdurate* are all employed to designate a morally depraved character; but *callousness* belongs properly to the heart and conscience; *hardened*, to both the heart and the understanding; *obdurate*, more particularly to the will. *Callousness* is the first stage of *hardness* in moral depravity; it may exist in the infant mind, on its first tasting the poisonous pleasures of vice, without being acquainted with its remote consequences. A *hardened* state is the work of time; it arises from a continued course of vice, which becomes, as it were, habitual, and wholly unfits a person for admitting any other impressions; *obduracy* is the last stage of moral *hardness*, which supposes the whole mind to be obstinately bent on vice. A child discovers himself to be *callous* when the entreaties, threats, or punishments of a parent cannot awaken in him a single sentiment of contrition; a youth discovers himself to be *hardened* when he begins to take a pride and a pleasure in a vicious career; a man shows himself to be *obdurate* when he betrays a settled and confirmed purpose to pursue his abandoned course without regard to consequences.

Hard, Hardy, Insensible, Unfeeling. —*Hard* may be applied to either that which makes resistance to external impressions or that which presses with a force upon other objects. *Hardy*, which is only a variation of *hard*, is applicable only in the first case: thus, a person's skin may be *hard* which is not easily acted upon; but the person is said to be *hardy* who can withstand the elements: on the other hand, *hard*, when employed as an active principle, is only applied to the moral character; hence the difference between a *hardy* man who endures everything and a *hard* man who makes others endure.

Insensible and *unfeeling* are but modes of the *hard;* that is, they designate the negative quality of *hardness*, or its incapacity to receive impression: *hard*, therefore, is always the strongest term of the three; and of the two others *unfeeling* is stronger than *insensible*. *Hard* and *insensible* are applied physically and morally; *unfeeling* is employed only as a moral characteristic. A horse's mouth is *hard* when it is insensible to the action of the bit; a man's heart is *hard* which is insensible to the miseries of others; a man is *unfeeling* who does not regard the feelings of others. The heart may be *hard* by nature, or rendered so by the influence of some passion; but a person is commonly *unfeeling* from circumstances. Shylock is depicted by Shakespeare as *hard*, from his strong antipathy to the Christians: people who enjoy an uninterrupted state of good health are often *unfeeling* in cases of sickness. As that which is *hard* mostly hurts or pains when it comes in contact with the soft, the term *hard* is peculiarly applicable to superiors or such as have power to inflict pain: a creditor may be *hard* toward a debtor. As *insensible* signifies a want of sense, it may be sometimes necessary: a surgeon, when performing an operation, must be *insensible* to the present pain which he inflicts. As *unfeeling* signifies a want of feeling, it is always taken for a want of good feeling: where the removal of pain is required, the surgeon shows himself to be *unfeeling* who does not do everything in his power to lessen the pain of the sufferer.

Hard, Difficult, Arduous.—*Hard* is here taken in the sense of causing trouble and requiring pains, in which sense it is a much stronger term than *difficult*, which, from the Latin *difficilis*, compounded of the privative *dis* and *facilis*, signifies merely not easy. *Hard* is therefore positive, and *difficult* negative. A *difficult* task cannot be got through with without exertion, but a *hard* task requires great exertion. *Difficult* is applicable to all trivial matters which call for a more than usual portion either of labor or thought; *hard* is applicable to those which are of the highest importance and accompanied with circumstances that call for the utmost stretch of every power. It is a *difficult* matter to get admittance into some circles of society that are select: it is *difficult* to decide between two fine paintings which is the finer; it is a *hard* matter to come to any conclusion on metaphysical subjects. A child mostly finds it *difficult* to learn his letters; there are many passages in classical writers which are *hard* to be understood by the learned.

Arduous, from the Latin *arduus,* lofty, signifying set at a distance or out of reach, expresses more than either *hard* or *difficult.* What is *difficult* may be conquered by labor and perseverance without any particular degree of talent; but what is *arduous* cannot be effected without great mental powers and accomplishments. What is *difficult* is so in various degrees, according to circumstances; that which is *difficult* to one person may be less so to another; but that which is *arduous* is difficult in a high degree, and positively *difficult* under every circumstance.

See also HERCULEAN.

Hard - hearted, Cruel, Unmerciful, Merciless.—*Hard-hearted* signifies having a hard heart, or a heart not to be moved by the pains of others. *Cruel,* in Latin *crudelis,* allied to *crudus,* raw flesh, and *cruor,* blood, that is, delighting in blood like beasts of prey, signifies ready to inflict pain: as a temper of mind, therefore, *cruel* expresses much more than *hard-hearted;* the latter denotes the want of that sensibility toward others which ought to be the property of every human heart; the former, the positive inclination to inflict pain and the pleasure from so doing. *Hard-hearted* is employed as an epith t of the person; *cruel,* as an epithet to things as well as persons; as a *cruel* man, a *cruel* action. *Hard-hearted* respec s solely the moral affections; *cruelty,* in its proper sense, respects the infliction of corporeal pains, but is extended in its application to whatever creates moral pains: a person may be *cruel,* too, in his treatment of children or brutes by beating or starving them; or he may be *cruel* toward those who look up to him for kindness.

The *unmerciful* and *merciless* are both modes of characteristics of the *hard-hearted.* An *unmerciful* man is *hard-hearted,* inasmuch as he is unwilling to extend his compassion or mercy to one who is in his power; a *merciless* man, which is more than an *unmerciful* man, is *hard-hearted,* inasmuch as he is restrained by no compunctious feelings from inflicting pain on those who are in his power. Avarice makes a man *hard-hearted* even to those who are bound to him by the closest ties; it makes him *unmerciful* to those who are in his debt. There are many *merciless* tyrants in domestic life, who show their dispositions by their *merciless* treatment of their poor brutes.

Hardly, Scarcely.—What is *hard* is not common, and in that respect *scarce:* hence the idea of unfrequency assimilates those terms both in signification and application. In many cases they may be used indifferently; but where the idea of practicability predominates *hardly* seems most proper; and where the idea of frequency predominates *scarcely* seems preferable. One can *hardly* judge of a person's features by a single and partial glance; we *scarcely* ever see men lay aside their vices from a thorough conviction of their enormity: but it may with equal propriety be said in general sentences, *hardly* one in a thousand, or *scarcely* one in a thousand, would form such a conclusion.

HARDIHOOD. See AUDACITY.

HARDINESS. See AUDACITY.

HARDSHIP. See GRIEVANCE.

HARLEQUIN. See ZANY.

HARM. See EVIL; INJURY; SCATHE.

HARMLESS. See GUILTLESS.

HARMONIOUS. See EUPHONIOUS.

HARMONY. See CONCORD; MELODY.

HARSH, ROUGH, SEVERE, RIGOROUS. *Harsh* (see ACRIMONY) and *rough* (see ABRUPT) borrow their moral signification from the physical properties of the bodies to which they belong. The *harsh* and the *rough* both act painfully upon the taste, but the former with much more violence than the latter. An excess of the sour mingled with other unpleasant properties constitutes *harshness:* an excess of astringency constitutes *roughness.* Cheese is said to be *harsh* when it is dry and biting: *roughness* is the peculiar quality of the damascene. From this physical distinction between these terms we discover the ground of their moral application. *Harshness* in a person's conduct acts upon the feelings and does violence to the affections: *roughness* acts only externally on the senses: we may be *rough* in the tone of the voice, in the mode of address, or in the manner of handling or touching an object; but we are *harsh* in the sentiment we convey and according to the persons to whom it is conveyed: a stranger may be *rough* when he has it in his power to be so: only a friend or one in the tenderest relation can be *harsh.*

Severe (see AUSTERE). *Rigorous,* from the Latin *rigor* and *rigere,* to stiffen, designates unbending, inflexible. These terms mark different modes of treating those that are in one's power, all of which are the reverse of the kind. *Harsh* and *rough* are epithets of that which is unamiable: they indicate the *harshness* and *roughness* of the humor: *severity* and *rigor* are not always to be condemned; they spring from principle, and are often resorted to by necessity. *Harshness* is always mingled with anger and personal feeling: *severity* and *rigor* characterize things more than the temper of persons. A *harsh* master renders every burden which he imposes doubly *severe* by the grating manner in which he communicates his will: a *severe* master simply imposes the burden in a manner to enforce obedience. The one seems to indulge himself in inflicting pain: the other seems to act from a motive that is independent of the pain inflicted. A *harsh* man is therefore always *severe,* but with injustice: a *severe* man, however, is not always *harsh. Rigor* is a high degree of *severity.* One is *severe* in the punishment of offences: one is *rigorous* in exacting compliance and obedience. *Severity* is always more or less necessary in the army, or in a school, for the preservation of good order: *rigor* is essential in dealing with the stubborn will and unruly passions of men.

HARSHNESS. See ACRIMONY.

HASTEN, ACCELERATE, SPEED, EXPEDITE, DESPATCH. *Hasten* comes from Anglo-Saxon *hœst,* Modern English *haste,* meaning originally violence. Old French *haste* is from the same Teutonic root. *Accelerate,* from *celer,* quick, signifies literally to quicken for a specific purpose. *Speed,* from Anglo-Saxon *spowan,* to succeed, meant originally to increase, to become prosperous —whence the phrase, *speed* the parting guest. *Expedite* (see DILIGENT). *Despatch* comes from Spanish *despachar,* from Latin *dis,* away, and a root found in the past participle *pactus,* from *pangere,* to fix.

Quickness in movement and action is the common idea of all these terms, which vary in the nature of the movement and the action. To *hasten* expresses little more than the general idea of quickness in moving toward a point; thus, he *hastens* who runs to get to the end of his journey: *accelerate* expresses, moreover, the idea of bringing something to a point; thus, every mechanical business is *accelerated* by the order and distribution of its several parts. It may be employed, like the word *hasten*, for corporeal and familiar actions: a tailor *accelerates* any particular work that he has in hand by putting on additional hands; or a compositor *accelerates* the printing of a work by doing his part with correctness. The word *speed* includes not only quick, but forward movement. He who goes with *speed* goes effectually forward, and comes to his journey's end the sooner. This idea is excluded from the term *haste*, which may often be a planless, unsuitable quickness. Hence the proverb, "The more *haste* the worse *speed*."

Expedite and *despatch* are terms of higher import, in application to the most serious concerns in life; but to *expedite* expresses a process, a bringing forward toward an end: *despatch* implies a putting an end to, a making a clearance. We do everything in our power to *expedite* a business: we *despatch* a great deal of business within a given time. *Expedition* is requisite for one who executes; *despatch* is most important for one who determines and directs. An inferior officer must proceed with *expedition* to fulfil the orders or execute the purposes of his commander; a general or minister of state *despatches* the concerns of planning, directing, and instructing. Hence it is we speak only of *expediting* a thing; but we may speak of *despatching* a person as well as a thing.

Hasten, Hurry.—*Hasten* (see above). *Hurry* is a word of imitative origin, indicating the sound of swift movement.

To *hasten* and *hurry* both imply to move forward with quickness in any matter; but the former may proceed with some design and good order, but the latter always supposes perturbation and irregularity. We *hasten* in the communication of good news when we make efforts to convey it in the shortest time possible; we *hurry* to get to an end when we impatiently and inconsiderately press forward without making choice of our means. To *hasten* is

opposed to delay, or a dilatory mode of proceeding; it is frequently indispensable to *hasten* in the affairs of human life: to *hurry* is opposed to deliberate and cautious proceeding: it must always be prejudicial, and unwise to *hurry;* men may *hasten;* children *hurry.*

As epithets, *hasty* and *hurried* are both employed in another sense; but *hasty* implies merely an overquickness of motion which outstrips consideration; *hurried* implies a disorderly motion which springs from a distempered state of mind. Irritable people use *hasty* expressions; they speak before they think: deranged people walk with *hurried* steps; they follow the blind impulse of undirected feeling.

HASTINESS. See RASHNESS.

HASTY. See ANGRY; CURSORY; SUDDEN.

HATE, DETEST. The alliance between these terms in signification is sufficiently illustrated in the articles referred to. Their difference consists more in sense than application. To *hate* (see ANTIPATHY) is a personal feeling directed toward the object independently of its qualities; to *detest* (see ABHOR) is a feeling independent of the person, and altogether dependent upon the nature of the thing. What one *hates* one *hates* commonly on one's own account; what one *detests* one *detests* on account of the object: hence it is that one *hates*, but not *detests*, the person who has done an injury to one's self; and that one *detests*, rather than *hates*, the person who has done injuries to others. Joseph's brethren *hated* him because he was more beloved than they; we *detest* a traitor to his country because of the enormity of his offence.

In this connection to *hate* is always a bad passion: to *detest* always laudable; but, when both are applied to inanimate objects, to *hate* is bad or good, according to circumstances; to *detest* always retains its good meaning. When men *hate* things because they interfere with their indulgences, as the wicked *hate* the light, it is a bad personal feeling, as in the former case, but when good men are said to *hate* that which is bad it is a laudable feeling, justified by the nature of the object. As this feeling is, however, so closely allied to *detest*, it is necessary further to observe that *hate*, whether rightly or wrongly applied, seeks the injury or destruction of the object: but *detest* is confined simply to the shunning of the object, or thinking of it with very great pain. God *hates* sin, and on that account punishes sinners; conscientious men *detest* all fraud, and therefore cautiously avoid being concerned in it.

Hateful, Odious.—*Hateful* signifies, literally, full of that which is apt to excite *hatred*. *Odious*, from the Latin *odi*, I hate, has the same sense originally.

These epithets are employed in regard to such objects as produce strong aversion in the mind; but when employed, as they commonly are, upon familiar subjects, they indicate an unbecoming vehemence in the speaker. *Hateful* is properly applied to whatever violates general principles of morality; lying and swearing are *hateful* vices; *odious* is more commonly applied to such things as affect the interests of others and bring *odium* upon the individual; a tax that bears particularly hard and unequally is termed *odious*, or a measure of government that is oppressive is denominated *odious*.

Hatred, Enmity, Ill-will, Rancor.—These terms agree in this particular, that those who are under the influence of such feelings derive a pleasure from the misfortune of others; but *hatred* (see AVERSION) expresses more than *enmity* (see ENEMY), and this more than *ill-will*, which signifies either an evil will or a willing of evil. *Hatred* is not contented with merely wishing *ill* to others, but derives its whole happiness from their misery or destruction; *enmity*, on the contrary, is limited in its operations to particular circumstances: *hatred*, on the other hand, is frequently confined to the feeling of the individual; but *enmity* consists as much in the action as in the feeling. He who is possessed with *hatred* is happy when the object of his passion is miserable, and is miserable when he is happy; but the *hater* is not always instrumental in causing his misery or destroying his happiness: he who is inflamed with *enmity* is more active in disturbing the peace of his *enemy*, but

c.e.s.—14

oftener displays his temper in trifling than in important matters. *Ill-will*, as the word denotes, lies only in the mind, and is so indefinite in its signification that it admits of every conceivable degree. When the will is evilly directed toward another in ever so small a degree it constitutes *ill-will*. *Rancor* comes from Latin *rancius*, evil smelling.

HAUGHTINESS, DISDAIN, ARROGANCE. *Haughtiness* denotes the abstract quality of *haughty*, which comes from Old French *haut*, originally *halt*, from *altus*, high. It meant originally, "high and mighty." *Disdain* (see CONTEMN). *Arrogance* (see that word).

Haughtiness is founded on the high opinion we entertain of ourselves; *disdain*, on the low opinion we have of others; *arrogance* is the result of both, but, if anything, more of the former than the latter. *Haughtiness* and *disdain* are properly sentiments of the mind, and *arrogance* a mode of acting resulting from a state of mind: there may therefore be *haughtiness* and *disdain* which have not betrayed themselves by any visible action; but *arrogance* is always accompanied with its corresponding action: the *haughty* man is known by the air of superiority which he assumes; the *disdainful* man, by the contempt which he shows to others; the *arrogant* man, by his lofty pretensions. *Haughtiness* and *arrogance* are both vicious; they are built upon a false idea of ourselves; but *disdain* may be justifiable when provoked by what is infamous: a lady must treat with *disdain* the person who insults her honor.

See also PRIDE.

Haughty, High, High-minded.—*Haughty* and *high*, derived from the same source as *haughty*, characterize both the external behavior and the internal sentiment; *high-minded* marks the sentiment only, or the state of the mind. With regard to the outward behavior, *haughty* is a stronger term than *high;* a *haughty* carriage bespeaks not only a *high* opinion of one's self, but a strong mixture of contempt for others: a *high* carriage denotes simply a *high* opinion of one's self: *haughtiness* is therefore always offensive, as it is burdensome to others;

but *height* may sometimes be laudable, inasmuch as it is justice to one's self: one can never give a command in a *haughty* tone without making others feel their inferiority in a painful degree; we may sometimes assume a *high* tone in order to shelter ourselves from insult.

With regard to the sentiment of the mind, *haughty*, whether it shows itself in the outward behavior or rests in the mind, is always bad; *height* as an habitual temper, and still more *high-mindedness*, which more strongly marks the personal quality, are expressly inconsistent with Christian humility; but a man may with reason be too *high* or too *high-minded* to condescend to a mean action.

HAUL. See DRAW.

HAUNT. See FREQUENT.

HAVE, POSSESS. *Have* comes from Anglo-Saxon *habban*, a widely distributed Teutonic word. *Possess*, in Latin *possessus*, participle of *possideo*, compounded of Latin *pot*, as in *potes*, able, and *sedere*, to sit, means to remain master, to be able to keep.

Have is the general, *possess* is the particular term: *have* designates no circumstance of the action; *possess* expresses a particular species of having. To *have* is sometimes to have in one's hand or within one's reach; but to *possess* is to *have* as one's own; a clerk *has* the money which he has fetched for his employer; the latter *possesses* the money, which he *has* the power of turning to his use. To *have* is sometimes to *have* the right to, to belong; to *possess* is to *have* by one and at one's command: a debtor *has* the property which he has surrendered to his creditor; but he cannot be said to *possess* it, because he *has* it not within his reach and at his disposal: we are not necessarily masters of that which we *have;* although we always are of that which we *possess:* to *have* is sometimes only temporary; to *possess* is mostly permanent: we *have* money which we are perpetually disposing of: we *possess* lands which we keep for a permanency: a person *has* the good graces of those whom he pleases; he *possesses* the confidence of those who put everything in his power.

HAZARD, RISK, VENTURE, JEOP-
ARD. All these terms denote actions performed under an uncertainty of the event: but *hazard* (see CHANCE) bespeaks a want of design and choice on the part of the agent; to *risk* (see DANGER) implies a choice of alternatives; to *venture*, which is the same as *adventure* (see EVENT), signifies a calculation and balance of probabilities: one *hazards* and *risks* under the fear of an evil; one *ventures* with the hope of a good. He who *hazards* an opinion or an assertion does it from presumptuous feelings and upon slight grounds; chances are rather against him than for him that it may prove erroneous: he who *risks* a battle does it often from necessity; he chooses the least of two evils; although the event is dubious, yet he fears less from a failure than from inaction: he who *ventures* on a mercantile speculation does it from a love of gain; he flatters himself with a favorable event, and acquires boldness from the prospect. He who *jeopards* a cause (from Old French *jeu*, Latin *iocus*, a game, and *partitus*, parted, meaning a divided game, one in which the outcome is dubious) threatens its downfall or disaster. *Jeopard* means to *hazard*, with a presumption, however, in favor of an unfortunate outcome. There are but very few circumstances to justify us in *hazarding;* there may be several occasions which render it necessary to *risk*, and very many cases in which it may be advantageous to *venture*.

HEAD. See CHIEF; TOPIC.

HEADSTRONG. See OBSTINATE.

HEADY. See OBSTINATE.

HEAL. See CURE.

HEALING. See SANITARY.

HEALTHY, WHOLESOME, SALUBRIOUS, SALUTARY. *Healthy* signifies not only having *health*, but also causing *health*. *Wholesome*, like the German *heilsam*, signifies making whole, keeping whole or sound. *Salubrious* and *salutary*, from the Latin *salus*, safety or *health*, signify likewise contributive to *health* or good in general.

These epithets are all applicable to such objects as have a kindly influence on the bodily constitution: *healthy* is the most general and indefinite; it is applied to exercise, to air, situation, climate, and most other things but food, for which *wholesome* is commonly substituted: the life of a farmer is reckoned the most *healthy;* and the simplest diet is the most *wholesome. Healthy* and *wholesome* are rather negative in their sense; *salubrious* and *salutary* are positive, that is, *healthy* and *wholesome* which does no injury to the *health;* that is *salubrious* which serves to improve the *health;* and that is *salutary* which serves to remove a disorder: climates are *healthy* or *unhealthy,* according to the constitution of the person; water is a *wholesome* beverage for those who are not dropsical; bread is a *wholesome* diet for man; the air and climate of southern France have been long famed for their *salubrity,* and have induced many invalids to repair thither for the benefit of their *health;* the effects have not been equally *salutary* in all cases

Wholesome and *salutary* have likewise an extended and moral application; *healthy* and *salubrious* are employed only in the proper sense: *wholesome* in this case seems to convey the idea of making whole again what has been unsound; but *salutary* retains the idea of improving the condition of those who stand in need of improvement: correction is *wholesome* which serves the purpose of amendment without doing any injury to the body; instruction or admonition is *salutary* when it serves the purpose of strengthening good principles and awakening a sense of guilt or impropriety: laws and punishments are *wholesome* to the body politic, as diet is to the physical body; restrictions are *salutary* in checking irregularities.

See also SOUND.

HEAP, PILE, ACCUMULATE, AMASS. To *heap* signifies to form into a *heap,* from Anglo-Saxon *heap,* a crowd, a pile. To *pile* is to form into a *pile,* from Latin *pila,* originally a pillar, a pier of stone. To *accumulate,* from the Latin *cumulus,* a heap, signifies to put *heap* upon *heap. Amass* comes from French *à masse,* Latin *ad massa,* literally in a mass, meaning to gather to one's self in a mass.

To *heap* is an indefinite action; it may be performed with or without order: to *pile* is a definite action done with design and order; thus we *heap* stones, or *pile* wood: to *heap* may be to make into large or small *heaps:* to *pile* is always to make something considerable in height: children may *heap* sticks together; men *pile* loads of wood together.

To *pile* is used always, to *heap* mostly, in the physical, *accumulate* and *amass* in the physical or moral acceptation. To *accumulate* is properly to bring or add *heap* to *heap,* which is a gradual and unfinished act; to *amass* is to form into a mass, which is a single complete act; a man may *accumulate* guineas or anything else in small quantities, but he properly *amasses* wealth, and in a figurative sense he *amasses* knowledge. To *accumulate* and to *amass* are not always the acts of conscious agents: things may *accumulate* or *amass;* water or snow *accumulates* by the continual accession of fresh quantities; ice *amasses* in rivers until they are frozen over: so in the moral acceptation, evils, abuses, and the like, *accumulate:* corruption *amasses.*

HEAR, HEARKEN, OVERHEAR. To *hear* is properly the act of the ear; it is sometimes totally abstracted from the mind, when we *hear* and do not understand: to *hearken* is an act of the ear and the mind in conjunction; it implies an effort to *hear,* a tendency of the ear: to *overhear* is to *hear* clandestinely, or unknown to the person who is heard, whether designedly or not. We *hear* sounds: we *hearken* for the sense; we *overhear* the words: a quick ear *hears* the smallest sound; a willing mind *hearkens* to what is said; a prying curiosity leads to *overhearing.*

HEARSAY. See FAME.

HEARTEN, ANIMATE, CHEER, COMFORT, ENCOURAGE. *Hearten* is a compound of the English *heart* and the suffix *en. Heart,* in Anglo-Saxon *heorte,* allied to Latin *cor,* implies the vital, inner, or chief part of anything, in persons the seat of the faculties. To *hearten* another is to bestow upon him an influence directly from the heart; figuratively a spoken word or a voluntary act, when the person is disheartened, that is, timely, sincere, and thoroughly meant.

To *animate* either a person, animal, or drooping plant is to impart new life to the subject by an infusion that goes directly to the heart; to inspire a person with energy, courage, ardor, to stimulate: to *cheer,* to comfort, console, invigorate, brace up, produce a joyous, hopeful state of mind: to *comfort,* to give consolation in time of affliction, sickness, or trouble, support, assistance, relief in time of misfortune or danger: and to *encourage,* to incite to renewed effort, to urge forward, to give confidence also to promote, help forward, advance.

While there is an apparent similarity in the import of all these terms, there are variant shades of meaning connected with each, which are critically considered in the articles on ANIMATE, CHEER, and ENCOURAGE.

HEARTINESS. See ZEAL.

HEARTLESS, BRUTAL, CRUEL, PITILESS, UNFEELING. *Heartless* (for derivation see HEARTEN) means literally without heart, and is applied to a variety of conditions that exhibit the worst features of human life, with nothing in extenuation. Of the terms here mentioned *brutal* and *pitiless* are the severest. *Brutal* is associated with the actions of a savage, an irresponsible, conscienceless creature, scarcely a whit better than a wild animal, whose attacks are liable to occur at any moment and to be repeated indefinitely, if death does not ensue from the first.

A person who is naturally *brutal* or who becomes so by evil influences is capable of deeds of violence and inhumanity with and without provocation. The *cruel* person may in his conduct reach the state of *brutality,* for he is disposed to injure or take pleasure in the injury of others, but his acts are generally studied ones, thought out in advance, showing a disposition or a growing gratification to injure others, while the *brutal* one is more apt to act on a momentary impulse.

Pitiless, however, implies a combination of whatever is *brutal* and *cruel,* for those whom these terms designate are destitute of compassion, are merciless, insistent in inflicting injury upon others, deaf to appeals for consideration, pity, and even life itself, unmoved by any sentiment or sympathy, and absolutely *unfeeling* toward their victims.

A further discussion of the general conditions which the above terms imply will be found in the article on CRUEL.

HEARTY, WARM, SINCERE, CORDIAL. *Hearty, i. e.,* having the heart in a thing, and *warm* (see FIRE) express a stronger feeling than *sincere* (see CANDID); *cordial,* from *cor,* the heart, *i. e.,* according to the heart, is a mixture of the *warm* and *sincere.* There are cases in which it may be peculiarly proper to be *hearty,* as when we are supporting the cause of religion and virtue; there are other cases in which it is peculiarly proper to be *warm,* as when our affections ought to be roused in favor of our friends; in all cases we ought to be *sincere* when we express either a sentiment or a feeling; it is peculiarly happy to be on terms of *cordial* regard with those who stand in any close relation to us. The man himself should be *hearty;* his heart should be *warm;* professions should be *sincere;* a reception *cordial.*

HEAT. See FIRE.

HEATHEN. See GENTILE.

HEAVE, SWELL. *Heave* is used either transitively or intransitively, as a reflective or a neuter verb; *swell* is used only as a neuter verb. *Heave* implies raising, and *swell* implies distension: they differ, therefore, very widely in sense, but they sometimes agree in application. The bosom is said both to *heave* and to *swell,* because it happens that the bosom *swells* by *heaving;* the waves are likewise said to *heave* themselves or to *swell,* in which there is a similar correspondence between the actions: otherwise most things which *heave* do not *swell,* and those which *swell* do not *heave.*

HEAVENLY. See CELESTIAL; GODLIKE.

HEAVINESS. See GLOOM; WEIGHT.

HEAVY, DULL, DROWSY. *Heavy* is allied to both *dull* and *drowsy,* but the latter have no close connection with each other.

Heavy and *dull* are employed as epithets both for persons and for things; *heavy* characterizes the corporeal state of a person; *dull* qualifies the spirits or the understanding of the subject. A person has a *heavy* look whose temperament seems composed of gross and weighty materials which weigh him down and impede his movements; he has a *dull* countenance in whom the ordinary brightness and vivacity of the mind is wanting.

Heavy and *drowsy* are both employed in the sense of sleepy; but the former is only a particular state, the latter particular or general; all persons may be occasionally *heavy* or *drowsy;* some are habitually *drowsy* from disease: they likewise differ in degree, the latter being much the greater of the two; and occasionally they are applied to such things as produce sleepiness.

Heavy, Burdensome, Weighty, Ponderous.—*Heavy,* from *heave,* signifies the causing to heave, or requiring to be lifted up with force; *burdensome* signifies having a *burden; weighty,* having a *weight;* and *ponderous,* from the Latin *pondus,* a weight, has the same original meaning.

Heavy is the natural property of some bodies; *burdensome* is incidental to some. In the vulgar sense things are termed *heavy* which are found difficult to lift, in distinction from those which are light or easy to be lifted; but those things are *burdensome* which are too troublesome to be carried or borne: many things, therefore, are actually *heavy* that are never *burdensome;* and others are occasionally *burdensome* that are never *heavy:* that which is *heavy* is so whether lifted or not; but that which is *burdensome* must be *burdensome* to some one carrying it: hard substances are mostly *heavy;* but to a weak person the softest substance may sometimes be *burdensome* if he is obliged to bear it; things are *heavy* according to the difficulty with which they are lifted; but they are *weighty* according as they *weigh* other things down. The *heavy* is therefore indefinite; but the *weighty* is definite and something positively great: what is *heavy* to one may be light to another; but that which is *weighty* exceeds the ordinary weight of other things: *ponderous* expresses even more than *weighty,* for it includes also the idea of bulk; the *ponderous,* therefore, is that which is so *weighty* and large that it cannot easily be moved.

HECTOR, BULLY. These words have a similar meaning. Hector comes from Greek "Εκτωρ, the celebrated hero of Troy and a mighty warrior. To *hector* was to treat others as Hector treated his foes in battle. *Hector* now differs from *bully* in suggesting a repeated exercise of argument and force —something irritating and harassing, and less definitely indicating the display of superior brute force. *Bully* comes from Old Low German. The oldest sense in English is "dear one," a lover. It now signifies a person who gets his own will by a display of force, especially against those whom he knows to be much weaker than himself; it carries the suggestion of a perfectly safe threat of force. The *bully* generally knows that he will not be called upon to live up to his fierce protestations; that the mere display will make his victim yield. *Hector* does not suggest this element in the verb to *bully.* One may *hector* one's equal or superior; one *bullies* one's inferiors.

HEED, CARE, ATTENTION. *Heed* (see ATTEND) applies to matters of importance to one's moral conduct; *care* (see CARE) to matters of minor import: a man is required to take *heed;* a child is required to take *care:* the former exercises his understanding in taking *heed;* the latter exercises his thoughts and his senses in taking *care:* the former looks to the remote and probable consequences of his actions, and endeavors to prevent the evil that may happen; the latter sees principally to the thing that is immediately before him. When a young man enters the world he must take *heed* lest he be not ensnared by his companions into vicious practices; in a slippery path we must take *care* that we do not fall.

Heed has, moreover, the sense of thinking on what is proposed to our notice, in which it agrees with *attention* (see ATTEND); hence we speak of giving *heed* and paying *attention:* but the former is applied only to that which is conveyed to us by another, in the shape of a direction, a caution, or an instruction; but the latter is said of everything which we are said to perform. A good child gives *heed* to his parents when they caution him against any dangerous or false step; he pays *attention* to the lesson which is set him to learn. He who gives no *heed* to the counsels of others is made to repent his folly by bitter experience; he who fails in paying *attention* cannot learn.

HEEDLESS. See NEGLIGENT.

HEIGHTEN, RAISE, AGGRAVATE. To *heighten* is to make *higher* (see HAUGHTY). To *raise* is to cause to *rise* (see ARISE). To *aggravate* (see that word) is to make *heavy*. *Heighten* refers more to the result of the action of making *higher; raise* to the mode; we *heighten* a house by *raising* the roof, where *raising* conveys the idea of setting up aloft, which is not included in the word *heighten*. On the same ground a head-dress may be said to be *heightened* which is made *higher* than it was before; and a chair or a table is *raised* that is set upon something else: but in speaking of a wall we may say that it is either *heightened* or *raised*, because the operation and result must in both cases be the same. In the improper sense of these terms they preserve a similar distinction: we *heighten* the value of a thing; we *raise* its price: we *heighten* the grandeur of an object; we *raise* a family.

Heighten and *aggravate* have connection with each other only in application to offences: the enormity of an offence is *heightened*, the guilt of the offender is *aggravated*, by particular circumstances. The horrors of a murder are *heightened* by being committed in the dead of the night: the guilt of the perpetrator is *aggravated* by the addition of ingratitude to murder.

HEINOUS, FLAGRANT, FLAGITIOUS, ATROCIOUS. *Heinous* comes from Old French *haïnos*, from *haïr*, to hate, from the Teutonic root also found in English *hate*. *Flagrant*, in Latin *flagrans*, burning, is a figurative expression denoting excessive and violent in its nature. *Flagitious*, in Latin *flagitiosus*, from *flagitium*, signifies peculiarly infamous. *Atrocious*, in Latin *atrox*, cruel, signifies exceedingly black in guilt.

These epithets, which are applied to crimes, seem to rise in degree. A crime is *heinous* which seriously offends against the laws of men; a sin is *heinous* which seriously offends against the will of God; an offence is *flagrant* which is in direct defiance of established opinions and practice: it is *flagitious* if a gross violation of the moral law or coupled with any grossness; a crime is *atrocious* which is attended with any aggravating circumstances. Lying is a *heinous* sin; gaming and drunkenness are *flagrant* breaches of the Divine law; the murder of a whole family is in the fullest sense *atrocious*.

HELICOPTER. See AIRCRAFT.

HELP, ASSIST, AID, SUCCOR, RELIEVE. *Help* is in Anglo-Saxon *helpan*, German *helfen*. *Assist*, in Latin *assisto*, or *ad* and *sisto*, signifies to place one's self by another so as to give him our strength. *Aid*, in Latin *adjutare*, a frequentative of *ad* and *juvare*, to help, signifies to profit toward a specific end. *Succor*, in Latin *succurrere*, to run to the help of any one. *Relieve* (see ALLEVIATE).

The idea of communicating to the advantage of another in case of need is common to all these terms. *Help* is the generic term; the rest specific: *help* may be substituted for the others, and in many cases where they would not be applicable. The first three are employed either to produce a positive good or to remove an evil; the latter two only remove an evil. We *help* a person to prosecute his work, or *help* him out of a difficulty; we *assist* in order to forward a scheme, or we *assist* a person in the time of his embarrassment; we *aid* a good cause, or we *aid* a person to make his escape; we *succor* a person who is in danger; or we *relieve* him in time of distress. To *help* and *assist* respect personal service, the former by corporeal, the latter by corporeal or mental labor: one servant *helps* another by taking a part in his employment; one author *assists* another in the composition of his work. We *help* up a person's load; we *assist* him to rise when he has fallen; we *speak* of a *helper* or a *helpmate* in mechanical employments, of an *assistant* to a professional man.

To *assist* and *aid* are used for services directly or indirectly performed: but the former is said only of individuals; the latter may be said of bodies as well as individuals. One friend *assists* another with his purse, with his counsel, his interest, and the like: one person *aids* another in carrying on a scheme; or one king, or nation, *aids* another with armies and subsidies. We come to the *assistance* of a person when he has met with an accident; we come to his *aid* when contending against numbers. *Assistance* is given, *aid* is sent.

To *succor* is a species of immediate *assistance*, which is given on the spur of the occasion; the Good Samaritan went to the *succor* of the man who had fallen among thieves; so in like manner we may *succor* one who calls us by his cries; or we may *succor* the poor whom we find in circumstances of distress. So likewise one may *succor* a nation.

The word *relieve* has nothing in common with *succor*, except that they both express the removal of pain; but the latter does not necessarily imply any mode by which this is done, and therefore excludes the idea of personal interference. To *help* is commonly an act of good-nature or discretion; to *relieve*, an act of humanity or generosity.

All these terms, except *succor*, may be applied to things as well as persons; we may walk by the *help* of a stick, read with the *assistance* of glasses, learn a task quickly by the *aid* of a good memory, and obtain *relief* from medicine.

HELPER. See ACCOMMODATOR.

HELPING. See AUXILIARY.

HERCULEAN, BRAWNY, POWERFUL, STRONG, VIGOROUS. *Herculean,* an adjective derived from Hercules (in Greek Ἡρακλῆς, the hero of Grecian mythology who was said to be possessed of superhuman strength, implies, both as to persons and objects, the quality of extraordinary strength. Applied to persons, *brawny* designates a tough, muscular condition, and relates particularly to the arms, calves of the legs, the breast, back, and such other parts as are employed in strenuous actions. *Powerful,* in this sense means might, force, both in an unusually high development; *strong,* having the power or ability to exert great bodily force, the mental or physical capability to bear or endure great burdens, sorrow, suffering; and *vigorous,*

the condition resulting from sound health, the possession of mental or physical energy, derived from the Latin *vigere,* to be lively.

Herculean, Difficult, Hard, Perilous, Toilsome.—This application of the term implies actions that require the power, strength, or courage of Hercules to perform or encounter that which is exceedingly great in magnitude and difficult or dangerous in the performance. *Difficult* implies that which is arduous, not easily managed or comprehended, more or less perplexing, that which requires much labor and skill to overcome or accomplish; *hard,* that which is compact and solid, not easily pierced or broken, unyielding, and, hence, necessitating continuous application and labor and involving mental or physical fatigue; *perilous,* that which is beset with danger to the performer, which exposes him to injury or hazard, to the extent of his life; and *toilsome,* that which requires much time, labor, and ingenuity, the exertion of bodily strength, with efforts of some continuance or duration, producing weariness, exhaustion, fatigue, and other results of over-labor.

HERESY. See HETERODOXY.

HERETIC, SCHISMATIC, SECTARIAN or SECTARY, DISSENTER, NON-CONFORMIST. A *heretic* is the maintainer of *heresy* (see HETERODOXY); the *schismatic* is the author or promoter of *schism;* the *sectarian* or *sectary* is the member of a *sect;* the *dissenter* is one who *dissents* from an established religion; and the *non-conformist* one who does not *conform* to an establishment. A man is a *heretic* only for matters of faith and doctrine, but he is a *schismatic* in matters of discipline and practice. The *heretic,* therefore, is not always a *schismatic,* nor the *schismatic* a *heretic.* Whoever holds the doctrines that are common to the Roman Catholic and reformed churches is not a *heretic* in the Protestant sense of the word, although he may in many outward formalities be a *schismatic.* Calvinists are not *heretics,* but many among them are *schismatics;* on the other hand, there are many members of the establishment who hold, though they do not avow, *heretical* notions.

The *heretic* is considered as such with

regard to the Catholic Church or the whole body of Christians, holding the same fundamental principles; but the *schismatic* and *sectarian* are considered as such with regard to particular bodies of Christians. *Schism,* from the Greek σχίζειν, to split, denotes an action, and the *schismatic* is an agent who splits for himself in his own individual capacity: the *sectarian* does not expressly perform a part, he merely holds a relation; he does not divide anything himself, but belongs to that which is already cut or divided. The *schismatic,* therefore, takes upon himself the whole moral responsibility of the *schism;* but the *sectarian* does not necessarily take an active part in the measures of his *sect;* whatever guilt attaches to *schism* attaches to the *schismatic;* he is a voluntary agent, acting from an erroneous principle, if not an unchristian temper: the *sectarian* is often an involuntary agent; he follows that to which he has been incidentally attached. It is possible, therefore, to be a *schismatic* and not a *sectarian;* as also to be a *sectarian* and not a *schismatic.* Those professed members of the establishment who affect the title of evangelical and wish to palm upon the Church the peculiarities of the Calvinistic doctrine, and to ingraft their own modes and forms into its discipline, are *schismatics,* but not *sectarians;* on the other hand, those who by birth and education are attached to a *sect* are *sectarians,* but not always *schismatics.* Consequently, *schismatic* is a term of much greater reproach than *sectarian.*

The *schismatic* and *sectarian* have a reference to any established body of Christians of any country; but *dissenter* is a term applicable only to the inhabitants of Great Britain, and bearing relation only to the established Church of England: it includes not only those who have individually and personally renounced the doctrines of the Church, but those who are in a state of *dissent* or difference from it. *Dissenters* are not necessarily either *schismatics* or *sectarians,* for British Roman Catholics are all *dissenters,* although they are the reverse of what is understood by *schismatic* and *sectarian:* it is equally clear that all *schis-*

matics and *sectarians* are not *dissenters,* because every established community of Christians, all over the world, have had individuals, or smaller bodies of individuals, setting themselves up against them: the term *dissenter* being in a great measure technical, it may be applied individually or generally without conveying any idea of reproach; the same may be said of *nonconformist,* which is a more special term, including only such as do not *conform* to some established or national religion: consequently, all members of the Romish Church, or of the Kirk of Scotland, are excluded from the number of *non-conformists;* while on the other hand, all British-born subjects not adhering to these two forms, and at the same time renouncing the established form of their country, are of this number, among whom may be reckoned Independents, Presbyterians, Baptists, Quakers, Methodists, and all other such *sects* as have been formed since the Reformation.

HESITATE, FALTER, STAMMER, STUTTER. *Hesitate* (see DEMUR). *Falter* or *faulter* seems to signify to commit a *fault* or blunder. *Stammer* comes from a root found in *stand;* it meant to stand fixed, amazed, and is related to German *stumm,* dumb. It now signifies the confusion and hesitation of speech incident to extreme amazement. *Stutter* is a frequentative of *stut,* once common in the sense of *stutter.* "I *stutte;* I can not speake my wordes redyly," writes Palgrave. The original root of *stutter* meant to strike against, hence to trip in the speech.

A defect in utterance is the idea which is common in the signification of all these terms: they differ either as to the cause or the mode of the action. With regard to the cause, a *hesitation* results from the state of the mind and an interruption in the train of thoughts; *falter* arises from a perturbed state of feeling; *stammer* and *stutter* arise either from an incidental circumstance or more commonly from a physical defect in the organs of utterance. A person who is not in the habit of public speaking, or of collecting his thoughts into a set form, will be apt to *hesitate* even in familiar conversation; he who first addresses a public assembly will be apt to *falter*. Children who first begin to read will *stammer* at hard words: and one who has an impediment in his speech will *stutter* when he attempts to speak in a hurry.

With regard to the mode or degree of the action, *hesitate* expresses less than *falter; stammer* less than *stutter*. The slightest difficulty in uttering words constitutes a *hesitation;* a pause or the repetition of a word may be termed *hesitating:* but to *falter* supposes a failure in the voice as well as the lips when they refuse to do their office. *Stammering* and *stuttering* are confined principally to the useless moving of the mouth; he who *stammers* brings forth sounds, but not the right sounds, without trials and efforts; he who *stutters* remains for some time in a state of agitation without uttering a sound.

See also SCRUPLE.

HETERODOXY, HERESY. *Heterodoxy,* from the Greek ἕτερος and δόξα, signifies another or a different doctrine. *Heresy,* through French and Latin from the Greek αἵρεσις, a choice, signifies an opinion adopted by individual choice.

To be of a different persuasion is *heterodoxy;* to have a faith of one's own is *heresy,* the *heterodoxy* characterizes the opinions formed; the *heresy* characterizes the individual forming the opinion: the *heterodoxy* exists independently and for itself; the *heresy* sets itself up against others. As all division supposes error either on one side or on both, the words *heterodoxy* and *heresy* are applied only to human opinions, and strictly in the sense of a false opinion, formed in distinction from that which is better founded; but the former implies any opinions, important or otherwise; the latter refers only to matters of importance: the *heresy* is therefore a fundamental schism. There has been much *heterodoxy* in the Christian world at all times, and among these have been *heresies* denying the most serious doctrines which have been acknowledged by the great body of Christians since the Apostles.

HETEROGENEOUS, from Greek ἕτερος, other, and γέγος, kind, meant literally of a different kind. It signifies that which is made up of different kinds of elements, and is opposed to *homogeneous.* It has no real synonymes except the more general words listed under *different,* which see.

HIDDEN. See SECRET.

HIDE. See CONCEAL; COVER; SKIN.

HIDEOUS, GHASTLY, GRIM, GRISLY. *Hideous* comes from Old French *hidos,* which is probably derived from Latin *hispidosus,* rough, shaggy. *Ghastly* comes from Anglo-Saxon *gœstan,* to terrify, allied to *aghast.* *Grim* is derived from Anglo-Saxon *grim,* fierce. *Grisly,* Anglo-Saxon *grislic,* is formed with the suffix *lic* from *grisan,* to shudder.

An unseemly exterior is characterized by these terms; but the *hideous* refers to natural objects, and the *ghastly* more properly that which is supernatural, or what resembles it. A mask with monstrous grinning features looks *hideous;* a human form with a visage of death-like paleness is *ghastly.* The *grim* is applicable only to the countenance; dogs or wild beasts may look very *grim: grisly* refers to the whole form, but particularly to the color; as blackness or darkness has always something terrifying in it, a *grisly* figure having a monstrous assemblage of dark color is particularly calculated to strike terror. *Hideous* is applicable to objects of hearing also, as a *hideous* roar; but the rest to objects of sight only.

HIGH, TALL, LOFTY. *High* is allied to German *hoch.* *Tall* comes from Middle English *tal,* seemly, obedient, valiant, which was a general word of approval. *Lofty* comes from Scandinavian *loft,* an upper room, allied to Anglo-Saxon *lyft,* air, sky, meaning high in the air.

High is the term in most general use, which seems likewise in the most unqualified manner to express the idea of extension upward, which is common to them all. Whatever is *tall* and *lofty* is *high,* but everything is not *tall* or *lofty* which is *high.* *Tall* and *lofty* both designate a more than ordinary degree of *height;* but *tall* is peculiarly applicable to what shoots up or stands up in a perpendicular direction, while *lofty* is said of that which is extended in breadth as well as in *height,* that which is lifted up or raised by an accretion of matter or an expansion in the air. By this rule we say that a house is *high*, a chimney *tall*, a room *lofty*. With the *high* is associated no idea of what is striking; but the *tall* is coupled with the aspiring, or that which strives to outtop: the *lofty* is always coupled with the grand and that which commands admiration.

High and *lofty* have a moral acceptation, but *tall* is taken in the natural sense only: *high* and *lofty* are applied to persons or what is personal, with the same difference in degree as before: a *lofty* title or *lofty* pretension conveys more than a *high* title or a *high* pretension. Men of *high* rank should have *high* ideas of virtue and personal dignity, and keep themselves clear from everything low and mean: a *lofty* ambition often soars too *high* to serve the purpose of its possessor, whose fall is the greater when he finds himself compelled to descend.

See also HAUGHTY.

HIGHEST. See SUPREME.

HIGH-FLOWN, BOMBASTIC, SWOLLEN. *High-flown* is a compound of the English *high* and *flown; high*, in Anglo-Saxon *heah*, implies that which is elevated; *flown*, from *fly*, in Anglo-Saxon *fleógan*, implies to move or pass through the air. *High-flown*, in most common usage, is applied to the various terms of language as employed in speech and writing that are extravagant, inflated, above the customary quality, in a pretentious flowery or affected style.

Bombastic is from *bombast*, originally a soft, loose stuff used to swell out garments, and is applied to high-sounding words, big and puffing, without much meaning or relation to a subject under discussion.

Swollen and *bombastic* are terms more closely allied, each implying language that is puffed up; hence used to make one appear consequential, as possessing greater intelligence than others.

Swollen is a general word which may under certain conditions have the meaning of *bombastic* or *high-flown*. *Bombastic* and *high-flown*, on the other hand, are specific words applied to language and manner.

HIGH-MINDED. See HAUGHTY.
HIGH-SOUNDING. See LOUD.
HILARITY. See MIRTH.
HIND. See COUNTRYMAN.
HINDER, PREVENT, IMPEDE, OBSTRUCT. *Hinder* comes from Anglo-Saxon *hindrian*, to keep back or behind. *Prevent*, from *præ* and *venire*, to come before, signifies to *hinder* by coming before, or to cross another by the anticipation of his purpose. *Impede*, from *in* and *pedes*, signifies to come between a person's feet and entangle him in his progress. *Obstruct*, from *ob*, in the way of, and *struere*, to heap together, signifies to set up something in his way, to block the passage.

Hinder is the most general of these terms, as it conveys little more than the idea which is common to them all, namely, that of keeping one from his purpose. To *hinder* is commonly said of that which is rendered impracticable only for the time being, or merely delayed; *prevent* is said of that which is rendered altogether impracticable. A person is *hindered* by the weather and his various engagements from reaching a place at the time he intended; he is *prevented* but not *hindered* by ill health from going there at all. If a friend calls, he *hinders* me from finishing the letter which I was writing; if I wish to *prevent* my son from reading any book I keep it out of his way. To *hinder* is an act of the moment, it supposes no design; *prevent* is a premeditated act, deliberated upon, and adopted for general purposes: the former is applied only to the movements of any particular individual, the latter to events and circumstances. I *hinder* a person who is running, if I lay hold of his arm and make him walk: it is the object of every good government to *prevent* offences rather than to punish offenders. In ordinary discourse these words come very close in sense when the circumstances of the case do not sufficiently define whether the action in hand be altogether suspended or suspended only for a time; but the above explanation must make it very clear that to *hinder*, in its proper sense and application, is but to stop in the progress, and *prevent* to stop at the outset.

HINT

To *impede* and *obstruct* are a species of *hindering* which is said rather of things than of persons: *hinder* is said of both; but *hinder* is commonly employed in regard to trifling matters, or such as retard a person's proceedings in the smallest degree; *impede* and *obstruct* are acts of greater importance, or produce a still greater degree of delay. A person is *hindered* in his work, although neither *impeded* nor *obstructed;* but the quantity of artillery and baggage which is attached to an army will greatly *impede* it in its march; and the trees which are thrown across the roads will *obstruct* its march. *Hindrances* always suppose the agency of a person, either of the one who *hinders* or the one who is *hindered:* but *impediments* and *obstructions* may be employed with regard to the operations of nature on inanimate objects. Cold *impedes* the growth of plants; a dam *obstructs* the course of water.

See also RETARD.

Hinder, Stop.—*Hinder* refers solely to the prosecution of an object: *stop,* signifying to make to stand, refers simply to the cessation of motion; we may be *hindered,* therefore, by being *stopped;* but we may also be *hindered* without being expressly *stopped,* and we may be *stopped* without being *hindered.* If the *stoppage* does not interfere with any other object in view, it is a *stoppage,* but not a *hindrance;* as when we are *stopped* by a friend while walking for pleasure: but if *stopped* by an idler in the midst of urgent business, so as not to be able to proceed according to our business, this is both a *stoppage* and a *hindrance:* on the other hand, if we are interrupted in the regular course of our proceeding, but not compelled to stand still or give up our business for any time, this may be a *hindrance,* but not a *stoppage:* in this manner, the conversation of others in the midst of our business may considerably retard its progress, and so far *hinder,* but not expressly put a *stop* to, the whole concern.

HINT, SUGGEST, INTIMATE, INSINUATE. *Hint* and *suggest* (see ALLUDE). To *intimate* is to make one *intimate,* or specially acquainted with, to communicate one's most inward thoughts.

Insinuate, from the Latin *sinus,* a bend, is to introduce by a winding course into the mind of another.

All these terms denote indirect expressions of what passes in one's own mind. We *hint* at a thing from fear and uncertainty; we *suggest* a thing from prudence and modesty; we *intimate* a thing from indecision; a thing is *insinuated* from artifice. A person who wants to get at the certain knowledge of any circumstance *hints* at it frequently in the presence of those who can give him the information; a man who will not offend others by an assumption of superior wisdom *suggests* his ideas on a subject, instead of setting them forth with confidence; when a person's mind is not made up on any future action, he only *intimates* what may be done; he who has anything *offensive* to communicate to another will choose to *insinuate* it rather than declare it in express terms. *Hints* are thrown out; they are frequently characterized as broken: *suggestions* are offered; they are frequently termed idle or ill-grounded: *intimations* are given, and are either slight or broad: *insinuations* are thrown out, they are commonly designated as slanderous, malignant, and the like.

To *hint* is taken either in a bad or an indifferent sense; it is commonly resorted to by tale-bearers, mischief-makers, and all who want to talk of more than they know. To *suggest* is oftener used in the good than the bad sense: as to *suggest* doubts, queries, difficulties, or improvements in matters of opinion is truly laudable, particularly for young persons; but to *suggest* anything to the disadvantage of another is even worse than to speak ill of him openly, for it bespeaks cowardice as well as ill-nature. To *intimate* is taken either in a good or an indifferent sense; it commonly passes between relatives or persons closely connected in the communication of their half-formed intentions or of doubtful intelligence; but to *insinuate* is always taken in a bad sense; it is the resource of an artful and malignant enemy to wound the reputation of another, whom he does not dare openly to accuse. A person is said to take a *hint,* to follow a *suggestion,* to receive an *intimation*, to disregard an *insinuation*.

See also KEY.

HIRE. See ALLOWANCE.

HIRELING, MERCENARY. *Hireling*, from *hire*, and *mercenary*, from *mercenarius*, based on *merx*, pay, are applied to any one who follows a sordid employment; but *hireling* may sometimes be taken in its proper and less reproachful sense, for one who is *hired* as a servant to perform an allotted work; but in general they are both reproachful epithets, the former having particular reference to the meanness of the employment, and the latter to the sordid character of the person. *Hireling* papers are those which are in the pay of a party; a *mercenary* principle will sometimes actuate men in the highest station.

HIT. See BEAT; STRIKE.

HOARD. See GARNER; TREASURE.

HODGE-PODGE. See OLIO.

HOIST. See LIFT.

HOLD, KEEP, DETAIN, RETAIN. *Hold* comes from Anglo-Saxon *healdan*, to *hold*; *keep* from Anglo-Saxon *cepan*, to observe, notice, attend to. *Detain* and *retain* both come from the Latin *tenere*, to *hold*. The first signifies, by virtue of the particle *de*, meaning from, to *hold* from another; the second, by virtue of the particle *re*, to *hold* back for one's self.

To *hold* is a physical act; it requires a degree of bodily strength or at least the use of the limbs; to *keep* is simply to have by one at one's pleasure. The having in one's power so that it shall not go is the leading idea in the signification of *hold*; the durability of having is the leading idea in the word *keep*: we may *hold* a thing only for a moment; but what we *keep* we *keep* for a time. On the other hand, we may *keep* a thing by *holding*, although we may *keep* it by various other means: we may, therefore, *hold* without *keeping*, and we may *keep* without *holding*. A servant *holds* a thing in his hand for it to be seen, but he does not *keep* it; he gives it to his master, who puts it into his pocket, and consequently *keeps*, but does not *hold* it. A thing may be *held* in the hand, or *kept* in the hand; in the former case the pressure of the hand is an essential part of

the action, but in the latter case it is simply a contingent part of the action: the hand *holds*, but the person *keeps* it. What is *held* is fixed in position, but what is *kept* is left loose, or otherwise, at the will of the individual. Things are *held* by men in their hands, by beasts in their claws or mouths, by birds in their beaks; things are *kept* by people either about their persons or in their houses, according to convenience.

Detain and *retain* are modes of *keeping;* the former signifies *keeping* back what belongs to another; the latter signifies *keeping* a long time for one's own purpose. A person may be either *held*, *kept*, *detained*, or *retained:* when he is *held* he is *held* contrary to his will by the hand of another; as suspected persons are *held* by the officers of justice, that they may not make their escape: he is *kept*, if he stops in any place, by the desire of another; as a man is *kept* in prison until his innocence is proved, or a child is *kept* at school until he has finished his education: he is *detained* if he be *kept* away from any place to which he is going or from any person to whom he belongs; as the servant of another is *detained* to take back a letter, or one is *detained* by business, so as to be prevented from attending to an appointment: a person is *retained* who is *kept* for a continuance in the service of another; as some servants are said to be *retained*, while others are dismissed.

Things are *held* in the improper sense: they are *kept*, *detained*, and *retained* in the proper sense. A money-lender *holds* the property of others in pledge; the idea of a temporary and partial action is here expressed by *hold*, in distinction from *keep*, which is used to express something definite and permanent: the money-lender *keeps* the property as his own if the borrower forfeits it by breach of contract. When a person purchases anything he is expected to *keep* it or pay the value of the thing ordered, if the tradesman fulfil his part of the engagement. What is *detained* is *kept* either contrary to the will, or without the consent, of the possessor: when things are suspected to be stolen, the officers have the right of *detaining* them until inquiry be instituted. What is *retained* is continued to be *kept;* it supposes, however, some alteration in the terms or circumstances under which it is *kept:* a person *retains* his seat in a train, notwithstanding that he finds it disagreeable: or a lady *retains* some of the articles of millinery which are sent for her choice, but she returns the rest.

All are used in a moral application except *detain;* in this case they are marked by a similar distinction. A person is said to *hold* an office, by which simple possession is implied: he may *hold* it for a long or a short time, at the will of others, or by his own will, which is not marked: he *keeps* a situation or he *keeps* his post, by which his continuance in the situation or at the post is denoted: but to say he *retains* his office signifies that he might have given it up, or lost it, had he not been led to continue in it. In like manner, with regard to one's sentiments or feelings, a man is said to *hold* certain opinions, which are ascribed to him as a part of his creed; he *keeps* the opinions which no one can induce him to give up; he *retains* his old attachments, notwithstanding the lapse of years and change of circumstances which have intervened and were naturally calculated to wean him from them.

See also CONTAIN.

Hold, Occupy, Possess.—*Hold* (see above). *Occupy,* in Latin *occupo,* or *ob* and *capere,* to hold or keep near, so that it cannot be held by others, or fill a space so that it cannot be filled by any other object. *Possess,* from Latin *possessus,* past participle of *possideo,* or *potis* and *sedeo,* signifies to sit as master of.

We *hold* a thing for a long or a short time; we *occupy* it for a permanence: we *hold* it for ourselves or others; we *occupy* it only for ourselves: we *hold* it for various purposes; we *occupy* only for the purpose of converting it to our private use. Thus a person may *hold* an estate, or, which is the same thing, the title-deeds to an estate, *pro tempore,* for another person's benefit; but he *occupies* an estate if he enjoys the fruit of it. On the other hand, to *occupy* is only to *hold* under a certain compact; but to *possess* is to *hold* as one's own. The

tenant *occupies* the farm when he *holds* it by a certain lease and cultivates it for his subsistence: but the landlord *possesses* the farm, *possessing* the right to let it and to receive the rent. We may *hold* by force, or fraud, or right; we *occupy* either by force or right; we *possess* only by right.

Hence we say, figuratively, to *hold* a person in esteem or contempt, to *occupy* a person's attention or a place, or to *possess* one's affection.

Hold, Support, Maintain.—*Hold* is here, as in the former article, a term of very general import. *Support* (see COUNTENANCE) and *maintain* (see ASSIST) include the idea of holding with other collateral ideas in their signification.

Hold and *support* are employed in the proper sense, *maintain* in the improper sense. To *hold* is a term unqualified by any circumstance; we may *hold* a thing in any direction, *hold* it up or down, in a straight or oblique direction: *support* is a species of *holding* up; to *hold* up, however, is a personal act or a direct effort of the individual; to *support* may be an indirect and a passive act; he who *holds* anything up keeps it in an upright posture by the exertion of his strength; he who *supports* a thing only bears its weight or suffers it to rest upon himself: persons or voluntary agents can *hold* up; inanimate objects may *support:* a servant *holds* up a child that it may see; a pillar *supports* a building.

In the figurative application a person is said to *hold* power for himself, but to *support* the authority of another, or to have one's own mind *supported* by circumstances or reflections. To *maintain* is to *hold* firmly or with vigor.

These terms are all applied to the opinions with a similar distinction. Opinions are *held* and *maintained* as one's own; they are *supported* when they are another's. We *hold* and *maintain* whatever we believe. We *support* the belief or doctrine of another or what we ourselves have asserted and *maintained* at a former time. What is *held* is *held* by the act of the mind within itself and as regards itself, without reference to others; but what is *maintained* and *supported* is openly declared to be *held;* it is *maintained* with others or against others; it is *supported* in an especial manner against others; it may be *maintained* by simple declaration or assertions; it is *supported* by argument.

What is *held* may be *held* by means of the affections, as to *hold* a person dear, or *hold* a thing in esteem; to *maintain* and *support* are applied only to speculative matters with which the understanding is engaged, as to *maintain* or *support* truth or error, to *maintain* or *support* a cause.

HOLIDAY. See FEAST.

HOLINESS, SANCTITY. *Holiness,* from Anglo-Saxon *halig,* allied to *hal,* whole, and *health,* has altogether acquired a Christian signification; it respects the life and temper of a Christian. *Sanctity,* based on the Latin *sanctus,* holy, has merely a moral signification, which it derives from the *sanction* of human authority.

Holiness is to the mind of a man what *sanctity* is to his exterior, with this difference, that *holiness* to a certain degree ought to belong to every man professing Christianity; but *sanctity,* as it lies in the manners, the outward garb, and deportment, is becoming only to certain persons and at certain times. *Holiness* is a thing not to be affected; but *sanctity,* consisting in externals, is from its very nature exposed to falsehood. It becomes those who fill a sacred office, but no others.

HOLLOW, EMPTY. *Hollow,* from *hole,* signifying like a hole, concerns the body itself; the absence of its own materials produces hollowness. *Empty* concerns foreign bodies; their absence in another body constitutes emptiness. *Hollowness* is therefore a preparative to *emptiness,* and may exist independently of it; but *emptiness* presupposes the existence of *hollowness:* what is *empty* must be *hollow;* but what is *hollow* need not be *empty.* *Hollowness* is often the natural property of a body; *emptiness* is a contingent property: that which is *hollow* is destined by nature to contain; but that which is *empty* is deprived of its contents by a casualty: a nut is *hollow* for the purpose of receiving the fruit; it is *empty* if it contain no fruit.

They are both employed in a moral acceptation and in a bad sense; the *hollow,* in this case, is applied to what ought to be solid or sound, and *empty* to what ought to be filled; a person is *hollow* whose goodness lies only at the surface, whose fair words are without meaning; a truce is *hollow* which is only an external cessation from hostilities: a person is *empty* who is void of understanding and knowledge; an excuse is *empty* which is unsupported by fact and reason; a pleasure is *empty* which cannot afford satisfaction.

HOLY, PIOUS, DEVOUT, RELIGIOUS. *Holy* (see HOLINESS). *Pious,* in Latin *pius,* signifies having a regard for the gods. *Devout,* in Latin *devotus,* from *devovere,* to engage by a vow, signifies *devoted* or consecrated. *Religious,* in Latin *religiosus,* comes from *religio,* meaning attention to the worship of the gods.

A strong regard for the Supreme Being is expressed by all these epithets; but *holy* conveys the most comprehensive idea; *pious* and *devout* designate most fervor of mind; *religious* is the most general and abstract in its signification. A *holy* man is in all respects heavenly-minded; he is more fit for heaven than earth: *holiness,* to whatever degree it is possessed, abstracts the thoughts from sublunary objects and fixes them on things that are above. Our Saviour was a perfect pattern of *holiness;* his apostles after him, and innumerable saints and good men, both in and out of the ministry, have striven to imitate his example by the *holiness* of their life and conversation.

Pious is a term more restricted in its signification, and consequently more extended in application than *holy: piety* is not a virtue peculiar to Christians; it is common to all believers in a Supreme Being; it is the homage of the heart and the affections to a superior Being: from a similarity in the relationship between a heavenly and an earthly parent, devotedness of the mind has in both cases been denominated *piety.* *Piety* toward God naturally produces *piety* toward parents; for the obedience of the heart, which gives rise to the virtue in the one case, seems instantly to dictate the exercise of it in the other. The difference between *holiness* and *piety* is obvious from this, that our Saviour and his apostles are characterized as *holy*, but not *pious*, because *piety* is swallowed up in *holiness*. On the other hand, Jew and Gentile, Christian and heathen, are alike termed *pious* when they cannot be called *holy*, because *piety* is not only a more practicable virtue, but because it is more universally applicable to the dependent condition of man.

Devotion is a species of *piety* peculiar to the worshipper; it bespeaks that devotedness of mind which displays itself in the temple when the individual seems by his outward services solemnly to *devote* himself, soul and body, to the service of his Maker. *Piety*, therefore, lies in the heart and need not *appear* externally; but *devotion* requires to be marked by some external observance: a man *piously* resigns himself to the will of God in the midst of his afflictions; he prays *devoutly* in the bosom of his family.

Religious is a term of less import than either of the other terms; it denotes little more than the simple existence of *religion*, or a sense of *religion*, in the mind: the *religious* man is so more in his principles than in his affections; he is *religious* in his sentiments, inasmuch as he directs all his views according to the will of his Maker; and he is *religious* in his conduct, inasmuch as he observes the outward formalities of homage that are due to his Maker.

When applied to things, these terms preserve a similar distinction: we speak of the *holy* sacrament; of a *pious* discourse, a *pious* ejaculation; of a *devout* exercise, a *devout* air; a *religious* sentiment, a *religious* life, a *religious* education, and the like.

Holy, Sacred, Divine.—*Holy* is here, as in the former article, a term of higher import than either *sacred*, which is in Latin *sacer*, or *divine* (see GOD-LIKE). Whatever is most intimately connected with religion and religious worship, in its purest state, is *holy*, unhallowed by a mixture of inferior objects, and elevated in the greatest possible degree, so as to suit the nature of an infinitely perfect and exalted Being. Among the Jews, the *holy* of holies was that place which was intended to approach the nearest to the heavenly abode, consequently was pre-served as much as possible from all contamination with that which is earthly: among the Christians, that religion or form of religion is termed *holy* which is esteemed purest in its doctrine, discipline, and ceremonies.

Sacred is less than *holy;* the *sacred* derives its sanction from human institutions and is connected rather with our moral than our religious duties; what is *holy* is altogether spiritual, and abstracted from the earthly. The laws are *sacred*, but not *holy;* a man's word should be *sacred*, though not *holy:* for neither of these things is to be reverenced, but both are to be kept free from injury or external violence. The *holy* is not so much opposed to, as it is set above, everything else; the *sacred* is opposed to the profane: the Scriptures are properly denominated *holy*, because they are the word of God, and the fruit of His *Holy* Spirit; but other writings may be termed *sacred* which appertain to religion, in distinction from the profane, which appertain only to worldly matters.

Divine is a term of even less import than *sacred;* it signifies either belonging to a deity or being like a deity; but from the looseness of its application it has lost in some respects the dignity of its meaning. The *divine* is often contrasted with the human: but there are many human things which are denominated *divine:* Milton's poem is entitled a *divine* poem, not merely on account of the subject, but from the exalted manner in which the poet has treated his subject: what is *divine*, therefore, may be so superlatively excellent as to be conceived of as having the stamp of inspiration from the Deity, which, of course, as it applies to human performances, is but a hyperbolical mode of speech.

HOMAGE, FEALTY, COURT. *Homage*, in Old French *homage*, from Latin *homo*, a man, signifies a man's, that is an inferior's, act of acknowledging superiority. *Homage*, in the technical sense, was an oath taken, or a service performed, by the tenant to his lord, on being admitted to his land; or by inferior princes to a sovereign, whereby they acknowledged his sovereignty and promised fidelity: in its extended and figurative sense it comprehends any solemn mark of deference, by which the superiority of another is acknowledged. *Fealty*, through Old French *fealte*, from Latin *fidelatem*, based on *fidelis*, loyal, trusty, is a lower species of *homage*, consisting only of an oath; it was made formerly by tenants, who were bound thereby to personal service under the feudal system. *Court*, which derives its meaning from the verb to *court*, woo, and seek favor, is a species of *homage*, complaisance, or deference, which is assumed for a specific purpose; it is not only voluntary, but depends upon the humor and convenience of the courtier.

Homage is paid or done to superior endowments; *court* is paid to the contingent, not the real, superiority of the individual. *Fealty* is figuratively employed in the sense of fidelity to one's sovereign. *Homage* consists in any form of respect which is admitted in civil society; the Romans did *homage* to the talents of Virgil by always rising when he entered the theatre; men do *homage* to the wisdom of another when they do not venture to contradict his assertions or call in question his opinions. *Court* is everything or nothing, as circumstances require; he who pays his *court* consults the will and humor of him to whom it is paid, while he is consulting his own interest.

HOME. See DOMICILE.

HONEST. See FAIR; SINCERE.

HONESTY, PROBITY, UPRIGHTNESS, INTEGRITY. *Honesty* is the most familiar and universal term; it is applied alike to actions and principles, to a mode of conduct or a temper of mind: a person may be *honest*, a principle *honest*, or an action *honest;* the other terms are applied to the person, as a person of *probity*, *uprightness*, and *integrity:* a man is said to be *honest* who in his dealings with others does not violate the laws; a servant is *honest* who does not take any of the property of his master or suffer it to be taken; a tradesman is *honest* who does not sell bad articles; and people in general are denominated *honest* who pay what they owe and do not adopt any methods of defrauding others.

Honesty is a negative virtue; all the other terms denote positive virtues and higher characteristics. *Probity*, from *probus*, good, and *probo*, to prove, signifying tried virtue or solid goodness, is applied not merely to the commercial dealings of men, but to all the concerns of life where truth and goodness are called into exercise. *Probity* refers to the rights of men, giving to every one his due, whether as regards his property, reputation, honor, or any other thing on which a value is set. *Honesty* is opposed to direct fraud, *probity* to any species of insincerity.

Uprightness, from *upright* or *up* and *right*, signifies bearing up in a straight and undeviating course in opposition to every temptation which may offer. *Uprightness*, therefore, supposes an independent and positive principle which forms the rule of life. Any person may be said to be *upright* in all situations where confidence and intelligence are required, but more particularly a judge who scrupulously adheres to the dictates of an unbiassed conscience.

Integrity, from *integer*, whole or sound, signifying soundness of principle, (as in Horace, "*integer vitæ, scelerisque purus*") is applied, like *uprightness*, to cases where a particular trust is reposed; but *integrity* is taken absolutely, that is, without any reference to the outward circumstances which might tend to produce the contrary characteristic. He who faithfully discharges his trust and consults the interests of others rather than his own is justly styled a man of *integrity*. This virtue is to be looked for especially in those who fill any office.

Honesty, Honor.—These terms both regard the principle which actuates men in the adjustment of their rights with one another. The words are both derived from the same source, namely, the Hebrew *hon*, substance or wealth, which, being the primitive source of esteem among men, became at length put for the measure or standard of esteem, namely, what is good. Hence *honesty* and *honor* are both founded upon what is estimable, with this difference, that *honesty* is confined to the first principles or laws upon which civil society is founded, and *honor* is an independent principle that extends to everything which by usage has been admitted as estimable or entitled to esteem. An *honest* action, therefore, can never reflect so much credit on the agent as an *honorable* action, since in the performance of the one he may be guided by motives comparatively low, whereas in the other case he is actuated solely by a fair regard for the *honor* or the esteem of others. To a breach of *honesty* is attached punishment and personal inconvenience in various forms; but a breach of *honor* is only followed by disgrace or the ill opinion of others. On the other hand, *honesty* is founded on the very first principles of human society, and *honor* on the incidental principles which have been attached to them in the progress of time and culture; the former is positive and definite, and he who is actuated by this principle can never err; but the latter is indefinite and variable, and, as it depends upon opinion, it will easily mislead. We cannot have a false *honesty*, but we may have false *honor*. *Honesty* always keeps a man within the line of his duty; but a mistaken notion of what is *honorable* may carry a man very far from what is right, and may even lead him to run counter to common honesty.

See also GLORY.

HONOR, REVERENCE, RESPECT. These terms agree in expressing the act of an inferior toward his superior; but *honor* (see GLORY) expresses less than *reverence* (see ADORE), and more than *respect* (see ESTEEM).

To *honor* is only an outward act; to *reverence* is either an act of the mind or the outward expression of a sentiment; to *respect* is mostly an act of the mind, though it may admit of being expressed by some outward act. We *honor* God by adoration and worship, as well as by the performance of His will; we *honor* our parents by obeying them and giving them our personal service: we *reverence* our Maker by cherishing in our minds a dread of offending Him and making a profane use of His holy name and word: we reverence our parents by holding a similar sentiment in a less degree.

To *honor*, when applied to things, is taken in the sense of holding in *honor;* and *respect*, to have *respect* for, with the same distinction between them.

Honor, Dignity. — *Honor* may be taken either for that which intrinsically belongs to a person or for that which is conferred on him. *Dignity,* based on the Latin *dignus,* worthy, signifying worthiness, may be equally applied to what is extrinsic or intrinsic in a man.

In the first case *honor* has a reference to what is esteemed by others; *dignity* to that which is esteemed by ourselves: a sense of *honor* impels a man to do that which is esteemed *honorable* among men; a sense of *dignity* to do that which is consistent with the worth and greatness of his nature: the former impels a man to elevate himself as an individual; the latter to raise himself to the standard of his species: the former may lead a person astray, but the latter is an unerring guide. It is *honor* which makes a man draw his sword upon his friend: it is *dignity* which makes him despise every paltry affront from others, and apologize for every apparent affront on his own part. This distinction between the terms is kept up in their application to what is extraneous of a man: *honor* is that which is conferred on him by others; but *dignity* is the worth or value which is added to his condition: hence we always speak of *honors* as conferred or received; but *dignities* as possessed or maintained. *Honors* may sometimes be casual; but *dignities* are always permanent: an act of condescension from the sovereign is an *honor;* but the *dignity* is that which exalts the man. Hence it is that *honors* are mostly civil or political; *dignities* may also be ecclesiastical.

HOPE, EXPECTATION, TRUST, CONFIDENCE. Anticipation of futurity is the common idea expressed by all these words. *Hope* is in Anglo-Saxon *hopa.* *Hope* is that which is welcome; *expectation* (see AWAIT) is either welcome or unwelcome: we *hope* only for that which is good; we *expect* the bad as well as the good. In bad weather we *hope* it will soon be better; but in a bad season we *expect* a bad harvest, and in a good season a good harvest. *Hope* is simply a presentiment; it may vary in degree, more according to the temper of the mind than the nature of the circumstances; some *hope* where there is no ground for *hope*, and others despair where they might *hope: expectation* is a conviction that excludes doubt; we *expect* in proportion as that conviction is positive: we *hope* that which may be or can possibly be; we *expect* that which must be or which ought to be. The young man *hopes* to live many years; the old man *expects* to die in a few years.

Hope and *expectation* consist in looking for some good, *trust* (see BELIEF) and *confidence* (see CONFIDE) in a dependence on a person or thing to bring about the good. We may, therefore, have either *hope* or *expectation* grounded on *trust* or *confidence*, or we may have them where there is no room for either *trust* or *confidence*; a person may *hope* that something good may turn up because the future is uncertain; we may *expect* that it will rain to-day; a person may *trust* to the skill of another, or *confide* in his promises. *Trust* and *confidence* denote the same sentiment, but *trust* is applied to objects generally, *confidence* to particular objects; we may *trust* partially, but we *confide* entirely; we may *trust* strangers, we *confide* in friends or those we are partial to.

Trust and *confidence* may both be applied to a man's self, or that which belongs to him, with a similar distinction.

HOPEFUL. See SANGUINE.

HOPELESS. See DESPERATE.

HORRIBLE. See FEARFUL.

HORRID. See FEARFUL.

HOST. See ARMY.

HOSTILE. See ADVERSE.

HOSTILITY. See ENMITY.

HOT, FIERY, BURNING, ARDENT. These terms characterize either the presence of *heat* or the cause of *heat*. *Hot*, Anglo-Saxon *hat*, is the general term which marks simply the presence of *heat; fiery, i. e.,* having fire, goes further, it denotes the presence of *fire*, which is the cause of *heat; burning, i. e.,* in a state of burning, denotes the action of *fire*, and consequently is more expressive than the two; *ardent* (see FERVOR), which is literally the same in signification, is employed either in poetry or in application to moral objects: a room is *hot;* a furnace or the tail of a comet *fiery;* a coal *burning;* the sun *ardent.*

In the figurative application, a temper is said to be *hot* or *fiery;* rage is *burning;* the mind is *ardent* in pursuit of an object. Zeal may be *hot, fiery, burning,* and *ardent,* but in the first three cases it denotes the intemperance of the mind when *heated* by religion or politics; the last is admissible so long as it is confined to a good object.

See also FIRE.

HOUSE. See FAMILY.

HOWEVER, YET, NEVERTHELESS, NOTWITHSTANDING. These conjunctions are in grammar termed adversative, because they join sentences together that stand more or less in opposition to each other. *However* is the most general and indefinite; it serves as a conclusive deduction drawn from the whole. "The truth is, *however,* not yet all come out"; by this is understood that much of the truth has been told, and much *yet* remains to be told: so likewise in similar sentences, "I am not, *however,* of that opinion"; where it is implied either that many hold the opinion or much may be said of it, but, be that as it may, I am not of that opinion: "*however,* you may rely on my assistance to that amount"; that is, at all events, let whatever happen, you may rely on so much of my assistance: *however,* as is obvious from the above examples, connects not only one single proposition, but many propositions either expressed or understood. *Yet, nevertheless,* and *notwithstanding* are mostly employed to set two specific propositions either in contrast or direct opposition to each other; the latter two are but species of the former, pointing out the opposition in a more specific manner.

There are cases in which *yet* is peculiarly proper, others in which *nevertheless,* and others in which *notwithstanding* are preferable. *Yet* bespeaks a simple contrast; "Addison was not a good speaker, *yet* he was an admirable writer; Johnson was a man of uncouth manners, *yet* he had a good heart and a sound head"; *nevertheless* and *notwithstanding* could not in these cases have been substituted. *Nevertheless* and *notwithstanding* are mostly used to imply effects or consequences opposite to what might naturally be expected to result. "He has acted an unworthy part, *nevertheless* I will be a friend to him as far as I can"; that is, although he has acted an unworthy part, I will be no less his friend as far as lies in my power. "*Notwithstanding* all I have said, he still persists in his own imprudent conduct"; that is, all I have said *notwithstanding* or not restraining him from it, he still persists. "He is still rich, *notwithstanding* his loss"; that is, his loss *notwithstanding*, or *not standing* in the way of it, he is still rich. From this resolution of the terms, more than from any specific rule, we may judge of their distinct applications, and clearly perceive that in such cases as those above cited the conjunctions *nevertheless* and *notwithstanding* could not be substituted for each other, nor *yet* for either: in other cases, *however,* where the objects are less definitely pointed out, they may be used indifferently. "The Jesuits piqued themselves always upon their strict morality, and *yet* [*notwithstanding* or *nevertheless*] they admitted of many things not altogether consonant with moral principle. You know that these are but tales, *yet* [*notwithstanding, nevertheless*] you believe them."

HUDDLE. See JUMBLE.

HUE. See COLOR.

HUG. See CLASP.

HUGE. See ENORMOUS.

HUMAN, HUMANE. Though both derived from *homo*, a man, they are thus far distinguished that *human* is said of the genus and *humane* of the species. The *human* race or *human* beings are opposed to the irrational part of the creation; a *humane* race or a *humane* individual is opposed to one that is cruel and fond of inflicting pain. He who is not *human* is divested of the first and distinguishing characteristics of his kind; he who is not *humane*, of the most important and elevated characteristic that belongs to his nature.

HUMANITY. See BENEVOLENCE.

HUMBLE, LOWLY, LOW. *Humble* is here compared with the other terms as it respects both persons and things. A person is said to be *humble* on account of the state of his mind: he is said to be *lowly* and *low* either on account of his mind or his outward circumstances. A *humble* person is so in his principles and in his conduct; a *lowly* person is so in the tone of his feelings, or in his station and walk of life; a *low* person is so either in his sentiments, in his actions, or in his rank and condition; but persons may sometimes be *low* from particular circumstances who are not *low* in condition. *Humility* should form a part of the character, as it is opposed to arrogance and assumption; it is most consistent with the fallibility of our nature. *Lowliness,* in the Christian belief, should form a part of our temper, as it is opposed to an aspiring and lofty mind; it is most consistent with the temper of our Saviour, who was meek and *lowly* of mind.

The *humble* and *lowly* are always taken in a good sense; but the *low* either in a bad or an indifferent sense. A *lowly* man, whether as it regards his mind or his condition, is so without any moral debasement; but a man who is *low* in his condition is likewise conceived to be *low* in his habits and his sentiments, which is being nearly akin to the *vicious*. The same distinction is preserved in applying these terms to inanimate or spiritual objects. A *humble* roof, a *humble* office, a *humble* station are associated with the highest moral worth; while a *low* office, a *low* situation, a *low* birth, seem to exclude the idea of worth.

See also ABASE.

Humble, Modest, Submissive.—These terms designate a temper of mind the reverse of self-conceit or pride. The *humble*, in Latin *humilis*, low, from *humus*, the ground, signifying the lowest position, is so with regard to ourselves or others. *Modesty* (see MODEST) is that which regards ourselves only: *submissiveness*, from *submissus*, signifying putting under, is that which regards others. A man is *humble* from a sense of his comparative inferiority to others in point of station and outward circumstances; or he is *humble* from a sense of his imperfections and a consciousness of not being what he ought to be: he is *modest*, inasmuch as he sets but little value on his qualifications, acquirements, and endowments. *Humility* is a painful sentiment; for when it concerns others it is coupled with fear; when it concerns our own unworthiness it is coupled with sorrow: *modesty* is a peaceful sentiment; it serves to keep the whole mind in due bounds. When *humility* and *modesty* show themselves in the outward conduct, the former bows itself down, the latter shrinks: a *humble* man gives freely to others from a sense of their deserving; a *modest* man demands nothing for himself, from an unconsciousness of deserving in himself.

Between *humble* and *submissive* there is this prominent feature of distinction, that the former marks a temper of mind, the latter a mode of action: the former is, therefore, often the cause of the latter, but not so always; we may be *submissive* because we are *humble;* but we may likewise be *submissive* from fear, from interested motives, from necessity, from duty, and the like; and on the other hand, we may be *humble* without being *submissive*, when we are not brought into connection with others. A man is *humble* when in solitude he takes a review of his sinfulness; he is *submissive* to a master whose displeasure he dreads.

Humble, Humiliate, Degrade.—*Humble* and *humiliate* are both drawn from the same source (see above). *Degrade* (see above).

Humble is commonly used as the act either of persons or things: a person may *humble* himself or he may be *humbled: humiliate* is employed to characterize things; a thing is *humiliating* or a *humiliation*. No man *humbles* himself by the acknowledgment of a fault; but it is a great *humiliation* for a person to be dependent on another for a living when he has it in his power to obtain it for himself.

To *humble* is to bring down to the ground; it supposes a certain eminence, either created by the mind or really existing in the outward circumstances; to *degrade* is to set down lower; it supposes steps for descending. He who is most elevated in his own esteem may be most *humbled;* misfortunes may *humble* the proudest conqueror: he who is most elevated in the esteem of others may be the most *degraded;* envy is ever on the alert to *degrade*. A lesson in the school of adversity is *humbling* to one who has known nothing but prosperity: terms of peace are *humiliating:* low vices are peculiarly *degrading* to a man of rank.

HUMIDITY. See MOISTURE.
HUMILIATE. See HUMBLE.

HUMOR, TEMPER, MOOD. *Humor* literally signifies moisture or fluid, in which sense it is used for the fluids of the human body; and as far as these *humors* or their particular state is connected with, or has its influence on, the animal spirits and the moral feelings, so far is *humor* applicable to moral agents. *Temper* (see DISPOSITION) is less specific in its signification; it may, with equal propriety, under the changed form of temperament, be applicable to the general state of the body or the mind. *Mood*, which is but a change from *mode* or manner, has an original signification not less indefinite than the former; it is applied, however, only to the mind. As the *humors* of the body are the most variable parts of the animal frame, *humor* in regard to the mind denotes but a partial and transitory state when compared with the *temper*, which is a general and habitual state. The *humor* is so fluctuating that it varies in the same mind perpetually; but the *temper* is so far confined that it always shows itself to be the same whenever it shows itself at all: the *humor* makes a man different from himself; the *temper* makes him different from others. Hence we speak of the *humor* of the moment; of the *temper* of youth or of old age: so likewise we say, to accommodate one's self to the *humor* of a person; to manage his *temper:* to put one into a certain *humor;* to correct or sour the *temper*. *Humor* is not less partial in its nature than in its duration; it fixes itself often on only one object, or regards only one particular direction of feelings: *temper* extends to all the actions and opinions as well as feelings of a man: it gives a coloring to all he says, does, thinks, and feels. We may be in a *humor* for writing or reading; for what is gay or what is serious; for what is noisy or what is quiet; but our *temper* is discoverable in our daily conduct; we may be in a good or ill *humor* in company, but in domestic life and in our closest relations we show whether we are good or ill *tempered*. A man shows his *humor* in different or trifling actions; he shows his *temper* in the most important actions: it may be a man's *humor* to sit while others stand, or to go un-shaven while others shave; but he shows his *temper* as a Christian or otherwise in forgiving injuries or not harboring resentments; in living peace-ably, not indulging himself in con-tentions.

When applied to bodies of men *hu-mor*, as denoting a temporary or fluctu-ating feeling, is more commonly used than *temper*.

Humor and *mood* agree in denoting a particular and temporary state of feeling; but they differ in the cause, the former being attributable rather to the physical state of the body, and the latter to the moral frame of the mind; the former, therefore, is inde-pendent of all external circumstances, or at all events of any that are re-ducible to system; the latter is guided entirely by events, or the view which the mind takes of events. *Humor* is, therefore, generally taken in a bad sense unless actually qualified by some epithet to the contrary: *mood* is always taken in an indifferent sense. There is no calculating on the *humor* of a man; it depends upon his *mood* whether he performs ill or well: it is necessary to suppress *humor* in a child; we dis-cover by the melancholy *mood* of a man that something distressing has happened to him.

See also GRATIFY; QUALIFY; WIT.

Humor, Caprice.—*Humor* is general, *caprice* (see FANCIFUL) is particular: *humor* may be good or bad; *caprice* is always taken in a bad sense. *Humor* is always independent of fixed prin-ciple; it is the feeling or impulse of the moment: *caprice* is always opposed to fixed principle or rational motives of acting; it is the feeling of the indi-vidual setting at naught all rule and defying all reason. The feeling only is perverted when the *humor* predomi-nates; the judgment and will are per-verted by *caprice;* a child shows its *humor* in fretfulness and impatience; a man betrays his *caprice* in his inter-course with others, in the management of his concerns, or in the choice of his amusements.

Indulgence, according to a mode of speech now practically obsolete, ren-ders children and subordinate persons

humorsome; prosperity or unlimited power is apt to render a man *capricious:* a *humorsome* person commonly objects to be pleased or is easily displeased; a *capricious* person likes and dislikes, approves and disapproves the . same thing in quick succession.

Humorsome, Humorous, Capricious —*Humor*, when applied to things, has the sense of wit, whence the distinction between *humorsome* and *humorous*, the former implying the existence of *humor* or perverted feeling in the person; the latter implying the existence of *humor* or wit in the person or thing. *Caprice* is improperly applied to things to des-ignate their total irregularity and plan-lessness of proceeding, as, in speaking of fashion, we notice its *caprice* when that which has been laid aside is again taken into use; diseases are termed *capricious* which act in direct opposi-tion to all established rule.

HUNT, CHASE. The leading idea in the word *hunt* from Anglo-Saxon *huntian*, to capture, is that of searching after; the leading idea in the word *chase* is that of driving away or before one. In a strict sense, *hunt* denotes a search for objects not within sight; *chase* is a pursuit after such objects only as are within sight: we may *hunt*, therefore, without *chasing:* we may *chase* without *hunting:* a person *hunts* after, but does not *chase* that which is lost: a boy *chases*, but does not *hunt*, a butterfly. When applied to field sports, the *hunt* commences as soon as the huntsman begins to look for the game; the *chase* commences as soon as it is found: on this ground, perhaps, it is that *hunt* is used, in familiar dis-course, to designate the specific act of taking this amusement; and *chase* is used only in particular cases where the peculiar idea is to be expressed: a fox-*hunt*, or a stag-*hunt*, is said to take place on a particular day; or that there has been no *hunting* this season, or that the *hunt* has been very bad: but we speak, on the other hand, of the pleas-ures of the *chase*, or that the *chase* lasted very long; the animal gave a long *chase*.

HURL. See CAST.
HURRY. See HASTEN.
HURT. See DISADVANTAGE; IN-JURY; SORRY.

HURTFUL, Pernicious, Noxious, Noisome. Between *hurt*, signifying full of *hurt*, and *pernicious* there is the same distinction as between *hurting* and *destroying*: that which is *hurtful* may *hurt* in various ways; but that which is *pernicious* necessarily tends to destruction: confinement is *hurtful* to the health: bad company is *pernicious* to the morals, or the doctrines of free-thinkers are said to be *pernicious* to the well-being of society. *Noxious* and *noisome*, from *nocere*, to *hurt*, are species of the *hurtful:* things may be *hurtful* both to body and mind; *noxious* and *noisome* only to the body: that which is *noxious* inflicts a direct injury; that which is *noisome* inflicts it indirectly: *noxious* insects are such as wound; *noisome* vapors are such as tend to create disorders.

HUSBAND, Conserve, Economize. *Husband*, from the Icelandic *husbondi*, that contracted from *husbuandi*, compound of *hus*, a house, and *buandi*, a dwelling, all imply the male head of a household. In the present application the term signifies to manage one's affairs with frugality, to use one's resources so as to produce the best results.

Conserve, from Latin *conservare*, means primarily to save. We *conserve* our health and property by adopting such methods as will save them from depreciation, injury, loss, or destruction. We *economize* our health, time, and property by managing each with care, prudence, and a proper regard for their value. *Economize* has an original meaning similar to that of *husband*, being derived from the Greek word for house, and indicating the management of the household. *Husband*, however, means primarily prudence in saving, in gathering together, and conserving resources; *economize* signifies prudence in spending. See Economical.

HUSBANDMAN. See Farmer.

HUSBANDRY. See Cultivation.

HYDROPLANE. See Aircraft.

HYPNOTISM, Mesmerism, Animal Magnetism. The difference between these three words is not a difference in meaning, but a difference in the theory implied in them, and in fashionable and professional usage. *Hypnotism* replaced *mesmerism*, and *mesmerism animal magnetism* in professional usage as names for the same phenomenon. This phenomenon is a peculiar condition of the nervous system induced by a fixed, abstracted attention of the mental and visual eye on one object not of an exciting nature. It was called *animal magnetism* by F. A. Mesmer, because he believed in a magnetic force in animals, peculiar to living beings, by which one acts on another just as the magnet acts on steel; to this the inducing of the hypnotic state was due. The phenomenon was by others called *mesmerism*, after Mesmer (about 1766), because it was made known to the public everywhere chiefly through his somewhat spectacular methods of producing it. *Mesmerism* refers, then, primarily to the manner of inducing a hypnotic condition. The term *hypnotism*, from ὕπνος, sleep, and νεῦρον, nerve, was coined in 1842 by James Braid, who was the first to investigate the subject in a physiological way. This name was intended to imply that the phenomenon was due not to any occult magnetic force, inherent in organic life everywhere, but to a peculiar condition of the nerves. His name replaced *mesmerism* in popular usage.

HYPOCHONDRIACAL, Melancholic, Splenetic. These words all refer to an abnormal psychological condition supposed to be produced or accompanied by a disorder of the *spleen;* but they indicate slightly different psychological states.

Hypochondriacal (from Greek ὑπό and χόνδρια, the parts beneath the breastbone, *i. e.*, the spleen) is the adjective corresponding to *hypochondria*, a gloomy and irritable state of mind in which the subject believes that his health is in a very serious condition and that he is threatened with death. *Melancholic* (Greek μελαγχολία, black bile, referring to secretions of the spleen) refers simply to a state of morbid gloom. *Splenetic*, from Latin *splen*, Greek σπλήν, spleen, refers to a state of morbid gloom especially characterized by irritableness of temper, a disposition to take offence at everything.

HYPOCRITE, Dissembler. *Hypocrite*, in Greek ὑποκριτής, from ὑπό and κρίνομαι, signifies one playing a part on a stage. *Dissembler*, from *dissemble*, in Latin *dissimulo* or *dis* and *similis,* signifies one who makes himself appear unlike what he really is.

The *hypocrite* feigns to be what he is not; the *dissembler* conceals what he is; the former takes to himself the credit of virtues which he has not; the latter conceals the vices that he has; every *hypocrite* is a *dissembler;* but every *dissembler* is not a *hypocrite:* the *hypocrite* makes truth serve the purpose of falsehood; the *dissembler* is content with making falsehood serve his own particular purpose.

HYPOTHETICAL. See EMPIRICAL.

I

IDEA, THOUGHT, IMAGINATION. *Idea*, in Latin *idea*, in Greek ἰδέα, from the root found in Latin *videre*, to see, signifies the thing seen in the mind. *Thought* comes from Anglo-Saxon *thencan*, modern English *think*. *Imagination* signifies the thing *imagined*, from Latin *imago*, from the root *im*, found in *imitare*, English *imitate*.

The *idea* is the simple representation of an object; the thought is the reflection; and the *imagination* is the combination of *ideas*: we have *ideas* of the sun, the moon, and all material objects; we have *thoughts* on moral subjects; we have *imaginations* drawn from the *ideas* already existing in the mind. *Ideas* are formed; they are the rude materials with which the *thinking* faculty exerts itself: *thoughts* arise in the mind by means of association and combination, or recur in the mind by the power of the memory; they are the materials with which the *thinking* faculty employs itself: *imaginations* are created by the mind's reaction on itself; they are the materials with which the understanding seeks to enrich itself. The term *ideas* is used in all cases for the mental representation, abstractedly from the agent that represents them: hence *ideas* are attached to words; *ideas* are analyzed, confounded, and the like; in which cases the word *thought* could not be substituted. *Thought* belongs only to thinking and rational beings: the animals may be said to have *ideas*, but not *thoughts:* hence *thoughts* are either mean, fine, grovelling, or sublime, according to the nature of the mind in which they exist: hence we say with more propriety, to indulge a *thought* than to indulge an *idea;* to express one's *thoughts*, rather than one's *ideas*, on any subject: although the latter term *idea*, on account of its comprehensive use, may, without violation of any express rule, be indifferently employed in general discourse for *thought;* but the former term does not on this account lose its characteristic meaning. *Imagination* is not only the fruit of *thought*, but of peculiar *thought:* the *thought* may be another's: the *imagination* is one's own: the *thought* occurs and recurs; it comes and it goes; it is retained or rejected at the pleasure of the *thinking* being: the *imagination* is framed by the power which we term *imagination;* it is cherished with the partiality of a parent for its offspring. *Thoughts* are busied with the surrounding objects; *imaginations* are employed on distant and strange objects: hence *thoughts* are denominated sober, chaste, and the like; *imaginations*, wild and extravagant.

See also PERCEPTION.

Ideal, Imaginary.—*Ideal* does not strictly adhere to the sense of its primitive, *idea:* the *idea* is the representation of a real object in the mind; but *ideal* signifies belonging to the *idea* independently of the reality or the external object. *Imaginary* preserves the signification of its primitive, *imagination* (see FANCY) denotes what is created by the mind itself. The *ideal* is not directly opposed to, but abstracted from the real; the *imaginary*, on the other hand, is d rectly opposed to the real; it is the unreal thing formed by the *imagination*. *Ideal* happiness is the happiness which is formed in the mind without having any direct and actual prototype in nature; but it may, nevertheless, be something possible to be realized; it may be above nature, but not in direct contradiction to it: the *imaginary* is that which is opposite to some positive existing reality; the pleasure which a lunatic derives from the conceit of being a king is altogether *imaginary*.

See also UTOPIAN.

IDIOM. See LANGUAGE.

IDIOT. See FOOL.

IDLE, LAZY, INDOLENT. *Idle* comes from Anglo-Saxon *idel*, vain, empty. *Lazy* comes from Low German *lasich*, allied to loose, signifying languid, idle.

Indolent, in Latin *indolens,* from *in,* not, and *dolens,* from *dolere,* to grieve, signifies not grieving, lacking in feeling; hence, lacking in life and energy.

A propensity to inaction is the co `- mon idea by which these words are connected; they differ in the cause and degree of the quality: *idle* expresses less than *lazy,* and *lazy* less than *indolent:* one is termed *idle* who will do nothing useful; one is *lazy* who will do nothing at all without great reluctance; one is *indolent* who does not care to do anything or set about anything. There is no direct inaction in the *idler;* for a child is *idle* who will not learn his lesson, but he is active enough in that which pleases himself: there is an aversion to corporeal action in a *lazy* man, but not always to mental action; he is *lazy* at work, *lazy* in walking, or *lazy* in sitting; but he may not object to any employment, such as reading or thinking, which leaves his body entirely at rest: an *indolent* man, on the contrary, fails in activity from a defect both in the mind and the body; he will not only not move, but he will not even think, if it give him trouble; and trifling exertions of any kind are sufficient, even in prospect, to deter him from attempting to move.

Lazy is figuratively applied to other objects.

Idle is also applied to things in the sense of leisure and vanity, for which see the next analysis.

Idle, Leisure, Vacant.—*Idle* is opposed here to busy; *leisure* comes from Anglo-French *leisir,* originally the infinitive mood, signifying to be permitted, from Latin *licere.* He, therefore, who is *idle,* instead of being busy, commits a fault; which is not always the case with him who is at *leisure* or free from his employment. *Idle* is always taken in a sense more or less unfavorable; *leisure* in a sense perfectly indifferent: if a man says of himself that he has spent an *idle* hour in this or that place, in amusement, company, and the like, he means to signify he would have spent it better if anything had offered; on the other hand, he would say that he spends his *leisure* moments in a suitable relaxation: he

who values his time will take care to have as few *idle* hours as possible; but since no one can always be employed in severe labor, he will occupy his *leisure* hours in that which best suits his taste.

Idle and *leisure* are said in particular reference to the time that is employed; *vacant* (see FILL) is a more general term that simply qualifies the thing: an *idle* hour is one without any proper employment; a *vacant* hour is in general one free from the employments with which it might be filled; a person has *leisure* time according to his wishes; but he may have *vacant* time from necessity; that is, when he is in want of employment.

Idle, Vain.—These epithets are both opposed to the solid or substantial; but *idle* has a more particular reference to what ought or ought not to engage the time or attention; *vain,* in Latin *vanus,* signifying empty, seems to qualify the thing without any such reference. A pursuit may be termed either *idle* or *vain:* in the former case, it reflects immediately on the agent for not employing his time on something more serious; but in the latter case it simply characterizes the pursuit as one that will be attended with no good consequences: when we consider ourselves as beings who have but a short time to live, and that every moment of that time ought to be thoroughly well spent, we should be careful to avoid all *idle* concerns; when we consider ourselves as rational beings, who are responsible for the use of those powers with which we have been invested by God we shall be careful to reject all *vain* concerns: an *idle* effort is made by one who does not care to exert himself for any useful purpose, who works only to please himself; a *vain* effort may be made by one who is in a state of desperation.

IGNOMINY. See INFAMY.

IGNORANT, ILLITERATE, UNLEARNED, UNLETTERED. *Ignorant,* in Latin *ignorans,* from the privative *in,* and the root *gno,* signifying to know, signifies not knowing things in general, or not knowing any particular circumstance. *Unlearned, illiterate,* and *unlettered* are compared with *ignorant* in the general sense.

Ignorant is a comprehensive term;

it includes any degree from the highest to the lowest, and consequently includes the other terms, *illiterate*, *unlearned*, and *unlettered*, which express different forms of *ignorance*. *Ignorance* is not always to one's disgrace, since it is not always one's fault; the term is not, therefore, directly reproachful: the poor, *ignorant* savage is an object of pity rather than condemnation; but when *ignorance* is coupled with self-conceit and presumption, it is a real deformity: hence the word *illiterate*, which is mostly used in such cases, has become a term of reproach: an *ignorant* man who sets up to teach others is termed an *illiterate* preacher; and quacks, whether in religion or medicine, from the very nature of their calling, are altogether an *illiterate* race of men. The term *illiterate* is in all cases taken for one who is without education or even the knowledge of his letters; the words *unlearned* and *unlettered* are disengaged from any unfavorable associations. A modest man, who makes no pretensions to learning, may suitably apologize for his supposed deficiencies by saying he is an *unlearned* or *unlettered* man; the former is, however, a term of more familiar use than the latter. A man may be described either as generally *unlearned* or as *unlearned* in particular sciences or arts; as *unlearned* in history; *unlearned* in philosophy; *unlearned* in the ways of the world: a rustic poet's muse may be described as *unlettered*.

ILL. See BADLY; EVIL.

ILL-FATED. See HAPLESS.

ILLITERATE. See IGNORANT.

ILLNESS. See SICKNESS.

ILLUMINATE, ILLUMINE, ENLIGHTEN. *Illuminate*, in Latin *illuminatus*, participle of *illumino* (from Latin *in*, and *lumen*, light), and *enlighten*, coined with the French *en*, from the verb *lighten*, both denote the communication of light; the former in the natural, the latter in the moral sense. We *illuminate* by means of artificial lights; or, as in the case of mediæval manuscripts (though, in this sense, the term is now obsolete) by color: the sun *illuminates* the world by its own light: preaching and instruction *enlighten* the minds of men. *Illumine* is but a poetic variation of *illuminate;* as, the Sun of Righteousness *illumined* the benighted world; *illuminations* are employed as public demonstrations of joy; no nation is now termed *enlightened* but such as has received the light of the Gospel.

ILLUSION. See DELUSION; FALLACY.

ILLUSTRATE. See EXPLAIN.

ILLUSTRIOUS. See DISTINGUISHED; FAMOUS.

ILL-WILL. See HATRED.

IMAGE. See LIKENESS.

IMAGINARY. See IDEAL.

IMAGINATION. See FANCY; IDEA.

IMAGINE. See APPREHEND; THINK.

IMBECILITY. See DEBILITY.

IMBIBE. See ABSORB.

IMITATE, COPY, COUNTERFEIT. The idea of taking a likeness of some object is common to all these terms; but *imitate* (see FOLLOW) is the generic: *copy* (see that word) and *counterfeit*, through French *contrefait*, from the Latin *contra*, against, and *facere*, to make, signifying to make in opposition to the reality, are the specific terms: to *imitate* is to take a general likeness; to *copy*, to take an exact likeness; to *counterfeit*, to take a false likeness: to *imitate* is, therefore, almost always used in a good or an indifferent sense; to *copy* mostly, and to *counterfeit* still oftener, in a bad sense: to *imitate* an author's style is at all times allowable for one who cannot form a style for himself; but to *copy* an author's style would be a too slavish adherence even for the dullest writer.

To *imitate* is applicable to every object, for every external object is susceptible of *imitation;* and in man the *imitative* faculty displays itself alike in the highest and the lowest matters, in works of art and moral conduct: to *copy* is applicable only to certain objects which will admit of a minute likeness being taken; thus, an artist may be said to *copy* from nature.

To *counterfeit* is applicable to but few objects: we may *counterfeit* coin, which is an unlawful act, or we may *counterfeit* the person, the character, the voice, or the handwriting of any one for whom we would wish to pass, which is also an unlawful act except on the stage.

Imitate, Mimic, Ape, Mock. — To

imitate is here the general term: to *mimic*, from the Greek μῖμος, an actor or mimic, and to *ape*, signifying to *imitate* like an *ape* (Anglo-Saxon *apa*, German *affe*), are both species of vicious *imitation*. One *imitates* that which is deserving of *imitation*, or the contrary: one *mimics* either that which is not an authorized subject of *imitation* or which is *imitated* imperfectly or so as to excite laughter. A person wishes to make that his own which he *imitates*, but he *mimics* for the entertainment of others.

To *ape* is a serious, though an absurd, act of *imitation*. To *mock*, Old French *mocquer*, a Picard form for *moucher*, to wipe the nose, Latin *muccare*, to blow the nose (from Latin *mucus*, English *mucus*), indicating a vulgar gesture of contempt, signifies to laugh at, and is an ill-natured and vulgar act of *imitation*. The ape *imitates* to please himself; the mocker *mocks* to insult others.

IMMATERIAL. See INCORPOREAL; UNIMPORTANT.

IMMEDIATELY. See DIRECTLY; NOW.

IMMENSE. See ENORMOUS.

IMMINENT, IMPENDING, THREATENING. *Imminent*, in Latin *imminens*, from *minere*, to project, signifies resting or coming upon. *Impending*, from the Latin *pendere*, to hang, signifies hanging upon or over. *Threat*, Anglo-Saxon *threotan*, to afflict, vex, urge, is allied to Latin *trudere* (found in *intrude* and *obtrude*), signifying to push, work, urge.

All these terms are used in regard to some evil that is exceedingly near: *imminent* conveys no idea of duration; *impending* excludes the idea of what is momentary. A person may be in *imminent* danger of losing his life in one instant, and the danger may be over the next instant: but an *impending* danger is that which has been long in existence and gradually approaching; we can seldom escape *imminent* danger by any efforts of our own: but we may be successfully warned to escape from an *impending* danger. *Imminent* and *impending* are said of dangers that are not discoverable; but a *threatening* evil gives intimations of its own approach; we perceive the *threatening* tempest in the blackness of the sky; we hear the *threatening* sounds of the enemy's clashing sword.

IMMODERATE. See EXCESSIVE.

IMMODEST, IMPUDENT, SHAMELESS. *Immodest* signifies the want of modesty: *impudent* and *shameless* signify without *shame*. *Immodest* is less than either *impudent* or *shameless:* an *immodest* girl lays aside the ornament of her sex and puts on another garb that is less becoming; but her heart need not be corrupt until she becomes *impudent:* she lacks a good quality when she is *immodest;* she is possessed of a positively bad quality when she is *impudent*. There is always hope that an *immodest* woman may be conscious of her error, and amend; but of an *impudent* woman there is no such chance—she is radically corrupt. *Impudent* may characterize the person or the thing: *shameless*, from Anglo-Saxon *sceamu*, shame, and negative suffix, characterizes the person. A person's air, look, and words are *impudent* when contrary to all modesty: the person himself is *shameless* who is devoid of all sense of shame.

See also IMPERTINENT; INDECENT.

IMMUNITY. See PRIVILEGE.

IMPAIR, INJURE. *Impair* comes through Old French *empeirer*, from Late Latin *impeiorare*, compounded of the Latin *in* and *peior*, worse, signifying to make worse. *Injure*, from *in*, against, and *iur*, the stem of *ius*, right, signifies to make otherwise than it ought to be.

Impair seems to be in regard to *injury* as the species to the genus; what is *impaired* is *injured*, but what is *injured* is not necessarily *impaired*. To *impair* is a progressive mode of *injuring:* an *injury* may take place either by degrees or by an instantaneous act: straining of the eyes *impairs* the sight, but a blow *injures* rather than *impairs* the eye. A man's health may be *impaired* or *injured* by his vices, but his limbs are *injured* rather than *impaired* by a fall. A person's circumstances are *impaired* by a succession of misfortunes; they are *injured* by a sudden turn of fortune.

IMPART. See COMMUNICATE.

IMPARTIAL. See NEUTRAL.

IMPASSABLE. See IMPERVIOUS.

IMPEACH. See ACCUSE.
IMPEDE. See HINDER.
IMPEL. See ACTUATE; COMPEL; ENCOURAGE.
IMPENDING. See IMMINENT.
IMPERFECTION, DEFECT, FAULT, VICE. These terms are applied either to persons or to things. *Imperfection*, denoting either the abstract quality of *imperfect* or the thing which constitutes it *imperfect*, in a person arises from his want of *perfection* and the infirmity of his nature; there is no one without some point of *imperfection* which is obvious to others, if not to himself; he may strive to diminish it, although he cannot expect to get altogether rid of it: a *defect* (see BLEMISH) is a deviation from the general constitution of man; it is what may be natural to the man as an individual, but not natural to man as a species; in this manner we may speak of a *defect* in the speech, or a *defect* in temper. The *fault* and *vice* rise in degree and character above either of the former terms; they both reflect disgrace more or less on the person possessing them; but the *fault* always characterizes the agent, and is said in relation to an individual; the *vice*, from Latin *vitium*, a vice or fault, characterizes the action and may be considered abstractedly: hence we speak of a man's *faults* as the things we may condemn in him; but we may speak of the *vices* of drunkenness, lying, and the like, without any immediate reference to any one who practices these *vices*. When they are both employed for an individual their distinction is obvious: the *fault* may lessen the amiability or excellence of the character; the *vice* is a stain; a single act destroys its purity; a habitual practice is a pollution.

In regard to things, the distinction depends upon the preceding explanation in a great measure, for we can scarcely use these words without thinking on man as a moral agent, who was made the most perfect of all creatures, and became the most *imperfect;* and from our *imperfection* has arisen, also, a general *imperfection* throughout all the works of creation. The word *imperfection* is therefore the most unqualified term of all: there may be *imperfection* in regard to our Maker,

or there may be *imperfection* in regard to what we conceive of *perfection;* and in this case the term simply and generally implies whatever falls short in any degree or manner of *perfection*. *Defect* is a positive degree of *imperfection;* it is contrary both to our ideas of *perfection* and to our particular intention: thus, there may be a *defect* in the materials of which a thing is made; or a *defect* in the mode of making it: the term *defect*, however, whether said of persons or things, characterizes rather the object than the agent. *Fault*, on the other hand, when said of things, always refers to the agent: thus we may say there is a *defect* in the glass, or a *defect* in the spring; but there is a *fault* in the workmanship, or a *fault* in the putting together, and the like. *Vice*, with regard to things, is properly a serious or radical *defect;* the former lies in the constitution of the whole, the latter may lie in the parts; the former lies in essentials, the latter lies in the accidents: there may be a *defect* in the shape or make of a horse; but the *vice* is said in regard to his soundness or unsoundness, his docility or indocility.

Imperfection, Weakness, Frailty, Failing, Foible.—*Imperfection* has already been considered as that which in the most extended sense diminishes the moral *perfection* of man; the rest are but modes of *imperfection* varying in degree and circumstances. *Weakness* is a positive and strong degree of *imperfection* which is opposed to strength; it is what we do not so necessarily look for, and therefore distinguishes the individual who is liable to it. *Frailty* is another strong mode of *imperfection* which characterizes the fragility of man, but not of all men in the same degree; it differs from *weakness* in respect to the object. A *weakness* lies more in the judgment or in the sentiment; *frailty* lies more in the moral features of an action. It is *weakness* in a man to yield to the persuasions of any one against his better judgment; it is *frailty* to yield to intemperance or illicit indulgences. *Failings* and *foibles* (from Old French *foible*, English *feeble*, Latin *flebilis*, doleful, from *flere*, to weep) are the smallest degrees of *imperfection* to which the human character is liable: we all have our *failings* in temper, and our *foibles* in our habits and our prepossessions; and he, as Horace observes, is the best who has the fewest.

IMPERIOUS, LORDLY, DOMINEERING, OVERBEARING. All these epithets imply an unseemly exercise or affectation of power or superiority. *Imperious,* from *imperare,* to command, characterizes either the disposition to command without adequate authority or to convey one's commands in an offensive manner: *lordly* (from Anglo-Saxon *hlaford,* lord, from *hlaf,* bread—English *loaf*—and *weard,* guard, English *ward,* signifying the guardian of the loaf) characterizes the manner of acting the *lord:* and *domineering,* from *dominus,* a *lord,* denotes the manner of ruling like a *lord,* or rather of attempting to rule; hence a person's temper or his tone is denominated *imperious;* his air or deportment is *lordly;* his tone is *domineering.* A woman of an *imperious* temper commands in order to be obeyed; she commands with an *imperious* tone in order to enforce obedience. A person assumes a *lordly* air in order to display his own importance; he gives orders in a *domineering* tone in order to make others feel their inferiority. There is always something offensive in *imperiousness;* there is frequently something ludicrous in that which is *lordly;* and a mixture of the ludicrous and offensive in that which is *domineering.*

These terms are employed for such as are invested with some sort of power, or endowed with some sort of superiority, however trifling; but *overbearing* is employed for men in the general relations of society, whether superiors or equals. A man of an *imperious* temper and some talent will frequently be so *overbearing* in the assemblies of his equals as to awe the rest into silence and carry every measure of his own without contradiction.

See also COMMANDING.

IMPERTINENT, RUDE, SAUCY, IMPUDENT, INSOLENT. *Impertinent,* in Latin *in,* a privative prefix, and *pertinens,* belonging, signifies being or wanting to do what it does not belong to one to be or do. *Rude,* in Latin *rudis,* rude, signifies literally unpolished, and, in an extended sense, wanting all culture. *Saucy* comes from *sauce,* in Latin *sals, a,* feminine of *salsus,* salt, signifying literally full of sauce, pungent, and, in an extended sense, stinging like salt. *Impudent* (see ASSURANCE). *Insolent,* from the Latin *insolens,* is a word of doubtful origin, possibly compounded of *in,* against, and *solens,* from a root signifying to swell—referring here to the swelling of pride.

Impertinent is allied to *rude,* as regards one's general relations in society, without regard to station; it is allied to *saucy, impudent,* and *insolent* as regards the conduct of inferiors. He who does not respect the laws of civil society in his intercourse with individuals, and wants to assume to himself what belongs to another, is *impertinent:* if he carry this *impertinence* so far as to commit any violent breach of decorum in his behavior, he is *rude. Impertinence* seems to spring from a too high regard of one's self: *rudeness* from an ignorance of what is due to others. *Impertinent,* in comparison with the other terms, *saucy, impudent,* and *insolent,* is the most general and indefinite: whatever one does or says that is not compatible with one's station is *impertinent; saucy* is a sharp kind of *impertinence: impudent* an unblushing kind of *impertinence; insolence* is an outrageous kind of *impertinence,* it runs counter to all established order: thus, the terms seem to rise in sense. A person may be *impertinent* in words or actions: he is *saucy* in words or looks: he is *impudent* or *insolent* in words, tones, gesture, looks, and every species of action.

IMPERVIOUS, IMPASSABLE, INACCESSIBLE. *Impervious,* from the Latin *in, per,* and *via,* signifies not having a way through; *impassable,* not to be passed through; *inaccessible,* not to be approached. A wood is *impervious* when the trees, branches, and leaves are entangled to such a degree as to admit of no passage at all: a river is *impassable* that is so deep that it cannot be forded: a rock or a mountain is *inaccessible* the summit of which is not to be reached by any path whatever. What is *impervious* is so for a permanency; what is *impassable* is commonly so only for a time: roads are frequently *impassable* in the winter that are *passable* in the summer, while a thicket is *impervious* during the whole of the year: *impassable* is likewise said only of that which is to be passed by living creatures, but *impervious* may be extended to inanimate objects; a wood may be *impervious* to the rays of the sun.

IMPETUOUS. See VIOLENT.

IMPIOUS. See IRRELIGIOUS; SACRILEGIOUS.

IMPLACABLE, UNRELENTING, RELENTLESS, INEXORABLE. *Implacable,* from Latin *in,* privative, and *placere,* to please, signifies not to be softened or pleased. *Unrelenting,* from the Latin *lentus,* slow, slack, soft, signifies not rendered soft. *Inexorable,* from *oro,* pray, signifies not to be turned by prayers.

Inflexibility is the idea expressed in common by these terms, but they differ in the causes and circumstances with which it is attended. Animosities are *implacable* when no misery which we occasion can diminish their force, and no concessions on the part of the offender can lessen the spirit of revenge: the mind or character of a man is *unrelenting* when it is not to be turned from its purpose by a view of the pain which it inflicts: a man is *inexorable* who turns a deaf ear to every solicitation or entreaty that is made to induce him to lessen the rigor of his sentence. A man's angry passions render him *implacable;* it is not the magnitude of the offence, but the temper of the offended that is here in question; by *implacability* he is rendered insensible to the misery he occasions and to every satisfaction which the offender may offer him: fixedness of purpose renders a man *unrelenting* or *relentless;* an *unrelenting* temper is not less callous to the misery produced than an *implacable* temper; but it is not grounded always on resentment for personal injuries, but sometimes on a certain principle of right and a sense of necessity: the *inexorable* man adheres to this rule, as the *unrelenting* man does to his purpose; the former is insensible to any workings of his heart which might shake his purpose, the latter turns a deaf ear to all the solicitations of others which would go to alter his decrees: savages are mostly *implacable* in their animosities; Titus

Manlius Torquatus displayed an instance of *unrelenting* severity toward his son; Minos, Æacus, and Rhadamanthus were the *inexorable* judges of hell.

Implacable and *unrelenting* are said only of animate beings in whom is wanting an ordinary portion of the tender affections: *inexorable* may be improperly applied to inanimate objects; justice and death are both represented as *inexorable*.

IMPLANT, INGRAFT, INCULCATE, INSTIL, INFUSE. To *plant* is properly to fix plants in the ground; to *implant* is, in the improper sense, to fix principles in the mind. To *ingraft,* from *graft,* to make one plant grow on the stock of another, is to make particular principles flourish in the mind and form a part of the character. *Inculcate,* from Latin *in* and *culcare,* for *calcare,* or tread into, means to stamp into the mind. To *instil,* from French *instiller,* derived from Latin *in* and *stillare,* to drop into, is, in the improper sense, to make sentiments, as it were, drop into the mind. To *infuse,* from *in* and *fusus,* past participle of *fundere,* to pour, is, in the improper sense, to pour principles or feelings into the mind.

To *implant, ingraft,* and *inculcate* are said of abstract opinions or rules of right and wrong; *instil* and *infuse* of such principles as influence the heart, the affections, and the passions. It is the business of the parent in early life to *implant* sentiments of virtue in his child; it is the business of the teacher to *ingraft* them. *Instil* is a corresponding act with *implant;* we *implant* belief; we *instil* the feeling which is connected with this belief. It is not enough to have an abstract belief of a God *implanted* into the mind: we must likewise have a love, and a fear of Him, and reverence for His holy name and Word *instilled* into the mind. To *instil* is a gradual process which is the natural work of education; to *infuse* is a more arbitrary and immediate act. Sentiments are *instilled* into the mind, not altogether by the personal efforts of any individual, but likewise by collateral endeavors; they are, however, *infused* at the express will and with the express endeavor of some person. *Instil* is applicable only to permanent sentiments; *infuse* may be said of any partial feeling: hence we speak of *infusing* poison into the mind by means of insidious and mischievous publications; or *infusing* jealousy by means of crafty insinuations, or *infusing* ardor into the minds of soldiers by means of spirited addresses coupled with military successes.

IMPLICATE, INVOLVE. *Implicate*, from *plicare*, to fold, denotes to fold into a thing; and *involve*, from *volvere*, to roll, signifies to roll into a thing: by which explanation we perceive that to *implicate* marks something less entangled than to *involve:* for that which is folded may be folded only once, but that which is rolled is turned many times. In application, therefore, to human affairs, people are said to be *implicated* who have taken ever so small a share in a transaction; but they are *involved* only when they are deeply concerned: the former is likewise especially applied to criminal transactions, the latter to those things which are in themselves troublesome: thus a man is *implicated* in the guilt of robbery who should stand by and see it done, without interfering for its prevention; he who is in debt in every direction is strictly said to be *involved* in debt.

IMPLORE. See BEG.

IMPLY. See SIGNIFY.

IMPORT. See SIGNIFICATION.

IMPORTANCE, CONSEQUENCE, WEIGHT, MOMENT. *Importance*, from *in* and *portare*, to carry, signifies the carrying or bearing with or in itself. *Consequence*, from the present participial stem of *consequi*, to follow, or result, signifies that which follows or results from a thing. *Weight*, Anglo-Saxon *gewiht*, from *wegan*, to carry, or lift (compare the phrase *weigh* anchor), hence to weigh, signifies the quantity that a thing weighs. *Moment*, from *momentum*, Latin *movere*, to move, signifies the force that puts in motion.

Importance is what things have in themselves; they may be of more or less *importance*, according to the value which is set upon them: this may be real or unreal; it may be estimated by the experience of their past utility or from the presumption of their utility for the future: the idea of *importance*, therefore, enters into the meaning of the other terms more or less. *Consequence* is the *importance* of a thing from its *consequences*. This term, therefore, is peculiarly applicable to such things the *consequences* of which may be more immediately discerned either from the neglect or the attention: it is of *consequence* for a letter to go off on a certain day, for the affairs of an individual may be more or less affected by it; an hour's delay sometimes in the departure of a military expedition may be of such *consequence* as to determine the fate of a battle. The term *weight* implies a positively great degree of *importance:* it is that *importance* which a thing has intrinsically in itself, and which makes it *weigh* in the mind: it is applied, therefore, to such things as offer themselves to deliberation; hence the counsels of a nation are always *weighty*, because they involve the interests of so many. *Moment* is that *importance* which a thing has from the power in itself to produce effects or to determine interests: it is applicable, therefore, only to such things as are connected with our prosperity or happiness: when used without any adjunct, it implies a great degree of *importance*, but may be modified in various ways, as a thing of no *moment*, or small *moment*, or great *moment;* but we cannot say with the same propriety, a thing of small *weight*, and still less a thing of great *weight:* it is a matter of no small *moment* for every one to choose that course of conduct which will stand the test of a death-bed reflection.

IMPORTANT. See CRITICAL.

IMPORTUNATE. See PRESSING.

IMPORTUNITY. See SOLICITATION.

IMPOSE. See DECEIVE.

IMPOST. See TAX.

IMPRECATION. See MALEDICTION.

IMPRINT, IMPRESS, ENGRAVE. *Print* and *press* are both derived from Latin *primere*, the former from the infinitive, the latter from *pressus*, the past participle, signifying in the literal sense to press or to make a mark by pressing: to *impress* and *imprint* are figuratively employed in the same sense. Things are *impressed* on the mind so as to produce a conviction: they are *imprinted* on it so as to produce recollection. If the truths of Christianity be *impressed* on the mind, they will show themselves in a corresponding conduct: whatever is *imprinted* on the mind in early life or by any particular circumstance is not readily forgotten. *Engrave,* from French *en* and *grave,* imitating Old French *engraver,* from Latin *in* and Old High German *graban,* to cut, or dig, cognate with English *grave,* to dig, expresses more in the proper sense than either, *imprint,* or *impress* and the same in its moral application; for we may truly say that if the truths of Christianity be *engraven* in the minds of youth, they can never be eradicated.

IMPRISONMENT. See CONFINEMENT.

IMPROMPTU. See UNPREMEDITATED.

IMPROVE. See AMEND.

IMPROVEMENT. See PROGRESS.

IMPRUDENCE. See ASSURANCE.

IMPUDENT. See IMMODEST; IMPERTINENT.

IMPUGN, ATTACK. These terms are employed synonymously only in regard to doctrines or opinions; in which case, to *impugn,* from *in,* against, and *pugnare,* to fight, signifies to call in question, or bring arguments against; to *attack* is to oppose with warmth. Sceptics *impugn* every opinion, however self-evident or well-grounded they may be: infidels make *attacks* upon the Bible and all that is held sacred by the rest of the world. He who *impugns* may sometimes proceed insidiously and circuitously to undermine the faith of others: he who *attacks* always proceeds with more or less violence. To *impugn* is not necessarily taken in a bad sense: we may sometimes *impugn* absurd doctrines by a fair train of reasoning: to *attack* (see ATTACK) is sometimes objectionable, either in the mode of the action or its object, or in both; it is a mode of proceeding which may be employed either in the cause of falsehood or of truth: when there are no arguments where-with to *impugn* a doctrine, it is easy to *attack* it with ridicule and scurrility: it is one's duty to *attack* an absurd or an erroneous, or a criminal doctrine, in the interest of truth and progress.

IMPUTE. See ASCRIBE.

INABILITY, DISABILITY. *Inability* denotes the absence of *ability* (see ABILITY) in the most general and abstract sense. *Disability* implies the absence of *ability* only in particular cases: the *inability* lies in the nature of the thing, and is irremediable; the *disability* lies in the circumstances, and may sometimes be removed: weakness, whether physical or mental, will occasion an *inability* to perform a task; there is a total *inability* in an infant to walk and act like an adult: a want of knowledge or of the requisite qualifications may be a *disability;* in this manner minority of age or an objection to take certain oaths may be a *disability* for filling a public office.

INACCESSIBLE. See IMPERVIOUS.

INACTIVE, INERT, LAZY, SLOTHFUL, SLUGGISH. A reluctance to bodily exertion is common to all these terms. *Inactive* (see ACTIVE) is the most general and unqualified term of all; it expresses simply the want of a stimulus to exertion. *Inert* is something more positive, from the Latin *in,* privative, and *ars,* art, without skill or mind; it denotes a specific deficiency either in body or in mind. *Lazy* (see IDLE). *Slothful* comes from *sloth,* which is formed from the adjective *slow,* originally *slowth,* and signifies full of slowness; and *sluggish,* from *slug* (a Scandinavian word signifying to droop, and hence, to be *inactive,* drowsy, heavy), denote an expressly defective temperament of the body which directly impedes action.

To be *inactive* is to be indisposed to action, that is, to the performance of any office, to doing any specific business: to be *inert* is somewhat more; it is to be indisposed to movement; to be *lazy* is to move with pain to one's self: to be *slothful* is never to move otherwise than slowly: to be *sluggish* is to move in a sleepy and heavy manner. A person may be *inactive* from a variety of incidental causes, as timidity, ignorance, modesty, and the like, which combine to make him averse to enter upon any business or take any serious step; a person may be *inert* from temporary indisposition; but *laziness,* *slothfulness,* and *sluggishness* are inherent physical defects: *laziness* is, however, not altogether independent of the mind or the will; but *slothfulness* and *sluggishness* are purely the offspring of nature, or, which is the same thing, habit superinduced upon nature. A man of a mild character is frequently *inactive*.

Some diseases, particularly of the melancholy kind, are accompanied with a strong degree of *inertness*, since they seem to deprive the frame of its ordinary powers to action, and to produce a certain degree of torpor; hence the term is properly applied to matter to express the highest degree of *inactivity*, which will not move without an external impulse.

Lazy people move as if their bodies were a burden to themselves; they are fond of rest and particularly averse to be put in action; but they will sometimes move quickly, and perform much when once impelled to move.

Slothful people never vary their pace; they have a physical impediment in themselves to quick motion: *sluggish* people are with difficulty brought into action; it is their nature to be in a state of stupor.

INADEQUATE. See **INCAPABLE.**

INADVERTENCY, **INATTENTION,** **OVERSIGHT.** *Inadvertency,* from *advert,* to turn the mind to, is allied to *inattention* (see **ATTENTIVE**) when the act of the mind is signified in general terms; and to *oversight* when any particular instance of *inadvertency* occurs. *Inadvertency* never designates a habit, but *inattention* does; the former term, therefore, is unqualified by the reproachful sense which attaches to the latter: any one may be guilty of *inadvertencies,* since the mind that is occupied with many subjects equally serious may not be turned so steadily toward some others that may escape notice; but *inattention,* which designates a direct want of *attention,* is always a fault, and belongs only to the young, or such as are thoughtless by nature: since *inadvertency* is an occasional act, it must not be too often repeated, or it becomes *inattention.* An *oversight* is properly a species of *inadvertency,* which arises from looking over, or passing by, a thing: we pardon an *inadvertency* in another, since the consequences are never serious; we must be guarded against *oversights* in business, as their consequences may be serious.

c.e.s.—15

INANIMATE. See **LIFELESS.**
INANITY. See **VACANCY.**
INAPPRECIABLE. See **ATOMIC.**
INATTENTION. See **INADVERTENCY.**
INATTENTIVE. See **NEGLIGENT.**
INBORN. See **INHERENT.**
INBRED. See **INHERENT.**
INCAPABLE, **INSUFFICIENT,** **INCOMPETENT,** **INADEQUATE.** *Incapable,* that is, *not* having *capacity* (see **ABILITY**); *insufficient,* or *not sufficient,* or *not* having what is *sufficient; incompetent,* or *not competent* (see **COMPETENT**), are employed either for persons or for things: the first in a general, the last two in a specific sense: *inadequate,* or *not adequate* or *equalled,* is applied most generally to things.

When a man is said to be *incapable* it characterizes his whole mind; if he be said to have *insufficiency* and *incompetency,* it regards the particular objects to which the power is applied: he may be *insufficient* or *incompetent* for certain things; but he may have a *capacity* for other things: the term *incapacity,* therefore, implies a direct charge upon the understanding which is not implied by *insufficiency* and *incompetency.*

Incapable is applied sometimes, in colloquial discourse, to signify the absence of that which is bad; *insufficient* and *incompetent* always convey the idea of a deficiency in that which is at least desirable: it is an honor to a person to be *incapable* of falsehood, or *incapable* of doing an ungenerous action; but to be *insufficient* and *incompetent* are, at all events, qualities not to be boasted of, although they may not be expressly disgraceful. These terms are likewise applicable to things, in which they preserve a similar distinction: infidelity is *incapable* of affording a man any comfort: when the means are *insufficient* for obtaining the ends, it is madness to expect success; it is a sad condition of humanity when a man's resources are *incompetent* to supply him with the first necessaries of life.

Inadequate is relative in its signification, like *insufficient* and *incompetent;* but the relation is different. A thing is *insufficient* which does not suffice either for the wishes, the purposes, or the necessities of any one in particular or in general cases; thus, a quantity of materials may be *insufficient* for a particular building: *incompetency* is an *insufficiency* for general purposes in things of the first necessity; thus, a person may be *incompetent* to support a family: *inadequacy* is still more particular, for it denotes any deficiency which is measured by comparison with the object to which it referred; thus, the strength of an animal may be *inadequate* to the labor which is required, or a reward may be *inadequate* to the service.

INCESSANTLY, UNCEASINGLY, UNINTERRUPTEDLY, WITHOUT INTERMISSION. *Incessantly* and *unceasingly* are but variations of the same word, Latin *cessare*, to *cease*, a frequentative of *cedere*, to yield; *in* and *un* are both negative prefixes. *Uninterruptedly* (see DISTURB). *Intermission* (see SUBSIDE).

Continuity, but not duration, is denoted by these terms: *incessantly* is the most general and indefinite of all; it signifies without ceasing, but may be applied to things which admit of certain intervals: *unceasingly* is definite, and signifies never ceasing; it cannot, therefore, be applied to what has any cessation. In familiar discourse, *incessantly* is an extravagant mode of speech, by which one means to denote the absence of those ordinary intervals which are to be expected; as when one says a person is *incessantly* talking, by which is understood that he does not allow himself the ordinary intervals of rest from talking: *unceasingly*, on the other hand, is more literally employed for a positive want of cessation; a noise is said to be *unceasing* which literally never ceases; or complaints are *unceasing* which are made without any pauses or intervals. *Incessantly* and *unceasingly* are said of things which act of themselves; *uninterruptedly* is said of that which depends upon other things: it rains *incessantly* marks a continued operation of nature, independent of everything; but to be *uninterruptedly* happy marks one's freedom from every foreign influence which is unfriendly to one's happiness. *Incessantly* and the other two words are employed either for persons or things; *without intermission* is,

however, mostly employed for persons; things act and react *incessantly* upon one another; a man of a persevering temper goes on laboring *without intermission* until he has effected his purpose.

INCIDENT. See CIRCUMSTANCE; EVENT.

INCIDENTAL. See ACCIDENTAL.

INCINERATION. See CREMATION.

INCIPIENT. See ELEMENTARY.

INCITE. See ENCOURAGE; EXCITE

INCLINATION, TENDENCY, PROPENSITY, PRONENESS. All these terms are employed to designate the state of the will toward an object: *inclination* (see ATTACHMENT) denotes its first movement toward an object: *tendency*, through French from *tendere*, to stretch, is a continued *inclination: propensity*, from *propensus*, past participle of the Latin *pro*, forward, and *pendere*, to hang, denotes a still stronger leaning of the will; and *prone*, from the Latin *pronum*, accusative of *pronus*, inclined toward, characterizes a habitual and fixed state of the will toward an object. The *inclination* expresses the leaning, but not the direction of that leaning; it may be to the right or to the left, upward or downward; consequently we may have an *inclination* to that which is good or bad, high or low; *tendency* does not specify any particular direction; but it is frequently applied to those things which degenerate or lead to what is bad; excessive strictness in the treatment of children has a *tendency* to damp their spirit: *propensity* and *proneness* both designate a downward direction, and consequently refer only to that which is bad and low; a person has a *propensity* to drinking, and a *proneness* to lying.

Inclination is always at the command of the understanding; it is out duty, therefore, to suppress the first risings of any *inclination* to extravagance, intemperance, or any irregularity: as *tendency* refers to the thing rather than the person, it is our business to avoid that which has a *tendency* to evil: the *propensity* will soon get the mastery of the best principles and the firmest resolution; it is our duty, therefore, to seek all the aids which religion affords to subdue every *propensity: proneness* to evil is inherent in our nature, which we derive from our animal nature; it is the grace of God alone which can lift us up above this grovelling part of ourselves.

See also BENT; DISPOSITION.

INCLINE. See LEAN; MERGE.

INCLOSE, INCLUDE. From the Latin *includo* (from *in*, in, and *claudere*, to shut) are derived *inclose* and *include*, *inclose* being derived through Old French *inclore*, past participle *inclos*. The former expresses the proper, and the latter the improper signification: a yard is *inclosed* by a wall; particular goods are *included* in a reckoning: the kernel of a nut is *inclosed* in a shell; morality, as well as faith, is *included* in Christian perfection.

See also CIRCUMSCRIBE.

INCOHERENT. See INCONSISTENT.

INCOMPETENT. See INCAPABLE.

INCONGRUOUS. See INCONSISTENT.

INCONSIDERABLE. See UNIMPORTANT.

INCONSISTENT, INCONGRUOUS, INCOHERENT. *Inconsistent,* from *in*, privative, and *consistent* (Latin *con*, together, and *sistens*, participle of *sistere*, to cause to stand), marks the unfitness of being placed together. *Incongruous,* from *in*, privative, and *congruere*, to suit, a Latin word of uncertain origin, marks the unsuitableness of one thing to another. *Incoherent,* from *in*, privative, *con*, together, and *hærere*, to stick, marks the incapacity of two things to coalesce or be united to each other.

Inconsistency attaches either to the actions or sentiments of men; *incongruity* attaches to the modes and qualities of things; *incoherency,* to words or thoughts; things are made *inconsistent* by an act of the will; a man acts or thinks *inconsistently,* according to his own pleasure: *incongruity* depends upon the nature of the things; there is something very *incongruous* in blending the solemn service of the church with the extravagant rant of some self-styled religious leaders: *incoherence* marks the want of coherence in that which ought to follow sequently; extemporary effusions from the pulpit are often distinguished most by their *incoherence.*

INCONSTANT. See CHANGEABLE.

INCONTROVERTIBLE. See INDUBITABLE.

INCONVENIENCE, ANNOY, MOLEST. To *inconvenience* is to make *not convenient* (see CONVENIENT). To *annoy* comes from the Old French *anoi*, Modern French *ennui*, derived from the Latin phrase *in odio*, signifying in hatred, or dislike. To *molest,* from the Latin *moles*, a mass, or weight, signifies to press with a weight.

We *inconvenience* in small matters, or by omitting such things as might be *convenient;* we *annoy* or *molest* by doing that which is positively painful: we are *inconvenienced* by a person's absence; we are *annoyed* by his presence if he renders himself offensive: we are *inconvenienced* by what is temporary; we are *annoyed* by that which is either temporary or durable; we are *molested* by that which is weighty and oppressive; we are *inconvenienced* simply in regard to our circumstances; we are *annoyed* mostly in regard to our corporeal feelings; we are *molested* mostly in regard to our minds: the removal of a seat or a book may *inconvenience* one who is engaged in business; the buzzing of a fly or the stinging of a gnat may *annoy;* the impertinent freedom or the rude insults of ill-disposed persons may *molest.*

INCORPOREAL, UNBODIED, IMMATERIAL, SPIRITUAL. *Incorporeal* (see CORPOREAL for derivation) marks the quality of not belonging to the body or having any properties in common with it; *unbodied* (for derivation see CORPOREAL) denotes the state of being without the body or not inclosed in a body: a thing may therefore be *incorporeal* without being *unbodied;* but not *vice versâ:* the soul of man is *incorporeal,* but not *unbodied,* during his natural life.

Incorporeal is always used in regard to living things, particularly by way of comparison with *corporeal* or human beings: hence we speak of *incorporeal* agency, or *incorporeal* agents, in reference to such beings as are supposed to act in this world without the help of the body; but *immaterial* is applied to inanimate objects; men are *corporeal* as men, spirits are *incorporeal;* the body is the *material* part of man, the soul his *immaterial* part: whatever external object acts upon the senses is *material;* but the action of the mind on itself, and its results, are all *immaterial:* the earth, sun, moon, etc., are termed *material;* but the impressions which they make on the mind, that is, our ideas of them, are *immaterial.*

The *incorporeal* and *immaterial* have always a relative sense; the *spiritual* is that which is positive: God is a *spiritual,* not properly an *incorporeal* nor *immaterial* Being: the angels are likewise designated, in general, as the *spiritual* inhabitants of heaven; although, when spoken of in regard to men, they may be denominated *incorporeal.*

See also CORPOREAL.

INCREASE, GROW. *Increase,* from the Latin *in,* in, and *crescere,* to grow (whence *crescent* is derived), signifies to grow larger and stronger. *Grow,* Anglo-Saxon *growan,* signified to put forth green shoots; it is allied to the word *green.*

The idea of becoming larger is common to both these terms, but the former expresses the idea in an unqualified manner, and the latter annexes to this general idea also that of the mode or process by which this is effected. To *increase* is either a gradual or an instantaneous act; to *grow* is a gradual process: a stream *increases* by the addition of other waters; it may come suddenly or in course of time, by means of gentle showers or the rushing in of other streams; but if we say that the river or stream *grows,* it is supposed to *grow* by some regular and continual process of receiving fresh water, as from the running in of different rivulets or smaller streams. To *increase* is either a natural or an artificial process; to *grow* is always natural: money *increases* by artificial means; corn may either *increase* or *grow:* in the former case we speak of it in the sense of becoming larger or *increasing* in bulk; in the latter case we consider the mode of its *increasing,* namely, by the natural process of vegetation On this ground we say that a child *grows* when we wish to denote the natural process by which his body arrives at its proper size; but we may speak of his *increasing* in stature, in size, and

the like. For this reason likewise *increase* is used in a transitive as well as intransitive sense; but *grow* always in an intransitive sense: we can *increase* a thing, though not properly *grow* a thing, because we can make it larger by whatever means we please; but when it *grows* it makes itself larger.

In their improper acceptation these words preserve the same distinction: "trade *increases*" bespeaks the simple fact of its becoming larger; but "trade *grows*" implies that gradual *increase* which flows from the natural concurrence of circumstances. The affections which are awakened in infancy *grow* with one's growth; a natural and moral process is here combined. The fear of death sometimes *increases* as one *grows* old; the courage of a truly brave man *increases* with the sight of danger: a moral process is here indicated which is both gradual and immediate, but in both cases produced by some foreign cause.

See also ENLARGE.

Increase, Addition, Accession, Augmentation.—Increase is here, as in the former article, the generic term: there will always be *increase* where there is *augmentation, addition,* and *accession,* though not *vice versâ.*

Addition is to *increase* as the means to the end: the *addition* is the artificial mode of making two things into one; the *increase* is the result: when the value of one figure is added to another, the sum is *increased;* hence a man's treasures experience an *increase* by the *addition* of other parts to the main stock. *Addition* is an intentional mode of *increasing; accession* is an accidental mode: one thing is added to another and thereby *increased;* but an *accession* takes place of itself; it is the coming or joining of one thing to another so as to *increase* the whole. A merchant *increases* his property by *adding* his gains in trade every year to the mass; but he receives an *accession* of property either by inheritance or by any other contingency. In the same manner a monarch *increases* his dominions by *adding* one territory to another, or by various *accessions* of territory which fall to his lot. When we speak of an *increase* we think of the whole and its relative magnitude at different times; when we speak of an *addition* we think only of the part and the agency by which this part is joined; when we speak of an *accession* we think only of the circumstance by which one thing becomes thus joined to another. *Increase* of happiness does not depend upon *increase* of wealth; the miser makes daily *additions* to the latter without making any to the former: sudden *accessions* of wealth are seldom attended with any good consequences, as they turn the thoughts too violently out of their sober channel and bend them too strongly on present possessions and good-fortune.

Augmentation is a mode of *increasing* not merely in quantity or number, but also in value or in the essential ingredient of a thing; it is therefore applied for the most part to the *increase* of a man's estate, possessions, family, income, or whatever is desirable.

It may also be applied to moral objects, as hopes, fears, joys, etc., with a like distinction.

INCREDULITY. See UNBELIEF.

INCULCATE. See IMPLANT.

INCURSION. See INVASION.

INDEBTED, OBLIGED. *Indebted* is more binding and positive than *obliged*: we are *indebted* to whoever confers an essential service: we are *obliged* to him who does us any service. A man is *indebted* to another for the preservation of his life; he is *obliged* to him for an ordinary act of civility: a *debt*, whether of legal or moral right, must in justice be paid; an *obligation* which is only moral ought in reason to be returned. We may be *indebted* to things; we are *obliged* to persons only: we are *indebted* to Christianity, not only for a superior faith, but also for a superior system of morality; we ought to be *obliged* to our friends who admonish us of our faults in friendly wise. A nation may be *indebted* to an individual, but men are *obliged* to one another only as individuals: the English nation is *indebted* to Alfred for the groundwork of its constitution; the little courtesies which pass between friends in their social intercourse with one another lay them under *obligations* which it is equally agreeable to receive and to pay.

INDECENT, IMMODEST, INDELI-CATE. *Indecent* is the contrary of *decent* (see BECOMING), *immodest* the contrary of *modest* (see MODEST), *indelicate* the contrary of *delicate* (see FINE).

Indecency and *immodesty* violate the fundamental principles of morality: the former, however, in external matters, as dress, words, and looks; the latter in conduct and disposition. A person may be *indecent* for want of either knowing or thinking better. *Indecency* may be a partial, *immodesty* is a positive and entire breach of the moral law. *Indecency* belongs to both sexes; *immodesty* is peculiarly applicable to the misconduct of women.

Indecency is less than *immodesty*, but more than *indelicacy*: they both regard the outward behavior. It is a great *indecency* for a man to marry again very quickly after the death of his wife; but a still greater *indecency* for a woman to put such an affront on her deceased husband: it is a great *indelicacy* in any one to break in upon the retirement of such as are in sorrow and mourning.

INDEED. See AYE.

INDELICATE. See INDECENT.

INDEMNIFY, COMPENSATE, REIM-BURSE. These terms all mean to make good that which has been lost, but they differ somewhat in the extent of their application. *Compensate*, from Latin *con*, against, and *pensare*, to weigh, means, literally, to weigh one thing with another; it is the most general of these three terms. It signifies to give back an equivalent for something lost, taken, or injured. *Indemnify* and *reimburse* have a similar meaning, but a more special application. *Indemnify* is derived from Latin *in*, privative, *damnum*, loss, and French *fier*, English *fy*, from Latin *facere*, to make. Hence it literally means to make free from loss. It signifies to make a payment to compensate for the loss of life or property. *Reimburse* is adapted from French *rembourser* by substituting Latin *re*, again, and *in*, in, for *rem*. *Bourser* comes from Latin *bursa*, a purse, Greek βύρση, a hide (purses being usually made of leather), which appears in English as *purse*. Hence it signifies literally to make in purse again, and refers to the payment of money in return for money paid out.

We *compensate* another for the trouble that he has taken for us by an act of generosity or favor; the United States sought to *indemnify* itself for the loss of life and property through the attacks of German submarines on trading vessels; we *reimburse* a friend who has lent us money or paid our debts by returning a sum equivalent to that which he spent. To *indemnify* and to *reimburse* are forms of *compensation*.

INDICATE. See SHOW.

INDICATION. See MARK.

INDIFFERENCE, INSENSIBILITY, APATHY. *Indifference* signifies *no difference*, that is, having no *difference* of feeling for one thing more than another. *Insensibility*, from Latin *in*, privative, and *sentire*, to know through the senses, to feel, signifies incapability of feeling, *Apathy*, from Greek ἀπάθεια, from ἀ, not, and παθεῖν, to suffer (found in *pathetic, pathos, sympathy*, etc.), signifies incapability to suffer or to feel.

Indifference is a partial state of the mind; *insensibility* and *apathy* are general states of the mind; he who has *indifference* is not to be awakened to feeling by some objects, though he may by others; but he who has not *sensibility* is incapable of feeling; and he who has *apathy* is without any feeling. *Indifference* is mostly a temporary state; *insensibility* is either a temporary or a permanent state; *apathy* is always a permanent state: *indifference* is either acquired or accidental; *insensibility* is either produced or natural; *apathy* is natural. A person may be in a state of *indifference* about a thing of the value of which he is not aware, or acquire an *indifference* for that which he knows to be of comparatively little value: he may be in a state of *insensibility* from some lethargic torpor which has seized his mind; or he may have a habitual *insensibility* arising from the physical bluntness of his understanding or the deadness of his passions; his *apathy* is born with him, and forms a prominent feature in the constitution of his mind.

Indifferent, Unconcerned, Regardless. —*Indifferent* marks the want of inclination: *unconcerned*, that is, having no *concern* (see CARE), and *regardless*, that is, without *regard*, mark the want of serious consideration. *Indifferent* regards only the will; *unconcerned*, either the will or the understanding; *regardless*, the understanding only: we are *indifferent* about matters of minor consideration; we are *unconcerned* or *regardless* about serious matters that have remote consequences: an author will seldom be *indifferent* about the success of his work; he ought not to be *unconcerned* about the influence which his writings may have on the public, or *regardless* of the estimation in which his own character as a man may be held. To be *indifferent* is sometimes an act of wisdom or virtue; to be *unconcerned* or *regardless* is mostly an act of folly or a breach of duty.

See also NEUTRAL.

INDIGENCE. See POVERTY.

INDIGENOUS. See NATAL.

INDIGNATION. See ANGER.

INDIGNITY, INSULT. *Indignity*, from the Latin *dignus*, worthy, signifying unworthy treatment, regards the feeling and condition of the person offended; *insult* (see AFFRONT) regards the temper of the offending party. We measure the *indignity* in our own mind; it depends upon the consciousness we have of our own worth: we measure the *insult* by the disposition which is discovered in another to degrade us. Persons in high stations are peculiarly exposed to *indignities*: persons in every station may be exposed to *insults*. *Indignities* may, however, be offered to persons of all ranks; but in this case it always consists of more violence than a simple *insult*; it would be an *indignity* to a person of any rank to be compelled to do any office which belongs only to a beast of burden.

INDISCRETION. See LAPSE.

INDISPOSITION. See SICKNESS.

INDISPUTABLE. See INDUBITABLE.

INDISTINCT, CONFUSED. *Indistinct* is negative; it marks simply the want of *distinctness: confused* is positive; it marks a positive degree of *indistinctness*. A thing may be *indistinct* without being *confused;* but it cannot be *confused* without being *indistinct:* two things may be *indistinct* or not easily distinguished from each other; but many things, or parts of the same things, are *confused:* two letters in a word may be *indistinct,* but the whole of a writing or many words are *confused:* sounds are *indistinct* which reach our ears only in part, but they are *confused* if they come in great numbers and out of all order. We see objects *indistinctly* when we cannot see all the features by which they would be distinguished from other objects: we see them *confusedly* when every part is so blended with the other that no one feature can be distinguished; by means of great distance objects become *indistinct;* from a defect in sight objects become more *confused.*

INDIVIDUAL. See PARTICULAR.

INDOLENT, SUPINE, LISTLESS, CARELESS. For *indolent* (*in,* not, and *dolens,* suffering, or freedom from pain, hence ease, idleness). See IDLE. *Supine,* in Latin *supinus,* from *super,* above, signifies lying on one's back or with one's face upward, which, as it is the action of a lazy or idle person, has been made to represent the qualities themselves. *Listless,* without *list,* in German *lust,* desire, signifies without desire. *Careless* signifies without care or concern.

These terms represent a diseased or unnatural state of the mind when its desires, which are the springs of action, are in a relaxed and torpid state, so as to prevent the necessary degree of exertion. *Indolence* has a more comprehensive meaning than *supineness,* and this signifies more than *listlessness* or *carelessness: indolence* is a general indisposition of a person to exert either his mind or his body; *supineness* is a similar indisposition that shows itself on particular occasions: there is a corporeal as well as a mental cause for *indolence;* but *supineness* lies principally in the mind: corpulent and large-made people are apt to be *indolent;* but timid and gentle dispositions are apt to be *supine.*

The *indolent* and *supine* are not, however, like the *listless,* expressly without desire: an *indolent* or *supine* man has desire enough to enjoy what is within his reach, although not always sufficient desire to surmount the aversion to labor in trying to obtain it; the *listless* man, on the contrary, is altogether without the desire, and is, in fact, in a state of moral torpor, which is, however, but a temporary or partial state arising from particular circumstances; after the mind has been wrought up to the highest pitch, it will sometimes sink into a state of relaxation in which it ceases to have apparently any active principle within itself.

Carelessness expresses less than any of the above; for, though a man who is *indolent, supine,* and *listless* is naturally *careless,* yet *carelessness* is properly applicable to such as have no such positive disease of mind or body. *Carelessness* is rather an error of the understanding, or of the conduct, than the will; since the *careless* man would *care,* be concerned for, or interested about things if he could be brought to reflect on their importance or if he did not for a time forget himself.

INDUBITABLE, UNQUESTIONABLE, INDISPUTABLE, UNDENIABLE, INCONTROVERTIBLE, IRREFRAGABLE. *Indubitable* signifies admitting of no *doubt; unquestionable,* admitting of no *question* (for both see DOUBT); *indisputable,* admitting of no *dispute* (see CONTROVERT); *undeniable,* not to be *denied* (see DENY); *incontrovertible,* not to be *controverted; irrefragable* comes from *in,* against, and a root *frag,* meaning noise, found also, perhaps, in *suffrage,* and signifies not to be changed by a popular outcry. These terms are all opposed to uncertainty; but they do not imply absolute certainty, for they all express the strong persuasion of a person's mind rather than the absolute nature of the thing: when a fact is supported by such evidence as admits of no kind of doubt it is termed *indubitable;* when the truth of an assertion rests on the authority of a man whose character for integrity stands unimpeached it is termed *unquestionable* authority; when a thing is believed to exist on the evidence of every man's senses it is termed *undeniable;* when a sentiment has always been held as either true or false, without dispute, it is termed *indisputable;* when arguments have never been controverted they are termed *incontrovertible;* and when they have never been satisfactorily answered they are termed *irrefragable.*

INDUCE. See ACTUATE.

INDULGE. See FOSTER; GRATIFY.

INDULGENT, FOND. *Indulgence* (see GRATIFY) lies more in forbearing from the exercise of authority; *fondness* (see AMOROUS) in the outward behavior and endearments: they may both arise from an excess of kindness or love, but the former is of a less objectionable character than the latter. *Indulgence* may be sometimes wrong, but *fondness* is seldom right: an *indulgent* parent is seldom a prudent parent, but a *fond* parent does not rise above a fool: all who have the care of young people should occasionally relax from the strictness of the disciplinarián and show an *indulgence* where a suitable opportunity offers; a *fond* mother takes away from the value of *indulgence* by an invariable compliance with the humors of her children. However, when applied generally or abstractedly the words are both taken in a good sense.

INDUSTRIOUS. See ACTIVE.

INEFFABLE. See UNSPEAKABLE.

INEFFECTUAL. See VAIN.

INELEGANT. See UNGRACEFUL.

INEQUALITY. See DISPARITY.

INERT. See INACTIVE.

INEXORABLE. See IMPLACABLE.

INEXPRESSIBLE. See UNSPEAKABLE.

INFALLIBLE, CERTAIN, POSITIVE, SURE, UNERRING. *Infallible*, a compound of *in*, not, and *fallible*, failing, erring, from the Latin *fallere*, to deceive, in French *infaillible*, signifies the quality of being free from the liability of error. *Certain* (from Latin *certus*, sure, and the suffix *-anus*, allied to *cernere*, to discriminate) implies that which is fixed, stated, beyond a doubt, anything that is undeniable, indisputable, incontrovertible. *Positive* concerns that which is real, actual, substantial, existing in fact, and is applicable both to persons and to objects. When, however, the term is related to persons, as a belief or statement, while it may be advanced as absolutely *positive*, the premises or basic knowledge may be erroneous, and the conclusion, therefore, will not be *infallible*, though the person may believe it to be so.

Sure implies conditions similar to those that are *positive*, and, literally, those that are absolutely fixed, established beyond question, and *unerring*; yet in mortal mind the term at times appears to belie itself, to be fluctuating, as something that to-day has every evidence of being *sure* may to-morrow prove a delusion, but this is a mere mental misconstruction of the term. *Unerring* is a term that in common usage is frequently misapplied. God alone is *unerring*, incapable of mistakes or failure. We speak of a marksman taking an *unerring* aim, but his action is not completed till his shot has struck its object, and in the meantime a chance change of wind may alter its direction, and though the aim was direct the result is not an *unerring* shot.

Associated with *infallible* is the substantive *infallibility*, implying the state or quality of being exempt from error. At the Œcumenical Council of the Roman Catholic Church, held in Rome in 1870, a dogma was decreed to the effect that when the Roman Pontiff, speaking *ex cathedra*, or in the discharge of his office, "defines a doctrine regarding faith or morals to be held by the Universal Church, (he) is possessed of that *infallibility* with which the Divine Redeemer willed that his Church should be endowed," and "that therefore such definitions of the Roman Pontiff are irreformable."

See also OMNISCIENT.

INFAMOUS, SCANDALOUS. *Infamous*, like *infamy* (see INFAMY), is applied to both persons and things; *scandalous*, only to things: a character is *infamous*, or a transaction is *infamous;* but a transaction only is *scandalous*. *Infamous* and *scandalous* are both said of that which is calculated to excite great displeasure in the minds of all who hear it, and to degrade the offenders in the general estimation; but the *infamous* seems to be that which produces greater publicity and more general reprehension than the *scandalous;* consequently is that which is more serious in its nature and a greater violation of good morals. Some men of daring character render themselves *infamous* by their violence, their rapine, and their murders; the trick which was played upon the subscribers to the South Sea Company was a *scandalous* fraud.

Infamy, Ignominy, Opprobrium.— *Infamy* is the opposite to good *fame;* it consists in an evil report. *Ignominy*, from the privative *in* and Latin *gnomin* for *gnomen*, old form of *nomen*, name, signifies an ill name, a stained name. *Opprobrium*, a Latin word, compounded of *ob*, on, and *probrum*, disgrace, signifies the highest degree of reproach or stain.

The idea of discredit or disgrace in the highest possible degree is common to all these terms: but *infamy* is that which attaches either to the person or to the thing; *ignominy* is thrown upon the person; and *opprobrium* is thrown upon the agent rather than the action. *Infamy* causes either the person or the thing to be ill spoken of by all; abhorrence of both is expressed by every mouth, and the ill report spreads from mouth to mouth: *ignominy* causes the name and the person to be held in contempt; it becomes debased in the eyes of others; *opprobrium* causes the person to be spoken of in severe terms of reproach, and to be shunned as something polluted. The *infamy* of a treacherous proceeding is increased by the addition of ingratitude; the *ignominy* of a public punishment is increased by the wickedness of the offender; *opprobrium* sometimes falls upon the innocent, when circumstances seem to convict them of guilt.

INFANTINE. See CHILDISH.

INFECTION. See CONTAGION.

INFERENCE. See CONCLUSION.

INFERIOR. See SECOND; SUBJECT.

INFIDELITY. See UNBELIEF.

INFINITE. See BOUNDLESS.

INFIRM. See WEAK.

INFLUENCE, AUTHORITY, ASCENDENCY or ASCENDENT, SWAY. *Influence* (see CREDIT). *Authority*, in Latin *auctoritas*, from *auctor*, the author or prime mover of a thing (originally the *increaser* or *grower*, from *augere*, to increase), signifies that power which is vested in the prime mover of any business. *Ascendency*, from *ascend* (see ARISE), signifies having the upper hand. *Sway* comes from Middle English *sweiyen*, sway, a word with many Teutonic parallels, allied to *swagger*.

These terms imply power, under different circumstances: *influence* is altogether unconnected with any right to direct; *authority* includes the idea of right necessarily; superiority of rank, talent, or property, personal attachment, and a variety of circumstances give *influence;* it commonly acts by persuasion, and employs engaging manners, so as to determine in favor of what is proposed: superior wisdom, age, office, and relation give *authority;* it determines of itself, it requires no collateral aid: *ascendency* and *sway* are modes of *influence*, differing only in degree; they both imply an excessive and improper degree of *influence* over the mind, independent of reason: the former is, however, more gradual in its process, and consequently more confirmed in its nature; the latter may be only temporary, but may be more violent. A person employs many arts, and for a length of time, to gain the *ascendency;* but he exerts a *sway* by a violent stretch of power. It is of great importance for those who have *influence* to conduct themselves consistently with their rank and station: men are apt to regard the warnings and admonitions of a true friend as an odious assumption of *authority*, while they voluntarily give themselves up to the *ascendency* which a valet or a mistress has gained over them, who exert the most unwarrantable *sway* to serve their own interested and vicious purposes.

Influence and *ascendency* are said likewise of things as well as persons: true religion will have an *influence* not only on the outward conduct of a man, but on the inward affections of his heart; and that man is truly happy in whose mind it has the *ascendency* over every other principle.

INFORM, MAKE KNOWN, ACQUAINT, APPRISE. The idea of bringing to the knowledge of one or more persons is common to all these terms. *Inform*, from the Latin *informare*, to shape within, signifies the creative power of knowledge working within the soul; it is therefore the generic term, and the rest specific: to *inform* is to communicate what has lately happened, or the contrary; but to *make known* is to bring to light what has long been *known* and purposely concealed: to *inform* is to communicate directly or indirectly to one or many; to *make known* is mostly to communicate indirectly to many: one *informs* the public of one's intentions, by means of an advertisement in one's own name; one *makes known* a fact through a circuitous channel and without any name.

To *inform* may be done either personally or otherwise; to *acquaint* and *apprise* are immediate and personal communications. One *informs* the government, or any public body, or one *informs* one's friends; one *acquaints* (for derivation see ACQUAINTANCE) or *apprises* (from Old French *aprise*, instruction, compounded of Latin *ad*, and the past participle of *prehendere*, to seize, to take, signifying to take information to another) only one's friends or particular individuals: one is *informed* of that which concerns either the *informant* or the person *informed*; one *acquaints* a person with, or *apprises* him of, such things as peculiarly concern himself, but the latter in more specific circumstances than the former: one *informs* a correspondent by letter of the day on which he may expect to receive his order, or of one's own wishes with regard to an order; one *acquaints* a father with all the circumstances that concern his son's conduct: one *apprises* a friend of a bequest that has been made to him; one *informs* the magistrate of any irregularity that occurs; one *acquaints* the master of a family with the misconduct of his servants: one *apprises* a person of the time when he will be obliged to appear.

Inform may be applied figuratively to things; the other terms to persons only in the proper sense.

Inform, Instruct, Teach.—The communication of knowledge in general is the common idea by which these words are connected with one another. *Inform* is here, as in the preceding article, the general term; the other two are specific terms. To *inform* is the act of persons in all conditions; to *instruct* and *teach* are the acts of superiors, either on one ground or another: one *informs* by virtue of an accidental superiority or priority of knowledge; one *instructs* by virtue of superior knowledge or supe-

rior station; one *teaches* (Anglo-Saxon *tæcan*, to show how to do, from the root found in English *token*) by virtue of superior knowledge rather than of station: diplomatic agents *inform* their governments of the political transactions in which they have been concerned; government *instructs* (Latin *in* and *structus*, past participle of *struere*, to build up) its different functionaries and officers in regard to their mode of proceeding; professors and preceptors *teach* those who attend public schools to learn. To *inform* is applicable to matters of general interest: we may *inform* ourselves or others on anything which is a subject of inquiry or curiosity, and the *information* serves either to amuse or to improve the mind: to *instruct* is applicable to matters of serious concern, or to that which is practically useful; a parent *instructs* his child in the course of conduct he should pursue: to *teach* regards matters of art and science; the learner depends upon the *teacher* for the formation of his mind and the establishment of his principles.

To *inform* and to *teach* are employed for things as well as persons; to *instruct* only for persons: books and reading *inform* the mind; history or experience *teaches* mankind.

Informant, Informer. — These two epithets, from the verb to inform, have acquired by their application an important distinction, the *informant* being he who informs for the benefit of others, and the *informer* to the injury of others. What the *informant* communicates is for the benefit of the individual, and what the *informer* communicates is for the benefit of the whole. The *informant* is thanked for his civility in making the communication; the *informer* undergoes a great deal of odium, but is thanked by no one, not even by those who employ him. We may all be *informants* in our turn, if we know of anything of which another may be informed; but none are *informers* who do not inform against the transgressors of any law.

See also ATTACHÉ.

Information, Intelligence, Notice, Advice.—*Information* signifies the thing of which one is informed: *intelligence*, from the Latin *intellegere* (from *inter*, between, and *legere*, to choose, signifying to choose between, hence to discern or understand), indicates that by which one is made to understand: *notice*, from the Latin *notitia*, is that which brings a circumstance to our knowledge: *advice* (see ADMONITION) signifies that which is made known. These terms come very near to each other in signification, but differ in application: *information* is the most general and indefinite of all; the three others are but modes of *information*. Whatever is communicated to us is *information*, be it public or private, open or concealed: *notice, intelligence*, and *advice* are mostly public, but particularly the former. *Information* and *notice* may be communicated by word of mouth or by writing; *intelligence* is mostly communicated by writing or printing; *advices* are mostly sent by letter: *information* is mostly an informal mode of communication; *notice, intelligence*, and *advice* are mostly formal communications. A servant gives his master *information*, or one friend sends another *information* from the country; magistrates or officers give *notice* of such things as it concerns the public to know and to observe; spies give *intelligence* of all that passes under their notice; or *intelligence* is given in the public prints of all that passes worthy of notice: a military commander sends *advice* to his government of the operations which are going forward under his direction; or one merchant gives *advice* to another of the state of the market. *Intelligence*, as the first intimation of an interesting event, ought to be early; *advices*, as entering into details, ought to be clear and particular; official *advices* often arrive to contradict non-official *intelligence*.

Information and *intelligence*, when applied as characteristics of men, have a further distinction: the man of *information* is so denominated only on account of his knowledge; but a man of *intelligence* is so denominated on account of his understanding as well as experience and information. It is not possible to be *intelligent* without *information;* but we may be well *informed* without being remarkable for *intelligence:* a man of *information* may be an agreeable companion, and fitted to maintain conversation; but an *intelli-*

gent man will be an instructive companion, and most fitted for conducting business.

INFRACTION. See INFRINGE.

INFRINGE, VIOLATE, TRANSGRESS. *Infringe*, from Latin *infringere, frangere*, to break, signifies to break into. *Violate*, from a hypothetical adjective based on the Latin *vis*, force, signifies to break with force. *Transgress*, from *trans*, across, and *gredi* (past participle *gressus*), to step, signifies to go beyond, or farther than we ought.

Civil and moral laws and rights are *infringed* by those who act in opposition to them: treaties and engagements are *violated* by those who do not hold them sacred: the bounds which are prescribed by the moral law are *transgressed* by those who are guilty of any excess. It is the business of government to see that the rights and privileges of individuals or particular bodies be not *infringed;* policy but too frequently runs counter to equity; where the particular interests of states are more regarded than the dictates of conscience, treaties and compacts are *violated:* the passions, when not kept under proper control, will ever hurry on men to *transgress* the limits of right reason.

See also ENCROACH.

Infringement, Infraction.—*Infringement* and *infraction*, which are both derived from the Latin verb *infringo* or *frango*, are employed according to the different senses of the verb *infringe*, the former being applied to the rights of individuals, either in their domestic or public capacity, and the latter rather to national transactions. Politeness, which teaches us what is due to every man in the smallest concerns, considers any unasked-for interference in the private affairs of another as an *infringement*. Equity, which enjoins on nations as well as individuals an attentive consideration to the interests of the whole, forbids the *infraction* of a treaty in any case.

INFUSE. See IMPLANT.

INGENUITY, WIT. *Ingenuity* (see INGENUOUS). *Wit*, from the Anglo-Saxon *witt*, knowledge, German *wissen*, to know, signifies knowledge or understanding.

Both these terms imply acuteness of

understanding, and differ mostly in its mode of displaying itself. *Ingenuity* comprehends invention; *wit* is the fruit of the imagination, which forms new and sudden conceptions of things. One is *ingenious* in matters either of art or science; one is *witty* only in matters of sentiment: things may, therefore, be *ingenious*, but not *witty;* or *witty*, but not *ingenious;* or both *witty* and *ingenious*. A mechanical invention, or any ordinary contrivance, is *ingenious*, but not *witty:* we say, an *ingenious*, not a *witty* solution of a difficulty; a flash of *wit*, not a flash of *ingenuity:* a *witty* humor, a *witty* conversation, not an *ingenious* humor or conversation: on the other hand, a thought is *ingenious*, as it displays acuteness of intellect and aptness to the subject; it is *witty*, inasmuch as it contains point and strikes on the understanding of others. *Ingenuity* is expressed by means of words or shows itself in the act; mechanical contrivances display *ingenuity: wit* can be only expressed by words; some men are happy in the display of their *wit* in conversation.

Sometimes the word *wit* is applied to the operations of the intellect generally, which brings it still nearer in sense to *ingenuity*, but in this case it always implies a quick and sharp intellect as compared with *ingenuity*, which may be the result of long thought or be employed on graver matters.

INGENUOUS, I N G E N I O U S. It would not have been necessary to point out the distinction between these two words if they had not been confounded in writing as well as in speaking. *Ingenuous*, in Latin *ingenuus*, and *ingenious*, in Latin *ingeniosus*, are, either immediately or remotely, both derived from *inginere*, to be inborn; but the former regards the freedom of the station and consequent nobility of the character which is inborn: the latter regards the genius or mental powers which are inborn. Truth is coupled with freedom or nobility of birth; the *ingenuous*, therefore, bespeaks the inborn freedom, by asserting the noblest right, and following the noblest impulse, of human nature, namely, that of speaking the truth; *genius* is altogether a natural endowment, that is, born with us, indepen-

dent of external circumstances; the *ingenious* man, therefore, displays his powers as occasion may offer. We love the *ingenuous* character on account of the qualities of his heart; we admire the *ingenious* man on account of the endowments of his mind. One is *ingenuous* as a man or *ingenious* as an author: a man confesses an action *ingenuously;* he defends it *ingeniously.*

See also FRANK; NAÏVE.

INGRAFT. See IMPLANT.

INGRATIATE. See INSINUATE.

INGULF. See ABSORB.

INHABIT. See ABIDE.

INHERENT, INBRED, INBORN, IN-NATE. The *inherent*, from *hæreo*, to stick, denotes a permanent quality or property, as opposed to that which is adventitious and transitory. *Inbred* denotes that which is derived principally from habit or by a gradual process, as opposed to what is acquired by actual efforts. *Inborn* denotes that which is purely natural, in opposition to the artificial. *Inherent* is the most general in its sense; for what is *inbred* and *inborn* is naturally *inherent;* but all is not *inbred* and *inborn* which is *inherent*. Inanimate objects have *inherent* properties; but the *inbred* and *inborn* exist only in that which receives life; solidity is an *inherent*, but not an *inbred* or *inborn*, property of matter: a love of truth is an *innate* property of the human mind; it is consequently *inherent*, inasmuch as nothing can totally destroy it. That which is *inbred* is bred or nurtured in us from our birth; that which is *inborn* is simply born in us: a property may be *inborn*, but not *inbred;* it cannot, however, be *inbred* and not *inborn*. Habits, which are ingrafted into the natural disposition, are properly *inbred*. Propensities, on the other hand, which are totally independent of education or external circumstances, are properly *inbred*, as an *inborn* love of freedom; hence, likewise, the properties of animals are *inbred* in them, inasmuch as they are derived through the medium of the breed of which the parent partakes

Inborn and *innate*, from the Latin *natus*, born, are precisely the same in meaning, yet they differ somewhat in application. Poetry and the grave style have adopted *inborn;* philosophy has adopted *innate:* genius is *inborn* in some men; nobility is *inborn* in others: there is an *inborn* talent in some men to command, and an *inborn* fitness in others to obey. Mr. Locke and his followers are pleased to say there is no such thing as *innate* ideas: and if they mean only that there are no sensible impressions on the soul until it is acted upon by external objects they may be right: but if they mean to say that there are no *inborn* characters or powers in the soul which predispose it for the reception of certain impressions, they contradict the experience of the learned and the unlearned in all ages, who believe, and that from close observation of themselves and others, that man has, from his birth, not only the general character which belongs to him in common with his species, but also those peculiar characteristics which distinguish individuals from their earliest infancy: all these characters or characteristics are, therefore, not supposed to be produced, but elicited, by circumstances; and ideas, which are but the sensible forms that the soul assumes in its connection with the body, are, on that account, in vulgar language termed *innate*.

INHUMAN. See CRUEL.

INIMICAL. See ADVERSE.

INIQUITOUS. See WICKED.

INJUNCTION. See COMMAND.

INJURE. See IMPAIR.

INJURY, DAMAGE, HURT, HARM, MISCHIEF. All these terms are employed to denote what is done to the disadvantage of any person or thing.

The term *injury* (see DISADVANTAGE) sometimes includes the idea of violence, or of an act done contrary to law or right, as to inflict or receive an *injury*, to redress *injuries*, etc.

Injury is often taken in the general sense of what makes a thing otherwise than it ought to be: the other terms are taken in that sense only, and denote modes of *injury*. *Damage*, from *damnum*, loss, and a suffix, is that *injury* to a thing which occasions loss to a person or a diminution of value to a thing. *Hurt* comes from Old French *hurter*, to strike or dash against, hence to injure. Its ultimate origin is unknown; it signifies the *injury* which destroys the soundness or integrity of things: the *harm*

(see EVIL) is the smallest kind of *injury*, which may simply produce inconvenience or trouble: the *mischief* is a great *injury*, which more or less disturbs the order and consistency of things. *Injury* is applicable to all bodies indiscriminately, physical and moral; *damage* to physical bodies only; *hurt* to physical bodies properly, and to moral objects figuratively. Trade may suffer an *injury*, or a building may suffer an *injury*, from time or a variety of other causes: a building, merchandise, and other things may suffer a *damage* if they are exposed to violence.

Hurt is applied to the animal body; a sprain, a cut, or bruise are little *hurts*. It may be figuratively applied to other bodies which may suffer in a similar manner, as a *hurt* to one's good name.

Harm and *mischief* are as general in their application as *injury*, and comprehend what is physically as well as morally bad, but they are more particularly applicable to what is done intentionally by the person: whence ready to do *harm* or *mischief* is a characteristic of the individual.

As applied to things, *harm* and *mischief* are that which naturally results from the object; when a thing is said to do *harm* or *mischief*, that implies that it is its property.

See also INJUSTICE; SCATHE.

INJUSTICE, INJURY, WRONG. *Injustice* (see JUSTICE), *injury* (see DISADVANTAGE), and *wrong*, from Late Anglo-Saxon *wrang*, cognate with *wring*, meaning a hurt resulting from crushing or wringing, are all opposed to the right; but the *injustice* lies in the principle, the *injury* in the action that *injures*. There may, therefore, be *injustice* where there is no specific *injury*; and, on the other hand, there may be *injury* where there is no *injustice*. When we think worse of a person than we ought to think, we do him an act of *injustice*; but we do not, in the strict sense of the word, do him an *injury*: on the other hand, if we say anything to the discredit of another, it will be an *injury* to his reputation if it be believed; but it may not be an *injustice*, if it be strictly conformable to truth, and that which one is compelled to say.

The violation of justice, or a breach of the rule of right, constitutes the *in-*

justice; but the quantum of ill which falls on the person constitutes the *injury.* Sometimes a person is dispossessed of his property by fraud or violence; this is an act of *injustice;* but it is not an *injury* if, in consequence of this act, he obtains friends who make it good to him beyond what he has lost: on the other hand, a person suffers very much through another's inadvertency, which to him is a serious *injury,* although the offender has not been guilty of *injustice.*

A *wrong* partakes both of *injustice* and *injury;* it is, in fact, an *injury* done by one person to another in express violation of justice. The man who seduces a woman from the path of virtue does her the greatest of all *wrongs.* One repents of *injustice,* repairs *injuries,* and redresses *wrongs.*

INNATE. See INHERENT.

INNER. See INWARD.

INNOCENT. See GUILTLESS; UNOFFENDING.

INOFFENSIVE. See UNOFFENDING.

INORDINATE. See IRREGULAR.

INQUIRE. See ASK.

INROAD. See INVASION.

INSANITY. See DERANGEMENT.

INSCRUTABLE. See UNSEARCHABLE.

INSIDE, INTERIOR. The term *inside* may be applied to bodies of any magnitude, small or large; *interior* is peculiarly appropriate to bodies of great magnitude. We may speak of the *inside* of a nutshell, but not of its *interior:* on the other hand, we speak of the *interior* of St. Paul's or the *interior* of a palace. This difference of application is not altogether arbitrary: for *inside* literally signifies the side that is inward; but *interior* signifies the space which is more inward than the rest, which is enclosed in an enclosure, consequently cannot be applied to anything but a large space that is enclosed.

INSIDIOUS, TREACHEROUS. *Insidious,* in Latin *insidiosus,* from *insidiæ,* stratagem or ambush (from *insidere,* to lie in wait or ambush, from *in,* in, and *sedere,* to sit), signifies as much as lying in wait. *Treacherous* is derived through Old French *trecherie* from Late Latin *triccare,* based on Latin *tricæ,*

wiles, difficulties, by which the English *trick* may also be influenced, and signifies the disposition to deceive, to overcome by wiles.

The *insidious* man is not so active as the *treacherous* man; the former only lies in wait to insnare us when we are off our guard; the latter throws us off our guard by lulling us into a state of security, to get us more effectually into his power: an enemy may be denominated *insidious,* but a friend is *treacherous.* He who is afraid of avowing his real sentiments on religion makes *insidious* attacks either on its ministers, its doctrines, or its ceremonies: he who is most in the confidence of another is capable of being the most *treacherous* toward him.

See also TREACHEROUS.

INSIGHT, INSPECTION. The *insight* into a thing is what we receive: the *inspection* is what we give: one gets a view into a thing by an *insight;* one takes a view over a thing by an *inspection.* An *insight* serves to increase our own knowledge; *inspection* enables us to instruct or direct others. An inquisitive traveller tries to get an *insight* into the manners, customs, laws, and government of the countries which he visits; by *inspection* a master discovers the errors which are committed by his scholars, and sets them right.

INSIGNIFICANT. See UNIMPORTANT.

INSINUATE, INGRATIATE. *Insinuate* (see HINT) and *ingratiate,* from *gratus,* grateful or acceptable, are employed to express an endeavor to gain favor; but they differ in the circumstances of the action. A person who *insinuates* adopts every art to steal into the good-will of another; but he who *ingratiates* adopts unartificial means to conciliate good-will. A person of *insinuating* manners wins upon another imperceptibly, even so as to convert dislike into attachment; a person with *ingratiating* manners procures good-will by manifest efforts. *Insinuate* and *ingratiate* may differ in the motive, as well as the mode, of the action: the motive is, in both cases, self-interest; but the former is unlawful, and the latter allowable. In proportion as the object to be attained by another's favor is base, so is it necessary to nave recourse to *insinuation;* when the object to be attained is that which may be avowed, *ingratiating* will serve the purpose. Low persons *insinuate* themselves into the favor of their superiors, in order to obtain an influence over them: it is commendable in a young person to wish to *ingratiate* himself with those who are entitled to his esteem and respect. In modern use, however, *ingratiate* clearly has begun to assume somewhat the same unfavorable connotation of *insinuate.*

Insinuate may be used in the improper sense for unconscious agents; *ingratiate* is always the act of a conscious agent. Water will *insinuate* itself into every body that is in the smallest degree porous; there are few persons of so much apathy that it may not be possible, one way or another, to *ingratiate* one's self into their favor.

Insinuation, Reflection.—These both imply personal remarks, or such remarks as are directed toward an individual; but the former is less direct and more covert than the latter. An *insinuation* always deals in half-words; a *reflection* is commonly open. They are both levelled at the individual with no good intent; but the *insinuation* is general, and may be employed to convey any unfavorable sentiment; the *reflection* is particular, and commonly passes between intimates and persons in close connection. The *insinuation* concerns the honor, the moral character, or the intellectual endowments of the person: the *reflection* respects his particular conduct or feelings toward another. Envious people throw out *insinuations* to the disparagement of those whose merits they dare not openly question; when friends quarrel they deal largely in *reflections* on the past.

INSIPID, DULL, FLAT. *Insipid,* in Latin *insipidus,* from *in,* privative, and *sapere,* to taste, signifies without savor. *Dull* (see DULL). *Flat* (see FLAT).

A want of spirit in the moral sense is designated by these epithets, which borrow their figurative meaning from different properties in nature: the taste is referred to in the word *insipid;* the properties of colors are considered un-

der the word *dull;* the property of surface is referred to by the word *flat.* As the want of flavor in any meat makes it *insipid* and renders it worthless, so does the want of mind or character in a man render him equally *insipid* and devoid of the distinguishing characteristic of his nature: as the beauty and perfection of colors consist in their brightness, the absence of this essential property, which constitutes *dulness,* renders them uninteresting objects to the eye; so the want of spirit in a moral composition, which constitutes its *dulness,* deprives it at the same time of that ingredient which should awaken attention: as in the natural world objects are either elevated or *flat,* so in the moral world the spirits are either raised or depressed, and such moral representations as are calculated to raise the spirits are termed spirited, while those which fail in this object are termed *flat.* An *insipid* writer is without sentiment of any kind or degree; a *dull* writer fails in vivacity and vigor of sentiment; a *flat* performance is wanting in the property of provoking mirth, which should be its peculiar ingredient.

INSIST, PERSIST. Both these terms being derived from the Latin *sisto,* to stand, express the idea of resting or keeping to a thing; but *insist* signifies to rest on a point, and *persist,* from *per,* through or by, and *sisto* (see CONTINUE), signifies to keep on with a thing, to carry it through. We *insist* on a matter by maintaining it; we *persist* in a thing by continuing to do it: we *insist* by the force of authority or argument; we *persist* by the mere act of the will. A person *insists* on that which he conceives to be his right: or he *insists* on that which he conceives to be right: but he *persists* in that which he has no will to give up. To *insist* is, therefore, an act of discretion; to *persist* is mostly an act of folly or caprice: the former is always taken in a good or indifferent sense; the latter mostly in a bad sense. A parent ought to *insist* on all matters that are of essential importance to his children; a spoiled child *persists* in its follies from perversity of humor.

INSNARE, ENTRAP, ENTANGLE, INVEIGLE. The idea of getting any object artfully into one's power is common to all these terms: to *insnare* is to take in, or by means of, a *snare*, from Anglo-Saxon *sneare*, a cord, string, or noose; to *entrap* is to take in a *trap*, from Anglo-Saxon *treppe*, a step, a *trap* being a contrivance into which an animal steps—allied to *tramp;* to *entangle* is to take in a *tangle*, which is a Scandinavian word, a frequentative of *tang*, sea-weed, and means to twist around and around like sea-weed; to *inveigle*, or to take by means of making blind, is a vitiation of the French *aveugle*, blind, from Latin *ab*, without, and *oculum*, eye.

Insnare and *entangle* are used either in the natural or moral sense; *entrap* mostly in the natural, sometimes in the figurative, *inveigle* only in the moral sense. In the natural sense birds are *insnared* by means of bird-lime, nooses, or whatever else may deprive them of their liberty: men and beasts are *entrapped* in whatever serves as a *trap* or an enclosure; they may be *entrapped* by being lured into a house or any place of confinement; all creatures are *entangled* by nets, or that which confines the limbs and prevents them from moving forward.

In the moral sense, men are said to be *insnared* by their own passions and the allurements of pleasure into a course of vice which deprives them of the use of their faculties and makes them virtually captives; they are *entangled* by their errors and imprudences in difficulties which interfere with their moral freedom and prevent them from acting. They are *inveigled* by the artifices of others when the consequences of their own actions are shut out from their view, and they are made to walk like blind men.

INSOLENT. See IMPERTINENT.

INSOLVENCY, FAILURE, BANKRUPTCY. *Insolvency*, from Latin *in*, not, and *solvere*, to loose, to discharge one's obligations, hence to pay, signifies the state of not being able to pay. *Failure* (see that word). *Bankruptcy*, modified etymologically from French *banqueroute* by knowledge of the second element, from the two words *banka* and *rupta*, signifies literally a broken bank.

All these terms are in particular use in the mercantile world, but are not excluded also f:om general application.

Insolvency is a state; *failure*, an act consequent upon that state; and *bankruptcy* is an effect of that act. *Insolvency* is a condition of not being able to pay one's debts; *failure* is a cessation of business, from the want of means to carry it on; and *bankruptcy* is a legal surrender of all one's remaining goods into the hands of one's creditors, in consequence of a real or supposed *insolvency*. These terms are seldom confined to one person or description of persons. As an incapacity to pay debts is very frequent among others besides men of business, *insolvency* is said of any such persons; a gentleman may die in a state of *insolvency* who does not leave effects sufficient to cover all demands. Although *failure* is here specifically taken for a *failure* in business, yet there may be a *failure* in one particular undertaking without any direct *insolvency:* a *failure* may likewise imply only a temporary *failure* in payment, or it may imply an entire *failure* of the concern. As a *bankruptcy* is a legal transaction, which entirely dissolves the firm under which any business is conducted, it necessarily implies a *failure* to the full extent of the term; yet it does not necessarily imply an *insolvency;* for some men may, in consequence of a temporary *failure*, be led to commit an act of *bankruptcy* who are afterward enabled to give a full dividend to all their creditors.

INSPECTION, SUPERINTENDENCY, OVERSIGHT. The office of looking into the conduct of others is expressed by the first two terms, but *inspection* comprehends little more than the preservation of good order; *superintendence* includes the arrangement of the whole. The monitor of a school has the *inspection* of the conduct of his school-fellows, but the master has the *superintendence* of the school. The officers of an army *inspect* the men, to see that they observe all the rules that have been laid down for them; a general or superior officer has the *superintendence* of any military operation. Fidelity is peculiarly wanted in an *inspector*, judgment and experience in a *superintendent*. *Inspection* is said of things as well as persons; *oversight* only of persons; one has the *inspection* of books in order to ascertain their accuracy; one has the *oversight* of persons to prevent irregularity: there is an *inspector* of the customs and an *overseer* of the poor.

See also INSIGHT.

INSPECTOR. See CENSOR.

INSPIRE. See ANIMATE; THRILL.

INSPIRING. See ELECTRIC.

INSTANCE. See EXAMPLE.

INSTANT, MOMENT. *Instant,* from *instare,* to stand over, signifies the point of time that stands over us, or, as it were, over our heads. *Moment,* from the Latin *momentum,* from *movere,* to move, signifies properly movement, but is here taken for the small particle of time in which any movement is made.

Instant is always taken for the time present; *moment* is taken generally for either past, present, or future. A dutiful child comes the *instant* he is called; a prudent person embraces the favorable *moment.* When they are both taken for the present time, *instant* expresses a much shorter space than *moment;* when we desire a person to do a thing this *instant,* it requires haste: if we desire him to do it this *moment,* it only admits of no delay. *Instantaneous* relief is necessary on some occasions to preserve life; a *moment's* thought will furnish a ready wit with a suitable reply.

Instant, Jiffy.—*Jiffy* is a colloquial word of uncertain origin, differing in its meaning from *moment,* much as *instant* differs, but indicating a still briefer moment of time than *instant.* It cannot, however, be employed in serious writing.

INSTIGATE. See ENCOURAGE.

INSTIL. See IMPLANT.

INSTITUTE, ESTABLISH, FOUND, ERECT. To *institute,* in Latin *institutus,* participle of *instituo,* from *in* and *statuere,* to place or appoint, signifying to dispose or fix for a specific end, is to form according to a certain plan; to *establish* (see FIX) is to fix in a certain position what has been formed; to *found* (see FOUND) is to lay the foundation of anything; to *erect* (see BUILD) is to make *erect.* Laws, communities, and particular orders are *instituted;* schools, colleges, and various societies are *established:* in the former case something new is supposed to be framed; in the latter case it is supposed only to have a certain situation assigned to it. The order of the Jesuits was *instituted* by Ignatius de Loyola; schools were *established* by Alfred the Great in various parts of his dominions. The act of *instituting* comprehends design and method; that of *establishing* includes the idea of authority. The Inquisition was *instituted* in the time of Ferdinand; the Church of England is *established* by authority. To *institute* is always the immediate act of some agent; to *establish* is sometimes the effect of circumstances. Men of public spirit *institute* that which is for the public good; a communication or trade between certain places becomes *established* in course of time. An *institution* is properly of a public nature, but *establishments* are as often private: there are charitable and literary *institutions,* but domestic *establishments.*

To *found* is a species of *instituting* which borrows its figurative meaning from the nature of buildings and is applicable to that which is formed after the manner of a building; a public school is *founded* when its pecuniary resources are formed into a fund or *foundation.* To *erect* is a species of *founding,* for it expresses, in fact, a leading particular in the act of *founding:* nothing can be *founded* without being *erected;* although some things may be *erected* without being expressly *founded* in the natural sense; a house is both *founded* and *erected;* a monument is *erected,* but not *founded;* so in the figurative sense, a college is *founded* and consequently *erected:* but a tribunal is *erected,* not *founded.*

INSTRUCT. See INFORM.

INSTRUCTION. See ADVICE; EDUCATION.

INSTRUCTIVE. See DIDACTIC.

INSTRUMENT, TOOL. *Instrument,* in Latin *instrumentum,* from *instruo,* signifies the thing by which an effect is produced. *Tool* comes from Anglo-Saxon *tol,* an implement for working, signifying the thing with which one toils. These terms are both employed to express the means of producing an end. An *instrument* is a *tool* of delicate or elaborate mechanism. Applied figuratively to persons, *instrument* is used mostly in a good sense, *tool* only in a bad sense. Individuals in high stations are often the *instruments* in bringing about great changes in nations; spies and informers are the *tools* of government.

INSUFFICIENT. See INCAPABLE; UNSATISFACTORY.

INSULT. See AFFRONT; INDIGNITY.

INSUPERABLE. See INVINCIBLE.

INSURRECTION, SEDITION, REBELLION, REVOLT. *Insurrection,* from *insurrectus,* participle of *surgere* (English *surge*), to rise up, signifies rising up against any power that is. *Sedition,* in Latin *seditio,* compounded of *sed,* for *se* and *itio,* signifies a going apart, that is, the people going apart from the government. *Rebellion,* from Latin *re,* against, and *bellum,* war, signifies turning upon or against, in a hostile manner, that to which one has been before bound. *Revolt,* in French *révolter,* is most probably compounded of *re* and *volter,* from *volvere,* to roll, signifying to roll or turn back from, to turn against that to which one has been bound.

The term *insurrection* is general; it is used in a good or bad sense, according to the nature of the power against which one rises up: *sedition* and *rebellion* are more specific; they are always taken in the bad sense of unallowed opposition to lawful authority. There may be an *insurrection* against usurped power, which is always justifiable; but *sedition* and *rebellion* are levelled against power universally acknowledged to be legitimate. *Insurrection* is always open; it is a rising up of many in a mass; but it does not imply any concerted or any specifically active measure: a united spirit of opposition, as the moving cause, is all that is comprehended in the meaning of the term: *sedition* is either secret or open, according to circumstances; in popular governments it will be open and determined; in monarchical governments it is secretly organized: *rebellion* is the consummation of *sedition;* the scheme of opposition which has been digested in secrecy breaks out into open hostilities and becomes *rebellion.* *Insurrections* may be made by nations against a foreign dominion, or by subjects against their government: *sedition* and *rebellion* are carried on by subjects only against their government.

Revolt, like *rebellion,* signifies originally a warring or turning against the power to which one has been subject; but *revolt* is mostly taken either in an indifferent or a good sense for resisting a foreign dominion which has been imposed by force of arms.

Rebel and *revolt* may be figuratively applied to the powers of the mind when opposed to each other: the will *rebels* against the reason.

INTEGRAL. See WHOLE.

INTEGRITY. See HONESTY.

INTELLECT, GENIUS, TALENT. *Intellect,* in Latin *intellectus,* from *inter,* between, and the past participle of *legere,* to choose, meaning that which chooses between or judges, signifies the gift of understanding, as opposed to mere instinct or impulse. *Genius,* in Latin *genius,* from *gignere,* to be born, signifies that which is peculiarly born with us. *Talent* (see FACULTY).

Intellect is here the generic term, and includes in its meaning that of the two other terms; there cannot be *genius* and *talent* without *intellect,* but there may be *intellect* without any express *genius* o˙ *talent.* *Intellect* is the intellectual power improved and exalted by cultivation and exercise; in this sense we speak of a man of *intellect,* or a work that displays great *intellect; genius* is the particular bent of the *intellect* which is born with a man, as a *genius* for poetry, painting, music, etc.; *talent* is a particular mode of *intellect* which qualifies its possessor to do some things better than others, as a *talent* for learning languages, a *talent* for the stage, etc.

See also UNDERSTANDING.

INTELLECTUAL. See MENTAL.

INTELLIGENCE. See INFORMATION.

INTEMPERATE. See EXCESSIVE.

INTEND. See DESIGN.

INTENT, INTENSE. *Intent* and *intense* are both derived from the verb to *intend,* Latin *intendere,* signifying to stretch toward a point or to a great degree: the former is said only of the person or mind; the latter qualifies things in general: a person is *intent* when his mind is on the stretch toward an object; his application is *intense* when his mind is for a continuance closely fixed on certain objects; cold is *intense* when it seems to have reached its highest pitch.

See also TENOR.

INTERCEDE, INTERPOSE, MEDI-ATE, INTERFERE, INTERMEDDLE. *Intercede:* from *inter*, between, and *cedere*, to go, signifies literally going between; *interpose*, through French from Latin *inter*, between, and Late Latin *pausare*, to place, means placing one's self between; *mediate*, from Latin *mediatus*, past participle of *mediare*, based on *medius*, middle, means coming in the middle; *interfere*, through French from *inter*, between, and Latin *ferire*, to strike, means striking between; and *intermeddle*, through French from Latin *inter*, between, and *misculare* (the intercalated *d* being an Anglo-French development, which was brought over into Middle English) (Late Latin), Latin *miscere*, to mix, signifies meddling or mixing among.

One *intercedes* between parties that are unequal; one *interposes* between parties that are equal; one *intercedes* in favor of that party which is threatened with punishment; one *interposes* between parties that threaten each other with evil: we *intercede* with the parent in favor of the child who has offended, in order to obtain pardon for him; one *interposes* between two friends who are disputing to prevent them from going to extremities. One *intercedes* by means of persuasion; it is an act of courtesy or kindness in the person between whom and him on whose behalf the intercession is made to comply; one *interposes* by an exercise of authority; it is a matter of propriety or necessity in the parties to conform. The favorite of a monarch *intercedes* in behalf of some criminal, that his punishment may be mitigated; the magistrates *interpose* with their authority to prevent the broils of the disorderly from coming to serious acts of violence.

To *intercede* and *interpose* are employed on the highest and lowest occasions; to *mediate* is never employed but in matters of the greatest moment. As earthly offenders, we require the *intercession* of a fellow-mortal; as offenders against the God of heaven,

we require the *intercession* of a Divine Being: without the timely *interposition* of a superior, trifling disputes may grow into bloody quarrels; without the *interposition* of Divine Providence, we cannot conceive of anything important as taking place: to settle the affairs of nations, *mediators* may afford a salutary assistance; to bring about the redemption of a lost world, the Son of God condescended to be *Mediator*.

All these acts are performed for the good of others; but *interfere* and *intermeddle* are of a different description: one may *interfere* for the good of others or to gratify one's self; one never *intermeddles* but for selfish purposes: the first three terms are, therefore, always used in a good sense; the fourth in a good or bad sense, according to circumstances; the last always in a bad sense.

INTERCHANGE, EXCHANGE, RECIPROCITY. *Interchange* is a frequent and mutual *exchange* (see CHANGE); *exchange* consists of one act only; an *interchange* consists of many acts: an *interchange* is used only in the moral sense; *exchange* is used mostly in the proper sense: an *interchange* of civilities keeps alive good-will; an *exchange* of commodities is a convenient mode of trade.

Interchange is an act; *reciprocity* is an abstract property: by an *interchange* of sentiment, friendships are engendered; the *reciprocity* of good services is what renders them doubly acceptable to those who do them and to those who receive them.

INTERCOURSE, COMMUNICATION, CONNECTION, COMMERCE. *Intercourse*, through French, from Latin *intercursus*, signifies, literally, a running between. *Communication* (see COMMUNICATE). *Connection* (see CONNECT). *Commerce*, from *cum*, and *merces*, merchandise, signifies, literally, an exchange of merchandise, and generally an interchange.

Intercourse and *commerce* subsist only between persons; *communication* and *connection* between persons and things. An *intercourse* with persons may be carried on in various forms; either by an interchange of civilities, which is a friendly *intercourse;* an exchange of commodities, which is a *commercial intercourse;* or an exchange of words, which is a verbal and partial *intercourse:* a *communication,* in this sense, is a species of *intercourse,* namely, that which consists in the *communication* of one's thoughts to another, which may subsist between man and man or between man and his Maker.

A *connection* consists of a permanent *intercourse;* since one who has a regular *intercourse* for purposes of trade with another is said to have a *connection* with him, or to stand in *connection* with him. There may, therefore, be a partial *intercourse* or *communication* where there is no *connection,* nothing to bind or link the parties to each other: but there cannot be a *connection* which is not kept up by continued *intercourse.*

The *commerce* is a species of general but close *intercourse;* it may consist either of frequent meeting and regular co-operation or in cohabitation: in this sense we speak of the *commerce* of men one with another, or the *commerce* of man and wife, of parents and children, and the like.

As it regards things, *communication* is said of places in the proper sense; *connection* is used for things in the proper or improper sense: there is said to be a *communication* between two rooms when there is a passage open from one to the other; one house has a *connection* with another when there is a common passage or thoroughfare to them: a *communication* is kept up between two countries by means of regular or irregular conveyances; a *connection* subsists between two towns when the inhabitants trade with one another, intermarry, and the like.

INTERDICT. See FORBID.

INTEREST, CONCERN. The *interest* (from the Latin *interesse,* to be among, or have a part or a share in a thing) is more comprehensive than *concern* (see AFFAIR). We have an *interest* in whatever touches or comes near to our feelings or our external circumstances; we have a *concern* in that which demands our attention. *Interest* is that which is agreeable; it consists of either profit, advantage, gain, or amusement; it binds us to an object and makes us think of it: *concern,* on the other hand, is something involuntary or painful; we have a *concern* in that which we are obliged to look to, which we are bound to from the fear of losing or of suffering. It is the *interest* of every man to cultivate a philosophical temper: it is the *concern* of all to be on their guard against temptation.

INTERFERE. See INTERCEDE.
INTERIOR. See INSIDE; INWARD.
INTERLOPER. See INTRUDER.
INTERMEDDLE. See INTERCEDE.
INTERMEDIATE, INTERVENING. *Intermediate* signifies being in the midst, between two objects; *intervening* signifies coming between: the former is applicable to space and time; the latter either to time or circumstances. The *intermediate* time between the commencement and the termination of a truce is occupied with preparations for the renewal of hostilities; *intervening* circumstances sometimes change the views of the belligerent parties, and dispose their minds to peace.

INTERMENT. See BURIAL.
INTERMIT. See SUBSIDE.
INTERN, CONFINE, INTERNE. *Intern,* in French *interne,* from Latin *internus,* inward, from *inter,* within, between, and suffix *-nus,* Italian and Spanish *interno.* *Intern,* as a substantive, signifies a student residing at a school, a boarder; in the more common form, *interne,* a physician or surgeon living at a hospital or similar institution, in distinction from a visiting or consulting physician or surgeon; also, in war-times, to a person or a vessel detained at an appointed place, without permission to leave. *Intern,* as a verb, signifies to send and *confine* in the interior of a country. Prisoners of war are *interned* at places more or less remote from the field of action, and captured war-ships and some other vessels are *interned* also at a distance from home ports. The former are usually held till exchanged, the latter till the close of the war. In the summer of 1915 there were about seventy Teutonic vessels of all kinds *interned* in the ports of the United States, because of the European war.

INTERPOSE. See INTERCEDE.
INTERPRET. See EXPLAIN.
INTERROGATE. See ASK.
INTERVAL, RESPITE. *Interval,* in Latin *intervallum,* signifies, literally, the space between the stakes which formed

a Roman intrenchment; and, by an extended application, it signifies any space. *Respite*, Old French *respit*, comes from Latin *respectum*. It referred originally to the "respect had to a suit on the part of a judge," and so meant a delay, a reprieve.

Every *respite* requires an *interval;* but there are many *intervals* where there is no *respite*. The term *interval* concerns time only; *respite* includes the idea of ceasing from action for a time; *intervals* of ease are a *respite* to one who is oppressed with labor; the *interval* which is sometimes granted to a criminal before his execution is in the most proper sense a *respite*.

INTERVENTION, INTERPOSITION. The *intervention*, from *inter*, between, and the past participle of *venio*, to come, is said of inanimate objects; the *interposition*, from *inter*, between, and *positus*, past participle of *pono*, to place, is said only of rational agents. The light of the moon is obstructed by the *intervention* of the clouds; the life of an individual is preserved by the *interposition* of a superior: human life is so full of contingencies that when we have formed our projects we can never say what may *intervene* to prevent their execution; when a man is engaged in an unequal combat, he has no chance of escaping but by the timely *interposition* of one who is able to rescue him.

INTIMACY. See ACQUAINTANCE.

INTIMATE. See HINT.

INTIMIDATE. See FRIGHTEN; OVERAWE.

INTOXICATION, DRUNKENNESS, INFATUATION. *Intoxication*, from the Latin *toxicum* (Greek τοξικόν, a poison for arrows, from τόξα, arrows), signifies the state of being imbued with a poison. *Drunkenness* signifies the state of having drunk overmuch. *Infatuation*, from *fatuus*, foolish, signifies making foolish. or the state of being made foolish.

Intoxication and *drunkenness* are used either in the proper or the improper sense; *infatuation* in the improper sense only; *intoxication* is a general state; *drunkenness* a particular state; *intoxication* may be produced by various causes; *drunkenness* is produced only by an immoderate indul-

gence in some *intoxicating* liquor: a person may be *intoxicated* by the smell of strong liquors, or by vapors which produce a similar effect; he becomes *drunken* by the drinking of wine or other spirits. In another sense, a deprivation of one's reasoning faculties is the common idea in the signification of all these terms: *intoxication* and *drunkenness* spring from the intemperate state of the feelings; *infatuation* springs from the ascendency of the passions over the reasoning powers: a person is *intoxicated* with success, *drunk* with joy, *infatuated* by an excess of vanity, an impetuosity of character, or a passion for one of the opposite sex.

INTRANSIGENT, COMMUNIST, NIHILIST, SOCIALIST. *Intransigent*, in French *intransigeant* and Spanish *intransigente*, is a compound of the Latin *in*, not, and *transigo*, to agree or settle, and implies a person who is dissatisfied with present conditions, especially of a social character, and who refuses to come to an agreement with others on questions of public interest. These terms form a part of a considerable number of designations having a common import, yet conveying different impressions according to conditions in the countries where they are most in vogue.

An *intransigent*, *intransigeant*, and *intransigente*, applied to persons in France, Italy, and Spain, respectively, or an *irreconcilable*, representing at first a member of the Extreme Left in the Spanish Cortes and subsequently a member of the extreme Republican party in Spain, is one who opposes existing policies in a political, economical, and social sense.

The *communist* believes in the doctrine that all property should be held equally by all members of a community. The *nihilist* of Russia believed in destroying existing institutions and governmental forms and policies, and in founding a new order of things generally. The *socialist* of Germany, the United States, and other countries believes that society should be reconstructed on the basis of co-operation of labor and the community of property, so that there would be neither the really rich nor the really poor.

The principles underlying these various doctrines have had earnest and eminent advocates for many years, and, as in innumerable attempts to harmonize and improve social conditions, many of the propagandists, through over-zeal, have been guilty of criminal excesses, especially in France, Italy, and Russia.

A further exposition of movements for social betterment will be found in the article on SOCIALISM.

INTRENCH. See ENCROACH; TRENCH.

INTREPID. See BOLD.

INTRICACY. See COMPLEXITY.

INTRICATE. See KNOTTY.

INTRIGUING. See SCHEMING.

INTRINSIC, REAL, GENUINE, NATIVE. *Intrinsic,* in Latin *intrinsecus,* from *intra,* within, and *sequi,* to follow, signified literally following inward, that is, lying in the thing itself. *Real,* through French *réel,* or directly from Late Latin *realis,* from the Latin *res,* signifies belonging to the very thing. *Genuine,* in Latin *genuinus,* from *gignere,* to bring forth, signifies actually brought forth, or springing out of a thing. *Native,* in Latin *nativus,* and *natus,* born, signifies actually born, or arising from a thing.

The value of a thing is either *intrinsic* or *real:* but the *intrinsic* value is said in regard to its extrinsic value; the *real* value in regard to the artificial: the *intrinsic* value of a book is that which it will fetch when sold in a regular way, in opposition to the extrinsic value, as being the gift of a friend, a particular edition, or a particular type: the *real* value of a book, in the proper sense, lies in the fineness of the paper and the costliness of its binding, and, in the improper sense, it lies in the excellence of its contents, in opposition to the artificial value which it acquires in the minds of biblio-philes from being a scarce edition.

The worth of a man is either *genuine* or *native:* the *genuine* worth of a man lies in the excellence of his moral character, as opposed to his adventitious worth, which he acquires from the possession of wealth, power, and dignity: his *native* worth is that which is inborn in him, and, natural, in opposition to the meretricious and borrowed worth which he may derive from his situation, his talent, or his efforts to please.

INTRODUCE, PRESENT. To *introduce,* from the Latin *intro,* into, and *ducere,* to lead, signifies literally to bring within or into any place; to *present* (see GIVE) signifies to bring into the *presence* of. As they concern persons, the former passes between equals, the latter only among persons of rank and power: one literary man is *introduced* to another by means of a common friend; he is *presented* at court by means of a nobleman.

As these terms concern things, we say that subjects are *introduced* in the course of conversation; men's particular views upon certain subjects are *presented* to the notice of others through the medium of publication.

INTRUDE, OBTRUDE. To *intrude* is to thrust one's self into a place; to *obtrude,* a use now practically obsolete, is to thrust one's self in the way—both from *trudere,* to thrust. *Intrude,* therefore, literally corresponds to the slang phrase *butt in.* It is *intrusion* to go into any society unasked and undesired; it is *obtruding* to put one's self in the way of another by joining the company and taking a part in the conversation without invitation or consent.

An *intruder* is unwelcome because his company is not at all desired, but an *obtruder* may be no further unwelcome than as he occasions an interruption or disturbance.

In the moral application they preserve the same distinction. Thoughts which we wish to banish *intrude* sometimes on the mind; unpleasant thoughts *obtrude* themselves to the exclusion or interruption of those we wish to retain.

See also ENCROACH.

Intruder, Interloper. — An *intruder* thrusts himself in: an *interloper* (coined from *inter,* Latin, meaning within, and Dutch *looper,* English *leap*) runs in between and takes his station. The *intruder,* therefore, *intrudes* only for a short space of time, and in an unimportant degree; but the *interloper* deprives another of his essential rights and for a permanency. A man is an *intruder* who is an unbidden guest at the table of another; he is an *interloper* when he joins any society in such manner as to obtain its privileges without sharing its burdens. *Intruders* are always offensive in the domestic circle: *interlopers* in trade are always regarded with an evil eye.

INTRUST. See CONSIGN.

INUNDATE. See OVERFLOW.

INVADE. See ENCROACH.

INVALID, PATIENT. *Invalid*, in Latin *invalidus*, signifies, literally, one not strong or in good health; *patient*, from the Latin *patiens*, suffering, signifies one suffering under disease. *Invalid* is a general, and *patient* a particular, term; a person may be an *invalid* without being a *patient:* he may be a *patient* without being an *invalid.* An *invalid* is so denominated from his wanting the ordinary share of health and strength; but the *patient* is one who is laboring under some bodily suffering. Old soldiers are called *invalids* who are no longer able to bear the fatigues of warfare: but they are not necessarily *patients.* He who is under the surgeon's hands for any wound is a *patient,* but not necessarily an *invalid.*

INVASION, INCURSION, IRRUPTION, INROAD. The idea of making a forcible entrance into a foreign territory is common to all these terms. *Invasion,* from *in,* into, and *vado,* to go, expresses merely this general idea, without any particular qualification: *incursion,* from *in* and *cursus,* past participle of *curro,* to run, signifies a hasty and sudden *invasion: irruption,* from *in,* and *ruptus,* past participle of *rumpo,* to break, signifies a particularly violent *invasion; inroad,* from *in* and *road,* signifying the making a road or way for one's self, implies the going farther into a country and making a longer stay than by an *incursion. Invasion* is said of that which passes in distant lands; Alexander *invaded* India; Hannibal crossed the Alps and made an *invasion* into Italy: *incursion* is said of neighboring states; the borderers on each side the Tweed used to make frequent *incursions* into England or Scotland.

Invasion is the act of a regular army; it is a systematic military movement: *irruption* and *inroad* are the irregular movements of bodies of men; the former is applied particularly to uncultivated nations, and the latter, like *incursion,* to neighboring states: the Goths and Vandals made *irruptions* into Europe;

the Scotch and English used to make *inroads* upon each other.

These words preserve the same distinction in their figurative application. *Invade* signifies a hostile attack, and may be applied to physical objects or to spiritual objects; as to *invade* one's peace of mind, privileges, etc.

Inroad denotes the progress into any body of what is bad; as the *inroads* of disease into the constitution, into the mind.

INVECTIVE. See ABUSE.

INVEIGH. See DECLAIM.

INVEIGLE. See INSNARE.

INVENT, FEIGN, FRAME, FABRICATE, FORGE. All these terms are employed to express the production of something out of the mind, by means of its own efforts. To *invent* (see CONTRIVE) is the general term; the other terms imply modes of *invention* under different circumstances. To *invent,* as distinguished from the rest, is busied in creating new forms either by means of the imagination or the reflective powers; it forms combinations either purely spiritual or those which are mechanical and physical: the poet *invents* imagery; the philosopher *invents* mathematical problems or mechanical instruments.

Invent is used for the production of new forms to real objects, or for the creation of unreal objects; to *feign* is used for the creation of unreal objects or such as have no existence but in the mind: a play or a story is *invented* from what passes in the world: Mohammed's religion consists of nothing but *inventions:* the heathen poets *feigned* all the tales and fables which constitute the mythology or history of their deities. To *frame,* that is, to make according to a frame, is a species of *invention* which consists in the disposition as well as the combination of objects. Thespis was the *inventor* of tragedy: Psalmanazar *framed* an entirely new language, which he pretended to be spoken on the island of Formosa; Solon *framed* a new set of laws for the city of Athens.

To *invent, frame,* and *feign* are all occasionally employed in the ordinary concerns of life, and in a bad sense; *fabricate* is seldom, and *forge* never, used any otherwise. *Invent* is employed for that which is the fruit of one's own mind and mostly contrary to the truth; to *feign* is employed for that which is unreal; to *frame* is employed for that which requires deliberation and arrangement; to *fabricate* and *forge* are employed for that which is absolutely false and requiring more or less exercise of the *inventive* power. A person *invents* a lie, and *feigns* sorrow; *invents* an excuse, and *feigns* an attachment. A story is *invented*, inasmuch as it is new and not before conceived by others or occasioned by the suggestions of others; it is *framed*, inasmuch as it requires to be duly disposed in all its parts, so as to be consistent; it is *fabricated*, inasmuch as it runs in direct opposition to actual circumstances and therefore has required the skill and labor of a workman; it is *forged* (from Old French *forge*, a work-shop, Latin *fabrica*), inasmuch as it seems by its utter falsehood and extravagance to have caused as much severe action in the brain as what is produced by the fire in a furnace or *forge*.

See also CONTRIVE; FIND.

INVERT. See OVERTURN.

INVEST, ENDUE or ENDOW. To *invest*, from *vestire*, to clothe, whence English *vestments* is derived, signifies to clothe in anything. *Endue* or *endow*, from the Latin *induo*, signifies to put on anything. One is *invested* with that which is external: one is *endued* with that which is internal. We *invest* a person with an office or a dignity: a person is *endued* with good qualities. To *invest* is a real external action; but to *endue* may be merely fictitious or mental. The king is *invested* with supreme authority; a lover *endues* his mistress with every earthly perfection. *Endow* is but a variation of *endue*, and yet it seems to have acquired a distinct office: we may say that a person is *endued* or *endowed* with a good understanding; but as an act of the imagination *endow* is not to be substituted for *endue*: for we do not say that it *endows*, but *endues* things with properties.

See also BESIEGE.

INVIDIOUS, ENVIOUS. *Invidious*, in Latin *invidiosus*, from *invidia*; or *in*, not, and *videre*, to see, signifies looking at with an evil eye: *envious* is literally only a variation of *invidious*. *Invidious*, in its common acceptation, signifies causing ill-will; *envious* signifies having ill-will. A task is *invidious* that puts one in the way of giving offence; a look is *envious* that is full of envy. *Invidious* qualifies the thing; *envious* qualifies the temper of the mind. It is *invidious* for one author to be judge against another who has written on the same subject: a man is *envious* when the prospect of another's happiness gives him pain.

INVIGORATE. See STRENGTHEN.

INVINCIBLE, UNCONQUERABLE, INSUPERABLE, INSURMOUNTABLE. *Invincible* signifies not to be vanquished (see CONQUER): *unconquerable*, not to be conquered: *insuperable*, not to be overcome: *insurmountable*, not to be surmounted. Persons or things which can withstand all force are in the strict sense *invincible;* but as in this sense nothing created can be termed *invincible*, the term is employed to express strongly whatever can withstand human force in general: on this ground the Spaniards termed their Armada *invincible*. The qualities of the mind are termed *unconquerable* when they are not to be won over or brought under the control of one's own reason or the judgment of another: hence obstinacy is with propriety denominated *unconquerable* which will yield to no foreign influence. The particular disposition of the mind or turn of thinking is termed *insuperable*, inasmuch as it baffles our resolution or wishes to have it altered; an aversion is *insuperable* which no reasoning or endeavor on our own part can overcome. Things are denominated *insurmountable*, inasmuch as they baffle one's skill or efforts to get over them or put them out of one's way: an obstacle is *insurmountable* which in the nature of things is irremovable. Some people have an *insuperable* antipathy to certain animals; some persons are of so modest and timid a character that the necessity of addressing strangers is with them an *insuperable* objection to using any endeavors for their own advancement; the difficulties which Columbus had to encounter in his discovery of the New World would have appeared *insurmountable* to any mind less determined and persevering.

INVITE. See ATTRACT; CALL.

INVOLVE. See IMPLICATE.

INWARD, INTERNAL, INNER, INTERIOR. *Inward* signifies toward the inside, that is, not absolutely within: *internal* signifies positively within: *inner,* as the comparative of *inward,* signifies more *inward;* and *interior,* as the comparative of *internal,* signifies more *internal. Inward* is employed more frequently to express a state than to qualify an object; *internal* to qualify the objects: a thing is said to be turned *inward* which forms a part of the *inside:* it is said to be *internal* as one of its characteristics; *inward,* as denoting the position, is indefinite; anything that is *in* in the smallest degree is *inward;* thus what we take in the mouth is *inward* in distinction from that which may be applied to the lips; but that is properly *internal* which lies in the very frame and system of the body; *inner,* which rises in degree on *inward,* is applicable to such bodies as admit of specific degrees of enclosure: thus the inner shell of a nut is that which is enclosed in the *inward:* so likewise *interior* is applicable to that which is capacious and has many involutions, as the *interior* coat of the intestines.

IRE. See ANGER.

IRIDESCENT. See NACREOUS.

IRONY. See RIDICULE; WIT.

IRRATIONAL, FOOLISH, ABSURD, PREPOSTEROUS. *Irrational,* compounded of *in,* not, *ratio,* reason, and a suffix, signifies contrary to reason, and is employed to express the want of the faculty itself, or a deficiency in the exercise of this faculty. *Foolish* (see FOLLY) signifies the perversion of this faculty. *Absurd,* from *ab,* and *surdus,* deaf, signifies that to which one would turn a deaf ear. *Preposterous,* from *præ,* before, and *posterus,* behind, signifies, literally, that side foremost which ought to be behind, which is unnatural and contrary to common sense.

Irrational is not so strong a term as *foolish:* it is applicable more frequently to the thing than to the person, to the principle than to the practice; *foolish,* on the contrary, is commonly applicable to the person as well as the thing;

to the practice rather than the principle. Scepticism, to those who have faith, is the most *irrational* thing that exists; the human mind, from this viewpoint, is formed to believe, but not to doubt: he is, of all men, considered most *foolish* who stakes his eternal salvation on his own fancied superiority of intelligence and illumination. *Foolish, absurd,* and *preposterous* rise in degree: a violation of common sense is implied by them all, but they vary according to the degree of violence which is done to the understanding: *foolish* is applied to anything, however trivial, which in the smallest degree offends our understanding: the conduct of children is therefore often *foolish,* but not *absurd* and *preposterous,* which are said only of serious things that are opposed to our judgment: it is *absurd* for a man to persuade another to do that which he in like circumstances would object to do himself; it is *preposterous* for a man to expose himself to the ridicule of others and then be angry with those who will not treat him respectfully.

IRRECONCILABLE. See INTRANSIGENT.

IRREFRAGABLE. See INDUBITABLE.

IRREGULAR, DISORDERLY, INORDINATE, INTEMPERATE. *Irregular,* that is, literally, *not regular,* marks merely the absence of a good quality; *disorderly,* that is, literally, out of order, marks the presence of a positively bad quality. What is *irregular* may be so from the nature of the thing; what is *disorderly* is rendered so by some external circumstance. Things are planted *irregularly* for want of design: the best troops are apt to be *disorderly* in a long march. *Irregular* and *disorderly* are taken in a moral as well as a natural sense: *inordinate,* which signifies also put out of order, is employed only in the moral sense. What is *irregular* is, or ought to be, contrary to the rule that is established; what is *disorderly* is contrary to the order that has existed; what is *inordinate* is contrary to the order that is prescribed; what is *intemperate* is contrary to the temper or spirit that ought to be encouraged. Our habits will be *irregular* which are not conformable to the laws of social society; our practices will be *disorderly* when we follow the blind impulse of passion; our desires will be *inordinate* when they are not under the control of reason guided by religion; our indulgences will be *intemperate* when we consult nothing but our appetites. Young people are apt to contract *irregular* habits if not placed under the care of discreet and sober people and made to conform to the regulations of domestic life: children are naturally prone to become *disorderly* if not perpetually under the eye of a master: it is the lot of human beings of all ages and stations to have *inordinate* desires, which require a constant check so as to prevent *intemperate* conduct of any kind.

IRRELIGIOUS, Profane, Impious. As epithets to designate the character of the person they seem to rise in degree: *irreligious* is negative; *profane* and *impious* are positive, the latter being much stronger than the former. All men who are not positively actuated by principles of religion are *irreligious; profanity* and *impiety* are, however, of a still more heinous nature; they consist not in the mere absence of regard for religion, but in a positive contempt of it and open outrage against its laws; the *profane* man treats what is sacred as if it were *profane;* what a believer holds in reverence and utters with awe is pronounced with an air of indifference or levity, and as a matter of common discourse, by a *profane* man; he knows no difference between sacred and *profane,* but as the former may be converted into a source of scandal toward others; the *impious* man is directly opposed to the *pious* man; the former is filled with defiance and rebellion against his Maker, as the latter is with love and reverence.

When applied to things, the term *irreligious* seems to be somewhat more positively opposed to *religion;* an *irreligious* book is not merely one in which there is no religion, but that also which is detrimental to religion, such as sceptical or licentious writings: the epithet *profane* in this case is not always a term of reproach, but is employed to distinguish what is temporal from that which is expressly spiritual in its nature; the history of nations is *profane* as distinguished from the sacred history contained in the Bible: the writings of the heathens are altogether *profane* as distinguished from the moral writings of Christians or the believers in Divine Revelation. On the other hand, when we speak of a *profane* sentiment or a *profane* joke, *profane* lips, and the like, the sense is personal and reproachful; *impious* is never applied but to what is personal, and in the very worst sense; an *impious* thought, an *impious* wish, or an *impious* vow, is the fruit of an *impious* mind.

IRREPROACHABLE. See Blameless.

IRREVERENT. See Sacrilegious.

IRRITATE. See Aggravate; Worry.

IRRUPTION. See Invasion.

ISOLATE. See Segregate.

ISSUE. See Arise; Consequence; Event; Offspring; Rise; Sally.

J

JABBER, GABBLE, MUMBLE. These are all imitative words signifying methods of vocal expression. Between *jabber* and *gabble* there is little difference except that suggested by the sound of the words; they are both derived from *gab*, to talk, itself an imitative word which has an interesting history. They signify the utterance of rapid, inarticulate sounds. *Jabber* is more frequently used to indicate that which is inarticulate, and suggests a greater rapidity and sharpness of utterance. Parrots and monkeys are said to *jabber;* ducks and geese, to *gabble. Jabber* is used especially of the sound of a foreign language; we speak of *jabbering* French, *jabbering* Italian, etc. *Gabble* is contemptuously applied to the sound of any talk. *Mumble* suggests a different type of utterance. It is a frequentative of Middle English *mum*, which signifies the least sound made with closed lips; it means, literally, to keep saying "mum, mum."

See also BABBLE.

JADE. See WEARY.

JAGGED, CLEFT, DENTICULATED, SERRATED, UNEVEN. *Jagged* is the adjective form of the substantive *jag*, a Scandinavian word signifying notch or tooth, and means notched or toothlike, signifying an uneven edge. An object that has been *cleft* or split usually exhibits irregular or rough edges or surfaces, as a rock that has been blasted; one that has become *denticulated* (from the Latin *denticulus*, a small tooth) displays projecting points; one that is *serrated* (from the Latin *serro*, to saw) shows protuberances or an irregular edge, as the cutting edge of a fine saw; and whatever is *uneven* is more or less rough or ragged on its surface or edge.

The Sierra Madre Mountains in Mexico and the Sierra Nevada range in California are so called because they have *serrated* or saw-tooth ridges, and a leaf and other botanical growths that have sharp, straight-edged teeth, pointing to the apex, are termed *serrated*.

Jag also has the significance of a small load, and from this is derived two American slang terms: a person who is thoroughly intoxicated is said to have a *load* on or to be carrying a *load;* another who is but partially intoxicated is said to have a *jag* on.

JAM. See PACK.

JANGLE, JAR, WRANGLE. A verbal contention is expressed by all these terms, but with various modifications: *jangle* is an imitative word of Scandinavian origin; it conveys by its own discordant sound an idea of the discordance which accompanies this kind of war of words. *Jar* is also an imitative word, which has parallels in the various Teutonic tongues; it means to utter a harsh sound, and comes from Middle English *garren*, to chide, Anglo-Saxon *ceorian*, to murmur, etc. *Wrangle* is a frequentative of *wring;* its original sense was to keep twisting on or urging; hence to argue vehemently. There is in *jangling* more of cross-questions and perverse replies than direct differences of opinion; those *jangle* who are out of humor with one another; there is more of discordant feeling and opposition of opinion in *jarring:* those who have no good-will to each other will be sure to *jar* when they come into collision; and those who indulge themselves in *jarring* will soon convert affection into ill-will. Married people may destroy the good-humor of the company by *jangling*, but they destroy their domestic peace and felicity by *jarring*. To *wrangle* is technically what to *jangle* is morally: those who dispute by a verbal opposition only are said to *wrangle;* and the disputers who engage in this scholastic exercise are termed *wranglers;* most disputations amount to little more than *wrangling*.

JAR. See JANGLE.

JAUNT. See EXCURSION.

JEALOUSY, ENVY, SUSPICION. *Jealousy* comes from Late Latin *zelosus*, full of zeal, from Greek ζῆλος, zeal, and signifies *zealous* for that which is one's own, and hence fearful lest some one should take it away. *Envy*, in French *envie*, Latin *invidia*, from *invideo*, compounded of *in*, privative, and *video*, to see, signifies not looking at, or looking at in a contrary direction.

We are *jealous* of what is our own; we are *envious* of what is another's. *Jealousy* fears to lose what it has; *envy* is pained at seeing another have that which it wants for itself. Princes are *jealous* of their authority; subjects are *jealous* of their rights; courtiers are *envious* of those in favor; women are *envious* of superior beauty.

The *jealous* man has an object of desire, something to get and something to retain; he does not look beyond the object that interferes with his enjoyment; a *jealous* husband may therefore be appeased by the declaration of his wife's animosity against the object of his *jealousy*. The *envious* man sickens at the sight of enjoyment; he is easy only in the misery of others: all endeavors, therefore, to satisfy an *envious* man are fruitless. *Jealousy* is a noble or an ignoble passion, according to the object; in the former case it is emulation sharpened by fear; in the latter case it is greediness stimulated by fear; *envy* is always a base passion, drawing the worst passions in its train.

Jealousy is applicable to bodies of men as well as individuals; *envious*, to the individuals only. Nations are *jealous* of any interference on the part of any other power in their commerce, government, or territory; individuals are *envious* of the rank, wealth, and honors of one another.

Suspicion, from Latin *suspicere*, *sub*, under, and *specere*, to look, *i. e.*, to look from under one's eyelids out of fear of being seen to look, denotes an apprehension of injury, and, like *jealousy*, implies a fear of another's intentions; but *suspicion* has more of distrust in it than *jealousy*: the *jealous* man doubts neither the integrity nor the sincerity of his opponent; the *suspicious* man is altogether fearful of the intentions of another: the *jealous* man is *jealous* only of him who he thinks wishes for the same thing as he does, and may rob him of it: the *suspicious* man is *suspicious* or fearful that he may suffer something from another. *Jealousy* properly exists between equals

or those who have a common object of desire; but *suspicion* is directed toward any one who has the power as well as the will to hurt; rival lovers are *jealous* of each other, but one person is *suspicious* of another's honesty, or parties entering into a treaty may be *suspicious* of each other's good faith. *Jealousy* cannot subsist between a king and his people in any other than in the anomalous and unhappy case of power being the object sought for on both sides; a king may then be *jealous* of his prerogative when he fears that it will be infringed by his people; and the people will be *jealous* of their rights when they fear that they will be invaded by the crown. According to this distinction, *jealousy* is erroneously substituted in the place of *suspicion*.

Jealousy is concerned only in not losing what one wishes for; *suspicion* is afraid of incurring some positive evil.

JEER. See Scoff.

JEOPARD. See Hazard.

JEST, Joke, Make Game, Sport. *Jest* meant originally a story, a merry tale, from Old French *geste*, an exploit, from Latin *gesta*, past participle of *gerere*, to wage war—a *geste* being a tale of warlike deeds. *Joke* is derived from Latin *iocus*, a game. To *make game* signifies here to make the subject of game or play (see Play). To *sport* signifies here to *sport* with or convert into a subject of amusement.

One *jests* in order to make others laugh; one *jokes* in order to please one's self. The *jest* is directed at the object; the *joke* is practiced with the person or on the person. One attempts to make a thing laughable or ridiculous by *jesting* about it, or treating it in a *jesting* manner; one attempts to excite good-humor in others, or indulge it in one's self, by *joking* with them. *Jests* are therefore seldom harmless: *jokes* are frequently allowable. The most serious subject may be degraded by being turned into a *jest;* but melancholy or dejection of the mind may be conveniently dispelled by a *joke*. Court fools and buffoons used formerly to turn their *jests* upon every subject by which they thought to entertain their employers: those who know how to *joke* with good-nature and discretion may contribute to the mirth of the company: to *make game* of is applicable only to persons: to make a *sport* of or *sport* with is applied to objects in general, whether persons or things; both are employed, like *jest*, in the bad sense of treating a thing more lightly than it deserves.

JIFFY. See INSTANT.

JILT. See COQUET.

JITNEY. See AUTOMOBILE.

JOCOSE. See FACETIOUS; JOCULAR.

JOCUND. See LIVELY.

JOIN. See ADD.

JOKE. See JEST.

JOLLITY. See MIRTH.

JOURNEY, TRAVEL, VOYAGE. *Journey*, through the French *journée*, a day's work, from Latin *diurnata*, the feminine past participle of Late Latin *diurnare*, to sojourn, based on *diurnus*, daily, signifies the course that is taken in the space of a day, or in general any comparatively short passage from one place to another. *Travel* is the same word as *travail*, to labor; it may be derived from Late Latin *trepalium*, a kind of rack for torturing martyrs made of three beams—*tres pali*. *Voyage* is derived through French from Latin *viaticum*, provisions for a journey, based on *via*, a way, and originally signified any course or passage to a distance, but is now confined to passages by sea.

We take *journeys* in different counties in England; we make a *voyage* to the Indies, and *travel* over the continent. *Journeys* are taken for domestic business; *travels* are made for amusement or information: *voyages* are made by captains or merchants for purposes of commerce. We estimate *journeys* by the day, as one or two days' *journey*; we estimate *travels* and *voyages* by the months and years that are employed. The Israelites are said to have *journeyed* in the wilderness forty years, because they went but short distances at a time. It is a part of polite education for young men of fortune to *travel* into those countries of Europe which comprehend the grand tour, as it is termed. A *voyage* round the world, which was at first a formidable undertaking, has now become familiar to the mind by its frequency.

JOVIALITY. See GLEE; MIRTH.

JOY, GLADNESS, MIRTH. The happy condition of the soul is designated by all these terms; but *joy*, from the Latin *gaudia*, joys, and *gladness* (see GLAD) lie more internally; *mirth* (see FESTIVITY) is the more immediate result of external circumstances. What creates *joy* and *gladness* is of a permanent nature; that which creates *mirth* is temporary: *joy* is the most vivid sensation in the soul; *gladness* is the same in quality, but inferior in degree: *joy* is awakened in the mind by the most important events in life; *gladness* springs up in the mind on ordinary occasions: the return of the prodigal son awakened *joy* in the heart of his father; a man feels *gladness* at being relieved from some distress or trouble: public events of a gratifying nature produce universal *joy*; relief from either sickness or want brings *gladness* to an oppressed heart; he who is absorbed in his private distresses is ill prepared to partake of the *mirth* with which he is surrounded at the festive board. *Joy* is depicted on the countenance or expresses itself by various demonstrations: *gladness* is a more tranquil feeling, which is enjoyed in secret and seeks no outward expression: *mirth* displays itself in laughter, singing, and noise.

See also PLEASURE.

JOYFUL. See GLAD.

JUDGE, UMPIRE, ARBITER, ARBITRATOR. *Judge*, through French *juge*, from Latin *judico* and *judex*, from *jus*, right, and *dicare*, to point out, signifies one pronouncing the law or determining right. *Umpire* is derived through Old French *nomper*, from Latin *non*, not, and *par*, equal, signifying a third man called into decide between two equals. *Arbiter* and *arbitrator*, from *arbitrari*, to think, signify one who decides.

Judge is the generic term, the others are only species of the *judge*. The *judge* determines in all matters disputed or undisputed; he pronounces what is law now as well as what will be law for the future; the *umpire* and *arbiter* are *judges* only in particular cases that admit of dispute; there may be *judges* in literature, in arts, and civil matters; *umpires* and *arbiters* are *judges* only in private matters. The *judge* pronounces, in matter of dispute, according to a written law or a prescribed rule; the *umpire* decides in all matters of contest; and the *arbiter* or *arbitrator* in all matters of litigation, according to his own judgment. The *judge* acts under the appointment of government; the *umpire* and *arbitrator* are appointed by individuals: the former is chosen for his skill; he adjudges the palm to the victor according to the merits of the case: the latter is chosen for his impartiality; he consults the interests of both by equalizing their claims. The office of *judge* is one of the most honorable; an *umpire* is of use in deciding contested merits, as the *umpire* at the games of the Greeks; in poetry and the grave style the term may be applied to higher objects.

The office of an *arbiter*, although not so elevated as a *judge* in its literal sense, has often the important duty of a Christian peace-maker; and as the determinations of an *arbiter* are controlled by no external circumstances, the term is applied to monarchs, and even to the Creator as the sovereign *Arbiter* of the world.

Judgment, Discretion, Prudence.— These terms are all employed to express the various modes of practical wisdom, which serve to regulate the conduct of men in ordinary life. *Judgment* is that faculty which enables a person to distinguish right and wrong in general: *discretion* and *prudence* serve the same purpose in particular cases. *Judgment* is conclusive; it decides by positive inference; it enables a person to discover the truth: *discretion* is intuitive (see DISCERNMENT); it discerns or perceives what is in all probability right. *Judgment* acts by a fixed rule; it admits of no question or variation; *discretion* acts according to circumstances and is its own rule. *Judgment* determines in the choice of what is good: *discretion* sometimes only guards against error or direct mistakes; it chooses what is nearest to the truth. *Judgment* requires knowledge and actual experience; *discretion* requires reflection and consideration; a general exercises his *judgment* in the disposition of his army and in the mode of attack; while he is following the rules of military art he exercises his *discretion* in the choice of officers for different posts, in the treatment of his men, in his negotiations with the enemy, and various other measures which depend upon contingencies.

Discretion looks to the present; *prudence*, from Latin *providens*, foreseeing, calculates on the future: *discretion* takes a wide survey of the case that offers: it looks to the moral fitness of things, as well as the consequences which may follow from them; it determines according to the real propriety of anything, as well as the ultimate advantages which it may produce: *prudence* looks only to the good or evil which may result from things; it is, therefore, but a mode or accompaniment of *discretion;* we must have *prudence* when we have *discretion*, but we may have *prudence* where there is no occasion for *discretion*. Those who have the conduct or direction of others require *discretion;* those who have the management of their own concerns require *prudence.* For want of *discretion* the master of a school or the general of an army may lose his authority: for want of *prudence* the merchant may involve himself in ruin, or the man of fortune may be brought to beggary.

As epithets, *judicious* is applied to things oftener than to persons; *discreet* is applied to persons rather than to things; *prudent* is applied to both: a remark or a military movement is *judicious;* it displays the *judgment* of the individual from whom they emanate; a matron is *discreet* who, by dint of years, experience, and long reflection, is enabled to determine on what is befitting a given case; a person is *prudent* who does not inconsiderately expose himself to danger; a measure is *prudent* that guards against the chances of evil. Counsels will be *injudicious* which are given by those who are ignorant of the subject: it is dangerous to intrust a secret to one who is *indiscreet:* the impetuosity of youth naturally impels them to be *imprudent;* an *imprudent* marriage is seldom followed by *prudent* conduct in the parties who have involved themselves in it.

See also DECISION; SENSE.

JUDGMENT - SEAT. See TRIBUNAL.

JUGGLE, CONJURE. *Juggle,* based on Old French *jugleor,* juggler, Modern French *jongleur,* a story-teller or conjuror, and *joculari,* to jest, from *joculus,* a little jest, signifies, as a substantive, an imposition, deception, trick, and as a transitive, to deceive by artifice, to play tricks or amuse by feats of legerdemain. *Conjure*, from Latin *con*, together, and *jurare*, to swear, signifies to produce an apparently magical effect by the pronouncing of mysterious words which seem to have a supernatural power. *Juggle* and *conjure* produce similar effects by different means. To *juggle* implies almost supernatural skill of hand or mind; to *conjure* implies the help of supernatural powers. The magic is within the *juggler* himself; it is external to the *conjuror*, but under his control.

See also CHEAT.

JUICE. See LIQUID.

JUMBLE, HUDDLE. *Jumble* and *huddle* both imply a state of confusion and disorder. *Jumble* is a Scandinavian word—a frequentative of *jump*, and signifies to keep making things *jump* together so that they interfere with each other, and become inextricably confused. *Huddle* is a frequentative allied to Middle English *huden*, to hide, and partly influenced by the Dutch *hoetelen*, to do a thing clumsily; it suggests a number of things carelessly crowded together under a cover or in a hiding-place. *Jumble* suggests a more positive state of confusion than *huddle*. Things *huddled* are crowded close together without an attempt at adjustment, but without necessarily interfering with each other or losing their separate identities. Things *jumbled* together are so crowded that the parts of one are mixed with the parts of others, and the result is disorganizing confusion.

JUNTO. See COMBINATION.

JUST. See RIGHT.

JUSTICE, EQUITY. *Justice*, based on *ius*, right, is founded on the laws of society: *equity*, from *æquitas*, fairness, rightness, and equality, is founded on the laws of nature. *Justice* is a written or prescribed law, to which one is bound to conform and make it the rule of one's decisions: *equity* is a law in our hearts; it conforms to no rule, but to circumstances, and decides by the consciousness of right and wrong. The proper object of *justice* is to secure property; the proper object of *equity* is to secure the rights of humanity. *Justice* is exclusive; it assigns to every one his own; it preserves the existing inequality between men: *equity* is communicative; it seeks to *equalize* the condition of men by a fair distribution. *Justice* forbids us doing wrong to any one, and requires us to repair the wrongs we have done to others: *equity* forbids us doing to others what we would not have them do to us; it requires us to do to others what in similar circumstances we would expect from them.

JUSTIFY. See APOLOGIZE.

JUSTNESS, CORRECTNESS. *Justness*, from *jus*, law, is the conformity to established principle: *correctness*, from *rectus*, right or straight (see CORRECT), is the conformity to a certain mark or line: the former is used in the moral or improper sense only; the latter is used in the proper or improper sense. We estimate the value of remarks by their *justness*, that is, their accordance to certain admitted principles. *Correctness* of outline is of the first importance in drawing; *correctness* of dates enhances the value of a history. It has been *justly* observed by the moralists of antiquity that money is the root of all evil; partisans seldom state *correctly* what they see and hear.

JUTTING. See SALIENT.

JUVENILE. See YOUTHFUL.

K

KEEN. See Acute; Sharp; Trenchant.

KEEP, Preserve, Save. The idea of having in one's possession is common to all these terms; it is, however, the simple meaning of *keep* (see Hold): to *preserve*, from *præ*, beforehand, and *servare*, to *keep*, that is, to *keep* for future use, signifies to *keep* with care and free from all injury; to *save*, allied to *safe*, is to *keep* laid up in a safe place and free from destruction. Things are *kept* at all times and under all circumstances; they are *preserved* in circumstances of peculiar difficulty and danger; they are *saved* in the moment in which they are threatened with destruction: things are *kept* at pleasure; they are *preserved* by an exertion of power; they are *saved* by the use of extraordinary means: the shepherd *keeps* his flock by simply watching over them; children are sometimes wonderfully *preserved* in the midst of the greatest dangers; things are frequently *saved*, in the midst of fire, by the exertions of those present.

Keep, Observe, Fulfil.—These terms are synonymous in the moral sense of abiding by and carrying into execution what is prescribed or set before one for his rule of conduct; to *keep* is simply to have by one in such manner that it shall not depart; to *observe*, in Latin *observo*, compounded of *ob*, near, and *servare*, to *keep*, signifying to *keep* in one's view, to fix one's attention, is to *keep* with a steady attention: to *fulfil* (see Accomplish) is to *keep* to the end or to the full intent. A day is either *kept* or *observed:* yet the former is not only a more familiar term, but it likewise implies a much less solemn act than the latter; one must add, therefore, the mode in which it is *kept*, by saying that it is *kept* holy, *kept* sacred, or *kept* as a day of pleasure; the term *observe*, however, implies always that it is *kept* religiously: we may *keep*, but we do not *observe* a birthday; we *keep* or *observe* the Sabbath.

To *keep* marks simply a perseverance or continuance in a thing; a man *keeps* his word if he does not depart from it: to *observe* marks fidelity and consideration; we *observe* a rule when we are careful to be guided by it; to *fulfil* marks the perfection and consummation of that which one has *kept;* we *fulfil* a promise by acting in strict conformity to it.

Keeping, Custody.—*Keeping* is, as before, the general term. *Custody* is in Latin *custodia*, from *custos*, a guardian, literally a "hider," related to Greek κεύθειν, to hide. The first of these terms is, as before, the most general in its signification; the latter is more frequent in its use. The *keeping* amounts to little more than having purposely in one's possession; but *custody* is a particular kind of *keeping*, for the purpose of preventing an escape: inanimate objects may be in one's *keeping;* but a prisoner, or that which is in danger of getting away, is placed in *custody:* a person has in his *keeping* that which he values as the property of an absent friend: the officers of justice get into their *custody* those who have offended against the laws, or such property as has been stolen.

KEY, Clue, Hint. These words represent the same idea under different metaphors. A *key*, a *clue*, and a *hint* are all means of discovery. *Key*, from Anglo-Saxon *cœg*, is that which unlocks. *Clue* signified originally a ball of thread, from Anglo-Saxon *cliwen;* hence a single thread by which the ball may be unrolled or a web untangled. *Hint* comes from Middle English *henten*, to seize; it is that upon which one seizes as a possible aid to discovery. A *clue* is less certain than a *key;* and a *hint* less certain than a *clue*. If a detective has found the *key* to a mystery, he is certain that he has succeeded in his case; if he has found a *clue*, he is hopeful, but not certain. If he has a *hint* to work upon, he may find a definite *clue*, but he has no reason for great optimism as yet.

KILL, MURDER, ASSASSINATE, SLAY or **SLAUGHTER.** *Kill,* from Anglo-Saxon *cwelan,* to die, means to cause to die, and is related to the verb *quell.* *Murder,* in Anglo-Saxon *morth,* German *mord,* etc., is connected with the Latin *mors,* death. *Assassinate,* from Arabic *hashashin,* signifies to *kill* after the manner of an *assassin,* which word probably comes from the Levant, where, in the thirteenth century, there lived a prince who was called the "Old Man of the Mountains." He lived in a castle between Antioch and Damascus, and brought up young men, whom he fed on the intoxicating drug *hashish* (whence *assassin*) and trained to lie in wait and *kill* passengers. *Slay* comes from Anglo-Saxon *slean,* to smite.

To *kill* is the general and indefinite term, signifying simply to take away life; to *murder* is to *kill* with open violence and injustice; to *assassinate* is to *murder* by surprise or by means of lying in wait; to *slay* is to *kill* in battle: to *kill* is applicable to men, animals, and also vegetables; to *murder* and *assassinate* to men only; to *slay* mostly to men, but sometimes to animals; to *slaughter* only to animals in the proper sense, but it may be applied to men in the improper sense, when they are *killed* like brutes, either as to the numbers or to the manner of *killing* them.

KIND, SPECIES, SORT. *Kind* comes from Anglo-Saxon *cynd,* race, indicating those united by ties of blood. *Species,* in Latin *species,* from *specere,* to behold, signifies literally the form or appearance, and in an extended sense that which comes under a particular form. *Sort,* in Latin *sors,* a lot, signifies that which constitutes a particular lot or parcel.

Kind and *species* are both employed in their proper sense; *sort* has been diverted from its original meaning by colloquial use: *kind* is properly employed for animate objects, particularly for mankind, and improperly for moral objects; *species* is a term used by philosophers, classing things according to their external or internal properties. *Kind,* as a term in vulgar use, has a less definite meaning than *species,* which serves to form the groundwork of science: we discriminate things in a loose or general manner by saying that they are of the animal or vegetable *kind;* of the canine or feline *kind;* but we discriminate them precisely if we say that they are a *species* of the arbutus, of the pomegranate, of the dog, the horse, and the like. By the same rule we may speak of a *species* of madness, a *species* of fever, and the like; because diseases have been brought under a systematic arrangement: but on the other hand, we should speak of a *kind* of language, a *kind* of feeling, a *kind* of influence; and in similar cases where a general resemblance is to be expressed.

Sort may be used for either *kind* or *species;* it does not necessarily imply any affinity or common property in the objects, but simple assemblage, produced, as it were, by *sors,* chance: hence we speak of such *sort* of folks or people; such *sort* of practices; different *sorts* of grain; the various *sorts* of merchandise: and in similar cases where things are sorted or brought together, rather at the option of the person than according to the nature of the thing.

Kindred, Relationship, Affinity, Consanguinity.—The idea of a state in which persons are placed with regard to each other is common to all these terms, which differ principally in the nature of this state. *Kindred* signifies that of being of the same *kin* or *kind.* *Relationship* signifies that of holding a nearer *relation* than others (see CONNECT). *Affinity,* from Latin *ad,* to, and *finis,* border, signifies that of coming close to each other's boundaries. *Consanguinity,* from *sanguis,* the blood, signifies that of having the same blood.

The *kindred* is the most general state here expressed: it may embrace all mankind or refer to particular families or communities; it depends upon possessing the common property of humanity: the philanthropist claims *kindred* with all who are unfortunate, when it is in his power to relieve them. *Relationship* is a state less general than *kindred,* but more extended than either *affinity* or *consanguinity;* it applies to particular families only, but it applies to all of the same family, whether remotely or distantly related. *Affinity* denotes a close *relationship,* whether of an artificial or a natural *kind:* there is an *affinity* between the husband and the wife in consequence of the marriage tie; and there is an *affinity* between those who descend from the same parents or relations in a direct line. *Consanguinity* is, strictly speaking, this latter species of descent; and the term is mostly employed in all questions of law respecting descent and inheritance. See also AFFECTIONATE; GRACIOUS; RELATION.

KINDNESS. See BENEFIT; BENEVOLENCE.

KINETIC. ACTIVE, MOVABLE. These three terms signify "pertaining to motion," but they differ in their application. *Kinetic*, from Greek κινέω, I move, means "resulting from motion," or "associated with motion," and is a scientific term. *Kinetic* energy, for instance, is energy resulting from motion. *Active*, from Latin *actus*, past participle of *agere*, to do or drive, and a suffix, signifies a state of motion, and further suggests motion emanating from within, not the result of force applied from without. *Movable* means a capacity for being put in motion—suggesting that the motion is a result of an external impetus. Hence none of these terms can be substituted for the other—closely allied in their meaning as they seem to be.

KINGDOM. See EMPIRE.

KINGLY. See ROYAL.

KINSMAN. See RELATION.

KISS, OSCULATION. The difference between these two terms is not one of meaning, but of customary usage. *Kiss*, from Anglo-Saxon *coss*, is the familiar and homely word. It is employed in simple, sincere, emotional, or poetical expression. *Osculation*, from Latin *osculum*, a little mouth, is a self-conscious and humorous periphrasis. It may be employed in scientific writing, as when the physiologist writes that "promiscuous *osculation* is a contributory factor in this disease"; or it may be employed by the smart journalist as a humorous substitute for the familiar Anglo-Saxon term. In this case, as in many others, the Latin furnishes the dignified and impersonal word, whose dignity, however, may be made to look like pomposity; the Anglo-Saxon furnishes the familiar and natural term.

KLEPTOMANIA, THIEVERY. Here again the difference in meaning corresponds to a difference in derivation. *Kleptomania* is a scientific term, from Greek κλέπτω, I steal, and Latin *mania*, madness. *Thievery* comes from Anglo-Saxon *theof*, and indicates the act of taking another's property. *Thievery* is the general and popular word and carries with it the suggestion of moral condemnation. *Kleptomania* is a specialized scientific word, suggesting an abnormal psychological condition. *Kleptomania* is an irresistible tendency to theft actuating people who are not tempted to it by necessitous circumstances or any obvious and natural motive, and is regarded as a form of insanity. The *thief* steals because he wants or needs the object, or intends to exchange it for something that he wants or needs. The *kleptomaniac* takes objects with which he may be already well provided and makes no apparent use of the stolen goods. Often he steals only a particular kind of article—an article perhaps valueless in itself or useless to him.

KNACK, ADROITNESS, DEXTERITY. *Knack* is an imitative word. It meant originally (1) a snap; (2) a snap with the finger-nail; (3) a jester's trick, a piece of dexterity. *Knack* is usually employed now to indicate a kind of skill or dexterity which does not result from practice and training, but is an accidental gift or acquirement, or the result of some unexplained trick. There is always something inexplicable about a *knack;* it cannot be *imitated* or reduced to rules of procedure. *Dexterity*, on the contrary, from *dexter*, the right hand, signifies ease and skill in using the hand; hence, by extension, any ease and skill in making or doing something; it may be the result of inborn gifts or of training and practice. *Dexterity* is uniform and reliable; a *knack* is casual and may be uncertain. *Adroitness*, from French *à droit*, Latin *ad directum*, or, in a right manner, is practically synonymous with *dexterous;* it indicates special quickness and cleverness of action. For a further distinction between *adroit* and *dexterous* see CLEVER.

KNAVISH. See DISHONEST.

KNELL, TOLL. There is little difference between these two words. Both indicate the slow ringing of a bell to announce death or disaster. *Toll* suggests by its sound a more solemn and a slower ringing. *Knell* is also used as a substantive to indicate figuratively the death or end of anything.

KNOCK. See RAP.

KNOTTY, INTRICATE, PERPLEXING. These words all indicate the quality of being difficult under the image of entangled threads, but they differ from each other in the character of the image and the concreteness and vividness with which it is suggested to the mind. A *knot* is the interweaving of two threads at one point in such a fashion as to tie them tightly together; *knotty* means full of *knots*, difficult to unfasten. *Intricate*, from Latin *in* and *tricæ*, wiles or hindrances, did not originally suggest the image of interwoven threads so clearly as *perplexing*, from Latin *per*, through, and *plexus*, past participle of *plectere*, to weave, which meant woven through and through. Now *intricate*, which first meant full of hindrances, clearly suggests the physical image of interwoven threads, and *perplexing*, which first suggested the physical image, is given the more general application. *Intricate* is an objective word; *perplexing*, a subjective word. *Intricate* describes the external object; *perplexing* indicates the state of mind induced by it. An *intricate* question becomes *perplexing* the minute some individual mind tries to solve it. *Knotty* is also an objective word, but more obviously metaphorical than intricate, and suggesting a somewhat different image.

KNOW, BE ACQUAINTED WITH. To *know* is a general term; to *be acquainted with* is particular. We may know things or persons in various ways; we may *know* them by name only, or we may *know* their internal properties or characters; or we may simply *know* their figure; we may *know* them by report, or we may *know* them by direct intercourse: one is *acquainted with* either a person or a thing only in a direct manner and by an immediate intercourse in one's own person. We *know* a man to be good or bad, virtuous or vicious, by being a witness to his actions; we become *acquainted with* him by frequently being in his company.

Knowledge, Science, Learning, Erudition.—*Knowledge* signifies the thing

known, from Anglo-Saxon *cnawan*, allied to Latin *noscere*, to know. *Science*, in Latin *scientia*, from *scire*, to know, has the same original meaning. *Learning*, from *learn*, signifies the thing learned. *Erudition*, in Latin *eruditio*, comes from Latin *ē* for *ex*, out, and *rudis*, rude, and signifies to bring out of a state of rudeness or ignorance, that is, the bringing into a state of perfection.

Knowledge is a general term which simply implies the thing *known*: *science, learning*, and *erudition* are modes of *knowledge* qualified by some collateral idea: *science* is a systematic species of *knowledge* which consists of rule and order; *learning* is that species of *knowledge* which one derives from schools or through the medium of personal instruction; *erudition* is scholastic *knowledge* obtained by profound research: *knowledge* admits of every possible degree, and is expressly opposed to ignorance; *science, learning*, and *erudition* are positively high degrees of *knowledge*.

The attainment of *knowledge* is of itself a pleasure independent of the many extrinsic advantages which it brings to every individual, according to the station of life in which he is placed; the pursuits of *science* have a peculiar interest for men of a peculiar turn. *Learning* is less dependent on the genius than on the will of the individual; men of moderate talents have overcome the deficiencies of nature by labor and perseverance, and have acquired such stores of *learning* as have raised them to a respectable station in the republic of letters. Profound *erudition* is obtained by but few; a retentive memory, a patient industry, and deep penetration are requisites for one who aspires to the title of an *erudite* man. *Knowledge*, in the unqualified and universal sense, is not always a good; we may have a *knowledge* of evil as well as good: *science* is good as far as it is founded upon experience; *learning* is more generally and practically useful to the morals of men than *science*: *erudition* is always good, as is a profound *knowledge* of what is worth knowing.

KNOWN. See PUBLIC.
KNUCKLE. See QUAIL.

L

LABOR, Take Pains or Trouble, Use Endeavor. *Labor,* in Latin *labor,* toil. To *take pains* is to expose one's self to *pains* (see Pain); and to *take* the *trouble* is to impose *trouble* on one's self (see Affliction). *Endeavor* (see that word).

The first three terms suppose the necessity for a painful exertion; but to *labor* expresses more than to *take pains,* and this more than to *trouble:* to *use endeavor* excludes every idea of pain or inconvenience: great difficulties to be conquered; great perfection or correctness require *pains;* a concern to please will give *trouble;* but we *use endeavors* wherever any object is to be obtained or any duty to be performed. To *labor* is either a corporeal or a mental action; to *take pains* is principally an effort of the mind or the attention: to *take trouble* is an effort of either the body or mind: a faithful minister of the Gospel *labors* to instil Christian principles into the minds of his audience, and to heal all the breaches which the angry passions make between them: when a child is properly sensible of the value of improvement, he will take the utmost *pains* to profit by the instruction of the master: he who is too indolent to *take* the *trouble* to make his wishes known to those who would comply with them cannot expect others to *trouble* themselves with inquiring into his necessities: a good name is of such value to every man that he ought to *use* his best *endeavors* to preserve it unblemished.

See also Work.

LABORIOUS. See Active.

LABYRINTH, Maze. Intricacy is common to both the objects expressed by these terms; but the term *labyrinth* has it to a much greater extent than *maze:* the *labyrinth,* from the Greek λαβύρινθος, of Egyptian origin, was a work of antiquity which surpassed the *maze* in the same proportion as the ancients surpassed the moderns in all other works of art; it was constructed on so prodigious a scale, and with so many windings, that when a person had once entered he could not find his way out without the assistance of a clue or thread. *Maze* is a word of doubtful origin; it was at first used to signify dreamy thought, dreamy perplexity, and then a structure of interweaving paths which induced such a state of mind. It is a modern term for a structure similar to a labyrinth, on a smaller scale, which is frequently made by way of ornament in large gardens. From the proper meaning of the two words we may easily see the ground of their metaphorical application: political and polemical discussions are compared to a *labyrinth;* because the mind that is once entangled in them is unable to extricate itself by any efforts of its own: on the other hand, that perplexity and confusion into which the mind is thrown by unexpected or inexplicable events is termed a *maze,* because, for the time, the brain is bereft of its power to pursue its ordinary functions of recollection and combination.

LACK. See Want.

LACONIC, Brief, Concise, Pithy. All of these terms indicate speech which contains no unnecessary words, but they differ from each other in the idea that they suggest in addition to that common to them all. *Brief,* from Latin *brevis,* means simply short; the opposite of long—containing few words. *Concise,* from Latin *concidere, concisus,* from *con,* an intensive prefix, and *cædere,* to cut, means cut off, or cut short—made shorter than it might naturally be—and suggests therefore a deliberate concentration in a small space. *Pithy* adds to this idea—it means full of pith. It does not necessarily mean short; but is usually connected with that idea—suggesting the concentration of much substance in a little space. *Laconic* comes from Λακωνικός, from Λάκων, a Laconian or inhabitant of Laconia—

Laconians or Spartans being noted for their brevity of speech. It suggests not only the character of the speech—brief, to the point—but the manner of utterance.

LADING. See FREIGHT.

LAG. See LINGER.

LAMBENT, FLICKERING, GLEAMING, TWINKLING. *Lambent,* from the Latin *lambo,* to lick, signifies licking or playing about like flames, hence, touching lightly, or gliding over. The term is most generally applied to light from any source as affected by exterior influences. Thus, we say that a light is *flickering* when it is moving with an unsteady and quick motion, swaying because of a sudden commotion in the air, and *flickering out,* especially the light from a candle or a lamp, when the wick or the oil is nearly consumed: *gleaming,* when it emits shooting or darting rays or exhibits unusual brightness; and *twinkling,* when it is burning unsteadily, shining with a tremulous, quivering effect; or exhibiting quick, spasmodic spurts, as the *twinkling* of the stars. The term is often used in poetry to imply that which touches lightly or glides over.

LAMENT. See BEWAIL; COMPLAIN; DEPLORE; GRIEVE; WAIL.

LAND, COUNTRY. *Land,* Anglo-Saxon *land,* signifies an open, even space, and refers strictly to the earth. *Country,* through Old French *contree,* from Late Latin *contrata,* the region lying opposite, comes from *contra,* opposite. Compare German *gegend,* from *gegen,* opposite. The term *land,* therefore, in its proper sense, excludes the idea of habitation; the term *country* excludes that of the earth, or the parts of which it is composed: hence we speak of the *land* as rich or poor, according to what it yields: of a *country,* as rich or poor, according to what its inhabitants possess: so, in like manner, we say, the *land* is ploughed for receiving the grain; or a man's *land,* for the ground which he possesses or occupies: but the *country* is cultivated; the *country* is under a good government; or a man's *country* is dear to him.

In an extended application, however, these words may be put for one another: the word *land* may sometimes be put for any portion of *land* that is under a government, as the *land* of liberty; and *country* may be put for any spot of earth or line of *country,* together with that which is upon it; as a rich *country.*

LANDSCAPE. See VIEW.

LANGUAGE, TONGUE, SPEECH, IDIOM, DIALECT. *Language,* through Middle French *language,* based on *langue,* from the Latin *lingua,* a *tongue,* and a suffix, signifies, like the word *tongue,* that which is spoken by the *tongue,* Anglo-Saxon *tunge. Speech* is the act of speaking, or the word *spoken. Idiom,* in Latin *idioma,* Greek ἰδίωμα, from ἴδιος, *proprius,* proper, or peculiar, signifies a peculiar mode of speaking. *Dialect,* through French from Latin *dialectus,* Greek διάλεκτος, from διαλέγομαι, to speak in a distinct manner, signifies a distinct mode of speech.

All these terms mark the manner of expressing our thoughts, but under different circumstances. *Language* is the most general term in its meaning and application; it conveys the general idea without any modification, and is applied to other modes of expression besides that of words, and to other objects besides persons; the *language* of the eyes frequently supplies the place of that of the *tongue;* the deaf and dumb use the language of signs; birds and beasts are supposed to have their peculiar *language: tongue, speech,* and the other terms are applicable only to human beings. *Language* is either written or spoken; but a *tongue* is conceived of mostly as something to be spoken: whence we speak of one's mother *tongue.*

Speech is an abstract term, implying either the power of uttering articulate sounds, as when we speak of the gift of *speech,* which is denied to those who are dumb; or the words themselves which are spoken, as when we speak of the parts of *speech;* or the particular mode of expressing one's self, as that a man is known by his *speech. Idiom* and *dialect* are not properly a *language,* but the properties of *language:* idiom is the peculiar construction and turn of a *language,* which distinguishes it altogether from others; it is that which enters into the composition of the *language,* and cannot be separated from it. A *dialect* is that which is engrafted on a *language* by the inhabitants of particular parts of a country, and admitted by its writers and learned men to form an incidental part of the *language;* as the *dialects* which originated with the Ionians, the Athenians, the Æolians, and were afterward amalgamated into the Greek *tongue.* Whence the word *dialect* may be extended in its application to denote any peculiar manner of speech adopted by any community.

LANGUID. See FAINT.

LANGUISH. See FLAG.

LAPSE. See SLIP.

LARGE, WIDE, BROAD. *Large* (see GREAT) is applied in a general way to express every dimension; it implies not only abundance in solid matter, but also freedom in the space, or extent of a plane superficies. *Wide,* in Anglo-Saxon *wid,* signifies an open space unencumbered by any obstructions. *Broad,* in Anglo-Saxon *brad,* has a similar meaning. Many things are *large,* but not *wide;* as a *large* town, a *large* circle, a *large* ball, a *large* nut: other things are both *large* and *wide;* as a *large* field, or a *wide* field: a *large* house, or a *wide* house: but the field is said to be *large* from the quantity of ground it contains; it is said to be *wide* both from its figure and the extent of its space in the cross directions; in like manner, a house is *large* from its extent in all directions; it is said to be *wide* from the extent which it runs in front: some things are said to be *wide* which are not denominated *large,* that is, either such things as have less bulk and quantity than extent of plane surface; as ell-*wide* cloth, a *wide* opening, a *wide* entrance, and the like; or such as have an extent of space only one way; as a *wide* road, a *wide* path, a *wide* passage, and the like. What is *broad* is in sense, and mostly in application, *wide,* but not *vice versâ:* a ribbon is *broad;* a ledge *broad;* a ditch is *broad;* a plank is *broad;* the brim of a hat is *broad;* or the border of anything is *broad;* on the other hand, a mouth is *wide,* but not *broad;* apertures in general are *wide,* but not *broad. Large* is opposed to small; *wide* to close; *broad* to narrow. In the moral application, we speak of *largeness* in regard to liberal-ity; *wide* and *broad* only in the figurative sense of space or size: as a *wide* difference; or a *broad* line of distinction.

Largely, Copiously, Fully.—*Largely* is here taken in the moral sense, and, if the derivation given of it be true, in the most proper sense. *Copiously* comes from the Latin *copia,* plenty, signifying in a plentiful degree. *Fully* signifies in a *full* degree; to the *full* extent, as far as it can reach.

Quantity is the idea expressed in common by all these terms; but *largely* has always a reference to the freedom of the will in the agent; *copiously* qualifies actions that are done by inanimate objects; *fully* qualifies the actions of a rational agent, but it denotes a degree or extent which cannot be surpassed. A person deals *largely* in things, or he drinks *large* draughts; rivers are *copiously* supplied in rainy seasons; a person is *fully* satisfied or *fully* prepared. A bountiful Providence has distributed His gifts *largely* among His creatures: blood flows *copiously* from a deep wound when it is first made: when a man is not *fully* convinced of his own insufficiency he is not prepared to listen to the counsel of others.

LASH. See WHIP.

LASS. See VIRGIN.

LASSITUDE. See FATIGUE.

LAST, LATEST, FINAL, ULTIMATE. *Last* and *latest* are both from *latst,* the superlative of Anglo-Saxon *læt,* slow—Modern English *late*—allied to Latin *lassus,* which is found in English words like *lassitude. Final* (see that word). *Ultimate* comes from Latin *ultimatus,* participle of *ultimare,* based on *ultimus,* the last.

Last and *ultimate* concern the order of succession: *latest,* the order of time; *final,* the completion of an object. What is *last* or *ultimate* is succeeded by nothing else: what is *latest* is succeeded at no great interval of time; what is *final* requires to be succeeded by nothing else. The *last* is opposed to the first; the *ultimate* is distinguished from that which immediately precedes it; the *latest* is opposed to the earliest; the *final* is opposed to the introductory or beginning. A person's *last* words are those by which one is guided; his *ultimate* object is sometimes remote or concealed from the view; a conscientious man remains firm to his principles to his *latest* breath; the *final* determination of difficult matters requires caution. Jealous people strive not to be the *last* in anything; the *latest* intelligence which a man gets of his country is acceptable to one who is in distant quarters of the globe; it requires resolution to take a *final* leave of those whom one holds near and dear.

See also UTTERMOST.

Lastly, At Last, At Length.—*Lastly*, like *last*, implies the order of succession: *at last* or *at length* refers to what has preceded. When a sermon is divided into many heads, the term *lastly* comprehends the *last* division. When an affair is settled after much difficulty, it is said to be *at last* settled; and if it be settled after a protracted continuance, it is said to be settled *at length*.

LAST-TERMS. See ULTIMATUM.

LATENT. See SECRET.

LATEST. See LAST.

LAUDABLE, PRAISEWORTHY, COMMENDABLE. *Laudable*, from the Latin *laudare*, to praise, is in sense literally *praiseworthy*, that is, *worthy of praise* or to be *praised* (see PRAISE). *Commendable* signifies entitled to *commendation*, from Latin *con*, together, and *mandare*, to place in the hands of—that is to say, worthy of trust, hence worthy of praise.

Laudable is used in a general application; *praiseworthy* and *commendable* are applied to individuals: things are *laudable* in themselves; they are *praiseworthy* or *commendable* in this or that person. That which is *laudable* is entitled to encouragement and general approbation; an honest endeavor to be useful to one's family or one's self is at all times *laudable*, and will insure the support of all good people. What is *praiseworthy* obtains the respect of all men: as all have temptations to do that which is wrong, the performance of one's duty is in all cases *praiseworthy*, but particularly so in those cases where it opposes one's interests and interferes with one's pleasures. What is *commendable* is not equally as important as the former two; it entitles a person only to a temporary or partial expression of good-will and approbation; the performance of those minor and particular duties which belong to children and subordinate persons is in the proper sense *commendable*.

LAUGH, RIDICULE. *Laugh* is the Anglo-Saxon word, from *hlihan*, an imitative word; *ridicule*, from *ridiculus*, is the Latin term, from *ridere*, to smile or laugh.

Both these verbs are used here in the sense for *laughter*, blended with more or less of contempt: but the former displays itself by the natural expression of *laughter*: the latter shows itself by a verbal expression: the former is produced by a feeling of mirth on observing the real or supposed weakness of another; the latter is produced by a strong sense of the absurd or irrational in another: the former is more immediately directed to the person who has excited the feeling; the latter is more commonly produced by things than by persons. We *laugh* at a person to his face; but we *ridicule* his notions by writing or in the course of conversation: we *laugh at* the individual; we *ridicule* that which is maintained by him.

Laughable, Ludicrous, Ridiculous, Comical, Comic, Droll.—*Laughable* signifies exciting, or fit to excite, *laughter*. *Ludicrous*, in Latin *ludicrus*, from *ludus*, a game, signifies belonging to a game or sport. *Ridiculous*, exciting, or fit to excite, *ridicule*.

Either the direct action of *laughter* or a corresponding sentiment is included in the signification of all these terms: they differ principally in the cause which produces the feeling; the *laughable* consists of objects in general, whether personal or otherwise; the *ludicrous* and *ridiculous* have reference more or less to that which is personal. What is *laughable* may excite simple merriment independently of all personal reference, unless we admit what Mr. Hobbes, and after him Addison, have maintained of all *laughter*, that it springs from pride. But without entering into this nice question, I am inclined to distinguish between the *laughable* which arises from the reflection of what is to our own advantage or pleasure, and that which arises from reflecting on what is to the disadvantage of another. The tricks of a monkey or the humorous stories of wit are *laughable* from the nature of the things themselves, without any apparent allusion, however remote, to any individual but the one whose senses or mind is gratified. The *ludicrous* and *ridiculous* are, however, species of the *laughable* which arise altogether from reflecting on that which is to the disadvantage of another; but the *ludicrous* has in it less to the disadvantage of another than the *ridiculous*. It is possible, therefore, for a person to be in a *ludicrous* situation without any kind of moral demerit, or the slightest depreciation of his moral character; since that which renders his situation *ludicrous* is altogether independent of himself; or it becomes *ludicrous* only in the eyes of incompetent judges. "Let an ambassador," says Mr. Pope, "speak the best sense in the world, and deport himself in the most graceful manner before a prince, yet if the tail of his shirt happen, as I have known it happen to a very wise man, to hang out behind, more people will *laugh* at that than attend to the other." This is the *ludicrous*. The same can seldom be said of the *ridiculous;* for as this springs from positive moral causes, it reflects on the person to whom it attaches in a less questionable shape and produces positive disgrace. Persons very rarely appear *ridiculous* without being really so; and he who is really *ridiculous* justly excites contempt.

Droll and *comical* are in the proper sense applied to things which cause *laughter*, as when we speak of a *droll* story, or a *comical* incident, or a *comic* song. They may be applied to the person; but not so as to reflect disadvantageously on the individual, as in the former terms.

LAVISH. See EXTRAVAGANT.

LAW. See MAXIM; ORDINANCE.

LAWFUL, LEGAL, LEGITIMATE, LICIT. *Lawful* is the adjective corresponding to *law*, a Scandinavian word from the root found in *lie*, a *law* being that which is *laid* down, which is fixed or established. *Legal* comes from Latin *legalis*, from *lex*, from the root found in *legere*, to collect—*law* being the *collection* of the customs and judgments of the people in one standard code of action. *Legitimate* has the same derivation. They

differ, therefore, according to the sense of the word *law; lawful* signifies the *law* in general, defined or undefined; *legal*, only the *law* of the land which is defined; *legitimate*, the laws or rules of science as well as civil matters in general. *Licit*, from the Latin *licet*, it is allowed, is used only to characterize the moral quality of actions; the *lawful* properly implies conformable to or enjoined by *law;* the *legal* what is in the form or after the manner of *law*, o. binding by *law:* it is not *lawful* to coin money with the king's stamp; a marriage was formerly not *legal* in England which was not solemnized according to the rites of the Established Church: men's passions impel them to do many things which are *unlawful* or *illicit;* their ignorance leads them into many things which are *illegal* or *illegitimate*. As a good citizen and a true Christian, every man will be anxious to avoid everything which is *unlawful:* it is the business of the lawyer to define what is *legal* or *illegal:* it is the business of the critic to define what is *legitimate* verse in poetry; it is the business of the linguist to define the *legitimate* use of words: it is the business of the moralist to point out what is *illicit*.

LAX. See LOOSE.

LAY, TAKE HOLD OF, CATCH, SEIZE, SNATCH, GRASP, GRIPE. To *lay* or *take hold of* is here the generic expression; it denotes simply getting into one's possession, which is the common idea in the signification of all these terms, which differ in regard to the motion in which the action is performed. To *catch* is to *lay hold of* with an effort. To *seize* is to *lay hold of* with violence. To *snatch* is to *lay hold of* by a sudden effort. One is said to *lay hold of* that on which one places his hand; he *takes hold of* that which he secures in his hand. We *lay hold of* anything when we see it falling; we *take hold of* anything when we wish to lift it up; we *catch* what attempts to escape; we *seize* it when it makes resistance; we *snatch* that which we are particularly afraid of not getting otherwise. A person who is fainting *lays hold of* the first thing which comes in his way; a sick person or one that wants support *takes hold of* another's arm in walking; various artifices are employed to *catch* ani-

LEAN

477

their prey the moment they come
within their reach; it is the rude sport
of a school-boy to *snatch* out of the
hand of another that which he is not
willing to let go.

To *lay hold of* is to get in the possession. To *grasp* and to *gripe* signify to
have or keep in the possession; an
eagerness to keep or not to let go is
expressed by that of *grasping;* a fearful anxiety of losing and an earnest
desire of keeping are expressed by the
act of *gripping.* When a famished man
lays hold of food he *grasps* it, from a
convulsive kind of fear lest it should
leave him: when a miser *lays hold of*
money he *gripes* it from the love he
bears to it, and the fear he has that
it will be taken from him.

See also LIE; PUT.

LAZY. See IDLE; INACTIVE.

LEAD, CONDUCT, GUIDE. *Lead* is
the Anglo-Saxon word, originally *lǽ-
dan,* corresponding to Latin *ducere,*
found here in *conduct,* from *cum,* with,
and *ducere,* to lead. For the origin of
guide see CHAPERON.

All these terms are employed to denote the influence which a person has
over the movements or actions of some
person. To *lead* is an unqualified action: one *leads* by helping a person onward in any manner, as to *lead* a child
by the hand, or to *lead* a person through
a wood by going before him. To *conduct* and *guide* are different modes of
leading, the former by virtue of one's
office or authority, the latter by one's
knowledge or power; as to *conduct* an
army, or to *conduct* a person into the
presence of another; to *guide* a traveller
in an unknown country. These words
may therefore be applied to the same
objects: a general *leads* an army, inasmuch as he goes before it into the field;
he *conducts* an army, inasmuch as he
directs its operations; the stable-boy
leads the horses to water; the coach-
man *guides* the horses in a carriage.

Conduct and *guide* may also be applied in this sense to inanimate objects;
as the pilot *conducts* the vessel into the
port, the steersman *guides* a vessel by
the help of the rudder.

In the moral application of these
terms, persons may *lead* or *guide* other
persons, but they *conduct* things; as to

lead a person into a course of life; to
guide him in a course of reading or
study; to *conduct* a lawsuit, or any
particular business. To *lead,* being a
matter of purely personal influence,
may be either for the benefit or injury
of the person *led.*

To *conduct,* supposing judgment and
management, and to *guide,* supposing
superior intelligence, are always taken
in the good sense, unless otherwise
qualified.

Things as well as persons may *lead,
conduct,* and *guide,* with a similar distinction. Whatever serves as a motive of action, or as a course and
passage to a place or an object, *leads.*
Whatever influences our conduct
rightly *conducts.*
Whatever serves as a rule or *guide
guides.*
As persons may sometimes be false
guides, so things may furnish a false
rule.

LEADER. See CHIEF.

LEADING. See CARDINAL; SU-
PREME.

LEAGUE. See ALLIANCE.

LEAN, MEAGRE. *Lean* is the Anglo-
Saxon word, from *hlæne,* originally
bending or stooping, hence inclined to
bend, or thin; *meagre* is probably a
Latin word from *macer,* thin, Greek
μακρός, long, though it early appears.
in Anglo-Saxon as *mæger,* probably borrowed from the Continent.

Lean denotes want of fat; *meagre*
want of flesh: what is *lean* is not always *meagre;* but nothing can be *meagre*
without being *lean.* Brutes as well as
men are *lean,* but men only are said
to be *meagre: leanness* is frequently
connected with the temperament;
meagreness is the consequence of star-
vation and disease. There are some
animals by nature inclined to be *lean;*
a *meagre,* pale visage is to be seen
perpetually in the haunts of vice and
poverty.

Lean, Incline, Bend.—Lean, in Anglo-
Saxon *hlænan* (see above), is derived
from the root found in *incline,* from
the Latin, Greek κλίνω, I bend. *Bend*
(see that word).

In the proper sense, *lean* and *incline*
are both said of the position of bodies;
bend is said of the shape of bodies:
that which *leans* rests on one side, or

C.E.S.—16*

in a sideward direction; that which *inclines leans* or turns only in a slight degree: that which *bends* forms a curvature; it does not all *lean* the same way: a house *leans* when the foundation gives way: a tree may grow so as to *incline* to the right or the left, or a road may *incline* this or that way; a tree or a road *bends* when it turns out of the straight course. In another sense, the judgment *leans*, the will *inclines*, the will or conduct *bends*, in consequence of some outward action. A person *leans* to this or that side of a question which he favors; he *inclines*, or is *inclined*, to this or that mode of conduct; he *bends* to the will of another. It is the duty of a judge to *lean* to the side of mercy as far as is consistent with justice: whoever *inclines* too readily to listen to the tales of distress which are continually told to excite compassion will find himself in general deceived; an *unbending* temper is the bane of domestic felicity.

LEARNED. See ACADEMIC.

LEARNING. See KNOWLEDGE; LETTERS.

LEAVE, QUIT, RELINQUISH. *Leave* is derived from Anglo-Saxon *læfan*, to leave, corresponding to the Latin *linquere*, found in *relinquish*. *Quit*, in French *quitter*, from the Latin *quietus*, rest, signifies to rest or remain, to give up the hold of. *Relinquish* (see ABANDON).

We *leave* that to which we may intend to return; we *quit* that to which we return no more: we may *leave* a place voluntarily or otherwise; but we *relinquish* it unwillingly. We *leave* persons or things; we *quit* and *relinquish* things only. I *leave* one person in order to speak to another; I *leave* my house for a short time; I *quit* it not to return to it.

Leave and *quit* may be used in the improper as well as the proper sense. It is the privilege of the true Christian to be able to *leave* all the enjoyments of this life, not only with composure, but with satisfaction; dogs have sometimes evinced their fidelity, even to the remains of their masters, by not *quitting* the spot where they are laid; prejudices, particularly in matters of religion, acquire so deep a root in the mind that they cannot be made to *relinquish*

their hold by the most persuasive eloquence and forcible reasoning.

See also CEASE; DESIST.

Leave, Take Leave, Bid Farewell or Adieu.—*Leave* is here general as before; it expresses simply the idea of separating one's self from an object, whether for a time or otherwise; to *take leave* and *bid farewell* imply a separation for a perpetuity. *Farewell* is a native English expression meaning "May you fare well"; *adieu* is French, from the phrase *à Dieu*, Latin *ad Deum*, meaning "I commit you to God's keeping."

To *leave* is an unqualified action; it is applied to objects of indifference, or otherwise, but supposes in general no exercise of one's feelings. We *leave* persons as convenience requires; we *leave* them on the road, in the field, in the house, or wherever circumstances direct; we *leave* them with or without speaking; but to *take leave* is a parting ceremony between friends, on their parting for a considerable time; to *bid farewell*, or *adieu*, is a still more solemn ceremony, when the parting is expected to be final. When applied to things, we *leave* such as we do not wish to meddle with; we *take leave* of those things which were agreeable to us, but which we find it prudent to give up; and we *bid farewell* to those for which we still retain a great attachment. It is better to *leave* a question undecided than to attempt to decide it by altercation or violence; it is greater virtue in a man to *take leave* of his vices than to let them *take leave* of him; when a man engages in schemes of ambition, he must *bid adieu* to all the enjoyments of domestic life.

Leave, Liberty, Permission, License.—*Leave* as here used is a word of different origin, from Anglo-Saxon *leof*, dear, found in English *lief*—meaning here pleasure, hence freedom of will, literally permission "to do as you please." *Liberty* is also taken for *liberty* granted, from Latin *liber*, free. *Permission* signifies the act of *permitting* (see ALLOW) or the thing *permitted*. *License*, in Latin *licentia*, from *licet*, it is lawful, signifies the state of being *permitted* by law or authority.

Leave and *liberty* may sometimes be taken as well as given; *permission* and *license* are never to be taken, but must always be granted, and that in an especial manner—the former by express words, the latter by some acknowledged and mostly legal form. *Leave* is employed only on familiar occasions; *liberty* is given in more important matters: the master gives *leave* to his servant to go out for his pleasure; a gentleman gives his friends the *liberty* of shooting on his grounds: *leave* is taken in indifferent matters, particularly as it respects *leave* of absence; *liberty* is taken by a greater, and in general an unauthorized, stretch of one's powers, and is, therefore, an infringement on the rights of another. What is done without the *leave* may be done without the knowledge, though not contrary to the will of another; but *liberties* which are taken without offering an apology are always calculated to give offence. *Leave* respects only particular and private matters; *liberty* respects general or particular matters, public or private; as *liberty* of speech, *liberty* of the press, and the like.

Leave and *permission* are both the acts of private individuals in special cases. The *permission* is a more formal and less familiar act than *leave;* the *permission* is often an act of courtesy passing between equals and friends; the *leave* is properly said of what passes from superiors to inferiors: a person obtains *leave* of absence. The *license* is always general, or resting on some general authority; as the *licenses* given by government, and poetic *licenses*. Whenever applied to individuals it carries with it the idea of a special authority; as a *license* given by a landlord to the tenant to assign his lease.

Leavings, Remains. — *Leavings* are the consequences of a voluntary act: they signify what is left: *remains* are what follow in the course of things; they are what *remains;* the former is therefore taken in the sense to signify what has been left as worthless; the latter is never taken in this sense. When many persons of good taste have the liberty of choosing, it is fair to expect that the *leavings* will be worth little or nothing, after all have made their choice. By the *remains* of beauty which are discoverable in the face of a female we may be enabled to estimate what her personal gifts were.

LEGAL. See LAWFUL.

LEGENDARY, FABULOUS, MYTHICAL, TRADITIONAL. These are all adjectives signifying the quality of old stories handed down from generation to generation either in oral or written form. *Legendary* comes from the gerundive of Latin *legere*, to collect or read; it signifies worthy of being collected and read, or characteristic of old collections of tales. *Fabulous*, from Latin *fabula*, a story, signifies storylike, with an emphasis upon the difference between the story which is the product of the untrammelled imagination and the plain reality. *Mythical* comes from Greek μῦθος, a fable. *Tradition* comes from Latin *tradere*, to hand down—signifying that which is handed down by word of mouth. *Legendary* and *traditional* differ from each other in the indication of the means of communication; the one is written, the other is generally oral, though these distinctions are not strictly observed. We speak of "written *tradition*" and denominate as *legends* stories that have never been written. *Traditional* has more of truth and seriousness than *legendary*. A *tradition* is preserved as a record of some fact, and the changes that it undergoes are usually due to natural mistakes and failures of memory; a *legend* is usually handed down because it is interesting—it makes a good story worthy of being read, and hence it may be improved by the imaginations of successive generations. *Mythical* suggests less of fact and veracity. A *mythical* hero, a *mythical* land are those which exist only in the imagination of those who tell about them. *Mythical* sometimes refers especially to the *myths* or old stories of the divinities and heroes preserved by various nations. It therefore suggests stories of the supernatural, and has some of the dignity of a *tradition* or *legend*. *Fabulous* has none of this traditional credibility and seriousness; something *fabulous* is a deliberate creation of the imagination transcending all bounds of reality. However, there are several curious modifications of these words. *Fabulous*, while suggesting the wildly extravagant, the apparently impossible, etc., does not arouse the same degree of incredulity that is aroused by *mythical*. *Mythical* wealth is wealth which is said to exist but does not; *fabulous* wealth is wealth transcending all bounds of probability, with the implication that it does really exist. *Mythical* indicates that which is believed but does not exist; *fabulous* that which is not believed but does exist. There is always a distinct difference in the significance of these four words; they are interchangeable only within some definite limits. The *traditional* splendor of a noble family, for instance, means *splendor* enduring from generation to generation both in memory and in reality; *legendary* splendor means splendor described in old stories, existent long ago, but not now; *mythical* splendor means that which is said to be but is not; *fabulous* splendor, splendor now existent but so great as to seem impossible.

LEGITIMATE. See LAWFUL.

LEISURE. See IDLE.

LENITY. See CLEMENCY.

LESSEN. See ABATE.

LET, LEAVE, SUFFER. The removal of hindrance or constraint on the actions of others is implied by all these terms; but *let*, like the German *lassen*, to leave, is a less formal action than *leave*, and this than *suffer*, from the Latin *suffero*, to bear with, signifying not to put a stop to. I *let* a person pass in the road by getting out of his way: I *leave* a person to decide on a matter according to his own discretion, by declining to interfere; I *suffer* a person over whom I am expected to exercise a control to go his own way. It is in general most prudent to *let* things take their own course: in the education of youth, the greatest art lies in *leaving* them to follow the natural bent of their minds and turn of the disposition, and at the same time not *suffering* them to do anything prejudicial to their character or future interests.

LETHARGIC. See SLEEPY.

LETTER, EPISTLE. According to the origin of these words, *letter,* in Latin *literæ*, signifies any document composed of written *letters*; and *epistle*, in Greek ἐπιστολή, from ἐπιστέλλω, to send signifies a *letter* sent or addressed to any one; consequently the former is the generic, the latter the specific term. *Letter* is a term altogether familiar; it may be used for whatever is written by one friend to another in domestic life, or for the public documents of this description which have emanated from the pen of writers, as the *letters* of Madame de Sévigné, the *letters* of Pope or of Swift; and even those which were written by the ancients, as the *letters* of Cicero, Pliny, and Seneca; but in strict propriety those are entitled *epistles*, as a term most adapted to whatever has received the sanction of ages, and by the same rule, likewise, whatever is peculiarly solemn in its contents has acquired the same epithet, as the *epistles* of St. Paul, St. Peter, St. John, St. Jude; and by an analogous rule, whatever poetry is written in the *epistolary* form is denominated an *epistle* rather than a *letter*, whether of ancient or modern date, as the *epistles* of Horace, or the *epistles* of Boileau; and, finally, whatever is addressed by way of dedication is denominated a dedicatory *epistle*. Ease and a friendly familiarity should characterize the *letter:* sentiment and instruction are always conveyed by an *epistle*.

See also CHARACTER.

Letters, Literature, Learning.—*Letters* and *literature* signify knowledge, derived through the medium of written *letters* or books; that is, information: *learning* (see KNOWLEDGE) is confined to that which is communicated, that is, scholastic knowledge. The term men of *letters* or the republic of *letters* comprehends all who devote themselves to the cultivation of their minds: *literary* societies have for their object the diffusion of general information: *learned* societies propose to themselves the higher object of extending the bounds of science and increasing the sum of human knowledge. Men of *letters* have a passport for admittance into the highest circles; *literary* men can always find resources for themselves in their own society: *learned* men, or men of *learning*, are more the objects of respect and admiration than of imitation.

LEVEL. See AIM; EVEN; FLAT.

LEVITY. See LIGHTNESS.

LEXICON. See DICTIONARY.

LIABLE. See SUBJECT.

LIBERAL. See BENEFICENT; FREE.

LIBERATE. See EMANCIPATE; FREE.

LIBERTY. See FREEDOM; LEAVE.

LICENSE. See LEAVE.

LICENTIOUS. See LOOSE.

LICIT. See LAWFUL.

LIE, LAY. By a vulgar error these verbs have been so confounded as to deserve some notice. To *lie* is neuter, and designates a state: to *lay* is active, and denotes an action on an object; it is properly to cause to *lie;* a thing *lies* on the table; some one *lays* it on the table; he *lies* with his fathers; they *laid* him with his fathers. In the same manner, when used idiomatically, we say a thing *lies* by us until we bring it into use; we *lay* it by for some future purpose: we *lie* down in order to repose ourselves; we *lay* money down by way of deposit: the disorder *lies* in the constitution; we *lay* a burden upon our friends.

See also UNTRUTH.

LIFE. See ANIMATION.

LIFELESS, DEAD, INANIMATE. *Lifeless* and *dead* suppose the absence of life where it has once been; *inanimate* supposes its absence where it has never been; a person from whom life has departed is said to be *lifeless* or *dead;* the material world consists of objects which are by nature *inanimate*. *Lifeless* is negative: it signifies simply without life or the vital spark: *dead* is positive; it denotes an actual and complete change in the object. We may speak of a *lifeless* corpse when speaking of a body which sinks from a state of *animation* into that of *inanimation;* we speak of *dead* bodies to designate such as have undergone an entire change. A person, therefore, in whom *animation* is suspended is, for the time being, in appearance at least, *lifeless,* although we should not say *dead*.

In the moral acceptation, *lifeless* and *inanimate* denote the want of that *life* or *animation* which is requisite or proper; *dead* implies the total want of moral feeling which ought to exist.

See also ABIOGENIC.

LIFT, HEAVE, HOIST. These are all Teutonic words that have come into modern English through different Teutonic languages. *Lift*, Middle English *liften,* is a Scandinavian word associated with German *luft,* air, meaning to raise in the air. *Heave* is an Anglo-Saxon word from the root found also in Latin *capere,* to take. *Hoist* is a Dutch word, from Middle Dutch *hyssen,* to lift up.

The idea of making high is common to all these words, but they differ in the objects and the circumstances of the action; we *lift* with or without an effort: we *heave* and *hoist* always with an effort; we *lift* a child up to let him see anything more distinctly; workmen *heave* the stones or beams which are used in a building; sailors *hoist* the long-boat into the water. To *lift* and *hoist* are transitive verbs; they require an agent and an object: *heave* is intransitive; it may have an inanimate object for an agent: a person *lifts* his hand to his head; when whales are killed, they are *hoisted* into vessels; the bosom *heaves* when it is oppressed with sorrow; the waves of the sea *heave* when they are agitated by the wind.

Lift, Raise, Erect, Elevate, Exalt.— The idea of making a thing higher than it was before is common to these verbs. To *lift* (see LIFT) is to take up from a given spot by a direct application of force. To *raise,* a Scandinavian word, meaning to cause to rise, to *erect,* from the Latin *erectum,* supine of *erigo;* to *elevate,* from *elevatus,* participle of *elevare,* based on *e,* out, and *levare,* to raise, signify to make higher by a variety of means, but not necessarily by moving the object from the spot where it rests. We *lift* a stool with our hands, we *raise* a stool by giving it longer legs; we *erect* a monument by heaping one stone upon another; a mountain is *elevated* so many feet above the surface of the sea. Whatever is to be carried is *lifted;* whatever is to be situated higher is to be *raised;* whatever is to be constructed above other objects is to be *erected;* and when the perpendicular height is to be described, it is said to be *elevated*. A ladder is *lifted* upon the shoulders: a standard ladder is *raised* against a wall; a scaffolding is *erected;* a pillar is *elevated* above the houses.

Lift and *raise* may sometimes be applied to the same objects: a stone may either be *lifted* or *raised*, but *lift* is the more ordinary term; so when *raise* and *erect* are applied to the same objects, *raise* is the more familiar expression. *Elevate* is most usual in scientific language. All these terms, except *erect*, have likewise a moral application; *exalt*, from *altus*, high, has no other. In this case *lift* is seldom used in a good sense; to *raise* is used in a good or an indifferent sense; to *elevate* is mostly, and *exalt* always, used in the best sense. A person is seldom *lifted* up for any good purpose, or from any merit in himself; it is commonly to suit the ends of party that people are *lifted* into notice or *lifted* into office; a person may be *raised* for his merits, or *raise* himself by his industry, in both of which cases he is entitled to esteem; so likewise one may be *lifted* up by pride, or *raised* in one's mind or estimation; one is *elevated* by circumstances, but still more so by one's character and moral qualities; one is rarely *exalted* but by means of superior endowments.

In modern building construction the term *elevator* is synonymous with *lift*.

LIGHTNESS, LEVITY, FLIGHTINESS, VOLATILITY, GIDDINESS. *Lightness*, from Anglo-Saxon *leoht*, light, signifies an abstract quality. *Levity*, in Latin *levitas*, from *levis*, light, signifies the same. *Volatility*, in Latin *volatilitas*, from *volare*, to fly, signifies flitting, or ready to fly swiftly on. *Flightiness*, from *flighty* and *fly*, signifies a readiness to fly. *Giddiness* is from Anglo-Saxon *gidig*, insane, possibly from Anglo-Saxon *god*, God, meaning possessed by a god, in which case it has the same origin as *enthusiasm*, from Greek ἔγθεος, a god within.

Lightness and *giddiness* are taken either in the natural or metaphorical sense; the rest only in the moral sense; *lightness* is said of the outward carriage or the inward temper; *levity* is said only of the outward carriage: a light-minded man treats everything *lightly*, be it ever so serious; the *lightness* of his mind is evident by the *lightness* of his motions. *Lightness* is common to both sexes; *levity* is peculiarly striking in women; and in respect to them, they are both exceptional qualities in the highest degree: when a woman has *lightness* of mind, she may easily tend

toward vice; when there is *levity* in her conduct, she exposes herself to public criticism. *Volatility*, *flightiness*, and *giddiness* are degrees of *lightness* which rise in signification on one another; *volatility* being more than *lightness*, and the others more than *volatility: lightness* and *volatility* are defects as they relate to age; those only who ought to be serious or grave are said to be *light* or *volatile*. When we treat that as *light* which is weighty, when we suffer nothing to sink into the mind, or make any impression, this is a defective *lightness* of character; when the spirits are of a buoyant nature, and the thoughts fly from one object to another, without resting on any for a moment, this *lightness* becomes *volatility:* a *light-minded* person sets care at a distance; a *volatile* person catches pleasure from every passing object. *Flightiness* and *giddiness* are the defects of youth; they bespeak that entire want of command over the feelings and animal spirits which is inseparable from a state of childhood; a *flighty* child, however, fails only from a want of attention; but a *giddy* child, like one whose head is in the natural sense *giddy*, is unable to collect itself so as to have any consciousness of what passes: a *flighty* person makes mistakes; a *giddy* person commits extravagances.

See also EASE.

LIKE. See EQUAL.

LIKENESS, RESEMBLANCE, SIMILARITY, SIMILITUDE. *Likeness* denotes the quality of being *alike* (see EQUAL). *Resemblance*, from *resemble*, compounded of *re* and *semble*, in French *sembler*, Latin *simulo*, from *similis*, like, signifies putting on the form of another thing. *Similarity*, from a hypothetical Latin *similaritas*, extended from *similis*, and allied to English *same*, denotes the abstract property of *likeness*.

Likeness is the most general, and at the same time the most familiar, term of the three; it implies either external or internal properties: *resemblance* implies only the external properties: *similarity* the circumstances or properties: we speak of a *likeness* between two persons; of a *resemblance* in the cast of the eye; of a *resemblance* in the form or figure; of a *similarity* in age and disposition. *Likeness* is said only of that which is actual; *resemblance* may be said of that which is apparent: a *likeness* consists of something specific; a *resemblance* may be only partial and contingent. A thing is said to be, but not to appear, *like* another; it may, however, have the shadow of a *resemblance:* whatever things are *alike* are *alike* in their essential properties; but they may *resemble* one another in a partial degree or in certain particulars, but are otherwise essentially different. We are most *like* the Divine Being in the act of doing good; there is nothing existing in nature which has not certain points of *resemblance* with something else.

Similarity or *similitude*, which is a higher term, is in the moral application, in regard to *likeness*, what *resemblance* is in the physical sense: what is *alike* has the same nature; what is *similar* has certain features of *similarity:* in this sense feelings are *alike*, sentiments are *alike*, persons are *alike;* but cases are *similar*, circumstances are *similar*, conditions are *similar*. *Likeness* excludes the idea of difference; *similarity* includes only the idea of casual *likeness*.

Likeness, Picture, Image, Effigy.—In the former article *likeness* is considered as an abstract term, but in connection with the words *picture* and *image* it signifies the representation of *likeness*. *Picture*, in Latin *pictura*, from *pingere*, to paint, signifies the thing painted. *Image*, in Latin *imago*, from the root *im*, found also in *imitari*, English *imitate*, signifies an imitation. *Effigy*, in Latin *effigies*, from *ex*, from, and *fingere*, to fashion, signifies that which is fashioned from or after the *image* of another thing.

Likeness and *picture*, as terms of art, are both applied to painting; but the term *likeness* refers us to the object of the art, namely, to get the *likeness;* and the *picture* to the mode of the art, namely, by painting; whence in familiar language an artist is said to take *likenesses* who takes or paints the portraits of persons; or in general terms an artist may be said to be happy in taking a *likeness* who can represent on paper the *likeness* of any object, but particularly that of persons. In other connections the word

picture is most usually employed in regard to works of art, as to sketch a *picture*, to finish a *picture*, and the like.

As a *likeness* may be given by other means besides that of painting, it may be taken for any *likeness* conveyed; as parents may be said to stamp or impress a *likeness* on their children. *Picture* may be figuratively taken for whatever serves as a *picture*, as a *picture* of happiness. *Image*, as appears from its derivation, signifies nothing more than *likeness*, but has been usually applied to such *likenesses* as are taken, or intended to represent spiritual objects, whether on paper or in wood or stone, such as the graven *images* which were the objects of idolatrous worship: it has, however, been extended in its application to any *likeness* of one object represented by another; as children are sometimes the *image* of their parents.

A *likeness* and a *picture* contain actual *likenesses* of the things which they are intended to represent; but an *effigy* may be only an arbitrary *likeness*, as where a human figure is made to stand for the figure of any particular man without any *likeness* of the individual. This term is applied to the rude or fictitious *pictures* of persons in books, and also to the figures of persons on tombstones or on coins, which contain but few traces of *likeness*. Or to the still ruder representations of individuals who are held up to public odium by the populace.

LIKEWISE. See ALSO.

LIMB. See MEMBER.

LIMIT, EXTENT. *Limit* is a more specific and definite term than *extent:* by the former we are directed to the point where anything ends; by the latter we are led to no particular point, but to the whole space included: *limits* are in their nature something finite; *extent* is either finite or infinite: we therefore speak of that which exceeds *limits* or comes within the *limits;* and of that which comprehends the *extent* or is according to the *extent:* a plenipotentiary or minister must not exceed the *limits* of his instruction; when we think of the immense *extent* of this globe, and that it is among the smallest of an infinite number of worlds, the mind is lost in admiration and amazement: it does not fall within the *limits* of a periodical work to enter into historical details; a complete history of any country is a work of great *extent*.

See also BOUND; FIX; TERM.

LIMITED. See FINITE.

LINEAGE. See FAMILY.

LINGER, TARRY, LOITER, LAG, SAUNTER. *Linger* is a frequentative of Middle English *lengen*, from Anglo-Saxon *lang*, Modern English *long*, meaning to keep lengthening the time it takes to do something. *Tarry* comes from Middle English *tarien*, to irritate, worry, or vex; hence to hinder or delay. *Loiter* comes from Middle Dutch *leuteren*, to trifle. *Lag* is a Celtic word meaning late or sluggish. *Saunter* is a word of uncertain origin, perhaps connected with *adventure*, indicating idle, planless going.

Suspension of action or slow movement enters into the meaning of all these terms: to *linger* is to stop altogether, or to move but slowly forward; to *tarry* is properly to suspend one's movement: the former proceeds from reluctance to leave the spot on which we stand; the latter from motives of discretion: one will naturally *linger* who is going to leave the place of his nativity for an indefinite period; those who have much business to transact will be led to *tarry* long in a place: to *loiter* is to move slowly and reluctantly; but, from a bad cause, a child *loiters* who is unwilling to go to school: to *lag* is to move slower than others, to stop while they are going on; this is seldom done for a good purpose; those who *lag* have generally some sinister and private end to answer: to *saunter* is altogether the act of an idler; those who have no object in moving either backward or forward will *saunter* if they move at all.

LIQUID, LIQUOR, JUICE. *Liquid* (see FLUID) is the generic term: *liquor*, which is but a variation from the same Latin verb, *liquere*, to be moist, whence *liquid* is derived, is a *liquid* which is made to be drunk: *juice*, in French *jus*, Latin *ius*, broth, soup, is a *liquid* that issues from bodies. All natural bodies consist of *liquids* or solids, or a combination of both: *liquor* serves to quench the thirst as food satisfies the hunger; the *juices* of bodies are fre-

quently their richest parts; water is the simplest of all *liquids*; wine is the most inviting of all *liquors*; the orange produces the most agreeable *juice*.

LIQUIDATE. See FLUID.

LIQUOR. See LIQUID.

LIST, ROLL, CATALOGUE, REGISTER. *List* is derived through French *liste*, from Old High German *lista*, a border, hence a strip, a long strip on which names were written. *Roll*, from Latin *rotula*, a little wheel, signifies in general anything *rolled* up, particularly paper with its written contents. *Catalogue*, in Latin *catalogus*, Greek κατάλογος, from καταλέγω, to write down, signifies a written enumeration. *Register*, from *re* back, *gerere* (past participle *gestum*), to bring, signifies something brought back, a record returned by a messenger or official.

A collection of objects brought into some kind of order is the common idea included in the signification of these terms. The contents and disposition of a *list* is the most simple; it consists of little more than names arranged under one another in a long, narrow line, as a *list* of words, a *list* of plants and flowers, a *list* of voters, a *list* of visits, a *list* of deaths, of births, of marriages: *roll*, which is figuratively put for the contents of a *roll*, is a *list* rolled up for convenience, as a long *roll* of saints: *catalogue* involves more details than a simple *list;* it specifies not only names, but dates, qualities, and circumstances. A *list* of books contains their titles; a *catalogue* of books contains an enumeration of their size, price, number of volumes, edition, etc.; a *roll* of saints simply specifies their names; a *catalogue* of saints enters into particulars of their ages, deaths, etc.: a *register* contains more than either, for it contains events, with dates, actors, etc., in all matters of public interest.

See also ENROLL.

LISTEN. See ATTEND.

LISTLESS. See INDOLENT.

LITERATURE. See LETTERS.

LITTLE, SMALL, DIMINUTIVE. *Little* comes from Anglo-Saxon *lytel*, from a Teutonic base meaning to stoop. For *small* see ATOMIC. *Diminutive* comes from Latin *minus*, and signifies made less. What is *little* is so in the ordinary sense in respect to size; it is properly opposed to great: the *small* is that which is less than others in point of bulk; it is opposed to the large: the *diminutive* is that which is less than it ought to be; as a person is said to be *diminutive* in stature who is below the ordinary stature.

In the moral application, *little* is frequently used in a bad sense, *small* and *diminutive* may be extended to other than physical objects without any change in their signification.

LIVE. See ABIDE; BE; EXIST.

LIVELIHOOD, LIVING, SUBSISTENCE, MAINTENANCE, SUPPORT, SUSTENANCE. The means of *living* or supporting life is the idea common to all these terms, which vary according to the circumstances of the individual and the nature of the object which constitutes the means. *Livelihood* was originally *livelode*, literally *life-leading*—from Anglo-Saxon *lif*, life, and *lad*, a way, literally a *leading*. *Subsistence* comes from Latin *sub*, under, and *sistere*, to cause to stand—meaning that which bears one up. *Support*, from *sub* and *portare*, to bear, and *sustenance*, from *sub* and *tenere*, to hold, have similar origins. *Maintenance* comes from *manus*, hand, and *tenere*, to hold, and signifies to hold in hand, to control and support. A *livelihood* is that which is sought after by the day; a laborer earns a *livelihood* by the sweat of his brow: a *subsistence* is obtained by irregular efforts of various descriptions; beggars meet with so much that they obtain something better than a precarious and scanty *subsistence*: *living* is obtained by more respectable and less severe efforts than the former two; tradesmen obtain a good *living* by keeping shops; artists procure a *living* by the exercise of their talents; *maintenance*, *support*, and *sustenance* differ from the other three, inasmuch as they do not comprehend what one gains by one's own efforts, but by the efforts of others: *maintenance* is that which is permanent: it supplies the place of *living*: *support* may be casual and vary in degree: the object of most public charities is to afford a *maintenance* to such as cannot obtain a *livelihood* or *living* for themselves; it is the business of the parish to give *support*, in time of sickness and distress, to all who are legal parishioners. *Maintenance* and *support* are always granted; but *sustenance* is that which is taken or received: the former comprehend the means of obtaining food; *sustenance* comprehends that which sustains the body and supplies the place of food.

LIVELY, SPRIGHTLY, VIVACIOUS, SPORTIVE, MERRY, JOCUND. The activity of the heart when it beats high with a sentiment of gayety is strongly depicted by all these terms: the *lively* is the most general and literal in its signification; life, as a moving or active principle, is supposed to be inherent in spiritual as well as material bodies; the feeling, as well as the body which has a power of moving arbitrarily of itself, is said to have life; and in whatever object this is wanting, this object is said to be dead: in like manner, according to the degree or circumstances under which this moving principle displays itself, the object is denominated *lively*, that is, having life. *Sprightly*, originally *spritely*, from Latin *spiritus*, spirit, signifies full of spirit or the active breath of life; and *vivacious*, in Latin *vivax*, from *vivere*, to live, is the same as *lively*. *Liveliness* is the property of childhood, youth, or even maturer age; *sprightliness* is the peculiar property of youth; *vivacity* is a quality compatible with the sobriety of years: an infant shows itself to be *lively* or otherwise in a few months after its birth; a girl, particularly in her early years, affords often a pleasing picture of *sprightliness*; a *vivacious* companion recommends himself wherever he goes. *Sportiveness*, that is, fondness of or readiness for sport, is an accompaniment of *liveliness* or *sprightliness*; a *sprightly* child will show its *sprightliness* by its *sportive* humor; *mirth*, i. e., *merriness* (see CHEERFUL), and *jocundity*, from *jocundus* or *jucundus*, and *juvo*, to delight or please, signifying the state of being delighted, are the forms of *liveliness* which display themselves in social life; the former is a familiar quality, more frequently to be discovered in vulgar than in polished society: *jocundity* is a form of *liveliness* which poets have ascribed to nymphs and goddesses and other aerial creatures of the imagination.

The terms preserve the same sense when applied to the characteristics or actions of persons as when applied to the persons themselves: imagination, wit, conception, representation, and the like are *lively;* a person's air, manner, look, tone, dance, are *sprightly;* a conversation, a turn of mind, a society, is *vivacious;* the muse, the pen, the imagination, are *sportive;* the meeting, the laugh, the song, the conceit, are *merry;* the train, the dance, are *jocund.*

LIVING, BENEFICE. *Living* signifies, literally, the pecuniary resource by which one lives. *Benefice,* from Late Latin *beneficium,* based on classical *benefacio,* signifies whatever one obtains as a benefit: the former is applicable to any situation of life, but particularly to that resource which a parish affords to the clergyman; the latter is applicable to no other object: we speak of a *living* as a resource immediately derived from the parish, in distinction from a curacy, which is derived from an individual; we speak of a *benefice* in respect to the terms by which it is held, according to the ecclesiastical law: there are many *livings* which are not *benefices,* although not *vice versâ.*

See also LIVELIHOOD.

LOAD.   See   CLOG;   FREIGHT; WEIGHT.

LOATH.   See AVERSE.

LOATHE.   See ABHOR.

LOATHING.   See DISGUST.

LOCALIZE.   See SEGREGATE.

LOCKOUT.   See CLOSE.

LODGE.   See HARBOR.

LODGINGS, APARTMENTS. For the derivation of *lodging* see HARBOR. A *lodging,* or a place to *lodge* or dwell in, comprehends single rooms, or many rooms, or in fact any place which can be made to serve the purpose; *apartments* only suites of rooms: *apartments,* therefore, are, in the strict sense, *lodgings;* but all *lodgings* are not *apartments:* on the other hand, the word *lodgings* is mostly used for rooms that are let out to hire or that serve a temporary purpose; but the word *apartments* may be applied to the suites of rooms in any large house: hence the word *lodging* becomes on one ground restricted in its use, and *apartments* on the other: all *apartments* to let out for hire are *lodgings,* but *apartments* not to let out for hire are not *lodgings.*

LOFTINESS.   See PRIDE.

LOFTY.   See HIGH.

LOITER.   See LINGER.

LONELY.   See ALONE.

LONG.   See DESIRE.

LONGING.   See YEARN.

LOOK, GLANCE. *Look* (see AIR) is the generic, and *glance* (see GLANCE) the specific term; that is to say, a casual or momentary *look:* a *look* may be characterized as severe or mild, fierce or gentle, angry or kind: a *glance* as hasty or sudden, imperfect or slight; so likewise we speak of taking a *look* or catching a *glance.*

Look, See, Behold, View, Eye.—*Look,* from Anglo-Saxon *locian,* signified originally to peep through a hole. *See* is in Anglo-Saxon *seon,* to perceive by the eye. *Behold,* compounded of the intensive *be* and *hold,* signifies to hold or fix the eye on an object. *View,* from Middle French *veuë,* participle of *veoir,* based on the Latin *video,* signifies simply what is seen. To *eye,* from the noun *eye,* Anglo-Saxon *eage,* allied to Latin *oculus,* eye, naturally signifies to examine with the *eye.*

We *look* voluntarily; we *see* involuntarily: the eye *sees;* the person *looks:* absent-minded people often *see* things before they are fully conscious that they are at hand: we may *look* without *seeing,* and we may *see* without *looking:* nearsighted people often *look* at that which is too distant to strike the visual organ. To *behold* is to *look* at for a continuance; to *view* is to *look* at in all directions; to *eye* is to *look* at earnestly and by side glances; that which is *seen* may disappear in an instant; it may strike the eye and be gone; but what is *looked* at must make some stay; consequently lightning, and things equally fugitive and rapid in their flight, may be *seen,* but cannot be *looked* at. To *look* at is the familiar as well as the general term, in regard to the others; we *look* at things in general which we wish to *see,* that is, to *see* clearly, fully, and in all their parts; but we *behold* that which excites a moral or intellectual interest; we *view* that which demands intellectual attention; we *eye* that which gratifies any particular passion:

an inquisitive child *looks* at things which are new to it, but does not *behold* them; we *look* at plants or finery or whatever gratifies the senses, but we do not *behold* them: on the other hand, we *behold* any spectacle which excites our admiration, our astonishment, our pity, or our love: we *look* at objects in order to observe their external properties; but we *view* them in order to find out their component parts, their internal properties, their powers of motion and action, etc.: we *look* at things to gratify the curiosity of the moment or for mere amusement; but the jealous man *eyes* his rival in order to mark his movements, his designs, and his successes; the envious man *eyes* him who is in prosperity, with a malignant desire to *see* him humbled.

Look, Appear.—*Look* is here taken in the neuter sense: in the preceding article it denotes the action of persons striving to see; in the present case it denotes the action of things figuratively striving to be seen. *Appear*, from the Latin *ad*, to, and *parere*, to come in sight, signifies to be present or at hand, within sight.

The *look* of a thing implies the impressions which it makes on the senses, that is, the manner in which it *looks;* its *appearance* implies the simple act of its coming into sight; the *look* of anything is therefore characterized as good or bad, mean or handsome, ugly or beautiful; the *appearance* is characterized as early or late, sudden or unexpected: there is something very unseemly in the *look* of a clergyman affecting the airs of a fine gentleman; the *appearance* of the stars in an evening presents an interesting view even to the ordinary beholder. As what *appears* must *appear* in some form, the signification of the term has been extended to the manner of the *appearance*, and brought still nearer to *look* in its application: in this case the term *look* is rather more familiar than that of *appearance:* we may speak either of regarding the *look* or the *appearance* of a thing, as far as it may impress others; but the latter is less colloquial than the former: a man's conduct is said to *look* rather than to *appear* bad; but on the other hand, we say a thing assumes an *appearance*, or has a certain *appearance*.

Look is always employed for what is real; what a thing *looks* is that which it really is: *appear*, however, sometimes refers not only to what is external, but to what is superficial. If we say a person *looks* ill, it supposes some positive and unequivocal evidence of illness: if we say he *appears* to be ill, it is a less positive assertion than the former; it leaves room for doubt and allows the possibility of a mistake. We are at liberty to judge of things by their *looks*, without being accused of want of judgment; but as *appearances* are said to be deceitful, it becomes necessary to admit them with caution as the rule of our judgment. *Look* is employed mostly in regard to objects of sense; *appearance* concerns natural and moral objects indifferently: the sky *looks* dark; an object *appears* through a microscope greater than it really is; a person's conduct *appears* in a more culpable light when interpreted by an enemy.

Looker-on, Spectator, Beholder, Observer.—The *looker-on* and the *spectator* are both opposed to the agents or actors in any scene; but the former is still more abstracted from the objects he sees than the latter.

A *looker-on* is careless; he has no part, and takes no part, in what he sees; he *looks on* because the thing is before him and he has nothing else to do: a *spectator* may likewise be unconcerned, but in general he derives amusement, if nothing else, from what he sees. A clown may be a *looker-on* who with open mouth gapes at all that is before him, without understanding any part of it, but he who *looks on* to draw a moral lesson from the whole is in the moral sense not an uninterested *spectator*. The *beholder* has a nearer interest than the *spectator;* and the *observer* has an interest not less near than that of the *beholder*, but somewhat different: the *beholder* has his feelings roused by what he sees; the *observer* has his understanding employed in that which passes before him: the *beholder* indulges himself in contemplation; the *observer* is busy in making it subservient to some proposed object: every *beholder* of our Saviour's sufferings and patience was struck with the conviction of His divine character, not excepting even some of those who were His most prejudiced adversaries; every calm *observer* of our Saviour's words and actions was convinced of His divine mission.

LOOSE, Vague, Lax, Dissolute, Licentious. *Loose* is a Scandinavian word. *Vague,* in Latin *vagus,* signifies wandering. *Lax,* in Latin *laxus,* is allied to *lack. Dissolute,* in Latin *dissolutus,* participle of *dissolvere,* signifies *dissolved* or set free. *Licentious* signifies having the *license* or power to do as one pleases (see Leave).

Loose is the generic, the rest are specific terms; they are all opposed to that which is bound or adheres closely: *loose* is employed either for physical, moral, or intellectual objects; *vague* only for intellectual objects; *lax* sometimes for what is intellectual, but oftener for the moral; *dissolute* and *licentious* only for moral matters: whatever wants a proper connection, or linking together of the parts, is *loose;* whatever is scattered and remotely separated is *vague:* a style is *loose* where the words and sentences are not made to coalesce so as to form a regularly connected series; assertions are *vague* which have but a remote connection with the subject referred to: by the same rule, *loose* hints thrown out at random may give rise to speculation and conjecture, but cannot serve as the ground of any conclusion; ignorant people are apt to credit every *vague* rumor and to communicate it as a certainty. Opinions are *loose,* either inasmuch as they want logical precision or as they fail in moral strictness; suggestions and surmises are induced by the wanderings of the imagination; opinions are *lax,* inasmuch as they have a tendency to lessen the moral obligation or to *loosen* moralities. A *loose* man injures himself, but a *lax* man injures society at large. *Dissoluteness* is the excess of *looseness; licentiousness* is the consequence of *laxity* or the freedom from external constraint. *Looseness* of character, if indulged, soon sinks into *dissoluteness* of morals; and *laxity* of discipline is quickly followed by *licentiousness* of manners.

See also Slack.

LOQUACIOUS. See Talkative; Voluble.

LORDLY. See Imperious.

LORD'S DAY. See Sabbath.

LORD'S - SUPPER, Eucharist, Communion, Sacrament. The *Lord's-Supper* is a term of familiar and general use among Christians, as designating in literal terms the supper of our Lord, that is, either the last solemn supper which He took with His disciples previous to His crucifixion or the commemoration of that event which conformably to His commands has been observed by the professors of Christianity. *Eucharist* is a term of peculiar use among the Roman Catholics, from the Greek εὐχαρίζομαι, I give thanks, because personal adoration, by way of returning thanks, constitutes in their estimation the chief part of the ceremony. As the social sentiments are kept alive mostly by the common participation of meals, so is brotherly love, the essence of Christian fellowship, cherished and warmed in the highest degree by the common participation in this holy festival: hence, by distinction, it has been denominated the *communion.* As the vows which are made at the altar of our Lord are the most solemn which a Christian can make, comprehending in them the entire devotion of himself to Christ, the general term *sacrament,* signifying an oath, has been employed by way of distinction for this ordinance. The Roman Catholics have employed the same term for six other ordinances; but the Protestants, who attach a similar degree of sacredness to no other than baptism, apply this appellation only to these two.

LOSE, Miss. *Lose* is in Middle English *lesen. Miss* comes from Anglo-Saxon *missan,* to fail to hit, from a base meaning to escape, avoid, etc., allied to Latin *mittere,* to send. To *miss,* probably from the participle *mis,* wrong, signifies to put wrong.

What is *lost* is supposed to be entirely and irrevocably gone; but what is *missed* may be only out of sight or not at hand at the time when it is wanted; health or property may be *lost;* one *misses* a coach, or one *misses* what has been mislaid. Things may be *lost* in a variety of ways independent of the person *losing;* but *missing* is mostly by the instrumentality of the person who *misses*. We *lose* an opportunity which it is not in our power to use; we *miss* an opportunity when we suffer it to pass without using.

LOSS, DAMAGE, DETRIMENT. *Loss* signifies the act of *losing* or the thing *lost*, from Anglo-Saxon *los*, destruction. *Damage*, in French *dommage*, Latin *damnum*, loss, signifies the thing taken away. *Detriment* (see DISADVANTAGEOUS).

Loss is here the generic term; *damage* and *detriment* are species or modes of *loss*. The person sustains the *loss*, the thing suffers the *damage* or *detriment*. Whatever is gone from us which we wish to retain is a *loss;* hence we may sustain a *loss* in our property, in our reputation, in our influence, in our intellect, and every other object of possession: whatever renders an object less serviceable or valuable, by any external violence, is a *damage;* as a vessel suffers a *damage* in a storm: whatever is calculated to cross a man's purpose is a *detriment;* the bare want of a good name may be a *detriment* to a young tradesman; the want of prudence is always a great *detriment* to the prosperity of a family.

LOT. See DESTINY.

LOUD, NOISY, HIGH - SOUNDING, CLAMOROUS. *Loud* comes from Anglo-Saxon *klud*, heard from afar. *Noisy*, from *noise*, is derived from Old French *naise*, a debate or quarrel (something that gives rise to *noise* in our sense), perhaps from *nausea*. *High-sounding* signifies the same as pitched upon an elevated key, so as to make a great noise, to be heard at a distance. *Clamorous*, from the Latin *clamare*, to cry, signifies crying with a loud voice.

Loud is here the generic term, since it signifies a great sound, which is the idea common to them all. As an epithet for persons, *loud* is mostly taken in an indifferent sense; all the others are taken for being *loud* beyond measure; *noisy* is to be lawlessly and unseasonably *loud; high-sounding* is to be *loud* only from the bigness of one's words; *clamorous* is to be disagreeably and painfully *loud*. We must speak *loudly* to a deaf person in order to make ourselves heard: children will be *noisy* at all times if not kept under control: flatterers are always *high-*

sounding in their eulogiums of princes: children will be *clamorous* for what they want if they expect to get it by dint of *noise;* they will be turbulent in case of refusal if not under proper discipline. In the improper application *loud* is taken in as bad a sense as the rest; the *loudest* praises are the least to be regarded: the applause of a mob is always *noisy; high-sounding* titles serve only to excite contempt where there is not some corresponding quality: it is the business of a party to be *clamorous*, as that serves the purpose of exciting the ignorant.

LOVE, FRIENDSHIP. *Love* (see AFFECTION) is a term of very extensive import; it may be taken either in the most general sense for every strong and passionate attachment or only for such as exist between the sexes, in either of which cases it has features by which it is easily distinguished from *friendship*—from Anglo-Saxon *freond*, modern English *friend*, from the verb *freogan*, to love.

Love exists between members of the same family; it springs out of their natural relationship, and is kept alive by their close intercourse and constant interchange of kindnesses: *friendship* excludes the idea of any tender and natural relationship; nor is it, like *love*, to be found in children, but is confined to maturer years; it is formed by time, by circumstances, by congruity of character and mutual sympathy. *Love* always operates with ardor; *friendship* is remarkable for firmness and constancy. *Love* is peculiar to no station; it is to be found equally among the high and the low, the learned and the unlearned: *friendship* is of nobler growth; it finds admittance only into minds of a loftier make: it cannot be felt by men of an ordinary stamp. Both *love* and *friendship* are gratified by seeking the good of the object; but *love* is more selfish in its nature than *friendship;* in indulging another it seeks its own gratification, and when this is not to be obtained it will change into the contrary passion of hatred; *friendship*, on the other hand, is altogether disinterested, it makes sacrifices of every description, and knows no limits to its sacrifice.

Lover, Suitor, Wooer.—*Lover* signifies literally one who *loves*, and is applicable to any object; there are *lovers* of money and *lovers* of wine, *lovers* of things individually and things collectively, that is, *lovers* of particular women in the good sense, or *lovers* of women in the bad sense. The *suitor* (from French *suite*, based ultimately on Latin *sequi*, to follow) is one who *sues* and strives after a thing; the word is equally undefined as to the object, but may be employed for such as *sue* for favors from their superiors, or *sue* for the affections and person of a woman. The *wooer* (from Anglo-Saxon *wogian*, to court, of obscure origin) is only a species of *lover*, who *woos* or solicits the kind regards of a female. When applied to the same object, namely, the female sex, the term *lover* is employed for persons of all ranks, who are equally alive to the tender passion of *love*: *suitor* is a title adapted to that class of life where all the genuine affections of human nature are adulterated by a false refinement or entirely lost in other passions of a guilty nature. *Wooer* is a tender and passionate title, which is adapted to that class of beings that live only in poetry and romance. There is most sincerity in the *lover*, he simply proffers his *love;* there is most ceremony in the *suitor*, he proffers his *suit;* there is most ardor in the *wooer*, he makes his vows.

LOVELY. See AMIABLE.

LOVING. See AMOROUS.

LOW, MEAN, ABJECT. *Low* (see HUMBLE). *Mean* comes from Anglo-Saxon *gemœne*, German *gemein*, common. *Abject*, in French *abject*, Latin *abjectus*, from *ab*, down, and *jacere*, to cast, signifies literally, cast down or brought very low.

Low is a much stronger term than *mean;* for what is *low* stands more directly opposed to what is high, but what is *mean* is intermediate: the *low* is applied only to a certain number or description; but *mean*, like common, is applicable to the great bulk of mankind. A man of *low* extraction falls below the ordinary level; he is opposed to a noble man: a man of *mean* birth does not rise above the ordinary level; he is upon a level with the majority. *Abject* expresses more than either of the others, for it denotes the lowest depression in a person's outward condition or position, as *abject* poverty.

When employed to designate character, they preserve the same distinction; the *low* is that which is positively sunk in itself; but the *mean* is that which is comparatively *low*, in regard to the outward circumstances and relative condition of the individual. Swearing and drunkenness are *low* vices; boxing and cudgelling are *low* games; a misplaced economy in people of property is *mean;* a condescension for our own petty advantages to those who are beneath us is *meanness*. A man is commonly *low* by birth, education, or habits; but *meanness* is a defect of nature which debases a person in spite of every external advantage. *Abject*, as a characteristic, is applied particularly to the spirit. Slavery is most apt to produce an *abject* spirit by depriving a man of the use of those faculties which elevate him above the brutes; poverty, fear, or any base passion may have the same effect.

LOWER. See REDUCE; STRIKE.

LOWLY. See HUMBLE.

LUCID. See CLEAR.

LUCKLESS. See HAPLESS.

LUCKY. See FORTUNATE.

LUCRE. See GAIN.

LUDICROUS. See LAUGHABLE.

LULL. See QUELL.

LUNACY. See DERANGEMENT.

LUSTRE. See BRIGHTNESS.

LUSTY. See CORPULENT.

LUXURIANT. See EXUBERANT.

M

MADNESS, FRENZY, RAGE, FURY.
Madness (see DERANGEMENT). *Frenzy*,
in Latin *phrenesis*, Greek φρένησις,
from φρήν, the midriff, heart, senses,
signifies a disordered psychology. *Rage*
is in French *rage*, Latin *rabies*, madness.
Fury comes from Latin *furia*, madness.

Madness and *frenzy* are used in the
physical and moral sense; *rage* and *fury*
only in the moral sense: in the first
case, *madness* is a confirmed derangement in the organ of thought; *frenzy*
is only a temporary derangement from
the violence of any disease or other
cause: the former lies in the system,
and is, in general, incurable; the latter
is only occasional, and yields to the
power of medicine. In the moral
sense of these terms the cause is put
for the effect, that is, *madness* and
frenzy are put for that excessive violence of passion by which they are
caused; and as *rage* and *fury* are species
of this passion, namely, the passion of
anger; they are, therefore, to *madness*
and *frenzy* sometimes as the cause is to
the effect: the former, however, are
much more violent than the latter,
as they altogether destroy the reasoning faculty, which is not expressly implied in the signification of the latter
terms. Moral *madness* differs both in
degree and duration from *frenzy:* if
it spring from the extravagance of *rage*,
it bursts out into every conceivable
extravagance, but is only transitory;
if it spring from disappointed love, or
any other disappointed passion, it is
as permanent as direct physical *madness; frenzy* is always temporary, but
even more impetuous than *madness;*
in the *frenzy* of despair men commit
acts of suicide, in the *frenzy* of distress
and grief people are hurried into many
actions fatal to themselves or others.

Rage refers more immediately to the
agitation that exists within the mind;
fury refers to that which shows itself
outwardly: a person contains or stifles
his *rage;* but his *fury* breaks out into
some external mark of violence: *rage*
will subside of itself; *fury* spends itself;

a person may be choked with *rage*, but
his *fury* finds a vent: an *enraged* man
may be pacified; a *furious* one is deaf
to every remonstrance. *Rage*, when
applied to persons, commonly signifies
highly inflamed anger; but it may be
employed for inflamed passion toward
any object which is specified; as a *rage*
for music, a *rage* for theatrical performances, a fashionable *rage* for any
whim of the day. *Fury*, though commonly signifying *rage* bursting out,
yet may be any impetuous feeling displaying itself in extravagant action;
as the divine *fury* supposed to be produced in the priestess of Apollo by
the inspiration of the god, and the
bacchanalian *fury*, which expression
depicts the influence of wine upon the
body and mind. In the improper application, to inanimate objects, the
words *rage* and *fury* preserve a similar
distinction: the *rage* of the heat denotes the excessive height to which it
is risen; the *fury* of the winds indicates their violent commotion and turbulence; so in like manner the *raging*
of the tempest characterizes figuratively its burning anger; and the *fury* of the
flames marks their impetuous movements, their wild and rapid spread.

See also DERANGEMENT.

MAGISTERIAL, MAJESTIC, STATE-
LY, POMPOUS, AUGUST, DIGNIFIED.
Magisterial, from *magister*, a master,
and *majestic*, from *majestas*, are both
derived from *magis*, more, or *major*,
greater, that is, more or greater than
others; but they differ in this respect,
that the *magisterial* is something assumed, and is therefore often false;
the *majestic* is natural, and consequently always real: an upstart, or an intruder into any high station or office,
may put on a *magisterial* air in order
to impose on the multitude; but it
will not be in his power to be *majestic*,
which never shows itself in a borrowed
shape; none but those who have a
superiority of character, of birth, or
outward station can be *majestic*.

Stately and *pompous* (see MAGNIFI-

CENCE) are most nearly allied to *magisterial; august* (from Augustus, the title of the Roman Cæsars) and *dignified* to *majestic:* the former being merely extrinsic and assumed, the latter intrinsic and inherent. *Magisterial* implies the authority which is assumed; *stately* regards splendor and rank; *pompous* regards personal importance, with all the appendage of greatness and power: a person is *magisterial* in the exercise of his office and the distribution of his commands; he is *stately* in his ordinary intercourse with his inferiors and equals; he is *pompous* on particular occasions of appearing in public: a person demands silence in a *magisterial* tone; he marches forward with a *stately* air; he comes forward in a *pompous* manner, so as to strike others with a sense of his importance.

Majestic is an epithet that characterizes the exterior of an object; *august* is that which marks an essential characteristic in the object; *dignified* serves to characterize a person's action as tending to give dignity: a woman's form is termed *majestic* when it has something imposing in it suited to the condition of majesty or the most elevated station in society; a monarch is entitled *august* in order to describe the extent of his empire; a public assembly is denominated *august* to bespeak its high character and its weighty influence in the scale of society; a reply is termed *dignified* when it upholds the individual and personal character of a man as well as his relative character in the community to which he belongs: the former two of these terms are associated only with grandeur of outward circumstances; the last is applicable to men of all stations who have each in his sphere a *dignity* to maintain which belongs to man as an independent moral agent.

MAGNETIC. See ELECTRIC.

MAGNIFICENCE, SPLENDOR, POMP. *Magnificence,* from *magnus,* great, and a weak form of *facere,* to do, signifies doing largely or on a large scale. *Splendor,* in Latin *splendor,* from *splendere,* to shine, signifies brightness of exterior. *Pomp,* in Latin *pompa,* Greek πομπή, a procession, from πέμπειν, to send, signified a sending, an escort-

ing, which, of course, was usually splendid and gorgeous, because men honored with an escort were usually deemed worthy also of a certain *splendor* and ceremony in the accoutrements of the escort.

Magnificence lies not only in the number and extent of the objects presented, but in their degree of richness as to their coloring and quality; *splendor* is but a characteristic of *magnificence,* attached to such objects as dazzle the eye by the quantity of light or the beauty and strength of coloring; the entertainments of the Eastern monarchs and princes are remarkable for their *magnificence,* from the immense number of their attendants, the crowd of equipages, the size of their palaces, the multitude of costly utensils, and the profusion of viands which constitute the arrangements for the banquet; the entertainments of Europeans present much *splendor,* from the richness, the variety, and the brilliancy of dress, of furniture, and all the apparatus of a feast, which the refinements of art have brought to perfection. *Magnificence* is seldomer unaccompanied with *splendor* than *splendor* with *magnificence,* since quantity, as well as quality, is essential to the one; but quality more than quantity is an essential to the other: a large army drawn up in battle array is a *magnificent* spectacle, from the immensity of their numbers and the order of their disposition; it will in all probability be a *splendid* scene if there be much richness in the dresses; the *pomp* will here consist in such large bodies of men acting by one impulse and directed by one will, hence military *pomp;* it is the appendage of power when displayed to public view: on particular occasions a monarch seated on his throne, surrounded by his courtiers and attended by his guards, is said to appear with *pomp.*

See also GRANDEUR.

MAGNIFICENT. See SUPERB.

MAGNITUDE. See SIZE.

MAIDEN. See VIRGIN.

MAIM. See MUTILATE.

MAIN. See CARDINAL; CHIEF.

MAINTAIN. See ASSERT; HOLD; SUSTAIN; UPHOLD.

MAINTENANCE. See LIVELIHOOD.

MAJESTIC. See MAGISTERIAL.

MAKE, FORM, PRODUCE, CREATE. The idea of giving birth to a thing is common to all these terms, which vary in the circumstances of the action: to *make* (see ACT) is the most general and unqualified term; to *form* (see FORM) signifies to give a *form* to a thing, that is, to *make* it after a given *form;* to *produce* (see AFFORD) is to bring forth into the light, to call into existence; to *create* (see CAUSE) is to bring into existence by an absolute exercise of power; to *make* is the simplest action of all, and comprehends a simple combination by the smallest efforts; to *form* requires care and attention and greater efforts; to *produce* requires time and also labor: whatever is put together so as to become another thing is *made;* a chair or a table is *made:* whatever is put into any distinct *form* is *formed;* the potter *forms* the clay into an earthen vessel: whatever emanates from a thing so as to become a distinct object is *produced;* fire is often *produced* by the violent friction of two pieces of wood with each other. The process of *making* is always performed by some conscious agent, who employs either mechanical means or the simple exercise of power: a bird *makes* its nest; man *makes* various things by the exercise of his understanding and his limbs; the Almighty has *made* everything by His word. The process of *forming* does not always require a conscious agent; things are *formed* of themselves or they are *formed* by the active operations of other bodies; melted lead, when thrown into water, will *form* itself into various little bodies; hard substances are *formed* in the human body, which give rise to the disease termed the gravel. What is *produced* is oftener *produced* by the process of nature than by any express design; the earth *produces* all kinds of vegetables from seed; animals, by a similar process, *produce* their young. *Create,* in this natural sense of the term, is employed as the act of an intelligent being and that of the Supreme Being only; it is the act of *making* by a simple effort of power, without the use of materials and without any process. Hence it has been extended in its ap-plication to the *making* of anything by an immediate exercise of power. The *creative* power of the human mind is a faint image of that Power which brought everything into existence out of nothing.

They are all employed in the moral sense and with a similar distinction: *make* is indefinite; we may *make* a thing that is difficult or easy, simple or complex; we may *make* a letter or *make* a poem; we may *make* a word or *make* a sentence. To *form* is the work either of intelligence or of circumstances: education has much to do in *forming* the habits, but nature has more to do in *forming* the disposition and the mind altogether; sentiments are frequently *formed* by young people before they have sufficient maturity of thought and knowledge to justify them in coming to any decision. To *produce* is the effect of great mental exertion, or it is the natural operation of things: no industry could ever *produce* a poem or a work of the imagination, but a history or a work of science may be *produced* by the force of mere labor. All things, both in the moral and intellectual world, are linked together upon the same principle of cause and effect by which one thing is the *producer* and the other the thing *produced:* quarrels *produce* hatred, and kindness *produces* love, as heat *produces* inflammation and fever, or disease *produces* death. What is *created* is not made by any natural process, but is called into existence by the *creating* power; small matters *create* jealousies in jealous minds.

MALADY. See DISORDER.

MALEDICTION, CURSE, IMPRECATION, EXECRATION, ANATHEMA. *Malediction,* from Latin *male,* ill, and *dicere,* to say, signifies a saying ill, that is, declaring an evil wish against a person. *Curse,* Anglo-Saxon *cursian,* is the native English term corresponding to *malediction. Imprecation,* from Latin *in,* in, and *precari,* to pray, signifies a praying down evil upon a person. *Execration,* from the Latin *execror,* that is, *e sacris excludere,* signifies the same as to excommunicate, with every form of solemn *imprecation. Anathema,* in Greek ἀνάθεμα, signifies a setting up, hence a devotion, a curse, and thus a putting out of a religious community as a penance.

The *malediction* is the most indefinite and general term, signifying simply the declaration of evil; *curse* is a solemn denunciation of evil: the former is employed mostly by men; the latter by some superior being as well as by men: the rest are species of the *curse* pronounced only by men. The *malediction* is caused by simple anger; the *curse* is occasioned by some grievous offence: men, in the heat of their passions, will utter *maledictions* against any object that offends them; God pronounced a *curse* upon Adam and all his posterity, after the fall.

The term *curse* differs in the degree of evil pronounced or wished; *imprecation* and *execration* always imply some positive great evil, and, in fact, as much evil as can be conceived by man in his anger; the *anathema* concerns the evil which is pronounced according to the canon law, by which a man is not only put out of the Church, but held up as an object of offence. The *malediction* is altogether an unallowed expression of private resentment; the *curse* was admitted, in some cases, according to the Mosaic law; and that, as well as the *anathema*, at one time formed a part of the ecclesiastical discipline of the Christian Church; the *imprecation* formed a part of the heathen ceremony of religion; but the *execration* is always the informal expression of the most violent personal anger.

MALEFACTOR. See CRIMINAL.

MALEVOLENT, MALICIOUS, MALIGNANT. These words have all their derivation from *malus*, bad, that is, *malevolent*, wishing ill; *malicious* (see MALICE), having *malice*; and *malignant*, from *malus* and *gignere*, to be born, having an inborn disposition that is bad.

Malevolence has a deep root in the heart and is a settled part of the character; we denominate the person *malevolent* to designate the ruling temper of his mind: *maliciousness* may be applied as an epithet to particular parts of a man's character or conduct; one may have a *malicious* joy or pleasure in seeing the distresses of another: *malignity* is not so often employed to characterize the person as the thing;

the *malignity* of a design is estimated by the degree of mischief which was intended to be done.

Malice, Rancor, Spite, Grudge, Pique. —*Malice,* in Latin *malitia,* from *malus,* bad, signifies the very essence of badness lying in the heart; *rancor* (see HATRED) is only continued *hatred;* the former requires no external cause to provoke it, it is inherent in the mind; the latter must be caused by some personal offence. *Malice* is properly the love of evil for evil's sake, and is, therefore, confined to no number or quality of objects, and limited by no circumstance; *rancor* depends upon external objects for its existence, and is confined to such objects only as are liable to cause displeasure or anger; *malice* will impel a man to do mischief to those who have not injured him and are perhaps strangers to him; *rancor* can subsist only between those who have had sufficient connection to be at variance.

Spite, from Old French *despit,* from Latin *de,* down, and a weakened form of *specere,* to look—to look down on, to despise—denotes a petty kind of *malice,* or disposition to offend another in trifling matters; it may be in the temper of the person, or it may have its source in some external provocation: children often show their *spite* to one another.

Grudge, from Old French *groucher,* to murmur, from an imitative base *gru;* and *pique,* from *pike,* denoting the prick of a pointed instrument, are employed for that particular state of *rancorous* or *spiteful* feeling which is occasioned by personal offences: the *grudge* is that which has long existed; the *pique* is that which is of recent date; a person is said to owe another a *grudge* for having done him an injury; or he is said to show *pique* to another who has made him an affront.

MALICIOUS. See MALEVOLENT; SATANIC.

MALIGNANT. See MALEVOLENT; VIRULENT.

MANAGE. See CONCERT; CONDUCT; WIELD.

MANAGEMENT. See CARE; ECONOMY.

MANGLE. See MUTILATE.

MANIA. See DERANGEMENT.

MANLY, MANFUL. *Manly*, or like a man, is opposed to juvenile, and of course applied properly to youths; but *manful*, or full of manhood, is opposed to effeminate and is applicable more properly to grown persons: a premature *manliness* in young persons is hardly less unseemly than a want of *manfulness* in one who is called upon to display his courage.

MANNER. See AIR; CUSTOM; WAY.

MANNERS, MORALS. *Manners* concern the minor forms of acting with others and toward others; *morals* include the important duties of life: *manners* have therefore been denominated minor *morals*. By attention to good *manners* we render ourselves good companions; by an observance of good *morals* we become good members of society: in the former instance we gain the good-will of others, in the latter their esteem. The *manners* of a child are of more or less importance, according to his station in life; his *morals* cannot be attended to too early, let his station be what it may.

See also ETIQUETTE.

MANŒUVRING. See TACTICS.

MARGIN. See BORDER.

MARINE. See MARITIME.

MARINER. See SEAMAN.

MARITIME, MARINE, NAVAL, NAUTICAL. *Maritime* and *marine*, from the Latin *mare*, sea, cognate with English *mere*, signifies belonging to the sea; *naval*, from *navis*, a ship, signifies belonging to a ship; and *nautical*, from *nauta*, a sailor, signifies belonging to a sailor or to navigation. Countries and places are denominated *maritime* from their proximity to the sea or their great intercourse by sea; hence England is called the most *maritime* nation in Europe. *Marine* is a technical term, employed by persons in office, to denote that which is officially transacted with regard to the sea in distinction from what passes on land; hence we speak of the *marines* as a species of soldiers acting by sea, as contrasted with the *maritime* society: or of *marine* stores. *Naval* is another term of art as opposed to military, and used in regard to the arrangements of government or commerce: hence we speak of *naval* affairs, *naval* officers, *naval* tactics, and the like. *Nautical* s a scientific term connected with the science of navigation or the management of vessels: hence we talk of *nautical* instruction, of *nautical* calculations. The *maritime* laws of England are essential for the preservation of the *naval* power which it has so justly acquired. The *marine* of England is one of its glories. The *naval* administration is one of the most important branches of our government in the time of war. *Nautical* tables and a *nautical* almanac have been expressly formed for the benefit of all who apply themselves to *nautical* subjects.

MARK, PRINT, IMPRESSION, STAMP. *Mark* comes from Anglo-Saxon *mearc*, possibly allied to *mearc*, signifying a boundary or limit, though this seems to be a different word. *Print* and *impression*, both from the Latin *premere*, to press, signify the visible effect produced by *printing* or pressing. *Stamp* signifies the effect produced by *stamping*, from Anglo-Saxon *stempan*, to stamp on with the feet.

The word *mark* is the most general in sense: whatever alters the external face of an object is a *mark;* a *print* is some specific *mark*, or a figure drawn upon the surface of an object; an *impression* is the *mark* pressed either upon or into a body; a *stamp* is the *mark* that is *stamped* in or upon the body. The *mark* is confined to no size, shape, or form; the *print* is a *mark* that represents an object: the *mark* may consist of a spot, a line, a stain, or a smear; but a *print* describes a given object, as a house, a man, etc. A *mark* is either a protuberance or a depression; an *impression* is always a sinking in of the object: a hillock or a hole are both *marks;* but the latter is properly the *impression:* the *stamp* is an *impression* made in a specific manner and for a specific object, as the *stamp* of a seal on wax. The *mark* is occasioned by every sort of action, gentle or violent, artificial or natural; by the voluntary act of a person, or the unconscious act of inanimate bodies, by means of compression or friction; by a touch or a blow, and the like: all the others are occasioned by one or more of these modes. The *print* is occasioned by artificial means of compression, as when the *print* of letters or pictures is made on paper; or by accidental and natural compression, as when the *print* of the hand is made on the wall, or the *print* of the foot is made on the ground. The *impression* is made by means more or less violent, as when an *impression* is made upon wood by the axe or hammer; or by gradual and natural means, as by the dripping of water on stone. The *stamp* is made by means of direct pressure with an artificial instrument.

Mark is of such universal application that it is confined to no objects whatever, either in the natural or moral world; *print* is mostly applied to material objects, the face of which undergoes a lasting change, as the *printing* made on paper or wood; *impression* is more commonly applied to such natural objects as are particularly solid; *stamp* is generally applied to paper or still softer and more yielding bodies. *Impression* and *stamp* have both a moral application: events or speeches make an *impression* on the mind; things bear a certain *stamp* which bespeaks their origin. Where the passions have obtained an ascendency, the occasional good *impressions* which are produced by religious observances but too frequently die away; the Christian religion carries with itself the *stamp* of truth.

Mark, Sign, Note, Symptom, Token, Indication.—*Mark* (see above). *Sign,* in Latin *signum,* signifies the thing that points out. *Symptom,* in Latin *symptoma,* Greek σύμπτωμα, from πίπτειν, to fall out in accordance, signifies what presents itself to confirm one's opinion. *Token* (see BETOKEN). *Indication,* in Latin *indicatio,* from *indicare,* to point out, signifies the thing which points out.

The idea of an external object which serves to direct the observer is common to all these terms; the difference consists in the objects that are employed. Anything may serve as a *mark,* a stroke, a dot, a stick set up, and the like; it serves simply to guide the senses; the *sign* is something more complex; it consists of a figure or representation of some object, as the twelve *signs* of the zodiac, or the *signs* which are affixed to houses of entertainment, or to shops. *Marks* are arbitrary; every one chooses his *mark* at pleasure: *signs* have commonly a connection with the object that is to be observed: a house, a tree, a letter, or any external object may be chosen as a *mark:* but a tobacconist chooses the *sign* of a redman; the innkeeper chooses the head of the reigning prince. *Marks* serve in general simply to aid the memory in distinguishing the situation of objects or the particular circumstances of persons or things, as the *marks* which are set up in a garden to distinguish the ground that is occupied; they may, therefore, be private and known only to the individual that makes them, as the private *marks* by which a tradesman distinguishes his prices: they may likewise be changeable and fluctuating, according to the humor and convenience of the maker, as the private *marks* which are employed by the military on guard. *Signs,* on the contrary, serve to direct the understanding; they have either a natural or an artificial resemblance to the object to be represented; they are consequently chosen, not by the will of one, but by the universal consent of a body; they are not chosen for the moment, but for a permanency, as in the case of language, either oral or written, in the case of the zodiacal *signs,* or the *signs* of the cross, the algebraical *signs,* and the like. It is clear, therefore, that many objects may be both a *mark* and a *sign,* according to the above illustration: the cross which is employed in books, by way of reference to notes, is a *mark* only, because it serves merely to guide the eye or assist the memory; but the figure of the cross, when employed in reference to the cross of our Saviour, is a *sign,* inasmuch as it conveys a distinct idea of something else to the mind; so likewise little strokes over letters, or even letters themselves, may merely be *marks,* while they point out only a difference between this or that letter, this or that object; but this same stroke becomes a *sign* if, as in the first declension of Latin nouns, it is a *sign* of the ablative case; and a single letter affixed to different parcels is merely a *mark* so long as it simply serves this purpose; but the same letter, or suppose it were a word, is a *sign* when it is used as a *sign*. A *mark* may be something accidental, and mean nothing; but a *sign* is that to which a meaning is always given: there may be *marks* on a wall occasioned by the elements or otherwise, but a *sign* is always the *sign* of something: a *mark*, if it consist of a sensible object, is only visible, but *signs* may be the object of hearing, smell, or any other sense: many things, therefore, may be *signs* which are not *marks;* when words are spoken and not written they are *signs* and not *marks;* and in like manner, the cross made on the forehead of a child in baptism is a *sign*, but not a *mark*.

When *mark* and *sign* are both taken to denote something by which one forms a judgment, the former serves either to denote that which has been or which is, the latter to designate that which is or will be, as persons bear the *marks* of age, or the *marks* of violence; or we may judge by the *marks* of a person's foot that some one has been walking in a particular place; hoarseness is a *sign* that a person has a cold; when mariners meet with certain birds at sea, they consider them as a *sign* that land is near at hand.

So likewise in application to moral objects or matters of a purely intellectual nature; as a *mark* of honor, or a *mark* of distinction; an outward and visible *sign* of an inward and spiritual grace.

So likewise in application to objects which serve as characteristics of the person, the *mark* illustrates the spring of the action; the *sign* shows the state of the mind or sentiments; it is a *mark* of folly or weakness in a man to yield himself implicitly to the guidance of an interested friend; tears are not always a *sign* of repentance.

Note is rather a *sign* than a *mark;* but it is properly the *sign* which consists of *marks*, as a *note* of admiration (!); or, in the moral sense, the *sign* by which the object is known; as persons of *note*, that is, which have a *note* upon them, or that by which they are known.

Symptom is rather a *mark* than a *sign;* it explains the cause or origin of complaints by the appearances they assume, and is employed as a technical term only in the science of medicine: as a foaming at the mouth and an abhorrence of drink are *symptoms* of canine madness; motion and respiration are *signs* of life; but it may likewise be used figuratively in application to moral objects.

Token is a species of *mark* in the moral sense, *indication* a species of *sign:* a *mark* shows what is, a *token* serves to keep in mind what has been: a *gift* to a friend is a *mark* of one's affection and esteem: if it be permanent in its nature it becomes a *token;* friends who are in close intercourse have perpetual opportunities of showing each other *marks* of their regard by reciprocal acts of courtesy and kindness; when they separate for any length of time they commonly leave some *token* of their tender sentiments in each other's hands, as a pledge of what shall be as well as an evidence of what has been.

Sign, as it respects *indication*, is said in abstract and general propositions: *indication* itself is employed only for the *sign* given by any individual; it bespeaks the act of the persons: but the *sign* is only the face or appearance of the thing. When a man does not live consistently with the profession which he holds, it is a *sign* that his religion is built on a wrong foundation; parents are gratified when they observe the slightest *indications* of genius or goodness in their children.

Mark, Trace, Vestige, Footstep, Track. —The word *mark* has already been considered at large in the preceding article, but it will admit of further illustration when taken in the sense of that which is visible, and serves to show the existing state of things; *mark* is here, as before, the most general and unqualified term; the other terms varying in the circumstances or manner of the *mark*. *Trace*, Middle French *tracer*, to follow, comes ultimately from Latin *trahere*, to drag. *Vestige*, in Latin *vestigium*, signifies, literally, a print of the foot. *Footstep* is taken for the place in which the foot has stepped, or the *mark* made by that step. *Track*, French *trac*, a beaten way, comes from a Teutonic verb meaning to scrape or shove.

The *mark* is said of a fresh and uninterrupted line: the *trace* is said of that which is broken by time: a carriage in driving along the sand leaves *marks* of the wheels, but in a short time all *traces* of its having been there will be lost; a *mark* is produced by the action of bodies on one another in every possible form; the spilling of a liquid may leave a *mark* on the floor; the blow of a stick leaves a *mark* on the body; but the *trace* is a *mark* produced only by bodies making a progress or proceeding in a continued course: the ship that cuts the waves and the bird that cuts the air leave no *trace* of their course behind; so men pass their lives, and after death leave no *traces* that they ever were. The *vestige* is a species of *mark* or *trace* caused by the feet of men, or, which is the same thing, by the works of active industry; as the *vestige* of buildings: there are *traces* of the Roman roads still visible in England; there are many *vestiges* of Roman temples in Italy.

In an extended and moral application they are similarly distinguished. The *mark* serves to denote as well that which is as that which has been; as *marks* of desolation, or *marks* of antiquity: *trace* and *vestige* show the remains of something that has been; the former in reference to matters of intellectual research generally, the latter in reference to that which has been built up or pulled down, as there are *traces* of a universal affinity in all known languages; there are *vestiges* of ancient customs in different parts of England.

Footstep is employed only for the *steps* of an individual: the *track* is made by the *steps* of many; it is the line which has been beaten out or made by stamping: the *footstep* is now commonly and properly employed only for men and brutes; but the *track* is applied to inanimate objects, as the wheel of a carriage. When Cacus took away the oxen of Hercules, he dragged them backward that they might not be *traced* by their *footsteps:* a *track* of blood from the body of a murdered man may sometimes lead to the detection of the murderer.

In the metaphorical application they do not signify a *mark*, but a course of conduct; the former implies one's moral feelings or mode of dealing; the latter one's mechanical and habitual manner of acting: the former is the consequence of having the same principles; the latter proceeds from imitation or constant repetition. A good son will walk in the *footsteps* of a good father. In the management of business, it is rarely wise in a young man to leave the *track* which has been *marked* out for him by his superiors in age and experience.

Mark, Badge, Stigma.—*Mark* is still the general and the two others specific terms; they are employed for whatever serves to characterize persons externally, or betoken any part either of their character or circumstances: *mark* is employed either in a good, bad, or indifferent sense; *badge* in an indifferent one; *stigma* in a bad sense: a thing may either be a *mark* of honor, of disgrace, or of simple distinction; a *badge* is a *mark* simply of distinction; the *stigma* is a *mark* of disgrace. The *mark* is that which is conferred upon a person for his merits, as medals, stars, and ribbons are bestowed by princes upon meritorious officers and soldiers; or the *mark* attaches to a person, or is affixed to him, in consequence of his demerits; as a low situation in his class is a *mark* of disgrace to a scholar; or a fool's cap is a *mark* of ignominy affixed to idlers and dunces; or a brand in the forehead is a *mark* of ignominy for criminals: the *badge* is that which is voluntarily assumed by one's self according to established custom; it consists of dress by which the office, station, and even religion of a particular community is distinguished: as the gown and wig are the *badge* of the legal profession; the gown and surplice that of clerical men: the uniform of charity children is the *badge* of their condition; the peculiar habit of the Quakers, or the Friends, is the *badge* of their religion: the *stigma* consists not so much of what is openly imposed upon a person as what falls upon him in the judgment of others; it is the black *mark* which is set upon a person by the public, and is consequently the strongest of all *marks*, and one which every one most dreads and every good man seeks least to deserve.

Mark, Butt.—The word *mark* has this additional meaning in common with the word *butt*, that it implies an object aimed at: the *mark* is literally a *mark* that is said to be shot at by the *marksman* with a gun or a bow.

It is also metaphorically employed for the man who by his peculiar characteristics makes himself the object of notice; he is the *mark* at which every one's looks and thoughts are directed: the *butt*, derived through French from an Old Low German word meaning to beat, allied to English *beat*, is a species of *mark* in this metaphorical sense; but the former calls forth only general observation, the latter provokes the laughter and jokes of every one. Whoever renders himself conspicuous by his eccentricities, either in his opinions or his actions, must not complain if he become a *mark* for the derision of the public: it is a man's misfortune rather than his fault if he become the *butt* of a company who are rude and unfeeling enough to draw their pleasures from another's pain.

Mark, Note, Notice.—*Mark* is here taken in the intellectual sense, fixing as it were a *mark* upon a thing so as to keep it in mind, which is in fact to fix one's attention upon it in such a manner as to be able to distinguish it by its characteristic qualities: to *mark* is therefore altogether an intellectual act: to *note* has the same end as that of *marking*, namely, to aid the memory, but one *notes* a thing by making a written *note* of it; this is therefore a mechanical act: to *notice*, on the other hand, from *notitia*, knowledge, is a conscious operation, signifying to bring to one's knowledge, perception, or understanding by the use of our senses. We *mark* and *note* that which particularly interests us: the former is that which serves a present purpose; *notice* that which may be of use in future. The impatient lover *marks* the hours until the time arrives for meeting his mistress: travellers *note* whatever strikes them of importance to be remembered when they return home: *notice*, which is a species of noting in small matters, may serve either for the present or the future; we may *notice* things merely by way of amusement, as a child will *notice* the actions of animals; or we may *notice* a thing for the sake of bearing it in mind, as a person *notices* a particular road when he wishes to return by the same way. See also Show.

MARKSMAN. See Sharpshooter.

MARRIAGE, Wedding, Nuptials. *Marriage*, from to *marry*, denotes the act of *marrying*; *wedding* and *nuptials* denote the ceremony of being *married*. To *marry* is based on Latin *maritus*, from a root found also in *masculine*, signifying a man, and means to be joined to a male; hence *marriage* comprehends the act of choosing and being legally bound to a man or a woman; *wedding*, from *wed*, and the Anglo-Saxon *weddian*, to promise or betroth, implies the ceremony of *marrying*, inasmuch as it is binding upon the parties. *Nuptials* comes ultimately from *nupta*, participle of the Latin *nubere*, to veil, because the Roman ladies were veiled at the time of *marriage*: hence it has been put for the whole ceremony itself. *Marriage* is an institution which, by those who have been blessed with the light of Divine Revelation, has always been considered as sacred: with some persons, particularly among the lower orders of society, the day of their *wedding* is converted into a day of riot and intemperance: among the Roman Catholics in England it has been the practice to have their *nuptials* solemnized by a priest of their own persuasion as well as by the Protestant clergyman.

It is customary among many Italians in the United States to have a civil marriage first and a religious one later, the couple living apart in the interval.

Marriage, Matrimony, Wedlock.—*Marriage* is oftener an act than a state: *matrimony* and *wedlock* both describe states.

Marriage is taken in the sense of an act when we speak of the laws of *marriage*, the day of one's *marriage*, the congratulations upon one's *marriage*, a happy or unhappy *marriage*, the fruits of one's *marriage*, and the like; it is taken in the sense of a state when we speak of the pleasures or pains of *marriage*; but in this latter case *matrimony*, which signifies a *married* life abstractedly from all agents or acting persons, is preferable; so likewise, to think of *matrimony*, and to enter into the holy state of *matrimony*, are expressions founded upon the signification of the term. As *matrimony* is derived from *mater*, a mother, because *married* women are in general mothers, it has particular reference to the domestic state of the two parties; broils are but too frequently the fruits of *matrimony*, yet there are few cases in which they might not be obviated by the good sense of those who are engaged in them. Hasty *marriages* cannot be expected to produce happiness; young people who are eager for *matrimony* before they are fully aware of its consequences will purchase their experience at the expense of their peace. *Wedlock* is the Old English word for *matrimony*, and is in consequence admitted in law, when one speaks of children born in *wedlock;* conformably to its derivation, it has a reference to the bond of union which follows the *marriage:* hence one speaks of living happily in a state of *wedlock*, of being joined in holy *wedlock*.

MARTIAL, WARFARE, WARLIKE, MILITARY, SOLDIER - LIKE. *Martial*, from Mars, the god of war, is the Latin term for belonging to war: *warlike* signifies, literally, like *war* (Old French *werre*, Modern French *guerre*, from Old High German *werra*, broil, confusion, allied to English *worse*). In sense these terms approach so near to each other that they may be easily admitted to supply each other's place; but custom, the lawgiver of language, has assigned an office to each that makes it not altogether indifferent how they are used. *Warfare*, from *war* and the Anglo-Saxon verb *faran*, modern *fare*, to go, means an expedition of war; hence is the carrying on of war, either by land or sea or both. It is also improperly applied to strife between political and other factions. *Martial* is both a technical and a more comprehensive term than *warlike;* on the other hand, *warlike* designates the temper of the individual more than *martial:* we speak of *martial* array, *martial* preparations, *martial* law, a court *martial;* but of a *warlike* nation, meaning a nation which is fond of war; a *warlike* spirit or temper, also a *warlike* appearance, inasmuch as the temper is visible in the air and carriage of a man. *Military*, from *miles*, signifies belonging to a soldier, and

soldier-like, like a soldier (*soldier* being derived from Late Latin *soldum*, pay, from *solidus*, originally an adjective meaning hard; then "hard cash" or money, and signifying originally one who fights for money). *Military*, in comparison with *martial*, is a term of particular import, *martial* having always a reference to war in general: and *military* to the proceedings consequent upon that: hence we speak of *military* in distinction from naval, as *military* expeditions, *military* movements, and the like; but in characterizing the men we should say that they had a *martial* appearance; but of a particular place that it had a *military* appearance, if there were many soldiers. *Military*, compared with *soldier-like*, is used for the body, and the latter for the individual. The whole army is termed the *military:* the conduct of an individual is *soldier-like* or otherwise.

MARVEL. See WONDER.

MASK. See CLOAK.

MASSACRE. See CARNAGE.

MASSAGE. See PRESS.

MASSIVE. See BULKY.

MASTER. See POSSESSOR.

MATCH. See TALLY.

MATERIAL. See CORPORAL; TANGIBLE.

MATRIMONY. See MARRIAGE.

MATTER, MATERIALS, SUBJECT. *Matter* and *materials* are both derived from the same source, namely, the Latin *materia*, stuff for building. *Subject*, in Latin *subjectum*, participle of *subicere*, to lie under, signifies the thing lying under and forming the foundation.

Matter, in the physical application, is taken for all that composes the sensible world, in distinction from that which is spiritual or discernible only by the thinking faculty; hence *matter* is always opposed to mind. In regard to *materials*, it is taken in an indivisible as well as a general sense; the whole universe is said to be composed of *matter*, though not of *materials:* on the other hand, *materials* consist of those particular parts of *matter* which serve for the artificial production of objects; and *matter* is said of those things which are the natural parts of the universe: a house, a table, and a chair consist of *materials*, because they are works of art; but a plant, a tree, an animal body, consist of *matter*, because they are the productions of nature.

The distinction of these terms in their moral application is very similar; the *matter* which composes a moral discourse is what emanates from the author; but the *materials* are those with which one is furnished by others. The style of some writers is so indifferent that it disgraces the *matter* by the manner; periodical writers are furnished with *materials* for their productions by the daily occurrences in the political and moral world. Writers of dictionaries endeavor to compress as much *matter* as possible into a small space; they draw their *materials* from every other writer.

Matter seems to bear the same relation to *subject* as the whole does to any particular part: the *subject* is the groundwork of the *matter;* the *matter* is that which derives from the subject: the *matter* is that which we get by the force of invention; the *subject* is that which offers itself to notice: many persons may, therefore, have a *subject* who have no *matter*, that is, nothing in their own minds which they can offer by way of illustrating this *subject:* but it is not possible to have *matter* without a *subject;* hence the word *matter* is taken for the substance and for that which is substantial; the *subject* is taken for that which engages the attention: we speak of a *subject* of conversation and *matter* for deliberation; a *subject* of inquiry, a *matter* of curiosity. Nations in a barbarous state afford but little *matter* worthy to be recorded in history; people who live a secluded life and in a contracted sphere have but few *subjects* to occupy their attention.

MATURE. See RIPE.

MAXIM, PRECEPT, RULE, LAW. *Maxim* (see AXIOM) is a moral truth that carries its own weight with itself. *Precept* (see COMMAND), *rule* (see GUIDE), and *law* (see LAWFUL), signifying the thing laid down, all borrow their weight from some external circumstance: the *precept* derives its authority from the individual delivering it; in this manner the *precepts* of our Saviour have a weight which gives

them a decided superiority over everything else: the *rule* acquires a worth from its fitness for guiding us in our proceeding: the *law*, which is a species of *rule*, derives its weight from the sanction of power. *Maxims* are often *precepts*, inasmuch as they are communicated to us by our parents; they are *rules*, inasmuch as they serve as a rule for our conduct; they are *laws*, inasmuch as they have the sanction of conscience. We respect the *maxims* of antiquity as containing the essence of human wisdom; we reverence the *precepts* of religion as the foundation of all happiness; we regard the *rules* of prudence as preserving us from errors and misfortunes; we respect the *laws* as they are the support of civil society.

MAY. See CAN.

MAZE. See LABYRINTH.

MEAGRE. See LEAN.

MEAN, PITIFUL, SORDID. For the derivation of these words see LOW, for *mean;* PITY for *pitiful;* and BARE for *sordid.* The moral application of these terms to the characters of men, in their transactions with one another, is what constitutes their common signification. Whatever a man does in common with those below him is *mean;* it evinces a temper that is prone to sink rather than to rise in the scale of society: whatever makes him an object of pity, and consequently of contempt for his degraded character, makes him *pitiful:* whatever makes him grovel and crawl, intent on low, vile aims, is *sordid*, from the Latin *sordes*, dirty. *Meanness* is in many cases only relatively bad as it respects the disposal of our property: for instance, what is *meanness* in one might be generosity or prudence in another: the due estimate of circumstances is allowable in all, but it is *meanness* for any one to attempt to save, at the expense of others, that which he can conveniently afford either to give or pay: hence an undue spirit of seeking gain or advantage for one's self to the detriment of others is denominated a *mean* temper: it is *mean* for a gentleman to do that for himself which according to his circumstances he might get another to do for him. *Pitifulness* goes farther than *meanness:* it is not merely that which degrades, but unmans the person; it is that which is weak as well as low: when the fear of evil or the love of gain prompts a man to sacrifice his character and forfeit his veracity he becomes truly *pitiful;* Blifil in *Tom Jones* is the character whom all pronounce to be *pitiful. Sordidness* is peculiarly applicable to one's love of gain; although of a more corrupt, yet it is not of so degrading a nature as the former two: the *sordid* man does not deal in trifles like the *mean* man; and has nothing so low and weak in him as the *pitiful* man. A continual habit of getting money will engender a *sordid* love of it in the human mind; but nothing short of a degraded character leads a man to be *pitiful.* We dislike a *mean* man: we hold a *pitiful* man in profound contempt: we hate a *sordid* man. *Meanness* descends to that which is insignificant and worthless: *pitifulness* sinks into that which is despicable: *sordidness* contaminates the mind with what is foul.

See also BASE; COMMON; DESIGN; LOW.

MEAN, MEDIUM. *Mean*, as here used, is but a contraction of *medium*, which signifies in Latin the middle path. The term *mean* is used abstractedly in all speculative matters: there is a *mean* in opinions between the two extremes: this *mean* is doubtless the point nearest to truth. *Medium* is employed in practical matters; computations are often erroneous from being too high or too low; the *medium* is in this case the one most to be preferred. The moralist will always recommend the *mean* in all opinions that widely differ from each other: our passions always recommend to us some extravagant conduct either of insolent resistance or *mean* compliance; but discretion recommends the *medium* or middle course in such matters.

MEANING. See SIGNIFICATION.

MEANS. See WAY.

MECHANIC. See ARTIST.

MEDDLE. See INTERMEDDLE, under INTERCEDE.

MEDDLESOME. See PRAGMATICAL.

MEDIATE. See ARBITRATE; INTERCEDE.

MEDIOCRITY. See MODERATION.

MEDITATE. See CONTEMPLATE.

MEDIUM. See MEAN.

MEDLEY. See DIFFERENCE; MIXTURE.

MEEK. See SOFT.

MEET. See FIT.

MEETING, INTERVIEW. *Meeting,* from to *meet,* is the act of *meeting* or coming into the company of any one: *interview,* compounded of *inter,* between, and *view,* to view, is a personal view of each other. A *meeting* is an ordinary concern, and its purpose familiar; *meetings* are daily taking place between friends: an *interview* is extraordinary and formal; its object is commonly business; an *interview* sometimes takes place between princes or commanders of armies.

See also ASSEMBLY.

MELANCHOLIC. See HYPOCHONDRIACAL.

MELANCHOLY. See DEJECTION; SPLENETIC.

MELODY, HARMONY, ACCORDANCE. *Melody,* from Greek μελῳδία, from Greek μέλος, a song, and ῳδή, a song, signifies something intended to be sung. *Harmony,* in Latin *harmonia,* Greek ἁρμονία, concord, from ἁρμός, a joining, signifies the agreement of sounds. *Accordance* denotes the act or state of *according* (see AGREE).

Melody signifies any measured or modulated sounds measured after the manner of verse into distinct members or parts; *harmony* signifies the suiting or adapting different modulated sounds to one another; *melody* is therefore to *harmony* as a part to the whole: we must first produce *melody* by the rules of art; the *harmony* which follows must be regulated by the ear: there may be *melody* without *harmony,* but there cannot be *harmony* without *melody:* we speak of simple *melody* where the modes of music are not very much diversified; but we cannot speak of *harmony* unless there be a variety of notes to fall in with one another. A voice is *melodious,* inasmuch as it is capable of producing a regularly modulated note; it is *harmonious,* inasmuch as it strikes agreeably on the ear and produces no discordant sounds. The song of a bird is *melodious* or has *melody* in it, inasmuch as there is a combination of sounds in it which are admitted to be regular, and consequently agreeable to the musical ear; there is *har-mony* in a concert of voices and instruments. *Accordance* is, strictly speaking, the property on which both *melody* and *harmony* are founded; for the whole of music depends on an *accordance* of sounds. The same distinction marks *accordance* and *harmony* in the moral application. There may be occasional *accordance* of opinion or feeling; but *harmony* is an entire *accordance* in every point.

MEMBER, LIMB. *Member* is the Latin term, from *membrum*, and *limb* the corresponding native English term from a root signifying a joint.

Member is a general term applied either to the animal body or to other bodies, as a *member* of a family, or a *member* of a community: *limb* is applicable to animal bodies; *limb* is therefore a species of *member;* for every *limb* is a *member*, but every *member* is not a *limb*. The *members* of the body comprehend every part which is capable of performing a distinct office; but the *limbs* are those jointed *members* that are distinguished from the head and the body: the nose and the eyes are *members*, but not *limbs;* the arms and legs are properly denominated *limbs*.

MEMOIRS. See ANECDOTES.
MEMORABLE. See SIGNAL.
MEMORIAL. See MONUMENT.

MEMORY, REMEMBRANCE, RECOLLECTION, REMINISCENCE. The same root, in Latin *memor*, mindful, *memini*, I remember, etc., is found in three of these words—*memory*, *remember*, and *reminiscence*. *Re*, in *remember* and *reminiscence*, signifies *again*—to call to mind again being the meaning of the words. *Recollection*, from *re* and *collect* (Latin *con* and *legere*, to bring together), signifies to bring together in the mind again.

Memory is the power of recalling images once made on the mind; *remembrance, recollection*, and *reminiscence* are operations or exertions of this power which vary in their mode. The *memory* is a power which exerts itself either independently of the will or in conformity with the will; but all the other terms express the acts of conscious agents, and consequently are more or less connected with the will. In dreams the *memory* exerts it-

self, but we do not say that we have any *remembrance* or *recollection* of objects. *Remembrance* is the exercise of *memory* in a conscious agent; it may be the effect of repetition or habit, as in the case of a child who *remembers* his lesson after having learned it several times; or of a horse who *remembers* the road which he has been continually passing; or it may be the effect of association and circumstances, by which images are casually brought back to the mind, as happens to intelligent beings continually as they exercise their thinking faculties. In these cases *remembrance* is an involuntary act; for things return to the mind before one is aware of it, as in the case of one who hears a particular name and *remembers* that he has to call on a person of the same name; or of one who, on seeing a particular tree, *remembers* all the circumstances of his youth which were connected with a similar tree. *Remembrance* is, however, likewise a voluntary act, and the consequence of a direct determination, as in the case of a child who strives to *remember* what it has been told by its parent, or of a friend who *remembers* the hour of meeting another friend in consequence of the interest which it has excited in his mind: experience teaches us, indeed, that scarcely anything in ordinary cases is more under the subservience of the will than the *memory;* for it is now become almost a maxim to say that one may *remember* whatever one wishes.

The power of *memory*, and the simple exercise of that power in the act of *remembering*, are possessed in common, though in different degrees, by man and animal; but *recollection* and *reminiscence* are exercises of the *memory* that are connected with the higher faculties of man, his judgment and understanding. To *remember* is to call to mind that which has once been presented to the mind; but to *recollect* is to *remember* afresh, to *remember* what has been *remembered* before, to recall with an effort what may have been forgotten. *Remembrance* busies itself with objects that are at hand; *recollection* carries us back to distant periods: simple *remembrance* is engaged in things that have but just left the mind, which are more or less easily recalled, and more or less faithfully represented; but *recollection* tries to retrace the faint images of things that have been so long unthought of as to be almost obliterated from the *memory*. In this manner we are said to *remember* in one half-hour what was told us in the preceding half-hour, or to *remember* what passes from one day to another; but we *recollect* the incidents of childhood; we *recollect* what happened in our native place after many years' absence from it. *Remembrance* is that homely, every-day exercise of the *memory* which renders it of essential service in the acquirement of knowledge or in the performance of one's duties; *recollection* is that exalted exercise of the *memory* which affords us the purest of enjoyments and serves the noblest of purposes; the *recollection* of all the minute incidents of childhood is a more sincere pleasure than any which the present moment can afford.

Reminiscence is altogether an abstract exercise of the *memory*, which is employed on purely intellectual ideas in distinction from those which are awakened by sensible objects: the mathematician makes use of *reminiscence* in deducing unknown truths from those which he already knows. *Reminiscence* among the disciples of Socrates was the *remembrance* of things purely intellectual, or of that natural knowledge which the souls had had before their union with the body; while the *memory* was exercised upon sensible things, or that knowledge which was acquired through the medium of the senses. *Reminiscence*, in its familiar application, signifies any event or circumstance long past, which is brought or comes to the mind, and which is usually of a pleasurable nature.

The Latins said that *reminiscence* belonged exclusively to man because it was purely intellectual, but that *memory* was common to all animals because it was merely the terminal point of the senses. That divine, though pagan philosopher, the high-winged Plato, fancied that our souls were at the first infusion *abrasæ tabulæ*, and that all our future knowledge was but a *reminiscence*.

MENACE. See THREAT.
MEND. See AMEND.
MENIAL. See SERVANT.
MENTAL, INTELLECTUAL, INTELLIGENT. There is the same difference between *mental* and *intellectual* as between *mind* and *intellect:* the *mind* comprehends the thinking faculty in general, with all its operations; the *intellect* includes only that part of it which consists of understanding and judgment: *mental* is therefore opposed to corporeal; *intellectual* is opposed to sensual or physical: *mental* exertions are not to be expected from all; *intellectual* enjoyments fall to the lot of comparatively few. Objects, pleasures, pains, operations, gifts, etc., are denominated *mental;* subjects, conversation, pursuits, and the like are entitled *intellectual*. It is not always easy to distinguish our *mental* pleasures from those corporeal pleasures which we enjoy in common with animals; the latter are, however, greatly heightened by the former in whatever degree they are blended: in a society of well-informed persons, the conversation will turn principally on *intellectual* subjects.

Intelligent, from *intelligens*, understanding or knowing, is a characteristic of the person: an *intelligent* being or an intelligence denotes a being purely spiritual or abstracted from matter.

When applied to individuals, it denotes having a quick understanding of things, as an *intelligent* child.

MENTION, NOTICE. *Mention*, from *mens*, mind, signifies here to bring to mind. *Notice* (see MARK). These terms are synonymous only inasmuch as they imply the act of calling things to another person's mind. We *mention* a thing in direct terms: we *notice* it indirectly or in a casual manner; we *mention* that which may serve as information; we *notice* that which may be merely of a personal or incidental nature. One friend *mentions* to another what has passed at a particular meeting: in the course of conversation he *notices* or calls to the *notice* of his companion the badness of the road, the wideness of the street, or the like.

MERCANTILE, COMMERCIAL. Both *mercantile* and *commercial* come from Latin *merx*, pay, salable goods.

Mercantile, from the same source, signifies the actual transaction of business, or a transfer of merchandise by sale or purchase; *commercial* comprehends the theory and practice of *commerce:* hence we speak in a ·peculiar manner of a *mercantile* house, a *mercantile* town, a *mercantile* situation, and the like; but of a *commercial* education, a *commercial* people, *commercial* speculations, and the like.

MERCENARY. See HIRELING; VENAL.

MERCIFUL. See GRACIOUS.

MERCY. See CLEMENCY; PITY.

MERGE, COMBINE, INCLUDE, UNITE. These words all signify the union of two or more things, but they differ in the closeness of the union and the character of the image under which it is suggested. *Merge,* from Latin *mergere,* to sink into water, to dip, signifies the closest union—the absolute swallowing up of one thing by another. *Include* suggests a similar idea—from Latin *in,* in, and *claudere,* to close—signifying to enclose. *Merge,* however, suggests more clearly the loss of identity of the thing *merged* or swallowed up, and is a stronger word. *Unite,* from Latin *unire,* based on *unus,* one, signifies to make one; it differs in the relation implied between the two or more objects. The lesser can only be *included* or *merged* in the greater. Two equal things may be *united.* *Combine* (see ASSOCIATION and CONNECT) signifies a relation that is not so close as that indicated in *unite*—as is explained in the article on CONNECT.

MERRIMENT. See GLEE.

MERRY. See LIVELY.

MERRY-ANDREW. See ZANY.

MESSAGE, ERRAND. *Message,* from the Latin *missus,* participle of *mittere,* to send, and a suffix, signifies the thing sent. *Errand* comes from Anglo-Saxon *œrende,* a message.

The *message* is properly any communication which is conveyed; the *errand* on which one person sends another is that which causes one to go: servants are the bearers of *messages,* and are sent on various *errands.* A *message* may be either verbal or written; an *errand* is limited to no form and to no circumstance: one delivers the *message,* and goes the *errand.* Sometimes the message may be the *errand,* and the *errand* may include the *message:* when that which is sent consists of a notice or intimation to another, it is a *message;* and if that causes any one to go to a place, it is an *errand:* thus it is that the greater part of *errands* consists of sending *messages* from one person to another.

METAMORPHOSE. See TRANSFIGURE.

METAPHOR. See FIGURE.

METHOD. See ORDER; SYSTEM; WAY.

MILITARISM, MILITANCY, MILITARY, MILITANT. *Militarism* and *militancy* both come from Latin *miles,* a soldier, but they differ in their application. *Militarism,* and its corresponding adjective, signify the state of being under arms and prepared to engage in war. It refers to formal and governmental preparation for war. *Militancy,* and its adjective *militant,* signify merely the general disposition to fight for a cause, and may have nothing to do with the actual science of warfare. A *militant* individual is one who is ready to fight, either physically or with the pen or the tongue, for his cause; a *military* man is a man who is or has been a part of a regularly constituted army.

See also PREPAREDNESS.

MIMIC. See IMITATE.

MINARET. See TURRET.

MIND. See ATTEND; SOUL.

MINDFUL, REGARDFUL, OBSERVANT. *Mindful* signifies that which we wish from others; *regardful* that which in itself demands *regard* or serious thought, particularly what *regards* the interests and feelings of others; *observant* implies both that which is communicated by others and that which carries its own obligations with itself: a child should always be *mindful* of its parents' instructions; they should never be forgotten: every one should be *regardful* of his several duties and obligations; they ought never to be neglected: ᴏne ought to be *observant* of the religious duties which one's profession enjoins upon him; they cannot with propriety be passed over. By being *mindful* of what one hears from the wise and good, one learns to be wise and good; by being *regardful* of what is due to one's self and to society at large, one learns to pass through the world with satisfaction to one's own mind and esteem from others; by being *observant* of all rule and order, we afford to others a salutary example for their imitation.

MINGLE. See MIX.

MINISTER, AGENT. *Minister* comes from *minus*, less, as *magister* comes from *magis*, more, the one being less, and the other more, than others: the *minister*, therefore, is literally one who acts in a subordinate capacity; and the *agent* (from *ago*, to act) is the one who takes the acting part: they both perform the will of another, but the *minister* performs a higher part than the *agent*: the *minister* gives his counsel and exerts his intellectual powers in the service of another, but the *agent* executes the orders or commissions given him: a *minister* is employed by government in political affairs; an *agent* is employed by individuals in commercial and pecuniary affairs, or by government in subordinate matters: a *minister* is received at court and serves as a representative for his government; an *agent* generally acts under the directions of the *minister* or some office of government: ambassadors or plenipotentiaries or the first officers of the state are *ministers;* but those who regulate the affairs respecting prisoners, the police, and the like are termed *agents*. A *minister* always holds a public character and is in the service of the state; the *agent* may be acting only for another individual, as a commercial *agent*.

See also CLERGYMAN.

Minister, Administer, Contribute.—To *minister*, from the noun *minister*, in the sense of a servant, signifies to act in subservience to another, and may be taken either in a good, bad, or indifferent sense, as to *minister* to the spiritual wants or to *minister* to another's caprices and indulgences when we encourage them unnecessarily. *Administer*, that is, to *minister* for a specific purpose, is taken in the good sense of serving another to his advantage: thus the Good Samaritan *administered* to the comfort of the man who had fallen among thieves. *Contribute* (see CONDUCE) is taken in either a good or bad sense; we may *contribute* to the relief of the indigent or we may *contribute* to the follies and vices of others. Princes are sometimes placed in the unfortunate situation that those who should direct them in early life only *minister* to their vices by every means in their power: it is the part of the Christian to *administer* comfort to those who are in want, consolation to the afflicted, advice to those who are feeble, and support to those who cannot uphold themselves: it is the part of all who are in high stations to *contribute* to the dissemination of religion and morality among their dependents; but there are, on the contrary, many who *contribute* to the spread of immorality and a contempt of all sacred things by the most pernicious example of irreligion in themselves.

MINUTE. See ATOMIC; CIRCUMSTANTIAL.

MIRACLE. See WONDER.

MIRTH, MERRIMENT, JOVIALITY, JOLLITY, HILARITY. These terms all express that species of gayety or joy which belongs to company, or to men in their social intercourse. *Mirth* refers to the feeling displayed in the outward conduct: *merriment* and the other terms refer rather to the external expressions of the feeling, or the causes of the feeling, than to the feeling itself: *mirth* shows itself in laughter, in dancing, singing, and noise; *merriment* consists of such things as are apt to excite *mirth:* the more we are disposed to laugh the greater is our *mirth;* the more there is to create laughter the greater is the *merriment:* the tricks of Punch and his wife and the jokes of ꞓ clown cause much *mirth* among the gaping crowd of rustics; the amusements with the swing or the merry-go-round afford much *merriment* to the visitants of a fair. *Mirth* is confined to no age or station; but *merriment* belongs more particularly to young people or those of the lower station; *mirth* may be provoked wherever any number of persons is assembled; *merriment* cannot go forward anywhere so properly as at fairs or public places. *Joviality* or *jollity*, and *hilarity*, are species of *merriment* which belong to the convivial board: *joviality* or *jollity* may accompany the pleasures of the table or any social entertainments; *hilarity* is the same thing qualified by the cultivation and good sense of the company; we may expect to find much *joviality* and *jollity* at a public dinner of plain people; we may expect to find *hilarity* at a public dinner of gentlemen: eating, drinking, and noise constitute the *joviality;* the conversation, the songs, the toasts, and the public spirit of the company contribute to *hilarity.*

See also FESTIVITY; GLEE; JOY.

MISANTHROPICAL, CYNICAL. *Misanthropical* and *cynical* both indicate a hostile attitude to mankind in general. *Misanthropical*, from Greek μισεῖν, to hate, and ἄνθρωπος, man, means hating mankind. *Cynical* comes from Greek κυνικός, which originally meant doglike, currish, snappish, and was the designation of a sect of Greek philosophers who affected to disbelieve in human goodness. *Misanthropical* implies a morbid psychological condition—often a nervous horror or fear of others, which has some definite external cause. *Cynical* indicates an intellectual attitude—a disbelief in the goodness of others, and a consequent tendency to sneer. The *misanthrope* makes himself miserable; the *cynic* makes others miserable.

The *misanthropical* man separates himself from the rest of human society; the *cynical* man moves among men sneering. *Cynicism* is often a characteristic of men of the world who have seen much of the shams and self-ishness of society. The *misanthropical* man is often one who has suffered from some great shock to his belief in human nature.

MISCARRIAGE. See FAILURE.
MISCELLANY. See MIXTURE.
MISCHANCE. See CALAMITY.
MISCHIEF. See EVIL: INJURY; SCATHE.

MISCONSTRUE, MISINTERPRET. *Misconstrue* and *misinterpret* signify to explain in a wrong way; but the former connotes the sense of one's words or the application of one's actions: those who indulge themselves in a light mode of speech toward children are liable to be *misconstrued;* a too great tenderness to the criminal may be easily *misinter-*

preted in favor of the crime. These words may likewise be employed in speaking of language in general; but the former implies the literal transmission of foreign ideas into our native language; the latter the general sense which one affixes to any set of words, either in a native or foreign language: the learners of a language will unavoidably *misconstrue* it at times; in all languages there are ambiguous expressions which are liable to *misinterpretations. Misconstruing* is the consequence of ignorance; *misinterpretations* of particular words are oftener the consequence of prejudice and voluntary blindness, particularly in the explanation of the law or of the Scriptures.

MISDEED. See OFFENCE.
MISDEMEANOR. See CRIME; OFFENCE.
MISERABLE. See UNHAPPY.
MISERLY. See AVARICIOUS.
MISFORTUNE. See CALAMITY; EVIL.
MISHAP. See CALAMITY.
MISINTERPRET. See MISCONSTRUE.
MISMANAGE. See BUNGLE.
MISS. See LOSE.
MISTAKE. See ERROR.
MISUSE. See ABUSE.
MITIGATE. See ALLAY.

MIX, MINGLE, BLEND, CONFOUND. *Mix* is in Anglo-Saxon *miscian*, from Latin *miscere*, to intermingle. *Mingle* comes from Anglo-Saxon *mengan*, to mix, allied to *among*. *Blend* is a Scandinavian word meaning to mix together.

Mix is here a general and indefinite term, signifying simply to put together: but we may *mix* two or several things; we *mingle* several objects: things are *mixed* so as to lose all distinction, but they may be *mingled* and yet retain a distinction: liquids *mix* so as to become one, and individuals *mix* in a crowd so as to be lost; things of different sizes are *mingled* together if they lie in the same spot, but they still may be distinguished. To *blend* is only partially to *mix*, as colors *blend* which fall into each other: to *confound* is to *mix* in a wrong way, as objects of sight are *confounded* when they are erroneously taken to be joined. To *mix* and *mingle* are mostly applied to material objects, except in poetry; to *blend* and *confound* are mental operations, and principally employed on spiritual subjects: thus, events and circumstances are *blended* together in a narrative; the ideas of the ignorant are *confounded* in most cases, but particularly when they attempt to think for themselves.

Mixture, Medley, Miscellany.—*Mixture* is the thing *mixed. Medley* comes from Old French *medler*, to mix or confuse. *Miscellany*, in Latin *miscellaneus*, from *miscere*, to *mix*, signifies also a *mixture*.

The term *mixture* is general; whatever objects can be *mixed* will form a *mixture:* a *medley* is a *mixture* of things not fit to be *mixed;* and a *miscellany* is a *mixture* of many different things. Flour, water, and eggs may form a *mixture* in the proper sense, but if to these were added all sorts of spices it would form a *medley. Miscellany* is a species applicable only to intellectual subjects: the *miscellaneous* is opposed to that which is systematically arranged; essays are *miscellaneous* in distinction from works on one particular subject.

MOAN. See GROAN; WAIL.

MOB. See PEOPLE.

MOBILITY. See PEOPLE.

MOCK. See DERIDE; IMITATE.

MODE. See WAY.

MODEL. See COPY.

MODERATION, MEDIOCRITY. *Moderation* (see MODESTY) is the characteristic of persons; *mediocrity* (that is, the mean or medium) characterizes their condition: *moderation* is a virtue of no small importance for beings who find excess in everything to be an evil; *mediocrity* in external circumstances is exempt from all the evils which attend either poverty or riches.

MODERN. See NEW.

MODEST, BASHFUL, DIFFIDENT. *Modest*, in Latin *modestus*, from *modus*, a measure, signifies setting measure to one's estimate of one's self. *Bashful* signifies ready to be *abashed* (see ABASH). *Diffident* (see DISTRUSTFUL).

Modesty is a habit or principle of the mind; *bashfulness* is a state of feeling: *modesty* is at all times becoming; *bashfulness* is observed only in young girls or other young persons in the presence of their superiors: *modesty* discovers itself in the absence of everything assuming, whether in look, word, or action; *bashfulness* betrays itself by a downcast look and a timid air: a *modest* deportment is always commendable; a *bashful* temper is not desirable.

Modesty is a proper distrust of ourselves; *diffidence* is a culpable distrust. *Modesty*, though opposed to assurance, is not incompatible with a confidence in ourselves; *diffidence* altogether unmans a person and disqualifies him for his duty: a person is generally *modest* in the display of his talents to others; but a *diffident* man cannot turn his talents to his own use.

See also HUMBLE.

Modesty, Moderation, Temperance, Sobriety.—*Modesty*, in French *modestie*, Latin *modestia*, and *moderation*, in Latin *moderatio*, both come from *modus*, a measure, limit, or boundary, that is, forming a measure or rule. *Temperance*, in Latin *temperantia*, from *tempus*, time, signifies the observance of proper times and seasons—propriety, self-control. *Sobriety* (see ABSTINENT).

Modesty lies in the mind and in the quality of feeling; *moderation* in the desires: *modesty* is a principle that acts discretionally; *moderation* is a rule or line that acts as a restraint on the views and the outward conduct: he who thinks *modestly* of his own acquirements, his own performances, and his own merits will be *moderate* in his expectations of praise, reward, and recompense; he, on the other hand, who overrates his own abilities and qualifications will equally overrate the use he makes of them, and consequently be *immoderate* in the price which he sets upon his services: in such cases, therefore, *modesty* and *moderation* are to each other as cause and effect; but there may be *modesty* without *moderation*, and *moderation* without *modesty. Modesty* is a sentiment confined to one's self as the object, and consisting solely of one's judgment of what one is and what one does; but *moderation*, as is evident from the above, extends to objects that are external of ourselves: *modesty*, rather than *moderation*, belongs to an author; *moderation*, rather than *modesty*, belongs to a tradesman or a man who has gains to make and purposes to answer.

Modesty shields a man from mortifications and disappointments, which assail the self-conceited man in every direction: a *modest* man conciliates the esteem even of an enemy and a rival. *Moderation* protects a man equally from injustice, on the one hand, and imposition, on the other: he who is *moderate* himself makes others so.

Moderation is the measure of one's desires, one's habits, one's actions, and one's words; *temperance* is the adaptation of the time or season for particular feelings, actions, or words: a man is said to be *moderate* in his principles who adopts the medium or middle course of thinking; it rather qualifies the thing than the person: he is said to be *temperate* in his anger, if he does not suffer it to break out into any excesses; *temperance* characterizes the person rather than the thing. A *moderate* man in politics endeavors to steer clear of all party spirit, and is consequently so *temperate* in his language as to provoke no animosity. *Moderation* in the enjoyment of everything is essential in order to obtain the purest pleasure: *temperance* in one's indulgences is always attended with the happiest effects to the constitution; as, on the contrary, any deviation from *temperance*, even in a single instance, is always punished with bodily pain and sickness.

Temperance and *sobriety* have already been considered in their proper application (see ABSTINENT), which will serve to illustrate their improper application. *Temperance* is an action; it is the *tempering* of our words and actions to the circumstances: *sobriety* is a state in which one is exempt from every stimulus to deviate from the right course; as a man who is intoxicated with wine runs into excesses and loses that power of guiding himself which he has when he is *sober* or free from all intoxication, so is he who is affected by any passion, in like manner, hurried away into irregularities which a man in his right senses will not be guilty of: *sobriety* is, therefore, the state of being in one's right or *sober* senses; and *sobriety* is, with regard to *temperance*, as a cause to the effect; *sobriety* of

mind will not only produce *moderation* and *temperance*, but extend its influence to the whole conduct of a man in every relation and circumstance, to his internal sentiments and his external behavior: hence we speak of *sobriety* in one's mien or deportment, *sobriety* in one's dress and manners, *sobriety* in one's religious opinions and observances. *Sober* may also be applied figuratively.

MOISTURE, HUMIDITY, DAMPNESS. *Moisture* is a word of disputed origin. *Humid* comes from Latin *humidus*, from the verb *humere*, to be moist. *Dampness* comes from the same root as the German *dampf*, a vapor.

Moisture is used in general to express any small degree of infusion of a liquid into a body; *humidity* is employed scientifically to describe the state of having any portion of such liquid: hence we speak of the *moisture* of a table, the *moisture* of paper, or the *moisture* of a floor that has been wet; but of the *humidity* of the air or of a wall that has contracted *moisture* of itself. *Dampness* is that species of *moisture* that arises from the gradual contraction of a liquid in bodies capable of retaining it; in this manner a cellar is *damp*, or linen that has lain long may become *damp*.

MOLEST. See INCONVENIENCE; TROUBLE.

MOLLIFY, APPEASE, PACIFY, SOOTHE. These words all mean to change from a state of wrath or disturbed emotion to one of peace. *Mollify* comes from Latin *mollis*, soft, tender, and a weak form of *facere*, to make. It signifies to make soft or mild. *Appease* comes from Old French *a pais*, Latin *ad pacem*, at peace, or rather to a state of peace. *Mollify*, *pacify* (from Latin *pax*, peace, and a weak form of *facere*, to make), and *appease* differ from each other in the degree of emotion suggested and the extent of the peace produced. To *mollify* is not so strong a word as to *pacify*, and to *pacify* does not suggest such dangerous wrath as *appease*. *Appease* is used especially with reference to persons or powers greater than ourselves. Men offered sacrifices in olden times to *appease* the gods; in the old fairy-tales beautiful maidens were offered as victims to *appease* the voracity of dragons and sea-monsters, etc. *Pacify* suggests a less dangerous anger or emotion. We *appease* the wrath that is dangerous to us; we *pacify* that which is merely annoying or vexatious—as when we *pacify* a crying child. *Mollify* and *soothe* are more general expressions. To *mollify* is to make gentle that which was violent. To *soothe*, from Anglo-Saxon *sooth*, truth, meant to "say sooth"—to agree with or say "yes" to. *Soothe* is more suggestive of physical action than *mollify*. We may *soothe* a wound by the application of healing salves, for instance, as well as *soothe* a ruffled temper with gentle words. *Mollify* has only the moral application. *Mollify* implies emotional excitement hostile to others which should be allayed; *soothe* merely implies any kind of disturbance. We *mollify* others for our own sakes; we *soothe* them for their own.

MOMENT. See IMPORTANCE; INSTANT.

MONAD. See UNIT.

MONARCH. See PRINCE.

MONASTERY. See CLOISTER.

MONEY, CASH. *Money* comes from the Latin *moneta*, a surname of Juno, in whose temple at Rome money was coined. *Cash*, from the French *casse*, a chest, signifies that which is put in a chest.

Money is applied to everything which serves as a circulating medium; *cash* is, in a strict sense, put for coin only: bank-notes are *money;* guineas and shillings are *cash;* all *cash* is therefore *money*, but all *money* is not *cash*. The only *money* the Chinese have are square bits of metal with a hole through the center by which they are strung upon a string: travellers on the Continent must always be provided with letters of credit, which may be turned into *cash*, as convenience requires.

MONOPLANE. See AIRCRAFT.

MONOPOLIZE, ABSORB, APPROPRIATE, ENGROSS. These words all mean to take complete or exclusive possession of something. *Appropriate* is the least emphatic. It comes from Latin *ad*, to, and *proprius*, one's own, and means to make completely one's own. *Absorb* (for derivation see AB-

SORB) goes further. It means not only to make one's own, but to swallow up entirely, so that the identity of the thing *absorbed* is lost. *Engross* and *monopolize* have similar meanings expressed under commercial figures. *Engross* is from the French *en gros*, in the *gross*, and means to buy up by the wholesale. *Monopolize* has a similar meaning. It comes from Greek μόνος and πωλεῖν, to sell, and means to obtain the exclusive right of selling. In ordinary usage there is little difference between *monopolize* and *engross*. *Monopolize* perhaps carries more of the suggestion of exclusiveness; *engross* more of absorption.

MONSTER. See WONDER.

MONSTROUS. See ENORMOUS.

MONUMENT, MEMORIAL. *Monument*, in Latin *monumentum* or *monimentum*, from *moneo*, to advise or remind, and a suffix, signifies that which puts us in mind of something. *Memorial*, from *memory*, signifies the thing that helps the memory.

From the above it is clear that these terms have, in their original derivation, precisely the same signification, but differ in their collateral acceptations: *monument* is applied to that which is purposely set up to keep a thing in mind; *memorials* are any objects which are calculated to call a thing to mind: a *monument* is used to preserve a public object of notice from being forgotten; a *memorial* serves to keep an individual in mind: the *monument* is commonly understood to be a species of building, as a tomb which preserves the *memory* of the dead, or a pillar which preserves the *memory* of some public event: the *memorial* always consists of something which was the property, or in the possession, of another, as his picture, his handwriting, his hair, and the like. The *Monument* at London was built to commemorate the dreadful fire of the city in the year 1666: friends who are at a distance are happy to have some token of each other's regard, which they likewise keep as a *memorial* of their former intercourse.

The *monument*, in its proper sense, is always made of wood or stone for some specific purpose; but in the improper sense anything may be termed a *monument* when it serves the purpose of reminding the public of any circumstance: thus, the pyramids are *monuments* of antiquity; the actions of a good prince are more lasting *monuments* than either brass or marble. *Memorials* are mostly of a private nature, and at the same time such as remind us naturally of the object to which they have belonged; this object is generally some person.

But it may likewise refer to some thing, if it be of a personal nature, or that by which persons are individually affected: our Saviour instituted the Sacrament of the Lord's-Supper as a *memorial* of His death.

MOOD. See HUMOR.

MORAL. See VIRTUOUS.

MORALLY. See ETHICAL.

MORALS. See MANNERS.

MORATORIUM. See DELAY.

MORBID. See SICK.

MOREOVER. See BESIDES.

MORTAL. See DEADLY.

MORTIFICATION. See VEXATION.

MORTIFY. See ABASH; SNUB.

MORTUARY. See NECROPOLIS.

MOTION, MOVEMENT. These are both abstract terms to denote the act of *moving,* but *motion* is taken generally and abstractedly from the thing that *moves; movement,* on the other hand, is taken in connection with the agent or thing that *moves:* hence we speak of a state of *motion* as opposed to a state of rest, of perpetual *motion,* the laws of *motion,* and the like; on the other hand, we say, to make a *movement,* when speaking of an army, a general *movement* when speaking of an assembly.

When *motion* is qualified by the thing that *moves* it denotes continued *motion;* but *movement* implies only a particular *motion:* hence we say, the *motion* of the heavenly bodies; the *motion* of the earth; a person is in continual *motion,* or an army is in *motion;* but a person who rises or sits down or goes from one chair to another makes a *movement;* the different *movements* of the springs and wheels of any instrument.

MOTION PICTURE. See MOVING PICTURE.

MOTIVE. See CAUSE; PRINCIPLE.

MOTOR. See AUTOMOBILE.

MOULD. See FORM.

MOUNT. See ARISE.

MOURN. See GRIEVE.

MOURNFUL, SAD. *Mournful* (from Anglo-Saxon *meornan,* to grieve, Modern English *mourn*) signifies full of what causes *mourning; sad* (see DULL) signifies either a painful sentiment or what causes this painful sentiment. The difference in the sentiment is what constitutes the difference between these epithets: the *mournful* awakens tender and sympathetic feelings: the *sad* oppresses the spirits and makes one heavy at heart; a *mournful* tale contains an account of others' distress; a *sad* story contains an account of one's own distress; a *mournful* event befalls our friends and relatives; a *sad* misfortune befalls ourselves. Selfish people find nothing *mournful,* but many things *sad:* tender-hearted people are always affected by what is *mournful,* and are less troubled about what is *sad.*

MOVABLE. See KINETIC.

MOVABLES. See GOODS.

MOVE. See GO; STIR; THRILL.

MOVEMENT. See MOTION.

MOVIES. See MOVING PICTURE.

MOVING, AFFECTING, PATHETIC. The *moving* is in general whatever moves the affections or the passions; the *affecting* and *pathetic* are what move the affections in different degrees. The good or bad feelings may be *moved;* the tender feelings only are *affected.* A field of battle is a *moving* spectacle: the death of a friend is an *affecting* spectacle. The *affecting* acts by means of the scenes as well as the understanding; the *pathetic* applies only to what is addressed to the heart: hence, a sight or a description is *affecting;* but an address is *pathetic.*

MOVING PICTURE, MOTION PICTURE, CINEMATOGRAPH, PHOTOPLAY, MOVIE. As is the case with most names of recent inventions, these terms differ not in meaning, but in application and usage. They all indicate the invention whereby figures in motion are photographed, so that the movement is reproduced when the picture is thrown on a screen. *Moving picture* was the name first used for this invention, but *motion picture* has also come into general usage and has been adopted by many of the corporations producing these pictures. *Moving picture* seems to a purist a more desirable term, because *moving* is an adjective form, whereas in the case of *motion picture* a substantive is made to do duty as an adjective. But some people contend that *motion picture* is a more accurate word, since the pictures themselves do not move; they are merely photographs of *motion*. The two terms, however, are used interchangeably. *Movie* is a popular abbreviation of *moving picture*, and one which, perhaps, deserves to receive general recognition as a new word, inasmuch as it is a spontaneous popular coinage to indicate a new invention, rather than a scientific name laboriously patched together out of Greek and Latin. *Cinematograph* is the technical term corresponding to *moving picture*, from Greek κίνειν, to move, and γράφειν, to mark or write. This is frequently shortened to *cinema*, which is also becoming a popular term for the *moving picture*, and is used among educated people sometimes as a more elegant substitute for *movie*. *Photoplay* differs somewhat from the other terms in its application. It is applied to a particular *moving-picture* drama, a play in pictures. The other words are rather indiscriminately used to indicate individual *moving-picture* plays, *moving-picture* houses, or the representations of the *moving picture*.

MULCT. See FINE.

MULTIPLANE. See AIRCRAFT.

MULTITUDE, CROWD, THRONG, SWARM. The idea of many is common to all these terms, and peculiar to that of *multitude*, from the Latin *multus; crowd* comes from Anglo-Saxon *crudan*, to push; and *throng* from Anglo-Saxon *thringan*, to press; and *swarm*, like the German *schwärmen*, to fly about, signifies running together in numbers. These terms vary, either in regard to the object or the circumstance: *multitude* is applicable to any object; *crowd, throng*, and *swarm* are in the proper sense applicable only to animate objects: the first two in regard to persons; the last to animals. A *multitude* may be either in a stagnant or a moving state; all the rest denote a *multitude* in a moving state: a *crowd* is always pressing, generally eager and tumultuous; a *throng* may be busy and active, but not always pressing or incommodious: it is always inconvenient, sometimes dangerous, to go into a *crowd;* it is amusing to see the *throng* that is perpetually passing in the streets of the city: the *swarm* is more active than either of the two others; it is commonly applied to bees which fly together in numbers, but sometimes to human beings, to denote their very great numbers when scattered about; thus the children of the poor in low neighborhoods *swarm* in the streets.

MUMBLE. See JABBER.

MUNIFICENT. See BENEFICENT.

MUNITIONS. See AMMUNITION.

MURDER. See KILL.

MURMUR. See COMPLAINT.

MUSE. See CONTEMPLATE; THINK.

MUSTER. See ASSEMBLE.

MUTABLE. See CHANGEABLE.

MUTE. See SILENT.

MUTILATE, MAIM, MANGLE. *Mutilate*, in Latin *mutilatus*, from *mutilus*, Greek μύτιλος, curtailed, docked, signifies to take off any necessary part. *Maim*, in Anglo-French *mahaym*, is a word of unknown origin. *Mangle*, in Anglo-French *mahangler*, is a frequentative of it.

Mutilate has the most extended meaning; it implies the total or partial loss of any limb: *mangle* is applied to irregular wounds in any part of the body: *maim* is confined to wounds in the limbs, particularly the hands. Men are exposed to the danger of *mutilation* by means of cannon-balls; they run the risk of being *mangled* when attacked with the sword; they frequently get *maimed* when boarding vessels or storming places.

Mutilate and *mangle* are applicable to moral objects; *maim* is employed in the natural or figurative sense. In this case *mangle* is a much stronger term than *mutilate;* the latter signifies to lop off an essential part; to *mangle* is to *mutilate* a thing to such degree as to render it useless or worthless. Every sect of Christians is fond of *mutilating* the Bible by setting aside such parts as do not favor its own scheme; and among them all the sacred Scriptures become literally *mangled* and stripped of all their most important doctrines.

MUTINOUS. See TUMULTUOUS.

MUTUAL, RECIPROCAL. *Mutual,* in Latin *mutuus,* from *muto,* to change, signifies exchanged so as to be equal, or the same, on both sides. *Reciprocal,* in Latin *reciprocus,* meant, literally, back and forth, from *reco,* back, and *proco,* forward. *Mutual* supposes a sameness in condition at the same time: *reciprocal* supposes an alternation or succession of returns. Exchange is free and voluntary; we give in exchange, and this action is *mutual:* return is made either according to law or equity; it is obligatory, and when equally obligatory on each in turn it is *reciprocal.* Voluntary disinterested services rendered by one person to another are *mutual:* imposed or merited services, returned from one to the other, are *reciprocal:* friends render one another *mutual* services; the services between servants and masters are *reciprocal.* The husband and wife pledge their faith to each other *mutually;* they are *reciprocally* bound to keep their vow of fidelity. The sentiment is *mutual,* the tie is *reciprocal.*

Mutual applies mostly to matters of will and opinion: a *mutual* affection, a *mutual* inclination to oblige, a *mutual* interest for each other's comfort, a *mutual* concern to avoid that which will displease the other—these are the sentiments which render the marriage state happy: *reciprocal* ties, *reciprocal* bonds, *reciprocal* rights, *reciprocal* duties—these are what every one ought to bear in mind as a member of society, that he may expect of no man more than what in equity he is disposed to return.

Mutual applies to nothing but what is personal; *reciprocal* is applied to things remote from the idea of personality, as *reciprocal* verbs, *reciprocal* terms, *reciprocal* relations, and the like.

MYSTERIOUS, MYSTIC. *Mysterious* and *mystic* are but variations of the same original, Greek μύστης, one who is initiated into a secret religious order; the former, however, is more commonly applied to that which is supernatural or veiled in an impenetrable obscurity; the latter to that which is natural, but concealed by an artificial or fantastical veil; hence we speak of the *mysterious* plans of Providence: *mystic* schemes of theology or *mystic* principles.

See also SECRET.

MYTHICAL. See LEGENDARY.

N

NAB, Appropriate, Clutch, Grasp, Seize. *Nab* is a Scandinavian word signifying to snatch at. Although the term has a wide range of usage and has long been recognized in polite language, in itself it is very near slang. A person by cunning, deceit, sharp practice may *nab* or *appropriate* from another credit for an achievement, some property, or other possession-conquering nations *appropriate, seize,* take possession of territory belonging to a defeated opponent as a spoil of war, and this has heretofore been considered right and proper.

To *appropriate* may be a slow action, one resulting from a more or less prolonged parley or negotiation, but to *seize* implies the real meaning of to *nab.* To *clutch* also implies a swift action, as a drowning person will *clutch* at anything likely to save his life, a falling person will *clutch, seize,* lay hold of any near-by object that will save a complete fall. To *grasp* implies actions both good and indefensible. It is a delight to *grasp* the hand of a friend; it is a great accomplishment to possess the intellectual capacity to *grasp* the spirit, truth, intent of a subject readily; but it is not justifiable to *grasp,* lay hold of greedily, take sudden possession of that which belongs to another without warrant or justification.

NACREOUS, Iridescent, Opalescent, Pearly, Polychromatic. These words all signify characterized by an interplay of colors, and derive their names and their respective differences from various substances. *Nacreous,* from *nacre,* mother-of-pearl (probably an Oriental word), takes its name from the inner covering of an oyster-shell and of certain other shells. It indicates a shining substance of the silvery gray color of the pearl, but shimmering with *iridescent* colors that appear and vanish as the light strikes it. *Iridescent,* from Latin *iris,* Greek ἶρις, the rainbow, signifies, literally, having all the colors of the rainbow. *Polychromatic,* from Greek πολύ, much, and χρῶμα, color, has a similar literal meaning less metaphorically expressed. But *iridescent* suggests both changefulness and light as well as color—an interplay of colors like light. *Polychromatic* is a more prosaic word; it merely means having many colors. *Opalescent* (from Latin *opalus,* English *opal,* the name of a precious stone) means resembling an *opal*—that is, having an interplay of soft milky-hued colors shot with flashes and gleams of fiery light. *Pearly,* from *pearl* (French *perle,* a word of unknown origin), means resembling the lustrous silvery white or silvery gray of the pearl which is sometimes touched with the faintest glow of color.

NAÏVE, Ingenuous, Artless. These words all refer to an absence of pretence and sophistication, and are used, in a good sense, to describe naturalness and simplicity. Of these three words *naïve* is the most inclusive and the most difficult to define. It is an imperfectly naturalized French word (from Latin *nativus,* native, inborn) which is almost always used in English with a feeling that it expresses something that cannot be described in blunt English terms.

Ingenuous (from Latin root *gen,* indicating birth) meant originally the simplicity and frankness of a well-born youth, and indicates a quality of character.

Artless means without *art,* and indicates primarily a mental characteristic. We say that a child is *artless,* that a young girl is *artless,* but that a youth is *ingenuous. Artless* conveys the impression of a certain innocence and ignorance of the world; *ingenuous,* the impression of an inborn disposition. *Naïve* expresses the idea involved in *artless* with a certain subtlety. It really differs from artless mainly in indicating a difference in the *perceiver,* rather than the quality *perceived.* It is faintly suggestive of that slight shade of tender-hearted amusement—of that complete sympathy of the heart, combined with a certain intellectual superiority and detachment—with which the educated or experienced man views an expression of *artlessness*. There are only a few words in English whose effectiveness depends so entirely upon an atmosphere undefinable and untranslatable; the other words of this character are also French.

NAKED. See BARE.

NAMBY-PAMBY. See SIMPLE.

NAME, CALL. *Name* comes from Anglo-Saxon *nama*, a name, allied to Latin *nomen*, a name. *Call* is a Scandinavian word. To *call* signifies properly to address one loudly, consequently we may *name* without *calling*, when we only mention a *name* in conversation; and we may *call* without *naming*.

The terms may, however, be employed in the sense of assigning a *name*. In this case a person is *named* by his *name*, whether by the proper patronymic or by some habitual variant; he is *called* according to the characteristics by which he is distinguished. The Emperor Tiberius was *named* Tiberius; he was *called* a monster. William the First of England is *named* William; he is *called* the Conqueror.

Name, Appellation, Title, Denomination.—*Name* (see above). *Appellation*, in French *appellation*, Latin *appellatio*, comes from Latin *ad*, to, and a stem meaning to speak, allied to Anglo-Saxon and Modern English *spell*. *Title*, in French *titre*, comes from Latin *titulus*, a superscription on a tomb. *Denomination* signifies that which *denominates* or distinguishes.

Name is a generic term, the rest are specific. Whatever word is employed to distinguish one thing from another is a *name;* therefore, an *appellation* and a *title* are a *name*, but not *vice versâ*. A *name* is either common or proper; an *appellation* is generally a common *name* given for some specific purpose as characteristic. Several kings of France had the *names* of Charles, Louis, Philip; but one was distinguished by the *appellation* of Stammerer, another by that of the Simple, and a third by that of the Hardy, arising from particular characters or circumstances. A *title*

is a species of *appellation*, not drawn from anything personal, but conferred as a ground of political distinction. An *appellation* may be often a term of reproach; but a *title* is always a mark of honor. An *appellation* is given to all objects, animate or inanimate; a *title* is given mostly to persons, sometimes to things. A particular house may have the *appellation* of "the Cottage," or "the Hall," as a particular person may have the *title* of Duke, Lord, or Marquis.

Denomination is to particular bodies what *appellation* is to an individual, namely, a term of distinction, drawn from their peculiar characters and circumstances. The Christian world is split into a number of different bodies or communities, under the *denominations* of Catholics, Protestants, Calvinists, Presbyterians, etc., which have their origin in the peculiar form of faith and discipline adopted by these bodies.

Name, Denominate, Style, Entitle, Designate, Characterize.—To *name* signifies simply to give a *name* to, or to address or specify by the given *name;* to *denominate* (from Latin *nomen*, name) is to give a specific *name* upon specific ground, to distinguish by the *name;* to *style*, from the noun *style* or manner (see DICTION), signifies to address by a specific *name;* to *entitle* is to give the specific or appropriate title. Adam *named* everything; we *denominate* the man who drinks excessively "a drunkard"; subjects *style* their monarch "His Majesty"; books are *entitled* according to the judgment of the author.

To *name, denominate, style,* and *entitle* are the acts of conscious agents only. To *designate*, signifying to mark out, and *characterize*, signifying to form a *characteristic*, are usually said only of things, and agree with the former only inasmuch as words may either *designate* or *characterize:* thus the word "capacity" is said to *designate* the power of holding; and "finesse" *characterizes* the people by whom it was adopted.

See also NOMINATE.

Name, Reputation, Repute, Credit.—*Name* is here taken in another sense for a name acquired in public by any peculiarity or quality in an object. *Reputation* and *repute*, from *reputo*, or *re*, back, and *putare*, to think, signifies the thinking of or the state of being thought of, or esteemed by, by the public. *Credit* signifies the state of being believed or trusted in general, from Latin *credere*, to believe or trust.

Name implies something more specific than *reputation;* and *reputation* something more substantial than *name;* a *name* may be acquired by some casualty or by some quality that has more show than worth; *reputation* is acquired only by time and built only on merit: a *name* may be arbitrarily given, simply by way of distinction; *reputation* is not given, but acquired, or follows as a consequence of one's honorable exertions. A physician sometimes gets a *name* by a single instance of professional skill, which by a combination of favorable circumstances he may convert to his own advantage in forming an extensive practice; but unless he have a commensurate degree of talent, this *name* will never ripen into a solid *reputation*.

Name and *reputation* are of a more extended nature than *repute* and *credit*. The *name* and *reputation* are given by the public at large; the *repute* and *credit* are acquired within a narrow circle. Strangers, or it may be distant countries, hear of the *name* and the *reputation* of anything; but only neighbors and those who have the means of personal observation can know its *repute* and *credit*. It is possible, therefore, to have a *name* and *reputation* without having *repute* and *credit*, and *vice versâ*, for the objects which constitute the former are sometimes different from those which produce the latter. A manufacturer has a *name* for the excellence of a particular article of his own manufacture a book has a *name* among would-be *connoisseurs* and pretenders to literature: a good writer, however, seeks to establish his *reputation* for genius, learning, industry, or some praiseworthy characteristic: a preacher is in high *repute* among those who attend him: a master gains great *credit* from the good performances of his scholars. There is also this distinction between *reputation* and *repute*, that *reputation* signifies the act of reputing or the state of being reputed, *repute* signifies only the state of being reputed.

Name and *repute* are taken either in a good or bad sense; *reputation* mostly, and *credit* always, are taken in the good sense only: a person or thing may get a good or an ill *name;* a person or thing may be in good or ill *repute; reputation* may rise to different degrees of height, or it may sink again into nothing; *credit* may likewise be high or low, but both *reputation* and *credit*, absolutely taken, imply that which is good.

NAP. See SLEEP.

NARRATION. See RELATION.

NARRATIVE. See ACCOUNT; RELATION.

NARROW. See CONTRACTED.

NATAL, NATIVE, INDIGENOUS. *Natal*, in Latin *natalis*, from *natus*, born, signifies belonging to one's birth, or the act of one's being born; but *native*, in Latin *nativus*, likewise from *natus*, signifies having an origin or beginning. *Indigenous*, in Latin *indigenus*, from *indu*, Old Latin, within, and *genitus*, born, signifies born in a given place.

The epithet *natal* is applied only to the circumstances of a man's birth, as his *natal* day; his *natal* hour; a *natal* song; a *natal* star. *Native* has a more extensive meaning, as it comprehends the idea of one's relationship by origin to an object; as one's *native* country, one's *native* soil, *native* village, or *native* place, *native* language, and the like.

Indigenous is a particular term used to denote the country where races of men are supposed to have first existed. It is also applied to plants in the same sense.

Native, Natural.—*Native* is to *natural* as a species to the genus: everything *native* is, according to its strict signification, *natural;* but many things are *natural* which are not *native*. Of a person we may say that his worth is *native*, to designate that it is some valuable property which is born with him, not foreign to him, or ingrafted upon his character; but we may say of his disposition that it is *natural*, as opposed to that which is acquired or otherwise. The former is mostly employed in a good sense, in opposition to what is artful, assumed, and unreal; the other is used in an indifferent sense, as opposed to whatever is the effect of habit or circumstances. When children display themselves with all their *native* simplicity, they are interesting objects of notice: when they display their *natural* turn of mind, it is not always that which tends to raise human nature in our esteem.

See also INTRINSIC.

Naturally, In Course, Consequently, Of Course.—The connection between events, actions, and things is expressed by all these terms. *Naturally* signifies according to the *nature* of things, and applies, therefore, to the connection which exists between events according to the original constitution or inherent properties of things: *in course* signifies *in the course* of things, that is, in the regular order that things ought to follow: *consequently* signifies by a *consequence*, that is, by a necessary law of dependence, which makes one thing follow another: *of course* signifies on account *of* the *course* which things most commonly or even necessarily take. Whatever happens *naturally* happens as it should do; whatever happens *in course,* or *in* due *course,* happens as we establish it: whatever follows *consequently* follows as we judge it logical; whatever follows *of course* follows as we expect it. Children *naturally* imitate their parents: people *naturally* fall into the habits of those they associate with: both these circumstances result from the *nature* of things: whoever is made a peer of the realm takes his seat in the upper house *in course;* he requires no other qualifications to entitle him to this privilege, he goes thither according to the established *course* of things; *consequently,* as a peer, he is admitted without question; this is a decision of the judgment by which the question is at once determined: *of course* none are admitted who are not peers; this results necessarily from the constituted law of the land.

NATION. See PEOPLE.

NATIONAL. See PUBLIC.

NATURALIZE, ACCLIMATE, ORIENT. These words all mean to become at home in a new country. But *naturalize,* from the very beginning when it was coined as French *natural-*iser, has meant to acquire the standing of a *natural*-born citizen, to be placed on the same footing before law as a *native* of the country. It is sometimes used with an extended application to refer to the adaptation of plants, etc., to a new country. *Acclimate* means to become accustomed to the *climate* of a new country. It may also be used figuratively in an extended sense to mean simply to become accustomed to. *Orient* is used as a verb to mean to adjust to new conditions—from French [*s'*]*orienter.* It referred originally to the placing of churches so that the altar was at the east (Latin *oriens,* the place of the rising sun); hence it came to mean to place with reference to the points of the compass; to get one's bearings.

NAUGHT. See ZERO.

NAUSEA. See DISGUST.

NAUTICAL. See MARITIME.

NAVAL. See MARITIME.

NEAR. See CLOSE.

NEAT. See TIDY.

NECESSARIES. See NECESSITIES.

NECESSARY, EXPEDIENT, ESSENTIAL, REQUISITE. For *necessary* see NECESSITY. *Expedient* comes from Latin *ex,* out, and *pedem* (accusative), foot, and signified originally taking the foot out, hence aiding movement and action. *Essential* means containing that essence or property which cannot be omitted, from Latin *essentia,* being, derived from a supposititious stem from *esse,* the infinitive of the verb to be. *Requisite* signifies literally required (see DEMAND).

Necessary is a general and indefinite term; things may be *necessary* in the course of nature; it is *necessary* for all men once to die; or things may be *necessary* according to the circumstances of the case, or our views of *necessity;* in this manner we conceive it *necessary* to call upon another. *Expedient, essential,* and *requisite* are modes of relative *necessity:* the *expediency* of a thing is a matter of discretion and calculation, and therefore not so self-evidently *necessary* as many things which we so denominate: it may be *expedient* for a person to consult another, or it may not, according as circumstances may present themselves. The *requisite* and the *essential* are more obviously *necessary* than the *expedient;* but the former is less so than the latter: what is *requisite* may be *requisite* only in part or entirely; it may be *requisite* to complete a thing when begun, but not to begin it; the *essential,* on the contrary, is that which constitutes the *essence,* and without which a thing cannot exist. It is *requisite* for one who would have a good library to select only the best authors; exercise is *essential* for the preservation of good health. In all matters of dispute it is *expedient* to be guided by some impartial judge; it is *requisite* for every member of the community to contribute his share to the public expenditure as far as he is able: it is *essential* to a teacher to know more than those he teaches.

Necessities, Necessaries. — *Necessity,* in Latin *necessitas,* and *necessary,* in Latin *necessarius,* from *necesse,* signify that which is indispensable. *Necessity* is the mode or state of circumstances or the thing which circumstances render *necessary;* the *necessary* is that which is absolutely and unconditionally *necessary.* Art has ever been busy in inventing things to supply the various *necessities* of our nature, and yet there are always numbers who want even the first *necessaries* of life. Habit and desire create *necessities;* nature only requires *necessaries:* a voluptuary has *necessities* which are unknown to a temperate man; the poor have in general little more than *necessaries.*

Necessity, Need. — *Necessity* (see NECESSARY). *Need* is in Anglo-Saxon *nied,* and is the native English word corresponding to the Latin word *necessitas.*

Necessity implies the thing wanted; *need* the condition of the person wanting. There would be no *necessity* for punishments if there were not evildoers; he is peculiarly fortunate who finds a friend in time of *need.* *Necessity* is more pressing than *need:* the former places one in a positive state of compulsion to act; it is said to have no law, it prescribes the law for itself; the latter yields to circumstances and leaves in a state of deprivation. We are frequently under the *necessity* of going without that of which we stand most in *need.*

From these two nouns arise two epithets for each, which are worthy of observation, namely, *necessary* and *needful, necessitous* and *needy.* *Necessary* and *needful* are both applicable to the thing wanted; *necessitous* and *needy* to the person wanting: *necessary* is applied to every object indiscriminately; *needful* only to such objects as supply temporary or partial wants. Exercise is *necessary* to preserve the health of the body; restraint is *necessary* to preserve that of the mind; assistance is *needful* for one who has not sufficient resources in himself: it is *necessary* to go by water to the Continent: money is *needful* for one who is travelling. The dissemination of knowledge is *necessary* to dispel the ignorance which would otherwise prevail in the world; it is *needful* for a young person to attend to the instructions of his teacher, if he wishes to improve.

Necessitous and *needy* are both applied to persons in want of something important; but *necessitous* may be employed to denote an occasional want, as to be in a *necessitous* condition in a foreign country for want of remittances from home; *needy* denotes a permanent state of want, as to be *needy* either from extravagance or misfortune.

NECESSITATE. See COMPEL.

NECROPOLIS, BURIAL - GROUND, CEMETERY, GRAVEYARD, MORTUARY. These words all indicate places where the dead are laid away. *Burial-ground* and *graveyard* are the native English terms; of these two *graveyard* is the more familiar word. It has more intimate and solemn associations than the analogous term *burial-ground.* We speak of the *burial-ground* of the Indians, for instance, in indicating an object of merely archæological interest. We speak of an English *graveyard* with some sympathetic realization of what it has meant to a community of people like ourselves. *Cemetery,* from Latin *cœmeterium,* Greek κοιμητήριον, a sleeping-place, is a term which has largely replaced the older term *graveyard* in ordinary speech now. Being a more modern and sophisticated term, it naturally has somewhat different connotations. We should speak of an old *burial-ground* in a little town as a *graveyard;* of the park-like *burial-grounds* in or near our cities as *cemeteries*. But this distinction is not always observed. *Necropolis*, from Greek νεκρός, dead, and πόλις, a city, means literally a city of the dead. It is a term applied to large and elaborate cemeteries near cities, or to burial-places of special dignity. *Mortuary*, from Latin *mortuus*, dead, is the term applied to a building or a room where dead bodies are kept for a time.

NEFARIOUS. See WICKED.

NEGLECT, OMIT. *Neglect* (see DISREGARD). *Omit*, in Latin *omitto*, or *ob* and *mitto*, signifies to put aside.

The idea of letting pass or slip, or of not using, is comprehended in the signification of both these terms; the former is, however, a culpable, the latter an indifferent action. What we *neglect* ought not to be *neglected:* but what we *omit* may be *omitted* or otherwise, as convenience requires.

These terms differ likewise in the objects to which they are applied; that is *neglected* which is practicable or serves for action; that is *omitted* which serves for intellectual purposes: we *neglect* an opportunity, we *neglect* the means, the time, the use, and the like; we *omit* a word, a sentence, a figure, a stroke, a circumstance, and the like.

Negligent, Remiss, Careless, Thoughtless, Heedless, Inattentive.—*Negligence* (see DISREGARD) and *remissness* concern the outward action: *careless, heedless, thoughtless,* and *inattentive* the state of mind.

Negligence and *remissness* consist in not doing what ought to be done; *carelessness* and the other mental defects may show themselves in doing wrong, as well as in not doing at all; *negligence* and *remissness* are, therefore, to *carelessness* and the others as the effect to the cause; for no one is so apt to be *negligent* and *remiss* as he who is *careless,* although *negligence* and *remissness* arise from other causes, and *carelessness, thoughtlessness,* etc., produce likewise other effects. *Negligent* is a stronger term than *remiss:* one is *negligent* in *neglecting* the thing that is expressly before one's eyes; one is *remiss* in forgetting that which was enjoined some time previously: the want of will renders a person *negligent;* the want of interest renders a person *remiss:* one is *negligent* in regard to business, and the *performance* of bodily labor; one is *remiss* in duty, or in such things as require mental exertion. Servants are commonly *negligent* in what concerns their master's interest; teachers are *remiss* in not correcting the faults of their pupils. *Negligence,* therefore, is the fault of persons of all descriptions, but particularly those in low condition; *remissness* is a fault peculiar to those in a more elevated station: a clerk in an office is *negligent* in not making proper memorandums; a magistrate, or the head of an institution, is *remiss* in the exercise of his authority to check irregularities.

Careless denotes the want of care in the manner of doing things; *thoughtless* denotes the want of thought or reflection about things; *heedless* denotes the want of heeding or regarding things; *inattentive* denotes the want of attention to things. One is *careless* only in trivial matters of behavior; one is *thoughtless* in matters of greater moment, in what concerns the conduct. *Carelessness* leads children to make mistakes in their mechanical exercises, in whatever they commit to memory or to paper; *thoughtlessness* leads many who are not children into serious errors of conduct, when they do not think of, or bear in mind, the consequences of their actions. *Thoughtless* is applied to things past, present, or to come; *careless* to things present or to come.

Careless is applied to such things as require permanent care; *thoughtless* to such as require permanent thought; *heedless* and *inattentive* are applied to passing objects that engage the senses or the thoughts of the moment. One is *careless* in business, *thoughtless* in conduct, *heedless* in walking or running, *inattentive* in listening: *heedless* children are unfit to go by themselves; *inattentive* children are unfit to be led by others.

NEGOTIATE, TREAT, TRANSACT. The idea of conducting business with others is included in the signification of all these terms; but they differ in the mode of conducting it and the nature of the business to be conducted *Negotiate,* from Latin *negotium* (from *neg*— for *ne*—not, and *otium,* leisure, signifying that which one does when one is not at leisure—*i. e.*, business), is applied in the original mostly to merchandise or traffic, but it is more commonly employed in the complicated concerns of governments and nations. *Treat*, from the Latin *tractare*, frequentative of *trahere*, to draw, signifies to turn over and over or set forth in all ways: these two verbs, therefore, suppose deliberation; but *transact*, from *transactus*, participle of *transago*, to carry forward or bring to an end, supposes more direct agency than consultation or deliberation; this latter is therefore adapted to the more ordinary and less entangled concerns of commerce. A congress carries on *negotiations* for the establishment of good order among different states; individual states *treat* with each other to settle their particular differences. To *negotiate* mostly applies to political concerns, except in the case of *negotiating* bills: to *treat*, as well as *transact*, is said of domestic and private concerns: we *treat* with a person about the purchase of a house, and *transact* our business with him by making good the purchase and paying down the money.

As nouns, *negotiation* expresses rather the act of deliberating than the thing deliberated: *treaty* includes the ideas of the terms proposed and the arrangement of those terms: *transaction* expresses the idea of something actually done and finished. *Negotiations* are sometimes very long pending before the preliminary terms are even proposed or any basis is defined; *treaties* of commerce are entered into by all civilized countries, in order to obviate misunderstandings and enable them to preserve an amicable intercourse; the *transactions* which daily pass in a great metropolis like that of London are of so multifarious a nature, and so infinitely numerous, that the bare contemplation of them fills the mind with astonishment. *Negotiations* are long or short; *treaties* are advantageous or the contrary; *transactions* are honorable or dishonorable.

See also TREAT.

NEIGHBORHOOD, VICINITY. *Neighborhood*, from *neighbor* (Anglo-Saxon *neah*, nigh, near, and *gebur* or *bur*, a husbandman, the same word as

Dutch *Boer*, English *boor*), signified originally the place near by where other farmers live. *Vicinity*, from *vicus*, a village, signifies the place which does not exceed in distance the extent of a village.

Neighborhood, which is of Saxon origin, is employed in reference to the inhabitants, or in regard to inhabited places, to denote nearness of persons to each other or to objects in general: but *vicinity*, which in Latin bears the same acceptation as *neighborhood*, is employed in English to denote nearness of one object to another, whether person or thing; hence the propriety of saying a populous *neighborhood*, a quiet *neighborhood*, a respectable *neighborhood*, a pleasant *neighborhood*, and to be in the *neighborhood*, either as it signifies the people or the country; but to live in the *vicinity* of a manufactory, to be in the *vicinity* of the metropolis or of the sea.

NEOPHYTE. See TYRO.

NEUTRAL, IMPARTIAL, INDIFFERENT. These words all indicate a disposition not to take sides in a quarrel, but they differ in the amount of sympathy for the combatants implied in them. *Indifferent* signified originally not making a distinction or difference between things—implying such a lack of sympathy or interest that one thing seems much like another. Here it indicates a lack of interest in either combatant. *Neutral*, from Latin *ne*, not, and *uter*, which of two, means not asking which is right. It implies complete intellectual detachment, but not necessarily lack of sympathy for one or both of the parties. It is the term applied to the non-combatant nations in time of war. *Impartial* means not taking the part of either side. By derivation it has the same meaning as the other words, but it implies distinct sympathy with one or both combatants, which is not allowed to influence judgment.

NEVERTHELESS. See HOWEVER.

NEW, NOVEL, MODERN, FRESH, RECENT. *New*, from Anglo-Saxon *neowe*, is the native English word corresponding to Latin *novus*, whence *novel* is derived. *Modern* signifies belonging to the present *mode*, from Latin *modus*, manner. *Fresh* is derived from a

Teutonic root which appears in Anglo-Saxon *fersc*, fresh; but its form is due to the feminine form of this same word in Old French—*freis*, masculine, *fresche*, feminine.

All these epithets are applied to what has not long existed; *new* expresses this idea simply without any qualification; *novel* is something strange or unexpected; the *modern* is the thing of to-day as distinguished from that which existed in former time; the *fresh* is that which is so *new* as not to be the worse for use, or that which has not been before used or employed; the *recent* is that which is so *new* as to appear as if it were just made or done. According to this distinction, *new* is most aptly applied to such things as may be permanent or durable, as *new* houses, *new* buildings, *new* clothes, and the like; in such cases it is properly opposed to the old; the term may, however, be applied generally to whatever arises or comes first into existence or notice, as *new* scenes, *new* sights, *new* sounds.

Novel may be applied to whatever is either never or but rarely seen; the freezing of the river Thames is a *novelty;* but the frost in every winter is something *new* when it first comes.

Modern is applied to that which is *new*, or springs up in the day or age in which we live; as *modern* books, *modern* writers, *modern* science; a book is *new* which is just formed into a book and has not been used; it is *modern* at the time when it is first published; so likewise principles are *new* which have never been broached before; they are *modern* if they have been published lately or within a given period: the *modern* is opposed to the ancient.

Fresh is said of that which may lose its color, vigor, or other perfection; as a *fresh* flower, the *freshness* of youth, etc.

So pleasures or passions are *fresh* which have not lost their power by satiety; they are *new* if they have but just sprung into activity.

Recent is applied to those events or circumstances which have just happened, as a *recent* transaction, or an occurrence of *recent* date.

News, Tidings.—*News* implies anything *new* that is related or circulated; *tidings*, in its Anglo-Saxon form, meant simply anything that happened; but it acquired the Scandinavian sense of *news*, especially *news* that arrived in due time and season, that is timely. *News* is unexpected; it serves to gratify idle curiosity: *tidings* are expected; they serve to allay anxiety. In time of war the public are eager for *news;* and they who have relatives in the army are anxious to have *tidings* of them.

NICE. See EXACT; FINE.

NIGGARDLY. See AVARICIOUS; ECONOMICAL.

NIGH. See CLOSE.

NIGHTLY, NOCTURNAL. *Nightly*, immediately from the word *night*, and *nocturnal*, from *nox*, night, signify belonging to the night, or the night season; the former is therefore more familiar than the latter: we speak of *nightly* depredations to express what passes every night, or *nightly* disturbances, *nocturnal* dreams, *nocturnal* visits.

NIHILIST. See INTRANSIGENT.

NIMBLE. See ACTIVE.

NINNY, NINCOMPOOP. These are slang or colloquial terms meaning a simpleton, and are not clearly distinguished from one another. *Ninny* comes probably from Italian *ninna*, a lullaby to put a child to sleep, based on *ninno*, child. The origin of *nincompoop* is supposed to be due to a vitiation of the Latin phrase *non compos mentis*. These words have been in the English language for centuries, but are so little differentiated from one another that it would be pedantry to make a distinction. Possibly *ninny* suggests more of silliness; *nincompoop* more of obtuseness, dulness.

NIP, BITE, PINCH. A *nip* is something between a *bite* and a *pinch*. In *biting* the substance taken between the teeth is cut; in *pinching*, which usually refers to a pressure upon a substance caught between two fingers or an instrument acting like the two fingers, it is simply bruised. To *nip* is to give a sharp, quick *pinch*.

NOBLE, GRAND. *Noble*, in Latin *nobilis*, from *nosco*, to know, signifying knowable, or worth knowing, is a term of general import; it simply implies the quality by which a thing is distinguished for excellence above other things: the *grand* (see GRANDEUR) is, properly speaking, one of those qualities by which an object acquires the name of *noble;* but there are many *noble* objects which are not denominated *grand.* A building may be denominated *noble* for its beauty as well as its size; but a *grand* building is rather so called for the expense which is displayed upon it in the style of building. A family may be either *noble* or *grand;* but it is *noble* by birth; it is *grand* by wealth and an expensive style of living. *Nobleness* of acting or thinking comprehends all moral excellence that rises to a high pitch; but *grandeur* of mind is peculiarly applicable to such actions or traits as denote an elevation of character, rising above all that is common.

NOCTURNAL. See NIGHTLY.

NOISE, CRY, OUTCRY, CLAMOR. *Noise* is any loud sound; *cry, outcry,* and *clamor* are particular kinds of *noises,* differing either in the cause or the nature of the sounds. A *noise* proceeds either from animate or inanimate objects; the *cry* proceeds only from animate objects. The report of a cannon and the loud sounds occasioned by a high wind are *noises,* but not *cries; cries* issue from birds, beasts, and men. A *noise* is produced often by accident; a *cry* is always occasioned by some particular circumstance: when many horses and carriages are going together they make a great *noise;* hunger and pain cause *cries* to proceed both from animals and human beings. *Noise,* when compared with *cry,* is sometimes only an audible sound; the *cry* is a very loud *noise;* whatever disturbs silence, as the proverbial falling of a pin in a perfectly still assembly, is denominated a *noise;* but a *cry* is that which may often drown other *noises,* as the *cries* of people selling things about the streets.

A *cry* is in general a definite sound, but *outcry* and *clamor* are irregular sounds; the former may proceed from one or many, the latter from many in conjunction. A *cry* after a thief becomes an *outcry* when set up by many at a time; it becomes a *clamor* if accompanied with shouting, bawling, and *noises* of a mixed and tumultuous nature.

These terms may all be taken in an improper as well as a proper sense. Whatever is obtruded upon the public notice, so as to become the universal subject of conversation and writing, is said colloquially to make a *noise;* in this manner a new and good performer at the theatre makes a *noise* on his first appearance.

A *noise* may be either for or against; but a *cry, outcry,* and *clamor* are always against the object, varying in the degree and manner in which they display themselves: *cry* implies less than *outcry,* and this less than *clamor.* When the public voice is raised in an audible manner against any particular matter it is a *cry;* if it be mingled with intemperate language it is an *outcry;* if it be vehement and exceedingly noisy it is a *clamor:* partisans raise a *cry* in order to form a body in their favor; the discontented are ever ready to set up an *outcry* against men in power; a *clamor* for peace in time of war is easily raised by those who wish to thwart the government.

NOISOME. See HURTFUL.

NOISY. See LOUD.

NOMENCLATURE. See DICTIONARY.

NOMINATE, NAME. *Nominate* comes from Latin *nomen,* name; *name* (see NAME). To *nominate* and to *name* are both to mention by *name;* but the former is to mention for a specific purpose; the latter is to mention for a general purpose: persons only are *nominated;* things as well as persons are *named:* one *nominates* a person in order to propose him, or appoint him, to an office; but one *names* a person casually, in the course of conversation, or one *names* him in order to make some inquiry respecting him. To be *nominated* is a public act; to be *named* is generally private: one is *nominated* before an assembly; one is *named* in any place: to be *nominated* is always an honor; to be *named* is either honorable or the contrary, according to the circumstances under which it is mentioned: a person is *nominated* for an office; he is *named* whenever he is spoken of.

NON-CONFORMIST. See HERETIC.

NON-PUTREFYING. See ASEPTIC.

NONSENSE. See TWADDLE.

NORMAL, TYPICAL. *Normal* and *typical* are both words which are commonly misused. They are taken to mean *average, ordinary,* whereas they really mean the reverse. The *normal* person is one that conforms to the *norm,* Latin *norma,* a carpenter's rule; that is to say, to the standard of humanity in any or all respects. This *standard,* how ver, is not obtained by taking the a rage of all people. As is shown by the medical standard in accordance with which the candidates for the army are tested, only one in four or five men corresponds sufficiently to the standard. *Normal* indicates what people would be if their development were not in any way hindered. *Typical,* from Greek τύπος, a mark, blow, stamp, has the same meaning as *normal,* with a slight difference of connotation in ordinary usage. A *typical* man is one who represents the standard to which others approximate more or less. The *typical* American is not the average or ordinary American. He is the one who represents the distinctive characteristics of Americans in their most characteristic form. *Normal* is generally used with reference to a particular standard—a standard of health, for instance. *Typical* is used with reference to distinguishing characteristics. A *normal* physique, for instance, is one that corresponds to the general standard, one that every one ought to have. A *typical* soldier's physique is one that represents the characteristics of the soldier unmodified by other influences.

NOTE. See MARK.

NOTED. NOTORIOUS. *Noted* (see DISTINGUISHED) may be employed either in a good or a bad sense; *notorious* is never used but in a bad sense: men may be *noted* for their talents or their eccentricities; they are *notorious* for their vices: *noted* characters excite many and divers remarks from their friends and their enemies; *notorious* characters are universally shunned.

NOTHING. See ZERO.

NOTICE, REMARK, OBSERVE. To *notice* (see ATTEND) is either to tal e or to give *notice*: to *remark,* compounded of *re* and *mark* (see MARK), signifies to reflect or bring back any *mark* to our own mind, or communicate the same to another; to *mark* is to *mark* a thing once, but to *remark* is to *mark* it again. *Observe* (see LOOKER-ON) signifies either to keep a thing present before one's own view or to communicate one's view to another.

In the first sense of these words, as the action concerns ourselves, to *notice* and *remark* require simple attention, to *observe* requires examination. To *notice* is a more cursory action than to *remark:* we may *notice* a thing by a single glance, or on merely turning our head; but to *remark* supposes a reaction of the mind on an object; we *notice* a person passing at any time; but we *remark* that he goes past every day at the same hour: we *notice* that the sun sets this evening under a cloud, and we *remark* that it has done so for several evenings successively: we *notice* the state of a person's health or his manners in company; we *remark* his habits and peculiarities in domestic life. What is *noticed* and *remarked* strikes on the senses and awakens the mind; what is *observed* is looked after and sought for: the former are often involuntary acts; we see, hear, and think because the objects obtrude themselves uncalled for; but the latter is intentional as well as voluntary; we see, hear, and think of that which we have watched. We *remark* things as matters of fact; we *observe* them in order to judge of them or draw conclusions from them: we *remark* that the wind lies for a long time in a certain quarter; we *observe* that whenever it lies in a certain quarter it brings rain with it. People who have no particular curiosity may be sometimes attracted to *notice* the stars or planets when they are particularly bright; those who look frequently will *remark* that the same star does not rise exactly in the same place for two successive nights; but the astronomer goes further and *observes* all the motions of the heavenly bodies, in order to discover the scheme of the universe.

In the latter sense of these words, as concerns the communications to others of what passes in our own minds, to *notice* is to make known our sentiments by various ways; to *remark* and *observe* are to make them known only by means of words: to *notice* is a personal act toward an individual, in which we direct our attention to him, as may happen either by a bow, a nod, a word, or even a look; but to *remark* and *observe* are said only of the thoughts which pass in our own minds and are expressed to others: friends *notice* each other when they meet; they *remark* to others the impression which passing objects make upon their minds: the *observations* which intelligent people make are always entitled to *notice* from young persons.

See also INFORMATION; MENTION.

NOTION. See CONCEPTION; OPINION; PERCEPTION.

NOTORIOUS. See NOTED; PUBLIC.

NOTWITHSTANDING. See HOWEVER.

NOURISH, NURTURE, CHERISH. To *nourish* and *nurture* are but variations from the same verb *nutrio*. *Cherish* (see FOSTER). Things *nourish*, persons *nurture* and *cherish:* to *nourish* is to build up bodily strength to supply the physical necessities of the body; to *nurture* is to extend one's care to the supply of all its physical necessities, to preserve life, occasion growth, and increase vigor: the breast of the mother *nourishes;* the fostering care and attention of the mother *nurtures.* To *nurture* is a physical act; to *cherish* is a mental as well as a physical act: a mother *nurtures* her infant while it is entirely dependent upon her; she *cherishes* her child in her bosom and protects it from every misfortune, or affords consolation in the midst of all its troubles when it is no longer an infant.

NOVEL. See FABLE; NEW.

NOVICE. See TYRO.

NOW, IMMEDIATELY, STRAIGHTWAY.

Now is the general term, meaning at this present moment. *Immediately* suggests more of emphasis and action. It means in the moment following a given moment. *Now* is static; *immediately* suggests action, movement. *Straightway* has the same meaning as *immediately,* but a slightly different connotation. It is a somewhat archaic word associated with Biblical phraseology, and suggestive of poetry or a distinctly literary style.

NOXIOUS. See HURTFUL.

NUMB, BENUMBED, TORPID. *Numb* and *benumbed* come from the past participle of Anglo-Saxon *niman,* Middle English *nomen,* to take, and signify overtaken, hence overpowered, unable to move. There are but few things *numb* by nature, but there may be many things which may be *benumbed. Torpid,* in Latin *torpidus,* from *torpere,* to languish, is most commonly employed to express the permanent state of being *benumbed,* as in the case of some animals, which lie in a *torpid* state all the winter; or, in the moral sense, to depict the *benumbed* state of the thinking faculty; in this manner we speak of the *torpor* of persons who are *benumbed* by any strong affection or by any strong external action.

NUMBER. See RECKON.

NUMERAL, NUMERICAL. *Numeral,* or belonging to number, is applied to a class of words in grammar, as a *numeral* adjective or a *numeral* noun: *numerical,* or containing number, is applied to whatever may concern number; as a *numerical* difference, where the difference consists between any two numbers or is expressed by numbers.

NUPTIALS. See MARRIAGE.

NURTURE. See NOURISH.

O

OBEDIENT, SUBMISSIVE, OBSE-QUIOUS. *Obedient* (see DUTIFUL). *Submissive* denotes the disposition to submit (see YIELD). *Obsequious*, in Latin *obsequius*, from *obsequor*, or the intensive of *ob*, near, and *sequi*, to follow, signifies following diligently and with a fixed intention to please.

One is *obedient* to command, *submissive* to power or the will, *obsequious* to persons. *Obedience* is always taken in a good sense; one ought always to be *obedient* where *obedience* is due: *submission* is relatively good; it may, however, be indifferent or bad: one may be *submissive* from interested motives or meanness of spirit, which is a base kind of *submission;* but to be *submissive* for conscience' sake is the bounden duty of a Christian: *obsequiousness* is never good; it is an excessive concern about the will of another which has always interest for its end. *Obedience* is a course of conduct conformable either to some specific rule or the express will of another; *submission* is often a personal act immediately directed to the individual. We show our *obedience* to the law by avoiding the breach of it; we show our *obedience* to the will of God, or of our parent, by making that will the rule of our life: on the other hand, we show *submission* to the person of the magistrate; we adopt a *submissive* deportment by a downcast look and a bent body. *Obedience* is founded upon principle and cannot be feigned; *submission* is a partial bending to another, which is easily affected in our outward behavior: the understanding and the heart produce *obedience;* but force or the necessity of circumstances gives rise to *submission*.

Obedience and *submission* suppose a restraint on one's own will, in order to bring it into accordance with that of another; but *obsequiousness* is the consulting the will or pleasure of another; we are *obedient* from a sense of right; we are *submissive* from a sense of necessity; we are *obsequious* from a desire of gaining favor: a love of God is followed by *obedience* to His will; they are coincident sentiments that reciprocally act on each other so as to serve the cause of virtue: a *submissive* conduct is at the worst an involuntary sacrifice of our independence to our fears or necessities, the evil of which is confined principally to the individual who makes the sacrifice; *obsequiousness* is a voluntary sacrifice of ourselves to others for interested purposes.

OBJECT, SUBJECT. *Object*, in Latin *objectus*, participle of *obicere*, to lie in the way, signifies the thing that lies in one's way. *Subject*, in Latin *subjectus*, participle of *subicere*, to lie under, signifies the thing forming the groundwork.

The *object* puts itself forward; the *subject* is in the background: we notice the *object;* we observe or reflect on the *subject: objects* are sensible; the *subject* is altogether intellectual: the eye, the ear, and all the senses are occupied with the surrounding *objects;* the memory, the judgment, and the imagination are supplied with *subjects* suitable to the nature of the operations.

When *object* is taken for that which is intellectual, it retains a similar signification; it is the thing that presents itself to the mind; it is seen by the mind's eye: the *subject*, on the contrary, is that which must be sought for, and when found it engages the mental powers: hence we say an *object* of consideration, an *object* of delight, an *object* of concern; a *subject* of reflection, a *subject* of mature deliberation, the *subject* of a poem, the *subject* of grief, of lamentation, and the like. When the mind becomes distracted by too great a multiplicity of *objects*, it can fix itself on no one individual *object* with sufficient steadiness to take a survey of it; in like manner, if a child have too many *objects* set before it for the exercise of its powers, it will acquire a familiarity with none: such things are not fit *subjects* of discussion. See also AIM; FIND FAULT.

Object, Oppose.—To *object* is to cast in the way, to *oppose*, from French *opposer* (Latin *ob*, against, and Late Latin *pausare*, to place, formed on Greek πάυσις, pause), is to place in the way; there is, therefore, very little original difference, except that casting is a more momentary and sudden proceeding, placing is a more premeditated action; which distinction, at the same time, corresponds with the use of the terms in ordinary life: to *object* to a thing is to propose or start something against it; but to *oppose* it is to set one's self steadily against it: one *objects* to ordinary matters that require no reflection; one *opposes* matters that call for deliberation and afford serious reasons for and against: a parent *objects* to his child's learning the classics or to his running about the streets; he *opposes* his marriage when he thinks the connection or the circumstances not desirable.

Objection, Difficulty, Exception.—*Objection* (see DEMUR) is here a general term; it comprehends both the *difficulty* and the *exception*, which are but species of the *objection*: an *objection* and a *difficulty* are started; an *exception* is made: the *objection* to a thing is in general that which renders it less desirable; but the *difficulty* is that which renders it less practicable; there is an *objection* against every scheme which incurs a serious risk: the want of means to begin or resources to carry on a scheme is a serious *difficulty*.

Objection and *exception* both concern the nature, the moral tendency, or moral consequence of a thing; but an *objection* may be frivolous or serious; an *exception* is something serious: the *objection* is positive; the *exception* is relatively considered, that is, the thing *excepted* from other things, as not good, and consequently *objected* to. *Objections* are made sometimes to proposals for the mere sake of getting rid of an engagement: those who do not wish to give themselves trouble find an easy method of disengaging themselves, by making *objections* to every proposition. We take *exception* at the conduct of others when we think it not sufficiently respectful.

OBJECTIVE, ACTUAL. *Objective* signifies outside of consciousness, belonging to that which is presented to consciousness, as opposed to consciousness itself. *Actual*, based on *actus*, past participle of Latin *agere*, to do or act, signifies really existing as distinguished from an idea in the mind—that which is as compared with what we should like to have it. According to these definitions, the two terms seem to have the same meaning, but *objective* is much more limited in its application than *actual*. That which is *objective* is simply outside of ourselves; that which is *actual* is that which really exists. Though, in one sense, *actual* implies that contrast between the thing beheld and the mind beholding indicated in *objective*, that which is within the mind may also be thought of as *actual*. We speak of "my *actual* thought," "my *actual* feeling"—implying a contrast between reality and unreality within the mind itself. Again that which is *objective* is not necessarily *actual* or really existent—as a whole school of philosophers have pointed out. In common speech *actual* is a word of frequent and various uses; *objective* is a rather special and scientific term.

OBLATION. See OFFERING.

OBLIGATION. See DUTY.

OBLIGE. See BIND; COMPEL.

OBLIGED. See INDEBTED.

OBLIGING. See CIVIL.

OBLITERATE. See BLOT.

OBLIVION. See FORGETFULNESS.

OBLONG, OVAL. *Oblong*, in Latin *oblongus*, from the intensive syllable *ob*, across, or over, signifies very long, longer than it is broad. *Oval*, from the Latin *ovum*, an egg, signifies egg-shaped. The *oval* is a species of the *oblong*: what is *oval* is *oblong*; but what is *oblong* is not always *oval*. *Oblong* is peculiarly applied to figures formed by right lines, that is, all rectangular parallelograms, except squares, are *oblong*; but the *oval* is applied to curvilinear *oblong* figures, as ellipses, which are distinguished from the circle: tables are oftener *oblong* than *oval*; garden beds are as frequently *oval* as they are *oblong*.

OBLOQUY. See REPROACH.

OBNOXIOUS, OFFENSIVE. *Obnoxious*, from *ob*, against, or in the way of, and *noxious*, signifies either being in the way of what is noxious or being very noxious or hateful. *Offensive,* from *ob,* against, and a stem *fend,* meaning to dash, signifies apt to give offence or displeasure. The *obnoxious* conveys more than the *offensive,* implying (though this use is now obsolete) to receive as well as to give offence; a man may be *obnoxious* to evils as well as *obnoxious* to persons.

In the sense of giving offence, *obnoxious* implies as much as hateful, *offensive* little more than displeasing: a man is *obnoxious* to a party to whose interests or principles he is opposed; he may be *offensive* to an individual merely on account of his manners or any particular actions. Men are *obnoxious* only to their fellow-creatures, but they may be *offensive,* though not *obnoxious,* to their Maker.

Persons only are *obnoxious* to others, things as well as persons are *offensive;* dust is *offensive* to the eye; sounds are *offensive* to the ear; advice, or even one's own thoughts, may be *offensive* to the mind.

See also SUBJECT.

OBSCURE. See DARK; ECLIPSE.

OBSEQUIES. See FUNERAL.

OBSEQUIOUS. See OBEDIENT.

OBSERVANCE. See FORM; OBSERVATION.

OBSERVANT. See MINDFUL.

OBSERVATION, OBSERVANCE. These terms derive their use from the different significations of the verb: *observation* is the act of observing objects with the view to examine them (see NOTICE): *observance* is the act of observing in the sense of keeping or holding sacred (see KEEP). From a minute *observation* of the human body, anatomists have discovered the circulation of the blood and the source of all the humors; by a strict *observance* of truth and justice a man acquires the title of an upright man.

See also REMARK.

Observe, Watch. — *Observe* (see GUARD). *Watch* (see NOTICE).

These terms agree in expressing the act of looking at an object; but to *observe* is not to look after so strictly as is implied by to *watch;* a general *observes* the motions of an enemy when they are in no particular state of activity; he *watches* the motions of an enemy when they are in a state of commotion; we *observe* a thing in order to draw an inference from it: we *watch* anything in order to discover what may happen: we *observe* with coolness; we *watch* with eagerness: we *observe* carefully; we *watch* narrowly: the conduct of mankind in general is *observed;* the conduct of suspicious individuals is *watched.*

See also KEEP; NOTICE; SEE.

OBSERVER. See LOOKER-ON.

OBSOLETE. See OLD.

OBSTACLE. See DIFFICULTY.

OBSTINATE, CONTUMACIOUS, STUBBORN, HEADSTRONG, HEADY. *Obstinate,* in Latin *obstinatus,* participle of *obstino,* from *ob* and the stem found in *stare,* to stand, signifies standing in the way of another. *Contumacious* (see CONTUMACY). *Stubborn,* Middle English *stoburn,* comes from Anglo-Saxon *stybb,* Modern English *stub,* and signified originally like a stick or stub remaining in the ground; hence not easily moved. *Headstrong* signifies strong in the head or the mind; and *heady,* inclined, so to speak, to follow one's own head.

Obstinacy is a habit of the mind; *contumacy* is either a particular state of feeling or a mode of action; *obstinacy* consists in an attachment to one's own mode of acting; *contumacy* consists in contempt of others: the *obstinate* man adheres tenaciously to his own ways, and opposes reason to reason; the *contumacious* man disputes the right of another to control his actions, and opposes force to force. *Obstinacy* interferes with a man's private conduct and makes him blind to reason; *contumacy* is an offence against lawful authority; the *contumacious* man sets himself against his superiors: when young people are *obstinate* they are recalcitrant to education; when grown people are *contumacious* they are troublesome subjects to the king.

The *stubborn* and the *headstrong* are species of the *obstinate:* the former lies altogether in the perversion of the will; the latter in the perversion of the judgment: the *stubborn* person wills what he wills; the *headstrong* person thinks what he thinks. *Stubbornness* is mostly inherent in a person's nature; a *headstrong* temper is commonly associated with violence and impetuosity of character. *Obstinacy* discovers itself in persons of all ages and stations; a *stubborn* and *headstrong* disposition betrays itself mostly in those who are expected to conform to the will of another. *Heady* may be said of any who are full of conceit and bent upon following their own desires.

OBSTRUCT. See HINDER.

OBTAIN. See ACQUIRE; GET.

OBTRUDE. See INTRUDE.

OBTUSE, BLUNT, DULL. All these words have the same original meaning; they are all opposed to sharp. *Obtuse* is the opposite of the sharp point of an angle of less than forty-five degrees; *blunt* (of unknown origin) is the opposite of a sharp point; *dull* is the opposite of a sharp edge, such as the blade of a knife. *Dull* and *obtuse* are also given a mental application (see DULL), *obtuse* referring to particular cases of *dulness*, not to the general character indicated by *dull*. *Blunt* has a moral application, referring to the manners and disposition of one who is not finely responsive or adaptable to the feelings and conditions of those around him, who offends by rude telling of unsavory truth, etc.

OBVIATE. See PREVENT.

OBVIOUS. See APPARENT; TANGIBLE.

OCCASION, OPPORTUNITY. *Occasion*, in Latin *occasio*, from *obcasio*, from *ob*, in the way of, and *cadere*, to fall, signifies that which falls in the way so as to produce some change. *Opportunity*, in Latin *opportunitas*, from *opportunus* (*ob*, near, and *portus*, harbor), signifies near the harbor or in accordance with the desires or needs.

These terms are applied to the events of life; but the *occasion* is that which determines our conduct and leaves us no choice; it amounts to a degree of necessity: the *opportunity* is that which invites to action; it tempts us to embrace the moment for taking the step. We do things, therefore, as the *occasion* requires, or as the *opportunity* offers. There are many *occasions* on which a man is called upon to uphold his opinions. There are but few *opportunities* for men in general to distinguish themselves.

Occasion, Necessity. — *Occasion* includes, *necessity* excludes, the idea of

choice or alternative. We are regulated by the *occasion*, and can exercise our own discretion; we yield or submit to the *necessity*, without even the exercise of the will. On the death of a relative we have *occasion* to go into mourning if we do not wish to offer an affront to the family; but there is no express *necessity*: in case of an attack on our persons there is a *necessity* of self-defence for the preservation of life.

Occasional, Casual.—These are both opposed to what is fixed or stated; but *occasional* carries with it more the idea of infrequency, and *casual* that of unfixedness, or the absence of all design. A minister is termed an *occasional* preacher who preaches only on certain *occasions;* his preaching at a particular place or on a certain day may be *casual*. Our acts of charity may be *occasional*, but they ought not to be *casual*.

OCCULT. See SECRET.

OCCUPANCY, OCCUPATION. These words derive their meaning from the different acceptations of the primitive verb *occupy*, the former being used to express the state of holding or possessing any object, the latter to express the act of taking possession of, or the state of being in possession. He who has the *occupancy* of land enjoys the fruits of it: the *occupation* of a country by force of arms is of little avail unless one has an adequate force to maintain one's ground. Both words are employed in regard to houses and lands, but when the term *occupation* is taken in the sense of a business it is sufficiently distinguished to need no illustration.

See also BUSINESS.

OCCUPY. See HOLD.

OCCUR. See TRANSPIRE.

OCCURRENCE. See EVENT.

ODD, UNEVEN. *Odd,* in Swedish *udda,* connected with the Dutch *oed,* and German *oede,* empty, deserted, signifying something wanted to match, seems to be a mode of the *uneven;* both are opposed to the even, but *odd* is said only of that which has no fellow; the *uneven* is said of that which does not square or come to an even point: of numbers we say that they are either *odd* or *uneven;* but of gloves, shoes, and everything which is made to correspond we say that they are *odd* when they are *single*; but that they are *uneven* when they are both different: in like manner, a plank is *uneven* which has an unequal surface or disproportionate dimensions; but a piece of wood is *odd* which will not match or suit with any other piece.

See also PARTICULAR.

ODIOUS. See HATEFUL.

ODOR. See SMELL.

OFFENCE, TRESPASS, TRANSGRESSION, MISDEMEANOR, MISDEED, AFFRONT. *Offence* is here the general term, signifying merely the act that *offends* (see DISPLEASE) or runs counter to something else.

Offence is properly indefinite; it merely implies an object without the least suggestion of the nature of the object; *trespass* and *transgression* have a positive reference to an object *trespassed* upon or *transgressed; trespass* is contracted from *trans* and *pass* (from Latin *passus*, step), that is, a stepping beyond; and *transgress*, from *trans* and *gressus* (participle of *gredi*), a going beyond. The *offence*, therefore, which constitutes a *trespass* arises out of the laws of property; a passing over or treading upon the property of another is a *trespass:* the *offence* which constitutes a *transgression* derives from the laws of society in general, which fix the boundaries of right and wrong: whoever, therefore, goes beyond or breaks through these bounds is guilty of a *transgression.* The *trespass* is a species of *offence* which peculiarly applies to the land or premises of individuals; *transgression* is a species of moral as well as political evil. Hunters are apt to commit *trespass* in the eagerness of their pursuit; the passions of men are perpetually misleading them and causing them to commit various *transgressions;* the term *trespass* is sometimes employed improperly as regards time and other objects; *transgression* is always used in one uniform sense as regards rule and law; we *trespass* upon the time or patience of another; we *transgress* the moral or civil law.

An *offence* is either public or private; a *misdemeanor,* the negative of *demeanor,* is a coined word from French *de,* Latin *de,* intensive, and French *mener,* to conduct—ultimately from Late Latin *minare,* to drive cattle, from *minari,* to threaten—so that the word meant successively to drive with threats, to lead or conduct, to conduct one's self, and hence came to refer to manners and action. *Misdemeanor* is properly a private *offence,* although improperly applied for an *offence* against public law, for it signifies a wrong *demeanor* or an *offence* in one's *demeanor* against propriety; a *misdeed* is always private, it signifies a wrong *deed,* or a *deed* which *offends* against one's duty. *Riotous* and disorderly behavior in company are serious *misdemeanors;* every act of drunkenness, lying, fraud, or immorality of every kind, is a *misdeed.*

An *offence* is that which affects persons or principles, communities or individuals, and is committed either directly or indirectly against the person; an *affront* (from *ad,* to, and *frontem,* brow) is altogether personal, and is made directly in the presence of the person affronted; it is an *offence* against another to speak disrespectfully of him in his absence; it is an *affront* to push past him with violence and rudeness. In this sense, whatever *offence* is committed against our Maker is properly an *affront;* and whatever *offends* Him indirectly may also be denominated an *affront,* as far as His will is opposed and His laws violated.

Offender, Delinquent.—The *offender* is he who *offends* in anything, either by commission or omission; the *delinquent* (from *delinquere,* to fail) signifies properly he who fails by omission, but it is extended to signify failing by the violation of a law. Those who go into a wrong place are *offenders;* those who stay away when they ought to go are *delinquents:* there are many *offenders* against the Sabbath who commit violent and open breaches of decorum; there are still more *delinquents* who never attend a public place of worship.

Offending, Offensive.—*Offending* signifies either actually *offending* or calculated to *offend; offensive* signifies calculated to *offend* at all times; a person may be *offending* in his manners to a particular individual, or use an *offending* expression on a particular occasion

without any imputation on his character; but if his manners are *offensive*, it reflects both on his temper and education.
See also OBNOXIOUS; UMBRAGE.

OFFER, BID, TENDER, PROPOSE. *Offer* (see GIVE) is employed for that which is literally transferable, or for that which is indirectly communicable: *bid* (see ASK) and *tender*, like the word *tend*, from *tendere*, to stretch, signifying to stretch forth by way of *offering*, belong to *offer* in the first sense. *Propose*, from French *proposer*, Latin *pro*, before, and French *poser*, to place (from Late Latin *pausare*, Greek παῦσις, *not* from Latin *ponere*), to place or set before, likewise characterizes a mode of *offering*, and belongs to *offer* in the latter sense. To *offer* is a voluntary and discretionary act; an *offer* may be accepted or rejected at pleasure; to *bid* and *tender* are specific modes of *offering* which depend on circumstances: one *bids* with the hope that one's offer will be accepted; one *tenders* from a prudential motive and in order to serve specific purposes. We *offer* money to a poor person as an act of charity or good-nature; we *bid* a price for the purchase of a house, as a commercial dealing subject to the rules of commerce; we *tender* a sum of money by way of payment, as a matter of discretion in order to fulfil an obligation. By the same rule one *offers* a person the use of one's horse; one *bids* a sum at an auction; one *tenders* one's services to the government.

To *offer* and *propose* are both employed in matters of practice or speculation; but the former is a less definite and decisive act than the latter; we *offer* an opinion by way of promoting a discussion; we *propose* a plan for the deliberation of others. Sentiments which differ widely from the major part of those present ought to be *offered* with modesty and caution; we should not *propose* to another what we would be unwilling to do ourselves. We commonly *offer* by way of obliging; we commonly *propose* by way of arranging or accommodating. It is an act of puerility to *offer* to do more than one is enabled to perform; it does not evince a sincere disposition for peace to *propose* such terms as we know cannot be accepted.

Offering, Oblation. — *Offering*, from *offer*, and *oblation*, from *oblatio* and *oblatus*, come both from *offero*, the one from the infinitive, the other from the past participle. The former is, however, a term of much more general and familiar use than the latter. *Offerings* are both moral and religious; *oblation* is religious only; the money which is put into the sacramental plate is an *offering;* the consecrated bread and wine at the sacrament are an *oblation*. The *offering* in a religious sense is whatever one *offers* as a gift by way of reverence to a superior; the *oblation* is the *offering* which is accompanied with some particular ceremony. The wise men made an *offering* to our Saviour, but not properly an *oblation;* the Jewish sacrifices, as in general all religious sacrifices, were in the proper sense *oblations*.

OFF-HAND. See UNPREMEDITATED.

OFFICE, PLACE, CHARGE, FUNCTION. *Office*, in Latin, *officium*, from *officio*, signifies either the duty performed or the situation in which the duty is performed. *Place* comprehends no idea of duty, for there may be sinecure *places* which are only nominal *offices* and designate merely a relationship with the government: every *office*, therefore, of a public nature is in reality a *place*, yet every *place* is not an *office*. The *place* of secretary of state is likewise an *office*, but that of ranger of a park is a *place* only, and not always an *office*. An *office* is held; a *place* is filled: the *office* is given or intrusted to a person; the *place* is granted or conferred: the *office* reposes a confidence and imposes a responsibility; the *place* gives credit and influence: the *office* is bestowed on a man from his qualification; the *place* is granted to him by favor or as a reward for past services; the *office* is more or less honorable; the *place* is more or less profitable.

In an extended application of the terms *office* and *place*, the latter has a much lower signification than that of the former, since the *office* is always connected with the state or is something responsible; but the *place* may be a *place* for menial labor: the *offices* are multiplied in time of war; the *places* for domestic service are more numerous in a state of peace and prosperity. The *office* is frequently taken not with any reference to the *place* occupied, but simply to the thing done; this brings it nearer in signification to the term *charge* (see CARE). An *office* imposes a task or some performance: a *charge* imposes a responsibility; we have always something to do in an *office*, always something to look after in a *charge;* the *office* is either public or private, the *charge* is always of a private and personal nature: a person performs the *office* of a magistrate or of a minister; he undertakes the *charge* of instructing youth or of being a guardian, or of conveying a person's property from one place to another.

The *office* is that which is assigned by another; *function* is properly the act of discharging or completing an *office* or business, from *functus,* participle of *fungor, viz., finem* and *ago,* to put an end to or bring to a conclusion; it is extended in its acceptation to the office itself or the thing done. In its strict sense, therefore, the *office* is performed only by conscious or intelligent agents who act according to their instructions; the *function,* on the other hand, is an operation either of unconscious or of conscious agents acting according to a given rule. The *office* of a herald is to proclaim public events or to communicate circumstances from one public body to another: a minister performs his *functions,* or the body performs its *functions.*

The word *office* is sometimes employed in the same application by the personification of nature, which assigns an *office* to the ear, to the tongue, to the eye, and the like. In this case the word *office* is applied to what is occasional or partial; *function* to that which is habitual and essential. When the frame becomes overpowered by a sudden shock, the tongue will frequently refuse to perform its *office;* when the animal *functions* are impeded for a length of time, the vital power ceases to exist.

See also BUSINESS.

OFFICIOUS. See ACTIVE.

OFFSPRING, PROGENY, ISSUE. *Offspring* is that which springs from; *progeny,* that which is brought forth or out of; *issue,* that which *issues* or proceeds from; all used in relation to the family or generation of the human species. *Offspring* is a familiar term applicable to one or many children; *progeny* is employed only as a collective noun for a number; *issue* is used in an indefinite manner without particular regard to number. When we speak of the children themselves we denominate them the *offspring;* when we speak of the parents, we denominate the children their *progeny.* A child is said to be the only *offspring* of his parents, or he is said to be the *offspring* of low parents; a man is said to have a numerous or a healthy *progeny,* or to leave his *progeny* in circumstances of honor and prosperity. The *issue* is said only in regard to a man that is deceased: he dies with male or female *issue,* with or without *issue;* his property descends to his male *issue* in a direct line.

OFTEN, FREQUENTLY. *Often,* or its contracted form *oft,* is an English word of unknown origin. *Frequently,* from Latin *frequens,* crowded or numerous, signifies a plurality or number of objects.

An ignorant man *often* uses a word without knowing what it means; ignorant people *frequently* mistake the meaning of the words they hear. A person goes out very *often* in the course of a week; he has *frequently* six or seven persons to visit him in the course of that time. By doing a thing *often* it becomes habitual: we *frequently* meet the same persons in the route which we *often* take.

OLD, ANCIENT, ANTIQUE, ANTIQUATED, OLD-FASHIONED, OBSOLETE. *Old,* in Anglo-Saxon *eald,* is perhaps from a root signifying to nourish, found in the word *alma,* fostering, in our phrase *alma mater. Ancient,* in French *ancien,* Late Latin *antianus* and *antique, antiquatus,* all come from the Latin *ante,* before, signifying in general before our time. *Old-fashioned* signifies after an *old fashion. Obsolete* comes from the Latin verb *obsolescere,* to decay.

Old signifies what has long existed and still exists; *ancient,* what existed at a distant period, but does not necessarily exist at present; *antique,* that which has been long *ancient,* and of which there remain but faint traces; *antiquated*, *old-fashioned*, and *obsolete*, that which has ceased to be any longer used or esteemed. A *fashion* is *old* when it has been long in use; a custom is *ancient* when its use has long been past; a bust or statue is *antique* when the model of it only remains; a person looks *antiquated* whose dress and appearance are out of date; manners which have gone quite out of *fashion* are *old-fashioned;* a word or custom is *obsolete* which has grown out of use.

The *old* is opposed to the new; some things are the worse for being *old*, other things are the better. *Ancient* and *antique* are opposed to modern: all things are valued the more for being *ancient* or *antique;* hence we esteem the writings of the *ancients* above those of the moderns. The *antiquated* is opposed to the customary and established; it is that which we cannot like, because we cannot esteem it: the *old-fashioned* is opposed to the fashionable: there is much in the *old-fashioned* to like and esteem; there is much that is ridiculous in the fashion: the *obsolete* is opposed to the current; the *obsolete* may be good; the current may be vulgar and mean.

See also ELDERLY.

OLDER. See SENIOR.

OLD TIMES. See FORMERLY.

OLIO, FARRAGO, HODGE-PODGE. These are terms borrowed from various languages signifying a mixed food of some sort, and hence, figuratively, any *jumble* or *mixture.* They differ from each other in the exact character of the mixed dish indicated and in the frequency and extent of their use as figurative terms. *Olio*, a mistaken form for *olia*, is intended to represent Spanish *olla*, Latin *olla*, a round earthen pot or dish, and hence that which is frequently served in the dish—*i. e.*, a mixture of different kinds of meat and vegetables. *Farrago* is a mixed food served to cattle. *Hodge-podge* is a corruption of *hotch-pot*, from French *hocher*, to shake, and *pot* (Anglo-Saxon *pott*). The Scotch form of *hodge-podge*, besides implying a mixture of various ingredients, means a thick broth of meat and vegetables. Of these three terms *hodge-podge* is the only one which has come into general colloquial use.

OMEN, PROGNOSTIC, PRESAGE. All these terms express some token or sign of what is to come. *Omen*, in Latin *omen*, *prognostic*, in Greek προγνωστικόν, from πρό, before, and γνοστικός, good at knowing, signifies the sign by which one judges a thing beforehand, because a *prognostic* is rather a deduction by the use of the understanding. *Presage* (see AUGUR).

The *omen* and *prognostic* are both drawn from external objects; the *presage* is drawn from one's own feelings. The *omen* is drawn from objects that have no necessary connection with the thing they are made to represent; it is the fruit of the imagination and rests on superstition: the *prognostic*, on the contrary, is a sign which partakes in some degree of the quality of the thing denoted. *Omens* were drawn by the heathens from the flight of birds or the entrails of beasts—*"Aves dant omina dira,"* TIBULLUS—and often from different incidents; thus Ulysses, when landed on his native island, prayed to Jupiter that he would give him a double sign by which he might know that he should be permitted to slay the suitors of his wife; and when he heard the thunder and saw a maiden supplicating the gods in the temple he took these for *omens* that he should immediately proceed to put in execution his designs. *Prognostics* are discovered only by an acquaintance with the objects in which they exist, as the *prognostics* of a mortal disease are known to none so well as the physician; the *prognostics* of a storm or tempest are best known to the mariner.

In an extended sense, the word *omen* is also applied to objects which serve as a sign, so as to enable a person to draw a rational inference, which brings it nearer in sense to the *prognostic* and *presage;* but the *omen* may be said of that which is either good or bad; the *prognostic* and *presage*, when it expresses a sentiment, mostly of that which is unfavorable. It is an *omen* of our success if we find those of whom we have to ask a favor in a good humor; the spirit of discontent which pervades the countenances and discourse of a people is a *prognostic* of some popular commotion. The imagination is often filled with strange *presages.*

When *presage* is taken for the outward sign, it is understood favorably, or in an indifferent sense.

OMIT. See NEGLECT.

OMNIPRESENT. See UBIQUITOUS.

OMNISCIENT, ALL - KNOWING, ALL-SEEING, ALL-WISE, INFALLIBLE. *Omniscient,* a Latin compound of *omnis,* all, and *sciens,* knowing, from *scio,* to know, in French *omniscient,* Spanish *omnisciente,* is the adjective form of *omniscience,* one of three attributes of God, the others being *omnipresence,* everywhere, and *omnipotence,* infinite power: it signifies universal, unbounded, infinite knowledge and infinite wisdom. In the application of the terms to God, the only proper one, *all-wise,* implies the quality we accord Him of possessing all the wisdom that has ever existed or ever can exist; *all-knowing,* the quality of possession of the fullest possible knowledge of all things; *all-seeing,* literally, the quality of seeing every person and thing; as a substantive, the Being who alone can see all persons and things—God; and *infallible,* the quality of being supremely perfect, incapable of erring or failing in anything, of being at all times and under all conditions certain, sure, and indisputable.

See also INFALLIBLE.

ON, UPON. There is now little difference between these two words; euphony and rhythm generally determine the choice between them on the part of a good writer. *Upon* is preferred when motion into position is indicated, as in the sentence "Place the book *upon* the table"; *on* is preferred when merely rest or support is to be indicated, as in the sentence, "The book is *on* the table."

ONCE, ERST, FORMERLY. *Once,* from Anglo-Saxon *an,* one, means literally at *one* time, referring to a particular time in the past. *Erst* is the superlative corresponding to the preposition and conjunction *ere,* Anglo-Saxon *ær,* before, and also means at a time before this. It is now used only in poetry or in poetic prose. *Formerly* is from the comparative form answering to *erst.* It means before this time. It differs from *once* in emphasizing not the one time in the past, but the relation of that time to the present.

C.E.S.—18

ONE, SINGLE, ONLY. *Unity* is the common idea of all these terms; and at the same time the whole signification of *one,* which is opposed to none; *single,* in Latin *singulus,* each or one by itself, probably contracted from *sine angulo,* without an angle, because what is entirely by itself cannot form an angle, signifies that *one* which is abstracted from others, and is particularly opposed to two, or a double which may form a pair; *only,* contracted from Anglo-Saxon *an-lic,* literally *one-like,* signifying in the form of unity, is employed for that of which there is no more. A person has *one* child is a positive expression that bespeaks its own meaning: a person has a *single* child conveys the idea that there ought to be or might be more, that more were expected, or that once there were more: a person has an *only* child implies that he never had more.

See also SOLITARY.

ONSET. See ATTACK.

ONWARD, FORWARD, PROGRESSIVE. *Onward* is taken in the literal sense of going nearer to an object: *forward* is taken in the sense of going from an object, or going farther in the line before one: *progressive,* from *pro,* forward, and *gressus,* past participle of *grede,* itself from *gradus,* a step, has the sense of going gradually, or step by step, before one. A person goes *onward* who does not stand still; he goes *forward* who does not recede; he goes *progressively* who goes *forward* at certain intervals. *Onward* is taken only in the proper acceptation of travelling; the traveller who has lost his way feels it necessary to go *onward* with the hope of arriving at some point; *forward* is employed in the improper as well as the proper application; a traveller goes *forward* in order to reach his point of destination as quickly as possible; a learner uses his utmost endeavors in order to get *forward* in his learning: *progressively* is employed only in the improper application to what requires time and labor in order to bring it to a conclusion; every man goes on *progressively* in his art, until he arrives at the point of perfection attainable by him.

OPALESCENT. See NACREOUS.

OPAQUE, DARK. *Opaque,* in Latin

opacus, corresponds in meaning to the native English *dark* (Anglo-Saxon *deorc*); the word *opaque* is to *dark* as the species to the genus, for it expresses that species of *darkness* which is inherent in solid bodies, in distinction from those which emit light from themselves or admit of light into themselves; it is therefore employed scientifically for the more vulgar and familiar term *dark*. On this ground the earth is termed an *opaque* body in distinction from the sun, moon, and other luminous bodies: any solid substance, as a tree or a stone, is an *opaque* body, in distinction from glass, which is a clear or transparent body.

OPEN. See CANDID; FRANK; PUBLIC; TANGIBLE.

OPENING, APERTURE, CAVITY. *Opening* signifies in general any place left *open* without defining any circumstances; the *aperture* is generally a specific kind of *opening* which is considered scientifically: there are *openings* in a wood when the trees are partly cut away; *openings* in streets by the removal of houses; or *openings* in a fence that has been broken down; but anatomists speak of *apertures* in the skull or in the heart, and the naturalist describes the *apertures* in the nests of bees, ants, beavers, and the like; the *opening* or *aperture* is the commencement of an enclosure; the *cavity* is the whole enclosure: hence they are frequently as a part to the whole: many animals make a *cavity* in the earth for their nests, with only a small *aperture* for their egress and ingress.

OPERATE. See ACT.

OPINIONATED, OPINIONATIVE, CONCEITED, EGOTISTICAL. A fondness for one's opinion bespeaks the *opinionated* man: a fond conceit of one's self bespeaks the *conceited* man: a fond attachment to himself bespeaks the *egotistical* man: a liking for one's self or one's own is evidently the common idea that runs through these terms; they differ in the mode and in the object.

An *opinionated* man is not only fond of his own *opinion*, but full of his own *opinion*; he has an *opinion* on everything, which is the best possible *opinion*, and is therefore delivered freely to every one, that they may profit in forming their own *opinions*. A *conceited* man has a *conceit* or a fond *opinion* of his own talent; it is not only high in comparison with others, but it is so high as to be set above others. The *conceited* man does not want to follow the ordinary means of acquiring knowledge: his *conceit* suggests to him that his talent will supply labor, application, reading, and study, and every other contrivance which men have commonly employed for their improvement; he sees by intuition what another learns by experience and observation; he knows in a day what others want years to acquire; he learns of himself what others are contented to get by means of instruction. The *egotistical* man makes himself the darling theme of his own contemplation; he admires and loves himself to that degree that he can talk and think of nothing else; his children, his house, his garden, his rooms, and the like, are the incessant theme of his conversation, and become invaluable from the mere circumstance of belonging to him. An *opinionated* man is the most unfit for conversation, which affords pleasure only by an alternate and equable communication of sentiment. A *conceited* man is the most unfit for co-operation, where a junction of talent and effort is essential to bring things to a conclusion; an *egotistical* man is the most unfit to be a companion or friend, for he does not know how to value or like anything out of himself.

Opinion, Sentiment, Notion.—*Opinion*, in Latin from *opinor*, think or judge, is the work of the head. *Sentiment*, from *sentio*, feel, is the work of the heart. *Notion*, in Latin *notio*, from *nosco*, to know, is a simple operation of the thinking faculty.

We form *opinions*, we have *sentiments*: we get *notions*. *Opinions* are formed on speculative matters; they are the result of reading, experience, and reflection: *sentiments* are entertained on matters of practice; they are the consequence of habits and circumstances: *notions* are gathered from sensible objects and arise out of the casualties of hearing and seeing. One forms *opinions* on religion as respects its doctrines; one has *sentiments* on religion as respects its practice and its precepts. The heathens formed *opinions* respecting the immortality of the soul, but they amounted to nothing more than *opinions*. Christians entertain *sentiments* of reverence toward God as their creator, and of dependence upon Him as their preserver.

Opinions are more liable to error than *sentiments*. The *opinion* often springs from the imagination, and in all cases is but an inference or deduction which falls short of certain knowledge: *opinions*, therefore, as individual *opinions*, may be false; *sentiments*, on the other hand, depend upon the moral constitution or habits; they may, therefore, be good or bad, according to the character or temper of the person. *Notions* are still more liable to error than either; they are the immature decisions of the uninformed mind on the appearances of things. The difference of *opinion* among men on the most important questions of human life is a sufficient evidence that the mind of man is very easily led astray in matters of *opinion*: whatever difference of *opinion* there may be among Christians, there is but one *sentiment* of love and good-will among those who follow the example of Christ rather than their own passions: the *notions* of a Deity are so imperfect among savages in general that they seem to amount to little more than an indistinct idea of some superior invisible agent.

OPPONENT. See ENEMY.

OPPORTUNE, AUSPICIOUS, FAVORABLE, SEASONABLE, TIMELY. *Opportune,* the adjective form of *opportunity,* from the Latin *opportunus,* signifies that which is fit or convenient, either as to a time, place, or occasion. *Auspicious* is a term applied only to things, and such as are casual or only indicative of good, those having promise of success or happiness, that are propitious, the term being derived from *auspicium,* an augury from birds, from *avis,* a bird, and *specere,* to inspect, hence, omens of success.

Favorable implies a condition that is propitious, advantageous, friendly, one that is wholly acceptable, as a *favorable* reply, a *favorable* day or time; *seasonable* (from Late Latin *satio,* a sowing, from *satus,* past participle of *serere,*

to sow, signifying the right time for sowing the seed), that which occurs or is done in a good or proper time, and so is specially welcome, that which belongs to a particular period of time, a benefit received in the time of need, in the nick of time; and *timely,* that which comes to pass at the right time, when most needed, when expected or promised. Differences between the terms *seasonable* and *timely* are critically considered in the article on TIMELY.

OPPORTUNITY. See OCCASION.

OPPOSE, RESIST, WITHSTAND, THWART. The action of setting one thing up against another is obviously expressed by all these terms, but they differ in the manner and the circumstances. To *oppose* (see CONTRADICT) is the most general and unqualified term; it simply denotes the relative position of two objects, and when applied to persons it does not necessarily imply any personal characteristic: we may *oppose* reason or force to force; or things may be *opposed* to each other which are in an *opposite* direction, as a house to a church. *Resist,* signifying, literally, to stand back, away from, or against, is always an act of more or less force when applied to persons; it is mostly a culpable action, as when men *resist* lawful authority; *resistance* is, in fact, always bad, unless in case of actual self-defence. *Opposition* may be made in any form, as when we *oppose* a person's admittance into a house by our personal efforts: or *oppose* his admission into a society by a declaration of our opinions. *Resistance* is always a direct action, as when we *resist* an invading army by the sword, or *resist* the evidence of our senses by denying our assent; or, in relation to things, when wood or any hard substance *resists* the violent efforts of steel or iron to make an impression.

With in *withstand* has the force of against, *re* in *resist* the force of back, but *stand* corresponds to *sist,* from Latin *sistere,* to stand. *Thwart* is a Scandinavian word originally an adverb (compare *athwart,* meaning across), signifying across, in the contrary direction, and thence developing into a verb meaning to cross, to work against. These words are modes of *resistance* applicable only to conscious agents. To *withstand* is negative; it implies not to *yield* to any foreign agency: thus, a person *withstands* the entreaties of another to comply with a request. To *thwart* is positive; it is actively to cross the will of another: thus humorsome people are perpetually *thwarting* the wishes of those with whom they are in connection. It is a happy thing when a young man can *withstand* the allurements of pleasure. It is a part of a Christian's duty to bear with patience the untoward events of life that *thwart* his purposes.

See also COMBAT; OBJECT.

OPPOSITE. See ADVERSE.

OPPROBRIUM. See INFAMY.

OPPUGN. See CONFUTE.

OPTIMISTIC, CHEERFUL, SANGUINE. All these terms mean in general hopeful, inclined to look on the bright side of things, but they differ in the suggested source of the hopefulness. *Optimistic* expresses an intellectual attitude, *cheerful* a moral attitude, and *sanguine* a quality of temper having a physical basis. *Optimistic* comes from Latin *optimus*, best, and means seeing the best in everything. For *cheerful* see CHEER. *Sanguine*, from Latin *sanguis*, blood, meant originally full blooded, and describes the attitude to life of the full-blooded people, of abounding animal spirits, who find easy what is hard for others, and are self-confident and bold, being conscious of their own capacity to face life and make the best of a situation. *Sanguine*, being founded on a physical condition, indicates a hopefulness that is really less enduring and stable than that indicated in *optimistic* or *cheerful*.

OPTION, CHOICE. *Option* is immediately of Latin derivation (from *optare*, to wish), and is consequently a term of less frequent use than the word *choice*, for the derivation of which see CHOOSE. The former term implies an uncontrolled act of the mind; the latter a simple leaning of the will. We speak of *option* only as regards one's freedom from external constraint in the act of *choosing:* one speaks of *choice* only as the simple act itself. The *option* or the power of *choosing* is given; the *choice* itself is made: hence we say a thing is at a person's *option*, or it is his own *option*, or the *option* is left to him, in order to designate his freedom of *choice* more strongly than is expressed by the word *choice* itself.

OPULENCE. See RICHES.

ORACULAR, AUTHORITATIVE, DOGMATICAL, PROPHETIC. *Oracular*, in Latin *oracularis*, from *oraculum*, an oracle, and that from *oro*, to speak, implied in its ancient sense that which related to an announcement from the gods in answer to some inquiry, a prophetic declaration, also to the places where such announcements were made, and to the deities making them. Such responses were closely allied to augury, but with this difference, that auguries could be taken anywhere, while the *oracular* places were defined and limited. From the common belief that the responses or answers were given by or through the influence of a certain divine afflatus, the people came to look upon them as *authoritative*, as proceeding from a source that could not be questioned, and, consequently placed implicit confidence in them.

Now, in ordinary language, that is *authoritative* which proceeds from a source that has the power to act, command, determine, and this source may be beneficial to all under its jurisdiction. *Authoritative*, therefore, has in general a good significance. *Dogmatical*, from Greek δόγμα (English *dogma*), an opinion, indicates an attempt to be *authoritative*—to express opinions with a show and assumption of authority not recognized by others; it has in general a somewhat derogatory implication. These words are allied to *oracular* through the common idea of expressing a judgment with a show of authority.

Prophetic implies an occurrence foretold, predicted, or presaged, and here again we revert to the ancient oracles, as their chief announcements were declarations of what was about to happen and what the inquirers should and should not do. The *prophets* of Holy Writ were men divinely inspired, who frequently uttered predictions of coming events, both as warnings and encouragement to the people.

ORAL. See VERBAL.

ORATION. See ADDRESS.

ORATORY. See ELOCUTION.

ORB. See CIRCLE.

ORDAIN. See APPOINT.

ORDER, METHOD, RULE. *Order* (see DISPOSE) is applied in general to everything that is disposed; *method,* in French *méthode,* Latin *methodus,* Greek μέθοδος, from μετά and ὁδός, or a way after, signifying the ready or right way to do a thing; and *rule,* from Latin *regula,* a rule, and *regere,* to govern, direct, or make straight (the former expressing the act of making a thing straight or that by which it is made so, the latter the abstract quality of being so), are applied only to that which is done; the *order* lies in consulting the time, the place, and the object, so as to make them accord; the *method* consists in the right choice of means to an end; the *rule* consists in that which will keep us in the right way. Where there are a number of objects there must be *order* in the disposition of them; where there is work to carry on, or any object to obtain, or any art to follow, there must be *method* in the pursuit; a tradesman or merchant must have *method* in keeping his accounts; a teacher must have a *method* for the communication of instruction: the *rule* is the part of the *method;* it is that on which the *method* rests; there cannot be *method* without *rule,* but there may be *rule* without *method;* the *method* varies with the thing that is to be done; the *rule* is that which is permanent and serves as a guide under all circumstances. We adopt the *method* and follow the *rule.* A painter adopts a certain *method* of preparing his colors according to the *rules* laid down by his art.

Order is said of every complicated machine, either of a physical or a moral kind: the *order* of the universe, by which every part is made to harmonize with the other part, and all individually with the whole collectively, is that which constitutes its principal beauty: as rational beings, we aim at introducing the same *order* into the moral scheme of society: *order* is, therefore, that which is founded upon the nature of things, and seems in its extensive sense to comprehend all the rest. *Method* is the work of the understanding, mostly as it is employed in the mechanical process; sometimes, however, as respects intellectual objects. *Rule* is said either of mechanical and physical actions or moral conduct. The term *rule* is, however, as before observed, employed distinctly from either *order* or *method,* for it applies to the moral conduct of the individual. The Christian religion contains *rules* for the guidance of our conduct in all the relations of human society.

As epithets, *orderly, methodical,* and *regular* are applied to persons and even to things according to the above distinction of the nouns: an *orderly* man, or an *orderly* society, is one who adheres to the established *order* of things; the former in his domestic habits, the latter in their public capacity, their social meetings, and their social measures. A *methodical* man is one who adopts *method* in all he sets about; such a one may sometimes run into the extreme of formality, by being precise where precision is not necessary: we cannot speak of a *methodical* society, for *method* is altogether a personal quality. A man is *regular,* inasmuch as he follows a certain *rule* in his moral actions, and thereby preserves a uniformity of conduct: a *regular* society is one founded by a certain prescribed *rule.* So we say, an *orderly* proceeding, or an *orderly* course, for what is done in due *order:* a *regular* proceeding, or a *regular* course, which goes on according to a prescribed *rule:* a *methodical* grammar, a *methodical* delineation, and the like, for what is done according to a given *method.*

See also APPOINT; CLASS; COMMAND; DIRECTION; DISPOSE; PLACE; SUCCESSION.

ORDINANCE, DECREE, EDICT, LAW, RULE. *Ordinance,* in Old French *ordenance,* from the Latin *ordo,* order, signifies a *rule* of action, an observance commanded, a religious rite or ceremony, a canon of the church, an enactment by a legislative body. Specifically, the term means an orderly disposition or arrangement, hence, a rule, custom, rite, ceremony, or observance established by an authority having jurisdiction over whatever may be affected by its action. Sovereigns, high political bodies, and courts issue *decrees,* which are simply orders to produce specified results.

The term *edict* (from Latin *e* for *ex*, out, and *dictum*, participle of *dicere*, to speak, signifying a formal "speaking out," to be heard by many people) is also applied to rules and laws promulgated in the same manner as a *decree*, but with this difference: a *decree* (from Latin *de*, from, and *cretum*, past participle of *cernere*, to separate, meaning to separate truth from falsehood, good from bad, hence to judge) may be the award of an umpire, an arbitration, or a special authority designated to determine a question in controversy, and may be the subject of review by a higher authority, while an *edict* is the proclamation of that which takes on the form and force of a law, a mandate, a command.

A *law* emanates from a regularly constituted authority, and has a power behind it to insure its respect and observance, as a law or act of the United States Congress can be sustained, if necessary, by the entire army and navy of the country. The relation of the term *law* to other synonymous terms is discussed in the articles on LAWFUL and MAXIM. A *rule* differs from the preceding terms in that it is a direction, a standard or guide; in law, an order by a court on a motion affecting parties to a suit, to regulate the practice of a court, or to establish a principle by a decision. This term is also further discussed in the article on ORDER.

ORDINARY. See COMMON.

ORGIES. See SATURNALIA.

ORIENT, EASTERN. *Orient* is the Latin term; *eastern*, the Anglo-Saxon word. The former comes from the present participle of the verb *oriri*, to rise, signifying the quarter where the sun rises. *Eastern* also signifies the quarter where the sun rises; it may be allied to the stem of the Latin *aurora*, signifying the dawn. *Orient* differs from *eastern* in the poetic and imaginative connotations that it has acquired. *Eastern* is the literal term, signifying from the east as a quarter of the heavens or of the earth. *Orient* signifies characteristic of the east—suggesting either the light and splendor of the sunrise or the rich lands of the east, whence came pearls and gold and spice and gorgeous fabrics in the old days.

ORIFICE, PERFORATION. *Orifice*, in Latin *orificium* or *orifacium*, from *os*, mouth, and *facere*, to make, signifies a made mouth, that is, an opening made, as it were. *Perforation*, in Latin *perforatio*, from *per*, through, and *forare*, cognate with English *bore*, to pierce, signifies a piercing through.

These terms are both scientifically employed to designate certain cavities in the human body; but the former signifies that which is natural, the latter that which is artificial: all the vessels of the human body have their *orifices*, which are so constructed as to open or close of themselves. Surgeons are frequently obliged to make *perforations* into the bones: sometimes *perforation* may describe what comes from a natural process, but it denotes a cavity made through a solid substance; but the *orifice* is particularly applicable to such openings as most resemble the mouth in form and use. In this manner the words may be extended in their application to other bodies besides animal substances, and applied to other sciences besides anatomy: hence we speak of the *orifice* of a tube, the *orifice* of any flower, and the like; or the *perforation* of a tree by means of a cannon-ball or an iron instrument.

ORIGIN, ORIGINAL, BEGINNING, RISE, SOURCE. *Origin* and *original* are both derived from the Latin *oriri*, to rise, the former designating the abstract property of *rising*, the latter the thing that is *risen;* the first of its kind from which others *rise*. *Origin* refers us to the cause as well as the period of beginning; *original* is said of those things which give an *origin* to another: the *origin* serves to date the existence of a thing; the term *original* serves to show the author of a thing, and is opposed to the copy. The *origin* of the world is described in the first chapter of Genesis; Adam was the *original* from whom all the human race has sprung.

Origin has regard to the cause, *beginning* simply to the period of existence: everything owes its existence to the *origin;* it dates its existence from the *beginning;* there cannot be an *origin* without a *beginning;* but there may be a *beginning* where we do not speak of an *origin*. We look to the *origin* of a thing in order to learn its nature: we look to the *beginning* in order to learn its duration. When we have discovered the *origin* of a quarrel, we are in a fair way of becoming acquainted with the aggressors; when we trace a quarrel to the *beginning*, we may easily ascertain how long it has lasted.

Origin and *rise* are both employed for the primary state of existence, but the latter is a much more familiar term than the former: we speak of the *origin* of an empire, the *origin* of a family, the *origin* of a dispute, and the like; but we say that a river takes its *rise* from a certain mountain, that certain disorders take their *rise* from particular circumstances which happen in early life: it is, moreover, observable that the term *origin* is confined solely to the first commencement of a thing's existence; but *rise* comprehends its gradual progress in the first stages of its existence; the *origin* of the noblest families is in the first instance sometimes ignoble; the largest rivers take their *rise* in small streams. We look to the *origin* as to the cause of existence: we look to the *rise* as to the situation in which the thing commences to exist, or the process by which it grows up into existence.

The *origin* and *rise* are said of only one object; the *source* is said of that which produces a succession of objects: the *origin* of evil in general has given *rise* to much idle speculation; the love of pleasure is the *source* of incalculable mischief to individuals, as well as to society at large: the *origin* exists but once; the *source* is lasting: the *origin* of every family is to be traced to our first parent, Adam; we have a never-failing *source* of consolation in religion.

See also FIRST; GERM; PRIMARY.

ORNATE, ADORNED, DECORATED, EMBELLISHED. For the distinction between *adorned*, *decorated*, and *embellished* see the article on ADORN where the verbs of which these are participles are critically discussed. *Ornate* differs from these words in intensity, and in not so distinctly suggesting the application of something external in order to beautify. That which is *ornate* is very much *adorned, decorated,* or em-

bellished; ornate is, as it were in meaning, if not in form, the superlative of these words. Moreover, *ornate* suggests gorgeousness and elaborateness inherent in the very design or material, not simply applied from without.

ORNITHOPTER. See AIRCRAFT.
ORTHODOX. See EVANGELICAL.
OSCILLATE. See WAG.
OSCULATION. See KISS.
OSTENSIBLE. See COLORABLE.
OSTENTATION. See SHOW.
OSTRACIZE. See PROSCRIBE.

OUT, ABROAD, BEYOND. All of these terms signify external to something. *Out*, Anglo-Saxon *ut*, signifies external to something enclosed. We speak of being *out* of the house, *out* of the city; of taking valuables *out* of a chest, etc. *Beyond*, from Anglo-Saxon *geond*, modern English *yond*, compounded with the prefix *be*, means external to some line or limit—on the other side of. *Abroad*, from Anglo-Saxon *a* (on) and *brad*, broad, means in the whole breadth of the land. It means out in the open, and suggests not the definite bounds, but the freedom and space beyond the bounds.

OUTCRY. See NOISE.
OUTDO. See EXCEED.
OUTLINE. See SYLLABUS.
OUTLINES. See SKETCH.
OUTLIVE, SURVIVE. To *outlive* is literally to live out the life of another, to live longer: to *survive*, in French *survivre*, Latin *super*, beyond, and *vivere*, to live, is to live beyond any given period; the former is employed to express the comparison between two lives; the latter to denote a protracted existence beyond any given term: one person is said properly to *outlive* another who enjoys a longer life; but we speak of *surviving* persons or things, in an indefinite or unqualified manner: it is not an unqualified blessing to *outlive* all our nearest relatives and friends; no man can be happy in *surviving* his honor.

OUTRAGE. See AFFRONT.
OUTSIDE. See SHOW.
OUTWARD, EXTERNAL, EXTERIOR. *Outward*, or inclined to the *out*, after the manner of the *out*, indefinitely describes the situation; *external*, from the Latin *externus* and *extra*, is more definite in its sense, since it is em-

ployed only in regard to such objects as are conceived to be independent of man as a thinking being: hence, we may speak of the *outward* part of a building, of a board, of a table, a box, and the like; but of *external* objects acting on the mind, or of an *external* agency. *Exterior* is still more definite than either, as it expresses a higher degree of the *outward* or *external*, the former being in the comparative and the latter two in the positive degree: when we speak of anything which has two coats, it is usual to designate the outermost by the name of the *exterior;* when we speak simply of the surface, without reference to anything behind, it is denominated *external:* as the *exterior* coat of a walnut, or the *external* surface of things. In the moral application, the *external* or *outward* is that which comes simply to the view; but the *exterior* is that which is prominent and which consequently may conceal something: a man may sometimes neglect the *outside* who is altogether mindful of the inward: a man with a pleasing *exterior* will sometimes gain more friends than he who has more solid merit.

OVAL. See OBLONG.

OVER. See ABOVE; YONDER.

OVERAWE, DAUNT, FRIGHTEN, INTIMIDATE. *Overawe,* a compound of the English *over* and the verb *awe* (see AWE), signifies, as a transitive, to restrain by fear or by superior influence. *Awe,* as a substantive, implies a fear that is reverential, or a feeling of emotion inspired by the contemplation of something sublime, and, as a transitive, to strike, inspire, or impress with feelings of reverential respect, or to hold one back or restrain him from some improper act by fear or respect. *Overawe,* in contradistinction, implies not only the usual quality of *awe,* but it assumes also the quality of a threat, an action that produces apprehension of something serious to come if something else is or is not done previously. To *daunt* (see DISMAY) a person is to check him in some proceeding by alarming him, to thwart, deter, or prevent him in a purpose, and, in an extreme sense, to appall, dismay, cow, and subdue him; to *frighten* one is to affright, terrify, shock with sudden fear, and

scare him; to *intimidate* (from Latin *timeo,* I fear, *timidus,* fearful) one is to put him into a state of fear, and this term applies not only to an act that frightens a person, but to a series of actions that may affect him in his business and social relations, and on its application serves to *restrain* or check him in his regular course.

The last term has had a very frequent application of late to certain workmen who have been *intimidated* from pursuing their regular occupation by others striving to force them to join in a labor strike or some disturbing labor proceeding, the importunities to do so usually being backed up by various threats in case of a refusal. Thus operators in an industrial plant may be *restrained* from continuing at work by *intimidations,* threats, insinuations, and other acts that cause a fear of consequences, and by these acts are *overawed* into doing what is demanded of them.

OVERBALANCE, OUTWEIGH, PREPONDERATE. To *overbalance* is to throw the balance over on one side. To *outweigh* is to exceed in weight. To *preponderate,* from *præ,* before, and *pondus,* a weight, signifies also to exceed in weight. Although these terms approach so near to each other in their original meaning, yet they have now a different application: in the proper sense, a person *overbalances* himself who loses his balance and goes on one side; a heavy body *outweighs* one that is light when they are put into the same pair of scales. *Overbalance* and *outweigh* are likewise used in the improper application; *preponderate* is never used otherwise: things are said to *overbalance* which are supposed to turn the scale to one side or the other; they are said to *outweigh* when they are to be weighed against each other; they are said to *preponderate* when one weighs down everything else: the evils which arise from innovations in society commonly *overbalance* the good; the will of a parent should *outweigh* every personal consideration in the mind, which will always be the case where the power of religion *preponderates.*

OVERBEAR, BEAR DOWN, OVERPOWER, OVERWHELM, SUBDUE. To *overbear* is to *bear* one's self *over* another, that is, to make another *bear* one's weight; to *bear down* is literally to bring down by *bearing* upon; to *overpower* is to get the *power* over an object; to *overwhelm*, from *whelm*, a Scandinavian word signifying to overturn, to cover with water, meant literally to drown, to submerge entirely; to *subdue* (see CONQUER) is, literally, to lead underneath, in the elliptical sense of leading beneath a yoke. A man *overbears* by carrying himself higher than others, and putting to silence those who might claim an equality with him; an *overbearing* demeanor is most conspicuous in narrow circles, where an individual, from certain casual advantages, affects a superiority over the members of the same community. To *bear down* is an act of greater violence: one *bears down* opposition; it is properly the opposing force to force until one side yields, as when one party bears another down. *Overpower*, as the term implies, belongs to the exercise of power which may be either physical or moral: one may be *overpowered* by another who in a struggle gets one into his power, or one may be *overpowered* in an argument when the argument of one's antagonist is such as to bring one to silence. One is *overborne* or *borne down* by the exertion of individuals; *overpowered* by the active efforts of individuals, or by the force of circumstances; *overwhelmed* by circumstances or things only: *overborne* by another of superior influence; *borne down* by the force of his attack; *overpowered* by numbers, by entreaties, by looks, and the like; and *overwhelmed* by the torrent of words or the impetuosity of the attack.

Overpower and *overwhelm* denote a partial superiority; *subdue* denotes that which is permanent and positive: we may *overpower* or *overwhelm* for a time or to a certain degree; but to *subdue* is to get an entire and lasting superiority. *Overpower* and *overwhelm* are said of what passes between persons nearly on an equality; but *subdue* is said of those who are, or may be, reduced to a low state of inferiority: individuals or armies are *overpowered* or *overwhelmed;* individuals or nations are *subdued*.

In the moral or extended application, *overbear* and *bear down* both imply force or violence, but the latter even more than the former: one passion may be said to *overbear* another, or to *overbear* reason. Whatever *bears down* carries all before it.

To *overbear*, *overwhelm*, and *subdue* are likewise applied to the moral feelings, as well as to the external relations of things; but the former two are the effects of external circumstances; the latter follows from the exercise of the reasoning powers: the tender feelings are *overpowered;* the mind is *overwhelmed* with painful feelings; the unruly passions are *subdued* by the force of religious contemplation: a person may be so *overpowered* on seeing a dying friend as to be unable to speak; a person may be so *overwhelmed* with grief, upon the death of a near and dear relative, as to be unable to attend to his customary duties; the passion of anger has been so completely *subdued* by the influence of religion on the heart that instances have been known of the most irascible tempers being converted into the most mild and forbearing.

See also IMPERIOUS.

OVERCOME. See CONQUER; QUELL.

OVERFLOW, INUNDATE, DELUGE. What *overflows* simply *flows over;* what *inundates* (from *in* and *unda*, a wave) *flows* into; what *deluges* (through French from *de*, for *dis*, apart, away, and *luere*, to wash) washes away.

The term *overflow* bespeaks abundance; whatever exceeds the measure of contents must *flow over*, because it is more than can be held: to *inundate* bespeaks not only abundance, but vehemence; when it *inundates* it *flows* in faster than is desired, it fills to an inconvenient height: to *deluge* bespeaks impetuosity; a *deluge* irresistibly carries away all before it. This explanation of these terms in their proper sense will illustrate their improper application: the heart is said to *overflow* with joy, with grief, with bitterness, and the like, in order to denote the superabundance of the thing; a country is said to be *inundated* by swarms of inhabitants when speaking of numbers who intrude themselves to the annoyance of the natives; the town is said to be *deluged* with publications of different kinds when they appear in such profusion and in such quick succession as to supersede others of more value.

OVERHEAR. See HEAR.

OVERPOWER. See BEAT; OVERBEAR.

OVERRULE, SUPERSEDE. To *overrule* is, literally, to get the superiority of rule; and to *supersede* (from *super* and *sedere*), is to get the upper or superior seat; but the former is employed only as the act of persons; the latter is applied to things as the agents: a man may be *overruled* in his domestic government, or he may be *overruled* in a public assembly, or he may be *overruled* in the cabinet; large works in general *supersede* the necessity of smaller ones, by containing that which is superior both in quantity and quality.

OVERRULING. See PREVAILING.

OVERRUN. See OVERSPREAD.

OVERSIGHT. See INADVERTENCY; INSPECTION.

OVERSPREAD, OVERRUN, RAVAGE. To *overspread* signifies simply to cover the whole surface of a body; but to *overrun* is a mode of spreading, namely, by running; things in general, therefore, are said to *overspread* which admit of extension; nothing can be said to *overrun* but what literally or figuratively runs: the face is *overspread* with spots; the ground is *overrun* with weeds. To *overrun* and to *ravage* (based on French *ravir*, Late Latin *rapire, f.. rapere*) are both employed to imply the active and extended destruction of an enemy; but the former expresses more than the latter: a small body may *ravage* in particular parts; but immense numbers are said to *overrun*, as they run into every part; the Barbarians *overran* all Europe and settled in different countries; detachments are sent out to *ravage* the country or neighborhood.

OVERTHROW. See BEAT; OVERTURN.

OVERTURN, OVERTHROW, SUBVERT, INVERT, REVERSE. To *overturn* is simply to turn over, an act which may be more or less gradual; but to *overthrow* is to throw over, which will be more or less violent. To *overturn* is to turn a thing either with its side or its bottom upward; but to *subvert* is to turn that under which should be upward: to *reverse* is to turn that before which should be behind; and to *invert* is to place

that on its head which should rest on its feet. These terms differ accordingly in their application and circumstances: things are *overturned* by contrivance and gradual means; infidels attempt to *overturn* Christianity by means of ridicule and falsehood: governments are *overthrown* by violence. To *overturn* is said of small matters; to *subvert* only of national or large concerns: domestic economy may be *overturned*; religious or political establishments may be *subverted*: that may be *overturned* which is simply set up; that is *subverted* which has been established: an assertion may be *overturned*; the best sanctioned principles may by artifice be *subverted*.

To *overturn*, *overthrow*, and *subvert* generally involve the destruction of the thing so *overturned*, *overthrown*, or *subverted*, or at least render it for the time useless, and are, therefore, mostly unallowed acts; but *reverse* and *invert*, which have a more particular application, have a less specific character of propriety: we may *reverse* a proposition by taking the negative instead of the affirmative; a decree may be *reversed* so as to render it nugatory; but both of these acts may be right or wrong, according to circumstances: likewise, the order of particular things may be *inverted* to suit the convenience of parties; but the order of society cannot be *inverted* without *subverting* all the principles on which civil society is built.

See also BEAT.

OVERWHELM, CRUSH. To *overwhelm* (see also under OVERBEAR) is to cover with a heavy body, so that one should sink under it: to *crush* (see BREAK) is to destroy the consistency of a thing by violent pressure: a thing may be *crushed* by being *overwhelmed*, but it may be *overwhelmed* without being *crushed*; and it may be *crushed* without being *overwhelmed*: the girl Tarpeia, who betrayed the Capitoline Hill to the Sabines, is said to have been *overwhelmed* with their arms, by which she was *crushed* to death: when many persons fall on one he may be *overwhelmed*, but not necessarily *crushed*: when a wagon goes over a body, it may be *crushed*, but not *overwhelmed*.

OWN. See ACKNOWLEDGE.

OWNER. See POSSESSOR.

P

PACE, STEP. *Pace*, derived from Latin *passus*, step, is the Latin term corresponding to the native English *step* (from Anglo-Saxon *steppan*), signifying a stretch of the legs.

As regards the act, the *pace* expresses the general manner of passing on or moving the body; the *step* implies the manner of setting or extending the foot: the *pace* is distinguished by being either a walk or a run, and in regard to horses a trot or a gallop: the *step* is distinguished by being long or short, to the right or left, forward or backward. The same *pace* may be modified so as to be more or less easy, more or less quick; the *step* may vary as it is light or heavy, graceful or ungraceful, long or short: we may go a slow *pace* with long *steps*, or we may go a quick *pace* with short *steps*: a slow *pace* is best suited to the solemnity of a funeral; a long *step* must be taken by soldiers in a slow march.

As regards the space passed or *stepped* over, the *pace* is a measured distance, formed by a long *step;* the *step*, on the other hand, is indefinitely employed for any space *stepped* over, but particularly that ordinary space which one *steps* over without an effort: a thousand *paces* was the Roman measurement for a mile; a *step* or two designates almost the shortest possible distance.

PACIFIST, CONSCIENTIOUS OBJECTOR, SLACKER. These are words which the European war brought into special prominence in England and America. *Pacifist* and *conscientious objector* signify one who does not believe in war, but *pacifist* puts the attitude in positive terms, *conscientious objector* in negative terms. A *pacifist* is one who believes in the establishment of world peace with some provision for an international court of arbitration, a league of nations to support the decrees of such a court, etc. *Conscientious objector* was coined to describe those persons who, without having any theory concerning the establishment of a pa-cific world, believe that war is morally wrong for them and refuse to fight. It referred primarily to members of such religious sects as the Quakers. The two terms are practically interchangeable. *Conscientious objector*, being the more inclusive term, now seems to be gaining ground. *Slacker* is a slang term describing a man who refuses to do his share of the fighting, who is *slack* in his duty. It is a term of contempt often applied by others to those who would call themselves *conscientious objectors* or *pacifists*.

PACIFY. See APPEASE; MOLLIFY; QUELL.

PAGAN. See GENTILE.

PAIN, PANG, AGONY, ANGUISH. *Pain* is connected with the Latin *pœna*, a penalty. *Pang* is a word of uncertain origin. *Agony* comes from the Greek ἀγωνία, a contest, signifying the labor or *pain* of a struggle. *Anguish*, from the Latin *angere*, to choke (whence *anger* and *anxiety* are also derived), signifies the *pain* arising from choking.

Pain, which expresses the feeling that is most repugnant to the nature of all sensible beings, is here the generic, and the rest specific, terms: *pain* and *agony* are applied indiscriminately to what is physical and mental; *pang* and *anguish* mostly signify that which is mental: *pain* signifies either an individual feeling or a permanent state; *pang* is only a particular feeling: *agony* is sometimes employed for the individual feeling, but more commonly for the state; *anguish* is always employed for the state. *Pain* is indefinite with regard to the degree; it may rise to the highest or sink to the lowest possible degree; the rest are positively high degrees of *pain*: the *pang* is a sharp *pain;* the *agony* is a severe and permanent *pain;* the *anguish* is an overwhelming *pain*.

PAINT, DEPICT. *Paint* and *depict* both come from the Latin *pingere*, to represent forms and figures: as a verb, to *paint* is employed either literally to represent figures on paper or to represent circumstances and events by means of words; to *depict* is used only in this latter sense, but the former word expresses a greater exercise of the imagination than the latter: it is the art of the poet to *paint* nature in lively colors; it is the art of the historian or narrator to *depict* a real scene of misery in strong colors.

As nouns, *painting* describes rather the action or operation, and *picture* the result. When we speak of a good *painting*, we think particularly of its execution as to drapery, disposition of colors, and the like; but when we speak of a fine *picture*, we refer immediately to the object represented, and the impression which it is capable of producing on the beholder: *paintings* are confined either to oil-*paintings* or *paintings* in colors: but every drawing, whether in pencil, in crayon, or in India ink, may produce a *picture;* and we have likewise *pictures* in embroidery, *pictures* in tapestry, and *pictures* in mosaic.

Painting is employed only in the proper sense; *picture* is often used figuratively: old *paintings* derive a value from the master by whom they were executed; a well-regulated family, bound together by the ties of affection, presents the truest *picture* of human happiness.

PAIR. See BOTH; COUPLE.

PALATE, TASTE. *Palate,* in Latin *Taste, palatum,* signifies the roof of the mouth. Middle English *tasten,* Old French *taster,* from a Late Latin *taxitare* (ultimately from Latin *tangere,* to touch), meant originally to touch, especially to touch lightly, then to touch lightly with the tongue.

Palate is, in an improper sense, employed for *taste,* because it shares with the tongue the sense of *taste,* but *taste* is never employed for *palate:* a person is said to have a nice *palate* when he is nice in what he eats or drinks; but his *taste* extends to all matters of sense, as well as those which are intellectual. A man of *taste,* or of a nice *taste,* conveys much more as a characteristic than a man of a nice *palate:* the former is said only in a good sense, but the latter is particularly applicable to the epicure.

PALE, PALLID, WAN. *Pale,* in French *pâle,* and *pallid,* in Latin *pallidus,* both come from *pallere,* to turn pale. *Wan* is in Anglo-Saxon *wann,* signifying dark, black, colorless.

Pallid rises upon *pale,* and *wan* upon *pallid:* the absence of color in any degree, where color is a requisite quality, constitutes *paleness;* but *pallidness* is an excess of *paleness,* and *wan* is an unusual degree of *pallidness: paleness* in the countenance may be temporary; but *pallidness* and *wanness* are permanent; fear or any sudden emotion may produce *paleness;* but protracted sickness, hunger, and fatigue bring on *pallidness;* and when these calamities are combined and heightened by every aggravation, they may produce that which is specifically termed *wanness.*

PALLIATE. See EXTENUATE; GLOSS.

PALLID. See PALE.

PALPITATE, FLUTTER, PANT, GASP. *Palpitate* is a frequentative of Latin *palpare,* to move quickly and frequently. *Flutter,* from Anglo-Saxon *floterian,* to *float* about, meant to drift back and forth, but it now signifies to fly backward and forward in an agitated manner. *Pant* comes through Old French *pantaisier,* to breathe with difficulty, from popular Latin *phantasiare,* to be oppressed with the nightmare, from Greek φαντασία, a vision, whence *fantasy* and *fancy* are derived. *Gasp* is in Middle English *gaspen,* but its further origin is not clear.

These terms agree in a particular manner, as they signify the irregular action of the heart or lungs: the former two are said of the heart, and the latter two of the lungs or breath; to *palpitate* expresses that which is strong; it is a strong beating of the blood against the vessels of the heart: to *flutter* expresses that which is rapid; it is a violent and alternate motion of the blood backward and forward: fear and suspense produce commonly *palpitation,* but joy and hope produce a *fluttering; panting* is, with regard to the breath, what *palpitating* is with regard to the heart; *panting* is occasioned by the inflated state of the respiratory organs, which renders this *palpitating* necessary: *gasping* differs from the former, inasmuch as it denotes a direct stoppage of the breath, a cessation of action in the respiratory organs.

PANEGYRIC. See ENCOMIUM.

PANG. See PAIN.

PANT. See PALPITATE.

PARABLE, ALLEGORY. Both these terms imply a veiled mode of speech, which serves more or less to conceal the main object of the discourse by presenting it under the appearance of something else, which accords with it in most of the particulars: the *parable*, in French *parabole*, Greek παραβολή, from παρά, beside, and βάλλειν, to cast, signifying a placing beside or a comparison of something with something else; the *allegory* (see FIGURE) in describing historical events. The *parable* substitutes some other subject or agent, who is represented under a character that is suitable to the one referred to. In the *allegory* are introduced strange and arbitrary persons in the place of the real personages, or imaginary characteristics and circumstances are ascribed to real persons. The *parable* is principally employed in the sacred writings; the *allegory* forms a grand feature in the productions of the eastern nations.

PARADE. See SHOW.

PARAMOUNT. See SUPREME.

PARASITE. See FLATTERER.

PARASOL. See UMBRELLA.

PARDON. See EXCUSE; FORGIVE.

PARDONABLE. See VENIAL.

PARE. See PEEL.

PARK. See FOREST.

PARLIAMENT. See ASSEMBLY.

PARODY. See CARICATURE; TRAVESTY.

PARSIMONIOUS. See AVARICIOUS.

PARSIMONY. See ECONOMY.

PARSON. See CLERGYMAN.

PART, DIVISION, PORTION, SHARE. *Part*, in Latin *pars*, a division, is a term not only of more general use, but of more comprehensive meaning than *division* (see DIVIDE); it is always employed for the thing *divided*, but *division* may be employed either for the act of *dividing* or the thing that is *divided*: but in all cases the word *division* has always a reference to some action and the agent by whom it has been performed; whereas *part*, which is perfectly abstract, has altogether lost this idea. We always speak of the *part* as opposed to the whole, but of the *division* as it has been made of the whole. A *part* is formed of itself by accident or made by design; a *division* is always the effect of design: a *part* is indefinite as to its quantity or nature; it may be large or small, round or square, of any dimension, form, size, or character; but a *division* is always regulated by some certain principles; it depends upon the circumstances of the *divider* and the thing to be *divided*. A page, a line, or a word is a *part* of any book; but the books, chapters, sections, and paragraphs are the *divisions* of the book. Stones, wood, water, air, and the like are *parts* of the world; fire, air, earth, and water are physical *divisions* of the globe; continents, seas, rivers, mountains, and the like are geographical *divisions*, under which are likewise included its political *divisions* into countries, kingdoms, etc.

A *part* may be detached from the whole; a *division* is always conceived of in connection with the whole; *portion*, from Latin *portio*, connected with *pars*, a part, and *share* (from Anglo-Saxon *scearu*, a fragment, based on *sceran*, German *scheren*, to sheer, allied with Old Irish *scaraim*, I separate) are particular species of *divisions* which are said of such matters as are assignable to individuals; *portion* refers to individuals without any distinction; *share* to individuals specially referred to. The *portion* of happiness which falls to every man's lot is more equal than is generally supposed; the *share* which partners have in the profits of any undertaking depends upon the sum which each has contributed toward its completion. The *portion* is that which simply comes to any one; but the *share* is that which belongs to one by a certain right. According to the ancient customs of Normandy, the daughters could have no more than a third *part* of the property for their *share*, which was *divided* into equal *portions* between them.

See also SEGREGATE.

Part, Piece, Patch.—*Part* in its strict sense is taken in connection with the whole; *piece*, in French *pièce*, may be ultimately of Celtic origin. *Patch,* Middle English *pacche,* of uncertain origin, is that *piece* which is distinguished from others.

Things may be divided into *parts* without any express separation; but when divided into *pieces* they are actually cut asunder. Hence we may speak of a loaf as divided into twelve *parts* when it is only conceived to be so; and divided into twelve *pieces* when it is really so. On this ground we talk of the *parts* of a country, but not of the *pieces;* and of a *piece* of land, not a *part* of land; so, likewise, letters are said to be the component *parts* of a word, but the half or the quarter of any given letter is called a *piece.* The chapters, the pages, the lines, etc., are the various *parts* of a book; certain passages or quantities drawn from the book are called *pieces:* the *parts* of matter may be infinitely decomposed; various bodies may be formed out of so ductile a *piece* of matter as clay. The *piece* is that which may sometimes serve as a whole; but the *patch* is that which is always broken and disjointed, a something imperfect: many things may be formed out of a *piece;* but the *patch* serves only to fill up a chasm.

Partake, Participate, Share. — *Partake* and *participate,* the one English, the other from Latin *participare,* based on an extended form of *pars,* and *capere,* or, to take a part, signify, literally, to take a part in a thing, and may be applied either in the sense of having a part in more than one object at the same time or having a part with others in the same object. In the first sense *partake* is the more familiar and ordinary expression, as a body may be said to *partake* of the essence of a salt and an acid. *Participate* is also used in the same sense, sometimes in poetry.

In the sense of having a part with others in the same object, to *partake* is a selfish action, to *participate* is either a selfish or benevolent action; we *partake* of that which pleases ourselves, we *participate* in that which pleases others, or in their pleasures.

To *partake* is the act of taking or getting a thing to one's self; to *share* is the act of having a title to a *share,* or being in the habit of receiving a *share:* we may, therefore, *partake* of a thing without *sharing* it, and *share* it without *partaking.* We *partake* of things mostly through the medium of the senses: whatever, therefore, we take a *part* in, whether gratuitously or casually, of that we may be said to *partake;* in this manner we *partake* of an entertainment without *sharing* it: on the other hand, we *share* things that promise to be of advantage or profit, and what we *share* is what we claim; in this manner we *share* a sum of money which has been left to us in common with others.

PARTICULAR, SINGULAR, ODD, ECCENTRIC, STRANGE. *Particular,* in French *particulier,* Latin *particularis,* from *particula,* a particle, signifies belonging to a particle or a very small part. *Singular,* in French *singulier,* Latin *singularis,* from *singulus,* every one, signifies, literally, unmatched (see ODD). *Eccentric,* through Late Latin from Greek ἐκ, out, and κέντρον, centre, signifies out of the centre or direct line. *Strange,* in Old French *estrange,* Latin *extraneus,* from Greek ἐξ, out of, and a suffix, signifies out of some other part, or not belonging to this part.

All these terms are employed either as characteristics of persons or things. What is *particular* belongs to some small *particle* or point to which it is confined; what is *singular* is *single,* or the only one of its kind; what is *odd* is without an equal or anything with which it is fit to pair; what is *eccentric* is not to be brought within any rule or estimate, it deviates to the right and the left; what is *strange* is different from that which one is accustomed to see, it does not admit of comparison or assimilation. A person is *particular* as regards himself; he is *singular* as regards others; he is *particular* in his habits or modes of action; he is *singular* in that which is about him; we may be *particular* or *singular* in our dress; in the former case we study the minute points of our dress to please ourselves; in the latter case we adopt a mode of dress that distinguishes us from all others.

One is *odd, eccentric,* and *strange,* more as it regards established modes, forms, and rules, than individual circumstances: a person is *odd* when his actions or his words bear no resemblance to those of others; he is *eccentric* if he irregularly departs from the customary modes of proceeding; he is *strange* when that which he does makes him new or unknown to those who are about him. *Particularity* and *singularity* are not always taken in a bad sense; *oddness, eccentricity,* and *strangeness* are never taken in a good one. A person ought to be *particular* in the choice of his society, his amusements, his books, and the like; he ought to be *singular* in virtue, when vice is unfortunately prevalent: but *particularity* becomes ridiculous when it concerns trifles; and *singularity* becomes culpable when it is not warranted by the most imperious necessity. As *oddness, eccentricity,* and *strangeness* consist in the violation of good order, of the decencies of human life, or the more important points of moral duty, they can never be justifiable and are often unpardonable. An *odd* man with whom no one can associate, and who likes to associate with no one, is an outcast by nature. An *eccentric* character, who distinguishes himself by the frequent breach of established rule, is a being who is bound to incur the hostility of the world. A *strange* person, who makes himself a *stranger* among those to whom he is bound by the closest ties, is a being as unfortunate as he is misunderstood.

When applied to characterize inanimate objects, these words are mostly used in an indifferent, but sometimes in a bad sense: the term *particular* serves to define or specify, it is opposed to the general or indefinite; a *particular* day or hour, a *particular* case, a *particular* person, are expressions which confine one's attention to one precise object in distinction from the rest; *singular,* like the word *particular,* marks but one object, and that which is clearly pointed out in distinction from the rest; but this term differs from the former, inasmuch as the *particular* is said only of that which one has arbitrarily made *particular;* but the *singular* is so from its own properties: thus a place is *particular* when we fix upon it and mark it out in any manner so that it may be known from

others; a place is *singular* if it have anything in itself which distinguishes it from others. *Odd,* in an indifferent sense, is opposed to even, and applied to objects in general; an *odd* number, an *odd* person, an *odd* book, and the like: but it is also employed in a bad sense to mark objects which are totally dissimilar to others; thus an *odd* idea, an *odd* conceit, an *odd* whim, an *odd* way, an *odd* place. *Eccentric* is applied in its proper sense to mathematical lines or circles which have not the same centre, and is never employed in an improper sense: *strange,* in its proper sense, marks that which is unknown or unusual, as a *strange* face, a *strange* figure, a *strange* place; but in the moral application it is like the word *odd,* and conveys the unfavorable idea of that which is uncommon and not worth knowing; a *strange* noise designates not only that which has not been heard before, but that which it is not desirable to hear; a *strange* place may signify not only that which we have been unaccustomed to see, but that which has also much in it that is objectionable.

Particular, Individual. — *Particular* (see PECULIAR). *Individual,* in French *individuel,* Latin *individuus,* with a suffix, signifies that which cannot be divided.

Both these terms are employed to express one object; but *particular* is much more specific than *individual;* the *particular* confines us to one object only of many; but *individual* may be said of any one object among many. A *particular* object cannot be misunderstood for any other while it remains *particular;* but the *individual* object can never be known from other *individual* objects while it remains only *individual. Particular* is a term used in regard to *individuals,* and is opposed to the general: *individual* is a term used in regard to collectives, and is opposed to the whole or that which is divisible into parts.

See also CIRCUMSTANTIAL; EXACT; SPECIAL.

PARTICULARLY. See ESPECIALLY.

PARTISAN. See FOLLOWER.
PARTNER. See COLLEAGUE.
PARTNERSHIP. See ASSOCIATION.

PARTY. See FACTION.

PASS, PASSPORT, SAFE-CONDUCT, SAFEGUARD. *Pass*, in French *passer*, from Late Latin *passare*, from *passus*, a step, Spanish *pasar*, Italian *passare*, all virtually mean to step, to go; permission to go or come, evidenced by a ticket or other document issued by a competent authority.

A *passport* is a warrant of protection issued by a government to one of its citizens to enable the bearer to visit or travel in another country without molestation. An *emergency passport* may be issued to a citizen of the United States happening to be in a foreign country, under specific circumstances, by certain representatives of the United States in that country.

A *safe-conduct* may be an official warrant issued as above, or a convoy or guard to protect the bearer in or passing through a hostile or a foreign country. To *safeguard* a person, a ship, or an important interest is to provide the subject with ample protection in any of the above forms.

In the second year of the European war (1915) it was discovered that many *passports* issued by the United States government had been forged and had got into the hands of spies of the Teutonic powers. This led the government to adopt more rigorous regulations for the issue of such documents.

PASSAGE. See COURSE.
PASSING OVER. See DEATH.
PASSIONATE. See ANGRY.
PASSIVE. See PATIENT.
PASSWORD. See SHIBBOLETH.
PAST. See BYGONE.
PASTIME. See AMUSEMENT.
PATCH. See PART.
PATHETIC. See MOVING.

PATIENCE, ENDURANCE, RESIGNA- TION. *Patience* applies to any troubles or pains whatever, small or great; *resignation* is employed only for those of great moment, in which our dearest interests are concerned: *patience*, when compared with *resignation*, is somewhat negative; it consists in the abstaining from all complaint or indication of what one suffers: but *resignation* consists in a positive sentiment of conformity to the existing circumstances, be they what they may. There are perpetual occurrences which are apt to harass the temper, unless one regards them with *patience;* the misfortunes of some men are of so calamitous a nature that if they have not acquired *resignation* they must inevitably sink under them. *Patience* applies only to the evils that actually hang over us; but there is a *resignation* connected with a firm trust in Providence which extends its views to futurity and prepares us for the worst that may happen.

As *patience* lies in the manner and temper of suffering, and *endurance* in the act, we may have *endurance* and not *patience:* for we may have much to *endure,* and consequently *endurance:* but if we do not *endure* it with an easy mind and without the disturbance of our looks and words, we have not *patience:* on the other hand, we may have *patience,* but not *endurance:* for our *patience* may be exercised by momentary trifles which are not sufficiently great or lasting to constitute *endurance.*

Patient, Passive, Submissive. — *Patient,* from the Latin *patiens,* signifies, literally, suffering, and is applied to things in general, but especially to what is painful. *Passive,* from the Latin *passivus* and *passus,* signifying, literally, suffered or acted upon, applies to those matters in which persons have to act; he is *patient* who bears what he has to suffer without any expressions of complaint; he is *passive* who abstains altogether from acting when he might act.

Patience is a virtue springing from principle; *passiveness* is always involuntary, and may be supposed to arise from want of spirit.

Patience is therefore applicable to conscious agents only; *passiveness* is applicable to inanimate objects which do not act at all, or at least not adversely.

Passive and *submissive* both refer to the will of others; but *passive* signifies simply not resisting; *submissive* signifies positively conforming to the will of another.

See also INVALID.

PATTERN. See COPY; EXAMPLE.
PAUSE. See DEMUR.
PAY. See ALLOWANCE.

PEACE, QUIET, CALM, TRANQUIL- LITY. *Peace* is derived through French from Latin *pax*. *Quiet* (see EASY). *Calm* (see ABATE; CALM). *Tranquillity* is in Latin *tranquillitas*, from *tranquillus*, at rest.

Peace is a term of more general application and more comprehensive meaning than the others; it applies either to communities or individuals; but *quiet* applies only to individuals or small communities. Nations are said to have *peace*, but not *quiet;* persons or families may have both *peace* and *quiet*. *Peace* implies an exemption from public or private broils; *quiet* implies a freedom from noise or interruption. Every well - disposed family strives to be at *peace* with its neighbors, and every affectionate family will naturally act in such a manner as to promote *peace* among all its members: the *quiet* of a neighborhood is one of its first recommendations as a place of residence.

Peace and *quiet*, in regard to individuals, have likewise a reference to the internal state of the mind; but the former expresses the permanent condition of the mind, the latter its transitory condition. Serious matters only can disturb our *peace;* trivial matters may disturb our *quiet:* a good man enjoys the *peace* of a good conscience; but he may have unavoidable cares and anxieties which disturb his *quiet*. There can be no *peace* where a man's passions are perpetually engaged in a conflict with one another; there can be no *quiet* where a man is embarrassed in his pecuniary affairs.

Calm is a species of *quiet*, which affects objects in the natural or the moral world; it indicates the absence of violent motion as well as violent noise; it is that state which more immediately succeeds a state of agitation. As storms at sea are frequently preceded as well as succeeded by a dead *calm*, so political storms have likewise their *calms*, which are their attendants, if not their precursors. *Tranquillity*, on the other hand, is taken more absolutely: it expresses the situation as it exists at the present moment, independently of what goes before or after; it is sometimes applicable to society, sometimes to natural objects, and sometimes to the mind. The *tranquillity* of the state cannot be preserved unless the authority of the magistrates be upheld; the *tranquillity* of the air and of all the surrounding objects is one thing which gives the country its peculiar charms; the *tranquillity* of the mind in the season of devotion contributes essentially to produce a suitable degree of religious fervor.

As epithets, these terms bear the same relation to each other: people are *peaceable* as they are disposed to promote *peace* in society at large, or in their private relations; they are *quiet* inasmuch as they abstain from every loud expression, or are exempt from any commotion in themselves; they are *calm*, inasmuch as they are exempt from the commotion which at any given moment rages around them; they are *tranquil*, inasmuch as they enjoy an entire exemption from everything which can discompose. A town is *peaceable* as respects the disposition of the inhabitants; it is *quiet* as respects its external circumstances of freedom from bustle and noise: an evening is *calm* when the air is lulled into a particular stillness which is not interrupted by any loud sounds: a scene is *tranquil* which combines everything calculated to soothe the spirits to rest.

Peaceable, Peaceful, Pacific.—*Peaceable* is used in the proper sense of the word *peace*, as it expresses an exemption from strife or contest; but *peaceful* is used in its improper sense, as it expresses an exemption from agitation or commotion. Persons or things are *peaceable;* things, particularly in the higher style, are *peaceful:* a family is designated as *peaceable* in regard to its inhabitants; a house is designated as a *peaceful* abode as it is remote from the bustle and hurry of a multitude. *Pacific* signifies either making *peace* or disposed to make *peace*, and is applied mostly to what we do to others. We are *peaceable* when we do not engage in quarrels of our own; we are *pacific* if we wish to keep *peace* or make *peace* between others. Hence the term *peaceable* is mostly employed for individual or private concerns, and *pacific* most properly for national concerns: subjects ought to be *peaceable*, and monarchs *pacific*.

See also PACIFIST; UNRUFFLED.

PEARLY. See NACREOUS.

PEASANT. See COUNTRYMAN.

PECULIAR, APPROPRIATE, PARTICULAR. *Peculiar*, in Latin *peculiaris*, from *peculium*, private property, *pecunia*, money, and *pecus*, cattle, in which property consisted, is said of that which belongs to persons or things; *appropriate*, signifying belonging, fitting (see ASCRIBE), is said of that which belongs to things only: the faculty of speech is *peculiar* to man, in distinction from all other animals; an address may be *appropriate* to the circumstances of the individual. *Peculiar* and *particular* (see PARTICULAR) are both employed to distinguish objects; but the former distinguishes the object by showing its connection with others; *particular* distinguishes it by a reference to some acknowledged circumstance; hence we may say that a person enjoys *peculiar* privileges or *particular* privileges: in this case *peculiar* signifies such as are confined to him and enjoyed by none else; *particular* signifies such as are distinguished in degree and quality from others of the kind.

See also UNIQUE.

PEDAGOGIC. See DIDACTIC.

PEEL, PARE. *Peel*, from the French *peler*, derived from Latin *pellis*, a skin, is the same as to skin or to take off the skin: to *pare*, from the Latin *parare*, to trim or make in order, signifies to smooth. The former of these terms denotes a natural, the latter an artificial, process: the former excludes the idea of a forcible separation; the latter includes the idea of separation by means of a knife or sharp instrument: potatoes and apples are *peeled* after they are boiled; they are *pared* before they are boiled; an orange and a walnut are always *peeled* but not *pared;* a cucumber must be *pared* and not *peeled:* in like manner, the skin may sometimes be *peeled* from the flesh, and the nails are *pared*.

See also SKIN.

PEEVISH. See CAPTIOUS: SPLENETIC.

PELLUCID, TRANSPARENT. *Pellucid*, in Latin *pellucidus*, is compounded of *per*, through, and *lucidus*, shining. *Transparent*, in Latin *transparens*, from *trans*, through or beyond, and *parere*, to appear, signifies that which admits light through it. *Pellucid* is said of that which is pervious to the light or of that into which the eye can penetrate; *transparent* is said of that which is throughout bright: a stream is *pellucid;* it admits of the light so as to reflect objects, but it is not *transparent* for the eye.

See also DIAPHANOUS.

PENALTY. See FINE.

PENETRATE, PIERCE, PERFORATE, BORE. To *penetrate* (see DISCERNMENT) is simply to make an entrance into any substance; to *pierce* is commonly assumed to come through Old French *pertuisier*, from Latin *per*, through, and *tundere*, to beat. *Perforate* comes from the Latin *per*, through, and *forare*, to pierce, which is the same word as the native English *bore*. To *penetrate* is a natural and gradual process; in this manner rust *penetrates* iron, water *penetrates* wood; to *pierce* is a violent, and commonly artificial, process; thus an arrow or a bullet *pierces* through wood. The instrument by which the act of *penetration* is performed is in no case defined; but that of *piercing* commonly proceeds by some pointed instrument: we may *penetrate* the earth by means of a spade, a plough, a knife, or various other instruments; but one *pierces* the flesh by means of a needle, or one *pierces* the ground or a wall by means of a pickaxe.

To *perforate* and *bore* are modes of *piercing* that vary in the circumstances of the action and the objects acted upon; to *pierce*, in its peculiar use, is a sudden action by which a hollow is produced in any substance; but to *perforate* and *bore* are commonly the effect of mechanical art. The body of an animal is *pierced* by a dart; but cannon is made by *perforating* or *boring* the iron: channels are formed underground by *perforating* the earth; holes are made in the ear by *perforation;* holes are made in the leather, or in the wood, by *boring;* these last two words do not differ in sense, but in application, the latter being a term of vulgar use, though sometimes used in poetry.

To *penetrate* and *pierce* are likewise employed in an improper sense; to *perforate* and *bore* are employed only in the proper sense. The first two bear the same relation to each other as in the former case: *penetrate* is, however, employed only as the act of persons; *pierce* is used in regard to things. There is a power in the mind to *penetrate* the looks and actions, so as justly to interpret their meaning; the eye of the Almighty is said to *pierce* the thickest veil of darkness. Affairs are sometimes involved in such mystery that the most enlightened is unable to *penetrate* either the end or the beginning; the shrieks of distress are sometimes so loud as to seem to *pierce* the ear.

See also THRILL.

Penetration, Acuteness, Sagacity.— As characteristics of mind, these terms have much more in them in which they differ than in what they agree: *penetration* is a necessary property of mind; it exists to a greater or less degree in every rational being that has the due exercise of its rational powers; *acuteness* is an accidental property that belongs to the mind only, under certain circumstances. As *penetration* (see DISCERNMENT) denotes the process of entering into substances physically or morally, so *acuteness*, which is the same as sharpness, from *acutus*, sharp, denotes the fitness of the thing that performs this process: and as the mind is in both cases the thing that is spoken of, the terms *penetration* and *acuteness* are in this particular closely allied. It is clear, however, that the mind may have *penetration* without having *acuteness*, although one cannot have *acuteness* without *penetration*. If by *penetration* we are commonly enabled to get at the truth which lies concealed, by *acuteness* we succeed in piercing the veil that hides it from our view; the former is, therefore, an ordinary, and the latter an extraordinary, gift.

Sagacity is in Latin *sagacitas*, from *sagire*, to perceive by the senses. The term has been applied to animals which discover an intuitive wisdom, and also to children, or uneducated persons, in whom there is more *penetration* than may be expected from the narrow compass of their knowledge; hence, properly speaking, *sagacity* is natural or uncultivated *acuteness*.

PENITENCE. See REPENTANCE.

PENMAN. See WRITER.

PENURIOUS. See ECONOMICAL.

PENURY. See POVERTY.

PEOPLE, NATION. *People* is derived through French from the Latin *populus.* The simple idea of numbers is expressed by the word *people:* but the term *nation*, from *natio* and *natus*, born, marks the connection of numbers by birth; *people* is, therefore, the generic, and *nation* the specific, term. A *nation* is a *people* connected by birth; there cannot, therefore, strictly speaking, be a *nation* without a *people:* but there may be a *people* where there is not a *nation.* The Jews, when considered as an assemblage, under the special direction of the Almighty, are termed the *people* of God, but when considered in regard to their common origin, they are denominated the Jewish *nation.* The Americans, when spoken of in relation to the British, are a distinct *people*, because they have a distinct *government*; but they are not a distinct *nation*, because they have a common descent. On this ground the Romans are not called the Roman *nation*, because their origin was so various, but the Roman *people*, that is, an assemblage living under one form of government.

In a still closer application, *people* is taken for a part of the state, namely, that part of a state which consists of a multitude, in distinction from its government; whence arises a distinction in the use of the terms; for we may speak of the British *people*, the French or the Dutch *people*, when we wish merely to talk of the mass, but we speak of the British *nation*, the French *nation*, and the Dutch *nation*, when public measures are in question, which emanate from the government or the whole *people.* The English *people* have ever been remarkable for their attachment to liberty: the abolition of the slave-trade is one of the most glorious acts of public justice which were ever performed by the British *nation.* Upon the same ground republican states are distinguished by the name of *people:* but kingdoms are commonly spoken of in history as *nations.* Hence we say the Spartan *people*, the Athenian *people*, the *people* of Genoa, the *people* of Venice, but the *nations* of Europe, the

African *nations,* the English, French, German, and Italian *nations.*

People, Populace, Mob.—*People* and *populace* are evidently changes of the same word to express a number. The signification of these terms is that of a number gathered together. *People* is said of any body supposed to be assembled, as well as really assembled: *populace* is said of a body only when actually assembled. The voice of the *people* is sometimes too loud to be disregarded; the *populace* in England are fond of dragging their favorites in carriages.

Mob and *mobility* are from the Latin *mobilis,* signifying movableness, which is the characteristic of the multitude: hence Virgil's *mobile vulgus.* (The word *mobile* was used in this sense in England at the end of the seventeenth century.) The term *mob,* therefore, designates not only what is low, but tumultuous. A *mob* is at all times an object of terror that mostly goes from bad to worse. *Mobility,* as an adjective, is used in its etymological sense to-day.

People, Persons, Folks.—The term *people* has already been considered in two acceptations under the general idea of an assembly; but in the present case it is employed to express a small number of individuals: the word *people,* however, is always considered as one undivided body, and the word *person* may be distinctly used either in the singular or in the plural; as we cannot say one, two, three, or four *people:* but we may say one, two, three, or four *persons:* yet, on the other hand, we may indifferently say, such *people* or *persons;* many *people* or *persons;* some *people* or *persons,* and the like.

With regard to the use of these terms, which is altogether colloquial, *people* is employed in general propositions, and *persons* in those which are specific or referring directly to some particular individuals: *people* are generally of that opinion; some *people* think so; some *people* attended: there were but few *persons* present at the entertainment; the whole company consisted of six *persons.*

As the term *people* is employed to designate the promiscuous multitude, it has acquired a certain meanness of acceptation which makes it less suit-

able than the word *persons,* when *people* of respectability are referred to: were I to say of any individuals I do not know who the *people* are, it would not be so respectful as to say, I do not know who those *persons* are: in like manner one says, from *people* of that stamp one can expect nothing better; *persons* of their appearance do not frequent such places.

Folks, Anglo-Saxon *folc,* is a homely and familiar word; it is not unusual to say good *people* or good *folks;* and in speaking jocularly to one's friends the latter term is likewise admissible: but in the serious style it is never employed except in a disrespectful manner: such *folks* (speaking of gamesters) are often put to sorry shifts.

See also PUBLIC.

PERCEIVE, DISCERN, DISTINGUISH. To *perceive,* in Latin *percipio,* or *per,* an intensive prefix, through, or thoroughly, and a weak form of *capere,* signifying to take hold of, is a positive, to *discern* (see DISCERNMENT) a relative, action: we *perceive* things by themselves; we *discern* them amidst many others: we *perceive* that which is obvious; we *discern* that which is remote or which requires much attention to get an idea of it. We *perceive* by a person's looks and words what he intends; we *discern* the drift of his actions. We may *perceive* sensible or spiritual objects; we commonly *discern* only that which is spiritual: we *perceive* light, darkness, colors, or the truth or falsehood of anything; we *discern* characters, motives, the tendency and consequences of actions, etc. It is the act of a child to *perceive* according to the quickness of its senses; it is the act of a man to *discern* according to the measure of his knowledge and understanding.

To *discern* and *distinguish* (see DIFFERENCE) approach the nearest in sense to each other; but the former signifies to see only one thing, the latter to see two or more in quick succession so as to compare them. We *discern* what lies in things: we *distinguish* things according to their outward marks; we *discern* things in order to understand their essences; we *distinguish* in order not to confound them. Experienced and discreet people may *discern* the signs of the times; it is just to *distinguish* between an action done from inadvertence and that which is done from design. The conduct of people is sometimes so veiled by art that it is not easy to *discern* their object: it is necessary to *distinguish* between practice and profession.

See also SEE.

Perception, Idea, Conception, Notion. —*Perception* expresses either the act of *perceiving* or the impression produced by that act; in this latter sense it is analogous to an *idea* (see IDEA). The impression of an object that is present to us is termed a *perception;* the revival of that impression, when the object is removed, is an *idea.* A combination of *ideas* by which any image is presented to the mind is a *conception* (see COMPREHEND); the association of two or more *ideas* so as to constitute a decision is a *notion* (see OPINION). *Perceptions* are clear or confused, according to the state of the sensible organs and the *perceptive* faculty; *ideas* are faint or vivid, vague or distinct, according to the nature of the *perception; conceptions* are gross or refined according to number and extent of one's *ideas; notions* are true or false, correct or incorrect, according to the extent of one's knowledge. The *perception* which we have of remote objects is sometimes so indistinct as to leave hardly any traces of the image on the mind; we have in that case a *perception,* but not an *idea:* if we read the description of any object we may have an *idea* of it; but we need not have any immediate *perception:* the *idea* in this case being complex, and formed of many images of which we have already had a *perception.*

If we present objects to our minds, according to different images which have already been impressed, we are said to have a *conception* of them: in this case, however, it is not necessary for the objects really to exist; they may be the product of the mind's operation within itself: but with regard to *notions* it is different, for they are formed respecting objects that do really exist, although perhaps the properties or circumstances which we assign to them are not real. If I look at the moon, I have a *perception* of it;

if it disappear from my sight, and the impression remains, I have an *idea* of it; if an object, differing in shape and color from anything else which I may have seen, presents itself to my mind, it is a *conception;* if of this moon I conceive that it is no bigger than what it appears to my eye, this is a *notion* which, in the present instance, assigns an unreal property to a real object.

See also SENTIMENT.

PERCEPTIBLE. See TANGIBLE.

PEREMPTORY. See POSITIVE.

PERFECT. See ACCOMPLISHED; COMPLETE.

PERFECTLY. See QUITE.

PERFIDIOUS. See FAITHLESS.

PERFORATE. See PENETRATE; THRILL.

PERFORATION. See ORIFICE.

PERFORM. See EFFECT: EXECUTE.

PERFORMER. See ACTOR.

PERIL. See DANGER.

PERILOUS. See HERCULEAN.

PERIOD. See SENTENCE; TIME.

PERISCOPE. ALTISCOPE, TELESCOPE. *Periscope,* a compound of the Greek περί, around, and σκοπεῖν, look, signifies, literally, a general view or a view on all sides, and, specifically, spectacles with concavo-convex glasses constructed to increase the distinctness of objects when viewed obliquely. As a substantive the term has a distinctive application to a form of telescope by which an observer is enabled to see over a parapet, wall, and other parts of a fortification, known as an *altiscope,* from the Latin *altus,* high, and σκοπεῖν, to see. It consists of a telescopic tube with a right angle at the top and a reverse right angle at the bottom, with mirrors arranged at these points.

A *periscope,* with which term the world became more familiar during the great European war, is an improved form of the *altiscope,* having at the top a lenticular total-reflection prism instead of a mirror, and turning upon a vertical axis, so that it is capable of sweeping the entire horizon. It is the slender instrument that rises above the surface from the body of a submarine when sufficiently submerged to be out of sight, with which the navigator scans the horizon and directs the craft for attacking another vessel.

PERISH, DIE, DECAY. To *perish*, in French *périr*, in Latin *pereo*, compounded of *per* and *eo*, signifying to go thoroughly away, expresses more than to *die* (see DIE), and is applicable to many objects; for the latter is properly applied only to express the extinction of animal life, and figuratively to express the extinction of life or spirit in vegetables or other bodies; but the former is applied to express the dissolution of substances, so that they lose their existence as aggregate bodies. What *perishes*, therefore, does not always *die*, although whatever *dies* by that very act *perishes* to a certain extent. Hence we say that wood *perishes*, although it does not *die;* people are said either to *perish* or *die:* but as the term *perish* expresses even more than *dying*, it is possible for the same thing to *die* and not *perish;* thus a plant may be said to *die* when it loses its vegetative power; but it is said to *perish* if its substance crumbles into dust.

To *perish* expresses the end; to *decay* the process by which this end is brought about: a thing may be long in *decaying*, but when it *perishes* it ceases at once to act or to exist: things may, therefore, *perish* without *decaying;* they may likewise *decay* without *perishing.* Things which are altogether new, and have experienced no kind of *decay*, may *perish* by means of water, fire, lightning, and the like: on the other hand, wood, iron, and other substances may begin to *decay*, but may be saved from immediately *perishing* by the application of preventives.

PERJURE. See FORSWEAR.
PERMANENT. See DURABLE.
PERMISSION. See LEAVE.
PERMIT. See ADMIT; CONSENT.
PERNICIOUS. See DESTRUCTIVE; HURTFUL.

PERPETRATE, COMMIT. The idea of doing something wrong is common to these terms; but *perpetrate*, from the Latin *per*, intensive, and *patrare*, signifying thoroughly to compass or bring about, is a much more determined proceeding than that of *committing.* One may *commit* offences of various degrees

and magnitude; but one *perpetrates* crimes only, and those of the more heinous kind. Lawless banditti, who spend their lives in the *perpetration* of the most monstrous crimes, are not to be restrained by the ordinary course of justice; he who *commits* any offence against the good order of society exposes himself to the censure of others who, in certain respects, may be his inferiors.

PERPETUAL. See CONTINUAL.
PERPLEX. See DISTRESS; EMBARRASS.
PERPLEXING. See KNOTTY.
PERPLEXITY. See QUANDARY; WORRY.
PERSEVERE. See CONTINUE.
PERSIST. See CONTINUE; INSIST.
PERSONS. See PEOPLE.
PERSPICUITY. See CLEARNESS.

PERSUADE, ENTICE, PREVAIL UPON. *Persuade* (see CONVICTION) and *entice* (see ALLURE) are employed to express different means to the same end, namely, that of drawing any one to a thing: one *persuades* a person by means of words; one *entices* him either by words or actions; one may *persuade* either to a good or bad thing; but one *entices* commonly to that which is bad; one uses arguments to *persuade*, and arts to *entice*.

Persuade and *entice* comprehend either the means or the end, or both; *prevail upon* comprehends no more than the end: we may *persuade* without *prevailing upon*, and we may *prevail upon* without *persuading.* Many will turn a deaf ear to all our *persuasions*, and will not be *prevailed upon*, although *persuaded:* on the other hand, we may be *prevailed upon* by the force of remonstrance, authority, and the like; and in this case we are *prevailed upon* without being *persuaded.* We should never *persuade* another to do that which we are not willing to do ourselves; credulous or good-natured people are easily *prevailed upon* to do things which tend to their own injury.

See EXHORT.
PERTINACIOUS. See TENACIOUS.
PERVERSE. See AWKWARD.
PESSIMISTIC, DESPONDING, GLOOMY. *Pessimistic* is a term derived from the Latin *pessimus*, the worst. *Desponding* comes from Latin *de*, away,

and *spondere,* to promise, and means literally promising away, yielding up wholly, hence despairing. *Gloomy* comes from Middle English *gloumen,* to lower. These three words are used to describe a disposition which is inclined to "look on the dark side of things," to give up hope. *Pessimistic* describes an intellectual attitude; *desponding,* an emotional state. The *pessimistic* man believes that things are worse than they are; the *desponding* man, holding such a belief, yields up all hope. *Desponding* indicates an abnormal psychological condition, and is a much stronger word than *pessimistic.* We may feel *pessimistic* about all sorts of trivial matters; we become *desponding* when something vital to happiness has been taken away, thereby, as it were, destroying the emotional balance. *Gloomy* is a word descriptive of manner, mood, and temperament rather than of a distinct and positive emotional condition such as that indicated in *desponding.* The *gloomy* man resembles a lowering sky; the light and sunshine seem to have been obliterated. But the word means little more than a general absence of cheerfulness, and suggests rather a diffused sadness, oftentimes without cause or object, than an intense and absolute hopelessness.

See also OPTIMISTIC.

PEST. See BANE.

PESTILENTIAL. See CONTAGIOUS.

PETITION. See PRAYER.

PETTY. See TRIFLING.

PETULANT. See CAPTIOUS.

PHANTASM. See HALLUCINATION.

PHANTOM. See VISION.

PHOTOPLAY. See MOVING PICTURE.

PHRASE. See DICTION; SENTENCE.

PICK. See CHOOSE.

PICTURE, PRINT, ENGRAVING. *Picture* (see PAINT) is any likeness taken by the hand of the artist: the *print* is the copy of the painting in a *printed* state; and the *engraving* is that which is produced by an *engraver:* every *engraving* is a *print;* but every *print* is not an *engraving;* for the *picture,* as in the case of woodcuts, may be *printed* from something besides an *engraving.* The term *picture* is sometimes used for any representation of a likeness, without regard to the process by which it is formed: in this case it is employed mostly for the representations of the common kind that are found in books; but *print* and *engraving* are said of the higher specimens of the art. On certain occasions the word *engraving* is most appropriate, as to take an *engraving* of a particular object; on the other occasions the word *print,* as a handsome *print,* or a large *print.*

See also RADIOGRAPH.

PIECE. See PART.

PIERCE. See PENETRATE; THRILL.

PILE. See HEAP.

PILLAGE. See RAPINE; SACK; SPOLIATION.

PILLAR, COLUMN. *Pillar* comes from Latin *pila,* a pier of stone. *Column* is in Latin *columna,* allied to *collis,* hill, and *culmen,* a summit (whence our word *culminate*), indicating a shaft which reaches upward. Both words are applied to the same object, namely, to whatever is artificially set up in wood, stone, or other hard material; but the word *pillar,* having come first into use, is the most general in its application to any structure, whether rude or otherwise; the term *column,* on the other hand, is applied to whatever is ornamental, as the Grecian order of *columns.*

So in poetry, where simply a support is spoken of, the term *pillar* may be used.

But where grandeur or embellishment is to be expressed, the term *column.*

Both terms are applied to other objects having a similarity either of form or of use. Whatever is set up in the form of a *pillar* is so denominated; as, stone *pillars* in crossways, or over graves, and the like.

Whatever is drawn out in the form of a *column,* be the material of which it is composed what it may, it is denominated a *column;* as a *column* of water, smoke, etc.; a *column* of men, a *column* of a page.

Pillar is frequently employed in a moral application, and in that case it always implies a support.

PINCH. See NIP; PRESS.

PINE. See FLAG.

PINNACLE. See TURRET.

PIOUS. See HOLY.

PIQUE. See MALICE; UMBRAGE.

PITEOUS, DOLEFUL, WOFUL, RUEFUL. *Piteous* signifies moving *pity* (see PITY). *Doleful*, or full of *dole*, in Latin *dolor*, pain, signifies indicative of much pain. *Woful*, or full of *woe*, signifies likewise indicative of *woe* (see WOE). *Rueful*, or full of *rue*, comes from Anglo-Saxon *hreowan*, to be sorry, and signifies indicative of much sorrow.

The close alliance in sense of these words one to another is obvious from the above explanation; *piteous* is applicable to one's external expression of bodily or mental pain; a child makes *piteous* lamentations when it suffers from hunger or has lost its way; *doleful* applies to those sounds which convey the idea of pain; there is something *doleful* in the tolling of a funeral bell or in the sound of a muffled drum: *woful* applies to the circumstances and situations of men; a scene is *woful* in which we witness a large family of young children suffering from sickness and want; *rueful* applies to the outward indications of inward sorrow depicted in the looks or countenance. The term is commonly applied to the sorrows which spring from a gloomy or distorted imagination, and has therefore acquired a somewhat ludicrous acceptation; hence we find Cervantes's characterization of Don Quixote rendered in English as the knight of the *rueful* countenance.

Pitiable, Piteous, Pitiful. — These three epithets drawn from the same word have shades of difference in sense and application. *Pitiable* signifies deserving of *pity; piteous*, moving *pity; pitiful*, full of that which awakens *pity*; a condition is *pitiable* which is so distressing as to call forth *pity*; a cry is *piteous* which indicates such distress as can excite *pity*; a conduct is *pitiful* which marks a character entitled to *pity*. The first of these terms is taken in the best sense of the term *pity*; the last two in its unfavorable sense: what is *pitiable* in a person is independent of anything in himself; circumstances have rendered him *pitiable*; what is *piteous* and *pitiful* in a man arises from the helplessness and imbecility or worthlessness of his character; the former connotes that which is weak; the latter that which is worth-less in him: when a poor creature makes *piteous* moans, it indicates his incapacity to help himself, as he ought to do, out of his troubles; when a man of rank has recourse to *pitiful* shifts to gain his ends, he betrays the innate meanness of his soul.

See also CONTEMPTIBLE; MEAN.

Pity, Compassion. — *Pity* is contracted from Latin *pietas*, English *piety*, from *pius*, which signified attentive to all natural duties, and implied especially a religious devotion to the gods and to parents and family. *Compassion*, in Latin *compassio*, from *con*, with, and *passus*, past participle of *pati*, to suffer, signifies to suffer in conjunction with another.

The pain which one feels at the distress of another is the idea that is common to the signification of both these terms, but they differ in the object that causes the distress: the former is excited principally by the weakness or degraded condition of the subject; the latter by his uncontrollable and inevitable misfortunes. We *pity* a man of weak understanding who exposes his weakness: we *compassionate* the man who is reduced to a state of beggary and want. *Pity* is kindly extended by those in higher condition to such as are humble in their outward circumstances; the poor are at all times deserving of *pity*, even when their poverty is the positive fruit of vice: *compassion* is a sentiment which extends to persons in all conditions; the Good Samaritan had *compassion* on the traveller who fell among thieves. *Pity*, though a tender sentiment, is so closely allied to contempt that an understanding person is always loath to be the subject of it, since it can never be awakened but by some circumstance of inferiority; it hurts the honest pride of a man to reflect that he can excite no interest but by provoking a comparison to his own disadvantage: on the other hand, such is the general infirmity of our natures, and such our exposure to the casualties of human life, that *compassion* is a pure and delightful sentiment that is reciprocally bestowed and acknowledged by all with equal satisfaction.

Pity, Mercy.—The feelings one indulges, and the conduct one adopts, toward others who suffer through their own fault, are the common ideas which render these terms synonymous; but *pity* lays hold of those circumstances which do not affect the moral character or which diminish the culpability of the individual: *mercy* lays hold of those external circumstances which may diminish punishment. *Pity* is often a sentiment unaccompanied with action; *mercy* is often a mode of action unaccompanied with sentiment: we have or take *pity* upon a person, but we show *mercy* to a person. *Pity* is bestowed by men in their domestic and private capacity; *mercy* is shown in the exercise of power: a master has *pity* upon his offending servant by passing over his offences and affording him the opportunity of amendment; the magistrate shows *mercy* to a criminal by diminishing his punishment. *Pity* lies in the breast of an individual and may be bestowed at his discretion: *mercy* is restricted by the rules of civil society; it must not interfere with the administration of justice. Young offenders call for great *pity*, as their offences are often the fruit of inexperience and bad example rather than of depravity: *mercy* is an imperative duty in those who have the power of inflicting punishment, particularly in cases where life and death are concerned.

Pity and *mercy* are likewise applied to the animal creation with a similar distinction: *pity* shows itself in relieving real misery and in lightening burdens; *mercy* is displayed in the measure of pain which one inflicts. One takes *pity* on a poor animal to whom one gives food to relieve hunger; one shows it *mercy* by abstaining from beating it.

These terms are, moreover, applicable to the Deity, in regard to His creatures, particularly man. God takes *pity* on us as entire dependents upon Him: he extends His *mercy* toward us as offenders against Him: He shows His *pity* by relieving our wants; He shows His *mercy* by forgiving our sins.

PITHY. See LACONIC.

PITILESS. See HEARTLESS.

PLACE, STATION, SITUATION, POSITION, POST. *Place*, from Latin *platea*, Greek πλατεῖα, a broad way, is the abstract or general term that comprehends the idea of any given space that may be occupied: *station* (see CONDITION) is the *place* where one stands or is fixed: *situation*, in Latin *situs*, a place, and *position*, from *positus*, the past participle of *ponere*, to place, signify the object as well as the place; that is, they signify how the object is put, as well as where it is put. A *place* or *station* may be either vacant or otherwise; a *situation* and a *position* necessarily suppose some occupied *place*. A *place* is either assigned or not assigned, known or unknown, real or supposed: a *station* is a specifically assigned *place*. We choose a *place* according to our convenience, and we leave it again at pleasure; but we take up our *station* and hold it for a given period. One inquires for a *place* which is known only by name; the *station* is appointed for us, and is, therefore, easily found. Travellers wander from *place* to *place;* soldiers have always some *station*.

The terms *place* and *situation* are said of objects animate or inanimate; *station* only of animate objects, or those which are figuratively considered as such; *position* properly of inanimate objects, or those which are considered as such: a person chooses a *place;* a thing occupies a *place*, or has a *place* set apart for it: a *station* or *stated* place must always be assigned to each person who has to act in concert with others; a *situation* or *position* is chosen for a thing to suit the convenience of an individual: the former is said of things as they stand with regard to others; the latter of things as they stand with regard to themselves. The *situation* of a house comprehends the nature of the *place*, whether on high or low ground, and also its relation to other objects, that is, whether higher or lower, nearer or more distant: the *position* of a window in a house is considered as to whether it is straight or crooked; the *position* of a book is considered as to whether it stands leaning or upright, with its face or back forward. *Situation* is, moreover, said of things that come there of themselves; *position* only of those things which have been put there at will. The *situation* of some tree or rock, on some elevated *place*, is agreeable to be looked at or to be looked from. The faulty *position* of a letter in writing sometimes spoils the whole performance.

Situation and *position* when applied to persons are similarly distinguished; the *situation* is that in which a man finds himself, either with or without his own choice; the *position* is that in which he is placed without his own choice.

Place, situation, and *station* have an extended signification in respect to men in civil society, that is, either to their circumstances or actions; *post* has no other sense when applied to persons. *Place* is as indefinite as before; it may be taken for that share which we personally have in society either generally, as when every one is said to fill a *place* in society, or particularly for a specific share of its business, as to fill a *place* under government: *situation* is that kind of *place* which specifies either our share in its business, but with a higher import than the general term *place*, or a share in its gains and losses, as the prosperous or adverse *situation* of a man: a *station* is that kind of *place* which denotes a share in its relative consequence, power, and honor, in which sense every man holds a certain *station;* the *post* is that kind of *place* in which he has a specific share in the duties of society; the *situation* comprehends many duties, but the *post* includes properly one duty only, the word being figuratively employed from the *post* or particular spot which a soldier is said to occupy. A clerk in a counting-house fills a *place:* a clergyman holds a *situation* by virtue of his office; he is in the *station* of a gentleman by reason of his education as well as his *situation:* a faithful minister will always consider his *post* to be there where good is to be done.

See OFFICE; PUT.

Place, Dispose, Order.—To *place* is to assign a *place* to a thing; to *dispose* is to *place* according to a certain rule; to *order* is to *place* in a certain *order.* To *place* is an unqualified act both as to the manner and circumstances of the action; to *dispose* is a qualified act; it is qualified as to the manner; the former is an act of expediency or necessity; the latter is an act of judgment

or discretion. Things are often *placed* from the necessity of being *placed* in some way or another: they are *disposed* so as to appear to the best advantage. We may *place* a single object, but it is necessary that there should be several objects to be *disposed.* One *places* a book on a shelf, or *disposes* a number of books, according to their sizes, on different shelves.

To *order* and *dispose* are both taken in the sense of putting several things in some *order*, but dispose may be simply for the purpose of *order* and arrangement; *ordering*, on the other hand, comprehends command as well as regulation. Things are *disposed* in a shop to the best advantage, or, in the moral application, the thoughts are *disposed;* a man *orders* his family, or a commander *orders* the battle.

Place, Spot, Site.—A particular or given space is the idea common to these terms; but the former is general and indefinite, the latter specific. *Place* is limited to no size or quantity; it may be large: but *spot* implies a very small *place*, such as, by a figure of speech, is supposed to be no larger than a *spot:* the term *place* is employed upon every occasion; the term *spot* is confined to very particular cases: we may often know in a general way the *place* where a thing is, but it is not easy after a series of years to find out the exact *spot* on which some event has happened. The *place* where our Saviour was buried is to be seen and pointed out, but not the very *spot* where he lay.

The *site* is the *spot* on which anything stands or is situated; it is more commonly applied to a building or any *place* marked out for a specific purpose; as the *site* on which a camp had been formed.

PLACID. See CALM.

PLAIN. See APPARENT; EVEN; FRANK; SINCERE; TANGIBLE.

PLAN. See DESIGN; PREMEDITATE; SYLLABUS.

PLANNING. See SCHEMING.

PLAUSIBLE. See COLORABLE.

PLAY, GAME, SPORT. *Play* comes from Anglo-Saxon *plegian*, from *plega*, a fight, battle, sport. *Game* comes from Anglo-Saxon *gamen*, to play. *Sport* is derived from Old French *disport*, from the phrase *se desporter* (Latin *dis*, apart, and *portare*, to carry), meaning to carry one's self away from work or annoyance.

Play and *game* both include exercise, corporeal or mental, or both; but *play* is an unsystematic, *game* a systematic, exercise: children *play* when they merely run after each other, but this is no *game;* on the other hand, when they exercise with the ball according to any rule, this is a *game;* every *game*, therefore, is a *play*, but every *play* is not a *game:* trundling a hoop is a *play*, but not a *game:* cricket is both a *play* and a *game*. One person may have his *play* by himself, but there must be more than one to have a *game*. *Play* is adapted to infants; *games* to those who are more advanced in years. *Play* is sometimes taken for the act of amusing one's self with anything intellectual, and *game* for the act with which any *game* is *played*.

Play and *sport* signify any action or motion for pleasure, whether as it regards man or animals; but *play* refers more to the action, and *sport* to the pleasure produced by the action.

Game and *sport* both imply an object pursued, but *game* comprehends an object of contest which is to be obtained by art, as the Olympic and other *games* of antiquity.

Sport comprehends a pleasurable object to be obtained by bodily exercise; as field *sports*, rustic *sports*, and the like.

Game may be extended figuratively to any object of pursuit; as the *game* is lost, the *game* is over.

Sport is sometimes used for the subject of *sport* to another.

Playful, Sportive.—*Playful*, or full of *play*, and *sportive*, disposed to *sport*, are taken in a sense similar to the primitive. *Playful* is applicable to youth or childhood, when there is the greatest disposition to *play*. *Sportive* is applied in a good sense to persons of maturer years. A person may be said to be *sportive* who indulges in harmless *sport*.

PLAYER. See ACTOR.

PLEAD. See APOLOGIZE.

PLEADER. See DEFENDER.

PLEASANT. See AGREEABLE; FACETIOUS.

PLEASE. See SATISFY.

PLEASED. See GLAD.

PLEASING. See AGREEABLE.

PLEASURE, JOY, DELIGHT, CHARM. *Pleasure*, through French *plaisir*, from the Latin *placere*, to please or give content, is the generic term, involving in itself the common idea of the other terms. *Joy* (see GLAD). *Delight*, from French *déliter*, Latin *delectare*, a frequentative of *delicere*, to allure (whence our adjective *delicious* is derived), signifies what allures the mind.

Pleasure is a term of most extensive use; it embraces one large class of our feelings and sensations, and is opposed to nothing but pain, which embraces the second class or division: *joy* and *delight* are but modes or modifications of *pleasure*, differing as to the degree and as to the objects or sources. *Pleasure*, in its peculiar acceptation, is smaller in degree than either *joy* or *delight*, but in its universal acceptation it defines no degree: the term is indifferently employed for the highest as well as the lowest degree: whereas *joy* and *delight* can be employed only to express a positively high degree. *Pleasure* is produced by any or every object; everything by which we are surrounded acts upon us more or less to produce it; we may have *pleasure* either from without or from within: *pleasure* from the gratification of our senses, from the exercise of our affections, or the exercise of our understandings; *pleasures* from our own selves or *pleasures* from others: but *joy* is derived from the exercise of the affections; and *delight* either from the emotions or the understanding. In this manner we distinguish the *pleasures* of the table, social *pleasures*, or intellectual *pleasures;* the *joy* of meeting an old friend; or the *delight* of pursuing a favorite object.

Pleasures are either transitory or otherwise: *joy* is in its nature commonly short of duration; it springs from particular events; it is *pleasure* at high tide, but it may come and go as suddenly as the events which caused it: one's *joy* may be awakened and destroyed in quick succession. *Delight* is more fleeting even than *joy*, and much more intense than simple *pleasure;* *delight* arises from a state of outward circumstances which is naturally less durable than that of *joy;* but it is a state seldomer attainable and not so much at one's command as either *pleasure* or *joy.*

Pleasure, joy, and *delight* are likewise employed for the things which give *pleasure, joy,* or *delight. Charm* (see ATTRACTION) is used only in the sense of what *charms* or gives a high degree of *pleasure,* but not a degree equal to that of *joy* or *delight,* though greater than of ordinary *pleasure; pleasure* intoxicates; the *joys* of heaven are objects of a Christian's pursuit; the *delights* of matrimony are last'ng to those who are susceptible of true affection; the *charms* of rural scenery never fail of their effect whenever they offer themselves to the eye.

See also COMFORT.

PLEDGE. See DEPOSIT; EARNEST.

PLENIPOTENTIARY. See AMBASSADOR.

PLENITUDE. See FULNESS.

PLENTIFUL, PLENTEOUS, ABUNDANT, COPIOUS, AMPLE. *Plentiful* and *plenteous,* signifying the presence of *plenty, plenitude,* or *fulness,* differ only in use, the former being mostly employed in the familiar, the latter in the grave, style. *Plenty* fills; *abundance,* in Latin *abundantia* (from *abundo,* to overflow, compounded of the intensive *ab* and *unda,* a wave, signifying, literally, overflowing), does more, it leaves a superfluity; as that, however, which fills suffices as much as that which flows over, the term *abundance* is often employed promiscuously with that of *plenty;* we may say indifferently a *plentiful* harvest or an *abundant* harvest. *Plentiful* is, however, a more familiar term than *abundant:* we say, therefore, most commonly, *plenty* of provisions; *plenty* of food; *plenty* of corn, wine, and oil: but an *abundance* of words; an *abundance* of riches; an *abundance* of wit or humor. In certain years fruit is *plentiful,* and at other times grain is *plentiful;* in all cases we have *abundant* cause for gratitude to the Giver of all good things.

Copious, in Latin *copiosus,* from *copia,* or *con,* together, and *opes,* wealth, signifying having a store, and *ample,* from Latin *amplus,* spacious, are modes either of *plenty* or *abundance:* the former is employed in regard to

what is collected or brought into one place; the term *ample* is employed only in regard to what may be narrowed or expanded; a *copious* stream of blood, or a *copious* flow of words, equally designate the quantity which is collected, as an *ample* provision, an *ample* store, an *ample* share, marks that which may at pleasure be increased or diminished.

PLIANT. See FLEXIBLE.

PLOT. See COMBINATION.

PLUCK. See DRAW.

PLUNDER. See RAPINE; SACK; SPOLIATION.

PLUNGE, DIVE. *Plunge* comes .rom a hypothetical Latin *plumbicare,* based on *plumbum,* lead, through French *plonger,* and means to fall into the water like the lead thrown out to *plumb* the depth. *Dive,* from Anglo-Saxon *dyfan,* to immerse, is allied to *dip, deep,* etc.

One *plunges* sometimes in order to *dive;* but one may *plunge* without *diving,* and one may *dive* without *plunging:* to *plunge* is to dart head foremost into the water: to *dive* is to go to the bottom of the water or toward it; it is a good practice for bathers to *plunge* into the water when they first go in, although it is not advisable for them to *dive;* ducks frequently *dive* into the water without ever *plunging.* Thus far they differ in their natural sense; but in the figurative application they differ more widely: to *plunge,* in this case, is an act of rashness: to *dive* is an act of design: a young man hurried away by his passions will *plunge* into every extravagance when he comes into possession of his estate: a "nervy" speculator will often make a *plunge* in the stock or commodities markets for control of an interest.

POINT. See AIM.

POISE, BALANCE. For the derivations of *poise* and *balance* see COUNTERPOISE.

To *poise* is properly to keep the weight from pressing on either side; to *balance* is to keep the *balance* even. The idea of bringing into an equilibrium is common to both terms, but a thing is *poised* as regards itself; it is *balanced* as regards other things; a person *poises* a plain stick in his hand when he wants it to lie even; he *balances* the stick if it has a particular weight at each end: a person may *poise* himself, but he *balances* others: when not on firm ground it is necessary to *poise* one's self; when two persons are situated one at each end of a beam they may *balance* one another. In the moral application they are similarly distinguished.

See also COUNTERPOISE.

POISON, VENOM. *Poison*, in French *poison*, Latin *potio*, a drink, is a general term; in its original meaning it signifies any potion which acts destructively upon the system. *Venom*, in French *venin*, Latin *venenum*, is a species of deadly or malignant *poison:* a *poison* may be either slow or quick; a *venom* is always most active in its nature: a *poison* must be administered inwardly to have its effect; a *venom* will act by an external application: the juice of the hellebore is a *poison;* the tongue of the adder and the tooth of the viper contain *venom;* many plants are unfit to be eaten on account of the *poisonous* quality which is in them; the Indians are in the habit of dipping the tips of their arrows in a *venomous* juice, which renders the slightest wound mortal.

The moral application of these terms is clearly drawn from their proper acceptation: the *poison* must be infused or injected into the subject; the *venom* acts upon him externally: bad principles are justly compared to a *poison*, which some are so unhappy as to suck in with their mother's milk; the shafts of envy are peculiarly *venomous* when directed against those in elevated stations.

POLITE, POLISHED, REFINED. *Polite*, from Latin *polire*, to make smooth (see CIVIL), denotes a quality; *polished*, of a similar derivation, a state: he who is *polite* is so according to the rules of *politeness;* he who is *polished* is *polished* by the force of art: a *polite* man is, in regard to his behavior, a finished gentleman; but a rude person may be more or less *polished* and yet not free from rudeness. *Refined* rises in sense, both in regard to *polite* and *polished:* a man is indebted to nature, rather than to art, for his *refinement;* but his *politeness* or his *polish* is entirely the fruit of education. *Politeness* and *polish* do not ex-

tend to anything but externals; *refinement* applies as much to the mind as the body: rules of conduct and good society will make a man *polite;* lessons in dancing will serve to give a *polish;* *refined* manners or principles will naturally arise out of *refinement* of men.

As *polish* extends only to the exterior, it is less liable to excess than *refinement:* when the language, the walk, and deportment of a man are *polished,* he is divested of all that can make him offensive in social intercourse; but if his temper be *refined* beyond a certain boundary, he loses the energy of character which is essential for maintaining his dignity against the rude shocks of human life.

See also GENTEEL; WELL-BRED.

POLITICAL, POLITIC. *Political* has the proper meaning of the word *polity*, which, from the Greek πολῑτεία and πόλις, a city, signifies the government either of a city or a country. *Politic*, like the word *policy*, has the improper meaning of the word *polity*, namely, that of clever management, because the affairs of states are sometimes managed with considerable art and finesse: hence we speak of *political* government as opposed to that which is ecclesiastic; and of *politic* conduct as opposed to that which is unwise and without foresight: in *political* questions, it is not *politic* for individuals to set themselves up in opposition to those who are in power; the study of *politics*, as a science, may make a man a clever statesman, but it may not always enable him to be truly *politic* in his private concerns.

POLLUTE. See CONTAMINATE; DEBAUCH.

POLYCHROMATIC. See NACREOUS.

POMP. See MAGNIFICENCE.

POMPOUS. See MAGISTERIAL; THEATRICAL.

PONDER. See THINK.

PONDEROUS. See HEAVY.

POOR, PAUPER. *Poor* and *pauper* are both derived from the Latin *pauper*, Old French *povre*, poor. *Poor* is a term of general use; *pauper* is a term of particular use: a *pauper* is a *poor* man who lives upon alms or the relief of the parish: the former is, therefore, indefinite in its meaning; the latter conveys a reproachful idea. The word *poor* is used as a substantive only in the plural number; *pauper* is a substantive both in the singular and plural: the *poor* of the parish are, in general, a heavy burden upon the inhabitants: there are some persons who are not ashamed to live and die as *paupers*.

POPULACE. See PEOPLE.

PORTEND. See AUGUR.

PORTION. See DEAL; PART.

POSITION, POSTURE. *Position* (see also PLACE) is here the general term, *posture* the particular term. The *position* is that in which a body is placed in respect to other bodies: as the standing with one's face or back to an object is a *position;* but a *posture* is that *position* which a body assumes in respect to itself, as a sitting or reclining *posture*.

See also TENET.

POSITIVE, ABSOLUTE, PEREMPTORY. *Positive,* in Latin *positivus,* from *positus,* past participle of *pono,* to put or place, and a suffix, signifies placed or fixed, that is, fixed or established in the mind. *Absolute,* from Latin *ab,* away, and *solutus,* participle of *solvere,* to loosen, signifies uncontrolled by any external circumstances. *Peremptory,* in Latin *peremptorius,* from *peremptor,* a destroyer, *per,* utterly, and *emere,* to take, signifying to take away utterly, means removing all further question.

Positive and *absolute* are employed for either things or persons; *peremptory* for persons only, or for that which is personal. What is *positive* has a determinate existence; it is opposed to what is negative, indeterminate, or precarious; as *positive* good, *positive* pleasure or pain; what is *absolute* is without dependence or connection, it is opposed mostly to the relative or conditional, as *absolute* existence, *absolute* justice.

In regard to persons or what is personal, *positive* applies either to the assurance of a man or to the manner of his expressing that assurance; a person may be *positive* in his own mind (see CONFIDENT), or he may make a *positive* assertion; *absolute* applies either to the mode of acting or the circumstances under which one acts, as to have an *absolute* possession or command, to make an *absolute* promise; *peremptory* is applied to the nature of the action or the manner of performing it; a command may be *peremptory,* and a tone *peremptory.* A *positive* assertion will remove doubt if made by one entitled to credit; an *absolute* promise will admit of no reservation on the part of the person making it. A *peremptory* command admits of no demur or remonstrance; a *peremptory* answer satisfies or puts to silence.

See also ACTUAL; CATEGORICAL; CONFIDENT; DEFINITE; INFALLIBLE.

POSSESS. See HOLD.

POSSESSIONS. See GOODS.

POSSESSOR, PROPRIETOR, OWNER, MASTER. The *possessor* has the full power, if not the right, of the present disposal over the object of possession; the *proprietor* and *owner* have the unlimited right of transfer, but not always the power of immediate disposal. The *proprietor* and the *owner* are the same in signification, though not in application, the first term being used principally in regard to matters of importance; the latter on familiar occasions: the *proprietor* of an estate is a more suitable expression than the *owner* of an estate: the *owner* of a book is more becoming than the *proprietor*. The *possessor* and the *master* are commonly the same person when those things are in question which are subject to *possession;* but the terms are otherwise so different in their original meaning that they can scarcely admit of comparison: the *possessor* of a house is naturally the *master* of the house; and, in general, whatever a man *possesses* that he has in his power and is consequently *master* of; but we may have, legally, the right of *possessing* a thing over which we have actually no power of control: in this case, we are nominally *possessor,* but virtually not *master*. A minor, or insane person, may be both *possessor* and *proprietor* of that over which he has no control; a man is, therefore, on the other hand, appropriately denominated *master,* not *possessor,* of his actions.

POSSIBLE, PRACTICABLE, PRACTICAL. *Possible,* from the Latin *posse,* to be able, and a suffix, signifies properly able to be done: *practicable,* compounded of Latin *practicus*, Greek πρακτικός, from the verb signifying to do, and a suffix, signifies to be able to put in *practice:* hence the difference between *possible* and *practicable* is the same as between doing a thing at all or doing it as a rule. There are many things *possible* which cannot be called *practicable;* but what is *practicable* must, in its nature, be *possible.* The *possible* depends solely on the power of the agent; the *practicable* depends on circumstances: a child cannot say how much it is *possible* for him to learn until he has tried; schemes have sometimes everything apparently to recommend them to notice, but that which is of the first importance, namely, their *practicability.*

The *practicable* is that which may or can be *practiced;* the *practical* is that which is intended for *practice:* the former, therefore, applies to that which men devise to carry into *practice:* the latter to that which they have to *practice:* projectors ought to consider what is *practicable;* divines and moralists have to consider what is *practical.* The *practicable* is opposed to the *impracticable;* the *practical* to the theoretical or speculative.

POST. See PLACE.

POSTPONE. See DELAY.

POSTURE. See ACTION; POSITION.

POTENT. See POWERFUL.

POTENTATE. See PRINCE.

POUND. See BREAK.

POUR, SPILL, SHED. *Pour* meant originally to purify or clarify by pressure, or pouring out, from Late Latin *purare,* Latin *purus,* pure. *Spill* is a Scandinavian word meaning to destroy or shed. *Shed* comes from Anglo-Saxon *sceadan.*

We *pour* with design; we *spill* by accident: we *pour* water over a plant or a bed; we *spill* it on the ground. To *pour* is an act of convenience; to *spill* and *shed* are acts more or less hurtful; the former is to cause to run in small quantities, the latter in large quantities: we *pour* wine out of a bottle into a glass; but the blood of a person is said to be *spilled* or *shed* when his life is violently taken away: what is *poured* is commonly no part of the body whence it is *poured;* but what is *shed* is no other than a component part; hence trees are said to *shed* their leaves, animals their hair, or human beings to *shed* tears. Hence the distinction between these words in their moral application.

POVERTY, WANT, PENURY, INDIGENCE, NEED. *Poverty,* through French from Latin *paupertatem,* based on *pauper,* poor, which marks the condition of being *poor,* is a general state of fortune opposed to that of riches.

Poverty admits of different states or degrees which are expressed by the other terms. *Want,* from the verb to *want,* denotes, when taken absolutely, the *want* of the first necessaries, which is a permanent state, and a low state of *poverty;* but it may sometimes denote an occasional *want,* as a traveller in a desert may be exposed to *want;* or it may imply the *want* of particular things, as when we speak of our *wants.*

Penury, in Latin *penuria,* allied to Greek πεῖνα, hunger, signifying extreme *want,* is poverty in its most abject state, which is always supposed to be as permanent as it is wretched, to which those who are already poor are brought, either by misfortune or imprudence.

Indigence, in Latin *indigentia,* from *indigere,* from *ind,* for, and *egere,* to be in need, to *want,* signifies the state of *wanting* such things as one has been habituated to or which are suited to one's station, and is properly applied to persons in the superior walks of life.

Need (see NECESSITY) implies a present *want,* or the state of *wanting* such things as the immediate occasion calls for: a temporary state to which persons of all conditions are exposed.

POWER, STRENGTH, FORCE, AUTHORITY, DOMINION. *Power,* from Anglo-French *poër,* which in Middle English developed a *w;* Late Latin *potere,* to be able, is the generic and universal term, comprehending in it that simple principle of nature which exists in all subjects. *Strength,* or the abstract quality of strong, and *force* (see ENERGY) are modes of *power.* These terms are all used either in a physical or a moral application. *Power,* in a physical sense, signifies whatever causes motion: *strength* that species of *power* that lies in the vital and muscular parts of the body. *Strength* is therefore internal, and depends on the internal organization of the frame; *power* on the external circumstances. A man may have *strength* to move, but not the *power*, if he be bound with cords. Our *strength* is proportioned to the health of the body and the firmness of its make: our *power* may be increased by the help of instruments.

Power may be exerted or otherwise; *force* is *power* exerted or active; bodies have a *power* of resistance while in a state of rest, but they are moved by a certain *force* from other bodies. The word *power* is used technically for the moving *force*.

In a moral acceptation, *power*, *strength*, and *force* may be applied to the same objects with a similar distinction: thus we may speak of the *power* of language generally; the *strength* of a person's expressions to convey the state of his own mind; and the *force* of terms, as to the extent of their meaning and fitness to convey the ideas of those who use them.

Power is either public or private, which brings it into alliance with *authority* (see INFLUENCE). Civil *power* includes in it all that which enables us to have any influence or control over the actions, persons, property, etc., of others; *authority* is confined to that species of *power* which is derived from some legitimate source. *Power* exists independently of all right; *authority* is founded only on right. A king has often the *power* to be cruel, but he has never the *authority* to be so. Subjects have sometimes the *power* of overturning the government, but they can in no case have the *authority*.

Power is indefinite as to degree; one may have little or much *power: dominion* is a positive degree of *power*. A monarch's *power* may be limited by various circumstances; a despot exercises *dominion* over all his subjects, high and low. One is not said to get *power* over any object, but to get an object into one's *power:* on the other hand, we get a *dominion* over an object; thus some men have a *dominion* over the conscience of others.

Powerful, Potent, Mighty.—*Powerful* is full of *power; potent*, from the Latin *potens*, the present participle of the verb *posse* (whence *possible* is derived), sig-

nifies, literally, being able or having *power*, and *mighty* signifies having *might*. *Powerful* is applicable to strength as well as *power:* a *powerful* man is one who by size and build can easily overpower another; and a *powerful* person is one who has much in his *power: potent* is used only in this latter sense, in which it expresses a larger extent of *power:* a *potent* monarch is much more than a *powerful* prince: *mighty* expresses a still higher degree of *power; might* is *power* unlimited by any consideration or circumstance; a giant is called *mighty* in the physical sense, and genius is said to be *mighty* which takes everything within its grasp; the Supreme Being is entitled either *Omnipotent* or *Almighty;* but the latter term seems to convey the idea of boundless extent more forcibly than the former.

See also HERCULEAN.

PRACTICABLE. See POSSIBLE.

PRACTICE. See CUSTOM; EXERCISE.

PRAGMATISM, PRACTICALISM, HUMANISM. These words all refer to a recent philosophy, "the most recent and (philosophically speaking) fashionable 'ism' that the new century has produced, known by some as *Humanism*, and by others as *Pragmatism*" (*Academy*, August 4, 1906). The philosophy teaches that the whole meaning of a conception expresses itself in practical consequences, either in the shape of conduct to be recommended or of experiences to be expected, if it is true. In short, "if it works, it is true." This was called *practicalism* by some because the test of truth is its results in *practice* (ultimately from Greek πράττειν, to do; but William James, the American exponent of the philosophy, gave it the name *pragmatism*, from the same Greek verb πράττειν, which has the same meaning as *practicalism* but is a trifle more euphonious. *Humanism*, from Latin *humanus*, pertaining to man, from *homo*, man, is applied to the philosophy because it judges truth not by abstract or theoretical principles, but simply by its practical outcome in human life. But the objection to the title *humanism* is that the word has already been applied to the work of the scholars of the Renaissance who revived the ideal of a perfect "human" life, on the basis of the Greek and Roman art, as contrasted with the spiritual ideal of the mediæval theologians. Hence, when *humanism* is used for *pragmatism,* there is confusion. As is the case with most new words, the difference between the synonymes is not one of meaning, but of customary usage.

PRAISE, COMMEND, APPLAUD, EX-TOL. *Praise,* through French *preis,* is connected with our own word *price* (Latin *pretium*), signifying to give a value to a thing. *Commend,* in Latin *commendo,* compounded of *con,* together, and *mandare,* to put into the hands, signifies to commit to the good opinion of others. *Applaud* (see APPLAUSE). *Extol,* in Latin *ex,* beyond, and *tollere,* to lift, signifies to lift up very high.

All these terms denote the act of expressing approbation. To *praise* is the most general and indefinite; it may rise to a high degree, but it generally implies a lower degree: we *praise* a person generally; we *commend* him particularly: we *praise* him for his diligence, sobriety, and the like; we *commend* him for his performances, or for any particular instance of prudence or good conduct. To *applaud* is an ardent mode of *praising;* we *applaud* a person for his nobility of spirit: to *extol* is a reverential mode of *praising;* we *extol* a man for his heroic exploits. *Praise* is confined to no station, though with most propriety bestowed by superiors on equals: *commendation* is the part of a superior; a parent *commends* his child for an act of charity: *applause* is the act of many as well as of one; theatrical performances are the frequent subjects of public *applause:* to *extol* is the act of inferiors, who declare thus decidedly their sense of a person's superiority.

PRAISEWORTHY. See LAUDABLE.

PRANK. See FROLIC.

PRATTLE. See BABBLE.

PRAYER, PETITION, REQUEST, EN-TREATY, SUIT. *Prayer,* from the Old French *preier,* Latin *precari,* to pray, is a general term, including the common idea of application to some person for any favor to be granted: *petition,* based on *petere,* to seek; *request* (see ASK);

entreaty (see BEG); *suit,* from *sue,* in Anglo-French *suer,* Latin *sequi,* to follow after, denote different modes of *prayer,* varying in the circumstances of the action and the object acted upon.

The *prayer* is made more commonly to the Supreme Being; the *petition* is made more generally to one's fellow-creatures; we may, however, *pray* our fellow-creatures, and *petition* our Creator: the *prayer* is made for everything which is of the first importance to us as living beings; the *petition* is made for that which may satisfy our desires: hence our *prayers* to the Almighty concern all our circumstances as moral and responsible agents; our *petitions* the temporary circumstances of our present existence.

When the term *prayer* is applied to men, it carries with it the idea of earnestness and submission; the *petition* is a public act, in which many express their wishes to the Supreme Authority; the *request* and *entreaty* are individual acts between men in their private relations: the people *petition* the king or the parliament; a child makes a *request* to its parent; one friend makes a *request* to another. The *request* marks an equality, but the *entreaty* defines no condition; it differs, however, from the former in the nature of the object and the mode of preferring; the *request* is but a simple expression; the *entreaty* is urgent: the *request* may be made in trivial matters; the *entreaty* is made in matters that deeply interest the feelings: we *request* a friend to lend us a book; we use every *entreaty* in order to divert a person from those purposes which we think detrimental: one complies with a *request;* one yields to *entreaties.* It was the dying *request* of Socrates that they would sacrifice a cock to Æsculapius; Regulus was deaf to every *entreaty* of his friends, who wished him not to return to Carthage.

The *suit* is a higher kind of *prayer,* varying both in the nature of the subject and the character of the agent. A gentleman pays his *suit* to a lady; a courtier makes his *suit* to the prince: *suit* in legal nomenclature meant originally a *petition* or a *prayer.*

PREARRANGE. See PREMEDI-TATE.

PRECARIOUS. See DOUBTFUL.

PRECEDENCE. See PRIORITY.

PRECEDENT. See EXAMPLE.

PRECEDING. See ANTECEDENT.

PRECEPT. See COMMAND; DOCTRINE; MAXIM.

PRECEPTIVE. See DIDACTIC.

PRECINCT. See BORDER.

PRECIOUS. See VALUABLE.

PRECIPITATE. See SUDDEN.

PRECISE. See ACCURATE.

PRECLUDE. See PREVENT.

PRECONTRIVE. See PREMEDITATE.

PRECURSOR. See FORERUNNER.

PREDETERMINE. See PREMEDITATE.

PREDICAMENT. See SITUATION.

PREDICT. See FORETELL.

PREDOMINANT. See PREVAILING; SUPREME.

PRE-EMINENCE. See PRIORITY.

PRE-EMINENT. See SUPREME.

PREFACE. See PRELUDE.

PREFER. See CHOOSE; ENCOURAGE.

PREFERABLE. See ELIGIBLE.

PREFERENCE. See PRIORITY.

PREJUDICE. See BIAS; DISADVANTAGE.

PRELIMINARY. See PREVIOUS.

PRELUDE, PREFACE. *Prelude,* from the Latin *præ,* before, and *ludere,* to play; signifies the game that precedes another; *preface,* from the Latin *fari,* to speak, signifies the speech that precedes. The idea of a preparatory introduction is included in both these terms; but the former consists of actions, the latter of words: the throwing of stones and breaking of windows is the *prelude* on the part of a mob to a general riot, and apology for one's ill behavior is sometimes the *preface* to soliciting a remission of punishment. The *prelude* is frequently, though not always, preparatory to that which is in itself actually bad: the *preface* is either to guard against something objectionable or to secure something desirable. Intemperance in liquor is the *prelude* to every other extravagance; when one wishes to insure compliance with a request that may possibly be unreasonable, it is necessary to pave the way by some suitable *preface.*

In the extended application they are both taken in an indifferent sense.

PREMEDITATE, PLAN, PREARRANGE, PRECONTRIVE, PREDETERMINE, PROPOSE. *Premeditate,* from Latin *præ,* before, and *meditari,* to think, means to think over something beforehand. *Plan,* from Latin *planum,* a flat surface, means properly a drawing on a flat surface—hence an outline of what is to be done. It has, therefore, more specific reference to action than *premeditate. Precontrive* means to *contrive* beforehand. (For derivation and meaning see CONTRIVE.) It suggests a working out of petty details and adjustment of the relations of the parts of a plan, and is applied to comparatively small projects, whereas *plan* may be applied to anything. *Prearrange* (see CLASS) also suggests the adjustment beforehand, but not the petty ingenuity of *precontrive. Predetermine* is to *determine* beforehand (see DETERMINE), and *propose,* from Latin *pro,* before, and French *poser,* to place, has a similar meaning. But *propose* means merely to place the possibility of a future course before the mind; *predetermine* suggests also an action of the will.

PREMISE, PRESUME. *Premise,* from *præ* and *missum,* the past participle of *mittere,* signifies to set down beforehand; *presume,* from *præ* and *sumere,* to take, or take up, signifies to take up or accept beforehand. Both these terms are employed in regard to our previous assertions or admissions of any circumstance; the former is used for what is theoretical or belongs to opinions; the latter is used for what is practical or belongs to facts: we *premise* that the existence of a Deity is unquestionable when we argue respecting His attributes; we *presume* that a person has a firm belief in Divine revelation when we exhort him to follow the precepts of the Gospel. No argument can be pursued until we have *premised* those points upon which both parties are to agree; we must be careful not to *presume* upon more than what we are fully authorized to take for certain.

PREPARATORY. See PREVIOUS.

PREPARE. See FIT.

PREPAREDNESS, PREPARATION. *Preparedness* is a substantive developed recently in the United States from the past participle of the verb *prepare*, and means *prepared* for war. It has in itself no other meaning than is implied in the substantive corresponding to *prepare*, already in existence — *i. e.*, *preparation;* but it derives its special significance and vogue from the agitation for increased armaments. It cannot be substituted for *preparation* in other connections. *Preparation* is the normal substantive corresponding to *prepare*.

Thus we *plan* things ahead of the time when wanted or to be done; we *prearrange* family matters before our death; we *precontrive* or experiment with transactions before results are needed; we *predetermine* or settle a problem or future action in our minds before it is necessary to *accomplish* it; and we *propose* something that may become a settled matter in the future.

PREPONDERATE. See OVERBALANCE.

PREPOSSESSION. See BENT; BIAS.

PREPOSTEROUS. See IRRATIONAL.

PREROGATIVE. See PRIVILEGE.

PRESAGE. See AUGUR; OMEN.

PRESCRIBE. See APPOINT; DICTATE.

PRESCRIPTION. See USAGE.

PRESENT. See GIFT; INTRODUCE.

PRESERVATION. See SALVATION.

PRESERVE. See KEEP; SAVE.

PRESS, SQUEEZE, PINCH, GRIPE. *Press*, in Latin *pressus*, participle of *premere*, to press. *Squeeze* comes from Anglo-Saxon *cwiesan*, to crush, with the addition of *es*, from the Old French prefix *es* (Latin *ex*) which has a privative force. *Pinch* is a nasalized form of Italian *picciare* or *pizzare*, North French *pincher*, meaning to prick with a sharp-pointed instrument—a *pick* or *pike;* it is not now applied to a pricking, however. *Gripe*, a word now seldom used in this spelling, and generally substituted by the analogous *grip*, is in Anglo-Saxon *gripan*.

The forcible action of one body on another is included in all these terms. In the word *press* this is the only idea; the rest differ in the circumstances. We may *press* with the foot, the hand, the whole body, or any particular limb; one *squeezes* commonly with the hand; one *pinches* either with the fingers or an instrument constructed in a similar form; one *gripes* with teeth, claws, or any instrument that can gain a hold upon the object. Inanimate as well as animate objects *press* or *pinch;* but to *squeeze* and *gripe* are more properly the actions of animate objects; the former is always said of persons, the latter of animals; stones *press* that on which they rest their weight; a door which shuts of itself may *pinch* the fingers; one *squeezes* the hand of a friend; lobsters and many other shell-fish *gripe* whatever comes within their claws.

In the figurative application they have a similar distinction; we *press* a person, by importunity, to some coercive measure; an extortioner *squeezes* in order to get that which is given with reluctance or difficulty; a miser *pinches* himself if he contracts his subsistence; he *gripes* (in modern parlance, *grips*) all that comes within his possession.

Press, Massage. — *Massage*, from French *massage*, signifying kneading, ultimately from *massa*, dough, is a certain kind of pressing, technically defined as "motion with *pressure*" used in the treatment of certain forms of physical illness and weakness. It is therefore a special and somewhat technical word corresponding to the general word *press*.

Pressing, Urgent, Importunate. — *Pressing* and *urgent*, from to *press* and *urge*, are applied as qualifying terms either to persons or things; *importunate*, from the verb to *importune* (based on Late Latin *importunatus*, past participle of *importunari*, compounded of *in*, privative, and *portus*, port, no port, *i. e.*, difficult of access), is applied only to persons. In regard to *pressing*, it is said either of one's demands, one's requests, or one's exhortations; *urgent* is said of one's solicitations or entreaties; *importunate* is said of one's begging or applying for a thing. The *pressing* has more of violence in it; it is supported by force and authority; it is employed in matters of right: the *urgent* makes an appeal to one's feelings; it is more persuasive, and is employed in matters of favor: the *importunate* has some of the force, but none of the authority or obligation, of the *pressing;* it is employed in matters of personal gratification. When applied to things, *pressing* is as much more forcible than *urgent* as in the former case; we speak of a *pressing* necessity, an *urgent* case. A creditor will be *pressing* for his money when he fears to lose it; one friend is *urgent* with another to intercede in his behalf; beggars are commonly *importunate* with the hope of teasing others out of their money.

PRESUME. See PREMISE.

PRESUMPTION. See ARROGANCE; ASSUMPTION.

PRESUMPTIVE, PRESUMPTUOUS, PRESUMING. *Presumptive* comes from *presume,* in the sense of supposing or taking for granted; *presumptuous, presuming* (see ASSUMPTION), comes from the same verb in the sense of taking upon one's self, or taking to one's self, any importance: the former is therefore employed in an indifferent, the latter in a bad, acceptation: a *presumptive* heir is one *presumed* or expected to be heir; *presumptive* evidence is evidence founded on some *presumption* or supposition; so likewise *presumptive* reasoning; but a *presumptuous* man, a *presumptuous* thought, or *presumptuous* behavior, all indicate an unauthorized *presumption* in one's own favor. *Presumptuous* is a stronger term than *presuming,* because it has a more definite use; the former, from the termination *ous,* signifies full of *presumption;* the latter the inclination to *presume:* a man is *presumptuous* when his conduct partakes of the nature of *presumption;* he is *presuming,* inasmuch as he shows himself disposed to *presume:* hence we speak of *presumptuous* language, not *presuming* language: a *presuming* temper, not a *presumptuous* temper. In like manner, when one says it is *presumptuous* in a man to do anything, this expresses the idea of *presumption* much more forcibly than to say it is *presuming* in him to do it. It would be *presumptuous* in a man to address a monarch in a language of familiarity and disrespect; it is *presuming* in a common person to address any one who is superior in station with familiarity and disrespect.

PRETENCE, PRETENSION, PRETEXT, EXCUSE. *Pretence* comes from *pretend* (see FEIGN) in the sense of setting forth anything independent of ourselves. *Pretension* comes from the same verb in the sense of setting forth anything that depends upon ourselves. The *pretence* is commonly a misrepresentation; the *pretension* is frequently a miscalculation: the *pretence* is set forth to conceal what is bad in one's self; the *pretension* is set forth to display what is good: the former betrays one's falsehood, the latter one's conceit or self-importance; the former can never be employed in a good sense, the latter may sometimes be employed in an indifferent sense: a man of bad character may make a *pretence* of religion by adopting an outward profession; men of the least merit often display the highest *pretensions.*

The *pretence* and *pretext* alike consist of what is unreal; but the former is not so great a violation of truth as the latter: the *pretence* may consist of truth and falsehood blended; the *pretext* consists altogether of falsehood: the *pretence* may sometimes serve only to conceal or palliate a fault; the *pretext* serves to hide something seriously culpable or wicked: a child may make indisposition a *pretence* for idleness; a thief makes his acquaintance with the servants a *pretext* for getting admittance into a house.

The *pretence* and *excuse* are both set forth to justify one's conduct in the eyes of others; but the *pretence* always conceals something more or less culpable, and by a greater or less violation of truth; the *excuse* may sometimes justify that which is justifiable, and with strict regard to truth. To oblige one's self under the *pretence* of obliging another is a contemptible trick; *illness* is an allowable *excuse* to justify any omission in business. And even where the *excuse* may be frivolous it does not imply direct falsehood.

Pretension, Claim. — *Pretension* and *claim* (see ASK) both signify an assertion of rights, but they differ in the nature of the rights. The first refers only to the rights which are considered as such by the individual; the latter to those which exist independently of his supposition: there cannot, therefore, be a *pretension* without some one to pretend, but there may be a *claim* without any immediate *claimant:* thus we say a person rests his *pretension* to the crown upon the ground of being descended from the former king; in hereditary monarchies there is no one who has any *claim* to the crown except the next heir in succession.

The *pretension* is commonly built upon personal merits; the *claim* rests upon the laws of civil society: a person makes high *pretensions* who estimates his merits and consequent deserts at a high rate; he judges of his *claims* according as they are supported by the laws of his country or the circumstances of the case: the *pretension* when denied can never be proved; the *claim*, when proved, can be enforced.

PRETEXT. See PRETENCE.

PRETTY. See BEAUTIFUL.

PREVAILING, PREVALENT, RULING, OVERRULING, PREDOMINANT. *Prevailing* and *prevalent* both come from the Latin *prævalere*, to be strong above others. *Ruling, overruling,* and *predominant* (from *dominari*, itself derived from *dominus*, lord) signify *ruling* or bearing greater sway than others.

Prevailing expresses the actual state or quality of a particular object: *prevalent* marks the quality of *prevailing*, as it affects objects in general. The same distinction exists between *overruling* and *predominant*. A person has a *prevailing* sense of religion; religious feeling is *prevalent* in a country or in a community. There is always some *prevailing* fashion which some persons are ever ready to follow. The idea has of late years become *prevalent*.

Prevailing and *prevalent* mark simply the existing state of superiority: *ruling* and *predominant* express this state in relation to some other which it has superseded or reduced to a state of inferiority. An opinion is said to be *prevailing* as respects the number of persons by whom it is maintained: a principle is said to be *ruling* as respects the superior influence which it has over the conduct of men more than any other. Particular disorders are *prevalent* at certain seasons of the year, when they affect the generality of persons: a particular taste or fashion is *predominant* which supersedes all other tastes or fashions.

PREVAIL UPON. See PERSUADE.

PREVALENT. See PREVAILING.

PREVARICATE. See EVADE.

PREVENT, ANTICIPATE. To *prevent* is literally to come beforehand, from Latin *præ*, before, and *venire*, to come; and *anticipate* to take beforehand, from Latin *ante*, before, and a weakened form of the verb *capere*, to take. The former is employed for actual occurrences; the latter as much for calculations as for actions: to *prevent* is the act of a person toward other persons or things; to *anticipate* is the act of a being either toward himself or another. In this original and now obsolete sense God is said to *prevent* man with His favor by interposing so as to direct his purposes to the right object.

So also a man may *prevent* what is to happen by causing it to happen before the time.

We *anticipate* the happiness which we are to enjoy in future; we *anticipate* what a person is going to say by saying the same thing before him.

Prevent, in its modern use, is always taken in the sense of causing a thing not to be done: *anticipate* may also be so used, but with this distinction, that to *prevent* is to cause a thing not to be done or happen at all, and *anticipate* is to *prevent* another from doing it by doing it one's self.

Prevent, Obviate, Preclude.—All these terms imply the causing something not to take place or exist. To *prevent* (see HINDER) is to cause something to happen before, so as to render another thing impracticable. To *obviate*, from *ob*, before, opposite, and *via*, way, signifies coming in the way so as to render the thing unnecessary or of no value. *Prevent* applies to events or circumstances in life; *obviate* to mental acts or objects: bad weather *prevents* a person setting out according to a certain arrangement; a change of plan *obviates* every difficulty.

To *preclude*, from Latin *præ* and *cludere*, based on *claudere*, to shut, and signifying to shut out a possibility by the intervention of something else, is, like *obviate*, applied to mental objects.

To *prevent* and *preclude* are rather the act of the thing than of the person; to *obviate* is rather the act of the person than of the thing. Circumstances may *prevent* or *preclude* anything from happening: a person *obviates* a difficulty or objection; so, according to this distinction, we may say either to *obviate* a necessity or to *preclude* a necessity for anything, according as this is effected by any person or by any circumstance.

PREVIOUS, PRELIMINARY, PREPARATORY, INTRODUCTORY. *Previous*, in Latin *prævius*, compounded of *præ*, before, and *via*, way, signifies leading the way or going before. *Preliminary*, from *præ* and *limen*, a threshold, signifies belonging to the threshold or entrance. *Preparatory* and *introductory* signify belonging to a preparation or introduction.

Previous denotes simply the order of succession: the other terms, in addition to this, convey the idea of connection between the objects which succeed each other. *Previous* applies to actions and proceedings in general; as a *previous* question, a *previous* inquiry, a *previous* determination: *preliminary* is employed only for matters of contract: a *preliminary* article, a *preliminary* condition, are what precede the final settlement of any question: *preparatory* is employed for matters of arrangement; the disposing of men in battle is *preparatory* to an engagement; the making of marriage deeds and contracts is *preparatory* to the final solemnization of the marriage: *introductory* is employed for matters of science or discussion; as remarks are *introductory* to the main subject in question: compendiums of grammar, geography, and the like, as *introductory* to larger works, are useful to young people. Prudent people are careful to make every *previous* inquiry before they seriously enter into engagements with strangers: it is impolitic to enter into details until all *preliminary* matters are fully adjusted: one ought never to undertake any important matter without first adopting every *preparatory* measure that can facilitate its prosecution: in complicated matters it is necessary to have something *introductory* by way of explanation.

See also ANTECEDENT.

PREY. See BOOTY.

PRICE. See COST; VALUE.

PRIDE, VANITY, CONCEIT. *Pride* comes from Anglo-Saxon *pryte*, from *prut*, proud, valiant, notable, which seems to be of French origin. It meant valiant, notable; hence a consciousness of being valiant and notable. *Vanity*, Latin *vanitas*, comes from *vanus*, empty, signifying a pride that has no basis in reality. *Conceit* (see that word).

The valuing of one's self for the possession of any property is the idea common to these terms, but they differ either in regard to the object or the manner of the action. *Pride* is the term of most extensive import and application, and comprehends in its signification not only that of the other two terms, but likewise ideas peculiar to itself. *Pride* is applicable to every object, good or bad, high or low, small or great; *vanity* is applicable only to small objects: *pride* is therefore good or bad: *vanity* is always bad, it is always emptiness or nothingness. A man is *proud* who values himself for his possession of literary or scientific talent, for his wealth, his rank, his power, his acquirements, or his superiority over his competitors; he is *vain* of his person, his dress, his walk, or anything that is frivolous. *Pride* is the inherent quality in man; and, while it rests on noble objects, it is his noblest characteristic; *vanity* is the distortion of one's nature resulting from inherent tendency or an injudicious education: *pride* shows itself variously, according to the nature of the object on which it is fixed; a noble *pride* seeks to display itself in all that can command the respect or admiration of mankind; the *pride* of wealth, of power, or of other adventitious properties, commonly displays itself in unseemly deportment toward others; *vanity* shows itself in false pretensions.

Pride, in the limited and bad sense, is always associated with strength and produces more or less violence; *vanity* is coupled with weakness.

Conceit is that species of self-valuation that respects one's talents only; in so far, therefore, it is closely allied to *pride;* a man is said to be *proud* of that which he really has, but to be *conceited* of that which he really has not: a man may be *proud* to an excess of merits which he actually possesses; but when he is *conceited*, his merits are all in his own *conceit;* the latter is therefore obviously founded on falsehood altogether. As self-*conceit* is the offspring of ignorance and *vanity*, it is most frequently found in youth, but as it is the greatest obstacle to improvement, it may grow up with a person and go on with him through life.

Pride, Haughtiness, Loftiness, Dignity.—*Pride* is employed principally as respects the temper of the mind: *haughtiness* (see HAUGHTY) and *loftiness* (see HIGH) concerns either the temper of mind or the external behavior. *Dignity* (see HONOR) only the external behavior. *Pride* is, as before, the general term; the others are modes of *pride*. *Pride*, inasmuch as it consists purely of self-esteem, is a positive sentiment which one may entertain independently of other persons: it lies in the inmost recesses of the human heart, and mingles itself insensibly with our affections and passions. *Haughtiness* is that mode of *pride* which springs out of comparison of one's self with others; the *haughty* man dwells on the inferiority of others; the *proud* man, in the strict sense, dwells on his own perfections. *Loftiness* is a mode of *pride* which raises the spirit above objects supposed to be inferior; it does not set man so much above others as above himself, or that which concerns himself.

As respects the exterior, *pride* in the behavior is always bad. But it is taken in an indifferent sense in application to animals or unconscious agents.

Haughtiness in one's carriage, and *loftiness* in one's tone or air, are mostly unbecoming and seldom warranted.

Dignity, which arises from a proper consciousness of what is due to one's self, is always taken in a good sense. It is natural to some men, and shows itself at all times; on other occasions it requires to be assumed.

PRIMARY, PRIMITIVE, PRISTINE, ORIGINAL. *Primary*, from *primus* and the suffix *arius*, signifies belonging to or like the first. *Primitive*, from the same ordinal, signifies being the first. *Pristine*, in Latin *pristinus*, from *prius*, signifies in former times. *Original* signifies containing the *origin*, from the verb *oriri*, to rise or begin.

The *primary* denotes simply the order of succession, and is therefore the generic term; *primitive, pristine*, and *original* include also the idea of some other relation to the thing that succeeds, and are therefore modes of the *primary*. The *primary* has nothing to come before it; in this manner we speak of the *primary* cause as the cause which precedes secondary causes: the *primitive* is that after which other things are formed; in this manner a *primitive* word is that after which, or from which, the derivatives are formed: the *pristine* is that which follows the *primitive*, so as to become customary; there are but few specimens of the *pristine* purity of life among the professors of Christianity: the *original* is that which either gives birth to the thing or belongs to that which gives birth to the thing; the *original* meaning of a word is that which was given to it by the makers of the word.

See also FIRST.

PRINCE, MONARCH, SOVEREIGN, POTENTATE. *Prince*, in French *prince*, Latin *princeps*, from *primus* and *capere*, to take, signifies the man who takes the first place. *Monarch*, from Latin *monarcha* (built on Greek μονάρχης, from μόνος, alone, and ἄρχειν, to rule), signifies one having sole authority. *Potentate*, from *potens*, powerful, signifies one having supreme power. *Sovereign* is derived from Latin *superanus*.

Prince is the generic term, the rest are specific terms; every *monarch, sovereign*, and *potentate* is a *prince*, but not *vice versâ*. The term *prince* is indefinite as to the degree of power: a *prince* may have a limited or despotic power; but in its restricted sense it denotes a smaller degree of power than any of the other terms: the term *monarch* does not define the extent of the power, but simply that it is undivided, as opposed to that species of power which is lodged in the hands of many: *sovereign* and *potentate* indicate the highest degree of power; but the former is employed only as respects the nation that is governed, the latter in respect to other nations: a *sovereign* is supreme over his subjects; a *potentate* is powerful by means of his subjects. Every man having independent power is a *prince*, let his territory be ever so inconsiderable: Germany was divided into a number of small states, governed by their petty *princes*. Every one reigning by himself in a state of some considerable magnitude, and having independent authority over his subjects, is a *monarch;* kings and emperors, therefore, are all *monarchs*. Every *monarch* is a *sovereign* whose extent of dominion and number of subjects rises above the ordinary level; he is a *potentate* if his influence either in the cabinet or in the field extends very considerably over the affairs of other nations.

PRINCIPAL. See CHIEF; SUPREME.

PRINCIPALLY. See ESPECIALLY.

PRINCIPLE, MOTIVE. The *principle* (see DOCTRINE) may sometimes be the *motive;* but often there is a *principle* where there is no *motive*, and there is a *motive* where there is no *principle*. The *principle* lies in conscious and unconscious agents; the *motive* only in conscious agents; all nature is guided by certain *principles;* its movements go forward upon certain *principles:* man is put into action by certain *motives;* the *principle* is the prime *moving* cause of everything that is set in motion; the *motive* is the prime *moving* cause that sets the human machine into action. The *principle* in its restricted sense comes still nearer to the *motive*, when it refers to the opinions which we form: the *principle* in this case is that idea which we form of things so as to regulate our conduct; the *motive* is that idea which simply impels to action: the former is therefore something permanent, and grounded upon the exercise of our reasoning powers; the latter is momentary and arises simply from our capacity of willing and thinking: bad *principles* lead a man into a bad course of life; but a man may be led by bad *motives* to do what is good as well as what is bad.

See also CHIEF.

PRINT. See MARK; PICTURE.

PRIOR. See ANTECEDENT.

PRIORITY, PRECEDENCE, PRE-EMINENCE, PREFERENCE. *Priority* denotes the abstract quality of being before others; *precedence*, from *præ*, before, and *cedere*, to go, signifies the act of going before: *pre-eminence* signifies being more eminent or elevated than others: *preference* signifies being put before others. *Priority* implies simply the order of succession, and is applied to objects either in a state of motion or rest; *precedence* signifies *priority* in going, and depends upon a right or privilege; *pre-eminence* signifies *priority* in being, and depends upon merit; *preference* signifies *priority* in placing, and depends upon favor. The *priority* is applicable rather to the thing than the person; it is not that which is sought for, but that which is to be had: age frequently gives *priority* where every other claim is wanting. The immoderate desire for *precedence* is often nothing but a childish vanity; it is a distinction that results from rank and power; a nobleman claims a *precedence* on all occasions of ceremony. The love of *pre-eminence* is laudable inasmuch as it requires a degree of moral worth which exceeds that of others; a general aims at *pre-eminence* in his profession. Those who are anxious to obtain the best for themselves are eager to have the *preference:* we seek for the *preference* in matters of choice.

PRISTINE. See PRIMARY.

PRIVACY, RETIREMENT, SECLUSION. *Privacy* literally denotes the abstract quality of *private* (from the Latin adjective *privatus*, based on *privare*); but when taken by itself it signifies the state of being *private:* retirement literally signifies the abstract act of *retiring:* and *seclusion* that of *secluding* one's self: but *retirement* by itself frequently denotes a state of being retired or a place of *retirement; seclusion*, a state of being *secluded:* hence we say a person lives in *privacy*, in *retirement*, in *seclusion: privacy* is opposed to publicity; he who lives in *privacy*, therefore, is one who follows no public line, who lives so as to be little known: *retirement* is opposed to openness or freedom of access; he, therefore, who lives in *retirement* withdraws from the society of others, he lives by himself: *seclusion* is the excess of *retirement;* he who lives in *seclusion* bars all access to himself; he shuts himself from the world. *Privacy* is most suitable for such as are in circumstances of humiliation, whether from their misfortune or their fault; *retirement* is peculiarly agreeable to those who are of a reflective turn, but *seclusion* is chosen only by those who labor under some strong affection of the mind, whether of a religious or a physical nature.

PRIVATE-CARRIER. See Com-mon-carrier.

PRIVATE MEETING. See Cau-cus.

PRIVILEGE, Prerogative, Ex-emption, Immunity. *Privilege,* in Latin *privilegium,* compounded of *privus* and *lex,* signifies a law made for any individual or set of individuals. *Prerogative,* from Latin *prærogativa (sc., tribus* or *centuria),* based on *præ,* be-fore, and *rogare,* to ask, was applied to the tribe or century to whom it fell by lot to vote first in the *Comitia,* which was *asked first* whom it would have for consul: hence applied in our language to the right of determining or choosing first in many particulars. *Exemption,* from the verb to *exempt,* and *immunity,* from the Latin *immunis,* free of public .jervice, from *in,* not, and *munis,* not ready to serve, based on *munus,* a pub-lic office, are both employed for the ob-ject from which one is *exempt* or free.

Privilege and *prerogative* consist of positive advantages; *exemption* and *immunity* of those which are negative: by the former we obtain an actual good, by the latter the removal of an evil. *Privilege,* in its most extended sense, comprehends all the rest: for *prerogative, exemption,* and *immunity* are *privileges,* inasmuch as they rest upon certain laws or customs which are made for the benefit of certain individuals. In the restricted sense, the *privilege* may be enjoyed by many; the *prerogative,* which is a peculiar and distinguished *privilege,* can be en-joyed only by a few. As they con-cern the public, *privileges* belong to the subject or are granted to him; *preroga-tives* belong to the crown. It is the *privilege* of a member of Parliament to escape arrest for debt; it is the *prerog-ative* of the crown to be irresponsible for the conduct of its ministers; as respects private cases, it is the *privilege* of women to have the best places assigned to them; it is the *prerogative* of the man to address the woman.

Privileges are applied to every ob-ject which it is desirable to have;

prerogative is confined to the case of making one's election or exercising any special power; *exemption* is ap-plicable to cases in which one is ex-empted from any tribute or payment; *immunity,* because of its derivation above explained, is peculiarly applica-ble to cases in which one is freed from a service: all chartered towns or cor-porations have *privileges, exemptions,* and *immunities:* it is the *privilege* of the city of London to shut its gates against the king.

See also Right.

PRIZE. See Capture; Value.

PROBABILITY. See Chance.

PROBITY. See Honesty.

PROCEED. See Advance; Arise; Go.

PROCEEDING, Process, Prog-ress. The first two of these words are based on Latin *pro,* forward, and the verb *cedere,* in the sense of go; the last on *progredior,* to advance. The man-ner of performing actions for the at-tainment of a given end is the com-mon idea comprehended in these terms. *Proceeding* is the most general, as it simply expresses the general idea of the manner of going on; the rest are spe-cific terms, denoting some particularity in the action, object, or circumstance. *Proceeding* is said commonly of such things as happen in the ordinary way of doing business; *process* is said of such things as are done by rule: the former is considered from a moral point of view; the latter from a scientific or technical standpoint: Freemasons have bound themselves by a law of secrecy not to reveal any part of their *proceedings;* the *process* by which paper is made has undergone considerable im-provements since its first invention.

Proceeding and *progress* both refer to the moral actions of men; but the *proceeding* simply denotes the act of going on or doing something; 'he *progress* denotes an approximation to the end: the *proceeding* may be only a partial action comprehending both the beginning and the end; but the *progress* is applied to that which re-quires time and a regular succession of action to bring it to completion: that is a *proceeding* in which every man is tried in a court of law; that is a *progress* which one makes in learning, by the addition to one's knowledge: hence we do not talk of the *proceeding* of life, but of the *progress* of life.

Proceeding, Transaction.—*Proceeding* signifies, literally, the thing that *proceeds;* and *transaction* the thing *transacted:* the former, therefore, is used of something that is going forward; the latter of something that is already done: we are witnesses to the whole *proceeding;* we inquire into the whole *transaction.* The term *proceeding* is said of every event or circumstance which goes forward through the agency of men; *transaction* comprehends only those matters which have been deliberately *transacted* or brought to a conclusion: in this sense we use the word *proceeding* in application to a disturbance in the street; and the word *transaction* to some commercial negotiation that has been carried on between certain persons. The term *proceeding* marks the manner of *proceeding;* as when we speak of the *proceedings* in a court of law: *transaction* marks the business *transacted;* as the *transactions* on the Exchange. A *proceeding* may be characterized as disgraceful; a *transaction* as iniquitous.

Procession, Train, Retinue.—*Procession,* from the verb *proceed,* signifies the act of going forward or before, that is, in the present instance, of going before others, or one before another. *Train,* from Old French *train,* Low Latin *trahinare,* a derivative of classical *trahere,* to draw, signifies the thing drawn after another, as in the modern *train,* a succession of cars; and in the present instance the persons who are led after, or follow, any object. *Retinue,* from French *retenue,* past participle of *retenir* (from Latin *re* and *tenere,* to hold back, retain), signifies those who are retained as attendants.

All these terms are said of any number of persons who follow in a certain order; but this, which is the leading idea in the word *procession,* is but collateral in the terms *train* and *retinue:* on the other hand, the *procession* may consist of persons of all ranks and stations; but *train* and *retinue* apply only to such as follow some person or thing in a subordinate capacity: the former in regard to such as make up the concluding part of some *procession,*

the latter only in regard to the servants or attendants on the great. At funerals there is frequently a long *train* of coaches belonging to the friends of the deceased, which close the *procession;* princes and nobles never go out on state or public occasions without a numerous *retinue:* the beauty of every *procession* consists in the order with which every one keeps his place and the regularity with which the whole goes forward; the length of a *train* is what renders it most worthy of notice; the number of a *retinue* in eastern nations is one criterion by which the wealth of the individual is estimated.

PROCESS. See PROCEEDING.

PROCLAIM. See ANNOUNCE; DECLARE.

PROCLAMATION. See DECREE.

PROCRASTINATE. See DELAY.

PROCURE. See GET; PROVIDE.

PRODIGAL. See EXTRAVAGANT.

PRODIGIOUS. See ENORMOUS.

PRODIGY. See WONDER.

PRODUCTION, PRODUCE, PRODUCT. The term *production* expresses either the act of *producing* or the thing *produced; product* and *produce* express only the thing *produced:* the *production* of a tree from a seed is one of the wonders of nature; the *product* will not be considerable. In the sense of the thing *produced, production* is applied to every individual thing that is *produced,* whether by nature or art, as a tree is a *production* or a painting is a *production* of art or skill: *produce* and *product* are properly applicable to those *productions* of nature which are made to turn to account; the former in a collective sense, and in reference to some particular object, the latter in an abstract and general sense: the aggregate quantity of grain drawn from a field is termed the *produce* of the field; but corn, hay, vegetables, and fruits in general are termed *products* of the earth: the naturalist examines all the *productions* of nature; the husbandman looks to the *produce* of his lands; the topographer and traveller inquire about the *products* of different countries.

There is the same distinction between these terms in their improper as in their proper acceptation; the *production* is whatever results from an effort, physical or mental, as a *production* of genius, a *production* of art, and the like; the *produce* is the aggregate result from physical or mental labor: thus, whatever the husbandman reaps from the cultivation of his land is termed the *produce* of his labor; whatever results from any public subscription or collection is, in like manner, the *produce:* the *product* is employed properly in regard to the mental operation of figures, as the *product* from multiplication, but may be extended to anything which is the fruit of the brain.

Production, Performance, Work.— When we speak of anything as resulting from any specified operation, we term it a *production:* as the *production* of an author, signifying what he has *produced* by the effort of his mind: Homer's Iliad is esteemed as one of the finest *productions* of the imagination. When we speak of anything as executed or *performed* by some person, we term it a *performance*, as a drawing or a painting is denominated the *performance* of a particular artist. The term *production* cannot be employed without specifying or referring to the source from which it is *produced* or the means by which it is *produced*; as the *production* of art, the *production* of the inventive faculty, the *production* of the mind, etc.: but a *performance* may be spoken of without referring to the individual by whom it has been *performed;* hence we speak of this or that person's *performance;* but we may also say, a good *performance.* When we wish to specify anything that results from *work* or labor, it is termed a *work:* in this manner we speak either of the *work* of one's hands or of a *work* of the imagination, a *work* of time, a *work* of magnitude.

See also AFFORD; EFFECT; MAKE.

PROFANE. See IRRELIGIOUS; SACRILEGIOUS.

PROFESS, DECLARE. *Profess*, in Latin *professus*, participle of *profiteor*, compounded of *pro* and *fateri*, to speak, signifies to set forth or present to public view. *Declare* (see that word).

An exposition of one's thoughts or opinions is the common idea in the signification of these terms; but they differ in the manner of the action, as well as in the object: one *professes* by words or by actions; one *declares* by words only: a man *professes* to believe that on which he acts; but he *declares* his belief in it either with his lips or in his writings. A *profession* may be general and partial; it may amount to little more than an intimation: a *declaration* is positive and explicit; it leaves no one in doubt: a *profession* may, therefore, sometimes be hypocritical; he who *professes* may wish to imply that which is untrue: a *declaration* must be either directly true or false; he who *declares* expressly commits himself upon his veracity. One *professes* either as respects single actions or a regular course of conduct; one *declares* either passing thoughts or settled principles. A person *professes* to have walked to a certain distance, to have taken a certain route, and the like: a Christian *professes* to follow the doctrine and precepts of Christianity; a person *declares* that a thing is true or false, or he *declares* his firm belief in a thing.

To *profess* is employed only for what concerns one's self; to *declare* is also employed for what concerns others: one *professes* the motives and principles by which one is guided: one *declares* facts and circumstances with which one is acquainted: one *professes* nothing but what one thinks may be creditable and fit to be known; but one *declares* whatever may have fallen under one's notice or passed through one's mind, as the case requires; there is always a particular and private motive for *profession;* there are frequently public grounds for making a *declaration.*

See also BUSINESS.

PROFESSION. See BUSINESS; VOCATION.

PROFICIENCY. See PROGRESS.

PROFIT. See ADVANTAGE; GAIN.

PROFLIGATE, ABANDONED, REPROBATE. These words have all a close connection. *Profligate*, in Latin *profligatus*, participle of *profligo*, compounded of the prefix *pro*, forward, down, and *fligare*, to dash, signifies properly one dashed down and destroyed; hence, by extension, wretched and then vile, used as a term of extreme reproach: so Cicero called Catiline "most *profligate* and abandoned of all mortals." *Abandoned* (see ABANDON). *Reprobate* (see REPROVE) signifies one thoroughly hardened to reproof.

A *profligate* man is one completely overcome and ruined by his vices: an *abandoned* man is one *abandoned* to his passions: the *reprobate* man is one who has been reproved until he becomes insensible to reproof and cannot be diverted from following his evil course.

PROFUNDITY. See DEPTH.

PROFUSE. See EXTRAVAGANT.

PROFUSION, PROFUSENESS. *Profusion*, from the Latin *profundo*, to pour forth, is taken in relation to unconscious objects, which pour forth in great plenty; *profuseness* is taken from the same, in relation to conscious agents, who likewise pour forth in great plenty: the term *profusion*, therefore, is put for plenty itself, and the term *profuseness* as a characteristic of persons in the sense of extravagance. At the hospitable board of the rich there will naturally be a *profusion* of everything which can gratify the appetite; when men see an unusual degree of *profusion*, they are apt to indulge themselves in *profuseness*.

PROGENITORS. See FOREFATHERS.

PROGENY. See OFFSPRING.

PROGNOSTIC. See OMEN.

PROGNOSTICATE. See FORETELL.

PROGRESS, PROGRESSION, ADVANCEMENT. A forward motion is designated by these terms: but *progress* and *progression* simply imply this sort of motion; *advance* and *advancement* also imply an approximation to some object: we may make *progress* in that which has no specific termination, as *progress* in learning, which may cease only with life; but the *advance* is made only to some limited point or object in view; as an *advance* in wealth or honor, which may find a termination within the lifetime. *Progress* and *advance* are said of that which has been attained; but *progression* and *advancement* may be said of that which one is attaining: the *progress* or the *advance* has been made, or the person is in the act of *progression* or *advancement:* a child makes *progress* in learning by daily attention; the *progression* from

one stage of learning to another is not always perceptible; it is not always possible to overtake one who is in *advance;* sometimes a person's *advancement* is retarded by circumstances that are altogether contingent: the first step in any destructive course prepares for the second, and the second for the third, after which there is no stop, but the *progress* is infinite.

See also PROCEEDING.

Progress, Proficiency, Improvement.— *Progress* is a generic term, the rest are specific; *proficiency*, from the Latin *proficio*, compounded of *pro*, forward, and a weakened form of *facere*, to do, signifies a state of *progression*—that is to say, a *progress* already made; and *improvement*, from the verb *improve* (see AMEND), signifies an improved condition—that is, *progress* in that which *improves*. The term *progress* here, as in the former paragraph, marks the step or motion onward, and the two others the point already reached: but *progress* is applied either in the proper or improper sense: that is, either to those travelling forward or to those going on stepwise in any work; *proficiency* is applied, in the improper sense, to the ground gained in an art, and *improvement* to what is gained in knowledge, or understanding, or abilities; when idle people set about any work it is difficult to perceive that they make any *progress* in it from time to time; those who have a thorough taste for either music or drawing will show a *proficiency* in it which is astonishing to those who are unacquainted with the circumstances; the *improvement* of the mind can never be so effectually and easily obtained as in the period of childhood.

Progress and *proficiency* are applied to the acts of persons, but *improvement* denotes also the act or state of things; one must make *progress* or show *proficiency*, but things admit of *improvement*.

PROGRESSIVE. See ONWARD.

PROHIBIT. See BAN.

PROHIBITION. See EMBARGO.

PROJECT. See DESIGN.

PROJECTING. See SALIENT.

PROLETARIAT, THE MASSES, HOI POLLOI. *Proletariat*, from Latin *proletarius*, one who helped the state by his children only (from *proles*, offspring), is a word which has come into general usage as a result of the popular interest in political economy during the later nineteenth century. It refers to the lowest class in an organized society, the laborers who have no capital and are dependent on the work of their hands from day to day for subsistence. The term *the masses* (from *mass*, a lump of unorganized, unmolded matter, from Greek μάσσειν, to knead—that which may be or should be kneaded) is also a comparatively recent phrase. It has the same meaning as *proletariat*, but a slightly different meaning, emphasizing not the existence of the lower order, as a distinct order, but as a great multitude outside of the distinct classes. Having been used somewhat contemptuously, it has been adopted as a name of honor by some of the leaders among "the masses," as the title of one of their organs in America, *The Masses*, shows. *Hoi polloi* is the Greek phrase οἱ πολλοί, transliterated with Roman letters. It means, literally, "the many," and among the Greeks was opposed to "the few," as "the masses" were opposed by Gladstone to "the classes." It has much the same connotations as *the masses*, but is generally used in a somewhat flippant and frivolous tone, whereas the phrase *the masses* is becoming a word to conjure with, to be uttered in all seriousness.

See also MASSAGE under PRESS.

PROLIFIC. See FERTILE.

PROLIX. See DIFFUSE.

PROLONG. See DELAY.

PROMINENT, CONSPICUOUS. *Prominent* signifies hanging over; *conspicuous* (see DISTINGUISHED) signifies easy to be beheld: the former is, therefore, to the latter, in some measure, as the species to the genus; what is *prominent* is, in general, on that very account *conspicuous;* but many things may be *conspicuous* which are not expressly *prominent:* nothing is *prominent* but what *projects* beyond a certain line; everything is *conspicuous* which may be seen by many: the nose on a man's face is a *prominent* feature, owing to its projecting situation; and it is sometimes *conspicuous*, according to the position of the person: a figure in a *painting* is said to be *prominent* if it appears to stand forward or before the others; but it is not properly *conspicuous* unless there be something in it which attracts the general notice and distinguishes it from all other things; on the contrary, it is *conspicuous*, but not expressly *prominent*, when the colors are vivid.

PROMISCUOUS, INDISCRIMINATE. *Promiscuous*, in Latin *promiscuus*, compounded of the prefix *pro* and *miscere*, to mingle, signifies thoroughly mingled. *Indiscriminate*, from the Latin *in*, privative, and *discrimen*, a difference, signifies without any difference.

Promiscuous is applied to any number of different objects mingled together; *indiscriminate* is applied only to the action in which one does not discriminate different objects: a multitude is termed *promiscuous*, as characterizing the thing; the use of different things for the same purpose, or of the same things for different purposes, is termed *indiscriminate*, as characterizing the person: things become *promiscuous* by the want of design in any one; they are *indiscriminate* by the express intention of some one: plants of all descriptions are to be found *promiscuously* situated in the beds of a garden: it is folly to level any charge *indiscriminately* against all the members of any community or profession.

PROMISE, ENGAGEMENT, WORD. *Promise*, in Latin *promissus*, from *promitto*, compounded of *pro*, before, and the past participle of *mittere*, to send; that is, in this application, to pledge beforehand, is specific, and consequently more binding than the *engagement* (see BUSINESS): we *promise* a thing in a set form of words that are clearly and strictly understood; we *engage* in general terms that may admit of alteration: a *promise* is mostly unconditional; an *engagement* is frequently conditional. In *promises* the faith of an individual is accepted upon his word and relied upon as if it were a deed: in *engagements* the intentions of an individual for the future are all that are either implied or understood: on the fulfilment of *promises* often depend the most important interests of individuals; an attention to *engagements* is a matter of mutual convenience in the ordinary concerns of life: a man makes a *promise* of payment, and upon his *promise* it may happen that many others depend for the fulfilment of their *promises:* when *engagements* are made to visit or meet others, the failure to observe such *engagements* causes great trouble.

As a *promise* and *engagement* can be made only by *words*, the *word* is often put for either, or for both, as the case requires: he who breaks his *word* in small matters cannot be trusted when he gives his *word* in matters of consequence.

PROMOTE. See ENCOURAGE.

PROMPT. See DILIGENT; READY.

PROMULGATE. See PUBLISH.

PRONENESS. See INCLINATION.

PRONOUNCE. See UTTER.

PROOF, EVIDENCE, TESTIMONY. The *proof* (see ARGUMENT) is that which simply *proves;* the *evidence* is that which makes *evident* (see CLEAR); the *testimony,* from *testis,* a witness, is a species of *evidence* by means of witnesses. In the legal acceptation of the terms *proofs* are commonly denominated *evidence,* because nothing can be admitted as *proof* which does not tend to make *evident;* but as what is *proved* is made more certain or indubitable than what is made *evident, proof* is more than *evidence. Proof* is likewise taken for the act of *proving* as well as for the thing that *proves,* which distinguishes it still further from *evidence.*

Evidence comprehends whatever is employed to make *evident,* be it words or deeds, be it writing or discourse; *testimony* is properly *evidence* by words spoken, and more strictly understood by the person giving the *evidence.*

In an extended application of these terms they are employed with a similar distinction: the *proof* is the mark or sign which *proves:* the *evidence* is the mark or sign which makes *evident:* the *testimony* is that which is offered or given by things personified in *proof* of anything.

The *proof* is employed for facts or physical objects: the *evidence* is applied to that which is moral; *testimony* regards that which is personal. All that our Saviour did and said were *evidences* of his divine character, which might have produced faith in the minds

of many, even if they had not had such numerous and miraculous *proofs* of his power. One friend makes a present to another in *testimony* of his regard: the *proof* and the *testimony* are something external, or some outward mark or indication; the *evidence* may be internal or lie in the thing itself, as the internal *evidences* of Christianity.

See also EXPERIENCE.

PROP. See STAFF.

PROPAGANDA. See SPREAD.

PROPENSITY. See INCLINATION.

PROPER. See RIGHT.

PROPERTY. See ESTATE; GOODS; QUALITY.

PROPHESY. See FORETELL.

PROPHETIC. See ORACULAR.

PROPITIOUS. See AUSPICIOUS; FAVORABLE.

PROPORTION. See RATE; SYMMETRY.

PROPORTIONATE, COMMENSURATE, ADEQUATE. *Proportion,* from the Latin *proportio,* compounded of *pro,* suitable to, in ratio with, and *portio,* a share, signifies having a *portion,* suitable to, or in agreement with, some other object. *Commensurate,* from the Latin prefix *com,* based on *cum,* with, and *mensuratus,* the past participle of the post-classical *mensurare,* to measure, I measure, signifies measuring in accordance with some other thing, being suitable in measure to something else. *Adequate,* in Latin *adæquatus,* participle of *adæquare,* from *ad,* to, and *æquus,* equal, signifies made level with some other body.

Proportionate is here a term of general use; the others are particular terms, employed in a similar sense, in regard to particular objects: that is *proportionate* which rises as a thing rises and falls as a thing falls; that is *commensurate* which is made to rise to the same measure or degree; that is *adequate* which is made to come up to the height of another thing. *Proportionate* is employed either in the proper or improper sense; in recipes and prescriptions of every kind *proportionate* quantities must always be taken; when the task increases in difficulty and complication, a *proportionate* degree of labor and talent must be employed upon it. *Commensurate* and *adequate* are employed only in the moral sense, the former to denote suitability of things in point of measure, the latter to denote the equalizing of powers: a person's recompense should in some measure be *commensurate* with his labor and deserts: a person's resources should be *adequate* to the work he is engaged in.

PROPOSAL, PROPOSITION. *Proposal* comes from *propose*, based on Latin *pro* and *ponere*, meaning to put forward, in the sense of offer: *proposition* comes from *propose*, in the sense of setting down in a distinct form of words. We make a *proposal* to a person to enter into a partnership with him; we make a *proposition* to one who is at variance with us to settle the difference by arbitration.

PROPOSE. See OFFER; PREMEDITATE; PURPOSE.

PROPOSITION. See PROPOSAL; SENTENCE.

PROPRIETOR. See POSSESSOR.

PROROGUE, ADJOURN. *Prorogue,* from the Latin *prorogare,* from *pro,* publicly, and *rogare,* to ask, means to propose an extension of office, to defer. *Adjourn,* from *ad,* to or until, and the French *journée,* the day, signifies only to put off for a day, or some short period: the former is applied to national assemblies only, the latter is applied to any meeting.

PROSCRIBE, BANISH, CONDEMN, DENOUNCE, EXILE, EXPEL, OSTRACIZE, REJECT. *Proscribe,* in Latin *proscribere,* from *pro,* before, openly, and *scribere,* to write, is virtually to put beyond the protection of the law by a written order. *Banish, expel,* and *exile* are closely allied applications signifying the act of driving or forcing a person from his country as a punishment by authority. *Condemn* is to censure, blame, declare to be forfeited, pronounce or judge guilty. *Denounce* is to threaten or accuse publicly; in diplomacy it is the act of abrogating a treaty. *Ostracize* meant originally to banish by a vote written on a potsherd, from Greek ὀστρακίζειν, to banish by potsherds, based on ὄστρακον, a potsherd, a tablet for voting, allied with *oyster,* which originally signified a shell. *Ostracize* differs from *proscribe, banish,* etc., in indicating a cutting off of the victim from social intercourse by a

general, but often informal, withdrawing of favor on the part of a whole group or community. *Reject* is to discard, cast aside, all of which is applicable alike to persons and things.

In old Roman history, to *proscribe* a person was to publish his name as one doomed to death and forfeiture of property; in ancient Athens to *banish* a citizen was to throw a shell, inscribed with the name of the person, into an urn.

PROSECUTE. See CONTINUE.
PROSELYTE. See CONVERT.
PROSPECT. See VIEW.
PROSPER. See FLOURISH.
PROSPERITY. See WELL-BEING.
PROSPEROUS. See FORTUNATE.
PROTECT. See DEFEND; SAVE.

PROTEST, EXPOSTULATE, REMONSTRATE. These words all indicate the statement of an objection on the part of some one to the acts or statements of another. *Protest,* from Latin *pro,* publicly, and *testor,* I bear witness, is a more solemn and formal act than *expostulate* and *remonstrate.* In business, for instance, a *protest* is a formal declaration by the holder of a bill of exchange of its non-payment or nonacceptance. *Remonstrate,* from Latin *re,* against, and *monstrare,* to show, is a mild form of protest in which the protesting party brings up arguments against a proposed course. To *expostulate* is a friendly form of *remonstrating.*

See also ULTIMATUM.

PROTRACT. See DELAY.
PROUD. See HIGH-FLOWN.

PROVE, DEMONSTRATE, EVINCE, MANIFEST. *Prove,* in Latin *probare,* signifies to make good, *i. e.,* to make good by proofs, which is here the general term; the other terms imply different modes of *proving:* we *prove* in different ways and in different degrees. To *demonstrate,* from *monstrare,* to show, and the intensive syllable *de,* signifies to *prove* in a specific manner, that is, in a clear and undeniable manner; we may *prove* facts, innocence, guilt, and the like; we *demonstrate* the truth or falsity of a thing.

Prove and *demonstrate* may also be applied to that which a person may show of himself; *evince* (which is of less frequent use) and *manifest* are used only in this application. To *prove* in this case is to give a proof, as to *prove* one's valor; to *demonstrate* is to give a clear or ocular proof, as to *demonstrate* an attachment to a thing; to *evince* is to show by convincing proof, as to *evince* one's integrity by the whole course of one's dealings; to *manifest* is to make manifest, as to *manifest* one's displeasure or satisfaction.

In regard to things, to *prove* is to serve as a proof; to *evince* is to serve as a particular proof; to *manifest* is to serve as a public proof. The beauty and order in the Creation *prove* the wisdom of the Creator; a persistence in a particular course of conduct may *evince* either great virtue or great folly; the miracles wrought in Egypt *manifested* the Divine power.

PROVERB. See AXIOM.

PROVIDE, PROCURE, FURNISH, SUPPLY. *Provide,* in Latin *providere, i. e.,* to foresee, signifies, literally, to see before, but, figuratively, to get in readiness for some future purpose. *Procure* (see GET). *Furnish* is in French *fournir,* from Old High German *frumjan,* to provide. *Supply,* in French *suppléer,* from Latin *sub,* up, and *plere,* to fill, signifies to fill up a deficiency or make up what is wanting.

Provide and *procure* are both actions that have a special reference to the future; *furnish* and *supply* are employed for that which is of immediate concern: one *provides* a dinner in the expectation that some persons are coming to partake of it; one *procures* help in the expectation that it may be wanted; we *furnish* a room as we find it necessary for the present purpose; one *supplies* a family with any article of domestic use. Calculation is necessary in *providing;* one does not wish to *provide* too much or too little: labor and management are requisite in *procuring;* when a thing is not always at hand, or not easily obtained, one must exercise one's time, strength, or ingenuity to *procure* it: judgment is requisite in *furnishing;* what one *furnishes* ought to be selected with reference to the circumstances of the individual who *furnishes;* care and attention are required in *supplying;* we must be careful to know what a person really wants in order to *supply*

him to his satisfaction. One *provides* against all contingencies; one *procures* all necessaries; one *furnishes* all comforts; one *supplies* all deficiencies.

Provide and *procure* are the acts of persons only; *furnish* and *supply* are the acts of unconscious agents: one's garden and orchard may be said to *furnish* one with delicacies; the earth *supplies* us with food. So in the improper application: the daily occurrences of a great city *furnish* materials for a newspaper; a newspaper, to many people, *supplies* almost every other want.

Providence, Prudence. — Providence and *prudence* are both derived from the verb to *provide;* but the former expresses the particular act of providing, the latter the habit of providing. The former is applied both to animals and men; the latter is employed only as a characteristic of men. We may admire the *providence* of the ant in laying up a store for the winter; the *prudence* of a parent is displayed in his concern for the future settlement of his child. It is *provident* in a person to adopt measures of escape for himself in certain situations of peculiar danger; it is *prudent* to be always prepared for all contingencies.

Prudent, Prudential. — Prudent (see JUDGMENT) characterizes the person or the thing; *prudential* characterizes only the thing. *Prudent* signifies having *prudence; prudential,* that which accords with rules of *prudence* or as respects *prudence.* The *prudent* is opposed to the *imprudent* and inconsiderate; the *prudential* is opposed to the voluntary: the course is *prudent* which accords with the principles of *prudence;* the reason or motive is *prudential* as flowing out of circumstances of *prudence* or necessity. Every one is called upon at certain times to adopt *prudent* measures; those who are obliged to consult their means in the management of their expenses must act upon *prudential* motives.

See also WISDOM.

PROVIDENT. See CAREFUL.

PROVISION. See FARE.

PROVISIONAL, CONDITIONAL, CONTINGENT, HYPOTHETICAL. The adjective *provisional* is derived from the Latin *provisio,* foresight, and implies the act of providing beforehand, previous preparation, temporary arrangement. *Conditional* signifies within certain limits, prescribed. *Contingent*, as an adjective, signifies accidental, also partial, as a lawyer's *contingent* fee; as a substantive, a possibility, a quota of troops. *Hypothetical* implies that which is a supposition or conjecture, something assumed in an argument.

See also EMPIRICAL.

PROVOKE. See AGGRAVATE; AWAKEN; EXCITE.

PRY, SCRUTINIZE, DELVE INTO. *Pry* is in all probability changed from *prove*, in the sense of try. *Scrutinize* comes from the Latin *scruta*, broken pieces, and signifies to search carefully as if among rubbish or broken pieces.

Pry is taken in the bad sense of looking more narrowly into things than one ought: *scrutinize* and *delve into* are employed in the good sense of searching things to the bottom. A person who *pries* looks into that which does not belong to him, and too narrowly also into that which may belong to him; it is the consequence of a too eager curiosity or a busy, meddling temper: a person who *scrutinizes* looks into that which is intentionally concealed from him; it is an act of duty flowing out of his office: a person who *delves* penetrates into that which lies hidden very deep; he is impelled to this action by the thirst of knowledge and a laudable curiosity.

A love of *prying* into the private affairs of families makes a person a troublesome neighbor; it is the business of the magistrate to *scrutinize* all matters which affect the good order of society: there are some minds so imbued with a love of science that they delight to *delve into* the secrets of nature.

PUBLIC, COMMUNITY, PEOPLE, SOCIETY, WORLD. In these applications the term *public* is usually preceded by the article *the*, and implies personality. The *community* is a body of citizens embraced in a region of any size. *People* are persons generally, inhabitants, race, kindred, family. *Society* is a collection or union of people having a common interest, often applied to the more cultivated portion of a community in its social relations. The *world* includes all people on earth, in the universe; sometimes applied to a personal environment, as *the world about us*, or to special bodies of people, as *the world of finance*.

PUBLISH, PROMULGATE, DIVULGE, REVEAL, DISCLOSE. *Publish* (see ADVERTISE). *Promulgate*, from Latin *promulgare*, to make known, is a word of unknown origin. *Divulge*, in Latin *divulgare*, from *di*, for *dis*, apart, and *vulgare*, based on *vulgus*, people, signifies to make known among the people. *Reveal*, in Latin *revelare*, from *veli*, veil, signifies to take off the veil or cover. *Disclose* signifies to make the reverse of *closed*.

To *publish* is the most general of these terms, conveying in its extended sense the idea of making known; but it is in many respects indefinite: we may *publish* to many or few; but to *promulgate* is always to make known to many. We may *publish* that which is a domestic or a national concern; we *promulgate* properly only that which is of general interest: the affairs of a family or of a nation are *published* in the newspapers; doctrines, principles, precepts, and the like are *promulgated*.

We may *publish* things to be known, or things not to be known; we *divulge* things mostly not to be known: we may *publish* our own shame or the shame of another, and we may *publish* that which is advantageous to another; but we commonly *divulge* the secrets or the crimes of another.

To *publish* is said of that which was never before known or never before existed; to *reveal* and *disclose* are said of that which has been only concealed or lain hidden: we *publish* the events of the day; we *reveal* the secret or the mystery of a transaction; we *disclose* from beginning to end a whole affair which has never been properly known or accounted for.

See also ANNOUNCE; DECLARE.

PUERILE. See YOUTHFUL.

PULL. See DRAW.

PUNCTUAL. See EXACT.

PURCHASE. See BUY.

PURE. See CLEAN; VIRTUOUS.

PURIFY. See SANCTIFY.

PURPORT. See TENOR.

PURPOSE, PROPOSE. We *purpose* (see DESIGN) that which is near at hand or immediately to be set about; we *propose* that which is more distant: the former requires the setting before one's mind, the latter requires deliberation and plan. We *purpose* many things which we never think worth while doing; but we ought not to *propose* anything to ourselves which is not of too much importance to be lightly adopted or rejected. We *purpose* to go to town on a certain day; we *pro ose* to spend our time in a particular study.

PURSUE. See Continue; Follow.

PUSH, Shove, Thrust, Ram. All these words denote the giving an impulse to a body with more or less force, but differ as to the situation in which the impulse is given. *Push* (ultimately from Latin *pulsare*, to beat, a frequentative of *pellere*, to drive), and *shove*, Anglo-Saxon *scufan*, require the bodies which give and receive the impulse to be in contact: one person cannot *push* or *shove* another without coming into direct personal contact with him; as when a person touches another in passing, it may be a *push* more or less violent: to *shove* is a continued action, which causes the body to move forward; as to *shove* a load along the ground. A body may be both *pushed* and *shoved* along, but in the former case this is effected by repeated *pushes*, and in the latter case by a continuation of the same act. To *thrust*, like *push*, is a single act; but *thrusting* is commonly performed by some instrument, as a pole, a stick, a hand, or some part of a body. It is a Scandinavian word allied to *threat* and to Latin *trudere*, found in *intrude*.

A body may likewise, in a similar manner, *thrust* itself, but it always *pushes* or *shoves* some other body.

Ram (a word which may be allied to *ram*, a male sheep, signifying to butt or strike as the sheep strikes with his horns) means also to *thrust* into, but it implies a more sharp and energetic action than *thrust*. *Push* and *shove* do not imply injury to the object; *ram* does. The word is applied as a substantive to a solid beak or point projecting from the bows of a war-vessel and enabling it to *ram* or batter its opponent.

PUT, Place, Lay, Set. *Put* comes from Anglo-Saxon *potian*, to thrust, Middle English *putten*. *Place* (see that word). *Lay* is in Anglo-Saxon *licgan*, to cause to lie, Middle English *leggan*. *Put* is the most general of all these terms; *place, lay,* and *set* are but modes of *putting;* one *puts* things generally, but the way of *putting* is not defined; one may *put* a thing into one's room, one's desk, one's pocket, and the like; but to *place* is to *put* in a specific manner and for a specific purpose; one *places* a book on a shelf as a fixed *place* for it, and in a position most suitable to it. To *lay* and *set* are still more specific than *place*, the former being applied only to such things as can be made to lie; and *set* only to such as can be made to stand: a book may be said to be *laid* on the table when *placed* in a downward position, and *set* on a shelf when *placed* on one end: we *lay* ourselves down on the ground; we *set* a trunk upon the ground.

PUTREFY. See Rot.

Q

QUAIL, Cower, Cringe, Knuckle. *Quail* is from a Teutonic base, *kwal;* cf. Modern German *qual*, anguish or distress. *Cower*, represented in Middle English by *couren*, is Scandinavian; it meant originally to lie quiet, to sit hunched up. *Cringe*, Anglo-Saxon *cringan*, meant to fall before the foe in battle. *Knuckle*, in Middle English *knokil*, a diminutive form allied to Middle Dutch *knoke*, a bone or knuckle, meant to place one's knuckles on the ground in shooting or casting marbles; it developed the meaning of to acknowledge one's self beaten in a game, to yield. All these words indicate a movement of fear or submission before an attack. *Quail* is the strongest word. It implies an absolute sinking of heart, a loss of courage before an attack or a misfortune. *Cringe* has a similar meaning, but is a milder word; it refers to a temporary physical shrinking before a blow. *Cower* means to huddle together and shudder with fear. There is more of physical fear in *cower;* more of mental and moral abasement accompanying fear in *cringe*. *Knuckle* means to yield to another under pressure; it does not necessarily imply physical fear, however.

QUAKE. See Shake.

QUALIFICATION, Accomplishment. The *qualification* (see Competent) serves the purpose of utility; the *accomplishment* serves to adorn: by the first we are enabled to make ourselves useful; by the second we are enabled to make ourselves agreeable. The *qualifications* of a man who has an office to perform must be considered: of a man who has only pleasure to pursue, the *accomplishments* are to be considered. A readiness with one's pen and a facility at accounts are necessary *qualifications* either for a school or a counting-house; drawing is one of the most agreeable and suitable *accomplishments* that can be given to a young person.

Qualify, Temper, Humor. — *Qualify* (see Competent). *Temper*, from Latin *temperare*, is to regulate the temperament. *Humor*, from Latin *humor*, is to suit the *humor*. See Humor.

Things are *qualified* according to circumstances: what is too harsh must be *qualified* by something that is soft and lenitive; things are *tempered* by nature or by Providence, so that things perfectly discordant should not be combined; things are *humored* by contrivance: what is subject to many changes requires to be *humored;* a polite person will *qualify* a refusal by some expression of kindness; Providence has *tempered* the seasons so as to mix something that is pleasant in them all. Nature itself is sometimes to be *humored* when art is employed: but the *tempers* of man require still more to be *humored*.

See also Fit.

QUALITY, Property, Attribute. *Quality*, in Latin *qualitas*, from *qualis*, how constituted, signifies such as a thing really is. *Property*, from *proprius*, proper or one's own, signifies belonging to a thing as an essential ingredient. *Attribute*, in Latin *attributus*, participle of *attribuere*, to bestow upon, signifies the things bestowed upon or assigned to another.

The *quality* is that which is inherent in the thing and coexistent; the *property* is that which belongs to it for the time being; the *attribute* is the *quality* which is assigned to any object. We cannot alter the *quality* of a thing without altering the whole thing; but we may give or take away *properties* from bodies at pleasure, without entirely destroying their identity; and we may ascribe *attributes* at discretion.

See also Fashion.

QUANDARY, Dilemma. These words both indicate a state of embarrassment in which the victim does not "know which way to turn." *Quandary* is a word of uncertain origin, possibly derived from scholastic Latin. *Dilemma*, Latin *dilemma*, Greek δίλημμα, is a double proposition or argument in which one is caught between two difficulties. It differs from *quandary* in distinctly suggesting two difficulties and the impossibility of deciding between them. *Quandary* simply suggests a general state of confusion and doubt. *Quandary* is generally used in the phrase "in a *quandary.*"

QUANTITY. See DEAL.

QUARREL, BROIL, FEUD. *Quarrel,* from Latin *querela,* a complaint (see DIFFERENCE), is the general and ordinary term; *broil* is in Old French *brouiller,* to jumble or confuse, allied to Italian *broglio,* whence the English *imbroglio* is derived. *Feud,* Old French *feide,* is also allied to Anglo-Saxon *fæhd,* enmity, and *fâh,* hostile, modern English *foe.* The idea of a variance between two or more parties is common to these terms; but the first signifies the complaints and charges which are reciprocally made; *broil* the confusion and entanglement which arise from a contention and collision of interests; *feud* the hostilities which arise out of the variance. There are *quarrels* where there are no *broils,* and there are both where there are no *feuds;* but there are no *broils* and *feuds* without *quarrels.* The *quarrel* is not always openly conducted between the parties; it may sometimes be secret and sometimes manifest itself only in a coolness of behavior: the *broil* is a noisy kind of *quarrel,* it always breaks out in loud and most reproachful language: *feud* is a deadly kind of quarrel which is heightened by mutual aggravations and insults. *Quarrels* are very lamentable when they take place between members of the same family; *broils* are very frequent among profligate and restless people who live together: *feuds* were very general in former times between different families of the nobility.

Quarrel, Affray, Fray.—A *quarrel* is indefinite, both as to the cause and the manner in which it is conducted; an *affray* or *fray,* from *frico,* to rub, signifies the conflict of the passions and is a particular kind of *quarrel:* a *quarrel* may arise between two persons from a private difference; an *affray* always takes place between many upon some public occasion: a *quarrel* may be carried on merely by words; an *affray* is commonly conducted by acts of violence: many angry words pass in a *quarrel* between too hasty people; many are wounded, if not killed, in *affrays* when opposite parties meet.

See also BICKER.

QUARRELSOME. See QUERULOUS.

QUARTER. See DISTRICT.

QUARTERS, ABODE, CANTONMENT, POST, STATION. In these applications the term assumes the plural form and applies to both domestic and military concerns. *Abode* and *dwelling* imply any kind of habitation, lodging, or temporary residence. *Cantonment, post,* and *station* are specifically military terms, implying, respectively, a part of a town allotted to a body of troops for temporary or permanent occupation; a permanent military establishment, as an important fortress, and a region assigned for the permanent location of a naval squadron, as the *Atlantic station.* The term *headquarters* designates the *station* or building where a commander-in-chief and his staff are located.

QUELL, QUASH. *Quell* is derived from Anglo-Saxon *cwellan,* to kill. It means to overcome completely, to reduce to quietness and peace. *Quash* comes from Latin *quassare,* to shatter. In some connections it means to annul completely; in this sense it is used in legal procedure. It is also used to refer to the complete suppression of an idea or a proposal. The police *quell* a riot; the opposition on a board of directors may *quash* a plan that does not seem feasible. *Quell* implies an active disturbance; *quash* only an incipient disturbance.

QUERULOUS, PETULANT. Both of these words apply to a fretful and dissatisfied temper, but they differ somewhat in their indication of the way in which the dissatisfaction shows itself. *Querulous* comes from *querulus,* full of complaints, and like *quarrel* (see above) derived ultimately from Latin *queri,* to complain. It means weakly and futilely complaining. A *querulous* person does not rise to the height of a really energetic protest. He merely continues to object in an ineffectual and self-pitying tone. *Petulant* comes from Latin *petulare,* a diminutive of *petere,* to attack in a small way. It refers to small outbursts in which there are more of wilfulness and "temper" than of the feeble misery implied in *querulous.* A cheerful person may be *petulant;* he cannot be *querulous.* *Petulance* is characteristic of healthy but undisciplined youth; *querulousness* of feeble age.

See also DIFFERENCE; QUARREL.

QUESTION, QUERY. *Question* (see ASK). *Query* is but a variation of *quære* (seek!), from the verb *quærere*, the Latin imperative to seek or inquire.

Questions and *queries* are both put for the sake of obtaining an answer; but the former may be for a reasonable or unreasonable cause; a *query* is mostly a rational *question:* idlers may put *questions* from mere curiosity; learned men put *queries* for the sake of information.

QUICK. See SUDDEN.

QUICKNESS, SWIFTNESS, FLEETNESS, CELERITY, RAPIDITY, VELOCITY. These terms are all applied to the motion of bodies, of which *quickness*, from *quick*, denotes the general and simple idea which characterizes all the rest. *Quickness* is nearly akin to life (from Anglo-Saxon *cwic*, alive, lively—the older meaning of which is found in the phrase the "quick and the dead" in the Apostles' Creed) and is directly opposed to slowness. *Swiftness* comes from Anglo-Saxon *swifan*, to move quickly; and *fleetness* is allied to Anglo-Saxon *fleotan*, to float. *Swiftness* and *fleetness* express higher degrees of *quickness*. *Celerity*, from Latin *celer*, Greek κέλης, a racer; *velocity*, ultimately from *volo*, to fly; and *rapidity*, from *rapere*, to seize or hurry along, differ more in application than in degree. *Quick* and *swift* are applicable to any objects; men are *quick* in moving, *swift* in running: dogs hear *quickly*, and run *swiftly;* a mill goes *quickly* or *swiftly* round, according to the force of the wind: *fleetness* is the peculiar characteristic of winds or horses; a horse is *fleet* in the race, and is sometimes described to be as *fleet* as the winds: that which we wish to characterize as particularly *quick* in our ordinary operations we say is done with *celerity;* in this manner our thoughts pass with *celerity* from one object to another: those things are said to move with *rapidity* which seem to hurry everything away with them; a river or stream moves with *rapidity;* time goes on with *rapid* flight: *velocity* signifies the *swiftness* of flight, which is a motion that exceeds all others in *swiftness:* hence,

we speak of the *velocity* of a ball shot from a cannon, or of a celestial body moving in its orbit; sometimes these words, *rapidity* and *velocity*, are applied in the improper sense by way of emphasis to the very *swift* movements of other bodies: in this manner the wheel of a carriage is said to move *rapidly;* and the flight of an animal, or the progress of a vessel before the wind, is compared to the flight of a bird in point of *velocity*.

QUIET. See APPEASE; EASE; PEACE.

QUIT. See LEAVE; STRIKE.

QUITE, COMPLETELY, ENTIRELY, PERFECTLY, TOTALLY, WHOLLY. These terms are so similar and so interchangeable in all respects that there is no necessity for a discrimination between them. The original significance and derivation can be found under the corresponding adjective forms. *Quite*, of the same origin (Middle English *quite* as *quit*, and connoting a similar finality), is, strictly speaking, synonymous with the words here given rather than with *rather* or *very*, with which it is often interchanged, as when we say *quite* good, meaning not *entirely* good, but *rather* good.

QUIVER. See SHAKE.

QUIXOTIC. FANTASTIC, VISIONARY. Properly speaking, *Quixotic* has no synonymes because it signifies acts akin in nature to those of Don Quixote, the hero of Cervantes's romance of that name, champion of all persons in distress and observer of all the magnanimities of knighthood. Don Quixote being a character absolutely unique in literature, there is no adjective that corresponds to *Quixotic;* but *fantastic* (from Greek φαντασία, vision, unreal appearance), signifying that which resembles the strange world of dreams, and *visionary* (Latin *visio*), which has the same original meaning, but suggests not the oddness and waywardness of the dream world, but its unreality and its wistful appeal—these two words partly correspond to the quality of action and thought indicated in *Quixotic*, while suggesting none of the humor and pathos, the contrast between the noble intention and the awkward and ridiculous action, also implied in that word.

QUOTE. See CITE.

R

RACE, GENERATION, BREED. *Race* (see FAMILY). *Generation*, in Latin *generatio*, from *generare*, signifies the thing begotten. *Breed* signifies that which is *bred* (see BREED). These terms are all employed in regard to a number of animate objects which have the same origin; the first two are said only of human beings, the latter only of animals: the term *race* is employed in regard to the dead as well as the living; *generation* is employed mostly in regard to the living: hence we speak of the *race* of the Heraclidæ, the *race* of the Bourbons, the *race* of the Stuarts, and the like; but the present *generation*, the whole *generation*, a worthless *generation*, and the like (yet we also speak of past *generations*): *breed* is said of those animals which are brought forth and brought up in the same manner. Hence, we denominate some domestic animals as of a good *breed*, where particular heed is given to the animals from which they come, and special care is taken of those which are brought forth.

See also COURSE; FAMILY.

RACK. See BREAK.

RADIANCE, BRILLIANCY. Both these terms express the circumstance of a great light in a body; but *radiance*, from *radius*, a ray, denotes the emission of rays, and is, therefore, peculiarly applicable to bodies naturally luminous, like the heavenly bodies; and *brilliancy* (see BRIGHT) denotes the whole body of light emitted, and may, therefore, be applied equally to natural and artificial light. The *radiancy* of the sun, moon, and stars constitutes a part of their beauty; the *brilliancy* of a diamond is frequently compared with that of a star.

Brilliancy is applied to objects which shine or glitter like a diamond. It is also applied figuratively to moral objects.

RADIATE. See SHINE.

RADIOGRAPH, PICTURE, REPRESENTATION. A *radiograph*, from the Latin *radio*, a ray, and the Greek γράφω, to write, is a *picture* or *representation* of an object in shadowy form by the action of Röntgen or X-rays on certain sensitive salts. It is a modern aid of great value in surgical science.

RAGE. See ANGER; MADNESS.

RAISE. See HEIGHTEN; LIFT.

RALLY. See DERIDE.

RAM. See PUSH.

RAMBLE. See EXCURSION; WANDER.

RANCOR. See HATRED; MALICE.

RANGE. See WANDER.

RANK. See CLASS; FULSOME.

RANSACK. See RUMMAGE.

RANSOM. See REDEEM.

RAP. See KNOCK.

RAPACIOUS, RAVENOUS, VORACIOUS. *Rapacious*, in Latin *rapax*, from *rapere*, to seize, signifies seizing or grasping anything with an eager desire to possess. *Ravenous*, from the Latin *rapina*, from *rapere*, to seize, signifies the same as *rapacious*. *Voracious*, from *vorax*, based on *vorare*, to devour, signifies an eagerness to devour.

The idea of greediness, which forms the leading feature in the signification of all these terms, is varied in the subject and the object: *rapacious* is the quality peculiar to beasts of prey or what is like beasts of prey: *ravenous* and *voracious* are common to all animals when impelled by hunger. The beasts of the forest are *rapacious* at all times; all animals are more or less *ravenous* or *voracious*, as circumstances may make them: the term *rapacious* applies to the seizing of anything that is eagerly wanted; *ravenous* applies to the seizing of anything which one takes for one's food: a lion is *rapacious* when it seizes on its prey: it is *ravenous* in the act of consuming it. The word *ravenous* implies the haste with which one eats; the word *voracious* the quantity which one consumes: a *ravenous* person is loath to wait for the dressing or cooking of his food; he consumes it without any preparation: a *voracious* person not only eats in haste, but he consumes great quantities and continues to do so for a long time. Abstinence from food for an unusual length of time will make any healthy creature *ravenous;* habitual intemperance in eating or an abnormal appetite will produce *voracity.*

In an extended sense, *rapacity* is applied as a characteristic of persons to denote their eagerness to seize anything which falls in their way.

Ravenous denotes an excess of *rapacity,* and *voracious* is applied figuratively to moral objects.

See also GREEDY.

RAPIDITY. See QUICKNESS.

RAPINE, PLUNDER, PILLAGE. The idea of property taken from another contrary to his consent is included in all these terms: but the term *rapine,* from Latin *rapina* (see above), implies most violence; *plunder* (from a Germanic word signifying trash, baggage, plunder), meaning to strip a house even of its least valuable contents, includes removal or carrying away; *pillage,* derived from Latin *pilare,* to pull out hair, to strip entirely, means wholesale booty which is searched for and taken away. A soldier who makes a sudden incursion into an enemy's country and carries away whatever comes within his reach is guilty of *rapine:* he goes into a house full of property, and carries away much *plunder;* he enters with the rest of the army into a town, and, stripping it of everything that was to be found, goes away loaded with *pillage;* mischief and bloodshed attend *rapine:* loss attends *plunder;* distress and ruin follow wherever there has been *pillage.*

RAPTURE. See ECSTASY.

RARE, SCARCE, SINGULAR. *Rare,* in Latin *rarus. Scarce* comes from Low Latin *scarpsus,* a shortened form of *excarpsus,* for classical *excerptus,* to select, meaning picked out. *Singular* (see PARTICULAR).

Rare and *scarce* both imply number or quantity, which admit of expansion or diminution: *rare* is a thinned number; *scarce* is a quantity cut short. *Rare* is applied to matters of convenience or luxury; *scarce* to matters of utility or necessity: that which is *rare* becomes valuable and fetches a high price; that which is *scarce* becomes precious, and the loss of it is seriously felt. The best of everything

is in its nature *rare;* there will never be a superfluity of such things; there are, however, some things, as particularly curious plants or particular animals, which, owing to circumstances, are always *rare:* that which is most in use will, in certain cases, be *scarce;* when the supply of an article fails, and the demand for it continues, it naturally becomes *scarce.* An aloe in blossom is a *rarity,* for nature has prescribed such limits to its growth as to give but very few of such flowers: the paintings of Raphael and the distinguished painters of former days are daily becoming more *scarce,* because time will diminish their quantity, although not their value.

What is *rare* will often be *singular* and what is *singular* will often, on that account, be *rare:* but these terms are not necessarily applied to the same object: fewness is the idea common to both; but *rare* is said of that of which there might be more; while *singular* is applied to that which is single or nearly single in its kind. The *rare* is that which is always sought for; the *singular* is not always that which one esteems: a thing is *rare* which is difficult to obtain; a thing is *singular* for its peculiar qualities, good or bad. Indian plants are many of them *rare* in England, because the climate will not agree with them: the sensitive plant is *singular,* as its quality of yielding to the touch distinguishes it from all others.

See also UNIQUE.

RASH. See FOOLHARDY; SUDDEN.

RASHNESS, TEMERITY, HASTINESS, PRECIPITANCY. *Rashness* denotes the quality of being *rash.* Cf. Anglo-Saxon *ræscan,* to flash, to move quickly and abruptly; Modern German *rasch,* quick. *Temerity* comes from Latin *temere,* from a root meaning gloom, darkness; and signifies the tendency to act "in the dark"; without sufficient information or foresight. *Hastiness* (see ANGRY and CURSORY). *Precipitancy,* from the Latin *præcipiti,* a crude form of *præceps,* headlong, based on *præ,* before, and *caput,* head, means, literally, the quality of being headlong, and signifies the quality or disposition of taking things before they ought to be taken.

Rashness and *temerity* have a close

alliance with each other in sense; but they have a slight difference which is entitled to notice: *rashness* is a general and indefinite term, in the signification of which an unreasoned and impulsive swiftness of action is the leading idea: this may arise either from a vehemence of character or a temporary ardor of the mind: in the signification of *temerity,* the leading idea is want of consideration, springing mostly from an overweening confidence or a presumptuous character. *Rashness* is therefore applied to corporeal actions, as the jumping into a river without being able to swim, or the leaping over a hedge without being an expert horseman; *temerity* is applied to our moral actions, particularly such as require deliberation and a calculation of consequences. *Hastiness* and *precipitancy* are but modes or characteristics of *rashness,* and consequently employed only in particular cases, as *hastiness* in regard to our movements, and *precipitancy* in regard to our measures.

RATE, PROPORTION, RATIO. *Rate* (see ESTIMATE) and *ratio,* which has the same origin and original meaning as *rate,* are in sense species of *proportion* (see PROPORTION): that is, they are supposed or estimated *proportions,* in distinction from *proportions* that lie in the nature of things. The first term, *rate,* is employed in ordinary affairs; a person receives a certain sum weekly at the *rate* of a certain sum yearly: *ratio* is applied only to numbers and calculations; as two is to four, so is four to eight, and eight to sixteen; the *ratio* in this case being double: *proportion* is employed in matters of science, and in all cases where the two more specific terms are not admissible; the beauty of an edifice depends upon observing the doctrine of *proportions;* in the disposing of soldiers a certain regard must be had to *proportion* in the height and size of the men.

See also TAX; VALUE.

RATIFY, APPROVE, BIND, CONFIRM, CORROBORATE, SETTLE, SUBSTANTIATE. *Ratify,* from French *ratifier,* from Latin *ratus,* fixed, and *ficare,* a crude form of *facere,* to make, in its broadest sense implies the settlement or establishment of something. We *approve* something that has been considered without previous action or already done for us by another; we *bind* ourselves to a specific action, as in a contract; we *confirm* an agreement reached in consultation; we *corroborate* something that has been said or done before; we *settle* a proposal, controversy, business affair; and we *substantiate* or prove a prior assertion, declaration. All of these actions are or may be *confirmed* in writings signed by the parties in interest.

A *ratification* is the act or evidence of *ratifying.* As an act it is that by which a competent authority *confirms* or accepts something done by another. In the case of a person who has reached his or her majority, it is an approval of something done during the period of minority which gives validity to what was done.

RATIONAL. See REASONABLE.

RAVAGE, DESOLATION, DEVASTATION. *Ravage* takes its root from the Latin *rapere,* signifying a seizing or tearing away. *Desolation,* from *solus,* alone, signifies made solitary or reduced to solitude. *Devastation,* in Latin *devastatio,* from *devastare,* to lay waste, based on *vastus,* waste, signifies reducing to a waste or desert.

Ravage expresses less than either *desolation* or *devastation:* a breaking, tearing, or destroying is implied in the word *ravage;* but *desolation* signifies the entire unpeopling of a land, and *devastation* the entire clearing away of every vestige of cultivation. Torrents, flames, and tempests *ravage;* war, plague, and famine *desolate;* armies of barbarians, who overrun a country, carry *devastation* with them wherever they go.

Ravage is employed likewise in the moral application; *desolation* and *devastation* only in the proper application to countries. Disease makes its *ravages* on beauty; death makes its *ravages* among men in a more terrible degree at one time than at another.

See also OVERSPREAD; SACK.

RAVENOUS. See RAPACIOUS.

RAY, BEAM. *Ray* (see GLEAM) is indefinite in its meaning; it may be said either of a large or small quantity of light: *beam,* from Anglo-Saxon *beam,* is something positive; it can be said only of that which is considerable. We may speak of *rays* either of the sun or the stars or any other luminous body; but we speak of the *beams* of the sun or the moon. The *rays* of the sun break through the clouds; its *beams* are scorching at noonday. A room can scarcely be so shut up that a single *ray* of light shall not penetrate through the crevices; the sea, in a calm moonlight night, presents a beautiful spectacle, with the moon's *beams* playing on its waves.

RAZE. See DEMOLISH.

REACH. See EXTEND.

READY, APT, PROMPT. *Ready* (see EASY) is in general applied to that which has been intentionally prepared for a given purpose; *prompt* (see EXPEDITIOUS) is applied to that which is at hand so as to answer the immediate purpose; *apt*, from *aptus*, fit, is applied to that which is fit or from its nature has a tendency to produce effects.

When applied as personal characteristics, *ready* connotes the will or understanding, which is prepared for anything; as *ready* to serve a person, a *ready* wit; *prompt* denotes the vigor or zeal which impels to action without delay, or at the moment when wanted; and *apt*, a fitness to do anything from the habit or temper of the mind.

See also PREPAREDNESS.

REAL. See ACTUAL; INTRINSIC; TANGIBLE.

REALIZE. See FULFIL.

REALM. See STATE.

REASON. See ACCOUNT; ARGUMENT; CAUSE; CONSIDERATION.

REASONABLE, RATIONAL. *Reasonable*, or according to reason, and *rational*, having *reason*, are both derived from the same Latin word *ratio*, reason, which, from *ratus*, itself from *reor*, to think, signifies the thinking faculty. They differ principally according to the different meanings of the word *reason*. *Reasonable* is sometimes applied to persons in the general sense of having the faculty of *reason*. But more frequently the word *rational* is used in this abstract sense of *reason*.

In application to things *reasonable* and *rational* both signify according to *reason;* but the former is used in reference to the business of life, as a *reason-* *able* proposal, wish, etc.; *rational* to abstract matters, as *rational* motives, grounds, questions, etc.

See also FAIR.

REBATE. See ABATE.

REBELLION. See CONTUMACY; INSURRECTION.

REBOUND, REVERBERATE, RECOIL. To *rebound* is to bound or spring back: a ball *rebounds.* To *reverberate* (from Latin *verber*, a scourge) is to beat back: a sound *reverberates* when it echoes. To *recoil* is to *coil* (from Latin *culus*, hinder part) or whirl back: a snake *recoils.* The two former are used in an improper application, although rarely; but we may say of *recoil* that a man's schemes will *recoil* on his own head.

REBUFF. See REFUSE.

REBUKE. See CHECK.

RECALL. See ABJURE.

RECANT. See ABJURE.

RECAPITULATE. See REPEAT.

RECEDE, RETREAT, RETIRE, WITHDRAW, SECEDE. To *recede* is to go back; to *retreat* is to draw back; the former is a simple action, suited to one's convenience: the latter is a particular action, dictated by necessity: we *recede* by a direct backward movement; we *retreat* by an indirect backward movement; we *recede* a few steps in order to observe an object more distinctly; we *retreat* from the position we have taken in order to escape danger; whoever can advance can *recede;* but in general only those *retreat* whose advance is not free: *receding* is the act of every one; *retreating* is peculiarly the act of soldiers or those who make hostile movements.

To *retire* and *withdraw* signify fundamentally the same as *retreat*, that is, to draw back or off; but they agree in application mostly with *recede*, to denote leisurely and voluntary acts: to *recede* is to go back from a given spot; but to *retire* and *withdraw* have implication of the place or the presence of the persons: we may *recede* on an open plain, but we *retire* or *withdraw* from a room or from some company. In this application *withdraw* is the more familiar term: *retire* may likewise be used for an army; but it denotes a much more leisurely action than *retreat:* a general *retreats*, by compulsion, before an enemy, but he may *retire* from an enemy's country when there is no enemy present.

Recede, retreat, retire, and *withdraw* are also used in a moral application; *secede* is used only in this sense: a person *recedes* from his engagement or his pretentions; he *retires* from business or *withdraws* from a society. To *secede* is a public act; men *secede* from a religious or political body; *withdraw* is a private act; they *withdraw* themselves as individual members from any society.

RECEIPT, RECEPTION. *Receipt* comes from *receive,* in its application to inanimate objects, which are taken into possession. *Reception* comes from the same verb, in the sense of treatment of persons at their first arrival: in the commercial intercourse of men, the *receipt* of goods or money must be acknowledged in writing; in the friendly intercourse of men, their *reception* of each other will be polite or cold, according to the sentiments entertained toward the individual.

RECEIVE. See ADMIT; TAKE.

RECENT. See NEW.

RECIPROCAL. See MUTUAL.

RECITAL. See RELATION.

RECITE. See REPEAT.

RECKON, COUNT, ACCOUNT, NUMBER. The idea of estimating is common to these terms, which differ less in meaning than in application: *reckon* (see CALCULATE) is the most familiar; *account* and *number, i. e.,* to put in the *number,* are employed only in the grave style: we *reckon* it a happiness to enjoy the company of a particular friend; we ought to *account* it a privilege to be enabled to address our Maker by prayer; we must all expect to be one day *numbered* with the dead.

RECLAIM, REFORM. *Reclaim,* from the Latin prefix *re,* again, and *clamare,* to call, signifies to call back to its right place that which has gone astray. *Reform* signifies to *form* anew that which has changed its *form:* they are allied only in their application to the moral character. A man is *reclaimed* from his vicious actions by the force of advice or exhortation; he may be *reformed* by various means, external or internal. A parent endeavors to *reclaim* a child, but too often in vain; the offender is in general not *reformed.*

RECLINE, REPOSE. To *recline* is to lean back; to *repose* is to place one's self back and usually to rest: he who *reclines, reposes:* but we may *recline* without *reposing:* when we *recline* we put ourselves into a particular *position;* but when we *repose* we put ourselves into that position which will be most easy and enable us to rest.

RECOGNIZE, ACKNOWLEDGE. *Recognize,* in Latin *recognoscere,* is to take *cognizance* of that which comes again before our notice; to *acknowledge* (see ACKNOWLEDGE) is to admit to one's *knowledge* whatever comes freshly to our notice: we *recognize* a person whom we have known before; we *recognize* him either in his former character or in some newly assumed character; we *acknowledge* either former favors or those which have been just received: princes *recognize* certain principles which have been admitted by previous consent; they *acknowledge* the justice of claims which are preferred before them.

RECOIL. See REBOUND.

RECOLLECTION. See MEMORY.

RECOMPENSE. See COMPENSATION; GRATUITY.

RECONCILE. See CONCILIATE.

RECORD, REGISTER, ARCHIVE. *Record* is taken for the thing *recorded,* or the collection in which a thing is *recorded; register,* either for the thing *registered* or the place in which it is *registered; archive,* mostly for the place, and sometimes for the thing: *records* are either historical details or short notices, which serve to preserve the memory of things; *registers* are but short notices of particular and local circumstances; *archives* are always connected with the state: every place of antiquity has its *records* of the different circumstances which have been connected with its rise and progress and the various changes which it has experienced; in public *registers* we find accounts of families and of their various connections and fluctuations; in *archives* we find all legal deeds and instruments which involve the interests of the nation, both in its internal and external economy. In an extended application of these terms, *records* contain whatever is to be remembered at ever so distant a period; *registers,* that which is to serve present purposes;

archives, that in which any things are stored.

See also ENROLL.

RECOUNT. See RELATE.

RECOVER, RETRIEVE, REPAIR, RECRUIT. *Recover* comes from Latin *recuperare* (whence English *recuperate* is derived), compounded of *re*, again, and *cipere*, a weakened form of *capere*, to take, contaminated with *sabine; cuprus*, good, signifying to recover and make good again. *Retrieve*, from the occasional form of the Old French *retreuver*, Modern *retrouver*, is to find again. *Repair*, in French *réparer*, Latin *reparo*, from *re* and *parare*, to make ready or right again, signifies to make a thing as good as it was before. *Recruit* is an ill-formed word from French *recroître*, Latin *recrescere*, to grow again.

Recover is the most general term, and applies to objects in general; *retrieve, repair*, and the others are only partial applications: we *recover* things either by our own means or by chance; we *retrieve* and *repair* by our own efforts only: we *recover* that which has been taken or that which has been lost; we *retrieve* that which has not finally been impaired or consumed; we *repair* that which has been injured; we *recruit* that which has been diminished: we *recover* property from those who wish to deprive us of it; we *retrieve* our misfortunes or our lost reputation; we *repair* the damage done to our property; we *recruit* the strength which has been exhausted: we do not seek after that which we think *irrecoverable;* we give that up which is *irretrievable;* we do not labor on that which is *irreparable;* our power of *recruiting* depends upon circumstances; he who makes a moderate use of his resources may in general easily *recruit* himself when they are gone.

Recovery, Restoration. — *Recovery* is the regaining of any object which has been lost or missing; *restoration* is the getting back of what has been taken away or that of which one has been deprived. What is *recovered* may be *recovered* with or without the use of means; the *restoration* is effected by others' agency; that which is lost by accident may be *recovered* by accident; the *restoration* of a prince to his throne is mostly effected by his subjects.

In respect to health or other things, *recovery* signifies, as before, the regaining something; and *restoration*, the bringing back to its former state.

See also RECRUIT.

RECREANT, APOSTATE, RENEGADE. These words all signify one who repudiates a faith or a cause to which he has given his allegiance. *Recreant*, from Low Latin *recredere*, from Latin *re*, again, and *credere*, to believe, meaning to believe again, carries most condemnation. A *recreant* is thought of as cowardly and dastardly, and the word is applied not merely to one who repudiates a particular faith, but to one who is generally faithless and unreliable. *Renegade*, from Latin *re*, again, and *negare*, to deny, also signifies one who abandons a faith or a cause; but it does not carry so strong a suggestion of something cowardly and despicable. *Apostate* has a more limited significance. It is derived from Late Latin *apostata*, from Greek ἀποστάτης, off, στάτης, a standing, meaning a standing off, a separation, and it refers specifically to one who repudiates a religious belief. Julian, the *Apostate*, was so called because he reverted from Christianity to paganism.

RECREATION. See AMUSEMENT.

RECTIFY. See CORRECT.

RECTITUDE, UPRIGHTNESS. *Rectitude*, based on Latin *rectus*, straight, is properly rightness, which is expressed in a stronger manner by *uprightness:* we speak of the *rectitude* of conduct or of judgment; of *uprightness* of mind or of moral character, which must be something more than straight, for it must be elevated above everything mean or devious.

REDEEM, RANSOM. *Redeem*, in Latin *redimere*, is compounded of *red* and *emere*, to buy off, or back to one's self. *Ransom* comes from the substantive *redemptio*, redemption, corresponding to *redimere*.

Redeem is a term of general application; *ransom* is employed only on particular occasions: we *redeem* persons as well as things; we *ransom* persons only: we may *redeem* by labor or by anything which supplies an equivalent for money; we *ransom* persons with money only: we *redeem* a watch or whatever has been given in pawn; we *ransom* a captive: *redeem* is employed in the improper application; *ransom* only in the proper sense: we may *redeem* our character, *redeem* our life, or *redeem* our honor; and in this sense our Saviour *redeems* repentant sinners; but those who are *ransomed* recover only their bodily liberty.

REDEMPTION. See SALVATION.

REDRESS, RELIEF. *Redress*, like *address* (see ACCOST), in all probability from the Low Latin *drectus*, for *directus*, straight, right, and hence signifying to make straight or right, is said only with regard to matters of right and justice; *relief* (see HELP) to those of kindness and humanity: by power we obtain *redress;* by active interference we obtain *relief:* an injured person looks for *redress* to the government; an unfortunate person looks for *relief* to the compassionate and kind: what we suffer through the oppression or wickedness of others can be *redressed* only by those who have the power of dispensing justice; whenever we suffer, in the order of Providence, we may meet with some *relief* from those who are more favored. *Redress* applies to public as well as private grievances; *relief* applies only to private distresses: under a pretence of seeking *redress* of grievances, mobs are frequently assembled to the disturbance of the better disposed; under a pretence of soliciting charitable *relief*, thieves gain admittance into families.

REDUCE, LOWER. *Reduce* is to bring back or to a given point, *i. e.*, in an extended sense, to bring down; *lower* is to make *low* or *lower*, which proves the close connection of these words in their original meaning; it is, however, only in their improper application that they have any further connection. *Reduce* is used in the sense of lessen when applied to number, quantity, price, etc.; *lower* is used in the same sense when applied to price, demands, terms, etc.: the former, however, occurs in cases where circumstances as well as persons are concerned; the latter only in cases where persons act: the price of corn is *reduced* by means of importation; a person *lowers* his price or his demand when he finds it too high.

In the moral application, *reduce* expresses more than *lower;* a man is said to be *reduced* to an abject condition, but to be *lowered* in the estimation of others; to be *reduced* to a state of slavery, to be *lowered* in his own eyes.

REDUNDANCY. See EXCESS.

REEL. See STAGGER.

REFER, RELATE, RESPECT, REGARD. *Refer*, from the Latin *re* and *ferre*, signifies, literally, to bring back; and *relate*, from the participle *latus*, of the same verb, signifies brought back: the former is, therefore, transitive, and the latter intransitive. *Refer* is commonly said of circumstances that carry the memory to events or circumstances; *relate* is said of things that have a natural connection: the religious festivals and ceremonies of the Roman Catholics have all a *reference* to some events that happened in the early periods of Christianity; the notes and observations at the end of a book *relate* to what has been inserted in the text.

Refer and *relate* carry us back to that which may be very distant; but *respect* and *regard* (see ESTEEM) turn our views to that which is near. Whatever *respects* or *regards* a thing has a moral influence over it; it is the duty of the magistrates to take into consideration whatever *respects* the good order of the community; laws *respect* the general welfare of the community; the due administration of the laws *regards* the happiness of the individual. Neither of these verbs, as such, are in common use to-day, except in such fixed formulas as *in respect* or *in regard to, as respects* or *as regards* a given object or idea.

See also ALLUDE.

REFINED. See POLITE; WELL-BRED.

REFINEMENT. See CULTIVATION.

REFLECT. See CONSIDER; THINK.

REFLECTION. See INSINUATION.

REFORM, REFORMATION. *Reform* has a general application; *reformation* a particular application: whatever undergoes such a change as to give a new form to an object occasions a *reform;* when such a change is produced, or claimed to be produced, in the moral character either of persons or institutions, it is termed a *reformation:* the concerns of a state require occasional *reform;* those of an individual require *reformation;* the *Reformation* was the work of Martin Luther. When *reform* and *reformation* are applied to the moral character, the former has a more extensive signification than the latter; the term *reform* conveying the idea of a complete amendment; *reformation* implying only the process of amending or improving. A *reform* in one's life and conversation will always be accompanied by a corresponding increase of happiness to the individual; when we observe any approaches to *reformation,* we may cease to despair of the individual who shows such tendency.

See also RECLAIM.

REFRACTORY. See UNRULY.
REFRAIN. See ABSTAIN.
REFRESH. See REVIVE.
REFUGE. See ASYLUM.
REFUSE, DECLINE, REJECT, REPEL, REBUFF. *Refuse* (see DENY), from Latin *refundere,* signifies simply to pour back—that is, to send back—which is the common idea of all these terms. *Decline,* in Latin *declinare,* signifies, literally, to turn aside; *reject,* from *jactare,* to throw, to cast back; *repel,* from *pellere,* to drive, to drive back. *Rebuff* comes from Latin *re,* back, and *buffare,* a word of onomatopœic or imitative origin, like English *puff.*

Refuse is an unqualified action: it is accompanied by no expression of opinion; *decline* is a gentle and indirect mode of refusal; *reject* is a direct mode, and conveys a positive sentiment of disapprobation: we *refuse* what is asked of us for want of inclination to comply; we *decline* what is proposed from motives of discretion; we *reject* what is offered to us because it does not fall in with our views: we *refuse* to listen to the suggestions of our friends; we *decline* an offer of service; we *reject* the insinuations of the interested and evil-minded.

To *refuse* is said only of that which passes between individuals; to *reject* is said of that which comes from any quarter: requests and petitions are *refused* by those who are solicited; opinions, propositions, and counsels are *rejected* by particular communities: the king *refuses* to give his assent to a bill; the Parliament *rejects* it.

To *repel* is to *reject* with violence; to *rebuff* is to *refuse* with contempt or what may be considered as such. We *refuse* and *reject* that which is either offered or simply presents itself for acceptance: the act may be negative or not outwardly expressed; we *repel* and *rebuff* that which forces itself into our presence contrary to our inclination: it is in both cases a direct act of force; we *repel* the attack of an enemy, or we *repel* the advances of one who is not agreeable; we *rebuff* those who put that in our way which is offensive. Importunate persons must necessarily expect to meet with *rebuffs,* and are in general less susceptible to them than others; sensitive minds feel a *refusal* as a *rebuff.*

See also DREGS; GARNISH.

REFUTE. See CONFUTE.
REGAL. See ROYAL.
REGARD. See ATTEND; CARE; CONSIDER; ESTEEM.
REGARDFUL. See MINDFUL.
REGARDLESS. See INDIFFERENT.
REGIMEN. See FOOD.
REGION. See DISTRICT.
REGISTER. See ENROLL; LIST; RECORD.
REGRET. See COMPLAIN.
REGULATE. See DIRECT; GOVERN.
REHEARSE. See REPEAT.
REIGN. See EMPIRE.
REIMBURSE. See INDEMNIFY.
REJECT. See PROSCRIBE; REFUSE.
REJOINDER. See ANSWER.
RELATE (see REFER), RECOUNT, DESCRIBE. *Relate,* in Latin *relatus,* participle of *referre,* signifies to bring that to the notice of others which has before been brought to our own notice. *Recount* is properly to *count* again or *count* over again. *Describe,* from the Latin *scribere,* to write, is literally to write down.

The idea of giving an account of events or circumstances is common to all these terms, which differ in the object and circumstances of the action. *Relate* is said generally of all events, both of those which concern others as well as ourselves; *recount* is said particularly of those things in which the recounter has a special interest: those who *relate* all they hear often *relate* that which never happened; it is a gratification to an old soldier to *recount* all the events in which he had a part during the military career of his early youth. We *relate* events that have happened at any period of time immediate or remote; we *recount* mostly those things which have been long past: in *recounting*, the memory reverts to past scenes and *counts* over all that has deeply interested the mind. Travellers are pleased to *relate* to their friends the noteworthy or remarkable things they have seen in other countries; the *recounting* of our adventures in distant regions of the globe has a peculiar interest for all who hear them. We may *relate* either by writing or by word of mouth; we *recount* mostly by word of mouth. *Relate* is said properly of events or that which passes: *describe* is said of that which exists: we *relate* the particulars of our journey, and we *describe* the country we pass through. Personal adventure is always the subject of a *relation;* the quality and condition of things are the subject of the *description*. We *relate* what happened on meeting a friend; we *describe* the dress of the parties or the ceremonies which are usual on particular occasions.

Relation, Recital, Narration, Narrative.—*Relation*, from the verb *relate*, denotes the act of *relating* or the thing *related*. *Recital*, from *recite* (Latin *re*, again, and *citare*, to quote), denotes the act of *reciting* or the thing *recited*. *Narration*, from *narrate* (from Latin *narus, gnarus*, knowing), denotes either the act of *narrating* or the thing *narrated*. *Narrative*, from the same verb, denotes the thing *narrated*. *Relation* is here, as in the former paragraphs, the general, and the others the particular terms. *Relation* applies to every object which is related, whether of a public or private, a national or an individual nature, history is the *relation* of national events; biography is the *relation* of particular lives; *recital* is the *relation* or *repetition* of actual or existing circumstances; we listen to the *recital* of misfortunes, distresses, and the like. The *relation* may concern matters of indifference: the *recital* is always of something that affects the interests of some individual: the pages of the journalist are filled with the *relation* of daily occurrences which simply amuse in the reading: but the *recital* of another's woes often draws tears from the audience to whom it is made. *Relation* and *recital* are seldom employed without connection with the object *related* or *recited; narrative* is mostly used by itself: hence we say the *relation* of any particular circumstance; the *recital* of any one's calamities; but an affecting *narrative*, or a simple *narrative*.

See also CONNECTION.

Relation, Relative, Kinsman, Kindred.—*Relation* is here taken to express the person *related;* it is, as in the former paragraph, the general term both in sense and application; *relative* is employed only as respects the particular individual to whom one is *related; kinsman* designates the particular kind of *relation*, and *kindred* is a collective term comprehending all one's *relations* or those who are one's kin. In abstract propositions the word *relations* is used in a more extended and universal sense: a man who is without *relations* feels himself an outcast from society; in designating one's close and intimate connection with persons we use the term *relative;* our near and dear *relatives* are the first objects of our regard: in designating one's *relationship* and connection with persons, *kinsman* is preferable; when a man has no children, he frequently adopts one of his *kinsmen* as his heir: when the ties of *relationship* are to be specified in the persons of any particular family, they are denominated *kindred;* a man cannot abstract himself from his *kindred* while he retains any spark of human feeling.

RELATIONSHIP. See AFFINITY; KINDRED.

RELAX, REMIT. The general idea of lessening is that which allies these words to each other; but they differ very widely in their original meaning and somewhat in their ordinary application; *relax*, from *re*, again, and *laxare*, to loosen, signifies to make loose, and in its moral use to lessen anything in its degree of tightness or rigor; to *remit*, from *re*, again, and *mittere*, to send, signifies to take off in part or entirely that which has been imposed, that is, to lessen in quantity. In regard to our own attempts to act, we may speak of *relaxing* in our endeavors and *remitting* our labors or exertions, though the latter in this sense is now very rarely used: in regard to our dealings with others, we may speak of *relaxing* in discipline, *relaxing* in the severity or strictness of our conduct, of *remitting* a punishment or *remitting* a sentence. The discretionary power of showing mercy when placed in the hands of the sovereign serves to *relax* the rigor of the law; when the punishment seems to be disproportionate to the magnitude of the offence, it is but equitable to *remit* it.

RELENTLESS. See IMPLACABLE.

RELIANCE. See DEPENDENCE.

RELICS. See REMAINS.

RELIEF. See REDRESS.

RELIEVE. See ALLEVIATE; HELP.

RELIGIOUS. See HOLY.

RELINQUISH. See ABANDON; LEAVE; WAIVE.

RELISH. See TASTE.

RELUCTANT. See AVERSE.

REMAIN. See CONTINUE.

REMAINDER. See REST.

REMAINS, RELICS. *Remains* signifies, literally, what *remains: relics,* from *relictus,* the past participle of the Latin *relinquere,* to leave, signifies what is left. The former is a term of general and familiar application; the latter is specific. What *remains* after the use or consumption of anything is termed the *remains;* what is left of anything after a lapse of years is the *relic* or *relics.* There are *remains* of buildings mostly after a conflagration; there are *relics* of antiquity in most monasteries and old churches. *Remains* are of value, or not, according to the circumstances of the case; *relics* always derive a value from the person to whom they were supposed originally to belong. The *remains* of a person—that is, what corporeally *remains* of a person after the extinction of life—will be respected by his friend; a bit of a garment that belonged, or was supposed to belong, to some saint will be a precious *relic* in the eyes of many devout Roman Catholics. All nations have agreed to respect the *remains* of the dead; religion, under most forms, has given a sacredness to *relics*

in the eyes of its most zealous votaries; the veneration of genius, or the devotedness of friendship, has in like manner transferred itself from the individual himself to some object which has been his property or in his possession, and thus acquired *relics* equally precious.

Sometimes the term *relics* is used to denote what *remains* after the decay or loss of the rest, which further distinguishes it from the word *remains,* which simply signifies what is left.

See also LEAVINGS.

REMARK, OBSERVATION, COMMENT, NOTE, ANNOTATION, COMMENTARY. *Remark* (see NOTICE), *observation,* and *comment,* in Latin *commentum,* past participle of *comminisce* (from Latin *com,* a prefix based on *cum,* intensive, and the root found in Latin *memini, memoria,* English *memory,* signifying to remember), are either spoken or written: *note, annotation* (see NOTE), *commentary,* a variation of *comment,* are always written. *Remark* and *observation,* admitting of the same distinction in both cases, have been sufficiently explained in the articles referred to: *comment* is a species of *remark* which often loses in good-nature what it gains in seriousness; it is mostly applied to particular persons or cases, and more commonly employed as a mode of censure than of commendation; public speakers and public performers are exposed to all the *comments* which the vanity, the envy, and ill-nature of self-constituted critics can suggest; but when not employed in personal cases, it serves for explanation: the other terms are used in this sense only, but with certain modifications; the *note* is most general, and serves to call the attention to particular passages in the text and to illustrate them: *annotations* and *commentaries* are more minute; the former being that which is added by way of appendage; the latter being employed in a general form; as the *annotations* of the Greek scholiasts, and the *commentaries* on the sacred writings.

REMARKABLE. See EXTRAORDINARY.

REMEDY. See CURE.

REMEMBRANCE. See MEMORY.

REMEMBRANCER. See MONUMENT.

REMINISCENCE. See MEMORY.

REMISS. See NEGLIGENT.

REMISSNESS. See LAXNESS.

REMIT. See ABATE; FORGIVE; RELAX; WAIVE.

REMNANT. See REST.

REMONSTRATE. See EXPOSTULATE.

REMORSE. See REPENTANCE.

REMOTE. See DISTANT.

REMOVE. See TRANSFER; UNVEIL.

REMUNERATION. See COMPENSATION.

REND. See BREAK.

RENEGADE. See RECREANT.

RENEW. See REVIVE.

RENOUNCE. See ABANDON.

RENOVATE. See REVIVE.

RENOWN. See FAME.

REPAIR. See RECOVER.

REPARATION. See RESTORATION.

REPARTEE. See RETORT.

REPAY. See RESTORE.

REPEAL. See ABOLISH.

REPEAT, RECITE, REHEARSE, RECAPITULATE. The idea of going over any words or actions is common to all these terms. *Repeat*, from the Latin *re*, again, and *petere*, to seek, or go over again, is the general term, including only the common idea. To *recite*, *rehearse*, and *recapitulate* are modes of *repetition*, conveying each some accessory idea. To *recite* is to *repeat* in a formal manner; to *rehearse* (from Latin *re*, again, and Old French *hercer*, to harrow, from *herce*, derived from Latin *hirpex*, a harrow) is to *repeat* or *recite* by way of preparation; to *recapitulate*, from *capitulum*, a chapter, is to repeat the chapters or principal heads of any discourse. We *repeat* both actions and words; we *recite* only words: we *repeat* single words or even sounds; we *recite* always a form of words: we *repeat* our own words or the words of another; we *recite* only the words of another; we *repeat* a name; we *recite* an ode or a set of verses.

We *repeat* for purposes of general convenience; we *recite* for the convenience or amusement of others; we *rehearse* for some specific purpose, either for the amusement or instruction of others: we *recapitulate* for the instruction of others. We *repeat* that which we wish to be heard; we *recite* a piece of poetry before a company; we *rehearse* the piece in private which we are going to recite in public; we *recapitulate* the general heads of that which we have already spoken in detail. A master must always *repeat* to his scholars the instruction which he wishes them to remember; Homer is said to have *recited* his verses in different parts; players *rehearse* their different parts before they perform in public; ministers *recapitulate* the leading points in their discourse. To *repeat* is commonly to use the same words; to *recite*, to *rehearse*, and to *recapitulate* do not necessarily require any verbal sameness. We *repeat* literally what we hear spoken by another; but we *recite* and *rehearse* events, and we *recapitulate* in a concise manner what has been uttered in a particular manner. An echo *repeats* with the greatest possible precision; Homer *recites* the names of all the Grecian and Trojan leaders, together with the names and account of their countries and the number of the forces which they commanded; Virgil makes Æneas *rehearse* before Dido and her courtiers the story of the capture of Troy and his own adventures; a judge *recapitulates* evidence to a jury.

REPEL. See REFUSE.

REPENTANCE, PENITENCE, CONTRITION, COMPUNCTION, REMORSE. *Repentance*, from *re*, back, and *pænitere*, to be sorry, allied to Greek πεῖνα, hunger, signifies thinking one's self wrong for something past: *penitence*, from the same source, signifies simply sorrow for what is amiss. *Contrition*, from the past participle of *conterere*, to rub together, is to bruise, as it were, with sorrow; *compunction*, from *compungere*, to prick thoroughly; and *remorse*, from *remorsus*, the past participle of *remordere*, to have a gnawing pain; and hence to vex, to torment. All express modes of *penitence* differing in degree and circumstance. *Repentance* refers more to the change of one's mind with regard to an object, and is properly confined to the time when this change takes place; we, therefore, strictly speaking, *repent* of a thing but once; we may, however, have *penitence* for the same thing all our lives. *Repentance* supposes a change of conduct, at least as long as the sorrow lasts;

but the term *penitence* is confined to the sorrow which the sense of guilt occasions to the offender.

Repentance is a term of more general application than *penitence*, being employed in respect to offences against men as well as against God; *penitence*, on the other hand, is applicable only to spiritual guilt. *Repentance* has application to our interests here, *penitence* to our interests hereafter.

Penitence is a general sentiment which belongs to all men as offending creatures; but *contrition*, *compunction*, and *remorse* are awakened by reflecting on particular offences: *contrition* is a continued and severe sorrow, appropriate to one who has been in a continued state of peculiar sinfulness: *compunction* is rather an occasional but sharp sorrow, provoked by a single offence or a moment's reflection; *remorse* may be temporary, but it is a still sharper pain awakened by some particular offence of peculiar magnitude and atrocity. The prodigal son was a *contrite* sinner; the brethren of Joseph felt great *compunction* when they were carried back with their sacks to Egypt; David was struck with *remorse* for the murder of Uriah.

REPETITION, Tautology. *Repetition* is to *tautology* as the genus to the species, the latter being a species of *repetition*. There may be frequent *repetition* which is warranted by necessity or convenience; but *tautology* is that which nowise adds to either the sense or the sound. A *repetition* may or may not consist of literally the same words; but *tautology*, from the Greek ταυτό, the same, and λ᾽για, saying, supposes such a sameness in expression as renders the signification the same. In the liturgy of the Church of England there are some *repetitions* which add to the solemnity of the worship; in most extemporary prayers there is much *tautology* that destroys the religious effect of the whole.

REPINE. See Complain.

REPLY. See Answer.

REPORT. See Fame.

REPOSE. See Ease; Recline.

REPREHENSION, Reproof. Personal blame or censure is implied by both these terms, but the former is much milder than the latter, and is of

less frequent use. By *reprehension* the personal independence is not so sensibly affected as in the case of *reproof:* people of all ages and stations, whose conduct is exposed to the investigation of others, are liable to *reprehension;* but children only, or such as are in a subordinate capacity, are exposed to *reproof. Reprehension* amounts to little more than passing an unfavorable sentence upon the conduct of another: *reproof* adds to this words more or less severe. The master of a school may be exposed to the *reprehension* of the parents for any supposed impropriety: his scholars are subject to his *reproof*.

See also Reproach; Blame.

REPRESENTATION. See Radiograph; Show.

REPRESS, Restrain, Suppress. To *repress* is to press back or down: to *restrain* is to strain back or down: the former is the general, the latter the specific, term: we always *repress* when we *restrain*, but not *vice versâ*. *Repress* is used mostly for pressing down, so as to keep that inward which wants to make its appearance: *restraint* is an habitual *repression* by which a thing is kept in a state of lowness: a person is said to *repress* his feelings when he does not give them vent either by his words or actions; he is said to *restrain* his feelings when he never lets them rise beyond a certain pitch: good morals as well as good manners call upon us to *repress* every unseemly expression of joy in the company of those who are not in a condition to partake of our joy; it is prudence as well as virtue to *restrain* our appetites by a systematic inhibition, that they may not gain the ascendency.

To *restrain* is the act of the individual toward himself; *repress* may be an act directed to others, as to *repress* the ardor and impetuosity of youth; to *suppress*, which is to keep under, or keep from appearing or being perceptible, is also said in respect to ourselves or others: as to *repress* one's feelings; to *suppress* laughter, sighs, etc.

So likewise when applied to external objects, as to *repress* the impetuosity of the combatants, to *suppress* a rebellion, information, etc.

REPRIEVE, Respite. *Reprieve* is a doublet of *reprove*, from *reprobare*, to try a case a second time, with the implication of rejection, and hence to disallow a sentence. *Respite* comes through French from Latin *respectum*, English *respect*, and refers to the respect had to a suit.

The idea of a release from any pressure or burden is common to these terms; but the *reprieve* is that which is granted; the *respite* sometimes comes to us in the course of things: we gain a *reprieve* from any punishment or trouble which threatens us; we gain a *respite* from any labor or weight that presses upon us. A criminal gains a *reprieve* when the punishment of death is commuted for that of imprisonment for life; a debtor may be said to obtain a *reprieve* when, with a prison before his eyes, he gets such indulgence from his creditors as sets him free: there is frequently no *respite* for persons in a subordinate station, when they fall into the hands of a hard taskmaster; Sisyphus is feigned by the poets to have been condemned to the toil of perpetually rolling a stone up a hill as fast as it rolled back, from which toil he had no *respite*.

REPRIMAND. See CHECK.

REPRISAL. See RETALIATION.

REPROACH, CONTUMELY, OBLOQUY. The idea of contemptuous or angry treatment of others is common to all these terms; but *reproach* is the general, *contumely* and *obloquy* are the particular, terms: the last two terms are of infrequent use to-day. *Reproach* (see BLAME) is either deserved or undeserved; the name of Puritan is applied as a term of *reproach* to such as affect greater purity than others; the name of Christian is a name of *reproach* in Turkey: *contumely*, of uncertain origin, but probably connected with *contumacious*, from Latin *contumax* (proud, stubborn, perverse, offensive), self-supposedly from *contemnere*, to despise, condemn, is always undeserved; it is the insolent and contemptuous rejection by a worthless person of merit in distress; our Saviour was exposed to the *contumely* of the Jews: *obloquy*, from *ob*, against, and *loqui*, to speak, signifying to speak against or to the disparagement of any one, is always supposed to be deserved or otherwise; it is applicable to those whose conduct has ren-

dered them objects of general censure, and whose name, therefore, has almost become a *reproach*. A man who uses his power only to oppress those who are connected with him will naturally and deservedly bring upon himself much *obloquy*.

See also DISCREDIT.

Reproachful, Abusive, Scurrilous.— *Reproachful,* or full of *reproach,* when applied to persons, signifies full of *reproaches;* when to things, deserving of *reproach: abusive,* or full of *abuse,* is applied only to the person, signifying using *abuse: scurrilous,* in Latin *scurrilis,* from *scurra,* signifying a buffoon or saucy jester, is employed as an epithet either for persons or things in the sense of using *scurrility.* The conduct of a person is *reproachful* inasmuch as it provokes or is entitled to the *reproaches* of others; the language of a person is *reproachful* when it abounds in *reproaches* or partakes of the nature of a *reproach:* a person is *abusive* who indulges himself in *abuse* or *abusive* language: and he is *scurrilous* who adopts *scurrility* or *scurrilous* language. When applied to the same object, whether to the person or to the thing, they rise in sense; the *reproachful* is less than the *abusive,* and this less than the *scurrilous;* the *reproachful* is sometimes warranted by the provocation; but the *abusive* and *scurrilous* are always unwarrantable; *reproachful* language may be, and generally is, consistent with decency and propriety of speech: *abusive* and *scurrilous* language is an outrage against the laws of good-breeding, if not of morality. A parent may sometimes find it necessary to address an unruly son in *reproachful* terms; or one friend may adopt a *reproachful* tone to another; none, however, but the lowest orders of men, and those only when their anger is awakened, will descend to *abusive* or *scurrilous* language.

REPROBATE, CONDEMN. To *reprobate* is much stronger than to *condemn,* but of less frequent application: we always *condemn* when we *reprobate,* but not *vice versâ:* to *reprobate* is to *condemn* in strong and reproachful language. We *reprobate* all measures which tend to sow discord in society and to loosen the ties by which men are bound to each other; we *condemn* all disrespectful language toward *superiors*. We *reprobate* only the thing; we *condemn* the person also: any act of disobedience in a child cannot be too strongly *reprobated;* a person must expect to be *condemned* when he involves himself in embarrassments through his own imprudence.

See also PROFLIGATE.

REPROOF. See REPREHENSION.
REPROVE. See BLAME; CHECK.
REPUBLIC. See EMPIRE.
REPUGNANCE. See AVERSION.
REPUTATION. See CHARACTER; FAME; NAME.
REQUEST. See ASK; PRAYER.
REQUIRE. See DEMAND.
REQUISITE. See NECESSARY.
REQUITAL. See COMPENSATION; RETRIBUTION.
RESCUE. See SALVATION.
RESEARCH. See EXAMINATION.
RESEMBLANCE. See LIKENESS.
RESENTMENT. See ANGER; UMBRAGE.

RESERVE, RESERVATION. *Reserve* and *reservation*, from *servare*, to keep, and *re*, back, both signify a keeping back, but differ as to the object and the circumstances of the action. *Reserve* is applied in a good sense to anything natural or moral which is kept back to be employed for a better purpose on a future occasion; *reservation* is an artful keeping back for selfish purposes: there is a prudent *reserve* which every man ought to keep in his discourse with a stranger; equivocators deal altogether in mental *reservation*.

Reserve, Retain.—*Reserve*, from the Latin prefix *re* and *servare*, to keep, signifies to keep back. *Retain*, from *tenere*, to hold, signifies to hold back: they in some measure, therefore, have the same distinction as keep and hold.

To *reserve* is an act of more specific design; we *reserve* that which is the particular object of our choice: to *retain* is a simple exertion of our power; we *retain* that which has once come in our possession. To *reserve* is employed only for that which is allowable; we *reserve* a thing, that is, keep it back with care for some future purpose: to *retain* is often an unlawful act; a debtor frequently *retains* in his hands the money which he has borrowed.

To *reserve*, whether in the proper or improper application, is employed only as the act of a conscious agent; to *retain* is often the act of an unconscious agent: we *reserve* what we have to say on a subject until a more suitable opportunity offers; the mind *retains* the impressions of external objects by its peculiar faculty, the memory; certain substances are said to *retain* the color with which they have been dyed.

RESIDE. See ABIDE.
RESIDENCE. See DOMICILE.
RESIGN. See ABANDON; GIVE UP.
RESIGNATION. See PATIENCE.
RESIST. See OPPOSE.
RESOLUTE. See DECIDED; STALWART; UNSWERVING.
RESOLUTION. See COURAGE.
RESOLVE. See DETERMINE; SOLVE.
RESORT. See FREQUENT.
RESOURCE. See EXPEDIENT.
RESPECT. See ESTEEM; HONOR; REFER.
RESPECTFUL. See DUTIFUL.
RESPITE. See INTERVAL; REPRIEVE.
RESPONSE. See ANSWER.
RESPONSIBLE. See ANSWERABLE; GUARANTEE.

REST, REMAINDER, REMNANT, RESIDUE. *Rest* is the substantive based on the Latin *restare*, compounded of *re* and *stare*, to stand behind, in this case, though not in the former (see EASE), signifying what stands or remains back. *Remainder* literally signifies what remains after the first part is gone. *Remnant* is but a variation of *remainder;* it comes from the present participle of *remanere*, whence *remainder* is derived. *Residue*, from the neuter of the Latin adjective *residuus*, based on *re*, back, and *sedere*, to sit, signifies likewise what remains back.

All these terms express that part which is separated from the other and left distinct: *rest* is the most general, both in sense and application; the others have a more specific meaning and use: the *rest* may be either that which is left behind by itself or that which is set apart as a distinct portion: the *remainder, remnant,* and *residue* are the quantities which remain when the other parts are gone. The *rest* is said of any part, large or small; but the *remainder* commonly regards the smaller part which has been left after the greater part has been taken. A person may be said to sell some and give away the *rest:* when a number of hearty persons sit down to a meal, the *remainder* of the provisions, after all have been satisfied, will not be considerable. *Rest* is applied either to persons or things; *remainder* only to things: some were of that opinion, but the *rest* did not agree to it: the *remainder* of the paper was not worth preserving.

Remnant, from the Latin participle stem *remanent,* remaining, is a species of *remainder* after the greater part has been consumed or wasted: it is, therefore, properly a small *remainder,* as a *remnant* of cloth; and metaphorically applied to persons, as a *remnant* of Israel. A *residue* is another species of *remainder,* which resides or keeps back after a distribution or division of anything has taken place; as the *residue* of a person's property, that which remains undisposed of.

See also CESSATION; STAND.

RESTITUTION.   See RESTORA-TION.

RESTORATION, RESTITUTION, REPARATION, AMENDS. *Restoration* is employed in the ordinary application of the verb *restore: restitution,* from the Latin verb *restituere,* is employed simply in the sense of making good that which has been unjustly taken or which ought to be *restored. Restoration* of property may be made by any one, whether it be the person taking it or not: *restitution* is supposed to be made by him who has been guilty of the injustice. The dethronement of a king may be the work of one set of men and his *restoration* that of another; it is the moral duty of every individual who has committed any sort of injustice to another to make *restitution* to the utmost of his power.

Restitution and *reparation* are both employed in the sense of undoing that which has been done to the injury of another; but the former connotes only injuries that affect the property, and *reparation* those which affect a person in various ways. He who is guilty of theft or fraud must make *restitution* by either *restoring* the stolen article or its full value: he who robs another of his good name, or does any injury to his

person, has it not in his power so easily to make *reparation.*

Reparation and *amends* (see COMPENSATION) are both employed in cases where some mischief or loss is sustained; but the term *reparation* comprehends the idea of the act of *repairing,* as well as the thing by which we *repair; amends* is employed only for the thing that will *amend* or make better: hence we speak of the *reparation* of an injury; but of the *amends* by itself. The term *reparation* comprehends all kinds of injuries, particularly those of a serious nature; the *amends* is applied only to matters of inferior importance. It is impossible to make *reparation* for taking away the life of another. It is easy to make *amends* to any one for the loss of a day's pleasure.

See also RECOVERY.

Restore, Return, Repay. — *Restore* comes from Latin *restaurare,* to set up again. *Return* comes from Latin *re,* again, and Low Latin *tornare,* to turn a lathe. For *repay* see PAY.

The common idea of all these terms is that of giving back. What we *restore* to another may or may not be the same as what we have taken; justice requires that it should be an equivalent in value, so as to prevent the individual from being in any degree a sufferer; what we *return* and *repay* ought to be precisely the same as we have received: the former in application to general objects, the latter in application only to pecuniary matters. We *restore* upon a principle of equity: we *return* upon a principle of justice and honor; we *repay* upon a principle of undeniable right. We cannot always claim that which ought to be *restored;* but we cannot only claim, but enforce the claim in regard to what is to be *returned* or *repaid:* an honest man will be scrupulous not to take anything from another without *restoring* to him its full value. Whatever we have borrowed we ought to *return;* and when it is money which we have obtained, we ought to *repay* it with punctuality. We *restore* to many as well as to one, to communities as well as to individuals; a king is *restored* to his crown; or one nation *restores* a territory to another; we *return* and *repay* not only individually, but personally and particularly: we *return* a book to its owner; we *repay* a sum of money to him from whom it was borrowed.

Restore and *return* may be employed in their improper applications as respects the moral state of persons and things; as a king *restores* a courtier to his favor, or a physician *restores* his patient to health: we *return* a favor; we *return* an answer or a compliment. *Repay* may be figuratively employed in regard to moral objects, as an ungrateful person *repays* kindnesses with reproaches.

RESTRAIN, RESTRICT. *Restrain* (see COERCE) and *restrict* are but variations of the same Latin verb *restringere:* the first from the infinitive, the second from its past participle, *restrictus;* but they have acquired a distinct acceptation: the former applies to the desires as well as the outward conduct: the latter only to the outward conduct. A person *restrains* his inordinate appetite; or he is *restrained* by others from doing mischief: he is *restricted* in the use of his money. To *restrain* is an act of power; but to *restrict* is an act of authority or law: the will or the actions of a child are *restrained* by the parent, but a patient is *restricted* in his diet by a physician, or any body of people may be *restricted* by laws.

See also REPRESS.

RESTRAINT. See CONSTRAIN; EMBARGO.

RESTRICT. See BOUND; RESTRAIN.

RESULT. See CONSEQUENCE.

RETAIN. See HOLD; RESERVE.

RETALIATION, REPRISAL. *Retaliation,* from *retaliate,* in Latin *retaliatum,* participle of *retaliare,* compounded of *re* and *taliare,* to requite in kind (the etymology of *talis* is far from certain), signifies so much again, or like for like. *Reprisal,* a word much used in connection with the European war, is a verbal substantive based on *repris,* past participle of the French verb *reprendre,* in Latin *reprehendere,* to take again, signifies to take in return for what has been taken. The idea of making another suffer in return for the suffering he has occasioned is common to these terms; but the former is employed in ordinary cases; the latter

mostly in regard to a state of warfare or to active hostilities. A trick practiced upon another in return for a trick is a *retaliation;* but a *reprisal* always extends to the capture of something from another, in return for what has been taken. *Retaliation* is very frequently employed in the good sense for what passes innocently between friends: *reprisal* has always an unfavorable sense. Goldsmith's poem, entitled "Retaliation," was written for the purpose of *retaliating* on his friends the joke that they had played upon him; when the quarrels of individuals break through the restraints of the law and lead to acts of violence to each other's property, *reprisals* are made alternately by both parties.

RETARD, HINDER. To *retard,* from the Latin *tardus,* slow, signifying to make slow, is applied to the movements of any object forward, as in the Latin "Impetum inimici tardare": to *hinder* (see that word) is applied to the person moving or acting: we *retard* or make slow the progress of any scheme toward completion; we *hinder* or keep back the person who is completing the scheme: we *retard* a thing, therefore, often by *hindering* the person; but we frequently *hinder* a person without expressly *retarding,* and, on the contrary, the thing is *retarded* without the person being *hindered.* The publication of a work is sometimes *retarded* by the *hindrances* which an author meets with in bringing it to a conclusion; but a work may be *retarded* through the idleness of printers, and a variety of other causes which are independent of any *hindrance.* So in like manner a person may be *hindered* in going to his place of destination; but we do not say that he is *retarded,* because it is only the execution of an object and not the simple movements of the person which are *retarded.*

To *retard* stops the completion of an object only for a time, but to *hinder* is to stop it altogether.

See also DELAY.

RETINUE. See PROCESSION.

RETIRE. See RECEDE.

RETIREMENT. See PRIVACY.

RETORT, REPARTEE. *Retort,* from *re,* back, and *torquere,* to turn, signifying to twist or turn back, is an ill-natured reply: *repartee*, a misspelling of *repartie*, feminine of the past participle of the French *repartir*, from Latin *re*, again, and *partire*, to divide, hence to lunge, is to answer thrust with thrust, cut with cut. The *retort* is always in answer to a censure, for which one returns a like censure; the *repartee* is commonly in answer to the wit of another, where one returns wit for wit. In the acrimony of disputes it is common to hear *retort* upon *retort* to an endless extent; the liveliness of discourse is sometimes greatly increased by the quick *repartee* of those who take part in it.

RETRACT. See ABJURE.

RETREAT. See ASYLUM; RECEDE.

RETRIBUTION, REQUITAL. *Retribution*, from *retribuere*, to bestow, signifying a bestowing back or giving in return, is a particular term; *requital* (see REWARD) is general: the *retribution* comes from Providence; *requital* is the act of man: *retribution* is by way of punishment; *requital* is mostly by way of reward: *retribution* is not always dealt out to every man according to his deeds; it is a poor *requital* for one who has done a kindness to be abused.

RETRIEVE. See RECOVER.

RETROSPECT, REVIEW, SURVEY. A *retrospect*, which signifies, literally, looking back, from *retro*, behind, and *spicere*, to behold or cast an eye upon, is always taken of that which is past and distant; *review*, which is a view repeated, may be taken of that which is present and before us; every *retrospect* is a species of *review*, but every *review* is not a *retrospect*. We take a *retrospect* of our past life in order to draw salutary reflections from all that we have done and suffered; we take a *review* or a second view of any particular circumstance which is passing before us, in order to regulate our present conduct. The *retrospect* goes farther by virtue of the mind's power to reflect on itself and to recall all past images to itself; the *review* may go forward by the exercise of the senses on external objects. The historian takes a *retrospect* of all the events which have happened within a given period; the journalist takes a *review* of all the events that are pass-

ing within the time in which he is living.

The *review* may be said of the past as well as the present; it is a *view* not only of what is, but what has been: the *survey*, which is a looking over at once, from the French *sur*, upon, and Old French *veër*, for *voir*, to see, is entirely confined to the present; it is a *view* only of that which is, and is taken for some particular purpose. We take a *review* of what we have already *viewed*, in order to get a more correct insight into it; we take a *survey* of a thing in all its parts, in order to get a comprehensive view of it, in order to examine it in all its bearings. A general occasionally takes a *review* of all his army; he takes a *survey* of the fortress which he is going to besiege or attack.

RETURN, REVERT. *Return* is the English, and *revert* the Latin: *return* is therefore used in ordinary cases to denote the coming back to any point of time or place; as to *return* home, or to *return* at a certain hour, or to apply one's self again to the same business or employment; as to *return* to one's writing: to *revert* is to throw back with one's mind to any object; we may, therefore, say, to *return* or *revert* to any intellectual object, with this distinction, that to *return* is to go back to the point here one left off treating of any subject; to *revert* is simply to carry one's mind back to the same object. As an act of an unconscious agent, *return* is used as before.

Revert signifies either to fall back into the same state or to return by reflection to the same object; all things *revert* to their primitive order and regularity.

See also RESTORE.

REVEAL. See PUBLISH; UNVEIL.

REVELS. See SATURNALIA.

REVENGE. See AVENGE.

REVERBERATE. See REBOUND.

REVERE. See ADORE.

REVERENCE. See ADORE; AWE; HONOR.

REVERSE. See OVERTURN.

REVERT. See RETURN.

REVERY. See DREAM.

REVIEW. See RETROSPECT; REVISAL.

REVILE, VILIFY. *Revile*, from the Latin prefix *re* and old French *aviler*, to make vile, built on the Latin *vilis*, cheap, worthless, signifies to reflect upon a person, or retort upon him that which is vile: to *vilify* signifies to make a thing vile, that is, to set it forth as vile. To *revile* is a personal act; it is addressed directly to the object of offence, and is addressed for the purpose of making the person vile in his own eyes: to *vilify* is an indirect attack which serves to make the object appear vile in the eyes of others. *Revile* is said only of persons, for persons only are *reviled;* but to *vilify* is said of persons as well as things. To *revile* is uncharitable : to *vilify* is seldom justifiable, for we cannot *vilify* without using improper language; it is seldom resorted to except as a manifestation of ill-nature.

REVISAL, Revision, Review. *Revisal, revision,* and *review* all come from the Latin *videre,* to see, and signify looking back upon a thing or looking at it again: the terms *revised* and *revision* are, however, mostly employed in regard to what is written; *review* is used for things in general. The *revisal* of a book is the work of the author, or of a reviser, for the purposes of correction: the *review* of a book is the work of the critic, for the purpose of estimating its value. *Revisal* and *revision* differ neither in sense nor application, that except the former is more frequently employed abstractedly from the object *revised* and *revision* mostly in conjunction: whoever wishes his work to be correct will not spare a *revisal;* the *revision* of classical books ought to be intrusted only to men of profound erudition.

See also Retrospect.

REVIVE, Refresh, Renovate, Renew. *Revive,* from the Latin *vivere,* to live, signifies to bring to life again; to *refresh,* to make fresh again; to *renew* and *renovate,* to make new again. The restoration of things to their primitive state is the common idea included in these terms; the difference consists in their application. *Revive, refresh,* and *renovate* are applied to animal bodies; *revive* expressing the return of motion and spirits to one who was for the time lifeless; *refresh* expressing the return of vigor to one in whom it has been diminished; the air *revives* one who is faint; a cool breeze *refreshes* one who

is affected by the heat. *Revive* and *refresh* connote only the temporary state of a body; *renovate* the permanent state, that is, the health or powers of a body; one is *revived* and *refreshed* after partial exhaustion; one's health is *renovated* after having been considerably impaired.

Revive is applied likewise in the moral sense; *refresh* and *renovate* mostly in the proper sense; *renew* only in the applied sense. A discussion is said to be *revived* or a report to be *revived;* a clamor is said to be *renewed* or entreaties to be *renewed:* customs are *revived* which have long lain dormant and, as it were, dead; practices are *renewed* that have ceased for a time.

REVOKE. See Abjure; Abolish.

REVOLT. See Defection; Insurrection.

REWARD. See Compensation.

RHETORIC. See Elocution.

RICHES, Wealth, Opulence, Affluence. *Riches* comes from Old French *richesse,* wealth, from Middle High German *riche,* which is the same word as Anglo-Saxon *ric.* *Wealth,* Middle English *welthe,* extended from *weal,* prosperity, which is allied to *well.* *Opulence,* from the stem of the Latin *opes,* riches, denotes the state of having riches. *Affluence,* from the Latin *ad,* to, and *fluere,* to flow, denotes either the act of riches flowing in to a person or the state of having things flowing in.

Riches is a general term denoting any considerable share of property, but without immediate reference to a possessor; whatever serves to make one rich is denominated riches, inasmuch as it supplies us with the means of getting what is really good; *wealth* and the other terms refer to outward possessions.

Riches is a condition opposed to poverty; the whole world is divided into *rich* and poor, and *riches* are distributed in different degrees; but *wealth, opulence,* and *affluence* all denote a considerable share of *riches: wealth* is a positive and substantial share of this world's goods, but particularly of money or the precious commodities; it may be taken in the abstract or in application to individuals: *opulence* consists of any large share in possessions or property generally, as houses, lands, goods, and chattels, and is applicable to the present and actual condition of the individual. *Affluence* is a term peculiarly applicable to the fluctuating condition of things which flow in in great quantities to a person. We speak of *riches* as to their effects upon men's minds and manners; it is not every one who knows how to use them: we speak of *wealth* as it raises a man in the scale of society and contributes to his weal or wellbeing: we speak of *opulence* as the present actually flourishing state of the individuals; and of *affluence* as the temporary condition. *Wealth* and *opulence* are applied to communities as well as individuals.

RIDICULE, Satire, Irony, Sarcasm. *Ridicule* (see DERIDE) has simple laughter in it; *satire* comes from *satura lanx,* a full dish, a dish of mixed ingredients, indicating a poem full of topical and personal hits: the former is employed in matters of a trifling nature; but *satire* is employed either in personal or grave matters. *Irony,* in Greek εἰρωνεία, from εἴρων, a dissembler who says less than he thinks or means, is disguised *satire;* an *ironist* seems to praise that which he really means to condemn. *Sarcasm,* from the Greek σαρκασμός, a sneer, and σαρκάζειν, to sneer, both based on σάρξ, flesh, signifying biting or nipping *satire,* so, as it were, to tear the flesh, is bitter and personal *satire;* all the others may be successfully and properly employed to expose folly and vice; but *sarcasm,* which is the indulgence only of personal resentment, is never justifiable.

See also LAUGH.

RIGHT, JUST, FIT, PROPER. *Right,* from Anglo-Saxon *riht,* signifying upright, not leaning to one side or the other, standing as it ought, is here the general term: the others express modes of *right.* The *right* and wrong are defined by the written will of God, or are written in our hearts according to the original disposition of our nature: the *just,* in Latin *justus,* from *jus,* law, signifying according to a rule of right, and the unjust, are determined by the written laws of men; the *fit* and *proper,* in Latin *proprius,* signifying belonging to a given specific rule, are determined by the established principles of society.

Between the *right* and the wrong there are no gradations: a thing cannot be more *right* or more wrong; whatever is *right* is not wrong, and whatever is wrong is not *right:* the *just* and unjust, *proper* and improper, *fit* and unfit, on the contrary, have various shades and degrees that are not so easily definable by any forms of speech or written rules.

The *right* and wrong depend upon no circumstances; what is once *right* or wrong is always *right* or wrong, but the *just* or unjust, *proper* or improper, are relatively so according to the circumstances of the case: it is a *just* rule for every man to have that which is his own; but what is *just* to the individual may be unjust to society. It is *proper* for every man to take charge of his own concerns; but it would be improper for a man in an unsound state of mind to undertake such a charge. *Right* is applicable to all matters, important or otherwise; *just* is employed mostly in matters of essential interest; *proper* is rather applicable to the minor concerns of life. Everything that is done may be characterized as *right* or wrong: everything done to others may be measured by the rule of *just* or unjust: in our social intercourse, as well as in our private transactions, *fitness* and *propriety* must always be consulted. As Christians, we desire to do that which is *right* in the sight of God and man; as members of society, we wish to be *just* in our dealings; as rational and intelligent beings, we wish to do what is *fit* and *proper* in every action, however trivial.

See also STRAIGHT.

Right, Claim, Privilege.—*Right* signifies in this sense what it is *right* for one to possess, which is, in fact, a word of large meaning: for since the *right* and the wrong depend upon indeterminable questions, the *right* of having is equally indeterminable in some cases with every other species of *right.* A *claim* (see ASK) is a species of *right* to have that which is in the hands of another; the *right* to ask another for it. The *privilege* is a species of *right* peculiar to particular individuals or bodies.

Right, in its full sense, is altogether

an abstract thing which is independent of human laws and regulations; *claims* and *privileges* are altogether connected with the laws of society. Liberty, in the general sense, is an inalienable *right* which belongs to man as a rational and responsible agent; it is not a *claim*, for it is set above all question and all condition: nor is it a *privilege*, for it cannot be exclusively granted to one being nor unconditionally be taken away from another.

Between *right* and power there is often as wide a distinction as between truth and falsehood; we have often a *right* to do that which we have no power to do; and the power to do that which we have no *right* to do: slaves have a *right* to the freedom which is enjoyed by creatures of the same species as themselves, but they have not the power to use this freedom as others do. In England men have the power of thinking for themselves as they please; but by the abuse which they make of this power we see that in many cases they have not the *right*, unless we admit the contradiction that men have a *right* to do what is wrong; they have the power, therefore, of exercising this *right* only because no other person has the power of controlling them. We have often a *claim* to a thing which is not in our power to substantiate; and, on the other hand, *claims* are set up in cases which are totally unfounded on any *right*. *Privileges* are *rights* granted to individuals, depending either upon the will of the grantor, or the circumstances of the receiver, or both; *privileges* are therefore partial *rights* transferable at the discretion of persons individually or collectively.

RIGHTEOUS. See GODLY.

RIGID. See ASCETIC; AUSTERE.

RIGOROUS. See AUSTERE; HARSH.

RIM. See BORDER.

RIND. See SKIN.

RIPE, MATURE. *Ripe* is the English (from Anglo-Saxon *ripe*, fit for *reaping*), *mature* the Latin word: the former has a universal application both proper and improper; the latter has mostly an improper application. The idea of completion in growth is simply designated by the former term; the idea of moral perfection, as far, at least, as it is attainable, is marked by the latter: fruit is *ripe* when it requires no more sustenance from the parent stock; a judgment is *mature* which requires no more time and knowledge to render it perfect or fitted for exercise: in the same manner a project may be said to be *ripe* for execution or a people *ripe* for revolt; and, on the contrary, reflection may be said to be *mature* to which sufficiency of time has been given, and age may be said to be *mature* which has attained the highest pitch of perfection. *Ripeness* is, however, not always a good quality; but *maturity* is always a perfection: the *ripeness* of some fruit diminishes the excellence of its flavor: there are some fruits which have no flavor until they come to *maturity*.

RISE, ISSUE, EMERGE. To *rise* (see ARISE) may either refer to open or enclosed spaces; *issue* and *emerge* (see EMERGENCY) have both a reference to some confined body: a thing may either *rise* in a body, without a body, or out of a body; but it *issues* and *emerges* out of a body. A thing may either *rise* in a plain or a wood; it *issues* out of a wood: it may either *rise* in water or out of the water; it *emerges* from the water; that which *rises* out of a thing comes into view by becoming higher: in this manner an air balloon might *rise* out of a wood; that which *issues* comes from the very depths of a thing, and, as it were, comes out as a part of it; but that which *emerges* proceeds from the thing in which it has been, as it were, concealed. Hence, in the moral application, a person is said to *rise* in life without a reference to his former condition; but he *emerges* from obscurity: color *rises* in the face; but words *issue* from the mouth.

See also ORIGIN.

RISK. See HAZARD.

RITE. See FORM.

ROAD. See ROUTE.

ROAM. See WANDER.

ROBBERY. See DEPREDATION.

ROBUST. See STRONG.

ROLL. See LIST.

ROMANCE. See FABLE.

ROOM. See SPACE.

ROT, PUTREFY, CORRUPT. The dissolution of bodies by an internal process is implied by all these terms: but the first two are applied to natural bodies only; the last to all bodies, natural and moral. *Rot* is the strongest of all these terms; it denotes the last stage in the progress of dissolution: *putrefy* (the modern variant of *putrefy,* based on *putrid*) expresses the progress toward rottenness; and *corruption* the commencement. After fruit has arrived at its maturity or proper state of ripeness it *rots:* meat which is kept too long *putrefies:* there is a tendency in all bodies to *corruption;* iron and wood *corrupt* with time; whatever is made, or done, or wished by men is equally liable to be *corrupt* or to grow *corrupt.*

ROUGH. See ABRUPT; HARSH.

ROUND. See CIRCUIT.

ROUNDNESS, ROTUNDITY. *Roundness* and *rotundity* both come from the Latin *rotundus* and *rota,* a wheel, which is a perfectly round body: the former term is, however, applied to all objects in general; the latter only to solid bodies which are round in all directions: one speaks of the *roundness* of a circle, the *roundness* of the moon, the *roundness* of a tree; but the *rotundity* of a man's body which projects in a *round* form in all directions, and the *rotundity* of a full cheek or the *rotundity* of a turnip.

ROUSE. See AWAKEN.

ROUSING. See ELECTRIC.

ROUT. See BEAT.

ROUTE, ROAD, COURSE. *Route* comes through the French from the adjective of the Latin phrase, *via rupta,* or "broken road." *Road* comes from the Anglo-Saxon *rídan,* to ride, signifying the place where one rides, as *course,* from the Latin *cursus* (see COURSE), signifies the place where one walks or runs.

Route is to *road* as the species to the genus: a *route* is a circular kind of *road;* it is chosen as the circuitous direction toward a certain point, and may consist of more than one *road* successively: the *road* may be either in a direct or indirect line; the *route* is always indirect: the *route* is chosen only by horsemen or those who go to a considerable distance, as those who choose the "*route* to India"; the *road* may be chosen for the shortest distance; the *route* and *road* are pursued in their beaten and frequented track; the *course* is often chosen in the un-

beaten track: an army or a company go a certain *route,* foot-passengers are seen to take a certain *course* over fields: *course* often implies circular completion, as, the sun runs its *course.*

ROVE. See WANDER.

ROYAL, REGAL, KINGLY. *Royal* and *regal,* both from the adjective *regalis,* based on Latin *rex,* a king, though of foreign origin, have obtained more general application than the corresponding English term *kingly. Royal* signifies belonging to a king, in its most general sense; *regal* signifies appertaining to a king, in its particular application; *kingly* signifies properly like a king. A *royal* carriage, a *royal* residence, a *royal* couple, a *royal* salute, *royal* authority, all designate the general and ordinary appurtenances to a king: *regal* government, *regal* state, *regal* power, *regal* dignity, denote the peculiar properties of a king: *kingly* always implies what is becoming a king, or after the manner of a king; a *kingly* crown is such as a king ought to wear; a *kingly* mien that which is after the manner of a king.

RUB, CHAFE, FRET, GALL. *Rub,* Middle English *rubben,* is of Celtic origin; it is not allied to German *reiben,* from which *rive* is taken; it is the generic term, expressing simply the act of bodies moving in contact with and against others; to *chafe* (from Old French *chaufer,* from Low Latin *calef'-care,* a late form of the classical *calfacere,* to make hot) signifies to *rub* a thing until it is heated: to *fret* comes from Anglo-Saxon *frétan,* compounded of *for,* intensive prefix, and *etan,* meaning to eat away; to *gall* is a different word from the noun *gall,* and corresponds probably to Latin *galla,* a gall-nut, oak-apple—hence a tumor, a skin affection; hence to rub or itch. Things are *rubbed* sometimes for purposes of convenience; but they are *chafed, fretted,* and *galled* injuriously: the skin is liable to *chafe* from any violence; leather will *fret* from the motion of a carriage; when the skin is once broken animals will become *galled* by a continuance of the friction. These terms are likewise used in the moral sense, to denote the actions of things on the mind, where the distinction is clearly kept up: we meet with *rubs* from the opposing sentiments of others; the angry humors are *chafed;* the mind is *fretted* and made sore by the frequent repetition of small troubles and vexations; pride is *galled* by humiliations and severe degradations.

RUDE. See IMPERTINENT.

RUDIMENTARY. See ELEMENTARY.

RUEFUL. See PITEOUS.

RUGGED. See ABRUPT.

RUIN. See BANE; DESTRUCTION; FALL.

RULE. See GOVERN; GUIDE; MAXIM; ORDER.

RULING. See PREVAILING.

RUMMAGE, RANSACK. These two words both signify to look for something. *Rummage,* compounded of French suffix *age* and Dutch *ruim,* a ship's hold, allied to *room.* It meant to stow away and then to search among things stowed away. *Ransack* comes from Scandinavian *rann,* a house, and *sak,* a root allied to seek, signifying to search a house thoroughly and carry away. *Ransack* signifies a thorough *rummaging.* The difference between the two words is mainly one of degree.

RUMOR. See FAME.

RUPTURE, FRACTURE, FRACTION. *Rupture,* from *ruptura,* the feminine of the future participle of *rumpere,* to break or burst, and *fracture* or *fraction,* similarly derived from *frangere,* to break, denote different kinds of breaking, according to the objects to which the action is applied. Soft substances may suffer a *rupture;* as the *rupture* of a blood-vessel; hard substances a *fracture,* as the *fracture* of a bone.

Fraction is used only in respect to broken numbers, as the *fraction* of a unit.

Rupture is also used in an improper application; as the *rupture* of a treaty.

RURAL, RUSTIC. Although both these terms, from the Latin *rus,* country, signify belonging to the country, yet the former, from the genitive stem *ruris,* is used in a good, and the latter in a bad or an indifferent, sense. *Rural* applies to all country objects except man; it is, therefore, always connected with the charms of nature: *rustic* applies only to persons or what is personal, in the country, and is, therefore, always associated with the want of culture. *Rural* scenery is always interesting; but the *rustic* manners of the peasants have frequently too much that is uncultivated and rude in them to be agreeable; a *rural* habitation may be fitted for persons in a higher station; but a *rustic* cottage is adapted only for the poorer inhabitants of the country.

See also COUNTRYMAN.

S

SABBATH, SUNDAY. The term *Sabbath*, from the Hebrew *shabbâth*, to rest, through French *sabbat*, implies a sacred day of rest from customary occupations, the institution of which, under the name of the *seventh day*, is first mentioned in Genesis 11:2-3. Always in the Gospels and as a rule in the other books, *Sabbath* means the *seventh day* of the week.

Distinctions between the *Sabbath* and *Sunday* were at one time very sharply drawn, the *Sabbath* being considered a purely Jewish term, and *Sunday*, otherwise called the *Lord's Day*, a Christian one; but most of the old contentions were long ago abandoned. The elder Disraeli is authority for the statement that the term *Sabbath* meant Saturday in the Middle Ages, and that it was first used in England for *Sunday* in 1554.

Both Jews and Christians observe the *seventh day* of the week, but from a different start, the former recognizing Saturday as their *Sabbath* and the latter the following day as their *Sunday*.

SACK, DESPOIL, DEVASTATE. *Sack*, in French *sac*, waste or ruin, may be derived from Latin *saccus*, a bag or sack for carrying away things. *Despoil* comes from Latin *spoliare*, based on *spolium*, a skin stripped off, referring to the dress of a dead warrior. *Devastate*, from *devastare*, based on Latin *vastus*, signifying large, empty space, means to lay waste. *Sack* is a stronger word than *despoil*. It means to go through a conquered territory and carry off everything of value. *Despoil* means to strip off something valuable, but it does not imply such thorough and wholesale destruction. *Devastate* means literally to lay waste, and refers not merely to the carrying away of valuables, but to the utter destruction of everything. We may speak of a city *devastated* by fire, or a country *devastated* by storm—so that the word has a wider application than *sack* and does not refer merely to warfare. *Despoil* may refer to the action of individuals. An unscrupulous lawyer may *despoil* a widow of the property left to her, etc. But *sack* is applied specifically to the treatment of captured territory in warfare. See also RAPINE; RAVAGE.

SACRAMENT. See LORD'S-SUPPER.

SACRED. See HOLY.

SACRILEGIOUS, IRREVERENT, DESECRATING. *Sacrilegious*, from Latin *sacrilegium* (based on the crude stem *sacri* and *legere*, to gather up and steal sacred things), the robbing of a temple, is a much more positive word than *irreverent*, which simply means not *reverent* (for the derivation see ADORE); but it is a less positive word than *desecrating*, from Latin *de*, not, and *sacer*, sacred, which means depriving of sacredness, and has a more extended application. *Sacrilegious* means positively *irreverent*, implying an *irreverence* that reveals itself in a distinct speech or act which shows a lack of regard for things held holy. *Desecrating* means not merely a positive expression of the disregard for things sacred, but an expression of such violence that it destroys the sacred character. *Irreverent* applies to an attitude of mind, *sacrilegious* to manner and speech, *desecrating* to action, though these distinctions are not clearly observed. (*Sacrilegious* is often mispronounced, even by educated persons, as sacr*i*legious.) See also IRRELIGIOUS.

SAD. See DULL; MOURNFUL.

SAFE, SECURE. *Safe*, in Latin *salvus*, to be tranquil, implies exemption from harm or the danger of harm; *secure* (see CERTAIN) the exemption from danger: a person may be *safe* or saved in the midst of a fire, if he be untouched by the fire; but he is, in such a case, the reverse of *secure*. In the sense of exemption from danger, *safety* expresses much less than *security*: we may be *safe* without using any particular measures; but none can reckon on any degree of *security* without great precaution: a person may be very *safe* on the top of a coach in the daytime; but if he wishes to *secure* himself, at night, from falling off, he must be fastened.

SAFE-CONDUCT. See PASS.

SAFEGUARD. See PASS.

SAGACIOUS. See SAGE.

SAGACITY. See PENETRATION.

SAGE, SAGACIOUS, SAPIENT. *Sage* and *sagacious* come from different Latin words, despite their similarity of form and meaning, *sage* being derived ultimately from Latin *sapere*, to be wise; *sagacious* from *sagax*, connected with *sagire*, to perceive by the senses. *Sapient* is derived from the present participle of *sapere*.

The first of these terms has a good sense, in application to men, to denote the faculty of discerning immediately, which is the fruit of experience, and very similar to that *sagacity* in animals which instinctively perceives a thing without the deductions of reason; *sapient* is now employed only in regard to animals which are trained to particular arts; its use, therefore, in respect to human beings, is mostly in the lofty or burlesque style.

SAILOR. See SEAMAN.

SAINTLY. See HOLY.

SAINT-SIMONIANISM. See SOCIALISM.

SAKE, ACCOUNT, REASON, PURPOSE, END. These terms are all employed adverbially, to modify or connect propositions; hence one says, for his *sake*, on his *account*, for this *reason*, for this *purpose*, and to this *end*. *Sake*, from Anglo-Saxon *sacu*, strife, a side in a strife, hence a cause, is mostly said of persons; what is done for a person's *sake* is the same as in behalf of his cause; one may, however, say in regard to things, for the *sake* of good order, implying what good order requires; *account* is indifferently employed for persons or things; what is done on a person's *account* is done in his behalf and for his interest; what is done on *account* of indisposition is done in consequence of it, the indisposition being the cause: *purpose* is properly personal and refers to that which a person *purposes* to himself; if we ask, therefore, for what *purpose* a thing is done, it may be to know something of some other person's character and principles: *reason* and *end* are applied to things only: we speak of the *reason* as the thing that justifies: we explain why we do a thing when we say we do it for this or that *reason;* we speak of the *end* by way of explaining the nature of the thing: the propriety of a measure cannot be known unless we know what *end* it will answer.

SALARY. See ALLOWANCE.

SALIENT, OUTSTANDING. Both of these words indicate that which is a noticeable or prominent feature of something. *Outstanding* is really just an English translation of *salient*, from Latin *salire*, to leap, hence to stand out; and the difference between them is mainly the difference usually found between words of English and Latin derivation. *Outstanding* suggests the picture more clearly. The *outstanding* feature of an occurrence is that which strikes the attention most vividly, which stands out from the rest. *Salient* does not so clearly suggest the image, but it is a somewhat more polished word.

SALLY, ISSUE. *Sally*, from Latin *salire*, to leap, is a particular kind of *issuing*. (For *issue* see ARISE.) It referred to the going forth of a detachment of soldiers from a besieged place to attack the besiegers. *Issue* means, in general, to go forth. *Sally* means to go forth with a certain spirit and gallantry, with an attitude of adventurousness. *Sally* is applied figuratively to a humorous thrust, a witticism or jest; in this sense it is used mainly as a noun. Here, too, it keeps its fundamental implication of a spirited and unexpected attack.

SALUBRIOUS. See HEALTHY.

SALUTARY. See HEALTHY.

SALUTE, SALUTATION, GREETING. *Salute* (see ACCOST) concerns the thing; and *salutation*, which is a variation of *salute*, the person giving the *salute:* a *salute* may consist either of a word or an action; *salutations* pass from one friend to another: the *salute* may be either direct or indirect; the *salutation* is always direct and personal; guns are fired by way of a *salute:* bows are given as a *salutation*.

The *salutation* is a familiar and ordinary form of courtesy between individuals; *greeting* is frequently a particular mode of *salutation* adopted on extraordinary occasions, indicative of great joy or satisfaction in those who *greet*.

SALVATION, DELIVERANCE, PRESERVATION, SAVING, REDEMPTION, RESCUE. *Salvation*, in French *salvation*, from Latin *salvationem*, from *salvus*, whole, has both a physical and a moral application. In the physical application we seek or receive *deliverance* from impending or present peril from some power beyond our own. We gain *preservation* from something destructive by some act of our own or of others, and we may be the subject or object of a *rescue* from danger, restraint, or violence.

In the moral application we are taught that *salvation* is the spiritual *deliverance* from sin and death, through the *saving* mercy of Jesus Christ, who offered himself as a ransom for mankind, his death being the final act of man's *redemption*, or the releasing and setting free of all living in sin.

SANATIVE. See SANITARY.

SANATORY. See SANITARY.

SANCTIFY, CLEANSE, CONSECRATE, DEVOTE, HALLOW, PURIFY. *Sanctify*, in French *sanctifier*, from Latin *sanctificere*, compound of *sanctus*, holy, and a weakened form of *facere*, to make, signifies literally to make holy or sacred, and applies both to persons and objects of a religious character.

In the personal application, to *sanctify* is to make holy, to have one's heart and life made to conform to the will of God. Prior to this act comes that to *cleanse* or *purify* from sin, to convert from a former state, to regenerate or make anew.

To *consecrate* is to set a person or object apart from that which is ordinary for some sacred purpose. This is done by others, as the *consecration* of a religious edifice or some part thereof, and the *consecration* of a person to the calling of the ministry.

To *devote* one's self to a sacred purpose is the act of the individual, to *devote* an object is for one or others to give or apply it. To *hallow* a place or object is to *consecrate* or set it apart for a sacred purpose.

SANCTION. See COUNTENANCE; UPHOLD.

SANCTITY. See HOLINESS.

SANE. See SOUND.

SANGUINARY, BLOODY, BLOODTHIRSTY. *Sanguinary*, from *sanguis*, is employed both in the sense of *bloody*, or having *blood*, and *bloodythirsty*, or *thirsting* after *blood; sanguinary*, in the first case, relates only to *blood* shed, as a *sanguinary* engagement or a *sanguinary* conflict; *bloody* is used in the familiar application, to denote the simple presence of *blood*, as a *bloody* coat or a *bloody* sword.

In the second case, *sanguinary* is employed to characterize the tempers of persons only; *bloodthirsty* to characterize the tempers of persons to any other beings: revolutionists will be frequently *sanguinary*, because they are abandoned to their passions and follow a lawless course of violence: tigers are by nature the most *bloodthirsty* of all creatures.

SANGUINE, ARDENT, BUOYANT, CHEERFUL, CONFIDENT, ELATED, ENTHUSIASTIC, HOPEFUL, WARM. *Sanguine*, from the Latin *sanguis*, meaning blood. One who abounds in blood is said to have a *sanguine* temperament, and that gives birth to the conditions indicated by the other terms.

The *ardent* person is warm, glowing, passionate, eager, and zealous; the *buoyant* one is in a state of mental uplift and is seldom depressed; the *cheerful* one is abounding in good spirits, is happy himself, and strives to make others happy; the *confident* one feels assured of his own power and future; the *elated* one is exultant, apt to be excitable, and is easily raised in spirits.

Enthusiastic persons are generally *ardent*, frequently visionary, sometimes fanatical, and always zealous in their undertakings. *Hopeful* ones always look on the bright side of things, see the silver lining of clouds, and are full of anticipation, expectation, and trust; *warm* ones are full of zeal, ardor, affection, and welcome, and are apt to be easily irritated.

See also OPTIMISTIC.

SANITARY, SANATORY. *Sanitary*, in French *sanitaire*, a coined word from Latin *sanitas*, sanity, and *sanatory*, extended from *sanator*, a healer (hence *sanatorium*), are terms commonly used indiscriminately, but having different applications. *Sanitary* specifically signifies something pertaining to health, *sanatory* something conducive to health.

Whatever is conducive to health, such as curing or healing applications or treatment, is *sanatory;* whatever pertains to or is connected with the preservation of health is *sanitary.* Allied to these terms are *sanitation,* or the system of promoting healthful reforms, and *sanitarium* or *sanatorium,* a resort for hygienic, restful, or curative treatment.

SAP, UNDERMINE. *Sap,* Anglo-Saxon *sæp,* signifies the juice which springs from the root of a tree; but *sap,* in the sense of *undermine,* is probably derived from Latin *sappa,* a spade or mattock; hence signifies to come at the root of anything by digging: to *undermine* signifies to form a mine under the ground or under whatever is upon the ground: we may *sap,* therefore, without *undermining;* and *undermine* without *sapping:* we may *sap* the foundation of a house without making any mine underneath; and in fortifications we may *undermine* either a mound, a ditch, or a wall without striking immediately at the foundation: hence, in the moral application, to *sap* is a more direct and decisive mode of destruction; to *undermine* is a gradual, and may be a partial, action. Infidelity *saps* the morals of a nation; courtiers *undermine* one another's interests at court.

SAPIENT. See SAGE.
SARCASM. See RIDICULE.
SARCASTIC. See TRENCHANT.
SATANIC. See DIABOLIC.
SATIATE. See SATISFY.
SATIRE. See RIDICULE; WIT.
SATISFACTION. See COMPENSATION; CONTENTMENT.

SATISFY, PLEASE, GRATIFY. To *satisfy* (see CONTENTMENT) is rather to produce pleasure indirectly; to *please* (see AGREEABLE) is to produce it directly: the former is negative, the latter positive, pleasure: as every desire is accompanied by more or less pain, *satisfaction,* which is the removal of desire, is itself to a certain extent pleasure; but what *satisfies* is not always calculated to *please;* nor is that which *pleases* that which will always *satisfy:* plain food *satisfies* a hungry person, but does not *please* him when he is not hungry; social enjoyments *please,* but they are very far from *satisfying* those who do not restrict their indulgences. To *gratify* is to *please* in a high degree, to produce keen pleasure: we may be *pleased* with trifles, but we are commonly *gratified* with such things as act strongly either on the senses or the affections: an epicure is *gratified* with those delicacies which suit his taste; an amateur in music will be *gratified* by hearing a piece of Handel's composition finely performed.

See also COMPENSATION.

Satisfy, Satiate, Glut, Cloy.—To *satisfy* is to make enough: *satiate* is a frequentative, formed similarly from *satis,* enough, but signifying to have more than enough. *Glut,* in Latin *glutire,* allied to *gula,* the throat, signifies to take down the throat. *Satisfaction* brings pleasure; it is what nature demands; and nature, therefore, makes a suitable return: *satiety,* meaning that which exceeds the desire, is attended with disgust; *glutting* is an act of intemperance; it is what the inordinate appetite demands; it greatly exceeds the former in degree both of the cause and the consequence: *cloying* is the consequence of *glutting.* Every healthy person *satisfies* himself with a regular portion of food; children, if unrestrained, seek to *satiate* their appetites, and *cloy* themselves by their excesses; brutes, or men sunk to the level of brutes, *glut* themselves with that which is agreeable to their appetites. So, in the moral application, we *satisfy* desires in general or any particular desire; we *satiate* the appetite for pleasure; one *gluts* the eyes or the ears by anything that is horrible or painful or *cloys* the mind.

SATURNALIA, CARNIVAL, ORGIES. These words all indicate particular festivals, and hence, by extension, unrestrained license and riotous self-indulgence. *Saturnalia,* in Latin the neuter plural of *saturnalis,* pertaining to Saturn, was an ancient Roman festival in honor of the god Saturn, in which all classes, including slaves, took part. It was celebrated in December and was regarded as a period of unrestrained license.

Carnival (not, as commonly misunderstood, from Italian *carne, vale!* or "Farewell, oh flesh! nor, as Lord Byron tried to explain it, 'Farewell to flesh'") is derived from Latin *carnis*, flesh, and Latin *levare*, to lift, remove, take away, and is the festival immediately preceding Lent in Italy, celebrating the beginning of fleshless and fasting days by a riot of self-indulgence. *Orgy*, Latin *orgia*, from Greek ὄργια, secret rites, refers to the secret festivals in honor of Bacchus, the god of wine, celebrated by extravagant revels; the word is usually employed in the plural—*orgies*. In the figurative application of these words there is little difference. All indicate unrestrained riot; but there is more of harmless gayety in *carnival*, perhaps, and more of extravagance, violence, and shamelessness in *orgies*.

SAUCY. See IMPERTINENT.

SAUNTER. See LINGER.

SAVAGE. See CRUEL; FEROCIOUS.

SAVE, SPARE, PRESERVE, PROTECT. To *save* is to keep or make safe. *Spare* comes from Anglo-Saxon *spær*. *Preserve*, compounded of *præ*, before, and *servare*, keep (cf. German *hüten* . . . VOR.), signifies to keep away from. *Protect* (see DEFEND).

The idea of keeping free from evil is the common idea of all these terms, and the peculiar signification of the term *save;* they differ either in the nature of the evil kept off or the circumstances of the agent: we may be *saved* from every kind of evil; but we are *spared* only from those which it is in the power of another to inflict: we may be *saved* from falling or *saved* from an illness; a criminal is *spared* from punishment, or we may be *spared* by Divine Providence in the midst of some calamity.

We may be *saved* and *spared* from any evils, great or small; we are *preserved* and *protected* only from evils of magnitude: we may be *saved* either from the inclemency of the weather or the fatal vicissitudes of life: we may be *spared* the pain of a disagreeable meeting or we may be *spared* our lives; we are *preserved* from ruin or *protected* from oppression. To *save* and *spare* apply to evils that are actual and temporary; *preserve* and *protect* to those which are possible or permanent: we may be *saved* from drowning; a person

may be *preserved* from infection or *protected* from an attack. To *save* may be the effect of accident or design; to *spare* is always the effect of intentional forbearance; to *preserve* and *protect* are the effect of a special exertion of power, the latter in a still higher degree than the former: we may be *preserved*, by ordinary means, from the evils of human life; but we are *protected* by the government or by Divine Providence from the active attacks of those who aim to do us harm.

To *spare* and *protect* refer mostly to personal injuries; *save* and *preserve* are said of whatever one keeps from injury on account of its value; as to *save* one's good name, to *preserve* one's honor.

See also DELIVER; KEEP.

SAVING. See ECONOMICAL; SALVATION.

SAVOR. See TASTE.

SAW. See AXIOM.

SAY. See SPEAK.

SAYING. See AXIOM.

SCALE. See ARISE.

SCANDAL. See DISCREDIT.

SCANDALOUS. See INFAMOUS.

SCANTY. See BARE.

SCARCE. See RARE.

SCARCELY. See HARDLY.

SCARCITY, DEARTH. *Scarcity* (see RARE) is a generic term to denote the circumstance of a thing being *scarce*. *Dearth*, which is the same as dearness (Middle English *derthe*, formed from the adjective as *warmth, health, wealth* are formed), is a mode of *scarcity* applied in the literal sense to provisions mostly, as provisions are mostly dear when they are *scarce;* the word *dearth*, therefore, denotes *scarcity* in a high degree: whenever men want something and find it difficult to procure, they complain of its *scarcity:* when a country has the misfortune to be visited with a famine, it experiences the frightfulest of all *dearths*.

Dearth is figuratively applied to moral objects; as a *dearth* of intelligence, of talent, and the like.

SCATHE, DAMAGE, HARM, INJURY, MISCHIEF. *Scathe* is from a Teutonic root meaning to harm. These terms apply both to the body and material objects and to the individual mind.

SCATTER. See SPREAD.

SCEPTICISM, Agnosticism, Atheism. These words are all used to indicate a disbelief in the articles of a religion, especially of the Christian religion, but they differ considerably in the degree and kind of unbelief that they indicate. *Scepticism,* from Greek σκέπτομαι, I consider, means the disposition to doubt all things, to come to no intellectual conclusion, because of an insufficiency of evidence. It has a wider application than the other two words and refers to a general intellectual attitude in respect to all things and not merely to an attitude to religious questions. *Agnosticism* has a similar meaning. It was a word coined by Huxley in a heated controversy between the theologians of the old school and the evolutionary scientists of the new to express his own attitude—that of simple open-mindedness on the subject of all questions concerning which he had no scientific evidence, especially concerning articles of religious faith. The doctrines of the Church could not be proved, he said. They cannot therefore be declared a true *gnosis*—a matter of intellectual knowledge. *Agnostic* he coined by prefixing the privative *a* to the Greek *gnosis* to signify one who refused to consider statements not based, like the facts of natural science, on the evidence of the senses as matters of scientific fact. He wished to proclaim himself open to correction, however, ready to examine all evidence. *Agnosticism* has therefore the same fundamental meaning as *scepticism.* The *agnostic,* like the *sceptic,* says, "I will consider," but, practically and historically, the words have had a different meaning. The *sceptic* doubts all evidence; the *agnostic* admits the validity of a certain kind of evidence—the evidence of the senses. *Scepticism,* as applied to religion, has generally indicated positive disbelief; *agnosticism,* the position of the open-minded inquirer. *Atheism,* while often confused with the other terms, has an entirely different meaning. It signifies a disbelief in the existence of a God, or at least of a personal God. The consistent *agnostic* cannot be an *atheist,* because, if he cannot prove the existence of a God, he is equally unable to prove His non-existence.

SCHEMING, Artful, Contriving, Designing, Intriguing, Planning. *Scheming,* in Latin *schema,* Greek σχῆμα, form, from σχήσω, future of, from the verb ἔχειν, to hold, signifies holding in one's hands or one's mind the plan and means of future action. As acts of *contriving, designing,* and *planning,* the term may be used both in a proper or praiseworthy sense and in an improper and reprehensible one.

These terms in the proper sense imply acts intended to result in benefits to ourselves or others on material lines, in which we devise, invent, project, outline, or sketch that which is necessary to the accomplishment of the purpose in mind. In the improper sense these operations may be to the disadvantage or injury of others.

In being *artful* and in *intriguing* we become cunning, crafty, engaged in secret and underhand plots. We may be *artful* solely, or all by ourselves, but when we are *intriguing* we usually need confederates, as the plot or *scheme* in mind is generally of a more or less complicated nature, and, as more than one person is involved, the intriguer cannot hold all the strings in his hands.

See also Design.

SCHISMATIC. See Heretic.

SCHOLAR, Disciple. *Scholar* (see School, below) and *disciple* are both applied to such as learn from others: but the former is said only of those who learn the rudiments of knowledge; the latter of one who acquires any art or science from the instruction of another: the *scholar* is opposed to the teacher; the *disciple* to the master: children are always *scholars;* adult persons may be *disciples.* *Scholars* chiefly employ themselves in the study of words; *disciples,* as the *disciples* of our Saviour, in the study of things: we are the *scholars* of any one under whose care we are placed or from whom we learn anything, good or bad; we are the *disciples* only of those who are distinguished, and for the most part in the good sense, though not always so: children are sometimes too apt *scholars* in learning evil from one another. Philosophers of old had their *disciples,* and nowadays there are many who have been exalted into that character who have their *disciples* and followers.

SCHOLASTIC. See ACADEMIC.

SCHOOL, ACADEMY. The Latin term *schola* signified a loitering-place, a place for desultory conversation or instruction, from the Greek σχολή, leisure; hence it has been extended to any place where instruction is given, particularly that which is communicated to youth. *Academy* derives its name from the Greek ἀκαδήμεια, the name of a gymnasium near Athens (so named for the hero Academus), where the philosopher Plato first gave his lectures, and which afterward became a place of resort for learned men; hence societies of learned men have since been termed *academies.* The leading idea in the word *school* is that of instruction given and doctrine received; in the word *academy* is that of association among those who have already learned: hence we speak in the literal sense of the *school* where young persons meet to be taught, or in the extended and moral sense of the old and new *school,* the Pythagorean *school,* the philosophical *school,* and the like; but the *academy* of arts or sciences, the French *Academy,* being members of any *academy,* and the like.

SCIENCE. See KNOWLEDGE.

SCOFF, GIBE, JEER, SNEER. *Scoff* is from an Old Low German word which may have meant originally a playful *shove.* *Gibe* (also spelled *jibe*) is from the Scandinavian. *Jeer* is a word of doubtful origin. *Sneer,* Middle English *sneren,* is allied to *snarl.*

Scoffing is a general term for expressing contempt; we may *scoff* either by *gibes, jeers,* or *sneers;* or we may *scoff* by opprobrious language and contemptuous looks, with *gibing, jeering,* or *sneering:* to *gibe, jeer,* and *sneer* are personal acts; the *gibe* and *jeer* consist of words addressed to an individual: the former has most of ill-nature and reproach in it; the latter has more of ridicule or satire in it; they are both, however, applied to the actions of vulgar or unseemly people who practice their coarse jokes on others.

Scoff and *sneer* are directed either to persons or things as the object; *gibe* and *jeer* only toward persons; *scoff* is taken only in the proper sense; *sneer*

derives its meaning from the literal act of *sneering:* the *scoffer* speaks lightly of that which deserves serious attention: the *sneerer* speaks either actually with a *sneer* or as it were by implication with a *sneer:* the *scoffers* at religion set at naught all thoughts of decorum, they openly avow the little estimation in which they hold it; the *sneerers* at religion are more sly, but not less malignant; they wish to treat religion with contempt, but not to bring themselves into the contempt they deserve.

SCOPE. See TENDENCY.

SCORN. See CONTEMN.

SCORNFUL. See CONTEMPTUOUS.

SCOUT. See SPY.

SCREAM. See CRY.

SCREEN. See COVER.

SCRIBE. See WRITER.

SCRUPLE, HESITATE, WAVER. To *scruple* (see CONSCIENTIOUS) simply keeps us from deciding; the terms *hesitate* (see DEMUR) and *waver,* from Anglo-Saxon *wæfre,* restless, wandering, bespeak a fluctuating or variable state of the mind. We *scruple* simply from motives of doubt as to the propriety of a thing; we *hesitate* and *waver* from various motives, particularly such as affect our interests. Conscience produces *scruples,* fear produces *hesitation,* irresolution produces *wavering:* a person *scruples* to do an action which may hurt his neighbor or offend his Maker; he *hesitates* to do a thing which he fears may not prove advantageous to him; he *wavers* in his mind between going or staying, according as his inclinations impel him to the one or the other: a man who does not *scruple* to say or do as he pleases will be an offensive companion, if not a dangerous member of society: he who *hesitates* only when the doing of good is proposed shows himself a worthless member of society; he who *wavers* between his duty and his inclination will seldom maintain a long or doubtful contest.

SCRUTINIZE. See PRY.

SCRUTINY. See EXAMINATION.

SCUM. See DREGS.

SCURRILOUS. See REPROACHFUL.

SEAL, STAMP. *Seal* is a specific, *stamp* a general, term: there cannot be a *seal* without a *stamp;* but there may be many *stamps* where there is no *seal.* The *seal,* in Latin *sigillum,* the diminutive of *signum*, signifies a signet or little sign, consisting of any one's coat of arms or any device; the *stamp* is, in general, any impression whatever which has been made by *stamping* (from *stamp*, meaning to *step* heavily, Greek στέμβειν, to *stamp*), that is, any impression which is not easily to be effaced. In the improper sense, the *seal* is the authority; thus, to set one's *seal* is the same as to authorize, and the *seal* of truth is any outward mark which characterizes it: but the *stamp* is the impression by which we distinguish the thing; thus a thing is said to bear the *stamp* of truth, of sincerity, of veracity, and the like.

SEAMAN, WATERMAN, SAILOR, MARINER. All these words denote persons occupied in navigation; the *seaman*, as the word implies, follows his business on the sea; the *waterman* is one who gets his livelihood on fresh water: the *sailor* and the *mariner* are both specific terms to designate the *seaman*: every *sailor* and *mariner* is a *seaman*; although every *seaman* is not a *sailor* or *mariner*; the former is one who is employed about the laborious part of the vessel; the latter is one who traverses the ocean to and fro, who is attached to the water and passes his life upon it. Men of all ranks are denominated *seamen*, whether officers or men, whether in a merchantman or a king's ship: *sailor* is used only for the common men, or, in the sea phrase, for those before the mast, particularly in vessels of war; hence our *sailors* and soldiers are spoken of as the defenders of our country; a *mariner* is an independent kind of *seaman* who manages his own vessel and goes on an expedition on his own account; fishermen and those who trade along the coast are in a particular manner distinguished by the name of *mariners*.

SEARCH. See EXAMINE; RUMMAGE; SEEK.

SEASON. See TIME.

SEASONABLE. See OPPORTUNE; TIMELY.

SECEDE. See RECEDE.

SECLUSION. See PRIVACY.

SECOND, SUPPORT. To *second* is to give the assistance of a *second* person; to *support* is to bear up on one's own shoulders. To *second* does not express so much as to *support*: we *second* only by our presence or our word; but we *support* by our influence and all the means that are in our power: we *second* a motion by a simple declaration of our assent to it; we *support* a motion by the force of persuasions: so likewise we are said always to *second* a person's views when we give him openly our countenance by declaring our approbation of his measures; and we are said to *support* him when we give the assistance of our purse, our influence, or any other thing essential for the attainment of an end.

Second, Secondary, Inferior.—*Second* and *secondary* both come from the Latin *secundus*, changed from *sequundus* and *sequi*, to follow, signifying the order of succession: the former simply expresses this order; but the latter includes the accessory idea of comparative demerit: a person stands *second* in a list, or a letter is *second* which immediately succeeds the first; but a consideration is *secondary*, or of *secondary* importance, which is opposed to that which holds the first rank. *Secondary* and *inferior* both designate some lower degree of a quality: but *secondary* is applied only to the importance or value of things; *inferior* is applied generally to all qualities: a man of business reckons everything as *secondary* which does not forward the object he has in view; men of *inferior* abilities are disqualified by nature for high and important stations, although they may be more fitted for lower stations than those of greater abilities.

SECRECY. See CONCEALMENT.

SECRET, HIDDEN, LATENT, OCCULT, MYSTERIOUS. What is *secret* (see CLANDESTINE) is so far removed as to be out of observation; what is *hidden* (see CONCEAL) is so covered over as to be altogether concealed: as a corner may be *secret*; a hole underground is *hidden*.

What is *secret* is known to some one; what is *hidden* may be known to no one: it rests in the breast of an individual to keep a thing *secret*; it depends on the course of things if anything remains *hidden*: every man has more or less of that which he wishes to keep *secret*; the talent of many lies *hidden* for want of opportunity to bring it into exercise, as many treasures lie *hidden* in the earth for want of being discovered and brought to light. A *secret* may concern only the individual or individuals who hold it, and those from whom it is kept; but that which is *hidden* may concern all the world: sometimes the success of a transaction depends upon its being kept *secret;* the stores of knowledge which yet remain *hidden* may be much greater than those which have been laid open. The *latent,* from the stem of Latin *latens,* lying hid, is the *secret* or concealed in cases where it ought to be open: a *latent* motive is that which a person intentionally, though not justifiably, keeps to himself; the *latent* cause for any proceeding is that which is not revealed.

Occult, in Latin *occultus,* participle of *occulere,* compounded of *ob,* over, and the stem found in *celare,* to hide, signifying that which is covered over; and *mysterious* (see DARK) are species of the *hidden:* the former connotes that which has a veil naturally thrown over it; the latter that mostly which is covered with a supernatural veil: an *occult* science is one that is *hidden* from the view of persons in general, which is attainable but by few; *occult* causes or qualities are those which lie too remote to be discovered by the inquirer: the operations of Providence are said to be *mysterious,* as they are altogether past our finding out; many points of doctrine in our religion are equally *mysterious,* as connected with and dependent upon the attributes of the Deity.

SECRET AGENT. See SPY.
SECRETE. See CONCEAL.
SECTARIAN. See HERETIC.
SECULAR, TEMPORAL, WORLDLY. *Secular,* in Latin *sæcularis,* from *sæculum,* an age or division of time, signifies belonging to time or this life. *Temporal,* in Latin *temporalis,* from *tempus,* time, signifies lasting only for a time. *Worldly* signifies after the manner of the *world* (from Anglo-Saxon *weoruld,* which is compounded of *wer,* a man, and *eld,* an age, signifying the age of a man, a man's life, the scene of a man's life).

Secular is opposed to ecclesiastical; *temporal* and *worldly* are opposed to spiritual or eternal. The idea of the *world* or the outward objects and pursuits of the *world,* in distinction from that which is set above the *world,* is implied in common by all the terms; but *secular* is an indifferent term, applicable to the legitimate pursuits and concerns of men; *temporal* is used either in an indifferent or a bad sense; and *worldly* mostly in a bad sense, as contrasted with things of more value. The office of a clergyman is ecclesiastical, but that of a school-master is *secular,* which is frequently vested in the same hands; the Upper House of Parliament consists of lords spiritual and *temporal; worldly* interest has a more powerful sway over the minds of the great bulk of mankind than their spiritual interests.

SECURE. See CERTAIN; PREPAREDNESS; SAFE.
SECURITY. See DEPOSIT; FENCE; GUARANTEE.
SEDATE. See COMPOSED.
SEDIMENT. See DREGS.
SEDITION. See INSURRECTION.
SEDITIOUS. See FACTIOUS; TUMULTUOUS.
SEDUCE. See ALLURE.
SEDULOUS, DILIGENT, ASSIDUOUS. The idea of application is expressed by these epithets; but *sedulous,* from the Latin *sedulus,* probably from *sedere,* to sit (the etymology *se,* apart, and *dolus,* guile, free from guile, working honestly, is an error), is a particular, *diligent* (see ACTIVE) is a general term: one is *sedulous* by habit; one is *diligent* either habitually or occasionally: a *sedulous* scholar pursues his studies with regular and close application; a scholar may be *diligent* at a certain period, though not invariably so. One is *sedulous* from a conviction of the importance of the thing; one may be *diligent* by fits and starts, according to the humor of the moment.

Assiduous (Latin *ad,* near, and *sedere,* to sit) and *sedulous* both express the quality of sitting or sticking close to a thing, but the former may, like *diligent,* be employed on a partial occasion; the latter is always permanent: we may be *assiduous* in our attentions to a person; but we are *sedulous* in the important concerns of life. *Sedulous* peculiarly concerns the quiet employments of life, but may be applied to any pursuit requiring persevering attention; a teacher may be entitled *sedulous*: *diligent* implies the active employments; one is *diligent* at work: *assiduity* holds a middle rank; it may be employed equally for that which requires active exertion or otherwise: we may be *assiduous* in the pursuits of literature, or we may be *assiduous* in our attendance upon a person or the performance of any office.

SEE, PERCEIVE, OBSERVE. *See*, Anglo-Saxon *seón*, may be either a voluntary or involuntary action: *perceive*, through French from the Latin *percipere*, based on *per*, thoroughly, and a weakened form of *capere*, to take into the mind, is always a voluntary action; and *observe* (see NOTICE) is an intentional action. The eye *sees* when the mind is absent; the mind and the eye or other senses *perceive* in conjunction: hence, we may say that a person *sees*, but does not *perceive*: we *observe* not merely by a simple act of the mind, but by its positive and fixed exertion. We *see* a thing without knowing what it is; we *perceive* a thing, and know what it is, but the impression passes away; we *observe* a thing, and afterward retrace the image of it in our mind. We *see* a star when the eye is directed toward it; we *perceive* it move if we look at it attentively; we *observe* its position in different parts of the heavens. The blind cannot *see*, the absent cannot *perceive*, the dull cannot *observe*. *Seeing*, as a corporeal action, is the act only of the eye; *perceiving* and *observing* are actions in which all the senses are concerned. We *see* colors, we *perceive* the state of the atmosphere and *observe* its changes.

Seeing sometimes extends further in its application to the mind's operations, in which it has an indefinite sense; but *perceive* and *observe* have both a definite sense; we may *see* a thing distinctly and clearly or otherwise; we *perceive* it always with a certain degree of distinctness, and *observe* it with a positive degree of minuteness: we *see* the truth of a remark; we *perceive* the force of an objection; we *observe* the reluctance of a person. It is further to be remarked, however, that, when *see* expresses a mental operation, it expresses what is

purely mental; *perceive* and *observe* are applied to such objects as are seen by the senses as well as the mind. We *see* the light with our eyes, or we *see* the truth of a proposition with our mind's eyes; but we *perceive* the difference of climate, or we *perceive* the difference in the comfort of our situation; we *observe* the motions of the heavenly bodies.

See also LOOK.

SEED. See GERM.

SEEK, SEARCH. To *seek* and *search* (see EXAMINE) are both employed in the sense of looking after something that is not in sight: *seek* applies to that which is near at hand and easily found; *search*, to that which is remote, hidden, or not to be found without difficulty: to *search*, therefore, is properly to *seek* laboriously; we *seek* a person by simply going to the place where he is supposed to be; *search* is made from place to place when it is not known where he is: a school-boy *seeks* birds' nests; the botanist *searches* for plants.

These terms may also be applied to moral objects with the same distinction: as to *seek* peace, knowledge; to *search* the thoughts, to *search* into mysteries.

SEEM, APPEAR. The idea of coming to the view is expressed by both these terms; but the word *seem* rises upon that of *appear*. *Seem*, from Anglo-Saxon *séman*, to satisfy, conciliate, signifies literally to *appear* like, and is therefore a species of *appearance*; *appear*, from the Latin *ad*, to, and *parere*, to come in sight, signifies to be present or before the eye. Every object may *appear*; but nothing *seems*, except that which the mind admits to *appear* in any given form. To *seem* requires some reflection and comparison of objects in the mind one with another; it is, therefore, peculiarly applicable to matters that may be different from what they *appear*, or of an indeterminate kind: that the sun *seems* to move is a conclusion which we draw from the exercise of our senses and comparing this case with others of a similar nature; it is only by a further research into the operation of nature that we discover this to be no conclusive proof of its motion. To *appear*, on the contrary, is the express act of things themselves on us; it is, therefore, peculiarly applicable to such objects as make an impression on us: to *appear* is the same as to present itself: the stars *appear* in the firmament, but we do not say that they *seem;* the sun *appears* dark through the clouds.

They are equally applicable to moral as well as natural objects with the above-mentioned distinction. *Seem* is said of that which is dubious, contingent, or future; *appear*, of that which is actual, positive, and past. A thing *seems* strange which we are led to conclude as strange from what we see of it: a thing *appears* clear when we have a clear conception of it: a plan *seems* practicable or impracticable; an author *appears* to understand his subject or the contrary. It *seems* as if all efforts to reform the bulk of mankind will be found inefficient; it *appears*, from the long catalogue of vices which are still very prevalent, that little progress has hitherto been made in the work of reformation.

SEEMLY. See BECOMING.

SEGREGATE, SEPARATE. *Segregate* and *separate* both mean to divide from something, to set apart. But *segregate*, from Latin *se*, meaning apart, away, and *gregare*, from *gregem*, accusative, meaning flock, herd, signifies to set apart in a group by itself. It means not merely to *separate* (see SEPARATE) but, after *separation*, to keep in a *separate* group. It is therefore a word of more specific meaning and narrower application.

SEIZE. See NAB.

SEIZURE. See CAPTURE.

SELECT. See SEGREGATE.

SELF-CONCEIT. See SELF-WILL.

SELFISH. See GREEDY.

SELF-WILL, SELF-CONCEIT, SELF-SUFFICIENCY. *Self-will* signifies the *will* in one's self: *self-conceit*, conceit of one's self: *self-sufficiency*, *sufficiency* in one's self. As characteristics they come very near to each other, but that disposition of the will which refuses to submit to every control either within or without is born with a person, and is among the earliest indications of character; in some it is less predominant than in others, but, if not early checked, it is that defect in our natures which will always prevail; *self-conceit* is a vicious habit of the mind which is superinduced on the original character; it is that which determines in matters of judgment: a *self-willed* person thinks nothing of right or wrong; whatever the impulse of the moment suggests is the motive to action: the *self-conceited* person is always much concerned about right and wrong, but it is only that which he conceives to be right and wrong; *self-sufficiency* is a species of *self-conceit* applied to action: as a *self-conceited* person thinks of no opinion but his own; a *self-sufficient* person refuses the assistance of every one in whatever he is called upon to do.

SEMBLANCE. See SHOW.

SENIOR, ELDER, OLDER. These are all comparatives expressive of the same quality, and differ, therefore, less in sense than in application. *Senior* is employed not only in regard to the extent of age, but also to duration either in office or any given situation: *elder* is employed only in regard to age: an officer in the army is a *senior* by virtue of having served longer than another; a boy is a *senior* in a school either by virtue of his age, his standing in the school, or his situation in the class; when, therefore, age alone is to be expressed, *elder* is more suitable than *senior;* the *elder* children or the *elder* branches of a family are clearly understood to include those who have priority of age.

Senior and *elder* are both employed as substantives, *older* only as an adjective: hence we speak of the *seniors* in a school, or the *elders* in an assembly; but an *older* inhabitant, an *older* family. *Elder* has only a partial use; *older* is employed in general cases: in speaking of children in the same family we may say the *elder* son is heir to the estate; he is *older* than his brother by ten years.

SENSATION. See FEELING; SENTIMENT.

SENSE, JUDGMENT. *Sense.* (see FEELING) signifies in general the faculty of feeling corporeally or perceiving mentally; in the latter case it is synonymous with *judgment*, which is a special operation of the mind. The *sense* is that primitive portion of the understanding which renders an account of things; and the *judgment* that portion of the reason which selects or rejects from this account. The *sense* is, so to speak, the reporter which collects the details and exposes the facts; the *judgment* is the *judge* that passes sentence upon them. According to the strict import of the terms, the *judgment* depends upon the *sense*, and varies with it in degree. He who has no *sense* has no *judgment;* and he who loses *sense* loses *judgment:* since *sense* supplies the knowledge of things, and *judgment* pronounces upon them, it is evident that there must be *sense* before there can be *judgment.*

On the other hand, *sense* may be so distinguished from *judgment* that there may be *sense* without *judgment*, and *judgment* without *sense: sense* is the faculty of perceiving in general; it is applied to abstract science as well as general knowledge: *judgment* is the faculty of determining, that is, of determining mostly in matters of practice. By *sense* the mind perceives by an immediate act, by the *judgment* it arrives at conclusions by a process. It is the lot of many, therefore, to have *sense* in matters of theory who have no *judgment* in matters of practice; while others, on the contrary, who have nothing above common *sense* will have a soundness of *judgment* that is not to be surpassed. Nay, further, it is possible for a man to have good *sense* and yet not solid *judgment:* as they are both natural faculties, men are gifted with them as variously as with every other faculty. By good *sense* a man is enabled to discern, as it were, intuitively, that which requires another of less *sense* to ponder over and study; by solid *judgment* a man is enabled to avoid those errors in conduct which one of weak *judgment* is always falling into. There is, however, this distinction between *sense* and *judgment*, that the deficiencies of the former may be supplied by diligence and attention; but a defect in the latter is not so easily to be supplied by efforts of one's own. A man may improve his *sense* in proportion as he has the means of information; but the *judgment* once matured rarely makes any advances toward improvement afterward.

The words *sense* and *judgment* are frequently employed without any epithets to denote a positively large share of these faculties.

As epithets, *sensible* and *judicious* both denote the possession of these faculties in a high degree, but in their application they are distinguished as above. A writer or a speaker is said to be *sensible;* a friend, or an adviser, to be *judicious. Sense* displays itself in the conversation or the communication of one's ideas; *judgment* in the propriety of one's actions. A *sensible* man may be an entertaining companion, but a *judicious* man in any post of command is an inestimable treasure. *Sensible* remarks are always calculated to please and interest *sensible* people; *judicious* measures have a sterling value in themselves that is appreciated according to the importance of the object. Hence it is obvious that to be *sensible* is a desirable thing, but to be *judicious* is an indispensable requisite in those who have to act a part.

See also SIGNIFICATION.

Sensible, Sensitive, Sentient. — All these epithets, which are derived from the same source, have obviously a great sameness of meaning, though not of application. *Sensible* and *sensitive* both denote the capacity of being moved to feeling: *sentient* implies the very act of feeling. *Sensible* expresses either a habit of the body and mind or only a particular state referring to some particular object: a person may be *sensible* of things in general, or *sensible* of cold, *sensible* of injuries, *sensible* of the kindnesses which he has received from an individual. *Sensitive* signifies always an habitual or permanent quality; it is the characteristic of objects: a *sensitive* creature implies one whose *sense* is quickly to be acted upon; a *sensitive* plant is a peculiar species of plants, marked for the property of having *sense* or being *sensible* of the touch.

Sensible and *sensitive* have always a reference to external objects; but *sentient* expresses simply the possession of feeling or the power of feeling, and excludes the idea of the cause. Hence, the terms *sensible* and *sensitive* are applied only to persons or corporeal objects: but *sentient*, which conveys the most abstract meaning, is applicable to men and spirits; *sentient* beings, taken absolutely, may include angels as well as men; it is restricted in its meaning by the context only.

Sensible, Perceptible.—These epithets are here applied not to the persons capable of being impressed, but to the objects capable of impressing: in this case *sensible* (see FEEL) applies to that which acts on the *senses* merely; *perceptible* (see SEE), to that which acts on the *senses* in conjunction with the mind. All corporeal objects are naturally termed *sensible*, inasmuch as they are *sensible* to the eye, the ear, the nose, the touch, and the taste; particular things are *perceptible*, inasmuch as they are to be *perceived* or recognized by the mind. Sometimes *sensible* signifies discernible by means of the *senses*, as when we speak of a *sensible* difference in the atmosphere, and in this case it comes nearer to the meaning of *perceptible;* but the latter always refers more to the operation of the mind than the former: the difference between colors is said to be scarcely *perceptible* when they approach very near to each other, so likewise the growth of a body is said not to be *perceptible* when it cannot be marked from one time to another by the difference of state.

SENSIBILITY. See FEELING.

SENSITIVE. See SENSIBLE.

SENSUALIST, VOLUPTUARY, EPICURE. The *sensualist* lives for the indulgence of his senses: the *voluptuary* (from *voluptas*, pleasure) is devoted to his pleasures, and as far as these pleasures are the pleasures of sense the *voluptuary* is a *sensualist:* the *epicure*, from *Epicurus*, is one who makes the pleasures of sense his god, and in this sense he is a *sensualist* and a *voluptuary.* In the application of these terms, however, the *sensualist* is one who is a slave to the grossest appetites; the *voluptuary* is one who studies his pleasures so as to make them the most valuable to himself; the *epicure* is a species of *voluptuary* who practices more than ordinary refinement in the choice of his pleasures.

SENTENCE, PROPOSITION, PERIOD, PHRASE. *Sentence*, in Latin *sententia*, is but a variation of *sentiment* (see OPINION). *Proposition* (see PROPOSAL). *Period*, in Latin *periodus*, Greek περίοδος, from περί, about, and ὁδός, way, signifies the circuit or round of words which renders the sense complete. *Phrase*, from the Greek φράζειν, to speak, signifies the words uttered.

The *sentence* consists of any words which convey sentiment: the *proposition* consists of the thing set before the mind, that is, either our own minds or the minds of others; hence the term *sentence* has more special regard to the form of words, and the *proposition* to the matter contained: they are both used technically or otherwise, the former in grammar and rhetoric, the latter in logic. The *sentence* is simple and complex; the *proposition* is universal or particular. *Period* and *phrase*, like *sentence*, are forms of words, but they are solely so, whereas the *sentence* depends on the connection of ideas by which it is formed: we speak of *sentences* either as to their structure or their sentiment; hence the *sentence* is either grammatical or moral: but the *period* regards only the structure; it is either well or ill turned: the term *phrase* denotes the character of the words; hence it is either vulgar or polite, idiomatic or general: the *sentence* must consist of at least two words to make sense; the *phrase* may be a single word or otherwise.

See also DECISION.

Sentence, Doom, Condemn.—To *sentence*, or pass *sentence*, is to give a final opinion or decision which is to influence the fate of an object. *Condemn*, from *con* for *cum*, wholly, and *damnare*, to harm or punish, is to pass such a *sentence* as shall be to the hurt of an object. *Doom* comes from Anglo-Saxon *dom*, a thing set or decided on, from the verb *don*, to do, Modern English *do*.

When these terms are taken in the judicial sense, to *sentence* is indefinite as to the quantum of punishment, which may be great or small; a criminal may be *sentenced* to a mild or severe punishment: to *condemn* and *doom* are always employed to denote a severe punishment, and the latter still severer than the former. A person is *condemned* to the galleys, to transportation for life, or to death; he is *doomed* to eternal misery.

To *sentence* is always the act of some conscious agent; but to *condemn* and *doom* may be the effect of circumstances or brought about by the nature of things. A person is always *sentenced* by some one to suffer in consequence of his conduct; he is *condemned* or *doomed*, either by his misfortune or his fault, to suffer whatever circumstances impose upon him; immoral writers are justly *condemned* to oblivion or infamy; or persons may be *condemned* by their hard lot to struggle through life for a bare living; and some are *doomed* by a still harder lot to penury and wretchedness.

To *sentence* is to pass sentence in the judicial sense only; but the noun *sentence* is taken in the sense of a judgment, and has likewise a moral as well as a judicial application, in which latter case it admits of a further comparison with *condemn* or *condemnation*. The *sentence* is a formal and the *condemnation* an informal judgment: the *sentence* may be favorable or unfavorable: the *condemnation* is always unfavorable: critics pronounce their *sentence* on the merits or demerits of a work; the public may *condemn* a measure in any manner by which they make their sentiments known. To *doom*, which signifies only to determine the fate of a person, is not allied to the other terms in their moral application.

Sententious, Sentimental. — Sententious signifies having or abounding in *sentences* or judgments; *sentimental*, having *sentiment* (see OPINION). Books and authors are termed *sententious;* but travellers, society, intercourse, correspondence, and the like are characterized as *sentimental*. Moralists, whose works and conversation abound in moral *sentences*, like Dr. Johnson's, are termed *sententious;* novelists and romance-writers, like Mrs. Radcliffe, are properly *sentimental*. *Sententious* books always serve for improvement; *sentimental* works, unless they are of a superior order, are in general hurtful.

SENTIENT. See SENSIBLE.

SENTIMENT, SENSATION, PERCEPTION. *Sentiment* and *sensation* are obviously derived from the same source (see FEEL). *Perception*, from *perceive* (see SEE), expresses the act of *perceiving* or the impressions produced by *perceiving*.

The impressions which objects make upon the person are designated by all these terms; but the *sentiment* has its seat in the heart, the *sensation* is confined to the senses, and the *perception* rests in the understanding. *Sentiments* are lively, *sensations* are grateful, *perceptions* are clear. Gratitude is a *sentiment* most pleasing to the human mind: the *sensation* produced by the action of electricity on the frame is generally unpleasant; a nice *perception* of objects is one of the first requisites for perfection in any art.

The *sentiment* extends to manners and renders us alive to the happiness or misery of others as well as our own; it is that by which men are most nearly allied to each other: the *sensation* is purely physical, and the effect of external objects upon either the body or the mind: *perceptions* carry us into the district of science; they give us an interest in all the surrounding objects as intellectual observers. A man of spirit or courage receives marks of honor, or affronts, with very different *sentiments* from the poltroon; he who bounds his happiness by the present fleeting existence must be careful to remove every painful *sensation:* we judge of objects as complex or simple according to the number of *perceptions* which they produce in us.

See also OPINION.

SENTINEL. See GUARD.

SEPARATE, SEVER, DISJOIN, DETACH. To *separate* (see ABSTRACT) is the general term: whatever is united or joined in any way may be *separated*, be the junction natural or artificial; but to *sever*, which is but a variation of *separate*, is a mode of *separating* natural bodies or bodies naturally joined: we may *separate* in part or entirely; we *sever* entirely: we *separate* with or without violence; we *sever* with violence only: we may *separate* papers which have been pasted together or fruits which have grown together; but the *head* is *severed* from the body or a branch from the trunk.

To *separate* may be said of things which are only remotely connected; *disjoin*, signifying to destroy a junction, is said of that which is intimately connected so as to be joined: we *separate* as convenience requires; we **may** *separate* in a right or a wrong manner; we mostly *disjoin* things which ought to remain joined: we *separate* syllables in order to distinguish them; but they are sometimes *disjoined* in writing by an accidental erasure. To *detach*, from Latin *de*, from, and French *tacher*, perhaps from a German word akin to the English tack or nail, signifying to take from a nail, has an intermediate sense between *separate* and *disjoin*, applying to bodies which are neither so loosely connected as the former nor so closely as the latter: we *separate* things that directly meet in no point; we *disjoin* those which may meet in many points; we *detach* those things which meet in one point only.

Separate, *sever*, and *detach* may be applied to mental as well as corporeal objects; persons may be *separated* from each other by diversity of interests or opinions; they may be *severed* from each other when their affections are estranged toward each other; they may be *detached* from each other by circumstances after having been attached by any tie.

See also DIFFERENT; DIVIDE; SEGREGATE.

SEPARATION. See DIVORCE.

SEPULCHRE. See GRAVE.

SEPULTURE. See BURIAL.

SEQUEL, CLOSE. *Sequel* is a species of *close;* it is that which follows by way of termination; but the *close* is simply that which *closes*, or puts an end to anything. There cannot be a *sequel* without a *close*, but there may be a *close* without a *sequel*. A story may have either a *sequel* or a *close;* when the end is detached from the beginning so as to follow, it is a *sequel;* if the beginning and end are uninterrupted, it is simply a *close*. When a work is published in distinct parts, those which follow at the end may be termed the *sequel;* if it appears all at once, the concluding pages are the *close*.

SERENE. See CALM.

SERIES, COURSE. A *series*, in Latin *series*, from *serere*, to bind or connect, is applied to things which are connected with each other simply in order of time or number. *Course*, in Latin *cursus*, from *currere*, to run, signifying the line formed or the direction

taken in running, applies to things which are so connected as to form, as it were, a line; a *series* of events are such as follow in order of time; a *series* of numbers of any work are such as follow in numerical order; a *course* of events is such as tends to the same end; a *course* of lectures, such as is delivered on the same subject.

See also SUCCESSION.

SERIOUS. See EAGER; GRAVE.

SERRATED. See JAGGED.

SERVANT, DOMESTIC, MENIAL, DRUDGE. In the term *servant* is included the idea of the service performed: in the term *domestic*, ultimately from *domus*, a house, is included the idea of one belonging to the house or family: in the word *menial*, from Old French *meisnee* (from Low Latin *mansionata*), a household (compare the title of Ruskin's book *Love's Meinie*), there is a similar suggestion; *drudge* comes from an Anglo-Saxon root signifying to endure, and is allied to *drudgery*, meaning hard and unpleasant work. We hire a *servant* at a certain rate and for a particular service; we are attached to our *domestics* according to their assiduity and attention to our wishes; we employ as a *menial* one who is unfit for a higher employment; and a *drudge* in any labor, however hard and disagreeable.

SERVICE. See BENEFIT; UTILITY.

SERVITUDE, SLAVERY, BONDAGE. *Servitude* expresses less than *slavery*, and this less than *bondage*.

Servitude, based on *servire*, conveys simply the idea of performing a service without specifying the principle upon which it is performed. Among the Romans, *servus* signified a slave, because all who served were literally slaves, the power over the person being almost unlimited. The mild influence of Christianity has corrected men's notions with regard to their rights as well as their duties, and established *servitude* on the just principle of a mutual compact, without any infraction of that most precious of all human gifts, personal liberty. *Slavery*, which marks a condition incompatible with the existence of this invaluable endowment, is a term odious to the modern ear: it had its origin in the grossest state of society, the word being derived from the Late Latin *sclavus*, from *Sclavi* or *Slavi* (cf. the Russian *slava,* glory), a fierce and intrepid people who made a long stand against the Germans, and, being at last defeated, were made *slaves. Slavery,* therefore, includes not only *servitude,* but also the odious circumstances of the entire subjection of one individual to another. *Bondage* came through Anglo-French from the Scandinavian *bondi,* a tiller of the soil (compare *husband*), but it has been associated in the popular mind with the verb *bind;* it signifies *slavery* in its most aggravated form, in which, to the loss of personal liberty, is added cruel treatment; the term is seldom applied in its proper sense to any persons but the Israelites in Egypt. In a figurative sense we speak of being a *slave* to our passions, and under the *bondage* of sin, in which cases the terms preserve precisely the same distinction.

The same distinction exists between the epithets *servile* and *slavish,* which are employed only in the moral application. He who is *servile* has the mean character of a servant, but he is still a free agent; but he who is *slavish* is bound and fettered in every possible form.

SET. See **PUT.**

SETTLE. See **ARBITRATE; COMPOSE; FIX; RATIFY.**

SEVENTH DAY. See **SABBATH.**

SEVER. See **SEPARATE.**

SEVERAL. See **DIFFERENT.**

SEVERE. See **AUSTERE; HARSH; STRICT.**

SEX. See **GENDER.**

SHACKLE. See **CHAIN.**

SHADE, SHADOW. *Shade* and *shadow* both come from Anglo-Saxon *scæd, sceadu,* a shadow. Both these terms express that darkness which is occasioned by the sun's rays being intercepted by any body; but *shade* simply expresses the absence of the light, and *shadow* signifies also the figure of the body which thus intercepts the light. Trees naturally produce a *shade,* by means of their branches and leaves: and wherever the image of the tree is reflected on the earth that forms its *shadow.* It is agreeable in the heat of summer to sit in the *shade;* the constancy with which the *shadow* follows the man has been proverbially adopted as a simile for one who clings close to another.

In the moral application they are more widely distinguished in their signification. As a *shade* implies darkness, so to be in the *shade* is the same as to be in obscurity; as the *shadow* is but a reflection or appearance, so, in the moral sense, the *shadow* of a thing is that which is opposed to the substance.

SHAKE, TREMBLE, SHUDDER, QUIVER, QUAKE. *Shake* is in Anglo-Saxon *sceacan;* and *shudder* is a frequentative verb based on Old Low German expressing a similar idea. *Quake* is derived from Anglo-Saxon *cwacian,* having the same meaning. *Quiver* comes from Anglo-Saxon *cwifer* in the adverb *cwifer-lice,* eagerly. *Tremble* comes from Low Latin *tremulare,* from classical Latin *tremulus,* trembling.

To *shake* is a generic term, the rest are but modes of *shaking:* to *tremble* is to *shake* from an inward cause or what appears to be so: in this manner a person *trembles* from fear, from cold, or weakness; and a leaf which is imperceptibly agitated by the air is also said to *tremble:* to *shudder* is to *tremble* violently: to *quiver* and to *quake* are both to *tremble* quickly; but the former denotes rather a vibratory motion, as the point of a spear when thrown against wood: the latter a quick motion of the whole body, as in the case of bodies that have not sufficient consistency in themselves to remain still.

Shake, Agitate, Toss. — Shake (see above). *Agitate,* in Latin *agitare,* is a frequentative of *ago,* to drive, that is, to drive different ways. *Toss* is probably contracted from *torsi,* perfect of *torqueo,* to whirl.

A motion more or less violent is signified by all these terms, which differ both in the manner and the cause of the motion. *Shake* is indefinite, it may differ in degree as to the violence; to *agitate* and *toss* rise in sense upon the word *shake:* a breeze *shakes* a leaf, a storm *agitates* the sea, and the waves *toss* a vessel to and fro: large and small bodies may be *shaken;* large bodies are *agitated:* a handkerchief may be *shaken;* the earth is *agitated* by an earthquake. What is *shaken* and *agitated* is not removed from its place;

but what is *tossed* is thrown from place to place. A house may frequently be *shaken*, while the foundation remains good; the waters are most *agitated* while they remain within their bounds; but a ball is *tossed* from hand to hand.

To *shake* and *toss* are the acts either of persons or things; to *agitate* is the act of things when taken in the active sense. A person *shakes* the hand of another, or the motion of a carriage *shakes* persons in general and *agitates* those who are weak in frame: a child *tosses* his food about; or the violent motion of a vessel *tosses* everything about which is in it. To *shake* arises from external or internal causes; we may be *shaken* by others, or *shake* ourselves from cold: to *agitate* and *toss* arise from some external action, direct or indirect; the body may be *agitated* by violent concussion from without, or from the action of perturbed feelings; the body may be *tossed* by various circumstances, and the mind may be *tossed* to and fro by the violent action of the passions. Hence the propriety of using the terms in the moral application. The resolution is *shaken*, as the tree is by the wind; the *mind* is *agitated* like troubled waters; a person is *tossed* to and fro in the ocean of life, as the vessel is *tossed* by the waves.

SHALLOW. See SUPERFICIAL.

SHAME. See ABASH; DISHONOR.

SHAMELESS. See IMMODEST.

SHAPE. See FORM.

SHARE. See DIVIDE; PART; PARTAKE.

SHARP, ACUTE, KEEN. The general property expressed by these epithets is that of *sharpness*, or an ability to cut. The term *sharp*, in Anglo-Saxon *scearp*, to cut, is generic and indefinite; the two others are modes of *sharpness* differing in the circumstance or the degree: the *acute* is not only more than *sharp* in the common sense, but signifies also *sharp*-pointed: a knife may be *sharp*, but a needle is properly *acute*. Things are *sharp* that have either a long or a pointed edge; but the *keen* is applicable only to the long edge, and that in the highest degree of *sharpness:* a common knife may be *sharp;* but a razor or a lancet is properly said to be *keen*. These terms preserve the same distinction in their figurative use. Every pain is *sharp* which may resemble that which is produced by cutting; it is *acute* when it resembles that produced by piercing deep: words are said to be *sharp* which have any power in them to wound; they are *keen* when they cut deep and wide.

See also ACUTE; TRENCHANT.

SHARP-SHOOTER, MARKSMAN, SNIPER. *Sharp-shooter* is a compound of *sharp*, in Anglo-Saxon *scearp*, and English *shooter*. A *sharp-shooter*, as a *marksman*, is one skilled in shooting with a revolver or rifle at a target or other object. In warfare a *sharp-shooter* is an expert *marksman* selected to pick off an enemy at long range or under unusual conditions, and his employment is considered legitimate.

A *sniper*, on the contrary, is a sneaking soldier or other person, skilled in the use of a rifle, who fires from the roof or upper windows of a building on persons passing in the street below. On the occupation of Vera Cruz, Mexico, by United States forces in 1914, much annoyance was caused soldiers passing on the streets by shots from concealed *snipers*.

SHED. See POUR.

SHELTER. See ASYLUM; COVER; HARBOR.

SHIBBOLETH, CRITERION, PASSWORD, TEST. *Shibboleth*, in Hebrew *shibbóleth*, meaning an ear of corn, also a river, from *shábal*, to grow, to flow, signifies, specifically, the test-word or password used by the Gileadites, under Jephthah, after their victory over the Ephraimites, as recorded in Judges xii, 6. The latter were unable to pronounce the *sh*, and, in attempting to escape, gave the word as *sibbóleth*, by which they betrayed themselves, and were slaughtered mercilessly.

Figuratively, the term is now used as a watchword, password, testword, or countersign of a political party, sect, or other organization, and, as such, it implies a *criterion*, a standard, law, principle, or fact by which the quality of anything may be estimated, or, as applied to persons, that by which they may be identified or have their accounts of themselves established. A *watchword*, *password*, or *testword*, in military, naval, political, and society usage, is a word or phrase given to persons entitled thereto by which they can prove themselves when questioned.

For a critical comparison of *criterion* and *standard* see the article on the former term.

SHIFT. See EVASION.

SHINE, GLITTER, GLARE, SPARKLE, RADIATE. *Shine* is in Anglo-Saxon *scinan*. *Glitter* comes from Anglo-Saxon *glitinian*, to shine. *Glare* is derived from Anglo-Saxon *glær*, a pellucid substance, amber, where the *r* stands for an older *s*; hence *glare* is closely allied to *glass*. To *sparkle* signifies to produce *sparks;* and *spark* is in Anglo-Saxon *spearca*, and refers to the crackling sound of the firebrand. To *radiate* is to produce rays, from the Latin *radius*, a ray.

The emission of light is the common idea conveyed by these terms. To *shine* expresses simply this general idea: *glitter* and the other verbs include some collateral idea in their signification. To *shine* is a steady emission of light; to *glitter* is an unsteady emission of light, occasioned by the reflection on transparent or bright bodies: the sun and moon *shine* whenever they make their appearance; but a set of diamonds *glitters* by the irregular reflection of the light on them; or the brazen spire of a steeple *glitters* when the sun in the morning *shines* upon it. This is the same in the improper as the proper application.

Shine specifies no degree of light; it may be barely sufficient to render itself visible, or it may be a very strong degree of light: *glare*, on the contrary, denotes the highest possible degree of light: the sun frequently *glares* when it *shines* only at intervals; and the eye also *glares*.

To *shine* is to emit light in a full stream; but to *sparkle* is to emit it in small portions, and to *radiate* is to emit it in long lines. The fire *sparkles* in the burning of wood; or the light of the sun *sparkles* when it strikes on knobs or small points; or the eye *sparkles:* the sun *radiates* when it seems to emit its light in rays.

SHIPPER. See COMMON-CARRIER.

SHOCK, CONCUSSION. *Shock* de-

notes a violent jolt or agitation; *concussion*, a shaking together. The *shock* is often instantaneous, but does not necessarily extend beyond the act of the moment; the *concussion* is permanent in its consequences, it tends to derange the system. Hence the different application of the terms: the *shock* may affect either the body or the mind; the *concussion* affects properly only the body or corporeal objects: a violent and sudden blow produces a *shock* at the moment it is given, but it does not always produce a *concussion:* the violence of a fall will, however, sometimes produce a *concussion* in the brain, which in future affects the intellect.

As *shock* conveys no idea of separation, only of impression, it is equally applicable to the mind and the body. Sudden news of an exceedingly painful nature will often produce a *shock* on the mind; but time mostly serves to wear away the effect which has been produced.

SHOCKING. See FORMIDABLE.

SHOOT, DART. To *shoot* and *dart*, in the proper sense, are clearly distinguished from each other, as expressing different modes of sending bodies to a distance from a given point. From the circumstances of the actions arise their different application to other objects in the improper sense; as that which proceeds by *shooting* goes forth from a body unexpectedly and with great rapidity: so, in the figurative sense, a plant *shoots* up, or a star is said to *shoot* in the sky which seems to move in a *shooting* manner from one place to another.

SHORT, BRIEF, CONCISE, SUCCINCT, SUMMARY. *Short*, Anglo-Saxon *sceort*, comes from a root meaning to cut; it is the generic, the rest are specific terms: everything which admits of dimensions may be *short*, as opposed to the long, that is, either naturally or artificially; the rest are species of artificial *shortness*, or that which is the work of art: hence it comes that material, as well as spiritual, objects may be termed *short:* but *brief*, in Latin *brevis*, in Greek βραχύς, *concise*, from Latin *concisus*, signifying cut into a small body, *succinct*, in Latin *succinctus*, participle of *sub*, up, and *cingere*, to girdle, meaning to draw up the skirts under the girdle, and fasten that tightly, signifying therefore brought within a small compass, and *summary* (see ABRIDGMENT) are intellectual or spiritual only. We may term a stick, a letter, or a discourse *short;* but we speak of *brevity* only in regard to the mode of speech; *conciseness* and *succinctness* as to the matter of speech; *summary* as to the mode either of speaking or acting: the *brief* is opposed to the lengthy or prolix; the *concise* and *succinct* to the diffuse; the *summary* to the circumstantial or ceremonious. It is a matter of comparatively little importance whether a man's life be long or *short;* but it deeply concerns him that every moment be well spent: *brevity* of expression ought to be consulted by speakers, even more than by writers; *conciseness* is of peculiar advantage in the formation of rules for young persons; and *succinctness* is a requisite in every writer who has extensive materials to digest; a *summary* mode of proceeding may have the advantage of saving time, but it has the disadvantage of incorrectness and often of injustice.

SHOVE. See PUSH.

SHOW, POINT OUT, MARK, INDICATE. *Show,* Anglo-Saxon *scéawian,* to see, then to make to see, is here the general term, and the others specific: the common idea included in the signification of them all is that of making a thing visible to another. To *show* is an indefinite term; one *shows* by simply setting a thing before the eyes of another: to *point out,* to fix a *point* upon a thing, is specific; it is to *show* some particular *point* by a direct and immediate application to it: we *show* a person a book when we put it into his hands; but we *point out* the beauties of its contents by making a *point* upon them or accompanying the action with some particular movement which shall direct the attention of the observer in a specific manner. Many things, therefore, may be *shown* which cannot be *pointed out:* a person *shows* himself, but he does not *point* himself *out;* towns, houses, gardens, and the like are *shown;* but single things of any description are *pointed out.*

To *show* and *point out* are direct personal acts; to *mark,* i. e., to put a

mark on, is an indirect means of making a thing visible or observable: a tradesman *marks* the prices of the articles which he sets forth in his shop.

Show and *mark* denote the acts of conscious or unconscious agents; *point out,* that of conscious agents only: *indicate* (see MARK) that of unconscious agents only; in this case, what *shows* serves as an evidence or proof; what *marks* serves to direct or guide; what *indicates* serves as an index to *point out.* That *shows* the fallacy of forming schemes for the future; it *marks* the progress of time; it *indicates* decay.

In an extended moral application they preserve the same distinction; to *show* is to prove in a general way that a thing is or will be; to *indicate* is to *show* or *point out* in a particular manner that a thing is.

Show, Exhibit, Display. — To *show* is here, as before, the generic term; to *exhibit* (see GIVE) and *display,* from Old French *despleier,* derived from Latin *dis,* apart, and *plicare,* to fold, signifying to unfold or set forth to view, are specific: they may all designate the acts either of persons or things: the first, however, does this either in the proper or the improper sense; the latter two rather in the improper sense. To *show* is an indefinite action applied to every object: things are *shown* for purposes of convenience; as one *shows* a book to a friend: *exhibit* is applied to matters that are extraordinary or unusual; things are *exhibited* to attract notice, as to *exhibit* flowers or animals: we *show* to one or many; we *exhibit* or *display* in as public a manner, and to as great numbers, as possible; as to *show* the marks to the by-standers; to *exhibit* a figure upon a pole; to *display* one's finery.

They admit of the same distinction when applied to moral objects: we may *show* courage, dislike, or any other emotion: *exhibit* skill, prowess, etc., in the field of battle; *display* heroism, and whatever may shine forth.

When said of things, they differ principally in the manner or degree of clearness with which the thing appears to present itself to view: to *show* is, as before, altogether indefinite, and implies simply to bring to view; *exhibit* implies to bring inherent properties to light, that is, apparently by a process; to *display* is to set forth so as to strike the eye: the windows on a frosty morning will *show* the state of the weather; experiments with the air-pump *exhibit* the many wonderful and interesting properties of air; the beauties of the creation are peculiarly *displayed* in the spring season.

See also UNVEIL.

Show, Exhibition, Representation, Sight, Spectacle. — *Show* signifies the thing shown; *exhibition* signifies the thing exhibited; *representation*, the thing represented; *sight*, the thing to be seen; and *spectacle*, from the Latin *spectaculum*, based on *spectare*, stands for the thing to be beheld.

Show is here, as in the former article, the most general term. Everything set forth to view is *shown;* and, if set forth for the amusement of others, it is a *show*. This is the common idea included in the terms *exhibition* and *representation:* but *show* is a term of vulgar meaning and application; the others have a higher use and signification. The *show* consists of that which merely pleases the eye; it is not a matter either of taste or art, but merely of curiosity: an *exhibition*, on the contrary, presents some effort of talent or some work of genius; and a *representation* sets forth the image or imitation of something by the power of art: hence we speak of a *show* of wild beasts, an *exhibition* of paintings, and a theatrical *representation*. The conjurer makes a *show* of his tricks at a fair, to the wonder of the gazing multitude; the artist makes an *exhibition* of his works; *representations* of men and manners are given on the stage.

Shows, exhibitions, and *representations* are presented by some one to the view of others; *sights* and *spectacles* present themselves to view. *Sight*, like *show*, is a vulgar term, and *spectacle* the nobler term. Whatever is to be seen to excite notice is a *sight*, in which general sense it would comprehend every *show*, but in its particular sense it includes only that which casually offers itself to view; a *spectacle*, on the contrary, is that species of *sight* which has something in it to interest either the heart or the head of the observer:

processions, reviews, sports, and the like are *sights;* but battles, bull-fights, or public games of any description are *spectacles*, which interest and stimulate the feelings.

Show, Outside, Appearance, Semblance. — Where there is *show* there must be *outside* and *appearance;* but there may be the last without the former. The term *show* always denotes an action, and refers to some person or thing as agent; but the *outside* may be merely the passive quality of something. We speak, therefore, of a thing as mere *show*, to signify that what is shown is all that exists; and in this sense it may be termed mere *outside*, as consisting only of what is on the *outside*. In describing a house, however, we speak of its *outside*, and not of its *show;* as also of the *outside* of a book, and not of the *show*. *Appearance* denotes an action as well as *show;* but the former is the act of an unconscious agent, the latter of one that is conscious and voluntary: the *appearance* presents itself to the view; the *show* is purposely presented to view. A person makes a *show* so as to be seen by others; his *appearance* is that which shows itself in him. To look only to *show*, or to be concerned for *show* only, signifies to be concerned for that only which will attract notice; to look only to the *outside* signifies to be concerned only for that which may be seen in a thing, to the disregard of that which is not seen: to look only to *appearances* signifies the same as the former, except that *outside* is said in the proper sense of that which literally strikes the eye; but *appearances* extend to a man's conduct and whatever may affect his reputation.

Semblance, from Old French *semblance*, formed with suffix *ance* from Latin -*antia*, on Old French *sembl-*er, from Latin *simulare*, to make like, always conveys the idea of an unreal *appearance*, or at least is contrasted with that which is real; he who wears only the *semblance* of friendship would be ill deserving the confidence of a friend.

Show, Parade, Ostentation. — These terms are synonymous when they imply abstract actions: *show* is here, as in the preceding article, taken in the vulgar sense; *ostentation* and *parade* include the idea of something particular. *Show* consists simply in letting that be seen which a person might, if he pleased, keep out of view; *parade* is a studious effort to show, which serves to attract notice: in this manner a person may make a *show* of his equipage or furniture who sets it out to be seen; he makes a *parade* of his wealth if he sets it forth with any artifice or formality so as to make it more striking. *Ostentation* is, like *parade*, a studied show, but it refers rather to the intention of the person than to the method by which the *show* is made. *Show* and *parade* may, therefore, according to the circumstances, serve the purpose of *ostentation*. A person makes a *show* of his liberality, or a *parade* of his gifts, and thus he gratifies his *ostentation*.

When taken in reference to things, the *show* is opposed to the reality; it is that which shows itself: the *parade* and *ostentation* is that which is ceremonious and artificial: the former in respect to what strikes the eye, and the latter in respect to what strikes the mind.

Showy, Gaudy, Gay.—*Showy*, having or being full of *show*, is mostly an epithet of dispraise; that which is *showy* has seldom anything to deserve notice beyond that which catches the eye: *gaudy*, from Latin *gaudere*, to rejoice, signifies literally full of joy, and is applied figuratively to the exterior of objects, but with the annexed bad idea of being striking to an excess: *gay*, Old French *gai*, Old High German *wàhi*, fine, beautiful, is used in the same sense as an epithet of praise: it is in this sense that the *gay* science of the Provençal troubadours was taken. Some things may be *showy*, and in their nature properly so; thus the tail of a peacock is *showy:* artificial objects may likewise be *showy*, but they will not be preferred by persons of taste: that which is *gaudy* is always artificial, and is always chosen by the vain, the vulgar, and the ignorant; a maid-servant will bedizen herself with *gaudy*-colored ribbons. That which is *gay* is either nature itself or nature imitated in the best manner: spring is a *gay* season, and flowers are its *gayest* accompaniments.

See also THEATRICAL.

SHREWD. See ACUTE.
SHRIEK. See CRY.
SHRINK. See QUAIL; SPRING.
SHUDDER. See SHAKE.
SHUT. See BLOCKADE; CLOSE.

SICK, SICKLY, DISEASED, MORBID. *Sick* denotes a partial state, *sickly* a permanent state, of the body, a proneness to be *sick:* he who is *sick* may be made well; but he who is *sickly* is seldom really well: all persons are liable to be *sick*, though few have the misfortune to be *sickly:* a person may be *sick* from the effects of cold, violent exercise, and the like; but he is *sickly* only from constitution.

Sickly expresses a permanent state of indisposition unless otherwise qualified; but *diseased* expresses a violent state of derangement without specifying its duration; it may be for a time only or for a permanency: the person or his constitution is *sickly;* the person or his frame, or particular parts, as his lungs, his stomach, his brain, and the like, may be *diseased.*

Sick, sickly, and *diseased* may all be used in a moral application; *morbid* is used in no other except in a technical sense. *Sick* denotes a partial state, as before, namely, a state of disgust, and is always associated with the object of the *sickness;* we are *sick* of turbulent enjoyments, and seek for tranquillity: *sickly* and *morbid* are applied to the habitual state of the feelings or character; a *sickly* sentimentality, a *morbid* sensibility: *diseased* is applied in general to individuals or communities, to persons or to things; a person's mind is in a *diseased* state when it is under the influence of corrupt passions or principles; society is in a *diseased* state when it is overgrown with wealth and luxury.

Sickness, Illness, Indisposition.— *Sickness* denotes the state of being *sick; illness* that of being *ill* (see EVIL): *indisposition* that of being physically not well disposed. *Sickness* denotes the state generally or particularly; *illness* denotes it particularly: we speak of *sickness* as opposed to good health· in *sickness* or in health; but of the *illness* of a particular person: when *sickness* is said of the individual, it designates a protracted state: a person may be said to have much *sickness* in his family. *Illness* denotes only a particular or partial *sickness:* a person is said to have had an *illness* at this or that time, in this or that place, for this or that period. *Indisposition* is a slight *illness,* such a one as is capable of disturbing him either in his enjoyments or in his business; colds are the ordinary causes of *indisposition.*

SIGHT. See SHOW.

SIGN, SIGNAL. *Sign* and *signal* are both derived from the same source (see MARK), and the latter is but a species of the former. The *sign* enables us to recognize an object; it is, therefore, sometimes natural: *signal* serves to give warning; it is always arbitrary. The changes which are visible in the countenance are commonly the *signs* of what passes in the heart; the beat of the drum is the *signal* for soldiers to repair to their post. We converse with those who are present by *signs;* we make ourselves understood by those who are at a distance by means of *signals.*

See also WAFT.

Signal, Memorable.—*Signal* signifies serving as a sign, *memorable* signifies worthy to be remembered. They both express the idea of extraordinary, or being distinguished from every other thing: whatever is *signal* deserves to be stamped on the mind and to serve as a sign of some property or characteristic; whatever is *memorable* impresses upon the memory and refuses to be forgotten: the former applies to the moral character, the latter to events and times: the Scriptures furnish us with many *signal* instances of God's vengeance against impenitent sinners, as also of His favor toward those who obey His will; the Reformation is a *memorable* event in the annals of ecclesiastical history.

Signalize, Distinguish.—To *signalize,* or make one's self a sign of anything, is a much stronger term than simply to *distinguish;* it is in the power of many to do the latter, but few only have the power of accomplishing the former: the English have always *signalized* themselves for their unconquerable valor in battle; there is no nation that has not *distinguished* itself, at some period or another, in war.

Significant, Expressive.—The *signifi-*

c.e.s.—21

cant is that which serves as a sign; the *expressive* is that which speaks out or declares; the latter is, therefore, a stronger term than the former: a look is *significant* when it is made to *express* an idea that passes in the mind; but it is *expressive* when it is made to *express* a feeling of the whole mind or heart: looks are but occasionally *significant,* but the countenance may be habitually *expressive. Significant* is applied in an indifferent sense, according to the nature of the thing signified; but *expressive* is always applied to that which is good: a *significant* look may convey a very bad idea, but an *expressive* countenance always *expresses* good feeling.

The distinction between these words is the same when applied to things as to persons: a word is *significant* of whatever it is made to signify, but a word is *expressive* according to the force with which it conveys an idea. The term *significant,* in this case, simply explains the nature, but the epithet *expressive* characterizes it as something good: technical terms are *significant* only of the precise ideas which belong to the art; most languages have some terms which are peculiarly *expressive,* and consequently adapted for poetry.

Signification, Meaning, Import, Sense.—The *signification* (see EXPRESS) is that which is signified to another; the *meaning* is that which the person means to express: this latter word, therefore, is properly used in connection with the person *meaning.*

The *signification* of a word is that which it is made to signify, and the *meaning* is that which it is meant to express: in this sense, therefore, we may indifferently say the proper, improper, metaphorical, or general *signification* or *meaning* of words; but, in reference to individuals, *meaning* is more proper than *signification,* as to convey a *meaning,* to attach a *meaning* to a word, and not to convey or attach a *signification.*

On the other hand, it is more appropriate to say a literal *signification* than a literal *meaning.* There is also this further distinction between *signify* and *mean* that the latter is applied in its proper sense to things as well as words.

Import, from *in* and *portare,* to carry, signifying that which is carried or conveyed to the understanding, is most allied to *signification,* inasmuch as it is applied to single words. The *signification* may include the whole or any part of what is understood by a word; the *import* is the whole that is comprehended under a word. The *signification* of words may be learned by definition, but their full *import* can be collected only from examples.

Sense (see FEELING), signifying that which is perceived by the senses, is most nearly allied to the word *meaning,* inasmuch as they both refer to the mind of the individual; but the *sense* being that which is rational and consistent with *sense,* is that which is taken or admitted abstractedly.

Signify, Imply. — *Signify* (see EXPRESS). *Imply,* a coined word ultimately from the Latin *implicare,* to fold in, signifies to fold or involve an idea in any object.

These terms may be employed either as respects actions or words. In the first case *signify* is the act of the person making known by means of a *sign,* as we *signify* our approbation by a look; *imply* marks the value or force of the action; our assent is *implied* in our silence. When applied to words or marks, *signify* denotes the positive and established act of the thing; *imply* is its relative act: a word *signifies* whatever it is made literally to stand for; it *implies* that which it stands for figuratively or morally. The term house *signifies* that which is constructed for a dwelling; the term residence *implies* something superior to a house. A cross, thus +, *signifies* addition in arithmetic or algebra; a long stroke, thus ——, with a break in the text of a work, *implies* that the whole sentence is not completed. It frequently happens that words which *signify* nothing particular in themselves may be made to *imply* a great deal by the tone, the manner, and the connection.

Signify, Avail.—*Signify* is here employed with regard to events of life and their relative importance. *Avail* (see AVAIL) is never used otherwise. That which a thing *signifies* is what it contains; if it *signifies* nothing, it contains nothing and is worth noth-

ing; if it *signifies* much, it contains much or is worth much. That which *avails* produces; if it *avails* nothing, it produces nothing, is of no use; if it *avails* much, it produces or is worth much. We consider the end as to its *signification* and the means as to their *avail.* Although it is of little or no *signification* to a man what becomes of his remains, yet no one can be reconciled to the idea of leaving them to be exposed to contempt; words are but too often of little *avail* to curb the unruly wills of children.

See also DECLARE; DENOTE.

SILENCE, TACITURNITY. The Latins have the two verbs *silere* and *tacere:* the former of which is interpreted by some as signifying to cease to speak, and the latter not to begin to speak; others maintain the direct contrary. According to the present use of the words, *silence* expresses less than *taciturnity:* the *silent* man seldom speaks, the *taciturn* man will not speak at all. The Latins designated the most profound *silence* by the epithet of *taciturna silentia.*

Taciturnity is always of some duration, arising either from necessity or from a particular frame of mind.

Silence always supposes something occasional that is adopted to suit the convenience of the party.

Silent, Tacit. — *Silent* characterizes either the person or the thing: a person is *silent* as opposed to one that talks; a place is *silent* as opposed to one that is noisy. *Tacit* characterizes only the act of the person; a person gives a *tacit* consent, or there was a *tacit* agreement between the parties.

Silent, Dumb, Mute, Speechless.— Not speaking is the common idea included in the signification of these terms, which differ either in the cause or the circumstance: *silent* is altogether an indefinite and general term, expressing little more than the common idea. We may be *silent* because we will not speak or we may be *silent* because we cannot speak; but in distinction from the other terms it is always employed in the former case. *Dumb,* Anglo-Saxon *dumb,* Old High German *tump,* stupid or idiotic, denotes a physical incapacity to speak: hence persons are said to be born *dumb;* they may likewise be *dumb* from temporary physical causes, as from grief, shame, and the like; a person may be struck *dumb*. It is in the Old High German sense, which is that of the Modern German *dumm*, that the so-called Pennsylvania Dutch employ incorrectly the English *dumb*. *Mute*, in Latin *mutus*, dumb, signifies a temporary disability to speak from arbitrary and incidental causes: hence the office of *mutes*, or of persons who engage not to speak for a certain time; and, in like manner, persons are said to be *mute* who dare not give utterance to their thoughts.

Speechless, or void of speech, denotes a physical incapacity to speak from incidental causes; as when a person falls down *speechless* in an apoplectic fit or in consequence of a violent concussion.

The terms *silent, mute*, and *dumb* are also applied to things as well as persons, the former two in the sense of not sending forth a sound; as the *silent* grove, a *mute* tongue, or a *mute* letter: *dumb*, in the sense of being without words, as *dumb* show.

SILLY. See SIMPLE.

SIMILARITY. See LIKENESS.

SIMILE, SIMILITUDE, COMPARISON. *Simile* and *similitude* are both drawn from the Latin *similis*, like, the former signifying the thing that is like, the latter either the thing that is like or the quality of being like: in the former sense only it is to be compared with *simile*, when employed as a figure of speech or thought; everything is a *simile* which associates objects on account of any real or supposed likeness between them; but a *similitude* signifies a prolonged or continued *simile*. The latter may be expressed in a few words, as when we say the godlike Achilles; but the former enters into minute circumstances of *comparison*, as when Homer *compares* any of his heroes fighting and defending themselves against multitudes to lions who are attacked by dogs and men. Every *simile* is more or less a *comparison*, but every *comparison* is not a *simile:* the latter *compares* things only as far as they are alike, but the former extends to those things which are different: in this manner, there may be a *comparison* between large things and small, although there can be no good *simile*.

See also LIKENESS.

SIMPLE, SINGLE, SINGULAR. *Simple*, in Latin *simplex*, from a root *sim*, meaning the same one (appearing in *singuli, single*, etc.), and *plicare*, to fold, signifying composed of one and the same fold, is opposed to the complex, which has many folds, or to the compound, which has several parts involved or connected with each other. *Single* and *singular* (see ONE) are opposed, one to double and the other to multifarious: but the latter is generally used in the sense of odd, unusual, or eccentric. We may speak of a *simple* circumstance as independent of anything; of a *single* instance or circumstance as unaccompanied by any other; and a *singular* instance as one that rarely has its like. In the moral application to the person, *simplicity*, as far as it is opposed to duplicity in the heart, can never be excessive: but when it lies in the head it is a mental defect. *Singleness* of heart and intention is that species of *simplicity* which is altogether to be admired: *singularity* may be either good or bad, according to circumstances; to be *singular* in virtue is to be truly good; but to be *singular* in manner is affectation, which is at variance with genuine *simplicity*, if not directly opposed to it.

Simple, Silly, Foolish.—The *simple*, when applied to the understanding, implies such a contracted power as is incapable of combination; *silly*, which originally meant "timely," hence lucky, blessed, innocent, and finally simple or foolish, and *foolish, i. e.*, like a *fool*, rise in sense upon the former, signifying either the perversion or the total deficiency of understanding; the behavior of a person may be *silly* who from any excess of feeling loses his sense of propriety; the conduct of a person will be *foolish* who has not judgment to direct himself. Country people may be *simple*, owing to their want of knowledge; children will be *silly* in company if they have too much liberty given to them; there are some persons who never acquire wisdom enough to prevent them from committing *foolish* errors.

See also NAÏVE.

SIMULATION, DISSIMULATION. *Simulation*, ultimately from *similis*, is the making one's self like what one is not; and *dissimulation*, from *dissimilis*, unlike, is the making one's self appear unlike what one really is. The hypocrite affects the *simulation* of virtue to recommend himself to the virtuous; the dissembler resorts to *dissimulation* to conceal his vices when he wants to gain the simple or ignorant to his side.

SIMULTANEOUS. See SYNCHRONOUS.

SIN. See CRIME.

SINCERE, HONEST, TRUE, PLAIN. *Sincere* (see CANDID) is here the most comprehensive term: *honest* (see HONESTY), *true*, and *plain* (see EVEN) are but modes of *sincerity*.

Sincerity is a fundamental characteristic of the person; *honesty* is but a part of *sincerity;* it denotes simply the absence of intentional or fraudulent concealment; we look for a *sincere* friend to tell us everything; we look for an *honest* companion who will speak without disguise; truth is a characteristic of *sincerity*, for a *sincere* friend is a *true* friend; but *sincerity* is, properly speaking, only a mode of truth. *Sincere* and *honest* are personal characteristics; *true* is a characteristic of the thing, as a *sincere* man, an *honest* confession, a *true* statement.

A *sincere* man must needs be *plain*, because *plainness* consists in an unvarnished style; and the *sincere* man will always adopt that mode of speech which expresses his sentiments most truly; but a person may be occasionally *plain* in his speech who is not so from *sincerity*. The *plain*, whether it respects the language or the conduct, is that which is divested of everything extraneous or artificial, and so far *plainness* is an auxiliary to *truth* by enabling the *truth* to be better seen.

See also HEARTY.

SINGLE. See ONE; SIMPLE; SOLITARY.

SINGULAR. See PARTICULAR; RARE; SIMPLE.

SINK. See FALL.

SITE. See PLACE.

SITUATION, CONDITION, STATE, PREDICAMENT, FLIGHT, CASE. *Situation* (see PLACE) is said generally of objects as they concern others; *condition*, as they are concerned themselves: our *situation* consists of those external circumstances in respect of property, honor, liberty, and the like which affect our standing in society generally. Whatever affects our person immediately is our *condition:* a person who is unable to pay a sum of money to save himself from a prison is in a bad *situation:* a traveller who is left in a ditch robbed and wounded is in a bad *condition.*

Situation and *condition* are said of that which is contingent and changeable, the latter still more so than the former; *state*, from the past participle of *stare*, to stand, signifying that position in which one stands, is said of that which is comparatively stable or established. A tradesman is in a good *situation* who is in the way of carrying on a good trade: his affairs are in a good *state* if he is enabled to answer every demand and to keep up his credit. Hence it is that we speak of the *state* of health and the *state* of the mind, not the *situation* or *condition*, because the body and mind are considered as to their general frame, and not as to any relative or particular circumstances, as the passing *condition* of one's health or transient disposition of one's mentality, so likewise a *state* of infancy, a *state* of guilt, a *state* of innocence.

When speaking of bodies, there is the same distinction in the terms as in regard to individuals. An army may be either in a *situation*, a *condition*, or a *state*. An army that is on service may be in a critical *situation* with respect to the enemy and its own comparative weakness; it may be in a deplorable *condition* if it stand in need of provisions and necessaries: an army that is at home will be in a good or bad *state* according to the regulations of the commander-in-chief. Of a prince who is threatened with invasion from foreign enemies and with rebellion from his subjects we should not say that his *condition*, but his *situation*, was critical. Of a prince, however, who like Alfred was obliged to fly and to seek safety in disguise and poverty, we should speak of his hard *condition:* the *state* of a prince cannot be spoken of, but the *state* of his affairs and government may: hence, likewise, *state* may with most propriety be said of a nation: but *situation* seldom, unless in respect to other nations, and *condition* never. On the other hand, when speaking of the poor, we seldom employ the term *situation,* because they are seldom considered as a body in relation to other bodies: we mostly speak of their *condition* as better or worse, according as they have more or less of the comforts of life; and of their *state* as regards their moral habits.

These terms may likewise be applied to inanimate objects; and, upon the same grounds, a house is in a good *situation* as respects the surrounding objects; it is in a good or bad *condition* as respects the painting and exterior altogether; it is in a bad *state* as respects the beams, plaster, roof, and interior structure altogether. The hand of a watch is in a different *situation* every hour; the watch itself may be in a bad *condition* if the wheels are clogged with dirt, but in a good *state* if the works are altogether sound and fit for service.

Situation and *condition* are either permanent or temporary. The *predicament,* originally a term in logic signifying one of the most general classes into which things can be divided, from Latin *prædicare,* to assert or declare, signifies that which is predicated or asserted; a class or kind described by definite marks, originally it had no unfavorable connotation, but in modern parlance, when applied to circumstances, it expresses a temporary embarrassed *situation* conceivably but not necessarily occasioned by an act of one's own: hence we speak of being in or bringing ourselves into a *predicament.* *Plight,* in the sense of peril, is derived from Anglo-Saxon *pliht,* risk, danger, hence also a promise involving risk or peril: it has no connection with the English *plight* in the sense of fold, which is derived from the Latin *plicatus,* participle of *plicare,* to fold. It signifies any circumstance in which one is disagreeably entangled. *Case* signifies anything which may befall us or into which we fall, from *casus,* past participle

of *cadere,* to fall, mostly, though not necessarily, contrary to our inclination. Those latter two terms, therefore, denote a species of temporary *condition,* for they both express that which happens to the object itself, without reference to any other. A person is in an unpleasant *situation* who is shut up in a railway compartment with disagreeable company. He is in an awkward *predicament* when, in attempting to please one friend, he displeases another. He may be in a wretched *plight* if he is overturned in a car at night and at a distance from any habitation. He will be in evil *case* if he is compelled to put up with a spare and poor diet.

See also CIRCUMSTANCE.

SIZE, MAGNITUDE, GREATNESS, BULK. *Size* is short for *assize,* from *assise,* the feminine past participle of the French verb *asseoir,* to sit: from its meaning of the sitting of judges came the tax by them established, hence a fixed amount, and thence it developed the meaning of quantity or size in general; it is a general term including all manner of dimension or measurement; *magnitude,* from the Latin *magnitudo,* from *magnus,* great, answering, literally, to the English word *greatness,* is employed in science or in an abstract sense to denote some specific measurement; *greatness* is an unscientific term applied in the same sense to objects in general: *size* is indefinite, it never characterizes anything either as large or small; but *magnitude* and *greatness* always suppose something *great;* and *bulk* denotes a considerable degree of *greatness:* things which are diminutive in *size* will often have an extraordinary degree of beauty or some other adventitious perfection to compensate the deficiency; astronomers have classed the stars according to their different *magnitudes; greatness* has been considered as one source of the sublime: *bulk* is that species of *greatness* which destroys the symmetry, and consequently the beauty, of objects.

SKETCH, OUTLINES. A *sketch* may form a whole; *outlines* are but a part: the *sketch* may comprehend the *outlines* and some of the particulars; *outlines,* as the term bespeaks, comprehend only the line on the exterior: the *sketch,* in drawing, may serve as a landscape, as it presents some of the features of a country; but the *outlines* serve only as bounding lines, within which the *sketch* may be formed. So in the moral application, we speak of the *sketches* of countries, characters, manners, and the like, which serve as a description; but of the *outlines* of a plan, of a work, a project, and the like which serve as a basis on which the subordinate parts are to be formed: barbarous nations present us with rude *sketches* of nature; an abridgment is little more than the *outlines* of a larger work.

See also DELINEATE.

SKILFUL. See CLEVER.

SKILFULNESS. See KNACK.

SKIN, HIDE, PEEL, RIND. *Skin,* a Scandinavian word, is the term in most general use; it is applicable both to human creatures and to animals: *hide,* Anglo-Saxon *hÿd,* allied to Latin *cutis,* skin (whence *cuticle*), is used only for the *skins* of large animals: we speak of the *skins* of birds or insects, but of the *hides* of oxen or horses and other animals, which are to be separated from the body and converted into leather. *Skin* is equally applied to the inanimate and the animate world, but *peel,* Latin *pellis,* a skin, and *rind,* Anglo-Saxon *rinde,* the bark of a tree, possibly allied to *rim,* signifying that which goes round and envelops, belong only to inanimate objects: the *skin* is generally said of that which is interior, in distinction from the exterior, which is the *peel:* an orange has both its *peel* and its thin *skin* underneath; an apple, a pear, and the like has a *peel.* The *peel* is a soft substance on the outside; the *rind* is generally interior and of a harder substance: in regard to a stick, we speak of its *peel* and its inner *skin;* in regard to a tree, we speak of its bark and its *rind:* hence, likewise, the term *rind* is applied to cheese and other incrusted substances that envelop bodies.

SLACK, LOOSE. *Slack,* Anglo-Saxon *sleac,* meant originally fluid. *Loose* is a Scandinavian word allied to the verb *lose.* These two words differ more in application than in sense: they are both opposed to that which is close bound; but *slack* is said only of that which is tied or that with which

anything is tied; while *loose* is said of any substances the parts of which do not adhere closely: a rope is *slack* in contrast with the tight rope, which is stretched to its full extent; and in general cords or strings are said to be *slack* which fail in the requisite degree of tightness; but they are said to be *loose* in an indefinite manner, without conveying any collateral idea: thus the string of an instrument is denominated *slack* rather than *loose;* on the other hand, *loose* is said of many bodies to which the word *slack* cannot be applied: a garment is *loose,* but not *slack;* the leg of a table is *loose,* but not *slack.*

In the moral application, that which admits of additional activity is denominated *slack,* and that which fails in consistency and close adherence is *loose:* trade is *slack,* or a person's zeal, etc., becomes *slack* (hence the term of reproach *slacker,* which arose during the European war to denote persons unwilling to work to help the allied countries to victory); but an engagement is *loose* and principles are *loose.*

SLANDER. See ASPERSE.

SLANT, SLOPE. *Slant* is a Scandinavian word, meaning to slope or glide, and *slope,* from the root found in the verb *slip,* are both expressive of a sideward movement or direction: they are the same in sense, but different in application: *slant* is said of small bodies only; *slope* is said indifferently of all bodies, large and small: a book may be made to *slant* by lying in part on another book on a desk or a table, but a piece of ground is said to *slope.*

SLAUGHTER. See CARNAGE; KILL.

SLAVERY. See SERVITUDE; THRALLDOM.

SLAY. See KILL.

SLEEP, SLUMBER, DOZE, DROWSE, NAP. *Sleep* is in Anglo-Saxon *slǽpan. Slumber* comes through Middle English *slumeren,* from a Teutonic root meaning to be silent. *Doze* is a Scandinavian word allied to *dizzy* and to *daze. Drowse* comes from the Anglo-Saxon *drúsian,* to be sluggish. *Nap* is in Anglo-Saxon *hnæppian,* to doze.

Sleep is the general term, which designates in an indefinite manner that state of the body to which all animated beings are subject at certain seasons in the course of nature; to *slumber* is to *sleep* lightly and softly; to *doze* is to incline to *sleep* or to begin *sleeping;* to *nap* is to *sleep* for a time: every one who is not indisposed *sleeps* during the night; those who are accustomed to wake at a certain hour of the morning commonly *slumber* only after that time; there are many who, though they cannot *sleep* in a carriage, will yet be obliged to *doze* if they travel in the night; in hot climates the middle of the day is commonly chosen for a *nap*.

Sleepy, Drowsy, Lethargic. — *Sleepy* expresses either a temporary or a permanent state. *Drowsy* expresses mostly a temporary state; *lethargic,* from *lethargy,* in Latin *lethargia,* Greek λληθαργία, compounded of λήθη, forgetfulness, signifying a proneness to forgetfulness or *sleep,* describes a permanent or habitual state.

Sleepy, as a temporary state, expresses also what is natural or seasonable; *drowsiness* expresses an inclination to *s eep* at unseasonable hours; it is natural to be *sleepy* at the hour when we are accustomed to retire to rest; it is common to be *drowsy* when sitting still after dinner. *Sleepiness,* as a permanent state, is an infirmity to which some persons are subject constitutionally; *lethargy* is a disease with which people otherwise the most wakeful may be occasionally attacked.

SLENDER. See **THIN.**

SLIDE. See **SLIP.**

SLIGHT. See **CURSORY; DISREGARD; SNUB; THIN.**

SLIM. See **THIN.**

SLIP, SLIDE, GLIDE. *Slip,* from *slipan,* and *slide,* from *slidan,* and *glide,* from *glidan,* are all Anglo-Saxon words.

To *slip* is an involuntary, and *slide* a voluntary, motion: those who go on the ice in fear will *slip;* boys *slide* on the ice by way of amusement. To *slip* and *slide* are lateral movements of the feet, but to *glide* is the movement of the whole body and just that easy motion which is made by *slipping, sliding,* flying, or swimming: a person *glides* along the surface of the ice when he *slides;* a vessel *glides* through the water.

In the moral and figurative application, a person *slips* who commits unintentional errors; he who wittingly, and yet without difficulty, falls into the practice and habits which are recommended *slides* into a certain course of life: he *glides* through life if he pursues his course smoothly and without interruption.

See also **LAPSE.**

SLOPE. See **SLANT.**

SLOTHFUL. See **INACTIVE.**

SLOW, DILATORY, TARDY, TEDIOUS. *Slow,* in Anglo-Saxon *sláw,* may be allied to *læves,* in Latin signifying the left hand, the left hand being slow of movement. *Dilatory,* of the same derivation as the English *dilate,* comes from Latin *di-dis,* apart, and *latus,* carried, the past participle of *ferre, i. e.,* an action which is put off and brought over from the time of its conception or requirement. It means lengthening out the time required for any performance. *Tardy,* from the Latin *tardus,* signifies, literally, slow. *Tedious,* from the Latin *tædium,* weariness, signifies causing weariness.

Slow is a general and unqualified term applicable to the motion of any object or to the motions and actions of persons in particular, and to their dispositions also; *dilatory* relates to the disposition only of persons: we are *slow* in what we are about; we are *dilatory* in setting about a thing. *Slow* is applied to corporeal or mental actions; a person may be *slow* in walking or *slow* in conceiving: *tardy* is applicable to mental actions; we are *tardy* in our proceedings or our progress; we are *tardy* in making up accounts or in concluding a treaty. We may be *slow* with propriety or not, to our own inconvenience or that of others; when we are *tedious* we are always so improperly: "To be *slow* and sure" is a vulgar proverb, but a great truth; by this we do ourselves good and inconvenience no one; but he who is *tedious* is *slow* to the annoyance of others: a prolix writer must always be *tedious,* for he keeps the reader long in suspense before he comes to the conclusion of a period.

SLUGGISH. See **INACTIVE.**

SLUMBER. See **SLEEP.**

SLY. See **CUNNING.**

SMALL. See **ATOMIC; LITTLE.**

SMEAR, DAUB. *Smear* is allied to

Anglo-Saxon *smerien*, a weak verb from the substantive *smeru* fat or grease, and originally signified to cover with fat or grease. *Daub* comes from Old French *dauber*, to plaster, from Latin *de*, down, and *albare*, to whiten.

To *smear* in the literal sense is applied to such substances as may be rubbed like grease over a body; if said of grease itself, it may be proper; as coachmen *smear* the coach-wheels with tar or grease; but if said of anything else, it is an improper action, and tends to disfigure, as children *smear* their hands with ink or *smear* their clothes with dirt. To *smear* and *daub* are both actions which tend to disfigure; but we *smear* by means of *rubbing* over: we *daub* by rubbing, throwing, or any way covering over: thus a child *smears* the window with his finger or he *daubs* the wall with dirt.

By a figurative application *smear* is applied to bad writing or whatever is soiled or contaminated, and *daub* to bad painting or to whatever is executed coarsely or clumsily: indifferent writers who wish to excel are fond of retouching their letters until they make their performance a sad *smear;* bad artists, who are injudicious in the use of their brush, load their paintings with color and convert them into *daubs.*

SMELL, Scent, Odor, Perfume, Fragrance. *Smell*, Middle English *smel*, is allied to *smoulder*. *Scent*, changed from *sent*, comes from the Latin *sentire*, to perceive or feel. *Odor*, in Latin *odor*, allied with Greek ὄζειν, to smell. *Perfume*, compounded of *per* and *fumus*, a smoke or vapor, that is, the vapor that issues forth. *Fragrance*, in Latin *fragrantia*, comes from *fragrare*, to emit an odor; hence, in Latin, *fragum*, a strawberry.

Smell and *scent* are said either of that which receives or that which gives the *smell;* the *odor*, the *perfume*, and *fragrance*, of that which communicates the *smell*. In the first case, *smell* is said generally of all living things without distinction; *scent* is said only of such animals as have this peculiar faculty of tracing objects by their *smell:* some persons have a much quicker *smell* than others, and some have an acuter *smell* of particular ob-

jects than they have of things in general: dogs are remarkable for their quickness of *scent*, by which they can trace their masters and other objects at an immense distance; other animals are gifted with this faculty to a surprising degree, which serves them as a means of defence against their enemies.

In the second case, *smell* and *scent* are compared with *odor*, *perfume*, and *fragrance* either as respects the objects communicating the *smell* or the nature of the *smell* which is communicated. *Smell* is indefinite in its sense and universal in its application; *scent, odor, perfume*, and *fragrance* are species of *smell:* every object is said to *smell* which acts on the olfactory nerves; flowers, fruits, woods, earth, water, and the like have a *smell; scent* is most commonly applied to the *smell* which proceeds from animal bodies; the *odor* is said of that which is artificial or extraneous; the *perfume* and *fragrance* of that which is natural: the burning of things produces an *odor;* the *perfume* and *fragrance* arises from flowers or sweet-*smelling* herbs, spices, and the like. The terms *smell* and *odor* do not specify the exact nature of that which issues from bodies; they may both be either pleasant or unpleasant; but *smell*, if taken in certain connections, signifies a bad *smell*, and *odor* signifies that which is sweet: meat which is kept too long will have a *smell*, that is, of course, a bad *smell;* the *odors* from a sacrifice are acceptable, that is, the sweet *odors* ascend to heaven. *Perfume* is properly a widespreading *smell*, and when taken without any epithet never signifies anything but what is good; it is the sweetest and most powerful *perfume:* the *perfume* from flowers and shrubs is as grateful to one sense as their colors and conformation are to the other; the *fragrance* from groves of myrtle and orange trees surpasses the beauty of their fruit or foliage.

SMITE. See Strike.
SMOOTH. See Even; Unruffled.
SMOTHER. See Stifle; Suffocate.
SNEER. See Scoff.
SNIPER. See Sharp-shooter.
SNUB, Cut, Slight. These words

all signify to treat another with contempt. *Slight* means to treat as if of *slight* importance. We may *slight* a friend indirectly by failing to invite him to a social entertainment or to consult his wishes in some matter in which he feels that he has a right to an opinion. *Snub*, the original meaning of which is to cut off, something short, indicates a more crude and direct action. We *snub* another by obviously disregarding him or treating him with contempt. To *cut* is to *cut* a friend or acquaintance out of the circle of our interests entirely. We may *slight* an acquaintance by treating him with less consideration than he expects. We *snub* him by treating him with a positive lack of respect or consideration. We *cut* him by disregarding him altogether, by failing to recognize his existence at all.

See also ABASH.

SOAK, DRENCH, STEEP. *Soak*, from Anglo-Saxon *socian*, is related to *suck*. *Steep* is a Scandinavian word meaning to make to *stoop*, to overturn, hence to pour water over grain by turning the receptacle upside down. *Drench* is a variation of drink; it means, literally, to cause to drink.

The idea of communicating or receiving a liquid is common to these terms. A person's clothes are *soaked* in rain when the water has penetrated every thread; he himself is *drenched* in the rain when it has penetrated, as it were, his very body; *drench*, therefore, in this case only expresses the idea of *soak* in a stronger manner. To *steep* is a species of *soaking* employed as an artificial process; to *soak* is, however, a permanent action by which hard things are rendered soft; to *steep* is a temporary action by which soft bodies become penetrated with a liquid: thus salt meat requires to be *soaked;* fruits are *steeped* in brandy.

SOBER, GRAVE. *Sober* (see ABSTINENT) expresses the absence of all exhilaration of spirits: *grave* (see that word) expresses a weight in the intellectual operations which makes them proceed slowly. *Sobriety* is therefore a more natural and ordinary state for the human mind than *gravity:* it behooves every man to be *sober* in all situations; but those who fill the most important stations of life must be *grave*. Even in our pleasures we may observe *sobriety*, which keeps us from any excessive ebullition of mirth; but on particular occasions, where the importance of the subject ought to weigh on the mind, it becomes us to be *grave*. At a feast we have need of *sobriety;* at a funeral we have need of *gravity*.

Sobriety extends to many more objects than *gravity;* we must be *sober* in our thoughts and opinions, as well as in our outward conduct and behavior; but we can be *grave*, properly speaking, only in our looks and our outward deportment.

See also MODESTY.

SOBRIETY. See MODESTY.

SOCIABLE. See CYCLE; SOCIAL.

SOCIAL, SOCIABLE. *Social*, from *socius*, a companion, signifies belonging or allied to a companion, having the disposition of a companion; *sociable*, from the same, signifies able or fit to be a companion; the former is an active, the latter a passive, quality: *social* people seek others; *sociable* people are sought for by others. It is possible for a man to be *social* and not *sociable;* to be *sociable* and not *social:* he who draws his pleasures from society without communicating his share to the common stock of entertainments is *social*, but not *sociable:* men of a taciturn disposition are often in this case; they receive more than they give: he, on the contrary, who has talents to please company, but not the inclination to go into company, may be *sociable*, but is seldom *social;* of this description are humorists who go into company to gratify their pride and stay away to indulge their humor.

Social and *sociable* are likewise applicable to things, with a similar distinction; *social* intercourse is that intercourse which men have together for the purposes of society; *social* pleasures are what they enjoy by associating together: a family is *sociable;* fellow-travellers are *sociable:* a church gives a *sociable*.

See also CONVIVIAL.

SOCIALISM, COMMUNISM. Both of these words indicate a theory of government which holds that necessities of life should not be wholly in the control of the individuals strong enough to take possession of them, but should be equitably distributed by some central authority acting in accordance with the will of the whole community. But *communism*, from Latin *communis*, common, holds that all goods should be held in common, that the possessions or earnings of each individual should go into a common fund to be redistributed in accordance with the needs of all the members composing the community. This system has been carried out in some special social groups—in the monasteries, for example—and, to some extent, in the organization of the Russian *Zemstva*, and it obtains to-day in many families, especially those of the working classes. But it has never been successfully extended to the large and various community composing a state. *Socialism*, on the other hand, simply provides that all that is necessary to support life—*i. e.*, land and the machinery of production—shall be under the control of the community as a whole, so that no individual shall have it in his power to buy up any of the crops, like wheat, which are necessary to support life, and to control the selling price, or to keep in his possession large tracts of land not under cultivation, etc. *Socialists* differ in their ideas concerning the character and extent of the communal control; and *socialism* is often associated with doctrines of *pacifism*, etc., which bring it into disrepute. But, as a matter of fact, in moments of crisis, when national existence is threatened, the *socialistic* principle of the control of that which is necessary for the welfare of the whole community by the whole community, is promptly applied—as in the food-control regulations in the warring countries during the European war, and the regulation of conscription in the United States.

SOCIALIST. See INTRANSIGENT.

SOCIETY, COMPANY. *Society* and *company* (for both see ASSOCIATION) here express either the persons associating, the act of associating, or the state of being associated. In either case *society* is a general and *company* a particular term; as respects persons associating, *society* comprehends either all the associated part of mankind, as when we speak of the laws or *society*, the well-being of *society;* or it is said only of a particular number of individuals associated, in which latter case it comes nearest to *company*, and differs from it only as to the purpose of the association. A *society* is always formed for some solid purpose, as the Humane *Society;* and a *company* is always brought together for pleasure or profit, as has already been observed. Good sense teaches us the necessity of conforming to the rules of the *society* to which we belong: good-breeding prescribes to us to render ourselves agreeable to the *company* of which we form a part.

When expressing the abstract action of associating, the term *society* is even more general and indefinite than before; it expresses that which is common to mankind, and *company* that which is peculiar to individuals. The love of *society* is inherent in our nature; it is weakened or destroyed only by the defect of our disposition or by some mental or psychological derangement: every one naturally likes the *company* of his own friends and connections in preference to that of strangers. *Society* is a permanent and habitual act; *company* is only a particular act suited to the occasion: it behooves us to shun the *society* of those from whom we can learn no good, although we may sometimes be obliged to be in their *company*. The *society* of intelligent men is desirable for those who are entering life; the *company* of facetious men is agreeable in travelling.

See also COMMUNITY; FELLOWSHIP; PUBLIC.

SOFT, MILD, GENTLE, MEEK. *Soft* and *mild* have the same form and application in Anglo-Saxon as in Modern English. *Gentle* (see that word). *Meek* is a Scandinavian word.

All these terms denote the absence of an unpleasant action, sometimes also a positively pleasant action, and sometimes a positive readiness to yield to the action of other bodies. *Soft* is taken in these different senses, as a *soft* pressure or tread which is not easily felt or heard, and a *soft* substance that yields readily to the touch or pressure. *Mild* and *gentle* are mostly taken in the sense of not acting with an unpleasant force; as *mild* cheese, or *mild* fruits, *gentle* motion. *Meek* is taken in the passive sense of not resisting force by force. The first three terms have a physical and moral application; the last only a moral application. *Soft* is applied to such objects as act pleasantly in point of strength on the ear or the eye, as a *soft* voice, a *soft* light; or pleasantly, in point of smoothness, on the feeling, as a *soft* cushion, a *soft* skin. *Mild* and *gentle* are applied to objects that act not unpleasantly on the senses; as *mild* beer, not too strong either for the palate or the body; *mild* air, that is, not unpleasantly cold; *gentle* exercise, *gentle* motion, not violent or excessive in degree: so a *gentle* stream and a *gentle* rain. These terms are, agreeably to this distinction, applied to the same objects; a *soft* voice, *soft* music, as that which is positively pleasant; a *gentle* voice is one not loud.

A *soft* air or climate is positively pleasant; a *mild* air or climate is simply without any undue cold; a *gentle* wind is opposed to one that is boisterous.

Soft is sometimes applied to motion in the purely negative sense; as a *soft* step, *i. e.*, one made without great pressure of the foot; a *gentle* motion is one that is made slowly, not quick. It is necessary to tread *softly* when no noise is to be made, and to move *gently* when one is ill.

So likewise when these terms are applied to objects that act on the moral feelings, they admit of a similar distinction. Words are either *soft*, *mild*, or *gentle; soft* words are calculated to soften or diminish the angry feeling of others. The proverb says, "A *soft* answer turneth away wrath." A reproof is *mild*, inasmuch as it does not wound the feelings; a censure, or admonition, or reproach, is *gentle*, inasmuch as it is free from asperity. So likewise punishments are *mild* that inflict little pain; means of coercion are *gentle* that are not violent. Manners are *soft*, *mild*, and *gentle*, but *softness* in this case is not always commendable. Too much *softness* in the manners of a man is inconsistent with manly firmness. *Mildness* and *gentleness* are more generally commendable. *Mild*

manners are peculiarly becoming in superiors or those who have the power of controlling others, provided they do not interfere with good order. *Gentle* manners are becoming in all persons who take a part in social life. *Softness* of manner may likewise be assumed, but *mildness* and *gentleness* are always genuine, the former arising from the temper, the latter either from the temper or from good-breeding, of which it is the greatest mark.

When these terms are employed as characteristics of the person or his disposition, they are comparable with *meek*, which is used only in this sense. *Soft*, as far as it denotes a susceptibility of *soft* or tender emotions, may and ought to exist in both sexes; but it ought to be the peculiar characteristic of the female sex; *mildness*, as a natural gift, may disqualify a man for command, unless it be tempered by firmness and discretion. *Gentleness*, as a part of the character, is not so much to be recommended as *gentleness* from habit.

Meekness denotes the forbearance to use force, even in cases of peculiar provocation: in those who are called upon to direct or command it may be carried to an excess.

Gentle, *mild*, and *meek* are likewise applied to animals, the former to designate that easy flow of spirits which fits them for being guided in their movements, and the latter to mark that passive temper that submits to every kind of treatment, however harsh, without an indication even of displeasure. A horse is *gentle*, as opposed to one that is spirited; the former is devoid of that impetus in himself to move which renders the other ungovernable: the lamb is a pattern of *meekness*, and yields to the knife of the butcher without a struggle or a groan.

SOIL. See STAIN.

SOJOURN. See ABIDE.

SOLACE. See CONSOLE.

SOLDIER-LIKE. See MARTIAL.

SOLE. See SOLITARY; UNIQUE.

SOLEMN. See GRAVE.

SOLICIT. See BEG; BESPEAK.

SOLICITATION, IMPORTUNITY.
Solicitation is general; *importunity* is particular: it is *importunate* or trouble-

some *solicitation*. *Solicitation* itself is that which gives trouble to a certain extent, but it is not always unreasonable: there may be cases in which we may yield to the *solicitations* of friends, to do that which we have no objection to be obliged to do; but *importunity* is that *solicitation* which never ceases to apply for that which it is not agreeable to give. We may sometimes be urgent in our *solicitations* of a friend to accept some proffered honor; the *solicitation*, however, in this case, although it may even be troublesome, yet is sweetened by the motive of the action: the *importunity* of beggars is often a deliberate means of extorting money from the traveller.

SOLICITOR. See DRUMMER.

SOLICITUDE. See CARE.

SOLID. See FIRM; HARD; SUBSTANTIAL.

SOLITARY, SOLE, ONLY, SINGLE. All these terms are more or less opposed to several or many. *Solitary* and *sole*, both derived from *solus*, alone or whole, signify a thing left by itself; the former mostly in application to particular sensible objects, the latter in regard mostly to moral objects: a *solitary* shrub expresses not only one shrub, but one that has been left to itself: the *sole* cause or reason signifies that reason or cause which stands unsupported by anything else. *Only*, that is, *onely*, signifying the quality of unity, does not include the idea of desertion or deprivation, but it comprehends that of want or deficiency: he who has *only* one shilling in his pocket means to imply that he wants more or ought to have more. *Single*, which is an abbreviation of *singular* (see SIMPLE), signifies simply one or more detached from others, without conveying any other collateral idea: a *single* sheet of paper may be sometimes more convenient than a double one; a *single* shilling may be all that is necessary for the present purpose: there may be *single* ones, as well as a *single* one; but the other terms exclude the idea of there being anything else. A *solitary* act of generosity is not sufficient to characterize a man as generous: with most criminals the *sole* ground of their defence rests upon their not having learned to know and

do better: harsh language and severe looks are not the *only* means of correcting the faults of others: *single* instances of extraordinary talents now and then present themselves in the course of an age.

In the adverbial form, *solely*, only, and *singly* are employed with a similar distinction. The disasters which attend an unsuccessful military enterprise are seldom to be attributed *solely* to the incapacity of the general: there are many circumstances both in the natural and moral world which are to be accounted for *only* by admitting a Providence as presented to us in Divine revelation: there are many things which men could not effect *singly* that might be effected by them conjointly.

See also ONE.

Solitary, Desert, Desolate. — *Solitary* (see above). *Desert* is the same as *deserted*, from Latin *desertus*, *de*, privative, and the past participle of *serere*, to join, meaning disjoined, abandoned, forsaken. *Desolate*, in Latin *desolatus*, signifies made *solitary*.

All these epithets are applied to places, but with different modifications of the common idea of solitude which belongs to them. *Solitary* simply denotes the absence of all beings of the same kind: thus a place is *solitary* to a man where there is no human being but himself; and it is *solitary* to a brute when there are no brutes with which it can hold society. *Desert* conveys the idea of a place made *solitary* by being shunned, from its unfitness as a place of residence. All *deserts* are places of such wildness as seem to frighten away almost all inhabitants. *Desolate* conveys the idea of a place made *solitary*, or bare of inhabitants, and all traces of habitation, by violent means: *desolation* is solitude coupled with wretchedness; every country may become *desolate* which is exposed to the inroads of a ravaging army, and a person may be *desolate* who feels himself unable to associate with others.

SOLVE, RESOLVE. *Solve* and *resolve* both come from the Latin *solvere*, to loosen.

Between *solve* and *resolve* there is no considerable difference either in sense or application: the former seems merely to speak of unfolding in a general

SOUL

641

manner that which is wrapped up in obscurity; to *resolve* is rather to unfold it by the particular method of carrying one *back* (*re-*) to first principles; we *solve* a problem and *resolve* a difficulty.

SOME, ANY. *Some,* Anglo-Saxon *sum,* allied to *same,* is altogether restrictive in its sense: *any,* Anglo-Saxon *œnig* (*an,* one, with suffix *ig*), signifying *a one,* is altogether universal and indefinite. *Some* applies to one particular part in distinction from the rest: *any* to every individual part without distinction. *Some* think this and others that: *any* person might believe if he would; *any* one can conquer his passions if he uses his will-power. In consequence of this distinction in sense, *some* can be used only in particular affirmative propositions; but *any,* which is equivalent to all, may be either in negative, interrogative, or hypothetical propositions: *some* say so: does *any* one believe it? He will not give to *any.*

SOON, EARLY, BETIMES. All these words are expressive of time; but *soon* respects some future period in general; *early,* or *ere,* before, and *betimes,* or by the time, before a given time, respect some particular period at no great distance. A person may come *soon* or *early;* in the former case he may not be long in coming from the time that the words are spoken; in the latter case he comes before the time appointed. He who rises *soon* does nothing extraordinary; but he who rises *early* or *betimes* exceeds the usual hour considerably. *Soon* is said mostly of particular acts, and is always dated from the time of the person speaking, if not otherwise expressed; come *soon* signifies after the present moment: *early* and *betimes,* if not otherwise expressed, have always respect to some specific time appointed; come *early* will signify a visit, a meeting, and the like; do it *betimes* will signify before the thing to be done is wanted: in this manner, both are employed for the actions of youth. An *early* attention to duties will render them habitual and pleasing; we must begin *betimes* to bring the stubborn will into subjection.

SOOTHE. See ALLAY; MOLLIFY.

SOPHISTRY, FALLACY. *Sophistry* comes from Greek σοφιστής, a teacher of arts and sciences for money; a pretended lover of wisdom. It derives its name from the so-called *sophists,* the teachers of rhetoric, who travelled from city to city imparting the secrets of plausible and convincing speech, making "the worse appear the better cause." *Sophistry* applies to an argument or reason which has a deceptive appearance of rationality and truth; *fallacy,* from Latin *fallax,* deceitful, to a general statement which seems to be true partly because it has been generally accepted without question. *Sophistry* is often founded on a *fallacy,* that is, it is a chain of argument that is deceptive, beginning with a general statement, a *fallacy,* which seems to be true, but is not.

SORDID. See MEAN.

SORROW. See AFFLICTION.

SORRY, GRIEVED, HURT. *Sorry* and *grieved* are epithets somewhat differing from their primitives *sorrow* and *grief* (see AFFLICTION), inasmuch as they are applied to ordinary subjects. We speak of being *sorry* for anything, however trivial, which concerns ourselves; but we are commonly *grieved* for that which concerns others. I am *sorry* that I was not at home when a person called upon me; I am *grieved* that it is not in my power to serve a friend who stands in need. Both these terms connote only that which we do ourselves: *hurt* (see DISPLEASE and INJURY) that which is done to us, denoting painful feeling from *hurt* or wounded feelings; we are *hurt* at being treated with disrespect.

SORT. See KIND.

SOUL, MIND. These terms, or the equivalents to them, have been employed by all civilized nations to designate that part of human nature which is presumed to be distinct from matter. The *soul,* however, from Anglo-Saxon *sáwel,* is probably from a Sanskrit root meaning *light.* Like the *anima* of the Latin, which comes from the Greek ἄνεμος, wind or breath, it is represented to our minds by the subtlest or most ethereal of sensible objects, namely, breath or spirit, and denotes properly the quickening or vital principle. *Mind,* on the contrary, from

Anglo-Saxon *gemynd*, is that sort of power which is closely allied to, and in a great measure dependent upon, corporeal organization: the former is, therefore, the immortal, and the latter the mortal, part of us; the former connects us with spirits, the latter with brutes; in the former we distinguish consciousness and will, which is possessed by no other created being that we know of; in the latter we distinguish nothing but the power of receiving impressions from external objects, which we call ideas, and which we have in common with the brutes. Poets and philosophers speak of the *soul* in the same strain, as the active and living principle.

The ancients, though unaided by the light of Divine revelation, yet represented the *soul* as a distinct principle. The Psyche of the Greeks, which was the name they gave to the human *soul*, was feigned to be one of their incorporeal or celestial beings. The *anima* of the Latins was taken precisely in the modern sense of the *soul*, by which it was distinguished from the *animus* or mind. Thus the Emperor Hadrian is said on his dying bed to have addressed his soul in words which clearly denote what he thought of its independent existence.

The *mind*, being considered as an attribute to the *soul*, is taken sometimes for one faculty and sometimes for another; as for the understanding, when we say a person is not in his right *mind:* sometimes for the intellectual power; or for the intellectual capacity; or for the imagination or conception.

Sometimes the word *mind* is employed to denote the operations of the thinking faculty, the thoughts or opinions; or the will, choice, determination, as in the colloquial phrase, to have a *mind* to do a thing.

Sometimes it stands for the memory, as in the familiar expressions to call to *mind*, put in *mind*, etc.

Lastly, the *mind* is considered as the seat of all the faculties, and also of the passions or affections.

The *soul*, being the better part of a man, is taken for the man's self; as Horace says, in allusion to his friend Virgil, "et serves animæ dimidium meæ"; hence the term is figuratively extended, in its application, to denote a human being, or the individual in general. Also, what is excellent, the essential or principal part of a thing, the spirit.

SOUND, SANE, HEALTHY. *Sound* is the Anglo-Saxon word, *sund*, corresponding to Latin *sanus*, whence *sane* is derived. *Healthy* (see that word).

Sound is extended in its application to all things that are in the state in which they ought to be, so as to preserve their vitality; thus animals and vegetables are said to be *sound* when in the former there is nothing amiss in their breath, and in the latter in their root. By a figurative application, wood and other things may be said to be *sound* when they are entirely free from any symptom of decay; *sane* is applicable to human beings, in the same sense, but with reference to the mind; a *sane* person is opposed to one that is insane. The mind is also said to be *sound* when it is in a perfect state to form right opinions.

Healthy expresses more than either *sound* or *sane;* we are *healthy* in every part, but we are *sound* in that which is essential for life; he who is *sound* may live, but he who is *healthy* enjoys life. *Sound*, in the sense of noise, comes from Latin *sonus*, a sound; *tone*, from Latin *tonum*, Greek τόνος, a thing stretched, the string of a musical instrument, the sound made by the vibrating of the string.

Sound is that which issues from any body, so as to become audible; *tone* is a species of *sound* which is produced from particular bodies: a *sound* may be accidental; we may hear the *sounds* of waters or leaves, of animals or men: *tones* are those particular *sounds* or modulations of *sound* which are made either to express a particular feeling or to produce harmony; a sheep will cry for its lost young in a *tone* of distress; an organ is so formed as to send forth the most solemn *tones*.

SOURCE. See GERM; ORIGIN; SPRING.

SOURCELESS. See ABIOGENIC.

SOVEREIGN. See PRINCE.

SPACE, ROOM. For the derivation of *space* see *spacious* under AMPLE. *Room*, Anglo-Saxon *rúm*, meant originally a wide space, and is allied to Latin *rus* (whence *rural*, etc.), meaning wide open country.

These are both abstract terms, expressive of that portion of the universe which is supposed not to be occupied by any solid body: *space* is a general term which includes within itself that which infinitely surpasses our comprehension; *room* is a limited term which comprehends those portions of *space* which are artificially formed: *space* is either extended or bounded; *room* is always a bounded *space*: the *space* between two objects is either natural, incidental, or designedly formed; the *room* is that which is the fruit of design, to suit the convenience of persons: there is a sufficient *space* between the heavenly bodies to admit of their moving without confusion; the value of a house essentially depends upon the quantity of *room* which it affords: in a row of trees there must always be vacant *spaces* between each tree; in a car there will be *room* only for a given number of persons.

Space is taken only in the natural sense; *room* is also employed in the moral application; in every person there is ample *room* for amendment or improvement.

SPACIOUS. See AMPLE.

SPARE. See AFFORD; SAVE.

SPARING. See ECONOMICAL.

SPARK. See GALLANT.

SPARKLE. See SHINE.

SPEAK, SAY, TELL. *Speak* and *say* are Anglo-Saxon words whose meaning has not altered from the beginning—*speak* being derived from later Anglo-Saxon *specan*, and *say* from *secgan;* compare German *sprechen* and *sagen.* *Tell,* Anglo-Saxon *tellan,* is allied to Anglo-Saxon *talu,* a number, a narrative—modern English *tale.*

To *speak* may simply consist in uttering an articulate sound; but to *say* is to communicate some idea by means of words: a child begins to *speak* the moment it opens its lips to utter any acknowledged sound; but it will be some time before it can *say* anything: a person is said to *speak* high or low, distinctly or indistinctly; but he *says* that which is true or false, right or wrong: a dumb man cannot *speak;* a fool cannot *say* anything that is worth hearing: we *speak* languages, we *speak* sense or nonsense, we *speak* intelligibly or unintelligibly; but we *say* what we think at the time.

In an extended sense, *speak* may refer as much to sense as to sound, but then it applies only to general cases, and *say* to particular and passing circumstances of life: it is a great abuse of the gift of speech not to *speak* the truth; it is very culpable in a person to *say* that he will do a thing and not to do it.

To *say* and *tell* are both the ordinary actions of men in their daily intercourse; but *say* is very partial, it may comprehend single unconnected sentences or even single words: we may *say* yes or no, but we *tell* that which is connected and which forms more or less of a narrative. To *say* is to communicate that which passes in our own minds, to express our ideas and feelings as they rise; to *tell* is to communicate events or circumstances respecting ourselves or others: it is not good to let children *say* foolish things for the sake of talking: it is still worse for them to be encouraged in *telling* everything they hear: when every one is allowed to *say* what he likes and what he thinks, there will commonly be more *speakers* than hearers; those who accustom themselves to *tell* long stories impose a burden upon others which is not repaid by the pleasure of their company.

See also UTTER.

Speak, Talk, Converse, Discourse.—The idea of communicating with, or communicating to, another, by means of signs, is common in the signification of all these terms: to *speak* is an indefinite term specifying no circumstance of the action; we may *speak* only one word or many; but *talk,* which is but a variation of *tell,* is a mode of *speaking,* namely, for a continuance: we may *speak* from various motives; we *talk* for pleasure; we *converse* for improvement or intellectual gratification: we *speak* with or to a person: we *talk* commonly to others; we *converse* with others. *Speaking* a language is quite distinct from writing it: those who think least *talk* most: *conversation* is the rational employment of social beings, who seek by an interchange of ideas to purify the feelings and improve the understanding.

Conversation is the act of many together; *discourse*, in Latin *discursus*, expressing properly an examining or deliberating upon, like *talk*, may be the act of one addressing himself to others; parents and teachers *discourse* with young people on moral duties.

SPECIAL, Specific, Particular. *Special*, in Latin *specialis*, signifies belonging to the species; *specific*, in Latin *specificus*, from *speci-*, for *species*, a species, and a weakened form of *facere*, to make, signifies making a species; *particular*, belonging to a particle or small part. The *special* is that which comes under the general; the *particular* is that which comes under the *special*: hence we speak of a *special* rule; but a *particular* case. *Particular* and *specific* are both applied to the properties of individuals; but *particular* is said of the contingent circumstances of things, *specific* of their inherent properties: every plant has something *particular* in itself different from others, it is either longer or shorter, weaker or stronger; but its *specific* property is that which it has in common with its species: *particular* is, therefore, the term adapted to loose discourse; *specific* is a scientific term which describes things minutely.

The same may be said of *particularize* and *specify*: we *particularize* for the sake of information; we *specify* for the sake of instruction: in describing a man's person and dress we *particularize* if we mention everything singly which can be said about it; in delineating a plan it is necessary to *specify* time, place, distance, materials, and everything else which may be connected with the carrying it into execution.

SPECIES. See KIND.
SPECIFIC. See SPECIAL.
SPECIMEN. See COPY.
SPECIOUS. See COLORABLE.
SPECK. See BLEMISH.
SPECTACLE. See SHOW.
SPECTATOR. See LOOKER-ON.
SPECTRE. See VISION.
SPECULATION. See THEORY.
SPEECH. See ADDRESS; LANGUAGE.
SPEECHLESS. See SILENT.
SPEED. See HASTEN.

SPELLBOUND, Bewitched. These words have a similar meaning. Both are of Anglo-Saxon origin, and bear their original meaning on their face, as it were. *Spellbound* means bound by a *spell*, a *spell* being originally a narrative myth or fable, hence the absorption of one who listens to such narration; thence by extension an utterance or incantation, by which superhuman spirits were called upon to take the victim under their power. *Bewitched* means under the influence of a witch. *Spellbound* and *bewitched* are both used figuratively—*spellbound* to indicate a state of rapt attention in which all motion is suspended; *bewitched* to signify under a powerful influence, which seems in some way abnormal. *Bewitched* often describes absorbing and exclusive admiration of or devotion to a person or an idea.

SPEND, Exhaust, Drain. *Spend* comes from Anglo-Saxon *spendan*, to spend, shortened from Latin *dispendere*, from *dis*, out, and *pendere*, to weigh, meaning to weigh out money. *Exhaust*, from the Latin *ex*, out, and *haustus*, past participle of *haurire*, to draw water. *Drain*, in Anglo-Saxon *drenian*, originally meant to become *dry*, and is allied to *dry*.

The idea of taking from the substance of anything is common to these terms; but to *spend* is to deprive it in a less degree than to *exhaust*, and that in a less degree than to *drain*: every one who exerts himself in that degree *spends* his strength; if the exertions are violent he *exhausts* himself; a country which is *drained* of men is supposed to have no more left. To *spend* may be applied to that which is either external or inherent in a body; *exhaust* to that which is inherent; *drain* to that which is external of the body in which it is contained: we may speak of *spending* our wealth, our resources, our time, and the like; but of *exhausting* our strength, our vigor, our voice, and the like; of *draining*, in the proper application, a vessel of its liquid, or in the improper application, *draining* a treasury of its contents: hence arises this further distinction, that to *spend* and to *exhaust* may tend, more or less, to the injury of a body; but to *drain* may be to its advantage.

Inasmuch as what is *spent* or *exhausted* may be more or less essential to the soundness of a body, it cannot be parted with without diminishing its value or even destroying its existence; as when a fortune is *spent* it is gone, or when a person's strength is *exhausted* he is no longer able to move: on the other hand, to *drain*, though a more complete evacuation, is not always injurious, but sometimes even useful to a body, as when the land is *drained* of a superabundance of water.

Spend, Expend, Waste, Dissipate, Squander. — *Spend* and *expend* both come ultimately from Latin *pendere*, to weigh—*spend* indirectly through Anglo-Saxon, *expend* directly from Latin *ex*, out, and *pendere*, to weigh; but *spend* implies simply to turn to some purpose or make use of; to *expend* carries with it likewise the idea of exhausting; and *waste*, moreover, comprehends the idea of exhausting to no good purpose: we *spend* money when we purchase anything with it; we *expend* it when we lay it out in large quantities so as essentially to diminish its quantity: individuals *spend* what they have; government *expends* vast sums in conducting the affairs of a nation; all persons *waste* their property who have not sufficient discretion to use it well: we *spend* our time, or our lives, in any employment; we *expend* our strength and faculties upon some arduous undertaking; we *waste* our time and talents in trifles.

Dissipate, in Latin *dissipatus*, from *dissipare*, means to disperse, to throw in all directions. *Squander* meant originally to scatter abroad, and is a nasalized form allied to Lowland Scotch *squatter*, to splash about, scatter. Both these terms, therefore, denote modes of *wasting;* but the former seems peculiarly applicable to that which is *wasted* in detail upon different objects, and by a distraction of the mind; the latter respects rather the act of *wasting* in the gross, in large quantities, by planless profusion: young men are apt to *dissipate* their property in pleasure; the open, generous, and thoughtless are apt to *squander* their property.

SPHERE. See Circle.

SPILL. See Pour.

SPIRIT. See Animation; Unction.

SPIRITED. See Spirituous.

SPIRITUAL. See Incorporeal; Spirituous.

SPIRITUOUS, Spirited, Spiritual, Ghostly. *Spirituous* signifies having *spirit* as a physical property, after the manner of *spirituous* liquors: *spirited* is applicable to the animal *spirits* of either men or brutes; a person or a horse may be *spirited*.

What is *spiritual* is after the manner of a *spirit*, and what is *ghostly* is like a *ghost:* although originally the same in meaning, the former being derived from the Latin *spiritus*, and the latter from the Anglo-Saxon *gast*, German *geist*, and both signifying what is not corporeal, yet they have acquired a difference of application. *Spiritual* objects are mostly distinguished from those of sense. Hence it is that the *spiritual* is opposed to the temporal.

Ghostly is more immediately opposed to the carnal or the secular, and is a term, therefore, of more solemn import.

SPITE. See Malice.

SPLASH. See Dabble.

SPLENDID. See Superb.

SPLENDOR. See Brightness; Magnificence.

SPLENETIC. See Hypochondriacal.

SPLENIC FEVER. See Anthrax.

SPLIT. See Break.

SPOIL. See Booty; Bungle.

SPOLIATION. See Rapine; Ravage; Sack.

SPONTANEOUSLY. See Willingly.

SPORT. See Amusement; Jest; Play.

SPORTIVE. See Lively; Playful.

SPOT. See Blemish; Place.

SPOTLESS. See Blameless.

SPOUT. See Spurt.

SPRAIN. See Strain.

SPREAD, Scatter, Disperse. *Spread* applies equally to divisible or indivisible bodies; we *spread* our money on the table, or we may *spread* a cloth on the table; but *scatter*, like *shatter*, is a frequentative of *shake*, and is applicable to divisible bodies only; we *scatter* corn on the ground. To *spread* may be an act of design or otherwise, but mostly the former; as when we *spread* books or papers before us: *scatter* is mostly an act without design; a child *scatters* the papers on the floor. When taken, however, as an act of design, it is done without order; but *spread* is an act done in order; thus hay is *spread* out to dry, but corn is *scattered* over the land.

Things may *spread* in one direction, or at least without separation; but they *disperse* (see DISPEL) in many directions, so as to destroy the continuity of bodies: a leaf *spreads* as it opens in all its parts, and a tree also *spreads* as its branches increase; but a multitude *disperses*, an army *disperses*. Between *scatter* and *disperse* there is no other difference than that one is immethodical and often involuntary, the other systematic and intentional: flowers are *scattered* along a path which accidentally fall from the hand; a mob is *dispersed* by an act of authority: sheep are *scattered* along the hills; religious tracts are *dispersed* among the poor: the disciples were *scattered* as sheep without a shepherd after the delivery of our Saviour into the hands of the Jews; they *dispersed* themselves, after his ascension, over every part of the world.

To *spread* is the general, the other two are particular terms. To *spread* may be said of anything which occupies more space than before, whether by a direct separation of its parts or by an accession to the substance; but to *expand*, from Latin *expandere*, is to *spread* by means of extending or unfolding the parts; a mist *spreads* over the earth; a flower *expands* its leaves; a tree *spreads* by the growth of its branches; the opening bud *expands* when it feels the genial warmth of the sun. *Diffusion* is that process of *spreading* which consists literally in pouring out in different ways.

Spread and *expand* are used likewise in a moral application; *diffuse* is seldom used in any other application: *spread* is here, as before, equally indefinite as to the mode of the action; everything *spreads*, and it *spreads* in any way; but *expansion* is that gradual process by which an object opens or unfolds itself after the manner of a flower. Evils *spread*, and reports *spread;* the mind *expands*, and prospects *expand;* knowledge *diffuses* itself; or cheerfulness is *diffused* throughout a company.

Spread, Circulate, Propagate, Disseminate.—To *spread* is said of any object material or spiritual; the rest are mostly employed in the moral application. To *spread* is to extend to an indefinite width; to *circulate* is to *spread* within a circle: thus news *spreads* through a country; but a story *circulates* in a village or from house to house, or a report is *circulated* in a neighborhood.

Spread and *circulate* are the acts of persons or things; *propagate* and *disseminate* are the acts of persons only. The thing *spreads* and *circulates*, or it is *spread* and *circulated* by some one; it is always *propagated* and *disseminated* by some one. *Propagate*, from the Latin *propagare*, to increase by layers, from *propages*, a layer, from stem contained in *compages* (compare English *compact*), a fastening together, and *disseminate*, from *dis*, apart, and *semen*, a seed, are here figuratively employed as modes of *spreading*, according to the natural operations of increasing the quantity of anything which is implied in the first two terms. What is *propagated* is supposed to secure new adherents, as when doctrines, either good or bad, are *propagated* among the people so as to make them converts: what is *disseminated* is supposed to be sown in different parts; thus principles are *disseminated* among youth.

SPRIGHTLY. See CHEERFUL; LIVELY.

SPRING, FOUNTAIN, SOURCE. *Spring* denotes that which *springs;* the word, therefore, carries us back to the point from which the water issues. *Fountain*, through French from Low Latin *fontana*, based on classical *fons*, a fountain, signifies that from which anything is poured, and comprehends in it a collection or certain quantity of water, both natural and artificial: and *source* is from Old French *sorse*, the feminine past participle of the verb *sourdre* (with intercalated *d*), from *surgere*, to rise, and carries us back to the place whence the water takes its rise. *Springs* are to be found by digging a sufficient depth in all parts of the earth: in mountainous countries, and also in the East, we read of *fountains* which form themselves, and supply the surrounding parts with refreshing streams: the *sources* of rivers are mostly to be traced to some mountain.

These terms are all used in a figurative sense: *spring* is taken for that which is always flowing; *fountain* for that which contains an abundant supply for a stream, and *source* for the channel through which from the commencement any event comes to pass.

Spring, Start, Startle, Shrink.—The idea of a sudden motion is expressed by all these terms, but the circumstances and mode differ in all; *spring* is indefinite in these respects, and is therefore the most general term. To *spring* and *start*, Middle English *sterten*, to move suddenly, may be either voluntary or involuntary movements, but the former is mostly voluntary and the latter involuntary; a person *springs* out of bed, or one animal *springs* upon another; a person or animal *starts* from a certain point to begin running, or *starts* with fright from one side to the other. To *startle*, which is a frequentative of *start*, is always an involuntary action; a horse *starts* by suddenly flying from the point on which he stands; but if he *startles* he seems to fly back on himself and stops his course; to *spring* and *start*, therefore, always carry a person farther from a given point; but *startle* and *shrink* are movements within one's self; *startling* is a sudden convulsion of the frame which makes a person stand in hesitation whether to proceed or not; *shrinking*, from Anglo-Saxon *scrincan*, is allied to *shrug, shrimp*, etc., and means a contraction of the frame within itself; any sudden and unexpected sound makes a person *startle;* the approach of any frightful object makes him *shrink* back; *spring* and *start* are mostly employed only in the proper sense of corporeal movements; *startle* and *shrink* are employed in regard to the movements of the mind as well as the body.

See also ARISE.

Sprinkle, Bedew.—*Sprinkle* is from *sprenkle*, the frequentative form of Middle English *sprengen*, allied to Dutch *sprenkelen*, to sprinkle; it denotes either an act of nature or design: to *bedew* is to cover with *dew*, which is an operation of nature. By *sprinkling*, a liquid falls in visible drops upon the earth; by *bedewing*, it covers by imperceptible drops: rain *besprinkles* the earth; dew *bedews* it.

So likewise, figuratively, things are *sprinkled* with flour; the cheeks are *bedewed* with tears.

SPRINGING. See SALIENT.

SPROUT, BUD. *Sprout* is in Anglo-Saxon *sprutan*, meaning to germinate, allied to *spout*. *Bud* is a word of uncertain but probably Teutonic origin which does not appear in Anglo-Saxon, but is found in Middle English as *budden*, to *bud*. Cf. Dutch *bot*, a bud. To *bud* is to put forth *buds;* the noun *bud* is a variation from button, which it resembles in form. (Cf. the French *bouton*, which means both *bud* and button.) To *sprout* is to come forth from the stem; to *bud*, to put forth in *buds*.

SPRUCE. See FINICAL.

SPURIOUS, SUPPOSITITIOUS, COUNTERFEIT. Spurious comes from Latin *spuries*, false, of illegitimate birth. *Supposititious* is derived from Latin *suppositicius*, from the stem of *supponere*, suppose or substitute, and signifies to be supposed or conjectured, something not real but substituted, in distinction from being positively known. *Counterfeit* (see IMITATE).

All these terms are modes of the false; the former two indirectly, the latter directly; whatever is uncertain that might be certain, and whatever is conjectured that might be conclusive, are by implication false; that which is made in imitation of another thing, so as to pass for it as the true one, is positively false. Hence, the distinction between these terms and the ground of their applications. An illegitimate offspring is said to be *spurious* in the literal sense of the word, the father in this case being always uncertain; and any offspring which is termed *spurious* falls necessarily under the imputation of not being the offspring of the person whose name it bears. In the same manner an edition of a work is termed *spurious* which comes out under a false name or a name different from that on the title-page; *supposititious* expresses more or less of falsehood, according to the nature of the thing. A *supposititious* parent implies little less than a directly false parent; but in speaking of the origin of any person in remote periods of antiquity, it may be merely *supposititious* or conjectural from the want of information. *Counterfeit* respects rather works of art which are exposed to imitation: coin is *counterfeit* which bears a false stamp, and every invention which comes out under the sanction of the inventor's name is likewise a *counterfeit* if not made by himself or by his consent.

SPURT, SPOUT. To *spurt* meant originally to germinate and is the same word as *sprout;* Middle English *spruten. Spout.* Middle English *spouten,* to spurt out—the word has probably no relation to the English *spit;* they both express the idea of sending forth liquid in small quantities from a cavity; the former, however, does not always include the idea of the cavity, but simply that of springing up; the latter is, however, confined to the circumstances of issuing forth from some place; dirt may be *spurted* in the face by means of kicking it up, or blood may be *spurted* out of a vein when it is opened, water out of the mouth, and the like; but a liquid *spouts* out from a pipe. To *spurt* is a sudden action arising from a momentary impetus given to a liquid either intentionally or incidentally; the beer will *spurt* from a barrel when the vent-peg is removed: to *spout* is a continued action produced by a perpetual impetus which the liquid receives equally from design or accident; the water *spouts* out from a pipe which is denominated a *spout,* or .t will *spout* out from any cavity in the earth, or in a rock which may resemble a *spout;* a person may likewise *spout* water in a stream from his mouth.

Hence the figurative application of these terms; any sudden conceit which compels a person to an eccentric action is a *spurt,* particularly if it springs from ill-humor or caprice; a woman will sometimes take a *spurt* and treat her intimate friends very coldly, either from a fancied offence or a fancied superiority; to *spout,* on the other hand, is to send forth a stream of words in imitation of the stream of liquid, and is applied to those who affect to be speakers or who recite in an affected manner.

SPY, SCOUT. For the derivation of *spy* see EMISSARY. *Scout* is derived from Old French *escouter,* to listen, Latin *auscultare.* A *spy* and a *scout* are both agents sent out to gain information, but *spy* suggests secrecy and disguise; *scout* active and watchful movement. A *spy,* in times of war, enters directly into the camp of the enemy and gains what information he can by pretending to espouse the enemy's cause. A *scout,* on the other hand, is a kind of watchman, as it were, sent out to explore a territory and find out what he can without being caught. He depends upon quickness of movement, skill, and observation rather than upon deceit.

SQUALID, DIRTY, FOUL. *Squalid, dirty,* and *foul* all indicate a condition of uncleanness. *Dirty* signifies merely that which is not clean, that which is covered with dirt. *Foul,* Anglo-Saxon *ful,* adds to the idea of uncleanness the suggestion of something loathsome, offensive. *Squalid,* from Latin *squalidus,* adds to the idea of uncleanness the suggestion of misery and poverty. A palace may be *dirty* or *foul;* but it will not be *squalid.* A peasant's hut may be spoken of as *squalid.*

SQUANDER. See SPEND.

SQUEAMISH. See FASTIDIOUS.

SQUEEZE. See BREAK; PRESS.

STABILITY. See CONSTANCY.

STABLE. See FIRM.

STAFF, STAY, PROP, SUPPORT. From *staff* in the literal sense comes *staff* in the figurative application: anything may be denominated a *staff* which holds up after the manner of a *staff,* particularly as it respects persons; bread is said to be the *staff* of life; one person may serve as a *staff* to another.

The *staff* serves in a state of motion; the *stay* and *prop* are employed for objects in a state of rest: the *stay* makes a thing *stay* for the time being, it keeps it in its place; it is equally applied to persons and things: we may be a *stay* to a person who is falling by letting his body rest against us; in the same manner buttresses against a wall, and shores against a building, serve the purpose of *stays* while they are repairing. For the same reason that part of a woman's dress which serves as a *stay* to the body is denominated *stays:* the *prop* keeps a thing up as a permanency; every pillar on which a building rests is a *prop;* whatever, therefore, requires to be raised from the ground and kept in that state may be set upon *props.* *Support* (see HOLD) is a general term, and in its most general sense comprehends all the others as species: whatever *supports*, that is, bears the weight of an object, is a *support*, whether in a state of motion like a *staff* or in a state of rest like a *stay* or *prop.*

Staff, stay, and *prop* are applied figuratively in the sense of a *support*, with a similar distinction between them.

Support is applied in the proper sense to moral as well as tangible objects: hope is the *support* of the mind under the most trying circumstances; religion, as the foundation of all our hopes, is the best and surest *support* under affliction.

Staff, Stick, Crutch. — *Staff* is in Anglo-Saxon *stæf. Stick* is Anglo-Saxon *sticca*, something that could *stick* or pierce into another object. *Crutch* comes from Anglo-Saxon *cricc*, developing to *crick* (cf. *cricket*), and through *critch* to *crutch*, a bent stick, and hence a *crutch* or *staff.*

The ruling idea in a *staff* is that of firmness and fixedness; it is employed for leaning upon; the ruling idea in the *stick* is that of sharpness with which it can penetrate; it is used for walking and ordinary purposes; the ruling idea in the *crutch* is its form, which serves the specific purpose of support in case of lameness; a *staff* can never be small, but a *stick* may be large; a *crutch* is in size more of a *staff* than a common *stick.*

STAGGER, REEL, TOTTER. *Stagger* is a Scandinavian word from a root signifying to push allied to *stake.* To *reel* signifies to go around like a *reel*, a small spindle for winding yarn. *Totter* is for *tolter*, a frequentative of *tilt.*

All these terms designate an involuntary and an unsteady motion; they vary both in the cause and the mode of the action; *staggering* and *reeling* are occasioned either by drunkenness or sickness; *tottering* is purely the effect of weakness, particularly the weakness of old age: a drunken man always *staggers* as he walks; one who is giddy *reels* from one part to another: to *stagger* is a much less degree of unsteadiness than to *reel;* for he who *staggers* is only thrown a little out of the straight path, but he who *reels* altogether loses his equilibrium; *reeling* is commonly succeeded by falling. To *stagger* and *reel* are said as to the carriage of the whole body; but *totter* has particular reference to the limbs; the knees and the legs *totter*, and consequently the footsteps become *tottering.* In an extended application, the mountains may be said to *stagger* and to *reel* in an earthquake: the houses may *totter* from their very bases. In a figurative application, the faith or the resolution of a person *staggers* when its hold on the mind is shaken and begins to give way; a nation or a government will *totter* when it is torn by internal convulsions.

STAGNATE. See STAND.

STAIN, SOIL, SULLY, TARNISH. *Stain* (see BLEMISH). *Soil* comes through French from Latin *suillus*, a pig; from *sus*, a sow, and signifies to wallow as a sow. *Sully*, Anglo-Saxon *sylian*, means to bemire, from Teutonic *sol*, mud, Modern English *soil;* but its meaning may be influenced by the verb to *soil. Tarnish* comes through French from Old High German *tarnen*, to obscure, darken.

All these terms imply the act of diminishing the brightness of an object; but the term *stain* denotes something grosser than the other terms and is applied to inferior objects: things which are not remarkable for purity or brightness may be *stained*, as hands when *stained* with blood or a wall *stained* with chalk; nothing is *sullied* or *tarnished* but what has some intrinsic value; a fine picture or piece of writing may be easily *soiled* by a touch of the finger; the finest glass is the soonest *tarnished:* hence, in the moral application, a man's life may be *stained* by some gross immorality: his honor may be *sullied* or his glory *tarnished.*

See also ATTAINT; COLOR.

STALWART, ATHLETIC, BRAWNY. *Stalwart* comes from Anglo-Saxon *stæ-*

pol-wyrde, literally, foundation-worthy, capable of being used as a foundation, hence strong, steadfast. *Athletic*, from Greek ἀθλητής, one who contends for a prize, means characteristic of one trained for physical contests. *Brawny* means having brawn, from Old French *braon*, a slice of flesh, German *braton*, flesh for roasting, brawn referring especially to the fleshy, muscular portions of the arms or legs. All these words signify "in possession of physical strength." In the case of *stalwart* the idea of physical endurance and courage is added to that of strength; in the case of *athletic* the idea of a special training rendering the body flexible and self-controlled as well as strong is added; in the case of *brawny* the specific suggestion of large muscles and hardened flesh is added to the idea common to all three words.

STAMMER. See HESITATE.

STAMP. See MARK; SEAL.

STAND, STOP, REST, STAGNATE. To *stand*, in Middle English *standen*, cognate with German *stehen*, Russian *stat'* or *stoyát'*, Latin *stare*, Greek ἵστημι, to stand, Hebrew *sut*, to settle. *Stop*, in Saxon *stoppan*, etc., conveys the ideas of pressing, thickening, as in the Low Latin *stupare*, to stop up with food, from the classical *stupa*, meaning *tow*, and the Greek στύπη, whence it has been made in English to express immovability. *Rest* (see EASE). *Stagnate*, in Latin *stagnatus*, participle of *stagnare*, comes from *stagnum*, a pool, and that either from *stare*, to *stand*, because waters *stand* perpetually in a pool, or from the Greek στεγνός, an enclosure, because a pool is an enclosure for waters.

The absence of motion is expressed by all these terms; *stand* is the most general of all the terms; to *stand* is simply not to move; to *stop* is to cease to move: we *stand* either for want or inclination or power to move; but we *stop* from a disinclination to go on: to *rest* is to *stop* from an express dislike to motion; we may *stop* for purposes of convenience or because we have no farther to go, but we *rest* from fatigue.

To *stagnate* is only a species of *standing* as respects liquids; water may both *stand* and *stagnate;* but the former is a temporary, the latter a permanent, *stand:* water *stands* in a puddle, but it *stagnates* in a pond or in any confined space.

All these terms admit of an extended application; business *stands* still, or there is a *stand* to business; a mercantile house *stops*, or *stops* payment; an affair *rests* undecided, or *rests* in the hands of a person; trade *stagnates.*

See also BROOK.

STANDARD. See CRITERION.

STARE. See GAPE.

START. See SPRING.

STARTLE. See SPRING.

STATE, REALM, COMMONWEALTH. The *state* is that consolidated part of a nation in which lie its power and greatness. The *realm*, from Old French *realme*, Modern *royaume*, a kingdom, both based on a hypothetical Low Latin *regalimen*, is any state whose government is monarchial. The *commonwealth* is the grand body of a nation, consisting both of the government and people, which forms the *commonwealth, welfare*, or *wealth*.

The ruling idea in the sense and application of the word *state* is that of government in its most abstract sense; affairs of *state* may either concern the internal regulations of a country or the arrangements of different *states* with each other. The term *realm* is employed for the nation at large, but confined to such nations as are monarchial and aristocratical; peers of the *realm* sit in the English Parliament by their own right. The term *commonwealth* refers rather to the aggregate body of men and their possessions than to the government of a country: it is the business of the minister to consult the interests of the *commonwealth.*

Its political components constitute the *commonwealth* of Australia, and its counties the *commonwealth* of Massachusetts.

See also SITUATION.

STATELY. See MAGISTERIAL; ORNATE; SUPERB.

STATION. See CONDITION; PLACE.

STAY. See CONTINUAL; STAFF.

STEADINESS. See CONSTANCY.

STEAL AWAY. See ABSCOND.

STEEP. See SOAK.

STEP. See PACE.

STERN. See ASCETIC; AUSTERE.

STICK, CLEAVE, ADHERE. *Stick* is in Anglo-Saxon *stecan*, Low German *steken*, Latin *stigare*, Greek στίζειν, to prick, Hebrew *stock*, to press. *Cleave*, in Anglo-Saxon *cleofian*, Low German *kliven* Danish *klaebe*, is connected with our words *glue* and *lime*, in Latin *gluten*, Greek κόλλα, glue. *Adhere* (see AT-TACH).

These terms all express the being joined to a body so as not to part from it without an effort. *Stick*, which is the general and familiar expression, denotes a junction more or less close: things may *stick* very slightly, so as to come off with the smallest touch, or things may be made to *stick* together so fast that they cannot be separated; wet paper may *stick* for a time, and by means of glue may *stick* firmly.

What *sticks* may *stick* in any manner, but what *adheres*, when said of natural bodies, *adheres* by the *sticking* on the outer surface: a foot *sticks* in the mud: wax *adheres* to the fingers. *Adhesion*, denoting a property of matter, is a scientific term.

Cleave is seldomer used than either of the other terms, but always implies a close *adhesion* produced by some particular cause.

Stick and *adhere* may also be applied figuratively, with the like distinction.

As the act of conscious agents, *stick* is, as before, the familiar expression, whether applied to material or spiritual objects; a person may *stick* with his body or his mind to anything: in both cases it is an act of determination or perseverance.

A person *cleaves* or *adheres* to an object, in the former case out of feeling, in the latter case from principle: a drowning man will *cleave* to anything by which he can be saved; a conscientious man *adheres* to the truth.

See also ADHERE; FIX; STAFF.

STIFLE, SUPPRESS, SMOTHER. *Stifle* is a Scandinavian word, allied to Icelandic *stifla*, to dam up, make stiff, and to English *stiff*. *Suppress* (see REPRESS). *Smother* comes from Middle English *smorther*, a suffocating smoke, and means to have the effect of a suffocating smoke.

Stifle and *smother* in their literal sense will be more properly considered under the article on SUFFOCATE; they are here taken in a moral application. The leading idea in all these terms is that of keeping out of view: *stifle* is applicable to the feelings only; *suppress* to the feelings or to outward circumstances; *smother* to outward circumstances only: we *stifle* resentment; we *suppress* anger: the former is an act of some continuance; the latter is the act of the moment: we *stifle* our resentment by abstaining to take any measures of retaliation; we *suppress* the rising emotion of anger, so as not to give it utterance or even the expression of a look. It requires time and powerful motives to *stifle*, but only a single effort to *suppress;* nothing but a long course of vice can enable a man to *stifle* the admonitions and reproaches of conscience; a sense of prudence may sometimes lead a man to *suppress* the joy which an occurrence produces in his mind. In regard to outward circumstances, we say that a book is *suppressed* by the authority of government; that vice is *suppressed* by the exertions of those who have power: an affair is *smothered* so that it shall not become generally known, or the fire is *smothered* under the embers.

See also SUFFOCATE.

STIGMA. See MARK.

STILL. See APPEASE; QUELL.

STIMULATE. See ENCOURAGE.

STIPEND. See ALLOWANCE.

STIR, MOVE. *Stir* is in Anglo-Saxon *styrian*, to move. *Move* (see MOTION).

Stir is here a specific, *move* a generic, term: we may *move* in any manner, but to *stir* is to *move* so as to disturb the rest and composure either of the body or mind; the term *stir* is therefore mostly employed in cases where any motion, however small, is a disturbance: a soldier must not *stir* from the post which he has to defend; atrocious criminals or persons raving mad are bound hand and foot, that they may not *stir*.

See also THRILL.

STIR UP. See AWAKEN.

STOCK, STORE. *Stock* meant originally a stump remaining in the ground —a significance which it still retains; hence it developed the meaning of something fixed.

The ideas of wealth and stability being naturally allied, it is not surprising that *stock*, which expresses the latter idea, should also be put for the former, particularly as the abundance here referred to serves as a foundation, in the same manner as *stock* in the literal sense does to a tree. *Store* likewise implies a quantity; but it implies an accumulated quantity. Any quantity of materials which is in hand may serve as a *stock* for a given purpose; thus a few shillings with some persons may be their *stock*-in-trade: any quantity of materials brought together for a given purpose may serve as a *store;* thus the industrious ant collects a *store* of grain for the winter. The *stock* is that which must increase of itself; it is the source and foundation of industry; the *store* is that which we must add to occasionally; it is that from which we draw in time of need. By a *stock* we gain riches; by a *store* we guard against want.

The same distinction exists between these words in their moral application; he who wishes to speak a foreign language must have a *stock* of familiar words; *stores* of learning are frequently lost to the world for want of means and opportunity to bring them forth to public view.

As verbs, to *stock* and to *store* both signify to provide; but the former is a provision for the present use and the latter for some future purpose: a tradesman *stocks* himself with such articles as are most salable; a fortress or a ship is *stored:* a person *stocks* himself with patience or *stores* his memory with knowledge.

STOP. See Cessation; Check; Hinder; Stand.

STORE. See Stock.

STORY, Tale. The *story* (see Anecdote) is either an actual fact or something feigned; the *tale* (see Fable) is always feigned: *stories* are circulated respecting the accidents and occurrences which happen to persons in the same place; *tales* of distress are told by many merely to excite compassion. When both are taken for that which is fictitious, the *story* is either an untruth or falsifying of some fact or it is altogether an invention; the *tale* is always an invention. As an untruth,

the *story* is commonly told by children; and as a fiction, the *story* is commonly made for children: the *tale* is of deeper invention, formed by men of mature understanding, and adapted for persons of mature years.

STOUT. See Corpulent.

STRAIGHT, Right, Direct. *Straight* is the Middle English past participle of the verb which is now *stretch*, and meant literally *stretched*. *Straight* is applied, therefore, in its proper sense, to corporeal objects; a path which is *straight* is kept within a shorter space than if it were curved. *Right* and *direct*, from the *rectus*, the past participle of Latin *regere* (to rule, guide), meaning here regulated or made as it ought, are said of that which is made by the force of the understanding, or by an actual effort, what one wishes it to be: hence, the mathematician speaks of a *right* line, as the line which lies most justly between two points, and has been made the basis of mathematical figures; and the moralist speaks of the *right* opinion, as that which has been formed by the best rule of the understanding; and, on the same ground, we speak of a *direct* answer as that which has been framed so as to bring one soonest and easiest to the point desired.

STRAIN, Sprain, Stress, Force. *Strain* is derived through Old French *estraindre*, from Latin *stringere*, to pull tight, related to Anglo-Saxon *streccan*, to stretch: *sprain* comes from Old French *espreindre*, to press or wring, from Latin *exprimere*, to press out. To *strain* is to extend beyond its ordinary length by some extraordinary effort; to *sprain* is to *strain* so as to put out of its place or extend to an injurious length: the ankle and the wrist are liable to be *sprained* by a sudden wrenching; the back and other parts of the body may be *strained* by overexertion.

Strain and *stress* are kindred terms, as being both variations of stretch and *stringere;* but they differ now very considerably in their application: figuratively we speak of *straining* a nerve, or *straining* a point, to express making great exertions, even beyond our ordinary powers; and morally we speak of laying a *stress* upon any particular measure or mode of action, signifying to give a thing importance: the *strain* (see STRESS) may be put for the course of sentiment which we express and the manner of expressing it; the *stress* may be put for the efforts of the voice in uttering a word or syllable: a writer may proceed in a *strain* of panegyric or invective; a speaker or a reader lays a *stress* on certain words by way of distinguishing them from others. To *strain* is properly a species of *forcing;* we may *force* in a variety of ways, that is, by the exercise of *force* upon different bodies and in different directions; but to *strain* is to exercise *force* by stretching or prolonging bodies; thus to *strain* a cord is to pull it to its full extent; but we may speak of *forcing* any hard substance in, or *forcing* it out, or *forcing* it through, or *forcing* it from a body: a door or a lock may be *forced* by violently breaking it; but a door or a lock may be *strained* by putting the hinges or the spring out of their place. So, likewise, a person may be said to *force* himself to speak when by a violent exertion he gives utterance to his words; but he *strains* his throat or his voice when he exercises the *force* on the throat or lungs so as to extend them. *Force* and *stress,* as nouns, are in like manner comparable when they are applied to the mode of utterance; we must use a certain *force* in the pronunciation of every word; this, therefore, is indefinite and general; but the *stress* is that particular and strong degree of *force* which is exerted in the pronunciation of certain words.

STRAIT, NARROW. *Strait* is derived through French from Latin *strictus,* participle of *stringere,* to bind close, and signifies bound tight, that is, brought into a small compass: *narrow,* from Anglo-Saxon *nearu,* closely drawn, expresses a mode of nearness or closeness. *Strait* is a particular term; *narrow* is general: *straitness* is an artificial mode of *narrowness;* a coat is *strait* which is made to compress a body within a small compass: *narrow* is either the artificial or the natural property of a body, as a *narrow* ribbon or a *narrow* leaf. That which is *strait* is so by the means of other bodies, as a piece of water confined close on each side by land is called a *strait:* whatever is bounded by sides that are near each other is *narrow;* thus a piece of land whose prolonged sides are at a small distance from each other is *narrow.* The same distinction applies to these terms in their moral or extended use.

STRANGE. See PARTICULAR.

STRANGER, FOREIGNER, ALIEN. *Stranger,* in Old French *estrangier,* from Latin *extraneus,* based on the preposition *extra,* in Greek ἐξ, signifies out of, that is, out of another country: *foreigner,* from Old French *forain,* derived from Low Latin *foranens,* from classical *foras,* out of doors, and *alien,* from *alienus,* another's, have obviously the same original meaning: they have, however, deviated in their acceptations.

Stranger is a general term and applies to one not known or not an inhabitant, whether of the same or another country; *foreigner* is applied only to *strangers* of another country, and *alien* to one who has no political or natural tie. Ulysses, after his return from the Trojan war, was a *stranger* in his own house; the French are *foreigners* in England, and the English in France; neither can enjoy, as *aliens,* the same privileges in a *foreign* country as they do in their own: the laws of hospitality require us to treat *strangers* with more ceremony than we do members of the same family or very intimate friends: the lower orders of the English are apt to treat *foreigners* with an undeserved contempt; every *alien* is obliged, in time of war, to have a license for residing in a foreign country.

Stranger is sometimes taken for one not acquainted with an object or not experienced in its effects: *foreigner* is used only in the proper sense; but the epithet *foreign* sometimes signifies not belonging to an object: *alien* is applied in its natural sense to that which is unconnected by any tie.

STRATAGEM. See ARTIFICE.

STRATEGY. See TACTICS.

STRAY. See DEVIATE.

STREAM, CURRENT, TIDE. A fluid body in a progressive motion is the object described in common by these terms: *stream* is the most general, the other two are but modes of the *stream: stream,* in Anglo-Saxon *stream,* in German *strom*, comes from a root meaning to flow; a *current*, from *currere*, to run, is a *stream* running in a particular direction; and a *tide*, Anglo-Saxon *tid*, time, in German *zeit*, time, is a periodical *stream* or *current*. All rivers are *streams*, which are more or less gentle according to the nature of the ground through which they pass; the force of the *current* is very much increased by the confinement of any water, between rocks, or by means of artificial impediments: the *tide* is high or low, strong or weak, at different hours of the day; when the *tide* is high, the *current* is strongest.

From knowing the proper application of these terms, their figurative and moral application becomes obvious: a *stream* of air or a *stream* of light is a prolonged moving body of air or light: so a *stream* of charity, bounty, and the like is that which flows in a stream: a *current* of air is a particular *stream* of air passing through or between other bodies, as the *current* of air in a house; so the *current* of men's minds or opinions, that is, the running in a particular line: the *tide* being a temporary *stream;* fashion, or the ruling propensity of the day, may be denominated a *tide:* it is sometimes vain to attempt to stem the *tide* of folly, it is therefore wiser to get out of its reach.

See also FLOW.

STRENGTH. See POWER.

STRENGTHEN, FORTIFY, INVIGORATE. *Strengthen*, from *strength*, and *fortify*, from *fortis* and a weakened form of *facere*, signify to make strong: *invigorate* signifies to put in vigor (see ENERGY).

Whatever adds to the *strength*, be it in ever so small a degree, *strengthens;* exercise *strengthens* either body or mind; whatever gives *strength* for a particular emergency *fortifies;* religion *fortifies* the mind against adversity: whatever adds to the *strength*, so as to give a positive degree of *strength*, *invigorates;* morning exercise in fine weather *invigorates*.

STRENUOUS, BOLD. *Strenuous*, in Latin *strenuus*, from the Greek στρηνής, strong, undaunted, untamed, expresses much more than *bold; boldness* is a prominent idea, but it is only one idea which enters into the signification of *strenuousness;* this combines likewise fearlessness, activity, and ardor. An advocate in a cause may be *strenuous* or merely *bold:* in the former case he omits nothing that can be either said or done in favor of the cause, he is always on the alert, he heeds no difficulties or danger; but in the latter case he displays his spirit only in the undisguised declaration of his sentiments. *Strenuous* supporters of any opinion are always strongly convinced of the truth of that which they support, and deeply impressed with a sense of its importance; but the *bold* supporter of an opinion may be impelled rather by the desire of showing his *boldness* than maintaining his point.

STRESS, STRAIN, EMPHASIS, ACCENT. *Stress* and *strain* (for both see STRAIN) are general both in sense and application; the former (from Old French *estrecir,* based on a hypothetical derivative of Latin *strictus,* tightened) still more than the latter: *emphasis,* from the Greek ἔμφασις, composed of ἐν, in, and φάσις, an appearance, signifying making to appear, and *accent,* in Latin *accentus,* from *ad,* to, and *cantus,* a song, signifying to suit the tune or tone of the voice, are modes of the *stress.* *Stress* is applicable to all bodies the powers of which may be tried by exertion, as the *stress* upon a rope, upon a shaft of a carriage, a wheel or spring in a machine: the *strain* is an excessive *stress,* by which a thing is thrown out of its course; there may be a *strain* in most cases where there is a *stress:* but *stress* and *strain* are to be compared with *emphasis* and *accent,* particularly in the exertion of the voice, in which case the *stress* is a strong and special exertion of the voice on one word, or one part of a word, so as to distinguish it from another; but the *strain* is the undue exertion of the voice beyond its usual pitch, in the utterance of one or more words: we lay a *stress* for the convenience of others; but when we *strain* the voice it is as much to the annoyance of others as it is hurtful to ourselves. The *stress* may consist in an elevation of voice or a prolonged utterance; the *emphasis* is that species of *stress* which is employed to distinguish one word or syllable from another: the *stress* may be accidental; but the *emphasis* is an intentional *stress:* ignorant people and children are often led to lay the *stress* on small and unimportant words in a sentence; speakers sometimes find it convenient to mark particular words, to which they attach a value, by the *emphasis* with which they utter them. The *stress* may be casual or regular, on words or syllables; the *accent* is that kind of regulated *stress* which is laid on one syllable to distinguish it from another: there are many words in our own language, such as subject, object, present, and the like, where, to distinguish the verb from the noun, the *accent* falls on the last syllable for the former and on the first syllable for the latter.

In reference to the use of words, these terms may admit of a further distinction; for we may lay a *stress* or *emphasis* on a particular point of our reasoning, in the first case, by enlarging upon it longer than on other points; or, in the second case, by the use of stronger expressions or epithets. The *strain* or *accent* may be employed to designate the tone or manner in which we express ourselves, that is, the spirit of our discourse: in familiar language, we talk of a person's proceeding in a *strain* of panegyric or of censure; but, in poetry, persons are said to pour forth their complaints of love in tender *accents*.

STRETCH. See EXTEND.

STRICT, SEVERE. *Strict,* from *strictus,* bound or confined, characterizes the thing which binds or keeps in control: *severe* (see AUSTERE) characterizes in the proper sense the disposition of the person to inflict pain, and in an extended application the thing which inflicts pain. The term *strict* is, therefore, taken always in the good sense; *severe* is good or bad, according to circumstances: he who has authority over others must be *strict* in enforcing obedience, in keeping good order, and in requiring a proper attention to their duties; but it is possible to be very *severe* in punishing those who are under us and yet very lax in all matters that our duty demands of us.

Strict may with propriety be applied to one's self as well as others: *severe* is applied to one's self only to denote self-mortification.

STRICTURE. See ANIMADVERSION.

STRIFE, CONTENTION. *Strife* and *contention,* derived from the verbs *strive* and *contend* (see STRIVE), have this further distinction, that they are both taken in the bad sense for acts of anger or passion; in this case *strife* is mostly used for verbal *strife,* where each party *strives* against the other by the use of contemptuous or provoking expressions; *contention* is used for an angry *striving* with others, either in respect to matters of opinion or matters of claim, in which each party seeks to get the better of the other. *Strife* is the result of a quarrelsome humor; *contention,* of a restless, selfish, and greedy humor: *strife* is most commonly to be found in private life; *contention* but too frequently mingles itself in all the affairs of men.

See also DISCORD.

STRIKE, HIT, KNOCK, SMITE, RAP, CUFF, SLAP. These words all signify to give a blow to something, but they differ in respect to the kind of blow indicated. *Strike,* from Anglo-Saxon *strican,* to go, proceed, allied to German *streichen,* to stroke, means to give a smooth, swift blow in which the length of something hits another thing. *Hit,* on the other hand, is a Scandinavian word meaning to light on—to touch quickly and sharply with a point of something. The arrow *hits* the mark; the peasant *strikes* his horse with a stick. These distinctions are not generally observed, but they are certainly implied in the use of the two words. To *knock,* Anglo-Saxon *cnucian,* is to strike one thing against another so as to make a sound; it implies the use of something hard and knobby. To *rap,* from Danish *rap,* is to knock lightly. To *smite,* from Anglo-Saxon *smitan,* meant originally to smear or to rub, and was a sarcastic expression for *strike.* It implies the use of the flat surface of something in delivering the blow. It is a slightly archaic word in English, with a Biblical flavor, and is the strongest and most energetic of these terms. It implies the overcoming of another with blows. To *slap,* perhaps an onomatopœic word, is to strike with the flat surface of the hand. To *cuff,* from the Scandinavian, is to strike with the doubled fist, or perhaps with the palm of the hand, implying random, sidelong blows. The distinctions here suggested are not absolute distinctions carefully observed. The words are in many circumstances well-nigh interchangeable, and the meaning of one readily merges into another; but the differences mentioned seem to be implied in the general use of the several terms when they are used most carefully.

See also BEAT.

STRIP. See BEREAVE.

STRIVE, CONTEND, VIE. *Strive* comes through Old French *estriver*, from the Scandinavian. For *contend* see CONTEND. *Vie* is derived from Old French *envier*, Latin *invitare*, meaning to invite to a game, hence to contend in a game.

To *strive* is the act of individuals without regard to others; as when a person *strives* to get a living or to improve himself; to *contend* and *vie* both denote the act of an individual in reference to others; as to *contend* in a lawsuit, to *vie* in dress. To *strive* may sometimes be applied where there is more than one party, as to *strive* for the mastery; but in this case the efforts of the individual are more distinctly considered than when we speak of *contending* for a prize; for this reason these words may be applied in precisely the same connection, but still with this distinction.

Striving consists always of some active effort, as when persons *strive* at the oar; *contending* may proceed verbally, as when men *contend* for their opinions; and *vying* may be indicated by any expression of the wish to put one's self in a state of competition with another; as persons *vie* with each other in the grandeur of their houses or equipages.

Contend may be used in a moral application, as to *contend* with difficulties: and *vie* may be used figuratively, as one flower may be said to *vie* with another in the beauty of its colors.

See also ENDEAVOR.

STROKE. See BLOW.

STROLL. See WANDER.

STRONG, ROBUST, STURDY. *Strong* is in Anglo-Saxon *strang*, answering to German *streng*. *Robust*, in Latin *ro-*

bustus, from *robur*, signifies, literally, having the strength of oak. *Sturdy* comes through Middle English *sturdi*, from Old French *estourdi*, amazed, of unknown origin. It meant rash, hence the physical frame of one capable of an adventurous deed.

Strong is here the generic term; the others are specific, or specify strength under different circumstances; *robust* is a positive and high degree of strength arising from a peculiar bodily make: a man may be *strong* from the strength of his constitution, from the power which is inherent in his frame; but a *robust* man has strength from both the size and texture of his body, in bone and nerve he is endowed with great power. A little man may be *strong*, although not *robust;* a tall, stout man, in full health, may be termed *robust*. A man may be *strong* in one part of his body and not in another; he may be *stronger* at one time, from particular circumstances, than he is at another: but a *robust* man is *strong* in his whole body; and, as he is *robust* by nature, he will cease to be so only from disease.

Sturdiness lies both in the make of the body and the temper of the mind: a *sturdy* man is capable of making resistance, and ready to make it; he must be naturally *strong*, and not of slender make, but he need not be *robust:* a *sturdy* peasant presents us with a man who, both by nature and habit, is formed for withstanding the inroads of an enemy.

Things as well as persons may be said to be *strong*, as opposed to the weak; as a *strong* rope, a *strong* staff: *robust* and *sturdy* are said only of persons or things personal; as a *robust* make, a *robust* habit; a *sturdy* air, a *sturdy* stroke.

See also COGENT; HERCULEAN.

STRUCTURE. See EDIFICE.

STRUGGLE. See ENDEAVOR.

STUBBORN. See OBSTINATE.

STUDY. See ATTENTION.

STUPID, DULL. *Stupid*, in Latin *stupidus*, from *stupere*, to be amazed or bewildered, expresses an amazement which is equivalent to a deprivation of understanding: *dull*, Anglo-Saxon *dol*, foolish, is connected with the German *toll*, and denotes a simple deficiency. *Stupidity* in its proper sense is natural to a man, although a particular circumstance may have a similar effect upon the understanding; he who is questioned in the presence of others may appear very *stupid* in that which is otherwise very familiar to him. *Dull* is an incidental quality, arising principally from the state of the animal spirits: a writer may sometimes be *dull* in a large circle, while he is very lively in private intercourse.

See also DULL.

STURDY. See STRONG.

STUTTER. See HESITATE.

STYLE. See DICTION; NAME.

SUAVITY, URBANITY. *Suavity* is, literally, sweetness; and *urbanity* the refinement of the city, in distinction from the country: inasmuch, therefore, as a polite education tends to soften the mind and the manners, it produces *suavity;* but *suavity* may sometimes arise from natural temper, and exist, therefore, without *urbanity;* although there cannot be *urbanity* without *suavity.* By the *suavity* of our manners we gain the love of those around us; by the *urbanity* of our manners we render ourselves agreeable companions: hence also arises another distinction, that the term *suavity* may be applied to other things, as the voice or the style; but *urbanity* to manners only.

SUBDUE. See CONQUER; OVERBEAR; QUELL; SUBJECT.

SUBJECT, LIABLE, LIKELY, EXPOSED, OBNOXIOUS. *Subject*, in Latin *subjectus*, participle of *subicere*, to cast under, signifies thrown underneath. *Liable* is compounded with the suffix *able*, from Old French *lier*, to tie, Latin *ligare.* *Exposed* is the participle of the verb *expose*, from Latin *ex*, and French *poser*, for the derivation of which see COMPOSE. *Obnoxious*, in Latin *obnoxius*, compounded of *ob*, on account of, and *noxius*, hurtful, signifies in the way of hurting.

All these terms are applied to those circumstances in human life by which we are affected independently of our own choice. Direct necessity is included in the term *subject;* whatever we are obliged to suffer, that we are *subject* to; we may apply remedies to remove the evil, but often in vain: *liable* conveys more the idea of casualties; and *likely* that of mere proba-

bility; we are *likely* to encounter good fortune, but are *liable* to incur disasters: we may suffer that which we are *liable* to, but we may also escape the evil if we are careful: *exposed* conveys the idea of a passive state, into which we may be brought either through our own means or through the instrumentality of others; we are *exposed* to that which we are not in a condition to keep off from ourselves; it is frequently not in our power to guard against the evil: *obnoxious* signifies properly *exposed* to the harm of anything; as *obnoxious* to the multitude, that is, *exposed* to their resentment: a person may avoid bringing himself into this state, but he cannot avoid the consequences which will ensue from being thus involved. We are *subject* to disease or *subject* to death; this is the irrevocable law of our nature: delicate people are *liable* to catch cold; all persons are *liable* to make mistakes: a person is *exposed* to insults who provokes the anger of a low-bred man: a minister sometimes renders himself *obnoxious* to the people.

Subject, liable, and *exposed* may be applied to things as well as persons, with a similar distinction: things are *subject* by nature, as *subject* to decay; *liable* by accident, as *liable* to be broken; *exposed* by situation, or for want of protection, as *exposed* to the cutting winds. *Obnoxious* is said only of persons or that which is personal.

To *subject* and *expose*, as verbs, are taken in the same sense: a person *subjects* himself to impertinent freedom by descending to unseemly familiarities with his inferiors; he *exposes* himself to the derision of his equals by an affectation of superiority.

Subject, Subordinate, Inferior, Subservient.—*Subject* (see above). *Subordinate*, compounded of *sub* and *ordinem*, signifies to be in an order that is under others. *Inferior*, in Latin *inferior*, is the comparative of *inferus*, low, which has no relation to *infero*, to cast into. *Subservient*, compounded of *sub* and *servio*, signifies serving under something else.

These terms may express either the relation of persons to persons or things or of things to things. *Subject* in the first case respects the exercise of power; *subordinate* is said of the station and office; *inferior*, either of a man's outward circumstances or of his merits and qualifications; *subservient*, of one's relative services to another, but always in a bad sense. According to the law of nature, a child should be *subject* to his parents: according to the law of a realm, he must be *subject* to his prince: the good order of society cannot be rightly maintained unless there be some to act in a *subordinate* capacity: men of *inferior* talent have a part to act which, in the aggregate, is of no less importance than that which is sustained by men of the highest endowments: men of no principle or character will be most *subservient* to the base purposes of those who pay them best. It is the part of the ruler to protect the *subject*, and of the *subject* to love and honor the ruler: it is the part of the exalted to treat the *subordinate* with indulgence, and of the latter to show respect to those under whom they are placed: it is the part of the superior to instruct, assist, and encourage the *inferior;* it is the part of the latter to be willing to learn, ready to obey, and prompt to execute. It is not necessary for any one to act the degrading part of being *subservient* to another.

In the second instance *subject* has the same sense as in the preceding article, when taken in the relation of things to things; *subordinate* designates the degree of relative importance between things: *inferior* designates every circumstance which can render things comparatively higher or lower; *subservient* designates the relative utility of things under certain circumstances, but not always in the bad sense. All things in this world are *subject* to change: matters of *subordinate* consideration ought to be entirely eliminated when any great object is to be attained: things of *inferior* value must necessarily sell for an *inferior* price: there is nothing so insignificant that it may not be made *subservient* to some purpose.

Subject, Subjugate, Subdue.—Subject signifies to make subject. *Subjugate,* from *jugum,* a yoke, signifies to bring under the yoke. *Subdue* (see CONQUER).

Subject is here the generic, the two other specific terms: we may *subject*

either individuals or nations; but we *subjugate* only nations. We *subject* ourselves to reproof, to inconvenience, or to the influence of our passions; one nation *subjugates* another: *subjugate* and *subdue* are both employed with regard to nations that are compelled to submit to the conqueror: but *subjugate* expresses even more than *subdue,* for it implies to bring into a state of permanent submission; whereas to *subdue* may be only a nominal and temporary subjection: Cæsar *subjugated* the Gauls, for he made them *subjects* of the Roman Empire: but Alexander *subdued* the Indian nations, who revolted after his departure.

See also MATTER; OBJECT.

SUBJECTION. See THRALDOM.

SUBJOIN. See AFFIX.

SUBJUGATE. See SUBJECT.

SUBLIME. See GORGEOUS; GRANDEUR; GREAT; MAGNIFICENCE; MAJESTIC; SPLENDOR; SUPERB; THRILL.

SUBMARINE, SUBMERSIBLE, U-BOAT. These words do not differ in meaning, but there is a slight variation in their usage and application. They all indicate a boat propelled entirely under water. In the hands of the Germans, in the European war, the *submarine* became an exceedingly dangerous and lawless mode of offence, and the source of an infinite complication of international relations which eventually brought the United States into the war and necessitated a reconsideration of all the laws of honorable warfare and international usage. *Submarine* is the most general term. It means, literally, "under-sea" craft, from Latin *sub,* under, and *mare,* sea. *Submersible* is a descriptive term sometimes substituted for *submarine,* especially by newspaper reporters anxiously in search of something to break the monotony of the endless repetition of a term to which the war gave such a general currency. It means a boat that *submerges* or dips under the water, from Latin *sub,* under, and *mergere,* to dip. *U-boat,* a semi-transcription, semi-translation of the German *U* or *Unterseeboote,* was originally applied to German submarines of the type of the U-53 which visited the shores of the United States in the autumn of 1916, and attacked ships of the Allies lying just beyond the three-mile line. In popular usage it was soon applied to all German submarines armed to attack the ships of the Allies.

SUBMISSIVE. See COMPLIANT; HUMBLE; OBEDIENT; PATIENT.

SUBMIT. See COMPLY.

SUBORDINATE. See SUBJECT.

SUBORN. See FORSWEAR.

SUBSERVIENT. See SUBJECT.

SUBSIDE, ABATE, INTERMIT. *Subside*, from the Latin *sub* and *sedeo*, signifies to settle to the bottom. *Abate* (see that word). *Intermit*, from the Latin *inter* and *mitto*, signifies to leave a space or interval between.

A settlement after agitation is the peculiar meaning of *subside*. That which has been put into commotion *subsides*: heavy particles *subside* in a fluid that is at rest, and tumults are said to *subside*: a diminution of strength characterizes the meaning of *abate*; that which has been high in action may *abate*; the rain *abates* after it has been heavy, and a man's anger *abates*: alternate action and rest is implied in the word *intermit*; whatever is in action may sometimes cease from action; labor without *intermission* is out of the power of man.

SUBSIST. See BE.

SUBSISTENCE. See LIVELIHOOD.

SUBSTANTIAL, SOLID. *Substantial*, based on *sub*, under and *stare*, to stand, signifies to be present, to exist, and hence having a substance: *solid*, from Latin *solidus*, based on *solum*, the ground (which meant originally that which is whole, entire), signifies having a firm foundation. The *substantial* is opposed to that which is thin and has no consistency: the *solid* is opposed to the liquid or that which is of loose consistency. All objects which admit of being handled are in their nature *substantial*; those which are of so hard a texture as to require to be cut are *solid*. *Substantial* food is that which has a consistency in itself and is capable of giving fulness to the empty stomach: *solid* food is meat in distinction from drink: so *substantial* beings are such as consist of flesh and blood, and may be touched, in distinction from those which are airy or spiritual: the earth is *solid* which is so hardened as not to yield to pressure.

So in the moral application, the *substantial* is opposed to that which exists in the mind only and which is frequently fictitious; as a *substantial* benefit, as distinguished from that which gratifies the mind: the *solid* is that which rests on reason and has the properties of durability and reality, as a *solid* reputation.

SUBSTANTIATE. See RATIFY.

SUBSTITUTE. See CHANGE.

SUBTERFUGE. See EVASION.

SUBTLE. See CUNNING.

SUBTRACT. See DEDUCT.

SUBVERT. See OVERTURN.

SUCCEED. See FOLLOW.

SUCCESS. See TRIUMPH.

SUCCESSFUL. See FORTUNATE.

SUCCESSION, SERIES, ORDER. *Succession*, signifying the act or state of *succeeding* (see FOLLOW), is a matter of necessity or casualty: things *succeed* each other, or they are taken in *succession* either arbitrarily or by design: the *series* (see that word) is a connected *succession*; the *order* (see PLACE), the *ordered* or arranged *succession*. We observe the *succession* of events as a matter of curiosity; we trace the *series* of events as a matter of intelligence; we follow the *order* which the historian has pursued as a matter of judgment; the *succession* may be slow or quick; the *series* may be long or short; the *order* may be correct or incorrect. The present age has afforded a quick *succession* of events, and presented us with a *series* of atrocious attempts to disturb the peace of society under the pretence of self-protection. The historian of these times needs only pursue the *order* which the events themselves point out.

Successive, *Alternate*.—What is *successive* follows directly; what is *alternate* follows indirectly. A minister preaches *successively* who preaches every Sunday uninterruptedly at the same hour; but he preaches *alternately* if he preaches every other Sunday, or on one Sunday in the morning and the other Sunday in the afternoon, at the same place. The *successive* may be accidental or intentional; the *alternate* is always intentional; it may rain for three *successive* days or a fair may be held for three *successive* days: trees are placed sometimes in *alternate* order when every other tree is of the same size and kind.

SUCCINCT. See SHORT.

SUCCOR. See HELP.

SUDDEN, ABRUPT, PRECIPITATE. *Sudden,* from Old French *sodain,* Low Latin *subitanus* (for *subitaneus*), Latin *subitus,* is derived ultimately from Latin *subire,* past participle *subitus,* meaning to come upon one by stealth, to arrive or go unexpectedly. It denotes that which happens quickly and unexpectedly. *Abrupt* and *precipitate* express the same idea under a metaphor. *Abrupt* (see ABRUPT) means literally "broken off"—something so unrelated to other things that it seems like something suddenly broken off. An *abrupt* movement is a *sudden* movement with a certain sharpness and decisiveness in the *suddenness.* *Precipitate,* from Latin *præ,* before, and *cipiti,* the stem of *præceps,* based on *caput,* head, means literally head-foremost. It refers to something that is not merely *sudden,* but is a little ahead of time.

SUFFER. See ADMIT; BEAR; LEAVE; TOLERATE; UNDERGO.

SUFFICIENT. See ENOUGH.

SUFFOCATE, STIFLE, SMOTHER, CHOKE. *Suffocate,* in Latin *suffocatus,* participle of *suffocare,* compounded of *sub* and *faux,* throat, signifies to constrain or tighten the throat. For *stifle* and *smother* see STIFLE. *Choke,* from Middle English *choken,* is allied to Icelandic *koka,* to gulp, and *kok,* the throat.

These terms express the act of stopping the breath, but under various circumstances and by various means; *suffocation* is produced by every kind of means, external or internal, and is therefore the most general of these terms; *stifling* proceeds by internal means, that is, by the admission of foreign bodies into the passages which lead to the respiratory organs: we may be *suffocated* by excluding the air externally, as by gagging, confining closely, or pressing violently: we may be *suffocated* or *stifled* by means of vapors, close air, or smoke. To *smother* is to *suffocate* by the exclusion of air externally, as by means of any substance with which one is covered or surrounded, as smoke, dust, and the like: to *choke* is a mode of *stifling*

by means of large bodies, as by a piece of food lodging in the throat.

To *choke,* in an extended and figurative sense, is to interrupt the action of any body by the intervention of any foreign substance, as a garden is *choked* with weeds; to *stifle* is altogether to put a stop or end to a thing by keeping it down, as to *stifle* resentment, sighs, etc.: to *smother* is to *choke* or prevent free action by covering or surrounding, as good resolutions are *smothered* by unruly desires or appetites.

SUFFOCATION. See ASPHYXIA.

SUFFRAGETTE. See VOTE.

SUGGEST. See ALLUDE; HINT.

SUGGESTION. See DICTATE.

SUIT. See AGREE; FIT; PRAYER; TALLY.

SUITABLE. See BECOMING; CONFORMABLE; CONVENIENT; CORRESPONDENT.

SUITOR. See LOVER.

SULLY. See STAIN.

SUMMARY. See ABRIDGMENT; SHORT.

SUMMON. See CALL; CITE.

SUNDAY. See SABBATH.

SUNDRY. See DIFFERENT.

SUPERB, AUGUST, STATELY. These words have in common the idea of pride and dignity and external splendor. *Superb,* from Latin *superbus,* proud, is often used simply as a general superlative. It means excellent, with a special emphasis upon that which is externally striking and complete. *August* is derived from the name of the Roman Cæsars, *Augustus.* It denotes that which is impressive and awe-inspiring in the last degree—a union of dignity and power both unlimited. In this sense we speak of the *august* power of God, etc. *Stately* means full of *state,* something full of dignity, with special emphasis upon the idea of stability and endurance. It does not denote the complete and striking impression produced by that which is *superb* nor the awe inspired by that which is *august,* but lays a greater emphasis upon the single impression of external and stable dignity.

SUPERFICIAL, SHALLOW, FLIMSY. The *superficial* is that which lies only at the surface; it is therefore by implication the same as the *shallow,* which has nothing underneath. Hence **a**

person may be called either *superficial* or *shallow* to indicate that he has not a profundity of knowledge; but, otherwise, *superficiality* is applied to the exercise of the thinking faculty and *shallowness* to its extent. Men of freely expressed sentiments may be *superficial* thinkers, although they may not have understandings more *shallow* than others. *Superficial* and *shallow* are applicable to things as well as persons: *flimsy* is applicable to things only. *Flimsy* (from Welsh *llymsi?* cf. the American dialect word *limsy;* or perhaps connected with *film*) is a modern word. In the proper sense we may speak of giving a *superficial* covering of paint or color to a body; of a river or piece of water being *shallow;* of cotton or cloth being *flimsy.*

In the improper sense, a survey or a glance may be *superficial* which does not extend beyond the *superficies* of things; a conversation or a discourse may be *shallow* which does not contain a basis of sentiment; and a work or performance may be *flimsy* which has nothing solid in it to engage the attention.

SUPERFICIES. See SURFACE.
SUPERFLUITY. See EXCESS.
SUPERINTENDENCY. See INSPECTION.
SUPERIORITY. See EXCELLENCE.
SUPERSCRIPTION. See DIRECTION.
SUPERSEDE. See OVERRULE.
SUPINE. See INDOLENT.
SUPPLE. See FLEXIBLE.
SUPPLICATE. See BEG.
SUPPLY. See PROVIDE.
SUPPORT. See BEAR; COUNTENANCE; ESPOUSE; HOLD; LIVELIHOOD; SECOND; STAFF; SUSTAIN; UPHOLD.
SUPPOSE. See APPREHEND; THINK.
SUPPOSITION. See CONJECTURE.
SUPPOSITITIOUS. See SPURIOUS.
SUPPRESS. See QUELL; REPRESS; STIFLE.
SUPREME, PREDOMINANT, PREEMINENT. All these words mean surpassing in power or in importance. *Predominant,* from Latin *præ,* above, before, and *dominari,* to rule, meant ruling over others. *Pre-eminent,* from Latin *præ,* and *eminere,* to project, means projecting beyond others. *Pre-eminent* indicates a state of being, *pre-*

O.E.S.—22

dominant one of action. At the same time *pre-eminent* is a stronger word than *predominant.* That which is *predominant* asserts its power over others, that which is *pre-eminent* stands out so that all see and recognize the superiority. *Pre-eminent* implies a more lasting superiority than *predominant,* which implies a state of struggle in which the first place may be yielded to another. *Supreme,* from Latin *supremus,* means holding the first place of all, beyond rivalry and comparison, possessing neither a superior nor an equal. It expresses the highest possible degree of *pre-eminence.*

SURE. See CERTAIN; INFALLIBLE.
SURFACE, SUPERFICIES. *Surface,* compounded of French *sur,* for *super,* and *face,* from *faciem,* is a variation of the Latin term *superficies;* and yet they have acquired this distinction, that the former is the current and the latter the scientific term; of course the former has a more indefinite and general application than the latter. A *surface* is either even or uneven, smooth or rough; but the mathematician always conceives of a plane *superficies* on which he founds his operations.

Surface, in its moral application, is extended to whatever presents itself first to the mind of the observer.

Superficies may be applied in its proper and definite sense to other objects than those which relate to science.

SURGE. See WAVE.
SURMISE. See CONJECTURE.
SURMOUNT. See CONQUER.
SURPASS. See EXCEED.
SURPRISE. See SUDDEN; WONDER.
SURRENDER. See GIVE UP.
SURROUND, ENCOMPASS, ENVIRON, ENCIRCLE. *Surround,* from Old French *suronder,* meant originally to overflow, from *super,* over, and *unda,* a wave. *Encompass* is compounded of French *en,* in, and *compas,* from Low Latin *compassus,* a circle or circuit, and meaning a going around in a circle till the last step ends where the first began. To *encompass* is to enclose in a circle. *Environ* comes from Old French *en,* in, and *virer,* to turn, whence *veer* is derived. *Encircle* means to enclose within a circle. *Blockade* is formed, with the suffix *ade,* from *block,* derived through Old

French from Dutch. It now means a blocking of the coasts of a hostile country by encompassing it with ships which prevent merchant-vessels from getting through with supplies; but it has been used to signify any blocking up of all exit or entrance by surrounding troops or fortifications.

Surround is the most literal and general of all these terms, which signify to enclose any object either directly or indirectly. We may *surround* an object by standing at certain distances all round it; in this manner a person may be *surrounded* by other persons, and a house *surrounded* with trees, or an object may be *surrounded* by enclosing it in every direction and at every point; in this manner a garden is *surrounded* by a wall. To *encompass* is to *surround* in the latter sense, and applies to objects of a great or indefinite extent: the earth is *encompassed* by the air, which we term the atmosphere; towns are *encompassed* by walls. To *surround* is to go round an object of any form, whether square or circular, long or short; but to *environ* and to *encircle* carry with them the idea of forming a circle round an object; thus a town or valley may be *environed* by hills, a basin of water may be *encircled* by trees, or the head may be *encircled* by a wreath of flowers.

In an extended or moral sense we are said to be *surrounded* by objects which are in great numbers and in different directions about us: thus a person living in a particular spot where he has many friends may say he is *surrounded* by his friends, or *environed* by objects in such manner that he cannot escape from them; so likewise a particular person may say that he is *surrounded* by dangers and difficulties: but, in speaking of man in a general sense, we should rather say he is *encompassed* by dangers, which expresses in a much stronger manner our peculiarly exposed condition.

Blockade may be figuratively applied to any cutting off of supplies.

SURVEY. See RETROSPECT; VIEW.
SURVIVE. See OUTLIVE.
SUSCEPTIBILITY. See FEELING.
SUSPENSE. See DOUBTS.
SUSPICION. See DISTRUST; JEALOUSY.

SUSTAIN, SUPPORT, MAINTAIN. *Sustain,* from Old French *sustenir,* compounded of *sus* or *sub* and *tenere,* to hold, signifies to hold or keep up. *Support* (see COUNTENANCE). *Maintain* (see ASSERT).

The idea of keeping up or preventing from falling is common to these terms, which vary either in the mode or object of the action. To *sustain* and *support* are frequently passive, *maintain* is always active. To *sustain* and *support* both imply the bearing or receiving the weight of any object, the former in reference to any great weight, the latter to any weight however small.

Sustain and *support* may also imply an active exercise of power or means which brings them still nearer to *maintain;* in this case *sustain* is an act of the highest power, *support* of any ordinary power.

So in bearing up against any opposing force; but *support* is here an act for the benefit of others; *maintain* is an act for one's own benefit, as to *sustain* a shock, to *support* one another in battle; to *maintain* one's self in a contest.

Existence is said to be *sustained* under circumstances of weakness or pressure; it is *supported* by natural means, as the milk of the mother *supports* the babe; or indirectly by what supplies the means, as to *support* one's family by labor: what is *maintained* is upheld by pecuniary means, as to *maintain* a family, a fleet, etc.

In the moral application, what presses on the mind is *sustained*, or *supported*, with the like distinction: grievous losses or injuries are *sustained;* afflictions and disappointments *supported.*

Things are *supported* and *maintained* voluntarily; the former in respect to what is foreign to us, as to *support* an assumed character, the latter in respect to what belongs to us, as to *maintain* one's own character.

SUSTENANCE. See LIVELIHOOD.
SWAIN. See COUNTRYMAN.
SWALLOW. See ABSORB.
SWAY. See INFLUENCE; WILL.
SWEAR, TAKE OATH, TESTIFY. *Swear,* from Anglo-Saxon *swerian,* originally meant simply to speak loudly; it is the stem found in *answer.*

It now means to affirm by an appeal to the powers recognized as holy, to assert in the name of God. To *take oath* (from Anglo-Saxon *ath*) means to *swear* formally by going through the ceremony of taking an oath or making an appeal to God. To *take oath* is a somewhat more exact and specific term than *swear*, but it means the same thing. To *testify*, from Latin *testes*, a witness, and a weakened form of *facere*, to make, means literally to make, or bear witness. It is associated with *swear* and *take oath* through the fact that a formal bearing of witness is preceded by an oath.

SWELL. See HEAVE.

SWERVE. See DEFLECT; DEVIATE.

SWIFTNESS. See QUICKNESS.

SWING. See WAG.

SWOLLEN. See HIGH-FLOWN.

SYCOPHANT. See FLATTERER.

SYLLABUS, SYNOPSIS. A *syllabus*, from Late Latin *syllabus*, Late Greek σύλλαβος, a list, allied to συλλαβή, a syllable, literally "that which holds together," from Greek σύν, together, and the aorist stem of λαμβάνειν, to take, is an outline or summary of the main points of a subject, course, lecture, or treatise. A *synopsis*, from Greek σύν, together, ὄψις, sight, is a complete view of the subject in a brief space. The two words have almost the same meaning, but *synopsis* emphasizes the summing up, the inclusion of everything in a little space, and *syllabus* emphasizes the outlining of the points to be made. A *syllabus* of a course of lectures, for example, is the outline distributed beforehand. The *synopsis* of a lecture may be given in the newspaper afterward. But *synopsis* is often used interchangeably with *syllabus*, though *syllabus* cannot always take the place of *synopsis*.

SYMBOL. See FIGURE.

SYMMETRY, PROPORTION. *Symmetry*, in Latin *symmetria*, Greek συμμετρία, from σύν and μέτρον, signifies a measure that accords. *Proportion*, in Latin *proportio*, compounded of *pro*, as regards or in relation to, and *portio*, a part, signifies every portion or part according with the other or with the whole.

The signification of these terms is obviously the same, namely, a due admeasurement of the parts to each other and to the whole: but *symmetry* has now acquired but a partial application to the human body or to things nicely fitting each other; and *proportion* is applied to everything which admits of dimensions and an adaptation of the parts: hence we speak of *symmetry* of feature; but *proportion* of limbs, the *proportion* of the head to the body.

SYMPATHY, COMPASSION, COMMISERATION, CONDOLENCE. *Sympathy*, from the Greek σύμ for σύν, with, and πάθεια, feeling, has the literal meaning of fellow-feeling, that is, a kindred or like feeling or feeling in company with another. *Compassion* (see PITY); *commiseration*, from the Latin *cum*, with, and *miserari*, to pity; *condolence*, from the Latin *con* and *dolere*, to grieve, signify a like suffering or a suffering in company. Hence it is obvious that, according to the derivation of the words, the *sympathy* may be said either of pleasure or pain, the rest only of that which is painful. *Sympathy* preserves its original meaning in its application, for we laugh or cry by *sympathy;* this may, however, be a merely physical operation.

Compassion is altogether a moral feeling which makes us enter into the distresses of others: we may, therefore, *sympathize* with others, without essentially serving them; but if we feel *compassion* we naturally turn our thoughts toward relieving them

Sympathy, indeed, may sometimes be taken for a secret alliance or kindred feeling between two objects.

Compassion is awakened by various kinds of suffering, but particularly by those which are attributable to our misfortunes; *commiseration* is awakened by suffering arising from our faults; *condolence* is awakened by the troubles of life, to which all are equally liable. Poverty and want excite our *compassion;* we endeavor to relieve them: a poor criminal suffering the penalty of the law excites our *commiseration;* we endeavor, if possible, to mitigate his punishment: the loss which a friend sustains produces *condolence:* we take the best means of testifying it to him.

Compassion is the sentiment of one

mortal toward another; *commiseration* is represented as the feeling which our wretchedness excites in the Supreme Being. *Compassion* may be awakened in persons of any condition; *commiseration* is awakened toward those who are in an abject state of misery; *condolence* supposes an entire equality and is often produced by some common calamity.

SYMPTOM. See MARK.

SYNCHRONOUS, SIMULTANEOUS, CONTEMPORANEOUS. These words all mean occurring at the same time. *Simultaneous*, from Late Latin *simultim*, at the same time, contaminated by Latin *moment-aneous*, means occurring at exactly the same instant. *Synchronous*, from Greek σύν, together, and κρόνος, time, means happening within the same period of time, but not necessarily at exactly the same instant. *Synchronous* and *simultaneous* are applied to occurrences; *contemporaneous* to both events and people. *Contemporaneous* comes from Latin *con*, for *cum*, together, and *tempus*, time; it means living or happening within the same period, the period being thought of not merely as a division of time, as in the case of *synchronous*, but as an age, a generation, a period marked by certain characteristics distinguishing it from other periods.

SYNOD. See ASSEMBLY.

SYNTHETIC, CONSTRUCTIVE. *Synthetic*, from Greek σύν, with, and θετικός, skilled in putting together, from συνθέτης, a putter-together, and *constructive*, from Latin *con*, together, and *structus*, the past participle of *struere*, a heaping up, both mean putting together. *Synthetic* is opposed to *analytic*, and *constructive* to *destructive*. *Synthetic* refers merely to an intellectual process, *constructive* to moral attitude and practical building up. *Synthetic* is more limited in its application, but more exact within its own field. It means putting together the constituent elements of a conception in such a way as to form an intellectual whole, a single idea. *Constructive* means in general building up. *Constructive* criticism is that which not merely destroys an old method or standard, but builds up a new one. *Constructive* social work is that which builds up a new order of society instead of merely destroying what was bad in the old régime. It implies active creation, which is not necessarily purely intellectual, and is often consciously opposed to the idea of *destructive*.

SYSTEM, METHOD. *System*, in Latin *systema*, Greek σύστημα, from σύστημι, or σύν and ἵστημι, to stand together, signifies that which is put together so as to form a whole. *Method*, in Latin *methodus*, is from the Greek μεθ', for, μετά, after, and ὁδός, a way, the literal sense thus being a way after, or a way by which anything is effected.

System expresses more than *method*, which is but a part of *system: system* is an arrangement of many single or individual objects according to some given rule, so as to make them coalesce; *method* is the manner of this arrangement, or the principle upon which this arrangement takes place. The term *system*, however, applies to a complexity of objects, but arrangement, and consequently *method*, may be applied to everything that is to be put into execution. All sciences must be reduced to *system;* and without *system* there is no science: all business requires *method;* and without *method* little can be done to any good purpose.

T

TACIT. See SILENT.

TACITURNITY. See SILENCE.

TACTICS, GENERALSHIP, MANŒU-VRING, STRATEGY. *Tactics*, from Greek τακτικός, fit for arranging, means the art of handling troops on the field of battle. *Strategy*, from Greek στρατηγία, signifies the art of projecting and planning a military movement. *Strategy* represents an intellectual achievement; *tactics*, a practical carrying out of that which has been directed by strategy. *Manœuvring*, through French, from Late Latin *man(u)opera*, a working with the hand (*manus*, hand, and *opera*, work), means the making of adroit or artful moves on the field of battle, the control of the troops in such a way as to bring about a desired result. It differs from *tactics* in emphasizing simply skilful movement.

TACTILE. See TANGIBLE.

TAINT. See ATTAINT; CONTAMI-NATE.

TAKE, RECEIVE, ACCEPT. *Take*, Middle English *taken*, is a Scandinavian word signifying to lay hold of. *Receive*, in Old French *recever*, Latin *recipere*, from *re*, back, and a weakened form of *capere*, to take, signifies to take back; and *accept*, from *accipere*, of a similar derivation (*ac* = ad, for), signifies to *take* for a special purpose.

To *take* is the general term, *receive* and *accept* are modes of taking. To *take* is an unqualified action; we *take* whatever comes in the way; we *receive* only that which is offered or sent: we *take* a book from a table; we *receive* a parcel which has been sent; we *take* either with or without consent, we *receive* with the consent, or according to the wishes, of another: a robber *takes* money from a traveller; a person *receives* a letter from a friend.

To *receive* is frequently a passive act; whatever is offered or done to another is *received;* but to *accept* is an act of choice: many things, therefore, may be *received* which cannot be *accepted;* as a person *receives* a blow or an insult: so in an engagement one may be said to *receive* the enemy, who is ready to *receive* his attack; on the other hand, we *accept* apologies.

Some things are both *received* and *accepted*, but with the same distinction. What is given as a present may be both *received* and *accepted*, but the inferior *receives* and the superior *accepts*. What is *received* comes to a person either by indirect means or, if by direct means, it comes as a matter of right; but what is *accepted* is a matter of favor either on the part of the giver or receiver. Rent in law may be both *received* and *accepted;* it is *received* when it is due from the tenant after he has broken his contract with his landlord. A challenge may be *received* contrary to the wishes of the *receiver*, but it rests with himself whether he will *accept* it or not.

Animals and things, as well as persons, may *take;* things may *receive;* but persons only *accept*. An animal may *take* what is offered to it; things *take* whatever attaches to them, but they *receive* that which by an express effort is given to them. The chameleon is said to *take* its hue from the surrounding objects; marble *receives* its polish from the hands of the workman.

TAKE OATH. See SWEAR.

TALE. See FABLE; STORY.

TALENT. See ABILITY; GIFT; IN-TELLECT.

TALK. See SPEAK.

TALKATIVE, LOQUACIOUS, GAR-RULOUS. *Talkative*, ready or prone to *talk*, from Middle English *talken*, to talk, from *talen*, to tell tales, Anglo-Saxon *talian*, to reckon or compute. *Loquacious*, from *loquari*, to speak or talk, has the same original meaning. *Garrulous*, in Latin *garrulus*, from *garrire*, to blab, signifies prone to tell or make known.

These reproachful epithets differ principally in the degree. To *talk* is allowable, and consequently it is not altogether so unbecoming to be occasionally *talkative;* but *loquacity,* which implies an immoderate propensity to *talk,* is always bad, whether springing from affection or an idle temper: and *garrulity,* which arises from the excessive desire of communicating, is a failing that is pardonable only in the aged, who have generally much to tell.

See VOLUBLE.

TALL. See HIGH.

TALLY, MATCH. A *tally* was originally a piece of wood (Low Latin *talea,* French *taille*) on which notches were cut to indicate number; it was a way of keeping a reckoning. *Match* comes from the stem found in Anglo-Saxon *gemœcca,* a companion. To *tally* means to correspond exactly with something that serves as a standard of measurement. To *match* is to be like another thing, to fit something so that the result is a harmonious whole. It is therefore less specific than *tally.* *Tally* indicates an exact correspondence, one that satisfies the desire for accurate knowledge. *Match* may refer to a correspondence that merely satisfies the taste.

TAME. See GENTLE.

TANGIBLE, OBVIOUS, REAL. *Tangible* means literally *touchable,* that which can be handled, from Latin *tangere,* to touch. *Obvious,* from Latin *ob,* opposite, and *via,* way, means lying in the way of. A *tangible* object is not necessarily *obvious* nor an *obvious* one *tangible,* but the two words have in common the idea of easily perceived. In the one case the means of perception is the sense of touch; in the other case it may be any of the senses, but especially the sense of sight. *Tangible* is used figuratively to denote anything that may be readily grasped by the mind and proved to exist; in this sense we speak of a *tangible* reason, of *tangible* evidence, etc. *Real,* from Low Latin *realis,* derived from *res,* thing, and a suffix, is applied to those things which have an actual existence. Where the proof of existence is thought to be demonstrable by the senses, *real* means having a physical form.

TANTALIZE. See AGGRAVATE; TEASE.

TARDY. See SLOW.

TARNISH. See STAIN.

TARRY. See LINGER.

TARTNESS. See ACRIMONY.

TASK. See WORK.

TASTE, FLAVOR, RELISH, SAVOR. *Taste* comes from the Teutonic *tasten,* to touch lightly, and signifies either the organs which are easily affected or the act of discriminating by a light touch of the organ or the quality of the object which affects the organs; in this latter sense it is closely allied to the other terms. *Flavor* most probably comes through Old French *fleür, flaür,* from the Latin *flare,* to blow, to breathe, signifying the rarefied essence of bodies which affect the organ of *taste.* *Relish* was originally an after-taste, from Old French *reles,* that which is left behind, from *relaxare,* to loosen, to allow to rest, to leave behind. *Savor* comes through French from Latin *sapor,* smell, taste, the *v* being analogical from *savor.*

Taste is the most general and indefinite of all these; it is applicable to every object that can be applied to the organs of *taste,* and to every degree and manner in which the organs can be affected: some things are *tasteless,* other things have a strong *taste,* and others a mixed *taste.* The *flavor* is the predominating *taste* and consequently is applied to such objects as may have a different kind or degree of *taste;* an apple may have not only the general *taste* of apple, but also a *flavor* peculiar to itself; the *flavor* is commonly said of that which is good; as a fine *flavor,* a delicious *flavor;* but it may designate that which is not always agreeable; as the *flavor* of fish, which is unpleasant in things that do not admit of such a *taste.* The *relish* is also a particular *taste;* but it is that which is artificial, in distinction from the *flavor,* which may be the natural property. We find the *flavor* such as it is; we give the *relish* such as it should be or as we wish it to be: milk and butter receive a *flavor* from the nature of the food with which the cow is supplied: sauces are used in order to give a *relish* to the food that is dressed with them.

Savor is a term in less frequent use than the others, but, conforming to the Latin derivation, it is employed to designate that which smells as well as *tastes,* a sweet-smelling *savor;* so likewise, in the moral application, a man's actions or expressions may be said to *savor* of vanity.

Taste and *relish* may be, moreover, compared as the act or power of *tasting* or *relishing:* we *taste* whatever affects our *taste,* but we *relish* that only which pleases our *taste:* we *taste* fruits in order to determine whether they are good or bad; we *relish* fruits as a dessert or at certain seasons of the day.

So in the extended or moral application, the words are distinguished in the same manner.

Taste, Genius. — *Taste,* in another sense, designates the capacity to derive pleasure from an object: *genius* designates the power we have for accomplishing any object. He who derives particular pleasure from music may be said to have a *taste* for music; he who makes very great proficiency in the theory and practice of music may be said to have a *genius* for it. It is obvious, therefore, that we may have a *taste* without having *genius;* but it would not be possible to have *genius* for a thing without having a *taste* for it: for nothing can so effectually give a *taste* for any accomplishment as that capacity to learn it and that susceptibility to all its beauties, which are circumstances inseparable from *genius.*

TAUBE. See AIRCRAFT.

TAUNT. See TEASE; TWIT.

TAUTOLOGY. See REPETITION.

TAX, DUTY, CUSTOM, TOLL, IMPOST, TRIBUTE, CONTRIBUTION. The idea of something given by the people to the government is expressed by all these terms. *Tax* comes through French from the substantive based on Late Latin *taxare* (ultimately from *tangere*), to touch, to handle, also to rate, value, appraise, whence Low Latin *taxa,* a tax, signifying the handling and appraising of valuables. *Custom* signifies that which is given under certain circumstances, according to *custom,* from Old French *costume,* based on an assumed neuter plural, *consuetumina,* derived from classical *consuetudo,* custom. *Duty* signifies that which is given as a due or debt. *Toll,* in Anglo-Saxon *toll,* etc., Low Latin *tolonium,* classical *teloneum,* Greek τέλος, a custom, signifies a particular kind of *custom* or due.

Tax is the most general of these terms, and applies to or implies whatever is paid by the people to the government, according to a certain estimate: the *customs* are a species of *tax* which are less specific than other *taxes,* being regulated by *custom* rather than any definite law; the *customs* apply particularly to what was *customarily* given by merchants for the goods which they imported from abroad: the *duty* is a species of *tax* more positive and binding than the *custom,* being a specific estimate of what is *due* upon goods, according to their value; hence it is not only applied to goods that are imported, but also to many other articles inland: *toll* is that species of *tax* which serves for the repair of roads and havens, or the liberty to buy or sell at fairs or other places.

The preceding terms refer to that which is levied by authority on the people; but they do not directly express the idea of levying or paying: *impost,* on the contrary, signifies, literally, that which is imposed; and *tribute* that which is paid or yielded; the former, therefore, exclude that idea of coercion which is included in the latter. The *tax* is levied by the consent of many, the *impost* is imposed by the will of one, and the *tribute* is paid at the demand of one or a few: the *tax* serves for the support of the nation; the *impost* and the *tribute* serve to enrich a government. Conquerors lay heavy *imposts* upon the conquered countries; distant provinces pay a *tribute* to the princes to whom they owe allegiance. *Contribution* signifies the *tribute* of many in unison or for the same end; in this general sense it includes all the other terms; for *taxes* and *imposts* are paid alike by many for the same purpose; but, as the predominant idea in *contribution* is that of common consent, it supposes a degree of freedom in the agent which is incompatible with the exercise of authority expressed by the other terms: hence the term is with more propriety applied to those cases in which men voluntarily unite in giving toward any particular object, as charitable *contributions,* or *contributions* in support of a war; but it may be taken in the general sense of a forced payment, as in speaking of military *contribution.*

These words, *tax*, *tribute*, and *contribution*, have an extended application to other objects besides those which are pecuniary: *tax*, in the sense of what is laid on without the consent of the person on whom it is imposed; *tribute*, that which is given to another as his due; and *contribution*, that which is given by one in common with others for some common object.

Tax, Rate, Assessment. — *Tax*, according to the above explanation, and *rate*, from the Latin *ratus* and *reor*, to think or estimate, both derive their principal meaning from the valuation or proportion, according to which any sum is demanded from the people; but the *tax* is imposed directly by the government for public purposes, as the land-*tax* and the window-*tax;* and the *rate* is imposed indirectly for the local purposes of each parish, as the church-*rates*, and the poor-*rates*. The *tax* or *rate* is a general rule or ratio by which a certain sum is raised upon a given number of persons; the *assessment* is the application of that rule to the individual.

TEACH. See INFORM.

TEAR. See BREAK.

TEASE, VEX, TAUNT, TANTALIZE, TORMENT. *Tease* is developed from Anglo-Saxon *tœsan*, to card wool, to pluck or pull, to scratch, hence to irritate, and hence, in a figurative sense, meaning to vex or tease. *Vex* (see DISPLEASE). *Taunt* is from the French *tenter*, Latin *tentare*, to tempt, to try or test. *Tantalize* (see AGGRAVATE). *Torment*, from the Latin *tormentum* and *torquere*, to twist, signifies to give pain by twisting or gripping, hence, to distress or anguish.

The idea of acting upon others so as to produce a painful sentiment is common to all these terms; they differ in the mode of action and in the degree of the effect. To *tease* is applied to that which is most trifling; *torment* to that which is most serious. We are *teased* by a jocose friend, or we are *vexed* by the carelessness and stupidity of our servants; we are *taunted* by the sarcasms of others; we are *tantalized* by the fair prospects which present themselves only to disappear again; we are *tormented* by the importunities of troublesome beggars. It is the repetition of unpleasant trifles which *teases;* it is the crossness and perversity of persons and things which *vex;* it is the contemptuous and provoking behavior which *taunts;* it is the disappointment of awakened expectations which *tantalizes;* it is the repetition of grievous troubles which *torments*. We are *tormented* by that which produces bodily or mental pain; we are *teased, vexed, taunted,* and *tantalized* only in the mind. Irritable and nervous people are most easily *teased;* captious and fretful people are most easily *vexed* or *taunted;* sanguine and eager people are most easily *tantalized:* in all these cases the imagination or the bodily state of the individual serves to increase the pain: but persons are *tormented* by such things as inflict positive pain.

TEDIOUS. See SLOW; WEARISOME.

TEGUMENT, COVERING. *Tegument*, in Latin *tegumentum*, from *tegere*, to cover, is properly but another word to express the sense of *covering*, yet it is now employed in cases where the term *covering* is inadmissible. *Covering* signifies mostly that which is artificial; but *tegument* is employed for that which is natural; clothing is the *covering* for the body; the skin of vegetable substances, as seeds, is called the *tegument*. The *covering* is said of that which covers the outer surface: the *tegument* is said of that which covers the inner surface; the pods of some seeds are lined with a soft *tegument*.

TELESCOPE. See PERISCOPE.

TELL. See SPEAK.

TEMERITY. See RASHNESS.

TEMPER. See DISPOSITION; FRAME; HUMOR; QUALIFY.

TEMPERAMENT, TEMPERATURE. *Temperament* and *temperature* are both used to express that state which arises from the tempering of opposite or varying qualities; the *temperament* is said of animal bodies and the *temperature* of the atmosphere. Men of a sanguine *temperament* ought to be cautious in their diet; all bodies are strongly affected by the *temperature* of the air.

See also FRAME.

TEMPERANCE. See MODESTY.

TEMPERATE. See ABSTINENT.

TEMPLE, Church. These words designate an edifice destined for the exercise of religion, but with collateral ideas which sufficiently distinguish them from each other. The *templum* of the Latins signified originally an open, elevated spot (the name being derived through Latin *temulum*, from Greek τέμενος, a sacred enclosure, from τέμνειν, to cut), marked out by the augurs with their *lituus*, or sacred wand, whence they could best survey the heavens on all sides: the idea, therefore, of spacious, open, and elevated enters into the meaning of this word. The Greek ναός, from ναίω, to inhabit, signifies a dwelling-place, and, by distinction, the dwelling-place of the Almighty; in which sense the Hebrew word is also taken to denote the high and holy place where Jehovah peculiarly dwelleth, otherwise called the *holy heavens*, Jehovah's dwelling or resting-place; whence St. Paul calls our bodies the *temples* of God when the Spirit of God dwelleth in us. The Roman poets used the word *templum* in a similar sense.

The word *temple*, therefore, strictly signifies a spacious open place set apart for the peculiar presence and worship of the Divine Being: it is applied with particular propriety to the sacred edifices of the Jews, but may be applied to any sacred place without distinction of religion.

Church is an interesting word because it seems to have been a term taken over by the northern barbarians into the Teutonic tongues directly from Greek, some time before they were Christianized. There is nothing corresponding to it in Latin, the usual intermediary between Greek and English. It is in Greek κυριακόν, a church, neuter of κυριακός (from κύριος, Lord), and signifies literally House of the Lord. A *church* is therefore a building consecrated to the Lord, and from the earliest periods of building *churches* this was done by some solemn ordinance.

The word *church* has by a figure of speech been applied to any building consecrated to the service of God.

Church, in the sense of a religious assembly, is altogether a different word, bearing no affinity to the word *temple*.

TEMPORAL. See Secular.

TEMPORARY, Transient, Transitory, Fleeting. *Temporary,* from *tempus,* time, characterizes that which is intended to last only for a time, in distinction from that which is permanent; offices depending upon a state of war are *temporary,* in distinction from those which are connected with internal policy: *transient,* that is, passing, or in the act of passing, characterizes what in its nature exists only for the moment: a glance is *transient. Transitory,* that is, apt to pass away, characterizes everything in the world which is formed only to exist for a time and then to pass away; thus our pleasures, and our pains, and our very being, are denominated *transitory. Fleeting,* which is derived from Anglo-Saxon *fleotan,* to float, is but a stronger term to express the same idea as *transitory.*

See also Provisional.

TEMPORIZING. See Time-serving.

TEMPT. See Allure; Try.

TENACIOUS, Pertinacious. To be *tenacious* is to hold a thing close, to let it go with reluctance: to be *pertinacious* is to hold it out in spite of what can be advanced against it, the prepositive syllable *per* having an intensive force. A man of a *tenacious* temper insists on matters which he considers important; one of a *pertinacious* temper insists on every trifle which is apt to affect his opinions. *Tenacity* may be a virtue or a vice, depending on circumstances; *pertinacity* is usually a foible: the former, if reprehensible, is more excusable than the latter. We may be *tenacious* of that which is good, as when a man is *tenacious* of whatever may affect his honor; but we cannot be *pertinacious* in anything but our opinions, and that, too, in cases when they are least defensible. It commonly happens that people are most *tenacious* of being thought to possess that in which they are most deficient, and most *pertinacious* in maintaining that which is most absurd. A liar is *tenacious* of his reputation for truth: persons of an iconoclastic tendency are the most *pertinacious* objectors to whatever is established.

TENDENCY, Drift, Scope, Aim.

Tendency, from to *tend*, denotes the property of tending toward a certain point, which is the characteristic of all these words, but this is applied only to things; and *drift*, from the Anglo-Saxon *drifan*, modern English *drive*, to drive; *scope*, probably from a Late Latin *scopus*, Greek σκοπός, watcher, spy, from σκέπτομαι, look; and *aim*, from the verb to aim (see that word), all characterize the thoughts of a person looking forward into futurity and directing his actions to a certain point. Hence we speak of the *tendency* of certain principles or practices as being pernicious; the *drift* of a person's discourse; the *scope* which he gives himself either in treating of a subject or in laying down a plan; or a person's *aim* to excel, or *aim* to supplant another, and the like. The *tendency* of many writings in modern times has been to unsettle the opinions of men: where a person wants the services of another, whom he dares not openly solicit, he will reveal his wishes by the *drift* of his discourse; a man of a comprehensive mind will allow himself full *scope* in digesting his plans for every alteration which circumstances may require when they come to be developed: our desires will naturally give a cast to all our *aims;* and, so long as they are but innocent, they are necessary to give a proper stimulus to exertion.

See also INCLINATION.

TENDER. See OFFER.

TENDERFOOT. See NAÏVE; SIMPLE; TYRO.

TENDERNESS. See BENEVOLENCE.

TENET, POSITION. The *tenet* (Latin *tenet*, he holds) is the opinion which we hold in our minds; the *position* is that which we lay down for others. Our *tenets* may be hurtful, our *positions* false. He who gives up his *tenets* readily evinces an unstable mind; he who argues on a false *position* shows more tenacity and subtlety than good sense. The *tenets* of the different denominations of Christians are scarcely to be known or distinguished, inasmuch as they often rest upon such trivial points: the *positions* which an author lays down must be very definite and clear when he wishes to build upon

them any theory or system. See also DOCTRINE.

TENOR, DRIFT, PURPORT. These words all signify the apparent significance of something, generally of a speech or series of remarks in oral or written form. *Purport* means the meaning that another is intended to get, the general intent. *Tenor* and *drift* express this meaning also under rather obvious metaphors. *Tenor* comes from Late Latin *tenorem*, a holding on, and refers to the voice which, in a masculine chorus, carries the air, and hence seems to hold the whole musical composition together. The *tenor* of a speech is the general theme and meaning, something corresponding to the part of the musical whole which is sustained by the tenor voice. *Drift* expresses the same idea under a different metaphor. It refers to the movement of a current, which even in moments of deceptive tranquillity, or in a storm which drives the waves before the wind against the current, may be detected by the direction in which floating objects on the surface of the water are drifting or moving. The *drift* of a speech is the general direction in which its thought seems to be moving, the apparent intention and meaning.

TENTATIVE. See EMPIRICAL.

TERM, LIMIT, BOUNDARY. *Term*, in Latin *terminus*, from the Greek τέρμα, an end, is the point that ends and that to which we direct our steps: *limit*, from the stem of the Latin *limes*, a landmark, is the line which marks. *Boundary*, from Late Latin *bodina*, possibly of Celtic origin, is the obstacle which interrupts our progress and prevents us from passing.

We are carried either toward or away from the *term;* we keep either within *limits* or we overstep them: we contract or extend a *boundary*. The *term* and the *limit* belong to the thing; by them it is ended: the *boundary* is that which is made or conceived by the person *bounding*. The *term* is the point that terminates; the *limit* is either a line or point which marks where to stop; the *boundary* is a line which includes a space and points out the extent beyond which one may not pass. The Straits of Gibraltar was the *term* of Hercules's voyages: it was said, with more eloquence than truth, that the *limits* of the Roman Empire were those of the world: the sea, the Alps, and the Pyrenees are the natural *boundaries* of France.

So likewise in application to moral objects. We mostly reach the *term* of our prosperity when we attempt to pass the *limits* which Providence has assigned to human efforts: human ambition often finds a *boundary* set to its gratification by circumstances which were the most unlooked for and apparently the least adapted to bring about such important results. We see the *term* of our evils only in the *term* of our life: our desires have no *limits;* their gratification only serves to extend our prospects indefinitely: those only are happy whose fortune is the *boundary* of their desires.

See also ARTICLE; BOUND; WORD.

TERMINATE. See END.

TERRIBLE. See FEARFUL; FORMIDABLE.

TERRIFIC. See FEARFUL.

TERRITORY, DOMINION. Both these terms signify a portion of country under a particular government; but the word *territory* brings to our minds the land which is included; *dominion* conveys to our minds the power which is exercised: the *territory* speaks of that which is in its nature bounded; *dominion* may be said of that which is boundless. A petty prince has his *territory,* the monarch of a great empire has *dominions.* It is the object of every ruler to guard his *territory* against the irruptions of an enemy; ambitious monarchs are always aiming to extend their *dominions.*

See also EMPIRE.

TERROR. See ALARM.

TEST. See ATTEMPT.

TESTIFY. See DECLARE; SWEAR.

TESTIMONY. See PROOF.

THANKFULNESS, GRATITUDE. *Thankfulness,* or a *fulness* of *thanks* (from Anglo-Saxon *thanc,* a thought, hence a pleasant thought, a grateful remembrance), is the outward expression of a *grateful* feeling. *Gratitude,* from the Latin *gratitudo,* is the feeling itself. Our *thankfulness* is measured by the number of our words; our *gratitude* is measured by the nature of our actions. A person appears very thankful at the time who afterward proves very *ungrateful. Thankfulness* is the beginning of *gratitude: gratitude* is the completion of *thankfulness.*

THEATRICAL, DRAMATIC, STAGEY, HISTRIONIC. These words all signify belonging to the stage or the art of the stage, but they differ considerably in their meaning. *Theatrical,* from Latin *theatricus,* Greek θεατρικός, a dramatic show, means pertaining to the theatre, that is, exaggerated and artificial in such a way as to create an emotional and sensuous effect. *Theatrical* is sometimes applied in a derogatory sense to actions or manners which are artificial, but it always adds to the general idea of artificiality that of a deliberate effect, usually an emotional effect. *Dramatic* comes through Latin from the Greek word δρᾶμα, a deed, act, drama, meaning that which is done or acted, from δράω, I do, and means pertaining to an action represented on the stage—*i. e.,* a drama. *Dramatic* does not suggest artificiality; it merely indicates that which is emotionally striking and exciting—that in which the normal effect of action and feeling is heightened and emphasized without transcending the bounds of reality. *Theatrical* implies something falsely *dramatic,* wherein the effect does not arise naturally, but is created simply by a method of presentation. *Stagey* is a translation of *theatrical* into ruder and more downright terms. It means resembling the exaggerations of the *stage. Histrionic,* from Latin *histrio,* an actor, has an entirely different meaning. It means pertaining to the art of the actor, and is not used in a derogatory sense.

THEME. See TOPIC.

THEORY, SPECULATION. *Theory,* from the Greek θεωρία, from θεάομαι, to behold, and *speculation,* from the Latin *speculatus,* participle of *speculari,* to behold, based on *specula,* a watch-tower, are both employed to express what is seen with the mind's eye. *Theory* is the fruit of reflection, it serves the purposes of science; practice will be incomplete when the *theory* is false; *speculation* belongs more to the imagination; it has, therefore, less to do with realities; it is that which is rarely to be reduced to practice, and can, therefore, seldomer be brought to the test of experience.

Hence it arises that *theory* is contrasted sometimes with the practice, to designate its insufficiency to render a man complete; and *speculation* is put for that which is fanciful and unreal; a general who is so only in *theory* will acquit himself miserably in the field; a religionist who is so only in *speculation* will make a wretched Christian.

THERE. See YONDER.

THEREFORE, CONSEQUENTLY, ACCORDINGLY. *Therefore,* that is, for this reason, marks a deduction; *consequently,* that is, in *consequence,* marks a consequence; *accordingly,* that is, according to some thing, implies an agreement or adaptation. *Therefore* is employed particularly in abstract reasoning; *consequently* is employed either in reasoning or in the narrative style; *accordingly* is used principally in the narrative style. Young persons are perpetually liable to fall into error through inexperience; they ought, *therefore,* the more willingly to submit themselves to the guidance of those who can direct them: the world is now reduced to a state of little better than moral anarchy; *consequently* nothing but renewed ideals and good government can bring the people back to the use of their sober senses: every preparation was made, and every precaution was taken; *accordingly* at the fixed hour they proceeded to the place of destination.

THICK, DENSE. Between *thick* (Anglo-Saxon *thicce*) and *dense* (Latin *densus*) there is little other difference than that the latter is employed to express that species of *thickness* which is philosophically considered as the property of the atmosphere in a certain condition: hence we speak of *thick* in regard to hard or soft bodies, as a *thick* board or *thick* cotton; solid or liquid, as a *thick* cheese or *thick* milk: but we use the term *dense* mostly in regard to the air in its various forms, as a *dense* air, a *dense* vapor, a *dense* cloud, and figuratively a *dense* population.

THIEVERY. See KLEPTOMANIA

THIN, SLENDER, SLIGHT, SLIM. *Thin,* Anglo-Saxon *thine,* meant originally stretched out. *Slender,* Old French *esclendre,* is allied to Old Low German *slender,* a trailing gown, and is a nasalized form of the stem found in the verb *slide;* that which is long, trailing, is associated generally with the idea of *slenderness* in the modern sense. *Slight* is an Old Low German word meaning originally even or flat, then plain, smooth, simple; then trivial, of no real weight and importance—thence *slight* in the sense in which it is here used. *Slim* comes from Dutch; it meant originally oblique, hence weak, poor, bad, thin, slight. In most of these cases the present physical application develops out of a more general application. *Thin* is the generic term, the rest are specific: *thin* may be said of that which is small and short, as well as small and long; *slender* is always said of that which is small and long at the same time: a board is *thin* which wants solidity or substance: a poplar is *slender,* because its tallness is disproportioned to its magnitude or the dimensions of its circumference. *Thinness* is sometimes a natural property; *slight* and *slim* are applied to that which is artificial: the leaves of trees are of a *thin* texture; a board may be made *slight* by continually planing; a paper box is very *slim.* *Thinness* is a good property sometimes; *thin* paper is frequently preferred to that which is thick: *slightness* and *slimness,* which is a greater degree of *slightness,* are always defects; that which is made *slight* is unfit to bear the stress that will be put upon it; that which is *slim* is altogether unfit for the purpose proposed: a carriage that is made *slight* is quickly broken and always out of repair; paper is altogether too *slim* to serve the purpose of wood.

Thinness is a natural property of many bodies, whether solid or fluid; *slender* and *slight* have a moral and figurative application.

THINK, REFLECT, PONDER, MUSE. *Think* is a Teutonic word found in most of the Germanic tongues in some form. *Reflect,* in Latin *reflectere,* signifies literally to bend back, that is, to bend the mind back on itself. *Ponder,* from *pondus,* a weight, signifies to weigh. For the derivation of *muse* see AMUSE.

To *think* is a general and indefinite term; to *reflect* is a particular mode of *thinking;* to *ponder* and *muse* are different modes ot *rejlecting*, the former on grave matters, the latter on matters that interest either the affections or the imagination: we *think* whenever we receive or recall an idea to the mind; but we *reflect* only by recalling, not one only, but many ideas: we *think* if we only suffer the ideas to revolve in succession in the mind; but in *reflecting* we compare, combine, and judge of those ideas which thus pass in the mind: we *think*, therefore, of things past, as they are pleasurable or otherwise; we *reflect* upon them as they are applicable to our present condition: we may *think* on things past, present, or to come; we *reflect, ponder*, and *muse* mostly on that which is past or present. The man *thinks* of the days of his childhood and wishes them back; the child *thinks* of the time when he shall be a man and is impatient until it has come: the man *reflects* on his past follies and tries to profit by experience; he *ponders* over any serious concern that affects his destiny, and *muses* on the happy events of his childhood.

Think, Suppose, Imagine, Believe, Deem.—To *think* is here, as in the preceding article, the generic term. It expresses, in common with the other terms, the act of having a particular idea in the mind; but it is indefinite as to the mode and the object of the action. To *think* may be the act of the understanding or merely of the *imagination:* to *suppose* and *imagine* are rather the acts of the *imagination* than of the understanding. To *think*, that is, to have any thought or opinion upon a subject, requires reflection; it is the work of time: to *suppose* and *imagine* may be the acts of the moment. We *think* a thing right or wrong; we *suppose* it to be true or false; we *imagine* it to be real or unreal. To *think* is employed promiscuously in regard to all objects, whether actually existing or not, or. if existing, are above our comprehension: to *suppose* applies to those which are uncertain or precarious; *imagine*, to those which are unreal. *Think* and *imagine* are said of that which affects the senses immediately; *suppose* is said only of that which occupies the mind. We *think* that we hear a noise as soon as the sound catches our attention; in certain states of the body or mind we *imagine* we hear noises which were never made: we *think* that a person will come to-day, because he has informed us that he intends to do so; we *suppose* that he will come to-day, at a certain hour, because he came at the same hour yesterday.

In regard to moral points, in which case the word *deem* may be compared with the others, to *think* is a conclusion drawn from certain premises. I *think* that a man has acted wrong: to *suppose* is to take up an idea arbitrarily or at pleasure; we argue upon a *supposed* case merely for the sake of argument: to *imagine* is to take up an idea by accident or without any connection with the truth or reality; we *imagine* that a person is offended with us, without being able to assign a single reason for the idea; we *imagine* evils even more numerous than those which are real: to *deem* is to form a conclusion; things are *deemed* hurtful or otherwise in consequence of observation.

To *think* and *believe* are both opposed to knowing or perceiving; but *think* is a more partial action than *believe:* we *think* as the thing strikes us at the time; we *believe* from a settled deduction: hence it expresses much less to say that I *think* a person speaks the truth than that I *believe* that he speaks the truth. I *think* from what I can recollect that such and such were the words, is a vague mode of speech, not admissible in a court of law as positive evidence: the natural question which follows upon this is, Do you firmly *believe* it? an affirmative answer to which, when made with the appearance of sincerity, must be admitted as testimony. Hence it arises that the word *think* can be employed only in matters that require but little thought in order to come to a conclusion; and *believe* is applicable to things that must be admitted only on substantial evidence. We are at liberty to say that I *think* or I *believe* that the account is made out right; but we must say that I *believe*, not *think*, that the Bible is the word of God.

THOUGHT. See IDEA.

THOUGHTFUL, CONSIDERATE, DELIBERATE. *Thoughtful*, cr full of *thinking; considerate,* or ready to con-*sider* (see CONSIDER); and *deliberate,* ready to *deliberate,* rise upon one an-other in their signification: he who is *thoughtful* does not forget his duty; he who is *considerate* pauses and *considers* properly what is his duty; he who *de-liberates* considers *deliberately.* It is a recommendation to a subordinate per-son to be *thoughtful* in doing what is wished of him: it is the recommenda-tion of a confidential person to be *con-siderate,* as he has often to judge ac-cording to his own discretion; it is the recommendation of a person who is acting for himself in critical matters to be *deliberate,* from Latin *de* and *librare,* to weigh. There is this further distinction in the word *deliberate* that it may be used in the bad sense to mark a settled intention to do evil: young people may sometimes plead in extenuation of their guilt that their misdeeds do not arise from *deliberate* malice.

THOUGHTLESS. See NEGLIGENT.

THRALDOM, VASSALAGE. *Thral-dom* refers to the condition of the northern *thrall* (Icelandic *thræll*) or slave, who served in the household and on the land; *vassalage* to the condition of the feudal *vassal* or dependent who was bound to render his lord certain military and financial services. *Thral-dom* therefore suggests a more absolute state of servitude, an entire subjection to the will of another, with the impli-cation of something irksome and har-assing in the state. *Vassalage* indicates a partial subjection, a subjection of will and more or less personal dependence.

See also SERVITUDE.

THREAT, MENACE. *Threat* comes from Anglo-Saxon *threát,* a crowd, a pushing, and signifies a method of exerting force by word of mouth. *Menace* is of Latin extraction. They do not differ in signification; but, as is frequently the case, the Anglo-Saxon is the familiar term and the Latin word is employed only in the higher style. We may be *threatened* with either small or great evils; but we are *menaced* only with great evils. One individual *threatens* to strike another: a general *menaces* the enemy with an attack. We are *threatened* by things as well as persons: we are *menaced* by persons only (or things personified): a person is *threatened* with a look: he is *menaced* with a prosecution by his adversary.

THREATENING. See IMMINENT.

THRIFTY. See ECONOMICAL.

THRILL, STIR, VIBRATE. *Thrill,* from Anglo-Saxon *thyrlian,* meant originally to pierce. For the deriva-tions of *stir* and *vibrate* see those words. These three terms all indicate a move-ment in response to some impulse received from without, and are figura-tively applied to a psychological state. But the character of the movement differs. *Stir* is the most general of the three words. It means simply to be set in motion, and refers to any physical or psychological response to a stimulus. *Vibrate* refers to a regular motion to and fro, or up and down. *Thrill* indicates a sudden piercing, poignant movement which quickly spends itself. Figuratively applied to psychological states, to *vibrate* means simply to respond to a stimulus, to move in harmony with it, as a sounding-board may respond to the sound-waves and *vibrate* accordingly. To *thrill* indicates more definite but mo-mentary emotion, an electric current of feeling, as it were, suddenly quiver-ing through the whole nervous system.

THRIVE. See FLOURISH.

THRONG. See MULTITUDE.

THROW. See CAST.

THRUST. See PUSH.

THWART. See OPPOSE.

TIDE. See STREAM.

TIDINGS. See NEWS.

See also ADVICE; INFORMATION.

TIDY, NEAT, TRIM. These three words contain the same general idea of a combination of orderliness and cleanness, but they differ in the degree and kind of orderliness indicated. *Tidy,* from Middle English *tid,* time, empha-sizes the idea of a seasonable, and hence a seemly, order—a *tidy* room is a room in which everything is picked up and put in its proper place. *Neat* empha-sizes the idea of cleanness added to order. *Trim* adds to the notion of cleanness and order a suggestion of something more positively pleasing. A *trim* attire is one in which *neatness* and *tidiness* are made positively striking by effective arrangement and emphasis.

TIE. See BIND.

TILLAGE. See CULTIVATION.

TIME, SEASON. *Time* is here the generic term; it is taken either for the whole or the part: *season* is any given portion of *time*. We speak of *time* when the simple idea of *time* only is to be expressed; as the *time* of the day or the *time* of the year; the *season* is spoken of in reference to given circumstances, as the year is divided into four parts, called the *seasons*, according to the nature of the weather: hence in general *time* is called the *season* which is suitable for any particular purpose; youth is the *season* for improvement. It is a matter of necessity to choose the *time;* it is an affair of wisdom to choose the *season*.

Time, Period, Age, Date, Era, Epoch. —*Time* is, as before, taken either for *time* in general or *time* in particular; all the other terms are taken for particular portions of *time*. In the sense of a particular portion of *time*, the word *time* is applied generally and indefinitely.

Time included within any given points is termed a *period*, from the Greek περίοδος, signifying a course, round, or any revolution: thus, the *period* of day or of night is the space of *time* comprehended between the rising and setting, or setting and rising, of the sun: the *period* of a year comprehends the space which, according to astronomers, the earth requires for its annual revolution. So, in an extended and moral application, we have stated *periods* in our life for particular things: during the *period* of infancy a child is in a state of total dependence on its parents; a *period* of apprenticeship has been appointed for youth to learn different trades.

The *period* is sometimes taken not only for the space of time included between two points of *time*, but sometimes for the terminating point; in this sense, to put a *period* to a thing is to terminate its existence, to destroy it.

The *age* is the *period* comprehended within the life of one man, or of numbers living at the same time, and consequently refers to what is done by men living within that *period:* hence we speak of the different *ages* that have existed since the commencement of the world, and characterize this or that *age* by the particular degrees of vice or virtue, genius, and the like, for which it is distinguished.

The *date* is properly the point of *time* which is marked on a writing, either to show the *time* when it was written, as the *date* of a letter, or to show when any contract is to be performed, or thing done, as the *date* of a bill of exchange. As the *date* in the first case shows when anything has been done, the word *date* may be applied generally to the time of any past event, as a thing of late *date* or early *date;* so of a thing out of *date*, which is so long gone by that the *date* of it is not known.

As the *date* in the second case shows how long it will be before a thing is to be done, as a bill of short *date* shows that it has but a short time to run, so the term *date* may be applied to the duration of any event.

Era, in Latin *æra*, probably from *æs*, brass, signifying a brass counter used in computing; and *epoch*, from the Greek ἐποχή, from ἐπέχειν, to stop, signifying a resting-place; both refer to points of *time* that are in some manner marked or distinguished; but the former is more commonly employed in the literal sense for points of computation in chronology, as the Christian *era;* the latter is indefinitely employed for any *period* distinguished by remarkable events: the captivity of the Jews is an *epoch* in the history of that nation. The terms may also be figuratively employed in the latter sense, as an eventful *era*.

Timely, Seasonable.—The same distinction exists between the epithets *timely* and *seasonable* as between *time* and *season* in the preceding article. The former signifies within the time, that is, before the time is past; the latter according to the season, or what the season requires. A *timely* notice prevents that which would otherwise happen; a *seasonable* hint seldom fails of its effect because it is *seasonable*. We must not expect to have a *timely* notice of death, but must be prepared for it at any time; an admonition to one who is on a sickbed is very *seasonable* when given by a minister or a friend. The opposites of these terms are *untimely* or *ill-timed* and *unseasonable: untimely* is directly opposed to *timely*, signifying before the time appointed; as an *untimely* death; but *ill-timed* is indirectly opposed, signifying in the wrong *time;* as an *ill-timed* remark.

Time-serving, Temporizing. — *Time-serving* and *temporizing* are both applied to the conduct of one who adapts himself servilely to the time and season; but a *time-server* is rather active, and a *temporizer* passive. A *time-server* avows those opinions which will serve his purpose: the *temporizer* forbears to avow those which are likely for the time being to hurt him. The former acts from a desire of gain, the latter from a fear of loss. *Time-servers* are of all parties, as they come in the way: *temporizers* are of no party, as occasion requires. Sycophant courtiers must always be *time-servers:* ministers of state are frequently *temporizers.*

See also OPPORTUNE.

TIMID. See AFRAID.

TIMOROUS. See AFRAID.

TINGE. See COLOR.

TINT. See COLOR.

TIRE. See WEARY.

TIRESOME. See WEARISOME.

TITLE. See NAME.

TOGETHER. See SYNCHRONOUS.

TOIL. See WORK.

TOILSOME. See HERCULEAN.

TOKEN. See MARK.

TOLERATE, ENDURE, SUFFER. *Tolerate* comes ultimately from Latin *tollere*, to bear; *endure*, from Latin *durus*, firm, lasting; *suffer*, from Latin *sub*, up, and *ferre*, to bear. The words all indicate submission to something unpleasant, but they differ in the kind of submission and the extent of the unpleasantness indicated. *Tolerate* suggests something annoying borne with some patience; *endure*, something in the nature of positive suffering borne with courage and fortitude. *Suffer* may indicate merely the granting of permission, the submission of the will, or it may imply the bearing of positive pain—that is, it may be either a much stronger word than *endure* or merely a slightly more emphatic form of *tolerate*. In this last sense it is used in the Bible and in other somewhat archaic expressions.

TOLL. See TAX.

TOMB. See GRAVE.

TONE. See SOUND.

TONGUE. See LANGUAGE.

TOO. See ALSO.

TOOL. See INSTRUMENT.

TOPSY-TURVY, UPSIDE-DOWN. *Topsy-turvy*, earlier *topsy-tervy*, or *topside-tervy*, where *tervy* represented a Middle English *terven*, to roll or over-turn. *Upside-down* bears its meaning on its face. *Upside-down* is a prosaic and literal way of saying what is more humorously suggested in *topsy-turvy*. *Upside-down* means merely turned so that the upper part is where the lower part ought to be. *Topsy-turvy*, while implying the same inversion, adds the idea of general confusion. It is a humorous and colloquial word.

TORMENT, TORTURE. *Torment* and *torture* both come from *torquere*, to twist, and express the agony which arises from a violent twisting or griping of any part; but the latter, which is more immediately derived from the verb, expresses much greater violence and consequent pain than the former. *Torture* is an excess of *torment*. We may be *tormented* by a variety of indirect means; but we are said to be *tortured* mostly by the direct means of the rack or similar instrument. *Torment* may be permanent: *torture* is only for a time or on certain occasions. It is related in history that a person was once *tormented* to death by a violent and incessant beating of drums in his prison: the Indians practiced every species of *torture* upon their prisoners: whence the application of these terms to moral objects. A guilty conscience may *torment* a man all his life: the horrors of an awakened conscience are a *torture* to one who is on his death-bed.

TORPID. See NUMB.

TORTURE. See TORMENT.

TOSS. See SHAKE.

TOTAL. See WHOLE.

TOTALLY. See QUITE.

TOTTER. See STAGGER.

TOUCH. See CONTACT; STRIKE; THRILL.

TOUR. See CIRCUIT; EXCURSION.

TOWER. See TURRET.

TRACE. See DERIVE; MARK.

TRACK. See MARK.

TRACT. See ESSAY.

TRACTABLE. See DOCILE.

TRADE, COMMERCE, TRAFFIC, DEALING. The old Middle English sense of *trade* was *path;* the word is allied to *tread*. It meant the beaten path worn between merchant and customer, hence regular business. *Commerce* is derived from Latin *cum*, with, and *merx*, merchandise. It refers to an exchange of merchandise between two or more people. *Traffic* comes through French from Italian *trafficare*, a Low Latin *traficum, trafica*, based perhaps on *trans* and a hypothetical verb *vicare, vicis,* or "change across." To engage in exchange or *trade*.

The leading idea in *trade* is that of carrying on business for purposes of gain; the rest are but modes of *trade; commerce* is a mode of *trade* by exchange: *traffic* is a sort of personal *trade*, a sending from hand to hand; *dealing* is a bargaining or calculating kind of *trade*. *Trade* is either on a large or small scale, *commerce* is always on a large scale; we may *trade* retail or wholesale; we always carry on *commerce* by wholesale: *trade* is either within or without the country; *commerce* is always between different countries: there may be a *trade* between two towns; but there is a *commerce* between England and America, between France and Italy: hence it arises that the general term *trade* is of inferior import when compared with *commerce*. The *commerce* of a country, in the abstract and general sense, conveys more to our mind, and is a more noble expression, than the *trade* of the country, as the merchant ranks higher than the *tradesman*, and a *commercial* house than a *trading* concern. *Trade* may be altogether domestic and between neighbors; the *traffic* is that which goes backward and forward between any two or more points: in this manner there may be a great *traffic* between two towns or cities, as between London and the capitals of the different counties; we also speak of busy thoroughfares of a city as full of *traffic*. *Trade* may consist simply in buying and selling according to a stated valuation; *dealings* are carried on in matters that admit of a variation: hence we speak of *dealers* in wool, in corn, seeds, and the like, who buy up portions of these goods, more or less, according to the state of the market.

Trade, however, in its most extended sense, comprehends all the rest.

See also BUSINESS; DEAL.

TRADITIONAL. See LEGENDARY.

TRADUCE. See DISPARAGE.

TRAFFIC. See TRADE.

TRAIN. See PROCESSION.

TRAITOROUS. See TREACHEROUS.

TRAMONTANE, ULTRAMONTANE. *Tramontane*, in French *tramontain*, northerly, from Italian *tramontano*, that from Late Latin *transmontanus, across* or *beyond* the mountains, is both an adjective and a substantive. As an adjective it implies lying north or being *beyond* the mountains, that is, the Alps, as the Italians originally applied the term, hence *foreign*. Subsequently the term was applied by the French to the Italians, as being south, *beyond*, or on the other side of the mountains. In the latter application the term takes the form of *ultramontane*, from Latin *ultra*, beyond, and *montanus*, a mountain.

As a substantive *tramontane*, as well as *ultramontane*, signifies one living or coming *across* or from *beyond* or from the other side of the mountains, hence a stranger, one of *foreign* habitation.

Tramontane also implies the north wind (*tramontana*) in the Mediterranean, and a peculiar blighting wind, very harmful in the Archipelago: and *ultramontane*, in church history, the name given in the Vatican Council (1870) to the opinion of the church that the Papal utterances *ex cathedra* on matters of faith and morals are irrevocable.

TRANQUIL. See UNRUFFLED.

TRANQUILLITY. See PEACE.

TRANSACT. See NEGOTIATE.

TRANSCEND. See EXCEED.

TRANSCRIBE. See COPY.

TRANSFER, TRANSMIT. These words both signify to remove from one place to another, but there is a slight difference in meaning corresponding to the difference in derivation. *Transfer* comes from Latin *trans*, across, and *ferre*, to carry, and signifies to carry across an intervening space. *Transmit* comes from Latin *trans*, across, and *mittere*, to send, and signifies to send across. We use *transfer* wherever the idea of actually bearing or carrying is prominent. We speak of *transmitting* messages by telegraph; of *transferring* goods by freight.

TRANSFIGURE, TRANSFORM, METAMORPHOSE. *Transfigure* is to make to pass over into another figure: *transform* and *metamorphose* (from Greek μετά and μορφόω, or I change about) are to put into another form, the first being said only of spiritual beings, and particularly in reference to our Saviour; the other two terms being applied to that which has a corporeal form.

Transformation is commonly applied to that which changes its outward form; in this manner a harlequin *transforms* himself into all kinds of shapes and likenesses. *Metamorphosis* is applied to the form internal as well as external, that is, to the whole nature; in this manner Ovid describes, among others, the *metamorphoses* of Narcissus into a flower and Daphne into a laurel: with the same idea we may speak of a rustic being *metamorphosed*, by the force of art, into a fine gentleman.

TRANSFORM. See TRANSFIGURE.

TRANSGRESS. See INFRINGE.

TRANSGRESSION. See OFFENCE.

TRANSIENT. See TEMPORARY.

TRANSITORY. See EVANESCENT; TEMPORARY.

TRANSLATE. See TRANSFER.

TRANSLUCENT. See DIAPHANOUS.

TRANSMIT. See TRANSFER; WAFT.

TRANSPARENT. See PELLUCID.

TRANSPIRE, EXHALE, LEAK OUT. *Transpire* originally meant to be sent off as vapor, to be breathed out, from Latin *trans*, through, and *spirare*, to breathe. It is a synonyme of *exhale* (from Latin *ex*, out, and *halare*, to breathe) when used literally, and a synonyme of *leak out*, used figuratively. It is not a synonyme of *happen* or *occur*, though vulgarly employed as such. We speak of a secret *transpiring*, meaning that it is breathed out, becomes known. *Exhale* has the same literal meaning, but not the same figurative application. *Leak out* has a similar figurative application, but the metaphor is not that of vapor *exhaled*, but of water, or other liquid, dripping out.

TRANSPORT. See BEAR; ECSTASY.

TRANSPORTER. See COMMON-CARRIER.

TRAVEL. See GO.

TRAVESTY, BURLESQUE, CARICATURE, PARODY. *Travesty*, in French *travesti*, past participle of *travestir*, to disguise one's self, from the Latin *trans*, across, over, implying a change, and *vestire*, to clothe, signifies that which has a changed or unusual attire, disguised in garments so as to present a ridiculous appearance. As a substantive it signifies that which has been changed, transformed, from a lofty, serious style into a ridiculous, ludicrous one.

Burlesque, as an adjective, signifies the exciting to laughter by an extravagant contrast; as a substantive, a ludicrous, grotesque representation; as a verb, to ridicule or make ridiculous by a humorous, fantastic, sarcastic change in an original. *Caricature*, as a substantive, comes through Italian from Latin *carricare*, to load a car, hence to overweight, to "lay on thick," to *caricature*. It signifies a figure or description of a person or thing in which defects are greatly exaggerated in order to give the subject a ridiculous appearance, a representation in which the salient features of the original are changed to the extent of producing a ludicrous effect, without entirely, or even essentially, destroying the resemblance.

Though *travesty* and *parody* have a general relationship they differ in application. *Parody* changes the subject-matter in hand and the personalities, and mockingly imitates the style of the original, as Richelieu's parody of Corneille's *Cid; travesty* leaves the subject matter partially, and the personalities wholly, unaltered, producing its intended effect by substituting the grotesque in action or speech for the serious, noble, or heroic.

For further critical distinctions between the meaning and derivations of these words see CARICATURE.

TREACHEROUS, TRAITOROUS, TREASONABLE. These epithets are all applied to one who betrays his trust, *treacherous*, from Middle High German *trechen*, to draw, entice, and *traitorous*, from Latin *traditórem,* a traitor, based on *tradere,* to give up; but *treacherous* (see FAITHLESS) connotes a man's private relations; *traitorous,* his public relation to his ruler and his country: he is a *treacherous* friend and a *traitorous* subject. We may be *treacherous* to our enemies as well as our friends, for nothing can lessen the obligation to be faithful in keeping a promise; we may be *traitorous* to our country by abstaining to lend that aid which is in our power. *Traitorous* and *treasonable* are both applicable to subjects: but the former is extended to all public acts; the latter only to those which affect the supreme power: a soldier is *traitorous* who goes over to the side of the enemy against his country; a man is guilty of *treasonable* practices who meditates taking the life of the king or aims at subverting his government: a man may be a *traitor* and be guilty of *treason* under all forms of government.

See also INSIDIOUS.

TREASURE, HOARD. The idea of laying up carefully is common to these verbs; but to *treasure* is to lay up for the sake of preserving; to *hoard,* to lay up for the sake of accumulating; we *treasure* the gifts of a friend; the miser *hoards* up his money: we attach a real value to that which we *treasure,* a fictitious value to that which is *hoarded.* To *treasure* is used either in the proper or improper sense; we *treasure* a book on which we set particular value or we *treasure* the words or actions of another in our recollection; the miser *hoards* up whatever he can scrape together.

TREAT. See FEAST.

TREATISE. See ESSAY.

TREATMENT, USAGE. *Treatment* implies the act of treating and *usage* that of using: *treatment* may be partial or temporary, but *usage* is properly employed for that which is permanent or continued: a passer-by may meet with ill-*treatment,* but children and domestics are liable to meet with ill-*usage.* All persons may meet with good or ill *treatment* from others with whom they casually come in connection, but *usage* is applied more properly to those who are more or less in the power of others: children may receive good or ill *usage* from those who have the charge of them, servants from their masters or wives from their husbands.

TREATY. See CONVENTION.

TREMBLE. See QUAIL; SHAKE.

TREMBLING, TREMOR, TREPIDATION. The first two of these terms are derived from the same source (see AGITATION), and designate a general state of agitation: *trembling* is not only the most familiar, but also the most indefinite, term of the three; *trepidation* (from Latin *trepidare*) and *tremor* are species of *trembling.* *Trembling* expresses any degree of involuntary shaking of the frame, from the affection either of the body or the mind; cold, nervous affections, fear, and the like are the ordinary causes of *trembling: tremor* is a slight degree of *trembling,* which arises mostly from a mental affection; when one is agitated one's mind is thrown into a *tremor* by any trifling incident: *trepidation* is more violent than either of the two, and springs from the defective state of the mind; it shows itself in the action, or the different movements, of the body, rather than in the body; those who have not the requisite composure of mind to command themselves on all occasions are apt to do what is required of them with *trepidation.*

Trembling and *tremulous* are applied as epithets, either to persons or things; a *trembling* voice evinces *trepidation* of mind, a *tremulous* voice evinces a *tremor* of mind: notes in music are sometimes *trembling;* the motion of the leaves of trees is *tremulous.*

TREMENDOUS. See FEARFUL.

TRENCH, CHANNEL, DITCH, FURROW. These words all indicate a passage cut in the ground. *Furrow* is the passage made by a plough in the field for the receiving of the seed. A *trench* is a deeper and wider passage cut in the ground and thoroughly excavated; it now refers particularly to the protective fortifications developed underground by both sides in the European war. A *ditch* is a small *trench* into which water is drained and carried off. A *channel* serves the same purpose as a *ditch,* but usually refers to a natural passageway made by the action of a stream or is figuratively extended to refer to something resembling such a natural passage, as when we speak of *channels* of trade, *channels* of intercourse, etc.

TRENCHANT, SHARP. *Trenchant,* from French *trencher,* to cut (Latin *truncare*), to cut down the *trunk* of a tree, means *sharp,* but implies a positive action of the sharp instrument on something. It is now used mainly in the figurative sense, whereas *sharp* has a literal as well as a figurative significance. A *sharp* speech is that which hurts or cuts like the blade of a knife; a *trenchant* criticism is that which suggests a *sharp* instrument wielded by an energetic hand. There is more action and deliberate purpose in *trenchant* than in *sharp.*

TRESPASS. See OFFENCE.

TRIAL. See ATTEMPT; EXPERIENCE.

TRIBUNAL, BAR, BENCH, COURT, JUDGMENT-SEAT. *Tribunal* is a substantive, derived from Latin *tribunal,* based on *tribunus.* The term implies a place for making decisions, a high or principal resort for litigants, consistently with its Latin prototype, which meant a raised platform on which the seats of the *tribunes,* or magistrates, were placed.

In ordinary language the *bar* in a court-room applies to the railing which separates the space for spectators from the part reserved for the judge, jury, lawyers, court officers, and witnesses when testifying. A law student is *called to the bar* when he is summoned to this railing to be sworn as a practitioner, and after the ceremony he is *admitted to the bar* and permitted to take a place *within the bar.*

The *bench,* or, figuratively, the *judgment-seat,* is the seat of a judge, singly or with associates, when discharging judicial duties. Collectively judges and lawyers are spoken of as *the bench and bar.*

The *bar, bench,* and *court,* the latter applying to the judge, the judicial department, and the place of adjudication, have varied jurisdictions, according to the special purpose of a *court.* The *bar and bench* remain the lawyers and judges in all cases, but the *court,* as the judicial department of government, is generally divided into several parts, each having authority to deal with specific cases, and all ranging from trial to appeal.

The term *tribunal* has received a very broad application in recent years by its extension to the adjudication of international disputes, etc., the highest type of which is what is known officially as the Permanent Court of Arbitration of The Hague, and popularly as The Hague Tribunal.

TRIBUTE. See TAX.

TRICE, JIFFY. *Trice* is a Scandinavian word, but the phrase *in a trice* is imitated from Spanish *en un tris, tris,* an imitative word meaning here the cracking of glass—the phrase therefore signifying in the time that it takes to smash something. *Jiffy* is a somewhat colloquial word of unknown origin. There is little difference in the meaning of the two words. Both signify "in the least possible time"; but *jiffy* is a familiar and half-humorous term. *Trice* is more suitable in dignified writing.

TRICK. See ARTIFICE; CHEAT.

TRIFLE. See DALLY.

TRIFLING, TRIVIAL, PETTY, FRIVOLOUS, FUTILE. *Trifling* comes from Old French *truffle,* signifying a thing of small worth. *Trivial* is derived from Latin *trivium,* from *tres,* three, and *via,* way, a place where three roads met, signifying that which can be picked up on the most frequented part of the common highway; hence, worthless, of no account. *Petty* comes from French *petit,* small—a Celtic word. *Frivolous* is derived from Latin *frivola,* broken potsherds, and goes back ultimately to *fricare,* to rub away. *Futile* contains the same root as Latin *fundere,* to pour, and signifies that which is poured out as worthless.

All these epithets characterize an object as of little or no value: *trifling* and *trivial* differ only in degree, the latter denoting a still lower degree of value than the former. What is *trifling* or *trivial* is that which does not require any consideration and may be easily passed over as forgotten: *trifling* objections can never weigh against solid reason; *trivial* remarks only expose the shallowness of the remarkers: what is *petty* is beneath our consideration, it ought to be disregarded and held cheap; it would be a *petty* consideration for a minister of state to look to the small savings of a private family: what is *frivolous* and *futile* is disgraceful for any one to consider; the former in relation to all the objects of our pursuit or attachment, the latter only in regard to matters of reasoning; dress is a *frivolous* occupation when it forms the chief business of a rational being; the objections of anarchists against orderly government are as *futile* as they are mischievous.

TRIM. See TIDY.

TRIP. See EXCURSION.

TRIPLANE. See AIRCRAFT.

TRITE, BANAL, HACKNEYED. All these words signify that which through familiarity has bred contempt. *Trite* comes from Latin *tritus*, the past participle of *terere*, to rub or grind. It refers to something out of which all possible interest or meaning has been rubbed or ground. A *trite* remark is that which has been made many times. *Hackneyed* comes through French from an uncertain source; perhaps from Dutch *hacken*, to chop, and *negge*, a nag, with the implication of jolting. A *hackney* was originally a horse used for every-day riding, as opposed to a war-horse; *hackney* then came to signify a hired equipage (whence *hack* is derived), and through that something common. *Banal* is derived from Late Latin *bannum*, from a Germanic root *bannan*, to summon. It referred originally to the service demanded of all feudal vassals, and, through the idea of something common to all, developed the meaning of *commonplace*. Of these three words *hackneyed* expresses most distinctly the idea of worn out by usage. A *hackneyed* quotation, for example, may be an excellent quotation in itself, but it has been used so often that it has lost its significance. *Trite* conveys the same meaning, but does it less clearly and distinctly. However, it adds to the suggestion of constant use a general implication that the whole substance of the thing denominated *trite* is stale and uninteresting. A *hackneyed* remark is one which has been made before; a *trite* remark may not have been made before in exactly the same form, but it conveys an idea which has lost its force through familiarity. *Banal*

emphasizes the idea of staleness, obviousness, still further, and departs more widely from the simple idea of *hackneyed*. *Banal* means "what any ordinary person might think of"— implying not repetition so much as an utter lack of originality in the first place.

TRIUMPH, CONQUEST, EXULTATION, SUCCESS, VICTORY. *Triumph*, in old French *triumphe*, French *triomphe*, from Latin *triumphum*, accusative of *triumphus*, cognate with Greek θρίαμβος, a hymn to Bacchus, Spanish *triunfo*, Portuguese *triumfo*, Italian *trionfo*, implied originally a grand procession in which a victorious general entered Rome by the Porta Triumphalis, in a chariot drawn by four horses, wearing an embroidered robe, an undergarment decorated with palm leaves, and a wreath of laurel round his forehead.

As a substantive, in ordinary language, the term signifies a display of pomp of any kind; a public festivity, tournament, pageant, unusual celebration; the expression of joy, great gladness, *exultation* for some noteworthy *success*. As a verb, it signifies to win a *conquest*, prevail over an adversary, achieve a decisive advantage in battle or other encounter, to subdue opposition, to accomplish a *victory*.

In a reprehensible sense it signifies to boast, brag, chuckle, exult on an advantage gained over another or believed to be gained, to "crow" insolently over the discomfiture of another.

TROOP, COMPANY. In a military sense, a *troop* is among the horse what a *company* is among the foot; but this is only a partial acceptation of the terms. *Troop*, in French *troupe*, immediately from Low Latin *troppus*, may be a metathesized form of English *thorp*; cf. Icelandic *thorp*, German *dorf*; it signifies an indiscriminate multitude; *company* (see ACCOMPANY) is any number joined together and bearing one another *company*: hence we speak of a *troop* of hunters, a *company* of players; a *troop* of horsemen, a *company* of travellers.

TROUBLE, DISTURB, MOLEST. Whatever uneasiness or painful sentiment is produced in the mind by outward circumstances is effected either by *trouble* (see AFFLICTION), by *disturbance* (see COMMOTION), or by *molestation* (see INCONVENIENCE). *Trouble* is the most general in its application; we may be *troubled* by the want of a thing or *troubled* by that which is unsuitable; we are *disturbed* and *molested* only by that which actively *troubles*. Pecuniary wants are the greatest *troubles* in life, the perverseness of servants, the indisposition or ill behavior of children, are domestic *troubles:* but the noise of children is a *disturbance*, and the prospect of want *disturbs* the mind. *Trouble* may be permanent; *disturbance* and *molestation* are temporary, and both refer to the peace which is destroyed; a *disturbance* ruffles or throws out of a tranquil state, a *molestation* burdens or bears hard either on the body or the mind: noise is always a *disturbance* to one who wishes to think or to remain in quiet; talking, or any noise, is a *molestation* to one who is in an irritable frame of body or mind.

Troublesome, Irksome, Vexatious.— These epithets are applied to the objects which create *trouble* or *vexation*. *Troublesome* is here, as before, the generic term; *irksome* and *vexatious* are species of the *troublesome:* what is *troublesome* creates either bodily or mental pain; what is *irksome* creates a mixture of bodily and mental pain; and what is *vexatious* creates purely mental pain. What requires great exertion, or a too long-continued exertion or exertions, coupled with difficulties, is *troublesome:* in this sense the laying in stores for the winter is a *troublesome* work for the ants, and compiling a dictionary is a *troublesome* labor to the compiler: what requires any exertion which we are unwilling to make, or interrupts the peace which we particularly long for, is *irksome;* in this sense giving and receiving of visits is *irksome* to some persons; travelling is *irksome* to others: what comes across our particular wishes, or disappoints us in a particular manner, is *vexatious;* in this sense the loss of a prize which we had hoped to gain may be *vexatious*.

See also WORRY.

TRUANT, TRAMP, VAGRANT, VAGABOND. *Truant* means one who wilfully absents himself from his duties or his usual place—a wanderer out of the beaten track, with the suggestion of idleness and irresponsibility. A *vagrant* (from Old French *walcrer*, to wander about, Old High German *walchan* (cf. English *walk*), probably influenced by French *vagant*, wandering, based on Latin *vagari*, to wander) is a wanderer; *vagabond* comes from the same Latin word, but adds to the idea of wandering that of shiftlessness, uselessness, irresponsibility. A *tramp*, from the verb *tramp*, is one that *tramps* through the country begging from house to house. All these words have therefore in common the idea of *wandering* with the implication of idleness and irresponsibility.

TRUCE, ARMISTICE. *Truce* comes through Middle English *trews*, a plural form, from Anglo-Saxon *treowa*, a compact; cf. Anglo-Saxon *treowe*, Modern English *true*. It means a cessation of hostilities on both sides accompanied by a pledge to refrain from attack until further notice. The implication of *true* comes from this mutual pledge. *Armistice* is derived from Latin *arma*, arms, and *-stitum*, the form assumed in composition by *statum*, past participle of *sistere*, a secondary form of *stare*, to stand. It means a suspension of arms by mutual agreement. In ordinary usage there is really no difference between *armistice* and *truce*. *Truce* indicates perhaps an *armistice* of some duration. It is the more simple and practical of the two words, and has therefore a wider figurative application.

TRUCK. See EXCHANGE.

TRUE. See SINCERE.

TRUST. See BELIEF; CONFIDE; HOPE.

TRUSTWORTHY. See FAITHFUL.

TRUSTY. See FAITHFUL.

TRUTH, VERACITY. *Truth* belongs to the thing, *veracity* to the person: the *truth* of the story is admitted upon the *veracity* of the narrator.

TRY, TEMPT. To *try* (see also ATTEMPT) is a particular species of trial: we *try* either ourselves or others; we *tempt* others: we *try* a person only in the path of his duty; but we may *tempt* him to depart from his duty: it is necessary to *try* the fidelity of a servant before you place confidence in him; it is wicked to *tempt* any one to do that which we should think wrong to do ourselves; our strength is *tried* by frequent experiments; we are *tempted*, by the weakness of our principles, to give way to the violence of our passions.

TUG. See Draw.

TUMBLE. See Fall.

TUMID. See Turgid.

TUMULTUOUS, Tumultuary. *Tumultuous* signifies having tumult; *tumultuary* (a word but rarely used to-day), disposed for tumult: the former is applied to objects in general, the latter to persons only: in *tumultuous* meetings the voice of reason is the last thing that is heard; it is the natural tendency of large and promiscuous assemblies to become *tumultuary*.

Tumultuous, Turbulent, Seditious, Mutinous.—*Tumultuous* (see Bustle) describes the disposition to make a noise; those who attend the playhouses, particularly the lower orders, are frequently *tumultuous*: *turbulent* marks a hostile spirit of resistance to authority; when prisoners are dissatisfied they are frequently *turbulent*: *seditious* marks a spirit of resistance to government; in republics the people are often disposed to be *seditious*: *mutinous* marks a spirit of resistance against officers either in the army or navy; a general will not fail to quell the first risings of a *mutinous* spirit. Electioneering mobs are always *tumultuous;* the young and the ignorant are so averse to control that they are easily led by the example of an individual to be *turbulent;* among the Romans the people were in the habit of holding *seditious* meetings, and sometimes the soldiery would be *mutinous*.

TURGID, Tumid, Bombastic. *Turgid* and *tumid* both signify swollen (from Latin *turgere* and *tumere*, both meaning to swell), but they differ in their application: *turgid* is most commonly applied to what swells by a physical process, as a *turgid* vessel; *tumid* is said of that which seems to swell in an unnatural or unusual manner, as the *tumid* waves. They are both applied to words. *Bombastic*, from *bombast*, a kind of cotton, signifying puffed up like cotton, is, figuratively, applicable to words only; but the *bombastic* includes the sentiments expressed; *turgidity* is confined mostly to the mode of expression. A writer is *turgid* who expresses a simple thought in lofty language: a person is *bombastic* who deals in large words and introduces high sentiments in common discourse.

Tumid is rarely applied to the style.

TURN, Bend, Twist, Distort, Wring, Wrest, Wrench. *Turn* comes from Latin *tornare*, to turn a lathe, Greek τόρνος, a lathe. *Bend* (see that word). *Twist*, Anglo-Saxon *twist*, signified originally a rope of double thread, from root found in *twice*, and hence as a verb it signifies the motion involved in winding one thread about another. *Distort*, in Latin *distortus*, participle of *distorquere*, compounded of *dis*, apart, and *torquere*, to turn, signifies to turn violently aside.

To *turn* signifies in general to put a thing out of its place in an uneven line; to *bend*, and the rest, are species of *turning*: we *turn* a thing by moving it from one point to another; thus we *turn* the earth over: to *bend* is simply to change its direction; thus a stick is *bent* or a body may *bend* its direction to a certain point: to *twist* is to *bend* many times, to make many *turns*: to *distort* is to *turn* or *bend* out of the right course; thus the face is *distorted* in convulsions. To *wring* is to *twist* with violence; thus linen which has been wet is *wrung*: to *wrest* or *wrench* is to separate from a body by means of *twisting;* thus a stick may be *wrested* out of the hand or a hinge *wrenched* off the door.

The same distinction holds good in the figurative or moral application: we *turn* a person from his design; we *bend* the will of a person; we *twist* the meaning of words to suit our purposes; we *distort* them so as to give them an entirely false meaning; we *wring* a confession from one.

Turn, Bent.—These words are compared here only in the figurative application, as respects the state of a person's inclination: *turn* is, therefore, as before, indefinite as to the degree; it is the first rising inclination: *bent* is a positively strong *turn*, a confirmed inclination; a child may early discover a *turn* for music or drawing;

but the real *bent* of his genius is not until he has made progress in his education and has had an opportunity of trying different things: it may be very well to indulge the *turn* of mind; it is of great importance to follow the *bent* of the mind as far as respects arts and sciences.

Turn, Wind, Whirl, Twirl, Writhe.— To *turn* (see above) is, as before, the generic term; the rest are but modes of *turning; wind* is to *turn* a thing round in a regular manner; *whirl*, to *turn* it round in a violent manner; *twirl*, to turn it round in any irregular and unmeaning way; *writhe,* to turn round in convolution within itself. A worm seldom moves in a straight line; it is, therefore, always *turning:* sometimes it . lies, and sometimes it *writhes* in agony: a wheel is *whirled* round by the force of gunpowder: a top is *twirled* by a child in play.

TURRET, MINARET, PINNACLE, TOWER. *Turret,* in old French *tourette,* diminutive of French *tour,* a tower, Latin *turris,* a tower, implied, in ancient warfare, a movable structure of wood for carrying soldiers, implements, supplies, etc., that could be rolled on its wheels to an advantageous position for attacking a fortified place, a contrivance suggestive of the wooden horse of Troy.

A *minaret* (Spanish *minarete,* from Arabian *manárat,* a candlestick, lamp, lighthouse) is a tall, slender *turret* or tower attached to a mosque and surrounded with balconies from which the muezzin calls the people to prayer. In Tudor architecture a *turret* is a small tower attached to another tower or erected at the angles of a church or public building. A *pinnacle* (Latin *pinnaculum,* a double diminutive of *pinna,* a wing) is a small polygonal *turret* rising above the rest of a building and forming its highest point.

In modern and most common usage the term *turret* applies to a rotating cylindrical steel tower rising above the deck of a warship and bearing guns that can be trained to discharge in any required direction. The first vessel constructed with such a *turret* was Captain John Ericsson's *Monitor,* described by the Confederates as "a cheese-box on a raft," which was hastily built for the Federal navy in the early part of the American Civil War. This had a single *turret,* mounting two guns. The later development of the warship into the battleship, and then the dreadnaught and the superdreadnaught, has called for twin *turrets* on some vessels and a second set superimposed on the first or others.

TWADDLE, BALDERDASH. *Twaddle* and *balderdash* have practically the same meaning. They differ only in their original derivation and in the general effect created by the form and sound of the word. *Twaddle* is an imitative word, a variation of *tattle,* a frequentative signifying to say "Ta, ta, ta." *Balderdash* is a Scandinavian word which originally signified a jumbled mixture of liquids. *Twaddle* more distinctly suggests the act of talking; *balderdash,* the nonsensical character of the talk.

TWAIN. See BOTH.

TWEEDLE, ALLURE, COAX, DECOY, ENTICE. *Tweedle* is a term of unproved etymology, but is believed to be allied with *twaddle* (see that word) or *twiddle,* signifying, in music, to touch lightly, to play, as on a violin, with a tremulous, quivering motion, also to busy one's self with trifles. *Tweedle* is closely allied with *wheedle,* both terms as verbs signifying to *allure,* to tempt by the offer of something good, real, or apparent, to *coax* or cajole one to do or give something against his first impulse, to flatter in order to gain a point; to *decoy,* to lead or *allure* or to practice deception to gain an end, and to *entice* or attract with soft words with the intent of getting what might otherwise be unattainable, to *wheedle out* of a person that which one wishes to get or know.

A very familiar use of the term *tweedle* is in connection with the term *tweedledum* in the phrase *tweedledum and tweedledee,* implying a distinction without a difference, an attempt to distinguish things or parts where no difference actually exists. This expression is said to have arisen in the eighteenth century, when a controversy occurred between the admirers of Bononcini and those of Handel concerning the merits of those musicians. The controversy reached such a wide and animated state that John Byrom (1691–1763) alluded to it as follows:

"Some say, compared to Bononcini,
That Mynheer Handel's but a ninny;
Others aver that he to Handel
Is scarcely fit to hold a candle.
Strange all this difference should be
'Twixt *tweedledum* and *tweedledee.*"

TWILIGHT. See GLOAMING.

TWINKLING. See LAMBENT.

TWISTED. See WRY.

TWIT, GIBE, TAUNT. *Twit* comes from Anglo-Saxon *ætwitan*, to point to, to reproach. It means to annoy by reminding of something discreditable or assumed to be discreditable. To *gibe*, allied to the Swedish dialectical word *gipa*, to gape, to talk foolishly or rashly, means to speak in a sneering or sarcastic manner. *Taunt* (see TEASE) is an exaggerated form of *twitting*—something positively malicious, not merely teasing. *Twitting* is a particular form of *gibing*—a more specific word.

TWO. See BOTH.

TYPE. See FIGURE.

TYRANNICAL. See ABSOLUTE.

TYRO, AMATEUR, NEOPHYTE, NOVICE. *Tyro,* properly *tiro,* in Latin in similar form, Italian *tirone,* French *tiron,* perhaps from Greek τέρην, delicate, soft, signifies a *beginner* in learning, a *learner* of the first rudiments, one having only an imperfect or slight knowledge, a mere smattering of a subject, an apprentice to a trade. A *neophyte,* through Latin from Greek νεόφυτος, newly planted, is a recent convert, one recently baptized, or one newly admitted to the order of the priesthood, a term sometimes used by Roman Catholic missionaries to designate their converts in non-Christian lands.

A *novice,* from Latin *novitius,* a derivative of *novus,* new, in ordinary language, is one who is new to any business, profession, art, or vocation, one who is as yet unskilled, just at the bottom of the ladder. In ecclesiastical usage the term signifies the title given to men or women who have entered a religious house and desire to embrace its rules, and in this sense it is synonymous with *postulant,* specifically one who asks, demands, or requests, a French substantive from Latin *postulo,* to demand, Spanish and Italian *postulante.*

U

UBIQUITOUS, EVERYWHERE, OM-NIPRESENT, UNIVERSAL. *Ubiquitous,* from Latin *ubique,* everywhere, is simply the Latin corresponding to the native English *everywhere,* used as an adjective. It differs from *everywhere* in being distinctly an "educated" word, one found only in the vocabulary of the educated. *Omnipresent* differs from *ubiquitous* in meaning not merely everywhere, but present everywhere at the same time. *Omnipresence* is one of the attributes of God. *Universal* is a more general word which may be limited to correspond to *everywhere;* it means *everywhere* throughout the whole scheme of things.

UGLY, HOMELY, HIDEOUS, UN-SIGHTLY. *Ugly,* from Anglo-Saxon *oga,* fear, from the Teutonic root *agh,* which also appears in the English word *awe* (Gothic *agis,* Icelandic *agi*), and *ly,* like, signifies that which is hateful, and hence the opposite of beautiful. *Homely* meant originally *homelike,* that which belongs to the home. It came to signify that which is contrasted with the splendor and beauty of social life outside of the home—that which is not regarded outside of the circle of the hearth. It indicates the opposite of beautiful, but not a positive degree of unpleasantness. To be *homely* is to be only mildly *ugly* or merely not beautiful; it does not suggest the presence of something really disagreeable as does *ugly.* *Unsightly* and *hideous* characterize that which is *ugly* by the psychological reaction to it. *Unsightly* means not fit for the sight, something from which we turn away our eyes. *Hideous,* through French *hideux,* a development of O.d French *hisdos,* from Latin *hispidosus,* rough, bristly, meant originally something fearful, revolting—the superlative degree of ugliness characterized by its effect upon the onlooker. It is therefore the strongest of these words, as *homely* is the mildest.

ULTIMATE. See LAST.

ULTIMATUM, FINAL WORD, LAST TERMS. *Ultimatum,* in Latin the neuter singular of *ultimatus,* the past participle of *ultimare,* signifies, literally, to be the last, to come to an end, and, in ordinary language, the last word. The term is used in connection with many actions, but its strongest application is to diplomatic negotiations, in which it has the dual sense of a declaration and a demand. In an international controversy the term implies directly the most favorable terms which a negotiator is prepared or willing to offer, the rejection of which will be considered as putting an end to negotiation and placing upon the second party the responsibility for whatever consequences may follow. In critical cases an *ultimatum* implies the *last terms* or conditions that will be offered, the *final word,* the extreme end in a controversy, and a direct or suggestive threat that if rejected resort will be had to redressive measures, but, apart from these rather lame attempts at periphrasis, it really has no synonymes.

The *ultimatum* was frequently employed in the great European war. Just prior to the outbreak Austria sent an *ultimatum* to Serbia regarding the assassination of Archduke Francis Ferdinand and his wife; and later Japan sent one to Germany, Russia one to Bulgaria, and, it was believed that both the Entente and the Central Powers had sent one to Greece for the purpose of winning her active coöperation in the war. The United States had frequent occasion to send messages to the belligerents, but these were known officially as *protests,* though they contained the essence of an *ultimatum,* as they pointed out the possibility of a severance of friendly relations if unheeded.

The "note" to Austria-Hungary, under date of December 12, 1915, concerning the sinking of the steamship *Ancona* by a submarine flying the Austro-Hungarian flag, with the loss of many American lives, was more of the character of an *ultimatum*, for it demanded that "the Imperial and Royal Government denounce the sinking of the *Ancona* as an illegal and indefensible act, that the officer who perpetrated the deed be punished, and that reparation by the payment of an indemnity be made for the citizens of the United States who were killed or injured by the attack on the vessel." The "note" further expressed the expectation that the Austro-Hungarian Government would "accede to its demand promptly."

ULTRAMONTANE. See TRA-MONTANE.

UMBRAGE, PIQUE. *Umbrage* comes from Latin *umbra*, a shade. *Pique* comes through French from the Teutonic word found in *pick*, meaning a *prick*, the sensation produced by contact with a sharp point. Both words are used now in a figurative sense to indicate a slight and momentary feeling or expression of vexation or jealous annoyance. *Umbrage*, in the phrase, to take *umbrage*, indicates the more positive feeling of the two—a shadowing, as it were, of anger and jealousy. *Pique* indicates a slighter and more frivolous feeling, a temporary pang of jealousy that is not strong enough to become a real and effective emotion. Neither of them indicate serious or permanent states of feeling.

UMBRELLA, PARASOL. *Umbrella* comes from Latin *umbra*, and is a diminutive form, meaning a little shadow. It indicates a screen, composed of a kind of canopy held over the head by a handle, to ward off the rain. *Parasol*, borrowed through French from Portuguese, and compounded of *parar*, to ward off (English *parry*), and *sol*, sun, means a similar screen of lighter and gayer material carried to protect the bearer from the sun.

UMPIRE. See JUDGE.

UNAFFECTED. See NAÏVE.

UNBELIEF, INFIDELITY, INCREDULITY. *Unbelief* (see BELIEF) concerns matters in general; *infidelity* (see FAITHFUL) is *unbelief* as respects Divine revelation; *incredulity* is *unbelief* in ordinary matters. *Unbelief* is taken in an indefinite and negative sense; it is the want of *belief* in any particular thing that may or may not

be *believed*. The term *unbelief* does not of itself convey any reproachful meaning; it signifies properly a general disposition not to *believe*.

We may be *unbelievers* in indifferent as well as the most important matters, but the term *unbeliever* taken absolutely means one who disbelieves religious dogmas.

Infidelity is a more active state of mind; it supposes a violent and total rejection of that which is commonly *believed*: *incredulity* is also an active state of mind, in which we refuse *belief* in matters that may or may not be rejected. The Jews are *unbelievers* in the mission of our Saviour; the Turks, from the Christian point of view, are *infidels*, inasmuch as they do not believe in the Bible: Deists and atheists alike are likewise considered *infidels*, inasmuch as they set themselves up against the Christian revelation; well-informed people are always *incredulous* of stories respecting ghosts and apparitions.

See also DISBELIEF.

UNBLEMISHED. See BLAMELESS.

UNBODIED. See INCORPOREAL.

UNBOUNDED. See BOUNDLESS.

UNCEASINGLY. See INCESSANTLY.

UNCERTAIN. See DOUBTFUL.

UNCERTAINTY. See QUANDARY.

UNCLEAN. See SQUALID.

UNCONCERNED. See INDIFFERENT.

UNCONQUERABLE. See INVINCIBLE.

UNCOUTH. See UNGAINLY.

UNCOVER, DISCOVER, DISCLOSE. To *uncover*, like *discover*, implies to take off the covering; but the former refers mostly to an artificial, material, and occasional covering; the latter, of rarer application, to a natural, moral, and habitual covering: plants are *uncovered* that they may receive the benefit of the air; they are *discovered* to aid the researches of the botanist.

To *discover* and *disclose* (see PUBLISH) both signify to lay open, but they differ in the object and manner of the action: to *discover* is to remove the covering which hides a thing from view, whether it be there by accident or design; to *disclose* is to open that which has been closed: as many things may be covered which are not closed, such things may, by drawing aside the covering, be *discovered:* a country is properly *discovered,* or a plant growing in some heretofore unknown place may be *discovered;* whatever is *disclosed* must have been previously closed or enclosed in some other body; as to *disclose* the treasures which lie buried in the earth.

So, in the figurative or moral application, a plot may be *discovered,* but a secret which lies deep in the bosom may be *disclosed.*

See also BARE; DISCLOSE.

UNCTION, UNGUENT. Both of these words come from Latin *ungere,* to anoint, but *unguent* has kept its literal significance, and *unction,* while not wholly losing its original meaning, has developed a figurative application. An *unguent* is a soothing salve or oil applied to the skin; *unction* had originally the same meaning, but it is now used figuratively to signify that which is soothing or healing. Moreover, from its original significance of an oil for anointing, it has developed another figurative meaning, and refers to a kind of manner or speech, insincere suavity or exaggerated fervor—so that it is a variation of that which is expressed in popular speech by the figurative use of *oily,* in "an *oily* manner," an "*oily* address." In the phrase *extreme unction,* the word retains its literal significance with the addition of a figurative meaning. It signifies the anointing of the eyes, ears, nostrils, hands, and feet of a person mortally ill to signify the application of the oil of grace to the soul. The phrase means literally the "last anointing."

UNDAUNTED. See BOLD.

UNDENIABLE. See INDUBITABLE.

UNDER, BELOW, BENEATH. *Under,* like *hind* in *behind,* and the German *unter, hinter,* etc., are all connected with the preposition *in,* implying the relation of enclosure. *Below* denotes the state of being low; and *beneath,* Anglo-Saxon *beneothan,* allied to German *nieder* and English *nether,* has the same original signification. It is evident, therefore, from the above, that the preposition *under* denotes any situation of retirement or concealment; *below,* any situation of inferiority or lowness; and *beneath,* the same, only

in a still greater degree. We are covered or sheltered by that which we stand *under;* we excel or rise above that which is *below* us; we look down upon that which is *beneath* us: we live *under* the protection of government; the sun disappears when it is *below* the horizon; we are apt to tread upon that which is altogether *beneath* us.

UNDERGO, BEAR, ENDURE, EXPERIENCE, SUFFER. *Undergo,* a compound of the prefix *under* and the English *go,* signifies, literally, to go, move, or pass under or below something, and has numerous applications. We undertake, or take upon ourselves, an enterprise, duty, obligation; we *bear* up with or against sorrow, misfortune, pain; we *endure* or put up with physical suffering, wrongs, conditions that we cannot alter; we *suffer* from annoyances, ill-health, untoward circumstances, accidents, losses, the enmity or machinations of others; and we *experience,* pass through, partake of, are subjected to, much that is unpleasant, disastrous, burdensome, heart-breaking.

UNDERMINE. See SAP.

UNDERSTAND. See CONCEIVE.

UNDERSTANDING, INTELLECT, INTELLIGENCE. *Understanding* (see CONCEIVE), being the Saxon word, is employed to describe a familiar and easy power or operation of the mind in forming distinct ideas of things. *Intellect* (see that word) is employed to mark the same operation in regard to higher and more abstruse objects. The *understanding* applies to the first exercise of the rational powers: it is therefore aptly said of children and savages that they employ their *understandings* on the simple objects of perception; a child uses his *understanding* to distinguish the dimensions of objects or to apply the right names to the things that come before his notice.

Intellect, being a matured state of the *understanding,* is most properly applied to the efforts of those who have their powers in full vigor: we speak of *understanding* as the characteristic distinction between man and brute; but human beings are distinguished from one another by the measure of their *intellect.* We may expect the youngest children to employ an *understanding* according to the opportunities which they have of using their senses; we are gratified when we see great *intellect* in the youth whom we are instructing.

Intellect and *intelligence* are derived from the same word; but *intellect* is applied merely to human power and *intelligence* to the spiritual power of higher beings, as the *intelligence* of angels: so, when applied to human beings, it is taken in the most abstract sense for the *intellectual* power: hence we speak of *intelligence* as displayed in the countenance of a child whose looks evince that he has exerted his *intellect* and thereby proved that it exists.

UNDERTAKING. See **Attempt**.

UNDETERMINED, Unsettled, Unsteady, Wavering. *Undetermined* (see **Determine**) is a temporary state of the mind; *unsettled* is commonly more lasting: we are *undetermined* in the ordinary concerns of life; we are *unsettled* in matters of opinion: we may be *undetermined* whether we shall go or stay; we are *unsettled* in our faith or religious profession.

Undetermined and *unsettled* are applied to particular objects; *unsteady* and *wavering* are habits of the mind: to be *unsteady* is, in fact, to be habitually *unsettled* in regard to all objects. An *unsettled* character is one that has no settled principles: an *unsteady* character has an unfitness in himself to settle. *Undetermined* describes one uniform state of mind, namely, the want of determination: *wavering* describes a changeable state, namely, the state of determining variously at different times. *Undetermined* is always taken in an indifferent, *wavering* mostly in a bad, sense: we may frequently be *undetermined* from the nature of the case, which does not present motives for determining; but a person is mostly *wavering*, from a defect in his character, in cases where he might determine. A parent may with reason be *undetermined* as to the line of life which he shall choose for his son: men of soft and timid characters are always *wavering* in the most trivial, as well as the most important, concerns of life.

UNDIGNIFIED. See **Ungraceful**.

UNDULATE, Vibrate, Wave. *Undulate*, in Latin *undulatus*, from *unda*, a wave, allied to Greek ὕδωρ, water, and the English word *water* (as well as to the Russian root *vodá*, water, which appears in *vodka*), refers to the rise and fall of the waves of the sea, and hence to any alternate elevation and depression of a surface. *Vibrate*, Latin *vibrare*, means to move to and fro or up and down. It usually signifies a quicker and more regular motion than *undulate*, with lesser elevations and depressions. *Wave*, as verb, comes from Anglo-Saxon *wafian;* the noun *wave*, derived from the verb, took the place of the Middle English *wawe*, allied to *wag:* it means to move to and fro in response to an impulse received from without. A flag *waves* to and fro in the wind; we *wave* a handkerchief to a friend on the deck of a steamer. *Wave* does not suggest alternate elevation and depression as do *vibrate* and *undulate*. It merely suggests a movement to and fro.

UNEASINESS. See **Worry**.

UNEASY. See **Ungraceful**.

UNERRING. See **Infallible**.

UNEVEN. See **Jagged**; **Odd**.

UNEXAMPLED. See **Unprecedented**.

UNEXPECTED. See **Sudden**.

UNFAITHFUL. See **Faithless**.

UNFEELING. See **Hard**: **Heartless**.

UNFOLD, Unravel, Develop. To *unfold* is to open that which has been folded; to *unravel* is to open that which has been *ravelled* or tangled; to *develop* is to open that which has been wrapped in an *envelope*. The application of these terms, therefore, to moral objects is obvious: what has been *folded* and kept secret is *unfolded;* in this manner a hidden transaction is *unfolded* by being related circumstantially: what has been entangled in any mystery or confusion is *unravelled:* in this manner a mysterious transaction is *unravelled* if any circumstance is fully accounted for: what has been wrapped up so as to be entirely shut out from view is *developed;* in this manner the plot of a play or novel, or the talent of a person, is *developed*.

UNFORESEEN. See SUDDEN.

UNFUNDED, FLOATING. *Unfunded* is a compound of the prefix *un*, not, and *funded*, provided with funds, and signifies a monetary obligation that has not been paid through lack of necessary means. While the term implies a debt, comprising bills, notes, and other evidences, in varying amounts, and due at different dates, it is most commonly employed to designate the part of a debt remaining unpaid and standing against a corporation or government.

A *floating* debt is that *unfunded* one which constitutes the real debt, the part of an originally larger one that is still owing, is unpaid. The *unfunded* debt of a government arises from arrears in its receipts, from obligations on which money has been raised, to be repaid out of future receipts. It is thus distinguished from a *funded* debt, which is that part of a public debt for the payment of interest for the reduction of which funds are appropriated at necessary intervals.

UNGAINLY, UNCOUTH. *Ungainly* is compounded of the negative prefix *un* and Icelandic *gegn*, ready, serviceable: cf. Scotch *gane*, fit, meaning originally not fitting. *Uncouth*, from Anglo-Saxon *uncuth*, unknown, hence strange, signifies a lack of conformity to prevailing modes of conduct or style, hence roughness, lack of social grace, etc. (Compare the similar development of *outlandish*, which originally meant simply from another land.) *Ungainly* refers mainly to physical awkwardness, *uncouth* to awkwardness of speech or manner. An *ungainly* person is one who is so constructed physically that he does not move with ease or grace. *Uncouth* indicates a lack of education and social advantages.

UNGOVERNABLE. See UNRULY.

UNGRACEFUL, INELEGANT, UN-DIGNIFIED, UNEASY. *Ungraceful*, a compound term, signifies, in its application to a person or object, that which is not pleasing to the eye or appropriate to its particular use. A person is *ungraceful* who is awkward, clumsy, bungling, unhandy, rough, uncouth in manners, unrefined, unpolished; *undignified*, uncouth in speech, clownish, gawky, slouchy in action: *inelegant*, in the choice of language or attire; *uneasy*, overactive, restless, boorish, unmannerly, excessively nervous, in general bearing.

A material object is *ungraceful* when it is unbecoming, ill-fitted, inappropriate, lacking in harmonious, pleasing appearance, unsuitable, not conformable to surroundings. An article of attire is *ungraceful* that does not correspond with other associated articles or does not accord with the wearer's complexion or figure.

UNHAPPY, MISERABLE, WRETCHED. *Unhappy* is literally not to be happy; this is the negative condition of many who might be happy if they pleased. *Miserable*, from *misereri*, to pity, is to deserve pity; that is, to be positively and extremely *unhappy:* this is the lot only of comparatively few: *wretched*, from our word *wreck*, Anglo-Saxon *wrecca*, an outcast (compare the Anglo-Saxon verb *wreccan*, to persecute, from which our words *wreck* and the verb *wreak*, in the phrase *wreak vengeance*, are derived), signifies cast away or abandoned, that is, particularly *miserable*, which is the lot of still fewer. As happiness lies properly in the mind, *unhappy* is taken in the proper sense with regard to the state of the feelings, but is figuratively extended to the outward circumstances which occasion the painful feelings; we lead an *unhappy* life, or are in an *unhappy* condition: as that which excites the compassion of others must be external, and the state of abandonment must of itself be an outward state, *miserable* and *wretched* are properly applied to the outward circumstances which cause the pain, and improperly to the pain which is occasioned. We may measure the force of these words, that is to say, the degree of *unhappiness* which they express, only by the circumstances which cause the *unhappiness*. An *unhappy* man is indefinite, as we may be *unhappy* from slight circumstances or from those which are important; a child may be said to be *unhappy* at the loss of a plaything; a man is *unhappy* who leads a vicious life: *miserable* and *wretched* are more limited in their application; a child may be both *miserable* and *wretched* if it has some serious cause, either in its own mind or in its circumstances, to make it so: a man is *miserable* who is tormented by his conscience; a mother will be *wretched* whose child is taken from her.

UNIFORM. See EQUAL.

UNIMPORTANT, INSIGNIFICANT, IMMATERIAL, INCONSIDERABLE. The want of *importance*, of *consideration*, of *signification*, and of *matter* or substance, is expressed by these terms. They differ, therefore, principally according to the meaning of the primitives; but they are so closely allied that they may be employed sometimes indifferently. *Unimportant* regards the consequences of our actions: it is *unimportant* whether we use this or that word in certain cases: *inconsiderable* and *insignificant* respects those things which may attract notice: the former is more adapted to the grave style, to designate the comparative low value of things; the latter is a familiar term which seems to convey a contemptuous meaning: in a description, we may say that the number, the size, the quantity, etc., is *inconsiderable;* in speaking of persons, we may say they are *insignificant* in stature, look, talent, station, and the like; or, speaking of things, an *insignificant* production or an *insignificant* word: *immaterial* is a species of the *unimportant* which is applied only to familiar subjects; it is *immaterial* whether we go to-day or to-morrow; it is *immaterial* whether we have a few or many.

UNINTERRUPTEDLY. See INCESSANTLY.

UNION, CONFEDERATION, COALITION, FUSION. These are all words used to signify a governmental or political combination. *Union* is the most general word. It signifies a making different entities *one*, from Latin *unus*, one, and may refer to any combination. *Confederation, coalition,* and *fusion* are different forms of political *union. Confederation,* from Latin *con,* together, and *fœdus,* league, means a joining together, a *union* in which different groups surrender part of their individual rights or powers to a central authority, but without entirely losing their separate identities. In a *confederation* such as that of the United States, for example, the states delegate certain of their powers to the central government without merging their separate identities in one. *Coalition* is derived from the past participle of the Latin word *coalescere,* found in English *coalesce,* and meaning to grow together. It signifies a temporary union of representatives of political parties for the purpose of carrying through some project in which they are all interested. A *coalition* cabinet is a cabinet composed of leaders of various political parties united in a common cause. *Fusion,* from the past participle *fusus* of Latin *fundere,* to pour (meaning something poured together, so that separate identities are lost), refers to a *union* of political parties in support of a single candidate or platform.

UNIQUE. See UNPRECEDENTED.

UNITE. See ADD; CONNECT; MERGE.

UNITED. See SYNTHETIC.

UNIVERSAL. See COSMOS; GENERAL; PUBLIC; UBIQUITOUS.

UNLEARNED. See IGNORANT.

UNLESS, EXCEPT. *Unless,* which is equivalent to *in less than, on a less supposition,* is employed only for the particular case; but *except* has always a reference to some general rule, of which an *exception* is hereby signified: I shall not do it *unless* he ask me; no one can enter *except* those who are provided with tickets.

See also BUT.

UNLETTERED. See IGNORANT.

UNLIKE. See DIFFERENT.

UNLIMITED. See BOUNDLESS.

UNMERCIFUL. See HARD-HEARTED.

UNOFFENDING, INOFFENSIVE. Both of these words indicate the negative of *offending* or *offensive,* and mean not *offending.* But *inoffensive* refers to a general disposition; *unoffending,* to a particular case. An *inoffensive* person is in the nature of things *unoffending;* one who is *unoffending* in one matter may not always be *inoffensive. Inoffensive* often carries with it the faintest implication of contemptuous condescension on the part of the speaker. It may mean not able to *offend,* not having capacity or energy enough to *offend. Unoffending* does not suggest this idea.

UNPOLLUTED. See VIRGIN.

UNPRECEDENTED, EXCEPTION-

AL, UNEXAMPLED, UNRIVALLED, UNIQUE. *Unprecedented*, a compound of the English *un*, not, and *precedented*, antecedent, previous, former, or prior, signifies that which is so rare that there is nothing to be compounded with it, something that is *sui generis*, of its own kind, standing alone, wholly by itself. It is a stronger term than *exceptional*, which implies that which is unusual, and it is more closely allied with *unexampled* and *unrivalled*, each implying something without a counterpart or anything parallel with or equal to it. The distinction is seen, for instance, in a formal address. An *exceptional* address may be one of unusual cleverness, interest, and brilliancy, without being so rare as to reach the acme of intellectual effort, yet it may not be an *unexampled* one, much less an *unrivalled* one, as the just application of those terms depends on the varying viewpoints of the hearers. Strictly, *unexampled* implies that which is without the same likeness in its essentials, and *unrivalled*, that which is of the best, of the first water; but in common usage the terms are frequently erroneously applied to several objects or degrees of objects when in truth they belong to one only, as only one can be supreme. *Unique* expresses the same idea in positive rather than negative terms. That which is *unique* is the only one of its kind (from Latin *unus*, one). It is the superlative expression of the idea common to all these terms, and should not be compared; a thing is *unique;* it cannot be more or most *unique.*

UNPREMEDITATED, EXTEMPORANEOUS, IMPROMPTU, OFF-HAND, UNSTUDIED. *Unpremeditated*, a compound of the English *un*, not, and *premeditated*, from the Latin *præmeditatus, præ*, before, and *meditari*, to meditate, implying to think of before, in advance of an action. This term is a very common one in criminology, signifying the commission of an act on the spur of the moment, on a sudden provocation, without previous cause, plan, or thought, as a felonious attack upon another that may result in a charge of assault and battery or of some degree of homicide, justifiable or otherwise.

Extemporaneous, from the Latin phrase *ex tempore*, at the moment, and *impromptu*, from the phrase *in promptu*, in readiness, from *promere*, to bring forward, are most generally applied to a spoken address that is called forth by an unexpected invitation, permitting the person called upon no opportunity for preparation. *Off-hand* is a less dignified term, as it implies a certain degree of carelessness, an indifferent fitting of language to occasion, a feeling that "anything will answer." *Unstudied* is most akin to *unpremeditated*, yet it implies a different effort, as an *unpremeditated* act may be one not previously thought of, while an *unstudied* act may be one that would ordinarily be studied or planned beforehand, but in its special application was done without any previous preparation.

UNQUESTIONABLE. See INDUBITABLE.

UNRAVEL. See UNFOLD.

UNRELENTING. See IMPLACABLE.

UNRIVALLED. See UNPRECEDENTED.

UNRUFFLED, CALM, PEACEFUL, SMOOTH, TRANQUIL. *Unruffled*, a compound of the English *un*, not, and *ruffled*, parallel with Old Dutch *ruyffelen*, to wrinkle, and allied to *ruff, rumple*, etc., is applied both to objects and persons, implying that which is not agitated, not stirred up, not changed from a normal condition. The surface of a stream remains *unruffled* when it is not forced into ripples by the wind; a person, when under exciting conditions, displays neither agitation, nervousness, apprehension, nor fear. The sea, the atmosphere, a person, are *calm* when undisturbed by abnormal conditions; they are then said to be serene, placid, imperturbable. *Peaceful* and *peaceable* are terms frequently misapplied. The former signifies freedom from agitation or commotion, and thus belongs to the present group, while the latter signifies freedom from strife or contest.

Smooth and *even*, too, are likewise used erroneously, to imply a level condition; but they really signify more than that. *Smooth*, as distinguished from *even*, means that which is free from every degree of roughness, however small, while whatever is *even* may be free only from unusual roughness or irregularities. *Smooth,* therefore, in its truest application is in full accord with *unruffled. Tranquil,* however, admits of but one condition, that is, freedom from agitation, physical or mental, from disturbance, roughness of any character or degree, or from anything that would interfere with quietude, repose.

UNRULY, Ungovernable, Refractory. *Unruly* marks the want of disposition to be ruled; *ungovernable,* an absolute incapacity to be governed: the former is a temporary or partial error, the latter is an habitual defect in the temper: a high-spirited child will be occasionally *unruly;* any child of strong passions will become *ungovernable* by excessive indulgence: we say that our wills are *unruly* and our tempers are *ungovernable. Refractory,* from *refractus,* past participle of the Latin *refrangere,* to break open, marks the disposition to break everything down before it: it is the excess of the *unruly* with regard to children: the *unruly* is, however, negative; but the *refractory* is positive: an *unruly* child objects to be ruled; a *refractory* child sets up a positive resistance to all rule; an *unruly* child may be altogether silent and passive; a *refractory* child always commits himself by some act of insubordination in word or deed: he is *unruly* if in any degree he gives trouble in the *ruling;* he is *refractory* if he actively resists being ruled.

UNSATISFACTORY, Dissatisfying, Insufficient. All these terms mean not meeting the wishes or expectations. *Unsatisfactory,* however, is a less positive term than *dissatisfying.* That which is *unsatisfactory* fails to satisfy; that which is *dissatisfying* produces a positive emotional reaction which is the opposite to satisfaction. One fails to meet the conditions; the other definitely opposes them. *Insufficient* means literally not enough. It indicates a special kind of unsatisfactoriness. That which is *insufficient* is lacking in quantity; that which is *unsatisfactory* may be lacking in quality as well. That which is *insufficient* is *unsatisfactory;* that which is *unsatisfactory* may be much more than *insufficient.*

C.E.S.—23

UNSEARCHABLE, Inscrutable. These terms are both applied to things set above the understanding of man, but not altogether indifferently; for that which is *unsearchable* is not set at so great a distance from us as that which is *inscrutable:* for that which is *searched* is in common concerns easier to be found than that which requires a *scrutiny.* The ways of God are to us finite creatures more or less *unsearchable;* but the mysterious plans of Providence, as frequently evinced in the affairs of men, are altogether *inscrutable.*

UNSETTLED. See Undetermined.

UNSHACKLE. See Emancipate.

UNSIGHTLY. See Ugly.

UNSPEAKABLE, Ineffable, Unutterable, Inexpressible. *Unspeakable* and *ineffable,* from the Latin *ineffabilis,* based on *in,* not, and *effabilis,* utterable, from *effari,* to speak out, have precisely the same meaning; but the *unspeakable* is said of objects in general, particularly of that which is above human conception, and surpasses the power of language to describe; as the *unspeakable* goodness of God: *ineffable* is said of such objects as cannot be painted in words with adequate force; as the *ineffable* sweetness of a person's look: *unutterable* and *inexpressible* are extended in their signification to that which is incommunicable by signs from one being to another; thus grief is *unutterable* which it is not in the power of the sufferer by any sounds to bring home to the feelings of another; grief is *inexpressible* which is not to be expressed by looks, or words, or any signs. *Unutterable* is therefore applied only to the individual who wishes to give *utterance; inexpressible* may be said of that which is to be expressed concerning others: our own pains are *unutterable;* the sweetness of a person's countenance is *inexpressible.*

UNSPOTTED. See Blameless.

UNSTEADY. See Undetermined.

UNSTUDIED. See Unpremeditated.

UNSWERVING, Constant, Determined, Resolute. In the moral sense, *unswerving* implies the quality that makes a person steadfast in his course of life, in his friendships, in his varied dealings with others, always resolved, faithful, persevering, unhesitating, unwavering, wholly dependable. He is *constant* whose course of action is incessant, uninterrupted, regular, who remains true through all contingencies. *Determined* is a more vigorous term, as it implies a consideration of certain conditions, a decision as to a proper course to follow, and a persistent adherence to that course, despite allurements or seeming advantages to the contrary. A *resolute* person is one possessing the quality of more than ordinary firmness of purpose, one having a fixed, unalterable purpose, one constant in the pursuit of an aim, one who is unshaken on all occasions, undaunted, inflexible, stout-hearted under trying or adverse circumstances. The terms *determined* and *resolute* have various shades of meaning, which are more critically considered under the term DECIDED.

UNTOUCHED. See VIRGIN.

UNTOWARD. See AWKWARD.

UNTRUTH, FALSEHOOD, FALSITY, LIE. *Untruth* is an *untrue* saying; *falsehood* and *lie* are *false* sayings: *untruth* of itself reflects no disgrace on the agent; it may be unintentional or not: a *falsehood* and a *lie* are intentional *false* sayings, differing only in degree as to the guilt of the offender: a *falsehood* is not always spoken for the express intention of deceiving, but a *lie* is uttered only for the worst of purposes. Some persons have a habit of telling *falsehoods* from the mere love of talking: those who are guilty of bad actions endeavor to conceal them by *lies.* Children are apt to speak *untruths* for want of understanding the value of words: travellers, from a love of exaggeration, are apt to introduce *falsehoods* into their narrations: it is the nature of a *lie* to increase itself to a tenfold degree; one *lie* must be backed by many more.

Falsehood is also used in the abstract sense for what is *false. Falsity* is never used but in the abstract sense, ᵗor the property of the *false.* The former is general, the latter particular, in the application: the truth or *falsehood* of an assertion is not always to be distinctly proved; the *falsity* of any particular person's assertion may be proved by the evidence of others.

UNUSED. See VIRGIN.

UNUTTERABLE. See UNSPEAKABLE.

UNVEIL, DISCLOSE, REMOVE, REVEAL, SHOW. *Unveil,* a compound of the English *un,* not, and *veil,* a covering, the latter in Old French *veile,* French *voile,* from the Latin *velum,* a sail, from *vehere,* to carry (*i. e.,* that which carries or moves the boat), and hence any piece of cloth, or a covering, signifies, as a transitive, to remove a covering from something, to make clear something that was previously hidden or but slightly visible; as an intransitive, to come to light or become known. The term has many applications—among them: we *unveil* a memorial, statue, or painting by removing its temporary covering; we *unveil* a secret, conspiracy, plot, purpose, by making it known; we *unveil* a mental burden by confiding it to another.

Disclose, from the Latin *discludere,* to open, signifies the act of making known or public something that is concealed, to bring to light something not generally known, and *reveal,* from the Latin *revelare,* to draw back a cover, in French *révéler,* signifies to divulge something known to ourselves but not to others, to lay bare a mystery or a secret purpose, in a special sense, to make known something which could not become known without divine or supernatural instruction. *Remove* signifies to take away, put aside, disassociate, separate, as to displace something that covers or conceals something else; and *show* implies an exhibition, a display, a presentation to the view, of something that has not been generally seen, by an action that makes it visible.

UNWILLING. See AVERSE.

UNWORTHY, WORTHLESS. *Unworthy* is a term of less reproach than *worthless;* for the former signifies not to be *worthy* of praise or honor; the latter signifies to be without any worth, and consequently in the fullest sense bad. It may be a mark of modesty or humility to say that I am an *unworthy* recipient of your kindness; but it would be folly and extravagance to say that I am a *worthless* recipient of your kindness. There are many *unworthy* members in every religious community; but every society that is conducted upon proper principles will take care to exclude *worthless* members. In regard to one another, we are often *unworthy* of the distinctions or privileges we enjoy; in regard to our Maker, we are all *unworthy* of His goodness, though not *worthless* in His eyes.

UPBRAID. See BLAME.

UPHOLD, AID, MAINTAIN, SANCTION, SUPPORT, VINDICATE. *Uphold,* a compound of the English *up* and *hold,* from a widely distributed Germanic root, *hal,* signifying to raise, hence to grasp and keep, means to keep raised or elevated. The term is equally applicable to persons and objects. We *uphold* a person when we agree with him, stand by him, make his attitude our own, on some controversy, proposition, or position he has assumed; we *aid* him by helping, assisting him to retain the position or attitude he has taken; we *maintain* his actions or declarations by affirming or defending them, adopting them as consistent with our own judgment; we *sanction* what he does or says by confirming, assenting to, coinciding with, the act or saying; we *support* him by favoring, seconding, consenting to, or vouching for, his position; and we *vindicate* him when we corroborate, establish the validity, or defend successfully that which he has said or done. In a material sense, *uphold* and *support* are applied to one object set beneath another, to bear it up, sustain it, or keep it from falling, as a pillar, base, foundation, or any object on which another object rests, and *maintain* is applied to the province or duty of the object so used.

UPON. See ABOVE; ON.

UPRIGHT. See VIRTUOUS.

UPRIGHTNESS. See HONESTY; RECTITUDE.

UPROAR. See BUSTLE.

UPSIDE-DOWN. See TOPSY-TURVY.

URBANITY. See SUAVITY.

URGE. See ENCOURAGE.

URGENT. See PRESSING.

USAGE, CUSTOM, PRESCRIPTION. The *usage* is what one has been long used to do; *custom* is what one generally does; *prescription* is what is prescribed by usage to be done. The *usage* acquires force and sanction by dint of time; the *custom* acquires sanction by the frequency of its being done or the numbers doing it; the *prescription* acquires force by the authority which prescribes. Hence it arises that *customs* vary in every age, but that *usage* and *prescription* supply the place of written law.

See also TREATMENT.

USE. See EMPLOY; UTILITY.

USUALLY. See COMMONLY.

USURP. See APPROPRIATE.

UTILITY, USE, SERVICE, AVAIL. *Utility* and *use* both come ultimately from *utor.* *Service,* from the Latin *servire,* to employ or make use of. *Avail,* from *a* or *ad* and French *valoir,* Latin *valere,* signifies strength for a given purpose or to a given end.

All these terms imply fitness to be employed to advantage (see ADVANTAGE). *Utility* is applied in a general sense to what may be usefully employed: *use* to that which is actually so employed; things are said to be of general *utility,* or a thing is said to be of a particular *use.*

The word *use* refers us to the employment of things generally and the advantage derived from such *use; service,* the particular state or capacity of a thing to be usefully employed. It is proper, therefore, to say that prayers and entreaties are of *use;* but in speaking of tools, weapons, and the like, to say they are of *service.* Prudence forbids us to destroy anything that may be of *use;* economy enjoins upon us not to throw aside anything as long as it is fit for *service.*

All the preceding terms are taken absolutely; *avail* is a term of relative import; it respects the circumstances under which a thing may be fit or otherwise to be employed with efficacy. When entreaties are found to be of no *avail,* females sometimes try the force of tears.

UTOPIAN, CHIMERICAL, FANCIFUL, IDEAL, VISIONARY. *Utopian* was derived from the Greek οὐ, not, and τόπος, a place, literally nowhere, and has the sense of a good or happy place. The term *Utopia* was coined by Sir Thomas

More for his famous work, published in 1513, describing an imaginary island, where the most nearly perfect system of laws and institutions existed; hence *Utopian*, as an adjective, has come to apply to anything founded on or involving ideal perfection, and, as a substantive, to a person enthusiastic in efforts to promote schemes for unalloyed social happiness. The term has had a general acceptance ever since Sir Thomas coined it, as it seemed to apply admirably to a class of political and social propagandists who aimed at impracticable, ideal perfectibility.

The term *chimerical*, from the Latin *chimæra* and Greek χίμαιρα, takes us back to the annals of mythology, wherein the *chimera* is described as a fire-spouting monster with a lion's head, a serpent's tail, and a goat's body, that was killed by Bellerophon. Hesiod narrates that the monster was the daughter of Typhaon and Echidna. When the term was introduced into common English language, it was used to imply an unreal creature of the imagination, and hence any vain or idle fancy. As *fancy* (for derivation see FANCIFUL) signifies a notion, caprice, idea, creative imagination, or that which does not really exist, but is hoped to exist, so *fanciful* signifies whatever one would like to see, do, or possess, yet is incapable of in any of these respects. So, too, is the *ideal* a *visionary* condition impossible of realization, however desirable or beneficial that state might be, because existing only in the imagination, a mental image, a conception of what ought to be. This term is also applied to a person or object regarded as a standard of perfection, as possessing qualities far above the ordinary.

UTTER, SPEAK, ARTICULATE, PRONOUNCE. *Utter*, from *out*, Middle English *outen*, a verb formed from the adverb *out*, corresponding to the colloquial expression "out with it," signifies to send forth a sound: this, therefore, is a more general term than *speak*, which is to *utter* an intelligible sound. We may *utter* a groan; we *speak* words only or that which is intended to serve as words. To *speak*, therefore, is only a species of *utterance;* a dumb man has *utterance*, but not *speech*. *Articulate* and *pronounce* are modes of *speaking;* to *articulate*, from *articulation*, a joint, is to *pronounce* distinctly the letters or syllables of words; which is the first effort of a child beginning to *speak*. It is of great importance to make a child *articulate* every letter when he first begins to *speak* or read. To *pronounce*, from the Latin *pronunciare*, to speak out loud, is a formal mode of *speaking*. A child must first *articulate* the letters and the syllables, then he *pronounces* or sets forth the whole word; this is necessary before he can *speak* to be understood.

See also ANNOUNCE; DECLARE; SPEAK.

UTTERMOST, EXTREME, FARTHEST, LAST. *Uttermost*, from Anglo-Saxon *utor*, signifies the *extreme* outer edge of anything. It therefore is a more limited application of the idea contained in *extreme*. The same is true of its relation to *farthest* and *last*. *Farthest* and *last* have a meaning similar to that of *extreme*, but they emphasize the utmost limit suggested in *extreme* from different points of view. *Farthest* lays the stress on distance; *last* expresses the idea in terms of numbers, or rather from the standpoint of some one counting. *Last* is that which comes at the end of a series.

V

VACANCY, VACUITY, INANITY. *Vacancy* and *vacuity* both denote the space unoccupied, or the abstract quality of being unoccupied. *Inanity*, from the Latin *inanis*, denotes the abstract quality of emptiness or of not containing anything: hence the former terms *vacancy* and *vacuity* are used in an indifferent sense; *inanity* always in a bad sense: there may be a *vacancy* in the mind, or a *vacancy* in life, which we may or may not fill up as we please; but *inanity* of character denotes the want of the essentials that constitute a character.

VACANT. See EMPTY; IDLE.

VACILLATE, WAVER. *Vacillate*, from Latin *vacillare*, to waver, is the Latin word corresponding to the native English *waver*, a frequentative of *wave*. *Waver* is used with a literal as well as a figurative significance. *Vacillate* is now used only figuratively to indicate mental indecision, an inability to determine upon a course of action or an opinion and to stick to it. It has a more limited application than *waver*, but is more specific within its narrower field.

VAGARY, CROTCHET, FANCY, WHIM. *Vagary*, in Latin *vagari*, French *vaguer*, Italian *vagare*, as a transitive signifies to roam, stroll, wander; as a substantive, a wandering of the thoughts, a wild freak, a *whim*, an unsubstantial purpose, an imaginary concept, a capricious frolic; as a verb, to wander about or wind, as a river.

A *vagary*, in whatever form it may assume, is an outgrowth of an unsteady mind, in most instances harmless, though often annoying to others; in some instances a consequence of imbecility, delirium, or insanity.

A *caprice* (derived through French from Italian *capriccio*, from *caprio*, goat, meaning a sudden leap of the mind like the leap of a goat—compare *caper*), or sudden impulse of the mind, may take the form of an innocent frolic or of a questionable act; a *crotchet*, originally a musical term, "tune" or "air," hence a *fancy* or a *whim*, is usually a *fancy* made especially noticeable by the tenacity with which its possessor clings to and displays it, a thought or idea out of the ordinary, a bit of imagination, groundless but conjured up; and a *whim* may be a sudden flash of the mind, a more or less ridiculous impression, or the result of a progressive aberration.

VAGRANT. See TRUANT.

VAGUE. See LOOSE.

VAIN, INEFFECTUAL, FRUITLESS. These epithets are all applied to our endeavors; but the term *vain* (see IDLE) is the most general and indefinite; the other terms are particular and definite. What we aim at, as well as what we strive for, may be *vain;* but *ineffectual*, that is, not *effectual* (see EFFECTIVE), and *fruitless*, that is, without *fruit*, signifying not producing the desired fruit of one's labor, refer only to the termination or value of our labors. When the object aimed at is general in its import it is common to term the endeavor *vain* when it cannot attain this object: it is *vain* to attempt to reform a person's character until he is convinced that he stands in need of reformation; when the means employed are inadequate for the attainment of the particular end, it is usual to call the endeavor *ineffectual;* cool arguments will be *ineffectual* in convincing any one inflamed with a particular passion; when labor is specifically employed for the attainment of a particular object, it is usual to term it *fruitless* if it fail: peace-makers will often find themselves in this condition, that their labors will be rendered *fruitless* by the violent passions of angry opponents.

VALOR. See BRAVERY.

VALUABLE, PRECIOUS, COSTLY. *Valuable* signifies fit to be *valued; precious*, having a high price; *costly*, costing much money. *Valuable* expresses directly the idea of *value; precious* and *costly* express the same idea indirectly: on the other hand, that which is *valuable* is said only to be fit or deserving of *value;* but *precious* and *costly* denote that which is highly *valuable,* according to the ordinary measure of *valuing* objects, that is, by the *price* they bear; hence, the latter two express the idea much more strongly than the former.

They are similarly distinguished in their moral application: a book is *valuable* according to its contents, or according to the estimate which men set upon it, either individually or collectively. The Bible is the only *precious* book in the world that has intrinsic *value,* that is, set above all price. There are many *costly* things, which are *valuable* only to the individuals who are disposed to expend money upon them.

Value, Worth, Rate, Price.—*Value,* from the feminine past participle of the French *valoir,* Latin *valere,* to be strong, implies those essential qualities which constitute its strength. *Worth,* in Anglo-Saxon *weorth,* valuable, a Germanic word from the root *war,* to guard or keep, found in *wary, ward,* etc., signifies that which deserves to be kept and guarded, hence the good experienced or felt to exist in a thing. *Rate* (see PROPORTION). *Price,* through Old French from Latin *pretium,* signifies what a thing is sold for.

Value is a general and indefinite term, applied to whatever is conceived to be good in a thing: the *worth* is that good only which is conceived or known as such. The *value,* therefore, of a thing is as variable as the humors and circumstances of men; it may be nothing or something very great in the same object at the same time in the eyes of different men. The *worth* is, however, that *value* which is acknowledged; it is therefore something more fixed and permanent: we speak of the *value* of external objects which are determined by taste; but the *worth* of things as determined by rule. The *value* of a book that is out of print is fluctuating and uncertain; but its real *worth* may not be more than what it would fetch for waste paper. The *rate* and *price* are the measures of that *value* or *worth;* the former in a general, the latter in a particular, application to mercantile transactions. Whatever

we give in exchange for another thing, whether according to a definite or an indefinite estimation, is said to be done at a certain *rate;* thus we purchase pleasure at a dear *rate* when it is at the expense of our health: *price* is the *rate* of exchange estimated by coin or any other medium: hence *price* is a fixed *rate,* and may be figuratively applied in that sense to moral objects; as when health is expressly sacrificed to pleasure, it may be termed the *price* of pleasure.

Value, Prize, Esteem.—To *value* is in the literal sense to fix a *value* on a thing. *Prize,* signifying to fix a *price,* and *esteem* are both modes of *valuing.*

To *value* is to set any *value,* real or supposititious, relative or absolute, on a thing: in this sense men *value* gold above silver or an appraiser *values* goods. To *value* may be applied to either material or spiritual subjects, to corporeal or mental actions: *prize* and *esteem* are taken only as mental actions; the former in reference to sensible or moral objects, the latter only to moral objects: we may *value* books according to their market price, or we may *value* them according to their contents; we *prize* books only for their contents, in which sense *prize* is a much stronger term than *value;* we also *prize* men for their usefulness to society; we *esteem* their moral characters.

VANISH. See DISAPPEAR.
VANITY. See PRIDE.
VANQUISH. See CONQUER.
VARIABLE. See CHANGEABLE.
VARIATION, VARIETY. *Variation* denotes the act of *varying* (see CHANGE); *variety* denotes the quality of *varying,* or the thing *varied.* The astronomer observes the *variations* in the heavens; the philosopher observes the variations in the climate from year to year. *Variety* is pleasing to all persons, but to none so much as the young and the fickle: there is an infinite *variety* in every species of objects, animate or inanimate.
VARIOUS. See DIFFERENT.
VARNISH. See GLOSS.
VARY. See CHANGE; DIFFER.
VASSALAGE. See THRALDOM.
VAST. See ENORMOUS.
VAUNT. See GLORY.

VEHEMENT. See VIOLENT.

VEIL. See CLOAK.

VELOCITY. See QUICKNESS.

VENAL, MERCENARY. *Venal,* from the Latin *venalis,* signifies salable or ready to be sold, which, applied as it commonly is to persons, is a much stronger term than *mercenary.* A *venal* man gives up all principles for interest; a *mercenary* man seeks his interest without regard to principle: *venal* writers are such as write in favor of the cause that can promote them to riches or honors; a servant is commonly a *mercenary,* who gives his services according as he is paid: those who are loudest in their professions of political purity are the best subjects for a minister to make *venal;* a *mercenary* spirit is engendered in the minds of those who devote themselves exclusively to trade.

VENERATE. See ADORE.

VENIAL, PARDONABLE. *Venial,* from the Latin *venia,* pardon or indulgence, is applied to what may be tolerated without express disparagement to the individual or direct censure; but the *pardonable* is that which may only escape severe censure, yet cannot be allowed: garrulity is a *venial* offence in old age; levity in youth is *pardonable* in single instances.

VENOM. See POISON.

VENTURE. See HAZARD.

VERACITY. See TRUTH.

VERBAL, VOCAL, ORAL. *Verbal,* from *verbum,* a word, signifies after the manner of a spoken word; *oral,* from the stem of *os,* a mouth, signifies by word of mouth; and *vocal,* from the stem of *vox,* the voice, signifies by the voice: the former two of these words are used to distinguish speaking from writing; the latter to distinguish the sounds of the voice from any other sounds, particularly in singing: a *verbal* message is distinguished from one written on a paper or in a note; *oral* tradition is distinguished from that which is handed down to posterity by means of books; *vocal* music is distinguished from instrumental; *vocal* sounds are more harmonious than those which proceed from any other bodies.

See also ANNOUNCE; SPEAK.

VERDANT. See GREEN.

VERGE. See BORDER.

VERSATILE. See CHANGEABLE.

VERY. See QUITE.

VESTIGE. See MARK.

VEX. See DISPLEASURE; TEASE.

VEXATION, MORTIFICATION, CHAGRIN. *Vexation* (see DISPLEASURE) springs from a variety of causes, acting unpleasantly on the inclinations or passions of men; *mortification* (see HUMBLE) is a strong degree of *vexation,* which arises from particular circumstances acting on particular passions: the loss of a day's pleasure is a *vexation* to one who is eager for pleasure; the loss of a prize, or the circumstance of coming into disgrace where we expected honor, is a *mortification* to an ambitious person. *Vexation* arises principally from our wishes and views being crossed; *mortification,* from our pride and self-importance being hurt; *chagrin,* in French *chagrin* (compare the title of Balzac's novel, *La Peau de Chagrin*), comes originally from *shagreen,* a word of Oriental origin meaning a rough and granular skin used for polishing, hence by extension anything irritating, or a state of irritation; disappointments are always attended with more or less *vexation,* according to the circumstances which give pain and trouble; an exposure of our poverty may be more or less of a *mortification,* according to the value which we set on wealth and grandeur; a refusal of a request will produce more or less *chagrin,* as it is accompanied with circumstances more or less *mortifying* to our pride.

See also TROUBLESOME.

VIBRATE. See THRILL; UNDULATE; WAG.

VICE. See CRIME; IMPERFECTION.

VICINITY. See NEIGHBORHOOD.

VICISSITUDE. See CHANGE.

VICTOR. See CONQUEROR.

VICTORY. See TRIUMPH.

VIE. See STRIVE.

VIEW, SURVEY, PROSPECT. *View* (see LOOK) and *survey,* compounded of *vey* or *view* and *sur,* over (Coleridge uses the word *surview* to mean a complete view of a thing as a whole), mark the act of the person, namely, the looking over a thing with more or less attention: *prospect,* from the Latin *prospectus* and *prospicere,* to see before, designates the thing seen. We take a *view* or *survey;* the *prospect* presents itself: the *view* is of an indefinite extent; the *survey* is always comprehensive in its nature. Ignorant people take but narrow *views* of things; men take more or less enlarged *views,* according to their cultivation: the capacious mind of a genius takes a *survey* of all nature. The *view* depends altogether on the train of a person's thoughts; the *prospect* is set before him, it depends upon the nature of the thing: our *views* of advancement are sometimes very fallacious; our *prospects* are very delusive; both occasion disappointment; the former is the keener, as we have to blame the miscalculation upon ourselves. Sometimes our *prospects* depend upon our *views,* at least in matters of religion; he who forms erroneous *views* of a future state has not foreseen the *prospect* beyond the grave.

View, Prospect, Landscape. — *View* and *prospect,* though applied here to external objects of sense, have a similar distinction as in the preceding article. The *view* is not only that which may be seen, but that which is actually seen; hence the term *view* is mostly coupled with the person *viewing,* although a *prospect* exists continually, whether seen or not: hence we speak of our *view* being intercepted, but not our *prospect* intercepted; a confined or bounded *view,* but a lively or dreary *prospect,* or the *prospect* clears up or extends.

View is an indefinite term; it may be said either of a number of objects or of a single object, of a whole or of a part: *prospect* is said only of an aggregate number of objects; we may have a *view* of a town, of a number of scattered houses, of a single house, or of the spire of a steeple; but the *prospect* comprehends that which comes within the range of the eye. *View* may be said of that which is seen directly or indirectly; *prospect* only of that which directly presents itself to the eye: hence a drawing of an object may be termed a *view,* although not a *prospect. View* is confined to no particular objects; *prospect* mostly suggests rural objects; and *landscape* means only a *view* on land. *Landscape, landskip,* or *landshape,* denote any portion of country which is in a particular form: hence the *landscape* is a species of *prospect.* A *prospect* may be wide, and comprehend an assemblage of objects both of nature and art; but a *landscape* is narrow, and lies within the compass of the naked eye: hence it is also that *landscape* may be taken for the drawing of a *landscape,* and consequently for a species of *view:* the taking of *views* or *landscapes* is the last exercise of the learner in drawing.

See also AIM; LOOK; SPY.

VIGILANT. See WAKEFUL.

VIGOR. See ENERGY.

VIGOROUS. See HERCULEAN.

VILE. See BASE; SQUALID.

VILIFY. See REVILE.

VINDICATE. See ASSERT; AVENGE; DEFEND; UPHOLD.

VIOLATE. See INFRINGE.

VIOLENCE. See FORCE.

VIOLENT, FURIOUS, BOISTEROUS, VEHEMENT, IMPETUOUS. *Violent* signifies having force (see FORCE). *Furious* signifies having *fury* (see ANGER). *Boisterous* comes possibly from *bestir,* signifying ready to *bestir* or come into motion. *Vehement,* in Latin *vehemens,* compounded of *veho* and *mens,* signifies carried away by the mind or the force of passion. *Impetuous* signifies having an *impetus* (from *in,* on, and *petere,* to fly, hence to seek, to rush on, to fall upon).

Violent is here the most general term, including the idea of force or violence, which is common to them all; it is as general in its application as in its meaning. When *violent* and *furious* are applied to the same objects, the latter expresses a higher degree of the former: a *furious* whirlwind is *violent* beyond measure. *Violent* and *boisterous* are likewise applied to the same objects; but the *boisterous* refers only to the *violence* of the motion or noise: hence we say that a wind is *violent* inasmuch as it acts with great force upon all bodies; it is *boisterous* inasmuch as it causes the great motion of bodies: *impetuous,* like *boisterous,* is also applied to bodies moving with great *violence.*

These terms are all applied to persons, or what is personal, with a similar distinction: a man is *violent* in his opinions, *violent* in his measures, *violent* in his resentments; he is *furious* in his anger, or has a *furious* temper; he is *vehement* in his affections or passions, *vehement* in love, *vehement* in zeal, *vehement* in pursuing an object, *vehement* in expression: *violence* transfers itself to some external object on which it acts with force; but *vehemence* implies that species of *violence* which is confined to the person himself: we may dread *violence* because it is always liable to do mischief; we ought to suppress our *vehemence* because it is injurious to ourselves: a *violent* partisan renders himself obnoxious to others; a man who is *vehement* in any cause puts it out of his own power to be of use. *Impetuosity* is rather the extreme of *violence* or *vehemence:* an *impetuous* attack is an excessively *violent* attack; an *impetuous* character is an excessively *vehement* character. *Boisterous* is said of the manner and the behavior rather than the mind.

VIRGIN, Damsel, Girl, Lass, Maid, Maiden. All these words indicate a young unmarried woman. *Virgin*, Latin *virgo, virginis*, refers specifically to a lack of experience of sexual intercourse, and may be used simply as a synonyme of *pure, untouched*, etc., as when we speak of *virgin* soil, *virgin* forests, etc. *Damsel* comes from the Old French *damoisel*, a young page or squire, from Late Latin *dominicellus*, a little lord, the diminutive of *dominus*, lord. *Girl*, also, was originally applied to a boy; it meant a child in general. *Lass* may be of Scandinavian origin. *Maid* is an abbreviation of *maiden*, Anglo-Saxon *mægden*, an unmarried girl. Of these terms *girl* is the usual word; *virgin* carries the special emphasis upon chastity. *Lass* is archaic or colloquial; *maiden* is poetic, laying some emphasis upon the idea suggested in *virgin; maid* is poetic, but is also used colloquially to indicate a female servant. *Damsel* is also a somewhat poetic and archaic word, sometimes humorously applied to particularly unpoetic persons.

VIRTUOUS, Chaste, Good, Moral, Pure, Upright. *Virtuous*, in French *vertueux*, from Low Latin *virtuosus*, Latin *virtus*, indicated the proper character of a man (*vir*), the sum of all manly virtues. It now signifies

the person who is at heart morally *good*, who abstains from vice, acts in the spirit of the *moral* law, is brave, valorous, and strong in principles, efficient through the operation of inherent qualities, *pure* in deed and thought, *upright*, honest, impartial, prompt in all his dealings, and, when applied to women, one having excellent qualities, specifically being *chaste, pure*, unspotted. When applied to actions the term signifies that which is done in conformity with the moral or divine law or with duty, that which is beneficial to others, that which creates or promotes goodness, morality, purity, in the community.

VIRULENT, Malignant. *Virulent* comes from Latin *virus*, originally slime, but used to signify poison. *Malignant* comes from Latin *malus*, bad, and *gignere*, to be born, to be of a certain nature. (Compare *benignant* for a similar formation and contrary meaning.) Both words signify actively and violently hostile or evil. In accordance with their derivations, however, *virulent* indicates that which is poisonous, *malignant* that which is fatally hostile to life or peace. *Virulent* speech is speech so permeated by intense and morbid ill-will that it seems to be poisoned. *Venomous* has a similar meaning, but is not so strong a word as *virulent*. *Malignant* speech is that which is also hostile; but the emphasis is placed upon the ill-will itself, not upon its morbid and poisonous character. *Malignant* is applied more frequently to actions and facial expression, *virulent* mainly to speech and emotion.

VISAGE. See Face.

VISIBLE. See Apparent.

VISION, Apparition, Phantom, Spectre, Ghost. *Vision*, from the Latin *visus*, seeing or seen, signifies either the act of seeing or thing seen: *apparition*, from *appear*, signifies the thing that appears. As the thing seen is only the improper signification, the term *vision* is never employed but in regard to some agent: the *vision* depends upon the state of the visual organ; the *vision* of a person whose sight is defective will frequently be fallacious, he will see some things double which are single, long which are short, and the like.

In like manner, if the sight be miraculously impressed, his *vision* will enable him to see that which is supernatural: hence it is that *vision* is either true or false, according to the circumstances of the individual; and a *vision*, signifying a thing seen, is taken for a supernatural exertion of the *vision; apparition*, on the contrary, refers us to the object seen; this may be true or false, according to the manner in which it presents itself. Joseph was warned by a *vision* to fly into Egypt with his family; Mary Magdalene was informed of the resurrection of our Saviour by an *apparition:* feverish people often think they see *visions;* timid and credulous people sometimes take trees and posts for *apparitions.*

Phantom, from the Greek φάντασμα, based on φαίνω, to appear, is used for a false *apparition* or the *appearance* of a thing otherwise than what it is; thus the *ignis fatuus*, vulgarly called jack-o'-lantern, is a *phantom. Spectre*, formed from *specere*, to behold, and *ghost*, from Anglo-Saxon *gast*, a spirit, are the *apparitions* of immaterial substances. The *spectre* is taken for any spiritual being that appears, but *ghost* is taken only for the spirits of departed men who appear to their fellow-creatures: a *spectre* is sometimes made to appear on the stage; *ghosts* exist mostly in the imagination of the young and the ignorant.

VISIONARY. See ENTHUSIAST; QUIXOTIC; UTOPIAN.

VISITANT. See GUEST.

VITAL. See CRITICAL.

VITIATE. See DEBAUCH.

VIVACIOUS. See LIVELY.

VIVACITY. See ANIMATION.

VIVID. See CLEAR.

VOCABULARY. See DICTIONARY.

VOCAL. See VERBAL.

VOCATION, CALLING, EMPLOYMENT, OCCUPATION, PROFESSION. All these words refer to a man's habitual business. *Vocation* is the Latin word corresponding to Teutonic *calling*. It means the business to which the natural talents or tastes lead a man. *Employment* signifies a more temporary business than *occupation. Profession* implies a formal intellectual training and is applied to the occupations de-

manding such a training—as law, medicine, etc.

VOGUE, FASHION. *Vogue*, ultimately from a Germanic word allied to *wave* or *wag*, and *fashion*, from Latin *factionem*, a noun derived from *facere*, to make, have much the same meaning, but *vogue* is a somewhat more specific and sophisticated word applied to the fashion that makes a particular appeal to the wealthy and otherwise *élite* and is temporarily emphasized by them. (See FASHION.)

VCID. See EMPTY.

VOLATILITY. See LIGHTNESS.

VOLUBLE, FLUENT, GLIB, LOQUACIOUS, TALKATIVE. *Voluble*, a French term taken from the Latin *volubilem*, that from *volvere*, signifies that which is easily turned about, rolled, or fickle. *Fluent*, from Latin *fluere*, to flow, signifies a ready speech which resembles Tennyson's brook or a brimming river in its continuous movement. *Glib*, originally *slippery*, is allied to the verb *glide.* (Compare Dutch *glibbery*.) *Loquacious* is derived ultimately from the Latin *loqui*, to speak, through *loquax*, talkative, and corresponds to *talkative* in its derivation. These words all mean ready of speech, but there are slight shades of difference between them. *Fluent* simply indicates speech that is uttered easily, without hesitation. It is generally a term of praise, or, at least, merely indifferent, not derogatory. *Loquacious* may be derogatory. A *loquacious* person is one who talks a great deal or talks too much. *Talkative* has a similar significance, but, being of English derivation, it carries its meaning on the face of it more plainly than does *loquacious* and is a more homely word. *Voluble* means both *fluent* and *loquacious*, inclined to talk freely and uttering the words with great speed and readiness. *Glib* means ready of speech, with especial reference to plausible and conciliatory language.

VOLUNTARILY. See WILLINGLY.

VOLUNTARY. See GRATUITOUS.

VOLUPTUARY See SENSUALIST.

VORACIOUS. See RAPACIOUS.

VOTE, SUFFRAGE, VOICE. *Vote* comes from *votum*, the neuter past participle of Latin *vovere*, to vow, and has therefore the same derivation as English *vow;* it signified a formal expression of opinion. *Suffrage* comes from Latin *suffragium*. *Voice* is here figuratively taken for the *voice* that is raised in favor of a thing.

The *vote* is the wish itself, whether expressed or not; a person has a *vote*, that is, the power of wishing; but the *suffrage* and the *voice* are the wish that is expressed; a person gives his *suffrage* or his *voice*. The *vote* is the settled and fixed wish, it is that by which social concerns in life are determined; the *suffrage* is a *vote* given only in particular cases; the *voice* is the declared opinion or wish, expressed either by individuals or the public at large. The *vote* and *voice* are given either for or against a person or thing; the *suffrage* is commonly given in favor of a person: in all public assemblies the majority of *votes* decide the question; members of

most representative political bodies are chosen by the *suffrages* of the people; in the execution of a will, every executor has a *voice* in all that is transacted.

VOUCH. See AFFIRM.

VOYAGE. See JOURNEY.

VULGAR. See COMMON.

VULNERABLE, WEAK, EXPOSED. *Vulnerable,* from Latin *vulnus*, wound, means easily wounded. It is therefore a synonyme of *weak*, but only in a special sense. *Vulnerable* refers to only one kind of weakness, and, it is therefore much more limited in its application, but more specific within its own range of application. *Exposed* expresses the idea involved in *vulnerable* by an indirect reasoning from cause to effect, as it were. That which is *exposed* is easily hit by a missile; it is therefore *vulnerable*.

W

WAFT, BEAR, CONVEY, FLOAT, SIGNAL, TRANSMIT. *Waft*, a variant of WAVE (which see), signifies to *bear*, *convey*, transport something through a fluid or buoyant medium like the air or sea, to *float*, as on the water or through the air, to beckon or *signal* by moving a flag or other object in the air, to *transmit* (poetical) a message, good wishes, a blessing; also to turn quickly, as "*Wafting* his eyes to the contrary," Shakespeare's *Winter's Tale*, to buoy up, as "Their lungs being able to *waft* up their bodies," Browne's *Vulgar Errors*, and a breath or current, as of air, as "One wide *waft*," Thomson's *Winter*.

WAG, FLUCTUATE, OSCILLATE, SWING, VIBRATE. *Wag*, from *wegan*, to bear, carry, move (whence *weigh*, to raise or lift, hence, in our sense, to weigh, is derived), signified to move back and forth, to keep moving. *Fluctuate*, from Latin *fluctus*, signified to move like a flood, like the tides of the sea, for instance. *Oscillate* is derived from *oscillum*, literally "a little mouth," applied to an image of Bacchus suspended from a tree, and hence meant to swing like a pendulum. *Swing* is derived from Anglo-Saxon *swingan*, to shake. (Compare *swinge* from the same verb.) *Vibrate* comes from Latin *vibrare*, to shake, brandish, etc. *Wag* is a highly colloquial word meaning to move back and forth, especially applied to the conscious movements of living creatures. A dog *wags* his tail. *Oscillate* means to *swing* between two objects. *Fluctuate* means to rise and fall irregularly like the waves of the sea; *vibrate* to move with a regular alternate depression and elevation. *Swing* means simply to move back and forth as if suspended from something.

See also UNDULATE.

WAGES. See ALLOWANCE.

WAIL, CRY, DEPLORE, GRIEVE, LAMENT, MOAN, WEEP. *Wail*, from Scandinavian *væla*, signifies to cry woe, from *væ*, *vei*, woe, used as an interjection. Compare *woe*. *Cry*, Old French *crier*, Italian *gridare*; Latin *quiritare*, is a frequentative of Latin *queri*, to complain or lament, whence the word *querulous* is derived. *Deplore* comes from Latin *plorare*, to weep, to shed tears. For the derivation of *grieve* see *grief*; for lament see *bewail*; for *moan* see *groan*. *Weep* is derived from Anglo-Saxon *wepan*, to cry aloud, to raise an outcry. All of these terms indicate a different shade of *wailing*. When we *cry* we make either a low, partially suppressed noise or one that amounts to a shriek or scream, according to the intensity of the cause or our power of self-control; so, too, when we *deplore*, *grieve*, or *lament* for or over a distressing condition, the expressions may be entirely inaudible, more apparent in manner or a change of countenance, or be indicated by a *moan*, which is always a low and, generally, prolonged expression of pain or sorrow, or a grief or lamentation may reach the height of hysteria, with its paroxysms of loud laughter or weeping. Then, when we *weep* we express our grief or anguish by shedding tears, a silent action in itself, but this, too, may be accompanied by an outcry, where the cause is especially intense.

WAIT, WAIT FOR, AWAIT, LOOK FOR, EXPECT. *Wait, wait for, await*, Old French *waite*, *gaite*, a guard, allied to Anglo-Saxon *wacian*, to watch, whence the verb *watch* is itself derived, to see or look, and *expect*, from the Latin *ex*, out of, and *specto*, to behold, both signify originally the same thing as *look for*, that is, to look with concern for a thing.

All these terms express the action of the mind when directed to future matters of personal concern to the agent. *Wait, wait for*, and *await* differ less in sense than in application, the former two being in familiar use, and the latter only in the grave style: these words imply the looking simply toward an object in a state of suspense or still regard; as to *wait* until a person arrives or *wait* for his arrival; and *await* the hour of one's death, that is, to keep the mind in readiness for it.

Wait and *wait for* refer to matters that are remote and obscure in the prospect or uncertain in the event; *await* may be applied to that which is considered to be near at hand and probable to happen, and in this sense it is clearly allied to *look for* and *expect*, the former of which expresses the acts of the eye as well as the mind, the latter, the act of the mind only, in contemplating an object as very probable or even certain. It is our duty patiently to *await* the severest trials when they threaten us. When children are too much indulged and caressed, they are apt to *look for* a repetition of caresses at inconvenient seasons; it is in vain to *look for* or *expect* happiness from the conjugal state when it is not founded on a cordial and mutual regard.

See also ATTEND.

WAIVE, ABANDON, FOREGO, RELINQUISH, REMIT, RENOUNCE. *Waive,* a very common legal term, derived through Norman French from Old Norse, and ultimately from a Germanic root, *waibyan,* to fluctuate, to swing about, signifies, literally, to give up a claim to something, to abstain from insisting on some right or claim. The term implies a variety of actions. When we *abandon* a person, object, or purpose, it is to be assumed that we give him or it up permanently, unless a time period is specified; but when we *forego* an action it is to be supposed that we abandon it temporarily only, either for convenience or expediency, and are privileged to resume it subsequently.

We *relinquish* something by giving it up, parting with it, and this, too, may be either a permanent or temporary act; but when we *remit* anything in the sense of *waive,* we moderate a condition by giving up a part of it, or surrender the condition or object to the other party in interest, as a magistrate may *remit* or give up a fine he has imposed, for sufficient reason. To *renounce* a matter, however, admits of but one effect, the total final rejection of it, either by positive repudiation, absolutely disowning it, or by other means of separating ourselves from it.

WAKEFUL, WATCHFUL, VIGILANT. We may be *wakeful* without being *watchful;* but we cannot be *watchful* without being *wakeful. Wakefulness* is an affair of the body, and depends upon the temperament; *watchfulness* is an affair of the will, and depends upon the determination: some persons are more *wakeful* than they wish to be; few are as *watchful* as they ought to be. *Vigilance,* from the Latin *vigil,* expresses a high degree of *watchfulness:* a sentinel is *watchful* who on ordinary occasions keeps good *watch:* but it is necessary for him, on extraordinary occasions, to be *vigilant* in order to detect whatever may pass. We are *watchful* only in the proper sense of *watching;* but we may be *vigilant* in detecting moral as well as natural evils.

WALK. See CARRIAGE.

WALK-OUT. See STRIKE.

WAN. See PALE.

WANDER, STROLL, RAMBLE, ROVE, ROAM, RANGE. *Wander,* in German *wandern,* is a frequentative of *wenden,* to turn, signifying to turn frequently. To *stroll,* from a Germanic base found in the word to *strike,* allied with *straggle, struggle,* etc., refers to an indefinite finding one's way about—feeling one's way. *Ramble* is a frequentative of *roam. Rove,* Dutch *roover,* a robber, is derived from Anglo-Saxon *reafian,* to rob, whence *rob* itself is derived, as well as the verb *bereave.* It referred to the movements of pirates, wandering robbers, and hence came to refer rather to the wandering than to the robbing. *Range,* from Old High German *hring,* allied to *rank,* referred to something set in rows, *ranged* in an orderly fashion; from this meaning the special significance of moving about in a certain fashion arose because the word referred to the movements of armed troops, ranks of men, and, as in the case of *rove,* came to signify the action rather than the subject acting. The word suggests the scouring of the country by armed men.

The idea of going in an irregular and free manner is common to all these terms. To *wander* is to go in no fixed path; to *stroll* is to *wander* out of a path that we had taken. To *wander* may be an involuntary action; a person may *wander* to a great distance or for an indefinite length of time; in this manner a person *wanders* who has lost himself in a wood: to *stroll* is a voluntary action, limited at our discretion; thus when a person takes a walk he sometimes *strolls* from one path into another as he pleases: to *ramble* is to *wander* without any object, and consequently with more than ordinary irregularity; in this manner he who sets out to take a walk, without knowing or thinking where he shall go, *rambles* as chance directs: to *rove* is to *wander* in the same planless manner, but to a wider extent; a fugitive who does not know his road *roves* about the country in quest of some retreat: to *roam* is to *wander* from the impulse of a troubled mind; in this manner a lunatic who has broken loose may *roam* about the country; so likewise a person who travels about, because he cannot rest in quiet at home, may also be said to *roam* in quest of peace: to *range* is the contrary of to *roam;* as the former indicates a disordered state of mind, the latter indicates composure and fixedness; we *range* within certain limits, as the hunter *ranges* the forest, the shepherd *ranges* the mountains.

See also DEVIATE.

WANT, NEED, LACK. To be without is the common idea expressed by these terms; but to *want* (of Scandinavian origin) is to be without that which contributes to our comfort or is an object of our desire; to *need* (Anglo-Saxon *nyd,* from a root signifying to force—that which forces us to the last extremity), a Germanic word, is to be without that which is essential for our existence or our purposes; to *lack* expresses a little more than the general idea of being without, unaccompanied by any collateral idea. From the close connection which subsists between desiring and *want,* it is usual to consider what we *want* as artificial and what we *need* as natural and indispensable: what one man *wants* is a superfluity to another; but that which is *needed* by one is in like circumstances *needed* by all: tender people *want* a fire when others would be glad not to have it; all persons *need* warm clothing and a warm house in the winter.

To *want* and *need* may extend indefinitely to many or all objects; to *lack,* or be deficient, is properly said of a single object; we may want or *need* everything; we *lack* one thing, we *lack* this or that; a rich man may *lack* understanding, virtue, or religion; he who *wants* nothing is a happy man; he who *needs* nothing may be happy if he *wants* no more than he has; for then he *lacks* that which alone can make him happy, which is contentment.

See also POVERTY.

WARM. See HEARTY; SANGUINE.

WARMTH. See FIRE.

WARN. See GARNISH.

WARNING. See ADMONITION; CAVEAT.

WARPED. See WRY.

WARRANT. See GUARANTEE.

WARY. See CAUTIOUS.

WASTE. See DESTROY; SACK; SPEND.

WATCH. See GUARD; OBSERVE.

WATCHFUL. See WAKEFUL.

WAVE, BILLOW, SURGE, BREAKER. *Wave,* from the verb to *wave,* is applied to water in an undulating state; it is, therefore, the generic term, and the rest are specific terms: those *waves* which swell more than ordinarily are termed *billows,* which is allied to the words *bulge, bag, bowl, bulk, belly,* etc., from a root signifying to swell: those *waves* which rise higher than usual are termed *surges,* from the Latin *surgere,* to rise: those *waves* which dash against the shore or against vessels with more than ordinary force are termed *breakers.*

See also UNDULATE.

WAVER. See FLUCTUATE; SCRUPLE; VACILLATE.

WAVERING. See UNDETERMINED.

WAY, MANNER, METHOD, MODE, COURSE, MEANS. All these words denote the steps which are pursued from the beginning to the completion of any work. The *way* (Anglo-Saxon *weg,* allied to Latin *via*) is both general and indefinite; it is either taken by accident or chosen by design: the *manner,* from Old French *maniere,* manner, through a verb *manier,* to handle, from Latin *manus,* hand, and *method* (Latin *methodus,* from Greek μέθοδος, from μετά, after, and ὁδός, way, meaning after the manner of) are species of the *way* chosen by design. Whoever attempts to do that which is strange to him will at first do it in an awkward *way;* the *manner* of conferring a favor is often more than the favor itself; experience supplies men in the end with a suitable *method* of carrying on their business.

The *method* is said of that which requires contrivance; the *mode* (from Latin *modus,* a measure, manner, kind, way, from a root also found in the verb *mete),* of that which requires practice and habitual attention, the former being applied to matters of art and the latter to mechanical actions: the master has a good *method* of teaching to write; the scholar has a good or bad *mode* of holding his pen. The *course* (Latin *cursus,* from *currere,* to run—a way in which one runs) and the *means* are the *way* which we pursue in our moral conduct: the *course* is the *course* of measures which are adopted to produce a certain result; the *means* collectively for the *course* which lead to a certain end: in order to obtain legal redress we must pursue a certain *course* in law; law is one *means* of gaining redress, but we do wisely, if we can, to adopt the safer and pleasanter *means* of persuasion and cool remonstrance.

WAYWARD, Wilful. These words both indicate a disposition to follow one's own will, but *wayward* is a stronger word than *wilful.* The *wilful* boy does not easily yield his will to that of another; he wishes to have his own way, but the wish may go no further than a mere expression of it in speech or manner. A *wayward* boy deliberately goes his own way contrary to the wishes of others. He expresses his *wilfulness* in action.

WEAK, Feeble, Infirm. *Weak,* allied to the Middle English verb *weken,* from Anglo-Saxon *wican,* to make weak, is itself derived from an adjective, *wac,* weak, and related to the German *weichen,* to weaken. *Feeble,* Old French *fleble,* is derived from the Latin *flebilis,* from *flere,* to weep, and means *doleful,* a thing to be wept over, hence weak. *Infirm* (see Debility).

The Saxon term *weak* is here, as it usually is, the familiar and universal term; *feeble* is suited to a more polished style; *infirm* is only a species of the

weak: we may be *weak* in body or *mind;* but we are commonly *feeble* and *infirm* only in the body: we may be *weak* from disease or *weak* by nature; it equally conveys the gross idea of a defect: but the terms *feeble* and *infirm* are qualified expressions for *weakness:* a child is *feeble* from its infancy; an old man is *feeble* from age; the latter may likewise be *infirm* in consequence of sickness. We pity the *weak,* but their *weakness* often gives us pain; we assist the *feeble* when they attempt to walk; we support the *infirm* when they are unable to stand. The same distinction exists between *weak* and *feeble* in the moral use of the words: a *weak* attempt to excuse a person conveys a reproachful meaning; but the *feeble* efforts which we make to defend another may be praiseworthy, although *feeble.*

See also Vulnerable.

Weaken, Enfeeble, Debilitate, Enervate, Invalid.—To *weaken* is to make *weak,* and is, as before, the generic term: to *enfeeble* is to make *feeble:* to *debilitate* is to cause *debility:* to *enervate* is to *unnerve;* and to *invalidate* is to make not valid or strong: all of which are but modes of *weakening* applicable to different objects. To *weaken* may be either a temporary or a permanent act when applied to persons; *enfeeble* is permanent, either as to the body or the mind: we may be *weakened* suddenly by severe pain; we are *enfeebled* in a gradual manner, either by the slow effects of disease or age. To *weaken* is either a particular or a complete act; to *enfeeble,* to *debilitate,* and *enervate* are properly partial acts: what *enfeebles* deprives of vital or essential power; what *debilitates* may lessen power in one particular, though not in another; the severe exercise of any power, such as the memory or the attention, may tend to *debilitate* that faculty: what *enervates* acts particularly on the nervous system; it relaxes the frame and unfits the person for action either of body or mind. To *weaken* is said of things as well as persons; to *invalidate* is said of things only; we *weaken* the force of an argument by an injudicious application; we *invalidate* the claim of another by proving its informality in law.

WEAKNESS. See IMPERFECTION.

WEAL, WELFARE. Both of these words are derived from Anglo-Saxon *wela*, abundance, allied to Modern English *well* and *wealth*. *Weal* is simply the archaic and poetic term corresponding to *welfare* in ordinary speech.

WEALTH. See RICHES.

WEAN, ALIENATE, DETACH, WITHDRAW. These terms all suggest the abandonment of some object of affection or desire or something to which one has been accustomed; but they differ in the character of the metaphor under which the idea is suggested and the energy of the action. To *alienate* (for derivation and meaning see *alien*) and *wean* are the strongest of these terms. *Wean*, in Anglo-Saxon *wenian*, to accustom, German *entwöhnen*, to accustom to do without, signifies literally to accustom an infant to do without its mother's milk, and figuratively it suggests the detaching or withdrawing of something to which one is as accustomed as the child is to its daily nourishment. *Detach* (for derivation see *attach*) means, literally, to unfasten. *Withdraw* means to draw away. Both of these terms may be used literally of physical objects or figuratively of the mind, the affections, or the desires.

WEAPONS. See ARMS.

WEARINESS. See FATIGUE.

WEARISOME, TIRESOME, TEDIOUS. *Wearisome* is the general and indefinite term; *tiresome* and *tedious*, causing *tedium*, a specific form of *wearisomeness*: common things may cause *weariness*; that which acts painfully is either *tiresome* or *tedious*; but in different degrees the repetition of the same sounds will grow *tiresome;* long waiting in anxious suspense is *tedious:* there is more of the physical in *tiresome* and of the mental in *tedious*.

Weary, Tire, Jade, Harass.—To *weary* is a frequentative of *wear*, that is, to *wear* out the strength. To *tire*, Anglo-Saxon *tirian*, to be weary, may be used both as a transitive and an intransitive verb. To *jade* is derived from the noun *jade*, a term of contempt applied to a worn-out horse. *Harass* (see DISTRESS).

Long exertion *wearies;* a little exertion will *tire* a child or a weak man; forced exertions *jade;* painful exertions or exertions coupled with painful circumstances *harass:* the horse is *jaded* who is forced on beyond his strength; the soldier is *harassed* who in his march is pressed by a pursuing enemy. We are *wearied* with thinking when it causes us effort to think any longer; we are *tired* of our employment when it ceases to give us pleasure; we are *jaded* by incessant attention to business; we are *harassed* by perpetual complaints which we cannot redress.

WEDDING. See MARRIAGE.

WEDLOCK. See MARRIAGE.

WEEP. See CRY; WAIL.

WEEPING. See LACHRYMAL.

WEIGH. See COUNTERPOISE.

WEIGHT, HEAVINESS, GRAVITY. *Weight*, from to *weigh*, is that which a thing *weighs*. *Heaviness*, from *heavy* and *heave*, signifies the abstract quality of the *heavy*, or difficult to heave. *Gravity*, from the Latin *gravis*, likewise denotes the same abstract quality.

Weight is indefinite: whatever may be *weighed* has a *weight*, whether large or small: *heaviness* and *gravity* are the property of bodies having a great *weight*. *Weight* is opposed only to that which has or is supposed to have no *weight*, that is, what is incorporeal or immaterial; for we may speak of the *weight* of the lightest conceivable bodies, as the *weight* of a feather: *heaviness* is opposed to lightness; the *heaviness* of lead is opposed to the lightness of a feather. *Weight* lies absolutely in the thing; *heaviness* is relatively considered with respect to the person: we estimate the *weight* of things according to a certain measure; we estimate the *heaviness* of things by our feelings. *Gravity* is that species of *weight* which is scientifically considered as inherent in certain bodies; the term is therefore properly scientific.

See also HEAVY; IMPORTANCE.

Weight, Burden, Load.—*Weight* (for derivation see above). *Burden*, from *bear*, signifies the thing borne. *Load*, Anglo-Saxon *lad*, a way, journey, or conveyance, signified originally that which was carried on a journey, hence, in our sense, a *load*. It has been confused with the verb *lade*, which has a different derivation, and this confusion has influenced the meaning.

The term *weight* is here considered in

common with the other terms, in the sense of a positive *weight;* by which it is allied to the word *burden:* the *weight* is said either of persons or things; the *burden* more commonly respects persons; the *load* may be said of either: a person may sink under the *weight* that rests upon him; a platform may break down from the *weight* upon it: a person sinks under his *burden* or *load;* a cart breaks down from the *load.* The *weight* is abstractedly taken for what has *weight,* without reference to the cause of its being there; *burden* and *load* have respect to the person or thing by which they are produced; accident produces the *weight;* a person takes a *burden* upon himself or has it imposed upon him; the *load* is always laid on: it is not proper to carry any *weight* that exceeds our strength; those who bear the *burden* expect to reap the fruit of their labor; he who carries *loads* must be contented to take such as are given him.

In the moral application these terms mark the pain which is produced by a pressure; but the *weight* and *load* rather describe the positive severity of the pressure; the *burden* respects the temper and inclinations of the sufferer; the *load* is in this case a very great *weight:* a minister of state has a *weight* on his mind at all times, from the heavy responsibility which attaches to his station; one who labors under strong apprehensions or dread of an evil has a *load* on his mind; any sort of employment is a *burden* to one who wishes to be idle; and time unemployed is a *burden* to him who wishes to be always in action.

WELCOME. See ACCEPTABLE; ACCOST.

WELFARE. See WEAL.

WELL-BEING, WELFARE, PROSPERITY, HAPPINESS. *Well-being* may be said of one or many, but more of a body; the *well-being* of society depends upon a due subordination of the different ranks of which it is composed. *Welfare,* or *faring well,* respects the good condition of an individual; a parent is naturally anxious for the *welfare* of his child. *Well-being* and *welfare* consist of such things as more immediately affect our existence: *prosperity,* which comprehends both *well-*

being and *welfare,* includes likewise all that can add to the enjoyments of man. The *prosperity* of a state or of an individual, therefore, consists in the increase of wealth, power, honors, and the like; as outward circumstances more or less affect the *happiness* of man: *happiness* is, therefore, often substituted for *prosperity;* but it must never be forgotten that *happiness* properly lies only in the mind, and that consequently *prosperity* may exist without *happiness;* but *happiness,* at least as far as respects a body of men, cannot exist without some portion of *prosperity.*

See also FORTUNATE; HAPPINESS.

WELL-BRED, COURTEOUS, CULTIVATED, POLISHED, REFINED. *Well-bred,* a compound of two English terms, *well* and *bred,* from *breed,* meaning to generate, beget, signifies a person or animal born of a good breed, stock, or race, or one well-born. The term has a broad application in the personal sense, as it implies refinement and cultivation in either sex. A *courteous* person (*i.e.,* one who has courtly manners) is always polite and obliging: a *cultivated* one exhibits the training or refining of the intellectual and social faculties; a *polished* one possesses elegance and suavity of manners: and a *refined* one displays an unvarying good taste and an instinctive aversion to anything that is coarse or extreme in thought or expression.

These qualities are not always to be found in one person, for a *courteous* one may be such from cultivation, not from nature, education, or association; a *polished* one is not necessarily *courteous,* for he may be such from study, association, or imitation and still lack many of the qualities of good-breeding; but a *cultivated* one is apt to exhibit the best and most attractive features of a broad and universal training, a wide knowledge of both books and men, and a high regard for the niceties of polite society.

WHEEDLE. See COAX.

WHIM. See FREAK; VAGARY.

WHIMSICAL. See FANCIFUL.

WHINING. See QUERULOUS.

WHIP. See LASH.

WHIRL. See TURN.

WHOLE, ENTIRE, COMPLETE, TOTAL, INTEGRAL. *Whole* excludes subtraction; *entire* excludes division;

complete excludes deficiency: a *whole* orange has had nothing taken from it; an *entire* orange is not yet cut; and a *complete* orange is grown to its full size: it is *possible*, therefore, for a thing to be *whole* and not *entire:* and to be both, and yet not *complete:* an orange cut into parts is *whole* while all the parts remain together, but it is not *entire;* it may be *whole* as distinguished from a part, *entire* as far as it has no wound or incision in it; but it may not be a *complete* orange if it is defective in its growth. *Whole* is applied to everything of which there may be a part actually or in imagination; as the *whole* line, the *whole* day, the *whole* world: *entire* is applied only to such things as may be damaged or injured, or is already damaged to its fullest extent; as an *entire* building, or *entire* ruin: *complete* is applied to that which does not require anything further to be done to it; as a *complete* house, a *complete* circle, and the like.

Total, from Low Latin *totalis,* extended from *totus,* the whole, has the same significance, but only a limited application; as a *total* amount or a *total* darkness, as distinguished from a partial amount or a partial degree of darkness.

Integral, from *integer,* literally untouched, from *in* (not) and the root *tag* which appears in the Latin *tangere,* to touch, has the same signification, but is applied now to parts or numbers not broken.

See also ALL.

WHOLESOME. See HEALTHY.

WHOLLY. See QUITE.

WICKED, INIQUITOUS, NEFARIOUS. *Wicked* (see BAD) is here the generic term; *iniquitous,* from *iniquus, inœquus,* not equal, signifies that species of *wickedness* which consists in violating the law of right between man and man; *nefarious,* from the Latin *nefas,* not according to the law (from *fari,* to speak, a law being something spoken, decreed, either by man or a power above man. Compare *fatum,* fate, the thing spoken). The term *wicked,* being indefinite, is commonly applied in a milder sense than *iniquitous;* and *iniquitous* than *nefarious:* it is *wicked* to deprive another of his property unlawfully, under any circumstances; but it is *iniquitous* if it

be done by fraud and circumvention, and *nefarious* if it involves any breach of trust; any undue influence over another, in the making of his will, to the detriment of the rightful heir, is *iniquitous;* any underhand dealing of a servant to defraud his master is *nefarious.*

WIDE. See LARGE.

WIELD, BRANDISH. *Wield,* from Anglo-Saxon *wealdan,* to have power, means to exercise with skill and effect. It is used with reference to the skilful handling of a weapon—to *wield* a sword, to *wield* an axe—and, figuratively, of the exercising of any power, as when we say "He *wields* a great influence." *Brandish* resembles *wield* in its physical application. It meant, literally, to wield a sword, from Old French *brand,* sword, of Germanic origin. However, it does not imply such a skilful handling as *wield;* there is more show and flourish in *brandish.* To *brandish* a sword is to wave it in the air so that every one may see and fear; to *wield* a sword is to exercise it skilfully in the work for which it was intended. In its figurative application *brandish* means to make a great show of power and authority, to flourish threateningly.

WILFUL. See WAYWARD.

WILL, WISH. The *will* is that faculty of the soul which is the most prompt and decisive; it immediately impels to action: the *wish* is but a gentle motion of the soul toward a thing. We can *will* nothing but what we can effect; we may *wish* for many things which lie above our reach. The *will* must be under the entire control of reason or it will lead a person into every mischief: *wishes* ought to be under the direction of reason or otherwise they may greatly disturb our happiness.

Willingly, Voluntarily, Spontaneously.—To do a thing *willingly* is to do it with a good will; to do a thing *voluntarily* is to do it of one's own accord: the former implies one's *willingness* to comply with the wishes of another; we do what is asked of us; it is a mark of good-nature: the latter implies our freedom from foreign influence; we do that which we like to do; it is a mark of our sincerity. It is pleasant to see a child do his task *willingly;* it is pleasant to see a man *voluntarily* engage in any service of public good. *Spontaneously* (from a lost Latin substantive *spons*) is but a mode of the *voluntary*, applied, however, more commonly to inanimate objects than to the will of persons: the ground produces *spontaneously* when it produces without culture; and words flow *spontaneously* which require no effort on the part of the speaker to produce them. If, however, applied to the will, it bespeaks in a stronger degree the totally unbiassed state of the agent's mind: the *spontaneous* effusions of the heart are more than the *voluntary* services of benevolence. The *willing* is opposed to the unwilling, the *voluntary* to the mechanical or involuntary, the *spontaneous* to the reluctant or the artificial.

WILY. See CUNNING.

WIN. See ACQUIRE.

WIND. See TURN.

WISDOM, PRUDENCE. *Wisdom,* allied to German *wissen,* to know, is the general term; it embraces the whole of practical knowledge: *prudence* (see PRUDENT) is a branch of *wisdom. Wisdom* directs all matters present or to come. *Prudence,* which acts by foresight, directs what is to come. Rules of conduct are framed by *wisdom,* and it is the part of *prudence* to apply these rules to the business of life.

WISH. See DESIRE; WILL.

WIT, HUMOR, SATIRE, IRONY, BURLESQUE. *Wit,* like wisdom, according to its original, from Anglo-Saxon *witan,* to know (compare German *wissen*), signifies knowledge, but it has so extended its meaning as to signify that faculty of the mind by which knowledge or truth is perceived, and in a more limited sense the faculty of discovering the agreements or disagreements of different ideas. *Wit,* in this latter sense, is properly a spontaneous faculty, and is, as it were, a natural gift: labored or forced *wit* is no *wit.* Reflection and experience supply us with wisdom; study and labor supply us with learning; but *wit* seizes with an eagle eye that which escapes the notice of the deep thinker and elicits truths which are in vain sought for with any severe effort.

Humor is a species of *wit* which flows

out of the *humor* of a person. *Wit,* as distinguished from *humor,* may consist of a single brilliant thought; but *humor* runs in a vein; it is not a striking, but an equable and pleasing flow of *wit.* Of this description of *wit* Mr. Addison, who knew best how to explain what *wit* and *humor* were, and to illustrate it by his practice, has given us the most admirable specimens in his writings.

Humor may likewise display itself in actions as well as words, whereby it is more strikingly distinguished from *wit,* which displays itself only in the happy expression of happy thoughts.

Satire (from *satura lanx,* a full dish, a dish of mixed ingredients, applied figuratively to a species of poetry full of animadversions on different persons and events) and *irony,* from the Greek εἰρωνεία, simulation and dissimulation, are personal and censorious sorts of *wit,* the first of which openly points at the object and the second in a covert manner takes its aim.

Burlesque (perhaps from Latin *burrula,* diminutive of *burræ,* trifles, Italian *burlesco,* ludicrous) is rather a species of *humor* than direct *wit,* which consists in an assemblage of ideas extravagantly discordant. The *satire* and *irony* are the most ill-natured kinds of *wit; burlesque* stands in the lowest rank.

See also INGENUITY.

WITHDRAW. See RECEDE; WEAN.

WITHSTAND. See OPPOSE.

WITNESS. See DEPONENT.

WOFUL. See PITEOUS.

WONDER, ADMIRE, SURPRISE, ASTONISH, AMAZE. *Wonder* is a Germanic word whose ultimate derivation is unknown. *Admire* is derived from Latin *admirari,* to wonder at, and allied to *miracle,* a thing to be wondered at. *Surprise,* compounded of French *sur,* on, and *prise,* taken, the feminine past participle of *prendre,* from Latin *prehendere,* signifies to take on a sudden. *Astonish,* Old French *estoner,* Latin *ex* and *tonare,* to thunder (compare the word *thunderstruck,* a forceful and colloquial synonyme of *astonished*), signifies to strike as it were with the overpowering noise of thunder. *Amaze* signifies to be in a *maze,* so as not to be able to collect one's self.

That particular feeling which anything unusual produces on our minds is expressed by all these terms, but under various modifications. *Wonder* is the most indefinite in its signification or application, but it is still the least vivid sentiment of all: it amounts to little more than a pausing of the mind, a suspension of the thinking faculty, an incapacity to fix on a discernible point in an object that rouses our curiosity: it is that state which all must experience at times, but none so much as those who are ignorant: they *wonder* at everything, because they know nothing. *Admiration* is *wonder* mixed with esteem or veneration: the *admirer* suspends his thoughts, not from the vacancy, but the fulness, of his mind: he is riveted to an object which for a time absorbs his faculties: nothing but what is great and good excites *admiration*, and none but cultivated minds are susceptible of it: an ignorant person cannot *admire*, because he cannot appreciate the value of anything. *Surprise* and *astonishment* both arise from that which happens unexpectedly; they are species of *wonder* differing in degree, and produced only by the events of life: the *surprise*, as its derivation implies, takes us unawares; we are *surprised* if that does not happen which we calculate upon, as the absence of a friend whom we looked for; or we are *surprised* if that happens which we did not calculate upon; thus we are *surprised* to see a friend returned whom we supposed was on his journey: *astonishment* may be awakened by similar events which are more unexpected and more unaccountable: thus we are *astonished* to find a friend at our house whom we had every reason to suppose was many hundred miles off; or we are *astonished* to hear that a person has got safely through a road which we conceived to be absolutely impassable.

Surprise may for a moment startle; *astonishment* may stupefy and cause an entire suspension of the faculties; but *amazement* has also a mixture of perturbation. We may be *surprised* and *astonished* at things in which we have no particular interest: we are mostly *amazed* at that which immediately concerns us.

Wonder, Miracle, Marvel, Prodigy, *Monster.*—*Wonder* is that which causes wonder. *Miracle,* Latin *miraculum,* is allied to *admire,* which see above. *Marvel* is derived from Latin *mirabilia,* which has the same root—signifying wonder. *Prodigy,* from Latin *prod* for *pro,* and a supposititious word, *agium,* a saying, which also appears in *adage,* means a saying beforehand, hence a sign, token, or portent, something extraordinary. *Monster,* in Latin *monstrum,* comes from *moneo* to warn, because among the Romans any unaccountable appearance was considered as an indication of some future event. *Wonders* are natural: *miracles* are supernatural. The whole universe is full of *wonders;* the Bible contains an account of the *miracles* which happened in those days. *Wonders* are real; *marvels* are often fictitious; *prodigies* are extravagant and imaginary. Natural history is full of *wonders;* travels abound in *marvels* or in *marvellous* stories, which are the inventions either of the artful or the ignorant and credulous: ancient history contains numberless accounts of *prodigies. Wonders* are fitting to the laws of nature; they are *wonderful* only as respects ourselves: *monsters* are violations of the laws of nature. The production of a tree from a grain of seed is a *wonder;* but the production of a calf with two heads is a *monster.*

WOOD-ENGRAVING. See XYLOGRAPHY.

WOOER. See LOVER.

WORD, TERM, EXPRESSION. *Word* is here the generic term, the other two are specific. Every *term* and *expression* is a *word,* but every *word* is not denominated a *term* or *expression.* Language consists of *words;* they are the connected sounds which serve for the communication of thought. *Term,* from *terminus,* a boundary, signifies any *word* that has a specific or limited meaning; *expression* (see EXPRESS) signifies any *word* which conveys a forcible meaning. Usage determines *words;* science fixes *terms;* sentiment provides *expressions.* The purity of a style depends on the choice of *words;* the precision of a writer depends upon the choice of his *terms;* the force of a writer depends upon the aptitude of his *expressions.* The grammarian treats of the nature of *words;* the philosopher weighs the value of scientific *terms;* the rhetorician estimates the force of *expressions.*

See also PROMISE.

WORK, LABOR, TOIL, DRUDGERY, TASK. *Work,* in Saxon *weorc,* Greek ἔργον, is the general term, as including that which calls for the exertion of our strength: *labor* (for derivation see that term) differs from it in the degree of exertion required; it is hard *work: toil,* probably connected with *till,* expresses a still higher degree of painful exertion: *drudgery* (see SERVANT) implies a mean and degrading *work.* Every member of society must *work* for his support, if he is not in independent circumstances: the poor are obliged to *labor* for their daily subsistence; some are compelled to *toil* incessantly for the pittance which they earn: *drudgery* falls to the lot of those who are the lowest in society. A man wishes to complete his *work;* he is desirous of resting from his *labor;* he seeks for a respite from his *toil;* he submits to *drudgery.*

Task, from Latin *tasca,* a tax (*tax* being another form of the same word), is a *work* imposed by others, and consequently more or less burdensome. Sometimes taken in the good sense for that which one imposes on one's self.

WORLD. See PUBLIC.

WORLDLY. See SECULAR.

WORRY, ANXIETY. *Worry* comes from Anglo-Saxon *wyrgan,* to strangle, to harm. It has thus a metaphorical significance similar to that of *anxiety,* for which see CARE. As a substantive *worry* has almost the same meaning as *anxiety,* but being an Anglo-Saxon word, whereas *anxiety* is of Latin origin, it differs in quality and atmosphere. *Worry* is a more homely and emphatic word than *anxiety,* and suggests the psychological state more directly.

For a further discussion of the synonymes of *anxiety,* and hence of *worry,* see CARE.

WORSHIP. See ADORE.

WORTH. See DESERT; VALUE.

WORTHLESS. See UNWORTHY.

WRANGLE. See JANGLE.

WRATH. See ANGER.

WRENCH. See TURN.

WREST. See TURN.

WRETCHED. See UNHAPPY.

WRING. See TURN.

WRITER, PENMAN, SCRIBE. *Writer* is an indefinite term; every one who *writes* is called a *writer;* but none are *penmen* but such as are expert at their pen. Many who profess to teach *writing* are themselves but sorry *writers:* the best *penmen* are not always the best teachers of *writing.* The *scribe* is one who *writes* for the purpose of copying; he is, therefore, an official *writer.*

Writer and *penman* have an extended application to one who *writes* his own compositions; the former is now used for an author or composer, as the *writer* of a letter or the *writer* of a book; the latter for one who *pens* anything worthy of notice for the use of the public. *Scribe* may be taken for one who performs, as it were, the office of *writing* for another.

Writer, Author.—*Writer* refers us to the act of *writing; author* (from Latin *auctor,* an originator, literally one who makes a thing to grow, from *augure,* to increase) lays emphasis on the act of inventing. There are, therefore, many *writers* who are not *authors,* but there is no *author* of books who may not be termed a *writer:* compilers and contributors to periodical works are properly *writers,* though not always entitled to the name of *authors.* Poets and historians are properly termed *authors* rather than *writers.*

WRITHE. See TURN.

WRONG. See INJUSTICE.

WRY, DISTORTED, TWISTED, ASKEW, WARPED. All of these words signify a turning from a normal position. *Wry* means bent to one side and somewhat twisted in the bending. *Distorted,* from *torquere,* to turn, means turned out of a normal state or position, with the implication not simply of bending, but of turning round and round. *Twisted,* past participle of *twist,* meant originally wound round and round, as in the case of two threads wound around and around each other by *twisting. Askew* is from Old Low German; it means turned aside like a *shying* horse, and is derived from the root that appears in English *shy. Warped* means made uneven in outline, referring to a flat surface that has become somewhat arched or otherwise irregular.

X

XANTHOUS. See BLONDE.

XYLOGRAPHY, WOOD - ENGRAVING. *Xylography* is the technical term, *wood-engraving* the common term for the same process. The difference is therefore not one of meaning, but of usage. *Xylography,* a term compounded of the Greek ξύλον, wood, and γράφειν, to write or draw, signifies the art of the *wood-engraver* or the act of cutting designs or figures on wood for printing, an art that in recent years has been largely superseded by various processes for book and periodical illustration. The term is also applied to a mode of printing or graining from the natural surface of the wood, and to a process of decorative painting on wood.

Y

YEARN, CRAVE, LONG. *Yearn, crave,* and *long,* as verbs, all mean to desire intensely, but the quality of the desire differs. *Long* means simply to wish intensely. *Yearn,* from Anglo-Saxon *georn,* eager, has a special suggestion of tenderness; *crave* is used of physical appetite.

YES. See AYE.

YET. See BUT; HOWEVER.

YIELD. See AFFORD; BEAR; COMPLY; GIVE UP.

YIELDING. See COMPLIANT.

YONDER, BEYOND, YON. The first two words are derived from the Anglo-Saxon adverb *geond;* *yon* is the Saxon adjective *geon,* signifying a place removed by more or less distance. *Yonder* means at a distance; it is becoming slightly archaic now. *Yon* is a poetic abbreviation for *yonder. Beyond* differs from *yonder* in signifying a place on the other side of a given point. We may say in general that the village is *yonder,* or we may say quite specifically that it is *beyond* the river.

YOUTHFUL, JUVENILE, PUERILE. *Youthful* signifies full of *youth,* or in the complete state of *youth: juvenile,* from the Latin *juvenis,* signifies the same; but *puerile,* from *puer,* a boy, signifies, literally, *boyish.* Hence the first two terms are taken in an indifferent sense, but the latter in a bad sense, or at least always in the sense of what is suitable to a boy only: thus we speak of *youthful* vigor, *youthful* employments, *juvenile* performances, *juvenile* years, and the like: but *puerile* objections, *puerile* conduct, and the like. We expect nothing from a *youth* but what is *juvenile;* we are surprised and dissatisfied to see what is *puerile* in a man.

Z

ZANY, HARLEQUIN, MERRY-AN-
DREW. *Zany*, a substantive derived
from the Old Italian *zane*, in Modern
Italian *zanni*, the familiar form of
Giovanni or John, signifies a silly-
John, a former appellation of buffoon
and clown, a person who amuses others
professionally by jests, antics, odd
gestures, etc., especially by awkwardly
and ineffectually trying to mimic the
other actors. A *harlequin* (a word of
uncertain origin, but probably from
Old Low German *helle Kyn*, "kin of
hell," goblins, devils; thence by extension clown, buffoon) is the performer
in the Italian pantomime who wears
party-colored garments and carries a
talismanic wand with which he produces unexpected or ludicrous effects
while executing his part; he is the lover
of Columbine.

Merry-andrew is a term that is now
comparatively seldom used in the
United States, though at one time it
was quite common here and very popular in England. It is said to be derived from Andrew Borde, physician
to Henry VIII, "who, in order to instruct the people, used to address them
at fairs and other crowded places in an
eccentric and amusing manner," but
this is doubtful.

ZEAL, ARDOR, EARNESTNESS. All
of these words indicate energy and
intensity of interest. *Earnestness* indicates a general attitude of mind;
ardor is applied to warm emotions;
zeal indicates energy applied to the
carrying through of a cause or the
propagation of an idea.

ZENITH, ACME, APEX. *Zenith*, a
substantive from the Old French
cenith, derived from Arabic *samt*, pronounced *semt*, signifies the summit or
top of the heavens, the part directly
over a spectator's head. Figuratively,
it is the highest or culminating point
of anything seen or referred to. *Acme*,
Greek ἀκμή, has a similar meaning; it
means the point or top. *Apex*, Latin
apex, meant the summit or topmost
point of something. While the two
words had originally the same meaning, *acme* is now used with a figurative significance, whereas *apex* more
clearly retains its original literal
meaning.

ZEPPELIN. See AIRCRAFT.

ZERO, CIPHER, NAUGHT, NEUTRAL,
NOTHING. *Zero* is the same in form in
French and Italian, and is considered
a contraction of *zefiro* or *zifro*, from the
Arabian *sifr*, meaning a cipher. The
Old Latin treatises on arithmetic Lat-
inized the Arabic term as *zephyrum*,
which became *zefiro* in Italian, and
then *zero*. Low Latin *zifra*, Old French
cifre, Modern French *chiffre*, Italian,
Spanish, and Portuguese *cifra*, German
ziffer, all meaning nothing, the absence
of anything, all come from a parallel
Arabic form *zifra*. *Cipher* and *zero*,
therefore, are doublets, and each is indicated by the sign 0. In general these
terms mean no thing or *nothing*, and
stand for the *neutral* point between
any ascending and descending scale or
series, implying the extreme point of
depression.

In the thermometer and similar scales
the *zero* is the point or line from which
all the divisions are measured, up or
down. In the Centigrade and Réau-
mur thermometers *zero* marks the
freezing-point of water; in the Fahren-
heit scale it is placed at 32° below that
freezing-point. The *absolute zero* of
the temperature is the lowest possible
temperature which the nature of heat
permits, or $-273°$ Centigrade. *Zero* in
arithmetic is called *naught*, and implies no number; in algebra, no quantity; in mathematics it possesses no
value of its own, but when placed after
a number it increases the value of that
number tenfold.

While *zero* and *cipher* are distinctly
scientific terms, they, and more commonly the latter, have come to be
applied to persons and objects in a
depreciative sense, as a person is said
to be a mere *cipher* who possesses no
value in character, importance, influence, or otherwise, or who has got

down to *zero*, when he has expended all his money, energy, will-power: so an object, proposition, argument, objection, is said not to amount to a *cipher* when it is unquestionably worthless.

ZEST, GUSTO. *Zest*, in Old French the same, Modern French *zeste*, from the Latin *schistos*, that from the Greek σχίζω, meaning to peel, skin, or divide, the French form implying a piece of the skin of a citron or lemon, and the English form something that gives a special relish, an added taste, as the skin or rind of a citron or lemon, commonly used in cookery for flavoring. That is *zest*, therefore, that imparts to anything an increased taste, flavor, satisfaction, enjoyment, a piq-

uancy, or sharpness, tartness, spiciness. *Gusto*, from the Latin *gusto*, taste, meant the taste, the hearty enjoyment of food, hence any particularly hearty enjoyment. *Zest* and *gusto* both mean keenness of enjoyment, but *gusto* indicates a more pronounced pleasure than *zest*.

ZONE, GIRDLE, BELT. These words differ rather in the dignity of their usage than in their meaning. All signify a band encircling the waist used for support or ornament. *Zone* is a purely poetic word; *girdle* is more dignified and less homely than *belt*. *Zone* has also been extended to signify a region of the earth—a *belt*, as it were, around the earth.